THE CAMBRIDGE

History of the Book in Britain

*

VOLUME IV
1557–1695

Volume IV of *The Cambridge History of the Book in Britain* covers the years between the incorporation of the Stationers' Company in 1557 and the lapsing of the Licensing Act in 1695. In a period marked by deep religious divisions, civil war and the uneasy settlement of the Restoration, printed texts – important as they were for disseminating religious and political ideas, both heterodox and state approved – interacted with oral and manuscript cultures. By 1695 the monopoly of the Stationers' Company was effectively broken. Capital investment by booksellers, the growing market in the colonies and in leisure reading, and the lapse of government control, all served to undercut the earlier domination of printers.

At a time when religion and politics were inseparable, all sides sought to make use of the press for their own ends. Yet these years saw a growth in reading publics, from the developing mass market in almanacs, ABCS, chapbooks, ballads and news, to works of instruction and leisure, including music. At the same time author publication and new ways of financing learned and scientific works were developed. Atlases, maps and travel literature overlapped with the popular market but were also part of the project of empire. Alongside the creation of a literary canon and the establishment of literary publishing there was a tradition of dissenting publishing, while women's writing and reading became increasingly visible. These changes were intimately linked to developments in typography, binding, format, page size, layout and *mise-en-page*.

The volume gives particular attention to the relation of London publishing with the Continent and its interplay with bookselling in the English provinces, as well as to the very different histories of the book during these years in Wales, Ireland, Scotland and the American colonies.

THE CAMBRIDGE

History of the Book in Britain

The history of the book offers a distinctive form of access to the ways in which human beings have sought to give meaning to their own and others' lives. Our knowledge of the past derives mainly from texts. Landscape, architecture, sculpture, painting and the decorative arts have their stories to tell and may themselves be construed as texts; but oral tradition, manuscripts, printed books, and those other forms of inscription and incision such as maps, music and graphic images, have a power to report even more directly on human experience and the events and thoughts which shaped it.

In principle, any history of the book should help to explain how these particular texts were created, why they took the form they did, their relations with other media, especially in the twentieth century, and what influence they had on the minds and actions of those who heard, read or viewed them. Its range, too – in time, place and the great diversity of the conditions of text production, including reception – challenges any attempt to define its limits and give an account adequate to its complexity. It addresses, whether by period, country, genre or technology, widely disparate fields of enquiry, each of which demands and attracts its own forms of scholarship.

The Cambridge History of the Book in Britain, planned in seven volumes, seeks to represent much of that variety, and to encourage new work, based on knowledge of the creation, material production, dissemination and reception of texts. Inevitably its emphases will differ from volume to volume, partly because the definitions of Britain vary significantly over the centuries, partly because of the varieties of evidence extant for each period, and partly because of the present uneven state of knowledge. Tentative in so many ways as the project necessarily is, it offers the first comprehensive account of the book in Britain over one and a half millennia.

D. F. McKenzie · David McKitterick · I. R. Willison
General Editors

DICTIONARIUM

SAXONICO-LATINO-ANGLICUM.

A

A Augmentum initiale, nonnunquam otioſum, eóque per aphæreſin *Anglis* uſitatiſſimam hodie ſæpe præciſum. *E. G.* abæꞃan, to beare: abeodan, to bid: abꞃecan, to breake, & alia ſexcenta. Atqui hoc ipſum ex uſu & genio linguæ Græcæ ad *Anglos* derivatum. quod, inter alia plura haud vulgaria, me docuit Studiorum meorum fautor ille unicus, D. *Mericus Caſaubonus*, magni quidem patris non minor filius, ac de me, & omnibus iſtius linguæ ſtudioſis vir optimè meritus, in laudatiſſimo de quatuor linguis tractatu, pag. 235. Particulam hanc *Alexander Gillius*, in *Logonom. Angl.* c. 9. vocat *epitaticam*: ut in amate. *i. terreo*; aber, *vehementius affirmo pro vero*; *&c.*

A. (*ut* be, ꝼoꞃ, ᵹe, *&* ꞇo) verborum præteritis, præteriti temporis participiis, ac verbalibus, ſæpe præpoſitum: cujus in ſequentibus exemplorum ſatis. Hîc interim monendum, præpoſitiones hujuſmodi ſæpe commutari. Quæ hîc igitur deſiderantur, illic (in vocibus ſcil. à cæterarum unâ aut alterâ incipientibus) nonnunquam inveniantur.

A. Semper, uſque. Alwaies, ever. he biþ à ẏmbe ꝥ an. *operoſè hoc unum molitur ſemper.* *item.* in ævum, in æternum, in perpetuum, in ſeculum: for ever, for ay. à buꞇan end. *i. ſemper, abſque fine.* à ꞇo populde. *in ſeculum.*

AA. *idem.* ââ ſẏ Godeſ nama ecelice ᵹebleꞇſod. *Collaudetur nomen Dei in æternum.* ⁊ uꞇon dôn. ſpa uſ ðeaꞃꝼ iſ. helpan ââ ðam pa ðoſꞇ ðe helpeſ beſꞇ behoꝼaþ. *Nos verò (ut quidem par eſt) ut quiſque maximè opis indigeat, ita ei ſemper potiſſimùm opitulemur.* Hoc linguâ Danicâ vetere, *æ.* V. *Worm: Literaturæ Runicæ* c. 27. p. 160.

Aac. quercus, robur. an Oake. linguâ Danicâ vetere eik. *Wormius. Kiliano*, eycke, &c. *V.* ac.

Aad. Congeries, ſtrues, pyra, ligni congeries, rogus. a Pile, a Wood-pile. *Bed.* Hiſt. li. 3. c. 16.

Aalᵹeꝼeꞃ. Igniarium. a Firesteel: alſo, Tinder.

Aam. Cauter. a Searing iron.

A B

Abacen. Coctus, piſtus. Baked, or baken.

Abæꞃan. Pati, tolerare. to bear, ſuffer, indure. *it.* ut abeꞃan.

Abal. Solertia, ingenium, ſcientia. Cunning, wit, wiſdome, knowledge, ſubtilty. *it.* habilitas. aptneſſe, ability, ableneſſe. —— heꞇ ꝥ þu þiſſeſ oꝼæꞇeſ æꞇe, cꞃæð ꝥ þin abal ⁊ cꞃæꝼꞇ. ⁊ þin mod-ſeꝼa maꞃa puꞃde. ⁊ þin lichoma leohꞇꞃe micle. Diaboli Adamum tentantis verba ſunt, *Paraph. Saxon.* pag. 25. *i. e. Præcepit* [Deus] *ut fructum hunc tu comedas*: *dixit* [mihi] *ſcientiam & peritiam tuam, mentiſque tuæ intellectum* [inde] *auctum iri, & corpus tuum multò luculentius futurum.*

Abannan. Mandare, præcipere, jubere. to command. *P. S.* p. 194. aban ðu þa beoꞃnaſ. bꞃeᵹo Caldea. uꞇ oꝼ oꝼne. *Præcipe tu, Caldæorum Imperator,* [Nabuchodonoſor] *viris illis nobilibus*, [tribus pueris ſc.] *ut de fornace exeant.* *it:* edicere, denuntiare, proclamare, publicare. to publiſh, to proclaime. uꞇ abannan. edicto convocare, congregare, evocare. to call forth, ſummon, congregate, or call together. *Teutonicis* eâdem ſignificatione, & ab eodem fonte, bannen: barbarè, *bannire.* Hinc etiam noſtratium bannes, pro nuptiarum pacto publicato. Huc inſuper (quod ad originem attinet) referendum Gallorum *bannir*, Italorum *bandire*, noſtratium baniſh. *i.* proſcribere, in exilium agere; & inde derivata: ſed & noſtratium banning: *i.* diræ, ſiniſtra imprecatio, execratio. Videat hîc qui velit Cl. Equitis *Spelmanni*, & doctiſſ. *Voſſii* Gloſſ. in voce *bannum. it. Menagii* Les Origines de la Langue Françoiſe, in *ban.*

Abaꞃian. Denudare, prodere, oſtendere, manifeſtare. to make bare, to betray, to detect, to diſcloſe, to diſcover, to declare or make manifeſt. *Teuton.* eodem ſenſu baeren. *Kilian.*

Abbad. Abbas. an Abbat.

Abban-dune. *Abindoniæ* oppidum in agro *Bercerienſi.* Abingdon, *al.* Abbington, in Barkſhire. ab Abbatiâ ſic dictum, q.d. Abbatiæ mons, vel collis: olim autem (Cl. *Cambdeno* teſte) Sheoveſham: de quo loco, ex vetuſto libro Abbendonenſi, hæc (inter alia) idem commemorat *Cambdenus: Hic ſedes regia, huc cùm de regni præcipuis & arduis tractaretur: negotiis concurſus fiebat populi.* Hæc autem loco illi ad concilia annuatim celebranda ab Anglo-Saxonibus deſignato, venerabili Bedæ Cloſeſhooh, aliis Cleoveſho,

A quibuſdam

William Somner, *Dictionarium Saxonico-Latino-Anglicum* (1659), sig. A1[r], printed by William Hall in Oxford by subscription. Ruled compartments, type ornaments; text in Anglo-Saxon, Latin and English; roman, italic, black letter and Anglo-Saxon type, the latter founded by Nicholas Nicholls for the University in 1656 and first used in this book.

THE CAMBRIDGE

History of the Book in Britain

*

VOLUME IV

1557–1695

*

Edited by

JOHN BARNARD

and

D. F. McKENZIE

with the assistance of

MAUREEN BELL

CAMBRIDGE
UNIVERSITY PRESS

PUBLISHED BY THE PRESS SYNDICATE OF THE UNIVERSITY OF CAMBRIDGE
The Pitt Building, Trumpington Street, Cambridge, United Kingdom

CAMBRIDGE UNIVERSITY PRESS
The Edinburgh Building, Cambridge CB2 2RU, UK
40 West 20th Street, New York, NY 10011-4211, USA
477 Williamstown Road, Port Melbourne, VIC 3207, Australia
Ruiz de Alarcón 13, 28014 Madrid, Spain
Dock House, The Waterfront, Cape Town 8001, South Africa

http://www.cambridge.org

First published 2002

Printed in the United Kingdom at the University Press, Cambridge

Typeface Renard No.2 Roman 9.5/13 pt. *System* LaTeX [TB]

A catalogue record for this book is available from the British Library

ISBN 0 521 66182 x hardback

I. M.

D. F. McKenzie

Michael Treadwell

Contents

LITERATURE OF THE LEARNED

LITERARY CANONS

Illustrations

Plates

Figures

Contributors

HUGH AMORY was sometime Senior Rare Book Cataloguer, the Houghton Library, Harvard University

RANDALL ANDERSON is an independent scholar based in Blue Earth, Minnesota

J. H. BAKER is Downing Professor of the Laws of England at the University of Cambridge

NICOLAS BARKER is Editor of *The Book Collector*

JOHN BARNARD is Emeritus Professor of English Literature at the University of Leeds

PETER BEAL is English Manuscript Expert and a Director at Sotheby's and Visiting Professor of English at the University of Reading

MAUREEN BELL is Senior Lecturer in English at the University of Birmingham

JONQUIL BEVAN is Reader in English at Edinburgh University

JOHN BIDWELL is Astor Curator of Printed Books at the Pierpont Morgan Library, New York

T. A. BIRRELL is Emeritus Professor of English at the University of Nijmegen

MICHAEL G. BRENNAN is Reader in Renaissance Studies at the University of Leeds

PETER CAMPBELL is a typographer and critic

JAMES P. CARLEY is Distinguished Research Professor at York University, Toronto, and Professor, Centre for Medieval Studies, University of Toronto

MARY CHAN is Emeritus Professor of English at the University of New South Wales

PATRICK COLLINSON is Regius Professor of Modern History, Emeritus, and Fellow of Trinity College, Cambridge

C. Y. FERDINAND is Fellow Librarian at Magdalen College, Oxford

Mirjam M. Foot is Professor of Library and Archive Studies at University College, London

Ian Green is Professor of Early Modern History at the Queen's University of Belfast

Mark Greengrass is Professor of History at the University of Sheffield

Paul Hammond is Professor of Seventeenth-Century English Literature at the University of Leeds

P. G. Hoftijzer is Professor of the History of the Book at the University of Leiden

Arnold Hunt is a Postdoctoral Fellow at the University of Nottingham

Lynette Hunter is Professor of the History of Rhetoric at the University of Leeds

Adrian Johns is Professor of History at the University of Chicago

Philip Henry Jones is Lecturer in Library and Information Studies at the University of Wales, Aberystwyth

Elisabeth Leedham-Green is a Fellow of Darwin College, Cambridge

Harold Love holds a Personal Chair at Monash University

D. F. McKenzie was Professor of Bibliography and Textual Criticism at the University of Oxford

David McKitterick is Librarian and Fellow of Trinity College, Cambridge

B. J. McMullin, formerly Reader in Librarianship, is Honorary Research Associate in the Centre for the Book at Monash University

Carolyn Nelson is Editor, Wing Short-Title Catalogue Revision Project at Yale University Libraries

Graham Parry is Professor of English at the University of York.

Kate Peters is Lecturer in Archive Management at University College, London

John Pitcher is a Fellow of St John's College, Oxford

James Raven is Reader in Social and Cultural History in the University of Oxford

Joad Raymond is Lecturer in English Literature at the University of East Anglia

Julian Roberts is the retired Deputy Librarian and Keeper of Printed Books at the Bodleian Library

Matthew Seccombe is at Harvard Law School Library

R. C. Simmons is Professor of American History at the University of Birmingham

NIGEL SMITH is Professor of English at Princeton University
MICHAEL TREADWELL was Professor of English at Trent University
ALEXANDRA WALSHAM is Senior Lecturer in History at the University of Exeter
ROBERT WELCH is Dean of the Faculty of Arts and Professor of English at the University of Ulster
LAURENCE WORMS is an antiquarian bookseller, Ash Rare Books, London

Preface

D. F. McKenzie was the motive force behind this whole seven-volume project, and his was the informing mind in mapping out the shape of volume IV. He had seen and commented upon all but four of the chapters in this volume, in some cases proposing substantial revisions, most of which had been completed before his sudden and unexpected death in March 1999. Had he lived to read through the typescript once every chapter had been put together, he would undoubtedly have proposed further changes, corrections, revisions and improvements. He would also have co-operated in the writing of the Introduction. In all these ways this volume is the poorer: nevertheless, this volume stands, like the other projects he was involved with at his death, either on his own or in co-operation with others, as a testimony to the breadth of his vision as a scholar and to his ability to inspire those he taught and those with whom he worked.

Many of the points made in Lotte Hellinga's and J. B. Trapp's Preface to the preceding volume in this history about the scholarly and archival sources available to the book historian apply to this period. The *Short-Title Catalogue* (*STC*) and Wing's *Catalogue* (Wing) together give a degree of bibliographical control unique to printed books in English or manufactured in Britain. Since work began on this project the digital *Eighteenth Century Short Title Catalogue* has evolved into the *English Short Title Catalogue 1473–1800* (*ESTC*), available through the Web. More recently still, as this volume was being completed, Early English Books Online (EEBO) became generally available in research libraries. This, based on UMI's microfilms of books in the two *Short-Title Catalogues* provides digitized images of the texts of works printed between 1473 and 1700 along with bibliographical information. *ESTC* and EEBO for the pre-1701 period are interrelated projects and are substantially (if in some respects, unevenly) complete. Although it is, and will for the foreseeable future remain, necessary to check these printed and electronic reference sources against one another, the combination of immediate access to physically distant texts along with multiple search terms (including imprint information) will allow research to be undertaken which would otherwise have been too time consuming for consideration, and will suggest entirely new ways of investigating book and textual history.

The archives of the Stationers' Company give a unique account in these years of details of personnel, the workings of the book trade, and the registry of copies. Further information is to be found in the State Papers and the Commons and Lords Journals. For the period up until 1640 much of this evidence is accessible in printed form, a result of the early to mid-twentieth century focus on the scholarly editing of Elizabethan and Jacobean play texts by R. B. McKerrow, W. W. Greg and A. W. Pollard among others and the earlier heroic labours of Edward Arber. However, the period from 1641 to 1700 is much less well served. The forthcoming *Chronology and Calendar of Documents relating to the London Book Trade 1641–1700*, edited by D. F. McKenzie and Maureen Bell, will make the book history evidence from the Stationers' archives, the *Calendar of State Papers Domestic*, the Commons and Lords Journals, and in the printed volumes of the Historical Manuscripts Commission available, with indices and proper annotation.

In the meantime, the publication of the microfilm edition of the Stationers' Company's archives, accompanied by Robin Myers's indispensable guide,[1] has made their consultation easier: the imaginative use of this resource in recent work by, for instance, Adrian Johns, Ian Gadd and Jonathan Sanderson,[2] only proves the need for the *Chronology and Calendar*. It is also the case that work like that of Arnold Hunt on Royal patents or Peter Blayney on the bookshops in St Paul's churchyard[3] demonstrates the continuing importance of exploring archival sources. The value of this kind of work is not limited to the London trade: for instance, Ian Maxted's examination of the 'artisan dynasties' of Exeter's seventeenth-century book tradesmen and Jonathan Barry's account of the trade in Bristol[4] underline the need for further systematic work on the form taken by the book trade in the provinces (cathedral towns and cities are likely to prove the most rewarding locations) which would add to the account given of the sixteenth and seventeenth centuries by Peter Isaac's ongoing *British Book Trade Index*.

In a period in which manuscript and print culture existed side by side and often interacted, it should be noted that access to the manuscript archive, scattered through public and private libraries, remains problematic despite the pioneering *Index of English Literary Manuscripts* by Peter Beal and the recent

1 Myers 1990. 2 Johns 1998, Gadd 1999, Sanderson 1999. 3 Hunt 1997, Blayney 1990.
4 Maxted 1989, 1996 and forthcoming; Barry 1985, 1991.

books by Harold Love and Henry Woudhuysen:[5] the plea made in this volume by Love for a short title catalogue of manuscripts to parallel those for printed books seems, for the moment at least, far from realization.

As will be evident by now, during the time this volume has been in preparation the landscape of book history has been evolving. There is more serious interest in the subject now in universities in the English-speaking world than was the case a decade ago, as the establishment of the Society for the History of Authorship, Reading and Publishing and its new journal, *Book History*, demonstrate. Closer to home, since this volume was planned, a history of the book in Wales, edited by Philip Henry Jones and Eiluned Rees, has appeared,[6] and multivolume histories for Ireland and Scotland have been commissioned. A three-volume history of libraries in Britain and Ireland has been commissioned by Cambridge University Press with Peter Hoare as its general editor: Keith Manley and Giles Mandelbrote will jointly edit volume II covering the years 1640 to 1850. 'Book history', then, is a moving target. There is as yet no generally agreed methodology, though what can be written depends to a very large extent on the kinds of archival material which happen to have been preserved institutionally or accidentally in a given country or nation. From the beginning it was the intention to produce 'a history of the book in Britain' not 'the history'. When planning this volume, D. F. McKenzie and I realized very early on that it would have to reflect the current state of play in the subject, and that different contributors would employ different approaches, even while we attempted to give an overview of the period as a whole. We recognized that a degree of overlap between chapters was unavoidable, partly because differing aspects of the some material required discussion, partly because some readers would want to consult single chapters. It was also our hope that this volume would include, as has proved to be the case, new research, even though in many places the volume, of necessity, synthesizes previously published scholarship: we also hoped that it would identify areas calling for further research.

John Barnard

5 *IELM*; Love 1993; Woudhuysen 1996. 6 Jones and Rees 1998.

Acknowledgements

Among many debts of gratitude, apart from those to the contributors themselves, the greatest is to the two General Editors, David McKitterick and Ian Willison, whose generous, positive and, above all, prompt comments and suggestions have brought this volume to its final shape. At a personal and pragmatic level the unfailing support, encouragement and shrewd advice of Caroline Bundy at the Press has been of different but equal importance from the beginning of what turned out to be an altogether more complicated venture than either of us perhaps imagined: Andrew Brown has throughout been supportive. Maureen Bell, despite the press of prior commitments, found the time to assist me in the final stages of the volume following the unexpected death of D. F. McKenzie in March 1999: her enthusiasm, moral support and scholarship have been of inestimable help. Christine Ferdinand and Florence Treadwell, despite great and immediate personal difficulties, found and sent to us the drafts of the chapters by D. F. McKenzie and Michael Treadwell without which volume IV could not have been completed.

The Leverhulme Trust generously funded four Research Fellowships which, though strictly speaking independent of *The Cambridge History of the Book in Britain*, gave the project credibility at an early stage and, more importantly, have fed new research results into the various volumes published or to be published while also enabling all four Fellows to develop their careers. Two of these, Christine Ferdinand, who was attached to the University of Oxford from 1990 to 1993, and Maureen Bell, who held her Fellowship at the University of Leeds from 1990 to 1992, are contributors to the present volume. Jenny Rogers and Isobel Holland, also supported by the Leverhulme grant, undertook further research at Leeds in 1993.

In addition to scholarly advice, Robin Myers offered practical and tactful help at a critical juncture. Nicolas Barker's willingness to undertake further work at the last minute has been invaluable. David McKitterick has been uniformly patient, ready with suggestions and advice throughout the gestation of volume IV; Ian Willison has been throughout encouraging and full of ideas. Robin Alston gave John Barnard and Maureen Bell access to the typescript of Philip Rider's index to the *Short-Title Catalogue* early in their work; John Morrison and Caroline Nelson did the same for Wing's *Short-Title Catalogue*; Henry Snyder authorized the sending of *ESTC* records at an early stage, and Steve Tabor was of instrumental help in making them accessible. Terry Screeton of the University of Leeds Computing Service ensured the data could be successfully manipulated. Peter Isaac kindly allowed access to the *British Book Trade Index*. Alastair Mann gave invaluable and generous assistance. Bill Bell gave encouragement at various difficult points.

I am grateful to the Huntington Library and the William Andrews Clark Memorial Library for the award of two research fellowships which allowed me to spend three months in 1984 working in their collections. My particular thanks are due to C. W. Sheppard, Oliver Pickering and the staff of the Brotherton Collection, the University of Leeds. I am also very grateful for the practical support given by the School of English at Leeds. In particular, Joanne Heath's help was invaluable in setting up the preliminary working party of prospective contributors held at Pembroke College, Oxford, in September 1992, in dealing with the subsequent correspondence, and in setting up an effective filing system. Between 1996 and 1998 Clare Lewis, uncomplainingly and with great efficiency, saw to the regularization of incoming typescripts and disks, along with the continuing correspondence, and began compiling the Bibliography. Catherine Sowden helped ensure that the typescript finally reached the Press. Advice over recurrent IT problems was given by Chris Jowett, Technical Manager of the School of English at Leeds. Kathy Brownridge and Michelle Double of the University of Leeds Research Unit resolved unexpected difficulties over funding with expedition and clearheadedness. I would also like to thank my colleagues at Leeds, Michael Brennan, Paul Hammond and Lynette Hunter, who not only agreed to contribute but understood the need for this volume.

Maureen Bell would like to thank Christine Penney and Martin Killeen, Special Collections Librarians at the University of Birmingham, for their prompt and unfailing resourcefulness; her colleagues in the Department of English at Birmingham for their much appreciated support, both moral and practical, and in particular Tony Davies, Mark Storey, Marilyn Washbrook and the members of the postgraduate research seminars. As ever, George Parfitt encouraged and advised at every turn.

Finally, I am indebted to the support and unfailingly good advice of Hermione Lee.

John Barnard

Introduction

JOHN BARNARD

The cultural impact of printing and the trade in books was out of all proportion to its economic significance. The importation of white and brown paper for writing, printing and packaging probably generated more profit for its wholesalers than the total output of printed texts did for printers, booksellers, mercuries, bookbinders and related trades, put together. Yet although the British book trade in 1557 was unavoidably insular and parochial when compared with that on the Continent,[1] it offered native writers a closed market which meant that a higher proportion of works in the vernacular were published than was the case abroad. Paradoxically, Britain's off-shore position, which made it for the most part culturally dependent on the Continent for learned writing of all kinds, privileged the development of its own independent traditions within the 'four kingdoms'. Printing dramatically accelerated the flow of information in the vernacular, and increasingly did so across class, cultural and national boundaries in the English-speaking world. It played a vital role in a world in which oral, visual, manuscript and printed texts all existed side by side, interacting with one another. Print did not replace manuscript circulation or production:[2] as is the case today, the new technology supplemented earlier ones, partially or largely replacing them for some functions, reinforcing them for others.

Retrospectively, the history of the book in Britain from 1557 to 1695 looks like a triumphalist progress in which a dominant Protestant vernacular culture, and an emergent canon of English literature, were steadily created and successfully displaced an earlier Latinate and Catholic world looking towards Europe, a process which began in England and then expanded to Scotland, Wales and

I am very much indebted to Maureen Bell for her advice, criticism and help in the writing of this chapter. David McKitterick and Ian Willison made invaluable comments and suggestions, and Ian Gadd suggested improvements at the last minute.

1 See Hoftijzer, below.

2 See Love, Chan and Beal, below: Brennan, below, demonstrates the importance of manuscript texts for travel books.

Ireland, and, later, the new American colonies. By the late seventeenth century, the resolution of the Stuarts' struggles with anti-monarchical, republican and dissenting traditions through the 'Glorious Revolution' of 1688, together with the subsequent final lapsing of the Licensing Act in 1695, enabled English culture and literature, increasingly presenting itself as a 'British' polity after the Act of Union in 1707, to develop its colonial markets, leading to the eventual worldwide dominance of the English language. As this volume makes clear, such an outcome could not have been forecast in 1557, nor was it foreseen by those active in the printing and dissemination of Catholic Counter-Reformation texts, by the Royalist opposition of the 1640s and 1650s, by radical and non-conformist writers for the press, or by the readers and writers of texts in Wales, Ireland, Scotland (for many of whom the output of the London press represented a profound cultural and linguistic threat)[3] or, later, those in the American colonies.[4] In each of these countries the trade and book culture developed very differently. These were years of economic uncertainty[5] and of political contestation, whose eventual outcome was uncertain, and they were punctuated by recurrent crises – Elizabeth's Protestant succession, the Armada, the execution of Charles I, the Commonwealth and Protectorate, the Dutch Wars and the Exclusion Crisis.

Despite the belief of writers from Lord Bacon to Elizabeth Eisenstein,[6] the printing press was not, on its own, an agent of change. Throughout the period covered by this volume print, politics and religion were inextricably linked to one another. There was an ongoing battle between differing religious beliefs and between various sects and institutions, all opportunistically making the best use they could of the book trade, both in print and manuscript, sometimes learning propaganda techniques from one another, sometimes modifying opponents' texts either to refute them or to sanitize them for a different Christian audience, and sometimes inventing new genres (like the Marprelate tracts or Quaker witnessings).[7] The circulation, legal or clandestine, of texts in print or manuscript offered different openings for Protestants prior to Mary's death and for Catholics thereafter, as well as for Brownists, Familists, Quakers, Ranters, Levellers and the dissenting clergy.

The continuing attempts throughout the period to control the output of the London presses and the circulation of manuscripts and of unlicensed, pirated or subversive books or pamphlets, whether through licensing, the Stationers' Company, the Star Chamber, Parliamentary acts or, after the Restoration,

3 See Jones, Welch and Bevan, below. 4 See Amory, below.
5 See Raven, below. 6 Eisenstein 1979, but see Johns 1998 and below.
7 See Collinson, Hunt and Walsham, and Green and Peters, below.

through Sir Roger L'Estrange's appointment as Surveyor of the Press, were only intermittently successful. Censorship, far from being pervasive or by the 1630s virtually totalitarian in its repressiveness,[8] was essentially *ad hoc*, inconsistent, opportunistic and usually ineffective.[9] Members of the book trade, pursuing profit, colluded with one another in the evasion of authority. Company officials impounded books in order to sell them on themselves,[10] while other tradesmen published printed pamphlets anonymously, using shared printing and swift distribution networks to cover their tracks.[11] At the same time authors used indirection, allusions, parallels and fables in legitimately published works. There was no doubt a degree of self-censorship, but these practices meant that despite regulation and harassment by the various authorities, the expression of political and religious belief in drama, literature, sermons and other forms was relatively free.

Print was intimately involved in the development of new reading publics, for instance, the mass market in 'little books'[12] and books written for, and increasingly by, women.[13] In the same years a number of impressive works of scholarship were produced like Sir Henry Savile's Chrysostom, printed at Eton,[14] works which were nearly always uncommercial and therefore dependent on subsidy of one kind or another.[15] The same ability to reach both newly literate and educated readers is equally evident in the imaginative use made of illustrations to support or extend verbal texts, or to stand in their own right as images. Copperplate engraving, developed in the Low Countries and Germany in the mid-fifteenth century, had reached England by 1545, but only became common in the seventeenth century.[16] Engraved title pages were used to attract buyers to cheap books through portraits of the author in works of practical divinity, but engraved plates are a characteristic feature of many of the most ambitious seventeenth-century books. Field's Bible, emblem books, scientific and music books,[17] and works by antiquarians all made extensive use of the rolling press, and offered a livelihood to engravers and to artists like Wenceslaus Hollar (1607–77). The printing of plates and their sale was a separate trade from printing in England. Maps were increasingly manufactured

8 The standard view particularly among literary historians, most influentially Patterson 1984 and 1993. See also Hill 1985.

9 See Hamburger 1984–5 and McKenzie 1988, 'Censorship' and below, pp. 560–1, 566–7, 765–7. See also Lambert 1992b, Clare 1990, Clegg 1997 and 2001 and Wheale 1999, pp. 13, 170–8.

10 Hetet 1985, pp. 43–59.

11 McKenzie 1976a, pp. 22–32. For a detailed bibliographical examination of one such case, Marvell's *Mr Smirke* (1676), see Lynch 2000.

12 See Simmons and Hunter, below.

13 See Bell, below.

14 Eight vols. (Eton, 1610) (*STC* 14629–29a).

15 See Barker, Parry, McKitterick, below.

16 See Hind 1952–64, Griffiths 1998 and O'Connell 1999.

17 See Bell, ch. 31, Chan and Johns, below.

at home and though they might be included in printed books they were also sold separately.[18] Atlases, which required heavy investment and a substantial market, were initially dominated by the Dutch trade, but by the end of the seventeenth century, although it was commercially risky (as the case of Moses Pitt shows only too clearly[19]) London publishers were prepared to challenge Continental pre-eminence in this field.[20] At the other end of the market, Peter Stent, active from 1642 to 1665, set up a successful business selling a wide range of prints, including maps, portraits both historical and contemporary, and topical images, which were directed not at the connoisseur but at a new middling public.[21]

By 1557 the London trade in printed books was well established. Most of the important vernacular genres – law books, primers, Psalms, sermons, school books, ballads and almanacs – were by then clearly identified. This achievement had earlier required legislation discriminating in favour of native-born members of the London trade to break foreigners' initial domination of the book trade, backed up by the further protection offered by royal patents. In theory at least, these were granted to protect individuals who made substantial investments in ventures of national importance which could only realize a profit over a period of years. Hence patents were awarded for large books like the statutes and law books or the Bible, or shorter works which had to be printed and distributed in very large numbers, all categories of books which required substantial initial capital investment in paper and manufacture.[22] The sale of patents was, of course, also a valuable source of income for the Crown, but it was to impact in unforeseen ways upon the development of the trade.

Some of the audiences for books were remarkably conservative. Thomas Tusser's *A hundreth goode pointes of husbandrie*, first published as a twenty-six page quarto in 1557, enlarged to *Five hundreth points* and 192 pages in 1573,[23] has a history of continuous publication until 1672 and, less frequently, thereafter.[24] It was still a quarto, it still contained Tusser's original dedication to Lord Paget with its opening acrostic, and it was still printed in black letter rather than roman type. (By the late seventeenth century roman type had mostly displaced black letter except in texts like the Tusser aimed at a more 'popular' audience and in some specialist areas like law, though there was a continuing demand for psalters and primers in small formats in both 'white' and 'black

18 Worms, below. 19 Harris 1985. 20 Worms, below.
21 Globe 1985. 22 See Raven, below. 23 *STC* 24372, 24375.
24 Wing T3369: the Stationers' Company still had it for sale *c.* 1695 (Blagden 1960, p. 187). However, the book sold only twenty-six copies in 1676/7 (Barnard 1994, pp. 24, 33). There was a new edition, *Tusser redivivus*, in 1710, reprinted in 1744.

letter', and black-letter folio editions of the Book of Common Prayer were still in demand.[25]) Similarly, yearly almanacs and prognostications, first published at least as early as 1493, were an important staple for the book trade throughout the sixteenth and seventeenth centuries and thereafter.[26] Thus, John Dade produced a yearly almanac from at least 1589 until 1615, after which William Dade's name replaced his, and publication then continued until 1701[27] – an early example of an eponymous brand name. But while the substance and content of Tusser's and Dade's two books remained unchanged, the ownership of their copy changed significantly. In 1557 Tusser's work had appeared under the imprint of Richard Tottell, while the early editions of Dade's almanac were published by Richard Watkins and James Roberts, who had purchased a royal patent in 1571 for the exclusive right to print all almanacs.[28] Both Tottell and Watkins were printer-booksellers. By the end of the seventeenth century both these books had long been the property of the Stationers' Company, the result of a long-term policy to gain control of the trade's profitable staple products, short works in English in small formats with guaranteed repeat editions. The tension between an individual's or a patentee's rights and those of the Company, implicit in the change of ownership of both titles, is crucial to an understanding of the financial structuring of the trade.

The trade at large had two main roles. First, it imported, legally or illegally, books from the Continent. The legal imports were primarily in Latin and languages other than English, and were either cheap editions of the classics for educational needs or more expensive books for the educated and professional classes. Even more than most other sections of a trade which Britain had to learn from the Continent, the Latin trade was, along with that of London's paper merchants, one which had long been dominated by foreigners with the connections and the necessary credit with overseas production centres.[29] However, some native businessmen were already active in importing books by the mid-sixteenth century and gradually made their way into the trade, until by 1700 they were in the majority.[30] Theirs was a wholesale trade, and the London port books (the customs records) give a remarkably detailed analysis of the individuals and families involved. Although the evidence is scanty, their main business throughout the period was in large numbers of small format editions of the classics and smaller numbers of learned books in larger formats.[31] The kinds of

25 See Blagden 1960, p. 187, Wing B3679 (1687) and Barnard 1999a, p. 369.
26 Bosanquet 1917; Blagden 1958b; Capp 1979.
27 *STC*, Wing, *BLC*. 28 Bosanquet 1917, p. 42.
29 For the preceding period, see Christianson, Needham and King in Hellinga and Trapp 1999.
30 See Roberts, below, pp. 160–72. For paper imports, see below, Bidwell ch. 28.
31 Roberts, below. For imports and exports in the eighteenth century see Barber 1976.

more expensive books imported can be inferred from inventories, the library lists of individuals and libraries, and from the printed catalogues of books brought from overseas which begin with that of Henry Fetherstone (Featherstone) in 1628[32] and continue intermittently until the end of the century. It is clear from these different sources that books were imported from all over Europe.[33] But even by the end of the seventeenth century books in English or printed in Britain could provide only a limited proportion of those needed by a serious reader.[34] Congreve's library, much more strongly biased towards English literature than most, depended on Continental printing for 40 per cent of its titles.[35] Locke's library is probably more typical – of his three and a half thousand books fewer than half were printed in Britain (and most of those, 1,637, in London) and only 39 per cent were in English, a proportion marginally higher than the number of titles in Latin (37 per cent), with titles in French making up the third significant language. (Of the Latin titles barely more than a hundred (3 per cent) were London printed.)[36] Even more striking is the case of the self-educated dissenting radical, Samuel Jeake (1623–90) of Rye: about a sixth of the books in his library of over two thousand titles were produced on the Continent, though only sixty of those were printed after 1640, and about a quarter of his library was in languages other than English, mostly Latin.[37] Apart from books brought back by individuals from their travels abroad, the larger proportion of these overseas books had been imported by the London trade (usually unbound, to create work for English craftsmen) and then distributed through their shops in London, their stalls at fairs, or through provincial retailers to the country as a whole. Only Scotland's manufacturing and retail book trade had a history in large part independent of London.[38]

Books imported surreptitiously by one means or another included texts such as Catholic works or the Latin versions of Hobbes's works, banned by the authorities,[39] but profit was a more substantial motive than belief. Since paper was cheaper on the Continent and its booksellers and printers had a far larger market, throughout this period books printed abroad cost less, and were usually better printed, than the home product.[40] In consequence, Bibles printed in Holland could undercut those printed in England[41] just as Latin school books

32 Pollard and Ehrman 1965; see also McKitterick and Leedham-Green below, pp. 00–00.
33 See Leedham-Green and McKitterick, below, pp. 323–4. For Scottish imports, see Bevan, below, pp. 689–90, 697 and Kelly 1997.
34 Compare with the preceding period, Ford in Hellinga and Trapp 1999.
35 Based on Hodges 1955, pp. 115–16.
36 Harrison and Laslett 1971, pp. 19–20.
37 Hunter, Mandelbrote, Ovenden and Smith 1999, pp. xxxvii–viii.
38 See Bevan, below.
39 See Collinson, Hunt and Walsham and Green and Peters, below.
40 Further see Hoftijzer, below.
41 See Roberts, below p. 165, McMullin, below, pp. 466–8, and Hoftijzer, below, pp. 739–40.

printed abroad were superior in quality as well as being cheaper than their English equivalent: it was, inevitably, a trade impossible to police effectively.[42]

The market for books printed in English could not at first reach beyond Britain. Works printed in English or in Law French, languages not used outside these islands, offered the only possible source of income for the entrepreneurial production of books or texts before the establishment of the American colonies.[43] Unlike the Continent, where ambitious publishers like Jenson or Plantin could look to merchant bankers or institutions or the state for financial investment[44] and where Louis XIII under the influence of Richelieu founded the Imprimerie Royale in 1640, such enlightened support was largely lacking in Britain. This made the publication of substantial works of any kind (even the Bible) problematic and explains key features of the publishing practices and financial imperatives peculiar to the London trade throughout this period.[45] Since books in English had no substantial European market, and since books in Latin could always be produced more cheaply on the Continent, the buying public available was strictly limited. As Archbishop Parker told Cecil in 1572, John Day and other printers were 'loth . . . to printe any Lattin booke, because they will not heare be uttered [i.e., published], and for that Bookes printed in Englande be in suspition abroad.'[46] (Despite these commercial difficulties, there is an extensive body of neo-Latin literature published by contemporary writers in Britain up to the year 1640.[47])

In 1582 Christopher Barker, writing as the Queen's Printer since 1577, analysed the state of the London trade, paying particular attention to the monopolies previously granted (for a fee) by the Crown covering particular categories of books. He thought that Henry Bynneman's patent for publishing dictionaries was 'more Dangerous to the Patentee then profitable' which he thought required £10,000 capital 'at the least' (equivalent to over £1,500,000 in today's currency):

> if the printer should print many of the said volumes, he must neede stande betwixt two extremes, that is, if he print competent nombers of each to mayntayne his charges, all England Scotland *and much more* were not able to vtter them; and if he should print but a few of each volume, the prices should be exceading greate, and he in more Daunger to be vndone, then likely to gayne. . . . (my italics)[48]

42 For some examples of their distribution in the provinces, see Barnard and Bell, below, pp. 681–2.
43 See Amory, below. 44 Jardine 1996. 45 See Raven, below.
46 Oastler 1975, p. 19 (citing BL, Lansdowne MS. 15, no. 50).
47 See Binns 1990. Neo-Latin culture was centred in Oxford and Cambridge Universities (Binns 1990, pp. xxiv, 393): publication must frequently have been supported by the author or by patronage.
48 Arber, I, p. 116. For the currency equivalents see Bank of England 2001, p. 9.

Barker was quite right. Bynneman's attempted publication in the early 1580s of Morelius's Latin and Greek dictionary, first published at Paris in 1558, led to financial disaster.[49] The English book trade's cultural relationship with the Continent, despite the publication of a handful of notable scholarly works,[50] was unavoidably provincial. This was as true of the market in the late seventeenth century as it had been in the sixteenth century: in the 1670s Robert Scott, the main importer of French books, 'expected to sell no more than twenty to thirty copies of a new mathematics book from abroad'.[51] These three inherent structural problems – the lack of an external market for books in English, the cost of paper, and the consequently high production costs – ensured that scholarly publication was rarely if ever commercially viable and seriously inhibited efforts to establish a learned press at either Oxford or Cambridge.[52] Nevertheless, by 1662 books published by the London trade were thought sufficiently important for the Licensing Act to require stationers to give copies of their new books to the newly designated copyright libraries.[53]

The profitability of printing was also threatened by the excess of productive capacity among London printers evident throughout this period. Christopher Barker's report on patents and the trade in December 1582 is quite explicit: he believed that instead of twenty-two[54] printing houses in London, '8. or 10. at the most would suffise for all England, yea and Scotland too'.[55] At the same time, the trade seems to have been chronically under-capitalized, creating particular problems for the production of large books. A case in point is the writing, production and distribution of Foxe's 'Book of martyrs' (1563). Foxe's martyrology was thought absolutely central to English Protestantism's sense of itself, so much so that a copy was supposed to be placed in every cathedral and in important public offices.[56] Yet without the patronage of the printer John Day, who held the lucrative patent for ABCs with the primer,

49 *STC* 18101 (1583). See Eccles 1957; Barnard and Bell 1991, pp. 20–5. Richard Hutton, the armourer, the recovery of whose loan led to Bynneman's downfall and whose name appears on the title page of the 1584 edition, credits Bynneman with originating the project in his Latin dedication to Robert Dudley, Earl of Leicester (sig. *ij^v). Starnes 1954, p. 112, mistakenly believes that Hutton was the book's editor and translator.

50 For example, the Eton edition of Chrysostom mentioned above (p. 3) or Thomas James's 1605 catalogue of the Bodleian. Thomas Vautrollier, John Wolfe, François Bouvier and the Oxford printer, Joseph Barnes, exceptionally had a few books on sale at the Frankfurt book fair in the 1570s and 1580s: see McKitterick 1992, pp. 86, 417, and Schwetschke 1850–77.

51 McKitterick 1992, p. 376, citing John Collins to John Beale, 20 August 1672 (*Correspondence of scientific men of the seventeenth century*, ed. S. J. Rigaud, Oxford, 1841, I, p. 200).

52 See McKitterick, below.

53 Leedham-Green and McKitterick, below, p. 336.

54 Actually twenty-three (see below, p. 13): Barker seems not to have counted his own shop as Queen's Printer.

55 Arber, I, p. 144.

56 Collinson, Hunt and Walsham, below, p. 37.

Foxe would never have been able to complete the work, while its subsequent publication history strongly suggests that as a commercial venture this essential Protestant text was always problematic.[57] After Day's death the 1596 edition was financed by a group of ten trade partners,[58] and when the stationers gained the rights to Foxe's work in 1620, they experienced serious difficulties in providing a subsequent edition, a problem only solved when no fewer than sixteen men agreed to share the risk of a new three-volume folio edition (1632).[59] The same problems are evident in scholarly publishing. John Minsheu's multilingual dictionary, *Ductor in linguas* (made up of 726 folio pages using Greek, Anglo-Saxon and Hebrew characters as well as roman, black letter and italic) on which he began work in 1599, was given a royal patent in 1611. Minsheu, however, was unable to raise the capital to publish the book until 1617: in doing so he sought the support of the two universities, the Inns of Court, and 'diuers Honorable and Right Worshipfull Personages, Bishops, and others', including merchants and London citizens: even so money ran out in the course of printing and the work was done at different times by two different printers.[60] It was this difficulty which led to the publication of the second edition in 1625 by subscription, the first English example of this practice,[61] one revived in the 1650s and taken up by the trade in the 1670s and 1680s.[62]

The two events which define the chronological limits of this volume, the grant of a royal charter to the Stationers' Company in 1557 and the lapse of the Licensing Act in 1695, are usually seen as definitively marking the dominance of the London book trade throughout this period, initially in England, Wales and Ireland, and then in the emergent American colonies. Both are indeed significant moments, but it is important to recognize that the trade in these years is characterized by change as much as by continuity, with the Company and its members adapting to new circumstances – economic, social, political and (to a lesser extent) technological.[63]

It now seems that the incorporation of the Company by Queen Mary in 1557 should be seen in important part as a normal transition in the life of a City

57 Oastler 1975.

58 *STC* 11226. For the division of the twelve shares among the partners in April 1595, see Greg and Boswell 1930, pp. lxviii, 51, 55.

59 *STC* 11228: further see Jackson 1957, pp. 230–31, 243–4, 434–6, 481, 482.

60 Williams 1948, pp. 755–60: see also *Ductor in linguas* (1617), sig. $\pi 2^r$ (see also $A4^r$).

61 Williams 1948, p. 770, who points out that the first edition of 1617 was not, as is usually claimed (Clapp 1932 and most subsequent writers), the first example of subscription publication.

62 See Green and Peters, below, pp. 78–9, and McKenzie, below, p. 565.

63 For developments in typefounding, see Barker, ch. 29 below; on changing patterns of bookbinding, see Foot, below.

craft guild[64] rather than, as W. W. Greg influentially claimed,[65] a far-sighted realization on the part of the Crown and the book trade of a mutually beneficial relationship, one which simultaneously served the Crown's interest in press control and the Company's interest in a trade monopoly. A complicity of interests in controlling the trade was certainly apparent to, and exploited by, both sides; but at times of stress (most notably under the restored Stuart monarchy, particularly when James II attempted to pack the Company's senior membership[66]) the potential conflict between the government's political will and the Company's commercial interests could cause friction. What is most striking is the Company's continuity, which after initial difficulties in the early 1640s maintained itself throughout the Interregnum and the reign of Charles II, held together by its mutual interests, notwithstanding the tensions between the printers and booksellers within the Company.[67] Yet despite the attention paid to the trade by successive governments, the Stationers' Company was always one of the poorer City corporations – in 1557 it ranked fifty-sixth out of a total of sixty-three and was still ranked among the poorer Companies in 1692.[68] Even so, the proportion of 'gentlemen' and London citizens choosing to apprentice their sons to the trade grew substantially between the years 1601 and 1700.[69]

The Company's incorporation in 1557 was highly significant in several ways. Control of the English and Welsh book trade was centralized in London (apart from the few rights granted to the two universities), a situation quite unlike that in the Low Countries or Scotland, neither of which had a single regulatory body.[70] As is usually pointed out, the Company's main functions were the registration of its members' rights to publish particular titles (thus securing their perpetual ownership), the admission of apprentices, and the regulation of the trade. To enforce this the Company was given powers of search throughout the country and, crucially, the printing of books was restricted to London (though this was challenged by the two universities in the 1580s and again later), helping to ensure the metropolis's dominance of the national trade until 1695. In addition, the Company's membership was given a legal corporate existence, creating a cohesive group identity for its members.[71] But the single most important change was to give the Company the legal 'power to redefine the trades over which it had jurisdiction':[72] in effect, as Peter Blayney argues, it meant that the Stationers' Company had appropriated the craft of

64 Pollard 1937a, p. 35; Pollard 1937b, p. 236; Lambert 1992b, pp. 13–14; McKenzie 1997, pp. 40–2. The guild may date back to 1403.

65 Greg and Boswell 1930, p. lx. 66 Blagden 1960, p. 171.

67 Blagden 1958c. 68 Gadd 1999, pp. 125–6. 69 Ferdinand 1992.

70 See Bevan, below, p. 687. 71 Gadd 1999. 72 *Ibid.*, p. 37.

printing to itself.[73] There had been no place for the new technology of printing in the City's guild structure when it was first introduced: Caxton, a wealthy mercer, set up as an entrepreneurial publisher in Westminster, outside the City limits. The Stationers, whose guild dates back to 1403, were originally retailers dealing in the circulation of manuscript texts, a bespoke trade which did not call for the heavy initial investment and slow capital return required by printed books. By 1557 a small number of printers with capital resources who were also publishers, and who were by this time mostly Stationers, dominated the trade. Of the ninety-seven names given in the Charter of Incorporation the most powerful were the seventeen printers, with at least a further two operating outside the Company, John Kingston, a Grocer, and the Continental printer, Robert Caley.[74]

An immediate consequence of the Charter was that the new Company immediately found itself engaged in external and internal struggles, ones which lasted from 1557 to 1605 and beyond. Externally, the Stationers wanted to restrict the trade of printing, and consequent productive capacity, to its own members (hence the struggle in the last years of the sixteenth century with the Drapers' Company, whose members had previously been tolerated, a struggle only resolved when twelve Drapers were admitted to the Company in 1599[75]). Internally, the monopoly held by a small number of wealthy tradesmen who owned the rights to the most lucrative kinds of text generated severe tensions within the Company itself.

This tension provided one of the two main themes in the Company's first phase (the other, the registration of ownership in copies, is dealt with separately below, though the two are interlinked). In one very important respect the Company's legal powers were compromised.

The powers awarded to the Company in 1557 were those of a City of London corporation, but they were powers which could always be challenged by the royal prerogative embodied in a patent.[76] It is therefore significant that shortly before the Company was incorporated, several of its members had purchased rights to the most important genres and titles (suggesting that the wealthiest printer–publishers were insuring themselves against any future changes in trade organization). In the reign of Edward VI, William Cecil, as

73 *Ibid.* citing P. Blayney's ongoing research into the Company.

74 Arber, I, p. xxxiii, compared with the index of printers and booksellers given in *STC*, III.

75 Johnson 1988, Gadd 1999, pp. 180–2.

76 For a summary account of the various patents and patentees which eventually became the basis for the English Stock see *STC*, Appendices A-E. This, and the account in Blagden 1960, pp. 63–76, *passim*, need to be supplemented by and read in the light of Blayney 1997b, whose revisionary study of the Company is in progress.

secretary of state, was instrumental in granting patents to Richard Tottell (law books), William Seres (primers) and John Day (Ponet's catechism and ABCs): he had earlier been involved in the granting of the New Testament to Richard Jugge as King's Printer in 1550.[77] Seres and Day lost their rights under Mary but regained them following Elizabeth I's accession, and in 1571 the valuable right in almanacs was granted, again by Cecil, to Richard Watkins and James Roberts. Together these classes of books (apart from the Bible and law books) made up most of the relatively small number of titles whose sale could be guaranteed year in year out in predictable quantities. Significantly, these men were all originally printers by profession. However, under Sir Thomas Smith, who succeeded Cecil in 1572, additional patents were granted to Thomas Vautrollier and to Francis Flower (including Lily's grammar), neither of whom belonged to the Company. (Flower, the Queen's Printer in Latin from 1574, made no pretence at all of publishing himself, but farmed out his monopoly, assigning the working of his patent to five members of the trade who paid him, said Barker, an 'annewity'.[78]) Confusingly, these privileges, together with the monopoly awarded to the bookseller Thomas Marsh, overlapped with titles previously patented, just as some of those granted earlier could be argued to overlap with some of the longer established rights of the King's Printer.[79] In granting these privileges (for a price) the Crown was acting in the interests of the few against the many, and the patentees' wealth and power came directly from their monopolies. The trade as a whole was at the mercy of a small body of privileged men, ensuring that the Company was throughout the period a conservative and inward looking cartel.

As early as August 1577 a petition complaining about this injustice was sent to the government claiming that less than a dozen patentees were destroying the livelihoods of nearly two hundred tradesmen[80] (to whom should be added their apprentices). This upsurge of resentment took its most effective form by attacking the most vulnerable patent, John Day's rights in the small, and easily distributed, *ABC with the little catechism*, when in 1582 a group of men, led by John Wolfe (a member of the Fishmongers' Company) and Roger Ward, pirated the *ABC* and sold it in large numbers.[81] This brought matters to a head. By 1583 all of the most dependable, and therefore valuable, titles peculiar to

77 For this and what follows, see Blayney 1997b. 78 Arber, I, p. 115.

79 As Christopher Barker points out in his report on the trade in December 1582, Arber, I, pp. 114–16, 144. See too Blayney 1997b.

80 Blagden 1960, p. 66. The petition was signed by thirty-five Stationers, half of whom were printers and six senior members of the Company, together with ten freemen of other Companies who made their living through books, and another 104 who had become freemen since the Queen came to the throne.

81 See Barnard and Bell, below, p. 680; further see Arber, II, pp. 753–69, Judge 1934, pp. 29–60.

the English trade – law books, the Bible, prayerbooks, Psalms, almanacs, ABCs, primers and dictionaries – were controlled by eleven patentees, each holding grants limited to a specific number of years. A measure of their hold on the trade's productive capacity is that of the fifty-three presses owned by twenty-three printing houses in May 1583, no fewer than twenty presses (38 per cent) were owned by the six patentees who were active as printers (significantly the rebel, John Wolfe, had five presses, two in a 'secret Vau[l]t', as many as the Queen's Printer, Christopher Barker).[82]

This put the patentees on the defensive, and the resultant outcry led, remarkably, to a Royal Commission to resolve the conflict. In this context Christopher Barker's frequently cited report on the state of the trade in December 1582 is very informative, but needs careful interpretation. Barker was in an awkward position. He had originally been a Draper, but had changed trades, becoming Queen's Printer in 1577. By 1582 he was both a patentee and an Upper Warden in the Company so that his personal and official interests were split right down the middle. His report is heavily biased towards the patentees, the profitability of whose privileges he minimized as far as possible, but his broad outline of the trade seems accurate. In Henry VIII's time a small number of printers 'of good credit and compotent wealth' invested in the manufacture of books which they sold wholesale ('in grosse') to Stationer booksellers (Barker passes over the printers' own retail activities). However, the great increase of 'Printers and printing' in Edward VI's reign – the mid-century saw the rise of both cheap almanacs and popular printed ballads[83] – required new investment in equipment and personnel. Barker's claim that as a result publisher-booksellers by 1557 possessed 'many of the best Copies', and had therefore relegated printers to the role of mere employee,[84] can only be partially true. The longest standing patents, those held by Tottell, Day, Seres, and by Barker himself, were all in the hands of printers who also acted as publishers in their own right.

The eventual compromise between the two groups was based on the patentees giving up some of their legally owned titles to the Company for the benefit of the poor of the trade, or agreeing to share their printing with others. In 1584 or the following year John Wolfe was bought off, becoming one of the partners in the Days' *ABC* patent (ironically enough, once made a member of the Stationers' Company Wolfe was particularly energetic in pursuing pirates).[85]

82 Arber, I, p. 248. 83 Capp 1979, p. 20.

84 Arber, I, p. 114. In contemporary usage the term 'book seller' could mean someone who was purely a retailer, but it also described a stationer whose main business was as publisher: Blayney 1997a, pp. 389–92, makes this important point forcefully.

85 Blagden 1960, p. 69, Feather 1988, p. 37.

The agreement meant that from 1584 onwards the Company therefore owned copies on behalf of its members. This could not have been achieved without the Company's earlier legal incorporation. It was this compromise, reached in 1584, between rights owned through the Crown and ones owed to the City trade organization, which led to the foundation of what came to be known as the 'English Stock'. By 1594 at least the Company and the chief partners in the old Day and Seres privileges in prayers and Psalms appointed a Treasurer and four stock-keepers to look after the trade in these books,[86] and between 1603 and 1605 the English Stock was consolidated. On 29 October 1603 James I gave the Company the rights to the main classes of vernacular titles which had been the subject of dispute in 1582–4, and in 1605 the Company acquired Tottell's rights over law books, owned by Thomas Wight since 1597. The cost of all this was considerable, £1,000 being spent on the law patent alone: the £9,000 required to set up this new business (an 'Vnder Company' within the Company[87]) was raised for the most part (in theory, exclusively) through the Stationers' own membership. The creation of the English Stock gave the Stationers corporate rights to the most valuable titles, whose management required a warehouse and an organizational structure to undertake the considerable job of ordering first the printing, and then the wholesaling of successive editions of all the titles now under their control. In return investors received a dividend of between 6.25 per cent and 10 per cent before the Restoration and 12 per cent thereafter.[88] Ostensibly this was an idealistic arrangement to ensure that the poorer members of the printing trade were given work, but the 105 shares issued were based on the Company's own strict hierarchy.[89] The allocation of shares was geared to the relative ability to pay. The most expensive were restricted to senior officials who in consequence accounted for one third of the total sum raised. Many more who wanted to buy shares were disappointed: the dominance of the Company's senior members was assured.[90]

Essentially the creation of the English Stock was a response to the situation in the early 1580s when a minority of patentees had a stranglehold over the trade's staple products: this was replaced by a financial arrangement whereby the production and distribution of those very same texts were in effect owned and controlled by the Company's leading members from 1603–5 onwards. While this, given the excess of productive capacity, was undoubtedly fairer

86 Blagden 1960, p. 76.

87 Richard Atkyns's description, made in 1663, is cited by Gadd 1999, p. 108. Unlike other joint-stock ventures by City Companies, the English Stock took control of a trade, previously the preserve of the individual, be they Stationer or not (*ibid.*, p. 107).

88 Blagden 1958c, p. 16, Blagden 1960, p. 96.

89 Blagden 1960, p. 94.

90 Blagden 1960, pp. 92–5.

than the situation in 1582, it nevertheless demonstrates the increasing dominance of booksellers over printers: by the early seventeenth century, if not well before, smaller printers (the majority) depended upon swift turnover for a modest income rather than risking long-term investment.[91] By restricting the largest share in the Stock to its higher echelons, the Company ensured that its policies continued to be governed by an oligarchy (albeit a different and much larger body than in 1582) whose main interest in the Stock was the maintenance of the dividend. (The success of the English Stock encouraged the Company to use its monopoly over the same titles to set up the abortive Latin Stock in 1616,[92] followed in 1618 by the Irish Stock, aimed at dominating the Irish market, which also failed, though less spectacularly and more gradually.[93]) Nevertheless, the dividend from the English Stock was a powerful (if conservative) unifying force for the better-off members of the trade, and helped the Company's hierarchical and oligarchic structure hold off, though with difficulty, the subsequent attacks on its monopolies.

Arnold Hunt has shown that from 1603 to 1640 there were, including renewals and reversions of existing rights, over seventy royal book-trade patents taken out. Up to a point the Company was able to use these to its own or to its members' advantage, and to increase its hold on existing rights to titles. But the patent system posed a serious threat to the Company's monopolies. Patents given to individual authors for single works, or for abridgements of existing works, were used to challenge the Stationers' rights. On some occasions patents were created which the Company was obliged to buy out.[94] For instance, George Wither, with considerable success, used a patent granted to him for his metrical version of the Psalms in a running battle with the Stationers from 1623 to 1635.[95] The later attack on the Company's monopoly by Michael Sparke and his supporters, however, came from within the trade, and differs from the more opportunistic use made of the patent system.[96] The Company's subsequent legal struggles over the law patent with John Seymour

91 Lambert 1992, pp. 21–7.

92 Roberts, below, pp. 161–2; Blagden 1960, pp. 106–7; Jackson 1957, pp. xi–xii, *passim*. See also Plomer 1907c, p. 294. Its nominal capital was £4,800, but a further £5,496 had to be borrowed in 1621: it was wound up in June 1617 (Blagden 1960, p. 106, Plomer 1907c, pp. 288–9, 295).

93 Blagden 1960, pp. 108–9; Jackson 1957, pp. xii–xiii, *passim*. See also Plomer 1907c, pp. 295–7 and Welch, below, p. 704. For the founding of the Bible Stock in 1646 and its failure see McMullin, below, pp. 465–6.

94 Hunt 1997. Hunt plans to extend his study of patents to cover the years 1641 to 1695: the period 1695 to 1760 has been covered by Rogers 2000, when royal licences were one alternative to the increasing ineffectiveness of using the Stationers' Register to claim copyright (Rogers 2000, pp. 133–4).

95 Carlson 1966, Jackson 1957, pp. 156, 162, 192, 247.

96 Blagden 1960, pp. 131–4 and Treadwell, pp. 762–5 below.

in the 1660s and its continuing arguments with both the Universities of Oxford and Cambridge over conflicting and overlapping rights,[97] show the Company going to considerable legal trouble and expense to maintain its position in the later part of the seventeenth century. Indeed, the frequency with which the Company was forced after the Restoration to go to law to defend its interests, rather than being able to settle the cases on its own authority, suggests that its powers were at risk throughout the seventeenth century and in decline in the last decades.[98]

The Company's other main role, ensuring that the ownership of copies was properly recorded, duly enforced, and if necessary arbitrated, affected the whole trade from its incorporation. Entry in the Stationers' Register was legal proof of ownership. The Company's record of the ownership of copies was a prerequisite for stability in a risk-taking business, and formed a main source of the Company's authority until the later years of the seventeenth century. Consequently, titles which were expected, or proved to be, valuable properties sooner or later found their way into the Register.[99] In the earlier part of this period first-time entries were usually made by a single tradesman in his own name, and a normal pattern would be that on his death his accumulated copies were assigned to his wife or sold to one or more successors. The idea of several tradesmen pooling resources to spread the financial risk was slow to develop, despite the example set by groups of men banding together to publish large works like Foxe's 'Book of martyrs' (1596 and 1632),[100] or Rider's dictionary.[101] By the mid-1650s 'complex joint ownership was becoming more common, if not yet usual' (John Harrison's widow inherited a one-sixteenth share in Lancelot Andrewes's sermons in 1656, the same year that a one-fourth share in Joseph Caryl's works was transferred to Mary Simmons).[102] Even so, the trade was slow to see the full advantages offered by mutual investment as a way of raising capital,[103] though, as the example of the copies owned by Richard Bentley at his death in 1697 shows, the descent of copyright over time inevitably led to their division into fragments. Giles Mandelbrote has demonstrated that although 'Novel' Bentley (*fl.* 1674–97) commissioned new books for his staple trade in plays, novels and light

97 Blagden 1960, pp. 193–201; McKitterick 1992, pp. 63–72, 80–82, 112–14, 154–8, 344–5; Johnson and Gibson 1946, pp. 95–7; Treadwell below.

98 Bald 1942, p. 85, McKitterick 1992, p. 113, Hunt 1997, p. 37; Treadwell, pp. 764–5, below.

99 The decision to enter a title was selective despite the regulation: many were never registered. See Bell 1994a who significantly modifies the earlier findings of Greg 1956 and 1966.

100 See above, p. 8–9. 101 See below, pp. 17, 20 and n.

102 Feather 1994, p. 42, giving the examples cited above from E & R, II, pp. 78, 119.

103 Further on the broader economic picture see Raven, below.

literature, he had accumulated at least 380 shares or part shares in the course of his career, most of which make no appearance in the Stationers' Register.[104] Among the list of his copies the most remarkable block of titles is the group of sixty-eight books in which he had a one-twelfth share: these had originally been owned by John Bill (*d.* 1630) or his senior partner John Norton (*d.* 1612), and had descended through the hands of no fewer than six successive owners, with further divisions into fractions, before becoming Bentley's property.[105] The smallest share he had was a one-forty-eighth interest in Rider's dictionary, first published in 1589.[106] Bentley's prosperity came as much from his shrewd investment in part shares in long-selling titles as from his ability to pick out new books and authors.

This increase in multiple ownership is probably related to the development of a group of booksellers who combined together to protect their copies in the years 1679 to 1685, when the Printing Act was in abeyance, forming what became known as a 'conger' and in effect acting as wholesalers using smaller tradesmen to retail their books: subsequently congers were formed to minimize the risks of investing in new titles,[107] and became normal trade practice in the eighteenth century. Both the gradual division of profitable copies over time into smaller and smaller fractions and the complex ownership rights within congers, meant that a single entry in the Stationers' Register had become a wholly insufficient means of recording the actual complexities of ownership. (Indeed, the slowness with which congers became an accepted method of financing larger ventures may have been precisely due to the problem of having no dependable and tested method of legally recording those partnerships.) It was the increasing irrelevance of the Stationers' Register to the realities of trade practice, as much as anything else, which led to the Company's decreasing importance and power in the last two decades of the century.[108]

No dependable data exist for a reliable analysis of the economics of the book trade or even of the levels of production by London printers, and what evidence there is is contradictory. In particular, as D. F. McKenzie points out, the apparently near-geometric increase in the yearly number of titles recorded by the two short-title catalogues between 1557 and 1700[109] must seriously misrepresent the actual volume of production, since the numbers of apprentices bound and freed remained remarkably stable, and the productive capacity of

104 Mandelbrote 1997.
105 Mandelbrote 1997, pp. 61–2, nos. 104–67, 175, 374–6.
106 Mandelbrote 1997, no. 374.
107 Hodgson and Blagden 1956, pp. 78–9; Treadwell 1982a; Feather 1988, pp. 68–72; Treadwell, below, pp. 733–4.
108 See Treadwell, below.
109 See appendix 1, table 1, figure A1.

the trade, if measured by the number of presses recorded, shows only a relatively small increase until the years 1679 to 1685.[110] McKenzie's broad conclusion seems inescapable – the loss-rate of titles rapidly increases as the record goes backwards in time, though the extent of that loss remains almost wholly unquantifiable.[111]

There are, however, several counter-indications, beginning with the frequent, if impressionistic, comments by contemporaries amazed or horrified by the increasing flood of printed material. In 1595 Andrew Maunsell published *The first part of the catalogue of English printed bookes*, dedicated to the Stationers' Company, in response to 'dayly the great increase in all kind of Learning in this flourishing Realme of England' in which 'the mysticall Science of Printing, hath been and is, an excellent hand-maide and great furtherer to the same ...'[112] Both population and literacy increased. In 1556 England's population was just over three million: by 1696 it was over five million,[113] an increase of well over a half (62 per cent). Even more significant was the disproportionate increase in London's population from about 120,000 (4 per cent of England's population in 1550) to nearly 500,000, or 10 per cent of England's population, by 1700.[114] This, together with London's swift growth outside the City walls, points to the increasingly metropolitan character of English culture. David Cressy's study of literacy estimates that 5 per cent of women and 15 per cent of men were literate in 1550, figures which had increased to 30 per cent and 40 per cent respectively by 1700,[115] although this, since it is based on the ability to write their own name and people were taught to read before learning to write, seriously underestimates functional literacy in this period.[116] In addition, the population of Wales increased in the same period;[117] in 1687 Ireland had a population of over one and a half million and the American

110 See McKenzie, below: for the annual counts see appendix 2. The known figures are as follows: 1583, printing houses 23, presses 53; 1586, printing houses 25 (Arber, I, p. 246; V, p. lii); 1637, printing houses 24; 1649, printing houses ?40; 1663, printing houses 59; 1668, printing houses 33, presses 82; 1675, printing houses 33; 1685–6, printing houses 55, presses 145 (Treadwell 1987, pp. 143, 145, 146, 148 and 151, 160, 151).

111 An exception is that provided by the Stationers' Stock in the years 1663–1700, where figures for the high loss-rates of staples like Psalms, psalters, primers and ABCs, are available. See Barnard 1999b.

112 Sig. $\pi 3^r$.

113 E. A. Wrigley, R. S. Davies, J. E. Oppen, and R. S. Schofield, *English population history from family reconstitution 1580–1837* (Cambridge, 1997), table A9.1.

114 R. Finlay and B. Shearer, 'Population growth and suburban expansion', *London 1500–1700: the making of the metropolis*, ed. A. L. Beier and R. Finlay (London, 1986), pp. 35–59. V. Harding challenges these findings in 'The population of London, 1500–1700: a review of the published evidence', *London Journal*, 15 (1990), 122–3.

115 Cressy 1980, graph 8.1.

116 For corrective accounts, see Spufford 1981, pp. 100–1, and Thomas 1986.

117 See Jones, below, p. 719.

colonies had over 290,000 inhabitants by 1670.[118] The number of booksellers in the provinces also increased in the seventeenth century.[119] Over the same period, although the evidence is sparse, imports of paper into London increased substantially.[120] In 1560 imports, probably including brown paper, amounted to 26,432 reams, as against 87,931 reams of white paper alone in 1630, and 165,078 reams in 1699.[121] That is, there was a threefold increase by 1630, a figure doubled again by the end of the century, altogether a sixfold increase.[122] Unfortunately, the records of 'white paper' do not distinguish between paper for printing and higher quality writing paper, which make these figures of limited value. But consumption evidently increased. The very substantial growth in the Company's membership between the latter half of the sixteenth century and 1682, and the increasing specialization and variety within the book trade, both in terms of personnel and genre,[123] point in the same direction. So too does the spread in the habit of reading to wider sections of the community and the growth of 'popular' literature.[124] Tellingly, by the end of the period both institutional and personal libraries had substantially increased in number and in size.[125] All these factors point to an increase in the number of books published in London, but it is clear that the evidence of a tenfold rise evident from the extant books (610 London titles in 1556–60 as against 6,524 in 1691–5[126]) very substantially exaggerates that increase. As David McKitterick has said,

> The perfectly correct impression that contemporaries had of an ever-increasing number of new books has to be countered by the fact that the tally of newly printed sheets being put into circulation did not grow at the same pace. Moreover, as new books were added to those already in existence, the impression was further strengthened of increasing numbers.[127]

From the trade's point of view there was an important corollary: its critical dependence on reprinted titles. Between 1668 and 1709 as many as 27 per cent of the books advertised in the *Term Catalogues* were reprints.[128] This figure is even more remarkable since there was no need to advertise the routine

118 L. A. Clarkson, 'The Irish population revisited', *Irish population, economy, and society*, ed. J. M. Goldstrom and L. A. Clarkson (Oxford, 1981), p. 26, which revises earlier estimates downwards; S. E. Morison, *The Oxford history of the American people* (London and New York, 1965), pp. 131–2.

119 See appendix 1, table 9.

120 See Bidwell, below.

121 Coleman 1958, pp. 12–14 and table 1.

122 Bland 1999 (whose figures differ slightly from the source in Coleman 1958) believes that the new demands of Elizabethan bureaucracy were partly responsible for this increase.

123 For specialisation in genres see McKitterick 1992, pp. 4–7. The livery grew from 25–30 to 176 in these years: see Gadd 1999, pp. 23–4, 67–70.

124 Spufford 1981, Watt 1991, Fox 2000: see also Simmons and Hunter below, pp. 506–13 and pp. 531–2.

125 See Leedham-Green and McKitterick, below.

126 See appendix 1, table 1.

127 McKitterick 1997, p. 206.

128 Appendix 1, table 4.

reprinting of almanacs, Psalms, ABCs, primers, school books or Bibles. Profitability for individual booksellers and for the trade at large was reliant, then as now, on a sound backlist.

Together, these factors explain how, despite continuing undercapitalization, it was possible to accumulate substantial wealth through the book trade. The printer and monopolist Richard Tottell (*b.*? 1528*fl.* 1550–93) exploited his law patent, one requiring considerable initial investment in paper, types and skilled workmen, successfully enough to invest in the innovatory *Songes and sonettes*, and enabled his family to make the transition from trade to landowners.[129] A good example of how a shrewd bookseller could make his way in the trade in the early seventeenth century is provided by the career of Cuthbert Burby. The orphan son of a Bedfordshire husbandman, he was active as a publisher only between 1592 and his death in 1608, probably in his early forties: his estate, worth £2,423 8*s*., places him in the top 3 per cent of London freemen whose wealth is known between 1586 and 1614.[130] Burby's success depended on his knowledge of different areas of the trade. He began early to acquire copies or part shares, beginning in 1592: these included literary works, among them works by Shakespeare and Jonson, but his most valuable copies were those of religious works, often of titles previously published by others. Most notable perhaps was his involvement as an assignee in the rights of John Rider's English–Latin dictionary in 1604 in partnership with, among others, the Master and Wardens of the Company.[131] By May 1598 he was sufficiently wealthy to buy his way into the Livery, and only two years later was one of three appointed to act as stock-keeper for the Seres and Day printing privileges. Not surprisingly he invested in the English Stock and had two £100 shares on his death (by rights he should only have had one).[132] But for his early death, Burby would have become a significant figure in the Company's history. Later in the period, George Sawbridge, who was the Company's Treasurer from 1647 to 1679, died a rich man with an estate valued at nearly £11,000 with a further £15,000 owing to him.[133] This had been achieved partly through careful investment in copies but also through using the cover of his official role as Treasurer of the

129 Greening 1997. For the *Songs and sonetes*, see below, pp. 23–4.

130 Johnson 1992, pp. 71–3, citing CLRO, Common Serjeant's Book, no. 1, fols. 255, 403 and R. Grassby, 'The personal wealth of the business community in seventeenth-century England', *EcHR*, 2nd ser., 23 (1970), pp. 220–34 (p. 224).

131 Arber, I, p. 276 (Burby had been assigned the whole copy in 1603, *ibid.*, p. 225): the 1604 consortium did not publish the book until 1606 owing to a clash with the rival dictionary by Thomas Thomas (Jackson 1957, p. 18). See also Johnson 1992, pp. 74–8, citing the list of over forty-four copies transferred by Burby's widow, Elizabeth (Arber, III, pp. 420–1) and *STC*.

132 Johnson 1992, pp. 73–4.

133 Mandelbrote 1995, pp. 74–5. See also the comments on his wealth by Dunton 1818, p. 211.

English Stock to cheat the Company to his own advantage.[134] The example of Richard Bentley's accumulation of an interest in an extraordinarily wide range of titles has already been mentioned, and the long career of Dryden's publisher Jacob Tonson (1655–1736), who retired aged sixty-three to his country house at Barn Elms, was similarly based on the accumulation of copies, many of which were literary, and the most valuable of which was Milton's *Paradise lost*.[135] From Burby onwards it is noticeable that the ownership of copies, or specialization, or a combination of the two, had replaced patents as the source of affluence. And it is significant that Richard Bentley only became a member of the Stationers' Company under pressure in 1684,[136] and that neither he nor Tonson sought high office within the Company. It was by then largely irrelevant to a publisher's entrepreneurial success.

One highly profitable area of the trade was the marketing, by the seventeenth century on a very large scale, of ballads, chapbooks, and 'little books' of popular piety, which reached a nationwide readership through pedlars, fairs and markets.[137] The publishing of ballads in the last part of the sixteenth century had been undertaken by many members of the trade, but it became increasingly specialized and was taken over by five Partners in 1624, including Thomas Pavier and John Wright I.[138] These texts, like almanacs, reached a large market and had an important influence on popular culture, though the exact nature of their impact on the nation's religious awareness remains a matter of debate.[139] Nevertheless, these classes of books, frequently making use of woodcuts, influenced an increasingly wide range of the population, ensuring the presence of print in the countryside and alehouses.[140]

Other kinds of recreational literature in the vernacular were in circulation throughout these years. The 1550s and 1560s saw a continuing demand for the medieval romances, many in translation, a vogue which Caxton and de Worde[141] had initiated in the previous century. The fifty-five or so books owned by the Coventry mason, Captain Cox, in 1573 are dominated by this kind of text, all London produced, and he also had over a hundred 'auncient' ballads and songs in manuscript.[142] Frances Wolfreston (1607–77), wife of a Midlands country squire, owned a collection also dominated by books in English including much in the way of literature (48 per cent), and only 8 per cent were in

134 Blagden 1960, pp. 204–5 and McKitterick 1992, pp. 344–5. 135 Lynch 1971, p. 126.
136 Mandelbrote 1997, p. 57. 137 See Spufford 1981 and Watt 1991.
138 See Watt 1991, pp. 74–127. See also Blagden 1954.
139 See Collinson, Hunt and Walsh, below, pp. 33–5, and Watt 1991.
140 Watt 1991, pp. 163–5, 194–6, 219–20.
141 For the importance of de Worde's role, see Meale 1992.
142 Langham 1983, pp. 53–4, 131–43.

Latin or French.[143] The young Norfolk gentleman, John Buxton (1608–60), left a record of his domestic expenditure between 1627 and 1631. His book buying was habitual, and books 'for my library' are a consistent, if smallish, part of his outgoings. David McKitterick notes that his choice of books 'is remarkable for being wholly English':[144] there are literary works, including fifty plays, but (despite his avocation) few law books, while French and Latin works are represented by translations, mostly recent.[145] Although in the late 1630s he and his wife were buying more theological or devotional works,[146] his earlier buying habits set him apart from the serious buying of legal works which characterizes the collecting a few years earlier of Simonds D'Ewes, like Buxton a student at the Inns of Court.[147]

Clearly related to this is the gradual establishment of a canon of English literature in these years,[148] together with the consequent recognition of the writer's authority,[149] paralleled by the development of non-canonical vernacular literatures.[150] But it is important to note that apart from Chaucer, first published by Caxton, and the publication by individual booksellers of texts like Spenser's *Faerie queene*, Daniel's *Works* and the 'classic' folios of Jonson's works and Shakespeare's plays (1616 and 1623 respectively),[151] the most deliberate canon formation of contemporary literature was that undertaken in the 1650s by the Royalist publisher, Humphrey Moseley.[152] (His project was continued after the Restoration by Henry Herringman and Jacob Tonson[153] – the latter being responsible for giving Milton's *Paradise lost* its classic status in 1688.[154]) The 1640s and 1650s were a period not just of crisis but of innovation.[155] The employment of the press for propaganda on both sides, the invention of the periodical press,[156] the beginning of Parliamentary printing,[157] Peter Stent's popular prints, John Playford's new 'song book form' for music publishing, and the use of subscription to support the publication of large scholarly ventures like Dugdale's antiquarian researches[158] or Brian Walton's Polyglot Bible,[159] all represent new developments. So too the proselytizing activities of Hartlib circle (in both manuscript and print),[160] the popularization and demystification of the medical profession by Nicholas Culpeper and his bookseller, Peter

143 Morgan 1989, p. 201. 144 McKitterick 1997, p. 207.
145 *Ibid.*, pp. 206–7. 146 *Ibid.*, pp. 209–13.
147 Watson 1966, pp. 20–1 and 228–37. McKitterick 1997, pp. 206–7n further cites the libraries of William Smith, William Freke and Justinian Pagitt, all trained at the Inns of Court.
148 See Pitcher, Raymond and Hammond, below. 149 Helgerson 1983, Kewes 1998, Johns 1998.
150 See Smith, below. 151 See Pitcher, below. 152 Kewes 1995 and Reed 1927–30.
153 See Hammond, below. 154 See Raymond, below.
155 For an outline of London publishing in these years, see Barnard 2001.
156 See Nelson and Seccombe, below and Raymond 1996b. 157 Lambert 1981 and 1984.
158 See Parry, below. 159 See Parry, below, pp. 185–6. 160 See Greengrass and Peters, below.

Cole,[161] the substantial number of biblical commentaries published by future non-conformist divines, and the works published by Quakers[162] and by other anti-establishment groups and writers,[163] similarly point to the years of the Civil War and Interregnum as a time at which new publishing openings were being explored, new middling audiences being created, and in which public opinion was increasingly formed through the press. Some of these innovations, such as newspapers and Parliamentary printing, were temporarily checked by the Restoration. Some, like the serial publication of literary texts and subscription publication, were to be later taken up as trade practices (indeed, subscription publication was imitated, first in Holland and then in Germany and France.)[164] Others, such as Playford's music business, Stent's trade in cheap prints, or the market for cheap medical works in the vernacular, were permanent successes.

The example of two books demonstrates some of the changes which took place in the trade during the years covered by this volume. In 1557 Richard Tottell published the most important early anthology of near-contemporary and contemporary English poetry, *Songes and sonettes*. In 1694 Dryden published his *Annual miscellany*. The difference between the two books is instructive in several respects. Only Henry Howard, Earl of Surrey, who had died ten years earlier, is mentioned on Tottell's title page though his unsigned 'The Printer to the Reader' further identifies Sir Thomas Wyatt. The prominence accorded to the bookseller has led to the book being known as 'Tottell's miscellany' and it is quite clear that this volume was a publisher's venture (and was highly successful, going into three editions in its first year and reaching its tenth and final sixteenth-century edition by 1587). The 'stigma of print'[165] explains why many of the aristocratic authors remained anonymous and why Tottell names only the dead: but its success demonstrated the viability of publishing near-contemporary poetry in English. At the same time, the fact that Tottell can only have found his texts, one way or another, in manuscript demonstrates the vitality of an active pre-existent aristocratic (and Court-centred) circuit of writers and readers of poetry.[166] Tottell's venture proved the existence of a wider audience who could afford to buy (or who could borrow) his black-letter small quarto volume of 212 unnumbered pages. Only in the second edition are the leaves given folio numbers, with a 'Table' of first lines added at the end locating the individual poems.

161 Sanderson 1999. 162 See Greengrass and Peters, below, pp. 70–5. 163 See Smith, below.
164 Van Rooden and Wesselius 1986, Kirsop 1984, pp. 31–2, and Martin and Chartier 1984, pp. 271–2.
165 See Saunders 1951.
166 See Love, below, p. 113, on the way Tottell's text is sited between manuscript and print culture.

Dryden's anthology of 1694 is very different. Although none of the names of the 'Eminent Hands' is mentioned on the title page, which gives the publisher's name as Jacob Tonson along with his address, there is a three-and-a-half page list of contents naming the large majority of authors and giving page references for the individual poems and translations. Tonson's late-seventeenth-century octavo is able to utilize a type area more than 10 per cent larger than the sixteenth-century quarto, a result of the increasing size of the sheet over the years, and still have very similar proportions.[167] Yet rather than using this extra typographical space to save money by fitting in extra text, the normal procedure in most other genres such as play quartos[168] or periodicals, the opposite obtained in this case. Tonson's page contained only eighteen leaded lines and was set in English, whereas Tottell used long primer set solid giving forty-two lines to the page. In consequence, although Tottell's volume had a third fewer pages than Tonson's miscellany,[169] it contained over a quarter more lines of verse than the later, and larger, octavo.

Typographically then, there has been a switch from black letter to roman, and where Tottell's priority was to cram in as much text as possible, the Dryden–Tonson volume is strikingly uneconomic in its use of white space. For Tonson's contributors and purchasers, expense mattered less than appearance, and the pagination, list of contents and layout exploit typographical elements to make the *Annual miscellany* of 1694 an object valued as much for its aesthetic as its literary properties. This impression is heightened by the addition of an engraved title page. The morphological changes in the structure and appearance of these two anthologies are a direct reflection of the increasing specialization over the period. Whereas Tottell's was a speculative venture aimed at an as yet undefined audience, Dryden's and Tonson's octavo was produced for a well-established 'polite' reading public.

If these two works show a move from a style of book production still closely tied to that of the manuscript text to one which is decisively typographic, the relationship between the bookseller and the author has changed even more radically. Where Tottell as printer–bookseller was bringing texts, previously kept hidden in manuscript by the 'vngentle horders vp of such treasure',[170] before the public for the first time, Tonson was an entrepreneurial bookseller who steadily built up a list containing the major English poets and dramatists.

167 Pollard 1941. As the unique copy of the *Songes and sonettes* (Bodley Arch. G. f. 12(1)) is heavily cropped, the dimensions of the two type areas (13.0 x 8.5 cm as compared to 14.0 x 8.9 cm) are a more dependable comparator than page size.

168 Compare the 1597 edition of *Richard III* with that of 1700.

169 Tottell's volume has 214 pages as against the 327 pages for Dryden's miscellany.

170 *Songes and sonettes* (1557), sig. A1^{v}.

His collaboration with Dryden in the creation of this miscellany clearly signals the social recognition of the writer's authority. By the 1690s Dryden and Tonson, their contributors and the reading public, were working within a well-established literary market, one in which a young future Whig politician like Joseph Addison was only too pleased to have his poetry appear alongside that of Dryden, despite the older poet's Jacobitism.

By 1695 book buying had long been a habit among the middle and professional classes, as the changing binding fashions,[171] and the buying of books as luxury items, indicate. At the same time, many texts continued to be circulated in manuscript form, ranging from separates to the elaborate collections of political and bawdy verse produced by scriptoria.[172] Printed works for entertainment and for educational, religious, and self-help purposes reached well beyond that market; and printed news and ballads fed into the culture of coffee-houses and clubs, helping create public opinion as a recognizable force.

The travel publications of Richard Blome and John Ogilby, beginning in the 1670s,[173] demonstrate with particular clarity how the trade, from being in 1557 an off-shore under-capitalized monopoly, largely dependent on the Continent for texts through translation or importation and for new skills like engraving,[174] had moved towards an entrepreneurial and cultural independence, even though it remained one still insecurely based financially. The publication of travel literature in the last years of the century shows the shift from a peripheral, if creative, position of cultural dependency to the beginnings of a self-sustaining industry, one whose future development was intimately linked to the imperial project of which travel literature was an integral part. The book trade had become increasingly specialized and diverse, and entrepreneurial publishing by booksellers had relegated printers to the role of manufacturers. The patterns which can be discerned in the 1680s and 1690s – booksellers combining to invest in copies, subscription and part publication, the growing market in the colonies, the development of better defined (and sometimes overlapping) reading publics, the weakened authority of the Stationers' Company, the increasing anxieties over copyright and the beginnings of the provincial trade's involvement in London publishing ventures, all backed up by a burgeoning consumer economy and the consolidation of British trade regulation in the latter part of the seventeenth century (in particular, the Navigation Acts of 1651 and 1660)[175] – created the commercial and structural conditions for the development of the eighteenth-century book trade in London, the provinces and abroad.

171 See Foot, below. 172 Love, below, pp. 104ff. 173 Brennan, below, pp. 246–7.
174 See Hind 1952–64. 175 Raven, below, pp. 581–2 and 2000, pp. 186–7.

RELIGION
AND
POLITICS

1

Religious publishing in England 1557–1640

PATRICK COLLINSON, ARNOLD HUNT
and ALEXANDRA WALSHAM

The nature of religious books and the religious use of print

'What multitude of Bookes full of sinne and abominations have now filled the world!' complained the puritan divine Edward Dering in 1572, 'witlesse devises', 'baudie songes', 'unchast Fables'. Such conventional complaints about the prevalence of 'profane' and 'ungodly' literature would be routine for decades to come.[1] This may help us to define 'religious publishing' by means of exclusion. But the problem of inclusion remains. For the modern world, the term 'religious' marks off a more or less discrete area of life, but this is anachronistic for the period under review, in which the commodity which we might want to distinguish as 'religion' permeated much, if not all, of what is now secularized. This is a health warning to be attached to otherwise useful statistical analyses of religious publishing in the period covered by the *Short-Title Catalogue*, or in the Stationers' Register. 'Religious books', in conventional terms, are found to have been the single most important component of the publishing trade, comprising around half the total output of the industry, and outweighing political, scientific, practical and fictional works:[2] indeed, fiction had yet to establish its respectable credentials, often disguising itself as edification, or morality.[3]

Or so attention to titles, and to professed authorial intents, might suggest. But do we exclude from our tally of 'religious' titles almanacs, medical treatises, cookery books, 'news', all saturated with pious vocabulary? Nor can we solve our problem of demarcation by examining the supposed motives of publishers, as if we can identify 'religious' propagandists, altruistic precursors of the Society for Promoting Christian Knowledge. Religion was amongst other

1 'Edward Dering' (but thought to have been the work of John More), *A briefe and necessarie catachisme of instruction*, in *Maister Derings workes* (London, 1590), sig. A1^{v}.

2 See Appendix 1, table 4. See also Bland 1999, pp. 457–9.

3 Nelson 1973; Hunter 1997.

things a stock in trade, and a reliable staple. Just what was it that motivated the 'puritan' pamphleteer, Philip Stubbes?[4] Nor were clerical authors necessarily above commercial considerations. When the Derby curate Richard Kilby sent to the press a sensational autobiographical account of the lie which he claimed to have been living as a minister, *The burthen of a loaden conscience* (1608), it was a publishing sensation, running into twelve editions. This may for all we know have been the intended outcome. Kilby's motives puzzled his contemporaries.[5]

So far we have risked another anachronistic error, understanding 'publication' to mean the publication of religious 'books'. But in the context of a Reformation which saw the printing press as a mere acolyte to an army of well-trained pastors and preachers, to interpret 'religious publishing' in the narrow and specialized sense familiar to the twentieth century may be distorting and limiting. Apart from oral communication, there was a mass of both polemical and devotional material which, if 'published', was published scribally, surviving only in manuscript. Some of the most active preachers of the age never appeared in print, or never in their lifetimes. Archbishop Tobie Matthew's preaching diary (preserved in York Minster in an eighteenth-century copy), records a total of 1,992 sermons, none of which was published.[6] The most celebrated preacher of Caroline London, Richard Holdsworth, published only one sermon, at the express command of Charles I.[7] So we need to ask what the circumstances were in which some religious communicators were, in our sense, published, even becoming bestselling authors.[8] For example, Robert Cleaver and John Dod were preaching ministers in Oxfordshire who in the early years of James I were suspended from preaching for their non-conformity. It was evidently only in those circumstances that they published their very popular expositions of the Book of Proverbs, and of the Ten Commandments (a book in its nineteenth edition by 1639), overcoming an inhibition about appearing in print to which their colleague, Robert Harris, author of some forty items in the *Short-Title Catalogue*, frankly confessed, writing in the preface to his first attributed work in print that those who knew him would find it strange to

4 Walsham 1998, pp. 177–206.

5 P. Lake, 'Richard Kilby: a study in personal and professional failure', *The Ministry: clerical and lay*, Studies in Church History, no. 26, ed. W. J. Sheils and D. Wood (Oxford, 1989), pp. 221–35; J. H. Marsden, *College life in the time of James the First as illustrated by an unpublished diary of Sir Symonds D'Ewes* (London, 1851), p. 70.

6 Collinson 1982, p. 48. 7 *DNB*, art. Holdsworth.

8 Bestselling religious authors included Bishop Lewis Bayly (for *The practise of pietie*), Arthur Dent (for *The plaine mans path-way to heaven*), Richard Greenham, William Perkins, John Preston and Richard Rogers. Greenham, Perkins and Preston were all 'commodities', actively marketed after their deaths. Preston, who died in 1628, was the author of seventy-four items listed in the *STC*, all published between 1629 and 1640.

see him in the press, 'who have in others disliked this ouer-printing, and for my selfe alwaies affected (it may be too much) priuacie and retirednesse'.[9] This invites us to consider how far Dod and Cleaver were communicating with the world at large, how far with their own flocks, to whom they were no longer allowed to preach.

So the assumed impersonality of 'publication' may be another anachronism. Books were often targeted to a known audience, rather than broadcast to strangers. An extreme example of targeting is provided by the little books and pamphlets with which tiny groups of separatist Puritans, in voluntary exile in the Netherlands, even individual separatists, raked over their differences in the early years of the seventeenth century.[10] George Johnson's *A discourse of some trouble and excommunications in the banished English Church at Amsterdam* (Amsterdam, 1603), a highly personalized attack on the pastor and other officers of the congregation launched by the pastor's brother, was a very substantial book . One can only speculate about the motives for carrying on quarrels of this kind in the medium of print rather than in handwritten letters or face-to-face encounters, and also wonder how such publications were financed.[11]

What do we mean by a religious 'book'? Our definition must be sufficiently flexible to accommodate folios and fragmentary scraps, bound hardback volumes and fragile hybrid media, such as ballads, woodcut pictures, and engravings,[12] publications costing a few pence and other publications priced at well over a pound, at a time when five or six pounds was an annual income for much of the population. This brings us to aspects of our subject which transcend the study of religious books as inert objects, taking us into the sociology of religious readership. For religious propagandists, this was the practical problem of how to impart religious knowledge to 'simple, rude, and ignorant people, who cannot reade themselves': or, we might add, afford books. Part of the answer was that such people should 'lend their ears to such as can read good bookes'.[13] This was too important a matter to be left to chance. For untold thousands,

9 For Dod and Cleaver, see *STC* 6954–6979, for Harris, *STC* 12816–12856, and especially Harris's *Absaloms funerall* (1st edn, London, 1610, 2nd edn cited). We owe these suggestions and references to Jason Yiannikkou.

10 Most of these titles are covered in ch. 2, 'Schisms among separatists', in Milward 1978. Generically different were the English translations of the writings of the Familist prophet Hendrik Niclaes ('HN'), printed in Cologne in 1574–5 (*STC* 18548.5–18564.5), which were targeted rather than broadcast, but by a process of itinerant colporteurage. See C. Marsh, *The family of love in English society*, 1550–1630 (Cambridge, 1994).

11 Michael E. Moody, 'A critical edition of George Johnson's *A discourse of some troubles and excommunications in the banished English Church at Amsterdam* 1603', unpub. PhD thesis, Claremont Graduate School 1979. These publications were most probably financed from the profits of Bible production for the (illegal) English market.

12 See *STC*, I, pp. xxi–xxix; *OED*, sv 'book'.

13 William Tye, *A matter of moment, or, a case of waight* (London, 1608), sig. C4^{r}.

their chief, even only, exposure to religious literature would have been via the catechism class, for which, in addition to the more or less official Catechism of the established Church, many hundreds of unofficial catechisms were devised by enterprising authors.[14]

One such private initiative was the little book called *Short questions and answers*, which had achieved at least thirty editions by the 1630s, sometimes attributed to Robert Openshaw but in fact the work of Eusebius Pagit, a Northamptonshire minister who, significantly, wrote it when suspended from preaching and employed by a private family, the Ishams. In a preface reprinted over a period of more than fifty years, Pagit claimed that his catechising method had worked. In a four-month course of indoctrination, his 'principles and aunsweares' had been learned by 'gentlemen, yeomen, horsekeepers, shepheardes, carters, milkemaides, kitchenboyes and al in that household', or almost all.[15]

While such anecdotal evidence cannot prove the general success of catechising as evangelism, it should make us cautious about accepting the extreme view of one leading historian of the Reformation that the Protestantism purveyed from the pulpit was so unappealing in both content and presentation that the English people could not be converted to it.[16] It also calls in question what until recently has been almost a consensual assumption among social historians: that godly Protestantism divided local communities, attracting support from the gentlemen and yeomen who ruled the local roost but alienating their poorer neighbours, serving to polarize society between the church and the alehouse, the refuge of the poor and resistant to a culture of Bibles and other godly books, even acting as a mechanism for social control.[17]

This sharp dichotomy is an overstatement. The earliest English reformers, with their Bibles and religious debates, were at home in inns, taverns and other places of public resort and communal sociability. They also utilized traditional modes of communication, the stage, iconography and song. The first generation of Elizabethan Protestants continued in this tradition, exploiting oral, visual and theatrical media, which were themselves undergoing a slow transformation under the influence of print. The 1560s saw the publication, and presumably

14 Green 1986, Green 1996. 15 Collinson 1982, pp. 233–4.

16 C. Haigh, 'The Church of England, the Catholics and the people', in C. Haigh, ed., *The reign of Elizabeth I* (Basingstoke, 1984), pp. 195–219, and especially pp. 212–14. This rather extreme view is qualified in C. Haigh, *English Reformations: religion, society and politics under the Tudors* (Oxford, 1993).

17 K. Wrightson, *English society 1580–1680* (London, 1982), ch. 7; K. Wrightson and D. Levine, *Poverty and piety in an English village: Terling 1525–1700* (2nd edn, Oxford, 1995), esp. ch. 6; P. Clark, *The English alehouse: a social history 1200–1830* (London, 1983). For an objection to the equation of Puritanism with 'social control', see M. Spufford, 'Puritanism and social control?', in A. Fletcher and J. Stevenson, eds., *Order and disorder in early modern England* (Cambridge, 1985), pp. 41–57.

performance, of Protestant interludes and moralities, many of them, like the clergyman Lewis Wager's *The life and repentaunce of Marie Magdalene*, of Edwardian origin, plays which freely mingled 'mirth' (bawdy humour) with evangelical doctrine. Hiring the services of ballad-mongers and minstrels, Protestant publicists also hijacked popular lyrics and melodies, publishing hundreds of moralizing parodies of the musical hits of the day in the form of black-letter broadsides: *Row well ye mariners* engendered several Protestant offspring, as did the only one of these ditties still alive and well today, *Greensleeves*, which was 'moralized to the Scriptures' in more than one parodic version. Pictorial propaganda also played to the gallery: graphic satirical prints which adopted the boldly anti-Papal motifs of early sixteenth-century Lutheran cartoons. And we should not ignore the emotive, action-packed woodcuts which adorned successive editions of Foxe's 'Book of martyrs' (see below), which also seem to have been sold as separates (penny plain, twopence coloured) to be stuck on the wall.

Yet in or around 1580 mainstream Protestant ministers performed an abrupt about-face. They began to turn their backs on drinking houses and to spurn the genres they had earlier appropriated so creatively. In repudiating these mimetic cultural vehicles as inherently blasphemous, they were effecting a profound ideological shift from iconoclasm (denunciation of false images) to what has been called 'iconophobia', the rejection of all images whatsoever, especially if employed for a moral or religious purpose. This can be understood as in part a generational change, as Protestants entered their conservative middle age, shedding the cheap and flashy ballad and broadsheet for the more decorous and prolix book. Alternatively, it may be described in terms of 'the rise of Puritanism', a more profound internalization of Protestant values. And, more broadly, historians of discursive rhetoric like Father Walter Ong have described the transformative superimposition of a religion of the Word, literally words on the printed page, on minds and imaginations.[18]

The main outlines of this development are incontestable. But more recent work has made it clear that the mid-Elizabethan moral and cultural watershed was neither decisive nor complete. The alehouse remained a milieu in which sacred and secular could comfortably co-exist, decorated with woodcuts of Old Testament characters and painted cloths bearing improving texts like 'Fear God' as well as paper pictures of royalty and nobility and amorous ditties.[19]

18 Collinson 1988, ch. 4, 'Protestant culture and the cultural revolution'; Collinson 1986. See W. J. Ong, *Ramus: method and the decay of dialogue* (Cambridge, MA., 1958), and W. J. Ong, *Interfaces of the word: studies in the evolution of consciousness and culture* (Ithaca, 1977). See also King 1982, Watt 1991, ch. 2. On Lutheran broadsheets, see R.W. Scribner, *For the sake of simple folk: popular propaganda for the German Reformation* (Cambridge, 1981).

19 Watt 1991, ch. 5, esp. pp. 196, 216; and p. 326.

While a Suffolk preacher in 1595 could roundly condemn the idea of printing and singing the Psalms in the guise of popular ballads, other clergymen were still, in effect, asking why the Devil should have all the best tunes, several decades later. In 1631 William Slayter published a setting of the Psalms which employed solemn but well-known melodies such as 'Rogero' and 'Fortune my Foe' (a favourite at public executions). Slayter was reprimanded in the Court of High Commission, but several of his tunes had been used in godly ballads entered in the Stationers' Register in 1624. The Devonshire minister, John Downe, who died in the same year, 1631, re-worked Shakespeare's 'Sigh no more, ladies' to teach lessons about Christ's consolation of the despairing sinner: 'Sigh no more soule, oh sigh no more.'[20] Early Stuart engravers and artists likewise went on producing pictures quite acceptable to Protestant iconophobes: 'godly tables for good householders' to hang above their mantelpieces, and emblematic 'monuments', celebrating the nation's providential deliverances from popish tyranny in 1588 and 1605, the defeat of the Armada and the discovery of the Gunpowder Plot.[21]

Popular and cheap literary genres continued to serve pious and polemical ends, well into the seventeenth century. One product of the London presses which lent itself to a kind of literary piracy was the 'three-halfpenny' pamphlet, reporting 'strange, true and wonderful news' of monstrous births, heavenly apparitions, appalling murders and other portents. Entirely typical is a little tract describing the appearance of the Devil during a devastating storm at Hay on Wye in 1585. According to its anonymous author, this terrifying spectacle was a providential punishment for sin.[22] Rival presses competed for the right to cover particularly dramatic events, and some printers cheated by updating old favourites and re-issuing them with a new title but otherwise almost unaltered. No one was more unscrupulous in this respect than John Trundle, whose trademark was 'Read and Tremble'. The hack writers responsible for these pamphlets conventionally assumed the persona of a thundering Protestant preacher, but sometimes what the titillating woodcut on the cover disguised was an actual Puritan diatribe or sermon.[23]

20 Nicholas Bownde, *The doctrine of the sabbath* (London, 1595), p. 241; William Slayter, *Psalmes, or songs of Sion* (London, 1631); *Reports of cases in the Courts of Star Chamber and High Commission*, ed. S. R. Gardiner (Camden Society, London, 1886), p. 186; John Downe, *A treatise of the true nature and definition of iustifying faith* (Oxford, 1635), p. 396.

21 Watt 1991, chs. 4 and 6; Walsham 1999, ch. 5; A. Walsham, 'Impolitic pictures: providence, history and the iconography of protestant nationhood in early Stuart England', in *The Church retrospective*, Studies in Church history, no. 33 ed. R. N. Swanson, (Oxford, 1997), pp. 307–28.

22 *A most rare and true report, of such great tempests, straunge sightes, and wonderfull accidents, which happened by the providence of God, in Herefordshire, at a place called Hay* (London, 1585).

23 Walsham 1999, pp. 43–7, 50, 96. See also Johnson 1986.

The murder pamphlet was one genre which was particularly open to this kind of appropriation. Protestant divines like Henry Goodcole, the ordinary of Newgate Prison, and Thomas Cooper, chaplain to the Fleet, neatly grafted predestinarian precepts on to narrative structures more commonly associated with Anthony Munday and other Grub Street hacks. Tales of sudden death equally lent themselves to this kind of treatment, for these were not what we should call accidents but acts of God. The story of a sleeping carpenter incinerated by a flash of lightning was converted by a Hampshire preacher into a homily on the text, 'Unless ye repent ye shall likewise perish.'[24] In the 1630s, the Shrewsbury cleric Peter Studley, who prided himself on his anti-Puritan credentials, gained mileage out of a gruesome axe murder committed by Enoch ap Evan, a godly halfwit.[25] Come the Civil War, neither Royalists nor Parliamentarians had any scruples about exploiting prodigy literature and astrological almanacs as vehicles for crude religio-political propaganda.[26]

If the production of 'godly ballads' declined with the passing of the Elizabethan age, part of the reason may have been that forward-looking clergymen were switching from verse to prose, exchanging the folio broadside for the short quarto or octavo pamphlet. The trend in the publishing industry was towards cheap formats intended for reading rather than hearing or seeing, and this eventually introduced the penny-priced religious chapbook, the speciality of 'marketplace theologians' like the Wiltshire preacher John Andrews, who forged a new and fruitful alliance between zeal and profit. Well adapted to the pedlar's pack, these little devotional tracts helped to satisfy the spiritual thirst of country consumers, and the preponderance of religious titles in the output of the chapbook publishers suggests that they sold well. But this was not much before our watershed of 1640. Earlier in the century, the classics of practical divinity (see below), such as Arthur Dent's *Plain mans path-way to heaven* and Richard Sibbes's *Bruised reed*, were packaged in octavo and duodecimo formats, but they would still have cost about a shilling. When the penny godlies arrived, they were strong on the suddenness of death, the terrors of judgement and hellfire, the urgent need for repentance. Not much in evidence was the quest for personal assurance of salvation, the phenomenon which has been called 'experimental Calvinism'.[27]

24 Lake 1994; John Hilliard, *Fire from heaven. Burning the body of one John Hitchell of Holne-hurst* (London, 1613).

25 P. Lake, 'Puritanism, Arminianism and a Shropshire axe-murder', *Midland History*, 15 (1990), 37–64.

26 B. Capp, 'Popular culture and the English Civil War', *History of European Ideas*, 10 (1989), 31–41; H. Rusche, 'Prophecies and propaganda, 1641 to 1651', *EHR*, 84 (1969), 727–70; C. Durston, 'Signs and wonders and the English Civil War', *History Today*, 37 (1987), 22–8; Friedman 1993.

27 Watt 1991, pp. 306–15, and chs. 7–8 *passim*. See also Watt 1995, E. Duffy, 'The godly and the multitude in Stuart England', *The Seventeenth Century*, 1 (1986), 31–55; Spufford 1981, ch. 8.

Indoctrination, public and private: polemic and controversy

A large part of the story of indoctrination concerns English Bibles, a topic receiving separate treatment elsewhere in this volume. Famously, the author of the nineteenth-century *History of the English people*, J. R. Green, pronounced that in the lifetime of Shakespeare the English became the people of a book (an expression originally coined by the Prophet Mohammed to characterize Jews and Christians), and that that book was the Bible.[28] There is no better case study of the interaction of public and private interest, commerce and edification, than the English Bible. The translators, from Tyndale and Coverdale in the 1520s and 30s to the Protestant exiles who produced the Geneva Bible (1560), the most popular version until well into the seventeenth century, were private men but, beginning with Henry VIII's Great Bible of 1536, the public interest in Bible promulgation was paramount.[29]

A major part of religious publication was by authority, and nowadays would bear the imprint of Her Majesty's Stationery Office. This included successive editions of the Book of Common Prayer, produced in bulk by the royal printers, liturgies designed for one-off occasions (such as the fast days occasioned by outbreaks of plague), the Thirty-Nine Articles of Religion, and articles and injunctions generated by the process of ecclesiastical visitation. These were issued by the Crown in connection with royal visitations of the Church at large, in the name of archbishops, bishops and archdeacons in respect of provincial, diocesan and archidiaconal visitations, employing an authority which equally derived from the Crown as Supreme Governor of the Church.[30]

The *Actes and monuments* of John Foxe, known in its own day and ever since as Foxe's 'Book of martyrs', an immense and audaciously revisionist history of the Christian Church which came to a climax with the Marian persecution of English Protestants, was no less influential than the Bible and the Prayer Book in constructing a new, Protestant identity for the English people as an elect nation, if not the elect nation, in God's esteem and design.[31] In a sense

28 J. R. Green, *Short history of the English people* (London, 1878), p. 447.

29 Pollard 1911; A.G. Dickens, *The English Reformation* (2nd edn, London, 1989), pp. 151–60; D. Daniell, *William Tyndale: a biography* (New Haven and London, 1994); G. Hammond, *The making of the English Bible* (Manchester, 1992).

30 These categories are covered in *STC* as Liturgies, Church of England, including 'State Services', 'Gowrie Conspiracy', and 'Special Forms of Prayer on Various Occasions', including such items as *The order of prayer... to auert Gods wrath from vs, threatned by the late terrible earthquake* (1580) and *A thanksgiving for the safe delivery of the queene, and happy birth of the young prince* (1630) (*STC* 16279–16559); and 'England, Church Of' (*STC* 1026–10382).

31 Haller 1964; Loades 1997.

those people wrote themselves into the book which they read, for Foxe was dependent upon the stories and other information with which he was liberally supplied by his correspondents and which his book ingested, as it grew and changed its shape through the successive editions of 1563, 1570, 1576 and 1583.[32] After Foxe's death, there were further extensions to the text of the 'Book of martyrs' in 1610 and 1632, as well as abridgements.[33] This was largely a matter of private enterprise (the enterprise of Foxe's printer John Day first and foremost), although the Elizabethan government lent its political (but not financial) support to the venture, requiring copies to be set up in cathedral churches and in some of the principal offices of Court.[34] The publication history of the Bible and Foxe suggests the futility, or at least artificiality, of debates about whether the English Reformation was inspired 'from above' or 'from below'.[35]

Paradoxically, the 'Book of martyrs' was also, in a sense, written by its Catholic critics, for whom it was a book of lies, 'so many lines, so many lies'.[36] For the revised editions which Foxe prepared in his lifetime were partly a response to this criticism, and took it into account.[37] Religious controversy was the generator of some of the largest books to have come off the Elizabethan and Jacobean presses, controversy between Catholics and Protestants, controversy among the Protestants themselves, with non-conformist, Puritan critics of the Elizabethan religious settlement pitted against its conformist defenders, the bishops and their offsiders.

The story begins with the so-called 'Great Controversy' conducted between Bishop Jewel, an all but official spokesman for the Elizabethan Church of England, and some of the English Catholics, now regrouping themselves in Continental exile; mainly a debate between two fellow Devonians and Oxford contemporaries, John Jewel versus Thomas Harding, who was the

32 The Arts and Humanities Research Board of the British Academy is currently funding a collated, critical, electronic edition of these four massive texts, drawing attention to the extent and complexity of the changes made in successive editions, and the disabling limitations of the nineteenth-century editions of *Actes and monuments*.

33 Nussbaum 1997 and 1998. See also D. Nussbaum, 'Reviling the saints or reforming the calendar?', in Wabuda and Litzenberger 1998, pp. 113–36.

34 There is no basis for the oft-repeated statement that Foxe was set up, by order, in all parish churches. Many copies were acquired by parishes, some of them still surviving, but normally they originated as gifts, sometimes by Catholics, under duress.

35 C. Haigh, 'The recent historiography of the English Reformation', in Haigh 1987, pp. 19–33; P. Collinson, 'England', in *The Reformation in national context*, ed. R. Scribner, R. Porter and M. Teich (Cambridge, 1994), pp. 80–94; P. Collinson, 'The English Reformation, 1945–1995', in *Companion to historiography*, ed. M. Bentley (London and New York, 1997), pp. 336–60.

36 Quoted, Collinson 1994, p. 152.

37 Important work by Dr Thomas Freeman on Foxe's considerable indebtedness to his Catholic critics is forthcoming.

most redoubtable controversialist out of seven Catholic alumni of Winchester and New College who reassembled in Louvain in the early years of Elizabeth.[38]

The first shot was fired by Jewel, recently made Bishop of Salisbury, in a sermon preached at Paul's Cross in London on 26 November 1559 and subsequently repeated at Court. In Reformation and Counter-Reformation polemics, antiquity was the first and last court of appeal, Catholics demanding of Protestants, 'where was your church before Luther?' On this occasion, Jewel stole a march on the opposition, challenging the other side to prove, on the authority of Scripture or of the primitive Church, that any of the following four articles of Catholic belief and practice had been known in the first six Christian centuries: communion in one kind, common prayer in a tongue not understood by the people, the institution of the Papacy, and the doctrine of transubstantiation. If anyone could prove the antiquity of any of these things, Jewel undertook to 'geue ouer and subscribe vnto hym'.[39] After some preliminary skirmishes, Jewel had his response in Harding's *Answere to Maister Iuelles chalenge* (Antwerp, 1564), to which Jewel replied in 1565. But by this time, Jewel had published a semi-official and anonymous *Apologia ecclesiae Anglicanae* (1562), ably translated by Francis Bacon's mother as *An apologie or answere in defence of the Churche of England* (1564). This initiated a parallel controversy with Harding, who in 1565 published *A confutation of a booke intituled An apologie of the Church of England*, to which Jewel duly responded in a massive *Defence of the apologie* (1567, and enlarged in 1570). These volumes grew in bulk through the polemical convention of printing, slab by slab, the text undergoing confutation. Schoolroom syllogisms were larded with vulgar abuse. Harding denounced Jewel's 'impudencie in lying', 'his continuall scoffing', 'his immoderate bragging'. Jewel's icy urbanity was no less wounding. 'If ye shall happen to write hereafter, send us fewer words and more learning.'[40]

A. C. Southern counts sixty-four titles published in the course of this controversy.[41] And these were only the opening rounds, with polemical works on both sides growing in bulk and sophistication towards the end of the sixteenth century and beyond, as John Rainoldes of Oxford and William Whitaker of Cambridge entered the lists against such opponents as Cardinal Bellarmine.

38 Southern 1950 provides a survey of the 'Great Controversy'. See also Milward 1977, ch. 1, 'Anglican challenge'.

39 Southern 1950, p. 60.

40 *Ibid.*, p. 73; *Works of John Jewel, Bishop of Salisbury*, ed. J. Ayre, Parker Society, IV (Cambridge, 1850), p. 1092.

41 Southern 1950, pp. 61–6.

Andrew Willet's *Synopsis papismi* (1592) addressed 'three hundreds of popish errors', which became four hundred in 1594 and five hundred in 1600.[42]

From their earliest beginnings, the controversies between non-conformist and conformist tendencies within the established Church, which initially concerned vestments and other 'ornaments' of the Church, found expression in print. Soon after the suspension of thirty-seven London ministers for nonconformity in 1566, what we may call the first Puritan manifesto appeared from the press, *A briefe discourse against the outward apparell of the popishe church.* This anonymous publication was apparently the work of Robert Crowley, a printer-preacher with experience of the book trade. But it was said (by John Stow) that the materials were supplied by 'the whole multitude of London ministers, every one of them giving their advice in writing'.[43] If true, this makes a landmark in the use of the printing press for a collective, ideological purpose, and also marks the emergence of an organized Puritan movement, the reality of which has sometimes been questioned. Crowley was answered in *A briefe examination for the tyme of a certaine declaration, lately put in print in the name and defence of certaine ministers in London*, sometimes attributed to none other than Archbishop Parker himself. And of course the ministers attempted to have the last word in *An answere for the tyme*.[44]

This was but the overture to a controversy of the 1570s which came to rival in scope and scale Jewel versus Harding. In 1572 two hotheaded London preachers, Thomas Wilcox and John Field, employed a clandestine press to publish an anonymous manifesto which they called *An admonition to the Parliament*, raising the stakes in the developing dialogue between proponents of what was called 'further reformation' and defenders of the status quo. Field complained that hitherto critics of the Elizabethan Church had dealt with only 'shells and chippings', neglecting matters of real substance, including what would later appear to be the very foundation stones of Anglicanism, episcopacy and the Prayer Book. The events which followed suggest that the bishops had few friends, and that government proclamations were almost impotent in controlling the underground press.[45]

Nevertheless, this might have been a flash in the pan if the decision had not been taken to answer the sniper fire of Field and Wilcox with the artillery of

42 Andrew Willet, *Synopsis papismi, that is, a generall viewe of papistry: deuided into three hundred of popish errors* (London, 1592, augmented editions of 1594 and 1600).

43 Collinson 1967, pp. 77–8. 44 Milward 1977, p. 26.

45 *Puritan manifestoes: a study of the origin of the puritan revolt*, eds. W. H. Frere and C. E. Douglas (London, 1907, 1954); Collinson 1967, pp. 118–20; P. Collinson, 'John Field and Elizabethan Puritanism', in Collinson 1983, pp. 334–70.

an official riposte. By now Jewel was dead, and the task, and opportunity, of refuting the *Admonition* (soon followed by an anonymous *Second admonition*) fell to an ambitious academic and cleric, John Whitgift, master of Trinity College, Cambridge and destined to be Archbishop of Canterbury. Moderate voices condemned the Puritan libel ('surely the book was fond'), but urged Whitgift not to respond, on the proverbial grounds that the second blow makes the fray. But before the year was out, Whitgift's *Answere* had been published. The gauntlet was now taken up by the leading academic proponent of presbyterian Puritanism, Thomas Cartwright, whom Whitgift had hounded out of his Cambridge chair and Trinity fellowship: *A replye to an answere* (1573), another clandestine publication. Of course Whitgift came back with *The defense of the aunswere* (1574), which was an invitation for Cartwright to publish (on a Heidelberg press) his *Second replie* (1575), and even (from Basel) *The rest of the second replie* (1577), in itself a fat little book of hundreds of pages.[46]

The 'Admonition Controversy' proved to be the first and most substantial episode in two decades of press war between Puritans and bishops, which accompanied agitation, in Parliament and elsewhere in the public domain, for further reformation, and to curb the supposed 'tyranny' of 'antichristian' bishops. John Field, co-author of the *Admonition* which, in a sense, began it all, was a precocious organizer and publicist, who understood the power of the press to advance a radical and allegedly populist cause. Field, who had helped John Foxe with his 'Book of martyrs', now gathered material evidence of the sufferings and trials of the new, Puritan 'martyrs', and prepared them for publication. *A parte of a register contayninge sundrie memorable matters for the reformation of our church* appeared from a foreign press in 1593, five years after Field's death, but the bulk of this material ('The seconde parte of a register') remained unpublished (or at least unprinted) until modern times.[47]

The year 1593 was the end of the line, for the time being. In that year, Richard Bancroft summed up a career of anti-Puritan intelligence work, activity which helped him to the bishopric of London, and, after Whitgift's death, to St Augustine's chair. He was responsible for two anonymous books which have been described as so much 'ecclesiastical vitriol': *Daungerous positions and proceedings, published and practised within this iland of Brytaine* (Presbyterian Scotland, in Bancroft's perception, being more than half the problem), and *A suruay of the pretended holy discipline*. These were thoroughly nasty, occasional pieces of anti-Puritan propaganda, now forgotten.[48] More memorable was a

46 Collinson 1967, pp. 119–21; Milward 1977, ch. 2, 'Puritan Admonition'.
47 Collinson 1983, 'John Field'; Peel 1915. 48 Collinson 1995b.

book published in March 1593, the first four portions of a work calling itself *Of the lawes of ecclesiasticall politie* by a somewhat reclusive divine known as Richard Hooker. What the 'judicious' Hooker intended to achieve in this, one of the greatest books in the language, is still debated. But there is agreement that his magisterial work somehow transcended all earlier ecclesiological debates, including the Admonition Controversy, reducing the matters at stake to their epistemological essentials.[49]

Was Hooker's *Lawes* also conclusive? In a sense it was, since public interest in these matters was by now exhausted, or so Hooker's publisher alleged, and the book was only produced with the aid of a generous subsidy from two of Hooker's old pupils.[50] But the Anglican belief that after Hooker there was nothing more to be said is a pious and unsustainable legend. The accession of James I reactivated the Puritan cause, and the Jacobean press was soon busy turning out Puritan and anti-Puritan apologetics and polemics, as well as a flood of more consensual religious literature suggestive of the growing strength of a firm middle ground, wide enough to accommodate both conformists and non-conformists.[51] A bibliographical guide to Jacobean and immediately post-Jacobean religious controversies lists 160 items in the section called 'Anglican v. Puritan', and a further seventy-three titles classified as 'Schisms Among Separatists'.[52]

However, nobody writing about Puritan literature in the early decades of the seventeenth century would concentrate on books about contested ceremonies. While these were not dead issues (though ecclesiological issues of Church government almost were), the strength of evangelical publishing now lay in what came to be known as 'practical divinity', a spiritual resource, mostly to be found in the Puritan strongholds of Essex, East Anglia and the Midlands, and a literature devoted to helping individual Christians (and, it appears, small reading groups) to find their way to salvation along the *ordo salutis*. These books, and the lives of their authors, which often came to be enshrined in spiritual biographies that were sources of edification in themselves, defined for William Haller what he called *The rise of Puritanism* (1938), with its base line in about 1600, almost as if the Elizabethan struggles for a full reformation had never happened. Others

49 P. Lake, *Anglicans and Puritans? Presbyterianism and English conformist thought from Whitgift to Hooker* (London, 1988), pp. 145–230; P. Collinson, 'Richard Hooker and the Elizabethan establishment', in A. S. McGrade, ed., *Richard Hooker and the construction of Christian community*, Medieval and Renaissance Texts and Studies, no.165 (Tempe, 1997), pp. 149–81; M. E. C. Perrott, 'Richard Hooker and the problem of authority in the Elizabethan Church', *JEH*, 49 (1998), 29–60; and references given by Collinson and Perrott.

50 Sisson 1940, pp. 49–60.

51 N. Tyacke, *The fortunes of English Puritanism, 1603–1640* (London, 1989); Collinson 1982.

52 Milward 1978, pp. 1–71.

have seen this sea change in the character of the 'godly' book trade as a shrewd tacking exercise, seeking the same ends by different and less political means.[53]

The taproot of this practical divinity was in Christ's College, Cambridge, which produced that exemplary Elizabethan Puritan, Edward Dering,[54] and the most internationally celebrated of English Calvinist divines, William Perkins, the inventor, almost, of a Protestant pastoral casuistry, and the author of no less than 118 items in the *Short-Title Catalogue*.[55] But the most influential of the spiritual authors was a younger Christ's man, the son of a Chelmsford artisan and preacher for much of his life in the Essex village of Wethersfield, Richard Rogers.[56] Rogers's *Seven treatises, containing such directions as is gathered out of the holie scriptures, leading and guiding to true happiness* went through six editions between 1603 and 1630, with a further five editions of an abridgement by Stephen Egerton of this large and scarcely affordable book. The influence of *Seven treatises* can be traced in the lives of a whole generation of Puritan laymen. By 1670 it could be said: 'You might see Mr Rogers seven Treatises practised to the life in him.'[57] *A garden of spirituall flowers*, a less demanding anthology of the writings of Rogers, Perkins and other practical divines, had reached at least thirty editions by 1630.[58]

When the printer told Richard Hooker that he doubted whether his book would sell, he explained that the market for that kind of thing had been ruined by a large and indigestible tome, recently published. He probably had in mind the book by Bishop John Bridges called *A defence of the gouernment established in the church of England for ecclesiasticall matters* (1587). Bridges deserves to have an honoured place in the history of English literature, since he was the immediate provocation for the slim little publications we know as the Marprelate Tracts. The first two tracts printed in the name of the author (or authors?) who went under the pseudonym of Martin Marprelate professed to provide an epitome of Bridges's *Defence*, 'a very ..... portable book, if your horse be not too weake'.[59]

53 W. Haller, *The rise of Puritanism* (New York, 1938, repr. 1957); C. Hill, *Society and Puritanism in pre-revolutionary England* (London, 1966).

54 P. Collinson, 'A mirror of Elizabethan Puritanism: The life and letters of "Godly Master Dering"', in Collinson 1983, pp. 289–323.

55 Editions of Perkins's Works, *STC* 19646–19654; *The work of William Perkins*, ed. I. Breward (Appleford, 1970).

56 An abridged version of the diary of Richard Rogers was printed by M. M. Knappen in *Two Elizabethan Puritan diaries* (Chicago, 1933).

57 Collinson 1982, pp. 269–70; Ferdinand Nicholls, *The life and death of Mr Ignatius Jurdain* (London, 1654), p. 5; Giles Firmin, *The real Christian* (London, 1670), sig. 213^{r}.

58 *STC* 21204.4–213.10: R. Rogers, *A garden of spirituall flowers. Planted by Ri. Ro[gers], Will. Per[kins], Ri. Gree[nhame], M. M[osse?] and Geo. Web[be]* (London, 1609–30).

59 Sisson 1940, p. 4; *The Marprelate Tracts* [1588–1589](facsimile edn, Leeds, 1967), *An epitome*, sig. B.

The Marprelate Tracts are justly famous as a landmark in the history of English satire. For contemporaries, as well as for us, they provided delicious refreshment after so much theological tedium. But if delicious they were also seditious, and insofar as they spoke for the Puritan cause (most Puritan divines, including Thomas Cartwright, disowned them), they were an admission of failure. To subject the bishops, as they did, to merciless ridicule has been compared to the use of poison gas in warfare, which is liable with a change of wind to blow back into the faces and lungs of those using it.[60] Presently, Martin was answered 'in his own vein' in a series of anti-Martinist pamphlets, and even on the stage. This seems to have been Bancroft's idea. Although Francis Bacon believed that Bancroft's tactic was reprehensible, and so, apparently, did the government,[61] Martin Marprelate discredited the cause of further reformation and helped, for the time being, to destroy its credibility.[62]

The identity of Martin's printer is known, Robert Waldegrave, a specialist publisher for the Puritan cause who had been driven out of a legitimate trade into clandestine printing; and the locations of the Martinist press, private houses at East Molesey in Surrey, Fawsley in Northamptonshire, Coventry, and Lancashire, where the adventure came to an end. But who was Martin? It is typical of the concerns (almost the obsession) of what may be called the old bibliography (as distinct from D. F. McKenzie's newer 'sociology of texts'), that for many years discussion of the Marprelate Tracts was almost confined to the game of hunt the author. Was Martin the Welsh preacher John Penry, or the radical parliamentarian Job Throkmorton, or even the Welsh soldier Sir Roger Williams, Shakespeare's Fluellen, the preferred candidate of no less a scholar than John Dover Wilson?[63] Now, with what has been called the death of the author, a more rewarding approach proves to be through the Tracts' bibliographical character. What kind of publications were the Tracts? How did these lively fictions relate to the real world, and what effect did they have on the real world? It is probably significant that when Bishop John Woolton heard tell of the first of the Tracts, down in Exeter, he described it as 'a slaunderous libell latelie cast abroad in London intituled Martin Marprelate', which had been dispersed in 'written Pamphletes that he hath sent from hand to hand full of all malicious slaunders'. In other words, Woolton instinctively

60 C .S. Lewis, *English literature in the sixteenth century excluding drama* (Oxford, 1954, pbk. 1973), p. 409.

61 Francis Bacon, 'An advertisement touching the controversies of the Church of England', in *Francis Bacon: a critical edition of the major works*, ed. B. Vickers (Oxford, 1996), pp. 1–19, 494–512; E. K. Chambers, *The Elizabethan stage* (repr., Oxford, 1967), I, pp. 295, IV, pp. 228–33; Black 1997.

62 Collinson 1967, 1990, pp. 391–6.

63 Pierce 1908, McGinn 1966, Carlson 1981, Wilson 1912a. See also Collinson 1967, 1990, pp. 394–6.

connected 'Martin' with the widespread practice of slandering enemies and other unpopular figures in libellous ballads, which were 'published' in handwritten form, posted and deposited in public places, and performed as songs and playlets, a vicious part of the culture of the Elizabethan town and countryside. There had recently been a rash of pro-Puritan libelling of this kind in Devon and Cornwall, which led Woolton to believe that he knew who Martin was.[64] At this point one begins to wonder what it may mean to describe the Marprelate Tracts as 'literature'. Certainly we shall not find in our period a better illustration of the dynamic interaction of speech, manuscript and print.

But to canonize in print what otherwise might have been localized and ephemeral libels made all the difference. Martin was almost at once known nationally, even internationally.[65] And that meant that he was more than merely reflective of the street theatre and language of Elizabethan England. He helped create a culture. And the achievement was theatrical: first the theatre of the bishops in their vestments; then Martin's parodic theatre of the absurd which employed the patter of the improvisatory stage clown, Dick Tarleton; and finally Bancroft's all too clever idea of 'pillorying' Martin, 'lancing and worming' him in jigs and pantomimes. This seems to have created the stereotype of the stage Puritan, which was soon subtly refracted in the ambivalent character of Shakespeare's Malvolio and less subtly depicted in the anti-Puritan plays of Ben Jonson, and especially *Bartholomew fair*. The derogatory word 'Puritan' was much more in evidence after these events than before, and there is a sense in which Puritanism was created, or at least constructed, by the printed fictions of Martin and Mar-Martin.[66]

Catholic books

It became the conventional wisdom of the Reformation itself that Protestantism and the printing press were virtually symbiotic, Gutenberg's invention an act of Providence.[67] But the Reformation had no monopoly on religious publishing and Tridentine Catholicism too was a religion of the printed book.[68] In the repressive conditions which followed the accession of Elizabeth, English

64 Collinson 1995b, pp. 159–64; Fox 1998. 65 Black 1997.

66 Collinson 1995b; P. Collinson, 'Ben Jonson's *Bartholomew Fair:* theatre constructs Puritanism', in *The theatrical city: culture, theatre and politics in London, 1576–1649*, eds. D. L. Smith, R. Strier and D. Bevington (Cambridge,1995), pp. 157–69.

67 See, for example, John Foxe, *Actes and monuments*, ed. S.R. Cattley, (8 vols., London, 1837–41), III, pp. 718–22.

68 For a more extended discussion, see Walsham 2000.

Catholics were if anything more dependent on print, which was a powerful surrogate for personal pastoral discipline. The Spaniard Luis de Granada called devout Catholic books 'domme preachers'. One such dumb preacher was a little book called *A methode, to meditate on the Psalter*, a simple step-by-step guide to prayer and a teach-yourself religious manual, designed for a country in which priests were scarce and their very presence a capital crime.[69]

In the early years of Elizabeth's reign the Protestant book trade lagged behind the Romanist competition. After the 'Great Controversy' (see above) the momentum of publication was sustained, as William Allen established the English seminary at Douai (1568), as political circumstances dictated a hasty relocation to Rheims (1578), and as new presses were set up by the Jesuits at Seville, Valladolid and Eu in Normandy. (The latter removed in 1592 to St Omer in the Spanish Netherlands.)[70] There was also much surreptitious Catholic publishing in England and Wales. By 1581, London alone housed several secret establishments. Stephen Brinkley and his assistants, based first at Greenstreet House and later in a wood at Stonor Park, printed books for Robert Persons and Edmund Campion before they and their press were apprehended.[71] Mainstream printers and members of the Stationers' Company with Catholic sympathies, including John Wolfe, Gabriel Cawood and Valentine Simmes, ensured that popish books continued to be produced, dispersed, and covertly sold.[72] Much later, in the 1620s, there was quite a community of Catholic printers and vendors lurking in such districts as Gunpowder Alley, Clerkenwell Green, Holborn, Fetter Lane and Little Britain, if John Gee's infamous *Foot out of the snare* is to be trusted.[73] Outside the capital, where clandestine publishing was safer, recusant booksellers and binders remained a constant thorn in the authorities' side. Between 1615 and 1621, nineteen items were issued from a press at Birchley Hall near Wigan, the family residence of James Anderton, alias John Brerely.[74] And in Jacobean Staffordshire and Worcestershire, one Francis Ash carried on a profitable trade in pictures, manuals and tracts, unmolested.

69 Luis de Granada, *A memoriall of a Christian life. Wherein are treated all such things, as appertayne unto a Christian to doe*, trans. R. Hopkins (Rouen, 1586), p. 12; *A methode, to meditate on the psalter, or great rosarie of our blessed ladie* (Antwerp [English secret press], 1598).

70 Southern 1950, esp. chs. 2, 6; Rostenberg 1971, esp. ch. 2.

71 Pollen 1906, pp. 28, 182–3; Hicks 1942, pp. xxxi–xxxii; Southern 1950, pp. 353–6; Rostenberg 1971, pp. 23–4.

72 Brown 1989, pp. 138–9.

73 Harmsen 1992, pp. 201–4, 239, 453. For other secret presses, see the list in Allison and Rogers 1989–94.

74 A. F. Allison, 'Who was John Brerely? The identity of a seventeenth-century controversialist', *Recusant History*, 16 (1982–3), 17–41; [Michael Sparke], *A second beacon fired by Scintilla* (London, 1652), p. 6.

Many of those involved in illicit publishing resorted to deceit and subterfuge: fictitious imprints, false dates and misleading pseudonyms are very common indeed. Such devious devices were sanctioned by the papal hierarchy only in exceptional circumstances, for the Tridentine *Decretum de editione et usu sacrorum librorum* had forbidden the printing of books without identifying their authors.[75] But anonymity was a necessity if the Catholic enterprise to reconvert England was to succeed, and the printing of pamphlets and the dissemination of manuscripts was almost a condition of success.[76]

Even a superficial glance at the statistics of Catholic book production between 1558 and 1640 confirms this point. Allison and Rogers's catalogue of Catholic works in English printed abroad or secretly in England identified some 932 items dating from this eighty-year period, a remarkable corpus excluding texts in Latin and the Continental vernaculars, which make an additional tally of 1,619.[77] Even in the later Stuart period, when Catholic publishing activity had declined from its pre-Civil War peak, recusant writings still far outnumbered those of the Baptists, Quakers and other non-conformist sects, falling only a little behind those of the established Church.[78] Impressive as these figures are, they alert us to only one sector of what we may call English Counter-Reformation book culture. There was also a still vibrant tradition of scribal publication, ensuring that much devotional and controversial material circulated clandestinely through the Catholic underground.[79] The survival of large numbers of handwritten copies of politically sensitive texts like *Leicesters Commonwealth* (1585) (twenty-three versions in the British Library alone) and *A conference about the next succession* by 'Robert Doleman' (a pseudonym for Robert Persons?) attest to a powerful symbiosis and interdependence between manuscript and print.[80] Much like Foxe, recusant hagiographers built up their dossiers from eyewitness accounts of the exemplary conduct of Catholics on the scaffold, which disseminated widely among the devout.[81]

75 See PRO, SP 12/137/26 ('Facultates concessae Patribus Roberto Personio et Edmundo Campiano pro Anglia die 14 Aprilis, 1580'), 8, printed in A. O. P. Meyer, *England and the Catholic Church under Queen Elizabeth*, trans. J. R. McKee (London, 1967 edn), appendix XVII. For the Tridentine decree, see Schroeder 1978, p. 19.

76 Hicks 1942, p. 356.

77 Allison and Rogers 1989–94.

78 See the remarks of C. Hibbard, 'Early Stuart Catholicism: revisions and re-revisions', *Journal of Modern History*, 52 (1980), 13. For books printed after 1641, see Clancy 1974, 1996. See also Allison and Rogers 1989–94. The works listed in the latter are excluded by the terms of reference of *STC*.

79 Brown 1989. For just one example of scribal publication, see *A treatise of mental prayer in which is briefly declared the manner how to exercise the inward actes of vertues* ([St Omer], 1617), sig. *8^r. Prior to being printed, this was 'delivered from hand to hand, many copies therof being spread abroad'.

80 Clancy 1964, pp. 237, 239; Brown 1989, pp. 121, 128, and *passim*.

81 See *Concertatio ecclesiae Catholicae in Anglia adversus Calvinopapistas et puritanos sub Elizabetha regina quorundam hominum doctrina & sanctitate illustrium renovata*, ed. John Gibbons and John Fen (n.p., 1588); ed. and augmented, John Bridgewater, 1589 (first published, London, 1583). See BL, MS.

Problems of supply and distribution were critical. Scraps of evidence gleaned from official and unofficial sources suggest that the network of communication grew ever more elaborate and extensive, far more so than its Puritan counterpart. The merchants and factors who were cogs in this machine were persuaded or handsomely paid to hide prohibited literature among their freight, to land them on isolated spots on south-western or North Sea coasts, or to bribe customs officers to turn a blind eye.[82] There is much anecdotal and circumstantial evidence to suggest that there was little to prevent the importation of Catholic books. Boats could be hired at Dunkirk (a lawless port run by pirates) and landings made at places like Margate and the Isle of Sheppey.[83] 'Crates and packages' of books ('cofres y fardros de libros en ingles') were sent to the Spanish ambassador in the diplomatic bag,[84] while in 1636 Queen Henrietta Maria expressed surprise that the customs house should have taken an interest in recent imports in her name, since there was 'nothing but bookes'.[85] However, the authorities went through the motions. In May 1592, the Privy Council ordered searches of all vessels docking in London for 'traiterous and sedicious bookes', brought in 'wrapped upp amongest marchandizes', and in 1609 the activities of a Barking fisherman who conducted a profitable sideline in shipping 'papisticall' literature concealed beneath his catch did not go undetected.[86] As with hard drugs in the modern world, the attendant costs of this illicit trade were borne by the consumer, who in 1624 had to pay twelve shillings for a Rheims New Testament, and as much as sixteen for Tobie Matthew's translation of St Augustine's *Confessions*, a little octavo, the real value of which was more like thirty pence.[87]

At the centre of this complex system of communications stood the emigré Richard Verstegan. Based in Antwerp from 1589 until his death in 1620, he managed the propaganda and intelligence wings of the mission brilliantly, liaising with key figures in Rome and leading Jesuits in Spain.[88] On the domestic

Lansdowne 96, no. 26, where Dr Ely sends Gibbons Mr Haith's martyr life 'fayre wrytten in folio'. Much martyrological material remains in MS. Particularly important are Christopher Grene's 'Collectanea', preserved in Stonyhurst College, and St Mary's College, Oscott.

82 Rostenberg 1971, ch. 3.

83 L. Owen, *The running register: recording a true relation of the state of the English colledges, seminaries and cloysters in all forraine parts* (London, 1626), p. 111.

84 Henry Taylor to the Marquess of Valeda, March 28 1640; Lambeth Palace Library (uncatalogued; see the Library's Annual Report, 1993).

85 Robert Aston to Sir John Wostenholme, 14 May 1636; Bodleian Library, MS. Tanner 70, fol. 89.

86 *APC 1591–2*, pp. 486–7; BL, MS. Lansdowne 153, fol. 20^{r}, printed in Harris 1966, pp. 260–1. Cf. *CSPD 1581–90*, pp. 78, 91; HMC, *Salisbury*, x, pp. 203–4.

87 Harmsen 1992, p. 216. Gee's comment on George Musket's *The Bishop of London his legacy* ([St Omer], 1623) was 'they squeezed from some Romish Buyers, six or seven shillings apiece. A dear price for a dirty Lie' (p. 218). See also Owen, *The running register* (Gee 1624, p. 218), p. 14.

88 See Petti 1959, Introduction, for a biographical summary.

front, dozens of more obscure individuals played their parts in the distributive network, including seminary priests like Thomas Awfield who brought in over 300 copies of William Allen's *True, sincere and modest defence of the English Catholiques that suffer for their faith* (1584), before suffering himself.[89] Women were particularly active in this capacity. Ann Dowse, widow of High Holborn, was, according to John Gee, a famous female dealer in these wares, while the printer Roger Heigham regularly sent his wife over to England 'under the habite of a Dutchwoman'. 'Two more dangerous women' than Mrs Heigham and one Mistress Daubrigscourt, wrote the spy William Udall to control, could 'hardly be found'.[90] A brisk trade in 'naughty books' was conducted in the London prisons, and there was also a flourishing black market in literature confiscated and then resold by corrupt pursuivants.[91] Mainstream booksellers and stationers in Paul's Churchyard and its vicinity found it worth their while to act as middlemen in the same trade.[92]

What were these 'seditious' and 'superstitious' books? Much of the stock in trade was controversial and political: texts enshrining the militant resistance theory of the Allen-Persons party, texts in support of Mary Queen of Scots and invasion by Spain, texts appealing for toleration and a mitigation of persecution, texts addressing contentious issues like the succession, Papal power and the royal supremacy. Examples are the notorious *Treatise of treasons* (1572), Nicholas Sander's *De origine et progressu schismatic Anglicani* (1585), and William Allen's Armada-related *Admonition to the nobility and people of England* (1588). Then there was a vast array of polemical theology, Thomas Harding in the 1560s, handing on the baton to Thomas Stapleton, Matthew Kellison and William Bishop.[93] No theologian was more eminent than the Jesuit Cardinal Robert Bellarmine, whose *Disputationes de controversiis Christianae fidei* of 1586 was considered by learned Catholics to be impregnable.[94] A recent

89 On Thomas Awfield, see *The life and end of Thomas Awfeeld a seminary preest and Thomas Webley a dyers servant in London . . . traitours who were condemned as fellons for bringing seditious books into this realme and dispersing of the same* (London, [1585]), sigs. A4^{v}, A6^{r}; Southern 1950, pp. 35–6.

90 Harmsen 1992, p. 240; BL, MS. Lansdowne 153, fols. 30^{r}, 22^{r}, 32^{r}, 16^{r}, 17^{r}, printed in Harris 1966, pp. 237, 244, 253, 262, 264.

91 *The Ven. Philip Howard Earl of Arundel 1557–1595*, Pollen and MacMahon 1919, p. 75; Petti 1959, 7–8; BL, MS. Lansdowne 153, fols. 18^{r}, 17^{r}, 14^{r}, printed in Harris 1966, pp. 239, 264, 265.

92 See, for examples, *CSPD 1603–1610*, p. 272 (report of 'A stationer in London, a pretended protestant, scatters popish books'), *CSPD 1633–4*, p. 481 (case of William Pamplin, merchant, William Brooks, stationer, and Thomas Blomfield the younger, fined for dispersing popish books, Feb. 1634).

93 Southern 1950, ch. 3; Clancy 1964; P. Holmes , *Resistance and compromise: the political thought of the Elizabethan Catholics* (Cambridge, 1982), parts 1, 3, 4; Milward 1977, chs. 1, 3, 6; Milward 1978, chs. 3, 4.

94 Foley 1875–83, VII, part 2, p. 1011. For some of the literature generated by Bellarmine's works, see Milward 1977, pp. 152–6, and Milward 1978, pp. 101–9.

study of such works doubts their ability to change the allegiance of a Protestant reader. Their function was to defend, and to counterattack, not persuade.[95] Shorter manuals and pamphlets may have had more impact on those 'that hath little will, or little leasure to read', as John Sweet noted in 1617. Broadsheets displaying the multiplicity of corrupt Protestant sects distilled the essence of the Reformation schism into the space of a single sheet.[96]

As time went on, Catholic controversialists developed ingenious polemical strategies, such as disguising themselves as moderate Protestant, or neutral observers. A Lancashire gentleman writing under the pseudonym of John Brerely seems to have been the first to have made use of this method of refuting heretics out of their own mouths, a device mimicked by the missionary priest Richard Broughton in his *First part of protestants proofes for Catholikes religion and recusancy*,[97] and perhaps owing something to the tactics of Richard Bancroft in *Daungerous positions* and other anti-Puritan works. But the tables were soon turned, as Protestants like Thomas Bell took full advantage of the internecine squabbles between the seculars and the Jesuits during the Archpriest and Appellant controversies, a quarrel they had chosen, to their cost, to play out in the medium of print.[98] But such books may have had a very limited effect, since Catholics in principle required a special dispensation to read heretical literature,[99] while many leading figures in the English mission began to fear that works of controversy were having a detrimental effect, filling 'the heades of men with a spirite of contradiction and contention', and distracting them from more properly religious concerns.[100]

Of first priority, from this point of view, was the publication of works designed to cultivate piety, devotion and repentance. This was an enterprise

95 Questier 1996, ch. 2, esp. pp. 36–7, 39.

96 John Sweet, *Monsigr Fate Voi* (St Omer, 1617). p. 153. For example, Richard Bristowe, *Briefe treatise* (popularly known as his *Motives*) and *Demaundes to be proponed of Catholiques to the heretikes* (Antwerp, 1576). Examples of broadsheets are *Typus haereticae synagogue* [Paris, 1585], and *Speculum pro Christianis seductis* (Antwerp, 1590). See also 'A showe of the Protestants petigrew', possibly a book illustration, reproduced in Watt 1991, plate 14, p. 155.

97 John Brereley [James Anderton], *The apologie of the Romane church* ([English secret press], 1604); Richard Broughton, *The first part of Protestants proofes for Catholikes religion and recusancy* (Paris [English secret press], 1607). See also Milward 1977, pp. 151–5. It was the apostate priest Thomas Bell who claimed to have pioneered this technique in his *Thomas Bels motives: concerning Romish faith and religion* (Cambridge, 1593), sig. 2^{v}; BL, MS. Lansdowne 75, fol. 40^{r}.

98 Milward 1977, pp. 116–26. Bell's *The anatomie of popish tyrannie* (London, 1603) is a good example. On Richard Bancroft, then Bishop of London, the Appellants, and Catholic book production, see PRO, SP 14/8/21–5; Plomer 1907a, Jenkins 1947–8, Curtis 1964.

99 Hicks 1942, p. 356; Schroeder 1978, p. 73. See also *Elizabethan casuistry*, ed. P. J. Holmes, CRS, 67 (London, 1981), 49–50, 92–3.

100 William Rainolds, *A refutation of sundry reprehensions, cavils, and false sleightes* (Paris, 1583), sig. $a3^{v}$; Robert Persons, *The first booke of the Christian exercise, appertaining to resolution* ([Rouen], 1582), p. 2.

which gathered pace with the entry on the scene of the Society of Jesus and the new-style spirituality devised by its founder, Ignatius Loyola. There were many small godly books intended for the laity, but also small manuals designed to help priests consecrate the sacrament and say mass.[101] Here was instruction for those who remained faithful to Mother Church in the fundamentals of Catholic practice and ritual: how to pray, how to confess, how to receive the eucharist.[102] There were translations of the works of Spanish and Italian churchmen, Luis de Granada, Alonso de Madrid, Fulvio Androzzi and Luca Pinelli; and some of these texts made their way into Irish, Scots Gaelic and Welsh.[103] Typical of this genre are *Certayne sweete prayers* of the fourteenth-century Dominican mystic Henry Suso (1575–8), Vincenzo Bruno's *Short treatise of the sacrament of penance* (1597), and John Bucke's *Instructions for the use of beades* (1589). Compiled 'for the benefite of unlearned', this tiny portable manual is illustrated with woodcuts and includes an elaborate folding plate to guide the reader through his or her devotions.

Literally hundreds of primers, missals, psalters and breviaries were printed in this period. One of the most widely used in the early seventeenth century was the *Officium beatae Mariae Virginis*, a Tridentine version of a book of hours which had its origins in medieval monastic communities.[104] Catholic catechisms also abounded, a symptom of the emerging confessionalism of the Counter-Reformation. Laurence Vaux's *Cathechisme or Christian doctrine*, first published in 1567, and written after a 'simple and rude maner' to meet the needs of 'yong scollers' and uneducated laymen, was enduringly popular. It was also old-fashioned, making no concessions to the straitened condition of Catholics in Protestant England, and endorsing paraliturgical practices upon which the Council of Trent would have frowned, such as anointing women receiving extreme unction 'upon the bealy'.[105] More up-to-date was *Certayne*

101 See the Latin table of directions for the behaviour of a priest, before, at, and after the solemnising of mass (Douai, 1577), preserved in BL, MS. Lansdowne 96, no. 58, fol. 70^{r}, printed in Harris 1966, p. 259.

102 On devotional literature, see Southern 1950, ch. 4; White 1931; White 1951; J. R. Roberts, *A critical anthology of English Recusant devotional prose, 1558–1603* (Pittsburgh, 1966). See also Clancy 1989; Molloy 1967–8.

103 For just a handful of examples, see Jean Pierre Camus, *Crynnodeb o adysc Cristnogaul*... (Paris, 1609); Morys Clynnog, *Athrauaeth Gristogaul, le cair uedi cynnuys*... (Milan, 1568); Grifith Robert, *Ynglynion ar y pader* [Wales?, 1580–90?]; Pietro Teramamo, *Dechreuad a rhyfedhus esmudiad eglwys yr arglwdhes Fair or Loreto* (Loreto, 1635); and the publications of the Irish Franciscan Giolla Brighde O Heoghusa, Allison and Rogers 1989–94, pp. 581–3.

104 Blom 1982. See also Crichton 1982–3.

105 Laurence Vaux, *A catechisme or Christian doctrine, necessary for children and ignorant people* (Louvain, 1568), other editions 1574, [1581?], 1583, 1590, 1599, 1605, 1620. Reprinted by T. G. Law for the Chetham Society, ns 4 (1885), quotations from 'The Printer to the Reader', 'The Author to the Reader', and p. 68.

necessarie principles of religion by the Dutch Jesuit Peter Canisius (1578–9). It too presented itself as 'very commodious for Infants and sucking babes', 'little ones and younglings'.[106] The professed aim of such publications, which was to enlighten the unlearned laity, should not be discounted. We are not yet in the 1640s, when the Catholic community was retreating into gentry and noble households, and Richard Lascelles's *A little way how to heare masse with profit and devotion* could assume an aristocratic audience supplied with resident chaplains.[107]

It may be that many ostensibly apolitical works of devotion should actually be regarded as subtle and sophisticated exercises in sect formation and anti-Reformation polemic. One sub-genre which might be viewed in this light is the body of tracts dedicated to convincing the laity that steadfast recusancy was the only way for a committed English Catholic to obtain salvation. In denouncing schismatics and Church Papists who conformed to varying degrees with the heretical régime, missionary leaders and labourers were attempting to create a pristine public image for a proscribed religion to which compromise and equivocation had become vital for its long-term survival. Printed propaganda against conformity was designed to daunt the Protestant enemy as much as to bolster the morale of the Catholic rank and file.[108] The literature of martyrdom and persecution was also double-edged: emotive accounts of Calvinist cruelties and executions were as much an incentive to foreign intervention and a call for a Papal crusade as a method of strengthening the collective identity of the beleaguered and molested faithful. The martyrological documents collected in the *Concertatio ecclesiae Catholicae* (1583, 1589, 1594) amounted to a Catholic *Actes and monuments*, and the graphic engravings published by Verstegan and Cavaleriis proved as compelling on the Continent as they did in Britain.[109] Individuals caught distributing 'pectores of parseousnes' done upon 'the saints' were particularly galling to a

106 St Peter Canisius, *Certayne necessarie principles of religion, which may be entituled, A catechisme conteyning all the partes of the Christian and Catholique fayth* (Douai, [1578–9]), sig. ¶6^{r-v}.

107 Richard Lascelles, *A little way how to heare masse with profit and devotion* (Paris, 1644), dedicated to Lady Ann Brudenell.

108 Walsham 1993, pp. 44–9. The most famous of such tracts is Robert Persons, *A brief discours conteyning certayne reasons why Catholiques refuse to goe to church* (Douai [London secret press], 1580). See also Milward 1977, pp. 65–73.

109 See A. G. Petti, 'Richard Verstegan and Catholic martyrologies of the later Elizabethan period', *Recusant History*, 5 (1959–60), 64–90; White 1963, chs. 7–8; J. T. Rhodes, 'English Books of Martyrs and Saints of the late sixteenth and early seventeenth centuries', *Recusant History*, 22 (1994), 7–25. For Cavaleriis and Verstegan, see respectively *Ecclesiae Anglicanae trophaea sive sanctorum martyrum* (Rome, 1584) and *Theatrum crudelitatem haereticiorum nostri temporis* (Antwerp, 1587). Note also the MS relation of the martyrdom of a Spaniard in Morocco and certain verses by way of challenge to Foxe, 'the martyr maker', preserved in PRO, SP 12/157/48 (1582?).

government anxious to avoid being tarred with the same brush as Bloody Mary Tudor.[110]

It is by no means inappropriate to present English Counter-Reformation book production as one manifestation of a Europe-wide movement rivalling the much-emphasized 'Calvinist International'.[111] Evidence abounds that the Catholic priesthood of Elizabethan and early Stuart England was not narrowly parochial, but participated in a literary culture which stretched its tentacles to all parts of Western Christendom. Through their efforts, key works by fellow Jesuits and seculars were rendered familiar to English readers, and in turn their own writings were transmitted into other languages and regions. Edmund Campion's *Decem rationes*, for example, went through over sixty editions before 1632: some forty-five Latin, two Czech, one Dutch, four Flemish, four French, nine German, one Hungarian, two Polish, and only one in English.[112] British missionaries made their mark and used the story of English recusancy to edifying effect as far away as Goa and Lima.[113]

And what about making the Bible accessible to the unlettered? It went against the grain for Catholics to concede the utility of a vernacular translation of the Bible. As late as the mid-twentieth century, it was not difficult to find Roman Catholics who considered lay Bible reading undesirable. But soon even Cardinal William Allen decided, in effect, that if one could not beat them, it was better to join them. Nevertheless, when the Rheims New Testament appeared in 1582 it was hedged about with prescriptive annotations (plate 1.1).[114] Yet gradually clerical exiles began to move with the times, and to make a virtue out of necessity, treating the scriptural medium as a valuable auxiliary and a creative opportunity.

To balance the story so far told, it must be conceded that dependence upon printed books had its critics. Contemporaries feared that the provocation of print would lead to harsher persecution. Modern historians of Catholicism suggest that print led to petrification of the liturgy, a devaluation of the oral and visual, and the replacement of communal ritual by a private, inward-looking piety, intimately tied to the gentry household. Print was in many respects

110 *Recusant documents from the Ellesmere Manuscripts*, ed. A. G. Petti, CRS, 60 (1968), 51, 89.

111 Cf. Francis Higman's analysis of the international transmission of Calvinism in Pettegree, Duke and Lewis 1994, pp. 82–99.

112 Doyle, review of Allison and Rogers 1989–94, I, *Recusant History*, 20 (1990), 146. There is no comparable bibliography for the Reformed churches.

113 Birrell 1994, p. 115.

114 See Southern 1950, p. 233. *The New Testament of Jesus Christ, translated faithfully into English, out of the authentical Latin* was published in Rheims in 1582; the Old Testament only twenty-five years later, in *The holie bible faithfully translated into English*, 2 vols. (Douai, 1609–10).

conservative.[115] But in the short term, these side effects were not foreseen, and the clergy waxed lyrical about the fruits of both controversial and devotional works. 'There is nothing which helps . . . our cause so much', wrote Persons to Aquaviva, General of the Jesuits.[116] The director of the St Omer press, John Wilson, wrote in 1616: 'Books penetrate where the priests and religious cannot enter.'[117] Here, in a distinctly paradoxical sense, were the true origins of the Society for Promoting Christian Knowledge.

So far, we have regarded 'Catholic' books as books for Catholics, which might seem to be only reasonable. But that was by no means the whole story. Devotional writers liked to think of their literary efforts as 'sweet and savorie honie combes', 'good and wholesome foode', and not merely for Catholic palates.[118] Many of their books included prefaces addressed to the devout or impartial Christian reader. Thomas Wright's *Disposition or garnishment of the soule to receive worthily the blessed sacrament* (1596) was meant for 'the vew and censure of three sortes of persons: Catholicks, protestantes, & demi-Catholickes' (or 'Church Papists'). Each of these carefully defined groups was addressed in a separate preface.

No single Catholic text had a greater reputation as spiritual food than Robert Persons's *First booke of the Christian exercise*, later retitled *The Christian directory*. First published as a bulky duodecimo in 1582, this devotional manual transcended the war of words raging between Protestants and Papists and concentrated on the task of sparking off individual spiritual renewal. A free adaptation of a work by the Italian Jesuit, Gaspar Loarte,[119] it was a book which effected conversions, revolutionizing the life of Thomas Poulton, who reported that as he read it, 'a marvellous light broke in upon me.'[120] The runaway success of the *Christian directory* indicated that it met a genuine need, filling a notable gap in the existing range of Protestant literature, to which books like Richard Rogers's *Seven treatises* were a belated response. In 1584, the Yorkshire minister Edmund Bunny produced a bowdlerised version of Persons's popular tract, from which he carefully removed all references to purgatory and free will, but retained nine-tenth of the original text intact. This book went through more Protestant impressions than Catholic. By 1600 the

115 Pollen 1906, pp. 154–5; Bossy 1985, pp. 97–104.
116 Hicks 1942, p. 107. 117 *CSP Milan*, p. 654.
118 Luis de Granada, *Of prayer, and meditation*, sig. b7^{v}; Canisius, *A summe of Christian doctrine*, sig. *2.
119 Robert Persons, *The first booke of the Christian exercise, appertayning to resolution* (Rouen, 1582); reissued as *A Christian directorie* in 1585, and (with variant titles) in 1598, 1607,1622, 1637. Gaspar Loarte's *The exercise of a Christian life* was translated and published in English by William Carter in 1579. The book was also translated into French, Scots Gaelic, German, Latin and Italian.
120 Foley 1875–83, I, pp. 158–9.

ratio was 24:1.[121] The Jesuit writer Luca Pinelli's *Meditationi brevi del santissimo sacramento* received two English translations, one for Roman Catholics, edited by Henry Garnet and published in about 1600, another for Protestants, edited by Christopher Sutton and first published in 1601. Sutton's version omits references to transubstantiation and penance, moderates much of the real presence language, but retains largely unchanged most of the prayers and meditations, particularly those concerned with self-examination and repentance.[122] It was Bunny's 'Resolution' which converted the Elizabethan playwright Robert Greene and the great seventeenth-century Presbyterian divine, Richard Baxter.[123] This was by no means the only example of confessional confusion, or cross-fertilisation. *The life and death of... the Virgin Mary* by the water poet, John Taylor (1620), a work which claimed to be an expurgated version of a Roman Catholic original, was included both in an inventory of works 'of the Roman religion' and in the impeccably protestant library of the Northamptonshire gentlewoman Judith Isham, where it sat alongside Bishop Bayly's *Practise of piety* and Richard Sibbes's *The soules conflict*.[124] The hidden motive of John Cosin in publishing his *Collection of private devotions* (1627) was to prevent ladies of the Court from defecting to Rome. Sponsored by Charles I, the text was designed to resemble small Catholic books of devotion.[125] This might be seen as symptomatic of a more conciliatory attitude to the Church of Rome and a growing readiness to acknowledge the Catholic heritage of the Church of England, at least in so-called Arminian circles.[126]

In 1624, the annual letter of the Jesuit mission recounted the story of a poor Warwickshire woman who became a Catholic after she had understood a Protestant preacher to say that illiterate people like herself could not hope to gain salvation.[127] By emphasizing the bibliocentric print culture of post-Reformation English Catholicism, have we suggested that the Catholic mission made the same elitist mistake? It has been suggested that Counter-Reformation

121 *A booke of Christian exercise, appertaining to resolution... perused, and accompanied now with a treatise tending to pacification: by Edmund Bunny* (London, 1584). See Gregory 1994, at p. 253; and Milward 1977, pp. 74–5. But see also Houliston 1996. There were six partial editions of Bunny's text, and it was also translated into Welsh in 1632.

122 Luca Pinelli, *Briefe meditations of the most holy sacrament and of preparation, for receiving the same*, ed. Henry Garnet ([English secret press], *c.* 1600) and Christopher Sutton, *Godly meditations upon the most holy sacrament of the Lordes supper* (London, 1601).

123 Robert Greene, *The repentance of Robert Greene* (London, 1592), sig. B2^{v}; Richard Baxter, *Reliquae Baxterianae* (London, 1696), p. 3.

124 John Taylor, *The life and death of... the Virgin Mary* (London, 1620). The examples cited occur in CUL, MS. Dd.14.25 (3), p. 17, and Northamptonshire Record Office, I.L.4046. See Watt 1991, p. 292.

125 John Cosin , *A collection of private devotions: in the practise of the ancient church, called the houres of prayer* (London, 1627).

126 Milton 1995.

127 Foley 1875–83, VII, part 2, pp. 1109–10.

spirituality found its niche in the seigneurial household, and had as little appeal for a peasantry wedded to folk custom and superstitious magic as Calvinist sermons.[128]

But many aspects of this paradigm are now qualified and refined. Like Puritan preachers who saw elementary education as the key to evangelism, in 1611 a group of recusant prisoners in York were found to be conducting a dame school for local children under the very noses of their warders.[129] And like many Reformed ministers, particularly in the first half of Elizabeth's reign, Catholic publicists made adroit use of the oral and visual to gain access to the partially illiterate, disseminating printed pictures, circulating anti-Protestant prophecies, rhymes and miracles in manuscript and by word of mouth, and composing devotional and polemical songs to popular tunes which were clearly designed to counter the godly ballads of the opposition. A series of Welsh carols devised by the martyred priest Richard White between 1577 and 1584 dealt with such issues as the rosary, the sinfulness of attending heretical services, the evils of the Reformation, and the assassination of William of Orange.[130] This was an ingenious attempt to commandeer the indigenous Celtic bardic culture, and bears striking similarities to Dr Jane Dawson's account of the Calvinist assimilation of traditional 'oral literate' methods of cultural transmission in the Gaelic-speaking Scottish Highlands and Islands.[131] To succeed as a missionary religion, Catholicism, like Protestantism, had to adjust to the needs of a society only gradually being infiltrated by print. Both Churches, and both evangelistic and pastoral agencies, were multimedia in their outreach.

Religious books and their readers

The Essex preacher Richard Rogers intended his *Seven treatises* for 'the simpler sort, whom I do chiefly respect and regard through this my whole labour'. But it is unlikely that many of 'the simpler sort' could have afforded a 600-page

128 C. Haigh, 'The continuity of Catholicism in the English Reformation', in Haigh 1987, pp. 204–5, 207; C. Haigh 'From monopoly to minority: Catholicism in early modern England', *Transactions of the Royal Historical Society*, 5th ser., no. 31 (1981), 138 and *passim*. J. Bossy, *The English Catholic Community, 1570–1850* (London, 1975), p. 282.

129 J. C. H. Aveling, *Catholic recusancy in the city of York 1558–1791*, CRS Monograph Series, no. 2 (St Albans, 1970), p. 82.

130 For Richard White, see Pollen 1908, pp. 90–9. For pictures, see above pp. 33, 45, 50. For prophecies, see *CSPD 1591–4*, p. 184. William Weston SJ circulated 'a penned book of miracles', following the Jesuit exorcisms of 1585–6 (Samuel Harsnet, *A declaration of egregious popish impostures* (London, 1604), p. 1). For ballads and rhymes, note, e.g., John Rhodes, *An answere to a Romish rime lately printed: wherein are contayned Catholike questions to the Protestant. The which rime was put forth ... libell-like, scattered and sent abroad, to withdraw the simple from the fayth of Christ* (London, 1602).

131 J. Dawson, 'Calvinism and the Gaidhealtachd in Scotland', in Pettegree, Duke and Lewis 1994, pp. 231–53.

folio costing perhaps ten or twelve shillings, or have found the time and leisure to read it, and it became customary to recommend Stephen Egerton's abridgement, made in 1604, 'for the use of my selfe, and some private friends'. To his credit, Rogers acknowledged the problem, admitting that 'in the wealthy estate there are many more helpes' to godliness 'then are to be found in the needie and poore'. The wealthy had time and liberty to 'inioy the preaching of the word, have recourse to reading, Christian conference in good company, meditation also and prayer', to which 'for the most part' the poor had no access.[132] Even a book like Henry Scudder's *The Christians daily walke*, which claimed to be 'digested . . . with such brevitie and perspicuitie, as was necessary to make the Booke a *vade mecum*, easily portable, and profitable to the poore and illiterate', ran to 800 pages in duodecimo and would probably have cost about 1s. 6d.[133] Historians have disagreed about the accessibility of such books. While one suggests that a book of that price would have been 'available to almost anyone able to read and not forced to subsist on charity', another believes that a husbandman with an arable holding of thirty acres would have found even a twopenny pamphlet quite difficult to afford.[134] Peter Clark has calculated that in Kent ownership of books among men in the early seventeenth century reached about 40 per cent, and among women about 25 per cent.[135] But these figures, as well as having a bias towards the minority of the population which made a will, are based on inventories from Canterbury, Faversham and Maidstone and probably overestimate book ownership in rural areas.

To be sure, purchase has never been the only way to get hold of a book, and we know all too little about the lending and borrowing of books and their circulation in society more generally. A Cornish diarist recorded his acquisition of the *Admonition to the Parliament*, reading it, and passing it on to 'Ford the preacher'.[136] We may safely assume that the clergy, representing a different kind of poverty, could not afford to buy all the books that they needed, and there is evidence that they often borrowed from their more affluent patrons and other friends. When the sister of the godly Suffolk gentleman Sir Robert Jermyn wrote her will, she left copies of the Tremellius Bible, an essential but expensive resource for a learned preacher, to a number of neighbouring

132 Rogers, *Seven treatises* (1603), prefatory epistle by Ezekiel Culverwell, sig. A4^{r}; Richard Rogers, *The practice of christianitie* (1618). For the recommended use of Egerton's abridgement, see Henry Scudder, *The Christians daily walke* (7th edn, London, 1637), sig. A11^{r}; Jeremiah Lewis, *The doctrine of thankfulnesse* (London, 1619), p. 20.

133 Scudder, *The Christians daily walke*, sig. A11^{v}.

134 S. Foster, *The long argument: English Puritanism and the shaping of New England culture, 1570–1700* (Chapel Hill and London, 1991), p. 91; Watt 1991, pp. 260–1.

135 Clark 1976. 136 Collinson 1967, 1990, p. 149.

ministers.[137] An obvious answer to this problem was a library, on the lines of a college library, and it was an answer which was already being found in the more progressive of communities in this, the first age of parish libraries. The Jermyns would have attended as a matter of course the regular Monday lecture at Bury St Edmunds. This was a 'combination lecture' maintained by the clergy of the region on a rota, the ministers forming a kind of collegiate auditory, together with gentry and townsmen. In the 1590s, a sizeable theological library (which still exists) was assembled in Bury, mostly by gift, which may have been intended primarily for the use of the combination lecturers.[138] In London, the institution of Sion College was, in effect, a lending library for the clergy (only recently amalgamated with Lambeth Palace Library).

The ownership and availability of books does not tell us much about book use. Bishop Griffith Williams could complain: 'I may rather sit and wonder to see so little piety practised among us; I know the *Practice of Piety* [Bishop Lewis Bayly's bestseller] is almost in every house, in every hand, and it should be so; but it is not in many hearts, that have it in their *hands*.'[139] In 1600 Francis Bradley drew attention to a phenomenon with which we are still familiar: the family Bible lying in a corner, 'seldome used'.[140] Some historians even claim to have found a negative correlation between strong Protestantism and literacy.[141] That seems inherently unlikely. But we must never forget that many illiterate people would have had access to the written word through hearing it read aloud. 'Acoustic' reading was in all probability a widespread practice. It may be that the capacity to read silently, and privately, was not yet fully developed. But, as Roger Chartier has found in studying access to print in rural France, actual evidence of reading aloud is extremely rare.[142]

The evidence of who acquired or had access to books, and what books, is incomplete unless we ask how those books were read, and enter into the experience of religious reading. When and where did it take place? Was it purposeful?

137 Will of Frances Jermyn, Bury and West Suffolk Record Office, Register of Sudbury Wills, vol. 34.

138 J. Craig, 'The "Cambridge Boies": Thomas Rogers and the "Brethren" in Bury St Edmunds', in Wabuda and Litzenberger 1998, pp. 170–5. The work of Dr U. Leu on the library of Heinrich Bullinger, preserved in the Zentralbibliothek, Zurich, suggests that, just as the Zurich Prophezei was the ultimate source of English exercises of prophesying and combination lectures, so Bullinger's books bore the same relation to the Zurich 'exercise' as the Bury library to the Monday lecture.

139 Griffith Williams, *The best religion* (London, 1636), sig. v2^{v}.

140 Francis Bradley, *A godly sermon preached before the right worshipfull Edward Cooke* (London, 1600), p. 34.

141 M. Ingram, *Church courts, sex and marriage in England, 1570–1640* (Cambridge, 1987), pp. 115–16; Byford 1988, ch. 5, section 7; M. McIntosh, *A community transformed: Havering 1500–1620* (Cambridge, 1992), ch. 4, section 1.

142 Chartier 1987, pp. 155–8.

Critical? Public or private? Above all, was there anything distinctive about early modern, as opposed to modern, reading practices? Can any conclusions be drawn about the response to religious texts, other than its sheer diversity? We must begin, as early modern readers began, with the Bible, for it is in the case of Bible reading that we can be most confident that there were rules. Naturally, the Bible was to be read with faith and reverence. 'The Word which we read will not profit us, unless it be mixed with faith.'[143] It was also to be read 'after an orderly manner', not piecemeal. 'Read not here and there a chapter', warned Richard Rogers, 'but the Bible in order throughout.'[144] Many writers recommended a regular course of reading by which the whole Bible could be read in a year. Both Lewis Bayly and John White prescribed three chapters a day, morning, noon and night, which would leave only six chapters unread at the end of the year.[145] Nicholas Bownde's stricter régime of four chapters a day meant that the New Testament could be read twice over, while the Book of Psalms was to be read monthly, or quarterly.[146] Such systems appear to have been widely used. Thomas Taylor's funeral sermon for Mrs Mary Gunter, for example, declared that every year 'for the space of fifteene yeares together', she read through the whole Bible 'beginning her taske upon her birthday, and reading every day so many Chapters as to bring it about just with the year.'[147] But John Downame was afraid that this sort of reading could become mechanical. He recommended a more interactive reading, the reader using his pen to mark the chapters of 'greatest excellencie, and most profitable for our edification'. The whole Bible was useful, but some parts were more useful than others.[148] There is evidence that Foxe's *Actes and monuments* was another book read 'throughly'. A daily regime is suggested by the achievement of the Exeter worthy Ignatius Jordan, who, we are told, read the Bible 'above twenty times over', using a system of asterisks and other marks to apply the text to himself, and Foxe (a much longer book) 'seven times over'.[149] Perhaps no other book was read in quite that way. Nevertheless, godly books by human authors could be placed in the category of the Word of God. 'By reading of the word', explained John Stoughton, 'I meane not onely the reading of the word it selfe, but also all good bookes soundly written of any points of religion, whereby the

143 J. Downame, *A guide to godlynesse* (London, 1629), fol. 311^{v}, citing Hebrews 4.2: 'the word preached did not profit them, not being mixed with faith in them that heard it'.

144 Rogers, *A garden of spirituall flowers* (1625), sig. 2D1^{v}; Downame, *A guide*, fol. 316^{v}.

145 Bayly, *The practise of pietie* (40th edition, 1632), sig. M4^{r}; John White, *A way to the tree of life* (London, 1647), sig. Z2^{r}.

146 Nicholas Bownde, *The holy exercise of fasting* (Cambridge, 1604), sig. Y7^{v}.

147 Taylor, *Three treatises* (London, 1633), sig. H8^{r}.

148 Downame, *A guide*, fol. 316^{v}.

149 Samuel Clarke, *A collection of the lives of ten eminent divines* (London, 1662), p. 453.

better to helpe us in understanding of the Scriptures themselves.'[150] And such books, like the Bible, were to be read in order, from beginning to end, not, said Richard Rogers, 'a leafe of one and a chapter of another, as idle readers use to doe for novelties sake'.[151]

There was another kind of reading, very different from the faithful reading of the Bible, which was adversarial, as when the exemplary Protestant gentlewoman Lady Margaret Hoby was read to from Roman Catholic books.[152] The adversaria which fill the margins of books once possessed by the Suffolk iconoclast, William Dowsing, are testimony to this habit. Annotating his copy of *A true modest and just defence of the petition for Reformation*, he writes: 'this is but a popish distinction', 'your argument have no ground from scripture therefore your conclusion is false'.[153] For Catholics to peruse heretical works without priestly permission was a mortal sin, punishable by excommunication. But casuistry allowed for situations in which such reading might be excused, in order to confute a Protestant, or disabuse simple, deluded people.[154] Catholic prisoners might be forced to read Protestant works. The convert Francis Walsingham was supplied with tracts by Thomas Bell, a renegade, including his virulent *Survey of popery* and *Anatomy of popish tyranny*, and was told: 'By that time you have read these books, and marked them well, you will have no mind to be a Papist.' But Walsingham's faith was not shaken.[155] Sir Thomas Tresham, by contrast, seems to have found Foxe's 'Book of martyrs' a source of inspiration. Stories of the courage of Protestants burned at the stake armed him with evidence that his stubborn recusancy was not 'a fault but a singular commendation', and consoled him during long periods of incarceration.[156]

When Catholics read devotional works, they may have done so in ways distinctively different from their neighbours and peers. Poring over a spiritual book could be an act of worship, the printed item becoming as much an icon and object of reverence as an image or a pair of beads.[157] Augustine Baker's elderly father used a Latin primer as a mnemonic to the vocal prayer in which he engaged almost every spare moment in the day.[158] John Bossy has remarked

150 J. Stoughton, *Two profitable treatises* (London, 1616), sig. O5^{v}.
151 Rogers, *Seven treatises* (1603), sig. 2D1^{r}. 152 Meads 1930, p. 120.
153 J. Morrill, 'William Dowsing, the bureaucratic puritan', in *Public duty and private conscience in seventeenth-century England: essays presented to G. E. Aylmer*, J. Morrill, P. Slack and D. Woolf, eds. (Oxford, 1993), pp. 182–7.
154 See n. 110, above; also BL, MS. Lansdowne 96, fol. 44^{v}. Richard Verstegan obtained a licence to read 'hereticall bookes' early in 1590.
155 Foley 1875–83, II, pp. 345, 348–9. 156 HMC, *Various Collections*, 3 (London, 1904), 30.
157 See, for example, Foley 1875–83, VI, p. 719. One Mr Gardiner, lawyer, 'daily used and occupied as may seem, to pray upon' a Latin primer.
158 *Memorials of Father Augustine Baker and other documents relating to the English Benedictines*, ed. J. McCann and H. Connolly, CRS, 33 (London, 1933), 18, 53.

that if we are looking for a typographical piety practised by silent readers, we are more likely to find it among devout Catholics, reading spiritual books in pews and closets, than in the ranks of the reformed.[159]

This may prompt us to ask where people did their reading. The godly John Bruen of Chester 'went abroad into the field to meditate, as *Isaac* did in the evening', taking with him 'some part of the Bible, or his Sermon Notebooke'.[160] Some artisans seem to have carried their books into their workrooms, to read and meditate as they performed repetitive and mechanical tasks. Richard Baxter observed that the weavers of Kidderminster would prop a book before them, as they stood at the loom, perhaps reading aloud to edify others.[161] A Suffolk weaver who died in 1576 owned no fewer than sixty-seven books, kept in four 'hutches' – as well as all the gear for morris dancing.[162] Cobblers too had every opportunity to read on the job, agricultural workers doubtless less so. A more obvious place for private reading was the bedchamber. In his survey of book ownership in Kent, Peter Clark found that while most families kept their books in the hall, there was an increasing tendency for books to be stored in the bedchamber or in a closet adjacent to it.[163] Books might be kept and used in a room set aside for reading and writing, usually referred to in this period as a 'study', rather than a 'library', except in the case of large book collections. A 'Studdye Roome' in an inventory of 1610 contains 'a deske whereuppon the Book of Martyrs now standes', and two dozen other books.[164]

If the closet was inward-looking, the study was a window on a world of learning, where reading was accompanied by note-taking and reference to other books, and to an existing system of knowledge. The closet was associated with female, the study with male reading. The study was a place where passages from a book could be classified under various topic-headings and stored in a commonplace book. John Rainoldes told his pupils: 'Note in the margent or in some paper booke for that purpose, the summe and method of that which you read.'[165] The use of a commonplace book was typical of university-trained readers, but Nicholas Byfield's *Directions for the private reading of the Scriptures*,

159 Bossy 1985, p. 101.
160 William Hinde, *A faithfull remonstrance of the holy life and happy death of John Bruen* (London, 1641) sig. K7^{v}.
161 Baxter, *Reliquae Baxterianae*, p. 89.
162 P. Collinson, 'Christian Socialism in Elizabethan Suffolk: Thomas Carew and his *Caveat for clothiers*', in C. Rawcliffe, R. Virgoe and R. Wilson, eds., *Counties and communities: essays on East Anglian history presented to Hassell Smith* (Norwich, 1996), p. 168.
163 Clark 1976. On private reading, see Thornton 1997, pp. 96–7.
164 *Ancient inventories . . . illustrative of the domestic manners of the English in the sixteenth and seventeenth centuries* (London, 1854), p. 82, from an inventory of household goods at Cockesdon (unidentified).
165 *A letter of Dr Reinolds to his friend, concerning his advice for the studie of divinitie* (London, 1613), sig. A8^{r}.

first published in 1617 or 1618, was an attempt to make the practice more widespread among lay Bible readers. The British Library copy of his book contains a contemporary female ownership inscription, suggesting that he may have succeeded in reaching a non-graduate readership. Lady Margaret Hoby's diary refers to 'my Common place book', or 'my table book'.[166] But the commonplace book always smelt of academe, presupposing the existence of 'a Common memory-bank', 'a cultural memory shared by writer and reader', who shared a specific type of education.[167]

Private households contained within themselves a kind of public domain. Books were read aloud as part of a set form of household worship, or, in a more recreational manner, as an accompaniment to household chores, such as needlework. John White commended his patroness, Lady Mary Crofts of Saxham in Suffolk, for causing the Bible to be read aloud by female members of her household. 'He who hath seene your children and attendants about you, private, at worke, hath doubted which were the worke: the Reading of some, while others were working, or the working of others while some were reading.'[168] John Bruen of Chester 'set upon a deske, both in his Hall, and in his Parlour, two goodly fair Bibles of the best Edition, and largest Volume', apparently for recreational use as well as for household worship, since they were intended to take the place of cards or dice.[169] At the Protestant 'nunnery' of Little Gidding, bookishness was circular. Books which included Foxe were read aloud as female members of the household worked to prepare their own books, exquisite and unique biblical concordances.[170] These examples are from gentry households, but the practice of reading aloud may have filtered downwards to households of the middling sort, via books of practical divinity like *A garden of spirituall flowers*, which advocated the practice. In the family of the obsessively pious London artisan Nehemiah Wallington, wife, children, three servants and an apprentice, Sunday mornings consisted of Bible reading and exposition, catechizing, and a reading from the *Garden of spirituall flowers*, 'very useful to our souls'.[171] Similar customs seem to have pertained in the homes of Catholic gentry and nobility, like the Meynells of North Kilvington in Yorkshire.[172]

166 Nicholas Byfield, *Directions for the private reading of the Scriptures* (3rd edn, London, 1626), sigs. A9^r, E10^v; Meads 1930, pp. 67, 88.

167 Moss 1993. On the use of commonplace books, see Beal 1993; M. Todd, *Christian humanism and the puritan social order* (Cambridge, 1987), pp. 82–9.

168 John White, *Two sermons* (London, 1615), sig. A3^v.

169 W. Hinde, *A faithfull remonstrance* (1641), sig. I6^r.

170 Collinson 1995a.

171 P. Seaver, *Wallington's world* (Stanford, 1985), p. 40. See p. 79 for the size of Wallington's household in the 1620s.

172 *Miscellanea*, ed. E. E. Reynolds, CRS, 56 (London, 1964), xxiv–v.

Here sermons, the Bible and Puritan classics were replaced by the Office of Our Lady, primers and manuals of prayer, with often a formidable recusant matriarch filling the role of the austere Puritan paterfamilias, the very type of whom was Dame Dorothy Lawson of St Anthony's near Newcastle upon Tyne, who established the practice of reading pious books and saints' lives in the company of her servants and maids.[173]

At a more public level still, books were put to active use in Church, where not only the Bible, Prayer Book and Homilies were set up, chained, on lecterns, but sometimes books like Jewel's *Apologia*, and, of course, Foxe, which were accorded semi-sacred status. And, as we have seen at Bury St Edmunds, some privileged parishes acquired larger collections of books, whole parish libraries.[174] But increasingly the hotter sort of Protestants carried their own books, normally Bibles, to Church, and in a demonstrative and almost ritual fashion. The *Garden of spirituall flowers* advised the sermon goer to 'fold down a leafe in your Bible from whence the place is recited, that so at your leasure, after you returne from the Church, you may examine it'. This was the practice mocked in John Earle's satirical character book *Microcosmographie*, where we meet with the hypocritical 'she-puritan', whose devotion was much in 'the turning up her ey, and turning downe the leaf in her book when she heares named Chapter and Verse'.[175] In Elizabethan Colchester, a foulmouthed innkeeper defamed female sermon goers, with their Bibles under their arms, unaccompanied by their husbands, getting up to all kinds of mischief. But when parishioners carried prayer books to Church in order to follow the service they were liable to be accused of the opposite tendency, since this appeared to perpetuate the pre-Reformation private devotion of the little portable book of prayers called the 'portuise'.[176] (This neat polarity is disturbed by the evidence of Bibles and New Testaments bound up with editions of the Prayer Book and metrical Psalms. Were these 'Puritan' or 'Anglican' artefacts?) However, marking the texts quoted by the preacher, and looking them up afterwards, perhaps in company, do seem to have been practices which were part of the religious culture of Puritanism. In Harpsden, Oxfordshire, in the 1630s, a group of parishioners met together in a private house 'with a bible before them . . . there to make tryall what they could

173 William Palmes, *The Life of Mrs Dorothy Lawson of St Anthony's near Newcastle-on-Tyne* (London, 1855), p. 48.

174 *Parochial libraries* 1959; Birkby 1977. Early examples are at Wimborne (Dorset), Grantham (Lincolnshire) and Hereford (All Saints). See Glenn and Walsh 1988. On Ipswich, see Blatchly 1989. On Bury St Edmunds, see p. 57 above.

175 Rogers, *A garden of spirituall flowers* (1625), sig. G6^r; John Earle, *The autograph manuscript of Microcosmographie* (facsimile reprint of Bodl. MS. Eng. misc. f. 89) (Leeds, 1966), p. 117.

176 Byford 1988, p. 143; J. Maltby, *Prayer Book and people in Elizabethan and early Stuart England* (Cambridge, 1998), pp. 44–5.

remember that Sunday of the sermons they had hearde, and the bible beeinge open, they did looke out the proofes'. Other books were also read at these meetings, including the works of Richard Sibbes and John Preston, and the Book of Homilies. In spite of the impeccably orthodox Homilies, such gatherings were bound to be suspect as Puritan 'conventicles'.[177]

Reading was supplemented by memory. James Warre advised readers to memorize the names of the books of the Bible from the leaf in the front where they were normally listed. 'The want of which (as I have often observed) hath caused many (in *Church*) to tosse the leaves of their *Bibles* to and fro (to seeke the place he nominates) and oftentimes to close the *Booke* without finding the same.'[178] But this was not enough to locate particular passages in a book, and Ezekiel Culverwell devised a more elaborate memory aid, intended to help people memorize whole passages by means of constant re-reading, and a series of key words linked to important texts.[179] This presents interesting ambiguities. It was a system requiring a high level of literacy and of familiarity with the printed text of the Bible, but it was designed to train the reader's memory to the point where reference to the printed text became almost unnecessary. What may appear to us improbable feats of memory were not unknown in the seventeenth century. Thomas Stoughton described from personal knowledge the talents of 'a young gentlewoman' who 'before she was nine years old (not much above eight) could say all the New Testament by heart'. Being asked where any words were, she would very accurately name book, chapter and verse. Mrs Mary Gunter committed to memory 'many select Chapters, and speciall *Psalmes*', which she repeated to herself every week, because 'she knew not what daies of tryall or persecution might come, wherein she might be deprived of her Bible, and other good books and helpes'.[180] Bible reading took place within a framework established in the memory. Edward Vaughan's prescriptive system required readers to go through the Bible taking notes, and then to discard the notes, repeating the process from memory.[181]

Why do women readers figure so largely in the evidence we have been considering? One reason may be that women, particularly gentlewomen, spent more

177 E.R. Brinkworth, 'The study and use of Archdeacons' Court Records', *Transactions of the Royal Historical Society*, 4th ser., 25 (1943), 114, quoting the Oxford archdeaconry act book for 1633–4, now in the Oxfordshire Record Office.

178 James Warre, *The touchstone of truth* (London, 1630), sig. G7^{r}.

179 Ezekiel Culverwell, *A ready way to remember the scriptures* (London, 1637).

180 Thomas Stoughton, *Two profitable treatises* (London, 1616), sig. A6^{v}–7^{r} and Thomas Taylor, *The pilgrims profession* (London, 1622), pp. 155–6. James Ussher's two aunts, both blind from birth, were able to repeat any part of the Bible from memory. See Nicholas Bernard, *The life and death of the Most Reverend and Learned Father of our Church Dr James Usher* (London, 1656), sig. C3^{v}.

181 Edward Vaughan, *Three introductions* (London, 1594), sig. K4^{v}.

time at home and had more leisure for private reading. Women who found it difficult to travel to sermons may have been forced to rely more heavily on printed books. But over and above these practical considerations, private reading was regarded as a characteristically feminine activity. Hans Eworth's portrait of Lady Dacre depicts its subject with a prayer book in one hand and a quill pen in the other, apparently caught in the act of transferring her religious meditations to paper. Elizabeth Honig reads out of the painting the assumption that the cold, moist humours of women made them particularly prone to retain impressions in the memory.[182] Some religious books were specifically designed for women readers. The three works comprising Thomas Taylor's *Three treatises* consist of a group of sermons dedicated to a godly gentlewoman, Elizabeth Backhouse, and her daughters, a funeral sermon for our friend Mary Gunter, and a treatise entitled 'A glasse for gentlewomen to dresse themselves by', its subject, female apparell.[183]

But books were not simply aids to devotion. They were also items of property which could be lent, given, sold or bequeathed to others. This qualifies the point about reading as a feminine activity, for, as Natalie Zemon Davis points out, books were socially and sexually neutral objects. They could pass between the sexes, or cross social boundaries, and were therefore particularly suitable items to be lent or given.[184] Adam Winthrop's diary contains a list of books on all subjects, including religion, lent at various times to his Suffolk neighbours.[185] Clergymen with large libraries frequently lent or bequeathed books to their clerical neighbours, such gifts and loans implying a sense of professional and intellectual collegiality.[186] Books were handed down within the family. The will of Margaret Barret, a Suffolk widow, divides her books among her grandchildren. Dorothy Woodside was to have Arthur Dent's *Plain mans path-way*, Ambrose More Samuel Smith's *David's blessed man*, Michael More 'my book of the New Testament', John More 'my service book', and Margery More a copy of Henry Smith's sermons, with the proviso that 'my daughter Collyns is to have the use of the service book and the book of sermons during her life'.[187] These books were treasured possessions, and to pass them on to the next generation was a means of continuing the family tradition of religious

182 Elizabeth Honig, 'In memory: Lady Dacre and pairing by Hans Eworth', *Renaissance bodies: the human figure in English culture c. 1540–1660*, ed. L. Gent and N. Llewellyn (London, 1990), pp. 60–85.

183 Taylor, *Three treatises*. 184 Davis 1983.

185 *Winthrop Papers*, 1 (Massachusetts Historical Society, 1929), 71.

186 R. O'Day, *The English clergy: the emergence and consolidation of a profession 1558–1642* (Leicester, 1979), p. 185.

187 *The wills of the Archdeaconry of Sudbury, 1630–1635*, ed. N. Evans, Suffolk Record Society, 29 (1987), 159–60.

reading. John Bruen bequeathed his religious notebooks to his heirs with the explicit instruction 'to read over, if it were but once in all their life, the bookes that he hath thus written'. When John Bunyan and his first wife married, they were as poor as churchmice, without so much as a dish or a spoon. But Mrs Bunyan's dowry included Dent's *Plain mans path-way* and Bayly's *Practise of pietie*, both left to her by her godly father when he died.[188]

We should not ignore the multiplicity of non-literary uses to which books were put. Books were venerated as receptacles of spiritual power and revered for their totemic and thaumaturgic properties.[189] Bibles were employed as magical talismans to ward off evil spirits, and objects on which to take binding oaths. Opened at random, they were used as sortes to predict the future. Bibles were used to detect criminals, make decisions, discover secrets, and for all kinds of quasi-medicinal purposes. There was also powerful negative symbolism, indicative of threatening power, when religious books, including missals, primers and religious pictures were ritually burned, as happened from time to time at Cheapside and other locations, and especially next to the great national pulpit of Paul's Cross. Far beyond London, 'papistical' books were also burned in the market place at Perin in Cornwall.[190] Not only Catholic literature made bonfires. The same fate was shared by a pamphlet celebrating John Darrell's activities as a Puritan exorcist in Lancashire, by the writings of Elizabethan Separatists, and, in the 1630s, William Prynne's notorious *Histrio-mastix*.[191]

Finally we return to our questions about early modern religious reading practices, to hazard an answer. Is there any way that we can generalize about these practices, or is the evidence simply too diverse? We should certainly beware of suggesting that any mode of reading was 'typical'. Reading could take place in many different places and circumstances, and the theory that a shift from public to private reading occurred in this period carries little conviction. However, we can generalize about the practices of particular groups of readers. Writing about the twelfth century, and the circulation of St Bernard's sermons among Cistercian readers, Brian Stock has developed the useful notion of 'textual communities', groups of readers who respond to similar texts in similar ways.[192] Writing about the sixteenth and seventeenth centuries, it is possible to speak of a 'textual community' of people whose group identity as Protestants was founded on their respect for the Bible, whose interpretation of the Bible

188 W. Hinde, *A faithfull remonstrance* (1641), sig. H4ʳ; John Bunyan, *Grace abounding to the chief of sinners*, ed. R. Sharrock (Oxford, 1962), p. 8.

189 Cressy 1986. 190 *APC 1597–8*, p. 387; Petti 1955, p. 95.

191 Gillett 1932, p. 1. For specific orders for the incineration of books, see Loomie 1978, pp. 72–4; Foley 1875–83, VII, part 2, p. 1122.

192 Stock 1983.

often took place collectively, at sermons or private conferences, and who read the Bible in recognizably similar printed texts. Edward Vaughan's guide to the use of the Bible explains the meaning and use of the various sigla embodied in the text, presupposing a community of readers using identical printed editions.[193] The reading of Foxe's 'Book of martyrs', too, tended to consolidate, if not actually to construct, a textual community sharing common memories and united by a common history. It has been claimed that Foxe created a textual community of the whole nation.[194] But that is to ignore Catholicism, which, as we have seen, was another and in many respects a very different textual community, its dependence upon texts if anything even greater. And then there was that proportion of the population, which we have no means of measuring, who may not have been part of any textual community. But, beyond that, the persistence of oral forms of discourse, the continued proliferation of manuscripts together with printed books, the diversity of their subject matter and of the uses to which they were put, and the varying capacities, intellectual and financial, of those who owned, read, or simply heard them, makes one cautious in defining these reading communities more exactly.

193 Edward Vaughan, *Ten introductions: how to read . . . all the bookes . . . in the holie Bible* (London, 1594), f. 11^{v}.

194 Haller 1964.

2

Religious publishing in England 1640–1695

IAN GREEN and KATE PETERS

In publishing, as in Church and State, the 1640s and 1650s witnessed massive changes, and in the first part of this section some of the more striking changes will be considered: in broad terms and then through a specific example – the uses to which the Quakers put print in the early stages of the development of that movement. The speed and extent of those changes do, however, need to be kept in perspective: not all works then produced were radical or subversive – many were conservative or even reactionary. Moreover, there were a number of developments which took several decades rather than a few years to reach a peak in the later Stuart period. In the final part of this section some of the continuities between the edifying and instructive works published in the half century before 1640 and those published in the half century after 1640, and especially after 1660, will be discussed. For in the 1690s as much as the 1650s, works on 'divinity' comprised half of the output of English presses.[1]

Publishing in the 1630s had been characterized by the production of huge quantities of officially approved publications such as the Authorized Version of the Bible, the Book of Common Prayer, and the version of the metrical Psalms associated with Sternhold and Hopkins, but in the 1640s, owing to jealousies within the print trade and political turbulence, this production was either severely curtailed or brought to an abrupt end. Even the humbler *ABC with the catechisme* and *Primer and catechisme* fell under a cloud in the 1650s.[2] To some extent the gap thus created was filled by the publication of new formularies, such as the Westminster Confession and Catechisms and the *Directory*, but far fewer editions of these were produced than of their episcopalian precursors,

1 London 1658 and 1660; and appendix 1, table 4; and see Edward Arber's comments in *TC*, III, pp. vii–viii. See also Bland 1999, pp. 457–9. For definitions of 'religious' works, see above, pp. 29–31 and below, p. 80.

2 For relative production of these works, see *STC* s.v. Bible, Liturgies (Church of England, Book of Common Prayer), and Bible (Psalms, English, Metrical, Sternhold and Hopkins); and Wing s.v. Bible, Book of Common Prayer, and Bible (English Psalms). See also Green 2000 chs. 2, 5, 9; and on ABCs and primers, Green 1996, pp. 175–7.

reflecting the limited success of the Presbyterians in establishing their *classes* in the counties.[3]

Nor was disruption of the existing pattern confined to official titles or the works of authors associated with the old regime, such as Lancelot Andrewes and William Chillingworth.[4] Works by well-established 'godly' authors like Henry Smith, William Perkins, William Greenham, John Dod, Robert Cleaver and John Preston also fell out of favour, as interest shifted from assurance and other pastoral concerns to polemics and prophecy.[5] In addition there was a marked reduction in the 1640s in the production of large-scale commentaries on the scriptures by 'godly' scholars such as Andrew Willet, Thomas Godwin and John Weemes – works which had found a steady if unspectacular market before the wars. Joseph Caryl found that the later volumes of his mammoth commentary on Job did not sell nearly as well as earlier ones, and John Mayer, engaged in the final stages of his cumulative commentary on every book of both Testaments, had difficulty in finding publishers and readers for the last four volumes (published between 1647 and 1653), for which he blamed the instability of the times and the high cost of setting up large books.[6] There was a partial recovery in the 1650s, but most publishers found quicker returns from the many shorter works prompted by the political and religious turmoil of the 1640s and the emergence of new groupings in the late 1640s and 1650s.[7]

In two recent studies and a chapter later in this volume, Nigel Smith has made a powerful case for dramatic changes in the literature of the 1640s and 1650s. With the collapse of official censorship and the rapid increase in new works in the 1640s, there was, he suggests, a 'democratizing', a 'downward dissemination' of print. With the ending of the virtual stranglehold of the clergy on producing religious works, there was an unprecedented rise of lay authorship of such works, not least by new or newly important groups such as the Levellers, Baptists and Quakers; and with the disorientating effect of civil war and the relentless pursuit of spiritual fulfilment among the more radical Puritans such as the Seekers and Muggletonians who were not prepared

3 See Wing s.v. Westminster Assembly, and *Directory*; also Carruthers 1957, *passim*; and Green 1996, pp. 176–7.

4 Cf. *STC* and Wing s.v. L. Andrewes (e.g. *XCVI sermons*) and W. Chillingworth (e.g. *The religion of Protestants*).

5 Cf. *STC* and Wing s.v. authors named in the text.

6 *Ibid.*, s.v. A. Willet (e.g. the various *Hexapla*), T. Godwin or Godwyn (e.g. *Moses and Aaron*), J. Weemes (*The Christian synagogue*), and J. Caryl's multi-volume *Exposition* of Job; J. Mayer, *A commentary upon the whole Old Testament* (4 vols., 1653, 1647, 1653, 1652), I, sig. [A4^r]; II, sigs. A2^r–4^v; and IV, sig. A3^v.

7 For commentaries published in the late 1640s and 1650s compared to earlier and later decades, see *NCBEL* 1855–88; for shorter works, Thomason 1908, and Smith 1994, p. 24.

to observe the self-imposed restraints of more conservative believers, there was a dynamic for radically different uses of language, the reconstruction or renovation of many existing genres which some readers found to be outmoded, and the creation of new forms of literary expression such as the conversion narrative and new forms of worship such as the sung hymn.[8]

As Smith points out, however, the traffic was not all one way. The press was also used to great effect *against* the radicals by the more cautious elements of the day such as the Presbyterians and more conservative Independents, as in the case of Thomas Edwards's *Gangraena*, and even by Royalists, as in the case of the *Eikon Basilike* which sold an extraordinary number of editions in a very short space of time.[9] The extent of the 'democratizing' of print and 'downward dissemination' was also perhaps limited. On the one hand, it is almost certain that most of those lesser professionals, smaller merchants, and apprentices in the towns and yeomen in the country who swelled the ranks of some regiments of the Parliamentarian armies and of the Levellers, Fifth Monarchy Men and Quakers, had learned to read *before* 1642, even if they did enjoy much greater freedom to read and write thereafter.[10] On the other, the lowest ranks of all remained largely illiterate, and the disruption that the civil wars brought to many schools and the production of some school books may actually have led to a decline rather than an increase in the pool of new readers.[11] Moreover, 'downward dissemination' depends on how much of the new material was understood and accepted and, as Smith readily concedes, some of the more extreme mystical or prophetic examples of radical writing often appeared 'incomprehensible, ridiculous, or dangerous' to those who were not of the fellowship or did not understand the codes used among those who were.[12]

The very limited number of repeat editions of a high proportion of the new works produced in the 1640s and 1650s also suggests a limited dissemination; and of those new works which did get past a first edition, only a few would be reprinted again after 1660. (The fact that these included works by episcopalians such as Jeremy Taylor's *Holy living* (1650) and *Holy dying* (1651), and Richard

8 Smith 1994, pp. 23–4, Introduction, and chs. 1, 3, 8; and Smith 1989, *passim*.

9 Smith 1994, pp. 42–3, 112–13; M. Watts, *The Dissenters*, I: *From the Reformation to the French Revolution* (Oxford, 1985), pp. 111–15; Wing E228–9, and E268–311B.

10 Smith 1989, pp. 6–11; *The Clarke papers*, I, ed. C. H. Firth (London, 1891), pp. 22–3; B. Capp, *The Fifth Monarchy men* (London, 1972), pp. 82–7; B. Reay, *The Quakers and the English Revolution* (London, 1985), pp. 20–6; J. F. McGregor and B. Reay, eds., *Radical Religion in the English Revolution* (Oxford, 1986), pp. 18–19. For literacy rates, see Cressy 1977, pp. 4–21, and Cressy 1980, chs. 5–7; and Houston 1985, p. 33.

11 As previous note; and on school books, see above, n. 2, and Wing s.v. Lily's *Grammar* and E. Coote, *English schoolmaster*.

12 Smith 1989, p. 13; Smith 1994, p. 9.

Allestree's *The whole duty of man* (1658) is another indication of the limited and often temporary nature of the changes of the mid-century decades.[13]) Many of the religious works that were republished most often in the mid-seventeenth century were either repeat editions of older, pre-war works, such as John Andrewes's repentance tracts – *Andrewes golden chaine* and *A golden trumpet*[14] – or logical developments of an existing genre, such as new catechisms for the new groupings of the day, like Henry Jessey's (Baptist) *Catechisme for babes or little ones* (1652) and George Fox's (Quaker) *Catechisme for children* (1657), and new titles in the 'penny godly' category, for example those by 'John Hart' and 'Andrew Jones' which, as we shall see, are an excellent example of publishers' skill in recognizing and feeding a particular type of demand, albeit with material of a derivative nature which often showed a limited theological awareness.[15] That having been said, it remains the case that in terms of authorship, language, style, content and distribution, the character of religious publishing changed in many ways during the civil wars and Interregnum, and an excellent if hitherto less familiar illustration of a number of these changes is provided by the ways in which the early Quakers used the medium of print during the 1650s.

The alacrity with which the first Quakers turned to printed books and pamphlets to nurture their infant movement both reflected and contributed to the speed with which that movement grew and became recognized as a national phenomenon. In 1652 Thomas Aldam urged George Fox to use the press, because printed books would be 'verye servisable for weake frends, and Convinceing the world'.[16] And despite the youth and limited formal education of early Quaker authors – most were in their twenties, and almost all without a university education – Quaker publications rapidly rose from a handful of small quarto books and broadsides in 1652 to twenty-eight books in 1653 – when Richard Farnworth boasted that there were already enough Quaker books to secure 'the Downefall of Antichrists Kingdome' – and to an average of two books each week by 1655.[17] This level could not be sustained, but Quakers remained prolific publishers, averaging perhaps seventy-five titles a year

13 Cf. Wing s.v. Jeremy Taylor and Richard Allestree (first edition was entitled, *The practice of Christian graces*).

14 STC 588.5, and Wing A3122, 3123–23A.

15 Green 1996, pp. 83–5, 166, 199, 222–7, and Green 2000, ch. 8.

16 Thomas Aldam to George Fox, 1652, FHL, A. R. Barclay MS. 1: 71, fols. 206–207.

17 Peters 1996, chs. 1, 2; Richard Farnworth to Thomas Aldam, April 1653, London; FHL, Portfolio 36: 151. The figure for publications in the 1650s are based on an analysis of Wing's *STC* and differ from those in Barbour and Roberts 1973, pp. 568–73 (appendix 1, table 6 below); they will be discussed in greater detail in Peters (forthcoming).

between 1660 and 1699, which for a society of only 40,000–50,000 members, many of whom were probably illiterate, was remarkably high.[18]

Quaker books proclaimed an unequivocal Quaker identity, from the first broadside written by George Fox, which warned those who denounced 'Trembling, and Quaking, to beware what you doe', and offered a lengthy biblical exegesis on trembling, to books which appropriated the Quaker nickname more visually, and exploited it as a badge of oppression: 'From them who in the World in scorn is called Quakers, which suffers for the Righteous Seed sake.'[19] Another characteristic of Quaker publishing from the outset and throughout the later Stuart period was that it was carefully controlled by the movement's leadership, securing remarkable cohesion in style and content.[20] Fox himself played a key role: in December 1653 he requested that all manuscripts be sent to him before publication. But both then and later, especially when Fox was in jail, a small handful of men and women was responsible for the orchestration of the writing, approval, printing, distribution and later re-editing of Quaker books.[21]

Quaker publications, ranging from broadsides and short quarto pamphlets of eight pages to far weightier books of over one hundred pages, fulfilled a number of functions within the movement. Many early printed tracts originated as manuscript letters written by itinerant ministers to meetings they had visited or to each other, letters offering encouragement and providing news of how other meetings were faring. Thus many of the first authors – Fox, Farnworth, James Nayler, Francis Howgill, Edward Burrough and William Dewsbery – were the itinerant ministers who preached Quaker beliefs among the large rural parishes of northern England and then across the whole country. As they travelled, establishing meetings and appointing local figures to continue their work, they carried each others' books and manuscripts and wrote more of their own; as they were imprisoned for their preaching, they encouraged local sympathizers

18 Peters 1996, p. 68; Keeble 1987, pp. 129, 138, 306 n. 9, 308 n. 43. The high priority given to keeping records has probably ensured a much higher survival rate for Quaker publications than for other comparable groups of this period.

19 Peters 1996, ch. 4; George Fox, *An exhortation to you who contemne the power of God* [n.p., 1652]; *A Declaration of the marks and fruits of the false prophets* [London, 1655], p. 1.

20 For discussions of Quaker writing, see Maurice Creasey, '"Inward" and "outward": a study in early Quaker language', *JFHS*, supp. 30 (1962); H. Brinton, *Quaker journals. Varieties of religious experience among Friends* (Wallingford, Pennsylvania, 1972); Barbour and Roberts 1973; J. I. Cope, 'Seventeenth-century Quaker style', *PMLA*, 71, 2 (1956), 725–54; H. Ormsby-Lennon, 'From shibboleth to apocalypse: Quaker speechways during the Puritan revolution', in P. Burke and R. Porter, eds., *Language, self and society: a social history of language* (Cambridge, 1991); Smith 1995a; R. Bauman, 'Aspects of seventeenth-century Quaker rhetoric', *The Quarterly Journal of Speech*, 56 (1970), 67–74; R. Bauman, *Let your words be few: symbolism of speaking and silence among seventeenth-century Quakers* (Cambridge, 1983). The best discussion of post-Restoration Quaker publishing is O'Malley 1982 and O'Malley 1979.

21 Thomas Aldam to George Fox [December 1653], FHL, Sw MS. 3: 39; Keeble 1987, p. 111.

and fellow prisoners to join with them in helping to secure publication of their 'sufferings' and protesting against religious persecution, establishing a tradition which would burgeon during the more serious bouts of persecution after the restoration of the old order in 1660.[22]

Other early Quaker publications had other purposes, such as Richard Farnworth's conduct book, *An Easter-reckoning* (1653), which outlined proper relations in a godly commonwealth, beginning with children's 'dues or duty' to parents, wives' duties to their husbands, servants' duties to masters, magistrates' duties to God, and ending with instructions to alehouse keepers and warnings to 'whoremongers and adulterers'. Such a work may also have had a practical aspect in helping internal discipline within the early movement, for when Farnworth travelled to Lincolnshire in 1656 a group of locals came 'to Lay some Causes, before the Truth In mee; which was heard and determined', including cases of slander, theft and over-pricing.[23]

A more common type of early publication denounced the puritan ministry by listing the attributes of pharisees and false prophets. Quaker preachers seeking to attract new followers encouraged involvement through the repetition of key phrases, sometimes in rhyme, and asking audiences to judge their own ministers' behaviour against the examples of false ministry from the Bible.[24] Much evidence survives for itinerant Quakers travelling with a number of such tracts, and reading from them, displaying them at public meetings, or pinning them to the Church door. One letter went on to describe how 'Many people were made to Reede them and convinced it was truth and proved by Scripture and confessed to our frends it was truth.'[25] Another described how Quaker followers read books aloud in churchyards after sermons, and at market crosses on market days, adding triumphantly, 'And the priests is all on fier.'[26] Such tracts also demanded action: 'All people that read these things, never come more at the Steeple-house, nor pay your Priest more Tythes, till they have answered them.'[27]

22 Peters 1996, pp. 49–56; J. R. Knott, *Discourses of martyrdom in English literature, 1563–1694* (Cambridge, 1993).

23 Richard Farnworth and Thomas Aldam, *An Easter-reckoning, or, a free-will offering* (London, 1653), pp. 17–20; Richard Farnworth, 20 November 1656, FHL, Portfolio 36: 149–50.

24 The pamphlets which established this format, by Thomas Aldam and fellow prisoners at York Castle, *False prophets and false teachers described*, and *A brief discovery of the three-fold estate of Antichrist* (London, 1653), were among the first Quaker tracts published.

25 [Thomas Aldam] to Margaret Fell, 1653, FHL, A. R. Barclay MS. 2: 159. The paper concerned was probably Richard Farnworth's *A call out of Egypt and Babylon*, or a manuscript version of it, which offered 'six and twenty Errours of the Priests discovered'; Richard Farnworth, *A call out of Egypt and Babylon* (London, 1653).

26 Richard Farnworth to Margaret Fell, 2 December 1652, FHL, Sw Trs 2: 19.

27 George Fox, *A paper sent forth into the world* (London, 1654), p. 8.

Other Quaker publications attempted a more sophisticated critique of the Puritan ministry by using print as an extension of debates with such ministers. The fact that relatively uneducated Quaker authors formally disputed in public with highly educated ministers on the true authority of the Christian ministry, argued for a universal inner light of Christ and the establishment of religious liberty of conscience, and then published the result is evidence of the participatory, 'popular' nature of both religion and religious publishing in the Interregnum.[28] There is a distinct element of propaganda in these accounts in that they portray victories by honest Quakers over hypocritical Puritan ministers, or the poaching of new recruits from rival Baptist or Independent congregations.[29] In other cases, books were published when a rival account of a dispute was perceived to be damaging the local Quaker following, as when Richard Farnworth realized that Edmund Skipp's *The world's wonder* 'doth much harm', and beseeched his colleagues in London to speed up the publication of his own reply, confident that 'if my Answer to it were downe and abrod', it 'would be usefull'.[30] Quaker authors claimed to be bothered by hostile publications only when they had an adverse effect on their own followers and sympathizers, but the temptation to get sucked into polemical debate sometimes proved hard to resist.[31]

Early Quaker books were printed in relatively small numbers, in runs of 300, or even 100 for a pamphlet specific to a locality, though by 1656, runs of 600 were agreed. In addition, small quantities of books and pamphlets – perhaps one dozen copies – were sent to established Quaker meetings. Thus in 1656, Margaret Fell instructed that copies of one of her own books 'may goe forth amongst freinds as the Rist of Books does, the same Quantety to Every place', suggesting a very established system of distribution focused on Quaker meetings.[32] There is evidence that these books were read aloud in meetings, as well as lent or sold for private reading, again blurring the line between oral and literate cultures. Collections were also made at such meetings to underwrite the

28 A. Hughes, 'The pulpit guarded: confrontations between orthodox and radicals in revolutionary England', in A. Laurence, W. Owens and S. Sims, eds., *John Bunyan and his England, 1628–88* (London, 1990), pp. 44–8.

29 See, for example, the naming of three former Baptist preachers who defected from their Church in Wickhambrook, Suffolk, to the Quaker meeting at Littleport, Cambridgeshire: James Parnell, *The watcher: or, the stone cut out* (London 1655), sigs. F3^r–G3^r.

30 Richard Farnworth to George Fox, Bromyard, Herefordshire, 26 April 1655, FHL, Sw MS. 3: 55; Edmund Skipp, *The world's wonder, or, the Quakers blazing star* (London, 1655). Farnworth's response appeared as *Antichrist's man of war apprehended* (London, 1655).

31 John Audland to Edward Burrough, Bristol, 14 July 1655 [poss. 1656], FHL, A. R. Barclay MS. 2: 177, fol. 151; Keeble 1987, pp. 86–9.

32 Margaret Fell to John Stubbs, [1656], FHL, Spence MS. 3: 40.

costs of printing in London – another factor in explaining the rapid expansion of early Quaker publishing.[33]

It would be wrong to imply, however, that such publications were exclusively introspective, concerned only with building the movement. Debates with Puritan ministers went to the heart of wider arguments about the nature of religious orthodoxy and what type of settlement should emerge. Quakers argued in print for legislation in favour of liberty of conscience, the abolition of tithes and the establishment of a truly godly Commonwealth. They grounded their case in their own experiences of persecution and hostile magistrates, as in an account of a Quaker trial in Norwich, whose author warned members of the government of the 'tyranny and persecution . . . acted privately in their Names'.[34] The political implications of religious persecution were always highlighted by Quaker authors in their tracts, which the Quakers made sure came into the hands of Members of Parliament, Cromwell's household, and the army, as well as Quaker audiences in the provinces.[35]

Although Quakers faced hostility from an early date, and that hostility grew apace after 1656, they seem to have enjoyed ready access to the press in London, where the vast majority of their books were printed.[36] In the 1650s none of their publications was formally licensed, and only one, apparently arbitrarily, was registered with the Stationers' Company.[37] In the years between 1652 and 1656, over half of their books were produced quite openly by the publisher, Giles Calvert, already notorious for publishing works by Levellers, Diggers and Familists, and though not a Quaker himself, clearly sympathetic to their cause. Thereafter his role was taken by his brother-in-law, Thomas Simmonds, who also openly published their works.[38] There were early signs of government concern about Quaker manuscripts and tracts, and from her home at Swarthmoor Hall, Lancashire, Margaret Fell organized a national network of safe contacts

33 See O'Malley 1979, pp. 172–4.

34 Richard Hubberthorne *et al.*, *The testimony of the everlasting gospel* [Norwich], (1655), p. 3.

35 A copy of James Nayler's tract entitled *The power and glory of the Lord shining out of the North* (London, 1653), held by Cambridge University Library, states that it was 'rec'd from Col. Wm. West [Barebones M. P.] 20 August 1653' (CUL Syn. 7. 65.57, p. 26); Thomas Aldam to George Fox [March 1655], FHL, Sw MS. 3: 38 discusses distributing books on his way for an audience with Cromwell; for examples of publications aimed explicitly at Parliament, see Anthony Pearson, *To the Parliament of the Common-wealth of England* [n.p., 1653], and George Fox, *A message from the Lord, to the Parliament of England* (London, 1654).

36 B. Reay, 'Quakerism and society', in McGregor and Reay, eds., *Radical religion*, pp. 141–64; Peters 1996, p. 76.

37 This was John Stubbs and William Caton, *A true declaration of the bloody proceedings of the men in Maidstone* (London, 1655), entered by Calvert in the Stationers' Company register on 20 June 1655: Arber, I, p. 486.

38 For a useful short account of Giles Calvert's status with the Quakers, see Terry 1938, pp. 45–9. More detail on early Quaker publishers is found in Littleboy 1921, pp. 1–16, 66–80; and Mortimer 1947, pp. 107–25.

and trustworthy carriers to ensure safe passage for manuscripts and books, and identify safe distribution points for books.[39] The early links established between Calvert and the Quakers reveal much about how the print trade could help to spread religious ideas at this time. Travelling ministers were directed to Calvert's shop on arrival in London and introduced by him into the radical communities of London. He forwarded letters and parcels to itinerant Quakers, books to provincial distributors, and provided credit for travelling Quakers, as well as publishing their works – over 200 by his death in 1663.[40] Thereafter his widow, Elizabeth, and other radical printers played a similar role among the underground communities of religious dissenters, running considerable legal risks in the context of renewed persecution.[41]

For in the much harsher climate represented by the Clarendon Code, the Licensing Act, and the searches of Sir Roger L'Estrange, Quakers would need the framework for self-censorship, the good links with radical London printers, and the established distribution networks of 'dispersers' that had all been set up in relatively easier times in the 1650s to survive and carry on the fight.[42] This part of the story is better known. After 1660 Quaker publications were usually unlicensed and anonymous: not only did the Quakers not recognize the state's right to censor their works, but also they knew that a licence would be refused even if they did seek one, and Fox sought to reduce elements such as perfectionism which had led to the Friends being associated with the more flamboyant sectaries and prophets of the 1650s.[43] Instead the Quakers, as Neil Keeble has remarked, 'seem . . . to have organized themselves into a religious counterpart to the Stationers' Company', with sympathetic printers and stationers working closely with the Quaker leaders who authorized publication in the preparing of texts, the protection of copyright, and the warehousing and retailing of books throughout England and in the New World.[44] As a result, between 1660 and 1699, nearly 3,000 new Quaker titles by over 600 different authors were published, mainly short and cheap works compared to the average episcopalian or moderate dissenting work, but representing an unswerving faith in the power of print to spread the gospel of the light within.[45]

39 Hetet 1987, p. 130; George Taylor to Margaret Fell, 26 February 1655, FHL Sw MS. 1: 214; *CSPD 1655–56*, p. 308; Anthony Pearson to Edward Burrough, 21 February 1654, FHL, Sw MS. 3: 111; Peters 1996, pp. 86–90.

40 For examples of Calvert welcoming Quaker preachers to the capital, see FHL, A. R. Barclay MS. 1: 28, fol. 82; Sw MS. 1: 208; 1: 209; Spence MS. 3: 7, and forwarding letters to itinerant Quakers, see FHL, Sw MS. 3: 30; Sw Trs 4: 99; A. R. Barclay MS. 2: 157, fol. 88; Markey MS. p. 13; Keeble 1987, 121–2.

41 Bell 1987; Hetet 1987.

42 Keeble 1987, chs. 1, 3, and p. 131.

43 Keeble 1987, pp. 111, 113; Smith 1989, pp. 345–6.

44 Keeble 1987, pp. 121–3, 131–2.

45 Keeble 1987, pp. 111, 123, 129, 131, 134, 141, 144.

After 1662 moderate Puritans, Presbyterians and Independents were also marginalized in Church and State, but their university-educated ministers continued to publish regularly for supporters who were drawn more from the middling and lower-middling ranks than the Quakers were, and authors like Richard Baxter, John Owen, John Bunyan, Thomas Doolittle and many others published quite openly with the help of sympathetic licensers.[46] There has been a tendency to treat the non-conformist literature of the last four decades of the seventeenth century as different both in type and effect from the 'Anglican' variety,[47] but there is a case for treating them together here. It may readily be admitted that there were many Restoration churchmen who regarded devotion to the Church's teachings and practices as the best antidote to what they saw as the shameful increase of heresy, atheism, sedition and sin in recent decades. But one of their strategies – the publication and distribution of a wide variety of devotional works, expositions of the church catechism, and handbooks on preparing for communion – was not very different from that of those dissenting ministers who published dozens of expositions of the Westminster Shorter Catechism and their own handbooks on prayer and preparation for communion, such as Thomas Doolittle's *Treatise concerning the lords supper* which passed through twenty-seven editions between 1667 and 1726.[48] Equally it cannot be denied that some Dissenters – and their printers – were subjected to many handicaps and hardships after 1662, not least in the publication of polemical works or works complaining at their treatment by the authorities and arguing the need for change. But, as already noted, many non-conformist ministers published their work as a matter of course, and when they concentrated on trying to reach the as yet unconverted, as in many of Baxter's practical works and Bunyan's allegories, they usually secured licences.[49]

What is more, there are many cases of co-operation or overlap between the two traditions. The Stationers' Company regularly commissioned and sold copies of the Westminster Assembly's Shorter Catechism as well as the episcopalian equivalent; the *Term catalogues*, in which leading publishers advertised new books and reprints, regularly carried details of works by Presbyterians and Congregationalists alongside those by conformist clergy; and a publisher like Brabazon Aylmer issued works by conformists such as Isaac Barrow,

46 Keeble 1987, pp. 111–13, 117–18, 141–4; and for examples of their works regularly republished see Green 2000, appendix 1.

47 C. J. Sommerville, *Popular religion in Restoration England* (Gainesville, 1977), appendix 1 and *passim*; Keeble 1987, pp. 128–9, 139, and *passim*; and for works attributed to 'godly' as opposed to conformable clergy, see below, pp. 83–4.

48 J. Spurr, *The Restoration Church of England, 1646–1689* (New Haven and London, 1991), chs. 3–7; Green 1996, chs. 2–4; and Green 2000, ch. 5; Wing D1899–1905A and *BLC*.

49 Keeble 1987, chs. 3, 4, 6.

John Tillotson, Richard Kidder and Edward Fowler as well as dissenters like Baxter, Thomas Manton, William Bates, Edward Pearse and (after he had turned against the Quakers) George Keith. Moderate episcopalian clergy like Simon Patrick, Edward Stillingfleet and John Tillotson also sat alongside dissenters like Thomas Gouge, Baxter, Bates and Giles Firmin on the Welsh Trust which from 1674 to 1681 tried to raise educational standards and distribute religious books in Wales; and Tillotson, a future Archbishop of Canterbury, later wrote a fulsome preface to Gouge's collected works in recognition of his charitable efforts in this and other fields.[50] Moreover, given the limited number of dissenters, less than a quarter of a million or 5 per cent of the population, we must conclude from the very large sales of a work like John Bunyan's *The pilgrim's progress* that it had a sufficiently wide appeal to persuade many churchgoers as well as dissenters to buy it. In this context it is instructive that in the preface to the second of a pair of allegories published by the Baptist Benjamin Keach in the early 1680s the author said that he had been encouraged to learn that both works had 'found a kind acceptance generally amongst all sorts of Protestants, whether conformists or nonconformists'; and when publishers were preparing a second volume of Bunyan's works in 1707 it was noted that the first volume had 'met with very great encouragement amongst good people of all persuasions (ministers as well as others)'.[51] If members of the contemporary clergy and print trade drew no sharp lines between the edifying and practical works written by moderate dissenters and conformists, perhaps we should not be too ready to do so. Indeed, it may be suggested (though not all would agree) that the message contained in the majority of the religious works published between 1660 and 1700, especially at the lower levels of instruction and edification – a common stress on the need for faith and repentance and the use of the means provided to help the faithful: Word, prayer, and sacraments – drew together not only teachers of different generations but also of different standpoints on matters of Church government and practice.[52] Perhaps the vitality of religious publishing at this time – and it was arguably a golden age for 'Anglicans' as well as 'dissenters'[53] – was in no small measure the product of a creative tension between on the one hand a pastoral urge to help the faithful and appeal to the unconverted to change before it was too late, and on the other

50 Barnard 1994, pp. 9–10, 22, 27–8 (and for a comparison, above, n. 3); *TC*, I–III, *passim*; Keeble 1987, pp. 123–4; G. H. Jenkins, *The foundation of modern Wales: Wales 1642–1780* (Oxford, 1993), pp. 137, 198–9; for the Tillotson preface, see *TC*, III, pp. 476, 489.

51 Keeble 1987, pp. 137–8; I. M. Green 'Bunyan in context: the changing face of Protestantism in seventeenth-century England', in M. van Os and G. J. Schutte, eds., *Bunyan in England and abroad* (Amsterdam, 1990), pp. 19–20, 27; B. Keach, *The progress of sin* (1707), sig. A3^{r}; and *TC*, III, pp. 581.

52 This point is developed in Green 1996, pt 2, and Green 2000, ch. 10, and *passim*.

53 See above, n. 2, and Spurr, *Restoration Church*, pp. 225–6, 229–30, 273, 282–3, 286, 289–90.

a competitive urge to confirm or win over the loyalty of as many followers as possible.

The religious publications of the later Stuart period were also produced in a context that embodied on the one hand the revival of patterns found before the 1640s and on the other continuity with elements of the publishing history of the 1640s and 1650s. In what remains of this chapter, we will concentrate on two aspects of those publications: patterns of production, and patterns of consumption, though it seems clear that the former were in many ways strongly shaped by the latter.

After 1660 there was a rapid resumption of pre-war patterns of large-scale production of Bibles, prayer books, psalters, and official catechisms and primers, together with large quantities of visitation articles and episcopal queries (now often with printed forms for churchwardens' and clergy's replies), and the articles, canons, and homilies of the church.[54] The resumption was not a mirror image. Production of *The ABC with the catechisme* and *The primer and catechisme* may actually have increased, with batches of 5,000 or 10,000 copies of the *ABC* being delivered to the Stationers' Company warehouses two, three, or even four times a year in the early years of Charles II's reign, and the *Primer* being printed in even larger quantities. Conversely, Bible production probably did not quite reach the heights attained in the 1620s and 1630s, for a variety of reasons: over-production in the 1630s, the flood of Dutch Bibles smuggled in in the 1640s and 1650s, the development of a second-hand market, perhaps a growing tendency for families to pass folio and quarto copies from generation to generation, and a slowing of population growth.[55] The balance between on the one hand didactic, 'practical', and devotional works and on the other controversial or prophetic ones, which had swung towards the latter in the 1640s and 1650s, swung back to the former, as is shown by production of godly living and godly dying manuals like those of Taylor and Allestree which soon reached a peak to match the pre-war sales of works by Becon and Bayly.[56]

The temporary shift towards shorter works in the 1640s noted above was also reversed, though the largest projects of all continued to face difficulties, such as the multi-volume *Critici sacri* (1660) that accompanied Walton's *Polyglot* (1653–7). For such projects publishers increasingly banded together to share the costs and risks, as with the sermons of Thomas Manton in 1679 and John Tillotson in 1696. From the 1680s especially, authors, editors and publishers

54 Green 1996, ch. 4; Green 2000, chs. 2, 4.

55 Green 2000, ch. 2; the number of editions was lower than the 1630s, but print runs were larger, especially for smaller formats. For production of the *ABC* and *Primer* see Green 1996, pp. 176–7.

56 This comment is based on the sample of bestsellers and steady sellers in Green 2000, appendix 1, and analysed there in chs. 4–7.

sought subscriptions from the public in return for cheaper copies of the first edition, as with the first collected edition of Joseph Caryl's enormous *Exposition upon Job* (1676), Matthew Poole's *Annotations upon the Holy Bible* (1683–5), the collected works of John Bunyan in 1692, and the practical works of Richard Baxter in 1707.[57] Moreover, while lay authors like Sir Matthew Hale and later Daniel Defoe wrote a number of popular or influential works, and the private prayers of aristocratic ladies became fashionable too when published, the majority of works were again composed by regular clergy or preachers, whether conformist or nonconformist.[58]

Other patterns of production were less a resumption of a pre-war pattern than the *culmination* in the later seventeenth century of a trend that had begun before 1640 and carried on through the revolutionary decades into the later Stuart period. Some of these trends related to design and presentation. One was the tendency towards the use of ever smaller formats for an existing text, such as the Bible, which had begun with the switch from folio to quarto as the most popular format under Elizabeth, and thence to octavo under the early Stuarts, but did not reach its peak until the increasing predominance of duodecimos in the late seventeenth century.[59] Another was the increasingly common practice of using an eye-catching title like *Apples of gold*, *A string of pearls*, or *The happy ascetick*, or an illustration on the title page, which can be found in the early Stuart period but was increasingly commonplace not only in the 1650s but also under the later Stuarts in the works of conformists like Taylor, Allestree, Anthony Horneck and Samuel Crossman, as well as Dissenters like Thomas Brookes, John Hayward, John Flavell and Benjamin Keach.[60] Other trends were more a matter of style and function, often as a result of authors trying to help the less informed grasp the full meaning of what they were hearing, reading or saying. This included the development of a sermon style that avoided both the orotundity of some early Stuart Court preachers and the tendency of some of the 'godly' to make their sermons top-heavy with scripture texts or fine distinctions; the continuing effort to find a catechetical work that would meet the needs of a particular community; the

57 Wing P994A (and *CHB*, III, p. 93); Keeble 1987, pp. 125–6, 130–1; *TC*, II, p. 504, and III, pp. 474–5, 581.

58 Green 2000, ch. 1; and cf. Sir Matthew Hale, *Contemplations moral and divine* (fifteen editions 1676–1720), Daniel Defoe, *The family instructor* (eleven editions 1715–34), and Ann Morton, Countess of Douglas, *The Countess of Morton's daily exercise* (seventeen editions 1666–96).

59 Green 2000, ch. 2.

60 For titles see, for example, Thomas Brookes's *Apples of gold for young men and women* and *A string of pearls, or the best things reserved till last*, Thomas Fuller's *Good thoughts in bad times*, John Hall's *Jacob's ladder*, and Anthony Horneck's *The happy ascetick*; for illustrations see, for example, Jeremy Taylor's *The great exemplar*, Samuel Crossman's *Young mans calling*, Benjamin Keach's *War with the devil* and *The progress of sin*, and John Hayward's *The horror and terrors of the hour of death*.

provision of more and more aids to Bible study designed to help 'lambs' wade through the shallows of scripture (rather than help 'elephants' swim across its deeper waters); and the construction of collections of prayers and of guides to preparing for communion that all ranks, all ages and both sexes could use.[61] The attempt to be as brief and simple as possible in order to reach both the 'middling sort of people' and the 'plain man' with little or no formal education was the stimulus of a great many of the works produced in the later Stuart period, but it was the successful culmination of a process begun at least a century earlier.[62]

These and other developments can be seen clearly if we turn to an analysis of a sample of Protestant bestsellers and steady sellers in the period 1536–1700. This sample consists of 727 titles identified through the *Short-Title Catalogues* which were printed in England at least five times in a thirty-year period, and which by their character or avowed intention may be deemed 'religious' in the sense of expressing a personal statement of faith, imparting doctrinal or ecclesiastical information of a Protestant kind, or exhorting or helping others to adopt correct forms of Christian conduct. The growing demand for such works is indicated by the fact that only 338 of these titles appeared in the hundred years from 1536 to 1640 compared to 389 first published during the sixty years from 1641 to 1700.[63] The size of the later Stuart market for such works may have been even larger than these figures suggest in that the official limit for editions published in the last two-thirds of the seventeenth century was for most works 2,000 copies, a third higher than the 1,500 permitted from the 1580s to the early 1630s. While many works on their first appearance were probably printed in relatively small runs, once a work had proved its popularity it was regularly published in runs up to and exceeding the permitted maximum. Thus Michael Sparke's *Crums of comfort*, first published under James I, was produced at the old ceiling of 1,500 copies, to judge from the 60,000 copies claimed to have been sold by the fortieth edition in 1652; so also apparently were many of Baxter's early works. But in the 1640s and 1650s, the Dutch were said to be printing much larger runs of Bibles destined for England; John Rawlet's *Christian monitor* was published in runs of 5,000 copies to judge from the 95,000 said to have been published in nineteen editions between 1683 and 1695; and by the turn of the century examples of runs of 6,000 and 10,000 for bestselling catechisms and other titles can be cited.[64]

61 Green 2000, chs. 3–5, and Green 1996, chs. 2, 5.

62 Green 1996; and Green 2000, *passim*.

63 Green 2000, Appendix 1 for the sample, Preface for the definition, and ch. 4 for an explanation of how the sample was constructed, and its strengths and weaknesses.

64 Arber IV, p. 22; M. Sparke, *Crums of comfort* (1652), sig q5^{v}; Keeble 1987, pp. 128, 133; J. Rawlet, *The Christian monitor* (1696), note at end; Green 1996, pp. 194–5, 748–9; J. Bunyan, *The pilgrim's progress*, ed. J. B. Wharey and Rev. R. Sharrock (Oxford, 1960), p. lxxiv, for an alleged run of 20,000.

The sample of best and steady sellers can be used to provide a thumbnail sketch of the types of books with which Protestant readers of different types were likely to come into contact in the later seventeenth century. Titles such as the Authorized Version of the Bible, the Book of Common Prayer, and Sternhold and Hopkins's metrical version of the Psalms represent only about 6 per cent of the *titles* in the sample, but with sales recovering from the mid-century dip they continued to account for over 40 per cent of the *editions* printed of works in the sample as a whole; and since the maximum print runs permitted for such titles were generally twice those allowed for most other titles, the gross number of copies of these titles may actually have exceeded that of the rest put together.[65] Printed sermons, both individual texts and the collected works of a particular preacher, comprise approximately 15 per cent of the sample, but with relatively fewer titles after 1640 than before, and a slightly lower average number of repeat editions for full-sized sermons (eight per title, as opposed to nine before 1640).[66] Treatises and tracts comprise over a third of the works in the sample, with an average number of editions of 10.5.[67] However, if we divide these into different types, we find that those which appear to have passed through most repeat editions after 1640 were those which provided guidance on godly living (average twenty editions per title) and godly dying (sixteen), whereas those which passed through fewer editions than average (seven or eight) were, as before 1640, either controversial (whether the polemic was aimed against Catholics or fellow Protestants) or prophetic.[68] Catechisms continued to provide about 10 per cent of titles in the sample after 1640, and although the average number of repeat editions fell, this has to be set against the higher print runs of which publishers regularly took advantage.[69] An increasingly common type of publication in the Elizabethan and early Stuart period – collections of supplementary prayers for use in the home, in the family unit or privately – continued to sell in disproportionately high numbers in the later seventeenth century (only 6 per cent of the sample after 1640 but an average of thirteen editions per title), while the number of handbooks on preparation for communion not only quadrupled after 1640 but also passed through an above average number of editions (twelve).[70] Works that combined edification with a measure of entertainment or adopted a variety of approaches also went from strength to strength, rising from below a fifth of the pre-1640 sample to nearly a quarter thereafter. These included religious verse (at all levels from

65 See above, n. 2, and Green 2000, chs. 2, 5, 9.

66 Green 2000, ch. 4; if we add in the probably inflated claims for repeat editions of chapbook sermons by authors like 'John Hart' (see below, pp. 83–4), the average becomes higher, at 12.5 editions.

67 Green 2000, ch. 4.

68 Green 2000, chs. 4, 6.

69 Green 2000, ch. 4.

70 Green 2000, ch. 5.

Herbert and Quarles to Bunyan and Keach), improving dialogues, religious allegories, uplifting biographies, cautionary tales, and open letters, and works in which authors had chosen to combine verse and prose, or information and exhortation with prayers or a catechism or both, as in Samuel Crossman's *Young mans monitor* (1664), John Flavell's *Navigation spiritualiz'd* (1664) and *Husbandry spiritualized* (1669), Richard Baxter's *The poor man's family book* (1674), and William Burkitt's *Poor man's help* (1694).[71] What these last examples show, together with the use of smaller formats described above and the marketing of the so-called 'godlies' described in the next paragraph, is not simply the much greater diversity of religious works that were being written and published in the later Stuart period, but also the extent to which the focus of religious publishing had been widened, to embrace not just the gentry, professionals and richer manufacturers and merchants who had been the staple lay purchasers of the larger religious works published in the first century after the Reformation, but also the lower-middling ranks, sailors, husbandmen, servants, poorer families and older adolescents at whom a growing proportion of new titles was being targeted.

This brings us to two other types of publication at the bottom end of the market – the 'godly' ballad and the 'godly' chapbook. These, a very small but growing percentage of works in the sample, are almost certainly underrepresented given the low survival rate of cheap print, but may have passed through a much higher than average number of editions, especially in the case of chapbooks. Both were printed on the cheapest paper, often using black-letter type, and were distributed widely throughout England in the later seventeenth century through the highly efficient system set up by the ballad partners in the early Stuart period. Both have attracted much attention from historians recently, though it was booksellers rather than authors who controlled both genres, and compared to the works described earlier they offered a garbled doctrinal message or were designed to titillate rather than edify.[72]

The broadside ballad was printed on a single sheet or half-sheet, sold for a penny, and often pinned or pasted on a wall, but it had been abandoned as a vehicle for effective Protestant indoctrination as early as the 1580s. However, a diluted version of the so-called 'godly' ballad survived as a staple of the print trade for another hundred years and more.[73] As a result, with only a few exceptions,[74] there was a dearth of solidly Protestant – as opposed

71 Green 2000, ch. 7.

72 On this point, Green 2000, ch. 8 differs from Spufford 1981, ch. 8, and E. Duffy, 'The godly and the multitude in Stuart England', *The Seventeenth Century*, 1 (1986), pp. 31–55. On the distribution of these works, see Spufford 1981, ch. 5; and Watt 1991, chs. 1, 7.

73 Watt 1991, pt. 1.

74 These are discussed in Green 2000, ch. 8.

to generic Christian – teaching in later Stuart ballads, even in those ostensibly based on a scripture story;[75] and those anti-Catholic ballads which appeared at times of heightened political tension such as 1679–81 and 1688–90 were usually better at attacking alleged 'popish' abuses than stating orthodox Protestant truths.[76] Ballads cataloguing the sins of the age which had aroused divine anger in the form of plague or war usually devoted most space to describing the vices in question before concluding with a brief assurance that an act of repentance or charity or an appeal to God for help would undoubtedly bring results – a view that the genuine 'godly' would have denounced as suggesting that good deeds or the power of human will could secure salvation.[77] Ballads containing a list of improving aphorisms were characterized by a bland moralism which again drew a simple equation between merit and reward, while those which described edifying deathbed scenes or embodied the older mortality tradition often contained strong elements of pre-Reformation motifs such as the dance of death and the passing-bell.[78] Such ballads were produced by publishers and authors who were arguably less anxious to inculcate genuine Protestant teaching and piety than make a profit by exploiting the public's fears about sudden death by plague or Catholic plots, pandering to their baser instincts with stories of lust, murder, or the dreadful ends met by atheists and other deviants, or fanning their social aspirations by telling them what constituted genteel behaviour.[79]

Chapbooks were flimsy little pamphlets, again often in black letter and with a crude woodcut on the cover, and were usually either twenty-four pages long and sold for twopence, or forty-eight pages and sold for threepence in the later Stuart period. Their antecedents can be traced back to the 1620s, but from the 1650s to the 1680s they sold in enormous quantities – *if* we can accept publishers' claims on many title pages that this was the '54th' or the '57th' impression when hardly any earlier editions are extant.[80] The overtly devotional or didactic

75 E.g. anon., *A godly ballad of the just man Job* [1655–56] (Wing G933H), and *A most excellent ballad of Joseph, and the sacred virgin Mary* [1663–74] (Wing M2880).

76 E.g. anon., *A looking-glass for all true Protestants* [c.1680?], and *Englands deliverance* [c.1688] (neither in Wing).

77 E.g. anon., *A looking-glass for a Christian family* [1641–74] (Wing L3011A), and [John Vicars], *A letter for a Christian family* [1674–9] (Wing V314A).

78 E.g. anon., *The dying mans good counsel to his children and friends* [1674–9] (Wing D2955), *The religious mans exhortation to all persons of what degree soever* [1685–8] (Wing R908), *St. Bernard's vision* [*c.*1640] (*STC* 1910 and Wing S298B–299B), and [T. Hill], *The doleful dance* [1655–8] (Wing H2013A).

79 This point is developed in Green 2000, ch. 8.

80 The following reached over fifty editions with suspicious speed: John Hart, *The plain mans plain path-way to heaven*; Andrew Jones, *The black book of conscience*; and T[homas] P[assinger], *Gods call to uncoverted sinners*. By comparison, we can chart most of the early and intervening editions of regularly reprinted works like Arthur Dent's *Sermon of repentance* and *Plaine mans path-way*, Samuel Smith's *Great assize*, Bayly's *Practise of pietie*, and the popular catechisms of Perkins, Pagit and Openshaw, Egerton, and Ball.

chapbooks were referred to at the time as 'small godly books' or 'godlies', and it has been argued that they were the work of 'godly' ministers.[81] A closer look suggests that very few were either acknowledged by known clergy or can be convincingly proved to have been their work: in many cases what we have is a cut down and bowdlerized version of a published or unpublished work by an author who owing to distance from London, ejection from office, or having recently died was in no position to prevent such acts of piracy.[82] The early works of John Andrewes and John Hart, for example, may have been genuine, but the decline in the competence of handling doctrinal matter and the increase in the number of publishing tricks associated with the ballad trade or the old Elizabethan moralistic pamphlets suggests that the authors of the later works issued under their names were hacks set on by publishers seeking new money-spinning titles.[83]

In the majority of the 'godly' chapbooks that survive, entertainment predominates over edification, whether through an account of *The wicked life and penitent death of Tho. Savage* or *The dying Christians pious exhortations* or *An almanack for two days viz the day of death and the day of judgement*.[84] Some even had a socially levelling element in them – attacks on sins associated with the rich and a stress on death coming to all regardless of status – that was consonant with the types of reader being targeted by the publishers.[85] Only a minority of 'godlies' – usually described as 'sermon' on the title page – used the extra space to provide a more sophisticated statement of salvation, repentance, or heaven and hell, than that found in ballads, but even these tended to leave out caveats against relying on free will or deathbed repentance; and a surprising number also combined Calvinist-sounding references to God's people being chosen from eternity or making our election and calling sure, with distinctly non-predestinarian remarks such as 'those who call on the Lord in the Lord's Prayer are the Lord's people', suggesting their authors were either not well versed in theology or themselves not fully orthodox.[86]

81 Cf. Watt 1991, pt 3; Spufford 1981, ch. 8, and appendix 1, pp. 262–3; and Duffy, 'The godly and the multitude', pp. 44, 47–8.

82 E.g. Baxter's *A call to the unconverted* (1658) became T.P.'s *Gods call to unconverted sinners* (1662). Many other examples are given in Green 2000, ch. 8.

83 This point is developed in Green 2000; but cf. *Andrewes golden chaine* (1637) and Andrewes's *A golden trumpet* (1641) against his earlier works, and Hart's *A godly sermon of Peters repentance* (1663) and *The plain mans plain path-way* (1665) with earlier works attributed to him.

84 Wing W2078 [1680?]; D2950A [1681–4]; and A2895C [1680?].

85 E.g. Robert Johnson's *Dives and Lazarus*, first published under James I but still being published in black letter in the 1680s, and A. Jones, *Death triumphant* (1674).

86 E.g. N. Vincent, *The day of grace* (1687) (Wing V406aA), and T. Wadsworth, *Christ in the clouds* (1682) (Wing W185A); R. Hough, *Saints blessed for ever* (1695) (Wing H214A), sigs. A5^{r-v}. Further examples are given in Green 2000, ch. 8. For a similar phenomenon in almanacs, see Capp 1979, pp. 146–9.

What is notably absent from both 'godly' ballads and chapbooks is the teaching which appears in the most elementary services, prayers, catechisms and homilies published at the same time in England: the over-arching need for a lively faith in Christ and sincere repentance, and the careful and systematic use of the Word, prayer and sacraments. Instead there is a pandering to the obstinate semi-Pelagianism of the many who equated 'religion' with right living and good neighbourliness.[87] Any survey of religious publications has to give these supposedly 'godly' works due consideration alongside those of a more orthodox origin because they contain a measure of Christian teaching, and because some collectors of the time, like Samuel Pepys and Frances Wolfreston, seem to have bought and read both the genuine article and the fake or inferior copy. But historians should consider the latter as a sub-stratum rather than the main vein of religious publication of this period. Alert to the commercial success of these works, publishers did not place pure doctrine or genuine edification high on their list of priorities, and it shows.

The other main element of continuity with the pre-war period was provided by patterns of readership. There were probably changes in the relative *numbers* of the different types of purchaser or reader of religious publications, but the main *categories* of readership probably remained much the same, as may be deduced from a combination of sources: records of private and institutional libraries, probate inventories, diaries, letters, and other anecdotal evidence, and the comments about the intended or actual sale of their works made by authors or publishers on title pages or in prefaces.[88] As in the century before 1640, though perhaps on a somewhat smaller scale, there was a highly educated readership consisting mainly of clergymen and academics at the peak of their professions, but also some very well-read and curious laymen who wanted copies of the latest edition of the Bible, such as Walton's *Polyglot*, and the more advanced treatises of the day, such as the nine volumes of *Critici sacri* that accompanied the Polyglot; and who did not mind whether these treatises were printed in England or abroad or were in English or Latin or another ancient or learned language. We tend to know more about the collections of the senior clergy, a number of whose libraries were catalogued at the time, in many cases for auction, and from these catalogues we know that many of them, both conformists like Ralph Cudworth

87 Capp 1979, pp. 146–9; Green 1996, pt 2; and M. J. Ingram, *Church courts, sex and marriage in England, 1579–1640* (Cambridge, 1987), ch. 3, and 'From Reformation to toleration: popular religious cultures in England, 1540–1690', in T. Harris, ed., *Popular culture in England, c. 1500–1850* (London, 1995), pp. 108–14.

88 These are discussed in Green 2000, ch. 1.

and Brian Walton and nonconformists like Lazarus Seaman and John Owen, owned very large collections which were dominated by patristic writings, biblical commentaries, theology, philology, histories and controversy, many of them printed on the Continent, perhaps with a leavening of *literae humaniores*. However, compared to similarly large collections made by laymen such as Sir Edmund Dering and Samuel Pepys, clerical libraries were generally notable for the absence of lighter literature such as plays, satires, topical verses and prints.[89]

The average parish clergyman probably had much smaller collections of a few dozen books, and to judge from surviving records of purchases, like those of Giles Moore in Sussex, and probate inventories, such as that for Thomas Devey in Warwickshire, these smaller collections were dominated by Bibles and the best aids to Bible study they could afford, the fashionable sermons of the day such as Stillingfleet's and Tillotson's, devotional tracts, handbooks on how to prepare for communion, and other improving works by authors like Jeremy Taylor, Richard Baxter, Simon Patrick, Anthony Horneck and John Norris, catechisms, and the occasional piece of controversy that touched them closely, such as Eachard's *Grounds and occasions of the contempt of the clergy*.[90] Many clergy were unlikely to have been able to afford more expensive works or even much beyond the basics, but their position was helped by the expansion of library collections and the liberalizing of borrowing rules in university, college and cathedral libraries.[91] The seventeenth century also witnessed the creation of scores of smaller local collections in England and Wales, either by individual benefactors (often a previous incumbent) or bodies like the Trustees for Erecting Parochial Libraries, set up by Thomas Bray.[92] In short, a poorly paid ministry was not necessarily a poorly read one.

Among the laity there was a variety of readerships: a fairly buoyant but more catholic readership among the gentry and urban patriciate; a moderately well educated readership among the yeomanry in the countryside and the increasing numbers of merchants, traders and lesser professional families in the towns; a less well educated group of readers drawn from the smaller shopkeepers, artisans and apprentices in the towns and those husbandmen and labourers who

89 Lawler 1898, pp. xvii, xxiv–vi, and *passim*; and cf. Nuttall 1951–2. For Dering's library, see below, n. 96; for the collections begun by Pepys, see Latham 1978–94, III; and see also Lievsay and Davis 1954, pp. 141–60.

90 *The journal of Giles Moore*, ed. R. Bird (Sussex Record Society, 68, 1971), pp. 116–17, 180–92; Salter 1978, pp. 33–46; and Green 2000, appendix 1.

91 Wormald and Wright 1958, pp. 213–19, 225–9, 236–40, 243, 246–7; Kelly 1966, pp. 59–65; Kaufman 1963–4.

92 Kelly 1966, pp. 50, 70–6, 90–109.

could afford some money for the education of their children, and were prepared to spend a little on books; and sectional groups such as women, children, dissenters and recusants which regularly cut across the social divide.[93]

A number of the established public and grammar schools offering a classical syllabus to the sons of the gentry and urban patriciate went through a lean spell after the Restoration, as did the universities; but any decline was probably relative, at least before 1700. The aristocracy and gentry, both male and female, remained not only the best educated of the lay readerships, with the largest amounts of disposable wealth to buy and the greatest leisure to read books (if they chose to do so), but also the most likely source of funds for a charitable venture such as the Society for Promoting Christian Knowledge (SPCK) or Queen Anne's Bounty, or for a subscription list for Doddridge's *Family expositor*.[94] This gentry readership overlapped with other categories of reader, such as the clergy, and also had its internal variations, owing to the different educations given to boys and girls, and the 'godly' disposition of some readers and the conformist predisposition of others. But it is also notable for the catholicity of its tastes. Gentry bought copies not only of works designed for them, such as Jeremy Taylor's *Holy living* and *Holy dying*, and Allestree's *The gentlemans calling* (1660) and *The ladies calling* (1673), but also of works aimed at 'the meanest reader' such as Allestree's *Whole duty of man*, or even an example of what is now termed 'cheap print', such as a 'godly' ballad or chapbook.[95] Many also bought works of a non-Calvinist, Erasmian, or Grotian standpoint embodying the norms they had imbibed at school and university, even if on some matters they also leant towards the 'godly' or dissenters. As two examples of this, we may cite on the one hand the 2,000 volumes collected by Sir Edward Dering, and on the other the 100 volumes acquired by Frances Wolfreston, the wife of a middling gentleman in Staffordshire. Dering's collection included many plays, and classical and historical works, which reflected his strong early interests in the theatre and antiquarian research, but it was also particularly strong on works of religious controversy which dominated his later years, during which

93 These are discussed in Green 2000, ch. 1, and in the next few paragraphs.

94 R. O'Day, *Education and society 1500–1800* (London, 1982), chs. 11, 14; D. Hayton, 'Moral reform and country politics in the late seventeenth-century House of Commons', *Past and Present*, 128 (1990), pp. 48–91; R. Unwin, 'The Established Church and the schooling of the poor: the role of the SPCK, 1699–1720', in *The Churches and education*, ed. V. A. McClelland (History of Education Society 1984), pp. 24–32; I. Green, 'The First Years of Queen Anne's Bounty', in R. O'Day and F. Heal, eds., *Princes and paupers in the English Church 1500–1800* (Leicester, 1981), pp. 248–9; the 1,100 subscribers to the first volume of Doddridge's *Family expositor* (1739) show a strong preponderance of 'gentry'; see also n. 105 below.

95 The Taylor works were written for the pious wife of the Earl of Carbery; for ownership of works by Allestree, see Spurr, *Restoration Church*, pp. 30, 230, 281–3; and see n. 96. For ownership of cheaper works by Pepys and Wolfreston, see Spufford 1981, chs. 6 and 8, and Morgan 1989.

he switched back and forth between King and Parliament.[96] The majority of Wolfreston's collection consisted of plays and poetry, but there was a minority of religious books of varied origins and character. She evidently prized and read her humbler collection, to judge from her habit of writing her name on the cover and making comments in the margin or copying suitable verses onto blank pages.[97]

The numbers of the 'middling sort' of people – those who unlike the gentry had to work for their income using their hands or skills acquired through training, but who unlike the poorer sort were usually self-employed and financially independent – were probably increasing fast due to an easing of population pressure and an upturn in trade and agriculture in the later Stuart period. By then they may have comprised between a third and a half of the families in England, and in many cases had disposable wealth which they were prepared to put towards buying books for themselves and education for their children. By then also a relatively high proportion of the middling sort had learnt to read, either through the older established schools, or one of the many elementary schools (and later the more advanced dissenting academies) set up in the later Stuart period, or through informal means (like the young Adam Martindale, taught by his siblings and a sister's suitor).[98] In a sample of inventories from eight English regions for the period 1675–1725 it was found that between 24 and 30 per cent of householders in London, East Kent and Hampshire owned books, with somewhat lower proportions further north and west. Further analysis suggested book-owning was more common among householders in provincial towns than in villages, and among families in trade than in farming; and a sliding scale based on the value of the inventory indicated that nearly half of the inventories worth over £500 mentioned books while only 7 per cent of those below £10 did.[99] It is these richer households, especially in the towns and trade, together with those members of the yeomanry and urban oligarchies who left wills rather than leaving their relatives to rely on probate inventories, that we are considering when we talk here of an educated readership among the middling sort.

96 Krivatsy and Yeandle 1992, pp. 137–269. For another collection that combined works of classical and Christian origin, works by both 'godly' and conformists, and works aimed at both the well educated and (like Dent's *Plaine mans path-way*) at 'the ignorant and vulgar sort', see Fehrenbach 1992, pp. 79–135.

97 Morgan 1989, pp. 197–219.

98 J. Barry and C. Brooks, eds., *The middling sort of people: culture, society and politics in England 1550–1800* (London, 1994), p. 3; O'Day, *Education and society*, chs. 2, 9, 11, 14; but cf. J. Simon, 'Was there a Charity School movement? The Leicestershire evidence', in B. Simon, ed., *Education in Leicestershire 1540–1940: a regional study* (Leicester, 1968), pp. 55–100; *The life of Adam Martindale written by himself*, ed. R. Parkinson (Chetham Society, 4, 1845), pp. 5, 24–5; Spufford 1979.

99 L. Weatherill, *Consumer behaviour and material culture in Britain 1660–1760* (London, 1988), *passim*.

Both the gentry and the educated 'middling sort' were in the market for topical sermons, collections of orthodox prayers, handbooks on 'godly living' and 'godly dying', works combining edification and entertainment such as religious verse and improving biographies (and the occasional cautionary tale of a more lurid kind), condensed versions of larger theological works and simplified aids to Bible study, and copies of catechisms and small Bibles and prayer books for their children to take to school or church.[100] The main distinction between gentry and urban readers was perhaps that the former, who tended to have had a longer and more classical education, were more likely to have been attracted to the Erasmian tradition of religious writing that lived on in the improving epigrams, essays and more florid epitaphs of the day, and to the 'characters' and 'emblems' that came into fashion in the early Stuart period, while their urban counterparts were probably more attracted by edifying biographies and funeral sermons on people they had known, and warnings to citizens such as Thomas Vincent's *Gods terrible voice in the city of London* (1667), which explained how their sins were responsible for the recent disasters they had experienced.[101] A further distinction might also be drawn, but this time within both gentry and urban readerships, between a conformist end of a spectrum of those more likely to read the works of Jeremy Taylor, Richard Allestree, Simon Patrick and Anthony Horneck or buy one of the growing variety of pieces of Church music by authors like John Patrick, and a non-conformist end, of those more likely to read works by Richard Baxter, Joseph Alleine, John Janeway, John Flavell or John Bunyan, though some of these authors probably had a much broader readership than this suggests.[102] The rapid rise of the provincial book trade in England and Wales at the close of the seventeenth and in the early eighteenth century, with both printers and booksellers appearing in regional centres and offering, among other works, sermons, catechisms and Church music by local authors, was probably due in no small degree to the demands of these gentry and urban readers, together with local clergy and teachers, though in Wales there was in addition a strong demand for works in Welsh.[103]

This leaves us at least three other important sets of readers. The first of these comprised the smaller shopkeepers, skilled artisans and apprentices in the town, and those poorer husbandmen and labourers in the countryside who

100 Green 1996, ch. 4; and Green 2000, chs. 1–3, 5, 7.

101 Green 2000, chs. 4, 7; and see above, notes 89, 96; on the reading tastes of Londoners in particular, see Wright 1935, L. C. Stevenson, *Praise and paradox: merchants and craftsmen in Elizabethan popular literature* (Cambridge, 1984); and Clark 1983.

102 These authors' works are discussed in Green 2000, chs. 5–7, and 9; but see also above, pp. 76–9.

103 Feather 1981; Jenkins, *Foundation of modern Wales*, pp. 204, 210, 215–17, 231–3, 237; N. Temperley, *The music of the English parish church* (2 vols.; Cambridge, 1979), I, pp. 130–3, 144, 173, 178–80; Green 2000, ch. 9. On Wales, see also p. 45 above, and Jones, below.

had little disposable income, but who had acquired some reading skills and were not short of curiosity. Such people might acquire books in various ways other than purchase: through borrowing from a local minister or schoolteacher or a neighbour, as the young Richard Baxter did, and his father had done before him, or through marriage, like John Bunyan, or through inheritance, like the old shepherd known to John Clare who on Sundays took into the fields to read out loud a battered old Bible, heavily inscribed with details of his family history.[104] Another means was through the gift of cheap copies of the Bible or of small- to medium-sized pamphlets of an educational or improving type donated by an author like Richard Younge, Thomas Gouge, and Clement Ellis, or a local minister (conformist or non-conformist), or by members of the Welsh Trust, SPCK, and Charity School movement.[105] John Rawlet estimated that five shillings given by the rich would pay for a poor household to be given a Bible, a Book of Common Prayer, and a copy of Allestree's *Whole duty of man*.[106] The age of distributing religious works in large numbers had thus dawned long before the age of John Wesley, Hannah More and the Tractarian Movement, and the main recipients were, naturally enough, those with some literacy but limited funds of their own. However, those personal funds could be and occasionally were used to buy books, and it was at purchasers like these that were targeted an increasingly wide range of pamphlets, almanacs, and other works (in both English and Welsh) costing no more than a few pence each, like Thomas Passinger's *God's call to unconverted sinners* (a 'sermon' on repentance with a heavy debt to Baxter's *Call to the unconverted*) and Nathaniel Crouch's *Youths divine pastime* (forty scripture histories turned into verse and illustrated), or the 'godly' ballads and chapbooks discussed earlier.[107]

That publishers were aware of the different depths of pocket among their customers is well illustrated in the 1682 edition of Edward Pearse's *The great concern* – 'a serious warning to a timely and thorough preparation for death' – which contained at the start 'A proposition for the more profitable improvement of burials, by giving of books'. In this two publishers urged those who arranged funerals not to spend money on giving mourners biscuits and wine or memorial rings or gloves, but to give them books to make them think about their own latter end. Suitable titles were listed and graded according to the wealth of the organizers: 'for the poorer sort, books of 6d. price', such as *The*

104 Baxter 1985, p. 7; J. Bunyan, *Grace abounding*, ed. G. B. Harrison (London, 1928), p. 10; *John Clare's autobiographical writings*, ed. E. Robinson (Oxford, 1983), p. 33.

105 Ian Green hopes to write about Younge and Ellis's use of print on another occasion; Cressy 1980, p. 50; M. G. Jones, *The Charity School movement* (Cambridge, 1938), pp. 280–7, 373–5; and see n. 94 above, and Jenkins, *Foundation of modern Wales*, pp. 137, 198–207, 231–2, 237.

106 Rawlet, *Christian monitor*, p. 51.

107 Spufford 1981, ch. 5; and Watt 1991, chs. 1, 7.

guide to heaven and Bury's *Improvement of death*; then 'books of 1s.' (including the Pearse volume), 'books of 1s. 6d. and 2s.' (including works by dissenters like Bates and Baxter as well as a bishop, Simon Patrick); and, finally, 'for the richer sort, books of 4, 5 and 6s. price', such as the combined version of Taylor's *Holy living* and *Holy dying*.[108]

At the bottom of the ladder were those who were too poor or not sufficiently interested to buy a book or who were insufficiently literate to read one even if it was given to them. Such people were not necessarily beyond the reach of print. Heads of gentry and urban households might read the Bible or an improving work out loud to servants who were illiterate; children in elementary schools were urged to read the Bible to their parents, especially if they could not read; neighbours might read to each other, like the Sussex shopkeeper Thomas Turner who records in his diary reading works like Tillotson's sermons to a neighbour; and in Church the text of the Bible, and the official liturgy and short catechism were regularly declaimed from a printed copy, and the text of the metrical Psalms 'lined out' by the parish clerk.[109] There were, however, limits to what could be achieved by such means. Dissenters like Isaac Watts clearly expected everyone to be – or to want to be – literate, and many conformist clergy, weary of the repetition involved in oral catechizing, would clearly have preferred to have given their catechumens a copy of the text to take away and learn at home.[110] But the need for oral instruction and rote memorization was still strong in 1700, even if it was not quite as strong as in 1600 or 1500.

Cutting vertically across the various strata mentioned in previous paragraphs were groups such as women and children, both of whom had an increasingly large number of religious works targeted at them. Women were considered to have special roles – and weaknesses – and not only had many edifying books dedicated to them, but also bought and read them, and indeed wrote them in increasing numbers too. Some became steady sellers, like Elizabeth Joceline's *The mothers legacie, to her unborn childe* (1624), *The Countess of Morton's daily exercise* (1666), the *Meditations and prayers* written by Elizabeth Percy, Duchess of Northumberland, to accompany the receiving of the sacrament (1682), and Theodosia Alleine's uplifting biography of her husband, Joseph (1671).[111] Textbooks for schoolchildren had existed before the Reformation,

108 E. Pearse, *The great concern* (1682), sigs. A3^{v}-4^{v}.

109 Green 2000, chs. 2, 4, 9; *The diary of Thomas Turner of East Hoathly*, ed. F. M. Turner (London, 1925), pp. 20, 22, 25, 27, 29.

110 Green 1996, ch. 5.

111 For the targeting of female readers, see P. Crawford, *Women and religion in England 1500–1720* (London, 1993), pp. 79–80, and the references there; A. Laurence, *Women in England 1500–1700. A social history* (London, 1994), pp. 165–74, and references on pp. 285–6; and Green 2000, chs. 1, 10. The works cited in the text are all listed in Wing.

but to these and the new Protestant catechisms were added a growing number of other religious works designed specially for children and youth: catechisms, guidance on confirmation and how to prepare for first communion, verse such as John Bunyan's edifying 'country rhymes for children' (in *A book for boys and girls*, 1686), admonitory advice and stories of godly children who had died young (in Thomas Brookes's *Apples of gold for young men and women* (1657) and Thomas White's *Little book for little children* [1660?]), and the shortened, illustrated versions of stories from the Bible (in *Youths divine pastime* by Crouch already mentioned). The expansion and commercialization of providing suitable books for the young certainly pre-dates the eighteenth century, even if the variety of material was much greater by the end of that century.[112]

Recusants may be cited as another group that cut across social boundaries and age groups. The 1,348 books published by or for English Catholics between 1641 and 1700 probably represent less than 2 per cent of the 'English' books then issued, but this was impressive for a community consisting of perhaps little more than 1 per cent of the population in England, and reflected the centrality of primers and manuals to Catholic instruction and worship.[113] Moreover, whereas almost 80 per cent of books for English Catholics issued between 1558 and 1640 had been published abroad, from 1641 to 1700 this fell to below 20 per cent. However, nearly a third of the 1,348 titles, including a much larger number of pamphlets, broadsides and sermons than usual, were published between 1685 and 1689, by men like Henry Hills whose career blossomed under James II. Without this windfall, the average annual output of new titles was lower than for the period before 1640. Over the period as a whole primers, manuals and a growing variety of catechisms were probably the most commonly owned works. Inspiration for spiritual works came less from Spain than before, and more from France, the Low Countries and Germany; authors were less likely to be Jesuits, and more likely to be secular clergy, like John Gother; and there was a greater empasis on practical spirituality, which Clancy sees as proof that 'the market for English Catholic works' was 'moving down the socio-economic scale', as was true of Protestantism as well.[114]

112 J. H. Plumb, 'The new world of children in eighteenth-century England', as reprinted in N. McKendrick *et al.*, *The birth of a consumer society* (London: 1982), pp. 286–315; P. Demers, *Heaven upon earth: the form of moral and religious children's literature, to 1850* (Knoxville, TN, 1993). For other works mentioned, see above, and Green 1996, pp. 33–5, 195–6, and chs. 3–4 *passim*.

113 Clancy 1996, pp. vii–xii (as Clancy points out, many English Catholics lived abroad); J. A. Bossy, *The English Catholic community, 1570–1850* (London, 1976), ch. 8; Blom 1982, pp. 43–7.

114 Clancy 1996, pp. ix–xii; and for various Catholic catechisms published in London by a King's Printer (Henry Hills, who converted to Catholicism under James II) and others in the period 1685–8, and works by Gother in 1698 and 1701, see Green 1996, pp. 600–13, 616–17, 654–5, 680–1, 710–11, 718–19, 726–7.

We may end with a series of vignettes: children in a dame school laboriously learning their letters and then mastering their catechism from a well-thumbed *ABC with the catechisme*; John Bunyan's 'Christian' trudging away from the city marked 'Destruction' with his nose buried in a good book; William Coe, the gentleman-farmer of Mildenhall who was torn between sin and piety, turning to Thomas Comber's *Companion to the altar* and Jeremy Taylor's *The great exemplar* for inspiration; and Anne Mary Childe, who died in 1659 and on a marble monument in the local church is depicted with all her books shelved behind her, and underneath a verse including the lines 'How seasoned was my soul with heaven's kind looks / When I comparing was with text my godly books.'[115]

115 Green 1996, pp. 170–84; the frontispiece depicting Christian appears in the third and subsequent editions of *The pilgrim's progress* (1679 onwards); *Two East Anglian diaries 1641–1729: Isaac Archer and William Coe*, ed. M. Storey (Suffolk Records Society XXXVI, 1994), pp. 250, 253; and monument on the north wall of Blockley parish church, Gloucestershire.

ORAL TRADITIONS AND SCRIBAL CULTURE

3

Oral and scribal texts in early modern England

HAROLD LOVE

Parliamentary histories tell us that on 22 February 1671 Charles II, present at the Lords for the second reading of the Subsidy Bill, was an unwilling listener to a severe critique of his policies from John, Lord Lucas. Lucas spoke on behalf of peers who would have been severely taxed under the bill, and who also objected to the methods of collection proposed, which they saw as an attack by the Commons on the Lords' privileges. He and his kind had been loyal cavaliers in the past but were now beginning to exhibit 'country' inclinations that would flower mightily during the coming decade. Should the King upon a good occasion require a quarter or (in some versions) a half of his estate, Lucas would willingly give it; but the present predicament was not of this kind, nor was he able to meet even the more modest levy proposed:

> For in ye tyme of ye last usurping powers, though great Taxes were exacted from vs, wee had then meanes to pay, wee lett our Lands, & sold our Corne, & Cattell, & there was plenty of Money through ye Nation, now there is nothing of this. Bricke is required of vs, & noe Straw allow'd vs to make itt with, for that our Lands are throwne vpon our hands, our Corne, & Cattell of little value is notorious to all ye World . . .

Huge subsidies voted to the crown had been 'poured out into the Purses of priuate men', many of whom 'att his Maties returne were worth little, or nothing', but who nonetheless kept 'their Coaches, & sixe Horses, their Pages, & Lacqueys' while loyal cavaliers had 'scarce sufficient left, to buy them Bread'. Moreover, far from enabling the kingdom to defend itself, the new impositions furthered the plots of the French King to weaken it, just as Samson had been weakened by Delilah (a nip at the Duchess of Portsmouth). Finally, if the Lords were not able to moderate a money bill from the Commons, political power would have passed irrevocably to the other house.[1]

1 Oxford, Bodleian Library, MS. Don. b. 8, pp. 198–201. I would like to thank Meredith Sherlock for her much appreciated help in the preparation of this chapter.

So, at any rate, the histories. But before we take their words at face value we need to look more closely at the event and its written and printed outcomes. That Lucas spoke strongly is not to be doubted. Writing to William Popple shortly afterwards, Andrew Marvell reported, 'I think I have not told you that, on our Bill of Subsidy, the *Lord Lucas* made a fervent bold Speech against our Prodigality in giving, and the weak Looseness of the Government, the King being present... But all this had little Encouragement, not being seconded.'[2] Meanwhile, there were 'Copys going about every where'. Marvell would certainly have heard first-hand reports of what was said; on the other hand, since he was unlikely to have been present to hear it, his knowledge of the substance of the speech probably came from one of the 'Copys'.

These were scribal 'separates' of a kind that had been used for at least a century for the circulation of Parliamentary speeches and diurnals.[3] By the reign of Charles II this copying had long been professionalized, with both current and retrospective materials available to order. In the 1670s two booksellers in the Strand were known traders in Parliamentary separates, but any scrivener's or attorney's office might also have taken on such work in slack times.[4] The reliability of these accounts depended on their source. When they were put into circulation by the speakers themselves, they were (at least to begin with) in approved texts, though we have no way of telling how exactly they represented what had been spoken. Accounts compiled by other members, relying on memory or notes taken at the time, were derived from words actually uttered, though how faithfully these were reproduced depended on the skill and conscientiousness of the note-taker. Finally, a version might be assembled outside the house drawing on the written or verbal reports of those who had been present. The form taken by this would depend on the editorial skills of the compiler and the range and comprehensiveness of the sources available; but it might equally be influenced by the compiler's own political agenda. In all cases texts were liable to prove unstable in transmission. Regarding the copies of Lucas's speech, Marvell relates:

> one of them was brought into the Lords' House, and *Lord Lucas* was asked whether it was his. He sayed Part was, and Part was not. Thereupon they took

2 *The poems and letters of Andrew Marvell*, ed. H. M. Margoliouth, 3rd edn, rev. P. Legouis and E. E. Duncan-Jones (Oxford, 1971), II, pp. 322–3.

3 A surreptitious printed edition of Lucas's speech (Wing L3992) exists bearing the date 1670 (for 1670/71); however, it is shown in *CSPD 1671*, p. 94, that the real date of publication can be no earlier than the closing months of 1673. Another 1673 edition (Wing L3991) claims to have been printed at Middelburg. There are numerous surviving manuscript copies. That in the miscellany of the Sussex vicar, John Watson, is annotated at its close 'Communicat a Tho: Becivall Causidico. Martij 24. 1670/1' (BL, MS. Add. 18220, fols. 64^v–67^v).

4 Love 1993, pp. 9–22.

> Advantage, and sayed it was a Libel even against *Lucas* himself. On this they voted it a Libel, and to be burned by the Hangman. Which was done; but the Sport was, the Hangman burned the Lords' Order with it.[5]

Lucas's denial may have been strategic (he was later to be one of Shaftesbury's lieutenants in the Exclusion Bill campaign); but, taking his words at their face value, and remembering that the spoken speech would still be fresh in the memories of his hearers, we have to assume that the publicly circulated version was the work of an editor who had interpolated a few strokes that had not occurred to the speaker.

Viewed in this light, the delivery of the speech is an act of some complexity. Since Lucas must have realized that so flagrant a confrontation of the King would lead to the circulation of versions of his words in manuscript, the oral delivery becomes, in one sense, an act of scribal publication by dictation. Marvell's position as a reader of the speech is also far from simple. He was himself involved in the scribal circulation of oppositional writing, contributing verse satires to the campaign against Clarendon: Sir Roger L'Estrange, the official charged with the suppression of subversive writings, alleged that he used an old Cromwellian officer as his amanuensis.[6] As a poet he followed the example of Sidney, Donne and Carew (among many others) in avoiding print wherever possible and restricting his verse to the scribal medium; only in prose was he willing to enlist the services of the press. It is not beyond possibility that he was implicated in the circulation of Lucas's speech, since he was certainly a political associate of those who were (a passage in his *An account of the growth of popery* (Amsterdam [i.e. London], 1677) restates one of its arguments[7]). Marvell was also a newsletter writer on behalf of the corporation of Hull and possibly other clients – a scribal journalist who had no difficulty in laying his hands on separates that he thought might interest his employers. He would have understood better than most the way that the three media of voice, script and (from 1673) print intersected in this particular political event and how their earlier histories had equipped them with their particular roles in the communication of texts and ideas.

The oral text

In considering these media, one by one, we need to remind ourselves how many of the key texts of late-sixteenth- and early seventeenth-century England

5 *The poems and letters of Andrew Marvell*, II, p. 323. 6 Kelliher 1978, p. 113.

7 That Louis XIV was attempting 'by frequent levyes of men, and mony, to exhaust, and weaken our Kingdome' (p. 52). Lucas points to 'often Alarmes of Armyes, & Fleetes, to induce vs, to consume our Treasure in vaine preparations against them' (p. 199).

belonged solely or primarily to the oral-aural medium. Reviewing the domain of the spoken word, Isaac Barrow noted that

> The chief and most considerable sort of men manage all their concernments meerly by Words; by them Princes rule their Subjects, Generals command their Armies, Senatours deliberate and debate about the great matters of State: by them Advocates plead causes, and Judges decide them; Divines perform their offices, and minister their instructions; Merchants strike up their bargains, and drive on all their traffick. Whatever almost great or small is done in the Court or in the Hall, in the Church or at the Exchange, in the School or in the Shop, it is the Tongue alone that doeth it: 'tis the force of this little machine, that turneth all the humane world about . . . so that, in comparison thereof, the execution of what we determine and all other action do take up small room; and even that usually dependeth upon foregoing Speech, which persuadeth, or counselleth, or commandeth it.[8]

The point is not simply that speech was involved in these activities, but that, in a society where most agreements were arrived at face to face, there was little intervening role played by writing and even less by print. Much, much more was done than in our world by 'the Tongue alone' and by memory, which had to be ready to preserve accurate records of what the tongue had said. The deliberations of Parliament, as we have seen, were preserved, if at all, only in unofficial handwritten diaries and transcripts of speeches, and the baldest of annotations in the clerk's book. Even news in Shakespeare's time was an oral commodity to be bartered daily in the nave of St Paul's and on the Exchange. In a society where literacy was still relatively low, and the personal libraries of the literate generally very small by modern standards, memory was the principal way of possessing texts.[9] For the unlettered many, this was probably not a handicap, since an ancient oral culture of proverbs, anecdotes, ballads, genealogies, charms, spells, recipes and communal wisdom still retained its vitality. The principal forms of post-Reformation worship were, for many, improvised, oral productions, with Anglican attempts to subject liturgy to the discipline of a printed book meeting strong Puritan resistance. Even the orthodox sermon, which we encounter today in printed form, was often committed to writing only after having been wholly or substantially improvised in delivery, with the word-by-word 'division' of the text providing the structural framework. When Donne wrote to Thomas Roe from Chelsea on 25 November 1625, he was occupied in expanding the notes from which he had originally preached

8 *Several sermons against evil speaking* (London, 1678), pp. 9–10.

9 For literacy levels see Cressy 1980. For the libraries of the learned see Leedham-Green 1986. For reading for memorization see Ong 1982, pp. 31–3; Manguel 1996, pp. 55–65.

his sermons into a written text. A copy survives of what is either a set of these notes or a summary made by a listener: in either case the spoken text must have differed significantly from the subsequent printed one.[10]

Texts composed on paper might also be intended for the oral medium. Much of the poetry of the period, even when brought forward in the dignity of print, was composed as scripts for recitation rather than for silent reading. Some, written for delivery on a particular social or ceremonial occasion, might even, as Ted-Larry Pebworth has argued, be discarded once that occasion had passed, entering scribal transmission fortuitously if at all.[11] Timothy Raylor has nominated the writers' drinking clubs of Caroline London as one influential source of such evanescent performance verse. The 'Order of the Fancy', whose leading lights were James Smith and Sir John Mennes, specialized in improvised nonsense, with the best improviser occupying the place of honour; but it also gave rise to a body of written burlesque and parody that, after recitation to meetings and very restricted circulation in manuscript, only slid into print under the Protectorate in the royalist anthologies known as drolleries.[12] At a later date, Anthony Hamilton's depiction of the circulation of verse at the court of Charles II illustrates that lampoons, even when as scandalous as Rochester's, were habitually read aloud or sung rather than furtively scanned in corners.[13]

The Elizabethan and Jacobean drama is known to us through the many surviving printed texts of plays and a handful of manuscripts; but for its authors and practitioners it was an art of speech and action preserved in the trained memories of performers.[14] Shakespeare excuses himself in Sonnet 122 for giving away a manuscript of poems by explaining that, since they were 'within my braine / Full characterd with lasting memory', the written version was superfluous; further, that to 'import forgetfulnesse' in him would be an insult.[15] Which is to say no more than that he possessed a skill without which no actor of his time could hope to survive professionally in an age of large repertoires, doubled roles and intensely verbal plays (but which also mirrored a much wider conception of reading as a means to memorization rather than an end in itself). While the promptbook gave the primary form of the text, actors learned their roles from 'parts' or 'sides' that held their own lines and the sketchiest of cues, these being the only sections of the work they ever saw in inscribed form. Instructions for entrances, exits and movements – the kind of material that a

10 Stanwood 1978 and *John Donne's Gunpowder Plot sermon. A parallel text edition*, ed. S. Shami (Oxford, 1997).

11 Pebworth 1989. 12 Raylor 1994. 13 Love 1995.

14 Considered in Love forthcoming.

15 *The complete works: William Shakespeare*, ed. S. Wells and G. Taylor (Oxford, 1986), p. 869.

modern playwright would place in stage directions not meant for delivery – were cunningly incorporated into the spoken text, since it was on this, not any written record, that the performer relied for monitoring the progress of the performance.[16] Performers of polyphonic music were in a similar situation. In their notational form the works usually survive as parts, not as scores, and were probably still composed in this way, line layered upon line, rather than chord following chord. At best the parts of a short piece might be laid out separately on a single opening, though, seeing there was no division into bars, this did not really expedite cross-reference from part to part. To 'read' such a composition, it would have been necessary to memorize all the parts singly, beginning with the bass. Like the professional actor, the average professional singer or instrumentalist would rarely have seen an integrated, easily realizable written text of any piece performed. It was the memorized aural text that preserved the 'work'.

The broad distinctions that have been drawn in recent decades between the cognitive practices that characterize oral cultures, script cultures and print cultures are often now applied in an unexamined way that becomes an obstacle to an understanding of the intricate negotiations between the media that were a fact of life in early modern Britain (and which will be considered later in this chapter). But there can be no doubt that the change to a print-dominated culture was accompanied by kinds of neural de-skilling and re-skilling whose cultural effects were very considerable. At the same time as the textbook begins to supplant the master's patient induction of the student into the experience of the craft, we also begin to move from a world in which educated persons carried their favourite texts in their heads as a lifelong possession to one in which such abilities, while not extinguished, were increasingly regarded as exceptional, and knowledge seen as residing not in minds but in written and printed records.[17] The earlier ideal is splendidly enunciated by Sprat in his life of Cowley:

> The first beginning of his Studies was a familiarity with the most solid and unaffected Authors of Antiquity, which he fully digested not only in his memory but his judgment. By this advantage he learnt nothing while a Boy that he needed to forget or forsake when he came to be a man. His mind was rightly season'd at first, and he had nothing to do but still to proceed on the same Foundation on which he began.[18]

But a passage from Montaigne's 'Du pedantisme', here in Charles Cotton's translation, had already overturned this ideal:

16 Bradley 1992, pp. 23–5. 17 Godzich 1994, p. 101.

18 *Critical essays of the seventeenth century*, 2 vols., ed. J. E. Spingarn (London, 1908; repr. 1957), II, p. 121.

> And here I cannot but smile to think how I have paid myself in shewing the Foppery of this kind of Learning, who myself am so manifest an Example; for, do I not the same Thing throughout almost this whole Treatise? I go here and there, culling out of several Books the Sentences that best please me, not to keep them (for I have no Memory to retain them in) but to transplant them into this; where, to say the Truth, they are no more mine, than in their first Places. We are, I conceive, knowing only in present knowledge, and not at all in what is past, no more than in that which is to come.[19]

The transition to a culture in which knowledge was seen as residing in books not memories, and the defining skill of the scholar was that of knowing where to find the requisite passage in the requisite book from the totality of those physically available, is one that took several centuries to reach its present state of perfection (when computers do it for us), but whose beginnings can be seen in the growing influence during the seventeenth century of the Cartesian conception of knowledge as residing in clear, self-evident universals rather than complex, laboriously memorized particulars. The strong appeal to secular intellectuals of this epistemological model encouraged a contempt for university learning as pedantic and self-indulgent – a criticism that the 'gownmen' met by becoming even less learned, on the whole, than their predecessors. At the same time the new Lockean cult of clarity and simplicity in language was undermining the pride of scholars in their mastery of huge multilingual vocabularies. 'I am persuaded', wrote the far-from-unlearned third Earl of Shaftesbury early in the eighteenth century, 'that to be a *virtuoso* (so far as befits a gentleman) is a higher step towards the becoming a man of virtue and good sense than the being what in this age we call a scholar'.[20] From the mid-seventeenth century the alphabetical recording of information in commonplace books yields to more straightforward summarizing of whole texts in consecutive order. Roger North rejected commonplacing as a guide to legal learning in favour of the writing of abridgements.[21] Neither did he particularly admire retentive memories: knowledge for him was to be fixed through conversation or, in his own case, the writing and revision of 'polite' essays whose stylistic ideal was that of an elegant generality.

The manuscript book

Intermediate between the oral text and the printed text lies the domain of the handwritten text. Having discussed the nature and extent of this domain in my

19 *Montaigne's essays in three books with notes and quotations*, trans. Charles Cotton, 6th edn (London, 1743), I, p. 144.

20 *Characteristics of men, manners, opinions, times, etc.*, ed. J. M. Robertson (London, 1900; repr. Gloucester, Mass., 1963), I, pp. 214–15.

21 R. North, *The life of the right honourable Francis North, Baron of Guilford* (London, 1742), pp. 16–18.

Scribal publication in seventeenth-century England I will refrain as far as possible from duplicating evidence that is already present there. Since its appearance our knowledge has been greatly enhanced through more specialized studies by Arthur Marotti, Henry Woudhuysen and Peter Beal. The most comprehensive account of practices, techniques and operatives is that of Woudhuysen.[22]

As already indicated, in the late sixteenth and seventeenth centuries a new composition might be circulated in any one of oral, written or printed form, or in any two or all three of these. Further divisions, hardly less significant, existed within each of the three media. A satirical ballad might be read in printed form as a fugitive broadsheet, or as part of an assemblage of such sheets, or, at a later date, as part of a substantial anthology; in manuscript it might appear as a private transcript, a professionally inscribed 'separate', or as part of a manuscript anthology or personal miscellany, or be posted in some public place; orally it might be either recited or sung in a variety of social settings and for a variety of purposes.[23] From any of these forms it might enter memory to be recycled in due course in the same or any other form. This range of choices for the circulation of a text had existed since the arrival of printing in Britain and had been no less crucial for the Henrician scholar-courtiers whose subtle negotiations between the possibilities and advantages of manuscript and print (and various kinds of each) are explored in David Carlson's *English humanist books*.[24] But by the 1550s, thanks to rising literacy, they were having to be made by many more people, and by the 1630s it was not simply a question of which texts were appropriate for manuscript transmission and which not, but of a department of the book trade existing that was specifically responsible for their reproduction and circulation.

Carlson's study draws attention to a tenacious nexus between the presentation of texts in manuscript and the mechanisms of patronage. The careers of writers such as Donne, Carew, Corbett, Davies and Strode a century later illustrate how literary talents exercised within the scribal medium could still be converted into secretaryships and benefices.[25] A question mark hangs over the large collections of complimentary poems that appear in the printed collections of Ben Jonson, Robert Herrick and Richard Flecknoe. Was their function simply to enhance the value of the printed book as an article of presentation, or are we to assume a retrospective bringing together of materials that had already been individually presented in manuscript? Marotti sees Jonson as

22 Marotti 1995; Woudhuysen 1996, esp. part 1, pp. 1–203; Beal 1998. See also Elsky 1989, pp. 184–208.

23 Fox 1994; Bellany 1993; Marotti 1995, pp. 75–133; Love 1993, pp. 231–83.

24 Carlson 1992.

25 Woudhuysen 1996, pp. 88–103.

'returning to the socio-literary environment of manuscript transmission for the poems that were finally printed in the posthumous 1640–41 folio as *Underwood*'.[26] Sometimes the occasion itself answers our question: poems that announce themselves as New Year's gifts belong to the most solemn moment of the patron's calendar. The presentation of a printed book as a new-year's-gift was regarded as something to be apologized for.[27]

Medieval traditions of transmitting texts through handwritten copies, then, were not extinguished by the arrival of print but assumed a range of specialized roles, ranging from one-to-one presentation in the hope of advantage to the widespread scribal circulation of texts that were regarded as inappropriate for the press. Among these last were writings that might be considered heterodox, subversive or oppositional, and that could be printed only surreptitiously or in the relatively brief periods when the central government was unable to exercise effective censorship. Others performed the function that Dr Johnson was later to claim for '*small* Tracts and *fugitive* Pieces', of containing 'the first Relations of Transactions, while they are yet the Subject of Conversation, divide the Opinions, and employ the Conjectures of Mankind'.[28] But the medium might also be chosen because the number of copies of a text needed at any particular time was not sufficient to justify the services of the press, or because the writer wished to retain a 'reserved' status for the knowledge so transmitted. This was particularly so for the women writers whose use of manuscript has been explored by Margaret Ezell in *The patriarch's wife*. The Bristol prophet Grace Carric, after initially thinking she might print her narrative of a vision received in 1635, changed her mind on the grounds that it was 'very unfitt, that such diuine & miracalous truth should be made common in these times wherin so manie falasies and false printed papers are set fourth'. Moreover, for it to be read by 'the meaner sort, of voulgar people' might 'somewhat eclipse the truth hereof'.[29] This attitude is an exemplary case of what J. W. Saunders has called the 'stigma of print'.[30]

In many cases scribal transmission hardens into the more self-conscious practice of scribal publication. A frequent pattern was for a new work to pass through an initial phase of dissemination under the author's personal supervision, then a second stage of uncontrolled private copying, then a third stage of copying for sale by commercial scriptoria; and only then, often after a lapse of years, would it make a (generally unauthorized) appearance in print. At each of

26 Marotti 1995, p. 244. 27 Cf. Love 1993, p. 66; Marotti 1995, pp. 187–8.
28 Introduction to the *Harleian Miscellany* in *Johnson's prefaces and dedications*, ed. A. T. Hazen (New Haven, Conn., 1937), pp. 54–5.
29 Ezell 1987, p. 65.
30 Saunders 1951; Woudhuysen 1996, pp. 13–15.

these stages it was likely to be incorporated into a larger bibliographic unit: first the 'linked group' of a small number of related works, next the personal miscellany or commonplace book, and lastly the professionally copied anthology or aggregation. Publication in a form analogous to the modern print-defined sense is most obvious where booksellers or newsletter writers organized scribal editions of a particular text for sale to their customers. The newsletters themselves sometimes had a weekly circulation of a hundred or more, and were preferred by those who could afford them to the printed newspaper. In this case copying was often done by groups of clerks in scriptoria; however, on other occasions, publication in a sense more characteristic of the scribal medium took place through the introduction of texts into networks of readers where there was a strong likelihood of them being copied and recopied.

These networks, for which the term 'scribal communities' has been proposed, are found everywhere in late-sixteenth-century and seventeenth-century England.[31] They might form around a patron, within an institution (e.g. a university college or legal inn), or between a group of county neighbours or scattered sharers in a common enthusiasm (most instrumental music of the period, to take one instance, was made available in this last way).[32] Many began as a way of linking distant friends or family members. Quite a number owed their continuance to the persistence of a particular committed individual – Samuel Hartlib and Henry Oldenburg being two well-known examples. The correspondence of Constance Aston (daughter of Sir Walter) reveals her as an assiduous solicitor of verses for her miscellany. She extracts a promise of three new poems from her brother, Herbert, for 'sending your box to Mr Henry Thimbleby', then chides him for not reciprocating poems 'perpetually' sent by herself.[33] While theoretically private, networks almost invariably intersected through members being simultaneously involved in two or more: one might, for example's sake, imagine the case of a viol-playing collector of Parliamentary diurnals with a supplementary interest in prophecies or feudal tenures using exchanges from one collection to obtain new material for another one. The result was that texts could travel on occasion with surprising speed. A writer such as Sidney or Donne would soon discover, if he did not know to start with, that the communication of a new work to his own immediate scribal community could lead to hundreds of additional copies being made. The difference between scribal and print publication in this respect was that such multiplication

31 Love 1993, pp. 179–82; Marotti 1995, pp. 137–208.

32 Ashbee and Holman 1996, pp. 243–70.

33 Cited from Huntington MS. HM 904 in Ezell 1987, p. 72. Jane Barker's participation in a similar network is described in King 1994.

took place not simultaneously, but consecutively, and that the activity of production was dispersed, not centralized. But as a means of bringing texts to readers it was no less effective and probably more influential in so far as the scribal text always carried an aura of forbidden knowledge. Manuscript materials would tend to be read with care and then preserved, whereas the printed pamphlet, their closest counterpart, might merely be scanned then discarded.

In tracing the practice of scribal communication from the period before the invention of printing to the verge of the Enlightenment, it is particularly important to become aware of the point at which it ceases to be merely utilitarian and assumes a character that we can describe as political, irrespective of what is actually being communicated. This arose from the implicit claiming of a right to possess information and to express opinion about matters in the public domain in defiance of the wishes of the Crown. The Reformation in England had put close to a situation in which the Church, through its legal powers and control over education, exercised great influence over the public communication of ideologically significant knowledge, while at the same time possessing highly efficient internal means, which disappeared with the loss of its international links, for the transmission of news. However, instead of leading to an immediate freeing of the market for knowledge, for which the press offered the technological means, religious reform replaced it with the no less restrictive notion of a state monopoly of information about events, both outside and inside the kingdom. The print publication of overseas news was strictly supervised at all but those relatively brief periods when governments lost the power to enforce control, the assumption always being that these were matters affecting princes alone in which the public had neither the right nor the capacity to form opinions. More surprisingly, at most periods this exclusion applied also to home news: as late as the reign of Charles II the only way of gaining an informed overview of current happenings within Britain was to subscribe to a manuscript newsletter, preferably Henry Muddiman's or one of those compiled from the reports of official informants by the secretaries of state.[34]

For much of the reign of Elizabeth the governed seem to have been reasonably content with this situation, relying on traditional oral methods of obtaining current information; but the restriction on the circulation of printed news generated two kinds of deprivation. The first of these bore on commercial decisions, especially those involving investment. The great merchant adventurers had their own trusted overseas correspondents, independent of the Crown's information-gathering services, and might also subscribe to Continental *lettres*

34 Muddiman 1971; Fraser 1956.

à main. In their case it would have been desirable that information likely to confer a commercial advantage travelled no further than themselves; but, since their ventures were increasingly co-operative ones, conducted by companies rather than individuals, and since other merchants and members of the aristocracy and gentry had to make decisions over whether or not to be investors in these ventures, information itself became a subject of exchange, in which the old was to be advantageously bartered for the new. Those who failed to exchange would sooner or later be left in the dark. News about events within the British Isles was sought for the same reason, the weather in Yorkshire or a fire in a port city being of no less commercial importance than the intentions of the Great Turk. In this case the information itself would spread progressively by oral means or by letter: its value as an object of exchange lay in the extent to which it was not yet available to others.

The conflict between the desire of the central government to control the circulation of news and the informational needs of merchants and investors was never properly resolved. But added to this we observe a growing hunger for information of a non-economic kind which could not be delivered effectively by the oral medium. This included, pre-eminently, news of the struggles of Protestant states against the demonized forces of European Catholicism. The Crown, on the other hand, was usually concerned to temper such curiosity, because it might lead to demands for military intervention. Challenges to this state monopoly of news could lead to severe punishments. William Stansby was lucky to lose only his press and his place of business and Nathaniel Butter and Thomas Archer to spend short periods in prison for their attempts to print corantos of foreign news in the early 1620s. For a period after this their newsbooks were tolerated, but in 1632 an embargo was re-established on all printing of foreign news which held sway until the collapse of royal authority in 1641.[35] Titus Oates (discussed in another section of this book) deserves to be recognized as a newsman of genius, not for his ability at coining plausible lies about plots that had never actually existed, but in his masterstroke of presenting his immensely detailed 'narrative' to the nation at large through the press. Its success reveals much about the naivety of a readership that was unused to having information about contemporary events presented with such a degree of circumstantial detail and, for that reason, proved unable to assess it at its true value.

But while the Crown or Parliament could control the press for most of the time, along with most of what was said in the courts and from the pulpit, they

35 McKenzie 1976b, pp. 1–15.

had no way of monitoring the circulation of texts in manuscript, apart from such crude measures as searches of rooms at university colleges and opening letters sent through the public mails. Aware of their helplessness, they did all they could through the law to make such transmission dangerous. Legal opinions were given that not to destroy a treasonable libel was to be oneself guilty of treason. But while this had little real effect on the volume of texts in circulation, it gave a political colouring to what had originally been a purely utilitarian activity. To pass on a text with even the remotest bearing on matters of state in a handwritten copy was to deny a claim to a monopoly over information which, however inefficiently enforced by Tudor and Stuart rulers, never ceased to be asserted. Moreover, even such innocent exchanges as those of musical, astrological and heraldic manuscripts were establishing pathways which were then open to more subversive materials, beginning perhaps with the texts of prophecies (in which there was an intense interest at all periods) but quickly leading to court gossip, which could hardly be ignored, even if its political point of view was not that of the reader, since it might be the only source of information available about shifts of power at the great centre of patronage. And, again, information once acquired was to be traded for new through the exchange of newsletters and separates.

It will be appreciated, then, that the scribal text had a politics, and that this politics was also a geography. From this perspective the transmission of a separate might be compared with the way an anecdote passed from speaker to speaker. One can imagine maps of these transmissions, each one linked by a physical journey and branching as the text was conveyed to new recipients who might transmit it in their turn. Such maps would need a temporal as well as a spatial dimension, for manuscript texts, like anecdotes, must frequently have returned to the hands of those who had already read and perhaps transcribed them. Woudhuysen's impressively thorough study, *Sir Philip Sidney and the circulation of manuscripts*, is rich in evidence of this kind. It seems likely that Sidney never saw any of his writings in printed form: he was a writer for the scribal medium alone, and through it had become the most admired poet of his time. Woudhuysen explores the paths that led from the poet to the musical settings by William Byrd found in manuscripts associated with Sir Edward Paston, and asks the same questions of a number of personal miscellanies.[36] Here the evidence is almost too abundant. Because affiliations based on region, family, education (school and university), religion and politics could all give rise to manuscript transmission, it is often difficult to decide which one of

36 Woudhuysen 1996, pp. 249–57 and 257–66.

several possible links was operative in a given instance. In Sidney's lifetime most transmission probably arose from face-to-face encounters. The 1630s saw the establishment of efficient public postal services leaving the metropolis for given destinations on stated days, and in 1680 the introduction of the penny-post within the metropolis was a further aid to rapid dissemination.

The geography of print was of a simpler nature, mimicking, even as it further entrenched, the economic and informational hegemony of London. With the overwhelming body of book production centred not simply in the capital but in one small area of it, the characteristic movement of the printed text was a straightforward one, first outward from printing house to booksellers' shops and then to the libraries of its purchasers. This pattern also held for the grand manuscripts written to order for wealthy collectors; but the lesser and more portable pieces moved themselves by 'dangerous, wandering ways' from reader to reader, able to generate new copies (in effect new editions) wherever they reposed. Pathways of distribution were also pathways of influence and economic affiliation, reflecting a challenge by regional and interest groups to the growing monopolization of knowledge at the centre that was concomitant with the process known as 'the nationalization of the town-based economy'.[37] In practice, the centre came to be defined by such oppositional writings rather than by any secure sense of its existence as a positive, integrated presence. It could not be identified simply with the court, for that institution was itself a hotbed of scribal authorship and the source of many of the most pungently oppositional texts of our period. Court writing is by definition factional and was often violently so. Its escape into wider circulation was no doubt unintentional in some cases, but must often have been deliberate. The scribally circulated writing associated with the embryo court of Prince Henry is a case in the sense that praise of the prince was often to be construed as criticism of his father. In the earlier reigns the great favourites, Leicester, Essex, Raleigh, Cecil, Somerset and Buckingham offered one kind of focus for opposition but, as we progress through the seventeenth century, personal satires increasingly give way to 'shotgun' attacks on groups – the ministry, the Parliament, the Church hierarchy – reflecting a general movement towards collective leadership and bureaucratized government.[38] While readers of scribally transmitted texts still sought new material from London, and especially from the London newsletter writers (who were also traders in separates), their communications to each other travelled by horse, coach, carrier's wagon and boat across a variety of routes of their own devising that, in their linkings across the borders of parishes and

37 Habermas 1989, p. 17. 38 Marotti 1995, pp. 75–133; *POAS* (Yale), II, pp. 339–40.

counties, formed an alternative information system, different in its means and pace of transmission, in the nature of the physical records it conveyed, and in the character and substance of its messages, from the metropolitan one. With the loss of this system in the eighteenth century, despite its partial replacement by the spread of provincial printing and journalism, a social way of knowing and the political structures it had informed were also lost. Even the gentry had become metropolitanized.

But this was emphatically not true of the period under review; and it is misleading to think of scribal transmission as the characteristic mode of a dying political order or of a superseded technology. Unlike ancient lanes, scribal pathways were not a relic of an older agrarian economy but a constantly self-reorganizing informational web among a governing class which was energetically modernizing its own productive practices. Indeed, the expansion in the transmission of texts through manuscript that characterized the period after 1580 was itself the product of technological advance, being directly dependent on improved physical communication (better roads, faster ships, stronger animals, more efficient ways of delivering mail). A new generation of country houses built by squires who no longer felt obliged to keep open house for their tenants allowed members of gentry families to escape from the oral community of the hall and parlour into private spaces more suitable for reading and reflection. The chest gave way to the cabinet or escritoire as a repository for writings. The longer periods of education that were now thought necessary for the sons of the gentry if they were to seek preferment – and for their daughters, too, if they were to fulfil their enlarged domestic and religious duties – made them more fluent writers and readers. Even such small matters as the growing availability of wax as opposed to tallow candles had its effect on the volume of scribal communication: the study need no longer reek of the kitchen. While the press and the official mails could convey hundreds of copies of a printed tract or proclamation within a matter of days to all corners of the kingdom, by the reign of James I, if not earlier, it was likely that the issues involved had already been canvassed through manuscript letters, essays and poems whose circulation was hardly less rapid, and which carried much more weight because they possessed an air of privileged secrecy which made them more carefully attended to (as was inevitable when many of their readers would personally transcribe them) and likewise more trusted than the output of the state-supervised print media. It is true there were exceptions to this rule, in the period leading up to the civil wars and again during the Exclusion Bill crisis, when the press spoke with a freedom previously and subsequently reserved for the scribal medium; and yet this did not mean that the flow of separates during this period was any less insistent.

Some things could still be said only in the more secretive medium, which was also the *personal* medium, instinct with presence. All these distinctions can be fruitfully pursued in considering what it might have meant to read a work from a manuscript rather than its printed cousin.

In a volume whose narrative concludes with the triumph of a London print-based information system, it is salutary to be reminded of this older method by which messages sought their readers individually by avenues that had nothing to do with those of the book trade, and that, even as we read, is reconstituting itself in the world around us to the clicking of keyboards and the hum of computer fans.

Negotiating the media

We have seen that most characteristic forms of the manuscript book – the personal miscellany, the scribal anthology and the collection of materials such as lampoons or parliamentary diurnals originally issued separately – were a uniting of smaller units. The overriding tendency of scribal compilation was agglutinative. However, the medium was also host to substantial prose works by writers as varied as Spenser (the *View of the present state of Ireland*), Sidney (the two *Arcadias* and the letter to the Queen on the proposed French marriage), Raleigh, Sir John Harington, Sir John Davies, Sir Robert Cotton, Sir Robert Filmer, Sir Thomas Browne, Samuel Hartlib, Hobbes and Algernon Sidney, which for one reason or another were designed by their authors for manuscript transmission only. Here the point is that the restriction sometimes followed from the content not the form or hoped-for audience of the work, making them, in a sense, printed books manqué. But in the same way it is possible to argue that a considerable number of printed books really belong to scribal rather than print culture. In the 'Advertisement' to the Moseley re-issue of the 1645 edition of *Poems, & c. written by Mr. Ed. Waller* we find the following:

> Reader. This parcell of exquisit Poems, have pass'd up and downe through many hands amongst persons of the best quallity, in loose imperfect Manuscripts, and there is lately obtruded to the world an adulterate Copy, surruptitiously and illegally imprinted, to the derogation of the Author, and the abuse of the Buyer.[39]

Waller himself was in exile in France by this time. There is no evidence that he had any intention of printing his poems, but a good deal that he had presented

39 E. Waller, *Poems 1645. Together with poems from Bodleian MS Don. d. 55* (Menston, W. Yorks, 1971), sig. A4^r.

collections in manuscript to individual friends and patrons. The preface to one of these scribal collections was borrowed to supply a preface for the 1645 edition, while another, with a different selection and arrangement of poems and a dedicatory letter to Queen Henrietta Maria, is preserved in the Bodleian Library.[40] When he did finally return to England in 1655 he 'was troubled to find his name in print, but somewhat satisfied to see his lines so ill rendred that he might justly disown them, and say to a mistaking Printer, as one did to an ill Reciter, – *Male dum recitas, incipit esse tuum*'.[41] His fate was that of innumerable other authors whose writings had been intercepted in scribal transmission (usually in debased texts) by piratical booksellers. The 1640 edition of Carew's poems and the 1680 edition of Rochester's both represent a scribal miscellany rushed into print with minimal intervention in order to capitalize on the author's recent death.[42] The various *State poems* collections of the late-seventeenth and early eighteenth centuries and the printed compilations of state papers already mentioned represent the other phenomenon of printed anthologies of scribal separates or their immediate printed derivatives. A collection such as *Tottell's miscellany* (1557), on the other hand, though compiled from texts that had previously circulated only in manuscript, belongs to the print medium in the sense that language, metre and sequence have been modified editorially to meet the expectations of a new audience and technological culture.

The distinction just made between print culture and scribal culture arises from work by both anthropologists and media theorists in expounding the informational law whose clearest enunciation is James Carey's axiom 'structures of consciousness parallel structures of communication'.[43] Carey also cites Harold Innis's summation of the consequences of this law: 'changes in communication technology affected culture by altering the structure of interests (the things thought about), by changing the character of symbols (the things thought with), and by changing the nature of community (the arena in which thought developed)' – all clearly true of the period under consideration.[44] While Carey is careful to frame his principle non-causationally, Innis's phraseology implies that technological change precedes change of consciousness. The historical evidence is more complex. It can be argued plausibly that the social and intellectual conditions that made printing desirable had existed for some time in Europe prior to the development of the technology. In Japan, on the

40 Bodleian Library, MS Don. d. 55.

41 'The printer to the reader', 2nd edn (London, 1664), p. [A3^r].

42 *The poems of Thomas Carew*, ed. R. Dunlap (Oxford, 1949), pp. lxii–lxiv; Vieth 1963.

43 Carey 1992, p. 161.

44 Carey 1992, p. 160.

other hand, woodblock printing was practised for centuries in monasteries for the devotional replication of prayers without any wider social use being imagined for it. With this in mind, it will be helpful to consider the important test case offered by antiquarian research.

We should note for a start that the copying and transmission of antiquarian records was one of the major concerns of writers in the scribal medium, and that a huge mass of transcripts made for this purpose still survives from our period.[45] In the late sixteenth and early seventeenth centuries such work received great encouragement from Camden's Society of Antiquaries and its most influential alumnus, Sir Robert Cotton. Although *Britannia* and a number of other printed works drew on the research of these members, the papers actually written for the society's meetings mostly remained restricted to manuscript circulation. The programme of copying was so successful that, when part of the Cottonian collection of medieval manuscripts was destroyed by fire in 1731, much of the loss was able to be restored from transcripts, some of which survived in several copies. However, the preponderant part of this vast national enterprise had different aims from those of the metropolitan scholars whose intention was always that the assembling of ancient precedents should contribute to the creation of new politics.[46] The regional historian compiling the archival record of his county or parish was less concerned with *using* the past than with continuing it. Most were themselves custodians of estate records reaching back several generations, and of a kind that their own day-to-day economic and legal activity continued to supplement. Many were eager students of feudal tenures, by which their rights to property and income were still likely to be affected. The complicated nature of inheritance encouraged careful preservation of testamentary records and marriage contracts. Genealogies were not simply a matter of family pride but the basis of claims to property in fact or reversion. Scholarly work on these materials took place against the real-life background of incessant litigation over the ownership of land and rights to make use of it for such purposes as pasturing animals, felling timber and drawing water, even if one were not the owner. An ancient charter might confirm or deny some much-prized local privilege.

Research of this kind, as exemplified in the lives of busy local historians such as Sir Symon Archer, had a self-interested aspect which further encouraged the restriction of its fruits to the scribal medium, although such scholars could be generous in their contributions to the greater projects of county and national histories.[47] But the point for our study is not this so much as the fact that

45 Woudhuysen 1996, pp. 116–33; Douglas 1951. 46 Sharpe 1979.
47 For Archer, see P. Styles, *Sir Simon Archer 1581–1662* (Oxford, 1946).

the scholar's connection with his sources was still an experiential, time-bound one. We need therefore to consider what the effect of such documentary material became when it was presented in the alien form of a massive printed compilation.

The answer is simple. The documents might be the same, scarcely altered from the form in which they had been contributed by the parish or county historian, but their connection with the reader was of a completely new nature. For their meaning now had to be established in a totalizing way, which had little to do with the relationship of the local landowner to his own and his neighbours' private archives, but everything to do with an emerging science of history whose interests were political and philosophical and whose aim, whether stated or not, was the replacement of local and family allegiances by national patriotism in the form in which it was defined by the metropolis. The texts associated with the new technology replaced the experience of the past as a shared possession with information *about* the past, seen as an increasingly remote source of materials for the operations of discursive reason. In doing so, the two media present us with two quite different constructions of the past.

The past of script, in this sense, is a past of process in which the incompleteness of the single record leads to a continually reiterated search for complementary records, but one that can never be complete since there is no point of intellectual exit from the interweaving of contingencies embodied in the scribal record. The most that could be done towards ordering these materials was to assemble them, as Simonds D'Ewes did in his compilations of Parliamentary papers and the post-1688 scriptoria did in their giant retrospective anthologies of lampoons, into as complete a mass as was permitted by the brute facts of survival. But even here the use made of these materials was likely to be piecemeal and any ordering of them purely for convenience. The past of print, on the other hand, is one organized around coherent narratives and a sense of purposive linear development. Where these were lacking, because a particular editor had been too much in love with the fortuitous felicities of the muniment room to impose a philosophic discipline upon the material of a collection, the reader would supply the lack by reference to the wider text of printed national history. Moreover, the loss of particular records was immaterial so long as there were sufficient left to establish principles by which the reader could gain a generalized Cartesian overview of the disordered terrain through which the hunter after manuscripts was condemned to journey incessantly. This principle applied as strongly to collections of recent political materials (such as Rushworth, Fuller and Nalson) as it did to the purely antiquarian collections. They, too, were annihilating the experiential past by replacing it with *information* that could no longer be apprehended as part of a lived continuum but might be subsumed under philosophical master narratives.

Governing and guiding this print-moderated enterprise were three principles enunciated by Carey in 'Reconceiving "Mass" and "Media"': the non-contingency of starting points, indubitability in unravelling problems, and a belief that the world of problems was independent of and accessible to the mind of the knowing observer.[48] Against this view, Carey sets another that he describes as Viconian while confessing to 'twisting somewhat to the purpose here', that 'the world as such has no essence and therefore no real independence'; that 'the "real" is continuously adapted and remade to suit human purposes, including the remaking of humans themselves'; and that 'it is this world of human activity we can understand with greatest clarity'. This is also, as I see it, the perspective of the manuscript separate and book, always embedded in human transactions and making no claim to a totalizing finality either as individual documents or as statements of opinion. And it is this that I also see as the most important part of their contribution to the formation of the bourgeois public sphere, as it has been conceptualized by Habermas.[49] Older scholars, among them Innis, saw the public sphere as collateral with, if not actually the product of, print culture, especially the newsbook and newspaper. Habermas's innovation was to see it as an outcome of an oral phenomenon – of new kinds of conversation which began to be practised in the London coffee-houses of the late seventeenth century. The inscriptional culture most closely associated with the emergence of this new phenomenon of 'private people come together to form a public'[50] was not the promiscuously obtainable newspaper or even the printed pamphlet, but the scribal separate and newsletter.

Complementing the sociological approach to the interaction of consciousness and technology (whose outstanding exponent in Britain has been D. F. McKenzie[51]), Marshall McLuhan, Walter J. Ong, Jonathan Goldberg, Martin Elsky and Alvin Kernan have each explored some of the ways in which the physical experience of the three media of voice, script, and print can be seen as giving rise to metaphorical apprehensions of the nature of knowledge which then become hypostatized into ways of knowing.[52] While in an oral culture language is only manifest in the act of speech, which is always a social act, the introduction of writing produces a conception of language as something that can exist independently of human minds engaged in the act of communication. This conception is further extended by print with its huge physical

48 Carey 1992, pp. 70–1. 49 Habermas 1989, pp. 32–3. 50 Habermas 1989, p. 25.
51 Particularly in his Panizzi lectures (McKenzie 1986).
52 McLuhan 1962; Ong 1982; Goldberg 1990; Elsky 1989; Kernan 1987.

masses of mechanically multiplied letterpress. While the printed book makes the experience of language passive and linear, script can be allowed a degree of 'residual orality' (to use Ong's much-borrowed phrase), arising both from the social circumstances of its production and the fact that its mode of inscription is a manual, not a mechanical one.[53] Moreover, because the technology of replication was identical with that of creation, scribes were encouraged to supplement or revise the texts that passed through their hands.[54] These distinctions accord in a broad sense with what was suggested earlier about processes of neural de-skilling and re-skilling and are useful points of reference in trying to understand the changing phenomenology of reading. However, we need to be careful that they are not applied in an *a priori* way that obscures the fact that the engagement of sixteenth-century and seventeenth-century readers with the available media was an intricate, nuanced one that does not readily allow itself to be subsumed.

In its preservation of the more intimate relationship between author and reader characteristic of oral culture and enacted in our case through the exchange of separates within scribal communities, script rejected print-culture claims for words being the property of an author or copyright holder for a sense of texts as communally possessed. Compilers would routinely mix together work from a writer's wider scribal community with authentic material: much of Sidney's and Donne's verse survives in such communally constructed collections.[55] But the Carew and Rochester printed volumes referred to earlier, while following the texts and order of their scribally published sources, have suppressed the evidence for multiple authorship in an attempt to conform to the print-culture ideal that all works in an authored volume (which is to say owned, and therefore negotiable as an investment) should be by the same hand. The subsequent history of the Rochesterian text shows a steady imposition of print assumptions manifest in the suppression of indecency, the search for a rational system of ordering (which was at the same time a rejection of the scribal sources' delight in mixture), the rejection of spurious material, and the search for ways of packaging Rochester, the occasional writer *par excellence*, as a national literary classic.[56]

What this points to is a number of levels at which the choice of medium determined the form taken by the work. In a simple sense all printed texts of this period are printed manuscripts – there is no known case of an author using the

53 Ong 1982, pp. 115–16, 119. 54 Marotti 1995, pp. 135–71.

55 See Sullivan 1988, pp. 201–8; Beal, *IELM*, I. 1, pp. 243–568; Marotti 1995, pp. 147–59; Hobbs 1989; Hobbs 1992.

56 Walker 1992; Love 1996a.

typographical case as a means of inscription. But in writing for transmission through manuscript rather than the press, an author would automatically adopt different conventions and decorums that had come to be considered proper to the medium. Scribal authors, as we have seen, whether or not they revealed their identity, were usually addressing the immediate audience of the scribal community, whereas print publishing authors took their places on the great stage of the world and had to accept the standards of behaviour regarded as proper for members of their class in appearances on that stage. Since freedom in uttering subversive opinions was one of the great attractions of the scribal medium, these opinions might well be supplied – even when there was no particular need for them – as part of what readers expected from such productions. The scribal world was also in an important sense an anti-hierarchical, carnivalesque one: lords such as the second Duke of Buckingham and his friends the Earls of Rochester and Dorset would use language of the grossest obscenity, while commoners made free with the reputation of lords and ladies, with the (often transparent) anonymity of the medium providing a counterpart to the carnival mask. The print-publishing author also had to wear a mask, but in this case it was the mask of politeness and decorum, with critical views expressed, if at all, with the degree of indirection appropriate to the author's social standing. Scribally published writing had no need to be indirect or ironic and rarely was.[57]

Conclusion

In these and other ways we can allow a theoretical force to Carey's and Ong's contention that the choice of medium was a choice of alternative ways of constructing consciousness. But what has not been made clear is how far broad distinctions drawn between oral, script-literate and print-literate cultures (and these and today's electronographic literacy) are to be applied to cultures in which an individual might move continually between media, or even encounter the same text (a poem, a sermon, Lord Lucas's speech on the Subsidy Bill) in all three. Before considering this we will need to return to some issues arising from our earlier discussion of oral texts.

By the period covered by this volume the experience of the oral text was rarely free from some sense of its involvement with the other media. Even as apparently pure a vehicle of oral expression as the satirical ballad, composed in order to insult some local enemy and sung in the context of the skimmington

57 Love 1993, pp. 308–9.

or as tavern entertainment, would also frequently be taken to a literate person in order to be written down – a sense having somehow arisen that its existence was not fully actual until this had taken place.[58] Likewise, probably the most universal memorial possession of all, the responses of the Book of Common Prayer, were regulated from a printed book and had first come into the world in this form. The Bible, on the other hand, while it might be studied as a printed book, was in fact the product of centuries of manuscript transmission which had left its text riddled with variants and indeterminacies. Its appearance in the stability of a state-regulated translation into English and in the objectivity of the printed page was, as the Catholic Père Simon and the Deist Anthony Collins were equally keen to point out, a double deception.[59] But then the Bible, as well as being available in print, was also known aurally from being read aloud as part of worship.

From time to time scribal transcriptions of printed materials are encountered which may even record the publication details of the exemplar or attempt a facsimile of the title page. Or a printed book may have been heavily corrected or revised in script. These interweavings complicate attempts to apply monistic models of media-based consciousness and point to possibilities of confusion and conflict in an individual's actual experience of texts that were neither purely oral, purely chirographic, nor purely typographical. Raylor cites an occasion in 1655 in which Milton's friend, Robert Overton, was caught in possession of some verses satirizing Cromwell, written on the back of an old letter. Overton pretended that he had been given the poem by a friend who had told him that Cromwell had himself seen it and laughed at it, but his servant betrayed the truth that 'his master had copied the verses down after "hearinge a fidler's boy singe them in London"'. Raylor notes:

> The text of the poem in Overton's possession bears the signs of memorial reconstruction and would be consonant with the servant's account of Overton copying it after hearing it sung. Differences between it and the version later published in *Cleaveland Revived* suggest the possibility that distinct versions of the poem were in circulation, one for singing and one for reading . . . While the former is written in a rollicking ballad meter, suitable for singing, the latter adopts a more stately iambic form.[60]

A similar tendency can be seen in the transmission of Rochester's 'In the Isle of Britain', where the more 'literary' texts preserve a fairly strict iambic pentameter while the more heavily interpolated ones drift continually in the direction

58 Fox 1994, pp. 58–65. 59 Love 1993, pp. 299–307. 60 Raylor 1994, pp. 205, 290.

of anapestic tetrameter.[61] In each case the scribal text was feeling the pull of the oral medium.

In considering what these mixed texts might have meant to their readers, it is helpful to look at the practice of authors as they moved between the media. In an essay on Marvell's letters to the Corporation of Hull, N. H. Keeble points out how carefully their writer maintains a decorum that is quite different from that of his letters to William Popple, or from those of the scribally circulated satires, the lyrics written for the Fairfax family, or the printed prose tracts.[62] In a striking act of dissociation, Marvell, writing in the scribal medium, can speak of the author of the printed *The growth of popery* as if he were a different person altogether:

> Three or four printed Books since have described, as near as it was proper to go, the Man being a Member of Parliament, Mr *Marvell* to have been the Author; but if he had, surely he should not have escaped being questioned in Parliament, or some other Place.[63]

In fact Marvell's writings negotiate a variety of 'Mr Marvells'. In his constructing the persona of the constituency letters, Keeble tells us, 'Omission was as important . . . as inclusion: he is defined by the tales he did not, or could not, tell. However, if only some statements could be admitted to (and admitted by) the letters of this correspondent, as some are "only proper within the walls of the Parl^t house" . . . then, in other places – other genres – what here could not be said might be uttered with propriety'.[64]

Keeble's comment is a reminder that even within the medium of script there were varying decorums and varying levels of freedom. His vision of Marvell as a writer acutely conscious of what was to be said and not to be said in the medium or sub-medium currently employed raises the possibility of similar discriminations applied in reading. What intersections of media make confusing to us need not have confused contemporaries. Could it be that such variously encountered texts were seen as providing a distinct and desirable range of colourings along a communicative spectrum, and that to view the same work at one time as diffracted by print and at another by voice or script was a welcome source of variety and an aid to understanding? Could it also be that these varied apprehensions had something to do with the stages by which events and ideas are absorbed into communal consciousness and made sense of? Might there have been a succession by which a new, possibly unsettling idea was first encountered in script, then tested in conversation, and finally integrated into the

61 Love 1997, pp. 202–4. 62 Keeble 1990.
63 *The poems and letters of Andrew Marvell*, II, p. 357. 64 Keeble 1990, p. 129.

structure of printed knowledge? Or with the first two phases reversed? Among the scientists of the Royal Society and its informal predecessors, work began with collegiate oral discussion, was tested and promulgated through correspondence and manuscript essays, such as those left in large quantities by Isaac Newton, and print-published only after a consensus had been reached about its significance. Something similar seems to have gone on in the coffee-houses. At each stage there might be reluctance to take the matter further, arising not from diffidence but from a sense that results had already sufficiently been communicated. In yet other cases new ideas encountered in print might be digested through scribal and spoken texts. The uncovering of these sequences is one of the tasks that await future workers in the field covered by this chapter.

But there are also more fundamental tasks to be performed before study of the scribal heritage of the early modern period can be said to have achieved the same level of maturity as studies of the contemporary printed book. These have been admirably summarized by Woudhuysen:

> The subject still needs its *STC* to catalogue the books themselves, its McKerrow and its Gaskell to explain how they were physically produced, and its Greg and its Bowers to establish how they should be described, what can be deduced from their make-up, and how their role in the editing of texts might be freshly considered in theory and in practice. It also needs a series of facsimiles illustrating a wide range of scribal hands . . . Something is now understood about the nature of the manuscript medium and its attendant problems, but only a small part of the surviving evidence from the early modern period has so far been considered in any depth. This contrasts markedly with the study of the book in the Middle Ages.[65]

A major scholarly enterprise awaits and invites.

65 Woudhuysen 1996, p. 6.

4

John Donne and the circulation of manuscripts

PETER BEAL

John Donne (1572–1631) is clearly the most striking instance of a major Tudor-Stuart poet who flourished in the context of a manuscript culture. Although, with apparent reluctance, Donne allowed in his own lifetime the publication of one major verse composition, his *Anniversaries* (1611–12), as well as two occasional commendatory and elegiac poems,[1] and although a trickle of epigrams, miscellaneous verses and snippets from his works made their way into printed miscellanies of the period as his poetry came increasingly to be treated as a common commodity,[2] the vast majority of his poetical output was certainly confined to manuscripts. Moreover, the sheer quantity of manuscript copies of poems by him which still survive (4,000-odd texts in upwards of 260 manuscripts)[3] – and which must be only a fraction of the number once in existence – indicates beyond doubt that Donne was the most popular English poet from the 1590s until at least the middle of the seventeenth century.

Donne's own attitude to their circulation was – eventually, at any rate – one of considerable ambivalence, and sometimes outright concern. For the publication of his *Anniversaries*, for instance, Donne felt obliged to apologize for having, as he says, '*descended* to print anything in verse . . . and do not pardon myself'.[4] Publication in print, where poems could be made available to all and sundry without any discrimination was, perhaps, construed as at the very least a lapse in gentlemanly taste and decorum. This was just one of a number of social, political and psychological considerations which would explain the lack of enthusiasm he felt about the prospect of publishing some of his poems late in 1614, when, as he confided to his friend Sir Henry Goodyer, he

1 'Upon Mr Thomas Coryats Crudities', *Coryats Crudities* (1611) and 'Elegie upon the untimely death of the incomparable Prince Henry' in Joshua Sylvester's *Lachrymae lachrymarum* (1613).

2 Cf. Sullivan 1993.

3 I listed 4,018 manuscript texts in *IELM*, I.1, pp. 262–555, 566–8. These numbers have since increased significantly, with many additional discoveries by myself and others, virtually all of which will be represented in the current multivolume *Variorum edition of the poetry of John Donne*, Indiana.

4 Donne to George Garrard, 14 April 1612, in his *Letters to severall persons of honour* (1651), p. 238.

was under pressure from the Lord Chamberlain, the Earl of Somerset, to do so. He was, he said, under a 'necessity of printing', at his own cost, 'a few Copies' of his 'Poems' and dedicating them to Somerset – as a kind of 'valediction to the world' before being ordained as a priest. For this reason he appealed to Goodyer to let him have 'that old book' of his own poems ('of mine old rags'), since it was otherwise costing him 'more diligence to seek them, then it did to make them'.[5] As it happens, nothing more is heard of this proposed edition.

Moreover, as he grew older and his station in life changed, Donne would come to see that even the relatively controlled medium of *manuscript* circulation demanded circumspection and self-censorship. In 1600 or perhaps later, for instance, Donne promised to acquaint a correspondent (? Sir Henry Wotton) with all his (manuscript) writings provided that he received, as he said, firm assurance that 'no coppy shalbee taken for any respect of these or any other my compositions sent to yo*u*'. He confessed, in effect, that he had some 'feare' about the circulation of his 'satyrs' and 'p[er]haps shame' about the circulation of his 'elegies' and possibly prose *Paradoxes*.[6] Similarly, in mid-1611, Donne asked Goodyer to keep to one side some of the literary papers he had lent him, which Donne now intended to revise and even cull as he saw fit, these apparently including his now lost Latin epigrams.[7] And we also have the testimony of Ben Jonson (in his cups) in 1619 that 'since he was made Doctor' (in March 1615) Donne 'repenteth highlie & seeketh to destroy all his poems'[8] – a comment which reinforces the impression that, if he had been able to do so, Donne would gladly have called in all copies of his early secular verse. This concern seems to have affected his attitude to his manuscript writings in general and led to caution as to who might have access to them. One later notable instance when he imparted his own writings to anyone occurred in 1619, when he was taking stock of his situation before embarking on a voyage to Germany from which he was not sure he would ever return. Donne then gave to Sir Robert Kerr, later Earl of Ancrum, a number of his manuscript writings, including 'Poems, of which', he said, 'you took a promise': it was as a characteristically solemn act of entrusting them to a guardian for their preservation, but not for widespread distribution.[9]

5 Donne to Goodyer, 20 December 1614, in Donne, *Letters* (1651), pp. 196–7.
6 Letter copied in the 'Burley MS' (Leicestershire Record Office, DG. 7/Lit.2, f.308^{v}); printed in Simpson 1948, pp. 316–17.
7 Donne, *Poems* (1633), pp. 351–2.
8 'Conversations with Drummond, 1619', in *Ben Jonson*, ed. C. H. Herford and P. and E. Simpson (Oxford, 1925–52), I, p. 136.
9 Donne, *Letters* (1651), pp. 21–22.

Nevertheless, of course, for all his caution, Donne's texts did generally escape out of his control, though it is unwise to present a simple, homogeneous picture of the manuscript circulation of Donne's poems over a period of fifty years or more.

Donne was a 'coterie' poet, in the sense that his poems were initially read within – and indeed to some extent occasioned by – a select circle of relatively like-minded friends, acquaintances, and potential patrons (both men and women).[10] As a clever, young, somewhat rakish, man-about-town, at least in his early years in the 1590s–1600s, Donne could afford to be witty, outspoken, risqué – his verses finding a sympathetic response in his London circle of young gentlemen, university students, lawyers and Inns of Court men, and aristocrats in the precincts of the Court itself. From the establishment of a sympathetic audience and readership, even though perhaps originally limited and exclusive, and as his poems attracted increasing interest, even being valued as models of wit, it inevitably followed that their circulation would gather its own momentum. It would develop into a cycle of copying and recopying, both of individual poems and, eventually, of whole series or even would-be comprehensive collections of his poems, totally beyond the author's personal sphere or approval – an ever-widening circle extending from persons (or their families) within Donne's actual acquaintance to many other members of society, both in and out of London. Transmission was also subject to the common process of manuscript culture whereby texts were liable to be copied, and sometimes adapted, to suit the tastes, standards and requirements of *compilers* and *readers*, rather than out of any sense of reverence for the sanctity of the author's original.

We can surmise that, besides copies of individual poems, there was circulated in the 1590s a separate small collection of his *Satyres*, together with *The storme* and *The calme* (four quarto booklets of these poems survive).[11] It is also possible that his various *Songs and sonnets* were gathered together and copied as an independent collection at this time – they tend to appear as a group in later collections, though no separate manuscript of them is known at present.

There is much scope for speculation about the nature of the manuscript circulation of Donne's poems from around the time of his ordination (January 1615) onwards. Evidence would tend to suggest (not surprisingly) that his earlier, amorous lyrics and satires were most popular, with a reasonably receptive 'market' for his miscellaneous elegies, verse epistles, etc., while, but for the very occasional copy of a single poem, his ostensibly more serious, religious poems tended to be gathered only in later, more formal collections. It is clear that by

10 Cf. Marotti 1986; Pebworth 1989.   11 *IELM*, I.1, p.254.

the 1620s large manuscript collections of his poems were being prepared, and recopied, and these proliferated well into the 1630s and beyond.

By March 1631, John Donne – Dean of St Paul's, and one of the most celebrated and respected clerics and preachers of his time – was dead. It is surprising that it took as long as two years for a publisher to bring out a printed edition of his poems. But even the appearance of John Marriott's quarto edition of 1633 did not prevent Donne's texts from continuing to thrive in a manuscript culture. Many poems by him copied from manuscript sources appeared in commonplace books and miscellanies of the 1630s and 1640s (an especially fruitful period for the production of such compilations). In addition, various exempla of the editions of 1633, 1635 and 1669 were annotated by readers, many of their corrections and emendations being based on collation with yet other manuscript texts.

The situation as regards Donne's prose works is slightly more complicated in that Donne had specific reasons for publishing in print, before his ordination, two substantial anti-Catholic polemics – his very longest work, *Pseudo-martyr* (1610) and *Conclave Ignati or Ignatius his conclave* (1611). However, concern about potentially 'misinterpretable' elements in his bold and lengthy discourse on suicide *Biathanatos* (written probably in 1608) led to his deliberately restricting its readership to a very few 'friends' in his own lifetime.[12] Of his other theological writings, he was prevailed upon, again allegedly by friends, to publish his *Devotions* in 1624; a total of six of his many sermons – source of much of his fame in his later years – appeared between 1622 and 1627, and the remainder were published posthumously, principally by his son in 1640–61. Otherwise, a handful of early satires and *jeux d'esprit* (such as his *Courtier's library*, *paradoxes and problems*, 'Characters' and other *Juvenilia*) were similarly confined to manuscripts until after his death.

The survival of so many contemporary or near-contemporary manuscript texts of Donne's poems offers scholars special opportunities for the study of manuscript literary culture in this period. At the same time, it provides complex textual problems for modern editors who would seek to establish 'authentic' texts where, without Donne's original autograph manuscripts to help them, none would seem to exist, and where the very history of manuscript transmission would seem to militate against the notion of 'authority'. Editors as recently as the 1970s have been especially guided by an attractive group of manuscript volumes (generally classified as 'Group I'), which have all the hallmarks of careful copying, as well as of aesthetic presentation (among them,

12 Donne, *Letters* (1651), pp. 21–22. Cf. also Beal 1998, ch. 2, pp. 31–57.

the calligraphic 'Leconfield MS', now in the Keynes collection in Cambridge University Library, is perhaps the most visually appealing and seductive of the Donne manuscripts known to date). Nevertheless, for all their status as ostensibly 'good texts', these volumes represent relatively late and sophisticated collections of Donne's verse, and editors' decisions need to be qualified by reference to earlier copies. It is inevitable that some measure of textual error and contamination will arise over so long a period of multiple duplication, even setting aside the complicating factor that Donne *may* have revised certain poems at different times. But the period when editors could dismiss out of hand the vast majority of manuscript witnesses as being intrinsically corrupt or unauthoritative (often in deference to early printed texts no less so) is now fortunately past. The editors of the current multivolume Donne *Variorum edition* will make a boldly eclectic choice of copy-texts, ranging from individual poems from well-known 'major' collections (such as the 'Westmoreland MS', now in the Berg Collection, New York Public Library, copied by Donne's friend Rowland Woodward) to single copies and to texts in the middle of miscellaneous commonplace books. Despite the huge industry employed in the past few decades in editing Donne, the study of his texts and of their transmission remains a field as wide-open as ever.

5
Music books

MARY CHAN

The patent granted to William Byrd and Thomas Tallis in 1575 to print both music books (except Psalm books) and ruled music paper draws attention to the close relationship throughout the whole of this period between printed and manuscript production of music books. Any brief account of music books in this period must be indebted to the ground-breaking and detailed work of D. W. Krummel.[1] Krummel writes of music printing; but this is by no means the whole story for music books. The difficulties associated with the patent, the special skills of the typesetters and the special founts required, the smallness of the market (especially early in the period) and the costliness of printed music meant that much of the music circulating, especially in the sixteenth century and the first half of the seventeenth century, was in manuscript. Indeed, some genres, such as cathedral music and keyboard music, were barely attempted in print at all. When printed and manuscript books for the period are considered together it becomes clear that their history is intertwined and that, for both categories, contents, layout and method of production were determined by the social contexts of their composition and their audience. For music, perhaps more than for other kinds of texts, social issues of performance, occasion and patronage were significant in determining what was printed, what was copied, and how music circulated. This is true for all genres of music: even the seemingly obvious distinction, between sacred and secular, is blurred in, for example, manuscript collections made for private, family use which include both kinds together, or in the reformed Church's printed Psalm books where the early Psalm tunes were adapted from courtly and ballad tunes.

It is not possible to claim for much music in this period the status of an 'ideal' text. For manuscripts this is particularly the case. Not only were errors transmitted and, as Morley said in 1597, 'easilie augmented';[2] each manuscript, too, had its own purpose, its own circle of users, its own determinants of

1 Krummel 1975.

2 Thomas Morley, *A plaine and easie introdvction to practical mvsicke* (London, 1597), p. 151.

repertoire. In the case of manuscripts, one could confidently claim the status of 'ideal text' only for those few surviving autograph manuscripts made as presentation copies. Printed books, too, were subject to performers' needs, that is, to the market. For example, madrigal collections printed over the first twenty years of the seventeenth century tended to merge with the English fashion for consort song and to describe their contents as 'apt for voices or viols' as viol consorts became popular from the beginning of the seventeenth century. Another instance is the dance music Thomas Campion published at the end of the Description of *The Lord Hay's masque*. Three dance tunes were 'set forth with words that they [might] be sung to the Lute or Violl', one of the few instances of printed masque dance music, despite Ben Jonson's claim that dancing was 'the soule of masque'.

For the early part of the period Krummel has described in detail the ways in which the patent for music books, including ruled music paper, controlled the publication of printed music in the latter part of the sixteenth century. He draws attention to the fact that Thomas Tallis and William Byrd had no experience in music printing and no type founts, but had been given the 1575 patent because they were respected musicians. As printers they were reliant on Thomas Vautrollier who had imported music type from France. The book they printed in 1575, *Cantiones sacrae*, sold poorly. After the death of Tallis (1585) and Vautrollier (1587), Byrd permitted Thomas East, who had acquired one of Vautrollier's founts, to print for him. Krummel points out how East's enthusiasm and drive could be seen to be directly responsible for the flourishing of the English madrigal publications from the late 1580s to the end of the century. The printing of Psalm books in England was also controlled by patent. But the uncertainties and complexities of printing secular music did not obtain for Psalm books, especially once the metrical Psalm texts of Sternhold and Hopkins, published with a single vocal line, came to be accepted as 'standard'.

Nicholas Temperley has discussed the use of Psalm books in the parish churches. The reformed Church adopted first the tunes of the Catholic service as in John Marbeck's *Booke of common praier noted* (1550).[3] The metrical settings of the Psalms derived in England, as in France, from the courtly tradition of poetry;[4] probably (as in Scotland) the Psalms were first sung to familiar, ballad, tunes.[5] The practice of Psalm singing in Elizabethan parish churches was not related so much to Puritan propaganda as to the fact that the tunes were simple and there was little money available to support professional choirs

3 N. Temperley, *The music of the English parish church* (Cambridge, 1979), I, p. 15.

4 Temperley, *Parish church*, p. 22 and Shire 1969, pp. 25–33.

5 Temperley, *Parish church*, p. 26.

or to keep organs in good repair. Of John Day's first three publications of Church music: *The whole booke of psalmes* (1562) with monophonic tunes, and the part-books *The whole psalmes in foure partes* (1563) and *Certaine notes* (1560–5), containing the sung portions of the liturgy and anthems, only the first was reissued.[6] Throughout the seventeenth century, parish churches had only the very basic music provided by the Psalm book. Cathedral choirs relied on their own manuscript copies of part music; later, pre-Restoration, published collections of harmonized Psalms (which did not set the versions of Sternhold and Hopkins) were intended for domestic use.

The market for secular printed music was much smaller than the ready-made one for Psalms. Thomas Whythorne draws comparison (by inference) between England and Italy, the abundance and ready availability of whose printed music he envies.[7] In England, the market was, as a consequence of its smallness, far more closely tied to the practices of particular individuals or groups of performers. The case of madrigals is an instance. In 1588 Thomas East published Nicholas Yonge's *Musica transalpina*, Italian madrigals in English translation. Yonge, a singing-man at St Paul's Cathedral, claims in the dedication that the volume represents the repertoire of friends who daily gathered at his house to sing, and having few songs available in English he collected together 'certaine Italiane Madrigales translated most of them fiue yeeres agoe by a Gentleman for his priuate delight'.[8] Winifred Maynard makes the suggestion that one of the reasons why English madrigal verse never attracted the best poets, as it had done in Italy for instance, was because the English madrigal had its beginnings as a predominantly *musical* genre and that this emphasis continued in the collections that followed Yonge's.[9] In 1590, Thomas Watson published *The first sett, of Italian madrigalls Englished*. This collection, and its successor in 1597, went further than Yonge's in that the words were not even attempts at translation of the original, sometimes providing the 'sense of the originall dittie', but often matching the music to completely different words.[10]

Printed books for part-singing or part-playing meant that multiple copies of songs for the group were readily available without the need for manuscript copying and they were published with the demands of performance by various combinations of voices and instruments in mind. The books were sold as sets, each part having its own book, 'a bibliographical entity, usually with its own

6 Temperley, *Parish church*, pp. 53–4.

7 *The autobiography of Thomas Whythorne*, ed. J. M. Osborn (Oxford, 1961), p. 247.

8 For discussion of Yonge's book see Maynard 1986, pp. 40–1; on the significance of Yonge's dedication to Gilbert Talbot, see Price 1976 and 1981, pp. 102–3.

9 Maynard 1986 pp. 41–4.

10 For other 'Englished' madrigals see Hamessley 1992, pp. 177–221.

pagination, collation, and title-page'.[11] The madrigal collections printed in this format provided the model for the printing of other polyphonic music. Another popular format for printing music for part-singing was that of the table-book, particularly after 1600 when songs with lute or viol accompaniment displaced the madrigal in popularity and collections became multi-purpose: 'apt' for voices and viols or for a solo singer accompanied by a lute, or as part-songs. These books are in folio, the music arranged on the two facing pages of a single opening, printed right way up, upside down and sideways on the page so that the performers could sit around a single copy (see plate 5.1(a) and (b)). The cantus part, which typically has a line of lute tablature under the vocal line, was always printed on the left-hand page to accommodate the neck of the lute. Both formats, the part-book and the table-book, draw attention to the performance orientation of music printing. Similar performance requirements were also paramount in the printing of solo lute music. The folio format was necessary to allow a whole piece of music, with its six-line stave and room above for the note values, to a single page and thus avoid page turns.

Early seventeenth-century music publishing could not supplant the flourishing copyist trade, since for many there was no other way for the music of a particular composer to circulate or become known. The keyboard music of William Byrd is an instance here. For while music for instruments which played chords, such as the lute, the *lyra viol*, the cittern and the bandora, could be notated in tablature, keyboard music, which required a six-line stave and more than one part to a stave, was not set from moveable type in the first part of the seventeenth century.[12] Only two books of keyboard music were printed before the Restoration: *Parthenia* (1613) and its sequel, with music for keyboard and bass viol, *Parthenia inviolata* (1613–24). Both books were engraved, a form of publication little used in England in the early seventeenth century. Engraved books were seen as luxurious, having a status close to that of the presentation manuscript. *Parthenia* may, indeed, have been originally intended for presentation to its dedicatees, Princess Elizabeth and Prince Frederick, the Elector Palatine, on their wedding in 1613.

For most manuscript books, contexts are more explicit than for printed books and sometimes reveal an extensive network of private exchange;[13] thus they had a significant influence on the musical culture of the earlier part of the period. The format of any particular manuscript book, its contents and

11 Krummel 1975, p. 80.

12 For an instance of moveable 'fitted' type for printing more than one line of music on a stave, see Thomas Tomkins's *Musica deo sacra* (London, 1668), discussed in Krummel 1975, p. 99.

13 Price 1981, p. 177.

their ordering, can reveal more about the social and musical circumstances of its production than a printed book can. Manuscript books might reveal both a general purpose (the collection of certain pieces of music for performance by individuals or a group) and more specific characteristics, such as modification of a piece or pieces for the skills, or the number, of performers; or additions for a particular, if unspecified, performance. Some reveal quite specific information about even particular performances – as, for instance, the manuscripts relating to the Hilton–Ramsey group. Hilton's manuscript contains several ornamented versions of passages for particular songs entered on spare staves at the foot of the page and on one song the statement 'The treble I tooke & prickt downe as mr Thorpe sung it'; another manuscript belonging to the same group of musicians contains several entries of songs (bass and words) in shorthand, possibly taken at dictation (plate 5.2). These point to the immediacy of the copy: not an 'ideal' version of a particular piece of music but a response to the pressure of its occasion.[14]

Music writing with any speed and accuracy was a skill which took practice to acquire. Some amateur musicians had the time and leisure to make copies for themselves as, for example, the Norfolk gentleman Thomas Hammond.[15] Others did not copy their own music but employed copyists. There were workshops of copyists from early in the period, and the practice continued at least to the end of the seventeenth century. In 1695 an advertisement in *The London gazette* offered for sale 'Twelve Sonatas' by Archangelo Corelli 'fairly prick'd from the true Original'.[16] Both John Playford and John Carr offered manuscript copies of music for sale along with printed music. In *Choice ayres and songs* (1681) Playford advertises that he can supply consort music, hymns and Psalms to all who would purchase them 'fairly and true Prick'd'.[17] Recent scholarship has uncovered the provenance of many manuscript collections and has identified particular copyists and particular circumstances of their work. The purposes of manuscripts can be divided roughly into three categories: for performance (either by the copyist or by a patron), for teaching, or as records or presentation copies.

The work of the London clergyman, Thomas Myriell, dating from the early seventeenth century, contains examples of both presentation and working manuscripts.[18] His two large manuscript books appear to have been intended as presentation copies: entitled (on an engraved title page) 'Tristitiae remedium',

14 See Chan 1979 and Chan 1990; BL Add. MS. 11608; BL Egerton MS. 2013.

15 Crum 1957; Monson 1982, p. 78.

16 Tilmouth, 1961, p. 16.

17 See Thompson 1995, p. 613.

18 P. J. Willetts, 'The identity of Thomas Myriell', *Music & Letters*, 53 (1972), 431–3; Monson 1982, pp. 5–74.

containing anthems, motets and madrigals.[19] Several others of his manuscripts appear to have been compiled as working copies, reflecting the kind of private musical activity described by Nicholas Yonge in his Dedication to *Musica transalpina*.

Cathedrals regularly employed copyists for their music since printed sources were largely unavailable,[20] so several identifiable copyists were, like Myriell and John Merro,[21] a lay clerk at Gloucester Cathedral from 1609, associated with the Church. Pamela Willetts has identified a group of copyists associated with John Barnard, the minor canon of St Paul's Cathedral who was responsible for the first and only printed book of cathedral music, *The first book of selected Church music* (1641).[22] Stephen Bing (1610–81) was a minor canon at St Paul's Cathedral, and while much of the music he copied was for St Paul's, other manuscripts identify him as a copyist employed by Sir Christopher Hatton and working with other musicians and copyists under Hatton's patronage, such as George Jeffreys and John Lilly.[23] Bing, with John Lilly, was responsible for copying a set of viol music, probably under the direction of Hatton, which is thought to have been intended as a presentation set for King Charles I, a project left unfinished at the outbreak of Civil War in the 1640s.[24]

During the Commonwealth period Bing, like many other Church musicians, turned to music teaching.[25] Indeed, much of the music copied by professional musicians and copyists was intended for teaching purposes: many wealthy families employed their own musician as part of the household to teach music to family members, to copy, and to compose for household performance, and in some cases to provide music in the private chapel. The account books belonging to Dudley, fourth Baron North, record payments over several years (from 1652) to George Loosemore for teaching the viol to his children, and later payments to John Jenkins as well for music copying and for music lessons. Later accounts also note payments to a Mr Brown for 'pricking lessons' and some of the music he copied is listed in the inventory of Francis North (the Lord Keeper North's) possessions made on his brother's death in 1685.[26] The set

19 Brussels MS. II. 4109 and BL, Add. MSS. 29372–7 (6 part-books).

20 For rates paid to copyists at St Paul's Cathedral, Westminster Abbey and the Chapel Royal see Boyer and Wainwright 1995, p. 635. Outside England, cathedrals had difficulty maintaining choirs and organists: see I. Cheveton, 'Cathedral music in Wales during the latter part of the seventeenth century', *Welsh Music*, 8 (1986), 6–17.

21 Monson 1982, ch. 4.

22 Willetts 1991, pp. 28–42.

23 P. Aston, 'George Jeffreys', *The Musical Times* (July 1969), 772–6; Thompson 1989; P. Willetts, 'Stephen Bing: a forgotten violist', *Chelys*, 18 (1989), 3–17; Pinto 1990; Wainwright 1990; P. Willetts, 'John Lilly: a redating', *Chelys*, 21 (1992), 27–38; Boyer and Wainwright 1995.

24 Boyer and Wainwright 1995, p. 624.

25 Willetts, 'Stephen Bing', pp. 3–5.

26 Rougham manuscript in the private collection of Dr Thomas North: 'Mr Walker's accounts Lists and Inventorys'.

of Panmure manuscripts from Panmure House, near Dundee, the former seat of the Maules, was compiled for the instruction of James and Harrie Maule in the 1670s and 80s.[27] The music books belonging to Sir William Mure of Rowallan may have been prepared for the musical education of his children.[28] Anne Baylie's manuscript,[29] partly in the hand of Edward Lowe, organist at Christ Church from 1630 and Heather Professor of Music at Oxford from 1661, also contains amateurish attempts at music writing in Anne Baylie's own hand.

Much of the secular music printed throughout the seventeenth century must have had its origin in patronage or employment of this kind, although there must have always been a tension between the composer's interests and those of the music-making public. Harold Love makes the point that composers who hoped their pupils would purchase manuscript copies of their compositions would be unlikely to want those compositions in print.[30] Such control was clearly not always possible. Henry Lawes, introducing his *Ayres and dialogues* (1653), a volume of songs he claims were mostly composed while he was music master to the daughters of the Earl of Bridgewater, complains that he was compelled into print to protect the integrity of his music, some of which had been previously printed by the stationer without his knowledge.

Some composers, perhaps to avoid the very problem Lawes complains of, compiled or caused to be compiled manuscript volumes of their own work which were to stand as a record. John Wilson's manuscript book[31] which he 'gave to the public library at Oxon before his majesty's restoration but with this condition that no person should peruse it till after his death' is partly in his hand and partly in another's;[32] John Hingeston, some time before 1683, compiled and wrote out a set of seven part-books which he dedicated to Edward Lowe and presented to the Music School at Oxford.[33] Others, like Henry and William Lawes, compiled autograph volumes as a record of their work.[34] The manuscript which begins with a number of works by Robert Ramsey,[35] elegantly (if inaccurately) transcribed and formally attributed, might have been initially intended as such a collection, although the volume was soon taken over for less formal purposes.[36]

While there is a good deal of evidence both explicit and implicit that both professional and amateur musicians met together to perform music, the

27 McCart 1989, pp. 18–29. 28 Shire 1969, pp. 213–14.
29 Christ Church, Oxford Mus. 438. 30 Love 1993, p. 64. 31 Bodleian Library Mus. b. 1.
32 Quoted from Anthony Wood's *Fasti Oxonienses* in Cutts 1956.
33 Bodleian Library Mus. Sch. D. 205–11; L. Hulse, 'John Hingeston', *Chelys*, 12 (1983), 23–42.
34 Henry Lawes's manuscript is BL Add. 53723. See Willetts 1969. William Lawes's collection is six volumes in the Bodleian and British Libraries. See M. Lefkowitz, *William Lawes* (London, 1960), p. 30; P. Walls, *Music in the English courtly masque, 1604–1640* (Oxford, 1996), pp. 33, 177–90.
35 Bodleian Library Don. c. 57. 36 See Chan 1990, pp. 233–6.

identification of collections of music which represent what and how they performed is not always easy. Information about public concerts is available for the Restoration period and many of the later seventeenth-century printed collections or song sheets of single songs reflect the repertoire of these, as of the theatre music. Nevertheless, some evidence of concerts earlier in the century can be gleaned from manuscript collections. John Irving has identified a set of part-books belonging to a group of professional musicians meeting to play together in Worcester in the 1640s. Performers' annotations in the manuscripts might indicate public or semi-public performance.[37] Other evidence is suggested by the relationship between the contents of the three 'working' manuscripts belonging to the Hilton–Ramsey group referred to above (p. 131), and the contents of early publications by John Playford.[38] If Hilton's group did influence Playford, then not since *Musica transalpina* would the motive for printing have been so closely allied to collective performance. Nevertheless, there is some distance between the versions of the songs Playford published – for mostly amateur musicians – and those manuscript collections which may have provided the basic copies. Playford was acknowledged as an 'editor' and his printed versions are in many cases simplified, provided with attractive titles and thus far from a composer's (or even a professional performance's) 'ideal'. Krummel describes him as a 'sponsor' for music who 'exercised a heavier editorial hand than most'.[39]

Playford, the major publisher of the second half of the century, began his publishing in 1650 with the re-issue of William Child's *Psalms for 3 Voices* (1639), an engraved book for which he acquired the plates. He did not continue with engraving. Apart from Psalms, Playford did not publish religious music.[40] Major collections of religious music were published by others, however, in the 1650s and 1660s.[41] One of these, John Wilson's *Psalterium Carolinum* (1657), used the same typeface as John Barnard's enormous set of ten part-books for double choir of five voices published in 1641: *The first book of selected Church musick*. Prepared under the Anglican régime before the impeachment of Archbishop Laud in 1641, the book was left largely unsold and the intended *Second book* never published. Barnard's was the first and only early printed collection of cathedral music. It came too late, was too expensive, or not sufficiently versatile for many cathedral choirs to take up. It draws attention, by its size and its 'failure', to the long and lively tradition of copying cathedral music.

Krummel makes clear that while Playford published two-thirds of the music in London between 1650 and 1686 he had both competitors and associates;

37 Irving 1984. 38 Chan 1979 and 1990. 39 Krummel 1975, p. 123.
40 See Temperley 1972, pp. 331–78. 41 Krummel 1975, p. 124.

and imitators who published for the first time outside London. Two song anthologies were published in Oxford which Krummel describes as looking 'exactly like Playford's work': John Wilson's *Cheerful ayres* ([1659]) and William King's *Poems of Mr Cowley* (1668). John Forbes's *Songs and fancies* (1662, 1666, 1682) was the first Scottish print of secular music.[42]

Music in Scotland, as also in smaller centres throughout Britain, was largely dependent on London (and the Continent) for the supply of printed music books. Helena Shire has pointed out that, without a Court after 1603 (and before then not always an adult monarch to promote a Court culture) and with a post-Reformation Church which required only music of extreme simplicity and which excluded instruments and organs from the service, there were very few professional musical requirements. *A compendious book of Godly and spiritual songs* compiled by John Wedderburn (place and date of publication are uncertain) contains no music, but its texts of hymns and metrical Psalms are to be sung to popular ballad tunes.[43] The one surviving Scottish manuscript set of part-books from the sixteenth century, the 'St Andrews Psalter', was compiled 1562/66–1590 by Thomas Wode, one-time vicar of St Andrews. Two copies were made of the set of five part-books and one was obviously in use in the 1620s since additions have been made on it in later hands. Dr Shire points out that Wode might have intended to publish his collection of Psalms as a harmonized psalter for 'Wode says he was moved to make it from the fear lest all knowledge and skill of part-writing should disappear from the land "allutterlie"'.[44] Psalm books were, however, printed in Edinburgh and at least until 1625 most contained music.[45]

The last fifteen years of the seventeenth century saw the growth in popularity of engraving and the consequent competition between John Playford's son, Henry, who took over the business in 1686 or 1687, and John Walsh. Henry Playford was conservative, preferring to continue using his father's founts rather than use engraving which was more suited to the increasing demand for printed instrumental music. Engraving, usually associated with Italian music, was used, however, for Henry Purcell's *Sonnatas of III. Parts* (1683), and most notably for Grabu's *Albion and Albanus* (1687), published in score. Engraving was also used for single song sheets which grew in popularity in the 1690s, often as a means of quickly producing songs from the theatre. John Walsh established himself with this kind of printing. One innovation made by Henry Playford was the publication (1699–1702 when it was taken over by Walsh) of *Mercurius musicus*, the first periodical publication devoted solely to new music,[46] although

42 Krummel 1975, p. 125–6. 43 Mitchell 1897; Shire 1969, p. 12. 44 Shire 1969, pp. 23–5.
45 Krummel 1975, p. 75. 46 Harvey 1985.

earlier the *Gentleman's journal* (1692–4), for example, devoted one section to music at the end of each monthly issue. Many of Purcell's songs were published in this *Journal*. Indeed, despite the extreme popularity of his music, during his lifetime there appeared no collections devoted to his songs alone, apart from editions of plays with music, often published by subscription, an increasingly popular method. His songs appeared with others in anthologies.

Purcell's music was perhaps nowhere more widely disseminated than in the theatre; and it was during the same period, the latter years of the seventeenth century, that the printing of theatre music, both as individual song sheets and in collections of songs, grew in popularity. Music was performed publicly in other venues as well: there were concerts of which John Bannister's (from 1672) are perhaps the best known;[47] but there was also the annual Lord Mayor's Day pageant,[48] the St Cecilia Day concerts (1683–1703) and concerts on the Thames – the most spectacular being those held on the frozen river in the winter of 1683–4.[49] Nevertheless, music was available in the public playhouses every day and much of it was printed. In this, Restoration practice differed markedly from that of the early part of the seventeenth century where the music performed in the theatres was rarely published. Songs from plays had been sometimes printed in contemporary collections not specifically associated with the theatre as, for instance, Alfonso Ferrabosco II's setting of Ben Jonson's 'Come my Celia' from *Volpone* which appeared in his *Ayres* (1609) or the songs from plays performed by Paul's Boys in the collections of Thomas Ravenscroft.[50] Some songs from plays were printed later, in other contexts as, for example, the songs by Robert Johnson for Shakespeare's *The tempest* which were first printed in John Wilson's *Cheerfull ayres* ([1659]). Some play songs survive in manuscript commonplace books. Much of the instrumental music which was heard in plays in the early part of the period was presumably music already in circulation, not composed for a specific play. But in the Restoration, theatre music was a major genre and the theatre a major producer of music both vocal and instrumental, sometimes as interlude and sometimes as 'opera'. It is, therefore, surprising that between 1660 and 1700 there were only seven plays printed with both text and instrumental or vocal music although there were many publications of the music alone for individual plays.

47 See Tilmouth 1961, p. 2.

48 See M. Burden, '"For the lustre of the subject": music for the Lord Mayor's Day in the Restoration', *Early Music*, 23 (1995), 585–602.

49 J. K. Wood, '"A flowing harmony": music on the Thames in Restoration London', *Early Music* 23 (1995), 553–81 discusses the various occasions on which music was performed on the river, including the concerts held on ice in 1683–4 (p. 567).

50 W. J. Lawrence, 'Thomas Ravenscroft's theatrical associations', *MLR*, 19 (1924), 418–23.

By the end of the seventeenth century London was still the centre of music publishing. Engraving was now regarded not so much as a luxury but as the new way of printing, though copying continued to flourish both privately and as a way of publishing. John Walsh reflects the changing social fashions in his concentration on publication of music from the theatre, on the up-to-date and the ephemeral.[51] Roger North, writing in the late 1690s, sums up the trend for novelty (and the theatre's influence on this) which was to take music publishing into the eighteenth century:

> Now our gallants and yong ladys are for learning, not musick, or such habits as well as skill, as may make them capable of it; but this or that new song, or some tunes or lessons on the flaut, or violin, by which they mean, not the song, tune, or lesson, but the voice, manner or hand of the performer. When ought appears upon the stage finely performed, they must needs learne that...[52]

North's criticism describes a society eager for the new engraved song sheets of John Walsh whose business was to become the dominant one in the next century.

51 Krummel 1975, p. 164, suggests that the song sheets might have replaced the broadside ballads which (with one or two exceptions) were printed without music before the Restoration.

52 *Roger North's 'Cursory notes of musicke' (c.1698–c.1703): a physical, psychological and critical theory*, ed. with introduction, notes and appendices by M. Chan and J. C. Kassler (Sydney, 1986), p. 237.

LITERATURE OF THE LEARNED

6

The Latin trade

JULIAN ROBERTS

That branch of the English book trade which imported books from countries outside the King's (or Queen's) obedience has traditionally been termed the 'Latin trade'. It is not known when the term was first used, and is unknown to the *Oxford English Dictionary*. It was certainly current in the early seventeenth century, and when the Stationers' Company of London set up in 1616 an organization to import books from Continental Europe, it was known as the 'Latin Stock'.

The Latin trade was a specialized trade, governed by national and trade regulations, with its own specialized personnel; though Graham Pollard's dictum,[1] that it was in the hands of aliens who were Brothers of the Stationers' Company, must now be modified in the light of further evidence. Many such booksellers *were* aliens and some were Brothers of the Company; but native Englishmen were heavily involved for much of this period, and if they failed to match the skill and contacts of the aliens, they lost money. As far as the Latin trade is concerned, the limits of 1557 and 1695 are arbitrary. Although the Stationers' Charter of 1557 is silent on the importation of books, the new status of the Company may have emboldened native Englishmen into Continental ventures. The lapse of the Licensing Act in 1695 had little immediate effect upon importing by native booksellers, since for many of them the selling of foreign books was now normal practice, and the 'anglicization' of the trade was under way even by 1600. Nevertheless, the Revocation of the Edict of Nantes in 1685 precipitated a further influx of alien booksellers.

Speculation as to why the importation of foreign books was such a significant feature of the English book trade for two centuries after the introduction of printing is outside the scope of the present chapter, since the distortion was apparent even before Caxton's time. The failure to establish learned and, to a lesser extent, educational printing is one cause, and the absence of an English

1 Pollard and Ehrman 1965, p. 85.

papermaking industry is another. But our period almost coincides with the final establishment of the Protestant religion and its concomitant vernacular Bible and liturgy, and with the confirmation by Elizabeth I of the Stationers' Charter granted by Philip and Mary. The boost given by the Reformation to printing in English was already evident in the reigns of Henry VIII and Edward VI, and the guaranteed sales of English Bibles, Books of Common Prayer and Psalms undoubtedly strengthened the economic foundations of printing and bookselling. From 1557 to 1695 it was possible for a London Stationer to make a very good living.

Sources

The sources for the history of the Latin trade from 1557 to 1695 are not so very different from those for the earlier period; but the message from them is stronger. The importance of the customs rolls for its history has been recognized ever since H. R. Plomer's modest yet crucial article of 1924.[2] Paul Needham's chapter on the customs rolls in volume III of this *History* sets out both the value and the limitations of these records so fully that it is essential reading for students of the succeeding period. Our period coincides, however, with the phasing out of the cumbersome parchment rolls, and their substitution by parchment books (supplied by the Exchequer) under the customs reforms of the Marquis of Winchester. These reforms were completed in 1564 with the issue of a new book of orders. The port books, like their predecessors, are fiscal documents in that they are records of moneys received – in the case of imports – from petty customs and subsidies of tunnage and poundage. A typical entry will give the name of the ship and its port of origin, followed by the master's name and the port where the voyage began. Individual cargoes then follow the entry for the ship; each consists of the merchant's name and the quantity and nature of the goods and the duty paid. On unbound books, the usual commodity of the Latin trade, petty customs were 3*d.* in the pound. The unit of assessment was the maund (or basket) which was conventionally valued at £4, and which attracted duty of 12*d.* A fatt, dryfatt (or barrel) was reckoned as half a maund, valued at 40*s.*, attracting duty of 6*d.* Only in the later seventeenth century does the unit of assessment change to the hundredweight (cwt). It is thus clear that the unit of assessment very imprecise, since neither we nor the waiters or searchers (the lesser officials who actually went on board the ship) can know how many books were packed in maunds

2 Plomer 1924.

or fatts. The titles of the books are never specified, and the waiters' quest for seditious or heretical books must have been further hampered by the fact that the sheets were securely packed in waterproof bales and barrels. It cannot be stressed too firmly that the survival of port books, like that of customs rolls, is extremely haphazard. Some of them are illegible. Since aliens were liable both to petty customs *and* tunnage and poundage, while natives only paid the latter, the role of aliens in importation is likely to be exaggerated by the uneven survival of port books. There is also a major gap in the customs records during the Civil War and Commonwealth.

Nevertheless, port books do give a broad picture of those, both alien and native, involved in the trade, the volume and approximate value of the cargoes containing unbound books, and of the routes along which they were shipped. There are, indeed, precise records[3] in the Plantin-Moretus Museum at Antwerp of the books sold by Christophe Plantin and his successors[4] to English and Scottish merchants and to aliens who traded in England. But Plantin also sold large quantities of books to the Birckmanns of Cologne who had a shop at Antwerp. Many of these were destined for the English market by the Birckmanns, who were for much of the sixteenth century the largest importers of books into the Port of London; but none of the Birckmanns' records survives. Plantin himself recorded in April 1566 that some of his Birckmann sales were 'A la poulle Grasse a scavoir a Conradus Leur homme en Angleterre.'[5] This is presumably Conrad Molyar, a Brother of the Stationers' Company, one of the Birckmanns' factors, and ultimately a bookseller in Oxford.[6] One 'Andre', similarly styled in 1567, was presumably Andreas Fremonsheim (see below, p. 154).[7] The interest of the Plantin-Moretus ledgers does not decline with the death of Plantin in 1589, for they also record some of the earliest purchases on behalf of the Latin Stock in 1617. At the end of the seventeenth century, the 1681 list of the creditors of Daniel Elzevier atones for the absence of other Elzevier records, while the correspondence of Samuel Smith preserved by Richard Rawlinson brings the Latin trade into full daylight.

But the most copious witness to the activities of the trade from 1557 onwards is borne by the mass of surviving books and the abundant evidence of contemporary purchase. Margaret Lane Ford's survey in volume III of this *History* based upon 'a systematic search for printed books with marks of English and Scottish ownership' includes data on more than 4,300 books. The Elizabethan settlement encouraged and sustained the growth of both personal and institutional collections on an immensely greater scale than in earlier

3 P-MA. 4 Clair 1959. 5 P-MA 44, fol. 48.
6 Roberts 1997. 7 P-MA 45, fol. 45.

periods. The universities and their colleges accumulated libraries whose origins can be documented, even if their librarians were sometimes reticent over their links with the trade.

Regulation of the trade

Statutes, decrees and internal trade regulations determined who might import books, in what state they might be brought in, the duty to be paid by the various categories of merchant, and what might be done with them when they were landed. Throughout the period, the impress of the Act of 1534, 'Concerning printers and binders of books' (25 Henry VIII cap.15) can be discerned. Its main provisions were these: 'That no person or persons resiant or inhabitant within this realm, after the said feast of Christmas next coming [Christmas 1534] shall buy to sell again any printed books brought from any parts out of the king's obedience, ready bounden in boards leather or parchment' and secondly, 'that no person or persons resiant or inhabitant within this realm after the said feast of Christmas shall buy within this realm, of any stranger, born out of the king's obedience, other than of denizens, any manner of printed books, brought from any parts beyond the sea, except only by engross and not by retail'. The prohibition on the importation of bound books ensured that well into the seventeenth century consignments of printed books are described in the port books as unbound, or in the dog-Latin of the ports as 'libri non ligati', 'libri inligati' or 'libri non compacti'. This was not a move in the direction of censorship but of protectionism; to provide work for English binders. It is, after all, easier to censor a bound book than one in (presumably folded) sheets. Merchants, moreover, could pack more such unbound books into the barrels in which books were normally carried. The second provision of the Act was also protectionist and, as Graham Pollard saw,[8] formed part of the as yet unchartered Stationers' Company's policy of strengthening its control of the book trade of London and if possible beyond, while confining aliens to that part of the trade where their competence most notably lay, in buying books abroad in gross and carrying them to the port of London. The University of Cambridge was as dependent as that of Oxford on foreign booksellers of learned books, but it was also more prescient. In 1528 or 1529 it petitioned Cardinal Wolsey that it might be allowed to have three booksellers who would be aliens and thus more expert in the pricing of books and better qualified to buy them from foreign dealers in the markets of London and elsewhere in the realm.[9] In 1534

8 Pollard 1937 a and b. 9 McKitterick 1992, ch. 2, 'The Charter of 1534'.

it received a Charter allowing it these three stationers, printers or booksellers, whether alien or native. If the appointed stationers were natives, well and good; if those appointed were aliens – as indeed the first appointees were – their status would be at least as good as that enjoyed by denizated aliens. The disadvantages under which foreigners laboured in sixteenth- and seventeenth-century England might be alleviated in two ways: by naturalization, a road to full status as an English subject, which was open to those who could procure an Act of Parliament; or by denization, granted under letters patent, for which a fee might be – but sometimes was not – charged.

This latter path was followed by large numbers of alien booksellers after 1534, as the privileges accorded to foreign printers and booksellers in 1484 were gradually eroded. This was not, perhaps, what the Stationers had intended, since denizated aliens could sell by retail, their new status enabled them to own real property, and they could, at least from the mid-sixteenth century, sue in the courts. They were, however, liable to taxes from which natives were exempted, such as petty customs, while natives were only liable to duties payable under subsidies of tunnage and poundage.

The Charter of 1557 limited printing to members of the London Company, but laid down nothing about the importation and selling of books. Details of the later regulation of the trade, and of such censorship as existed, will be discussed below. Since the records of the Company, and in particular of its members, are reasonably full after 1557, it is possible to see how the Company accommodated those aliens who were qualified to sell books. Many men, usually bearing foreign names, were admitted as Brothers, upon payment of 2*s.* 6*d.* (as against the 3*s.* 4*d.* which was paid by those admitted to the freedom of the Company). Most of the major alien importers of the sixteenth century were Brothers of the Company, though it is not clear how long this category of membership was maintained. Denization seems always to have been necessary, and there were large-scale denizations of Huguenot refugees, including many booksellers, after the Revocation of the Edict of Nantes in 1685. The London Stationers were ultimately unable to control bookselling outside the City, though there was a perceptible drift of members of the Company into the provinces, and towards Oxford, unprotected by a charter such as that obtained by Cambridge, in the mid-sixteenth century.[10] Towns and cities would impose their own restrictions on trading within their limits, though customers might encounter itinerant booksellers at fairs held outside these limits.

10 Arber, v, p. lii.

The Stationers' Charter, in its silence on the subject of bookselling, tacitly admitted the right of booksellers in other towns and cities to operate. There was thus no restriction upon the right of provincial booksellers to bring in books directly from abroad. Nevertheless, this practice seems to have lapsed, at least until well into the next century, and we no longer find their names in the customs rolls or in the port books or, indeed, as purchasers in Plantin's records. Hermann Evans of Oxford brought in his last recorded consignment in 1556. It would be surprising if the privileged booksellers of Cambridge had not taken advantage of the proximity of such out-ports as Ipswich or King's Lynn, but there is no evidence from the port books that they did, and much evidence that their principal suppliers were from London, the Birckmanns and later Ascanius de Renialme. This situation seems to have obtained also in early seventeenth-century Oxford; the booksellers there relied mainly upon London-based importers to feed the healthy appetites for foreign books of the Bodleian Library and of the colleges, and did not themselves venture as far as Frankfurt, Leipzig, or even Amsterdam. Later, booksellers became more venturesome; both Samuel Smith and his partner Benjamin Walford went abroad, the former in 1687 and 1701, the latter in April 1695 and October 1697.[11] The timing of Walford's journeys suggests that he may have attended spring or autumn fairs. The Star Chamber Decree of 1586 regulated printing in fine detail, and again, said nothing about books from abroad. The decree was issued on 23 June 1586, and Archbishop Whitgift's permission, dated in October of that year, reads very much like hindsight:[12]

> whereas sundry books are from time to time set forth in the parts beyond seas, by such as are addicted to the errors of popery: yet in many respects expedient to be had by some of the learned of this realm: containing also oftentimes matter in them against the state of this land, and slanderous unto it; and therefore no fit books to pass through every man's hand freely: in consideration whereof, I have tolerated Ascanius de Renialme, merchant bookseller, to bring into this realm from the parts beyond seas, some few copies of every such sort of books: upon this condition only, that any of them be not shewed nor dispersed abroad, but first brought to me, or some other of her Majesty's Privy Council, that so they may be delivered, or directed to be delivered, furth unto such persons only, as by us, or some of us, shall be thought most meet men...

Ascanius was no doubt grateful to be 'tolerated' in what he had always done – though a Protestant – and would continue to do. The Stationers who set up the

11 Hodgson and Blagden 1956, p. 26.

12 John Strype, *The life and acts of John Whitgift Archbishop of Canterbury* (London, 1718, 1717), p. 269.

Latin Stock in 1616 took such toleration for granted, confident, no doubt, that such a system of inspection as that proposed by Whitgift was impracticable.

The brief rise and rapid fall of the Latin Stock is described below (pp. 161–2). The provision at its foundation, that its purpose was to import such books as might lawfully be brought into the country (if the wording is correctly reported) may have been intended to reassure authority; but authority, in the form of the privy council, called, in 1628 after the winding-up of the Stock, for a list of those who sold 'mart books' and old books.[13] The list drawn up by Adam Islip, Edmund Weaver and Humfrey Crosse contains the names of thirty-eight men, some of whom were not even Stationers. The trade was clearly centred in Duck Lane and Little Britain. Some others were Stationers whose names appear in the Poor Book; but they had been told to prepare a catalogue of their wares, and not to sell further until the privy council had seen it. It may be seen as an augury of the tightest control the trade was to experience, the Star Chamber Decree of 11 July 1637, 'concerning printing'.[14]

The Star Chamber Decree, 1637

Most of the provisions of the Decree did indeed concern printing, and need not be rehearsed; but its proposed draconian control of importing is relevant here.

Merchants bringing in books were to submit a true catalogue of them in writing to the Archbishop of Canterbury or the Bishop of London (ch. 5 of the Decree). The merchants were not to open, nor the customs officers to pass, any of the packages containing books except in the presence of the two bishops or their assistants, or of the Master and Wardens of the Stationers' Company (ch. 6). No one was to import books which had been previously entered in the Stationers' Register, or for which privileges[15] existed (ch. 7). (This last had been a grievance for some time.) No books in English were to be imported (ch. 11). No stranger or foreigner was to bring in or sell books printed abroad in any language unless he were a free Stationer of London, had been brought up in that profession, and had his whole means of subsistence in it (ch. 12) – which was perhaps a blow at the higglers of Duck Lane and Little Britain. Finally, no merchant or shipowner was to land or import books into any port except that of the City of London (ch. 32). The effectiveness of the Decree – if any – was short-lived, since the Court of Star Chamber was abolished in 1641.

13 Greg 1967, Calendar no. 226 and Documents pp. 240–1. 14 *STC* 7757. 15 Hunt 1997.

It would be gratifying to believe that the world of this mean and restrictive Decree had been swept away by John Milton's *Areopagitica, for the liberty of unlicens'd printing*, occasioned by a Parliamentary Ordinance of 1643. But the reality lay in the *Act against unlicensed and scandalous books and pamphlets and for the better regulating of printing* of 20 September 1649. The importer is to be fined £5 for each seditious book. Apart from this, there is no change from the Star Chamber Decree, except that the Archbishop of Canterbury and the Bishop of London are no longer in office, in Milton's words, 'to besot us to the gay imitation of a lordly *Imprimatur*, one from Lambeth House, another from the West End of Paul's'. Whoever lost the Civil War, it was not the Stationers' Company of London, for the packages might still not be opened without being viewed by the Master and Wardens; who must be given forty-eight hours' notice. The spirit in which the Act was applied may be gauged from its revival in January 1653, when 'it is now appointed that Lords Days and Days of Public Thanksgiving and Humiliation, if any shall happen within forty-eight hours shall not be accompted nor reckoned as part of the said forty-eight hours'.

The Licensing Act, 1662

The Licensing Act of 1662 does little more than restore the two bishops to their task of viewing imported books, while confirming the Stationers in theirs – and safeguarding their privileges. The Act does, however, recognize what must already have happened since at least 1628, by permitting the import (by Stationers, of course) of books ready bound, not formerly prohibited, which had been printed ten years before the date of importation.

The Stationers' Charter of 1684

Cyprian Blagden has given a detailed account of the events which led up to the granting of a new Charter on 22 May 1684.[16] The calling in, under *quo warranto* proceedings, of Charters granted to towns and companies formed part of Charles II's policy of ensuring the loyalty of those who elected members of Parliament, and the loyalty of Stationers was particularly desirable at a time when the Licensing Acts had, temporarily, lapsed. It seems that the Stationers' Company was the first to petition for, and be granted, a new Charter. Its provisions were in most respects more restrictive than any previous regulations, but the provision which most affected the import trade was that which extended

16 Blagden 1960, pp. 166–72.

the control of the Company beyond London to Westminster and four miles around, and the Company was not slow to proceed against hawkers, higglers, and the French booksellers who were settling beyond the limits of the City of London. The Stationers' triumph, ineffective in the short term, was also short-lived, since the *quo warranto* proceedings were reversed in 1690 and the Company's jurisdiction was once again confined to the City.

Such, then, were the general legal restraints upon importing which were in force – and there is no doubt that they were extensively evaded or ignored – until the Licensing Acts finally lapsed, and the House of Commons refused to renew them in 1695.

Censorship

From the general regulation of the Latin trade, it is a short step to the censorship of classes of imported books and that of individual authors or books; but arguments about the nature of sixteenth- and seventeenth-century censorship are only relevant here in so far as there was any attempt to control the import trade. Machinery, often rusty and underused, existed to do so, and derived from the Royal Injunctions of 1559.[17] These laid down a system for regulating domestic production so elaborate that the printing trade would surely have come to a halt, had it been enforced. A decision on importing was, however, deferred:

> And touching all other books of matters of religion, or policy, or governance, that hath been printed either on this side the seas or on the other side, because the diversity of them is great and that there needeth good consideration of the particularities thereof, her majesty referreth the prohibition or permission thereof to the order which her said commissioners within the City of London shall take and notify. According to the which her majesty straightly commands to her subjects/commands all manner her subjects, and specially the warden and company of stationers to be obedient.
>
> Provided that these orders do not extend to any profane authors and works in any language that hath been heretofore commonly received or allowed in any the universities or schools, but the same may be printed and used as by good order they were accustomed.

Nothing seems to have happened until 1566. A memorandum of January of that year from the Queen to the Marquis of Winchester (probably drawn up by Cecil)[18] places the responsibility of searching for seditious imports through the

17 *TRP*, 460. 18 Greg 1967, Calendar 34, Supplementary documents 2, pp. 114–15.

port of London upon officials appointed by the Bishop of London and for those through other ports upon the appropriate diocesan bishop. There is as yet no evidence that these powers were exercised – but it is clear that trade through ports other than London was envisaged. The Ordinances of 1566,[19] which exist in a manuscript and two printed versions, refer to 'divers disorders in the printing and uttering of books' and display the Privy Council's desire to impose political control over seditious books by harnessing the Stationers' expertise in detecting them. The Wardens of the Company, or those deputed by them, were enabled under clause 5 'in any ports, as other suspected places within this realm, to open and view all packs, dryfatts, maunds, and other things wherein books or paper shalbe contained, brought into this realm: and also to make search in all workhouses, shops, warehouses, and other places of printers, booksellers, or such as bring books into this realm to be sold . . . ' Blagden also refers to a draft bill of the same year, 1566, 'to avoid divers seditious books' and to a draft 'Act to restrain the printing, selling and uttering of unprofitable and hurtful English books'. Cyndia Susan Clegg[20] plausibly links these concerns to increased activity in English printing by recusant presses at Antwerp and Louvain which the government might well wish to suppress. The Stationers' energies were, however, principally directed against the secret printing of registered copies, and the only rewarded success of their agent Hugh Singleton against imported material – as opposed to his and Thomas Purfoot's several successes against unauthorized printing at home – was the two shillings the Company paid him for 'taking up of books at the waterside'; though what he seized may equally well have been piratical or seditious.

The role of Richard Carmarden

Since episcopal officials would hardly maintain a continuous presence at the waterside, the burden – such as it was – of searching fell upon the officials of the port and, in this context, the career of Richard Carmarden is relevant. Carmarden was a Merchant Taylor who earns his place in the printers' index to *STC* as the publisher of an edition of the Great Bible printed by Cardin Hamillon at Rouen in 1566.[21] According to the published port book[22] he imported forty reams of printed books and paid 40*s*. in duty. At some time he became a customs official, and appears frequently in the State Papers (Domestic) in connection with rating and with various commodities. He is named as Surveyor of the Customs in 1593, but perhaps more accurately in 1597 as Overseer of the

19 Blagden 1958a. 20 Clegg 1997. 21 *STC* 2098. 22 Dietz 1972.

Waiters of the Port. In the latter document,[23] addressed to Burghley as Lord Treasurer, he speaks of the latter's 'commandment unto me given charge and daily to all her Majesty's waiters to look narrowly after all books that come into this port from foreign parts'. A barrel of books had arrived from Zealand and had been stayed in the Queen's storehouse ' which is full of the like books of these enclosed'. Evidently the government relied for routine control of imports upon the zeal of customs officials, but did not respond quickly to the results of their zeal. Carmarden died in 1603 or 1604, and was succeeded in office by a son of the same name. His zeal too was insufficiently regarded; in 1615 he petitioned the King to the effect that the Stationers had been converting to their own use the fines and forfeitures from the seizure of unlawful books, and asked for the arrearages due to him.[24] As D. F. McKenzie remarked in his third Lyell Lecture 'Time and again commerce compromised censorship. While members of the Company *may* have worked to discover scandalous printing they also worked to conceal it.'[25]

Regulation by proclamation

This period is narrowly preceded by the most comprehensive – and in the event least successful – attempt to exclude specified imported books. The proclamation of 13 June 1555[26] recited a list of authors including Luther and all leading Protestant writers whose works might not be brought into the realm. Hughes and Larkin identify English editions of these works, but since importation of books in Latin, Dutch (i.e. German), English, Italian or French was forbidden, the proclamation was clearly aimed with equal force at imported texts. The offending texts were to be surrendered to the ordinary of the diocese. The penalties for possession of such seditious or heretical books were stiffened under another proclamation of 6 June 1558;[27] offenders were to be placed under martial law. The ensuing Protestant regime did not resort at once to proclamations on books (the Ordinances of 1566 already mentioned are not strictly a proclamation), but one of 1569[28] was aimed at books in English printed overseas. The issue and circulation of Pius V's Bull *Regnans in excelsis* of 2 February 1570 deposing Elizabeth I – and in consequence supporting Mary Stuart's succession – evoked proclamations ordering the arrest of those circulating such documents (1 July 1570[29] and 14 November 1570[30]). Thereafter the targets of proclamations were as likely to be imported Protestant books, such as those

23 Greg 1967, Calendar 148, Document 16. 24 Jackson 1957, pp. 352–53.
25 McKenzie 1988, p. 5. 26 *TRP*, 422. 27 *TRP*, 443.
28 *TRP*, 561. 29 *TRP*, 577. 30 *TRP*, 580.

of the Family of Love (3 October 1580[31]) or the works of Robert Browne and Robert Harrison (30 June 1583[32]) as those of recusant tendency (12 October 1584[33]). In the few proclamations of the two succeeding reigns which covered importing, the concerns of government about heresy and sedition were outweighed by those of the Stationers for their patents and privileges. That of 15 August 1624[34] had been designed to exclude 'popish scandalous books', but King James would not sign it until puritanical books and pamphlets were treated similarly. That of 25 September 1623,[35] while inveighing against the uttering of seditious books, was at least equally concerned to keep out books printed abroad but covered by existing patents and privileges. An early proclamation of Charles I[36] was designed to prevent the sale of Latin books, reprinted beyond the seas, which had been first printed in Oxford or Cambridge. This may indicate royal solicitude for such privileges as the Stationers had conceded to the universities. The likelihood is that some English booksellers were having Latin texts reprinted abroad, thus nullifying the concessions made to the university printers. Suspiciously large imports by Edmund Weaver from Ireland in 1626[37] may indicate use of the Irish Stock's press in Dublin for similar purposes. The republication in 1635 of John Selden's *Mare clausum* evoked a proclamation[38] forbidding importation of foreign-printed editions. Another of 1 May 1636[39] reiterated the King's (and no doubt Archbishop Laud's) concern that books in the learned tongues printed in the universities and in London were being reprinted abroad and imported. The probability is that London Stationers were responsible. After the Restoration, seditious and unlicensed books were denounced by proclamations, but these were not aimed at imported books as such.

The trade and the tradesmen from 1557

Although it was asserted at the outset of this chapter that the date 1557 was not particularly meaningful for the history of the Latin trade, it is nevertheless true that the ten years after the chartering of the Stationers' Company were, for reasons mostly unrelated, significant ones for the trade. Books and authors prohibited by the proclamations of 1555 and 1558 were now openly sought. The importation of liturgical books of the Sarum or Roman rites, which had been resumed during the Marian reaction, came abruptly to a halt. The reorganization of the customs at least provided a different and more usable kind of fiscal record of imports. The availability of newly published books at the biannual Frankfurt

31 *TRP*, 652. 32 *TRP*, 667. 33 *TRP*, 672. 34 *SRP*, I, p. 256. 35 *SRP* I, 247.
36 *SRP*, II, p. 5. 37 PRO E.190/31/3. 38 *SRP*, II, p. 216. 39 *SRP*, II, p. 219.

fairs became widely known through the printing of catalogues, at first by Georg Willer of Augsburg for the autumn fair in 1564. Although John Dee was the first recorded owner of the catalogues in England,[40] several extant sets attest their use at the end of the century and beyond.[41] There are also grounds for thinking that native Englishmen took a prominent part in importing at about this time. We might attribute this to a confidence born of a new Charter; and perhaps also to the temporary eclipsing of aliens who were for the most part Protestants.

The roll recording the subsidy of tunnage and poundage of 1556/7[42] includes a number of natives (indigenae): Nicholas Cliston (whose initial enthusiasm was not matched by success, since he died in Oxford in 1578/9 leaving much unsold stock),[43] John White, William Owen, Nicholas England, Thomas Barker, Anthony Smith and Francis Sparry (not all of whom were Stationers). Since the Petty Customs records are also extant,[44] the additional tax burden upon aliens can be seen. Francis Birckmann is by far the largest importer, native or alien, but Hermann Evans of Oxford (a denizated alien) also brought in a fatt of unbound books. He is the last provincial bookseller to be found in the customs records, but his subsequent absence may be due to his lack of commercial success in Oxford.

The Birckmanns of Cologne

The Birckmanns[45] were not only the largest importers for the next twenty years; they were also the most senior. The relationships of the several members of the family involved in the Latin trade are not always clear, but Franz I was recorded as paying petty customs in the customs roll for 1502/3.[46] In 1504 his name appears in the first of many imprints as the publisher (and therefore the importer) of pre-Reformation liturgical books of the Sarum rite. The Birckmanns supported (and doubtless profited from) reform also, since Franz I imported an English version of the New Testament. He died in 1529 or 1530, and this can, therefore, only have been Tyndale's. Heinrich Birckmann, a stationer denizated in 1535, was probably a brother, while a second brother, Arnold I, who died on 28 April 1541, is associated with his brother Franz

40 Roberts and Watson 1990, nos. 2110–12.

41 There are sets in York Minster Library dated 1596–1623 which belonged to Archbishop Tobie Matthew, and in the Library of Trinity College, Dublin, mainly from the library of Archbishop James Ussher. I am indebted to Bernard Barr and Charles Benson for information upon these. Copies in the Bodleian from 1602–28 were bequeathed by Robert Burton in 1640.

42 PRO E.122/86/6.

43 Gibson 1907, pp. 10–16.

44 PRO E.122/86/8.

45 Schmitz 1987 and Corsten 1962.

46 PRO E.122/80/2; Plomer 1924.

in the correspondence of Erasmus. Erasmus's references to the Birckmanns are nearly always harsh, though a picture of their international activities as booksellers, couriers of money (including Erasmus's income from England) and bearers of news, also emerges from these letters. They were to be found in Cologne, where there was a small printing shop, Antwerp (where they had a shop or warehouse in the Kammerstraat at the sign of the Fat Hen), and London. Franz II (probably, but not certainly the son of Franz I) appears in two imprints of 1530 (*STC* 16240 and 16240.5) but much more extensively in customs rolls up to 1557. A John Birckmann who also appears is occasionally described as a denizated alien; he was perhaps the son of Heinrich and thus a cousin of Franz II or, more probably, the son of Arnold I, and therefore a brother of Arnold II. By 1557 Arnold II (1523–74, son of Arnold I), was the head of the firm in London. He was then a Brother of the Stationers' Company and was on several occasions assessed for larger sums than other Brothers upon mayoral precepts to the Company; for example Arnold Birckmann contributed 2*s*. to the collection for Bridewell in 1556,[47] while Conrad Molyar gave 8*d*., and 11*s*. for a window for the new hall.[48] Except upon one well-known occasion,[49] Arnold is not recorded as an importer, and the name that appears in such port books as survive is that of the Widow Birckmann, or Agnes Birckmann; she was the widow of Arnold I, Agnes von Gennep, who outlived her husband by nearly forty years, dying on 6 November 1580. Arnold II died in 1574 in Cologne.

The Birckmanns employed a series of factors in London: Herry Harman (1541), Conrad Molyar or Mollar (previously servant to John Gypkyn in 1541, a Brother of the Stationers' Company, and from 1567 a university bookseller in Oxford),[50] Andreas Fremonsheim (about 1561) and Rumold Mercator (about 1568). With the exception of Molyar, all were undenizated aliens, yet the Birckmanns, while importing wholesale, clearly sold books by retail at their shop in St Paul's Churchyard. John Dee was one of their customers.[51] In 1604 a Dutch scholar, Johann Radermacher, recalled seeing Dee in their shop forty years earlier. Dee was evidently a good customer but a bad payer, for when he left for his long European travels in 1583, the factor Fremonsheim – who had catalogued Dee's library – unsuccessfully sued Dee's brother-in-law Nicholas Fromonds for an outstanding debt of £63. 13*s*. 8¼*d*. Dee in sharp contrast to Erasmus had praised the Birckmanns in a letter to Josias Simler of 4 July 1574; he offered to send Simler some manuscript readings 'per amicos meos, longe honestissimos, Birckmannos nimirum Colonienses'.[52]

47 Arber, I, p. 48. 48 Arber, I, p. 61. 49 See below p. 155. 50 Roberts 1997, p. 325. 51 Roberts and Watson 1990, pp.12–13. 52 Zentralbibliothek, Zurich, MS. F 59 fol. 389.

In 1564 also, Sir William Cecil wrote to the Marquis of Winchester,[53] with a special plea on behalf of Arnold Birckmann and Conrad Molyar. They were about to despatch into England five fatts and two maunds[54] of books from the Frankfurt fair via Antwerp, not knowing of the proclamation (of 23 March 1564) against trade with the Low Countries. Cecil asked that they might quietly discharge the books – and the four or five boxes of green ginger for Cecil's own use. This episode is revealing both of the diverse functions of international booksellers, and perhaps of the favours required of, and granted to, this particular merchant. The days of Antwerp as the seat of the English Staple were numbered, however; the port was closed temporarily in 1564, and again in 1568, when the Staple was moved to the less bookish Hamburg.

Both the changes in the trade-routes and the dominance (albeit waning) of the Birckmanns are illustrated by an extant port book, that of the Surveyor of Petty Customs from Michaelmas 1571 to Michaelmas 1572, covering imports by aliens.[55] Most of the shipments were from Hamburg, though Emden was also used, as were the French Channel ports. Agnes Birckmann was only the second largest importer, with 21½ fatts, worth £43. The largest importer was Pierre du Puis (denizated in 1568 and a Brother of the Stationers' Company in the following year) who brought in 31½ fatts, worth £63, while the other lesser importers, notably Robert Cambier (denizated in mid-stream on 14 February 1572), also bore French names.

The Birckmanns supplied books to Cambridge, both wholesale – since they unsuccessfully claimed £196 12*s*. 1*d*. from the bookseller Philip Scarlett in 1570,[56] (and Andrew Perne appeared in court for them in 1572) – and retail, since in 1577/8 the university paid 'Widdowe Brickman' £4 for some books which Sir Nicholas Bacon had ordered on its behalf. There is as yet no evidence that they supplied academic books to Oxford, though the presence there of their former factor Conrad Molyar (admitted as a bookseller on 27 January 1567) may well have given them an outlet. Perhaps the £4 payment to Agnes Birckmann reassured her into supplying more to Cambridge; on 29 May 1579, the Privy Council wrote to the Lord Mayor of London 'that wheras he hath arrested certaine drifattes and bales of bookes belonging to the Brickmans and other stationers, strangeres, delivered to the cariers of Cambridge to be conveyed thither, uppon pretence that they were forreine bought and solde and so forfeicted by the charter of that citie, he is required to forbeare to proceade

53 Greg 1967, Calendar 32.

54 A maund (basket) was normally reckoned, for customs purposes, to be the equivalent of two fatts (barrels). Thus the consignment probably consisted of two maunds of books and a fatt containing ginger.

55 PRO E.190/5/5.

56 I owe the details of this episode to Dr Elisabeth Leedham-Green.

against the stationers for anie bookes so appointed to be sent to the Universities'.[57] Whether this intervention was intended to favour the Birckmanns or Cambridge or both, this was the last break the firm was to get in England. Agnes Birckmann, widow for nearly forty years, died in November 1580, and the decision was taken to wind up its activities in London. One of the London factors, Rumold Mercator, was responsible for this. The other factor, Andreas Fremonsheim, had to take John Dee's brother-in law to court. The fact that Dee was pursued for the same amount ten years later[58] by John Norton suggests that the firm's assets, including debts owed to it, had passed into suitable English hands. The Birckmanns seem on the evidence to have enjoyed a favoured status, and it will shortly be argued that a successor to them was eventually found by the agency of Christophe Plantin, a bookseller most concerned, despite the political barriers, and disasters like the Spanish Fury of November 1576, to keep the English buying books.

Christophe Plantin

Plantin's ledgers are a unique source for individual titles despatched to London from 1558 until well into the seventeenth century. The opening of Plantin's career as a printer in 1555 shortly precedes the new ventures by native Englishmen into the business of importing noted as one possible outcome of the chartering of the Stationers' Company. Colin Clair[59] has provided a very valuable overview of Plantin's huge sales to English customers and to the numerous émigré French booksellers who worked in London. One of Clair's few errors is in mis-recording one of the earliest transactions with Nicholas England. Although Plantin did send a consignment of maps to Nicholas England as early as August 1558, the sale included a very large quantity of books, and England received further consignments in October 1558 and January 1559. Nicholas Cliston (Plantin always refers to him as Clifton) was another substantial customer in 1558. Nicholas England sent lists of books required, but also chose them 'estant present en Anvers' on his return from Frankfurt. During the 1560s England was in partnership (for importation) with Humfrey Toy, an arrangement which seems to have lasted until the former's death or retirement after 1567. The native Englishmen whose names appear in the published port book for 1567/78[60] were mostly customers of Plantin – Lucas Harrison, George

57 *APC 1579*, ns. 11, p. 144.
58 *The private diary of Dr John Dee*, ed. by J. O. Halliwell (Manchester, 1842), p. 54.
59 Clair 1959. 60 Dietz 1972.

Bishop and Humfrey Toy; only Garret Dewes, a substantial importer in that year, seems to have gone elsewhere. Plantin's ledgers record that Harrison and Bishop were present in Antwerp on 29 and 30 September.[61] They were probably on the way to or from Frankfurt. The same men had been equally active in 1566, and one of England's orders[62] included:

25 Plautus 16°
12 floresTerentij trilingues
50 Virgilius 8°
50 Apophthegmata Erasmi 8°
25 Epistole famil. Cicer.
50 Epistole selecte Ciceronis 8°
12 Sententie Ciceronis 16°
25 Terentius sine annotat.
5 Annotationes in eundem(?)
25 Grammatica greca Clenardi
12 Hesiodi opera et dies

This is a typical order destined for London; very large numbers of small-format classics, usually followed by large-format learned books in ones and twos. Although the Englishmen bought generously enough for Plantin to give them accounts (usually settled at the Frankfurt fair) there is some evidence that they found the books hard to sell. Apart from Plantin's direct sales, many books also found their way to England via the Sign of the Fat Hen, and by special arrangements such as that (described in detail by Clair) concluded with Jean Desserans (denizated in 1566) and in which Thomas Vautrollier (denizated in 1562) also took part. This agreement ensured a copious flow of books to London until 1568. Plantin also supplied Robert Cambier, who has already been noted as a major importer from the port book of 1571/2.

Ascanius de Renialme

Plantin's earliest transaction with Ascanius de Renialme took place in 1576, when Jan Moerentorf, Plantin's son-in-law, paid Ascanius 255 florins and 18¾ stivers at Frankfurt. Ascanius was perhaps related to Charles de Regnialme,[63] described as 'frère de Bomberghen' in 1559, and Clair draws attention to Ascanius's letter of 1578, addressing Moerentorf as 'amy Jean', hardly the style

61 P-MA 45, fol. 139, 139^{v}. 62 P-MA 44, fol. 44^{v}. 63 P-MA 35, fol. 81.

of a complete stranger. Ascanius's establishment as a bookseller in London in 1578 was rapid and smooth. He is described in the *Returns of aliens*[64] as an Italian from the dominions of the Doge of Venice, who came to see the country with his wife, and remained there. He was admitted a Brother of the Stationers' Company on 27 June 1580. Italian he may have been, but all his connections were with the Netherlands, and he was a Protestant. His wife Elizabeth was from Middelburg, and she had evidently been married before, since she had a son, James Rimé or Rimius, who followed his stepfather into the Latin trade. In his will[65] Ascanius describes François Bouvier as his brother-in-law; Bouvier's wife Lucy also came from Middelburg, so she and Elizabeth de Renialme were sisters. Ascanius, his brother-in-law Bouvier, and Hercules Francis, rather than the native English, stepped (temporarily) into the breach made by the decline of the Birckmann business.

On the evidence it is now possible to concur, at least as regards the last twenty years of the sixteenth century, with Graham Pollard's dictum, quoted at the beginning of this chapter, that the Latin trade was in the hands of aliens who were Brothers of the Stationers' Company,[66] and Plantin's ledgers confirm this. The recurring names in the surviving port books are those of Hercules Francis, Bouvier and Ascanius de Renialme (or his widow Elizabeth). Hercules Francis had begun his career in Paris as Hercule François, servant to Jacques du Puis, but he was a Protestant and settled in London. He is named as a Brother of the Company in 1589/90 as 'Hercules ffrancis servant to mr du puys',[67] thus taking over from Baptiste or Pierre du Puis a very substantial business. He died in 1603 or 1604.

By far the largest importers were the brothers-in-law. There are extant port books for two half-years, Easter–Michaelmas 1589[68] and Easter–Michaelmas 1593.[69] In the former, Ascanius brought in 16½ fatts, Baptiste du Puis 11 fatts, Hercules Francis 1 fatt (as du Puis's factor?), and Bouvier only two. This is also the year of Giacomo Castelvetro's brief intervention in the trade.[70] One cannot tell how many of Ascanius's purchases were from Plantin direct and how many were from Frankfurt, which he is known to have frequented. In this, the year of Plantin's death, Ascanius paid him 515 florins 7½ stivers.[71] In 1593 Ascanius's imports amounted to 17½ fatts and Bouvier's 8½. If the

64 R. E. G. and E. F. Kirk, *Returns of Aliens*, Publications of the Huguenot Society, 10 (1900–8), pt 2 (1902), pp. 309, 354; pt 3 (1907), p. 50.

65 PRO Prob.11/95; see also Plomer 1903, pp. 35–6.

66 Pollard and Ehrman 1965, p. 85.

67 Stationers' Company Liber A, fol. 58ᵛ.

68 PRO E.190/8/2.

69 PRO E.190/9/5.

70 Roberts 1990.

71 P-MA 19. This 'Grand livre des libraires' contains a consolidated record of most of Ascanius's payments to Plantin and his successors.

establishment of Ascanius in London can be attributed to Plantin, it was not the least of that great man's commercial triumphs.

Ascanius enjoyed very warm relations with the London Stationers, and his will, with its abundant bequests to the Company and to some individual members, is a testimony to these. On 6 December 1591 the Company agreed that new books imported from Frankfurt – 'for the space of one monnethe after the Retorne of everie ffrankford mart' is the phrase in Register B[72] – might be offered to the printers of the University of Cambridge for possible reprinting.[73] The selection at the Fair and subsequent display at Stationers' Hall was perhaps one of those functions for which the Stationers relied upon their Brethren, and particularly upon Ascanius. He was only to be disappointed in one matter; despite support from the Stationers and from the government, he was unable to become a printer. He did not, as has been suggested, issue a printed catalogue; he and others referred to manuscript lists as 'catalogues'.[74]

The generous bequests in Ascanius's will were not confined to his fellows in the trade, and two members of his household were thus, briefly, to influence the Latin trade. There was a legacy of £100 to his stepson, James Rimé, conditional on his behaving well and exercising the trade of bookselling, and one of £10 to his servant Adrian Marois, again conditional on his good conduct to Ascanius's widow, and serving out his contract.

The turn of the century, with the death of Ascanius in 1600, that of Hercules Francis in 1603 or 1604, and the apparent retirement of François Bouvier might be seen as the end of alien domination of the Latin trade. As will be seen, this is a slight oversimplification.

One specialized clientele seems to have been served by the Brother (1 February 1580) and alien recorded as Jan Walteneel by Worman[75] and McKerrow, and by others under a variety of spellings. Despite his membership of the Dutch Church in London, he bought considerable quantities of 'Horae' and 'rouges et noires'[76] from the Officina Plantiniana, purchases which involved himself and his widow (after 1607) in considerable debts to it. How many of these found their way to England and how many to English Catholic communities on the Continent, is not clear.

72 Greg and Boswell 1930, pp. 39–40.

73 There are a few clear examples of this concession to the Cambridge press. Thomas had already reprinted a mart book in 1585 (*STC* 24529); other examples are *STC* 15702 and 12938.

74 Bouvier and Ascanius both sent (manuscript) catalogues to the Cambridge bookseller Hugh Burwell, and their letters to him are preserved in a binding in Gonville and Caius College library. (Information from Mr D. A. Pearson.)

75 Worman 1906.

76 This is the normal trade term for Roman Catholic liturgical books.

It is a fair speculation that the 'Heirs of Ascanius de Renialme' who appear as booksellers in Frankfurt in 1605? and 1607? (*STC* 12685 and 12685.3) were his stepson James Rimé and his servant Adrian Marois/Marius. As Ascanius had hoped, both entered the Latin trade, and both are recorded as major purchasers from the Officina Plantiniana and in the port books.[77] For example, on 12 May 1609, James Rimé's consignment on the Seahorse of Dort was 14 fatts or 7 maunds,[78] larger than anything recorded for his stepfather. Adrian Marius supplied the library of Trinity College, Dublin, with books to the substantial value of £28 16*s.* in 1608; Norton and Bill then sold only £27 8*s.* 4*d.* worth to the College.[79] Whether the 'Heirs' were in partnership is unclear, and it is possible that they were ultimately put out of business by the Latin Stock after 1616, or by the rise of John Norton and John Bill.

John Norton and John Bill

It has been suggested (above, p. 156) that John Norton acquired some of the Birckmanns' assets in the early 1580s. He was thus probably engaged in the Latin trade before 1600, but the absence of customs records for native Englishmen has meant that the extent of his trading does not appear until 1604,[80] when the arrival of nine fatts of books from Stade is neatly, if not precisely, confirmed by Sir Thomas Bodley's letter to Thomas James of 7 November.[81] Details of purchases by Norton and Bill from the Officina Plantiniana appear in the *Journal* for 1607.[82] The role of John Bill in particular in supplying the early needs of Bodley's new library is well known from Bodley's correspondence, and the Library continued to use his services until 1620–1, when Bill disposed of his foreign books to the Latin Stock. The curators of the Library decided in July 1615 to meet within a week of the arrival of the Frankfurt fair catalogues, and from spring 1617 what they saw was probably John Bill's own version of the catalogues (*STC* 11328 and after). The Library then shopped around, and Thomas James's successor John Rous and the Huguenot sub-librarian John Verneuil both travelled to London to buy books. Those for which they paid 'the Companie of the Stationers' no doubt came from the Latin Stock shop in the garden of the new Stationers' Hall in Ave Maria Lane. There were

77 An interesting family link within the trade is suggested by the presence of Henry Fetherstone (below, pp. 162–3) and 'Jeanne femme de Jacques Reymes' at the baptism of Adrian, son of Adrian Marie and Jeanne Behaut his wife, on 4 April 1613. W. J. C. Moens, *The registers of the French Church of Threadneedle Street, London, 1600–1639*, Publications of the Huguenot Society, 9 (1896), p. 89.

78 PRO E.190/14/5.

79 TCD Particular Book Mun/v/1/1, fol. 33.

80 PRO E.315/467.

81 Bodley 1926, p. 117.

82 P-MA 179.

purchases of this kind in 1620–1, 1621–2 and 1624–5, amounting in all to £23 3*s*. 6*d*.[83]

The Latin Stock

The setting up of the Latin Stock in January 1616 by a group of 112 Stationers was a bold attempt by the Company to monopolize the importing of books. Although occasional details relating to it appear, for example in Court Book C, the only record of its establishment was published in 1907 by H. R Plomer.[84] The Stock was set up by 112 Stationers, who agreed to become partners 'in buying and selling all sorts of books that might legally be bought and sold to the subjects of this Kingdom'. They also decided to have factors and agents 'beyond the seas . . . for the buying of all books as were printed in those parts'. According to Blagden,[85] the nominal capital was £4,500, but only 75 per cent of this sum was paid up. Nevertheless some of the members embarked upon a massive series of purchases, and some of these are recorded in the ledgers of the Officina Plantiniana.[86] In 1616 and 1617, Antwerp was visited by a number of English booksellers, who spent very heavily there. They were William Welby 'estant present en Anvers' on 3 August 1616, who spent 310 florins 13 stivers on what were clearly big books rather than school texts and grammars; and Samuel Nealand, very much at the outset of his bookselling career, who paid 328 florins 4 stivers for 'divers livres' which included many by Cardinal Bellarmine, on 26 August 'en compagnie de Thomas Thorp'. Thorp favoured Bellarmine also, and bought fifty of his *Scala mentis* and 200 of *Gemitus columbae*; on 16 March 1617, most significantly, he is described as 'de Compagnie de Londres', while on 13 December of that year he was buying 'pour la Compagnie de Londres'. John Parker, described by Plomer as 'associated with Henry Featherstone until 1619' was also 'estant present' in 1617; he bought his way into the Latin Stock in about 1619.

The Stock was in almost immediate collision with the highly experienced John Bill, and his publication from 1617 of a 'London' series of the Frankfurt fair catalogues[87] was perhaps his act of defiance, countered by another 'London' version printed by Felix Kyngston.[88] Evidently an accommodation was reached, by which in January 1621 the Stock bought up Bill's foreign books,[89] and the two parties agreed on a single 'London' version of the fair catalogues.[90]

83 Hampshire 1983, pp. 42, 43, 63. 84 Plomer 1907c, Roberts 2000.
85 Blagden 1960, pp. 106–7. 86 P-MA 223, 224, 226, 229.
87 *STC* 11328–11328.4, 11328.6, 11328.8, 11328.10. 88 *STC* 11328.7, 11328.9.
89 Jackson 1957, p. 132. 90 *STC* 11329.4–11330.8.

Despite the lavish expenditure in Antwerp – or perhaps because of it – the Stock could pay only one dividend, and that out of capital, in 1619. Nor did its members repeat their visits to Antwerp, and a few modest orders from Simon Waterson and Clement Knight in 1622, recorded in the ledgers of the Officina Plantiniana[91] may even have been placed by agents. There is a little evidence from the port books, in particular that for a subsidy of tunnage and poundage in 1625–6,[92] that a number of Stationers who were members of the Stock were active in importing; Simon Waterson, Edmund Weaver and Bonham Norton brought in 5½ maunds in that year. But Henry Fetherstone brought in 8¼, and his sales to the Bodleian put the £23 the Librarians spent with the Stock into proper perspective. After a series of transactions, mostly discreditable, the Company decided to wind up the Stock on 27 June 1627. At this point there was a dispute between Bill and the Stock; Bill claimed that he was owed £920, though he finally settled in December for £800 in cash and books.[93] His publication of spring and autumn fair catalogues for 1628 (without any English titles),[94] underlines what he perhaps saw as his triumph over a foolhardy venture. Blagden's verdict[95] is 'The kindest explanation is that men who were extremely competent in their own businesses made, during a period of general economic depression, a complete mess of an organization from which, as booksellers, they might expect direct competition if it were well enough managed to pay dividends to the partners.' Less kindly, it might be added that these businessmen were well versed in monopolies, but that monopolies are of little value if those operating them cannot prevent others from doing the same thing. John Bill died in 1630, and he and the Stock were outlived by a bookseller whose experience rivalled, and exceeded, that of Bill, and who succeeded him as the favoured supplier of the Bodleian Library.

Henry Fetherstone

Henry Fetherstone had been apprenticed to Bonham Norton, and was freed on 5 October 1607. Evidently writing with some experience of the trade and of the Frankfurt fairs in particular, Fetherstone addressed a number of petitions, unfortunately undated, to the University of Cambridge, at once describing the unsatisfactory nature of dealing at the fairs, and warning the university of the perils to university booksellers in particular from the intended creation of

91 P-MA 229, fol. 123, 209. 92 PRO E.190/31/3. 93 Jackson 1957, p. 199.
94 *STC* 1331, 11331.2. 95 Blagden 1960, p. 106.

a monopoly such as the Latin Stock. No documents like these[96] can, apparently, be found in Oxford's archives, but he can hardly have failed to alert that university, since the university library there was actively buying books (with Fetherstone as its principal supplier in the 1620s), whereas that at Cambridge was not.

Fetherstone's independence seems to have done him no lasting harm, since he was later Warden (1635–6 and 1639–40) and Master (1641–2) of the Company, despite 'his having given over trading' in 1631/2.[97] He was also the founder of a 'family' of Latin traders. In February 1619 his determination to keep the 'foreign' Robert Martin cost him a fine from the Company. Fetherstone had Martin translated to the Stationers' Company in 1622 at a cost of £6 13*s*. 4*d*. 'Foreign' in this context may mean 'not properly apprenticed'; but the name may well be French, and Martin an alien whose readiness to travel resulted in the series of six catalogues of imports from France and Italy issued between 1633 and 1650.[98] George Thomason was Fetherstone's apprentice, and possibly succeeded to his shop in 1637. Thomason in turn was in partnership with Octavian Pulleyn from 1635 to 1645. All sold books to the Bodleian. The appearance of books of some antiquity in these catalogues suggests that these and other 'mart books' were being imported ready bound, and that this provision of the 1534 Act was now, at long last, ignored.

Robert Martin's offerings of books from France and Italy may well point to a change in the trade routes, away from war-torn northern Europe to safer areas further south; Spanish books might be had in Venice without the perils that had attended John Bill's brief visit to Seville in 1604.[99] The decline of the Frankfurt fair was also a probable factor in the collapse of the Latin Stock, whose relatively inexperienced members relied on its continuance. The Bodleian accounts mention the autumn and spring marts for the last time in 1629–30,[100] but the Library was regularly spending sums of £40–£50 with Thomason until the Civil Wars in England diminished its own income. Lucien Febvre and H.-J. Martin saw an early decline for Frankfurt: 'Foreign booksellers largely ceased to attend the fair in those latter years [1625 to 1635] and there were hardly any French there after 1620–1625'.[101] Nevertheless, the buoyant sales by Martin, Thomason and Pulleyn at Oxford are confirmed by the port book for 1633–4 (imports by denizens).[102] The biggest importer was Humphrey Robinson (another of the Bodleian's suppliers), and the busiest port was Rouen. Rotterdam

96 McKitterick 1992, p. 144. 97 Hampshire 1983, p. 89.

98 Martin does not appear among the native English in paying the subsidy of tunnage and poundage in the port books of the 1630s.

99 Bodley 1926, no. 114, p. 118. 100 Hampshire 1983, p. 80.

101 Febvre and Martin 1976, p. 232. 102 PRO E.190/38/3.

was, surprisingly in view of Amsterdam's later importance, a more commonly named port.

The curators of the Bodleian Library would have welcomed the opportunity to broaden the geographical scope of their collections which the travels of Martin and Thomason frequently gave them,[103] and their task was simplified by the availability of printed catalogues. The Frankfurt catalogues (in, presumably, their 'English' versions) were used by the Library, but private buyers did likewise. The earliest Frankfurt catalogues held by the Bodleian were in fact Robert Burton's (bequeathed in 1640), and bear his marks.

Latin trade catalogues

The phenomenon of the publication and use of printed booksellers' catalogues is not English but European, as both Febvre and Martin and Pollard and Ehrman make clear. Where England was unusual was that it had not only growing institutional libraries and eager collectors, but also a chronic balance of payments deficit in the book trade. Thus, English book buyers made extensive use of foreign booksellers' catalogues. Bonaventure Elsevier's name occurs only once in the surviving records as an importer, in the largely illegible port book of imports by aliens in 1626–7,[104] when he brought in a maund of unbound books on 16 October 1627. But the firm's catalogues circulated widely. Two of the Bodleian's three copies of the 1674 catalogue are in identical sheepskin bindings, and one was presented by Daniel Elzevier. An English collector, Griffin Higgs, had a collection of thirty-one catalogues of the period 1627–40, some marked and all but four from one or other of the Elzeviers.[105]

Civil Wars and Restoration

The period of the Civil Wars, Commonwealth and early Restoration is one of the most poorly documented in the history of the Latin trade. There seem to be no port books, and purchasing by the Bodleian Library peters out, to revive a little with sales from local booksellers during the Commonwealth. The Library had to wait until 1663–4 before it could buy from Robert Scott and James Allestree on the scale that it had from Martin and Thomason before the Civil War. Richard Allestree the divine, and the first cousin of the bookseller James Allestree, was involved in the choice of books.

103 Hampshire 1983, pp. 92, 96, 105, 125, 131.
104 PRO E.190/32/1. 105 Morrish 1971 and 1990.

Holland Bibles

The importation of Bibles, Books of Common Prayer and metrical Psalms, mainly printed in Holland in defiance of the patents held by the King's Printers or, from 1603, by the English Stock of the Stationers' Company, does not strictly form part of the Latin trade, but because it was so widespread, apparently in the mid-seventeenth century, it deserves some mention here. These books were fairly easy to produce and were profitable, thanks both to an assured sale in England, and to the lower price of paper in Continental Europe. In the period up to, and immediately after 1640, they are relatively easy to detect from the use of woodcut title pages and initials. After that date, detection is more difficult (though not, it seems, to contemporaries), and there is abundant documentary evidence that the printing of such books went on, and that the rewards were the greater because Dutch printers were apparently using a form of stereotyping. *STC* records many such books,[106] most of which have false imprints and dates, and attributes many to the press of Jan Fredericksz Stam, who worked at Amsterdam from 1628 to 1657.[107] (See fig. 21.3.) Some of the books recorded as of later (i.e. post-1640) date are evidence of the legal confusion of the Civil War and Commonwealth period, when importation of 'Holland Bibles' was evidently on a huge scale. A memorandum quoted by John Johnson and Strickland Gibson,[108] referring to the 1670s, alleges that the King's Printers had in seven years seized £15,000 worth of Holland Bibles, many of which had been sold on, at great profit. Harry Carter[109] considered that the smuggling of Bibles had become less profitable by 1678, through improved efficiency by the Customs. The output of the Oxford Bible Press may also have contributed.

The trade after 1660

Samuel Pepys was an avid buyer of books, many of them foreign. In his early years he patronized Joshua Kirton, 'my bookseller' until the latter was ruined by the fire of 1666. On 26 September 1666 Pepys recorded 'But here by Mr Dugdale I hear the great loss of books in St Pauls churchyard, and at their hall also – which they value at 150000l; some booksellers being wholly undone and among others, my poor Kirton they say'.[110] On 5 October 'a great want thereof there will be of books, specially Latin books and foreign books'.[111] In 1667 John

106 *STC* 2174–80, 2328.5–2328.9, 2330–2330.9, 2499–2499.7.
107 Johnson 1954. See also below, pp. 466–8.
108 Johnson and Gibson 1946, pp. 78–9. 109 Carter 1975, p. 95.
110 Pepys 1970–83, VII, p. 297. 111 Pepys 1970–83, VII, p. 309.

Starkey was 'my new bookseller'. Pepys also browsed in Duck Lane, where he not only kissed William Shrewsbury's wife, but bought a 1527 *Legenda aurea*. He was in Duck Lane again in April 1668, 'and there did overlook a great many of Monsieur Fouquet's library, that a bookseller hath bought'. From 1681, Robert Scott had become important, and at the end of Pepys's life, Samuel Lowndes was his favoured supplier. The damage caused by the Great Fire, and the severe losses suffered by booksellers in particular, combined with the effects of two Dutch wars seem to have brought depression to the book trade in the years immediately after the Stuart Restoration.

If this was indeed so, the recovery came rapidly, and Robert Scott was one of its leaders. His large sales to the Bodleian have already been mentioned. His career has been studied by Leona Rostenberg.[112] She describes his catalogue of 1674 as 'splendid'; though Scott may not be wholly responsible for its splendour (see appendix below, p. 173). In titling it 'ex variis Europae partibus advectorum' he was perhaps following the pre-war example of Robert Martin's series, but the use of the international learned language was also a portent for the Latin trade. When he left off trade, his stock of about 25,000 volumes was sold from 13 February 1688 by his former apprentice Benjamin Walford, and it was thought sufficiently attractive for the catalogue to be available in a French edition from booksellers in France, the Netherlands and Germany.[113] The Latin trade was changing its nature, dramatically. London booksellers, native Englishmen, were buying extensively abroad, and selling abroad too; they were investing in the purchase of great foreign libraries, so that Pepys had access to Fouquet's books – presumably at William Shrewsbury's shop in Duck Lane – while Robert Scott could contemplate buying the de Thou library in 1680, and claimed he had bought from the library of Pierre de Montmaur for Charles II. Moses Pitt's sale of the library of Gijsbert Voet in November 1678 was one of the earliest of English auctions.[114] The principal practitioners were men of general culture and linguistic fluency, and publicized their stock by advertisement and by printed catalogues, where the learned and international character of the trade was emphasized by the use of Latin.

Moses Pitt

Importing was but one facet of the career of Moses Pitt, and it was not the one which led to his financial ruin and imprisonment for debt.[115] He was apprenticed in 1654 to Robert Littlebury, a member of the Haberdashers'

112 Rostenberg 1954. 113 Munby and Coral 1977, p. 8.
114 Munby and Coral 1977, p. 3. 115 Harris 1985.

Company, who also traded as a bookseller, and was made free of that company in 1661. His earliest recorded premises were at the White Hart in Little Britain, an address which suggests a trade in 'mart books', and which also protected him from the worst effects of the fire of 1666. Like Littlebury, Pitt appears in the port books as an importer, and perhaps on a larger scale than his master, since his 1681 debt to Daniel Elsevier was greater (see below). Pitt early specialized in scientific and mathematical books, was bookseller to the Royal Society, and appears as such in the correspondence of Henry Oldenburg. His principal innovation in the Latin trade was the publication of the first six numbers of the *Catalogus librorum in regionibus transmarinis nuper editorum*, from Easter Term 1676 to Hilary Term 1677, which ran in parallel with the *Term Catalogues*, and issues of it are sometimes bound with them. Later issues, to Hilary Term 1679, were published by George Wells and Samuel Carr or by Samuel Carr alone.

Expansion of the Latin trade

Two documents confirm that the Latin trade had ceased to be a specialized one, the province of a limited number of aliens, but one widely followed in the London and indeed provincial book trade.

The first is the port book, covering imports by denizens from Christmas 1681 to Christmas 1682.[116] It contains the names of about fifty importers, half of whom are Stationers, including some of the most prominent figures in the London trade, Awnsham Churchill, John Williams, Robert Littlebury, Henry Faithorne and John Kersey, Moses Pitt, Robert Scott, Abel Swalle, John Gellibrand, Henry Mortlock, Mark Pardoe and Samuel Smith. Richard Davis of Oxford also appears; he had been a regular supplier to the Bodleian for more than twenty years. Most of the books in 1681–2 were dispatched from Amsterdam and Rotterdam.

The other document tells the same story – over a longer period – and explains the dominance of these Dutch cities. It is a list of the debts owed to Daniel Elsevier (1626–80), published from the Notarial Archives of Amsterdam by I. H. van Eeghen.[117] The debts had been incurred over a long period, for there is a reference to the elder Octavian Pulleyn as 'verstorven en verdorven' – dead and rotten. Among the numerous British debtors are booksellers not only from London, but from Oxford, Cambridge and Edinburgh. On the assumption that there were approximately 12 florins to £1 sterling, most of these debts are

116 PRO E.190/116/1. 117 Van Eeghen 1960–78, III, pp.111–19.

under £100, but those of Mark Pardoe, Spencer Hickman and the Mearnes are much larger.

French immigrant booksellers

It would be wrong to suppose that participation by aliens in the Latin trade had ceased in the face of the growing versatility and sophistication of the native booksellers. The increasingly precarious position of French Protestants under Louis XIV led to widespread emigration even before the final Revocation of the Edict of Nantes on 17 October 1685. Protestants had already been excluded from the guilds of printers and booksellers, and those who left for England rapidly formed what Katherine Swift has called 'a closely knit group of booksellers who, from their shops in the Strand, supplied London with new French books . . . and antiquarian books, almost all imported from the Continent'.[118] One of the most important of this group seems to have anticipated the exodus. Jean de Beaulieu made four appearances (under a variety of spellings) in the port book for 1681 (imports by aliens)[119] and eleven in the similar book for 1682.[120] He is perhaps the man who is recorded in the *Livre des tesmoignages* of the French Church in Threadneedle Street[121] as bringing a 'Témoignage' from Amsterdam in 1682, and who became denizated in December 1687.[122] A sale of books from the stock of John de Beaulieu was held in 1699 (?).[123] His premises in Duke's Court, St Martin's Lane, and from 1684 in St Martin's Lane itself, were at some distance from those of his compatriots near the French Church in the liberty of the Savoy. All would originally have been outside the jurisdiction of the Stationers' Company but, under the new Charter of 1684,[124] the Company – in theory – extended its powers over London and Westminster and four miles around, and it was with the confidence of these new powers that in June 1684 the Court of Assistants summoned before it a number of booksellers trading outside the City limits. These included 'Mounsieur Buroe [Beaulieu?]' trading in Salisbury Exchange, and 'Mounsieur Boyer' trading in Duke's Court, St Martin's Lane.[125] Denization, however, was as necessary as it had been 150 years before; so great was the influx of French Protestants that from 1681 to 1688 refugees were denizated by Order in Council, though the regular procedure of enrolment on the Patent Rolls was also followed,

118 Swift 1990. 119 PRO E.190/105/3. 120 PRO E.190/114/7.

121 W. Minet, *Livre des tesmoignages de l'Eglise de Threadneedle Street 1669–1789*, Publications of the Huguenot Society of London, 21 (1909), p. 66.

122 *Ibid.*, p. 21. 123 Wing B1569, Munby and Coral 1977, p. 18.

124 Blagden 1960, pp. 166–72. 125 Stationers' Company, Court Book F, fol. 17.

for even larger numbers. The impact of these alien booksellers can be seen in the two port books for 1694 and 1696; both are for subsidies of tunnage and poundage, the earlier for imports by aliens, the second for imports by denizens (which here include denizated aliens). In the earlier,[126] David Delgas, agent for the Huguetans of Amsterdam, is by far the largest importer. In the later,[127] we find the expected names of the big London booksellers, John Churchill, Richard Chiswell, Robert Clavell, Samuel Smith, Samuel Buckley, but some new names also. They (often grossly mis-spelt) are of the French refugee booksellers from the Strand, Pierre de Varenne, Jean Cailloué and the widow Marret. Pierre de Varenne in particular went on to use the newly popular auction to sell his imports at Exeter Exchange in the Strand. The earlier sales, from 1693, were probably a means of raising money quickly, but they continued at Exeter Exchange and at inns and coffee-houses until 1724. Jacques/James Levi (denizated 5 March 1691), according to Swift,[128] son-in-law to Pierre de Varenne, continued the practice until the 1730s.[129] The vogue of these auctions suggests that the Latin trade itself may have been increasingly dominated by them after 1700. The catalogue[130] of Samuel Buckley's fixed-price auction of 14 November 1699 was distributed by a number of Stationers, but also by 'Peter Varennes at Seneca's head in the Strand', which suggests, at least, a truce.

Bennet, Smith and Buckley

But the most important practitioners of the Latin trade were, by 1695, Samuel Buckley and Samuel Smith. With Smith's name must be linked that of Thomas Bennet, because in publishing the outgoing correspondence of Bennet and of his apprentice and successor Henry Clements, Norma Hodgson and Cyprian Blagden[131] made abundant use of the incoming correspondence of Bennet's neighbour in St Paul's Churchyard, Samuel Smith.

Bennet, born in 1664/5, apprenticed to Henry Mortlock and freed in 1686, was, until his death in 1706, best known for his publication of theology of a High Church tendency; Dunton noted that he was 'very much devoted to the Church'. He had 'a considerable trade in Oxford'.[132] He does not seem to have supplied the Bodleian, and Dunton may be referring to his publication of editions of the classics by Oxford scholars. These, and theology formed

126 PRO E.190/149/4. 127 PRO E.190/158/1. 128 Swift 1990, p. 125.
129 Munby and Coral 1977 *passim*. 130 BL, SC 924. 1, Munby and Coral 1977, p. 18.
131 Hodgson and Blagden 1956. 132 Quoted in Hodgson and Blagden 1956, p. 6.

the core of his offers to the Dutch booksellers, such as Pieter van der Aa, the Waesberghes, J. H. Wetstein, and (later) Pieter Mortier with whom he dealt. He was able to tempt van der Aa in 1699 with a list of new classics from the Oxford and Cambridge presses – books which perhaps no longer earned John Locke's scathing condemnation of English editions: 'by this Act [the Licensing Act] and their patents [the Stationers] slobber them over as they can cheapest, so that there is not a book of them vended beyond seas, both for their badness and dearness'.[133] A notable feature of Bennet's imports was the English taste for 'old Elzivir', of which Bennet bought 119 volumes from Wetstein in 1684.[134] Samuel Buckley's [1697?] catalogue also includes a collection of Elseviers in duodecimo.

As Hodgson and Blagden point out, Bennet was not, at least judging by his 'scrappy and disconnected' correspondence, a major importer. (He did, however, buy heavily from David Delgas, who was.) His name has not been found in the port books. Unlike the next two booksellers, he was unable to correspond in French with his Dutch suppliers.

It is indeed quite otherwise with Samuel Smith.[135] According to Plomer he was apprenticed to Moses Pitt, who would have been, though technically a Haberdasher, a most appropriate master. D. F. McKenzie however says he was freed on 6 March 1682 'apparently never formally bound' by Samuel Gellibrand (who had died in 1675).[136] He advertised in the *Term catalogues* from Easter 1682 to Trinity 1707. He entered copies (at first of a rather 'light' nature) from April 1683, but later, with such names as Boyle, Ray, Sydenham and Morton, of a decidedly scientific bent, until 1696. From 1693 copies were entered to him and his future brother-in-law and partner Benjamin Walford. Smith published the *Philosophical Transactions* and was 'printer' (presumably bookseller) to the Royal Society. He died in 1707.

Although Hodgson and Blagden rightly stress the importance of Smith's incoming correspondence, in 375 leaves from 23 March 1683 to 9 October 1692, and describe it as 'an apparently complete series for a period of nine years', it would seem that even the omnivorous Richard Rawlinson[137] did not secure the beginning and end of Smith's transactions. For Smith was already a substantial importer in 1682, and the port book[138] records imports of 27½ cwt,

133 Peter King, Baron King, *Life of John Locke*, new edn (London, 1830), I, pp. 374–87.

134 Hodgson and Blagden 1956, p. 32.

135 Smolenaars and Veenhoff 1997. I am very grateful to Marja Smolenaars and Ann Veenhoff, whose detailed study of Samuel Smith has enabled them to provide me with accurate details for his birth, death and apprenticeship.

136 McKenzie 1974, p. 63.

137 Bodleian, MS. Rawlinson Letters 114.

138 PRO E.190/116/1.

plus some bound books. This was a smaller total than that achieved by some old-established importers like George Wells or Robert Littlebury. Similarly the port book for Christmas 1695 to Christmas 1696[139] (a year for which Smith's correspondence is no longer extant) displays Smith (and Smith and Co., which presumably signifies Smith and Walford) as a major importer, though second in bulk to the French refugee Cailloué. The figures for these two years should caution us against supposing that the spread and detail of Smith's transactions were unusual; he was one bookseller among many. Nevertheless, the letters, summarized according to bookseller and date by Hodgson and Blagden,[140] give a more accurate view of the kind of books destined for the English market than any documents since the ledgers of Christophe Plantin a century earlier. The letters are from twenty-six firms (counting Steven Swaart and his widow, specialists in English books in Amsterdam, as one firm). The centre of the trade is Amsterdam (and Thomas Bennet's smaller and later correspondence confirms this), though many of the cargoes were shipped from Rotterdam. The most copious letters are from the Wetsteins, the Waesberghes and J. D. Zunner of Frankfurt.

The nature of the orders for multiple copies had barely changed since Plantin; they were for small-format editions of the classics. Since the correspondence of other Latin traders has, apart from Bennet's, perished, it is hard to say whether the scientific, medical and legal bias of Smith's orders represent his specialism as bookseller and publisher to the Royal Society. That seems probable. It is also probable that the booksellers who occasionally added orders (for cash or in exchange) to their letters or invoices, were interested in new English scientific books. The single letter from Abraham Wolfgang of 27 July 1688 names books from the Oxford press and publications of other prominent Latin traders. J. D. Zunner sent a substantial order for books by Boyle on 25 May 1684. The growing (though not universal, as Thomas Bennet found) acceptability of English learned publications, even of Greek grammars, on the Continent, is a notable feature of the late seventeenth-century Latin trade, as is the role of Dutch, German and French Protestant booksellers in fostering a two-way trade. Smith also bought extensively at auctions in Holland.[141]

Richard Lapthorne, a Devonian resident in London, has recently been revealed[142] as a highly active agent and book-collector for a fellow-countryman, Richard Coffin of Portledge. He saw the Latin trade from a customer's angle, and was also an assiduous attender at auctions, both on Coffin's behalf and

139 PRO E.190/158/1. 140 Hodgson and Blagden 1956, appendix 4.
141 Smolenaars and Veenhoff 1997, p. 38. 142 Treadwell 1997.

as an amateur dealer. He tried Smith and Walford and Abel Swalle 'which are the great dealers in that sort of learning', unsuccessfully, for a newly published Danish book, and found that Thomas Bennet in fact had it in stock.

Samuel Buckley was characterized by Graham Pollard as 'the last of the old-style Latin Trade importers'.[143] His professional pedigree was immaculate, since he had been apprenticed to Samuel Smith. Like Smith, he was fluent in foreign languages; but while Smith and his partner Walford only issued two catalogues, Buckley brought out four between 1695 and [1700]. After a last book-buying trip to the Continent in 1701 – which included attendance at several auctions in Holland – he left the Latin trade for a new career as a newspaper editor and publisher. This change does not however herald any diminution of the trade, though increases in duty temporarily made it less attractive. Its practice was now widespread. The Stationers had relied on their new Charter of 1684 in attempting to impose their control over Westminster and beyond. In Blagden's words they 'were trying to swim against the tide of trading development',[144] particularly with a government proclaiming its support (on 25 April 1689) for the settlement of French Protestants. The Charter of 1684 was virtually cancelled in 1690, to the great benefit of the booksellers in the Strand and parts westward, and the lapse of the Licensing Acts in 1695 cost the Stationers the rights which, on paper at least, they had enjoyed in limiting imports to the port of London, and confining the trade to *bona fide* Stationers. Pre-publication censorship was at an end.

From 1696 the ledgers of the newly appointed Inspector-General of Customs enable estimates to be made of both import and exports of books. Hodgson and Blagden publish these (where extant) as their appendix 4 up to Christmas 1706, and it is clear that both sides of the trade flourished, and that the appetite of Continental Europe for English books remained keen. The figures are, over the longer term, distorted by the almost continuous state of war with France and swingeing duties on French goods. Nevertheless, the very close cultural links between Britain and France were maintained through Holland by the French emigré booksellers. The Huguetan catalogue which Pierre de Varenne adopted (see below, p.173) to advertise his own wares contained a section of 'Rubro-nigri' – the liturgical books which he had left his own country to avoid. He would still sell them, just as Jan Walteneel had sold the 'rouges et noirs' he bought in Antwerp a hundred years before. Censorship of imported, doctrinally troublesome books was barely a reality in 1595; by 1695 it was abolished.

143 Pollard and Ehrman 1965, p. 97. 144 Blagden 1960, p. 169.

Appendix

Latin trade catalogues

The catalogues in Pollard's table 8[145] are nearly all very rare, and some survive only in a single copy – a fact which suggests that other catalogues may have disappeared completely. But there is another aspect of them so far unremarked; some of those listed were not printed in England. One of the most substantial, Octavian Pulleyn's catalogue of 1657, does not look like an English book, and its opening section, 'Libri catholici', was hardly tactful marketing in 1657. While the catalogues of 1664 and 1677 attributed to Robert Scott seem to be 'ghosts', Pollard himself noted the deleted imprint 'Opera Fr. de Latte, bibliopolæ' on p. 204 of the 1674 catalogue; in other words, it was produced in France, with many section headings in French, and copies probably exist advertising the stock of de Latte or another French bookseller. Moses Pitt's catalogue seems to exist in two states; two Bodleian copies (258.c.36 and Broxb.100.9) have a rather chatty preface by Pitt and a priced list of English books on sigs. D3 and D4. Sig. C1 is a cancel, and the reason for the cancellation is evident from the third Bodleian copy (Johnson d.735(6)). Whoever compiled the original catalogue was offering a copy of Milton's *Pro populo Anglicano defensio*, 'An apology for regicide', specifically called in and suppressed by proclamation (13 August 1660). Furthermore, the printing of Pitt's catalogue reveals the use of a clumsily contrived 'w' – generally indicative of foreign (Dutch or French) origin. Pitt was abroad for a longish period in 1674, visiting Constantine Huygens at the Hague in May.[146]

No later examples of English booksellers' use of catalogues from foreign booksellers have come to light, though Pierre de Varenne took over two catalogues of 1700 and 1701, one certainly, the other probably from the Huguetans, substituting in manuscript his name and address for the originals.[147]

145 Pollard and Ehrman 1965, p. 99.

146 *The correspondence of Henry Oldenburg*, ed. and translated by A. R. and M. B. Hall (Madison, WI, 1965–86), XI, pp.18–22.

147 Bodleian, 4° Z. 21(8,9) Art.

7

Patronage and the printing of learned works for the author

GRAHAM PARRY

Patronage was a significant condition of publication in Elizabethan and early Stuart times.[1] A patron's name gave assurance that the book was a responsible work, accountable to a known figure in public life. The usual procedure involved the author seeking permission from a patron to offer the dedication of a particular work; acceptance implied approval of the subject of the book, and usually meant that the patron was willing to reward the author in some way, usually financial, as an acknowledgement for the honour implied by the dedication. Quite possibly, if the book proved contentious, the patron would offer some kind of protection to the author. By attracting dedications of certain kinds of works, a patron could demonstrate where his interests were most engaged in matters of religion, history, poetry or other aspects of learning. Patronage was widely accepted as a duty of wealth or station, but in Elizabethan times it was not a function that was avidly exercised by the nobility. There was no encouragement from the top. Queen Elizabeth, though the recipient of numerous dedications (some 180 are recorded), seems rarely to have condescended to reward their authors, either financially or by advancement to their careers. Her acceptance was usually their sole reward. Although some reviewers of the Elizabethan scene have deferentially suggested that the Queen had a policy of delegating patronage of letters to her leading noblemen, just as she delegated the patronage of her entertainments to avoid expense to the Exchequer, there is no clear evidence of such a policy. Elizabeth was parsimonious, and seems not to have considered the patronage of authors to be a royal concern. None the less, acceptance of a dedication by the Queen must have encouraged the booksellers to take up the volume in question.

During Elizabeth's reign the court as a whole effectively failed to act as a centre of patronage, and it fell to a few noblemen with an interest in letters to act as patrons in a consciously discriminating way, aware that in France or

1 For the earlier part of the period, see Williams 1962; Parry 1981; Peck 1990; Brown 1993; Marotti 1995: for the later years, see Robinson and Wallis 1975 and 1995–; Griffin 1996.

Italy, or indeed in ancient Rome (to which the whole patronage system looked back), intelligent and generous encouragement of authors had raised a noble and enduring literature. The interrelated families of the Earl of Leicester, Sir Philip Sidney and the Earl of Pembroke performed the functions of patronage most productively, patriotically intent as they were on fostering the growth of humane letters in England. The other figure in this period who stands out for his discriminating patronage is William Cecil, Lord Burghley.[2]

Burghley was Elizabeth's chief minister from 1572 until his death in 1598, and Chancellor of Cambridge University from 1559 onwards. He was a serious promoter of learning in England, like his rival Leicester. He attracted scholars into his service, and his residences at Cecil House in London and Burghley House in Lincolnshire became centres of humanist discussion, modest in comparison to their European equivalents, but significant for England. The educators John Cheke and Roger Ascham were amongst his friends, and the preface of Ascham's principal work *The scholemaster*, dedicated to Cecil by Ascham's widow in 1570, gives us a glimpse of the open-mindedness that made him a responsive patron. 'Though his head be never so full of most weightie affaires of the Realme, yet, at dinner time he doth seeme to lay them always aside: and ever findeth fitte occasion to taulke pleasantlie of other matters, but most gladly of some matter of learning: wherein he will curteslie hear the mind of the meanest at his table.' At that table might be found Arthur Golding, the translator, who dedicated his versions of Caesar, Pomponius Mela and of Leonardo Bruni's history of the Gothic Wars to his patron. Gabriel Harvey was another protégé for a while, as was George Puttenham whose *Art of English poesie* was offered to Cecil in 1589. All told, about ninety books bear Cecil's name as dedicatee,[3] and the large number of authors to whom he offered protection and support furnished him with books that spread right across the curriculum of Renaissance humanism, suitable indeed for the Chancellor of Cambridge. The range of books is strikingly similar to those produced under the patronage of Lord Leicester, who was also a major figure of state and a man concerned to advance learning in England: books on policy and politics (best exemplified by Thomas Chalenor's *De republica Anglorum* of 1579), history ancient and modern, translations of classical texts, works on medicine, astronomy, mathematics and chronology. In matters of religion, Cecil was almost indistinguishable from Leicester: he sponsored translations of Calvin's sermons and commentaries and he attracted English sermons of an orthodox Calvinist character; he encouraged anti-Jesuit polemics by writers such as Meredith Hamner and Anthony

2 For Burghley's patronage, see van Dorsten 1981. 3 Williams 1962.

Munday. Bishop Jewel dedicated his sermons to Cecil. One has a strong sense of Cecil as a pillar of the reformed Church.

Perhaps the most significant volume to be dedicated to Cecil was William Camden's *Britannia* (1586), the historico-topographical survey that had begun as an account of Britain as a province of the Roman Empire and had grown to be a book that traced the complex history of the island from Ancient British times to the Tudor era, a celebration of the antiquity of the nation and the richness of the land. Camden's early sponsors had been Philip Sidney and Fulke Greville, but it was Cecil (the patron of Westminster School where Camden was master) who received the dedication of the Latin first edition, a tribute to his encouragement of humanist scholarship. One might think Queen Elizabeth was the most appropriate dedicatee for such a work, but her lack of bounty towards scholars may have been a disincentive, and Camden's dedication to Burghley has an eloquent warmth of appreciation as he tells how much he owes both to his patron's library and to his patron's enthusiasm for the subject. If Burghley here seems to be envisaged as the chief custodian of the land, that impression was strengthened by John Norden's dedication of his *Speculum Britanniae* in 1593, the beginning of his county-by-county survey of the nation, with maps, that was intended as a development of Camden's work. Burghley favoured Norden's project, and persuaded the Privy Council to approve it, but Norden faltered and his ambition faded. Burghley, however, maintained his eminent role of patron until his death in 1598.

Burghley's patronage was complemented by that of Robert Dudley, Earl of Leicester, who was perhaps the most purposeful and generous of Elizabethan patrons. Eleanor Rosenberg's book *Leicester: patron of letters* has credibly identified a policy of encouraging writers across a wide spectrum in the interests of scholarship and reformation. He encouraged translation in order to fill the almost empty cabinets of English intellectual life with modern works and versions of the classics. Numerous polemical works vindicating the Protestant cause were translated from the French, including John Field's important *A treatise of the Church* from du Mornay's original, and certain of Calvin's sermons translated into English by Anthony Munday and Arthur Golding. Works on medicine, cosmography, horsemanship, military tactics and civil courtesy were printed with Leicester's name as dedicatee. Golding began his translations of *Ovid* for Leicester in 1565. Leicester believed strongly in the virtues of history, both as a way of arousing national pride and in order to inculcate a knowledge of statecraft. He sponsored the publication of Richard Grafton's *Chronicles* in 1563, and also the *Chronicles* of John Stow (1565, further editions 1566, 1570, 1573 and 1575) and Ralph Holinshed (1577 and 1587). He welcomed

Thomas Blundeville's book on the principles of historiography, *The true order and method of wryting and reading hystories*, translated from Italian sources in 1574. Modern Continental history was made available in the translation of Phillipe de Commines's *History* by Thomas Dannett (not published until 1596, but originally dedicated to Leicester) and Thomas Stocker's translation of *The civil warres in the Lowe Countries* in 1583. Support of Calvinistical Protestantism was a high priority for Leicester, as a large number of works defending the reformed Elizabethan Church and published under his patronage testify. The Puritan William Fulke was one of his protégés, bringing out works of commentary and prophecy in the 1560s and 70s; John Rainoldes was another. Works by Calvin and Peter Martyr and Beza were translated under Leicester's auspices, and Calvinist expositions of St Paul and St John. The sermons of the leading Anglican polemicist John Jewel were dedicated jointly to Leicester and Burghley in 1583. Allied to the many works of Protestant defence issued under the protection of Leicester's name were numerous attacks on Catholic, and particularly Jesuit, positions, in the 1580s; Meredith Hamner was the leading protagonist in these assaults.

By means of his extensive patronage, Leicester operated a cultural policy across a broad front, an exceptional achievement amongst the Elizabethan nobility. He seems genuinely to have taken an interest in his protégés, supporting them in numerous ways and advancing their careers where he could. His influential role in Elizabethan politics meant that he was able to place his favoured writers with some ease in the many posts in the administration of church and state that he could command, while his position as Chancellor of the University of Oxford from 1564 onwards allowed him to reward scholars with academic preferment.

In the latter years of Leicester's life, his nephew Sir Philip Sidney began to complement his patronage, but Sidney had neither the political power nor the social status of his uncle, and his early death in 1586 cut short the rise of a new Maecenas.[4] Sidney did, however, specifically encourage literary endeavour, advancing the 'New Poetry' of which he was a proponent by sponsoring the first work of Edmund Spenser to get into print, *The shepherd's calendar* in 1579. Sidney's relations with Spenser show neatly how a patron could help a cultural cause and secure the fortunes of an author: not only did Sidney promote Spenser's poetry, but he also managed to recommend Spenser as secretary to his friend Lord Grey de Wilton when Grey went to Ireland as Lord Deputy in 1580, thus ensuring Spenser's livelihood for the rest of his career. Sidney was

4 Woudhuysen 1996.

sustaining a wide range of intellectual activities at the time of his death, and showed many indications of being a more adventurous patron than Leicester. Many of the dedications he accepted were of a predictable character and similar to works offered to his uncle: books on statecraft, military tactics, horsemanship, medicine; historical accounts of Ireland, Wales, and Turkey; works of Puritan polemic, and anti-Catholic satire.

Evidence of Sidney's modernism, indications of his movement towards the uplands of Renaissance thought, come from his patronage of the wayward genius of Giordano Bruno, neo-platonist, hermeticist, metaphysician and theorist of the plurality of worlds. During Bruno's two-year stay in England, from 1583 to 1585, Sidney was one of his protectors, and gained access to Bruno's esoteric world. Bruno's admiration and gratitude to Sidney are expressed in his Ash Wednesday dialogue, *La cena de le ceneri*, and his dedication of two of his strenuously imaginative works to Sidney shows the two men had formed a vigorous intellectual relationship. *Lo spaccio de la bestia trionfante* (1584) and *De gli eroici furori* (1585) were both published in London with a false Paris imprint as the uneasy Bruno sought to make his movements confusing to authorities in several countries. Their publication in England, however, marked a moment of true internationalism of the kind that Sidney's cultural activities had long aspired to attain.

There were other contacts with Italian writers in England: Alberico Gentili, a Protestant refugee, dedicated his work on International Law, *De legationibus*, to Sidney in 1585, and his brother Scipio offered him paraphrases of the Psalms in classical metres. Sidney had a great admiration for Peter Ramus, the French scholar and logician whom he had met in 1572 in Paris, and he acted as a focus for Ramist works in England. A biography of Ramus was dedicated to him by his French disciple Théophile de Banos, and in 1584 William Temple published his work of Ramist dialectics with Sidney's name as dedicatee. Sidney's letter to Temple acknowledging the book conveys some idea of his generosity to scholars, assuring him 'that whyle I live yow shall have me reddy to make known by my best power that I bear yow good will, and greatly esteem those thinges I conceav in yow. When yow come to London or Court I prai yow let me see yow, mean whyle use me boldli, for I am beholding.'[5] Sidney was as good as his word, and eventually appointed Temple his secretary. Here is a case that shows the substantial reward that a patron could make to a client. Finally, one should not ignore Sidney's support for the rapidly enlarging projects of colonization and exploration that were a feature of his time. A friend of Drake

5 Quoted in Buxton 1954, p. 146.

and Raleigh, Sidney might have become active in colonization ventures had he lived longer; as it is, his patronage of Richard Hakluyt, who dedicated his *Divers voyages touching the discoverie of America* to Sidney in 1582, gave a clear indication of his interests.

After Sidney's hugely lamented death in 1586, his sister Mary (1561–1621), already active as a patron, continued the family tradition, and her marriage to Henry Herbert, second Earl of Pembroke in 1577, and her two sons William and Philip Herbert, third and fourth earls respectively, ensured its continuation.[6] The Sidney and Herbert families exhibited an exceptional concern for the encouragement of imaginative writing – plays, poetry and romance in particular. Shakespeare, Jonson, Massinger, Ford, Daniel and Drayton were all beneficiaries of the Herberts' desire to live in the midst of a flourishing literary culture. Playwrights and poets did occasionally need assistance from their patrons when they ran into trouble with the authorities and ended in prison, in debt or disgrace, but for the most part the significance of Pembroke patronage lay not so much in financial support, hospitality or the provision of sinecures (though all these favours were generously dispensed) but in the reassuring presence of men and women of the highest social rank who offered attention and respect to writers of variable talents right up until the Civil Wars.

The Stuart era was indeed a more friendly time for writers than Elizabethan times. King James was the most published monarch ever to hold the throne: he had written books on theology, statecraft and social issues; he was a poet of modest achievement. He was proud to be an author, and believed that writers contributed to the virtue of a kingdom. His love of plays and masques, exemplified by his support of his company of players the King's Men, must have been a significant factor in the exceptional brilliance of the drama at this time, and contributed to its intellectual vitality, for the possibility of performance at court was a constant stimulus to invention. James was not an active patron of letters in the sense of direct encouragement of authors, but given his pedantic character and his experience of learning, it was possible to believe that books were part of the glory of a kingdom. His relations with Ben Jonson over many years, enigmatic and sometimes strained, and his habit of wide-ranging curiosity, meant that he probably had more familiarity with authors than most monarchs, and possibly greater tolerance for their aspirations.

James's most distinctive involvement with book production was, of course, his patronage of the Authorized Version of the Bible, published in 1611. Initially proposed at the Hampton Court Conference in 1604, the project for a new

6 Brennan 1988; Lewalski 1993, esp. pp. 222–8 and notes.

translation was taken up with enthusiasm by the King, and he assiduously promoted the work. Some fifty biblical scholars and translators were employed, working in six groups and consulting frequently among themselves. The King kept in close touch with the work, providing instructions about the guiding principles: the Bishops' Bible should serve as a model as far as possible, the established ecclesiastical words should be retained. Above all, the language of the translation should be simple and clear and direct, avoiding ambiguity and consequent doctrinal confusion. The work was completed in six years, and dedicated deservedly to King James who had presided over the project and moved it successfully forward.

The most purposeful of Stuart patrons was King James's eldest son, the egregious Prince Henry. He encouraged and rewarded authors from an early age, and seems to have taken a serious interest in their productions. Like Cecil or Leicester, or like his admired Philip Sidney, Prince Henry accepted the dedication of books that reflected his own priorities and interests, and used the patronage of authors as a way of advertising his own agenda in matters of culture and religion. Contemporaries admired him for his heroic spirit, his steadfast Protestantism, his military bearing and for his love of the arts that produced a short-lived Italianate renaissance at his court. Authors of some moral gravity were attracted to him, and their dedications gave the Prince a distinctive character of noble vision and responsibility. George Chapman set the tone with his translations of Homer in 1609 and 1611, the prefatory material of both volumes attributing the full range of Homeric virtues to Prince Henry. Ben Jonson constructed masques that figured the Prince in fantasies of chivalry and romance. Michael Drayton characterized him as the good genius of Great Britain in *Poly-Olbion*, the poetic celebration of the richly historied land that he dedicated to Henry in 1612. Henry was also the presiding spirit of Henry Peacham's emblem book *Minerva Britanna* (1612) that emphasized the Prince's combination of classical and chivalric qualities as a national leader and moral exemplar. Resolute Protestants found their champion in Prince Henry, and dedicated their works calling for aggressive policies against the Catholic powers of Europe and the Jesuit presence at home. Sir Walter Raleigh, imprisoned in the Tower, took it upon himself to instruct the Prince in matters of statecraft and sea-power, and the prince seems to have responded favourably to the man who was the victim of King James's hostility. Raleigh was in the process of writing his immense *History of the world* for Prince Henry, tracing the course of God's providence throughout history, and which no doubt would have culminated in prophecies of the Prince's role in God's designs for mankind, had not Henry died in 1612, causing Raleigh to lay down his pen.

Prince Henry carried out the duties of a patron with some conscientiousness: he found places in his household for approved authors, such as Chapman, Drayton and John Florio, he granted pensions to others, and gave generous words of encouragement. Raleigh believed that the Prince would soon bring about his liberation from prison by interceding with his father. Prince Henry was a truly interactive patron, who understood the national desirability of a flourishing literary culture and the political utility of orchestrating a chorus of voices to express his own developing identity. One can well understand the universal lament among the community of writers and scholars at his unanticipated death in 1612.[7]

No patron so sympathetic to the welfare of writers arose again in the remainder of the century, and royal patronage was never again a significant factor in conditioning the status of authors. Indeed, the phenomenon of the major patron encouraging, protecting and facilitating the publications of a broad range of writers also faded in the seventeenth century. By the end of the third decade, the patronage system was in decline, as one can judge by the case of Ben Jonson, who, even with his reputation as the most excellent poet of the age, found it increasingly difficult to make ends meet. Jonson had long lived off the patronage system from pensions, gifts and hospitality from a number of noble families, and he had a known skill in ingratiating himself with aristocratic women who were susceptible to the arts; but by the 1630s these sources of support were failing, and his later years were impoverished.[8] Jonson's history reminds one that one should not overlook the significance of female patrons in early Stuart times. Mary Herbert, Countess of Pembroke, and sister to Sir Philip Sidney, had developed a remarkable reputation as an encourager of poets and writers from the early 1590s to her death in 1621, as she strove to continue her brother's tradition of fostering the art of letters in England. She gave active help to Samuel Daniel and to meritorious though minor figures such as Abraham Fraunce and Nicholas Breton; she assisted Spenser's rise to fame, and she encouraged her distant relative Sir John Harington to apply himself to poetry. Her status, her kinship and her own example as a writer made her the target of numerous dedications, but close inspection of the dedications and panegyrics addressed to her suggests that most of the authors were motivated by delusive hope: they had no direct acquaintance with her, and received little or no benefit from their offerings. Thomas Nashe, Gabriel Harvey, Barnabe Barnes, Thomas Churchyard, and the musician Thomas Morley all seem to have been celebrators of the Countess's virtues who remained unrewarded and unacknowledged. A

7 For Prince Henry's patronage, see Parry 1981, pp. 64–94, and Strong 1986, pp. 7–70.
8 For Jonson's relations with patrons, see Evans 1989.

more spirited and characterful patron was Lucy, Countess of Bedford, from the Harington family. A witty, thrusting and influential woman, she gave material help through employment or pensions to a number of significant writers. John Florio taught languages in her household, and dedicated to her his translation of Montaigne's *Essays* (1603), and also his dictionary of Italian and English *A worlde of wordes* (1598). She retained Samuel Daniel, as he worked on his philosophical poems on English history; he also dedicated to her the first Stuart masque, *The vision of the twelve goddesses*, in which the Countess had danced at court in 1604. Samuel Daniel benefited from her patronage as dedications of his historical poems witness, and George Chapman and Ben Jonson acknowledged her support. Her most eminent client was John Donne, who enjoyed a somewhat uneasy relationship with her, part friend, part dependent: the relationship between aristocratic patron and needy gentleman writer was almost always uncomfortable. The Countess for her part seems to have enjoyed the intellectual stimulus of her literary transactions, for she was an active judge of poetry, and she wrote verse herself, sometimes engaging in poetic competition with her clients. Her patronage of notable authors brought her a distinctive reputation for wit and advanced taste, assets in the cultural milieu of the Jacobean court. While her favoured poets received material benefits from her patronage, outsiders might sue in vain. The Countess was one of the nine dedicatees chosen by Amelia Lanyer for her book of religious meditations *Salve deus rex Judaeorum* (1611), as she targeted the most literate and religiously disposed ladies of the Jacobean Court for favour;[9] all, however, seem to have ignored her special pleas for assistance as a pious woman deserving encouragement. Effective patronage was not at all easy to secure if one did not already have an entrée to the patron's circle.

The decline of the patronage system by the 1630s – and indeed the unsatisfactory nature of the patron–client relationship as a whole – is feelingly expressed by some disillusioned remarks in Henry Peacham's *The truth of our times* (1638). Peacham was a man of letters with a wide angle on the world; a minor poet, emblematist, commentator on the times, and best known as the author of *The compleat gentleman* (1622). His mediocre talents had been fostered at different times by Prince Henry, the Earl of Dorset and the Earl of Arundel, but he had come to recognize that authors played an insignificant part in their patrons' lives. He advises an aspiring young writer that it is vain to expect 'the favour and support of some great personage for thy preferment', by dedications or panegyrics or by the presentation of a finely bound volume. He may receive a

9 Ezell 1993; Lewalski 1993; Lanyer 1993.

gratuity that will hardly cover his expenses, but as for more substantial aid – preferment, a place, a pension – it will all be airy promise: 'perhaps you shall be willed to come another time, but one occasion or another will so fall out, that come never so often, you loose but your labour, your great patron is not stirring, he is abroad at dinner, he is busy with such a lord; to be short, you and your labour are forgotten'.[10]

During the Civil Wars and throughout the Commonwealth years, aristocratic patronage faded, and authors were obliged to make the best deals they could directly with the booksellers, and live with the pressures of the market. But in the case of large learned and scholarly books, a new method of publication began to emerge, and that was by subscription. The first book published by subscription in England seems to have been the second edition of John Minsheu's *The guide into tongues*, published in 1625,[11] a dictionary in eleven languages. The potential of this system seems not to have been appreciated but in the 1650s publishing by subscription became established as a way of getting important works of scholarship and theology into print.

The career of the industrious antiquarian William Dugdale well illustrates both the problems of and the solution to the publication of scholarly projects on a grand scale.[12] His first production was *Monasticon Anglicanum*, the immense register of monastic foundations, their charters and land-holdings that had been begun in the 1620s by the Yorkshire antiquary Roger Dodsworth under the patronage of Sir Thomas, later Lord, Fairfax, who had provided preferment and pensions to Dodsworth. Dugdale had joined in as a collaborator in 1638, gradually taking on a greater share of the research. By 1653, enough material for two large folio volumes had been assembled, but in the reformist mood of the Commonwealth years, monasteries were a distinctly unfashionable subject. They suggested a sympathy with Catholicism and with a great property-owning Church. Fairfax had backed off from the project in the 1640s. Dodsworth and Dugdale approached the London booksellers with no real optimism, hoping only that they would offer enough money to cover the expenses incurred in transcribing the records and preparing a fair copy of the manuscript. The two authors decided to borrow money to finance the publication of the *Monasticon*, but Dodsworth died in August 1654, leaving Dugdale alone to bear the costs of printing. He was determined that the book should have fine illustrations (an unusual addition to a learned book at that time) as he wanted to record the magnificent buildings that the men of plain religion had tried so hard to destroy.

10 Henry Peacham, *The truth of our times* (London, 1638) pp. 32, 33–4. On Dugdale, see also Barker below, pp. 217–18.
11 F. B. Williams 1948, pp. 755–60.
12 Details of Dugdale's transactions may be found in Hamper 1827.

He hit upon the idea of asking supporters to subscribe the cost of an engraved plate, by Daniel King or Wenceslaus Hollar, at £5 a time, and have their arms and some appropriate words included. Such contributors could be counted on to purchase the printed volume. Subscribing an engraved plate was in effect an inexpensive form of patronage that allowed many individuals to associate themselves with the book, and allowed the book to represent a constituency of readers when it appeared. The first volume of the *Monasticon* contained fifty-two dedicated plates when it was published in 1655. Dugdale paid for the whole cost of the paper and printing of this volume, using the subscription money for the plates partly to offset these costs. He presumably sold numbers of unbound copies to one or more booksellers according to demand, or in some way reached an agreement with London booksellers to market the book for him. He sent only the first volume of the *Monasticon* to the press, hoping that income from volume I would help finance the costs of volume II. The print run is not known, but for such a large folio it was probably 1,000 copies.

At the same time Dugdale was undertaking the equally large task of preparing his *Antiquities of Warwickshire* (1656) for the press. For twenty years Dugdale had been collecting material for this scrupulously researched county history, which addresses the history, economy and social character of the county on a parish by parish basis.

Particular attention was paid to the gentry families of Warwickshire, for these were the people who were most likely to purchase the book, which was copiously illustrated by Hollar, who provided plates of the seats and tombs of significant families. Once more, Dugdale took on himself the whole expense of paper and printing, and also bore the costs of numerous engravings which were not subscribed by well-wishers. Once again, he was the owner and disseminator of the unbound copies, and obliged to make arrangements with booksellers to market the work. Such was his commitment to scholarship that he was willing to fund his expenses from his estate. Dugdale's correspondence shows that in 1658, even as he was paying off his printer for the costs of producing *Warwickshire*, he was also making advance payments towards the expenses of his next project, *The history of St Paul's* (1658), which he had rapidly compiled when he unexpectedly came into possession of large quantities of charters and other documents in 1656. This volume was a work of preservation, for the cathedral had been so badly damaged by Parliamentary troops in the Civil Wars and afterwards, when most of its furnishings were destroyed, that its pre-war condition was only a memory. Hollar once again supplied numerous etchings of the fabric and the monuments, and these plates could be paid for, at £5 a time, by interested parties. Perhaps because St Paul's had been the church of William Laud when he was Bishop of London, there are many Laudian sympathizers identifiable among the patrons of the plates. The publication of a cathedral history by a well-known royalist in Cromwellian times ensured a surge of sentiment in memory of the extinguished Church of England, so that purchasing the book must have been in part a declaration of support for that Church. Again, the book was printed at Dugdale's expense, and marketed by the author. Dugdale's lodgings in London by the late 1650s were becoming a book depository, as unsold copies of his books filled his upper chambers. The second volume of the *Monasticon*, published in 1661, extended this impressive series of scholarly works underwritten by the author and helped along by subscriptions for the plates. It was a heroic record, and testimony to Dugdale's devotion to learning; but it was clearly not a satisfactory method of getting such books into print, for it placed an almost intolerable financial and organizational strain on the author.

The successful way forward lay with a more efficient subscription system organized by sponsors or booksellers. An admirable pioneering example of this method was the Polyglot Bible that was printed between 1654 and 1657 under the general editorship of Brian Walton, later Bishop of Chester. This immensely learned work, which printed texts in nine languages in six large folios, was the supreme work of biblical scholarship in seventeenth-century England, involving the most learned Anglican scholars of the age, and begun in the 1640s at Oxford. By 1652, John Pearson, the eminent divine who also became Bishop of Chester, was soliciting subscriptions and circulating a printed prospectus that carried recommendations from Archbishop Ussher and the lawyer John Selden, along with a note that the project was approved by the Council of State. By the end of 1652, nearly £4,000 had been subscribed, and that sum was doubled the next year. Sympathizers were invited to make free gifts to the project, or to advance money to be repaid by copies of the work.[13] The sum of £10 was required for a set. Further advertising emphasized 'the public good' and 'the honour of the nation'. The Orientalist Abraham Whelock wrote to the Vice-Chancellor of Cambridge suggesting that each college should order a set, and that every nobleman and fellow-commoner at the university place a subscription. The Council of State was approached for a donation of £1,500, which sum was not forthcoming. Even without state help, enough money was raised to publish six noble and complex volumes in three years. The dedication of the Polyglot Bible was a confused and contentious business. Oliver Cromwell the Lord Protector wished to have the dedication, but Brian

13 The publication of the Polyglot Bible is described in Todd 1821. See also Barker below, pp. 218, 648–51.

Walton the chief editor did not want Cromwell to have that honour. Walton resented the fact that the Council of State had made no contribution to the work; he was moreover an Anglican and a Royalist. He himself wanted to dedicate the Bible to the exiled Prince Charles as Charles II of England, but this gesture was deemed too provocative by the other movers of the work. The work appeared without a dedication but with two prefaces, variously present in different copies, one acknowledging the Protector and the Council of State, the other making no mention of these parties, but not mentioning Charles either. The confused preliminaries of the work speak of the tensions and divided loyalties of the time, but the successful appearance of the Polyglot Bible gave a convincing demonstration of the merits of the subscription system.

The method was applied again to the publication of William Somner's Anglo-Saxon Dictionary in 1659, a highly important work of scholarship that made the study of that language accessible for the first time. By the 1670s, when Dr John Fell took over the lease of Oxford University Press and embarked on a career of scholarly publishing, the subscription system was seen as the natural way to launch such books, and Fell was prepared to publish learned works if three hundred subscribers could be found.[14] The subscription system first began to be applied to the publication of substantial literary works (as opposed to scholarly compilations) in the 1650s, when John Ogilby promoted his translation of Virgil, a richly illustrated folio, in this way in 1654. He followed up this successful venture with translations of the *Iliad* and the *Odyssey* published in the same way in 1660 and 1665. The illustrated folio edition of *Paradise lost* was published by subscription in 1688, the first work of English literature to be so marketed. The important translation of *Virgil* by John Dryden, issued in a handsome folio with engravings in 1697, a major event in publishing, firmly established the practice of subscription as the way to bring out significant works of 'polite' literature, as well as scholarship. Though Dryden had three patrons, Lord Normanby for the *Aeneid*, Chesterfield for the *Georgics* and Lord Clifford for the *Pastorals*, their gifts amounted to about £500, half of what Dryden received from the subscribers, who were recruited both by the publisher Jacob Tonson and by the author himself.[15]

The combination of subscription and aristocratic support that accompanied the production of Dryden's *Virgil* expresses the state of affairs at the end of the seventeenth century quite well. Aristocratic patronage was renewed at the Restoration, and remained an important factor in the business of bringing out a work of literature, but it was being supplemented by increasingly strong market

14 See Carter 1975, pp. 49–112, for Fell's activities as publisher of learned works.
15 See Barnard 1963, p. 140, and Barnard 2000.

forces that could be effectively directed by an astute bookseller. Dryden's career is highly instructive in this respect, for as the leading literary figure of his age, producing many kinds of literature – poetry, plays, critical essays, translations – his experience is central to an understanding of author–patron relationships in the Restoration period.[16] He was able to attract a good number of aristocratic patrons during the years from 1660 to 1668, including Lords Dorset, Orrery, Newcastle, Rochester and Mulgrave. These patrons were mostly associated with the Court, and Dryden's many dedications and epistles make clear the reciprocal benefits of patronage at this time. The patrons provided encouragement to Dryden by way of monetary gifts and access to the higher social circles where figures of power and influence were to be met. They provided protection as well as hospitality, and this role became more important as politics became more rancorous, particularly after the intensification caused by the Exclusion Crisis of 1679. Knowledge that a writer had the support of a significant social and political figure made rivals more wary of attacking him in print, or even in person. The gallery of noble patrons that Dryden could appeal to did much to enhance his standing in the literary society of the Restoration years. In return, the patrons received the credit of fostering some of the finer productions of contemporary literature, a reputation for liberality, judgement and taste, and the services, when needed, of a sharp writer for their cause. Beyond the level of aristocratic patronage, but partly as a result of it, Dryden was able to secure two prestigious pension-bearing posts, those of Poet Laureate and Historiographer Royal, that were in the gift of the King. These posts, together with the gifts from patrons, and the financial deals he made with booksellers, ensured Dryden a fair income until 1688.

With the Revolution that year, Dryden, a Tory, a Catholic and a supporter of James II, lost his official positions, and his principal patrons lost their political influence, but he was able to recover his position with the new Whig-dominated Williamite régime. He strengthened his links with one of his old friends and patrons, the Earl of Dorset, who had become a leading Whig politician and Lord Chamberlain to William and Mary's Court. Dorset was himself a poet, and Dryden dedicated to him the masterful 'Essay on Satire' that was placed as an introduction to his translations of Juvenal and Persius in 1693. Dryden turned to another old patron, Lord Mulgrave, now Marquis of Normanby, who although a supporter of the exiled James, had recovered power in the new régime thanks to his friendship with Queen Mary. To him Dryden dedicated the major work of his last years, his translation of the *Aeneid* (1697), the dedication, as long as a

16 For details of Dryden's patronage, see Griffin 1996, pp. 70–98.

book, taking the form of an essay on *Virgil* and the heroic poem.[17] In the years after 1688, Dryden was also concerned to develop a close relationship with the publisher Tonson, who was also a Whig, and who was a dominant figure in the book trade. These figures, patrons and publisher alike, with their Whig sympathies, were willing to respond to the disadvantaged Dryden because he was the finest writer of his time, and they acquired merit, as well as profit in Tonson's case, from their association with him. As already noted, Dryden's *Virgil* was marketed by subscription, as well as being supported by aristocratic patrons. At the end of the century, such patrons were still important, but they needed to be matched by publishers who were willing to show their commitment to an author by offering a mutually advantageous contract. Most significantly for the production of polite literature and scholarship, there now existed a large body of educated readers, ranging from the aristocracy through the gentry to the middle class, who were prepared to put their money forward through subscription, and ensure the viability of a venture. This was the system that would sustain literature and learning for much of the eighteenth century.

17 The circumstances of the production of Dryden's *Virgil* are examined in Barnard 2000.

8
University printing at Oxford and Cambridge

DAVID McKITTERICK

The presses at Cambridge and Oxford in the sixteenth and seventeenth centuries were distinctive. Geographically and commercially they were isolated. Their printers were unlike printers in London in that they could have no everyday dealings with other presses nearby, since there were none. They were privileged. The government of these presses, and of the men who worked them, was unlike that of any press in London. They were protected by university interests. They were all these before they were in any sense learned.

Each town is about fifty miles from London, and though the Thames could be exploited by those wishing to move bulky and heavy quantities of paper between London and Oxford, distance remained an obstacle. For Cambridge, there was no such river, only roads that became muddy and difficult in winter. In some respects, Oxford looked also to the west and to the north and south, at a crossing of the river and on a main route to the Cotswold towns and to Wales. Cambridge was on no such obvious route, and even in the nineteenth century visitors to Britain tended to choose Oxford before Cambridge in planning their tours.

Universities expect textual authority; they require established prices for their books; they expect to exert control. In other words, they require an economic and reliable means of producing texts for teaching and for the promotion of scholarship. These requirements are common to the manufacture of printed books in universities in Britain in the sixteenth and seventeenth centuries and to manuscript books in the University of Bologna three hundred years earlier.[1]

Universities met these needs in various ways. In 1470, the first press in France was established at the Sorbonne, but this never became a university press.[2] At Leiden, Willem Sylvius and his son Karel were succeeded briefly by Plantin when he served as printer to the university between 1583 and 1585, to be followed by his son-in-law Franciscus Raphelengius; in the following century,

1 Destrez 1935; Pollard 1978a; Bataillon, Guyot and Rouse 1988.
2 Veyrin-Forrer 1987, pp.161–87.

various members of the Elsevier family held this position.[3] Again, there was no suggestion of a university press in the sense gradually developed in England. The earliest presses at Oxford and at Cambridge, in the 1470s and the 1520s respectively, were short-lived, coming to an end because the books produced there could not be sold in sufficient quantities to sustain them. Printing was not properly established in either university until the 1580s.

The first printers at the Oxford and Cambridge presses were foreigners, from Germany; much of the manufacture and marketing of books in Britain remained dependent on foreigners or immigrants even at the end of the seventeenth century, when skilled immigrants were recruited to re-establish university printing on a new footing. In the sixteenth century, this foreign dependence prompted the course of events that in 1534 led Henry VIII to grant to the University of Cambridge a privilege to print 'omnimodos libros', all manner of books, and further allowed the university to continue to license booksellers in the town who were strangers, or foreigners. The university argued successfully that foreign skills, and foreign connections in the book trade, were essential.[4]

Yet, despite this licence, no printing took place at Cambridge until 1583, or at Oxford until 1585. Why was this? During much of the intervening period, the universities were under threat. The renaissance of the 1530s at Cambridge was a brief one. The excitement of new colleges at Oxford (Christ Church, 1525; Trinity, 1555; St John's, 1557) and at Cambridge (Magdalene, 1542; Trinity, 1546) was not sustained. Student entries declined in the mid-century, and finances were at a low ebb. At Oxford in the 1550s the entire university population amounted to under 1,200 people.[5] This period was also difficult for libraries. The library founded at Oxford by Sir Thomas Bodley in 1598 was, in his own words, a response to the sight of the old one then lying 'ruined and wast'. At Cambridge, the University Library possessed no works of the Continental reformers until Matthew Parker, Archbishop of Canterbury, presented a systematically chosen working collection in 1574.[6]

Such books as were needed were obtained from abroad, or from London stationers. Likewise, it was assumed that work originating in the two universities would be printed elsewhere. The lectures on Ephesians delivered by Martin Bucer at Cambridge were printed, posthumously, at Basel. The *Lucubrationes* of Walter Haddon, formerly Regius Professor of Civil Law at Cambridge,

3 Van Gulik 1975, pp. 367–93; Voet 1969–72, I, pp. 105–13; Lane *et al.* 1997; Willems 1880.

4 McKitterick 1992, pp. 22–37.

5 James McConica, 'Studies and faculties; introduction', *HUO*, III, pp. 151–6, at p. 153.

6 Oates 1986, pp. 93–118; Leedham-Green and McKitterick 1997, pp. 153–235. See also Leedham-Green and McKitterick, pp. 330, 334–6 below.

were edited by Thomas Hatcher, and printed at London by William Seres in 1567. Demosthenes, edited by Nicholas Carr, Regius Professor of Greek at Cambridge, was printed in 1571 by Henry Denham. The speech delivered to Queen Elizabeth at Woodstock in 1575 by Laurence Humfrey, Vice-Chancellor of Oxford, was printed by Henry Binneman. The lectures by Edward Lively, Regius Professor of Hebrew at Cambridge, on the Old Testament prophets, were printed likewise at London, by George Bishop in 1587. Undergraduate editions of the most basic texts were imported from towns on the Rhine, or from the Low Countries. The necessity of international trade, and particularly of family connections, was daily obvious.

The founders of the new presses at Oxford and Cambridge in the 1580s were both native Englishmen. One, Thomas Thomas, was a former university teacher; the other, Joseph Barnes, was a bookseller at Oxford. Both indicated something of their purpose in their earliest publications: to provide better for study and for teaching. To that end, Thomas edited and then printed a modestly priced edition of Ovid, followed in 1587 by his own Latin dictionary. The parallels with the Estienne family in Paris and Geneva, simultaneously printing and pursuing their scholarly work, were not lost on commentators, notwithstanding the much smaller scale of Thomas's enterprise. In so far as Thomas gained a contemporary national reputation, he was soon named as 'that puritan printer'; and in printing work by William Whitaker, Professor of Divinity, became the means of publishing one of the most influential theologians of his generation, with a European reputation.

These presses were established at a time when the universities were once again expanding, and expanding rapidly. In this we may find some of the reasons for printing at the two English universities at last becoming feasible. A local market, and (crucially) the means to maintain a flow of capital by way of trading links between local stationers and London, meant for the first time that presses could be maintained. At Oxford, Jesus College was founded in 1571. Two new colleges (Emmanuel, 1584; Sidney Sussex, 1596) were founded at Cambridge by the end of the sixteenth century. They came into being at a time when both universities were seeking a new way forward, politically and educationally. There were calls for better and cheaper printing than was available in England at the time. Nicholas Carr, Professor of Greek, and Thomas Hatcher, of King's College, had been forthright in attacking the printing trade.[7] Some of this was the perennial complaint of the scholar against the mechanic, but there was considerable justice in their case.

7 Nicholas Carr, *De scriptorum Britannicorum paucitate*, ed. T. Hatcher (London, 1576).

However, and not surprisingly, the advent of printers in the two university towns was not necessarily welcome. They represented a threat to the comfortable position of the Stationers' Company, whose dominance of printing in England to that point had ensured the prosperity of a coterie of its members. On Cecil's advice, plans to establish a press at Cambridge in the 1570s were abandoned because of the opposition of London stationers. A few years later, Thomas's plans to erect a press were immediately challenged by the Company. Jealousies, and sometimes open warfare, persisted throughout the seventeenth century, modified periodically only by treaties of convenience between London and the two university authorities.

It was partly as a consequence of these disputes that the universities themselves became drawn ever more into running the presses. At first, the presses at Oxford and at Cambridge were private enterprises. Like booksellers or other businessmen in the university towns, the printers had to be licensed by the university, with the respective universities having the added responsibility for licensing what was printed. In this way, what originated as a means of gown controlling town became a financial charge, involving legal fees and other expenses. The universities were obliged to protect their positions against London. It was this need for self-protection that gave the University Printers at Oxford and Cambridge a distinctive character, that made them more than the licensed agents of their universities, and gave them more than simply a title. In defending university interests against London interests, the presses found a distinctive identity that drew them closer to the administrative centres of the universities. At Oxford, this process was consolidated by the deliberate creation of a learned press under Laud. Both Oxford and Cambridge appointed senior members of the university to positions of responsibility. Cambridge appointed an Esquire Bedell (that is, one of its most senior officers) as a University Printer in about 1608, and from 1625 Thomas Buck, his successor at one remove, became a powerful voice in the press's affairs almost until his death in 1670. At Oxford, the law bedell was also to have charge of the press.

As private businessmen, Thomas, Barnes and their successors owned their presses, type and other equipment. They also decided on what was to be printed, on who was to pay for the printing, and on how to share costs. None of these decisions, apart from the licence required from the universities, was other than a private risk, taken if possible in conjunction with a bookseller. Thus, licensed and legally protected by the universities, successive University Printers were in most respects private and independent, meeting their own profits or losses. Prices of the books were also to be set by the university authorities, who thus retained a further measure of control. In the 1620s, the University Printer at

Cambridge, Cantrell Legge, faced financial ruin. Without any subsidy from the university authorities, printers could only work profitably like any other printer, in tandem with booksellers, either in their own town or in London.

From the first, Thomas sought to establish relationships with the more sympathetic London stationers, and especially with Thomas Chard. Barnes, at Oxford, who retired only in 1617, after a prolific career, worked frequently with his son, John Barnes, a London Stationer through whom he gained access to the Frankfurt book fair. But while arrangements might be made for many books to be financed and sold in this way, and especially for those by men such as Whitaker, William Perkins or John Rainolds who enjoyed an international reputation, many of those printed at the university towns could expect only relatively slight sales beyond their immediate locality. At his death in 1588, Thomas still possessed perhaps more than a quarter of an edition of Ramus's *Dialectica* that had been amongst his first books prepared for his university audience.

In order to provide a more sound financial basis, to pay for such essentials as new type, and indeed to subsidize the necessary work for educational purposes (for which the price was controlled), printers sought at various times to print the most popular of all books, and in particular the Bible, the Prayer Book, the metrical Psalms of Sternhold and Hopkins, elementary editions of classical texts, and almanacs. All challenged monopolies held in London either by the King's Printers or by the Stationers' Company. Consequently, the history of university printing in much of the seventeenth century is a tale of legal wrangling, of compromises, of covenants of forbearance with the Stationers' Company, or of trade alliances.

At Cambridge, Thomas's successor John Legate, printed a sixteenmo New Testament probably in 1590, and the Bible in octavo in 1591. These had to be closely modelled typographically on London printings, for they sought exactly the same market, throughout the country, and therefore had to compare in style, format and price. It is a measure of the difficulties encountered both in the trade and in the considerable investment required in printing so long a book as the Bible, that thereafter none was printed at Cambridge until 1629, and none at all was printed at Oxford for many years to come. Compromises with the demands of the Stationers' Company and the King's Printers, accepted by Cambridge in 1629 and by Oxford in 1636/7,[8] limited the powers of the University Printers, but they did provide a working relationship for Bible printing, backed by the authority of the King. In this way, Cambridge was permitted to print the larger

8 For the Cambridge agreement, see Greg 1967, pp. 203–5. The Oxford agreement is printed in Madan 1895–1931, I, pp.285–7; see also Johnson and Gibson 1946, pp.18–39.

formats of the Bible (but not, therefore, the most popular or profitable), the Book of Common Prayer, the Psalms in metre, and the books most used in grammar schools or by undergraduates. The result was that during the early 1630s, the University Printers at Cambridge, Roger Daniel and Thomas Buck, were among the country's principal suppliers of the basic classical texts and other books necessary for the grammar school and undergraduate. The folio Bible printed at Cambridge in 1629 shows many signs of careful revision, and that of 1638, edited by Samuel Ward and others, was referred to as the standard edition until the mid-eighteenth century. Almanac printing, begun by Legge in 1624 and at first hotly disputed by the Stationers' Company, became a further source of profit in one of the most lucrative of all markets, of major importance to the continuing existence of printing in Cambridge until the end of the century.

This acceptance in the more popular market involved a break with past practice. The books printed at the two university presses from the 1580s to the 1620s were on the whole characterized by a conservatism that reflected the universities' own predilections. Lists were dominated by Protestant dogma, by sermons, by theology, and by educational needs. There had been, of course, many exceptions, most obviously John Smith's *Map of Virginia* printed at Oxford in 1612. In Cambridge, for about thirty years from the early 1590s, the press's energies were largely devoted to printing the bestselling sermons of the Puritan William Perkins, or commentaries on the Bible by Andrew Willet. In addition, the two presses had from the beginning served more obviously local purposes, printing university collections of verse or other official documents. The first printed catalogue of the Bodleian Library was printed by Barnes in 1605, and a second in 1620, though this and other learned printing was hindered by lack of appropriate or sufficient type.

After 1629, the press at Cambridge thrived as never before. Supported by the assured income from printing for a predictable and large market, the list of books emanating from the press of Daniel and Buck diversified. Elementary texts of Cicero, Ovid and Demosthenes sat beside standard educational authors such as Corderius, Vives, Spagnuoli and Seton. Winterton's edition of the minor Greek poets, much republished until the end of the century, first appeared in 1635. In the 1630s, too, Buck and Daniel became familiar on the title pages of poetry and other imaginative literature: George Herbert's *Temple*, first published at Cambridge in 1633, some years after its author had left the university for a country parish, went quickly into several editions. A play by Thomas Randolph had been published in 1632, and was printed twice again by 1640; volumes by Phineas Fletcher appeared in the following year, and by

Richard Crashaw in 1634. The death of a member of Christ's College, and the subsequent verses written by a group of his friends, resulted in the printing of Milton's *Lycidas* in 1638. In another vein, Thomas Fuller's *Holie warre* first appeared in 1639, followed in 1642 by *The holy state*. All were works by authors either resident in or having some immediate connection with the university, though these authors tended to be printed subsequently not in Cambridge, but in London.

In Buck and Daniel, the university sought to combine the supervision of a university figure with the practical skill of a Londoner. Buck was a successful college bursar; Daniel had been trained in London. The appearance of many of the books published during these years betrayed Daniel's background in the engraving trade, as well as his ambitions and ideals. Engraved title pages were frequent, and the volumes by Fuller, and John Cruso's *Militarie instructions for the cavallrie* (1632) were heavily illustrated with copperplates. But Buck, the bursar, and Daniel, the craftsman, frequently quarrelled. It seems that Buck took the lead in promoting school books, whereas Daniel was more inclined to printing books which would (in his view) do honour to a university press. Oxford, with two printing houses, and a larger output, seemed to offer a preferable alternative in which the popular and scholarly strands could be separated.[9] It was a dual route that Cambridge never took except for a few years' overlap at the end of the century.

In the early seventeenth century, there was no generally accepted definition of a university press. The most obvious learned presses of individuals such as Amerbach or Froben in Basel, Aldus in Venice, the Estiennes in Paris and Geneva, Colines in Paris, Plantin in Antwerp, or John Day in London, had been private affairs. Institutional presses, most notably that of the Vatican and the Propaganda Fide press, had their own agendas.[10] Though a printer might describe himself as printer to the university, universities did not found presses.

The advent of Archbishop Laud at Oxford was therefore important in an institutional way. No printer in Britain had hitherto attempted a programme such as that by Robert Estienne to print new editions of classical texts from the royal – or any other – library.[11] One of Laud's ambitions was to 'set up a Greek press in London and Oxford'. Later on, he noted that this had been achieved for London, and so he drew attention to the distinction between the two centres, as well as the importance of there being learned printing in both. In London, the King's Printers became the subject for his experiment, and Patrick Young's editions of Nicetas (1637) and of Gilbert Foliot on the Song of

9 McKitterick 1992, p. 174. 10 Barberi 1965, pp. 432–56; Vervliet 1981.
11 Armstrong 1954, especially pp. 131–8.

Songs (1638) were the result. Appointed Chancellor of the University in 1629, Laud determined that the press there should become a learned one, suitably equipped with Greek and oriental types, and committed to the publication of texts from manuscripts in the Bodleian Library (he presented his own very substantial collection mainly of Greek and oriental manuscripts to the library in 1636–40).[12] To some extent he succeeded. The two Oxford printers at the time, John Lichfield and William Turner, were to be treated with the utmost caution: Laud had a low opinion of English printers, 'mechanic craftsmen' who 'for the most part look for profit and saving of labour, caring not at all for the beauty of letters or good and seemly workmanship'; and the patents enjoyed by the university were 'over the Heads' of the King's Printers and the London Stationers.[13]

Laud's statutes of 1634 provided for subsidy, but expected too much of the person to be appointed Architypographus:

> a man thoroughly acquainted with Greek and Latin literature and deeply learned in philological studies. His functions shall be to superintend the printing done in that place and to see that the material and equipment, that is to say, the paper, presses, type, and other implements of this workshop shall be the best of their kind. In all work that comes from the University's public printing office he shall determine size of type, quality of paper, and width of margins, correct correctors' mistakes, and take unremitting care of the good appearance and fine workmanship of the product.[14]

It was an ideal inspired by the reputations of the celebrated learned printers of the sixteenth century. But to expect it regularly, and to expect it of a university official whose other duties consisted of ordinary university administration, was unrealistic.

The Laudian press was to be funded from money received from students on entering the university, and on taking their degrees – the same fund that was to pay for building and maintaining the Schools quadrangle. Besides this, in 1636/7 Oxford reached a covenant of forbearance with the Stationers' Company, whereby the Company was to pay the University £200 a year in return for Oxford's not exercising its right to print the Bible, Lily's grammar and other steady sellers.

In 1633 John Lichfield, who the year before Laud's advent at Oxford had printed the fourth edition of Robert Burton's *Anatomy of melancholy*, now printed the *editio princeps* of the Greek *Epistola ad Corinthios* of Pope Clement I, a text found at the end of the Codex Alexandrinus: the manuscript had arrived in

12 Macray 1890, pp. 83–8. 13 Carter 1975, pp. 29–30. 14 Carter 1975, p. 31.

England only six years previously. In order to further oriental scholarship, the university equipped itself with Hebrew and Arabic matrices from Leiden, some of which were employed by Pococke for his *Specimen historiae Arabum* (1648). In order to meet the demands of mid-century scholarly preoccupations with the Old Testament and its background, more Hebrew was bought from London in 1652. Oxford was gradually accumulating (albeit not entirely satisfactorily, as was soon discovered) a range of types with which to tackle complicated Greek and middle eastern texts.

Laud's attempts at reform of the press were characterized by a lack of flexibility, and by a lack of understanding of how the book trade functioned. His requirements of the University Printer were impracticable from the beginning but he did not live to see the outcome. He was impeached in London in 1640, resigned the chancellorship of the university in 1641, and was executed in 1645. The importance of Oxford as a Royalist headquarters during the Civil War, bringing with it inescapable demands for printed propaganda, and the accidental burning of the printing house in 1644, both hindered the ambitions entertained by Gerard Langbaine (keeper of the university archives from 1644), Patrick Young, James Ussher and others for a learned press. Instead, printing at Oxford was dominated, to an extent quite unlike Cambridge, by proclamations and by political propaganda. Between 1643 and 1645, a weekly royalist newspaper, *Mercurius Aulicus*, was printed by Henry Hall, who later claimed to have been paid nothing for his work.

In so many ways a distraction from learned printing, the Civil War was nonetheless followed by a period in both universities when interest in natural philosophy was encouraged.[15] The Royal Society, founded in London, was in some respects a culmination of these activities, and the links between London and the universities are inevitably reflected in relationships between the printers and booksellers in these centres. Bacon's *Of the advancement and proficience of learning*, translated by Gilbert Watts of Lincoln College and printed at Oxford by Leonard Lichfield for two London booksellers, appeared in 1639–40 and proved to be a cornerstone. Apart from his poems, the Cambridge Platonist Henry More was little printed at Cambridge, though the local bookseller William Morden was energetic in promoting his work amongst London printers. Seth Ward, Professor of Astronomy at Oxford, was printed both in London and Oxford. Slightly later, the medical work of Thomas Willis, appeared likewise in both places. In the 1650s, mathematics was dominated by John Wallis, Professor of Geometry, whose most important work was all printed at

15 Webster 1975, especially pp.144–78.

Oxford. Oriental work has already been mentioned, and learned publishing in this area during the Interregnum is chiefly remarkable for the so-called London Polyglot Bible (1652–8), edited by a team led by Brian Walton of Magdalen College, Oxford, and Peterhouse, Cambridge. Published by subscription, it was printed in six large folio volumes not in either of the university towns, but in London.[16]

While Laud promoted his ideal at Oxford, at Cambridge the concept of a university learned press was worked out only very slowly. Here, there was no such attempt at institutional reform, and public ambitions were less. Attempts to obtain the matrices for Erpenius's oriental types following his death in 1624 proved futile, the equipment remaining at Leiden. When in 1632 a new edition of the Greek New Testament was printed, special type, of a larger size and better designed than that to hand, was cast from matrices borrowed from Oxford. More positively, when the University Librarian, Abraham Whelock, determined that a new edition of Bede should be printed, after manuscripts of the Anglo-Saxon text in the library of Corpus Christi College and the University Library, a special effort was made and new punches were cut.[17] Whelock's edition appeared in 1643, followed by Lambarde's' Αρχαιονομια in 1644. Whelock's skills encompassed Arabic and Persian (in 1632 he was appointed the University's first Professor of Arabic), and the lack of suitable type at Cambridge may have been a discouragement to his publishing. Some of his scholarship is to be seen in the Walton Polyglot Bible; his uncompleted edition of the Gospels in Persian was printed only posthumously, at London in 1657.

The distinction between university and private enterprise had been defined in a material way when in 1619 the University of Oxford accepted the Greek type presented by Sir Henry Savile, used for his folio edition of John Chrysostom printed at Eton in 1610–13. The new types bought subsequently for learned printing at Oxford likewise became the property of the university, not of the printer of the day. They were stored separately, in the old convocation house (a room adjacent to the university church). Under the guidance of the architypographus (from 1658 it was Samuel Clarke, one of the translators of the Walton polyglot), the university would agree to print works, with its own types if appropriate, and paid for partly by the Schools. Books were then published often through the agency of Richard Davis (*fl.* 1646–90), a local bookseller whose career spanned over forty years. Since by this method the

16 For early subscription publishing, see Parry, above, pp. 183–6, 188 and Clapp 1933, Pollard and Ehrman 1965, pp. 178–95.

17 For the background of earlier Anglo-Saxon types, see Lucas 1997, pp. 147–88, and Clement 1997, pp. 192–244.

university could not well increase its capital for further development, it was a process that permitted, but could not encourage, a learned press.

Much of the success of the Cambridge press during this period had been due to Roger Daniel, whose practical ability, connections in the book trade, and sympathy for learned work suited him ideally for his post. The university maintained its supervision partly through (as at Oxford) a system of licensing, but more particularly through Thomas Buck. For many practical purposes, Daniel could be his own man. His printing house was settled in the old Augustinian friary, near the centre of the town yet somewhat removed from the university's centre, but local jealousies, and his royalist sympathies, resulted in his being ejected in 1650, when he retired to London. He was charged with having neglected his work, and this was no more than an excuse. Cambridge preferred to appoint a less ambitious, and perhaps more amenable, person.

Between 1655 and the 1690s, only two men were active printers in Cambridge: John Field and (from 1669) John Hayes. Both were intimately connected with the London book trade, and the focus of attention moved from Cambridge to London. Before his appointment, Field had been much involved in Parliamentary printing, not always profitably. The appointment at Cambridge offered opportunities that had eluded him in London, and particularly the printing of the Bible and other privileged books. The printing of such books escalated. During the Interregnum, Bible printing had no longer been the preserve of a near-monopoly; but one result of a less disciplined and restrictive environment had been widespread concern amongst readers and (for more worldly business reasons) the book trade at the accuracy of the text.[18] The lectern Bible printed by Field in 1658–9 was based on the old text of 1638. It also became, when stock was acquired by the entrepreneurial John Ogilby in 1660, the most lavishly illustrated of all English Bibles published in the seventeenth century: its spectacular visual appearance owed less to Field's printing than to Ogilby's adding double-opening engravings after the most fashionable Italian, Flemish and Dutch painters.[19] Further, cheaper, Bibles followed.

More numerous, and affecting a vastly greater proportion of the population, over half of all sheet almanacs for the entire country were from Field's presses by the mid-1660s.[20] As demand soared for all kinds of almanacs in the following two decades, the fortunes of Field and his successor John Hayes moved with it. Like quantities of school books, they were not for local booksellers, but for the English Stock of the Stationers' Company, the largest publisher in the country. Although in the 1660s and 1670s there continued to appear a supply of learned

18 McKitterick 1992, pp. 319–27; Baillie 1997, pp. 65–91.

19 Schuchard 1975; van Eerde 1976.

20 Blagden 1958b, pp. 107–16; Capp 1979.

and sometimes pioneering books by members of the university, including John Ray's flora of Cambridgeshire (1660–3), John Spencer's work on comparative religion *Dissertatio de Urim et Thummim* (1669), Robert Sheringham's *De Anglorum gentis origine* (1670), Isaac Newton's edition of Varenius *Geographia generalis* (1672), and William Spencer's edition of Origen (1676), most printing was for London booksellers or publishers. Apart from the English Stock, the dominating figure here was George Sawbridge, publisher of Francis Gouldman's Latin dictionary, North's Plutarch (1676), and Schrevelius' *Lexicon manuale* and *Thesaurus graecae*. As treasurer of the English Stock and as a bookseller in his own right, Sawbridge was in a unique position of trust, which he abused blatantly. Shortly after Field's death in 1668 he secured the lease of the Cambridge printing house, and in effect became Hayes's partner. Thus, responsible in his capacity as treasurer of the English Stock, he was able to swindle his London colleagues by allocating orders to himself. The scam lasted more than ten years, and he proved adept in avoiding a final confrontation in London. To members of the university unaware of the extent of these irregularities, the press seemed a scandal on other grounds. As one critic put it, 'Cambridge should be busied about something better than Almanacks, and books for children.'[21] The example of Oxford, where John Fell and the architypographus Samuel Clarke were preparing for fundamental changes, was not to be ignored.

At Cambridge, the privileged books and the ordinary books were printed at the same premises, on the same presses, and by the same men.[22] But at Oxford in 1678 a separate Bible Press was established. This crucial development, which affected the running of the University Press until the twentieth century, came about as a result of a crisis. In 1675, Fell printed a folio Bible and Prayer Book. They were commercial failures. But the university's right to print these books, though of little use to itself in that it failed to sell them, was of potential value to booksellers. In 1678, the right to print Bibles, school books and other privileged books was sublet to a group of wealthy London stationers including Moses Pitt and Thomas Guy, who were thereby enabled to print in defiance of the King's Printers. These stationers, some of them deeply implicated in the thriving trade in unauthorized Bibles from the Netherlands, where Roger Daniel's name was heavily used to mislead, proceeded to print Bibles in large quantities, beginning with a quarto edition in 1679. In a fierce trade war, the price of Bibles collapsed. The smallest format could be had for as little as 1*s*. 4*d*. The Oxford imprint became widely known on Bibles, though the university itself took no financial part in their publication. Exact quantities produced

21 McKitterick 1992, p. 340. 22 McKitterick 1990, pp. 497–516.

at Oxford during this period are not recorded. They included perhaps 40,000 small Bibles and as many Testaments for Ireland alone, but this was a drop in the ocean. In 1679, the King's Printers alleged that the Oxford Press had in hand an edition of 30,000 copies just of a duodecimo New Testament.[23]

For the latter part of the seventeenth century, the name of John Fell, Dean of Christ Church, has become synonymous with learned printing at Oxford.[24] Already embroiled in such projects, in 1669 he wrote of a press 'which I hope by God's blessing may not only prove usefull to us poor Scholars but reflect some reputation and advantage on the Publick'.[25] In 1672, and on the expiry of a covenant of forbearance with the Stationers' Company, the university leased its right to print to Fell and to Thomas Yate, Principal of Brasenose College. Meanwhile, in 1669–70 Fell had been mainly responsible for beginning to obtain type and matrices from Holland; in 1676, Peter de Walpergen, a Dutch typefounder, also arrived in Oxford, at first residing in the Dean's lodgings at Christ Church, where he prepared punches and matrices for new typefaces. Fell proposed a press 'free from mercenary artifices'; but though in this respect his ambition was comparable with Laud's, he broke with the Laudian statutes by insisting on a printer rather than a university administrator or other academic figure. From 1667, the press became the everyday responsibility of John Hall, son of an Oxford printer.

The agenda of proposed books was specific, and ambitious. It included a folio Greek Bible, to be edited from the Codex Alexandrinus, the Targum, the Psalter and Gospels in Coptic, the Greek and Latin fathers, Anglo-Saxon ecclesiastical texts, ancient mathematicians, texts in Syriac, Arabic and Persian, numismatics and natural history.[26] In 1672, when this scheme was drawn up, it seemed as if such a programme was pursuable. The Greek Councils of the Church were already in hand, as were Robert Morison's illustrated herbal, a catalogue of the Arundel marbles, Wood's history of the university and Hyde's great catalogue of the Bodleian Library. Nevertheless, the diversity of subject-matter and language reflected ambitions rather than reality. Fell died in 1686. His own *magnum opus*, an edition of Cyprian, was published in 1682. By then, other projects had been added. The planned Greek New Testament appeared in the end in octavo rather than folio. Robert Plot's highly readable accounts of Oxfordshire and Staffordshire had demonstrated how a learned press could also be accessible to a wider audience than simply an academic one. After Fell's death, the programme he had set in train continued, Hickes's pioneering Old English grammar appearing in 1689. Of a planned eleven volumes of an atlas projected

23 Carter 1975, pp. 93–9. 24 Morison and Carter 1967.
25 Carter 1975, p. 51. 26 Carter 1975, p. 63.

by the London bookseller Moses Pitt, only four appeared, in 1680–3; but though this bears the imprint of Oxford it did not come from Fell's printing house.

Inevitably, the death of so energetic, opinionated, autocratic and commanding a figure required some adjustment. There had since the 1630s been a university committee charged with supervising expenditure on learned printing, using money received in compensation from the Stationers' Company. It was a strictly limited brief. But in 1690, Fell's executors made over to the university all the equipment acquired by him and his partners, and so for the first time the press in Oxford came under the control of the Delegates. The architypographus, John Hall, whose principal duties under Fell had been reflected in his title of warehouse-keeper, remained in everyday supervision until his death in 1707. In a separate development, in 1692 the university leased to the Stationers' Company its rights in printing the Bible and Prayer Book. When the first Bible to be printed under these new arrangements duly appeared in 1695, the new Bible partners styled themselves 'University Printers', but they had no direct connection with learned printing at Oxford. It was a title that more reflected testimony to the university's name than the reality of the situation, and it was to cause grief in the next century when Oxford-printed Bibles proved on occasion to be unduly inaccurate in their texts.

The assumption in 1690 by the Oxford Delegates of the power to print and to publish marks the beginning of the modern University Press. It was, in the words of the Press's official historian, a decision taken by accident.[27]

A similar assumption of responsibility at Cambridge a few years later was no accident. The Syndics (equivalent of the Oxford Delegates), who still today remain charged by the University with the operation of the University Press's printing and publishing, date from 1698. Cambridge had produced no figure such as Fell. There were several in the university who were dismayed to see the university's privilege to print employed on little more than maintaining profits for London booksellers, but their criticism lacked direction. In the 1690s this came to a head, and the principal move for reform came from Richard Bentley, who after graduating from St John's College spent some years as a private tutor and in the course of his duties came to reside at Oxford. There he witnessed at first hand the implications and possibilities of a learned press. The plans he drew up for his own university bear some of the same weaknesses as at Oxford, and in particular a failure to address questions of marketing and of continuing capital investment. But the principles to be applied were the same. A printer was to be engaged, type was to be acquired (it had to be from the Netherlands), and the

27 Carter 1975, p. 143.

libraries of the university contained many manuscripts requiring to be edited. The first book to be printed at the new Cambridge Press was dated 1699.[28]

The two university presses shared the same problems. At different times, and usually by different routes, they each faced the challenges posed by the London printers. But behind these difficulties lay further ones. First, the idea of a university press was a new one. Though universities had indeed, and for centuries, been accustomed to provide books for teaching, there was no tradition of publishing learned works or editions of manuscripts in the college and university libraries. In so far as there was any tradition in the latter, the precursor of the learned university presses was Matthew Parker, who in the 1560s and 1570s oversaw the editing and publication of various manuscripts in his own library bearing on the earlier history of the Church. Though Parker gave books to his university in his lifetime, and bequeathed his library to his college, Corpus Christi, at his death in 1575, other Cambridge fellows did not follow this example. Parker's programme of scholarly publication came from the presses of London: Matthew Paris from Reynold Wolfe in 1571, Aelfric's *Testament of antiquitie* [1566?], the Gospels in Anglo-Saxon (1571) and Asser's life of Alfred (1574) all from John Day, and Thomas Walsingham (1574) from Binneman. Two decades later, in a world less preoccupied with the recovery of an Anglican apologetic, Thomas pursued a quite different policy. It remained for Whelock in the 1640s to return to the manuscripts for which Parker had taken such pains. In Oxford, interest in building on the strengths of library holdings in this way was likewise intermittent, though when it did appear it was stronger, and more effective.

But there was a greater, and more fundamental difficulty in the universities' understanding of what they had licensed or created. In both universities, few people understood that to print and publish a book required more than text, type, press, ink and paper: that it also required the means to propagate, advertise, distribute and sell what had been printed. Arthur Charlett, Master of University College, Oxford, concluded sadly even of the books printed under Fell's guidance, 'the vending of books we never could compasse'.[29] Books printed at Oxford were expensive in comparison with the work of the cheapest London printers, and a venture into school book printing in 1672–3 lasted only a few months.

Relations with the larger extra-academic markets remained unsettled. At Cambridge, agreement with the Stationers' Company permitted a highly

28 McKenzie 1966; McKenzie 1976a, pp. 322–7.

29 Carter 1975, pp. 61, 151.

lucrative trade in printing almanacs, but at Oxford no such agreement was reached. Instead, from 1674 there appeared a distinctive series of elaborately engraved sheet almanacs: again it was a limited achievement in commercial terms, but one that achieved a success and respect of its own.[30] Meanwhile, books from the learned press stayed in print for years. A substantial residue of stock of Morison's herbal, with its costly engraved illustrations, was sold off in 1713 and two years later was in the hands of the London bookseller Paul Vaillant.[31] Though a few Cambridge books printed by Hayes in the last decades of the seventeenth century were published by subscription – as was the case with Barnes's edition of Euripides in 1694 – it was a hazardous undertaking, and was often disliked by the London booksellers who were liable to undermine such enterprise if they could.

By the late 1690s, both universities could boast learned presses, under their own control, run by professional printers, and with provision for their continued existence defined in an institutional manner. At Cambridge, John Hayes died in 1705, and with him died also the long association with the Stationers' Company whereby Cambridge had become little more than a cheap source of poorly printed books for a London publisher. In the hands of the new University Printer, Cornelius Crownfield, the University Press was created in its modern form. Many of the old problems persisted for both universities, but at least the central organization, defined by the direct link of supervisory committee with the academic body, was to remain unchanged in its essence for many years to come.

Finally, how large were the printing houses at Oxford and Cambridge? In the 1580s, in an effort to bring order into the trade and to control competition, the Star Chamber and the Stationers' Company laboured to limit the numbers of printers and of presses. The rules then laid down were frequently broken. In London in 1583 there seem to have been fifty-three presses divided between twenty-three printing houses; by 1615 the aim was to have thirty-three among nineteen.[32] In 1637, twenty-four master printers can be identified, permitted one or more presses each.[33] Such a situation, in which numbers were so strictly controlled for the sake of the profit of a few, placed intolerable demands on the less influential portions of the London book trade and greatly strengthened the case for increased printing at Oxford and Cambridge. At the end of the 1620s, the Stationers complained that there were four or five presses at Cambridge

30 Petter 1974. 31 Gibson and Johnson 1943, pp. 38–9; Carter 1975, p. 238.

32 Greg 1967, pp. 29, 54; Arber, I, p. 248; III, p. 699.

33 Greg 1967, p. 105; *STC* 7757; Arber, IV, pp. 528–36; Treadwell 1987, pp. 143, 156–7.

alone:[34] it was on these presses, at a time when the London presses were artificially limited, that Buck and Daniel built their highly successful business in almanacs and steady-selling educational books as well as in more advanced learning.

When the Bible press was established at Oxford, it was agreed that the London booksellers concerned should keep four presses at work. This soon increased, perhaps to as many as eight or nine. In 1684 there were thirteen presses and two proof presses in all at Oxford, distributed between the Bible press, the learned press, and Leonard Lichfield, as master printer. By the late 1680s, the Bible press may have possessed eleven. In the mid-1690s, the learned press possessed seven. The concentration was the largest in the country. At Cambridge, John Hayes had six presses in use in 1690, most of their time occupied with almanacs, school books or other work for the Stationers' Company. The Oxford and Cambridge Presses worked in competition or in conjunction with perhaps 145 presses distributed among about fifty-five printing houses in London in 1686.[35]

In Oxford and Cambridge, there were no other printers, with whom work could be shared. In London, shared printing was commonplace, and a normal event: it remained so for many years after the close of the period covered by this volume. For printing popular books, as well as for longer ones, it was essential. Exact comparisons between printing in the university towns and in London are not reliable as a guide to the expansion of particular businesses, but the rise in the number of printing presses at the universities over a comparatively short period is remarkable testimony to the increasing inadequacy of the London trade in responding to demand for printed matter.

Ultimately, it was not just a question of distance, of convenience or inconvenience from the London trade. The self-seeking jealousies so frequently aired by the Stationers' Company (and especially by the most powerful members of the English Stock), and by successive King's Printers, were reminders of how effective the university presses could be in encouraging and contributing to the growth in demand for printed books. They were not just learned presses. Had they been such, the Stationers would have tolerated them more readily; indeed, the Company stated as much in the 1580s, the 1630s and the 1690s. Though their strengths emerged only intermittently, in their independence from the London cliques they were always potentially, and sometimes actually, among the most powerful presses in the country.

34 Greg 1967, p. 196. 35 Treadwell 1987, pp. 151, 161.

9

Editing the past: classical and historical scholarship

NICOLAS BARKER

The publication of the bull *Regnans in excelsis* in 1570 had many unexpected side effects, one of which was to inaugurate a native school or habit of scholarship. Isolation in intellectual matters, hitherto the accidental product of geography, was now enforced. If the main and immediate effect was theological, in creating the need for a firm and sustainable base for the Church of England, it also brought about a significant change in thought about the history of the country. With these changes went a new independence of mind (not always beneficial) that spread to classical and legal studies, to mathematics and science – in short, a new approach to the medieval *omne scibile*. Previously, English scholars had felt themselves part of a European commonwealth of letters. Erasmus's English friends, William Grocyn, Thomas Linacre, John Colet, William Lily, Thomas More, looked abroad for company, and for the means of publication. Linacre, like Erasmus, worked at the Aldine press; More's *Utopia* was first published at Louvain, the second edition and his *Epigrammata* by Froben at Basel; Cuthbert Tunstall's *De arte supputandi* was printed and reprinted at Paris. Their work was part of the Erasmian concept of *bonae litterae*, in which textual scholarship was only part, as much devoted to the spread of learning by translation, from Greek to Latin or Latin to the vernacular, and by practical works, such as grammars and manuals. They bought their books abroad, as Bishop Richard Foxe and John Claimond did for Corpus Christi College, Oxford. They saw their primary task as educational: Richard Croke, the first Greek reader at Cambridge, Sir Thomas Smith and Roger Ascham, his successors, and Sir John Cheke, the first Regius Professor of Greek, were all important figures in public life, equally well known abroad.

The book trade, as such, had only a minor role in this. One-and-a-half centuries later, Bishop White Kennett, one of the first English scholars to take a bibliographical interest in the past, observed: 'What else was the reason that most of our old Historians were first printed beyond the seas; but only that cheaper methods and quicker sale made the Editors to gain abroad what they must have lost at home?'[1] The 'Editors' he had in mind were what we would rather call publishers, and it is true that of the 'old Historians' from Bede onwards, only Higden's *Policronicon* was printed in England before the mid-sixteenth century; it was left to foreigners to print the first editions of Geoffrey of Monmouth and Gildas's *De Excidio*.[2] The book trade itself had a different view of the same phenomenon. Archbishop Parker, who did so much to change it, remarked of John Day, his printer, 'loth he and other printers be to printe any Lattin booke, because they will not heare be uttered and for that Bookes printed in Englande be in suspition abroad'.[3] There were, however, other than commercial reasons for this apparent neglect.

Scholarship, in the sense of a critical approach to texts and sources, as opposed to uncritical accumulation, was essentially the new humanistic approach, which had already reached England in the fifteenth century. Poggio Bracciolini had spent four years in England (1419–23), which, if unrewarding to him in terms of manuscript discovery, left their mark on those he met. The other Italians who visited (Piero del Monte, Tito Livio Frulovisi) or wrote manuscripts (Leonardo Bruni, Pier Candido Decembrio) for Humfrey, Duke of Gloucester, reinforced this. At some point, before the middle of the century, the new scepticism confronted the traditional history of Britain that went back to Geoffrey of Monmouth and the 'vetustissimus liber' in which he said he found the tale of Brutus, Albion, Lucius and, most memorable of all, King Arthur. Writing *Granarium* about 1435, John Whethamstede, the humanist abbot of St Albans, listed four reasons for doubting the existence of Brutus, and did not mention Arthur at all. This text did not reach print until 1586, when Camden quoted part of it in the first edition of *Britannia*, but it no doubt represents scholarly opinion then and later in the century. That opinion might have been expected to grow and sweep away the old legendary history with other medieval lumber, as the light of the new learning and then the Reformation spread far and wide over legend and history, sacred and secular. But it did not. Caxton, who printed the *Chronicles of England* and the *Policronicon*, was a firm traditionalist, a position reinforced by the *Morte d'Arthur* in 1485. The date is significant: a legendary descent from Arthur reinforced the Tudor claim to the throne, and the first-born son of Henry VII and Elizabeth of York was deliberately christened Arthur. Thereafter, scepticism about the 'matter of Britain', at least in public, came dangerously close to treason. Loyal chroniclers, from Fabian to Stow, and a

1 In W. Somner, *A treatise of gavelkind* (2nd edn, London, 1726), p. 97.

2 The first edition of Geoffrey of Monmouth was printed by Jodocus Badius at Paris as *Britanniae utriusque Regum et principum origo et gesta insignia* (1508, reprinted 1517); the editor was Ivo Cavellatus, who took a pioneering interest in Celtic history, strangely neglected at the Sorbonne.

3 Oastur 1975, p. 19 (citing BL, Lansdowne MS. 15, no. 50).

new generation of Protestant antiquaries, rebutting Polydore, addressed the task of adapting legend to new circumstances.

Chief of these was John Leland, a scholar of St Paul's School under William Lily, and later at the Universities of Cambridge, Oxford and of Paris, where he met the famous French humanist, Guillaume Budé. He spent the troubled 1530s searching the libraries, especially those of the dispossessed monasteries, for books, especially the forgotten texts of those who had written about Britain. From this grew the further ambition to compile a biographical account of British writers, and the still greater one, the result of all his journeys, to write a topographical description of Britain itself. Able though he was (his Latin poetry was printed in his lifetime and after, and his collections, unpublished, fed generations of later historians), his ambition out ran his ability and ultimately his sanity. His notes remain, a vivid picture of Tudor England, the more so since he took particular interest in the physical remains of the past, from Offa's Dyke to what he firmly believed was Arthur's great seal, then exhibited in Westminster Abbey. Patriotism may have made him credulous, but it gave his narrative an irresistible vigour and charm.

Leland's legacy was confused by controversy. The *Historia majoris Britanniae* of the Scot John Mair, a thorough sceptic in the matter of Brutus and his Scottish equivalent, Scota, published in Paris in 1521, had escaped criticism, since it admitted Arthur. The Italian Polydore Vergil, who came to England in 1502, edited the earliest historical text on Britain, Gildas, *De excidio et conquestu Britanniae*, in 1525.[4] As a result he received the royal commission to write his *Anglica historia*. Though this too was printed abroad (at Basel in 1534), it aroused great criticism, mainly because it treated Arthur as the invention of Geoffrey of Monmouth. Polydore pointed out, reasonably enough, that there was no mention of him in Gildas or other contemporary historians, but nothing, not even admission of the coming of St Joseph of Arimathea to Glastonbury (a post-Galfridan invention that suited current orthodoxy, anxious to find a pre-Roman source for British Christianity), would assuage wounded national pride. When the *Historia Scotorum* of Hector Boece was published in 1527, its divergences, no less legendary, from the British history caused further uproar. All these doubts and differences were now vigorously repudiated by Leland's friend John Bale, who, taking a leaf out of the forged histories of Annius of Viterbo (irresistible in the sixteenth century), put the British history still further back, not just to Brutus but to Noah and the progeny of Japhet.

4 He collated two manuscripts, one belonging to Cuthbert Tunstall, whose chaplain, Robert Ridley, assisted him; this edition has a reasonable claim to be considered the first critical edition of any British historical text.

Paradoxically, then, it was those of an older generation, in scholarly terms, and of the old faith who preserved a critical as well as enquiring approach to the documents and archaeological remains of British history. When the legal antiquary and publisher John Rastell, Thomas More's brother-in-law, came to write *The pastyme of people* (1529), he was equally sceptical of the fabulous history of Britain in general as he was of Arthur's great seal in particular. When George Lily, son of the High Master of St Paul's and chaplain to Cardinal Pole, contributed his 'Anglorum Regum Epitome' to Paolo Giovio's *Descriptio Britanniae* (1548), he completely dismissed the 'Trojan' legend, a view that probably reflects the opinion of the older generation, his father, Colet and More; the map of Britain that he also produced, influential as the first 'modern' depiction of the country, may have been based on the work of More's protégé, the astronomer Nicolaus Kratzer. The best flavour of this humanist critical approach comes from John Twyne's conversation piece, first printed in 1590 but dating back to 1530, when John Foche, the last abbot of St Augustine's, Canterbury, entertained Nicholas Wotton and another monk, just returned from conducting Juan Vives from Louvain to Oxford, with Twyne himself. They talk of the Albionic cliffs, once joined to Europe (so that Vives's Channel crossing would have been unnecessary), and the earliest inhabitants, giants but primitive people, dwellers in caves and clad in skins. The heroic Brutus is dismissed, and so is Geoffrey and his lost book – he should have taken more care of it, if only to clear himself of inventing such tales. Twyne went on to suggest that the second colonists had been Phoenicians; he knew from Vives's commentary on St Augustine's 'City of God' that they had been drawn to Spain by its mineral wealth, whence it was a short step to the tin of Cornwall; he adduced far from implausible philological and ethnographic evidence.[5] No one followed him in this until Aylett Sammes published his extravagant but unfairly maligned *Britannia antiqua illustrata* in 1676.

The isolation enforced by *Regnans in Excelsis* may have curbed this sort of cosmopolitan speculation, but it also brought an end to serious consideration of the old British history. It was not compatible with a new interest, critical in every sense, in the history of Christianity in Britain. When More and Tyndale engaged in controversy, each expected the other to put their arguments to the sharpest test of historic accuracy. Bacon remarked on the impact of Luther, 'enforced to awake all antiquity, to make a party against the present time. So that the ancient authors, both in divinity and humanity, which had long time slept in libraries, began generally to be read and revolved.'[6] For the Anglican

5 Kendrick 1950, pp. 105–7.
6 *Of the proficience and advancement of learning*, ed. B. Montagu (London, 1838), p. 37.

Church in particular, the independent origin of Christianity in Britain was especially important. George Hickes, the greatest scholar of a later age, put it succinctly: 'I know not any work an antiquary can do more serviceable to the Church than this, which will show the faith and other chief doctrines of the English-Saxon Church to be the same as ours, and perfectly answer that never ending question, "Where was your church before Luther?".'[7] The line that stretches from Archbishop Matthew Parker to James Ussher, and from Ussher to Hickes, is one of the most impressive strands in British scholarship, but other interests besides ecclesiastical pointed in the same direction. Interest in the common law stretched back beyond the Norman Conquest, and John Selden wrote in *Analecta Anglo-Britannica*: 'To refer the original of our English laws to the Conquest is a huge Mistake, for they are of far more distant Date.'[8] And besides the Church and the law was a growing body of antiquaries interested in the history of their country, its documents and monuments, for its own sake.

Archbishop Parker's belief in the importance of Anglo-Saxon studies stretched from collecting the manuscripts that he left to Cambridge and Corpus Christi College to an informed interest in their printing with specially cut types, supervised by his printer John Day. But his enduring monument was the editing, with the aid of his chaplain, John Joscelyn, of Ælfric's 'Homilies' and grammar, the tenth-century chronicle and life of King Alfred of Asser, the *Flores historiarum* of 'Matthew of Westminster', Matthew Paris's *Historia major* and the chronicle of Thomas Walsingham, all of which appeared between 1566 and 1574. Publication went hand in hand with his equally systematic attempt to collect and preserve the manuscripts on which the published texts were based. Nor was Parker unique in his determination to explore and publish the relics of the Anglo-Saxon past in the 1560s. William Cecil, Lord Burleigh shared both these interests; returning a manuscript borrowed from his library, Parker wrote 'in the riches whereof... I reioice as moche as thei wer in myn owne. So that thei maye be be preserved within the realme, & not sent over seas by couetose statyoners, or spoyled in the poticarye shoppis.'[9] The interests of the book trade might lie elsewhere, but Archbishop and Secretary of State were at one in this endeavour. Already Laurence Nowell had transcribed, and his protégé William Lambarde published in 1568, the first text of the Old English laws as *Archaeonomia, sive de Priscis Anglorum Legibus*.[10]

7 George Hickes, letter to the Bishop of Bristol, 22 May 1714 (HMC, *Portland*, v. 445; cit. Douglas 1951, p. 19).

8 Douglas 1951, p. 53. 9 Wright 1958a, p. 156.

10 Nowell's collections are in BL, Cotton MSS. Vitell. D. vii and Domit. xviii.

These publications came out while William Camden was at Oxford and during the years of travel that preceded his appointment as master at Westminster School in 1575, the year that Parker died. This inspiration to a naturally curious mind was enhanced by the visit to London in 1577 of Abraham Ortelius, as great an antiquary as geographer, who (as he later recorded) urged him 'to restore Britain to Antiquity and Antiquity to Britain'. This task was to occupy the rest of his life. A major part of it was *Britannia*, the survey of the history and principal features, especially the antiquities, of every part of the realm, that grew from a small octavo in 1586 to a substantial folio by 1607, the last edition to appear in his lifetime. Unlike Leland, who had restricted himself to what he had seen in England and Wales, Camden covered the whole of the British Isles, using information from a growing band of local informants. Gently putting aside the old British history, he was an enthusiast for the Saxon sources made familiar by Parker and Laurence Nowell. *Britannia* became the pole-star of a new generation with a scholarly passion for the history of the country. At once a repository of newly discovered fact and a universal source of reference, it served as a model for many local histories, a genre whose popularity it did much to create.

In the same year that *Britannia* was published, 'divers Gentlemen in London, studious of Antiquities, fram'd themselves into a College or Society of Antiquaries'.[11] They included lawyers, heralds (among them Camden), civil servants and country gentlemen. Of the last, Sir Robert Cotton, come that year from Conington and Cambridge to Westminster (where he had previously been at school under Camden), was to have the greatest influence. Unlike Parker, he had no interest in publication, but devoted his life to preserving, by fair means or foul, documents of historic importance. Better than any one, he knew, as Parker had written to Cecil, 'if this opportunity be not taken in our time, it will not so well be done hereafter'.[12]

Everything was grist to Cotton's mill, from the greatest monuments, the Lindisfarne Gospels and *Beowulf*, to the political papers of his own time. If he did not publish, he was conspicuously generous in lending, too generous for his own good. Raleigh and Bacon were both among his beneficiaries, but *The History of the world*, the *Historie of the raigne of King Henry the Seventh*, still more Hayward's *First part of the life and reign of King Henry the IIII*, were, if commercially successful, politically dangerous. Cotton's possession of state papers and the use he made of them brought about his downfall. But the antiquaries never ceased to be grateful to him. Among those who borrowed manuscripts from

11 Wright 1958b, pp. 180–1.   12 *Correspondence of Matthew Parker*, p. 328.

Cotton was James Ussher, who 'constantly came over to England once in three years, spending one month of the summer in Oxford, another at Cambridge, and the rest of the time in London, spending his time chiefly in the Cottonian Library, the noble and learned master of which affording him free access, not only to that but his own conversation'. In 1622, writing to Ussher, Cotton records the return of eight manuscripts that he had borrowed.[13] He helped Camden with the fifth edition of *Britannia*, and the published works of John Selden, John Speed and John Weever attest his assistance.[14]

Although antiquity owed its largest debt to Parker and Camden, neither was exemplary, judged by modern standards, in their treatment of texts. Both saw themselves as publishers rather than editors in our sense of the word, and a critical judgement of age and authenticity of manuscripts and readings was second to the task of publication; to both, this had an ulterior purpose, Parker's explicit in *De antiquitate Britannicae ecclesiae* (1572),[15] Camden's implicit in the changing shape of *Britannia* as it grew. It was inevitable that Parker's corrupt texts, as yet unreprinted in England, should be included in the collection of English chronicles, *Rerum Britannicarum scriptores vetustiores*, printed by Jerome Commelin at Heidelberg in 1587, and again form part of Camden's *Anglica Hibernica Normannica Cambrica a veteribus scripta* (1603), better remembered for the first printing of much of Giraldus Cambrensis and the chronicle of Robert of Jumièges. A more respectable example was set by Sir Henry Savile, whose *Scriptores post Bedam* (1597) not only printed unpublished texts (if inaccurately transcribed) of William of Malmesbury, Henry of Huntington and Roger Hoveden, but also a part of the Anglo-Saxon chronicle from a manuscript destroyed in the Cottonian Library fire in 1731. Savile's work remained deservedly popular (it was reprinted at Frankfurt in 1601), but his most famous contribution to scholarship, one that achieved a European reputation, was the publication of the complete works of St John Chrysostom at the press he set up at Eton in 1610–13, using Greek types by Pierre Haultin specially purchased for the purpose, which he later left to the University of Oxford.

If other learned works were supplied to the British market from abroad (the imprints of books listed in contemporary inventories and in surviving collections show an interesting diversity of sources), those that were translated into English provide a different index of their penetration. The translations from the Greek and Latin classics published in England are striking, both in number and

13 R. Parr, *The life and times of the most reverend James Ussher, late lord archbishop of Armagh, primate and metropolitan of all Ireland* (London, 1686), pp. 11, 79.

14 In Selden's editions of *Fleta* (1647) and Eadmer's *Historiae novorum* (London, 1623), Speed's *History of Great Britaine* (London, 1611) and Weever's *Ancient funeral monuments* (London, 1631).

15 M. Parker, *De antiquitate Britannicae ecclesiae* (London, 1572), pp. 1–15.

variety, and Philemon Holland made a virtual profession of it (he also translated Camden's *Britannia* into English). Henry Savile's translation of Tacitus found many readers who may have seen in the *Histories* certain parallels with their own times. Among contemporary authors, Erasmus, not surprisingly, leads the field, but Boccaccio, Ficino, Osorius, Ramus and Vives also found translators. Sir Thomas Elyot translated Francesco Patrizi's *De regno et regis institutione* and Sir Thomas More a fragment of Pico della Mirandola. Calvin and Melanchthon both had an obvious vernacular market, as did Agrippa and Paracelsus. The international market for literary texts in Latin also left its mark, with the 'Mantuan', Giovanni Battista Spagnuoli, leading the way, but the native John Owen scarcely less popular. Dedekind, Casimir Sarbiewski, Angerianus, Palingenius and another native with an international reputation, John Barclay, were all translated into English.[16] English editions of the Greek and Latin classics were mainly directed to the school market, but Thomas Farnaby's Juvenal and Persius (1612), Seneca (1613), Martial (1615), Lucan (1618) and Virgil (1634), if intended for the same purpose and selling in edition after edition until well into the eighteenth century, also attracted the generally respectful notice of foreign editors. *Parthenicon Elizabethae Joannae Westoniae, Virginis nobilissimae, poëtriae florentissimae, linguarum plurimarum peritissimae* (Prague, 1605) recalls the career of that *rarissima avis* of British scholarship, Elizabeth Jane Weston, who earned the respectful admiration of Joseph Scaliger.

Savile and Camden died within a year of each other in 1622 and 1623, both leaving important legacies in the endowment of professorial chairs, Camden's at Oxford in history, Savile's in astronomy in both universities. The work that they had begun was continued. Sir Henry Spelman, a founder member of the Society of Antiquaries, had a seminal part in this process. Although much of the work that he did was published only towards the end of his life or after his death, he initiated scholarly study of feudal tenure (eventually published by Edmund Gibson as *Feuds and tenures by knight service* in 1698), instituted philological study of old and middle English, in *Archaeologus in modo glossarii* (1626), and began the work of collecting the records of English church councils, in the first part of *Concilia, decreta, leges, constitutiones, in re ecclesiarum orbis Britannici* (1639), that was eventually to reach fruition in the work of Archbishop Wake and David Wilkins, *Concilia* (1737). By introducing the young William Dugdale to Sir Symon Archer and Lord Hatton, he set him off on a career so rich in publication that it permeated a later generation of antiquarian work as thoroughly as Camden had earlier. Finally, at the end of his life, he founded the

16 Binns 1990.

lectureship at Cambridge for the study of 'domestique Antiquities touching our Church and reviving the Saxon tongue', which by enabling the work of Abraham Whelock and William Somner again had far-reaching influence on Old English studies.

James Ussher was one of those who persuaded Spelman to undertake this last benefaction. In an age of prodigious learned endeavour, Ussher's work was recognized by his contemporaries as outstanding. In editing the *Historia Brittonum* of Nennius he had examined no less than eleven manuscripts, setting a new critical standard for the treatment of the earliest witnesses of British history. He was a major contributor with Selden to *Historiae Anglicanae scriptores decem* (1652), edited by Roger Twysden. Like Parker he was determined to establish roots of a British Church independent of Rome, the theme of *A discourse of the religion anciently practised by the Irish*, published in 1623, two years before his translation to the archbishopric of Armagh, and of his *Treatise on the originall of bishops* (1641). But his main works were singularly free of any bias. His *Britannicarum ecclesiarum antiquitates* (1639) was based on an independent examination of all the sources that carefully distinguished the prejudices of time or place. In *Annales veteris et novi testamenti* (1650–4) he attempted to establish a universal biblical chronology by a comparison of sources, following the *De emendatione temporum* of Joseph Justus Scaliger (who had himself begun to learn Anglo-Saxon in his last years). The *Annales* made Ussher famous throughout Europe, and it was not to be superseded until the archaeological discoveries of the nineteenth century.

John Selden was the other British scholar to have a European reputation. His early work as an orientalist, *De diis Syriis* (1617), was first printed in London, and reprinted at Leiden in 1629 with the oriental types not then available for it in England. His edition of Eadmer's *Historia novorum* (1623) was remarkable for its long essay on Domesday, the first attempt at a comprehensive account of the text, and his contribution to *Analecta Anglo-Britannica* equally laid the basis for understanding Anglo-Saxon political institutions. The *History of tithes* (1618) and *Titles of honor* (1614) dealt with two important themes of medieval and later history. *Mare clausum* (1635) crossed swords with the great Dutch jurist Hugo Grotius, asserting the principle of sovereignty over the sea against Grotius's *Mare liberum*. He was not the only Englishman to do so. The *Adversaria miscellanea posthuma* (1659) of Thomas Gataker, chiefly remembered now for his *Marci Antonini de Rebus suis* (1652), covered a wide range of scholarly subjects, from Hebrew to classical texts. Two chapters dealt with Greek dramatic fragments, on which Grotius had written the standard work, *Excerpta ex tragicis et comicis Graecis*. Despite the title of the second, 'Hugonis Grotii Elogium', Gataker was politely critical, showing where Grotius had confused the text of a quotation with its source, with an equal sense of meaning and metre. If Britain had for a century been preoccupied with local texts and problems, Selden and Gataker showed that it could hold its own in the European arena.

The arrival in 1621 of Francis Junius from Heidelberg to become librarian and tutor in the Earl of Arundel's household provided a reciprocal influence. There he met Selden, at work on *Marmora Arundelliana* (1624), and soon fell under the spell of Anglo-Saxon. In thirty years in the Arundel household he found and read more Anglo-Saxon manuscripts and became more expert in the language than any of his predecessors, although his main work was done after 1651. His nephew Isaac Vossius followed him, invited to England by John Pearson in 1670, with whom he shared an interest in the epistles of St Ignatius; he became a canon of Windsor. Selden had found lack of oriental types a serious drawback, one which dogged the long career of William Bedwell (1563–1632), England's first Arabist, admired by both Isaac Casaubon and Thomas Erpenius.[17] Bedwell came to Semitic languages from mathematics, inspired by Lancelot Browne. Lancelot Andrewes, not yet a bishop, was his first patron, but despite his acquaintance with the book trade, which included Richard Field, John Bill and John Norton, father and son, he was never able to get into print the Arabic lexicon to which he devoted his life. The nearest he came to it was when he went to Holland in 1612, and negotiated with the Raphelengius brothers for the purchase of their Arabic types, only to find them defective when they eventually arrived. His published works, however, included mathematical tables (no small challenge to Field), an Arabic vocabulary and an index of the suras of the Koran. His lexicon was to find a posthumous as well as contemporary fame.

Bedwell's immediate disciples and beneficiaries were Edward Pococke at Oxford and Abraham Whelock at Cambridge, whose *Quattuor Evangeliorum Domini Nostri Jesu Christi versio Persica* (1657) made use of the Polyglot types. Whelock's earlier works appeared at Cambridge, while at Oxford Laud, Chancellor from 1629, set about a similar initiative there. Having persuaded his predecessor, the Earl of Pembroke, to buy the Barocci collection of Greek manuscripts for the Bodleian, he obtained a Charter for the university to print. New types were bought from Holland, and work begun on an edition of the Byzantine chronicle of John Malalas. It was, however, with Henry Savile's types that the first critical text to be published at Oxford was printed in 1633; this was Pope Clement I's *Ad Corinthios epistola prior*, edited by the King's librarian,

17 A. Hamilton, *William Bedwell the Arabist 1563–1632* (Leiden, 1985).

Patrick Young, from the fragments found at the end of the Codex Alexandrinus, given to Charles I in 1628 by the Patriarch Cyril Lucaris, come to discuss the possible union of the Greek and Anglican Churches.

Whelock was chosen by Sir Henry Spelman, who knew his skill in Anglo-Saxon, as his first lecturer; he had already set him the task of compiling a dictionary, following the example of Junius. He now wrote 'We have some Dictionaries MS. already of good use, done by skilful men in that language, all which I endeavour to get drawn into one Body', but 'in the mean tyme you would applie yourself to the antientest Authors of our Church and Church History'.[18] Whelock duly produced in 1643 the *editiones principes* of the Anglo-Saxon Chronicle and of the Saxon text of Bede's Ecclesiastical History, the first English translation of the Latin text of Bede. This remarkable work was reissued the following year with Lambarde's Ἀρχαιονομια, *sive de Priscis Anglorum legibus*, with a supplement by Sir Roger Twysden for the laws of William I and Henry I. The dictionary was not forgotten, and after Whelock's death in 1653 the task passed to William Somner, Registrar of the diocese of Canterbury and neighbour of Sir Edward Dering, at whose house the Surrenden Society (himself, Twysden, Dugdale, Hatton and Thomas Shirley) used to meet. He had already written *A treatise of gavelkind, both name and thing* in 1647, although it was not published until 1660, and compiled the glossary for the *Historiae Anglicanae scriptores decem*. He was allowed to use the stipend that Spelman had provided to further his work, and the *Dictionarium Saxonico-Latino-Anglicum* was finally published in 1659.

By now the Civil War that had swept away Laud had brought about other changes that affected the course of British scholarship. The last great monument of his era was the enormous folio edition of the *Historia major* of Matthew Paris, edited by William Wats, who had helped Spelman with the first part of *Archaeologus* (1626).War now brought to an end the patronage of Lord Arundel: not only Junius, but the Czech engraver, Wenceslaus Hollar, were forced to find other employment. Junius went to Holland, where he met another refugee, Thomas Marshall, then chaplain to the Merchant Adventurers at Dordrecht, formerly Ussher's pupil, who now became his. There Junius published *Caedmonis monachi paraphrasis poetica Geneseos* (1655), the first substantial Anglo-Saxon poetic text (not, in fact, by Caedmon), from the manuscript that he had acquired, and using types that he had cut in Holland. He and Marshall worked together on a diglot version of the Gospels in Anglo-Saxon and Gothic,

18 Douglas 1951, p. 54.

for which again special types were required. After the Restoration Marshall returned to Oxford as fellow of Lincoln College. Junius stayed on to complete their work in 1655,[19] before following Marshall to Oxford where he died in 1677, leaving his manuscripts and types to the university. Arundel's other protegé, Hollar, found another patron in William Dugdale, and between them they now transformed English antiquarian scholarship.

Dugdale had already under Archer's influence embarked on a history of Warwickshire. In 1638 through Spelman, who encouraged them both to collaborate, he met the Yorkshire antiquary, twenty years his senior, Roger Dodsworth, who had long been collecting the remains and documents of monastic foundations in the North. Two years later, he went with Lord Hatton and a herald-painter, Thomas Sedgwick, on a series of journeys to the Midlands and further north, to make a verbal and visual copy of monuments that Hatton, who foresaw the probable results of the Civil War, was determined to record.[20] This made a deep impression on Dugdale, and when war came, he was able, although a strong Royalist, to pursue his work among the public records in London, and also a vigorous correspondence with fellow-antiquaries, especially Dodsworth, rarely able to leave Yorkshire. He put together Dodsworth's collections with Spelman's, adding his own and others', and had as many of the sites as he could skilfully engraved by Hollar. The first volume of *Monasticon Anglicanum* came out in 1654, followed a year later by *The antiquities of Warwickshire illustrated from records, leiger-books, manuscripts, charters, evidences, tombes and armes*, to which Hollar added his prints, among them the great Beauchamp tomb at Warwick and the first depiction of a prehistoric flint implement. The *Monasticon* was at once recognised as the greatest monument of British scholarship yet to appear, rich in documentary evidence of all kinds; other volumes appeared in 1661 and 1673, a set fit to be put against the great French scholarly texts of Duchesne and Mabillon.

Dugdale has been criticized for passing off others' work as his own, but this is to misconstrue his role: he was, in the language of his time, an 'editor'; he it was who brought all this material together, and arranged the subscriptions that paid for plates and printing. It would have been an astonishing achievement in prosperous times, and to have brought it off when he did was miraculous. He followed it with *The history of St Paul's Cathedral* in 1658, the text based on documents that he found; it was largely (and again presciently) illustrated

19 *Quattuor D. N. Jesu Christi Evangeliarum versiones perantiquae duo, Gothica scilicet et Anglo-Saxonica* (Dordrecht, 1665). On Dugdale's subscription publication, see above pp. 183–5.

20 A. Wagner, N. Barker, and A. Payne, *Medieval pageant: Writh's Garter book: the ceremony of Bath and the Earldom of Salisbury roll* (London, 1993), pp. 31–2.

with Hollar's fine architectural plates. After the Restoration, with scholarly communication easier, Dugdale's publications multiplied. Alert to his skill, the promoters of the new Bedford Level engaged him to produce, again with Hollar's help for maps and plates, *The history of imbanking and drayning of divers fenns and marshes* (1662); *Origines juridiciales* came out in 1666, the great *Baronage or historical account of the lives and most memorable actions of our English nobility*, the first historical peerage (again based in part on Dodsworth's collections), in three volumes in 1675–6, *A perfect copy of all summons of the nobility* in 1685. Besides these, he found time to publish continuations of his old friend Sir Henry Spelman's work in *Glossarium archaiologicum* and *Concilia, decreta, leges, constitutiones, in re ecclesiarum orbis Britannici*, both edited by Charles Spelman and himself, in 1664. When he died in 1686, he left a body of work that no other historical writer could equal.

If the Civil War had been the main stimulus of the antiquarian studies whose focus was Dugdale, the plight of the Church of England produced another equally remarkable scholarly enterprise, the Polyglot Bible (see pp. 185–6, 648–51, below). This was only one, if the greatest, of any number of scholarly as well as pastoral enterprises undertaken by the dispossessed clergy, for whom William Chillingworth's *The religion of protestants a safe way of salvation* (1638) offered a hope not brought to fulfilment until the Restoration. Like Dugdale, they found publication difficult, since the traditional lines of communication within the trade were disturbed or broken. If Dugdale took the role of publisher into his own hands, not all the booksellers were passive: the success of Jeremy Taylor was largely achieved by Richard Royston's device of using the spare leaves at the end of the books he published in the 1650s to advertise Taylor's works, an innovation that still remains in frequent use. These difficulties notwithstanding, work proceeded. Edward Pococke, who had learned oriental languages as chaplain to the Turkey Merchants at Aleppo, had his *Specimen historiae Arabum* (1650) printed at Oxford, and followed it with *Porta Mosis*, the commentary on the Talmud of the great thirteenth-century scholar, Moses Maimonides; it was printed as it had been written with the Arabic text in Hebrew letters. The *Opera mathematica*, also printed at Oxford in 1656–7, of John Wallis, Savilian Professor for over fifty years, prefigured the invention of differential calculus and introduced ∞ as the symbol for infinity. In 1658 Edmund Castell borrowed (against a bond of £1,000) William Bedwell's Arabic dictionary for his *Lexicon Heptaglotta* (1669), the most imposing monument of the scholarship that had gone into the Polyglot Bible.[21]

21 Hamilton, *William Bedwell*, p. 93.

The achievements of the seventeenth century shaped the course of sacred and profane scholarship, in the British languages and history and (to an increasing degree) mathematics, astronomy and the other sciences. The Royal Society provided a focus for the latter, and the London trade catered to its *Transactions* as it did to Boyle, Hooke, Evelyn and Newton. The former continued to depend on individual initiative.[22] Laud's ambitions for Oxford were finally realised by John Fell, Dean of Christ Church and Bishop of Oxford. Like Laud, he realised that learning could not hope to rely on the trade, either for printing or publishing; the university must have its own press, and this Fell proceeded to supply, despite opposition from the university itself. He knew that a press must have proper types, and these he got from Holland, persuading Thomas Marshall to return there for the purpose. As to books, Fell's model was Richelieu's Imprimerie Royale, notably its great series of the Byzantine historians. He began, like Laud, with Clement *Ad Corinthios epistola* (1669), but the first great book to appear was a complete collection of the canons of the Eastern Church, Συνοδικον *sive pandectae canonum SS. Apostolorum*, edited by William Beveridge and published in two folio volumes of 1,588 pages in 1672. Over the next fifteen years, a host of learned publications, on Greek astronomy, natural history and topography, Anthony Wood's history of the university and *Marmora Oxoniensia*, Humphrey Prideaux's publication of the antique sculptures and inscriptions given to the university by the second Earl of Arundel, poured out. If the income Fell had hoped would support this academic work from printing privileged books did not materialize, there was no mistaking the quality of what was produced.

Fell's own magnum opus was the works of St Cyprian, listed in his first plan for the press as 'Cyprian according to the very many excellent uncollated Copies we have by us'. Cyprian was a man after his own heart, who had suffered persecution and believed in an independent episcopacy, as he had and did. Fell's edition was exemplary (the last editor, Wilhelm Hartel, found little to change in 1868–71), and it was published in a large folio of 856 pages in 1682. Part of it was a biography of the saint, 'Annales Cyprianici', by John Pearson, Bishop of Chester. He was educated at Eton where Wotton was provost and John Hales a fellow, and the library provided the roots of his great learning. He then followed his father to Queens' College, Cambridge, and into the Church, whose defence occupied the years up to 1660 (*An exposition of the Creed*, his most famous work, was published in 1659). His scholarly career began when he returned to Cambridge, first as Professor of Divinity, then as Master of Trinity College.

22 This point is implicit in Woolf 2000, pp. 245–54.

It was principally distinguished by his *Vindiciae epistolarum S. Ignatii* (1672), a work important not only as a study of a disputed early Christian text but also for the originality with which he treated it. He set out to establish the authenticity of the text, dividing his argument into two sections, the first disposing of the sceptics, the second advancing his own proofs, building his argument, using both historical and philological evidence to support each other. But his most striking display of his mastery of textual criticism came earlier, and like his life of St Cyprian was a contribution to another's book, famous in its time, Thomas Stanley's edition of Aeschylus (1663).[23] His insight into Greek usage was based on a rare familiarity with the scholia and the lexicographers, Hesychius (his *Adversaria Hesychiana* were published by Gaisford in 1844) and the Suda, but his conjectures were even more impressive, revealing an insight into the whole breadth of Greek literature. Only one other man was to achieve this degree of penetration and certainty in seventeenth-century England.

In the 1660s Lincoln College, Oxford, was the cradle of Anglo-Saxon studies; Thomas Marshall, now its Rector, had been joined by George Hickes, who was to revolutionize the study not merely of Anglo-Saxon but all the northern languages. An extraordinary number of those who followed came from the north-west counties. Camden's mother was a Cumbrian woman, Pearson's father came from Kendal, and there was a strong tradition of interest in antiquity in the counties of Lancashire, Westmorland and Cumberland. Sir Daniel Fleming, High Sheriff of Westmorland, and his son George Fleming, Archdeacon of Carlisle, maintained strong family links with Oxford.[24] It was their college, Queen's, that now became so famous for the quantity as well as quality of its scholars that it became known as 'a nest of Saxonists'. The first of these was William Nicolson, the future Bishop of Carlisle and author of *The English historical library*, the first bibliography of British history. He was 'so well skill'd in the Saxon language that Sr Joseph [Williamson] has founded a Saxon Lecture in our Colledge which he reades every Wednesday in Terme time', as Thomas Dixon wrote to Daniel Fleming in 1679.[25] Williamson, Secretary of State and President of the Royal Society, was one of the 'undertakers' who shared with Fell in the establishment of the Press, and was to be the great benefactor of the college. But it was Nicolson's successor, Edward Thwaites, who created the 'nest of Saxonists'. If *Heptateuchus, liber Job et evangelium Nicodemi Anglo-Saxonice* (1698), which revolutionized the study of Ælfric's writings, would have ensured

23 Pearson was first given full credit for this in E. Fraenkel, (ed.), Aeschylus, *Agamemnon* (Oxford, 1950), I, p. 40 and App. II.

24 J. R. Magrath, *The Flemings in Oxford*, I–III, Oxford Historical Society, XLIV, LXII, LXXIX (Oxford, 1904–24).

25 *Ibid.*, I, p. 302.

his reputation, his main work was written in the work his pupils produced, among them Alfred's translation of Boethius, the revised text of Somner's dictionary, and lastly Elizabeth Elstob's edition of Ælfric's *Homily on the birthday of St Gregory* (1709), whose engravings include the portrait of one who was as 'beautiful in his personage' as 'pleasant in his conversation'.

Another who fell under Thwaites's spell was Edmund Gibson, future Bishop of Lincoln and London, who came from Westmorland to Queen's College in 1689, and who produced only in 1692 the first edition of the Anglo-Saxon Chronicle to be based on more than one version; if injudiciously conflated, this provided the first evidence of four of the six different main versions. He now laid the foundations of the historical work that was to dominate the 'Convocation controversy', notably his *Synodus Anglicana* (1702) and *Codex juris ecclesiastici Anglicani* (1713). The other great Westmorland scholar of this age went not to Queen's but to St John's College, Cambridge. John Smith was one of those who contributed to the new enlarged edition of Camden's *Britannia* that Gibson edited in 1695, but his life was devoted to the great edition of Bede's *Ecclesiastical history*, the first critical edition and based on three of the five earliest manuscripts, which finally appeared after his death in 1722.[26] This was the latest of a series of publications of texts, printed at Oxford, on the early history of Britain. William Fulman produced *Rerum Anglicarum scriptores* in 1684, and Thomas Gale followed it with *Historiae Anglicanae scriptores quinque* in the same year, and *Historiae Britanniae, Saxonicae, Anglo-Danicae, scriptores XV* in 1691. If not always as critical as they should be, these were the texts that finally produced accurate versions of Gildas and Nennius, and the first English edition of Eddi's life of St Wilfrid.

Equally important in its time was *Anglia sacra*, the masterpiece of the short life of Henry Wharton. Wharton went from Norfolk to Caius College, Cambridge, in 1680, and thence to Lambeth, under Archbishop Sancroft. After editing an enlarged edition of Ussher's *Historia dogmatica* (1689) and *A treatise proving scripture to be the rule of faith writ by Reginald Pecock* (1688), to which he supplied a glossary of Middle English words, he turned his attention to the documentary history of cathedrals served by monastic houses. 'If such histories could be found of every episcopal see', he wrote, 'a perfect history of our bishops would then arise. I thereupon resolved to dispose them in such order as might effect the design; leaving out miracles, fables, and such like; but retaining their words and correcting their errors, and supplying omissions by notes at the bottom of

26 N. Sykes, *Edmund Gibson, Bishop of London 1669–1748: a study in politics & religion in the eighteenth century* (London, 1926).

the page.'[27] This extraordinarily modern *modus operandi* might seem a recipe for a lifetime of research: Wharton did it in two years. *Anglia Sacra* appeared in two folio volumes in 1691; it contained a prodigious number of new texts, including William of Malmesbury's life of Wulfstan and John of Salisbury's of Anselm; if in his haste he sometimes cut corners, his judgement was rarely at fault; if Mabillon had already edited Osbern's life of Dunstan, it was Wharton who for the first time collected all the texts on his life and put them in context. But his work, which would have added the collegiate cathedrals, was cut short by early death in 1695; what he did lived on to inspire William Stubbs in the nineteenth century. The accuracy of Wharton's work did not conceal the familiar ulterior motive of establishing the independence of the British Church. Not long before, Robert Brady published *An introduction to old English history* (1684), following it with a *History of England* in two volumes (1685, 1700). Regius Professor of Physic at Cambridge and physician in ordinary to Charles II and James II, he was from about 1670 keeper of the records in the Tower, and he knew his charges well. Like Wharton he had an ulterior motive, to defend the royal prerogative, but like him he had a still greater respect for his documents. If constitutional history since the Restoration had revolved round the nature of the 'contract' implicit in the Norman Conquest, Brady took a different line; he might trace the prerogative to Norman origins and Domesday itself, but he based his narrative on documents and complete, not partial, citation. If Wharton inspired Stubbs, Brady anticipated J. H. Round.

Junius's manuscripts had provided Gibson with part of his Anglo-Saxon Chronicle material, and it was Junius's types that provided the means with which the Oxford Press printed Hickes's *Institutiones grammaticae Anglo-Saxonicae, et Moeso-Gothicae* in 1689. Hickes, by now Dean of Worcester, had written this during the troubled times that led to the accession of William III, to whom (though firmly opposed to James II's absolutism) he would not swear the oath of allegiance. He was therefore deprived of his office, and led the rest of his life as one of the non-jurors, initially in peril of his life. His first refuge was with White Kennett, then Vicar of Ambrosden, near Oxford, who had supported the Revolution. He was busy on his own historical work, published by the Oxford Press as *Parochial antiquities attempted in the history of Ambrosden, Burcester and other adjacent parts* in 1695. This was more than parish history, but a deliberate attempt to collect all the documents relating to it, making it 'a microcosm of feudal history'.[28] Kennett was congenial to Hickes, despite their political

27 Wharton to Hugh Todd, 28 Oct. 1689, in Douglas 1951, p. 145.

28 G. Bennett, *White Kennett, Bishop of Peterborough: a study in the political and ecclesiastical history of the early eighteenth century* (London, 1957), p. 162.

difference, and 'to divert him from that Mischief... desired his Instruction in the *Saxon* and *Septentrional* Tongues... It was upon this frequent Discourse and Importunity of Mr *Kennett* that Dr Hicks then and there laid the Foundation of that noble Work which he brought to Perfection in about seven Years after.'[29] The extraordinary circumstances in which *Linguarum veterum septentrionalium thesaurus* was written brought Hickes much other help, help that crossed the lines of political allegiance, all punctually recorded; young scholars were set to work to transcribe, others sent transcriptions of manuscripts otherwise inaccessible from abroad. If Thwaites was 'auctoris adjutor maximus', Sir Andrew Fountaine, owner of a famous library and coin collection, provided the section on Anglo-Saxon coins, and the whole of the third volume was a catalogue of manuscripts in or containing Anglo-Saxon compiled by the young Humfrey Wanley, who was to become the greatest palaeographer of all. The great work in its entirety, when it came out, printed at Oxford again with the Junian types used for Hickes's earlier grammar, was the first attempt, on the grandest scale, of a comparative philology; adding Frankish and Icelandic grammar to Anglo-Saxon, it traced the roots of Old English in north European earth from which it had sprung.

The appearance of Hickes's work in 1703–5 was a European, not merely British, event. The dedication to Prince George of Denmark, husband of Queen Anne, showed how far the work transcended national as well as political boundaries. Runolf Jonas and Johan Peringskiöld had contributed to it, and Leibnitz had put his wide connections at Hickes's disposal. In his 'Dissertatio Epistolaris de Linguarum Veterum Septentrionalium Usu', which made up most of the second volume, he emphasized the importance of charters as a source for Anglo-Saxon history. In this Hickes showed that he had read and fully understood the importance of Jean Mabillon's *De re diplomatica* (1681). Mabillon now read the *Thesaurus* and was equally complimentary; copies were bought for the Escorial and the Biblioteca Laurenziana at Florence.

Thomas Gale was, perhaps, the only other English scholar to enjoy a similar reputation abroad. He too was a Yorkshire man, and from the North Riding, like Hickes; he was perhaps ten years older. He was successively Professor of Greek at Cambridge (1666), High Master of St Paul's School (1672) and Dean of York (1697), he had a high reputation and wide influence in his own time, justified by the range of his publications. He began with editions of the classics, including the *editio princeps* of the original Greek text of Iamblichus's *De Mysteriis*, printed from a manuscript brought to England by Isaac Vossius, invited by

29 W. Newton, *The life of White Kennett* (London, 1730), p. 12.

John Pearson. His *Opuscula mythologica, ethica et physica* (Cambridge, 1670–1; reprinted with wider circulation at Amsterdam, 1688) brought together uncommon Greek texts with his own good Latin translations; his texts were taken from previous editions, without critical assessment. The Latin editors of his time, William Baxter in his Horace (1701) and Thomas Creech's Lucretius (1682), followed the same course. The same was true of the historical texts that Gale published next; both he and William Fulman employed copyists without collating their work against the originals; the long list of errata that Gale provided was clearly the result of belated proof-reading. It was Wharton, his own copyist and a more critical editor, who saw through the false charters of 'Ingulf of Crowland' reprinted with less excuse from Savile's 1596 collection.

But if Gale was not as critical than modern standards would demand, he earned the respect of his contemporaries by the amount of work he produced. Pierre Huet, Bishop of Avranches, as famous for his critical judgement as for the quantity of his work, praised the versatility of Gale's work.[30] One of Huet's works was a treatise on the exact site of the biblical paradise, which Gale translated; through him it came to the hands of a Yorkshire parson, Marmaduke Carver, who produced his learned, *A discourse of the terrestial paradise* (London, 1666). Like Henry Oldenburg and Leibnitz, Gale believed profoundly in scholarly communication. Another exchange came about through Edward Bernard, Savilian Professor at Oxford, and general editor of *Catalogi librorum manuscriptorum Angliae in unum collecti* (1697/8), the collaborative union catalogue of the manuscript resources of British libraries that engaged a large number of British scholars and was the admiration of Europe. Mabillon, anxious to publish Eddi's life of Wilfrid for *Acta ordinis Sancti Benedicti*, pursued the suggestion made by Nicolas Heinsius in *Acta sanctorum* in 1675 that the text must survive in England and found a manuscript in the Cottonian Library, which he published. Gale, meantime, had discovered a more complete manuscript of the text in Salisbury Cathedral, which he published in *Historiae Britannicae, Saxonicae, Anglo-Danicae scriptores xv* in 1691. He was already in correspondence with Mabillon, and now sent him the supplementary material through Bernard, whose work on the *Catalogi* made him a clearing-house for such exchanges, and Mabillon published it with grateful acknowledgement to Gale.[31]

This sort of exchange recalls the international correspondence of Erasmus's time, and Gale maintained the habits and standards of an earlier age; this could lead to misunderstanding, as with Gibson over the 1695 *Britannia*. He believed in encouraging the young, such as the two pupils of Wakefield grammar

30 Nichols 1812–20, IV, p. 542. 31 Douglas 1951, pp. 60–1.

school who went on to greater things. One was John Potter, Regius Professor of Divinity at Oxford and future Archbishop of Canterbury, whose *Archaeologia Graeca* (1697–8) was praised by Gronovius; the other was his opposite as Regius Professor at Cambridge, Richard Bentley. But Gale had another gift, familiar a century before, but less so now. He was a considerable collector of manuscripts and had a fine library of printed books. Among the former were a famous manuscript of Photius (later used by Porson), and two of the Greek New Testament, used by John Mill; he left the library to his son Roger, who bequeathed the manuscripts to Trinity College, Cambridge, but the printed books (many with his notes) were dispersed. There was one other man who had as extensive a library at the time, Gale's exact contemporary Edward Stillingfleet, Dean of St Paul's and later Bishop of Worcester. Stillingfleet was the author of *Origines Britannicae* (1685), a history of 'the British churches from their first plantation to the conversion of the Saxons'; if he followed Ussher in seeking origins independent of Rome, he had a modern critical sense for his sources, dismissing legend and forgery. But Stillingfleet has a greater claim to the gratitude of posterity, for it was he who appointed as tutor to his younger son in 1682 the young Richard Bentley; in his library Bentley read and read, laying the foundations of a learning that none of his predecessors, not even Ussher, could have achieved.

It had been Laud's ambition for the press he had planned for Oxford to print the Byzantine chronicle of John Malalas from the unique Barocci manuscript in the Bodleian Library. After Laud's death Samuel Clarke as 'Architypographus' had pressed forward with it, and Fell, to whom Laud's wishes were sacred, urged the young Humphrey Prideaux to undertake it, but without success. After Fell's death in 1686, the task passed to John Mill, Principal of St Edmund Hall, with William Lloyd, future Bishop of St Asaph, and Humphrey Hody, Stillingfleet's chaplain, by whom it was finally brought out in 1691. The previous year, Mill happened to talk to Bentley, in Oxford with his pupil, about the edition, and invited him to read the proofs and comment on them. Bentley responded with 'Epistola ad Millium', printed as an appendix. It was a series of brilliant dissertations, displaying an equal depth of reading and philological insight on subjects ranging from Orphic theology to tragic scansion. Bentley's second masterpiece also came as a result of an invitation, from his friend William Wotton, anxious to disprove Sir William Temple's belief in the antiquity and therefore merit of the 'Epistles of Phalaris'. The argument was again philological and based on Bentley's extraordinarily wide reading. The sixth-century tyrant writes in Attic not his natural Doric; he refers to Thericlean cups more than a century before the lifetime of the potter Thericles, and quotes Euripides long before the poet lived. All this was delivered with a vigour that induced irritation and provoked attack, a response that called for a second edition of *A dissertation on the epistles of Phalaris* over four times as long as the first; every absurdity, ancient or modern, was pursued and annihilated. It was an achievement that Bentley equalled but never surpassed.

The last work of seventeenth-century British scholarship was the first of the new century. In 1675 Fell had brought out an edition of the Greek New Testament with Gale's help, including readings from over a hundred manuscripts. But he was not satisfied, and bestowed the task of a still more thorough recension of all the known witnesses in every language on John Mill. This was in 1678. For thirty years Mill laboured on; Bentley had found the text almost complete, but the 'prolegomena', summarizing the sources and providing a rationale of the text, required a gigantic effort, not to be completed until March 1707. Three months later Mill died. His monument lay in the 30,000 variant readings that he had amassed. The number shocked some of his contemporaries but not Bentley, who wrote in his *Remarks upon a late discourse of free-thinking* (by Anthony Collins): 'Make your 30,000 as many more, if numbers of Copies can ever reach that Sum: all the better to a knowing and serious Reader, who is thereby more richly furnish'd to select what he sees Genuine.'[32] Bentley's own plan for an edition went back to his days in Stillingfleet's household, when he wrote 'a sort of *Hexapla*, a thick volume in quarto', in which he wrote every word in the Hebrew Bible, with against each the interpretations in all the different languages and early commentators. His ultimate plan was

> to give an edition of the Greek testament exactly as it was in the best examplers at the time of the Council of Nice; so that there shall not be twenty words, not even particles, difference; and this shall carry its own demonstration in every verse, which I affirm cannot be so done of any other ancient book, Greek or Latin; so that this book, which, by the present management, is thought the most uncertain, shall have a testimony of certainty above all other books whatever, and an end be put to all Various Lections now and hereafter.[33]

'Iuxta exemplar Millianum' remained to canonize Mill's edition into the last century, but Bentley's, which reached 'Proposals' (1720) that bore the name of his collator, John Walker, never came to fruition. He alone could have done it, and with it British scholarship would have come of age. If rough with his opponents, Bentley was generous in praise of those whose work he could admire, like that on Ignatius of 'the most excellent Bishop Pearson',

32 R. Bentley, *Remarks upon a late discourse of free-thinking* (London, 1713), p. 76.

33 Letter to Archbishop Wake, 15 April 1716; quoted, A. Fox, *John Mill and Richard Bentley: a study of the textual criticism of the New Testament 1675–1729* (Oxford, 1954), p. 118.

'for though it has not pass'd the Hand of the Author; yet it's in every way worthy of him, for the very Dust of his Writings is Gold'.[34] Memorable words indeed, so memorable that Stubbs, contemplating the heroic figures of the Convocation controversy, Gibson and Kennett, Nicolson and Wake, heirs of Parker and Ussher, Laud, Fell and Hickes, unconsciously repeated them: 'The very dust of their writings is gold.'[35] If not every one of these heroes was touched with genius, 'An air of personal distinction surrounded them, and they were fashioned in no common mould.'[36] It was, indeed, a golden age of British scholarship.

34 R. Bentley, *A dissertation on the epistles of Phalaris* (2nd edn, London, 1699), pp. 424–5.
35 W. Stubbs, *Seventeen lectures* (Oxford, 1900), p. 381. 36 Douglas 1951, p. 283.

10

Maps and Atlases

LAURENCE WORMS

The production of printed maps and atlases in the British Isles has long been a specialized activity standing somewhat apart from the generality of book production. This has to a large extent been true ever since maps first began to appear as illustrations in London-printed books of the mid-sixteenth century. The reasons for this were primarily technical. Map publishing required skills in making and printing blocks or plates quite separate from those involved in the setting and printing of type. Map publishers were noticeably earlier than the book trade at large to adopt intaglio printing from engraved metal plates, a factor that from the beginning set them apart, for intaglio plates (unlike woodcuts which could be printed alongside ordinary letterpress) required a quite different type of printing press (the 'rolling-press') and, at least to some extent, specialized inks and papers. A further difference is that the trade in maps and atlases is inherently international, with maps requiring little in the way of translation. This led to extreme vulnerability to overseas competition, but also to extensive and in some ways atypical interrelationships between members of the domestic trade and their counterparts abroad.

The map trade is itself difficult to define. Individual maps might be sold separately, either in single sheets or as several sheets joined to make a wall map for display. Maps might also appear as book illustrations or as part of an atlas (here very loosely defined as any production of which the maps form an essential feature). Many survive only as part of a composite 'atlas factice' of maps from different sources assembled or 'published' in non-standard form. In such various ways they might come to be sold either by their surveyor, draughtsman or engraver, by a more or less specialist mapseller, by a maker of scientific instruments, by a bookseller, or by a printseller also stocking a wider range of engraved material. In terms of a study of the period this makes for much fragmentation. Even from the start, the map trade (however defined), although almost exclusively restricted to London throughout the period, spilled out from the usual and comparatively well-documented confines of the Stationers' Company.

Mapmakers and publishers are found who were nominally Grocers, Merchant Taylors, Leathersellers, Drapers or Weavers. This was in part historical accident, but it was perhaps also that the Stationers had less to offer purveyors of maps. The physical ownership of elaborately engraved and expensive printing-plates was of itself usually sufficient protection of copyright – and major projects in any case generally received the specific protection of a royal privilege. The censorship of maps, perhaps oddly in a fractious age, was rarely a concern of the authorities and, from the Stationers' side, there was perhaps little interest in an often marginal and unprofitable activity. The lack of overall coherence that regular affiliation to the Stationers might have provided has hindered studies of the map trade to the extent that many basic biographical sources are as yet unknown or untapped.[1] For some of the reasons already touched upon, the bibliographical aspect of maps and atlases is also fraught with unusual difficulties of analysis and dating.[2] Survival rates too are poor, horrendously so in the case of separately printed maps. Yet, however that may be, the surviving maps and atlases of this period offer some of its richest and most rewarding study.

The precursors

The use of maps was a relatively new phenomenon in the sixteenth century. There is little evidence even of the vocabulary – 'map', 'plat', 'plot', 'plan', 'chart' – being used in English, at least in cartographic senses, before this time, while 'atlas' itself was not a term that became familiar until the following century.[3] In 1557 maps were still little used even for the purposes of surveying or navigation. That they came into wider use was partly a matter of improved mapping theory and technique, but the use of printing to disseminate multiple copies was a crucial factor. The history of map printing in the British Isles before this date is simply told: there was virtually none. Caxton included diagrams of the medieval world in *The myrrour of the worlde* 1481 (*STC* 24762),[4] but with the exception of three woodcut battle plans in William Patten, *The expedicion into Scotlãde of the most woorthely fortunate prince Edward, Duke of Soomerset*... 1548, published by Richard Grafton, the only other maps known as book illustrations are the woodcut map of the Coverdale Bible (almost certainly printed abroad)

1 The most recent and reliable biographical summaries are given in Skelton 1970 and Tyacke 1978.

2 Tyacke 1992, pp. 130–41.

3 In their cartographic senses the *OED* gives 'carte' (or 'carete') 1502, with the form 'chart' 1571; 'plat' 1511; 'map' 1527 (although 'mapamonde' is found in Chaucer); 'plot' 1551; and 'plan' not until 1678. Some slightly earlier instances are now known.

4 Campbell 1987, nos. 67–8.

1535 (*STC* 2063.3)[5] and similar woodcut maps in New Testaments published by Reyner Wolfe in 1549 and Richard Jugge in 1552–3 (*STC* 2858, 2867, 2869–70).[6] There are suggestions of printed maps no longer extant, the best-documented of which are John Rastell's 110 'mappis of Europa', listed in his inventory of 1538,[7] and a world map by Sebastian Cabot, reported by Hakluyt to have been 'cut' by Clement Adams in about 1549, but the only surviving separately published maps are the wall maps of Spain and the British Isles (*STC* 11713.5, 11718.7) produced in London by the Flemish surgeon and instrument maker Thomas Geminus.[8] Dated 1555, they signal the early adoption in England of intaglio map printing from copperplates.

Early imports

This modest tally does not of course indicate the full extent of maps available. Manuscript maps were already increasingly being used for administrative and military purposes and there is considerable evidence for the circulation of maps and atlases printed abroad.[9] Specific instances of such imports are known, with surviving documentation showing the London bookseller Nicholas England taking a consignment of forty-three maps from Christopher Plantin of Antwerp in 1558. Similar shipments are later recorded to Plantin's London agent, Jean Desserans, and various other booksellers including George Bishop and Ascanius de Renialme.[10] The two great international figures of late sixteenth-century cartography, Abraham Ortelius (1528–98) and Gerard Mercator (1512–94), who produced in the Netherlands the first modern world atlases – Ortelius, *Theatrum orbis terrarum*, Antwerp 1570, and Mercator, *Atlas sive cosmographicae meditationes*..., Duisburg 1585–95 (the latter using the word 'atlas' to describe a collection of maps for the first time) – had professional and family ties with London. Their maps and atlases could readily be obtained there and such imports of Dutch and Flemish (and later French) material were to remain a pervasive feature of the trade throughout the period under review.

Early Elizabethan maps

The example of Geminus seems to have stimulated a brief flurry of similar wall maps. Records remain of two such maps of London itself. The first, dating from about 1560 and generally known as the 'lost' map, survives only in the form of

5 Ingram 1993, pp. 26–31. 6 Delano-Smith and Ingram 1991. 7 Roberts 1979.
8 Karrow 1993, pp. 250–4. 9 Delano-Smith 1995, pp. 67–93. 10 Clair 1959, pp. 28–45.

three of the original copper printing-plates.[11] What is probably a separate 'carde of London' (together with an unidentified 'mappe of Englonde and Skotlande') was entered for copyright at Stationers' Hall between 1562 and 1563 by the French refugee Giles Godet.[12] This may well be *Civitas Londinum* (*STC* 194.5), a woodcut wall map long erroneously attributed to Ralph Agas, that although only surviving in later states, is datable from internal evidence to just this time. The last of this group, also once 'lost', is Anthony Jenkinson's striking map of Russia, engraved in London by Nicholas Reynolds in 1562.[13] The unique surviving example, recently discovered in Poland, now stands as the earliest surviving wall map by an English mapmaker.

This first flowering of wall-map production seems to have petered out, but maps were beginning to appear as book illustrations with more regularity. Richard Jugge, after a hiatus under Mary, continued his map-illustrated Bibles and over sixty editions of London Bibles with maps were to appear before 1600, with an Edinburgh example from 1576–9 (*STC* 2125). Jugge also published a translation of Martin Cortés, *The arte of navigation* 1561, containing what is generally regarded as the earliest English map of the New World.[14] William Cuningham, *The cosmographical glasse, conteinyng the pleasant principles of cosmographie, geographie, hydrographie, or nauigation*... 1559, published by John Day, has a woodcut map of Norwich, the earliest English printed town plan. Copperplate maps for illustration made their first appearance with an engraved title to the *Stirpium aduerseria noua, perfacilis vestigatio* of Petrus Peña and Matthias de l'Obel 1570 (*STC* 19595). Jugge's 'Bishops' Bible' 1572 (*STC* 2107) has a particularly admired map engraved by the instrument maker Humphrey Cole, while an equally attractive coloured map of Cambridge by Richard Lyne appeared in Day's edition of John Caius, *De antiquitate Cantabrigiensis Academiae libri duo* 1574.

The first national atlases

Although increasing in numbers, such maps remained unusual. It is against this background that the first English atlas, the Christopher Saxton atlas of England and Wales of 1579 (*STC* 21805.1), needs be set (plate 10.1).[15] In cartographic

11 Howgego 1978, no. 1. Marks 1964. The third plate was discovered as this chapter was being prepared for press: the circumstance of its discovery in Germany probably tips the balance in favour of the view that the map was engraved outside England.

12 Arber, I, pp. 90–1, 211–13. Howgego 1978, no. 8.

13 Karrow 1993, pp. 317–20.

14 But see Burden 1996, no. 23, for a possibly earlier example.

15 Skelton 1970, no. 1. Ravenhill 1992.

terms the full survey of an entire country was itself a new development, with no comparable national atlas having yet been produced elsewhere. Perhaps arising from a proposal made by Laurence Nowell in 1563,[16] this daunting undertaking was commissioned by Thomas Seckford, Master of the Court of Requests, almost certainly at the behest of Lord Burghley. This was clearly in some manner an official exercise and Saxton (*fl.*1570–1610),[17] a previously obscure Yorkshire surveyor, received 'placarts' from the Privy Council requiring local authorities to render him assistance. His method, perhaps an early form of triangulation,[18] was of an accuracy that took England for a time to the forefront of European cartography. In terms of book production, the completed atlas, with thirty-five folio maps meticulously engraved in a flamboyant strapwork style between 1574 and 1579, was a larger and more elaborate book than any previously produced in the British Isles. It set a precedent for a new and distinct publishing genre, the county-atlas, that publishers were to imitate and attempt to emulate until the nineteenth century. Most of the engraving, and probably the printing, was undertaken by craftsmen trained abroad, but the assumption must be that Saxton himself oversaw its distribution. A ten-year privilege was granted to him for this purpose in 1577 and there is no apparent link with any regular member of the book trade. The atlas was followed by his magnificent twenty-sheet wall map of England and Wales, *Britannia insularum in oceano maximo*..., completed in 1583,[19] but the remainder of Saxton's career was concerned in the production of manuscript estate-maps, a new demand for which his atlas seems to have galvanized if not actually created.

Some measure of the swiftness and maturity of his achievement (and of Seckford's generosity as patron) is supplied by comparison with the somewhat later first national atlases of Scotland and Ireland. The Scottish divine Timothy Pont (*fl.* 1574–1611) began his survey of Scotland perhaps as early as the 1580s, but, lacking similar patronage to Saxton, only a single map may plausibly have been published in his lifetime (*A new description of the shyres Lothian and Linlitquo* engraved in Amsterdam before 1613 at the expense of the Edinburgh bookseller Andro Hart). The remainder of his work, completed by others, did not reach print until 1654, when it was published at Amsterdam by the eminent Dutch cartographer Joan Blaeu. Only 'after such troubles as the mind shudders to remember', as the preface remarks, did it finally take its place alongside Saxton.[20] Its eventual publication coincided exactly with the contracting of Sir William Petty (1623–87) in 1654 to undertake a survey of Ireland, principally

16 Barber 1983, pp. 16–21. 17 Evans and Lawrence 1979. 18 Ravenhill 1983.
19 Shirley 1980, no. 137. 20 Moir 1973–83, I, pp. 37–53.

for redistributing land forfeited in the wake of Cromwell's reconquest. Despite the limitations of his commission, Petty seems from the start to have intended privately to produce a full-scale atlas. The survey was largely completed by 1656 but, following the Pont precedent, it was to take thirty years and to cost Petty 'near £1000 to have it engraved in Amsterdam' before the finished atlas was privately published in London as *Hiberniae delineatio* [1685].[21]

The 'Waggoner'

The second English atlas, an edition of Lucas Waghenaer's sea charts published as *The mariners mirrour* in 1588, was produced at the direct behest of the Privy Council, with the Clerk to the Council, Anthony Ashley, translating the text from the original Dutch edition of 1584. The forty-five folio plates of the London edition were, as in the case of Saxton, produced by a team of engravers mainly from overseas. Regarded as 'perhaps the greatest single advance in the history of hydrographic publication',[22] the Waghenaer charts soon became a synonym for all maritime atlases, which were simply 'waggoners' to seamen for generations after. Despite its impact and importance, it exists in isolation. There were no further maritime atlases produced in England for seventy years. Demand was partly met by the production of manuscript charts or 'plats', typically drawn on vellum and mounted on hinged wooden boards for use at sea, an active trade in which sprang up at about this time. It was a trade perhaps stimulated by the appearance of the Waghenaer atlas in the same way that manuscript estate maps had been stimulated by the appearance of the Saxton atlas. As far as printed charts were concerned, the market was left wholly to the chart-makers of Amsterdam, who by the early seventeenth century routinely produced English-language editions of their 'waggoners', under such evocative titles as *The light of navigation . . .* or *The fierie sea-columne . . .*, with only the occasional and marginal involvement of English booksellers.[23]

Exiles and Grocers

A singular irony of this situation was that the pivotal figure in the establishment of Amsterdam as the European centre of cartographic publishing had shaped his early career in England. The Fleming Jodocus Hondius (1563–1612) was perhaps a dozen years in London in religious exile. The plates he engraved for *The mariners mirrour* are his earliest recorded work, although he had been

21 Skelton 1970, no. 106. Andrews 1987. 22 Skelton 1966.
23 See Koeman 1967–85, especially vol. IV, for further examples.

in London since at least 1583, producing *inter alia* maps of the continents, the recently discovered roundel maps 1589–90,[24] and the influential ornamented map of England, *Typus Angliae* 1590.[25] The Emery Molyneux globes he engraved in 1592 were the first engraved in England and the largest yet produced anywhere in Europe.[26] Although Hondius made his further career in Amsterdam, there producing the great atlases for which he is chiefly remembered, his years in England were the proving ground of his later achievement. Further evidence of an upsurge in serious cartographic publishing in England is offered in the career of Augustine Ryther (*fl.*1576–93). A member of the Grocers' Company and the founder there of a highly distinguished school of instrument makers,[27] Ryther was the only certainly native English engraver to work on the Saxton and Waghenaer atlases. He went on to publish his own atlas celebrating the Armada victory, *Expeditionis Hispanorum in Angliam vera descriptio*... 1590 (*STC* 24481a), engraved from designs by Robert Adams and charting the naval action. This was the third and last folio sixteenth-century English atlas and Ryther provides their sole evidence of continuity. He was almost certainly the engraver of Saxton's 1583 wall map and also engraved the Ralph Agas wall map of Oxford 1588 (*STC* 194.3) and the similar John Hamond map of Cambridge 1592 (*STC* 12734.7). In 1590 he produced the William Bowes pack of geographical playing cards,[28] decorated with miniature county maps. He further contributed important maps to theoretical works on navigation by Thomas Hood in 1590 and 1592 (*STC* 13697, 13696.5) and appears to have acquired Saxton's printing-plates, reissuing the county maps, which are sometimes bound together with his Armada charts. Ryther's apprentice, Charles Whitwell (*fl.*1590–1611), engraved both John Norden, *Surrey* 1594 and Philip Symondson, *A new description of Kent*... 1596, the former one of a proposed series of county maps with which Norden intended to improve on Saxton with additional information and descriptive text in guidebook style.[29] The latter is regarded as the most technically accomplished English map of the period.

This apparently promising position ended somewhat abruptly. Ryther was imprisoned, probably for debt, in 1595 and is heard of no more. Despite a desperate pursuit of patronage, Norden never progressed beyond the six

24 Schilder 1992, pp. 44–7. 25 Shirley 1980, no. 159. Schilder 1985, pp. 40–3.

26 Wallis 1951, pp. 275–90; Wallis 1962, pp. 267–79.

27 Joyce Brown, *Mathematical instrument-makers in the Grocers' Company 1688–1800* (London, 1979), pp. 58–61.

28 Skelton 1970, no. 2. Sylvia Mann and David Kingsley, 'Playing cards depicting maps of the British Isles, and of the English and Welsh counties', *Map collectors' series*, 87 (1972), 3–35, esp. 4–5.

29 Kitchen 1997, pp. 43–61.

maps he published between 1593 and 1598. Hondius departed for Amsterdam taking with him not only the Waghenaer plates but also his kinsman Pieter van den Keere, who had engraved maps for Hondius and Norden. Although both Hondius and Van den Keere retained strong and lasting connections with the London trade, they had in effect taken specialist map-publishing with them. It was not revived in England for sixty years, with such output of maps as there was passing to the wider book-trade and to more generalist printsellers.

The booksellers

The controversial John Wolfe (1548?–1601) seems to have been the printer of Ryther's Armada maps (as well as registering the copyright) and he subsequently produced in the 1590s a handsome series of map-illustrated travels, the most imposing of which was his folio translation of *John Huighen van Linschoten, his discours of voyages*... 1598, the nearest approximation to an English world atlas of the sixteenth century. He is the first bookseller that can be said to have commissioned maps in any routine way and was important in encouraging what might be termed the first generation of professional London copperplate engravers. John Norton (1556/7–1612) and his apprentice John Bill (1576–1630) were importers of (besides much else) maps and atlases from Ortelius. Norton had in stock in 1596 no less than seven copies of the *Theatrum orbis terrarum*, at that time the most expensive book ever produced.[30] He went on to publish his own miniature version, *An epitome of Ortelius*... [1601?] and subsequently (with Bill) a full-scale folio edition dated 1606.[31] The first, rivalled by the similar *Abraham Ortelius his epitome* 1603, published by James Shaw, was the earliest English-text world atlas proper. In numbers of maps these two pocket atlases far exceeded any previous London publication, but both were 'bought-in' productions, actually printed in Antwerp. Shaw thenceforth disappeared, but Norton, perhaps encouraged by his acquisition of the grammar patent, which also conferred certain rights in the field of maps and charts,[32] moved on to his folio Ortelius, *The theatre of the whole world*... The

30 Hessels 1887, I, pp. 696–7, letter 294. Hessels glosses the Norton referred to as John Norton's cousin, Bonham Norton. This is possible, but in this context unlikely.

31 The dating of both is suspect, but the former is bibliographically very closely related to the Latin-text edition published at Antwerp in 1601. The latter is dated 1606, although an internal reference to John Speed's *Theatre* (1611–[1612]) (see below) as 'lately set forth' has not been satisfactorily explained.

32 Skelton 1970, p. 242. *CSPD 1603–10*, p. 74. Mace 1993.

maps were again printed abroad from the original plates, but had text added in London. The finished atlas was an outstanding piece of work, the largest volume yet to appear under a London imprint and the most extensive of all the many editions of the *Theatrum*. It appears to have had only limited commercial success and a more original and lasting venture was the map-illustrated edition of William Camden, *Britannia, sive florentissimorum regnorum Angliа . . .*, that Norton published with George Bishop in 1607.[33] Soon reprinted in an English translation in 1610, the Camden with county maps became a regular feature of publishing for two hundred years. The maps in this case were simply copied from Saxton and Norden, but this was the first time a full set of folio maps had been engraved entirely by engravers permanently resident in London.

Despite this position of apparent strength, the number of similar books containing maps produced over the next three decades is noticeably small. Beyond the curious poetic maps of Michael Drayton's *Poly-Olbion* 1612–22,[34] and some maps of individual interest in such travel books as William Baffin, *A description of East India . . .* 1619, there is little of note to record. Henry Fetherstone, like Norton and Bill a major importer, published Samuel Purchas, *Hakluytus posthumus or Purchas his pilgrimes* 1625 with many 'maps and peeces cut in brasse or wood', some freshly engraved, but for the most part comprising second-hand Hondius plates originally produced for the Amsterdam *Atlas minor* 1607. John Bill produced a pocket-edition of Camden with county maps in 1626.[35] Also worthy of note is Robert Milbourne's edition of Sir Thomas Stafford, *Pacata Hibernia . . .* 1633, with maps of Irish towns and campaigns. The pugnacious Michael Sparke (1586?–1653) published John Smith, *The generall historie of Virginia . . .* 1624 and Luke Fox, *North-west Fox* 1635, both with maps of individual historic importance. Sparke further achieved distinction by using the word 'atlas' in the title of a British publication for the first time with the quarto *Historia mundi: or Mercator's atlas* 1635, but the maps were for the most part printed from the by now third-hand Hondius *Atlas minor* plates previously used by Fetherstone. Even the period after the Civil War saw little increase in this type of publication and there were no new 'bookseller' atlases until 1670, although Henry Seile's edition of Peter Heylyn, *Cosmographie* 1652, with its delightful maps of the continents, proved an enduring success. For the most important ventures in early seventeenth-century cartographic publishing it is necessary to look beyond the regular book trade to a small group of specialist printsellers.

33 Skelton 1970, no. 5. 34 Skelton 1970, no. 8. 35 Skelton 1970, no. 15.

The printsellers

The imprints of Hans Woutneel (*fl.*1586–1603) may be said to be the first printselling (as opposed to bookselling) imprints to arise in London.[36] He was an importer of a variety of engraved material, including maps from Ortelius, and towards the close of his recorded career he evidently intended to publish his own maps. He had engraved in Amsterdam (almost certainly by Hondius) a never completed series of folio county maps dated 1602–3 and prepared from the manuscripts of the herald and topographer William Smith (1550?–1618).[37] Woutneel also published *A descripsion of the kingdoms of England, Scotland & Ireland*... 1603, a wall map apparently to commemorate the Union of England and Scotland and intended to rival a similar and more finished map of the same type produced by the historian John Speed (1552–1629).[38] It was at about this point that Speed began on the preparation of his own famous series of county maps, eventually to appear as *The theatre of the empire of Great Britaine*... 1611–[1612] and designed as an atlas companion to his national history.[39] With sixty-seven folio maps it extended Saxton's coverage to encompass the whole of the British Isles and was thus the first British atlas. Speed freely admitted to having 'put my sickle into other mens corne' and the general geography relies wholly on earlier work, but he had none the less travelled the country himself and took pride in a new feature, the inclusion of seventy-three inset town plans, fifty from his own surveys. For most of the towns there is no earlier representation. An early proof of the map of Cheshire was engraved in London by William Rogers, but in the event most or all of the maps were sent to Hondius in Amsterdam for engraving and the plates shipped back to London. The finished work, engraved in typically formal but cluttered Jacobean style, struck a lasting chord with the public and the maps were many times reprinted both singly and in atlas form well into the eighteenth century. Originally published by the printselling partnership of John Sudbury (*fl.*1599; *d.*1621) and George Humble (*fl.*1603; *d.*1640), the latter receiving a royal privilege in 1608, it was the most successful cartographic publication of the time. It provided a platform for Humble later to produce Speed's *A prospect of the most famous parts of the world* 1627, the first full-scale general British world atlas. The plates, many spectacularly decorated with vignettes of cities, were again engraved in Amsterdam and Humble also acquired from Holland some earlier plates of miniature county maps engraved by Pieter van den Keere, which he

36 Gerard 1996. 37 Skelton 1970, no. 3.
38 Shirley 1980, nos. 255, 261. Schilder and Wallis 1989, pp. 22–6. 39 Skelton 1970, no. 7.

augmented and published as a pocket-edition of the *Theatre*, under the title *England Wales Scotland and Ireland described and abridged...from a farr larger voulume...* 1627.[40]

By now with map plates from his atlases covering all parts of the world, Humble seems to have had for some years a virtual monopoly on the sale of separate maps. Although rivals had entered the general field of printselling, there were perhaps none able or prepared to make a similar investment in plates. The field was in any case in some disarray as the result of an eccentric and long-contested monopoly granted to a royal favourite in 1619 covering everything (specifically including maps) printed on one side of the paper only.[41] A striking exception to the general position is provided by the impressive wall map by William Grent, *A new and accurate map of the world* 1625,[42] published by the printseller Thomas Jenner (*fl.*1618; *d.*1673). Jenner began to engage more heavily in maps at the time of the Civil War, bringing out an amplified version of *A direction for the English traviller* 1643 (first published by Matthew Simmons in 1635), with the original thumbnail county maps now enlarged,[43] as well as Wenceslaus Hollar's 'Quarter-master's map' of 1644, announced as 'useful for all commanders for quarteringe of souldiers & all sorts of persons that would be informed, where the armies be'.[44] Armed conflict has the inevitable effect of raising demand for maps and the old Saxton and Speed plates were brought out to provide atlases published respectively by the printsellers William Web of Cornhill and George Humble's son William.[45] While these productions had a sale, it is indicative of the continuing fragility of the trade that they were almost certainly less popular than two folio English county atlases produced by the rival Amsterdam publishing houses of Joan Blaeu and Joannes Janssonius in 1645 and 1646.[46] Although offering nothing new in the way of geographical detail, the standard of production, in terms of engraving, paper, colouring and decoration, was such as to leave the English productions looking distinctly outmoded. Despite an extensive stock of plates, which by now also included a pocket version of Speed's world atlas, again engraved by Van den Keere,[47] the younger Humble was

40 Skelton 1970, no. 17. The date and context of an earlier version (*STC* 23034.5) are uncertain.

41 Jackson 1957, pp. xvi–xxii; Greg 1967, pp. 65–66,102, 164–169, 172–175.

42 Shirley 1983, no. 313. The earliest known impression is dated 1625, although the inclusion of Jenner's early address at the White Bear on Cornhill suggests an earlier version now lost. This is probably the map entered under an identical title to the bookseller Henry Gosson in 1622 – Arber, IV, p. 79.

43 Skelton 1970, nos. 20–2, 25.

44 *The kingdome of England & principality of Wales exactly described...* 1644. Shirley 1980, no. 537.

45 Skelton 1970, nos. 27, 36.

46 Skelton 1970, nos. 28, 34.

47 *A prospect of the most famous parts of the world* 1646.

granted a special licence in 1653 to import cartographic publications from the Netherlands.[48]

The emergence of two new printselling establishments in the 1640s was to give domestic map publishing a slightly wider base. Although Peter Stent (1613?–65) rarely produced new maps, he built up a considerable working stock of older map plates including the Woutneel–Smith counties. He also issued in 1654 the earliest extant English catalogue to feature maps, the broadside *A catalogue of plates and pictures*.[49] Robert Walton (*fl.*1647; *d.*1688) operated in similar fashion, but also produced a number of new maps, of which one of the best examples is *A new plaine, and exact map of America*... 1658.[50] Some of his stock is listed in Thomas Porter, *A new book of mappes*... 1655, which itself contains the first new map of London actually engraved in London since Norden's map of 1593.[51] Richard Newcourt's wall map *London* 1658, engraved by the gifted William Faithorne on a much larger scale, was the most ambitious map of this type since the 1560s and still presents a charming view of the pre-fire city.[52] Farther afield, there is evidence from the offer of 'all sorts of globes, mapps of the world or in parts, either kingdoms, provinces or particular counties' contained in a catalogue put out by the Newcastle bookseller William London, that some kind of countrywide distribution arrangements were by now in place (*A list of the most vendible books in England*... 1657).

The weavers

The Restoration in 1660 finally marked the reassertion of greater ambition in cartographic publishing and the resurgence of a specialized map trade.[53] Although his career began a little earlier, this is first reflected by Joseph Moxon (1627–91). The son of a printer who had worked in Holland, he established himself as a globe and instrument maker as well as printer in the 1650s. His *A book of sea-plats*... 1657, marked the beginnings of a challenge to the long domination of Dutch sea charts and he was appointed Hydrographer to the King 'for making globes, maps and sea-plats' in 1662.[54] His work, sometimes sold by lottery or raffle, soon achieved some celebrity and it was to Moxon that Pepys went for globes both for his home and his office.[55]

48 Skelton 1970, p. 243. 49 Globe 1985. Griffiths 1998, p. 173. 50 Burden 1996, no. 330.
51 Inset on a larger map of the British Isles, engraved by Hollar and dated 1654. Howgego 1978, no. 10.
52 Howgego 1978, no.12. 53 Woodward 1978, pp. 159–86.
54 *CSPD 1661–1662*, p. 241. 55 Wallis 1978, p. 6.

Elected a Fellow of the Royal Society in 1678, Moxon gave an intellectual edge to British cartographic publishing that had been lacking since the 1590s. He achieved a wider fame with his *Mechanick exercises*... 1677–84, the first manual of printing, and incidentally in so doing established a precedent for the publication of works by monthly instalment,[56] an effective way of spreading costs and returns that was to provide a means to the publication of many eighteenth-century atlases. Moxon belonged to the Weavers' Company and was followed in his activities by an important group of other members of that Company. Robert Morden (*fl.*1667; *d.*1703), almost certainly one of Moxon's apprentices, offered the same range of stock – advertising 'all sorts of globes, spheres, maps large and small, sea-platts, and other mathematical instruments'. He is remembered principally for his small atlas *Geography rectified*... 1680 and his folio county maps for a new edition of Camden in 1695,[57] although his separately printed wall maps offer more substantial evidence of his merit. Almost the earliest member of the map trade to essay newspaper advertising,[58] Morden's advertisements reveal a distinctive pattern of publication, with the production of many individual maps based on the pooling of limited resources in ad-hoc partnerships with his colleagues. A frequent partner was William Berry (1639–1718), apprenticed to Moxon in 1656, who had success in the 1680s with a series of impressive two-sheet maps based on the influential work of the French cartographer Nicolas Sanson, 'corrected and amended' by himself and sometimes bound in atlas form. Philip Lea (*fl.*1683; *d.*1700), apprenticed to Morden in 1675, shared in map and globe production with his master, was consulted by Pepys on cartographic matters, and acquired the old Saxton plates which he overhauled, reworked and reissued 'with a great many additions and corrections'. Moxon's son, James Moxon (*fl.*1671; *d.*1708), was a map engraver who has a further interest in having worked in Edinburgh for a short time, there engraving and selling two maps compiled by the mathematician John Adair.[59] Another Weaver engraver, who extended the activity of this group well into the eighteenth century, was Sutton Nicholls (*fl.*1689–1729). Among much other work he collaborated with James Moxon on *Military geography in twelve mapps*... 1691, an innovative cartographic guide to the recent campaigns.

56 Wiles 1957, pp. 79–80. 57 Skelton 1970, no. 117.
58 Contemporary *London gazette* advertisements are fully transcribed in Tyacke 1978.
59 Moir 1973–83, I, pp. 65–78.

Ogilby and Blome

The more general book trade too was to evince a revived interest in maps. The Scotsman John Ogilby (1600–76), was in turn dancing-master, perhaps soldier, poet, founder of the Dublin theatre, translator, publisher and printer of lavish editions of the classics.[60] Ruined by the Great Fire, he ended a picaresque career with a short but dramatic intervention into cartographic publishing. Conceiving an 'English atlas' covering the world in several volumes, he restored his fortunes by a pioneering use of lotteries and rapidly produced a series of lavishly illustrated travel books, including *Africa: being an accurate description*... 1669, *Atlas Japannensis*... 1670, *Atlas Chinensis*... 1671, and *America: being the latest, and most accurate description*... 1670. Not perhaps atlases in the modern sense, although Ogilby called them so, they offered not just maps but a rich mixture of narrative and wonder, adapted and translated from the recently published works of Nieuhoff, Montanus and Dapper. His finest achievement was the completion of a complete road survey of England and Wales, published in folio as *Britannia. Volume the first*... 1675. Measured with the 'waywiser', a pedometer improved if not actually invented by Robert Hooke, the principal highways were depicted in the form of decorative scrolled strips, some having pictorial titles showing the 'waywiser' in motion. They gave as memorable and defining an image of Restoration England as Saxton had given of Elizabethan England a century earlier. Wholly original in concept and execution the *Britannia* provided a pattern for countless later publications.[61] As a final grace-note to an extraordinary career, Ogilby saw almost to completion *A new and accurate map of the City of London*... 1676, the first surviving genuinely detailed and accurate large-scale map of London, published by his kinsman and successor William Morgan (*fl.*1675; *d.*1690) just weeks after Ogilby's death.[62] Morgan himself went on to publish the impressive *London &c. actually survey'd* 1682, which extended the coverage of the earlier map to include the whole built-up area of the capital.

Richard Blome (1635–1705) shared Ogilby's passion for rich illustration and was as adroit as Ogilby in offering inducements to subscribers.[63] He announced in 1668 a programme of separate publications that would build into his own 'English atlas', and despite a reputation for 'progging tricks'[64] he managed to produce much of what he proposed, albeit in less elaborate form

60 Van Eerde 1976. Griffiths 1998, pp. 184–8.
61 Fordham 1926. 62 Hyde 1980, pp. 2–8. 63 Clapp 1932.
64 Anthony à Wood, *Athenae Oxonienses*, ed. P. Bliss (3rd edn, London, 1815), II, p. 298.

than promised. His *A geographical description of the four parts of the world*... 1670 represents an attractive world atlas, with maps based on Sanson. *Britannia: or, a geographical description*... 1673, although 'a most entire piece of theft out of Camden and Speed',[65] has a certain feverish charm, as does a smaller county atlas produced simply as *Speed's maps epitomiz'd*... 1681.[66]

Blome's final contribution was an abortive project advertised in the 1690s for producing a survey of London illustrated with 'ichnographical maps of the wards and parishes'.[67] The survey never materialized, but the maps, which may originally have been engraved for Ogilby, certainly existed. They eventually appeared, bearing traces of Blome's name imperfectly erased, as illustrations to John Stow, *A survey of the cities of London and Westminster*... 1720.

Maritime charts

Following Moxon's 'waggoner' a further attempt was made to break into maritime publishing by John Seller (1632–97), originally a compass maker and from his premises on the river at Wapping a supplier of instruments, almanacs and navigational texts.[68] His method of mounting from scratch a genuinely large-scale publishing operation was perhaps the only one open to him. He acquired quantities of disused Dutch printing plates (said to have been disposed of for scrap metal) and simply refurbished them for re-use.[69] It was not a method that impressed knowledgeable contemporaries, still less later commentators, yet, as Pepys noted, his importance was strategic and political – 'till Seller fell into it we had very few draughts, even of our own coasts, printed in England'.[70] The amount of new work he produced has often been underestimated and even padding out his ambitious folio atlases (*The English pilot*... 1671 on, *The coasting pilot* ... 1672 and *Atlas maritimus*... 1675) with refurbished plates he ran into financial difficulties. His plates then passed to others, the most important of whom were John Thornton and William Fisher. Thornton (1641–1708) was a prominent member of the still flourishing group of manuscript chart makers known variously as the Thames School or, from their livery company affiliation, the Drapers' School, that had appeared in the late sixteenth century.[71] He continued to produce manuscript charts but his increasing engagement in printed charts and atlases like *The English pilot. The fourth book*... 1689 (a continuation of Seller published with Fisher) was to mark the beginning of the final transition from manuscript to print in this area. This was not a rapid process

65 William Nicholson in 1696, cited in Skelton 1970, p. 142.
66 Skelton 1970, nos. 90, 104. 67 Tyacke 1978, no. 284.
68 Verner 1978, pp. 127–157; Shirley 1995, pp. 2–9. 69 Chappell 1935, p. 107.
70 Tanner 1926, p. 238. 71 Campbell 1973, pp. 81–106. Smith 1978, pp. 45–100.

and the work of another member of this school, William Hack (*fl.*1671–1702), indicates how large a manuscript trade still existed. Hack's work admittedly survives in improbable quantity, but comprises over 300 separate charts and a significant number of manuscript atlases, including at least fourteen versions of the 'Buccaneer's atlas' he produced under variations of the title *Atlas of the great south sea of America*. These alone contain over 1,600 charts.[72] The bookseller William Fisher (*fl.*1654; *d.*1692) founded a specialized concern that under the names of his successors, Richard Mount and Thomas Page, came to dominate eighteenth-century maritime publishing, a success based largely on the atlas *Great Britain's coasting pilot* 1693. Although not without its detractors, this handsome atlas of forty-eight folio charts was the first British maritime atlas based on original survey (conducted by Captain Greenvile Collins between 1681 and 1688) and finally held the key for the English chart trade to compete on equal terms with the Dutch. It was to remain in print for a hundred years.[73]

Abandoned projects

John Seller's later output was largely of miniature atlases, of which the earliest were the *Atlas minimus* . . . [1678] and the *Atlas caelestis* . . . [1680] (the first British celestial atlas). He did however attempt to undertake a full-scale survey of the country under the working title 'Atlas Anglicanus'.[74] Six new county maps were produced between 1676 and 1681, in collaboration with the surveyor John Oliver, before the project faltered to an end. Seller's business survived but more punishing in its failure was the eleven- or twelve-volume world atlas proposed by the bookseller Moses Pitt (1631?–97). Pitt specialized in scientific and travel books and encouraged by Robert Hooke he intended *The English atlas* to rival the great Dutch folio atlases of Janssonius and Blaeu. Using Seller's device of 'refreshing' old plates, Pitt, in association with Dutch partners, began an overhaul of the Janssonius *Atlas major* plates sold at auction in Amsterdam in 1676. Adding new maps and revising others he managed to produce four exquisite finished volumes containing some 177 maps between 1680 and 1683 before the patience of his backers finally ran out. Arrested for debt in 1686, Pitt is last heard of as the author of *The cry of the oppressed* 1691, grimly illustrated with interior scenes of the Fleet prison.[75]

72 Smith 1978, pp. 83–7.
73 Robinson 1962, pp. 40–3, 158–62. Verner 1969.
74 An *atlas factice* of this title, with sheets derived from a variety of sources, was actually assembled by Seller in 1694. Skelton 1970, pp. 217–18.
75 Rostenberg 1980, pp. 2–8.

Conclusion

Although never completed, Pitt's atlas, elegantly printed at Oxford on the finest paper, is a potent symbol of the occasional grandeurs and frequent failures in the atlas publishing of the period. In cartographic terms there had been a broad success, with the whole landmass of the British Isles and most of its coastline surveyed and published. The level of accuracy of some of this work was, even by the standards of the time, less than satisfactory, but it had been done, and a basis for future improvement established. Towards the end of the period particularly, London publishers like Thornton and Morden were also making a considerable contribution towards the early mapping of the Americas. Maps and atlases were conceived as much a matter of art as of science, and the handsome folios of Saxton and Speed, often surviving with vibrant contemporary hand colour, are among the most breath-taking examples of the craftsmanship of the period. They are matched by the baroque extravaganzas of Ogilby, as well as the magnificence of the little-known and seldom exhibited wall maps.

The failures were ones neither of art nor science. What beset the map trade was chronic undercapitalization, or as Morden succinctly put it 'irresistible poverty'. The costs of engraving, copper and paper were too great for any but the most successful productions to show a profit.[76] This explains the large numbers of miniature atlases, the long continuance in use and endless refurbishing of old plates, and the prevalence of the ad-hoc 'atlas factice'.[77] Even the extensive use of refurbished plates could not save Seller's *English pilot* or Pitt's *English atlas*. If the costs of production were high, the costs of a new field or marine survey were equally beyond the means of the map trade. The only original surveys that met with success were those like Saxton and Collins that had received official backing. It was to be another hundred years before the permanent establishment of publicly funded surveying and publishing bodies like the Ordnance Survey and the Hydrographic Office of the Admiralty, but the necessity was clearly understood by that shrewd observer of the contemporary scene, Mr Secretary Pepys,

> This work is never well to be done at the charge of private people, it being too chargeable and what will never answer their expense and care, and so will either never be done well, or not at all by them; and it is certain that till now never

76 Some actual costings are given in Tyacke 1973, pp. 70–7.

77 Several complete county atlases in this composite form are known assembled by the printseller John Overton (1640–1713), who took over Stent's plates in 1665. Some perhaps display sufficient uniformity of content to be classed as published editions. Skelton 1970, nos. 89, 91, 107, 111, 121.

anything was done in this nation in it [but] at the cost and by encouragement of the Crown ...[78]

78 From Pepys's report of a conversation concerning maritime atlases with the master-mariner, Thomas Phillips: Chappell 1935, p. 108.

I am most grateful to Sarah Tyacke and Ashley Baynton-Williams for the loan of their notes.

11

The literature of travel

MICHAEL G. BRENNAN

Various kinds of 'private' and 'public' forms of book production were commonly utilized to preserve experiences of travel. The compilation of manuscript volumes, which far exceeded the production of printed books, is of crucial importance in any consideration of the readership of travel literature between 1557 and 1695. Indeed, no first-hand significant account of travels in Europe by an Englishman reached print before 1600 despite the frequent publication in these years of translations of major works by foreigners (translation remained a key source for texts throughout the period). Some of these manuscripts were probably written as private reference manuals and some circulated only in manuscript. On some occasions conflicting accounts might be circulating simultaneously in manuscript and print. In print the choices available to an author or bookseller ranged from sensationalist single sheet ballads,[1] hastily printed newsletters, crudely printed pamphlets, populist publications and handy pocket guides in slim octavo and duodecimo, to expensive and lavishly illustrated quartos and folios aimed at the wealthy individual purchaser or institutional libraries. Later, following the Restoration, accounts of individual journeys were usually published in folio. But from the mid-1570s there had been a large selection of guide books, including cheaply printed narratives, available to anyone travelling in Europe for education or pleasure as opposed to business.

A small number of travel publications was financed by the authors themselves, like Coryate and, probably, Sir James Ware;[2] by collaborative publishing as was the case for the editions of Hakluyt in the 1590s,[3] or sponsored by a City Company with overseas trading interests.[4] Others appeared only through the personal support of influential royal, court and city patrons or, later in the period, subscription or lottery publication. Although a systematic study of the stationers involved in the production of travel literature still awaits

1 See below, p. 271. 2 See below, pp. 254, 256.
3 See below, p. 261. 4 See below, p. 260.

compilation, it is clear that a wide range of printers and booksellers, such as the Eliot's Court syndicate in the Little Old Bailey,[5] responded to the commercial, political and intellectual potential of such writings and their publications created an expanding archive, which drew on the manuscript tradition. Such stationers (along with their readers) were attracted by the sheer diversity of 'travel writing', a term which at this period encompassed both the reiteration of the routinely familiar in Britain and Western Europe and pioneering accounts of attempts by land and sea to locate *terra incognita* in Africa, the Americas, Russia, and the Far East. Demand was such that books might be up to the minute reports, like those of Frobisher's voyages, years out of date, or verging on the fabulous. Consequently, distinctions between geographical fact and speculative (or even superstitious) hypothesis often became blurred. Such writings also readily embraced antiquarian, anthropological, political and religious materials, leading to a distinct sense of generic eclecticism within the form. This broadly defined genre encouraged the development of reliable observation at home and abroad and facilitated the creation of a network of informants for local history.[6] After the Restoration the number of accounts of European journeys increased markedly, and travel literature became increasingly concerned with reliable factual reporting. Furthermore, travel writing could be used either as a means of categorizing the national identities of both authors and foreigners, or as a sometimes fictive framework (later more readily related to prose fiction), for the defining of the self as observer and narrator. In this sense, the literature of travel, incorporating a wide spectrum of literary styles, was projected by both its authors and publishers as offering something for most kinds of readers.

Travel literature contributed, sometimes unconsciously but more deliberately as time passed, to the project of empire.[7] This is most explicit in the works written on Ireland but is also evident in those on the Americas which encouraged colonization through emigration and plantation.[8] More generally, printed travel literature functioned as propaganda while meeting the fascinated public interest in the swift expansion of England's overseas interests and validated

5 This syndicate, formed by Edmund Bollifant, Arnold Hatfield, John Jackson, and Ninian Newton succeeded to the printing materials of Henry Bynneman (*d.* December 1583). They also farmed out work to other printers whose names did not necessarily appear on the title page of their publications. As partners died or left the syndicate, they were replaced by new ones up to the early 1650s. The imprint of members of the Eliot's Court Press appears on a significant proportion of travel works from this period, as indicated by examples cited in this chapter. See Plomer 1922–3 together with the syndicate's publications listed by *STC*, III, pp. 58–9.

6 See below, pp. 248–50.

7 See the discussion of the Hakluyts, Purchas, Hariot and Spenser in Canny and Low 1998.

8 See below, pp. 251–2, 259–65.

the country's growing maritime empire, on occasions justifying commercial motives with the more idealistic notion of spreading Christianity.[9]

1 England and Ireland

This (highly selective) survey of the various kinds of travel writing circulating in both manuscript and print between 1557 and 1695 begins with the development of mid-sixteenth-century domestic travel writing as an offshoot of the growing antiquarian fascination with the history (as opposed to the legends) of the British Isles. Two such books, both originally printed abroad, exerted a major influence over their English readers. Polydore Vergil's *De divisione Britanniae* (Basel, 1534–1651) and John Bale's *Descriptiones Angliae* (Wesel, 1548–59) established many of the basic methodologies for reliable historical research and the recording of observations on landscape and society adopted by Tudor travellers in both domestic and foreign locations.[10] The practice of compiling detailed topographical works from first-hand observation was continued by such noted historians as Sir John Prise, Robert Talbot, and members of Matthew Parker's circle. Thomas Twyne's translation of *The breviary of Britain* (1573) by Humphrey Llwyd and William Harrison's the 'Island of Britain' in Holinshed's *Chronicles* (1577–87), typified the growing emphasis within the English book trade on the provision of detailed and reliable geographical information set within an historical perspective. The culmination of this form of topographical writing came with William Camden's synoptic landmark of antiquarian scholarship, *Britannia* (Eliot's Court Press, 1586–1639), which reached an even wider audience through Philemon Holland's elegant English translation, *Britain: or a chorographical description* (Eliot's Court Press, 1610–95). Camden's extensive travels, along with his reliance for extra information upon correspondence with a network of cartographers, topographers, and local historians, confirmed the Tudor fascination with first-hand exploration of the native landscape and its history.[11] Camden remained a pervasive influence over successive generations of writers, who travelled both in England and abroad. Fynes Moryson, for example, based the 'England' section of his *Itinerary* (1617) almost entirely upon information derived from *Britannia* and also carried over these methods of description into his analyses of foreign countries.

9 See below, p. 265

10 Bale also completed the work of the itinerant antiquarian scholar, John Leland, who travelled between numerous monastic libraries (1535–43), gathering materials for his intended 'Description of Britain', as described in his *Laborious journey . . . for England's antiquities*, ed. J. Bale (1549). (The place of publication for all works referred to in this chapter is London, unless stated otherwise. Date ranges note first and last edition before 1700.)

11 McKisack 1971, pp. 1–11, 11–25, 98–103, 126–54.

Alongside these broad historical surveys of the landscape of Britain developed an archly patriotic form of topographical writing (disseminated in both manuscript and print), which sought to encapsulate the distinctive character of specified regions. William Lambard's *Perambulation of Kent* (1576–1656), first printed in a run of 600 copies, may be compared with other less familiar examples in manuscript, such as Sampson Erdeswicke's acute observations on Cheshire (1574) and Staffordshire (*c.* 1593–1603).[12] The first edition of John Norden's eclectic *Speculum Britanniae: Middlesex* (Eliot's Court Press, 1593–1637), intended as an accumulative and long-term publishing project, was steadily supplemented by both manuscript and printed descriptions of other counties, such as 'Cornwall' (*c.* 1584, printed 1728) and *Hartfordshire* (1598, BL copy annotated by John Stow).[13] Of no less importance were Norden's maps which (unlike John Speed's) included roads; and his *England, an intended guide for English travellers* (1625), also provided its readers with forty plates of triangular distance tables. Other cheaper works were merely cobbled together (presumably illegally) from existing printed sources. For example, *A direction for the English traveller* (1635–43), later revived as *A book of the names of all parishes* (1657–77), copied the tables from Speed's *England, an intended guide* and included some old maps from a folio letterpress instruction sheet of 1595 (see *STC* 1072.5), originally issued with ten engraved plates, of which four were county maps of England and Wales to be cut up as playing cards. The *Survey of Cornwall* (1602), by Richard Carew, a poet and active member of the Society of Antiquaries, led the way for other discursive Stuart surveys, such as William Burton's *Leicestershire* (1622), Tristram Risdon's 'Devon' (1630), Thomas Gerard's 'Somerset' (1633), and William Grey's *Northumberland* (1649).[14] Worthy of special mention here is Michael Drayton's lyrical and patriotic panegyric in verse of the English landscape, *Poly-Olbion* (1613–22), the major topographical poem of the Jacobean period. From the early 1580s individual experiences of travel within England were also written up with increasing frequency, usually in slim manuscript volumes or loose sheets, to be preserved and sometimes circulated as 'private' family books. Typical of such records are Laurence Bostock's brief diary of his journey to Chester (1581), Justinian Pagit's peregrination through the Midlands (1630), an anonymous record of a trip to the West of England (1637), a short survey by Lieutenant Hammond of twenty-six counties

12 The errata list of Lambard's *Perambulation* states the number of copies printed. See also Arber, II, p. 789. Erdeswicke: Cheshire, BL, Harl. MS. 473, printed 1847; *'View' or 'Survey' of Staffordshire*, ed. T. Harwood (1844).

13 See Arber, II, p. 16, for Norden's patent to print *Speculum Britanniae*, 'with privilege for ten years'.

14 Risdon's 'Devon' was first printed in 1714. Gerard's 'Somerset', printed Somerset Record Soc., 1900.

(1634–5), Sir William Brereton's sixty closely written leaves bound in parchment, recording his northern perambulations (1635), and Peter Mundy's observations on English towns (1634, 1639).[15]

A revival of interest in the geographical documentation of England during the 1650s and 1660s prompted stationers to scrabble around for suitable publications. For example, an old manuscript on Chester by William Smith was resurrected as *The vale-royal of England* (1656) by the engraver, Daniel King, partly as a vehicle for his own copperplate engravings; and a 'Survey of Staffordshire' (*c.* 1591–1603), probably by Sampson Erdeswicke, was entered in the Stationers' Register for 1656–7 (no printed copy known). At the same period, Sir William Dugdale was compiling materials for his monumental *Antiquities of Warwickshire* (1656), a publication that marked a genuine turning point in local history book production through its respect for primary documentation and the tracing of manorial descent. Many other volumes of variable quality (both in their printing and content) were being produced by the presses under the Protectorate, including Richard Hawkins's *The national excellencies of England* (1658); John Evelyn's sociological *Character of England* (1659); *England described* (1659), mostly lifted from Camden's *Britannia* by the Parliamentarian, Edward Leigh; and meticulously detailed surveys of Kent by Richard Kilburne (1657) and the Royalist herald, John Philipott (1659–64). The Restoration was marked by Edward Walker's *Iter Carolinum* (1660), a sombre parody of travel writing, intended as a hagiographical record of Charles I's military itinerary and personal sufferings during the 1640s. Outside court politics, a preoccupation with botany, natural history, and local archaeology began to figure more prominently within the literature of travel, as in Joshua Childrey's influential but derivative *Britannia Baconia* (1660); Robert Plot's excellent natural histories of Oxfordshire (1677) and Staffordshire (1686), both inspired by Childrey's work; and the anonymous *England's remarks* (1678–82). The compilation of personal 'tourist memoirs' also remained popular, including Thomas Kirk's 'Journeyings through Northumberland and Durham' (1677, printed 1847) and James Brome's *Three years' travels over England and Wales* (1694–1707). Such was the public appetite for this kind of literature that some of the printed accounts offered for sale by stationers were decades out of date, while others were

15 Bostock, BL, Harl. MS. 2113. Pagit, BL, Harl. MS. 1026. [Anon] to West of England, BL Harl. MS. 6494. Hammond, BL, Lansdowne MS. 213, printed Camden Misc., 1936. Brereton, printed Chetham Soc., 1844. Mundy, Hakluyt Soc. edn, 1919, 1925. See pp. 260–1 below for the way in which the original publications of Hakluyt, and subsequently Purchas, were extended over the years: the publications of the Hakluyt Society (1847–) include edited texts of other voyages along with some of those printed by Hakluyt. For the authorised bibliography of the society's publications see Hair 1996.

distinctly eccentric. The strange *Northern memoirs* (1694) of the Cromwellian trooper, Richard Franck, well represents both of these categories. The travels therein recounted had been undertaken in the mid-1650s, written up in about 1658, re-edited in the 1680s, and finally published in 1694, after Franck's return from a period in America. Printed at his own expense, Franck's bizarre memoirs were cast as a rambling euphuistic dialogue between Theophanis, Agrippa, Aquila, and Arnoldus (Franks).

Many other personal narratives of travel through England after 1660, still valuable for their wealth of local detail, survive in manuscript volumes, such as Edward Browne's antiquarian journal of his Derbyshire tour with Sir Thomas Browne (1662), Thomas Baskerville's record of various parts of England (from 1681), and Robert Plot's trip with Sir Thomas Browne into Kent (1693).[16] Along with the casual tourist, other regular travellers who noted down their observations as they travelled the roads of England included tradesmen, state and local officials, circuit judges, and preachers. In this last category, one of the most memorable accounts of hardships endured was George Fox's renowned Quaker *Journal* (1694), commemorating his 'sufferings, Christian experience and labours of love in the work of the ministry', as he travelled through England (from *c.* 1643), Scotland (from 1657), Ireland (from 1659), the West Indies and North America (1671–2), and Holland (1677, 1684).[17]

In contrast to the predominantly historical and geographical concerns of writings prompted by travels through England, both printed and manuscript commentaries on the Irish landscape were focused at this period almost exclusively upon the opportunities afforded by an ongoing English programme of aggressive and exploitative colonialism. Elizabethan printed tracts and books on Ireland were also preoccupied with attempts to impose Protestantism on the country from the time of the Anglicized 'Reform Parliament' (1560) until the collapse of the Tyrone Rebellion (1603). *The letter sent by J. B. Gentleman, to R. C. Esquire* (1572), a brief printed advertising tract, supported the ultimately unsuccessful plans by Sir Thomas Smith to establish an English colony with a capital called Elizabetha in the Ards, County Down. Smith also published

16 Browne, BL, Sloane MS. 1900, printed 1836. Baskerville, HMC, *Portland.*, II, 263–314; BL, Harl. MSS. 1483, 4716, 6344. Plot, BL Sloane MS. 1899.

17 *The short journal and itinerary journals of George Fox. In commemoration of the tercentenary of his birth (1624–1924)*, ed. Norman Penney with an introduction by Edmund Harvey (Cambridge, 1925). Comparable kinds of missionary-inspired travel narratives were compiled by Elias Wilson in his seven-page, *Strange... news from Italy* (1673), an account of four Yorkshire Quakers preaching in France, Italy, and Turkey (where they were martyred); in *William Penn's travels... for the service of Christ* (1694); and in the series of deranged tracts penned by the fanatical Irish Quaker, John Perrot, who travelled to Rome in 1660 to preach against Catholicism, resulting in his deserved incarceration in a madhouse.

(probably at his own expense), a colonial prospectus in a single folio sheet, *The offer and order... by Sir Thomas Smith* (1572), extolling the potential gains to be made by settlers and mentioning that the Letters Patent and Indentures for this project could be inspected by prospective investors at the sign of the Sun in Paul's Churchyard (the shop of Antony Kitson). A year earlier, Edmund Campion had adopted a more scholarly perspective in his judicious 'History of Ireland' (1571), adapted and continued by Richard Stanihurst (who was born in Dublin) in Holinshed's *Chronicles* (1577–86) as 'The description of Ireland'. Various other forms of written records were used to describe the Irish landscape and its inhabitants. Sir William Gerard, a Lord Chancellor of Ireland, travelled to England in 1578 to present personally to the Privy Council his notes on Ireland in the form of an official manuscript report. Similarly William Herbert's colonialist tract, 'A description of Munster', compiled a decade later, was ultimately filed among other official State Papers.[18] Probably the most visually memorable publication on Ireland from the 1580s was John Derricke's *The image of Ireland* (printed 1581 but not entered until July 1582), a series of semi-allegorical verses with twelve striking woodcuts (now surviving as a complete set only in the Edinburgh University Library copy), illustrating Irish native life and, implicitly, the potency of English rule.

Circulated widely in manuscript but not printed until 1633 (see under Sir James Ware below), Edmund Spenser's *Present state of Ireland* (*c.* 1596) presented itself as a humanist tract, based upon a Ciceronian dialogue between Eudox, interested in Ireland but uninformed, and Iren, the experienced traveller in the country. Spenser's colonial sentiments (he was then serving as secretary to Lord Grey of Wilton, Lord Deputy of Ireland) were keenly supported by Robert Payne's slim octavo *Description of Ireland* (1589–90), published after the Munster settlement was already well underway; and by *Solon his folly* (Oxford, 1594), by Richard Beacon, formerly Queen's Attorney at Munster. The latter tract was cast as an elegant classical debate over how Athens (England) should develop a colonialist policy towards Salamina (Ireland), while advocating harshly repressive measures to eradicate Irish nationalism and the transportation of the English poor to colonize Ireland.

Other important printed works of this period include Sir Thomas Stafford's folio, *Pacata Hibernia* (1599–1602, printed 1633), relating to Sir George Carew's governorship of Munster and eventually published as a piece of political panegyric from the perspective of a long-term Irish resident. (Stafford may also have been Carew's illegitimate son.) Two re-issues of this substantial work appeared

18 Gerard, 1578, printed *Analecta Hibernica*, 1931. Herbert, PRO CSP Ireland, 1586–8.

in 1633 and 1634, according to their cancel title pages, with 'part of the impression made over, to be vented for the benefit of the children of J. Mynshew, deceased'.[19] Of equal importance to these printed works, several manuscript accounts by Englishmen of Irish experiences also survive, such as Sir John Harington's 'Irish Journal' on the 1599 expedition of Robert Devereux, Earl of Essex, and his 'Short view of Ireland' (*c.* 1605), based upon his personal experiences as a planter in Munster in 1587 and then as a soldier in 1599; and 'A treatise of Ireland' (*c.* 1600) by John Dymmock, another member of Essex's retinue.[20] The ex-soldier Barnaby Rich, who was in Ireland at various periods between 1573 and 1617, penned a series of popular quarto pamphlets promulgating a ruthlessly colonialist view, including *A short survey of Ireland* (1609), the polemical *A new description of Ireland* (1610–24), published to coincide with the Ulster plantation and defended in *A true and a kinde excuse* (1612), and *The Irish hubbub* (1617). Some of Rich's other tracts circulated only in manuscript, such as 'The anatomy of Ireland' (1615), which (like Spenser's and Beacon's tracts) cloaked the exploitative nature of its proposals within the elegance of the classical dialogue form.

Englishmen residing in Ireland continued to record their personal views of both the Irish landscape and English rule. Although Fynes Moryson is best known for his extensive European and Middle Eastern travels between 1591–5 and 1596–7, he also served in Ireland as secretary to Lord Deputy Mountjoy. Moryson compiled an account of his experiences (printed Dublin, 1735), characterized by his suspicion of the Irish nomadic culture and the supposed natural sloth of the natives. The informed account of Ireland in Camden's *Britannia* (1607) was compiled by an English Jesuit, William Good, who had been briefly based at Limerick during the 1560s. Thomas Gainsford, who had served in the wars against Hugh O'Neill and had been involved in the Ulster plantation (1610), provided a lively personal perspective on the lush Irish countryside and its inhabitants in *The glory of England* (1618–22); and William Lithgow, who was in Ireland from August 1619 until February 1620, offered in his *Total discourse* (1632) a notably hostile account of the Irish. Luke Gernon, appointed as Second Justice of Munster in 1619, wrote 'A Discourse of Ireland' (*c.* 1620), in the form of a long letter to an unnamed friend permeated with an arrogant condescension towards the Irish and an unquestioning confidence in English authority.[21]

19 The children of John Minsheu (*d.c.*1625) were beneficiaries of the Stationers' Company from *c.*1626 until at least 1639. See *STC*, III, p. 120.

20 Harington, 'Irish journal', printed *Nugae antiquae*, 1804; 'Short view of Ireland', ed. W. D. Macray (1879). Dymmock, 'A treatise of Ireland', ed. R. Butler (1843).

21 Gernon, 'A discourse of Ireland', ed. C. L. Falkiner (1904).

Renewed English interest in Irish history during the 1630s was marked by the publication of Sir James Ware's *Ancient Irish histories* (1633, printed in London by Thomas Harper for the Dublin Society of Stationers, probably at Ware's expense), which included Campion's and Spenser's accounts of Ireland.[22] In 1635 Sir William Brereton rounded off his Continental travels with a brief tour of Ireland in 1635 and compiled the first notable English tourist account of the country. But the minority pursuit of tourism was soon abruptly curtailed by the turmoil of the 1641 Rebellion. The surveyor John Woodhouse produced two invaluable printed reference works, *A guide for strangers in Ireland* (1647) and *The map of Ireland* (1653), which also listed the benefits accrued to the Protestant occupiers of forfeited papist lands. G.N.'s *A geographical description of Ireland* (1642) provided over 100 pages of detailed descriptions, strongly advocating absolute English rule as a route to peace for the '5 Provinces, and 32 Counties'; while hastily printed newsletters recounted exciting incidental details of the struggle for power, such as *A new remonstrance of Ireland* (1641), covering the period 5 May to 2 June, by 'C.I. an eye-witness'.

The Cromwellian Act of Settlement (1652) sought to repay the creditors of the Commonwealth with confiscated lands amounting to virtually all of Ireland except for Connaught. The Dutchman, Gerard Boate, never himself visited Ireland but outlined, in parallel with the topographical and geographical elements of his *Irelands Natural History* (1652–7), the profits to be gained from colonial residence in Ireland. Boate died before his tract could be published but it was seen through the press, 'for the benefit of the adventurers and planters therein', by Boate's brother, Arnold, with a dedication to Oliver Cromwell by Samuel Hartlib. William Petty, the Physician General of the British troops in Ireland, completed the first scientific map survey of Ireland, called the 'Down survey' – not for the use of travellers but primarily for the carving up of the land among Cromwell's supporters. Petty also compiled a detailed economic and administrative tract, *The political anatomy of Ireland* (1672, printed 1691). Other kinds of first-hand accounts of the country from this period include *The moderate cavalier* (Cork?, 1675), a printed verse miscellany ('fit for all Protestants houses in Ireland', according to its title page) by the ex-soldier William Mercer; and Thomas Dineley's informative account of his own travels, 'Observations in a voyage through the kingdom of Ireland in 1681'.[23] The interests of Catholic Ireland were finally crushed by the defeat of James II at the Battle of the Boyne (1690). Many of the survivors of the Stuart and Irish opposition were then exiled

22 See also Ware's *De Hibernia* (1654), *De praesulibus Hiberniae* (Dublin, 1665) and for Ireland more fully, below ch. 34.

23 Dineley, 'Observations', ed. J. Graves (1870).

to the Continent by the Treaty of Limerick (1691) which paved the way for the anti-Catholic penal laws of 1695.[24] This conclusive period in the anglicizing of Ireland was powerfully recorded in the authoritative *An exact description of Ireland* (1691) by Laurence Echard, a Cambridge educated historian and Archdeacon of Stow.

2 Western Europe and the Mediterranean

While a considerable number of translations of major works on the historical and political institutions of Western European countries were published during the last decade of Elizabeth's reign, such as Ludovico Guicciardini's *Low Countries* (1593), Contarini's *Venice* (1599), and Conestaggio's *Portugal and Castile* (1600), no significant first-hand account of travels in Western Europe by an Englishman reached print during this period. Instead, the recording of such experiences was confined exclusively to the compilation of 'private' manuscript volumes. Some of the most informative of these accounts include the slim journal (1547–55) of Sir Thomas Hoby, the diplomat and translator of Castiglione's *The courtier*; the observations (1563) of Richard Smith, a member of Sir Edward Unton's entourage; and the manuscript journals of Sir John North (1575), Sir Stephen Powle (1579–81), Sir Arthur Throckmorton, and Henry Piers (1595–8).[25] Such Elizabethan travellers were assisted by a veritable library of guide books from the mid-1570s. For those embarking by ship, there were translations from Latin of Hieronymus Turler's *The traveller* (1575) and from the Dutch of Cornelius Anthonisz by Robert Norman of *The safeguard of sailors* (1584–1600, augmented by E. Wright, 1605–71), detailing depths, tides and distances by sea. For those on land, there were invaluable reference books such as *The post of the world* (1576) by Richard Rowlands (Verstegen), who ran a printing press at Antwerp before moving to Paris; John Browne's *The marchants avizo* (1589–1640); and Giovanni Botero's renowned *The traveller's breviat* (1601–30), translated from Italian by Robert Johnson, with valuable information not only

24 Two contrasting perspectives on these troubles are provided by the manuscript journal (ed. R. Caulfield, 1857), of Roland Davies, Dean of Cork, recording his travels in England and Ireland between 1688 and 1691; and the journal (ed. R. H. Murrey, Oxford, 1912) of 'Captain' John Stevens, a Jacobite supporter who landed at Bantry Bay in May 1689 and witnessed the defeat at the Boyne and the fall of Limerick in October 1691, before fleeing to the Continent where he eked out a living translating Spanish and Portuguese works of history.

25 Hoby, in Italy, written *c.*1564, BL Egerton MS. 2148, Camden Misc. edn, 1902. Smith, in Italy, BL, Sloane MS. 1813, see *Papers of the British School at Rome*, 7 (1914). North, in Flanders, Germany, Switzerland, Italy, Bodl. Addit. MS. C 173. Powle, in Geneva, Basel, Strasbourg, Bodl. Tanner MS. 309. Throckmorton, in Low Countries, Germany, Czechoslovakia, Italy, France, see A. L. Rowse, *Ralegh and the Throckmortons* (1962), pp. 80–94. Piers, in Low Countries, Germany, Italy, written *c.*1605, Bodl. Rawl. MS. D 83.

on Europe but also on Spanish and Portuguese commercial activities in Persia, East Africa, India and China.

The reign of King James saw a significant growth in Western European travel, due partly to greater accessibility engendered by peace-time conditions from 1604 and, increasingly, to an escalating hostility towards Catholic subjects, some of whom viewed travel abroad as a convenient form of educational self-exile. As recorded in their manuscript accounts, younger members of the aristocracy, both Catholic and Protestant, also began more commonly to undertake the 'giro' or cultural itinerary (the precursor of the 'Grand Tour'), usually following some of the long familiar pilgrimage and trade routes through France, Spain, Italy, Germany and the Low Countries. Two youthful Cecils, William Lord Cranbourne (1608–10), and William Lord Roos (1610), left juvenile but engaging accounts of their travels. Sir Charles Somerset (1611–12), a son of the Catholic Earl of Worcester and a member of Prince Henry's circle, left England as anti-papist hysteria grew in 1610 and later compiled a sophisticated narrative of his experiences, probably intended as a manuscript reference manual on travel and statecraft for his family and court circle.[26] Other informative accounts of similar experiences were compiled by (possibly) Sir Thomas Berkeley (1610), Thomas Wentworth, later Earl of Strafford (1612), and Sir Thomas Puckering (1614).[27]

Printed accounts of individual travels through Western Europe first began to be published at this period. One of the earliest, Thomas Coryate's *Crudities* (1611), adopted an eccentric narrative style to record a rich blend of personal observation and, probably, a pinch of fictional reconstruction. It also appears from both the title page (William Stansby 'for the author') and a commendatory acrostic poem by Ben Jonson that Coryate himself bore the brunt of the publication costs (although the work was registered under the names of Edward Blount and his frequent partner, William Barrett). William Lithgow, a Protestant Scotsman, saw into print successive editions of his informative *Painefull peregrinations* (1614–23), later enlarged as *Total discourse* (1632–92); and also compiled a moving printed verse dialogue *The pilgrims farewell* (Edinburgh, 1618, printed by Andro Hart, at the 'expences of the author'), on the 'joys and miseries of peregrination'.[28] The adventure-packed *Travels* (1614) of William

26 Lord Cranborne, in France, Italy, Germany, see HMC, *Salisbury*, XXI.104–13, 237–49, written in schoolboy French. Lord Roos, in Spain, PRO SP 94/17. Somerset, in France, Italy, Germany, Low Countries, Flanders, Brotherton MS. Trv. q. 3, University of Leeds, ed. M. G. Brennan (Leeds, 1993).

27 Berkeley (?), in Flanders, Germany, Switzerland, Italy, BL Sloane MS. 682. Wentworth, in France, Sheffield Public Library, Wentworth Woodhouse MSS. Puckering, in Venice, BL, Harl. MS. 7021.

28 For the withdrawal of the 1616 edition by order of the Stationers' Company in June 1616. See Jackson 1957, pp. 355–6.

Davies, a merchant navy barber-surgeon, provided grimly detailed accounts of his captivity as a Florentine galley-slave, a voyage to the Amazon, and imprisonment by the Inquisition. Similarly, James Wadsworth, the son of a lapsed Jesuit and later a renegade Catholic informer against papists, recounted in *The English Spanish pilgrim* (1629–30) how in 1622 he had embarked on a Jesuit mission to Spain, only for his ship to be captured by Moorish pirates and its passengers sold into slavery at Algiers. On a less sensational but no less absorbing level, Fynes Moryson's *Itinerary* (1617), one of the most authoritative works of travel writing printed during the Jacobean period, documented his travels through much of Western Europe, as well as Turkey and the British Isles.[29] A miscellany of historically based translations also began to appear on the English bookmarket, most notably: Jean Le Petit's, *The Low-Country Common-wealth* (1609) and Pierre d'Avity's *Estates, empires, & principalities of the world* (1615), both translated by Edward Grimeston; and Thomas de Fougasses's, *General history of Venice*, translated by W. Shute (1612).

As the concept flourished of undertaking European travel for education and pleasure (rather than just for business and diplomacy), so the range of basic guidebooks proliferated. These included Sir Robert Dallington's politically inspired *View of France* (1604, first issue unauthorized, ed. Sir F. Mitchell without reference to Dallington), promptly reissued under its author's supervision as *A method for travel* (1605), and his *Survey of the great duke's state of Tuscany* (1605); Sir Thomas Palmer's, *How to make our travels... more profitable* (1606), imitating Zwinger's *Methodus apodemica* (1577) and containing Ramist-like charts of possible routes; Gabriel Richardson's, *Of the state of Europe* (Oxford, 1627); *Profitable instructions [for] travellers*, a compendium of old travel advice by Robert Devereux, Earl of Essex, Sir Philip Sidney, and William Davison (1633); *Instructions for foreign travel* (1642–50) by the merchant and diplomat, James Howell; and Peter Heylin's *Survey of France* (1656), based on his experiences there in 1625. Travel itself became a lively topic for literary discussion, whether from the hostile perspective of Joseph Hall's, *Quo vadis? a just censure of travel* (1617), or from the more favourable point of view taken in discursive essays 'Of travel' by Sir Francis Bacon (1625) and Henry Peacham (*Complete gentleman*, 1622–61; and *Truth of our times*, 1638).

A sprinkling of printed narratives of personal European travels also appeared during Charles I's reign, such as Sir Thomas Overbury's *Travels in the Low Countries* (1609, printed 1626–51); John Raymond's, *An itinerary... through Italy* (1648); and Owen Feltham's, *Three months observations of the Low-Countries*

29 See Arber, v, p. lviii, for Moryson's patent to publish this work.

(1648–52), a pirated edition of his *Brief character of the Low-Countries* (1652–71). The convention of compiling personal manuscript volumes, recording itineraries through Western Europe, was still thriving, typical of which are those by (possibly) Thomas Abdy (1633–5), Sir William Brereton (1634–5), and Peter Mundy in Spain (1611–17) and later in the Low Countries, Poland and Russia (1639–48).[30] Predictably, the outflux to the Continent of royalist émigrés during the English Civil War (along with the movement of others seeking education and adventure) engendered a proliferation in this kind of unpublished travel book. Of the numerous manuscripts surviving, the following merit special mention: Joseph Colston (1641–5), who had gone abroad to study medicine at Padua but prolonged his trip, probably due to the political situation at home; John Bargrave (1646–7), who remained abroad for most of the Commonwealth and Protectorate; Dr Isaac Basire (1647–9), one of Charles I's chaplains; Robert Lord Willoughby (1648–9); the Royalist William Edgeman with Sir Edward Hyde and Lord Cottington (1649–51); Robert Montagu, Lord Mandeville, later Earl of Manchester (1649–51), who began his diary as a naive and immature fifteen-year old; the Royalist artist, Richard Symonds (1649–52); Philip Stanhope, Earl of Chesterfield (1650–2); Sir John Reresby (1654–9), who chose to travel abroad during the Commonweath; and Francis Mortoft (1658–9).[31]

The most renowned European travel memoirs from this period are undoubtedly those of John Evelyn, whose discriminating narratives contain a wealth of detail and shrewd interpretation.[32] However, even this classic among travel diaries cannot always be regarded as a source of informed, first-hand commentaries on foreign locations and raises the issue of originality in travel writing of the period. Evelyn's description of Paris, for example, was largely written up during his retirement in the 1670s (rather than at the time of his main visit to the city in 1643), and was heavily dependent on Claude de Varenne's *Le voyage de France* (Paris, 1643) for much of its specific detail. For Evelyn, as for many of his contemporaries, the compilation of a travel narrative was regarded as the production of an informed personal commentary, filtered through an extensive

30 Abdy, in France, Italy, Bodl. Rawl. MS. D 1285. Brereton, in the Low Countries, Chetham Soc. edn, 1844. Mundy, Hakluyt Soc. edn, 1907–25.

31 Colston, in France, Italy, BL, Sloane MS. 118. Bargrave, in Italy, Camden Soc. edn, 1867. Basire, in France, Italy, ed. L. Monga and C. Hassel, 1987. Lord Willoughby, in France: HMC Ancaster MSS., pp. 341–8. Edgeman, in Flanders, France, Spain, Bodl. Clarendon MS. 137. Lord Mandeville, in France, Switzerland, Germany, Bodl. Rawl. MS. D 76. Symonds, in France, Italy, BL, Egerton MSS. 1635, 1636; BL, Harl. MSS. 943, 1278; Bodl. Rawl. MS. D 121. Earl of Chesterfield, in France, Italy, BL, Add. MS. 19253. Reresby, in Italy, ed. A. Browning (1936). Mortoft, in France, Italy, Hakluyt Soc. edn, 1925.

32 Evelyn, in the Low Countries (1641); France, Italy, Switzerland (1643–7), ed. E. S. de Beer (Oxford, 1955).

and expected (but often unacknowledged) use of earlier sources. In contrast to this kind of heavy literary dependence, the merchant and prolific traveller, Peter Mundy, was one of the few writers always to give precedence to his own observations. His huge diary, although still greatly underestimated, is of considerably more importance than Evelyn's, in terms of both its sheer quantity of reliable personal observation and geographical coverage, including valuable material on France (1608–10), Spain (1615, 1621, 1625), Turkey (1617–20), India, Surat and Japan (1628–39), the Low Countries, Russia, Prussia and Poland (1640–7), and India (1655).[33]

After the Restoration, informative manuscript accounts of travels continued to be compiled, such as the diary of Robert Moody (1660–2), a servant to Banister Maynard.[34] There was also a distinct increase in the number printed works on Continental travel. Some printed volumes offered translations of major European works of scholarship, such as Franciscus Schottus's *Itinerario d'Italia*, written for the Jubilee Year of 1600 and translated from Latin by Edmund Warcupp as *Italy in its original glory* (1660) – the source of much of Evelyn's Italian commentaries – and François Misson's, *A new voyage to Italy*, translated from French (1695–9). Other publications made available to the reading public detailed accounts of individual itineraries, although these now tended to be expensive, folio productions. These included *The voyage of Italy* (according to its title page, 'Newly printed at Paris, to be sold in London', 1670–86) by the Roman Catholic priest, Richard Lassels; John Ray's 'topographical, moral and physiological' tour through the Low Countries, Germany, Italy, and France, *Observations . . . made in a journey . . . with a catalogue of plants* (1673) and his miscellaneous *Collection of curious travels* (1693), dedicated to the President of the Royal Society (of which Ray was a leading member); *A journey into Greece* (1682) by George Wheler and Jacob Spon; Gilbert Burnet's *Some letters . . . of travels through Switzerland, Italy and Parts of Germany* (Amsterdam and Rotterdam, 1686–98); and William Bromley's, *Remarks in the grand tour* (1692–3).

3 Collections of voyages and the American New World

The three monumental collections of voyages from this period, by Richard Eden, Richard Hakluyt, and Samuel Purchas, utilized the printed word to fuel a growing domestic fascination with the expansion of English interests overseas.

33 Mundy's manuscripts include Bodl. Rawl. A 315 (partly autograph) and BL, Harl. MS. 2286 (a scribal transcript given to Sir Paul Pindar), Hakluyt Soc. edn, 1907, 1914, 1919, 1925, 1936.

34 Moody, in France, Italy, Germany, Low Countries, Bodl. Rawl. MS. D 84.

Eden's first major publication, *A treatise of New India* (1553), translated from Sebastian Münster's *Cosmographia*, was essentially historical in character and enthusiastically recounted the exploits of Columbus, Vespucci, Magellan, and the Portuguese in the East. Eden, a friend of Sebastian Cabot, predictably emphasized the riches that had been derived by the Spanish from the New World but in this 1553 translation he neither adopted the word 'colony' nor advocated direct English involvement in overseas colonization. However, only two years later appeared his *Decades of the New World or West India* (1555), the first major printed collection of voyages in English.[35] Although tactfully acknowledging Spanish authority, Eden's preface to the *Decades* sought to convert his foreign sources into aggressive propaganda for English acquisitive exploration and colonization. Eden, always aware of the practical needs of mariners, also translated influential navigational handbooks by Martín Cortés (1561) and Jean Taisnier (1576). He died in 1576, on the eve of completing a considerably expanded second edition of the *Decades*. Fortunately, the fruits of these revisions were not lost since Eden's protégé, Richard Willes, completed the planned new edition as *The history of the travel in the West and East Indies* (1577). Its publication was specifically timed with an eye to Frobisher's second and third voyages (1577, 1578), sponsored by the Company of Cathay (perhaps a contributor to the printing costs) in search of the Northwest Passage.[36] Consequently, the publication of Willes's 1577 edition (with the pro-Spanish tone of the 1555 edition silently removed) served to alert English readers for the first time to the lucrative potential of Cathay trade, just as Eden's 1555 volume had been the first English printed text to offer American exploration and colonization as a viable activity for Marian England.

The Richard Hakluyt cousins (one a lawyer, the younger a clergyman) concentrated their interests on two focal points for English colonialism: eastern North America and India. The publication of the clergyman's *Divers voyages touching the discovery of America* (1582), promoted the use of northern routes for English trade with the East Indies and the resettlement of England's poor and petty criminals as New World colonialists. In 1584 Hakluyt put forward colonial plans for the east coast of North America in his widely circulated and influential manuscript tract, 'Discourse of Western planting' (printed 1877).

35 Eden's *Decades* (1555) included accounts of exploration compiled by Peter Martyr, Oviedo y Valdés, and López de Gómara, as well as the Pigafetta-Magellan narrative, details of the Cabot voyages, several descriptions of Russia, and an account of the first two English voyages to West Africa.

36 In support of this preoccupation with the Northwest Passage, Willes's 1577 edition included much new material on Asia, such as Varthema's travels, Galeotto Pereira's description of China, and Giovanni Maffei's account of Japan, as well as narratives of Jenkinson's journeys in Russia and Central Asia.

While resident in Paris from 1583 to 1588 as chaplain to the English Ambassador, Hakluyt revised and extended Martyr's *Decades* in a notable Latin edition (1587) and assembled, in Boies Penrose's apt phrase, his 'great prose epic of the Elizabethan period', the *Principal navigations, voyages, and discoveries of the English nation* (1589), which chronicled in three sections (1: Levant, Middle and Far East, West Africa 2: Northeast Passage, Russia, Central Asia 3: New World voyages and early colonialism) the great English maritime tradition with the intention of stimulating colonial ambitions.[37] A much expanded second edition (1598) of the first volume was followed by the second (1599) and third volumes (1600), all of these 1590s volumes being financed by a publishing syndicate headed by Christopher Barker (Queen's Printer, 1577–87) and including George Bishop, Ralph Newbery (both shareholders in the Queen's Printing House) and (from 1598 onwards) Christopher Barker's son, Robert (Queen's Printer, 1600–3, King's Printer, 1603–17). Samuel Purchas, another clergyman, continued Hakluyt's work in his four volume *Hakluytus Posthumus, or Purchas his Pilgrimes* (1625), through which the bookseller Henry Fetherstone sought to cash in on the commercial success of Hakluyt's publications and Purchas's own earlier *Pilgrimage* (1613–25), a religious world gazetteer. Fetherstone reprinted much of Hakluyt's material, along with more recent Virginia and East India voyages, enabling Purchas to lend his support to the now well established English colonialist activities in the New World and India.

In addition to the translated works included in the collections by Eden, Hakluyt, and Purchas, the English book market was kept well supplied with individual publications of translations of foreign works of exploration. For example, the stationer, Thomas Hackett, himself translated Jean Ribaut's accounts of the French Huguenot colonies in Florida as *The whole and true discovery of terra Florida* (1563). This tract had already been circulating in manuscript (in support of a possible Anglo-Huguenot venture in Florida) and it was probably published with the author's active involvement since Ribaut was in England at the time. But only three years later Hackett performed a total volte-face by publishing what virtually amounted to an anti-colonialist tract, a translation of Nicholas Le Challeux's horrific account of the massacre of Ribaut's surviving colonialists under René de Laudonnière by the Spanish in *Last voyage . . . into terra Florida* (1566). Two years later Hackett was once more back in step with other optimistic English colonialists through his edition of André Thevet's *New found Worlde, or Antarctike* (1568), which contained alluringly attractive

37 Penrose 1955, p. 318. This essay has drawn extensively upon Penrose's pioneering researches into travel writing.

descriptions of not only Florida, but also Brazil, Canada, Madagascar, and the East Indies. Some writers managed effectively to corner specific sections of the translation market for themselves. John Frampton, a former merchant, specialized in the translation and adaptation for English purposes of Spanish materials.[38] Thomas Nicholas, a Levant merchant formerly based in the Canary Islands who, like Frampton, had suffered under the Inquisition, concentrated on stories of the fall of Mexico and Peru.[39] Hakluyt was also a prolific sponsor of translations and under his influence John Florio translated Jacques Cartier's *Two navigations to New France* (1580). While in Paris Hakluyt himself translated Laudonnière's *Florida* (1587) and later compiled an English version of Ferdinando de Soto's *Virginia richly valued* (1609–11). In an astute commercial move, the Levant merchant, Michael Lok (one of Frobisher's original sponsors in the 1570s), rendered Hakluyt's own edition of Martyr's *Decades* into English (1612).

Cheap printed narratives of English voyages also abound in this period and may be represented by those relating to John Hawkins and his son Richard, Frobisher, Drake, and Cavendish. John Hawkins's own account of the sensational 1567 San Juan de Ulúa incident, *The troublesome voyage* (1569), was supplemented by *The travels of an English man* (1591), an exciting narrative by Job Hortop, who had survived this Spanish slaughter of English mariners only later to be captured, imprisoned at Seville and committed to the galleys. In post-Armada England, such acts of naval heroism (sometimes barely distinguishable from open piracy) rapidly became the stuff of popular legend. *Sir Richard Hawkins in his voyage into the South Sea 1593* (1622), prefaced with a dedication to Prince Charles by Hawkins (who died while the volume was at press), commemorated his various triumphs and setbacks in the 'Dainty' against the Spanish and provided a jingoistic celebration of English fortitude in the face of Spanish imperialism.

Sir Humphrey Gilbert's pioneering (although entirely mistaken), *Discourse of a discovery for a new passage to Cataia* (written in the mid-1560s, widely circulated in manuscript and then edited for the press in 1576 by the poet, George Gascoigne), provided a significant impulse for Frobisher's three epic voyages

38 Frampton's translations include: Nicolás Monardes, *Joyful news out of the New Found World* (1577–96); Martín Fernández de Enciso's *A brief description of... West India* (1578); and Bernardino de Escalante's *Discourse of... navigation* (1579).

39 Nicholas translated López de Gómara's *Conquest of the West India* (1578), intended as colonialist propaganda in the wake of the Frobisher voyages; and Zárate's *Discovery and conquest of Peru* (1581) in support of Sir Francis Drake's ventures. One Nicholas Lichefield (possibly a pen-name of Thomas Nicholas) also translated from the Portuguese the first book of Lopes de Castanheda's *Discovery and conquest of the East Indies* (1582).

(1576, 1577, 1578, Hakluyt Soc. edn, 1867) – as did Thevet's *New found worlde, or Antarctike* (1568), which Frobisher had with him on his first voyage. The ex-soldier and hack-poet, Thomas Churchyard, borrowed from Gilbert's earlier colonialist policies in Ireland the idea of transporting England's poor to the New World, as advocated in doggerel verse in his *Commendation of Sir Humphrey Gilbert's venturous journey* (1578). This sustained promulgation of Gilbert's views in both manuscript and print demonstrates how a closely knit group of family and friends could sometimes manipulate the book trade to their own advantage, as in *The worlds hydrographical description* (1595), by John Davis (his voyages: 1585, 1586, 1587, Hakluyt Soc. edn, 1878), a trusted associate of Adrian Gilbert, Sir Humphrey's younger brother and half-brother to Sir Walter Raleigh. As with John and Richard Hawkins, Frobisher's daring exploits fired the popular taste for tales of English naval heroism (as well as his investors' more hard-headed hopes for huge financial returns), prompting stationers to rush into print with thrilling accounts of his various voyages by Dionyse Settle (1577), providing the first published eye-witness account by an Englishman of America; Thomas Ellis (1578), recording the third voyage into northern waters and contact with eskimos; and George Best (1578), who compiled the major account of Frobisher's achievements.

The narratives of Francis Drake's voyages, one of the most revered of English mariners (even though he was out of favour at court between 1589 and 1593), were variously utilized by stationers and their sponsors as popular adventure stories, anti-Spanish polemic, stimulants for later colonialist ventures, and, above all, in the creation of that most powerful of imperialist tools, the image of the quasi-mythical 'great Englishman'. Drake's seamanship in both circumnavigating the world (1577–80, printed Hakluyt), thereby proving the possibility of access to the East without recourse to a northern passage, and crushing the Armada (1588), along with his numerous morale-boosting acts of piracy and plunder against the Spanish, were endowed by writers with an almost epic potency during the early years of the development (and validation through print) of an English maritime empire. Drake's renowned 1585 incursions against the Spanish were described by Walter Bigges in *Sir Francis Drakes West Indian voyage* (1589–96) and those of 1587 in Henry Haslop's *News out of the coast of Spain* (1587). His last voyage in 1596 with Sir John Hawkins, leading to his death off Portobello, was recounted in Henry Savile's *A libel of Spanish lies*, which also provided a text of the libel letter, by Bernaldino Delgadillo, in both Spanish and English (1596). A record of his circumnavigation, based upon the journal of the ship's chaplain, Francis Fletcher, *The world encompassed* (assembled *c.* 1595, printed 1628–34, by his nephew, Sir Francis Drake, Bt), confirmed his already legendary status.[40] At the beginning of Charles I's reign Drake's example was still considered powerful enough in print to inspire 'this dull age', as in Philip Nichols's *Sir Francis Drake revived* (1626–8, also sponsored by Drake's nephew), recounting the Panama raid of 1572–3. This tract pointedly borrowed its title from *Franciscus Dracus redivivus* (Amsterdam, 1596), which had held Drake up as a champion of Dutch and English Potestantism against the Catholic forces of Spain.

When considering narratives of individual voyages, it is also important to note that several (sometimes conflicting) accounts of the same voyage might well be circulated, sometimes simultaneously, in both manuscript and print. For example, distinct versions by five participants and one contemporary commentator are known of Thomas Cavendish's 1591–3 failed voyage.[41] The first three were printed by Purchas in 1625: (1) Cavendish's own paranoid self-justification written at sea before he died, printed from a manuscript owned by Hakluyt and used as the printer's copy. (Another manuscript survives, possibly a transcript of Cavendish's original papers.) (2) The memoirs of Anthony Knivet, whom Cavendish had put ashore to die, recalling his long years as a Portuguese captive. (3) Purchas's own sensational introduction to the original, censored printing of Cavendish's narrative. (4) John Davis's tract in his own defence, printed as *The seaman's secrets* (1595) – Cavendish had accused him of wilfully trying to destroy the voyage; and (5) John Jane's history of the voyage, printed in the third volume of Hakluyt (1600), supporting Davis's case. (6) Finally, the writer Thomas Lodge, who had served as a gentleman volunteer on board Cavendish's ship, the 'Leicester', mentions the voyage in the prefatory matter to his prose romance, *A Margarite of America* (1596).

In terms of colonial texts, a distinct literary form in themselves, Raleigh's Roanoke colony prompted *A brief and true report of the new found land of Virginia* (1588, with copperplate engravings by Théodore de Bry, who reprinted the text in his own *Americae descriptio*; also reprinted in Hakluyt) by the mathematician, Thomas Hariot, who had been sent by Raleigh to map Virginia in 1585–6. Despite the failure of this venture, other publications continued to highlight the rich potential of the New World, such as John Brereton's *Discovery of the north part of Virginia* (Eliot's Court Press, 1602), based upon his experiences as one of the first group of intended settlers in New England; and the *Discovery of the land of Virginia* (Eliot's Court Press, 1605), by James Rosier,

40 A manuscript copy of part of Fletcher's journal was made by a London pharmacist, John Conyers, in 1677, although the original manuscript is now lost.

41 See Edwards 1988.

who sailed with George Weymouth's East India Company voyage in search of a Northwest passage to India. The Jamestown settlement of 1607, the first permanent English colony in North America, also prompted a wide range of publications, such as *Good news from Virginia* (1613) by Alexander Whitaker, whose idealistic missionary zeal for the colony was unmistakable. In contrast, Ralph Hamor's *Present estate of Virginia* (1615) was rather more concerned with the practicalities of settlement and the potential for commercial investment, as befits an author who had himself spent four hard years in the colony. By far the most influential accounts, however, were from the pen of Captain John Smith, the settlers' self-appointed historiographer, who wrote *A true relation of... Virginia* (1608), followed by *A map of Virginia* (Oxford, 1612), published with a collection of individual reports from the colony, collected together by William Symonds. Smith's attention then turned further north, producing *A description of New England* (1616), which explored the possibilities of establishing regular trade in fishing, mining, and furs along the coasts of Massachusetts and Maine. (Some copies of this volume included the insertion of an additional single leaf, detailing Prince Charles's proposed new names for New England locations.) Smith followed this with *New Englands trials* (1620–2), which played down missionary intentions in favour of purely commercial considerations. (1,000 copies of this promotional publication were distributed free to some thirty of the chief trading companies in London.) Finally Smith produced his most important work, *The general history of Virginia* (1624, advertised in a 1623 prospectus), which was supplemented by *The true travels... of Captain John Smith* (1630) and *Advertisements for the unexperienced planters of New England* (1631).

4 Russia, the Levant, and the Middle East

English travel writing concerning Russia, the Levant, and the Middle East begins in this period with attempts by the Merchant Adventurers to discover a northeast route to Cathay through the ill-fated voyage (1553–4) of Sir Hugh Willoughby and Richard Chancellor.[42] The Muscovy (Russia) Company was granted its Charter by Philip and Mary in 1555 and prospered for the next three years. Still in the hope of finding a Cathay route, it sponsored the pioneering expedition (1558–63, printed Hakluyt, Hakluyt Soc. edn, 1886) of Anthony Jenkinson overland from Moscow to Turkestan and Persia. Hakluyt

42 Willoughby and his crew froze to death trying to shelter on the Lapland coast and his journal survived only because it was discovered, along with his corpse, by Russian fishermen during the next summer. See BL, Cotton Otho E.VIII. Chancellor was more successful, recording in his own journal how he located the mouth of the White Sea and travelled overland from Archangel to Moscow in order to establish trade with the court of Ivan Vassilivich (the Terrible).

edited texts of the journeys of some of Jenkinson's successors, Arthur Edwards (1565), Lawrence Chapman (1568–9), and Thomas Bannister (1569), in the hazardous trans-Caspian trade to Persia. Choosing the medium of verse, George Turbenville, penned his *Poems describing Russia* (lost 1568 edition, but some poems reprinted in *Tragical tales*, 1587, pp. 145ff., and in Hakluyt) while resident at Moscow as secretary to the English Ambassador, Thomas Randolph.[43] The first edition of *Russe Common Wealth* (1591–1643), by the diplomat and poet, Giles Fletcher, who had led an embassy to the Czar in 1588, although suppressed by the Muscovy Company (reprinted only in part in Hakluyt and Purchas), marked the culmination of this phase of English interest in the Russian empire. In the later period, however, four printed works on Russia also merit special mention: *Voyage... in Rushia* (1605), a tract relating to the death of Boris Godonov by Sir Thomas Smith, an energetic member of both the Muscovy and East India Companies; William Russell's *Bloody massacre in the city of Moscow* (1607); Henry Brereton's *News of the present miseries of Rushia* (1614); and John Milton's *Brief history of Moscovia* (*c.* 1640s, printed 1682), a compilation of notes lifted entirely from Hakluyt and Purchas and therein 'more akin to a foreign-office briefing than to a book'.[44]

Eventually, London merchants (with booksellers following in their wake) began to switch their interests away from trans-Caspian routes in favour of reviving sea traffic between England and the Levant. The new Turkey Company (1581), led by the merchants Sir Edward Osborne and Richard Staper, hoped to establish direct English trade links with India, via Syria, Mesopotamia and the Persian Gulf. The wanderings of Ralph Fitch in Southern Asia (1583–91, printed Hakluyt) gained much valuable information for this venture; as did the journey of John Newbery through Iraq and Persia (1580–2, printed Purchas). Two other influential volumes at this period were Thomas Washington's translation of Nicolas de Nicolay's, *Navigations... made into Turkey* (1585, with illustrations copied from the Antwerp 1576 edition) and John Wolfe's Italian edition of Pigafetta's *Itinerario* from Vienna to Constantinople (1585). By 1592 the Turkey Company's charter had expired and it amalgamated with the Venice Company to form a new Levant Company, under the governorship of Osborne with its main trading station at Aleppo. From then on, the Levant and Middle East figured prominently in the English book trade's concerns with commerce overseas.

43 For other printed verses on experiences of travel, see Robert Baker's account of two Guinea voyages in 1562–3 (printed Hakluyt) and Richard Rich's heroic verses on the survival of colonialists shipwrecked on Bermuda, in *News from Virginia* (1610).

44 *Complete prose works of John Milton*, VIII: *1666–1682*, ed. Maurice Kelley (New Haven and London, 1982), p. 463.

Sometimes the activities of a small group of individuals could fuel the stationers' preoccupation with certain key geographical areas. Interest in Persia, for example, escalated through the popularity of printed accounts of the travels of the remarkable Sherley brothers, such as *A true report of Sir Anthony Sherley's journey* (1600) and William Parry's *Travels of Sir Anthony Sherley* (1601).[45] John Cartwright's *The preachers travels* [on Robert Sherley] (1611) was followed by Sir Anthony's own *Relation of his travels into Persia* (1613). Increasing public interest in the Sherleys also began to prompt publications in a variety of other literary forms. Anthony Nixon, an industrious pamphleteer, was commissioned (probably by Thomas Sherley) to produce *The three English brothers* (1607), which borrowed extensively from Parry's text; a play was compiled (lifting material from Nixon's pamphlet before its publication) by Day, Rowley and Wilkins, *The travels of the three English brothers* (1607); the dramatist Thomas Middleton produced, *Sir Robert Sherley, sent ambassadour* (1609), a prose translation of a Latin work; and Purchas (1625) also printed extensive materials on the Sherleys, by which time accounts of their adventures (especially Robert's and Anthony's) had become as much mythic as historical records.

Individual travellers, from a wide range of occupational backgrounds, also compiled, either for publication or for manuscript circulation, personal (and sometimes highly idiosyncratic) accounts of their experiences. Most famously, Fynes Moryson's *Itinerary* (1617), covered not only Europe but also the Middle East. John Sanderson, a merchant based at Constantinople, recorded his experiences of the Ottoman Empire and the Holy Land in his *Travels* (1584–1602, Hakluyt Soc. edn, 1931). The organ-builder and member of the Blacksmiths' Company, Thomas Dallam, left a carefully compiled tradesman's journal of his visit to Constantinople to install an instrument for Mohammed III.[46] Other informative printed accounts included Henry Timberlake's narratives of his travels (or, more accurately, pilgrimage) in Syria and Palestine, *The travels of two English pilgrims* (1603–31, reprinted in R. B., *Two journeys to Jerusalem*, 1683–95); *The travels of certain Englishmen into Africa, Asia*, ed. Theophilus Lavender (1609–12), by William Biddulph, chaplain to the English merchants at Aleppo; and *News from Aleppo* (1628) by Charles Robson, another of the Aleppo chaplains. *Relation of a Journey Begun . . . 1610* (1615, reprinted in Purchas as *Sandys Travels*, 1652–73), by George Sandys (later Treasurer of the Virginia Company) provided valuable accounts in four books of travels through Greece and Turkey, Egypt,

45 For the unlicensed printing of the former tract, the stationers Ralph Blower and William Jaggard were fined and had their copies impounded. Arber, II, pp. 831, 833. See also BL, Sloane MS. 105, ed. E.D. Ross, 1933.

46 BL, Add. MS. 17480, Hakluyt Soc. edn, 1893.

the Holy Land, and the Mediterranean islands.[47] Publishing interest in the Levant and Persia was renewed during the 1630s and 1640s with the ongoing financial success of the Levant Company. Sir Thomas Herbert's *Relation of some years travel* (1634–77) and Henry Blount's *Voyage into the Levant* (1636–71) were both substantial works by ardent royalists. (Many of the Company's overseas factors remained staunch monarchists during the 1640s and 1650s.) Other historically based studies, such as Michel Baudier's influential quarto *History of the grand seigneurs*, translated by Edward Grimeston (1635), supplemented English knowledge of Turkish court life and society. A smattering of other informative and culturally aware accounts remained hidden away from public readership in manuscript, including those by Peter Mundy and Robert Bargrave, a Levant merchant.[48]

After the Restoration, the commerce of the Levant Company suffered significantly from the Dutch wars and from the incursions of the Dutch East India Company but these conflicts served only to fuel English readers' interests in the area. Stationers eagerly fed this demand with the familiar blend of original works and translations. The former category included major works of historical and geographical scholarship, *The present state of the Ottoman Empire* (1667–86) and *The history of the Turkish Empire* (1680–7) by Sir Paul Rycaut, consul of the Levant Company at Smyrna; and Thomas Smith's *Remarks upon the... Turks* (1678). But by far the greater number of important works were translations. The travels and commercial experiences of Jean Baptiste Tavernier (Baron d'Aubonne), the son of a Dutch map seller resident in Paris, became widely known in England through the translations by John Phillip of his *Six voyages through Turkey into Persia and the East Indies* (1677–88) and *A new relation of the inner part of the Seraglio* (1684). Three other major French works appeared in translation between 1685 and 1695: *Travels into Persia and the East-Indies* (1686–91) by Jean Chardin, who (like Tavernier) was primarily interested in the diamond trade; A. Lovell's translation of Jean de Thevenot's *Travels* through Turkey and Persia (1687), whose father, Melchisedek Thevenot, had himself been a celebrated collector of travel accounts; and the missionary, Nicolas Sanson's *Present state of Persia*, translated by John Savage (1695). Such was popular demand that even totally outdated materials on the region found their way into print, such as Ogier Ghiselain de Busbeq's, *Embassy into*

47 Sandys' *Relation* (1615) also contained material on Africa, as did Edward Webbe's *Troublesome travels* (1590–1600), William Biddulph's *Travels*, ed. Theophilus Lavender (1609–12), William Lithgow's *Painefull peregrinations* (1614–92), Richard Jobson's *Golden trade* (1623), and Sir Thomas Herbert's *Some years travel* (1634–77).

48 Mundy: Turkey: 1617–39, Hakluyt Soc. edn, 1907, 1914. Bargrave: Bodl. Rawl. MS. C 799, Hakluyt Soc. edn, 1999.

Turkey (1694), translated from a 1589 edition with reference to the 1660 Latin version.

5 India and the East Indies

Both Hakluyt and Purchas gave considerable prominence to Indian travel narratives in their collections. Probably the most important is the diary (1583–91, printed Hakluyt) of Ralph Fitch, the first Englishman to describe his impressions of Burma and Siam, as well as his imprisonment by the Portuguese at Ormuz and Goa. There is also the account (1608–13) of William Hawkins, the nephew of Sir John Hawkins and the first East India Company representative at Surat; and the diary (1608–11) of his agent William Finch, who obtained important trading privileges from the Great Mogul.[49] Sir Thomas Roe, a veteran of voyages to the West Indies and South America, compiled an informative journal (1615–19) of his trade embassy to Jahángir, Mogul of Hindustan, and his homeward journey through Persia. Roe's memoirs may also be compared with those (1616–17) of his naval chaplain, Edward Terry.[50] The journal (1608–17) of John Jourdain, who visited Surat and Agra and was President of the Council of India in 1618 before being killed by the Dutch (1619), covers large areas of India and southern Arabia and offers an interesting comparison with Robert Coverte's printed quarto *An Englishman that travelled by land through many kingdoms* (1612–31), an account of his epic journey through India, Afghanistan, and Persia after being shipwrecked.[51] Coryat's two publications from India, *Greeting from the court of the Great Mogul* (1616) and *Mr Thomas Coriat to his friends in England sendeth greeting: from Agra*, edited with verses by J. Taylor (1618), were circulated in the form of printed comic newsletters. The title page of the former, specifically addressed to 'the sireniacall gentlemen, that meet the first Friday of every month, at the Mermaid in Breadstreet', was adorned with a woodcut of Coryat perched on an elephant; while the latter pictured him precariously astride a camel.

The Portuguese dominance of the East Indies' spice trade, with trading posts centred at Goa, Malacca, and Ormuz, began to be threatened by the Dutch and then by the English during Elizabeth's reign. In England translations at first provided the main source of written information about this little known area, such as Fernam Lopes de Castanheda's *Discovery of the East Indies* (1582),

49 Hawkins: BL, Egerton MS. 2100, printed Purchas, Hakluyt Soc. edn, 1878. Finch's diary, printed Purchas, was brought back to England after his death by a servant, Thomas Styles.

50 Roe: BL, Add. MS. 6115, selections printed Purchas, Hakluyt Soc. edn, 1899. Terry: selections printed Purchas and as *A voyage to East India* (1655).

51 Jourdain, BL, Sloane MS. 858, Hakluyt Soc. edn, 1905.

translated by Nicholas Lichefield (Thomas Nicholas?) and dedicated to Sir Francis Drake; and the *Voyage and travel [1563–81] ... into the East India*, translated by Thomas Hickock from the Italian of the Venetian merchant, Cesare Federici (1588 and Hakluyt). The Dutchman Jan Linschoten had sailed from Lisbon to Goa as a young man in 1583 and compiled a detailed account of his experiences, the *Itinerario*, which was translated by William Phillip and printed by John Wolfe in a well-illustrated volume as a *Discourse of voyages into the East & West Indies* (1598, Hakluyt Soc. edn, 1885). Several other Dutch accounts of voyages were translated into English, such as another collaborative venture between Phillip and Wolfe, *A voyage made by certain ships of Holland into the East Indies* (1598), usually attributed to its Dutch publisher, Bernardt Langenes.

The twelve early voyages of the English East India Company between 1601 and 1612 also gave rise to several narratives of considerable merit. As propaganda for the first expedition, William Walker translated from the Dutch an account of Jacob van Neck's voyage (1601), whose exploits in 1598 had already been advertised by a lively newsletter, *A true report* (1599). Hakluyt himself translated Antonio Galvano's *Discoveries of the world* (Eliot's Court Press, 1601), detailing Portuguese commerce in the East Indies up to 1555 (and heavily reliant upon the work of Martyr and Gómara). The expedition for the Company by Sir James Lancaster, an Armada veteran, was detailed in the anonymous *Voyage of the fleet to the East Indies* (1603, Hakluyt Soc. edn, 1877); while Henry Middleton's voyage and exploits at Java were recounted in *The last East-Indian voyage* (1606, Hakluyt Soc. edn, 1856) and in Edmund Scott's *Exact Discourse ... of the East Indians* (1606). Furthermore, the insistence of the directors of the East India Company that detailed logs of every voyage be kept, resulted in an important manuscript collection of marine journals of the early voyages, preserved in the India Office Library. Some of the most important are the voyages of Peter Floris to Bengal and Siam (1611–15), and the naval battles of Surat with the Portuguese of Thomas Best (1612–14) and Nicholas Downton (1614–15).[52]

Other informative accounts of individual travel experiences continued either to be printed, such as *The preachers travels* (1611) by John Cartwright (previously chaplain to Weymouth's 1602 northwest passage voyage) and a translation of Henri de Feynes' *Survey of all the East Indies* (1615); or to be preserved in manuscript, as with Nicholas Withington's 'Travels [of] a factor in the East Indias' (1612–16, Hakluyt Soc. edn, 1934), recording his capture by the natives on an overland trip to meet Robert Sherley's boat at the mouth of the Indus. But news of the Dutch massacre of the English agents at Amboyna (in the

52 Floris: Marine Logs XIII, Hakluyt Soc. edn, 1934. Best: Marine Logs XV, Hakluyt Soc. edn, 1934. Downton: printed Purchas, Hakluyt Soc. edn, 1939.

Moluccas or Spice Islands) reached England in 1624 and overshadowed the merely geographical concerns of travellers and merchants in the East Indies. Predictably, the English press exploited to the full the sensational potential of this atrocity. Francis Coles, a well known publisher of ballads, rushed out a single-sheet folio ballad, *News out of East India . . . Amboyna* (1624), embellished with a crude woodcut illustrating the horrific torture and slaughter of the factors. This single sheet also served as an advertising flyer for a more substantial quarto account, *True relation of the unjust, cruel, and barbarous proceedings against the English at Amboyna* (1624, unique copy in the library of Magdalene College, Cambridge), published by Nathaniel Newbery.

The Amboyna massacre fuelled a prolonged English hostility towards the Dutch. As late as the mid-1660s their activities in the East Indies were still attracting virulent hostility from English presses, as in the *Second part of Amboyney* (1665), a miscellany of narratives detailing various acts of outrage and exploitation attributed to the Dutch. During the previous three decades, a sporadic trickle of more informative volumes on the East Indies had also appeared in English bookshops, including Christopher Farewell's recollections of his four years of travels in Asia, *An East-India colation* (1633); William Bruton's, *News from the East-Indies* (1638); a brief but invaluable gazetteer, *The East-India trade* (1641); and John Darell's *Mr Courteen's catastrophe and adieu to East-India* (1652), relating to Sir William Courteen's Goa venture.[53] Stationers also responded to public interest in the East Indies with a range of more populist publications, most notably Henry Cogan's lively translation, printed in a handsome folio edition, of Mendes Pinto's *Voyages* (1653–92), the vivid memoirs of a Portuguese adventurer. Read both as travelogue and prose fantasy, Pinto's picaresque accounts were often regarded as semi-fictitious (earning him the sobriquet, 'Mendax Pinto'), a quality which would have enhanced rather than diminished their sales.

The total eclipse of the Portuguese in the East Indies and Orient took place between 1656 and 1665. Following their martyrdom and expulsion from Japan (1638–40), Bombay was also ceded to the English, and Quilon, Cochin, and Cananor fell to the Dutch, along with other Portuguese strongholds in Ceylon and on the Coromandel Coast. As with many other geographical areas, post-Restoration interest in the East Indies was fed almost entirely by translations. These included Adam Olearius's *Voyage and Travels [1638–40] into the East Indies*, translated from German by John Davies and published in a handsome folio dedicated to the revived Muscovy Company (1662–9); Pietro Della Valle's *Travels*

53 In manuscript, Peter Mundy compiled detailed accounts of his time in Surat and India (Hakluyt Soc. edn, 1907, 1914), culminating in his return to India in 1655 (Hakluyt Soc. edn, 1936).

[1623–6] into East India and Arabia deserts (1665), translated from Italian by G. Havers and printed with an account of Sir Thomas Roe's 1615 embassy to the East Indies as its second part; François Bernier's *Late revolution of the empire of the Great Mogol* (1671–6), translated by Henry Oldenbourg, the first secretary of the Royal Society; Jean de Thevenot's *Travels* to the East Indies (1687); and, in handy duodecimo volumes, translations of Alexandre de Chaumont's, *A relation of the late embassy to the court of the King of Siam* (1687) and Guy Tachard's *Relation of the voyage to Siam* by six Jesuits (1688). Finally, a major source on the discovery of India by Manuel de Faria y Sousa was translated from a 1666 Portuguese edition by the antiquary 'Captain' John Stevens as *The Portuguese Asia* (1695). In the case of Japanese materials, the English book trade's dependency was even more highly specialized. Following the martyrdom and expulsion of the Portuguese from Japan (1638–40) to prevent the spread of Christianity, all Europeans except the Dutch were excluded until 1850. Hence, Dutch texts became, by necessity, the exclusive focus for English translators.[54]

The careers of Richard Blome (*d.* 1705) and John Ogilby (1600–76) illustrate just how popular and lucrative travel literature eventually became towards the end of this period. Blome, formerly an heraldic painter and cartographer, arranged (as 'undertaker') the publication of lavish octavo and folio volumes by subscription. These works, often prefaced with fulsome dedications to Charles II and produced by the best printers and illustrators available, included Sir Thomas Linch's *The island of Jamaica* (1672, reprinted in 1678 with *The present state of Algiers*); *The present state of . . . America* (1687, dedicated to James II); and ambitious proposals (1695) for the descriptions of London and Westminster. Blome's edition of *The four parts of the world* (1670), by the French missionary and cosmographer, Nicolas Sanson, included in its preliminaries Charles II's royal copyright warrant for twenty-one years and commendations from the likes of John Evelyn, Sir Kenhelm Digby, and Nicholas Mercator. Blome's most famous work, *Britannia* (1673–7), although attractively printed, was largely cobbled together from Camden and Speed. Before exploiting the commercial potential of geographical works, John Ogilby had earned a precarious living. After the Restoration he was invested with the honorific title of 'King's Cosmographer and Geographic Printer' and began under royal patronage to

54 See, for example, Roger Manley's translation from the 1636 Dutch edition of *A true Description of . . . Japan and Siam* (1663–71), by Frans Caron and Joost Schouten; John Ogilby's *Atlas Japannensis* (1670) from the Dutch edition by Arnoldus Montanus; John Morrison's 1684 editions of Jan Janszoon Struy's epic travels between 1647 and 1672 through Europe, Russia, the Levant, the Far East, and (briefly) Japan (bk 1, chapter 12); and a Latin translation from a 1649 Dutch edition of Bernard Varen's *Descriptio regni Japoniae et Siam* (Cambridge, 1673).

concentrate his considerable entrepreneurial energies upon travel and topography. Although neither a bookseller nor printer, in addition to his *Britannia* (1675), he published in handsome folio editions with lavish illustrations (some sold by subscription lottery with his own books as the prizes), a translation of Olfert Dapper's *Africa* (1669); collections drawn from numerous sources on *America* (1670) and *Asia* (1673); important works on China and Japan; and numerous maps and cheap guide books for English localities, such as *Itinerarium Angliae* (1675) and the *Pocket book of roads* (1679).[55] The success of Blome's and Ogilby's publications demonstrate how by the end of James II's reign travel writing, through its cultural, commercial, and political uses, had become a central aspect of the English book trade.

55 Ogilby published a lavish folio translation of Jan Nieuhof's account of the Dutch East India Company's embassy to China (1669–71), with Olfert Dapper's *Atlas Chinensis* as volume two of the 1671 edition. This volume also included useful selections from the *Antiquities of China* by the German Jesuit, Athanasius Kircher, best known for his important *China monumentis* (Amsterdam, 1667). See van Eerde 1976. The English book trade depended almost entirely at this period on Jesuit missionaries for materials on China, including *China and France* (1676) by Johann Grueber, who also explored Tibet; a *New History of China* (1688) by Gabriel de Magaillans; and *Travels . . . to discover a new way by land into China* [bk III, 'Roads into China'] (1693) by Philip Avril. For further discussion of Blome and Ogilby, see above, pp. 25, 241–2.

12

Science and the book

ADRIAN JOHNS

Books and things

The period covered by this volume saw the most profound transformation in natural knowledge ever to take place in Britain. At the beginning of Elizabeth I's reign, Aristotelianism held sway, and natural philosophy was a largely contemplative enterprise pursued at universities. A century and a half later, scholasticism had been eclipsed for good. The intervening years saw the flourishing of mechanical and mathematical approaches to creation, the invention of experimental philosophy, the advent of the Royal Society, and the achievements of Francis Bacon, William Harvey and Robert Boyle. The greatest of all works of natural knowledge, Isaac Newton's *Philosophiae naturalis principia mathematica* ('Mathematical principles of natural philosophy', 1687), had just appeared, and its enormous influence was beginning to be felt. If this was not quite a 'scientific revolution' – because what emerged from it was not yet modern science – it was nonetheless a change out of all recognition from anything that had gone before. What this dramatic transformation owed to the contemporary culture of the book, and what, if any, consequences it held for that culture, are the questions addressed in this chapter.

Many of those involved in creating the new philosophy of the period, and until recently most of their historians, would not have hesitated to answer these questions in dismissive terms. What was so admirable about the new philosophy, they were given to insisting, was that it abandoned the culture of the book altogether. It repudiated words in favour of things. Proponents called for the wholesale rejection of 'bookish' learning and its replacement by practical knowledge gained through direct experience. The exhortation was repeated across nations, confessions and philosophical schools. The pansophic philosopher, Comenius wrote, should 'not delay . . . by reading authors, but proceed to search into the very mines of things real'. William Gilbert introduced his enormously influential *De magnete* ('On the magnet', 1600) by praising 'true philosophers' – that is, those who 'not only in books but in things themselves look for knowledge'. Paracelsians and alchemists, too, urged their students to abandon books and venture into the world in search of understanding. Petrus Severinus wanted them to 'burn up your books' and buy stout shoes, while Gabriel Plattes declared that 'it is a great while since I read any books'. And when the Royal Society pioneered experimental philosophy in the Restoration, its own apologist even denied that it had a library. Such unanimity at a time of unprecedented epistemic upheaval was remarkable indeed. It seemed that the new philosophy, whatever it might be, could be recognized primarily – and perhaps only – by its rejection of the book.[1]

But in practice such pronouncements always had to be qualified. All of them were themselves made in printed books, of course, and those books were presumably not meant to be included in their own condemnations. More broadly, Gilbert's remark in particular was inspired by an 'ocean of books' flooding late-Elizabethan London, and no natural philosopher could ignore this unprecedented tide of printed works. Paracelsians might exalt the sympathetic experience of nature and deride the text-bound philosophies of the schoolmen, but they did so in some of the most elaborately beautiful printed works of their age. Comenius himself rather sadly admitted that he had never managed to follow his own advice. Plattes too, whilst he certainly recommended that alchemists reject most books, thought it essential to compile and use a 'Concordance' to the good ones that did exist. And Thomas Sprat, finally, was proved wrong: the Royal Society did create a library, and he himself boasted that its members were 'Read', as well as 'Travell'd', 'Experienc'd' and 'Stout'.[2]

Moreover, as well as playing an inescapable role in the everyday work of natural philosophers, books remained central to how they themselves characterized that work. Even as they affected to despise the books of humans, natural philosophers stayed incorrigibly fond of the notion that they were 'reading' a 'book of nature'. This was a hoary motif, but not necessarily a hollow one. On the contrary: its prominence in this period – greater, perhaps, than in any other before or since – came about partly because it ceased to be merely metaphorical and took on distinct critical bite. Attempting to stipulate the characteristics of sound philosophizing, writers of all opinions articulated its nuances in increasingly pointed detail. For example, natural historians like Ulisse Aldrovandi 'read' their collections in the light of Ovid and Cicero. Such reading

1 Young 1932, pp. 47–48; S. Shapin, *The scientific revolution* (Chicago, 1996), p. 68; Debus 1966, p. 20; G. Plattes, 'A caveat for alchymists', in *Chymical, medicinal, and chyrurgical addresses made to Samuel Hartlib, Esquire* (London, 1655), p. 61; T. Sprat, *Observations on Monsieur de Sorbier's voyage into England* (London, 1665), p. 242.

2 G. Naudé, trans. J. Evelyn, *Instructions concerning erecting of a library* (London, 1661), sig. A4^{v}.

resembled that exemplified in countless commonplace books. Omnivorous of discrete items of knowledge, and tolerant of their discontinuity, it was concerned for the mythical, historical, symbolic and sometimes occult meanings of natural things more than for taxonomy or causal philosophizing. In action, it generated a distinct brand of encyclopaedic natural history.[3] But there were other kinds of reading too. Mechanical philosophers and mathematicians could adopt Galileo's dictum, and insist that the book of nature was written in mathematical characters. This called for a very different reader, in that it would be 'humanly impossible to understand a single word' without bringing mathematical skills to bear on what was assumed to be a coherent, geometrical subject.[4] Paracelsians in turn voiced their own characterizations of the reading process, often drawing on the notion that God had inscribed 'signatures' into created things. These were signs – not only visible marks, but also smells, sounds, and textures – by which an adept could identify the natural powers and medicinal virtues imbued in particular objects. 'All herbs, plants, trees and other things issuing from the bowels of the earth are so many magic books', taught Oswald Croll. A proficient adept, then, should read the book of nature as an exegete would Scripture, tapping into a cornucopia of divine hints.[5] In each case, a representation of reading practices tied a philosophy of nature to an account of proper investigatory conduct.

Such representations could be put to use in three principal ways. They served to differentiate between rival methods of inquiry, to cast distinctions between competing claims about Creation, and to form moral judgements of those who proposed such claims. The notion of reading a book of nature thereby took on consequential moral force. For example, Nehemiah Grew recommended experimental philosophy by portraying a model virtuoso, John Wilkins, holding the Bible in one hand and Grew's own book in the other. The latter served as a commentary on the former, 'by which, in part God reads the World his own Definition, and their Duty to him'. Grew later introduced the main principles of his *Anatomy of plants* by informing Charles II of the novel insight that vegetables and animals shared similar organs, such as lungs. 'A *Plant* is, as it were, an *Animal* in Quires', he announced, 'as an *Animal* is a *Plant*, or rather several *Plants* bound up into one *Volume*'. On the other hand, the mid-seventeenth-century

3 Findlen 1994, p. 56. For commonplacing in bookish natural philosophy, see Blair 1997, pp. 49–81, and Moss 1996, pp. 268–72.

4 Galileo Galilei, 'The Assayer,' in Drake 1957, p. 238. For an interpretation of this passage, see Biagioli 1993, pp. 306–7.

5 H. C. Agrippa, *Three books of occult philosophy*, trans. J. Freake, ed. D. Tyson (St Paul, MN), 1997, p. 102; R. Turner, *Paracelsus of the supreme mysteries of nature* (London, 1656), sigs. B1^r–2^v; Hannaway 1975, pp. 63–4, 113. See also M. Foucault, *The order of things* (London, 1974), pp. 17–45.

physician Nathaniel Highmore rejected Sir Kenelm Digby's atomistic matter theory because it allowed for no way of encoding and reading signatures, thus outlawing a major aspect of the devout physician's practice. And Glaswegian professor George Sinclair condemned Descartes for forcing experiments into compliance with his own '*fancies*', declaring that this was 'to study *Natural History*, as *Hereticks* do the *Scripture*'.[6]

What was really striking, then, was the sheer diversity of ways, both practical and conceptual, in which natural philosophers across Europe put the book to use. Just as impressive was the range of printed materials they generated – or hoped to generate. At one extreme stood the tickets and ephemera on which an institution like the Royal Society came to depend for its weekly functioning; at the other, the projects of the great natural historians like Aldrovandi. Neither of these extremes has tended to survive, the one because such materials were discarded as soon as they had been used, the other because they were beyond the capacity of contemporary printers to produce in the first place. Only thirteen of Aldrovandi's 400 manuscript volumes had been published by the time the project was cancelled in the 1670s, for example, at which rate the last would not have appeared until well after the year 3000.[7] In Britain, especially, naturalists' grand schemes to print eternal monuments of learning all too often came to nothing. The nearest thing here to Aldrovandi's titanic work was probably Robert Fludd's *Utriusque cosmi . . . historia* ('Survey of both worlds', 1617–26), but even to begin this universal 'Naturall history' proved beyond any domestic printing house. Printed on the Continent, it fizzled out after a comparatively trifling nine years and seven volumes.[8] Later, the Royal Society too would attempt to publish a natural history fit to circulate among the courts of Europe; far from creating the splendid ambassador for itself that it had envisaged, the Society's venture into publishing failed so resoundingly that it almost caused its own bankruptcy. The scientific book in Britain, when it succeeded, was to be a more modest affair. With occasional exceptions, it spoke to 'modest' readers engaged principally in disputes with each other. The 'matters of fact' central to experimental philosophy would certainly depend on astute employment of the printed page – but in the form of the first learned periodical, not the last omniscient encyclopaedia.

6 N. Highmore, *The history of generation* (London, 1651), pp. 12–13; G. Sinclair, *The hydrostaticks* (Edinburgh, 1672), p. 316; N. Grew, *The anatomy of plants* (London, 1682), sig. $\pi 2^{v}$; N. Grew, *The anatomy of vegetables begun* (London, 1672), sigs. $A4^{r}$–7^{r}.

7 According to my own whimsical extrapolation from Findlen 1994, pp. 25–26, 30.

8 R. Fludd, *Utriusque cosmi . . . historia*, 7 vols. (Oppenheim, 1617–26); R. Fludd, *Doctor Fludds answer unto M. Foster* (London, 1631), pp. 21–2. Fludd called his series a natural history in his *Mosaicall philosophy* (London, 1659), p. 3.

Despite the conventional avowal, then, the relation between new natural knowledge and the book was by no means one of absolute disjunction. Real distinctions were being drawn, but at a more local and practical level: not between embrace and repudiation of the book itself, but between different kinds of books, between different readers, and between proper and improper uses of the printed word. Natural philosophers in fact thought long and hard about how properly to create, circulate and interpret books – and when to refrain from doing so altogether. They engaged personally with the intricate details of their manufacture. And at the same time, they also reflected at a more conceptual level on the processes and powers of reading. At a moment of extraordinary dissensus in all natural knowledge, the stakes in doing so were peculiarly high. They included the distinction of legitimate authors from the countless impostors clamouring for attention in early modern England, and hence the identification of knowledge itself.

Science in a Stationers' commonwealth

Citizens of around 1600 who wished to find out about the natural world could not simply ask a scientist. They had instead to choose between a dizzying array of potential informants. Physicians, lawyers, university dons, alchemists, mechanical philosophers, sailors, Paracelsians, pastors and craftsmen all sought to advance their own claims. As if this were not enough, an indeterminate number of international transients passed through London, hoping to make connections, or at least a quick profit; Giordano Bruno and Cornelius Drebbel were only the best known of them.[9] The resulting printed cacophony was what so horrified the Queen's physician in 1600. 'Intoxicated' by reading, William Gilbert warned, even the most talentless aspired to 'write numerous books' and to 'profess themselves philosophers, physicians, mathematicians, and astrologers'. At the same time, the populace treated those men who did possess authoritative credentials of scholarly learning with increasing disdain. The outcome could surely be a 'confused world of writings' that survived only by feeding ravenously on itself.[10]

In that world, natural knowledge faced a crisis of credit. In whom should readers vest their faith, and on what grounds?[11] As Gilbert asserted, the book participated in this crisis in a profound sense. The bitter struggles between so

9 Deborah Harkness is currently engaged in a study of these people, who were perhaps too transient and various to be called a community. For Bruno's surreptitious use of London printers, see Woodfield 1973, pp. 20–1, 62–8.

10 William Gilbert, *On the Magnet* [1600], trans. P. F. Mottelay (New York, 1958), p. xlviii.

11 S. Shapin, *A social history of truth* (Chicago and London, 1994).

many competing practitioners determined the existence, character and influence of the books that came into being. More broadly, they conditioned the proprieties of creating and using such books. And at the most abstract level, they decided what kind of thing a natural-philosophical book was and should be. The most important element in this determination was the necessity that the book span what were often represented as two distinct social worlds: those of craft and patronage.

In Renaissance natural philosophy, patronage played a central part in both discriminating between claimants and deciding the fate of their claims. Across Europe, newly powerful royal courts offered legitimation for people and practices not welcomed in traditional institutions. A court could harbour such oxymoronic creatures as the 'philosopher and mathematician', for instance, of which Galileo Galilei was the leading specimen.[12] England's relatively weak monarchy could follow suit to only a limited degree. There was no royal mathematician or philosopher here until John Flamsteed in 1675, and even Flamsteed was only made Astronomer Royal, not Philosopher. Yet naturalists and mathematicians nonetheless made use of sophisticated patronage strategies in search of support and accreditation. Their books were not just dedicated to patrons, but physically presented to them as gifts. Despite being printed, these presentation volumes became bespoke objects, the individuality of which mattered as much as their uniformity. As Edmund Waller told Thomas Hobbes, such 'gifts' were 'proportioned to the use & inclination of the receaver'.[13] More elaborate ones had individually coloured engravings and special bindings. They were often distributed along with accompanying devices such as sectors, globes and models of the heavens, some of which were deemed essential to their reception – so that there is a risk of anachronism inherent in the modern rare-books library, which tends to isolate the books from these materials. The combination could prove very fruitful indeed. In 1610, Galileo skilfully ratified his celestial discoveries by circulating copies of his *Sidereus nuncius* ('Starry messenger') to the courts of Europe alongside telescopes, through which patrons might be persuaded to look for themselves to confirm his reports. Thomas Harriot's failure to exploit such opportunities is a major reason why he has ever since remained in comparative obscurity, even though he made similar observations to Galileo's, and at much the same time.[14]

Yet books, even courtly ones, were also mechanic products. For one to come into existence at all, someone needed to negotiate the printing house.

12 Biagioli 1993, pp. 7–8.
13 T. Hobbes, *Correspondence*, ed. N. Malcolm (Oxford, 1994), I, pp. 294–5.
14 For Galileo, see Biagioli 1990; for Harriot, see Alexander 1995.

Naturalists might attempt to embrace the conventions of polite learning current in France, the Holy Roman Empire and Italy, but to do so they had to engage with a community of printers and booksellers – contemporaries called them 'Stationers' – that operated according to different criteria. This was also true of their Continental counterparts, of course (Galileo and Johannes Kepler were both expert in dealing with the book trade), but in England the supposed supremacy of courtly conventions in this process was harder to sustain. Natural philosophers' books fell subject to Stationers' calculations of viability, to Stationers' schedules of production, and to Stationers' distribution networks. Not just their existence, but their character and reception depended on the Stationers. In short, the creation and circulation of natural knowledge in print occurred within what George Wither famously called a 'Stationers commonwealth'.[15]

The Stationers maintained a network of largely domestic printing houses of modest size. These premises relied for their daily continuance on small-scale projects that brought in ready money. Yet traditional scholarly works, such as the books of mathematics or natural philosophy produced by university scholars, might be hundreds of pages long, and produced no short-term financial sustenance. To secure a regular income printers would therefore print several books simultaneously, sometimes divide up a given book among several printing houses, and lay major projects aside in order to produce pamphlets. John Flamsteed complained of this when the printers of his great *Historia coelestis Britannica* ('British survey of the heavens,' 1712 and 1725) delayed it in favour of newspapers.[16] It was a frequent source of complaint, but often had to be suffered if Stationers were to undertake a large work at all.

Gentlemen who experienced this kind of practice were apt to condemn the Stationers as simple agents of interest. But in reality things were not so straightforward. In fact, the Stationers maintained an elaborate civility, policed by regular searches and adjudicated by the monthly court that met in Stationers' Hall. They prized this régime as epitomizing the civil nature of their craft. In deciding whether and what to print, a master-printer referred primarily to this civility, and perceived his interests in its terms. To become a work of 'science', any book therefore had to sustain its credit (that is, both its financial viability and its epistemic reputation) in this realm, as well as in those of scholars and patrons. It was a demanding challenge. How demanding was revealed in their different ways by four enterprises that exploited the world of print to the full: natural history, medicine, magic and the mathematical sciences.

15 G. Wither, *The schollers purgatory* (London[?], 1624), title page.
16 F. Baily, *An account of the Reverend John Flamsteed* (London, 1835), p. 262.

The uses of natural history

Natural history was both one of the most successful enterprises of the Renaissance and one of the most problematic. Aldrovandi and others spent decades collecting natural and wondrous objects, and displaying them in cabinets of curiosity to which the learned thronged from throughout Europe. But the mass of natural facts they made available for philosophizing was widely criticized as at once inconsistent, insufficient and excessively credulous.[17] The combination made for particular problems in Britain. As we have seen, this country could boast no real counterpart to Aldrovandi, not least because its Stationers could not generally undertake such lavish works. But a growing literature did develop that addressed the problem of deciding the credit of prospective natural facts on the basis of printed or other testimony. Bacon's own natural histories were partly intended to exemplify this enterprise, and Joshuah Childrey's *Britannia Baconica* (1661) claimed to train its reader in discriminating between truth and falsity in '*credulous Writers*'. In some cases, such critical postures were underwritten largely by the difficulty of preserving the plausibility and hence the financial viability of what were always expensive books to produce. John Ray thus found himself forced not only to distinguish between different portrayals of species (selecting those of eye-witnesses before those simply copied from Gesner or Aldrovandi), and not only to issue ever more detailed rules to his engravers to ensure verisimilitude (some of which they seem to have ignored), but also to display this kind of work clearly to future readers. He had to do this in order to distinguish his own volume from earlier, equally costly ones. For Ray, the credit of these portrayals was a commercial necessity as well as an epistemic good.[18]

Natural history's reliance on images was at once its greatest asset and its greatest problem. Engravings might well be beautiful and eye-catching, and they suited courtly tastes very well. But they were expensive to produce, subject to the ('mechanick') engraver's interpretative skills, and vulnerable to unauthorized reproduction. Francis Aston even preferred that Ray's *History of plants* be printed with no images at all rather than permit 'old figures' to be re-used. Engravings were also the source of the Royal Society's troubles in printing its edition of Francis Willughby's *Historia piscium* ('Survey of fishes,' 1686). It is telling evidence for the importance of natural history that when it sought to

17 S. Shapin, *The scientific revolution* (Chicago, 1996), pp. 85–9. On the history of the fact in this period see also L. Daston and K. Park, *Wonders and the order of nature 1150–1750* (New York, 1998), pp. 215–53, and Daston, 'The factual sensibility', *Isis*, 79 (1988), 452–70.

18 J. Childrey, *Britannia Baconica* (London, 1661), sigs. A8^r–B^r; F. Willughby *Ornithology*, ed. J. Ray, (London, 1678), sigs. A2^r–(a)^r.

produce a printed ambassador for its activities, the Society chose to undertake such a work rather than an experimental discourse or a piece of mathematics. Yet the book was not a success. Even though Fellows sponsored individual engravings, its illustrations proved both prohibitively expensive and subject to 'scruples' as to their accuracy. Their credit, in both senses of the word, crumbled. The volume was a flop in commercial, scholarly, and patronage terms (plate 12.1).[19] The Parisian Académie Royale des Sciences's virtually contemporary *Memoirs for a natural history of animals*, by contrast, overcame such problems, but only by remaining outside the commercial world altogether. Copies were 'Presents only from the King, or Academy, to Persons of the greatest Quality', remarked Alexander Pitfield, its English translator, 'and were hereby rendered unattainable by the ordinary Methods for other Books.' Its images were creditable because their selected engravers were carefully trained and closely overseen. They reliably reflected the views of a collective of gentlemen free from interest and possessed of 'eyes to see these sorts of things'. Credit in natural history images was thus attainable if one could operate outside the world of 'mechanick' calculations. This was a solution of sorts, but its absolutist tinge made it both unwelcome and impracticable in England. Pitfield's translation was again a Stationers' product, reflecting its different political and cultural environment, and again he felt forced to vouch nervously for the worth of the illustrations. An important element in his success (and that of scientific illustration in general in the late seventeenth century) was the identity of his engraver, Richard Waller. Waller was a respected virtuoso as well as a skilled engraver, and the credit of the one identity underwrote the work of the other.[20]

Natural history books found diverse uses in the hands of different readers. In the British book trade, even courtly works became vulnerable to repeated appropriation at the hands of Stationers and their allies. Beginning as a patronage gift to Charles I, Peter Heylyn's *Cosmographie*, for example, became successively a tribute to Laudianism in the dark days of Cromwell's rule, a staple of Tory nostalgia in the Restoration, and a piece of allegedly Jacobite propaganda under William III. In its latter guise it led indirectly to the ousting of Edmund Bohun as licenser of the press, and his emigration to become a naturalist in Carolina. At the same time, the *Cosmographie* varied in size from a modest quarto, through an ungainly folio, to a portable octavo suitable for carrying into coffee-houses to aid in virtuosic conversations.[21] In these more modest formats natural-history

19 E.g., Gunther 1923–67, XII, pp. 85–86, 89–90, 92–93, 95.

20 A. Pitfield, trans., *Memoirs for a natural history of animals* (London, 1688), 'The Publisher to the Reader', sigs. a^{r}–b2^{v}; Ezell 1984.

21 Johns 1996, pp. 106–24.

volumes could have uses extending, as it were, into the field. Childrey's *Britannia Baconica* thus announced itself as a 'Portable-book' small enough to be carried around the country and used as a guide to remarkable curiosities.[22] Cheaper as well as smaller, such texts facilitated an expansion in the readership for natural history, and thereby in the constituency prepared to investigate local phenomena and submit reports to London virtuosi. But even lavish folios could have a practical impact. Most strikingly of all, with such herbals as John Gerard's *Herball* (1597) and John Parkinson's *Paradisi in sole Paradisus terrestris* (1629) books and gardens became figuratively interchangeable. A medical student in 1649 was thus advised to read a work by Parkinson on the grounds that 'you enter into him, as in to a fair well ordered garden, where you may readily pick out which herb you will'. Gardeners were sometimes ordered to dig up beds and replant them so as to match the latest classifications of the natural order promulgated in these expensive, thousand-page tomes (plate 12.2). With such practical innovations the concept of reading a book of nature led to the reshaping of physical environments in the image of a printed page.[23]

Medicine: practice and credibility in the vernacular

Books like Parkinson's served at least two purposes. As well as offering comprehensive taxonomies of flora, they also provided extended information about the medical 'virtues' of the plants they described. This undoubtedly explains a large part of their appeal. For if natural history books experienced ambiguous fortunes in Britain, works of medicine thrived as never before. And it was vernacular medicine in particular that so flourished. Encouraged by the spread of Paracelsianism, the number of English medical books of all kinds increased relentlessly, reaching some 85–90 per cent of total medical publications by the mid-seventeenth century. The College of Physicians, since 1518 the corporate overseer of London's medical practitioners, attempted to restrain this growth. The College's power over the medical marketplace had always been more theoretical than actual, however, and it was never very successful in these efforts. In the 1640s-50s in particular, when it lost all influence over the licensing of books, vernacular publishing flourished.[24]

The implicit calculation that inspired the College to seek such influence over the trade in medical books is simple enough, and it demonstrates why vernacular publishing caused its Fellows so much anxiety. There were at any

22 J. Childrey, *Britannia Baconica* (London, 1661), sigs. A8^{v}–B1^{r}.
23 Cunningham 1996, pp. 50–1; see also Hunt 1994.
24 For the College's responses to the medical marketplace see Cook 1986 and Henry 1991.

given time about 20–40 Fellows active in the capital's medical marketplace. The population of London, however, stood at around 200,000 in 1600, and was increasing rapidly. Unable to find a collegiate physician – and unable to afford his services if they could – the ill were therefore likely to seek out alternatives. There were many available, from graduate physicians, through surgeons and apothecaries, to local cunning-men; the ability to treat ailments was also a recommended duty for housewives. These alternative practitioners rested their legitimacy either on rival licensing authorities or on none at all, and were only loosely classifiable within the tripartite structure of physicians, surgeons and apothecaries. They made creative use of print to bolster their reputations and to garner custom among a broad urban readership. A vernacular work by such a practitioner could easily be published in an impression of around 1,000 copies, and dozens of editions appeared on the streets in the course of the sixteenth and seventeenth centuries. On the one hand, they alerted readers to their writers' claims and credentials; on the other, they simultaneously fostered scepticism about traditional authorities. They even encouraged readers to concoct their own remedies, especially after Nicholas Culpeper published his unauthorized translation of the College's own pharmacopoeia in 1649 (plate 12.3). By the beginning of the eighteenth century a popular and profitable literature of lay medicine was in the offing. The result threatened to be an ever-growing population of practitioners, independent of collegiate control and committed to self-perpetuation through the deployment of printed recipes.[25]

Vernacular medical books are often characterized as 'popular' medicine. Indeed, along with almanacs – by far the biggest sellers of all – they were probably the only works of natural knowledge to command a really sizeable readership.[26] But in fact their uses by the variegate communities of the medical marketplace allow for no such neat classification, whether in terms of content or circulation. They were not slavish popularizations of élite knowledge, their use was not restricted to the lay or provincial readers generally reckoned 'popular', and collegiate physicians themselves sometimes credited their recommendations.[27] Practising surgeons, for example, constituted the principal market for works like Richard Wiseman's richly produced *Severall chirurgicall treatises* (1676), a text authoritative enough to attract the jocularly ghoulish nickname of 'Wiseman's book of martyrs'. Before long the College of Physicians itself was being confronted by candidates for high office who vaunted their

25 Webster 1975, pp. 264–9. For books of secrets, see Eamon 1994, esp. pp. 250–66, 305–14.

26 Capp 1979; Blagden 1958b; Sanderron 1999.

27 Fissell 1992; Slack 1979. Fissell's argument is in part a specific application of more general points made by Roger Chartier about the historiography of popular culture, most recently in Chartier 1995, pp. 83–97.

unorthodox iatrochemical views in learned Latin.[28] On the other hand, licentiates were not slow to retaliate with frequent pamphlets of their own, attacking with their own weapons the 'empirics' who wrote, read and used vernacular books. But they found themselves on disconcertingly level ground when would-be patients came to distinguish between legitimate and spurious claimants. At a time when credit could no longer be assured simply by licensing – whether of books or men – in no field did Gilbert's prophecy come closer to realization than his own. The history of the medical book in Britain became a history of pamphlet wars.[29]

Natural magic: reading and experience

As the College of Physicians' oversight declined, so the increase in vernacular medical publishing threatened to change not only the language of medical knowledge, but its character too. In particular, Paracelsian and alchemical texts were issued in unprecedented numbers.[30] These often contained recipes for concocting curative agents, which readers were urged to attempt for themselves. Licentiates warned that the resulting mixtures were more likely to prove dangerous than beneficial, especially if the recipes were read without a knowledgeable physician in attendance. But their warnings were probably widely ignored, where they were heard at all. The idea that natural knowledge could be encapsulated in discrete practical procedures, recorded in print and replicable by any reasonable reader, was fast becoming familiar. With it was arriving a new kind of engagement with natural knowledge in print. This development was most clearly articulated in a field closely connected to medicine: natural magic.

A new philosophy would require a new kind of engagement with books. But the character of that new engagement remained unclear. Reading practices varied as widely as did strategies of manufacture and distribution, and, although the critical techniques of scholasticism were falling into disfavour, no agreed replacement had emerged. The advent of vernacular pharmacopoeias and Paracelsian works aimed at a lay readership provoked reflection on the alternatives. Practitioners of natural magic in particular advanced a powerful and popular notion. They exhorted their readers to go out into the world to gather knowledge by experience, and maintained that such experience could be

28 Debus 1966, pp. 52–81.

29 For the uses of print by various medical practitioners later in the seventeenth century, see Cook 1986, pp. 38–45.

30 Dobbs 1975, pp. 49–53.

captured and communicated in recipe-like texts. On the other hand, however, the more philosophical among them – alchemists in particular – maintained that subjectivity retained an inescapable role in the garnering of experience, if only because the microcosm/macrocosm analogy stated that every event in one's body had a direct counterpart in the natural world. Prayer, meditation and fasting were therefore just as essential for a successful trial as sound practical techniques and good furnaces. Indeed, alchemists tended to claim that a practitioner working to obtain the philosophers' stone sought to purify himself at the same time as redeeming the matter in his alembic, in what amounted to a personal transmutation.[31]

'Chymists' like George Starkey and Robert Fludd (a licensed physican in his own right) were acutely aware of the problems involved in any attempt to convey skilled knowledge by textual means alone. 'You may consume the greatest part of your Life' in reading, Helvetius warned, 'before you can gather thence . . . the direct manual Operation.' Alchemists were notorious for their claims to abjure open communication, their warnings against casual revelations of knowledge to the vulgar, and the obscurity of their prose when they did publish. Yet they affirmed that books could embody instructions for practical enterprises, and they produced the most beautiful and sumptuous books of their age. The resolution of this apparent paradox lay in how they conceived of the act of reading itself. In fact, alchemists argued that one could only read a book of chymistry properly in two circumstances: if one were a true 'adept' already, or else if one were in training with such an adept. In other circumstances, barring direct divine intervention, the resulting concoction would be either futile or dangerous. This conception bore fruit in practice. Apprentices in natural magic like Elias Ashmole were indeed trained by existing adepts, called 'fathers', who fulfilled this function. The 'apprentice' spent a long initiation period poring over texts, meditating on images, and practising chymical processes. At length he would be reduced to nothing, reborn, and redeemed as an adept. Ashmole himself was quite explicit about the character of the change wrought in him by this process of reading guided by an alchemical father. To extract truth amounted to the new adept's first transmutation.[32]

31 E.g., J. H. Helvetius, *The golden calf which the vvorld adores* (London, 1670), pp. 24–26, 41, 45–46. For the continuing importance of natural magic in early modern science, see P. H. Smith 1994 and Webster 1982.

32 Josten 1966, I, pp. 76–9; II, pp. 567–8, 574. A fine reconstruction of a student alchemist's reading practice is presented in Newman 1994a, pp. 115–69. For alchemical secrecy, see Newman 1994b, and R. Boyle, 'An epistolical discourse . . . inviting all true lovers of vertue and mankind, to a free and generous communication of their secrets and receits in physick', in *Chymical, medicinal, and chyrurgical addresses made to Samuel Hartlib, Esq.* (London, 1655), pp. 146–7; but for Boyle's own

Alchemists and chymists represented their prolonged engagement with the page in appropriate terms. In alchemical books, they said, the truth was 'latent'. It lay hidden, 'even as our Tincture of Philosophers is both included, and retruded, in External Minerals, and Metallic Bodies'. This suggests a reason both for the notorious obscurity of alchemical books and for their famously elaborate images. These works were deliberately arcane, not just to conceal their knowledge from the vulgar, but as an essential element in the transmutative development of the apprentice-adept. Their truths *must* be 'latent' in order to be transmuted. Michael Maier's *Atalanta fugiens* provides a ready example. Maier's book incorporated musical harmonies containing deliberate misprints. The misprints certainly shielded their truths from the uninformed, but that was not their major purpose. The real point was that a true adept would perceive immediately how to remedy (transmute) these printed notes so as to achieve the appropriate harmonies. Moreover, Maier's book also indicates another important element of the adept's reading experience. Since God had been munificent, a chymist or natural magician sought not one true meaning in any natural phenomenon, but as many meanings as possible. This implied a need to embody multiple truths such that the imagination could apprehend them simultaneously. In nature, God had used signatures to achieve this. The most successful magical practitioners followed suit by creating artificial images, as exemplified most lavishly in works like Maier's (or, to cite a British author, Fludd's). These extraordinary pictures were not simply 'illustrations', but an independent, and indeed primary, means of capturing and conveying knowledge (plate 12.4).[33]

The mathematical sciences and the problems of authorship

The impact of new uses of the book may have been striking in medicine and natural magic, but even more impressive was a transformation wrought in the visibility, conduct and standing of the so-called 'mathematical sciences'. That transformation spanned almost exactly the period of this volume. The first English primer in geometry, Robert Recorde's *Pathway to knowledge*, appeared in 1551, and with Isaac Newton's *Principia* in 1687 mathematics announced

extensive involvement in alchemical work, writing, and publishing, see L. Principe, *The aspiring adept: Robert Boyle and his alchemical quest* (Princeton, 1998).

33 J. H. Helvetius, *The golden calf which the vvorld adores* (London, 1670), pp. 67–9, 102–4, 117–18; M. Maier, *Atalanta fugiens* (Oppenheim, 1618); B. T. Moran, *The alchemical world of the German court* (Stuttgart, 1991), pp. 102–14; Hannaway 1975, p. 61.

itself to be the key to all natural knowledge. In the interim, mathematical practitioners learned to use print to good effect. Like magical practitioners – and some of the best mathematicians, William Oughtred among them, practised natural magic too – they recognized that the problems of conveying skills in print could be severe. But they were even more successful than the chymists in confronting those problems. In doing so, they permanently changed the epistemological status of their enterprise.[34]

The mathematical sciences comprised a set of numerical and mechanical practices ranging across such fields as navigation, surveying, fortification and shipbuilding. From astrology to instrument-making, 'the mathematicals', as Elizabethans called them, provided vocations for a large and growing number of practitioners distributed across the capital and beyond. They furnished valuable services to clients ranging from noblemen to navigators, surveying properties, draining farmland and forecasting futures. But from around 1550 they also began to advance the claim that they could supply natural-philosophical knowledge better than that emanating from the universities. Here was where their problems began.[35]

It may seem obvious today that mathematics has a principal part to play in understanding natural phenomena. But in early modern Europe this was widely denied. Aristotelians in particular tended to regard the application of mathematics to nature with suspicion, since it seemed to embody a fundamental category mistake. The point of natural philosophy was to consider nature in its substantial whole, and to provide causal accounts of *why* phenomena occurred as they did; mathematics treated quantity, at best but one aspect of such phenomena, and had nothing to say on the crucial matter of causation. In Aristotelian terms, the mathematicals were therefore 'mixed' sciences, in that they applied mathematical techniques to inappropriate, non-mathematical objects. They might produce tangible effects, but not real, philosophical knowledge. Add to that their grubbily practical character, not to mention their association with the mercenary self-interest of the craftsman, and learned gentlemen had good reason to suspect their claims to both epistemic and civil worth. What qualified these men to issue such challenges in print to existing knowledge? Were they not exhibiting both personal immodesty and social irresponsibility – not to mention profound philosophical error?[36]

34 R. Recorde, *The pathway to knowledge* (London, 1551), sigs. ξii^{v}, aii^{r-v}. For Oughtred, see Aubrey 1982, p. 229.

35 S. Johnston 1991; Bennett 1991. For a survey of practitioners, see E. G. R. Taylor, *The mathematical practitioners of Tudor and Stuart England* (Cambridge, 1954), pp. 165–307.

36 Dear 1995, e.g., pp. 3, 36, 161–79. See also Bennett 1986 and R. S. Westman, 'The astronomer's role in the sixteenth century: a preliminary study', *History of Science*, 18 (1980), 117–27.

Such challenges required responses on a personal level as well as a philosophical one. Mathematical practitioners answered them by using the raw materials of personal character, political thought, history and epistemology to forge credibility for both themselves and their enterprise. New representations of authorship were thus central to their efforts. 'Unlearned Mechanician[s]' like Robert Norman might concede that they lacked the traditional legitimacy accorded by a university education. But they argued that scholastic disputations were in any case no basis for reputation, since they exhibited only contumacious incivility, not harmonious certainty. At the same time, they tried hard to distinguish themselves from the 'mere mechanicks' who perpetuated vulgar errors and hoarded craft secrets. This was a particularly important distinction, since it implied that authorship itself, far from being evidence of immodesty, showed these new mathematical practitioners to be civil members of the commonwealth. A mathematician might then appeal to the conventions of patronage, claiming that a nobleman had requested him to publish. This invoked an obligation powerful enough to make reticence, normally a virtue, into a social offence. In Digges's words, such a request 'provoked, or rather inforced' authorship. The resulting book then enjoyed the protection of the patron's personal credit, which supplemented or even supplanted that of the writer.[37] And enough exemplars could also be corralled from the past to constitute a veritable apostolic succession of mathematical authors, proving the persona to be a commendable one. Practitioners identified themselves with Archimedes, Pythagoras and Roger Bacon, and reinterpreted Aristotle, Plato and Galen to show that each had acknowledged the centrality of geometry to knowledge of all kinds. John Dee, in the most influential of all such arguments, appropriated Vitruvius to laud both the scope of the mathematical sciences and the virtues of their model practitioner. In such hands, mathematical authorship and its genealogy took shape simultaneously. Not for the only time in the period of the scientific revolution, a new persona for the investigator of nature was inaugurated with the claim that it was in fact extremely ancient.[38]

Surviving in the Stationers' commonwealth was never straightforward, but for mathematicians, like natural historians, it was unusually problematic. Mathematics required special typography and skills – as Thomas Hood remarked, it

37 S. Johnston 1991, pp. 321–2, 325–6; R. Norman, *The newe attractive* (London, 1581), sigs. Aii^{v}, Aiii^{r}, Bi^{r}–ii^{r}; Digges 1579, sigs. Aiii^{r}–aii^{v}, pp. 188–91.

38 Norman, *The new attractive*, sig. Aii^{v}; R. Recorde, *The pathway to knowledge* (London, 1551), sigs. ς i^{r}–iii^{r}; L. Digges, *An arithmeticall militare treatise, named Stratioticos*, ed. T. Digges (London, 1579), sigs. Aiii^{r}–aii^{v}; J. Dee, 'Mathematicall praeface', in *The elements of geometrie of the most auncient philosopher Euclide of Megara*, trans. H. Billingsley (London, 1570), sigs. [☞ 4^{r}]–A4^{v}; Bennett 1982, pp. 12–13. The importance of apostolic successions in the legitimation of mathematics is displayed in Dear 1995, pp. 93–123.

was 'an harder matter to print these mathematicall works trew, then bookes of other discourse' – and the market was generally insufficient to provide the secure prospect of a return. Even someone as well-connected as Dee consequently found that the greater part of his writings could never be printed at all. He was dismayed to discover that just one volume would cost 'more hundred pounds, Charges, to be prepared for the print (in respect of the Tables, and Figures therto requisite): than you would easily beleve'. London's printers declared the prospect too 'dreadfull' to entertain. They refused to undertake the work at all unless Dee himself financed the process – a demand that helped fuel his requests for a court appointment. In this, at least, his experience was representative. True, scholars' complaints took on a conventional air, serving as they did to underline the modesty of the writer; but the convention itself rested on repeated and painful experience. Stationers did indeed remain reluctant to undertake mathematical works throughout the period. In the Restoration, John Collins – who had been apprenticed as a Stationer before becoming a mathematical author and facilitator for would-be virtuosi – proposed drawing up a list of works lost forever as a result of his erstwhile peers' caution. The edition of Kinckhuysen's *Algebra* once mooted by Isaac Newton would have made an especially noteworthy entry, given the origins of its failure in a combination of Stationer's misgivings and scholar's reluctance to appear 'ambitious'.[39]

Even if one did successfully engage a printer, moreover, further dangers awaited. Printers' expertise, coupled with their self-regard as an autonomous craft, generated some that were particularly resented. Richard Norwood declared that as a result of his printers' creativity in setting texts he could not guarantee the fidelity of an early table of logarithms. Moreover, he complained, rivals had been allowed to enter the printing house, whence they had absconded with copies and pirated the tables at their own presses.[40] Dee, too, found that this was not a realm in which one's work, once passed to the printing house, remained the unambiguous fruit of one's own authorship. Practitioners thus found that their efforts to represent theirs as a civil as well as useful enterprise, productive of natural knowledge as well as technique and mechanical prowess, risked being stymied by the necessary involvement of the Stationers. In ways like these the character of the master printer and the printing house impinged

39 T. Hood, *The making and use of the geometricall instrument, called a sector* (London, 1598), p. 52; J. Dee, *General and rare memorials pertayning to the perfect arte of navigation* (London, 1577), sig. ε*ii^{r-v}; S. J. Rigaud (ed.), *Correspondence of scientific men of the seventeenth century* (Oxford, 1841), I, pp. 122, 147–56, 178; II, pp. 14–16; R. S. Westfall, *Never at rest: a biography of Isaac Newton* (Cambridge, 1980), pp. 222–32; Oldenburg 1965–86, V, pp. 468–72.

40 R. Norwood, *Trigonometrie* (London, 1631), sig. A4^{r}.

even on mathematics – then, as now, conventionally esteemed as perhaps the most asocial form of knowledge.

The character of scientific dispute itself came to reflect such concerns. In particular, dispute was typically cast in terms of plagiarism. As Dee himself dryly remarked, opponents suggested any number of rival sources for his *Propaedeumata aphoristica*, in an attempt to prove that 'any Man els, was the Author'; meanwhile others proceeded to publish as their own ideas that were properly Dee's. Both tried 'craftily' to appropriate the patronage rewards 'of Credit, Commendation, or liberall consideration' due to Dee himself. In general, he considered himself 'dammageably discredited' by the 'Counterfeting' of 'Forgers' prepared to use the press to destroy himself and his authorial reputation. The resulting charge-sheet included not only necromancy but torture, and more than a hint of treason.[41]

Dee's complaints sound to us extreme, even paranoid; but similar expressions of outrage were just as plentiful in the writings of, say, Robert Hooke and Isaac Newton. In between, countless mathematicians – and, from mid-century, philosophers – reported having their papers lost, plagiarized, and subjected to unauthorized publication, occasionally several times over. Again, the prominence of such complaints was partly conventional. Claims of piracy could readily be used to defend the act of publishing as emanating from a reluctant gentleman, his hand forced by the risk of misrepresentation. But the convention referred to an experience that was common enough for it to remain plausible. The problem of credit that piracy generated was thus substantial. From the mathematical sciences it spread throughout natural philosophy and beyond. One reader was reduced to addressing Thomas Hobbes himself to ask him 'whether *Le corps politique* is the French translation of your *Leviathan* . . . and whether you approve of this translation[, for] it has been printed in Holland'. In fact, it was an unauthorized translation with no stated place of origin, and its original, a work entitled *De corpore politico*, was itself an unauthorized printing of just the second half of the *Elements of law*. To such readers and writers, such repeated reappropriations were endemic and lasting characteristics of the printing trades, which they accounted piratical to the core. It may well be that no renowned author escaped unscathed – and it is certain that none could predict beforehand that he would be so fortunate.[42]

In the service of accuracy, natural philosophers and mathematicians consequently felt the need to 'play the Stationer', as it were, and intervene in the

41 J. Dee, *General and rare memorials pertayning to the perfect arte of navigation* (London, 1577), 'A brief notc scholasticall', sigs. Δii^{r}–iii^{r}, εi^{r}–εiii^{v}.

42 T. Hobbes, *Correspondence*, ed. N. Malcolm (Oxford, 1994), I, pp. 314–16.

printing house itself. Any would-be author must attend in person. Finding a printer who was mathematically literate – as Thomas Salusbury tried to do for his translation of Galileo's *Dialogue on the two great world systems* – was an insufficient substitute for this close involvement. Salusbury complained publicly that even William Leybourn, a surveyor, tutor, and mathematical author in his own right, was not up to the task. But intervening personally meant qualifying the very independence that a gentleman most sought to protect. As well as having to enter spaces not particularly deferential to outsiders' views, he also had to accept that the resulting book had been subject to a civility that was not his own. Some sought to use intermediaries, such as John Collins or Henry Oldenburg, for this task. Isaac Newton himself needed his Edmond Halley to shepherd the *Principia* through the press. But even these agents, expert though they might become, had to rest content with compromising with the Stationers. Halley thus found that his initial plan to publish the *Principia* himself, handling its printing and distribution directly, met with potentially fatal opposition from the booksellers. He had to accommodate them by appointing an established bookseller as undertaker of the publication. The title of the work was decided by his first plan, Newton conceding to it in order to protect Halley's investment; but its very existence was conditional on the second. 'I am contented to lett them go halves with me', Halley told Newton of the booksellers, 'rather than have your excellent work smothered by their combinations'. In Halley's London, authorship – even of what is arguably the greatest work in the history of science – was compromised by the very measures deemed necessary to protect and legitimate it.[43]

The Stationers' civility mentioned above was of little help in this situation. In fact, it reinforced the status of the problem as central to the realm of print in early modern Britain. There were indeed social mechanisms in place to structure the decisions of the printer and bookseller, and the propriety of those decisions was in principle ensured by the Stationers' Company's oversight. But the character of the trade's conventions meant that it was the master printer or (increasingly) the bookseller who made the crucial decisions, rather than the author or an intermediary like Halley. Licensing and privileges – the two measures by which the state intervened directly in the working of the book trade – did not materially alleviate this situation, since each acknowledged the Stationer as the proprietor of a given work. In practice, moreover, enforcement of each depended on participants in the trade. In this sense, at least, both

43 T. Salusbury (ed.), *Mathematical collections and translations*, 2 vols. (London, 1661–65), I, sig. *2^r; Cohen 1971, pp. 132–3, 136–7. For the importance of independence of mind to a learned gentleman, see S. Shapin, *The social history of truth* (Chicago and London, 1994), pp. 168–72. For the use of intermediaries in publishing on the Continent, see Goldgar 1995, pp. 35–53.

licensing and privileges therefore amounted to joining the Stationers in lieu of beating them. This was why loud voices could be heard from the scholarly community condemning the very protocols that were intended in part to protect their prized publishing ventures. John Locke thought the powers of the Stationers constituted a major reason to oppose the renewal of the Licensing Act, so that the threat of some future licenser objecting to any assertion of 'the motion of the Earth' stood in tandem with the power of patentee Stationers to monopolize classical writers like Cicero. Thomas Hobbes was not particularly concerned for the freedom of philosophizing, but he too fell foul of the Stationers' conventions over patenting. He even pondered appealing to his enemies in the Royal Society to publish his works for him. Hobbes's last written words, penned in a letter shortly before his death in 1679, were these: 'The priviledge of stationers is (in my opinion) a very great hinderance to the advancement of all humane learning'.[44]

John Dee proposed a solution to these problems of print, as a significant part of his general claim to state patronage. Dee argued for establishing a new philosophical home in Winchester. Remote from London and the Court, this new house would be less prone to casual visitors than his existing Mortlake premises, and better suited to entertaining the kind of wandering scholar 'loath to be seene or heard of publickly in court or city'. 'Mechanicall servants' could construct instruments under Dee's oversight, and protect their secrets from the eyes of 'vulgar sophisters'. Dee likewise argued for 'a printing house to be set up' there, devoted to 'good, rare, and antient bookes in Greeke and Latine, and some of my owne'. Produced in isolation from the ways of the Stationers, these books would now be printed 'with my owne ordering and oversight'. No Stationer would ever again be given the chance to refuse Dee's projects, and interferers would be unable to commit offences within the printing house. Moreover, the implications would extend beyond Britain itself. By circulating the resulting books independently of the Stationers' networks, Dee would gain an international reputation for 'ability and credit', and would be 'better able to allure and win unto me rare and excellent men from all parts of Christendome'. In short, he proposed to solve the problems of authorship not by going himself to the printing house, but by bringing the printing house to him. He would subdue the craft under his own domestic authority. The master printer, for once, would be a guest in the gentleman's home.[45]

44 *The correspondence of John Locke*, ed. E. S. De Beer (Oxford, 1976–89), pp. 785–96; Hobbes, *Correspondence*, I, pp. 314–16; II, pp. 771–3.

45 J. Crossley (ed.), *Autobiographical tracts of Dr John Dee* (London, 1851), pp. 39–41. For the importance of the household in Dee's work and life, see Harkness 1997.

Dee's proposed printing house was never established. But its character deserves notice. In a sense, the proposal was but one of a succession of attempts by mathematical practitioners not just to use print, but to affect its nature. Beginning with Regiomontanus – whose plan to print the classics of mathematical science predated even the great humanist projects of Aldus Manutius – these proposals tracked the rise of the mathematical sciences themselves. They culminated in Dee's own time with the great Danish astronomer Tycho Brahe. Brahe's extravagant feudal fiefdom of Uraniborg included a printing house and paper mill as well as a castle, observatory and alchemical laboratory. Dee, who was in intermittent contact with Brahe, was certainly aware of his efforts. Yet although the press at Uraniborg did at least come into existence, it too was not as successful as had been hoped. Brahe faced repeated setbacks, and did not complete his astronomical printing. Exiled in 1597, he took his press with him to Prague, where he continued to search in vain for reliable operators. In the end the greater part of his work remained unprinted until long after his death. Even so, Tycho Brahe became an iconic figure in the mathematical sciences, in at least three respects. To British practitioners following Dee, he was emblematic of the nobility of their practice. To those ambitious of employing the press in the service of the new philosophy, he was a model to emulate. And in our own day his unrealized aspirations have been taken for the reality of a print culture.[46]

Tycho Brahe's plans revealed the aspiration of mathematical practitioners; his failures showed how difficult it would be to realize those aspirations. Like Brahe, Dee aspired to remove the scientific book from the Stationers' commonwealth. His project was the first of repeated British proposals for a press devoted to learning. Very few ever got beyond the most provisional of drafts. But three did. William Laud's Oxford Press, devoted primarily to patristic and classical learning, was the first of these. Laud's successor, John Fell, made the Oxford Press a notable scholarly and typographical success. Yet even Fell could not realize his ambition to produce a corpus of ancient mathematical works; his idea came to no more than had Regiomontanus's two centuries earlier. Richard Bentley's printing house in Cambridge was a more important exception to the rule, thanks in large part to Bentley's own determination to make it a success. In 1713 it produced the second edition of Isaac Newton's *Principia*. Like the Oxford Press, the Cambridge Press had long been in the shadow of the Stationers' Company, from which it only really emerged towards the end of the seventeenth century. A different approach was that of the third institution

46 Johns 1998, pp. 6–21.

to show success: the Royal Society. Realizing the futility of attempting isolation, the Society engaged closely with the London book trade. Its fortunes are discussed later in this chapter.[47]

In Britain, the presses at Oxford and Cambridge came as close as it was possible to get to a new Uraniborg. Their patchy success showed the continued difficulty of establishing such an institution. Yet what if Uraniborg could be built not out of bricks, mortar, and a very large moat, but out of social conventions? Towards the end of our period, after a century of failures to discipline the press into conformity with learning, one mathematical practitioner tried to do just that. Joseph Moxon's *Mechanick exercises on the whole art of printing* is justly renowned as the first comprehensive account of early modern printing in all its aspects. But this renown obscures its contemporary purpose. In fact, the *Mechanick exercises* drew upon all the conventions developed by the mathematical scientists over the preceding century to make the Stationers' commonwealth a safe place for natural philosophy.

Moxon was first and foremost a wholehearted devotee of the mathematicals. A proficient globe-maker, he curried favour with Fellows of the Royal Society like Evelyn and Hooke, and was eventually elected a Fellow himself. He printed or published works on the mathematical sciences well into the 1680s, the *Mechanick exercises* among them. The new publication was licensed by the Society, and Moxon represented it as contributing to its programme.[48] Its discussion reflected this. The focus of Moxon's portrayal of the printing house was the master printer. The master was the 'Soul' of the enterprise, with lesser workmen mere 'members of the Body' subject to his natural authority. Borrowing directly from Dee, Moxon modelled this figure on the Vitruvian architect. He would 'Philosophize with himself' when establishing a printing house, using considerations of number, weight and measure to ensure the deft management of space and light. The press itself, similarly, should not be a product of artisanal trial and error, but 'a Machine invented upon mature consideration of Mechanick Powers, deducted from Geometrick Principles' – a 'harmonious design', in short, constructed according to 'the Rules of Architecture'. This was why Moxon recommended a particular press that he attributed to Willem Jansen Blaeu, a fellow mathematical practitioner who had worked with Tycho Brahe himself in Uraniborg. Blaeu's design was just that – a *design*, rather than a product of unreflective craft – and it originated with the foremost

47 Feingold 1997, pp. 435–6; McKenzie 1966, e.g., I, pp. 119–26.

48 Moxon 1962, pp. xxxiii–iv, xlv–xlix, 14, 409–41, 481; J. Moxon, *Tutor to astronomy & geography*, (4th edn. London, 1686), p. [272]; Birch 1756–7, III, pp. 441–2, IV, p. 26; Hooke, *The diary of Robert Hooke ... 1672–1680*, ed. H.W. Robinson and W. Adams (London, 1935), pp. 337–8, 448; Jagger 1995, pp. 193–208; Stationers' Company, Court Book D, fols. 87^r, 101^v, 212^r.

authority in the mathematical sciences.[49] Finally, Moxon made similar stipulations of the characters to be printed with it. He himself manufactured type, providing letter for both John Wilkins's universal character and Robert Boyle's Irish Bible schemes; he publicized his principles in the first specimen-sheet of characters ever printed in Britain. Those principles were once again derived directly from the mathematical sciences. Moxon insisted that characters must be generated out of 'Mathematical Regular Figures'. Only by applying this principle could a master hope to approach the letters of the ancients, which had been constructed strictly from 'Circles, Arches of Circles, and Straight Lines'. He recommended using the microscopes of his virtuosi friends to construct such letters, and mathematical instruments to measure and perfect their proportions.[50]

For a purportedly objective treatment, Moxon's text had some curious omissions. It is particularly noteworthy that booksellers were entirely absent. Booksellers had in fact long dominated the Stationers' commonwealth, to the extent that some printers wanted to secede and form their own company. Yet Moxon knew what he was doing. He was himself an outsider to the Company, which wanted his press destroyed. He regarded his title of Hydrographer Royal, obtained to protect his printing of charts from press-pirates, as authorizing his printing work despite his not being a Stationer himself. Moxon sympathized with the complaints of both printers and mathematical authors about the arbitrary character of booksellers' power, and shared an ambition to reconstruct the conventions of the trade in order to remedy the situation. An alliance of royal power (through grants of privilege like his own) with printers' traditional craft skills seemed a good way to achieve this end. Using such an alliance, it might just be possible to replace the booksellers' interested calculations with the civility of scholarship and the honest technique of the master-craftsman. So the omission reflected an aspiration to reconstruct the book trade in the image of a harmonious state.

The booksellers were well aware of such arguments, and countered them by claiming that they alone possessed the knowledge and contacts to act as intermediaries between gentlemen and craftsmen. For Moxon's project to be feasible, then, gentlemen authors must be persuaded that it was possible for them to understand the tactics of book-making. So printing must be subjected to

49 Moxon 1962, pp. xxii, 10–12, 15–17, 40–1, 45–9, 82–4, 327, 373–4, Appendix IV, p. 395; Dee, 'Mathematicall praeface', sigs. a3^{r}, d3^{r}–4^{v}.

50 J. Moxon, *Regulae trium ordinum literarum typographicarum* (London, 1676), pp. 3–4; Moxon 1962, pp. xxxv, xxxviii, 357ff.

geometrical rules, he insisted, and taught, not through the Stationers' opaque apprenticeship régime, but openly, by the reading of 'Experiments' such as those in the *Mechanick exercises*. He recognized, of course, that '*Craft* of the hand' could not be taught by reading alone. To gain practical skills, reading must be guided by an existing master, and one needed 'Practice and exercise' to acquire the required dexterity. Nonetheless, Moxon maintained that his tracts would enable lay readers to become 'conversant' in the craft's 'Rules'. A gentleman could understand the culture of a printing house even while remaining personally innocent of the manual labour of printing. Learned civility could overcome booksellers' conventions, as institutionalized in the Stationers' régime. The century-long struggle of mathematical practitioners against the contemporary culture of the book would end with their victory. Craftsman and scholar would meet in harmony. In short, printing would become what Moxon called a 'science'.[51]

The Royal Society and the reform of printed knowledge

The Interregnum saw an unprecedented peak in the publication of vernacular medicine, natural magic, and the mathematical sciences. Experience, not book-learning, was everywhere exalted. But the result was not everything that the best-known proponents of new knowledge, the followers of Samuel Hartlib, envisaged. The characteristics of the Stationers' commonwealth combined with the diversity of reading practices to produce a crisis in the credit of printed claims of all kinds. Riven with charges of plagiarism, piracy and seditious potency, the book trade of the mid-seventeenth century created scepticism about the science in its texts more than it did new knowledge. Hartlib's own proposals were hard to distinguish from the hare-brained schemes pouring forth from contemporary projectors. In medicine, William Walwyn pointed to a similar problem of credit, cautioning readers against the dangers of imbibing drugs 'much over-boasted in Books'. Such concoctions were 'in no measure to be trusted to', Walwyn warned. A recognized practitioner must be in attendance when the new medical books were put to use; otherwise they were more likely to kill than cure. Walwyn was no friend to the College of Physicians, but, as

51 J. Moxon, *Mechanick exercises: or the doctrine of handy-works* (3rd edn, London, 1703), sigs. A2^{r}–[A4]^{v}; Blagden 1960, pp. 148ff.; Moxon 1962, pp. 19–21, 21–4, 25, 87, 97, 87–120; J. Moxon, *Proves of several sorts of letters* (Westminster, 1669). The argument for an alliance of royal power and craft skill against booksellers' 'interest' was a complex one adopted by several writers in the Restoration: it is reconstructed in Johns 1998, pp. 297–320.

Culpeper remarked, this had long been the main argument used by the College against vernacular medical publishing in general.[52]

In 1652, the Paracelsian William Rand proposed to Hartlib a way of avoiding the plight of the many natural philosophers who found themselves 'rook't' by Stationers. Rand moved beyond the piecemeal, individual proposals of a Dee or a Brahe by suggesting a collective response. He proposed replacing the Stationers' civility with that of a community of scholars. 'Learned men in a body or Collegiate association', he remarked, 'with leave of the Magistrate[,] might well print their owne Inventions.' They could then ensure that their works appeared 'in such a Manner & with such reputation of correctednes &c that hardly any others would print them'.[53] The problems of credit and piracy would be circumvented simultaneously. It was, he averred, 'but a modest request'. Modest it may have been, but it came to no more than his parallel plan for an organization to rival the Royal College of Physicians. Only in the last third of our period would enduring mechanisms come into existence that provided a reasonable chance of disciplining the Stationers' commonwealth. Those mechanisms were the creation of a new learned institution: the Royal Society.[54]

The Royal Society of London for Improving of Natural Knowledge, to give it its full title, obtained its first charter from Charles II in 1662. The new Society, deriving from less formal meetings in Oxford and London since as far back as 1645, was devoted primarily to the development of natural knowledge by 'experiments'. The term itself was not new; it had been used by mathematical practitioners before 1600. But the idea that it could characterize an entire enterprise – in other words, that there could be such a thing as 'experimental philosophy' – was new indeed. Thanks to the work of a number of historians, the experimental conduct of the virtuosi in the Society has become relatively familiar.[55] As well as the contrivance and display of experiments themselves, however, Fellows devoted much time to the receipt, reading, and distribution of printed and written materials, and these activities are much less well known. Their practices of reading and experimenting intermeshed, and were intended to be both novel and normative. 'Books and experiments do well together', as one admirer put it, and at the Society the figure of the experimental philosopher was defined partly by their conjunction.[56]

52 Jenner 1994, pp. 352–4; W. Walwyn, *The writings of William Walwyn*, ed. J. R. McMichael and B. Taft (Athens, GA, 1989), p. 457; N. Culpeper, *A physical directory* (London, 1650), sigs. B1^r–2^v.

53 Sheffield University, HP 62/17/1A-2B.

54 Cook 1986, pp. 128–9.

55 Most notably in S. Shapin and S. J. Schaffer, *Leviathan and the air-pump: Hobbes, Boyle and the experimental life* (Princeton, 1985).

56 S. J. Rigaud, (ed.), *Correspondence of scientific men of the seventeenth century* (Oxford, 1841), I, p. 158. An example of someone separated from books was Leeuwenhoek, whom Molyneux found 'a very

Experimental philosophy necessarily impinged upon the Stationers' commonwealth, if only because relations between scholars were customarily lubricated by exchanges of books. In a much stronger sense, however, it depended on reports of experiences being reproduced and distributed to readers not only in the Royal Society but across Europe. Since few people could actually be present at an experiment, they necessarily relied on such reports; and the enterprise itself required that recipients trust them as authentic pieces of testimony. The reports had then to become the foci of further conversations, responses and experimental labours. Making local work into universal knowledge depended on the success and continuation of these exchanges. Ambivalent about the conduct of the Stationers, and disdainful of what they castigated as bookcraft, the virtuosi therefore sought new ways of engaging with print and its products. They developed protocols of appraisal, circulation and publication to guard works both manuscript and printed, and where necessary to guide the transition into print. And they developed unwritten conventions guiding the assessment of books and papers once they were printed. The Royal Society announced itself as the first place where natural philosophy could be conducted on the basis of materials read, printed, distributed and appraised by a community honour-bound to respect propriety.

We can see how the Society sought to achieve this end by tracing a typical response to an incoming book or manuscript. Such a submission might be made for a variety of reasons: to announce one's membership of the republic of letters, as a gesture of civility to the fellowship, or, in Newton's case, as a means of 'securing his invention to himself'. Fellows were in fact obliged to submit copies of any work they published. The work would then be 'presented' to the Society. That is, it would be formally announced at a regular meeting, perhaps by the Society's omnicompetent secretary, Henry Oldenburg. The niceties of such an announcement derived from those of courtly patronage régimes, and here too, as in a royal court, the character of a contribution's future reception largely depended on them. Academies revived the reciprocal relation between presentation and legitimation familiar from courtly settings, with the major difference that the prince was not present in person. His absence allowed for more emphatic pronouncements of authorship than had been possible a century earlier for Dee. Robert Hooke could be altogether more assertive – and

civil complaisant man, and doubtless of great natural abilities; but . . . quite a stranger to letters, master neither of Latin, French, or English, or any other of the modern tongues besides his own.' This was 'a great hinderance to him in his reasonings upon his observations; for being ignorant of all other mens thoughts, he is wholly trusting to his own, which, I observe, now and then lead him into extravagancies, and suggest very odd accounts of things, nay, sometimes such, as are wholly irreconcileable with all truth' (Birch 1756–7, IV, p. 366).

he was, to the extent of becoming notorious for his exaggerated claims and repeated allegations of plagiarism against all comers. But in this Hooke was far more representative than his enemies liked to imply. After a century or more of debate, authorship had emerged as among the central foci and engines of natural-philosophical debate.[57]

The presentation of a book occurred in almost every weekly gathering. Before long it became an essential stimulus to the Society's work. Above all, presentation was a 'public' act. It manifested the Society's collective rationality, and as such formed the entry point into a sequence of further actions representative of its experimental civility. The Society would reciprocate with a letter of thanks, for example, or even election to a fellowship. And in many cases it would institute a 'perusal' of the work. This was a rather ritualistic procedure of appraisal, useful both as a gesture of homage to the author and as a spur to the imaginations of those listening at the time. Typically, one or two selected Fellows would be chosen to read the work; they would leave with it at the end of the day, and report back a week or two later. Perusal of this kind became as regular an occurrence as experimentation. When the Society 'read' a book, in fact, its 'reading' was generally nothing more than the reported perusal of these delegates. Henry Stubbe even claimed that the virtuosi had not read Sprat's apologetic *History of the Royal Society*, 'but, as in other cases, gave their *assent* and *applauds* upon trust'.[58]

Perusal evidently signalled regard for the contributor and his claims. But it also led into philosophical conversation, experimental work, and, quite possibly, extended dispute. Accordingly, the Fellows conducting a perusal did so with particular issues in mind. One indication is given by Aglionby's dismissive verdict of a medical text: 'there was a great deal of reading in it', he reported, 'but little experiment'.[59] Another, more extensive, response was prompted by Hooke and Pope's perusal of the Florentine Accademia del Cimento's experimental reports. They declared that the trials 'had also been considered and tried in England, and even improved beyond the contents of that book', but that they had nevertheless been described 'with much accuracy and politeness'. However, only 'some of them' had included 'an acknowledgment of the origin, whence they were derived'. Taking his cue from this remark, Robert Boyle proceeded to prosecute the contested or insecure experiments. Pope commented further

57 Birch 1756–7, IV, p. 347. Fellows were also required to identify themselves as such on title pages, largely, one assumes, in an attempt to establish the Society as achieving substantial results – something that many in Restoration London were disposed to doubt.

58 H. Stubbe, *A reply unto the letter written to Mr. Henry Stubbe in defense of the history of the Royal Society* (Oxford, 1671), p. 19.

59 Birch 1756–7, IV, p. 253.

on the book's account of sound, thereby generating extended conversation about Italian and English measures of distance, and Richard Waller undertook to create an English translation. Waller's edition of the *Essayes of natural experiments* was eventually published under the Society's auspices. It was then again presented to the Society, and Denis Papin constructed a new three-month series of experiments developing its themes.[60] A perusal had here given rise to mild questioning over authorship, and thence to conversation and new experimentation – and finally to the publication of another book that was used to restart the cycle all over again. In tracing such processes, we come close to seeing how the Royal Society stimulated its weekly production of experimental philosophy.[61]

Along with perusal went registration: the entry of the contribution into a manuscript volume. The point of this, Boyle remarked, was to 'secure' authors against the 'usurpations' of rivals. Among natural philosophers, usurpation had become a common blanket term for plagiarism and piracy. The register, as the chief instrument for its detection and prevention, now became the keystone of experimental propriety. It guaranteed the sanctity of authorship itself. The disputes pursued in the early history of the Society – indeed, virtually the Society's early history itself – came to be defined by the régime it facilitated. These included Thomas Hobbes's definitive battles of the early 1660s (which Hobbes claimed to be prosecuting because of Oldenburg's improprieties in registering his mathematical work), Hooke's many struggles with Isaac Newton and others, and Newton's own agonized relations with Leibniz, which continued past 1700. 'Scientific' disputes almost always now took the form of contests for priority.[62] The register had civilized such accusations, but only at the expense of making them central to the experimental life.

Yet no such system could isolate natural philosophers altogether from the Stationers' commonwealth. That Sprat's *History* included a long section framed as an extension of the register was implicitly an admission that the press must be put to use. Indeed, the Society often recommended that submissions be printed. It would not generally act as publisher itself, however, and was far more likely to encourage its Fellows to subscribe to a publication in an effort to underwrite the costs of a reluctant Stationer. It might even guarantee to buy a specific number of copies. When Martin Lister wanted to produce a work on insects, for example, but found that the Stationers refused to undertake it, the

60 Birch 1756–7, IV, pp. 331–2, 335–7, 379.

61 Indeed, Robert Boyle castigated his colleagues when they perused a presented text *without* doing experiments: Birch 1756–7, IV, p. 329.

62 Meli 1993, pp. 96–125, presents an especially thorough and consequential reconstruction of the reading practices applied by Leibniz to Newton's *Principia* in perhaps the most important of all such disputes.

Society resolved to pay for the impression by buying fifty copies for the virtuosi and another hundred for other recipients. To reciprocate, Lister volunteered to engrave the plates and donate them to the Society.[63] This was the kind of deal frequently done when publishing proposals came up. By contrast, the only occasion when the Society tried to act as undertaker itself was a sobering failure. Francis Willughby's *Historia piscium* came to the Fellows' attention as a consequence of Lister's entomology project, since it was in thanking the Society for its help that Lister mentioned the existence of the manuscript.[64] A lavish work of natural history like Willughby's would make an ideal ambassador for the Society, it was felt, and would surely be admired across Europe. In the event, however, the book proved expensive to produce, aesthetically unimpressive, slow to sell, and of imperceptible scholarly impact. Persistent legend has it that the *Historia piscium* even imperilled the publication of Newton's *Principia*, which followed shortly after (plate 12.5).

By stark contrast, the Society's most successful initiative was in fact not the Society's at all. This was its 'public register', the *Philosophical transactions*. The *Transactions* was an entirely original kind of enterprise: a periodical devoted to natural knowledge. Launched by Oldenburg in 1665, it survived difficult times to inaugurate a new social economy of science as the definitive element in the republic of letters. The comprehensive *magnum opus* was not entirely displaced (the *Principia* was still to come), but the regular publication in series of briefer, discrete reports now mirrored more accurately the actual processes of work in natural philosophy. It served a vital purpose in securing authorship beyond the Society itself, and in circulating works throughout Europe. Most important of all, the *Philosophical Transactions* manifested the civilities of experimental philosophy both at home and abroad (plate 12.6).

The Society intervened in the world of the Stationers in two broader ways. It became a corporate licenser; and it appointed named 'printers' (in fact, booksellers) for its Fellows' projects, granting them patent rights in return for an undertaking that they would abstain from producing unauthorized editions. Its aim in both respects was simple. Unlike other licensing authorities, the Society's intent was not to suppress books. Nor did it mean to endorse any specific philosophical or technical claims in the books to which it gave its licence. Rather, its imprimatur vouched for the authenticity of the object itself. Without making itself a party in philosophical disputes, the Society underwrote the propriety of the records in which such debate could occur.[65] These,

63 Birch 1756–7, IV, p. 124. 64 Birch 1756–7, IV, pp. 127, 371, 373.

65 See, for example, William Petty's remarks (W. Petty, *Discourse made before the Royal Society... concerning the use of duplicate proportion* (London, 1674), sigs. A3^{v}–4^{r}, A8^{r-v}), that the work was

it was saying, could be trusted to be reliable reports of their authors' words and opinions: they were not unauthorized editions, piracies, plagiarisms, epitomes or unreliable translations by nameless third parties. Their authors had volunteered to act according to accepted norms of genteel conduct. The privileging of 'printers' served the same end, since the granting of patent rights came only with a guarantee that no translations, reprints or epitomes would be issued without the Society's consent. To modern ears, used to these qualities being taken for granted, it may all seem unnecessary. But in the seventeenth century it was essential.

In effect, then, the Royal Society moved not just to exploit the possibilities offered by print, but to remake those possibilities. It was neither a straightforward achievement nor an easy one, and its implications extended from the most intimate aspects of experimental practice to the most fundamental of new knowledge about the natural world. In mid-seventeenth century Britain, the learned book was surrounded by doubts about its viability, credibility and authorship. None of these problems, we may note, is characteristic of today's scientific book, which partakes of an established disciplinary identity and is subject to broadly uncontested conventions of authorship, manufacture, distribution and appraisal. An essential aspect of the scientific book in this period is therefore that by our lights it was not *scientific* at all. The Royal Society alone could not make it so. But the Society's innovations did contribute significantly to a reconfiguration of intellectual authorship and of learned civility – and finally even of print itself – that made the later development of the scientific book possible. The ambitions of Regiomontanus, Dee, Brahe, Moxon and Hartlib were finally to be realized, not by defeating the Stationers, but by joining them.

'a Sample' of the Royal Society's labours, and that 'the *Society* have been pleased to order it to be published; (I dare not say, as approving it, but as committing it to Examination.)'

13

Samuel Hartlib and the commonwealth of learning

M. GREENGRASS

Does Samuel Hartlib deserve prominence in a history of the book in Britain? He wrote little and claimed even less in print, a modest publisher with an indifferent commercial record. He was not a scholar, held no university degree, and did not own a large library. Yet he is an exemplary and contextual figure in the history of the book. He was a specialist in the collection, organization and distribution of knowledge, and his convictions tell us a good deal about how he interpreted the place of books in the commonwealth of learning. Moreover, his role as a publicist during England's mid-century 'troubles' illustrates the complex interplay between printing, scribal publication and private correspondence, enabling Hartlib to serve as a vital point of contact between England and the *république des lettres*. Hartlib and his English associates preferred the term 'Common-wealth of Learning'.[1] It expressed their somewhat naïve transactional view of information flow and commodified knowledge, and stressed the significance of public access to it. The chance survival of Hartlib's papers, lost from sight shortly after his death until their rediscovery in 1933, enables us to recover the aspirations and activities of this 'intelligencer'.[2]

'The greatest instrument of public edification'

Samuel Hartlib was a self-effacing publicist who side-stepped the civilities that we have come to see as significant in the verification of science in the seventeenth century.[3] Asserting no gentility or prior knowledge as to where truth might lie or be found, 'Albureth' (the magus-like anagram he occasionally adopted) placed the reliability and verifiability of knowledge in the public

1 E.g. [Francys Lodowyck (var. Lodwick)], *A common writing* (1646), preface 'To the Reader', sig. A3; Dury 1958, p. 71.

2 Greengrass and Leslie 1995; Greengrass 1998.

3 S. Shapin, *A social history of truth* (Chicago, and London, 1994).

domain. His role was as an 'instrument' to render it public, and thereby of benefit to all. 'I find my selfe obliged to becom a conduit pipe... towards the Publick' he wrote in 1650.[4] 'As for myself', he said three years later, 'I claim nothing but the contentment to be the Publisher thereof, that I may be instrumentall to advance the comforts of many thereby'.[5] Others who benefited from Hartlib's activities as a 'well-willer' to the public accepted his assessment at face value. He was 'born and framed to be an Instrument of God for stimulating, sharpening and uniting men's inborn talents' (Comenius), 'that painfull and great instrument' (Petty), 'the incitement of great good to this Iland' (Milton), 'the greatest instrument of public edification' (Dury).[6]

Hartlib's life in England was one of conviction interwoven by opportunism. Its essential details are well known from studies published this century.[7] He had been born in around 1600 in the Baltic city of Elbing (Eblag) in Polish Prussia into a notable merchant family. He was brought up and educated in a Brandenburg and Silesia that were beginning to experience what some historians have characterized as the 'Second Reformation'.[8] The term refers to that small clutch of German states and cities that became attracted to Calvinism despite its being formally outlawed in the Empire by the peace of Augsburg (1555). It had initially been most influential in the Rhineland. By the turn of the century, however, it had spread to Oderland Germany where Johann Sigismund, Elector of Brandenburg (*r.*1608–19), attempted to introduce Calvinism to his state.

Hartlib studied first at the Calvinist Academy at Brieg in Silesia before going on to the University of Königsberg, a battleground for the Calvinist enterprise in this, a newly acquired territory. During the early phases of the Thirty Years War, however, the Calvinist states of the Rhineland found themselves vulnerable to Habsburg forces and, by the latter years of the 1620s, the war-theatre had moved towards the Baltic.[9] Many Calvinist Protestants took refuge in the Low Countries. Hartlib came to England (in part, no doubt, because his mother had been English) and settled in London in 1628. There he lived more or less permanently, until his death in March 1662, first at Dukes Place, then Angel

4 S. Hartlib, 'Preface to the Reader' in *Discours of husbandrie used in Brabant and Flanders* (1650), sig. A4^r. Hartlib was echoing Dury's description of him as a 'conduit pipe of things communicable' – see appendix to Turnbull 1920, p. 79.

5 *A design for plentie* (London, 1653), sig. A2^v.

6 *The complete prose works of John Milton*, gen. ed. D. M. Wolfe (New Haven, 1953–82), II, p. 363; [William Petty], *The advice of W. P. to Mr Samuel Hartlib* (London, 1648), p. 1; Turnbull 1947, p. 67.

7 Turnbull 1920 and 1947; Trevor-Roper 1967; above all, Webster 1975.

8 Schilling 1986; on the 'Second reformation' in Brandenburg, see also Nischan 1994.

9 Greengrass 1993; but the problem of the displaced Calvinists that resulted is an important subject that has yet to be properly explored.

Court, Charing Cross, before finally settling in Axe Yard, Westminster, with his son (also Samuel) in 1658 – a close neighbour of Samuel Pepys.[10]

What could a foreigner in London do? The possibilities were limited. 'Strangers' were subject to punitive taxation and legally restricted. At moments of political tension they were the victims of xenophobia.[11] Hartlib exploited the advantages afforded to him by his knowledge of languages, his education and his network of foreign contacts. Having tried and failed to run a school in Chichester in 1630, he returned to London and established a manuscript newsletter service, employing copyists to despatch news bulletins in manuscript separates to subscribers. He employed his contacts abroad as well as those among the exiles in London.[12] They were supplemented by information from John Dury, a Protestant divine of Scottish descent, whose self-appointed mission was to reconcile the confessional differences between Protestant states as a prelude to a more general Christian reunion.[13] In July 1631, Dury set off on what would turn into half a lifetime of peregrination. As he went, he sent back names and addresses of contacts that Hartlib, his London 'factor', could use.

At the same time, Hartlib acted as an agent for others, especially for patents – a significant role amongst the London stranger community for whom technology transfer was a passport to financial security and social integration.[14] He collected money to sustain Dury's mission, to support foreign scholars in Britain, and to assist various exiles overseas. Over £1,400 passed through Hartlib's hands as a charity agent in the five years from 1637 to 1641. From his accounts, we can reconstruct the support he received. It included prominent ministers like Stoughton, Puritan grandees like Wharton and Robartes as well as well-established London merchants and provincial gentlemen. But there were also subscriptions from instrument makers, schoolmasters, college manciples and a 'Gardiner-Florist' from Stepney – an indication of the broad social constituency that Hartlib drew on thereafter.[15]

10 Pepys 1970–83, v, p. 30 – the entry for 29 January 1664 recalls that there had been a time when Hartlib had been Pepys's social superior 'in all respects'.

11 Scouloudi 1985, introduction, pp. 1–55.

12 Grell 1989, esp. ch. 5 contains valuable details on many of Hartlib's contacts in London.

13 On Dury's life, see Batten 1944; Rae 1998.

14 In his diary, Hartlib noted how to get copies of existing patents from the Broad Seal Office (HP29/3/56A – Ephemerides, 1635), noted how it saved money to register several inventions in one patent, and kept a petition for a patent (the one he had prepared for the Moravian exile in London, Christopher de Bergh) as a pro forma for use in the future. When Sir Richard Carew, an energetic gentleman projector, sought a patent in 1640 for his 'Warming stone or Gambathoes' it was to Hartlib that he wrote to seek assistance (HP71/17/1A).

15 The subscription lists and accounts are analysed in Greengrass 1995, pp. 75–9.

Amongst the individuals whom Hartlib assisted in the 1630s was the Moravian educationalist, Jan Amos Komenský (Comenius).[16] Hartlib had been in correspondence with him since around 1632 and had come to appreciate the potential of his encyclopaedic endeavours. Hartlib's first publication, an unauthorized printing of Comenius's pansophic manifesto, the *Conatuum Comenianorum praeludia* (Oxford, 1637) was, in part, intended to raise enthusiasm and subscriptions for the projected enterprise. It was also probably a 'cloak' for illegal collections of money without letters patent. Just under 300 copies of the printing were distributed free of charge by Hartlib. Along with them went a request for critical response and an appeal for funds.[17] Despite the recent events of the Thirty Years War, it said, God's providence had provided new light for mankind. Comenius's vision was a revelation. Pansophy offered a key to the books of nature and of God; its potential must be fostered by public subscription.[18] Hartlib's publishing activities thus began as a by-product of his pansophic and charitable endeavours.

On the eve of the English Civil War, it was ambitious proposals for the reformation of learning, based on Comenius' beguiling metaphysics, that dominated Hartlib's activities. He had already conceived of the desirability of a 'vniversal, learned, corresponding Intelligency'.[19] In a sermon preached before the Long Parliament on Sunday 29 November 1640, John Gawden had commended the works of Comenius and, partly on this basis, Hartlib used his influence in the corridors of Westminster to propose the reform of Chelsea College as a 'Universal College of the Learned'.[20] Comenius, who had finally arrived to stay with Hartlib in London in October 1641, was seen as its potential dean.[21] Hartlib published Comenius's proposals for pansophic method (the *Prodromus*) in *A reformation of schooles* (1642).[22] At the same time, he signed (along with John Dury) an extraordinary 'fraternal covenant'.[23] By this solemn, private agreement, dated 13 March 1642, they committed one another to spend their lives in a conjoint, godly promotion of three defined objectives, all to the mutual

16 On Comenius, see the standard study of Blekastad 1969.

17 HP18/20/1A–2B; 18/20/1A–2B.

18 *Ibid.* – 'Dei glora, Orbis salus in eo agitur... Tale enim revera futurum erit novum hoc Comenii opus, Libri Naturae et Scripturae clavis, artium, omnium vitae humanae utilium compendium exactissimum, uno verbo, Pansophia... Eripiemus, sat scio, facile, modo superfluis delitiarum nostrarum pauxillum detrahare coeperimus.'

19 The expression is used in his diary, or *Ephemerides*, for 1640 (HP30/4/46A).

20 John Gawden, *The love of truth and peace* (London, 1641), p. 41.

21 Young 1932.

22 J. A. Komenský, *A reformation of schooles* [London, 1641] (English Linguistics, 1500–1800; a collection of facsimile reprints, no. 143) (Menston, W. Yorks., 1969).

23 Edited in Turnbull 1947, pp. 458–60.

edification of the common good. These were the procuring of religious peace, the education of young people to Christian truth, and a complete reformation of ways of learning. This pact made them 'all three in a knot sharers of one anothers labours' and it shaped the rest of their lives.[24]

Their efforts were initially overtaken by the Civil War. Hartlib remained in London, acting as an unofficial agent for the Parliamentary cause and involved in military innovations.[25] Following the Parliamentary victory in 1646, he devoted himself to establishing an 'Office of Address' in London. Initially a scheme proposed by Dury, the Office of Address was to be a national agency.[26] Dury was insistent that it should be funded by the state.[27] It was to have two distinct branches, each with its own agent. The first, the 'Office of Address for Accommodations', was to function in London as a labour and trade exchange with the merchant publicist Henry Robinson at its head. The second, the 'Office of Address for Communications' was to maintain registers of information on 'Matters of Religion, of Learning, and of all Ingenuities'. Hartlib would be its agent, based in Oxford. It was not the first agency of its kind, as Hartlib knew. The title and some details came from Théophraste Renaudot's 'Bureau d'Adresse' in Paris, about which Hartlib had been informed as early as 1639.[28] But it was ambitious, and, in 1648, it seemed propitious. Hartlib busied himself in advancing the cause, drafting an Act of Parliament.[29] As comments came in, the scheme grew and evolved.[30] Those from William Petty were so extensive

24 [John Dury] *A motion tending to the pvblick good of this age, and of posteritie* (London, 1642), p. 42.

25 See Raylor 1993.

26 John Dury, *Considerations tending to the happy accomplishment of Englands Reformation in Church and State* (London, 1647).

27 HP58/14A–15B ('Reasons Why the State should not suffer the Office of public Entries or Addresses to bee in any other hand but such as they shall appoint to have it') – a memorandum probably for circulation around MPs in support of the proposed Act.

28 In 1611, two gentlemen of the privy chamber, Sir Arthur Gorges and Sir Walter Cope, had been accorded a patent to provide a 'publique Office Roome or place of resort or repaire of people for the Notice of borowing and Lending of Monoyes [etc] . . . and to keepe one or more Kalender or Kalenders, Register or Registers . . . '. A copy of the patent exists in Hartlib's papers (HP/48/2/1A–1B). HP30/4/33A (Ephemerides, 1639); and 64B (Ephemerides, 1640) for the first references to Renaudot's scheme in Hartlib's papers. Arnold Boate later forwarded printed pamphlets about the Paris establishment at Hartlib's request in 1648 – HP58/3A–4B (Arnold Boate to Hartlib, Paris, 26 July 1648).

29 Various scribal copies of the proposal prepared for distribution are to be found amongst Hartlib's papers as well as a translation into German – HP39/2/84A–98B; Hartlib received at least one set of (not particularly enthusiastic) replies from a German source (abstracted at HP59/9/8B). The draft act is at HP63/7/6A and it was hoped that Francis Rous would present it in Parliament (Braddick and Greengrass 1996, p. 324).

30 Cressy Dymock, who was much taken with the proposal, forwarded his independent reflections to Hartlib in early 1648 – mentioned HP31/22/21B (Ephemerides, 1648) – and Hartlib's papers contain both his own alternative projection of the office of address as a kind of delivery service (HP30/10/1A) and also his proposed 'Office of Address for servants', a recruiting agency (HP31/11/1A–6B).

that Hartlib rushed them into print to invite further reactions.[31] These were all accumulated into a revised proposal in which the Office of Accommodations was given pride of place.[32] His provincial correspondents were mostly enthusiastic about the proposal and, although MPs were never persuaded of the necessity for state funding, Hartlib was voted various substantial pensions.[33] He had struck a chord.

Under the Commonwealth and Protectorate, Hartlib was a respected figure. He employed secretaries to assist him in operating a kind of unofficial Office of Address. He had influence in high places. This was also the period of his most prolific, and most re-printed, publications.[34] They were mainly written by others, with Hartlib's prefaces occupying no more than 5 per cent of the print space. Frequently they were compilations (sometimes published as separates but occasionally vented together as a batch) around a particular subject about which he had sought information through his informal network. The subject matter was remarkably varied. It included agronomy, apiculture, silk manufacture, chemistry, mathematics, librarianship and the 'natural history' of Ireland. In their various ways, the subjects were 'models' of the putative reformed 'Commonwealth of Learning'. It is as 'Designs', 'Ideas', 'Patterns' and 'Projects' that we should read them. Come the Restoration, however, and Hartlib's star quickly waned. Those who live by the 'publick' must die by it too, especially in an age that reasserted the gentry civilities by which knowledge should be circulated and truth validated. Hartlib had grown uncomfortably close to the 'projectors', those readily portrayed as merchants seeking fortune at the public expense. He was easily parodied as a 'fanatick'.[35] His closeness to the previous régime ensured that he was marginalized and his petition to Charles II went unanswered. He died in penury in March 1662 after progressively debilitating ill-health, mainly forgotten, echoed satirically perhaps

31 [Petty], *The advice of W. P. to Mr. Samuel Hartlib*. The most critical comments on Petty's proposal came from Henry More – HP18/1/2A–3B (Henry More to Hartlib, 12 March 1648/9) – cited Greengrass, Leslie and Raylor 1994, p. 20.

32 [Samuel Hartlib], *A further discovery of the office of publick address for accommodations* (London, 1648).

33 E.g., HP60/14/14A (John Hall to Hartlib, Cambridge, 25 Jan. 1647/8) – 'I long for that business'; HP10/10/7A (Joshua Rawlin to Hartlib, Adesham, Kent, 15 May 1648), etc; Turnbull 1920, pp. 48–51 (for Hartlib's pensions).

34 Taking the seventy-two publications listed in Turnbull 1947 and amending it with reference to Leslie and Raylor 1992 and those listed under Hartlib's name in the Wing Catalogue, Sanderson 1994, Appendix C, undertook a calculation of the sheet-counts for each of them. The twenty-three publications up to the end of 1648 required 105.83 sheets in total (two not available to include in the count); the forty-nine publications from 1649 to 1660 required 440.9 sheets (one not available in the count).

35 Hartlib explained to Worthington in a letter of 17 December 1660 that he was upset by the publication of a mock-utopian work (J. Sadler's *Olbia*) which had been dedicated to him: 'They say it reflect upon me as if I were a refined Quaker, or a fanatick' (reprinted Webster 1979, p. 201). (U Cam. S. Hist. 10.65.52.)

in 1676 as the gimcrack inventor 'Sir Samuel Hearty' in Shadwell's play *The virtuoso*.[36]

The 'business of learning'

Technologia, the disposition of the arts and sciences (the *techne*) in general, was the information science of the first half of the seventeenth century, the study of knowledge systems in the context of how we know what we know, and how we convey it to others. It was the subject of whole volumes, of which perhaps the best-known example is William Ames's *Technometria* (London, 1633).[37] These works of philosophical pedagogy drew directly from contemporary writings on logic. As Howard Hotson has outlined, it was in the universities and Calvinist academies of central Europe that the reactions against Aristotelian logic had developed furthest.[38] They had adopted Ramism most thoroughly in the later sixteenth century. It offered a more practical training in how to analyse a text, prepare a memorandum and convince an audience than the abstruse densities of Aristotle's Organon. And when it became evident that there was still a need for training in logic to prepare students for the higher faculties (especially theology), Ramism transmogrified into 'methodical Peripateticism' as Bartholomäus Keckermann, its most distinguished exponent, termed it. Keckermann's writings, in particular his *Systema logicum* (1599), enjoyed a success equivalent to that of Ramus a generation previously. Like Ramus, he spawned a clutch of imitators. He offered the prospect of a systematic disposition of all the arts and sciences and a method for their comprehension. This method did not exclude Ramist 'topics' or a disposition to base all understanding upon observable experience, but it embraced them within clearly stated 'theses' and linked 'praecognita' from which a 'system of systems' or overall method of studying could eventually be derived.

These were deep rivers and they flowed slowly. Hartlib was not a professional logician, still less a philosopher; but he had been taught by an admirer of Keckermann's at Brieg and he knew their meanderings well. They influenced him, as they would influence Comenius too, at every turn. His private diary, or Ephemerides, documents his search for a 'right method', a 'true logick', especially during the critical decade of the 1630s (when it survives only for the years

36 *The complete works of Thomas Shadwell*, ed. M. Summers (London,1927), III, pp. 97 ff.

37 *Technometry*, ed. and trans. L. W. Gibbs (Philadelphia, 1979).

38 See H. Hotson, 'Philosophical pedagogy in reformed central Europe between Ramus and Comenius: a survey of the continental background of the "Three Foreigners"' in Greengrass, Leslie and Raylor 1994, pp. 29–50.

1634–5 and 1639–1643).[39] Here one finds the amateur Hartlib, enthusiastically engaging with those who offered the most systematic, comprehensive and alluring of methods – Baconian, Comenian, Acontian, Ramist, Keckermanian, Stresonian, Cartesian – yet hesitating between them. He responded directly to their aspirations but often relied on the comments of others to measure critically on what they had to offer, unwilling to choose one as against another. In the process, though, a subtle filtration was taking place and what emerged was a learning technology that ideally suited Hartlib's needs.

Its basic tenets are easily stated. The sum of human knowledge lay (as Comenius would often say) in three 'books' – those of nature, human reason, and divinely inspired scriptural wisdom.[40] This knowledge was a divine gift to us, a cornucopia or endless blessing when used aright. But it had become corrupted. The book of nature was neglected because traditional learning excluded its rich lessons. The book of reason was constrained by the absence of a right method of studies. The Word of God had become a battleground for contending theologians since the Reformation. As subjects developed their own specialist vocabularies and the use of the vernacular spread, the familiar tension in any advanced civil society between the contending but equally important needs for specialist and generally applicable knowledge had grown greater. The Garden of Eden, the Ark of the Covenant, the Temple of Solomon and the Tower of Babel were biblical narratives deployed in Hartlib's circle to demonstrate both the dangers and potential (when correctly comprehended), of human knowledge.[41] What was needed was a complete reformation of learning for, as Dury put it; 'except sciences bee reformed in order to this Scope, the increas of knowledge will increas nothing but strife, pride and confusion'.[42]

The remedy was to find new ways of learning. It should not be too difficult. God had given us all a talent. Keeping one's talent secret or hidden was an offence against God. So, too, was every kind of monopoly that constrained our talents. Talents were to be exported, traded and sent abroad, not hidden 'in a napkin'.[43] In this way what Petty called 'the businesse of Learning' would be transformed. Thus 'the wits and endevours of the world may no longer be as so many scattered coales or firebrands, which for want of union, are soone quenched . . . '.[44] It was a mercantilist conception of knowledge in which the

39 See S. Clucas, 'In search of "The True Logick": methodological eclecticism among the "Baconian reformers"' in Greengrass, Leslie and Raylor 1994, pp. 51–74.

40 E.g., J. A. Komenský (Comenius), *Via Lucis* (composed during his time in London but not published until 1668), ed. E.T. Campagnac as *The way of light* (Liverpool and London, 1938), ch. 16, para. 9.

41 Bennett and Mandelbrote 1998. 42 Dury 1958, p. 31.

43 Samuel Hartlib, *The reformed husband-man* (London, 1651), p.10.

44 [Petty], *The advice of W. P. to Mr. Samuel Hartlib*, p. 2.

lucriferous flow of raw and semi-finished articles would generate industry and ingenuity 'to the end that all Knowledge may abound in Love, and the discovery of one Truth may beget another'.[45] All the institutions of society had a part to play in this transformation, and particularly the state. Here, as elsewhere, Hartlib reflected his background in the 'Second Reformation', where Calvinism had become the servant for busy, modernizing statesmen. The state was a force for good, publicizing inventions, freeing the press, facilitating technology transfer, funding educational opportunities and encouraging colonization. And this reformation of knowledge became, in the heady days of 1647–9, but one part of a much larger transformation, a 'Reformation of our Church, State and Lives', a 'Universall Reformation fit for the Kingdom of God' a 'Generall Reformation' that would herald the coming of the millennium.[46]

The business of learning began with the process of reading. Humanist school-teacher manuals had already said a good deal about that. It should involve the practice of synopsis, a chosen passage excerpted into a book of commonplaces. Beyond that lay the matter of how one summarized a passage, digested its 'marrow', prior to comparing what one author had to say with another. Hartlib diligently enquired how to maximize this process of synoptic 'ordered reading' (or 'concinnation'). The result was a baffling array of techniques: the 'Pellian and Reineran analytical reading', the 'Ordered doctrinal reading of Streso' (or 'more Stresoniano'), 'Brook's Method of construing', the 'Marginal reading of Dury' (or 'methodus duraeus') and 'Brinsley's Army of Analytical Questions'.[47] Some of these had been developed by school teachers (Richerson, Brinsley, Brook, Pell); others emerged from the studies of Protestant theologians (Streso, Dury, Gawden). Hartlib noted the 'several ways of compendiating... reading' practised by scholars, approving of the practice of the Protestant theologian Matthias Bernegger who 'lays and spreads so many authors all along... a long kind of board et *repositorium*'.[48] One method that particularly captivated Hartlib in 1639–40 was 'Harrison's booke-invention'. Thomas Harrison was a London school master who had devised 'an excellent and the compleatest Art... of *excerpendi*'.[49] Hartlib described the technology thus: 'Hee aimes by it to gather (1) All the Authors (2) their Notions or Axiomes (3) their whole discurses... The ground of it [is] a passe port with as much paper vpon it as you please. Vpon it there bee slices of paper put on which can bee removed and transposed as one pleases which carries a world of conveniences in it.'[50] The result was 'an incredible easy compend for quotations', that Hartlib

45 Dury, *Considerations tending*, p. 49. 46 *Ibid.*, pp. 8; 31; 33; 35, and *passim*.
47 See Clucas, 'In *search*' and Howell 1956. 48 HP30/4/47B (Ephemerides, 1640).
49 HP30/4/46A (Ephemerides, 1640). 50 HP30/4/46A (Ephemerides, 1640).

praised for its 'Comportibility' since it offered 'Mobility to transpose your notions where you will to put in to find presently'. Harrison proposed a system of cross-referencing ('allegations by ciphers') and hoped to complete a 'special logick for the art of collecting'.[51]

Catalogues were the key. The development of the book index, the cross-referenced text and the printed catalogue is an often overlooked fusion of humanist learning technologies and print culture that reached its maturity in the seventeenth century. Hartlib's proposals for the reformation of learning depended upon these components and he was imaginative in suggesting ways of creating and printing catalogues.[52] He wanted summaries of the contents of new books to be made available in accordance with the best synoptic technologies as a way of improving their sales and undercutting the 'basenes of stationers'.[53] Later, the proposed Office of Address of 1647 would require the keeping of cross-referenced 'Registers' of all kinds. Petty's scheme of 1648 proposed that two agents be set to work 'perusing al Books and taking notice of all Mechanicall Inventions'.[54] Robert Child's proposed 'Chymical club' of 1650 aimed to do the same with alchemical literature.[55] Hartlib's friend from his brief stay in Chichester, the mathematician John Pell, praised the 'great vse of Indexes' which, he added, 'is observed by few'.[56] 'Perfect indexes' would prevent the proliferation of needless technical terms in different vernaculars. His own *Idea of mathematics* proposed 'A *catalog* of mathematicians and their workes' under three separate headings.[57] There would be 'a synopsis of all the severall *kindes* of mathematicall writings, either extant in print, or *accessible* manuscripts in public libraries'. This would be followed by a 'Chronicall *catalog* of *mathematicians names*'. Lastly there would be 'A *catalog* of the *writings themselves*' in chronological order, noting the numbers of pages and volumes and cross-referencing to previous and subsequent editions as well as to the first synoptic catalogue. A public library should act as a repository of copies of all the volumes to which it referred. In addition, it should keep 'a Catalog of all such workmen as are able and fit to be imployed in making Mathematicall instruments and representations, working upon wood, magnets, metalls, glasse, &c.'.

51 HP30/4/47A (Ephemerides, 1640).

52 HP29/2/26A (Ephemerides, 1634); cf his suggestion that all title pages be printed separately (as was the practice in France) so that they could the more readily be collected together as an automatic index (HP29/2/34A).

53 HP30/4/70B (Ephemerides, 1641).

54 (Petty), *The advice of W.P. to Mr. Samuel Hartlib*. p. 3.

55 HP28/1/61B (Ephemerides, 1650); the aim had already been stated by the projector, Gabriel Plattes whose advice was printed by Hartlib as the 'Caveat for Alchymists' in the *Chymical, medicinal and chyrugrical addresses*... (1655). He thought chemists most needed to 'labor first to collect the true experiments out of all bookes' before they 'fall to practice'.

56 HP30/4/55A (Ephemerides, 1640).

57 Wallis 1967, pp. 142–3.

Hartlib printed this proposal (which he had received thirty years previously) as an appendix to Dury's *Reformed librarie-keeper* in 1650. The latter had suggested something akin. Libraries, as currently constituted, buried knowledge on shelves, hid talent away. University librarians, thought Dury, lacked vision: 'but to speak in particular of Librarie-Keepers, in most Universities that I know; nay indeed in all, their places are but Mercenarie, and their emploiment of little or no use further, then to look to the Books committed to their custodie'.[58] The 'Reformed' librarian would be 'a Factor and Trader for helps to Learning'. He would keep catalogues of the 'Treasurie committed unto his charge' and 'trade' with those at home and abroad 'to multiplie the public stock' of knowledge 'of which hee is a Treasurer and Factor'. Each year, he should be required to 'give an account of his Trading, and of his Profit in his Trade' to the faculty, who would assist him in putting to one side those published works that made no new contribution to the stock of knowledge.

What then, was Hartlib's attitude to books and manuscripts? He was fascinated by their potential, but they were not objects to be revered. They were to be methodized, epitomized, gutted of their information. Books were important because they contained secrets; despite being published, the knowledge they contained often remained hidden, subterranean and precious. The adjectives he applies to the books of which he approves are telling. They are 'very rare', 'exquisite', 'precious'. Sometimes he noted the pages to be 'exscribed'. From his diary we can reconstruct something of his own itineraries in London as he visited the booksellers around St Paul's; from his correspondence we can follow the news of recent publications as it reached him, and see him abstract the details into his diary. Hartlib was one of the best-informed Londoners of the period, and especially on the subjects in which he had a lasting interest.

Real and important wisdom in books could easily be obscured by an over-elaborate rhetorical style. Hartlib was often critical of the written style of authors; 'ornate', 'indifferent', 'obtuse', 'Antick and Phantasticall', 'Absurd and pedantical' are some of the phrases he uses for authors who shrouded their lack of originality in rhetorical flourishes. Like Acontius, he sought 'the utmost brevity and perspicuity' and wished to 'dispense with all verbosity'. The Restoration rhetoric of the non-rhetorical, epitomized in Thomas Sprat's *History of the Royal Society*, had its antecedents in the Hartlib circle whose significance in the formation of the Royal Society Sprat would, however, assiduously marginalize.[59] In Hartlib's circle, too, lay the origins of that distinctive strand of political arithmetic, whose rhetoric involved an attempt to convince

58 Dury 1958, p. 16. 59 Wood 1980.

an ingenious public of a proposition on the basis of rationally costed, weighed and measured statistics.[60] Not all abstrusely written works were, however, to be rejected out of hand. Sometimes these abstractions resulted from our unfamiliarity with the subject-matter and we should not rush to conclusions.[61] The hidden riches of God's creation would not be instantly accessible. We should be assiduous and patient in the business of learning.

Hartlib had no interest in owning knowledge. It was more important to know where it was to be found and to encourage public access to it. With Dury, he advanced the case for some educational books to be printed and distributed freely at public expense.[62] 'By writing and dispensing freely of good bookes', he remarked in his diary in 1640, 'an insens[ible] impression will be made . . . vpon the world without any solemnity or pompe'.[63] He encouraged the establishment of public libraries, noting their foundation (for example, that of Sir Humphrey Chetham in Manchester) in his diary.[64] He was equally fascinated to learn of developments abroad and printed an account of the Wolfenbüttel library in 1651. One of the most important tasks ('speciall Correspondency') for the Agent of the Office of Communications, as foreseen in 1647, was to communicate with librarians abroad.[65] Although Hartlib had good relations with his printers (William Dugard and Richard Wodenothe – who, in different ways, shared his enthusiasms) he was opposed to anything but a limited degree of copyright assigned to authors or stationers.[66] In 1641, as the powers of the English Stationers' Company were challenged in the Long Parliament, Hartlib recorded in his diary that it was: 'a great injury that stationers have copies for ever. It should suffice they should enioy them for 5. 10. 15 years. Ot[h]erwise they never reprint them and by this means many good books are suppressed or perish altogether.'[67] He and his correspondents shared an equivalent dislike for the patent system for inventions and sought similar reforms. They were all (the rights of an author or inventor notwithstanding), shades of the Old Adam.[68] As Hartlib's correspondent, the Kentish gentleman Sir Cheney Culpeper told

60 Besides William Petty, and at a different level of sophistication, the writings of Hartlib's agricultural correspondents, especially Cressy Dymock, were especially noted for such devices. See Letwin 1963.

61 HP30/4/41A (Ephemerides, 1640).

62 Dury, *Considerations tending*, p. 50; cf. John Dury, *A seasonable discourse* (London, 1649), sig. D4^{v}, where he advocated 'a peculiar Presse for Printing of things to be distributed and communicated to the Schools and Universities, or universally to the chiefe learned men of the Land, to possesse them with those things which may season their spirits with thoughts of a Publicke concernment'.

63 HP30/4/38A (Ephemerides, 1640).

64 HP28/4/28A (Ephemerides, 1654).

65 Dury, *Considerations tending*, p. 49.

66 For Dugard, see Rostenberg 1965; for Wodenothe, see Sanderson 1994.

67 HP30/4/76B (Ephemerides, 1641).

68 For Hartlib, Milton and the question of authorial copyright, see Kevin Dunn, 'Milton among the monopolists: Aeropagitica, intellectual property and the Hartlib circle' in Greengrass, Leslie and Raylor 1994, ch. 9.

him in March 1646, monopolist 'Corporations of Merchantes', 'the monopoly of Power which the King claimes', the 'monopoly of Equity', and the 'great monopoly', that of the Church, must all be destroyed in the coming Great Instauration.[69] As in 'Macaria', the blueprint utopia published by Hartlib in the same month (October 1641) that Comenius arrived in London, the resulting brave new world would be a pluralist civil society in which free information flows were as essential to its flourishing health as free labour and the freedom of religious conscience.[70]

A much freer form of knowledge, however, lay to hand in the world around. Like many of his contemporaries, Hartlib firmly distinguished between knowledge which had been transferred by the written word and knowledge that has been acquired experientially. Experiential knowledge was always to be preferred. It demonstrated more clearly than any book ever could the 'first principles' of nature.[71] So the 'philosophic gardener', John Beale sought to match book culture with real observation in his *Herefordshire orchards*.[72] Such knowledge was less easily monopolized, more readily subjected to the searching proof of public verification. It was part of the cornucopia of God's boundless creation, a 'subterraneal treasure'. With 'Experimental Industriousness', a 'New World' of knowledge awaited man's colonization.[73] This preference explains why Hartlib's diary records the details of mechanical trades and popular medical remedies related to him by his barber and his maid. This is why John Beale accepted that tree-grafting was better learned from 'An Artist' who 'can teach more in a day than a book in a mon[e]th'.[74] It explains why Hartlib's London itineraries took him to the instrument makers of the city, the Deptford dockyards, the Rotherhithe 'glass-house', or the Küffler dye-works. This was what drove Hartlib to be instrumental in the inventive fancies of a succession of unlettered, self-taught and self-made individuals who, in their various ways, had found unique opportunities to advance their prospects during the civil war. The 'vulgar Baconianism' that persuaded Hartlib's well-born friend Sir

69 Braddick and Greengrass 1996, pp. 269–70. 70 Webster 1979.

71 To take one example, Hartlib cited Joachim Hübner approvingly in his diary as saying: 'People never consider the true way of studying which is either 1. To shew the first principles out of which the first inventors tooke their knowledge. 2. Or out of Bookes which have handled matters out of those principles. This notion is never distinctly apprehended by Men. Now hee that is directed to study the principles themselves hase a great advantage before the other. For this last must have much to doe to get the true meaning of his authors and to come as far as they did, and then hee can never come an inch further than the Principles which they follow. Wheras the other if hee get but any new principle will bee able to raise a world of other deductions which no body did before them' – HP30/4/31B (Ephemerides, 1639).

72 I.B. [John Beale], *Herefordshire orchards a pattern for all England* (London, 1657), pp. 13 and 19.

73 [Hartlib], *The reformed husband-man*, preface 'To the reader', sig. A2^{v}.

74 John Beale, *Herefordshire* (London, 1657), p. 31.

Cheney Culpeper to 'religiously condiscend to things & men of lowe degree, at leaste soe farre as to examine & knowe them' was based on a metaphysic of knowledge that went far beyond books and their contents.[75]

'The dutie of communication'

Harold Love has already examined the nature and significance of scribal networks and scribal publication, describing Hartlib as one of the 'too few writers [who] published extensively in both media... who moved freely between the printed pamphlet, the scribal separate and the personal letter as each was found appropriate to the task in hand'.[76] The survival of Hartlib's manuscripts enables us to explore the relationship between Hartlib's published works and his wider scribal networks, and to investigate the culture and significance of the latter. Hartlib regarded manuscript books as at least as important as printed ones. He carefully noted the comment of Thomas Goodwin to him that 'the best things are kept in mens studies in Manuscripts' and that there were 'more excellent Manuscripts now because this age is so much improved'.[77] As with printed books, Hartlib had bright ideas for how such potential could be harnessed to create a 'Common stock where Truths are to bee gathered preserved et increased'. Sermons, that potentially rich source of practical divinity, could be collected via stenographers whose activities in taking sermons down verbatim had so impressed Comenius during his visit to London.[78] Since manuscript books lay in private hands, he carefully noted the deaths of those who 'live in the spirit... scientifically' – men of science, Puritan divines and others known to have collections of manuscript books. This was in the hope that their 'legacies' (the 'Ana' of the eighteenth-century Republic of Letters) would become publicly available to give birth to seminaries of new knowledge and ideas. When he inherited, or had access to, the papers of Gabriel Plattes and Gerard Boate, he actively promoted their broader circulation both in manuscript and in print. In this respect, Hartlib was both part of, and distinctive within, the culture of scholarly scribal networks, where the attitudes were typically those of the gentleman collector. These were the privy assemblage of delicate trifles for their own sake, coupled with occasional hints in correspondence of the worth of the collection and the owner's willingness to show it to his friends. He might possibly part with a duplicate in exchange for another piece, or offer one as a gift to an esteemed correspondent in the anticipation of being accepted as a worthy

75 Trevor-Roper 1967; Braddick and Greengrass 1996, pp. 130, 266.

76 Love 1993, p. 147. 77 HP29/2/28B (Ephemerides, 1634); cf. Clucas 1991, p. 37.

78 Patera 1892, p. 39 ('Comenius ad amicos Lesznae in Polonia agentes', London, 8/18 October 1641).

virtuoso. It was a private, polite, unstructured set of non-continuous networks of communication, 'labyrinths' (as Comenius would have termed them) of knowledge that never led to science, which Hartlib sought to transform.

Hartlib worked within this scribal network culture.[79] His own substantial corpus of correspondents both at home and abroad was widely acknowledged.[80] Whilst we have yet to have Hartlib's 'circle' fully delineated, the recent study of Johann Moriaen, a key figure in his communication with the Netherlands, reveals its essential features, especially its diversity.[81] Hartlib accepted the common decorum of scribal network culture. He understood sensitivities in matters of conscience or political and military intelligence. He acknowledged the importance of not allowing the great secrets of nature into incompetent, or base hands.[82] He appreciated the indulgent tolerance and culture of courtesy that functioned between true *ingenui* ('correspondencie' was coterminous with agreement or 'harmonie'). He accepted and encouraged the *tesserae* of utopian prospectuses whose distinctive character was, in part, shaped by the private communication channels of scribal networks.[83] But Hartlib did so with a religious purpose and distinctive agenda. He sought to communicate knowledge and make it public in such a way that would ultimately have eroded its domestic economy (just as it would become eroded in the eighteenth century). There was a millenarian impulse behind this agenda. 'We have also an expresse promise concerning the latter times' wrote Comenius in the translation published by Hartlib in 1642. Citing the passage from Daniel 12: 4 that had appeared on the famous frontispiece to Bacon's *Instauratio magna* (1620), Comenius saw the total reformation of knowledge as an invitation to complete the prophecy and usher in the last days.[84] Behind Hartlib's extraordinary endeavours and commitments lay a sense that God's secret providence made the mid-century upheavals a time of opportunity for a wholesale reformation in which knowledge would play a central and determining role. 'And who can tell' wrote John Dury of the Office of Address in 1647, 'whether God . . . have reserved this *special secret* till this seasonable time' in advancing the godly cause of the 'reformation of true learning and wisdom'.[85]

This reformation must begin, of course, within each individual. In the 'Further Discoverie', a manuscript treatise probably written by Dury in 1648

79 Greengrass 1997.

80 E.g., Milton in the treatise *On education* (1644) in his preface to Hartlib, acknowledging '. . . the learned correspondence which you hold in foreigne parts, and the extraordinary pains and diligence which you have us'd in this matter both heer, and beyond the Seas' – *The complete prose works of John Milton*, II, p. 363.

81 Young 1998.

82 Newman 1994b, p. 63.

83 Dickson 1998.

84 Komenský, *A reformation of schooles*, p. 29.

85 [Hartlib], *The reformed husband-man*, p. 6.

but extensively edited by Hartlib prior to its circulation around members of the Long Parliament, the introduction addressed that question. '[B]ecause wee judge the time to be neere at hand, Wee prepare ouselves; wee trimme our lampes.'[86] But the wicks of knowledge would only be kept burning by communicating our talents to others and receiving their offerings in return; 'every one as he hath received any gift from ... God should communicat the same unto others'. We each have a 'duetie of Communication in Spirituall and Rationall matters'.[87] Such 'communicatio' (the common Latin rendering of the Greek 'koinonia' or 'shared communion') was, as Calvinist political theorists of the 'Second Reformation' had said, the foundation of all civil societies.[88] By fulfilling our duties we would advance the 'Accomplishment of our Reformation'. It would be a long, organic, interractive process, an 'instauration' (Calvin used the term a good deal more than 'reformation' to describe the processes of change advocated by the biblical prophets).[89] As Comenius put it, the reformation of learning was: 'like unto a tree arising from its living roots, which by its inbred vertue spreads it selfe into boughs, and leaves, and yeeldeth fruit. But that which we desire, is to have a living tree, with living roots, and living fruits of all the Arts, and Sciences, I meane Pansophy, which is a lively image of the Universe, every way closing, and agreeing with itselfe, every where quickning itselfe, and covering itselfe with fruit.'[90] This was a vision of a shared recovery of that traduced knowledge 'which Adam did bring into the world through lust' and which, so long as we did not give way to our 'self-seeking Affections', was ours by birthright.[91]

Communication, 'that which the Communion of Saints doth oblige Us unto', permeates Hartlib's activities as a publicist at every turn.[92] It explained his extensive diary, carefully indexed in the margin as to its subject-matter. Like Comenius and many English Puritans of the period, he thought it was a powerful instrument which, when re-read, would lead one closer towards 'God and His works of Creation' and the amendment of one's life.[93] But it was also a means of recording and ordering communication.[94] Communication underlined his willingness to put individuals in touch with one another and to forward unsolicited information to those who would find it important. It explained his interest in recipes for ink, new ways of blotting paper and new

86 HP47/10/2A–55B cited at 2B. 87 HP47/10/18B.

88 Althusius, *Politica methodice digesta* [1603], ed. C. J. Friedrich (Cambridge, Mass., 1932), pp. 15–6; cf. A. Black, *Guilds and civil society in European political thought from the twelfth century to the present* (London, 1984), ch. 11.

89 Wilcox 1994. 90 Komenský, *A reformation of schooles*, p. 24.

91 HP 47/10/4A; 20B. 92 Dury, *Considerations tending*, p. 6.

93 Greengrass 1996, pp. 48–9; Delany 1969, pp. 63–6; Ebner 1971.

94 HP31/2/10A–B (Ephemerides, 1648).

writing pens. It is not surprising that various individuals in the Hartlib circle should have sought to perfect a machine for 'double' or 'multiple' writing or that Hartlib should have been instrumental in organizing a public test of it in December 1647 before nine witnesses.[95] Amongst the latter was the famous developer of 'common writing', Francis Lodwick, whose schemes for a 'real character' Hartlib published and promoted that same year for their communicative possibilities.[96] The witnesses watched William Petty, its developer, transcribe the first chapter of St Paul to the Hebrews, including the verse: 'That the communication of thy faith may become effectual by the acknowledging of every good thing which is in you in Christ Jesus' (v. 6).

This ethos also lay at the heart of Hartlib's publishing energies. They were 'ideas' or 'patterns' of the processes of reformation. In the case of the *Commonwealth of bees* (1655), for example, the informatics analogy was very evident. The bees are Hartlib's correspondents. They collect the pollen of information in a providentially bountiful and free nature and bring it back in a spirit of public service to the hive of the office of address. There it will become the sweet rewards of the industrious commerce of letters, so much more virtuous than the slave sugar from New World colonies, the product of inquisitorial knowledge systems. Similar analogies existed with silkworms, fruit trees, fertilizers, colonization and the processes of chemical change.

Hartlib routinely edited and put into the public domain works that had come his way through his scribal network without the author's consent or permission. Comenius had been somewhat surprised when he received ten free copies of the *Conatuum praeludia* through the post via Danzig since he had never been consulted as to its publication.[97] The alchemist George Starkey, whose multiple publishing personae were clearly intended to exploit the labyrinthine world of scribal networks, expressed equal alarm that a tract he had written found its way into print through Hartlib without his consent.[98] Hartlib's most substantial publications, *Samuel Hartlib his legacie* (1651 and subsequent editions), *Chymical, medicinal, and chyrurgical addresses* (1655) and *The reformed commonwealth of bees* (1655) were, in reality, offshoots of his scribal network. They comprised letters solicited or received from individuals upon a particular subject that had been circulated for additional comments, the results edited and then launched upon the public.

As an editor, Hartlib was relatively scrupulous – his reputation as an 'intelligencer' depended on it. So, although he tended to edit out extensive rhetorical or allegorical flourishes from the material he eventually published in the

95 HP71/7/3A (22 December 1647). 96 Salmon 1972.
97 Greengrass 1995, p. 84. 98 Newman 1994a, p. 60.

Commonwealth of bees, his alterations were mainly at the level of standardization of punctuation, orthography and capitalization.[99] There are only a few cases where he altered (especially in translation) the sense of a passage. When Hartlib was informed that the *Discourse on the husbandry* that he published in 1650 was in fact a treatise composed by Sir Richard Weston and that he had relied on an inadequate copy, Hartlib sought to correct the damage.[100] The following year, he twice wrote to the author, asking him to make the printed copy 'compleat and sufficiently enlarged', albeit without receiving any reply. When it came to republishing it 'corrected and inlarged' in 1652, Hartlib carefully included his letters to Weston to shield himself from any allegations of sloppiness.[101]

Hartlib encouraged publications from others and they, in turn, sought his advice. We know something of his own publishing ventures. From the scattered, undated accounts that survive amongst Hartlib's papers relating to the publication and sales of the second and third editions of the *Legacie* in 1652 and 1655, it is clear that Hartlib bore the costs of printing and binding.[102] His printer (Richard Wodenothe) sold the copies from his shop and forwarded the proceeds back to Hartlib. From the fragmentary, mainly undated, correspondence of Wodenothe with Hartlib, it is evident that the former acted for him more generally in the book trade.[103] But printing was a risky venture in comparison with the more informal and less capital-intensive medium of scribal publication. Even in the case of the *Legacie*, Hartlib's most successful publication, he had 225 copies unsold from the second edition in 1655 and was probably reduced to selling them under an alternative cover to recoup the costs in 1659.[104] Meanwhile, the market for worthy enjoinders towards Protestant unification had also fallen flat and Dury mentioned in September 1654 that Richard Wodenothe was disappointed with the sales of his *An earnest plea for gospel communion* (1654).[105] In 1657, Wodenothe pleaded with Hartlib to intercede with Dury for the money that he was still due for that publication and asked them both to petition the Lord Protector for an office to stave off his

99 T. Raylor, 'Samuel Hartlib and the commonwealth of bees' in Leslie and Raylor 1992, ch. 5, esp. pp. 112–15.

100 HP46/7/13A–14B (William Spenser to Edward Barnett, Athorpe, 23 December 1650).

101 [Sir Richard Weston], *A discours of husbandrie used in Brabant*, 2nd ed. (London, 1652), sig.E2^{v} etc.

102 HP31/20/2A–7A. The third edition cost Hartlib 10*d*. per copy for a print run of 800 copies of about forty sheets per copy to a total outlay of £33 6*s*. 8*d*. Cf. Sanderson 1994, p.12.

103 HP33/6/9A (Wodenothe to Hartlib, no date). The printer refused to take Hartlib's copy of Harrington's *Oceana*: 'I shall not sell it [in] my Shop in a Twelve month.' He had already taken Heylin's *Cosmographia* from him: 'I feare that I shall loose 4. or 5s by that', lamenting 'the hazard in byinge bookes and my vncertain saile'.

104 It was issued under the title *The compleat husband-man* and printed and sold by Edward Brewster.

105 'it sticks on his hand' – HP4/3/37A (Dury to Hartlib, 30 Sep. 1654).

impending bankruptcy.[106] The 'dutie of communication' had generally proved to be a money and effort-consuming responsibility in a world 'governed by opinion' and there was apparently little to show for it all by 1660.

What, if anything, had Hartlib achieved? It is easy to overstate the importance of any individual or group in matters of cultural change. Many of the specific causes he promoted were unrealistic or unsuccessful. At best, his significance was indirect, instrumental and diffusive. Since all republics of letters are, by their nature, self-reflexive and voluntary, it is not so much the failure of Hartlib to gain state endorsement that counts but rather his success in persuading many individuals from disparate backgrounds to think a new way and talk a new language. He had no direct influence in the formation of the Royal Society (despite earlier claims to the contrary) yet by osmosis, through other individuals, and through shaping an agenda, he was not without significance.[107] In agricultural change, this was particularly noticeable.[108] Although he was not alone in advocating the possibilities of new husbandries, he was instrumental in advertising their potential and in engaging the enthusiasms of a minority of the English gentry in pursuit of them. Above all, he attached the English commonwealth of learning more firmly to the European republic of letters as it emerged from the divisive impact of the Reformation. Hartlib's interest in Paracelsian chemical medicine, Helmontian chemistry and the chemical processes pioneered by Johann Rudolph Glauber coincided with a renaissance of interest in such subjects and the rise of translations from European-based publications in England, which Hartlib undoubtedly facilitated.[109] Hartlib was instrumental in various areas of technological and scientific transfer. He created the mechanisms that allowed the currents of European scientific discourse to flow more freely to England. Whether in Cambridge, in the taxonomy of John Ray or the Cartesianism to which Newton reacted unfavourably, or further afield in the New England of John Winthrop Junior, Hartlib's intelligencing activities had not been in vain. He would find his successors amongst the Huguenot refugees in Augustan England, by which time the republic of letters had truly formed.[110]

106 HP33/6/3A–4B (Richard Wodenothe to Hartlib, London, 19 Nov. 1657).

107 See the balanced assessment in Hunter 1981.

108 J. Thirsk (ed.), *The agricultural history of England and Wales* (Cambridge, 1985), II, pp. 298–325, 533–89.

109 Webster 1975, ch. 4.

110 Goldgar 1995.

14

Ownership: private and public libraries

ELISABETH LEEDHAM-GREEN AND
DAVID McKITTERICK

The history of libraries between the mid-sixteenth century and the end of the seventeenth is one not simply of expansion and multiplication, but of changes in the relationships between readers and the book trade, in the ways books were organized, and in the values placed upon them by institutions or individuals. Books – new and old – were neglected as well as welcomed, while Britain became accustomed to using libraries on a scale unimagined at the beginning of our period.

When John Bateman, Fellow of the newly re-founded Gonville and Caius College, Cambridge, died in 1559, the university appraisers valued his goods at £48 17*s*.1*d*. He was probably not yet forty years old. His quarters comprised a chamber, an inner chamber, an upper chamber and a study. The chamber contained a table, a desk, sundry chairs and forms, a quantity of clothing, nearly all of it described as 'old', but he was well equipped with drinking glasses and table linen. There was also a 'pair of clavichords'. His inner chamber was his bedroom, with more chairs, two desks and a fireplace. The upper chamber contained a trestle table and eating utensils. The 'study' had two chairs, but no free-standing writing surface, a brush, a pen-case and an inkhorn. Here also were found some 500 books. We might perhaps describe the room as his library.

Bateman's collection was diverse. Over half was theological, not unnaturally since he was presumably studying for the degree of Bachelor of Divinity, at least until shortly before his death when the country turned Protestant again. The books are listed in no particular order except that, very typically, the multivolume editions of the Fathers had pride of place and head the inventory: Augustine in eight volumes, Jerome in three, Origen in two, Ambrose, Gregory, Basil, Athanasius each in one. Later on we find a seven-volume edition of Jerome. Eusebius, St Bernard, Tertullian are here also, and Augustine in epitome. A substantial portion of his theological books are anti-Lutheran, but this was no placid Catholic. He had, after all, come up to the Edwardian university. The text of the Bible is (unusually) present in force, with Bibles, Testaments or Psalters in twelve Latin versions, two Greek versions, two Graeco-Latin versions, and, wonderfully, two English versions, one French version and no fewer than six Hebrew versions.

In addition to theology he had standard texts in grammar (unusually including Syriac (two) and Hebrew (fourteen)), dialectic, rhetoric and philosophy. He was atypical in not having parted with the texts for the Bachelor of Arts course as soon as he had completed it. Perhaps he was teaching. There are a few texts in medicine, law, cosmography and mathematics, along with Aquinas, Scotus and a manual of chiromancy. Apart from his Bibles, seven of his theological works, one of his medical works, three legal texts and two grammars are in English. He had also Sir Thomas More's *Apology*, Elyot's *Governor* and *Image of governance*, Chaucer, Gower, a work of John Lydgate, two books of the story of Troy, and the poems of the Earl of Surrey, presumably *Songes and sonnettes*, as well as Guevara, Politian, the *Dialogus creaturarum* and Quintus Curtius in English translation. There are thirty-three English books listed, considerably more than appraisers usually noted in academical libraries at this time. By contrast, among the 1,489 books recorded in probate inventories as owned by 107 members of Oxford university dying between 1507 and 1576 only 153 books were in English, and ninety-three of those were theological.[1] The vast majority of these books, were, of course, printed on the mainland of Europe.

In academic circles, the demand for learned texts was constant. They had a significant re-sale value, and so were usually listed in some detail among the effects of the deceased. Vernacular texts tended to be smaller books, unrelated to the academic syllabus and of less, and less easily computed, value and so are underrepresented in the inventories. Bateman probably had more than thirty-three English books. The final item in his list reads 'divers other old bokes 6*s.* 8*d.*'. 'Thappologie of Sir Thomas More' was valued at 8*d.* and there are many books here valued at one or two pence. It would be rash to suppose that the members of the two universities did not own works of contemporary English literature. There is no lack of anecdotal evidence to the contrary and, after all, many contemporary English authors were themselves bred in the universities. Commonplace books, libraries in miniature, testify to the circulation of contemporary verses among the young gentlemen of the colleges and the Inns of Court into the late seventeenth century. In brief, while many of Bateman's books were such as might be found on the shelves of many of his contemporaries and in the stock of Cambridge booksellers, it is possible to pinpoint items which reveal his own predilections, academic and otherwise.

1 *PLRE* 5–112 in vols 2–4 (Leedham-Green 1986, I, pp. 234–44).

When Sir Edward Dering, MP for Kent, and a member of the Cotton circle, died in 1644 almost half of his quite substantial library of some 670 books was in English. He was a serious-minded reader – rather more than half of his English books treated of theology.[2] Only a few academics in the early seventeenth century owned libraries of such a size, and the range of vernacular literature available to them was significantly less, although, of course, it increased with the passage of time. Nonetheless, Sir Edward, as a country gentleman, who also moved in antiquarian circles in London, was a likelier customer for English works of vernacular history and geography, both of which feature prominently among his interests,[3] and he was also a keen purchaser of English literature, including play texts. He had easy access to the London booksellers and, as a man of influence, was no doubt in receipt of gifts from aspiring authors as well as from his learned friends. He had, moreover, a gentleman's house. By the end of the century, few great houses were without a library.

The evolution of the library as a distinct room in a gentleman's house awaits a full investigation. Andrew Perne's probate inventory, drawn up in 1589, shows that the majority of his books were arranged, presumably on shelves, in the Master's lodge at Peterhouse quite systematically, with grammar, philosophy, theology (Catholic and Lutheran separately), geometry and maps in the upper study, along with classical literature, and a scattering of natural philosophy. History, cosmography and civil law were shelved in the lower study, and Bibles, concordances and dictionaries on assorted shelves and flat surfaces in his chamber.[4] At a much more humble level John Edmunds, an MA of Cambridge, but one who had reverted to his father's status as a merchant of the town, had a room in his house set aside as his 'study' in 1596.[5] We have also fairly elaborate accounts of John Dee's and of Sir Robert Cotton's libraries; but Perne, Dee and Cotton are exceptional and for all their size, their libraries were, to a greater or lesser extent, rooms to be private in rather than rooms for entertaining in, such as were to become standard features of country houses. For much of the seventeenth century it was still quite usual, even in great houses, for books as items of relative rarity to be kept in closets and indeed in chests, and some of the earliest seventeenth-century bookcases are in the form of shelved cupboards. As bindings became finer, and books a more potent status-symbol, the cupboard doors disappeared or were replaced with wire mesh or, as in Pepys' bookcases, with glazing, though few, probably, went to the extent that he did

2 Three hundred and fourteen of his 676 books (46.5 per cent) were in English, of which 166 (52 per cent) were theological. For Dering's books see *PLRE* 4.1–631 (I, pp. 137–269).

3 Constituting between them 19 per cent of his English texts.

4 Leedham-Green 1986, I, pp. 423–4.

5 Cambridge University Archives: VC Ct.I.112^{v}.

to present his books in perfect alignment by providing the smaller ones with little blocks to stand on.[6]

The sources, however, exaggerate the contrast between the working libraries of relatively impoverished academics in the mid-sixteenth century and the gentleman's library of the next century. What we know of Dering's books is derived partly from his account books, which record items which the compilers of inventories *post mortem* scorned to list as too ephemeral: 'Divers other books'.

Any increase in the proportion of vernacular texts in Dering's library compared with Bateman's would be not just a function of their different tastes and opportunities. While the staple academic texts continued to appear in Latin, and, for the most part, to be printed overseas, the native book trade, both in production and in distribution, made available an ever-increasing range of more substantial books in English, as well as a host of pamphlets and newsletters of compelling interest, especially during the mid- and late seventeenth century. Of women as independent book-owners we have, as yet, little extensive evidence, notable exceptions being Frances Wolfreston (1607–76/7) and Elizabeth Puckering – both, by coincidence, of the West Midlands.[7]

Sears Jayne lists 258 private library catalogues dating from between 1550 and 1600, and 217 between 1600 and 1640.[8] A good many have come to light since, and many remain to be found. For most people, there are no such lists. The libraries of John Donne and Ben Jonson, for example, have been recovered only by searching for surviving books bearing their marks of ownership.[9] Jayne's list concentrates exclusively on English libraries, expressly excluding the rest of Britain and lists with fewer than fifteen named items. His examples range from the sixteen books owned by Robert Garrett of King's College in 1556 to the 352 manuscripts and 5,769 printed books of Archbishop Bancroft in 1612, besides the various lists of John Dee's and Robert Cotton's collections. In this narrow scope it is hard to generalize about private libraries so various in their range and in their generations.[10] Some, like Parker, D'Ewes[11] and Cotton,[12] as also less celebrated collectors, like Jaspar Gryffyth,[13] were bent on preserving ancient manuscripts, many of them the spoils of the dissolved monasteries; others were concerned to acquire for their legatee institutions the latest, or at least the best, texts of the world of scholarship – Perne in the

6 There is some discussion of the development of library rooms in Girouard 1978; for both rooms and furnishings, and fine illustrations, see Thornton 1978, pp. 303–15.

7 Jayne 1983, p. 46; Morgan 1989; McKitterick 2000.

8 Jayne 1983.

9 Keynes 1973; McPherson 1974.

10 See his comments on the difficulties of generalizing even in a much more confined sphere in Pearson 1992, especially pp. 226–7.

11 Watson 1966.

12 Tite 1994; Wright 1997.

13 Ovenden 1994.

fields of theology and history in which he was himself interested, John Nidd[14] in medicine which, so far as we can tell, he never practised and in which he was certainly not formally qualified. Gentlemen equipped themselves with works of heraldry and topography and with manuals of instruction for magistrates, with recent history and with courtesy books.

In the mid-sixteenth century the book trade was still largely concentrated in London, Oxford and Cambridge. Most of the owners of substantial libraries known to us either had access to one of these sources or acquired their books overseas, in the course of their travels or by dealing – directly or through the agency of friends – with Continental stationers. By the early seventeenth century, however, the provincial gentry could stock their shelves without travelling so far afield. The 1616 inventory of John Foster's shop in York shows that he was supplying not only the clergy of the cathedral and city, but also those of the surrounding towns and villages, besides tradesmen in the town. Foster's wares were sophisticated enough, moreover, to attract the custom of serious book collectors like Sir Edward Stanhope, even if only as an incidental supplier.[15]

From the decade of the Civil War, the number of outlets increased substantially,[16] but information on new British books and pamphlets had been increasingly accessible since 1595 with the advent of printed trade lists, and then in newsletters distributed throughout the country.[17] Foreign books were known to a more widely dispersed readership through the circulation of the Frankfurt fair catalogues, of which an English edition was printed annually by John Bill from 1617 to 1628,[18] although surprisingly few sets of these have survived.[19] From 1668, the *Term catalogues* offered a guide used by trade and customers alike. Lists of older books were further accessible with the publication of such aids as the Bodleian catalogues of 1605 and subsequently, while specialist collectors had access to an increasing number of subject indexes.[20]

Samuel Pepys, in London, could busily call on the booksellers, and commission his fine bookcases and fine bindings,[21] amassing finally a total of 3,000 volumes, comprising, as well as printed books, manuscripts, maps and volumes of prints and ballads. In distant Derbyshire, Sir William Boothby was at much

14 Leedham-Green 1986. I, pp. 576–84.

15 Barnard and Bell 1994, esp. table 3, p. 17 [41]. Sir Edward Stanhope was a substantial donor of books to the library of Trinity College, Cambridge. See Gaskell 1980 and *PLRE* 2.1–161 (Leedham-Green 1986, I, pp. 141–78).

16 For a convenient summary see Morgan 1990.

17 Frearson 1993a.

18 Pollard and Ehrman 1965. See their table 8 for a survey of surviving lists of books imported for sale between 1628 and 1700. On catalogues for the Latin trade see Roberts, above pp. 162–4, 170, 173.

19 The exception is the collector Tobie Mathew, whose books are distinguished in *A catalogue of the printed books in the library of the Dean and Chapter of York*, ed. J. Raine, York, 1896.

20 James 1605; Wheeler 1928; Taylor 1966.

21 Latham 1978–94.

the same time no less passionately busied in building up his own library of perhaps thousands of volumes, through the agency of booksellers both in London and in the provinces, including Michael Johnson in Lichfield.[22] He had a great thirst for religious texts and for newsletters, but he also ordered literature, including play texts, and historical works and seems to have owned manuscripts also.

The proliferation of genres in British seventeenth-century publishing, and of sources of information about books available, inspired and enabled the construction of highly personal private libraries. Between 1676 and 1695, at least 200 private libraries were sold at auction alone, ranging in size from the vast collections of the Earl of Anglesey or Duke of Lauderdale, or of the commoner Richard Smith, to groups of just a few hundred books. The advent of the wide-ranging library as an essential element of a gentleman's house and an index to his learning, cosmopolitan tastes and, in theory at least, his magnanimity, was signalled by John Evelyn's translation of Gabriel Naudé's *Instructions concerning erecting of a library* (1661; French edition 1627).[23] Pepys wisely commented that Naudé was 'above my reach',[24] and yet for the most part Naudé's instructions merely reflected what had been the practice of collectors for many decades, at least in scholarly circles. Andrew Perne's library, for instance, covered most branches of knowledge, and it embraced, as Naudé proposed, ancient and modern authorities, orthodox and heretical texts, books large and small, massive sets and books of excerpts. It was arranged by subject and supplemented by globes, coins, instruments and maps, and his bindings were plain. It is more than likely that he made it available to his friends. The only instruction that we do not know him to have anticipated is that on catalogues. Naudé advocated two, one by subject and one by author. None survives from Perne's lifetime, but the unnatural neatness and accuracy with which the books are entered in his probate inventory may perhaps suggest that he at least maintained a shelf-list.

Whether in volumes on their shelves, or in fragments of old manuscripts used to strengthen bindings, there was scarcely a major library in seventeenth-century England that did not contain a residue of medieval or monastic libraries. The dispersal of libraries after the dissolution of the monasteries was a piecemeal affair. At Hereford,[25] Worcester, Durham and some other cathedrals, books remained where they were.[26] In most places, the bulk of the libraries fell into private hands, some to be preserved for piety's sake, for the sake of

22 Beal 1997.

23 For a convenient edition, not however aiming faithfully to reproduce Evelyn's translation, see the annotated edition from the University of California Press (Berkeley and Los Angeles, 1950).

24 Pepys 1970–83, VI, p. 252.

25 Mynors and Thomson 1993.

26 Wright 1958a, p. 164.

some local association, or just for the needs of basic literacy.[27] On a larger scale, the majority of the surviving books from Norwich Cathedral Priory came to Cambridge University Library in the 1570s.[28] At Canterbury, successive cullings by a series of well-placed bibliophiles – Matthew Parker, John Whitgift and Thomas Nevile – led to the preservation of large groups of books at Corpus Christi College and Trinity College in Cambridge.[29] Books from Bury St Edmunds were preserved as a group, thanks to William Smart, of Ipswich, at Pembroke College, Cambridge.[30]

Parker (*d.*1575) was principally concerned to assemble manuscript evidences of the standing and antiquity of the English Church, and both manuscripts and printed books bearing on the antecedents and the settlement of the Elizabethan Church. His design in so doing had been recognized, and his powers of accumulation enhanced, by a privy council decree, published as a broadsheet in 1568, authorizing him to take possession of 'auncient recordes or monumentes, written of the state and affairs of [the] realmes of Englande and Irelande'. Single-minded though Parker may have been in his mission to justify, indeed to sanctify, the Elizabethan Settlement, he did not resist manuscripts of a different hue, and in addition to theology he acquired historical and biographical writings, treatises of astronomy and music, mathematics, alchemy, philosophy, politics and law, French romances, bestiaries, and works by Homer and Euripides, Cicero and Seneca, Chaucer, Langland and Wycliffe.[31]

In making his collection, Parker was concerned with preserving, for the benefit of posterity, *texts*, and that being his aim he treated many of his volumes in what we would now regard as a cavalier fashion, dismembering composite volumes and reassembling them to suit better his own purposes,[32] much as Sir Robert Cotton was to do two generations later.[33] Both certainly lent, and more often borrowed, manuscripts within a circle of like-minded friends, but in the interim other collectors, chiefly of printed books, conceived of making their treasures more widely accessible. Notable among these was John Dee (*d.*1608). Similar to Parker in that he had petitioned Queen Mary (albeit unsuccessfully) for a commission not only for the 'recovery and preservation of Ancient Writers and Monuments' dispersed at the Reformation, but also for the acquisition of further texts from beyond the seas, he was dissimilar in that from shortly after his return from Antwerp in 1564 he offered his own huge library

27 D. N. Bell 1994, pp. 116–20; Sharpe 1996, pp. 13–16; Carter 1998.

28 Ker 1949 ; Ker 1964; Oates 1986, pp. 137–8.

29 Ker 1964, pp. 30–4; James 1900–4; James 1909–13; Dickins 1972; Page 1993; de Hamel 1997.

30 M. R. James, *A descriptive catalogue of the manuscripts in the library of Pembroke College, Cambridge* (Cambridge, 1905); Ker 1964, pp. 17–19.

31 Page 1993; and for French MSS., Wilkins 1993.

32 Page 1993, *passim*.

33 Tite 1994.

at Mortlake (over 2,000 printed books and some 200 manuscripts in 1583) as a public resource, especially for those who came to him as students.[34] Dee's library had particular strengths, notably in astronomy, alchemy, cosmology, geography, mathematics, medicine, recent history, navigation and other practical matters. Archbishop Bancroft (*d.*1612), predictably, was more concerned with theology, but also with law, history, topography and classical texts, and his 352 manuscripts and 5,769 printed books, bestowed in his library at Lambeth, were bequeathed, in the first instance 'to the service of God and his church, of the kings and commonwealth of the Realme and particularly of the Archbishops of Canterbury'. It was approved as a public library by King James.[35]

Libraries in the universities suffered by neglect, as well as (in England) by the opinions enforced by Mary's and Edward VI's commissioners. Buying here was in fits and starts, and donations, great or small, were erratic. At Oxford, where in 1556 it was agreed that even the furniture should be sold, the university's very own library stood as an example of destruction: the cast-offs were secured and, more importantly, put to immediate use, by the Dean and Chapter at Christ Church.[36] In general, it was not until the 1580s that college libraries were again buying or acquiring on a large scale, and (at Merton College, for example) requiring changes to the furniture as the new stall system took the place of the old lecterns.[37] At Cambridge, the restoration of the University Library in the 1570s was led astutely by Perne and by Parker. In a carefully orchestrated campaign, the library was equipped with the standard texts of reformation theology and of the Church fathers, and with an up-to-date collection in other subjects.[38] Perne himself emphasized the renaissance by presenting a numismatic collection, no less important a part than books of such a library.[39]

At a more modest level, the reign of Elizabeth witnessed if not quite the conception then the early development of libraries for shared use in parishes.[40] Their fortunes varied. Much of the difficulty lay in assumptions about institutional libraries, and in particular a failure to acknowledge by practical means that such libraries require money to thrive, or even to survive. Before the seventeenth century, and indeed long afterwards for many places, the expectation was that libraries would live on donations, and in particular on bequests. Among the first parish libraries from which reasonable numbers of

34 Roberts and Watson 1990, appendix 3 and pp. 41–5; Sherman 1995.

35 Irwin 1964, pp. 228–30.

36 Oxford University Archives Registrum I, fol.157; Macray 1890, p. 12; Ker 1986, at pp. 465–6.

37 Ker 1959, pp. 459–515. 38 Leedham-Green and McKitterick 1997.

39 Oates 1986, pp. 139–40.

40 Kelly 1966, pp. 50, 68, appendix 2 ('Checklist of endowed libraries founded before 1800'). For parish libraries in England, see *Parochial libraries* 1959.

books survive are those at Guildford (founded by John Parkhurst, Bishop of Norwich, in 1573),[41] which was soon taken in by the local grammar school, Bury St Edmunds (1595),[42] Newcastle upon Tyne (by 1597), Grantham (1598)[43] and Ipswich (1599; likewise taken under the wing of the local grammar school).[44] At Edinburgh, the library given by Clement Litill to the town and its kirk in 1580 became the basis for the new university library under his brother four years later.[45] In Aberdeen, the common (or public) library founded in 1585 remained independent of the new Marischal College until the books were removed there in the 1630s.[46]

For whom were the earliest public libraries intended, and how far were they indeed public? The injunctions of 1559 to set up copies of the Bible and of the Paraphrases of Erasmus in every parish church were directed at clergy and lay people alike. George Bull, notable in his day chiefly for his work on the ante-Nicene fathers, was incumbent of a parish near Bristol in the 1650s, and spent two months each year in Oxford for the sake of the libraries. His biographer noted this with approval. 'It is a great Misfortune to a young Clergyman, when he is confined to a Country Cure, to be destitute of such Books as are necessary to enable him to make any considerable Advance in his Studies of Divinity . . . And if the solid Foundation of useful Knowledge is not laid, and the habit of Studying acquired, while men are in the prime of their days, they seldom make any Progress that will be able to distinguish them from Persons of ordinary Attainments.'[47] Bull's example became quoted, to a generation on the Continent of Europe to whom British scholarship was becoming increasingly familiar.[48]

Some of these early community libraries were meant (as at Oakham) for the local clergy, their heavy theological content befitting such a destination.[49] Others, often scarcely lighter in tone, were for the wider public. In 1598, Francis Trigge provided a library to be used 'by such of the cleargie and others as well beinge inhabitantes in or near Grantham and the Soake thereof'.[50] In 1653, Humphrey Chetham bequeathed the residue of his estate specifically for a library 'for the use of schollars', 'the same bookes there to remaine as a publick library forever'. Chetham's library became an exception to the fate that so often overtook libraries for which there was no continuing care. As a result of

41 Woodward and Christophers 1972. 42 Birkby 1977.
43 Glenn and Walsh 1988. 44 Blatchly 1989.
45 Finlayson and Simpson 1967; Finlayson 1980. 46 Mitchell 1954.
47 Robert Nelson, *The life of Dr George Bull, late Lord Bishop of St David's*, 2nd edn (1714), p. 43.
48 D. Maichelius, *Introductio ad historiam literariam de praecipuis bibliothecis Parisiensibus* (Leipzig, 1721), praefatio. For once, and most unusually, the example was quoted in English. A Latin translation was appended in a footnote.
49 Herbert 1982. 50 Roberts 1971, pp. 75–90; Glenn and Walsh 1988.

investing Chetham's bequest in land, an income was provided for the purchase of books, and the library could remain alive to the interests of succeeding generations.[51]

The parish library at Langley Marish near Slough, founded by Sir John Kederminster (*d.*1631) and kept in a room adjoining the church, was unusual in its elaborate decoration and in its expensive shelving arrangements.[52] It was more akin to a personal, domestic, library. Most parish or other local libraries were kept either in chests, or on plain shelves, or sometimes in a cupboard. At Turton (Lancashire) the books given by Humphrey Chetham in 1651 were protected by a case with shelves and folding doors, secured with iron bars.[53] The practice of chaining books continued even into the eighteenth century, and many copies survive of the Bible and of Foxe's *Book of martyrs*.[54] Two of the largest chained libraries belonging to parishes, at Wimborne and All Saints', Hereford, date their foundation from the late seventeenth century – that is, only a few years before a new impetus was given to the foundation of parish libraries by the energies of Thomas Bray and of the Society for Promoting Christian Knowledge, by activists such as James Kirkwood in Scotland, and by the Parochial Libraries Act of 1709.

It is easy to be over-serious about donors' intentions, or to seek to discover purpose in the presence of a particular book where none was ever thought. Libraries come about by accident as well as by design, and never more so than when they depend on donations rather than on careful spending from endowments. The school library of Bury St Edmunds (founded in 1550) is not untypical of its kind, in containing not only such necessities as Calepinus's *Lexicon* (1523) in a binding by John Siberch and various other classical texts also in Cambridge bindings, but also Martin Bucer's copy of Galen in five folio volumes (Basel, 1538).[55] Many other such apparent aberrations testify to the random element in most libraries.

Surviving school libraries from Edward VI's foundations attest that, as in parish libraries, money was not necessarily available for their increase in each generation. Moreover, as books passed out of fashion, or were replaced by new editions that were cheaper, and more usually bought privately than borrowed

51 Kelly 1966, pp. 77–9; H. S. A. Smith 1989. Kelly also offers (p. 81) a few examples of non-theological individual books given or bequeathed to churches, but these scarcely count as libraries.

52 Rouse 1941. Illustrated in Thornton 1978, colour plate xvii.

53 Illustrated in Streeter 1931, p. 305; see also Christie 1885, pp. 19–25, 57–60.

54 A convenient list of chained books is in Cox and Harvey 1908, pp. 332–40, superseding Blades 1890.

55 Books from the school library are now divided between Cambridge University Library and the West Suffolk Record Office, Bury St Edmunds. See also Bartholomew and Gordon 1910.

or bought corporately, so changing perceptions of the relationship between public and private collections often led to periods of neglect. It was commonly assumed, for example, that on the whole books in larger formats were more suitable for corporate libraries, and conversely those in smaller ones less so. Such a view was becoming obsolete by the end of the seventeenth century, thanks to the tendency of books generally to be printed more economically, using smaller type, smaller formats, and therefore less paper; but the fact that books could be bought more cheaply meant a greater emphasis on private ownership, to the neglect of many of the older libraries. The next century's charitable and educational interest in founding new libraries attempted to reverse this, often in different sections of the population.

In cases where libraries were bequeathed substantially to institutions, like those of Andrew Perne,[56] William Drummond of Hawthornden,[57] or, indeed, Samuel Pepys, we can seldom be certain as to the stage in the formation of the collection at which the owner began to regard his library no longer simply as his armory and his recreation but as his memorial, and as such an uncertain index of personal taste. Others were less obviously concerned with establishing a resource for the world at large. We may think of Sir Thomas Knyvett (*d.*1618),[58] Sir Henry Spelman, the legal historian (*d.*1641), or Sir Thomas Egerton, Lord Chancellor (*d.*1617) (some of whose books came to him with his third wife, Alice, née Spencer, Dowager Countess of Derby) and his son, the First Earl of Bridgewater (*d.*1649), all of whom probably formed their collections for their own and their immediate heirs' use and enjoyment.

Changes of emphasis in subjects for study, the greater numbers of books amongst which to choose, the political turmoil of the late 1630s and 1640s both in Britain and on the Continent, changes in the physical forms of books themselves and in the ways in which they were published, all contributed to a mood of uncertainty for institutional libraries. It is not surprising, given such a climate, that John Dury was scathing of librarians even in 1651:

> Their places are but Mercenarie, and their emploiment of little or no use further, then to look to the Books committed to their custodie, that they may not bee lost; or embezeled by those that use them: and this is all.[59]

In Dury's view, the librarian was to guard the public stock of learning, and to recommend it to others. He was a 'Factor and Trader for helps to learning'. To this end, he was to prepare catalogues, and engage in correspondence as a

56 Leedham-Green 1986, I, pp. 419–79; McKitterick 1991. 57 MacDonald 1971.
58 McKitterick 1978. 59 Dury 1651, p.17.

means of trading – not just of knowledge, but apparently of books too for the increase of stock. Dury's principal experience came from his prolonged travels abroad in German-speaking Europe, the Low Countries, and Scandinavia. As a member of the Hartlib circle he was one of those most engaged to promote ways of extending and exchanging knowledge.[60] He put into words what some others sought by their deeds.

The mid-century witnessed a profound change in attitude to both the preservation of knowledge and its dissemination. Not surprisingly, opinions differed. In 1667, the infant Royal Society was given the library of the Earls of Arundel, rich not just in modern learning but also in early printed books, notably from the library of the German humanist Willibald Pirckheimer. Further donations followed. The early interests of the Society were by no means confined to the sciences, but it was not long before the need for such a wide-ranging library was questioned. Donations leaned heavily to mathematics, natural philosophy and medicine.[61] Much of the wealth of the Arundel library proved to be misplaced: tolerated but neglected until in the nineteenth century many non-scientific books from it passed to the British Museum; others were sold later. The tale of the Arundel books is a reminder that libraries may change their purpose, and become redundant not simply because they are out of date. Created and imbued with life in precise and defined circumstances, libraries may by the passage of time, or else by some change in their ownership or administration, wither away and die, or else develop shapes unimagined by their creators.

Libraries reflect both everyday needs and (to some extent) theories of knowledge. The organization of the Bodleian was simple: theology, jurisprudence, medicine and arts, the books in each to be shelved according to size and then in alphabetical order of author. In some respects it was akin to Leiden, where the new university library, opened only a few years previously, was organized according to seven principal subjects.[62] By contrast, much of Cambridge University Library remained organized by donor.[63] The printed catalogue of its collections, the first such of any institutional library in Britain, published in 1574 and inserted into copies of Parker's *De antiquitate Britannicae ecclesiae*, reflected this order.[64]

60 Webster 1975 and Greengrass above, p. 314.

61 *Bibliotheca Norfolciana: sive catalogus libb. manuscriptorum & impressorum in omne arte & lingua* (1681); Mayhew and Sharp 1910; *The record of the Royal Society of London* 4th edn (1940), pp. 150–4.

62 [P. Bertius], *Nomenclator autorum omnium, quorum libri vel manuscripti, vel typis expressis exstant in bibliotheca academiae Lugduno-Batavae* (Leiden, 1595); Pol 1975, pp. 393–459.

63 Oates 1986, pp. 265–6.

64 Oates 1986, pp. 95–6. A summary list of institutional catalogues of European libraries between 1574 (Cambridge) and 1670 (Utrecht; Copenhagen) is given in Pollard and Ehrman 1965, pp. 257–8.

The first printed Bodleian catalogue (1605)[65] was fundamentally a shelf-list, of books from many sources and of a library already far larger than that at Cambridge. As helps to the reader or library user, special sections listed biblical commentaries in biblical order, commentaries on Aristotle by their subject, commentators on civil and canon law, and writers on Hippocrates and Galen. An index provided access by author. A new edition of the catalogue was published in 1620, now in alphabetical order of author in the face of so many more books; but far more influential was that of 1674, a folio volume associated with the name of Thomas Hyde. In interleaved form it was taken up by libraries in Britain and overseas as the basis for describing their own collections. Hyde was later criticized for insisting on an arrangement by author rather than by subject like the Le Tellier catalogue of 1693.[66] Thus, broadly speaking, conventions were gradually established for some matters, while the ordering on the shelves remained a matter for individual libraries: there remained no agreed schemes in Britain for the classification of printed or manuscript knowledge.[67]

Furnishings for institutional libraries remained frequently conservative. In the mid-sixteenth century, libraries at Oxford and Cambridge were undergoing a gradual change as expanding collections forced the abandonment of desks (still visible, for example, at Trinity Hall in Cambridge) in favour of the stall system (still in use in Duke Humfrey's library in the Bodleian). The practice of setting shelves at right angles to the windows persisted even to Sir Christopher Wren's otherwise revolutionary building for Trinity College, Cambridge, designed in the 1670s and completed in 1693.[68] In presenting his plans, Wren emphasized some of his principles: large windows set well above readers' heads so as to provide the best light; floor materials used in a way that would be both hard-wearing and provide the peace necessary to think; tables designed for easy consultation of books; and decorative sculpture, in the tradition of classical Rome (the example of Asinius Pollio, related by Pliny, was frequently quoted in library literature),[69] that would inspire modern generations. In the last he was to be frustrated by lack of funds, but he was following a well-established principle. The frieze in the Bodleian Library, depicting two hundred writers from classical times to the early seventeenth century had a direct bearing on the contents of the shelves below, and libraries as diverse as Bishop Cosin's

65 James 1605; Wheeler 1928; Norris 1939, pp. 142–59.

66 Philippe Dubois, *Bibliotheca Telleriana, sive catalogus librorum bibliothecae illustrissimi ac reverendissimi C. M. Le Tellier* (Paris, 1693).

67 Claude Jolly, 'Naissance de la "science" des bibliothèques', in Jolly 1988, pp. 381–5; Latham 1978–94, vol. 7, Introduction, pp. xviii–xx; R. Chartier, *The order of books: readers, authors and libraries in Europe between the fourteenth and eighteenth centuries* (Cambridge, 1994).

68 McKitterick 1995.

69 Pliny, *Hist. Nat.*, xxxv.ii.

at Durham (1668) and St John's College, Oxford (1636) could also point to comparable ideas in their decorative schemes.[70]

More fundamentally, those who fled abroad during the Interregnum returned with cosmopolitan knowledge of libraries in France and the Dutch Republic, and patriotism played an increasing part in discussions as the idea of a national library was promoted in England.

The Bodleian Library was *de facto* the British national library. In founding his new library, opened in 1602, Sir Thomas Bodley sought a living continuity. He arranged for the Stationers' Company to see it supplied with new books published in London; he stirred up other men's benevolence; he set out a programme of building that entailed nothing less than an entire new quadrangle three storeys in height; and he left his estate to provide an income for purchases.[71] Thanks not least to a stream of major collections including Archbishop Laud's western and oriental manuscripts, the Barocci collection given by the Earl of Pembroke (1629), the library of John Selden (*d.* 1654), quite apart from lesser gifts, its collections were unequalled. Purchases added further, whether from the Frankfurt book fair or (as in the case of the oriental manuscripts of Edward Pococke, in 1693) by private treaty.

The importance of national collections was acknowledged when in 1662 the first Licensing Act included the obligation for stationers to deposit copies of all new publications in the royal library, the Bodleian, and Cambridge University Library.[72] The legislation, continued in various forms to this day, was similar to provision made for the French royal library as early as the 1530s.[73] Although (as in France) it was widely ignored, it provided a foundation. When in 1694 Richard Bentley was appointed Royal Librarian, he sought to apply it more systematically, and so to establish a national library worthy of the name. At the same time, he campaigned for new buildings, and for the purchase of major libraries which came onto the market.[74] In all this he addressed needs and opportunities too often unheeded by subsequent generations. His efforts found little support at court, and the need was finally met – well after his death – by removing the royal library to the care of the nation, following the British Museum Act of 1753.

70 Masson 1972; Masson 1981. See also comparable questions at Leiden: *Nomenclator autorum omnium, quorum libri exstant in bibliotheca academiae Lugduno-Batavae* (Leiden, 1595), B2^{v}.

71 Bodley 1926; Bodley 1926–8; Philip 1983; Hampshire 1983; Philip and Morgan 1997.

72 13 and 14 Charles II, c. 33.

73 Estivals 1961. For the determined and politically driven expansion of the French royal library in the seventeenth century, see Delisle 1868–91 and Balayé 1988.

74 Richard Bentley, *A proposal for building a royal library, and establishing it by Act of Parliament* (1697), repr. in Bartholomew 1908, pp. 93–6.

It remained an anomaly that London, among the largest cities in Europe, had no library that could properly be called public. Sion College, opened in 1630, possessed a collection designed for the London clergy.[75] It was severely damaged in the Great Fire, when books from the old library of St Paul's Cathedral were also destroyed. The westward expansion of the population was acknowledged by Thomas Tenison's foundation in 1684 of a public library alongside the church of St Martin in the Fields. A pioneer of its kind, and in a building designed by Christopher Wren,[76] it was never intended to serve all London's needs. John Evelyn, familiar with France, where the royal library had long been open to the public, and where to collect books in the expectation of sharing them was to perform a public benefit, despaired at his own country. 'This greate & august citty of London, abounding with so many wits and letter'd persons, has scarce one library furnish'd and indow'd for the publiq.'[77] Glancing across the Thames, he found Lambeth Palace library ebbing and flowing like the river beside it, as archbishop succeeded archbishop. But it was hardly convenient to the population of the west end.[78]

Had Evelyn considered the cathedral libraries, he could have found some encouragement. The experiences of the mid-century prompted a determination to restore what had been neglected or damaged. Michael Honywood, fellow of Christ's College in Cambridge, returned from the Low Countries and was appointed Dean of Lincoln in 1660. There he caused a new library to be erected in the cloister, to the design of Wren; and on his death in 1681 he bequeathed his books to the cathedral. Many of them had been collected during his exile.[79] At Winchester, where in the 1570s Robert Horne had attempted to enforce injunctions to repair and improve the library, George Morley transformed matters in 1684 by his bequest of his own library and of money to equip a room especially for it. At York, Archbishop Dolben issued injunctions in 1685 designed to restore the library as a place of learning, and likewise left his own books on his death. At Exeter, a local doctor removed the books from the cathedral for safekeeping during the Interregnum, and the fresh start made after 1660 was encouraged by a large donation from Edward Cotton.[80] Gloucester Cathedral benefited from the duplicates in John Selden's collection. Lichfield Cathedral library was refounded thanks to the Second Duke of Somerset. John Cosin,

75 Pearce 1913. 76 Hoare 1963.

77 Evelyn to Samuel Pepys, 12 August 1689: *Diary and Correspondence of John Evelyn Esq.*, ed. H. B Wheatley (London, 1906), III, pp. 448–9.

78 Bill 1966; Cornforth 1988. For the library's fortunes after 1649, and its temporary sojourn at Cambridge, see Oates 1986, pp. 247–67, 303–13.

79 Griffiths 1970; Hurst 1982; a full account of Honywood's library is in preparation by Marika Keblusek.

80 Lloyd 1967.

Bishop of Durham (*d.*1672), presented many of his own books to Peterhouse in Cambridge, and established a public library for the bishopric.

By the end of the century, historical, literary and palaeographical needs had become fused, as in Edward Bernard's *Catalogi librorum manuscriptorum Angliae et Hiberniae* (1697). Like many such compilations, this was an amalgam of previously published information (the Cambridge University Library entries were taken straight from James's work of almost a century previously) and of new work – largely by Humfrey Wanley. It was a triumph of organization; but it was also triumphant in declaring the wealth of libraries in the British Isles, the collections and redistributions of a century and a half. In private owners such as John Moore,[81] Sir Hans Sloane[82] and Thomas Gale, Dean of York,[83] as well as in the newly reorganized university and cathedral libraries, the catalogue reflected the determination of contemporary collectors to link the needs of literary, historical, scientific and theological scholarship not just with bibliophily, but also with a willingness to collect for the sake of preservation, in the faith that books sometimes of little current account would become valued in ways not yet realized.

81 McKitterick 1986. 82 MacGregor 1994.
83 James 1900–4. Printed books from Gale's library were sold in three catalogues by Thomas Osborne and J. Shipton in 1757–8.

15

Monastic collections and their dispersal[1]

JAMES P. CARLEY

In 1556, one year before the *terminus a quo* for this volume, John Dee (1527–1608), magus and book collector, composed 'A Supplication to Q. Mary . . . for the recovery and preservation of ancient Writers and Monuments'.[2] Appealing to Mary's piety Dee first regretted the 'spoile and destruction' of the monastic libraries which, he pointed out, was still happening even in the time of Reconciliation, books 'enclosed in walls, or buried in the ground' and 'burnt, or sufferd to rott and decay'. To combat this lamentable state of affairs he proposed the establishment of a Library Royal and commissioners who would go about the country retrieving ancient books. Copies would be made and the originals then restored to their present owners if they desired them. Dee shrewdly recommended haste in this endeavour since malicious persons might otherwise hide the books in their possession. Even though immensely sympathetic to a return to the old order Mary did not adopt Dee's scheme and it foundered, as would all similar proposals over the next centuries.[3]

Two years after our *terminus ad quem* Edward Bernard's *Catalogi librorum manuscriptorum Angliae et Hiberniae* was published, listing the contents of the large institutional libraries as well as those of private individuals. By this time most of the major collections had been assembled and a stability insured.[4] Subsequently, of course, smaller libraries have been broken up, books moved

1 C. E. Wright remains the primary authority in this area: see Wright 1953; Wright 1958a; 1958b. In an essay of this scope it would neither be feasible nor productive to provide a list of all the known post-dissolution collectors of medieval manuscripts, and the reader is referred to Ker 1985 and the list of Andrew Watson's writings found in Carley and Tite 1997, pp. 473–6, for key examples. For general studies of antiquarianism see Fox 1956, Kendrick 1950, Levine 1987, McKisack 1971, Momigliano 1950, Parry 1995, Woolf 1990.

2 Printed by Roberts and Watson 1990, pp. 194–5.

3 See Fritze 1983, pp. 282–84 for a hypothesis, untenable in my opinion, concerning why Catholics were not interested in rescuing monastic books. In general, medieval manuscripts were not fashionable in the years immediately after the Dissolution and Catholics as well as reformers preferred printed 'humanist' books.

4 As N. R. Ker observed ('The migration of manuscripts from the English medieval libraries' in Ker 1985, p. 460): 'There is not, in fact, any large collection of English medieval manuscripts which was not either immobilized in 1697, or in a fair way to becoming immobilized'.

around, and there have been new finds in England and on the Continent, but the great age of migration of English medieval manuscripts was effectively over. Bernard thus provides a basic guide to the modern location of monastic survivors.

Dissolutions and removal of books from the monasteries did not begin with Henry VIII's Act of Supremacy: for example, Henry's pious grandmother, Lady Margaret Beaufort, endowed Christ's College, Cambridge in 1507 with lands from the dissolved Creek Abbey, also transferring books and jewels. In the 1520s Thomas Wolsey dissolved a number of small monasteries and used their incomes to endow Ipswich College and Cardinal College, Oxford; books were part of the booty. What was unique to Henry's Dissolution, however, was the scale and speed of the undertaking as well as the almost total disregard for the books. Even contemporary observers were shocked, John Bale noting shortly after Henry's death that '[T]o destroye all without consyderacyon, is and wyll be unto Englande for ever, a moste horryble infamy amonge the grave senyours of other nacyons.'[5] John Leland's commissions of 1533 and 1536 'to peruse and dylygentlye to searche all the lybraryes of monasterees and colegies of thys youre noble realme' and his enthusiastic praise for Henry's refurbished libraries at Westminster, Hampton Court and Greenwich notwithstanding, there was no official policy for rescue during the crucial years.[6]

Although many books were destroyed – manuscripts of Duns Scotus, as the notorious Richard Layton gloated, 'faste nailede up upon postes in all comon howses of easment' – thousands did survive and began to surface in collections in the second half of the sixteenth century. How does one account for this? Leland (*d.* 1556) and Bale (*d.* 1563) are, of course, crucial. Through Leland's efforts hundreds of manuscripts were brought to the royal palaces, even if they were not necessarily the ones modern scholars would have wished to have seen saved; he also built up his own large private library. Like Leland, Bale set out to produce a *De viris illustribus* for his country comparable to Johann Tritheim's *Catalogus scriptorum ecclesiasticorum* and he collected books as part of this endeavour. In Bale's case, however, there is a profound tension between an inclusivity engendered by patriotic considerations, that is, an impulse to preserve every known British author, and an exclusivity based on his religious

5 Bale 1549, sig. B 1ʳ.

6 Although Leland may have hoped single-handedly to create a national library, 'the reality', as N. R. Ker has concluded (Ker 1964, p. xii), 'was a rather small collection of selected books, not truly of the first interest and drawn from a restricted area'. Ker (1985) has also observed ('The migration', p. 464) that 'the kinds of books which had on the whole the best chance of surviving were historical, patristic, and biblical, and mainly of the twelfth and thirteenth centuries, and that the kinds of books which had the least chance of surviving were those containing the scholastic theology and philosophy of the later Middle Ages, and the law-books'. See also Ker 1954.

principles, that is, a desire to remove the most egregious papists of the past from the roster of illustrious writers.[7] Like Leland, Bale picked up books for himself, but by his own account much of his collection was abandoned when he fled to the Continent from Ireland in 1553.[8] Apart from Leland and Bale there were other lesser known individuals who had access to monastic libraries and carried off books: Sir John Prise (1502/3–55), appointed monastic visitor in 1535 and 1539, who gathered books primarily from the west of England and whose books ultimately were deposited at Jesus College, Oxford and Hereford Cathedral,[9] or Robert Talbot (*c.* 1505–58), prebendary of Norwich Cathedral, who annotated and perhaps owned Norwich Cathedral Priory books.[10] Certain books were taken away by departing religious, as in the case of the last prior at Lanthony, Richard Hart, who removed a large part of the library with him when the priory was dissolved. Richard Boreman, the last abbot of St Albans, sold former St Albans books to John Dee in the 1550s. In Yorkshire, where the wills of former religious have been analysed, there are many references to monastic books.[11] Nor were the books simply carried off as spoil; there are indications they were being held in trust, as it were, for future revival of the old houses.[12] Some books appear to have remained *in situ* at the abandoned monasteries for a number of years until they were discovered by interested parties such as R. Ferrar, who recovered two Anglo-Saxon manuscripts from Tavistock Abbey for Francis Russell, Second Earl of Bedford in 1566.[13] Monastic books could

7 Indeed Bale challenged Leland on his lack of discrimination: 'Unum fortasse displicebit, nec mihi interim placet, quod sine discrimine doctrinarum ac spirituum exploratione pleraque sint hic pertractata, et iniqua pro sanctis admissa'. Quoted in Brett and Carley 1990, p. xii. See also Ross 1991.

8 As was the case with other Marian exiles Bale may have taken his most treasured medieval manuscripts abroad with him. On his books in general see O'Sullivan 1995, and the references cited therein.

9 See Ker, 'Sir John Prise', in Ker 1985, pp. 471–95. A number of his books came from St Guthlac's Priory, Hereford.

10 See Ker, 'Medieval manuscripts from Norwich Cathedral Priory', in Ker 1985, p. 246. For other collectors of the period see Ker 1964, p. xii.

11 See Cross 1991. Cross, p. 262, suggests that the individuals were allowed to take books with them because the books were of little commercial value.

12 For example, the former prior of Monk Bretton, William Browne (*d.* 1557), was at the centre of a small community of dispersed monks, all of whom brought books with them. Browne explicitly left his books to the priory should it ever be restored. In his will drawn up in 1558 Edward Heptonstall left his books to the house at Kirkstall, should it ever be revived. Robert Hare (*d.* 1611) wished Cambridge, Trinity Hall MS. 1 to be returned to St Augustine's Canterbury in the event of its restoration. It is possible that former St Albans books were left to the revived community in 1558 by the nephew of a previous abbot Robert Catton.

13 See Ker 1957, nos. 21, 220. At some point after the dissolution of the monastery at Bury St Edmunds on 4 November 1539 John Leland received a letter authorizing him 'to see what bookes be lefte yn the library there, or translatid thens ynto any other corner of the late monastery'. Quoted in *The itinerary of John Leland in or about the years 1535–1543*, ed. L. Toulmin Smith (London, 1906–10), II, p. 148.

still be found in the buildings at St Augustine's Canterbury into the seventeenth century.[14]

Ushering in what Ker has characterized as the golden age of collecting (1560–1640),[15] are three important documents: a letter from Bale to Matthew Parker, dated 30 July 1560, in response for a request for information 'concernyne bokes of antiquite, not printed'; a list of texts relating to Anglo-Saxon history prepared by John Joscelyn *c.* 1565–66 and a list of writers on medieval English history drawn up by Joscelyn *c.* 1565.[16] These provide indications concerning what manuscripts were available and where they could be found in the 1560s. The information is limited, obviously, to individuals with whom Bale and Joscelyn might have come into contact, and thus it has a Protestant and a regional bias, but the owners do range from people associated with the court to religious officials and some individuals fairly far down on the social scale.

Bale's letter is addressed to Matthew Parker, Archbishop of Canterbury 1559–1575, to whom Joscelyn (*d.* 1603) was chaplain and Latin secretary; Parker is a key figure for the direction antiquarian studies took in the second half of the sixteenth century.[17] Like Bale and Dee, Parker wished to collect and have copied monastic manuscripts and he seems to have drawn up the draft of a broadsheet issued on the authority of the Privy Council on 7 July 1568, a document very similar in intent to Dee's earlier Supplication. The broadside was written approximately thirty years after the Dissolution, when the former religious and the first collectors were dying out, and Parker had an understandable sense of urgency, observing in the letter accompanying the draft that 'if this opportunity be not taken in our time, it will not so well be done hereafter'. One of the people Parker employed to collect materials was his domestic chaplain

14 See Watson 1986, pp. 135–6. For a detailed discussion of the history and subsequent fate of books from Christ Church Canterbury see Ramsay 1995. Ramsay notes (p. 378) that it wasn't until the early 1620s that the cathedral libraries began to be seriously viewed as repositories of what had survived from the medieval past. Christopher de Hamel (De Hamel 1997, pp. 271–3) traces the post-Suppression fate of a number of Christ Church books.

15 Ker 1964, p. xii. See also Ker, 1985, 'The Migration', p. 459, where he observes that 'In the eighteenth century, already, collectors had to look to the Continent for their best manuscripts. Indeed, the active period in the migration of manuscripts from the English medieval libraries to the modern collections was coming to an end in the middle of the seventeenth century'. There is, however, some evidence that books from English monastic houses were still readily available at the end of the seventeenth century. The non-Welsh component of the collection of Sir Thomas Mostyn (*d.* 1692) was made up primarily of English materials and it would seem that this is a result of what was for sale rather than reflecting a conscious policy on Mostyn's part: see Huws 1997, pp. 458–59.

16 All three are edited in Graham and Watson 1998. At the end of his letter to Parker Bale added that William, 1st Lord Paget, Sir John Mason and Robert Record were rumoured to own many 'notable monuments', but very few surviving manuscripts can be associated with these individuals.

17 See Page 1993. On the context of Parker's request to Bale see Jones 1981. On his printing enterprises see Clement 1997; also Robinson 1998.

Stephen Batman (*d.* 1584) who reported that by 1572 he himself had gathered 6,700 books.[18] Parker's motives in collecting manuscripts reflect his desire to justify the doctrines of the Church of England through appeal to historical precedents: in his view the Anglo-Saxon Church was much closer to his own reformed church on doctrinal matters than it was to the Church of Rome. As Batman pointed out, too, the 'choice' examples were not always returned after having been copied[19] and his collections formed the basis for the Parkerian bequest in 1575 to Corpus Christi College, Cambridge.[20]

Parker's motives for collecting and his manner of dealing with the monastic past in the light of the revived Anglicanism represents the expected norm for his period. Protestants of considerably more advanced views than Parker also gathered up monastic texts as witnesses to the iniquities of the Catholic faith.[21] At the opposite extreme, however, there were the Catholic collectors who still had hopes of a reconciliation with Rome. Small collections went to the Continent with their owners during Elizabeth's reign or earlier;[22] in the case of the Brigittine nuns of Syon, for example, some of the books in the cask of books and five crates of unbound books which they took with them from the Spanish Netherlands to Rouen in 1580 may well have derived from their original library.[23] There were other individuals, the most important of whom was Lord William Howard of Naworth Castle (1563–1640), who did not leave England and who actively sought out and preserved monastic materials.[24]

18 The figure is quoted by Wright 1953, p. 220, from Batman's *The doome warning all men to the judgement* (1581). Wright gives a list of possible sources for Parker's collection (pp. 220–4).

19 In his letter Bale, obviously alert to other possibilities, specifically requested that certain of the books he was sending Parker be returned to him again: 'I besyche your grace that at convenyent tyme, I maye have them restored agayne.'

20 Throughout our period the Oxford and Cambridge colleges became the final repository for collections put together by private individuals: Sir Thomas Pope gave monastic books he retrieved from the royal library to Trinity College, Oxford; Sir John White gave Southwick books to St John's College, Oxford; John Whitgift, Thomas Nevile and William Bowyer provided manuscripts for Trinity College, Cambridge, and so on. For the late sixteenth-century donors to Cambridge University Library see Leedham-Green and McKitterick 1997, pp. 153–66. Around 1605 Sir Thomas Bodley persuaded King James to grant him a warrant 'for the choice of any books that I shall like in any of his houses or librarys'. Bodley's plan was blocked by Sir Peter Young, father of Patrick Young, Keeper of the Royal Library from *c.* 1605 to 1649. (For a list of donors to Bodley's library from 1600 to 1695 see Hunt 1953, pp. 79–122.) Bodley was not the only individual to have designs on royal books and in December 1610 Young wrote to James Montague, Bishop of Bath and Wells, claiming that Richard Bancroft, who had just left his books to Lambeth, had borrowed more than 500 volumes from the royal library.

21 See, for example, the account of the books acquired by the Cooke family from Kirkstall Abbey (Barnard 1992, p. 86).

22 On the exile community see Coppens 1993, pp. 1–11; also Rogers 1997.

23 See de Hamel 1991, p. 128. Other libraries, such as that of Sir Thomas Copley, were abandoned when their owners fled England: see Carley 1997a, pp. 366–9.

24 On Howard see Reinmuth 1973–4. The other great Catholic collector of the period was John, Lord Lumley (1534–1609) who had almost 400 monastic manuscripts from a variety of houses. However, neither Lumley nor his father-in-law Henry Fitzalan, twelfth Earl of

Bernard's *Catalogi* provides a list of books still at Naworth at the close of the seventeenth century, but this does not represent the whole extent of the collection, which was assembled in part as a monument to the Catholic religion but which had an equally strong historical/antiquarian bias and which included some very fine English illuminated manuscripts – the Luttrell Psalter, the De Lisle Psalter, the Howard–Fitton Psalter, and the Gospels of Queen Margaret of Scotland.[25]

As has been well documented, the foundation of the Elizabethan Society of Antiquaries around 1586 represented a major development in antiquarian studies.[26] The direction of research as exemplified in the weekly meetings concerned political and legal topics, particular institutional origins, rather than the religious issues which had so exercised the Parkerian circle.[27] Many of the great Elizabethan antiquaries and collectors were members, including Arthur Agarde (*d.* 1615), Robert Beale (*d.* 1601), William Camden (*d.* 1623), Richard Carew (*d.* 1620), Sir Robert Cotton (*d.* 1631), Sir William Dethick (*d.* 1612), Sir John Doderidge (*d.* 1628), William Fleetwood (*d.* 1594), Michael Heneage (*d.* 1600), Joseph Holland (*d.* post 1605), William Lambarde (*d.* 1601), James Ley, Earl of Marlborough (*d.* 1629), Sir Henry Spelman (*d.* 1641), John Stow (*d.* 1605), Thomas Talbot (*fl.* 1580), Francis Tate (*d.* 1616), Francis Thynne (*d.* 1608). Around 1602 three of the members attempted to obtain a charter to establish an 'academy for the study of antiquity and history'.[28] Key to the academy was to be the library, which would have functioned as a national archive, 'well furnished with divers ancient bookes and rare monuments of antiquity, which otherwise may perish'. As in previous cases nothing came of

Arundel (1512–79), from whom a sizeable portion of his collection derived, seems to have been particularly interested in preserving monastic materials as such, although Arundel did acquire manuscripts at the time of the dissolution: see Jayne and Johnson 1956, pp. 3–4, 10–11. De Hamel 1997 lists former Christ Church Canterbury books which later surfaced in Catholic contexts.

25 Slightly later the Benedictine monk Augustine Baker (*d.* 1641) transcribed records and may have also collected original material for the English Congregation in exile. Certainly, he wrote to Cotton in 1629 on behalf of the English nuns at Cambrai, asking him 'to bestowe on them such bookes as you please, either manuscript or printed, being in English, conteining contemplation, Saints' lives or other devotions'. Quoted by Philip Jebb and David M. Rogers, 'Rebirth', in *The Benedictines in Britain* (1980), p. 94.

26 Apart from Wright the chief sources are Evans 1956, pp. 7–13; van Norden 1946; van Norden 1949–50.

27 However, Parker's close associate, William Cecil, first Lord Burghley (*d.* 1598), who had a group of scholars around him, such as Laurence Nowell (*d. c.* 1571), acquiring and interpreting medieval manuscripts, was concerned with the history of the establishment of civil institutions. On his library see Selwyn 1997, p. 397.

28 On this topic see Herendeen 1988, p. 205: 'Encompassing both antiquarian and historical work, the Society was meant to centralize materials for their better preservation and easier access and analysis, and in this we can see the joint influence of Leland and Camden, and how together they paved the way for the work of the Surrenden Society.'

the project and in 1607, as a result of James I's disfavour, the Society ceased to meet altogether.[29]

Ironically, the three greatest private libraries of the second generation of antiquaries were put together by precisely the individuals who had argued for a public collection: Dee, Parker and Cotton. They resulted from a failure of public schemes and, in some sense, were perceived by their owners as interim measures. Parker, of course, took care that what he put together would remain intact: there were elaborate regulations concerning annual audits and dire penalties for loss of books.[30] As a result, the Parker collection is still more or less the same as it was in 1575. Dee's collection had always been a more fluid one and even before the main sales of 1625 and 1626 books moved out of the library. The subsequent owners present a catalogue of the collecting world of the late sixteenth and early seventeenth century: Robert Bowyer, Lord Burghley, Sir Henry Savile, William Crashaw, George Carew, Sir Walter Cope, Lord William Howard, Henry Savile of Banke, Sir Robert Cotton, Sir Simonds D'Ewes, Thomas Allen, James Ussher, Brian Twyne, perhaps John Selden and Richard Holdsworth. Cotton's collection was the most impressive of them all and its sources the most wide-ranging.[31] It was, as Sharpe concludes, central to the politics and scholarship of early Stuart England. Cotton was a generous lender of materials and most of the antiquaries of his generation, including many from abroad, made use of his library.[32] A mark of just how important his collection had become by the end of his life is the fact that it came under suspicion and from 1629 Cotton was granted only limited access to it.[33] Although the library remained in the hands of his family after his death in 1631 it was destined for the nation – in 1629 he drew up an indenture to this effect – to which ultimately it was transferred, more or less intact, in 1702.

Although the sixteenth- and seventeenth-century antiquaries were anxious to salvage manuscripts their concerns did not stretch to preservation as we

29 In 1614 there was an attempt to refound the Society, but this was once again blocked by the King and for the next quarter of the century the College of Arms in some sense took the place of the dissolved Society. As Herendeen (1988) observes, p. 210, 'The work of John Philipot (Somerset Herald), William Dugdale (Garter King of Arms), John Weever (a close friend of the herald Augustine Vincent), and Simonds D'Ewes, is inseparable from the activities and collections of the College of Arms, and prepared the way for the permanent establishment of a Society of Antiquaries'.

30 See Page 1993, p. 2.

31 On Cotton see Sharpe 1979, Tite 1994, Wright 1997. The interconnectedness of the collecting world is indicated by the fact that Lord William Howard's daughter Margaret married Thomas, Cotton's eldest son and heir.

32 Indeed, in his will Camden stipulated that Cotton be permitted to go through his chambers and claim back any materials which belonged to him: see Parry 1995, p. 76; also Tite 1997.

33 In Wright 1997, p. 22, Sharpe observes that by the end of 1630 Cotton seems to have been restored to royal favour and that had he lived longer he would have had a career as political adviser.

know it. Parker had books disbound and reorganized; he tidied opening and closing pages; he had scripts imitated to fill in missing sections. Books were cut down and rebound in new combinations. Nor did he mutilate his own books only. Returning a manuscript to Burghley he observed:

> I had thought to have made up the want of the beginning of the Psalter, for it wanteth the first psalm, and three verses in the second psalm, and methought the leaf going before the xxvith psalm would have been a meet beginning before the whole Psalter . . . the first psalm written on the back side: which I was in mind to have caused Lylye to have counterfeited in antiquity, &c., but that I called to remembrance that ye have a singular artificer to adorn the same, which your honour shall do well to have the monument finished, or else I will cause it to be done and remitted again to your library. . . .[34]

Cotton's techniques were not dissimilar and in some ways he was even more violent in the treatment of his books than Parker had been.[35] Indeed, it is not until the eighteenth century that anything resembling a modern attitude towards the integrity of the codex begins to emerge. In this, as in so much else, Humfrey Wanley (1672–1726) is a pioneer, reacting in horror to D'Ewes's treatment of one of his own manuscripts:

> It seemeth a little extraordinary to me that Sir Simonds D'Ewes should . . . take his old Book, and cutt off the first leaf or leaves; rase off the 3 first lines in another place wherein were the conclusion of a former Chapter, & the Title of the next; write thereon a new Title for the Book . . . and that he should, to crown the matter, prefix a new Frontispiece or Title of his own Invention thereunto, to make the World believe that this was not to be deemed a book of that Kind that it proveth to be. Q. Whether it be fair for any Gentleman to do these things by an old History, although the Book be his own Property.[36]

Focused as they were on religious and political issues and questions of precedent, the antiquaries of our period seem to have had little interest in literary manuscripts as such: for the most part these were essentially working libraries. Certainly Cotton would not have counted the Beowulf or the Gawain manuscripts among his greatest treasures.[37] Service books, even the most exquisite, seem to have had little or any prestige during our period.

34 *Correspondence of Matthew Parker, DD. Archbishop of Canterbury*, ed. J. Bruce and T. T. Perowne (Cambridge, 1853), pp. 253–4. See also Parkes 1997, p. 124.

35 He and Patrick Young, for example, indulged in complex negotiations involving the radical dismemberment of medieval codices: see Carley and Tite 1992; also Carley 1997a.

36 BL, Harley MS. 266; quoted in Watson 1966, p. 50.

37 There are isolated examples of individuals collecting manuscripts in Middle English in the early seventeenth century or slightly before, such as Joseph Holland – on whom see Caldwell 1943 – and William Browne – on whom see Edwards 1997. Ley also owned Middle English texts.

Cotton dismembered for binding purposes the beautiful illuminated mid-fourteenth-century psalter, now reconstituted as BL manuscript Royal 13 D.I*.[38] The Harley Psalter received only a perfunctory reference in D'Ewes's catalogue and was probably bought for a mere five shillings.[39] Throughout the seventeenth century, then, presumably much continued to disappear, to be used for the ignoble purposes to which Bale had referred so much earlier. In a letter dated 10 July 1722, for example, Thomas Tanner described how he took possession of the important Glastonbury manuscript:

> I had this very book 30 years since in Oxford, when a student of Christ Church (Mr Clarges) sending for some tobacco at a Grocers had a parcell sent in one of the leaves. Some present being more curious than ordinary finding it to be something historical, rescued what remain'd the next morning from destruction.[40]

On the other hand, most lamentations over the dissolution of the monasteries seem implicitly to suggest that monastic collections remained in a static state throughout the Middle Ages like insects trapped in amber. In fact, the monasteries themselves had weeded out and recycled over the centuries: many medieval manuscripts have flyleaves or covers taken from much more ancient texts. By the 1530s printed books were beginning to push out the older manuscripts in the more lively establishments. Up-to-date scholarship would have rendered many of the old Bibles, commentaries and perhaps even histories valueless and therefore dispensable. Ironically it was the very destruction of the monasteries which led ultimately to the enshrinement of the libraries as cultural icons. In her study of the Dissolution and how it created a transformed view of the past Margaret Aston has observed that: 'The very process of casting off the past generated nostalgia for its loss. And with nostalgia came invigorated historical activity.'[41]

38 See Carley and Tite 1992. 39 See Watson 1966, p. 41.

40 BL, Add. MS. 22934; quoted in Carley 1994, p. 272. Even later, fragments from medieval manuscripts were thrown away during the process of rebinding and Philip Bliss (1787–1857) built up an important collection by trading fragments for pots of beer.

41 Aston 1973, p. 255.

LITERARY CANONS

16

Literature, the playhouse and the public

JOHN PITCHER

Books and performance

In 1576 the actor James Burbage constructed the first purpose built public theatre in Europe since the fall of ancient Rome. Burbage's new playhouse, situated in the district of Shoreditch in London, was called simply The Theatre. What followed from this, over the next fifty years and more, in cultural interactions of the most complex kind, was the emergence of two histories, one of material objects and the marketplace (since The Theatre was soon competing with rival playhouses in London), and the other of an eruption and opening in human consciousness manifested in and provoked by the drama that Shakespeare and his contemporaries wrote for the stage. The first history is of the physical spaces and economic conditions in which Elizabethan and Jacobean plays were performed, of the actors who played them, and the audiences who watched them. The second history is that of the plays themselves, as artefacts of words and spectacle shaped by and in turn shaping the imaginations and the psychological and social desires and needs of the dramatists and their audiences.

Other forms of human endeavour and achievement converged on this moment of public theatre, among them the resources of classical drama, poetry and rhetoric, and the conventions for the conduct of public and state ceremony in all aspects of English life, in royal courts, in the streets, and in the Church. One of the reasons for the astonishing success of the public stage was its capacity to assimilate and to exploit the many different cultural forms that were presented to it. At a formal level, it was able, for instance, to absorb and transform contemporary music and song, and the pavan and the jig; at the level of power and authority, it could show men and women contesting the domestic space of the family and of personal and dynastic heritage. Within its lifespan (from 1576 until the theatres were closed in 1642), the public stage took almost everything into itself and restaged it, from the humblest to the most elevated of human activities. Whether this made it as socially dangerous as contemporary critics claimed (showing actors as princes, but even more insidiously rendering princes as mere actors in power plays) is a matter for debate. What is not in doubt is the measure of excitement, agitation and hostility the theatres produced in contemporary culture as a whole, especially over the highly sensitive issues associated with social rank.

To its first audiences the most disturbing and alluring thing about the public stage was that it was a hybrid. As an entertainment it started on the same social level as baiting, blinding and killing bulls and bears, cockfighting, visiting brothels, and watching criminals being put to death. But it also aspired to respond to and cultivate other, less cruel and violent tastes, ones for poetry and well-plotted stories, for plausible dialogue and discoveries, and for the portrayal of gentleness and sorrow. Theatre audiences were mixed, alarmingly so to the London authorities who were responsible (without a modern police force) for keeping the peace. The indiscriminate mingling of godly citizens, the professional classes and the middling sort with their apprentices and servants, and with thieves and prostitutes, hardly encouraged the establishment social ideal that people should know their place and stay in it.

The most troubling aspect of the public stage as hybrid, however, was in its shameless joining of knowledges, vulgar with arcane, and high with low. The authorities tried to resist this union (by banning certain subjects, religious ones in particular) but they failed, because in this the theatres were allied to the other great agent for cultural and imaginative upheaval at this time, the printed book. It is characteristic of Shakespeare that he should be prescient enough to recognize this conjunction (and confrontation) of stage and book from the outset of his writing career, in one of his plays from the early 1590s, *Titus Andronicus*. In this gory Senecan tragedy set in late imperial Rome, the nobleman Titus is tested to the point of madness by the appalling things done to him and his family, for which he takes revenge. Two of his sons are beheaded, and their heads sent to him as a joke: he kills another of his sons himself, and he cuts off his own right hand. Most horrible of all is the rape of his daughter Lavinia, made even worse when the rapists cut out her tongue and cut off her hands to prevent her speaking or writing about the crime. In the chapbook source,[1] which Shakespeare follows closely elsewhere, the rape is revealed almost immediately: Lavinia at once takes a stick between her lopped wrists and scrawls the rapists' names in the dust. In the play, however, Lavinia's disclosure of what has happened to her is delayed throughout an

1 Given in *Narrative and dramatic sources of Shakespeare*, ed. G. Bullough (London, 1964–75), VI, pp. 34–44 (the chapbook was printed in the eighteenth century, but 'probably goes back to a sixteenth-century original', VI, p. 7).

entire Act, and the rape is not revealed until she has a book of Ovid's *Metamorphoses* in front of her. The discovery scene (IV. i), most of which Shakespeare invents, opens with her wildly pursuing her terrified young nephew across the stage:

> *Enter Lucius' son, and* LAVINIA *running after him, and the boy flies from her with his books under his arm. Enter* TITUS *and* [his brother] MARCUS.

Her father calms her and finds, through signs, that what she wants so desperately from young Lucius is his copy of Ovid. She claws at the book, frantically and clumsily turning over the leaves, searching for the passage which will tell all. 'Help her', says Titus, when she reaches it,

> what would she find? Lavinia, shall I read?
> This is the tragic tale of Philomel,
> And treats of Tereus' treason and his rape;
> And rape, I fear, was root of thy annoy.[2]

In book 6 of the *Metamorphoses*, Tereus raped his wife's sister Philomela, cut out her tongue and shut her away in a tower, but his plan to silence her failed when she made a tapestry in which she described her fate to her sister Progne. Philomela was released, and Progne took revenge on Tereus by murdering their son Itylus and serving him at a meal to his father. In the play, once the crime against Lavinia has been uncovered like this, through Ovid, Marcus teaches her how to write in the sand with a stick in her mouth, guiding it with her stumps. She writes *stuprum* ('rape') and the names of the rapists, and Titus begins his revenge, part of which, even though from the chapbook source, is closer to the pattern in Ovid or Seneca's *Thyestes* (Titus murders the rapists, grinds their flesh and bones, and feeds them to their vile mother).

Shakespeare brings the book of Ovid's *Metamorphoses* into *Titus Andronicus* for several reasons. Within the fiction, it heightens the tension (is this how Titus will discover the truth?), and it allows him to make the subtle psychological point that the well-read and high-born Lavinia is so traumatized by her ordeal that she cannot begin to communicate it except through an equally horrid fictional archetype in a book. There is also, outside the fiction of the play, a social provocativeness on Shakespeare's part about using Ovid like this, making the original audiences aware that he had put before them a hybrid of high and low art, élite Roman tragicomic poetry joined with a popular horror story in prose. To his contemporaries, there was nothing new about mutilation and awful deaths (one of the arts of the public executioner was to disembowel

2 *Titus Andronicus*, ed. J. W. Lever (London, 1953), IV. i. 46–9.

those convicted of treason and show them their own entrails before they died), nor about the stratification of knowledge which ensured that a small proportion of the population knew a lot (be it books of Ovid or histories of the world) while most people knew next to nothing. The monstrous newness of the public theatre, abetted by printed story books in verse and prose and by the scriptures in the vernacular, was that time and again it prompted the vulgar, standing alongside their betters, to imagine that there were ways up and through the caste layers of rank, and of learning, skills, and trades, and of pleasure.

In the figure of Lavinia tormented in front of the book it may be that Shakespeare showed even more of this than he intended. Lavinia's furious, ungainly scrabbling at the pages, in agony and frustration, is caused by the fact that she has the knowledge but cannot pass it on without a terrible effort. This is inside the fiction, but what might audiences watching this in the early 1590s have made of it, many of whom must have struggled to understand poetry in English, let alone Ovid in Latin, and who (without an education at grammar school or university) can hardly have had the story of Philomela by heart. Perhaps Lavinia's speechlessness and impotence looking at the book were for many of the audiences, rudely literate at best, a metamorphosed and grotesque but still strangely recognizable image of their own condition. Lavinia knows what the book holds but cannot say it, while they know that the book holds what they want to know but cannot read it.

Not surprisingly, there were attempts, from within Elizabethan élite book culture, to keep the public theatres at a distance, by demonizing them and accusing them of arousing and feeding the worst appetites of the vulgar. In one episode in the major poem of the period, *The faerie queene*, first published in 1590, Edmund Spenser takes on this same subject, the sexual degradation of a noblewoman, but the context he gives for her agony is pointedly that of a theatre audience. The woman is Amoret, who (in book III xii) has been made a captive by the magician Busirane, and who can only be rescued by the beautiful warrior maiden, Britomart. Busirane has wounded Amoret and used her vital spirits (writing spells in a manuscript book with her blood) to conjure up a phantasm that shows her being dragged along in a love pageant, her heart cut out of her body and on its strings. The boy god Cupid, unblindfolded, presides over the procession, riding on the back of a lion, relishing her pangs of love, represented in the figures around her, Fear, Cruelty, Desire and others. The pageant is an allegory or psychomachia of the virgin Amoret's feelings at the prospect of her marriage to Sir Scudamour, but it is also intended to indicate Britomart's mental and spiritual state as she watches it. The pageant – another hybrid, a learned one, joining a medieval love procession with a Renaissance triumph – is ushered in front of Britomart by a figure called Ease who enters (stanzas 3–4)

as on the ready flore
Of some Theatre, a graue personage,
That in his hand a branch of laurell bore,
With comely haueour and count'nance sage,
Yclad in costly garments, fit for tragicke Stage.

Proceeding to the midst, he still did stand,
As if in mind he somewhat had to say,
And to the vulgar beckning with his hand,
In signe of silence, as to heare a play,
By liuely actions he gan bewray
Some arguments of matter passioned . . .

For centuries spectacles such as this, anatomizing the mysteries and savagery of love, had been the preserve of courts, exclusive displays in shows or paintings or poems for the men and women at the very top of society. The vulgarization of this experience, disclosing it to the general public makes it, Spenser claims, into something prurient, even pornographic, a lubricious stage play for greedy, uncivilized eyes. From this juxtaposition of high moral art with barbarism, the élite readers of *The faerie queene* were supposed to see even more clearly how to distinguish between holy and unholy forms of love. The danger, as Spenser's critics were quick to point out, was that the publication of such images ('magnifying louers deare debate'[3]) might encourage vicious tastes in people of all ranks, especially the young and perhaps even women. The effect of *The faerie queene*, in other words, might not be at all cautionary or conservative, if it disturbed still further (as the theatre might) the dividing lines between the upper and lower parts of Elizabethan society.

It is impossible to determine how significant such risks were to the collective social imagination through this mingling of people in the theatres and among the readership for printed books of poems, prose fiction, and stage plays. For one thing, there are no reliable figures for the sizes of the audiences. Modern scholarship can give only approximate estimates of the yearly audiences who attended the London playhouses; it knows even less about how many purchased books of literature and drama in the vernacular. Over the half century from 1576 the public theatres, more than ten of them, were built in different sizes and designs, with standing and seating capacities that ranged from about nine hundred (at the select indoor Blackfriars) to perhaps three thousand (at the

3 *The faerie queene*, book IV, proem, line 5.

outdoor Globe).[4] The print runs for books of sophisticated Elizabethan poetry, or for texts of plays like *Titus Andronicus*, might vary according to the type of work (sonnets or epics), and to the size and format of the book with its consequences for the publishers' investment, but it is difficult to believe that they were ever much over 1,000 copies, and they may well have been considerably smaller, perhaps only a few hundred. In the case of playbooks it may have taken four years or more for booksellers in London and the provinces to dispose of a print run as small as 800 copies, even where the book was priced as low as sixpence.[5] *The faerie queene*, published as a substantial and well-printed quarto, was probably on sale for three or four times as much, and it probably sold just as slowly. Of course there would have been many more readers than there were buyers of poems, plays and novellas, but it is entirely feasible that the supply of such books, even of the quarto editions of *Romeo and Juliet*, *Hamlet* and *King Lear*, often exceeded the demand for them. Moreover, even where a play text was reprinted, the total number of copies sold must still have been small in comparison with the number of playgoers who watched the same play in one of the public theatres. *Titus Andronicus*, for instance, first published in 1594, was reprinted twice, once in 1600 and then again in 1611. The aggregate of copies sold over two decades was perhaps between 2 and 3,000. This was about the same as the maximum capacity at just *one* performance of *Titus Andronicus* in one of the bigger playhouses – and between January and June 1594 *Titus Andronicus* had been performed at least five times at the Rose.[6] Even though more precise figures are not available, either for booksales or for attendances at the theatre, and although we have no clear picture of how frequently specific plays were performed, it is reasonable to infer that interest in *Titus Andronicus* on stage was far, far greater than the appeal it had as a fiction in a printed book, perhaps by a factor of five or ten or possibly even more.

Estimates like these can only tell us about the scale of the audiences for books and performances. To know more, especially about contemporary tastes and social mix, we must turn to other forms of evidence. One revealing instance of an individual taking pleasure in the drama in print rather than in the theatre is that of the late-sixteenth-century aristocrat, Charles Blount, Baron Mountjoy, by far the most successful of the Elizabethan generals in Ireland. Mountjoy was a great reader and annotator of his books, and he was esteemed for his knowledge of and command in discussing theological niceties. He was an aristocrat, a man

4 The designs and capacities of the different theatres are outlined by Andrew Gurr in *Playgoing in Shakespeare's London* (Cambridge, 1987), pp. 13–33.

5 Blayney 1997a, pp. 411–12.

6 *The revels history of English drama 1576–1613*, ed. C. Leech and T. W. Craik (London, 1975), III, p. 65.

at arms, the lover of Penelope Rich (Sir Philip Sidney's Stella), and a student of letters, not to say a bookish man. His secretary, who served with him in the Irish campaigns, also reports of Mountjoy that he much enjoyed reading playbooks for recreation, and that he owned a number of printed quartos of the drama. Yet Mountjoy would never attend the theatre in person, certainly not the public playhouses.[7]

This may point to a number of things – to a contempt for the vulgarity of watching plays, or to a cautiousness about being seen by his social inferiors and being in proximity to them, or even to a dislike of the kind of high-born company (his own social equals) that frequented the playhouses. What is intriguing, however, is that Mountjoy was the great friend and ally of Robert Devereux, Earl of Essex, and very nearly his fellow-conspirator in the failed coup and rebellion of 1601 – the Essex, that is, who was a regular visitor at the public theatre, who used a private production of *Richard II* to bolster up his own spirits and those of his conspirators immediately before the attempted coup,[8] and who was so obviously, even hectically, theatrical himself. Perhaps it was Mountjoy who all along was the more intelligent of these two aristocrats, cunningly keeping himself out of the theatre and its inducements to play-acting and to hysterical overacting. Safe in his study or war tent, scribbling in the margins of his books, including playbooks, Mountjoy may have preserved very carefully the distinction between being a courtier and being a player. The explanation for his staying away from the public stage may have been more straightforward than this, however: it is quite possible that, educated traditionally through classical models (Roman poets, historians and dramatists), and through a book-based syllabus, Mountjoy simply did not respond to the enactment of thought and feeling in the physical space of the theatre.

Against this nobleman's personal separation of the drama in print and in performance, we may set a striking instance of how printed texts of Shakespeare were used for amateur performances by individuals at the other end of the social scale. These performances took place in 1607 and 1608 on board the *Dragon*, an East India Company merchant ship bound, with two others, the *Hector* and the *Consent*, for the East Indies. On 5 September 1607, off the coast of Sierra Leone, the captain of the *Dragon*, William Keeling, invited on board a local interpreter, Lucas Fernandez, a converted Negro, brother-in-law of the local king Borea. There some of the ship's company, in Keeling's words, 'gaue the tragedie of Hamlett'. At the end of the month there was another performance, this time of

7 Fynes Moryson, *An itinerary containing his ten yeeres travel*... (Glasgow, 1907–8), II, pp. 264ff. See also C. Falls, *Mountjoy: Elizabethan General* (London, 1955).

8 See Gurr, *Playgoing*, pp. 113–14.

Richard II, when William Hawkins, captain of the *Hector*, dined with Keeling. Six months later, on 31 March 1608, Keeling recorded yet another performance in his journal: 'I envited Captain Hawkins to a ffishe dinner, and had hamlet acted abord me', and then added, probably by way of justification, 'which I permitt to keepe my people from idlenes and unlawful games, or sleepe'.[9] Both plays dealt with dangerous subjects – regicide, usurpation, and the volatility of the mob – but Keeling used them to maintain ship's discipline. Under the scorching equatorial sun he wisely allowed his crew their London playbooks, their favourite melancholy princes, their swapping of roles in rank and gender, and their dressing up. Perhaps there was also a need to hold the men together as a group, which acting in and watching plays might achieve – the very opposite in fact of allowing them to divert themselves by *reading* the plays (or anything else) in solitude, separated from one another. The serious threat to social control in this is well illustrated in another example of recreation on the high seas, this time from February 1596 on board a warship under the command of George Clifford, Earl of Cumberland. While all the rest of the ship's company were at morning prayers, Cumberland noticed one 'young gallant' sitting apart 'reading Orlando Furioso'. After the service the Earl went up to him immediately. In front of all the crew, he told the young man that 'we might look that God would serve us accordingly if we served him not better', and he 'bade him be sure that if again he took him in the like manner he would cast his book overboard and turn himself out of the ship'.[10]

The difficult thing with examples like this is the danger of over-interpretation. However, we are clearly dealing with a highly unstable microculture, with no one dominant social or aesthetic pattern of behaviour. Snobbery there is, and so too a striking eclecticism in the materials on show and in individual taste. Everyone (including the dramatists) proclaims the moral and political dangers of permitting all and sundry to enter and to participate in this heady, theatricalized and largely secular life of the imagination, fed from above and below by élite and popular books. It appears that imaginative literature – some of it shaped for the public stage, some of it for book reading that set its face against the attractions of the stage – had begun to assume a prominence in the lives of many people at all ranks in early modern English society. This prominence was quite out of proportion to the number of poems and stories published in print, and even to the large number of performances staged in the London theatres. No one can dispute the tabulations that show us that while sermons and law books poured from the Elizabethan and Jacobean press, poems, plays

9 E. K. Chambers, *William Shakespeare: a study of facts and problems* (Oxford, 1930), II, pp. 334–5.
10 G. C. Williamson, *George, Third Earl of Cumberland (1558–1605)* (Cambridge, 1920), p. 281.

and stories in the vernacular only amounted to a smallish fraction of the total output of the printing houses. And yet within fifty years of the opening of The Theatre – a hybrid space open to both peers and prostitutes – a book would be published, the first folio of Shakespeare's plays, that would captivate many among the élite, from the ruling monarch down to clerics and lawyers and even to women. How this transformation in the social positioning of Shakespeare and contemporary writers came about depended to a large extent on what was happening to non-theatrical literature between the 1590s and the 1620s.

Books and literary genres

In the late Elizabethan period we see the arrival of the recognizably modern literary author, and the beginnings of the formation of the English literary canon. Neither thing happened overnight. Indeed the preparation for them can be traced throughout the sixteenth century. Much of the work of establishing the notion of an English author was done, not for important Tudor writers (Sir Thomas More or Wyatt or Surrey), but for Chaucer. A text of *The Canterbury tales* was published by Caxton as early as 1477. However, complete works did not appear in print until the series of large folio editions prepared by Pynson (1526), Thynne (1532, 1542, and ?1550), Stow (1561) and Speght (1598 and 1602). Chaucer's life, the kind of writer he was (medieval *rhetor* or laureate *auctor*), where he should be positioned in relation to Tudor court society and to militant Protestant politics, were topics debated vigorously by, among others, Leland, Fox and Ascham, but it was in these editions that the project to confirm Chaucer as the first vernacular classic was accomplished.[11] The task of printing his texts from manuscripts brought with it fundamental questions that the editors would have to answer sooner or later: which of the poems attributed to him were really his? What was the chronological order in which they were written? And what were their historical and personal contexts? The most satisfactory answers were provided by Thomas Speght, one of Spenser's contemporaries at Cambridge, whose editions included a glossary of old and obscure words and a comprehensive account of the poet's life. The texts in Speght, as in all the Tudor editions, were printed in double columns and in black letter, a typeface associated with medieval rather than modern styles. Intriguingly, his first edition was issued with two title pages, one with classical columns and figures and a quotation from Ovid, the other with gothic columns wrapped around with vines.[12]

11 For an overview of Chaucer's early reception see Pask 1996, pp. 9–52.

12 The title pages (*STC* 5077–78) are illustrated in Pask 1996, pp. 40–1. There were two issues, one of which, *STC* 5079, has variant imprint.

Chaucer's editors made him the pre-eminent English literary writer (emphasizing his Englishness and aligning him with the reforming spirit of the Lollards), but they set themselves and everyone else an almost insoluble problem. *Troilus and Criseyde* and *The Canterbury tales* were obviously works of genius, but could not be positioned within the Tudors' classical frame of things. They recognized his debts to the ancients, but his poems were irredeemably blurred when judged against the classical genres. They were neither epic nor tragedy nor comedy nor pastoral as the ancients understood them. Even in his debts to his Italian contemporaries, Petrarch and Boccaccio, Chaucer veered away from their classical elements. The only way to respond, as Francis Beaumont, one of his admirers at Cambridge, urged in a preface to the Speght edition of 1598, was to praise Chaucer as *sui generis*, an original poet with no rival, ancient or modern, in his psychological and moral realism. Chaucer's 'devise of his Caunterburie Pilgrimage', Beaumont argued, is completely

> his owne, without following the example of any that ever writ before him. His drift is to touch all sortes of men, and to discover all vices of that Age, and that he doth in such sort, as he never failes to hit every marke he levels at.[13]

From this it would not be an enormous step to the even more contentious idea, that living English writers, even ones who wrote for the public stage, might be similarly classified – in their own terms, that is, not those prescribed by neoclassical critics.

Gabriel Harvey, another Cambridge man and a friend of Spenser, put this idea into words, revealingly, in a manuscript note in his copy of Speght's 1598 edition of Chaucer. Harvey complains that too few contemporary writers have met the high standards set by Chaucer and the medieval and early Tudor poets. He then lists those that do, and the reputations they currently enjoy. Among these, Sidney's *Arcadia* and Spenser's 'Faerie Queene ar now freshest in request'. Robert, Earl of Essex, he continues, 'much commends [William Warner's epic] Albions England', while

> The Lord Montjoy makes the like account of Daniels peece of the Chronicle, touching the Vsurpation of Henrie of Bullingbrooke. Which in deede is a fine, sententious, & politique peece of Poetrie: as proffitable, as pleasurable. The younger sort takes much delight in Shakespeares Venus, & Adonis: but his Lucrece, & his tragedie of Hamlet, Prince of Denmarke, haue it in them, to please the wiser sort.

13 Quoted by Pask 1996, p. 37.

There is praise too for poets whose work is still in manuscript. Sir Edward Dyer's 'written deuises farr excell most of the sonets, and cantos in print', and his 'Amaryllis, & Sir Walter Raleighs Cynthia, how fine and sweet inuentions'.[14] Minor genres are also noted – Heywood's proverbs, Owen's epigrams, and Hakluyt's prose – and there is mention too of his contemporaries, Constable, Watson and Chapman, but there is nothing about Ben Jonson's plays or Donne's poems in manuscript, as might have been expected by this date (around 1600).

Harvey had an unusual if not bizarre personality, with a great capacity for quarrelling, but he was no fool. He was nearly fifty when he wrote this note, and some of his tastes seem rather old fashioned. However, he shrewdly saw that authors are made not only by their talent and achievements but by the likes and dislikes of their audiences. Samuel Daniel's *Civil wars* ('the Chronicle'), an epic or heroic poem about the Wars of the Roses first published in 1595 and modelled on Lucan's *Pharsalia*, is an enjoyable, 'politique peece of Poetrie', but what matters most is the endorsement of the poem by Lord Mountjoy, whose approval of Daniel is set against the commendation Warner receives from the Earl of Essex. Further contrasts flow from this, between Shakespeare's younger readers and theatregoers and his wiser ones, and between poetry in print and coterie writing in manuscript. The political comment in these antitheses is transparent. In 1600, Essex was a brooding Hamlet in disgrace, while his wiser friend and rival Mountjoy, although (as noted earlier) he kept away from the theatres, nevertheless remained in public view in Ireland, and was unlikely ever to take arms against the Queen. Like his poet and client Daniel, Mountjoy was a student of history who had pondered the terrible costs to medieval England of usurpation and civil war. Harvey's judgements about the merits of living writers, and how their work is being ranked by contemporaries, are therefore made *through* these political alignments: the discourse we now know as English literary criticism, here in its most rudimentary form, emerges out of a simple political commentary. Harvey wrote this note for personal reasons (including, towards the end, his failure to publish his own poetry), but he was also playing his part in a new public forum where the status of English authors would be debated, in print and in manuscript notes like this one. But tellingly, although he was well-versed in classical writers and in the literature of the Continent, Harvey avoids doing what other commentators do (Francis Meres, for example), when they weigh their contemporaries. Writers are not assigned a position relative to an established ancient authority or genre: Daniel is not praised for being like the epic poet Lucan, nor Shakespeare for being another Ovid

14 Chambers, *William Shakespeare: a study of facts and problems*, II, pp. 197–8.

(the usual comparisons). The standard is Chaucer, and the shape of the Elizabethan literary canon, chiefly created through books printed in the 1590s, is in many respects the one that has survived to the present day.

It was Ben Jonson, one of the authors Harvey failed to mention, who made this new forum of literary judgement visible within his writing, indeed central to it. Jonson may have derived the structure of his early satirical comedies from classical models, but their dominant pattern – of ignorant, unsophisticated foolishness being shown up by urbane, well-educated wit – confirms that the working of this forum was, in his eyes, the guarantee of an ordered, civilized life. At the conclusion of the final scene of *Every man in his humour*, Jonson's first major success performed in the late summer of 1598, there is a moment of exposure and humiliation that is entirely characteristic of the best and worst of his comedy. Despite his struggling and resistance, the character Matheo, the booby and wouldbe gentleman lover, is held fast as his pockets are searched by the wits, Prospero and Clement. What they find in them is a bundle of papers, with writing in Matheo's hand, some of it addressed to his lady, or she he would adore, Madonna Hesperida. 'What, all this verse?' Clement exclaims,

> Body of me, he carries a whole realm, a commonwealth of paper, in his hose!
> Let's see some of his subjects. [*Reads*]
> *Unto the boundless ocean of thy beauty*
> *Runs this poor river, charged with streams of zeal,*
> *Returning thee the tribute of my duty,*
> *Which here my youth, my plaints, my love reveal.*
> Good! Is this your own invention?

'No sir', Matheo confesses, 'I translated that out of a book called *Delia*.'[15] The passage Matheo has copied out is in fact the opening quatrain of the famous and influential sonnet sequence, *Delia*, by Samuel Daniel, which was first published in 1592. The sonnets appeared in print five times up to 1598,[16] and they were often alluded to, praised, and imitated by contemporary dramatists and the literati (including Shakespeare). Which of these characters, Matheo or Clement, victim or tormentor, surprises us more over this copying out of *Delia*? Could Matheo, fool as he is, really have hoped to pass off these familiar lines as his own (as he tries to elsewhere in the play with lines from Marlowe's *Hero and Leander*)? And is it possible that Clement, such a spark of fashion, who prides himself on his city knowledge and literary judgement, would not immediately recognize the signature of such well known poetry?

15 Quarto text, *Everyman in his humour: a parallel-text edition of the 1601 quarto and the 1616 folio*, ed. J. W. Lever (London, 1972), pp. 270–2.

16 *STC* 6243.2–6 (1592–8).

This backhanded compliment – the lines are good, but does anyone know who wrote them? – probably ignited the literary and personal quarrel between Daniel and Jonson, between established poet and newcomer, one which grew into an important debate about the aesthetics and politics of courtly art in the Jacobean masque, verse epistle and historiography. Daniel's reputation was at its height around this time – as Harvey's note suggests – and he too had recognized that the public forum itself could be a proper subject for a poem. In 1599 he published *Musophilus*, an ambitious and difficult poem cast as a colloquy between Musophilus ('the lover of poetry', and of learning more generally) and Philocosmus ('the lover of the world', the pragmatic and active man). The topics covered include Chaucer and the Elizabethan writers, the fact that too many trivial books are being published, the part the vulgar have in judging things, and the utility and limits of a liberal education in one of the universities. There is no winner in this debate; the dialogue ends inconclusively, and Daniel's version of the forum is far from what Jonson intended it should be – that is, a sort of public academy, with himself as its head, which, through naming and shaming, was to bring about a reformation of morals and manners, and of the abuses of the contemporary stage (particularly violations of neoclassical proprieties, in which Shakespeare was the chief culprit). Daniel was disgusted at Jonson's authoritarian rule-making, but he lacked resilience and withdrew, leaving the field to his opponent.

One indication of how much ground he gave up is in the title page of his folio collection of poems published in 1601 as *The works*, which includes *Delia*, *The civil wars*, and *Musophilus* (see plate 16.1). The title alone was a measure of his high standing (before this no living writer had issued a collection with this range of genres as his *Works*), and the engraved figures, classical columns, and arch of royal arms, designed for this book in particular, confirmed his credentials as an established English author. All the signs are that Daniel's folio was well received, especially among the élite (a copy was placed in the Bodleian in Oxford when King James visited the Library in 1605). By contrast, fifteen years later, when Jonson came to publish his folio *Workes*, a collection of poems, plays and masques with an even more considered and elaborate title page (see plate 16.2), his title was ridiculed by some people for its presumption: since play was not the same as work, how could stage plays be works?[17]

17 D. Riggs, *Ben Jonson: a life* (Cambridge, MA, 1989), pp. 226–8. The Bodleian presentation copy of Daniel's *Works* is Arch. G. d. 47 (title page reproduced as plate 16.1): evidence that Daniel gave the book in 1605 comes in part from the list of acquisitions kept by Thomas James, Bodley's Librarian (MS. Bodley 510, p. 296). The quarrel between Daniel and Jonson is considered by Loewenstein 1991, pp. 168–91.

The papers in Matheo's pockets, with poems written on them, have something further to tell about Elizabethan and Jacobean literary culture, and the growing public discussion about it. Knowing lines by heart from contemporary poets, or copying extracts from printed poems into a manuscript commonplace book or on to separate sheets of paper, was normal practice. In December 1596 Henry Colling, of Bury St Edmunds, a reader and collector of books, wrote down two stanzas of Shakespeare's *Venus and Adonis* in his papers, probably from memory,[18] and a few years later, in the Cambridge play, *The first part of the return from Parnassus* (1601), the young graduate and ninny Gullio (a character modelled on Matheo) evidently has other stanzas and couplets from Shakespeare's poem by heart, along with lines from Thomas Kyd's popular play, *The Spanish Tragedy*.[19] Sometimes the copying out of poetry was quite substantial. One of the Sloane manuscripts in the British Library contains the first forty-six sonnets of Daniel's *Delia*, not very neatly or very accurately, from the printed text of 1595.[20] Although the copy is contemporary with the printed editions, there is no question of this manuscript having any independent value as a textual witness, and it is not an exercise in calligraphic grace. The sonnets are crammed into the quarto-sized pages, with final couplets turned up into the side margins, and several lines have been omitted in a transcription that appears to have been done in some haste. Why was it done at all, though? The explanation is probably the simple one, that several of the surviving manuscripts of Tudor poems are in fact copies of printed texts. Books, even if issued in editions of 1,000 copies, were not able to satisfy all the demands of an expanding market for poetry, and wider distribution did not mean that everyone could obtain from print all the poems they wanted.[21]

This takes us back to the estimates of the print runs of play books. If the Daniel editions are anything to go by, it seems possible that books of English poetry by named authors sold more quickly and in larger quantities than plays from the public stage (five editions of *Delia* up to 1598, so perhaps 4,000 copies in six years, and still someone felt the need to copy from one of the editions). If we put together all the editions of Shakespeare's poems (*Venus and Adonis*, *The rape of Lucrece*, *The sonnets* and the falsely attributed *Passionate pilgrim*), and assume print runs of between 800 and 1,000, then upwards of 14,000 copies were in print before his death in 1616 (still meagre numbers in comparison with theatre audiences however). To books published by Daniel and Shakespeare we must

18 Kelliher 1990b, pp. 164–70.

19 *The three Parnassus plays*, ed. J. B. Leishman (London, 1949), lines 923–3, 983, 989, 995–1000 and 1002–3, 1452–3.

20 *IELM*, I. 1. 201, DaS6, copied from 6243.5 (1595).

21 See Kelliher 1990a, p. 259.

add editions of poetry by, among others, Sidney, Spenser and Michael Drayton, as well as the anthologies at the turn of the century that contained pieces by Marlowe and Raleigh. Almost all of these copies have perished, since they were small books. Once more, however, the production and sale of printed books give only part of the story: for many people poetry written in manuscript and privately circulated had the highest aesthetic and social cachet.

Scribal publication was the older form of publication, which print had not replaced, and certainly not in specific areas, including that of imaginative literature.[22] The first version of Sidney's *Arcadia*, for example, a prose romance the length of a modern novel, was completed around 1580. On Sidney's instructions, it was copied by hand by scribes who made ten or more copies, which were distributed among the Sidney family, friends and allies, and, beyond these, to courtiers and to members of the gentry. Sidney himself had no intention of putting any of his works into print, and it was not until the 1590s, more than five years after he had died in action fighting the Spanish, that his sister and others began to publish as printed books the sonnet sequence *Astrophil and Stella*, *A defence of poetry*, and the much revised and unfinished version of the *Arcadia*.[23] English poets had published lyrics and translations in manuscript throughout the sixteenth century (Wyatt, Surrey, and Raleigh are famous instances), but not until the final decade of Elizabeth's reign did scribal publication of poetry become truly an *alternative* to print, something socially superior because it was written for a closed, privileged community of readers.[24] The brilliance of John Donne and his upwardly mobile circle of young lawyers and minor courtiers ensured that their coterie poetry, begun in the 1590s, was superior on almost every other count too. Donne's social poise, his inventiveness in subject matter, his suave mastery of new metres and of classical elegy and satire, and his astonishing lexicon instantly made him tomorrow's man, a rival not only to Sidney and Daniel in print, but even to England's archpoet, Spenser. The circulation in manuscripts (single sheets as well as in compilations) of the *Songs and sonnets*, Donne's supreme achievement, was restricted at first to intimate friends, to other writers, and to people he wanted to impress, and it was some time before the poems (as distinct from his reputation as a poet) became more widely known. One reason that Matheo's papers are such a joke is that they are merely copied from printed books, because he has no access to the new poetry being written and passed around by the smart literary set headed by Donne. Later in life, and rather unwillingly,

22 See Love, ch. 3, above.
23 The *Old Arcadia* manuscripts are considered by Woudhyusen 1996, pp. 299ff.
24 Further, see Love above, ch. 3.

Donne had to write some of his poetry for print, but that involved a loss of exclusiveness.

Even as these clever, well-to-do males strove to keep out of printed books, others were taking a big step to get into them. Although there were precious few women writers in this period, and most of what they wrote remained in manuscript, a few (notably Amelia Lanyer) did venture to publish a book of poems.[25] Given what men thought of women *reading* poetry (something discussed below), their reaction to them writing it was probably hostile and dismissive – not that different presumably from their feelings about an uneducated weaver like Thomas Deloney publishing stories, or a London boatman like John Taylor issuing occasional verse and pamphlets. These were social novelties, in which daring intruders entered from the periphery, but there were innovations in the categories (or sub-genres) of writing as well. Elizabethan and Jacobean authors, even élite ones, were not slow to claim in print that they had invented this or that English literary form: Thomas Lodge, a doctor, claimed the verse epistle, and Sir William Cornwallis the essay.[26] In all, for about thirty years from around 1600, the literary scene in England was made out of many contradictory and competing mental and social energies – in print, in manuscript, and on the stage – some of which asserted and prized literary authorship (in Chaucer and in the living writers), some of which kept authorship hidden and disdained public attention (among the coterie poets and wits), and some of which sought to make literary authors the masters of all discourse and genres and all audiences (the Jonsonian dream in which authorship was identical with authority). Yet it was within this space, whatever its confusions and clamour, that writers and readers contrived something quite exceptional for themselves – an embryonic, undeveloped form of the modern public sphere.

Books and the civilizing process

One of the major transformations of the upper crust of European society – from late medieval warrior princes and their cadre into humanist overlords and bureaucrats at the Renaissance court – was more or less completed in England even before Queen Elizabeth was born. The role that book culture

25 See *The poems of Aemilia Lanyer: salve deus rex Judaeorum*, ed. S. Woods (New York and Oxford, 1993), pp. xxx–xxxvi.

26 In *A fig for Momus*, 1595, A3^{v}, Lodge declares that his epistles '*are in that kind, wherein no Englishman of our time hath publiquely written*', while Cornwallis writes in 1601 that 'I holde neither *Plutarche's* nor none of those auncient short manner of writings nor *Montaigne's* nor such of this latter time to bee rightly tearmed Essayes . . . But mine are Essaies', *Essayes by Sir William Cornwallis, the younger*, ed. D. C. Allen (Baltimore, 1946), p. 190.

and its champions Erasmus and More had in this phase of the civilizing process is well known.[27] By the end of the sixteenth century books of all kinds were continuing to reshape the outlook and manners of the English élite but, as we have seen, the spectrum of people whose lives were influenced by literary writing and the public stage was widening rapidly. It also seems that everyone – citizens of London, clerics, and women as much as writers and courtiers – wanted their say about the stories, poems and literary authors that were important to them. Frequently the ways in which vernacular literature was being used or judged was made one of the topics in a story or a play. As early as 1592, for example, in a pamphlet in prose called *The cobler of Caunterburie*, which follows Chaucer's *Canterbury tales* in some respects, a group of citizens chat and tell jokes on a journey by boat down the Thames from Billingsgate to Gravesend. The conversation turns to a pamphlet of stories called *Tarltons newes*, which is praised by some people in the group but criticized by others. One of the citizens declares that most of the stories in the book are stolen out of Boccaccio,[28] which suggests a familiarity with both native and foreign prose fiction, especially since *The Decameron* was not translated in full in England until 1620. How many of London's citizens really had this command of stories it is impossible to say, but what is not in doubt is that putting the right name to this or that story mattered even to the urban middling sort (the attributions of poems in coterie manuscript circulation, to Donne and to others, even though often wrong, point to a similar concern to attach a name to contemporary literature).

Hangers-on and servants in big houses were easy targets for ridicule on the Jacobean stage, particularly if they could be shown to be taking modern literature too seriously. One of the characters in *The scornful lady*, a play written by Beaumont and Fletcher around 1610, is mocked for doing just that. When (in II. i) Roger, the curate in a grand country house, finds himself being edged out of his suit to the fickle Abigail by smarter, more upmarket young men, he asks himself, in despair,

> Did I for this consume my quarters in meditation, vowes, and wooed her in *Herocyall Epistles*? Did I expound *The Owle*, and undertooke, with labour and expence the recollection of those thousand Peeces, consum'd in Cellors and Tobacco shops of that our honour'd Englishman *Nicholas Breton*?[29]

27 See N. Elias, *The civilizing process*, 2 vols., trans. E. Jephcott (Oxford, 1978–82).

28 *The cobler of Caunterburie: and, Tarltons newes out of Purgatorie*, ed. G. Creigh and J. Belfield (Leiden, 1987), p. 23.

29 *The dramatic works in the Beaumont and Fletcher canon*, gen. ed. F. Bowers (Cambridge, 1966–96), II, p. 481.

Roger has been wooing Abigail by writing verse letters to her imitated from Drayton's *England's heroical epistles* (1597) and by offering her the dubious pleasure of his exposition of *The owl*, another poem by Drayton, a notoriously obscure satire on the court published in 1604. These endeavours are preposterous enough – what would Abigail want with old-fashioned or unintelligible stuff like this? – but there is worse to follow. Roger's tastes in vernacular poetry are so hopelessly out of date that he is a devotee of Breton, a minor Elizabethan poet whose books by 1610 (so Beaumont and Fletcher suggest) have all been broken up and are being used as wrapping paper around twists of tobacco (or worse), from which the curate has made up a copy of Breton for his sweetheart. Roger is educated, probably a graduate, but he simply has no idea of what is good or bad in modern English poetry. He is obviously a descendant of Ben Jonson's character Matheo, but there is something even more desperate and sad and more real-life about him because of the way he clings to reading poetry as something to do, something (however small) to be good at doing. The contemporary readership of literature and drama probably included a sizeable number of curates, tutors, clerks, schoolmasters and even the upper reaches of the household staff – unimportant people, that is, putting up with the humbling constraints of their duties and abilities, possibly relieved to have something about which they were fairly free to speak (because it was not explicitly or directly political or religious), whatever the jibes and sneers at them from the younger set of dramatists who were out to flatter their social and intellectual betters.

The forum even contained women. In *Epicoene or the silent woman* (1609), one of Jonson's most disturbing gender comedies, there is a group of collegiate ladies (played on stage of course by male actors in drag), who are monsters of fashion, manipulation, and superficial learning (their names tell us enough – two of them are Madam Haughty and Madam Centaure). According to their detractors (in II. ii), these ladies delight in cosmetics, approve of abortion, and refuse their husbands sex unless they are paid for it. Most perverse of all, women like this also have views on living writers, and 'censure poets and authors and styles, and compare 'em, Daniel with Spenser, Jonson with tother youth [Shakespeare], and so forth'. Jonson tries to make out that the collegiate ladies are freaks – disturbing hybrids, women with too much male in them – and that only his satirical comedy can purge the sick topsy-turvyness they represent. His real unhappiness, though, is with women voicing any opinions at all (a silent woman would be a miracle), and most men in Elizabethan and Jacobean society would have concurred with this. From a male perspective, books of English poems, plays and stories could only make the situation worse since women were able to understand them without knowing Latin or Italian or French. They might also lay claim to a place in the forum (as they do in *Epicoene*), and even begin to conduct their lives differently on account of what they read. The moralists reproved men for letting their wives and daughters read erotic poems like *Venus and Adonis*, or Ovid in translation, because the lustful play they saw there would stimulate their desires and erotic imagination.[30] As some shrewder men realized, the danger was much less simple. There was not much chance that intelligent women who had read English poetry and drama would take Venus or Cressida or Cleopatra as their role models, but they might well come to expect the men in their lives, particularly their suitors in marriage, to have read Shakespeare or Chaucer or even a love story by John Lyly or by an Italian in translation.

Evidence of early modern women buying or borrowing or inheriting books of English literature is indeed substantial. In his account book for 1611, Thomas Screvin, steward to the Manners family, Earls of Rutland, noted, among payments for 'a perspective glasse', and a 'plaster for the gowte for my lord', three pounds given 'to Mr Cotgrave that presented his French Dictionary to my Lady', and the purchase, also for 'my Lady', of Marlowe's *Hero and Leander* along with Bishop Joseph Hall's *Heaven upon earth or of true peace and tranquilitie of minde*, which indicate the diversity and seriousness of the Countess's interests.[31] Moreover, it was another woman, Mrs Frances Wolfreston, living a quiet, provincial life in the Midlands on quite a different social level, who preserved for us the only surviving copy (now in the Bodleian) of the 1593 first edition of that book so dangerous to ladies, *Venus and Adonis*.[32]

In the past two decades social historians and students of early modern book culture have paid increasing attention to real-life readers of books of poetry and drama like Lady Rutland and Mrs Wolfreston. They have studied what imaginative literature was being read in this period, who read it, how it was annotated, and (as far as is possible) what part it played in individual lives. The evidence is piecemeal and scattered, found in library lists, inventories, account books, wills, diaries, commonplace books and in the margins of books themselves,[33] and extends to academics, statesmen and minor courtiers, lawyers, physicians, schoolmasters, undergraduates and law students, clerks, women

30 Wright 1935, pp. 109ff. 31 HMC, *Rutland*, 12th Report, IV, p. 490.

32 Morgan 1989, pp. 202 and 218. McKitterick 2000, p. 368, cites the cases of women with small estates like Ann Lumley, the widow of a Banbury weaver, who had books in their possession when they died.

33 Further, see above pp. 55–66, 89–93, ch. 14 and below ch. 20. See also, Leedham-Green 1986, Kiessling 1988, Jardine and Grafton 1990, *PLRE*, Coppens 1993, McKitterick 1997 and Raven, Small and Tadmor 1996. One book-collector in the 1570s who was not part of the court or city set is Captain Cox, a stone mason (Langham 1983, pp. 53–4 and 97–8).

who kept manuscript commonplace books,[34] country gentlemen, judges, merchants and craftsmen, and, of course, writers themselves, both amateur and professional. These studies, important as they are, do not as yet answer the one overriding question: did the Elizabethan literature and drama we now prize so highly have any common or unifying effect on these disparate and divided men and women, the first audiences of Shakespeare and Jonson and the others? Did their books of poems and plays and novellas civilize them, or give them any sense of belonging with one another to a community, however much in flux, that was enlarging and becoming conscious of itself? Not a social grouping alone, like the exclusive one that read Donne's lyrics, but rather a parasocial one, an imagined community that stretched across hierarchies of rank and gender, and conceived of the pleasures and comprehension of the literary arts as unrestricted to this or that type of person.

The best response to this question at present is a series of observations and guesses, even though there are cultural historians who would argue, as postmoderns, that we ought not to be asking this question in the first place since it runs the risk of falsifying the reality of what were mutually hostile sections in early modern society – in essence those with and those without power and choice (chiefly women and the underclasses). Against this objection, there are other key areas of convergence in this period – towards the Tudor nation state, a national Church, even the beginnings of the British Empire and a modern economy – that invite us to examine, in parallel, how another social and abstract category, the literary sphere, may have emerged around the same time. We need to keep matters in perspective, of course – the big issues of the day were not concerned with the readership of Shakespeare's plays, but how God was to be worshipped properly, how the poor were to be fed and the plague controlled, and how the power of Spain could be checked. All the same, the expression of opinion, pretty well confined in the cases of sermons and Parliamentary speeches, was probably rather more possible on the public stage and in books of literature, if only because the censors were often myopic and inconsistent. Thus the literary sphere may indeed have presented special opportunities for comment on, say, how the country was being governed (think of the astonishing disclosures in *King Lear* about the depths of evil to which the élite could sink).

The Elizabethans and Jacobeans do not seem to have had a particularly clear notion of a literary sphere or even a public one, and for the most part their

34 See Beal 1993, Burke 1997 and Larson forthcoming: McKitterick 2000, p. 365, cites S. Clarke, *The lives of sundry eminent persons in this later age*... (1693), pp. 157, '154' [162], 173 on Mary, Countess of Warwick's commonplace book. See also Bell, below, ch. 20.

vocabulary was not able to describe the idea of it. Opinion, for instance, was a highly elastic term, generally pejorative, shading into popular appeal, the fickle approval, that is, which the great might fleetingly enjoy from the many. Early modern words for lots of people taken together always stink of fear – the vulgar, the multitude, the crowd – and the abstract term *the public*, as it is used in modern democracies (public opinion), had certainly not yet arrived. What we can see, however, in the language of the body politic (where social categories were likened to human organs and limbs), is their understanding of a wholeness, held together by a regulatory system that took in but also redistributed and expelled (like digestion in the body). Among the forces which would have allowed the early modern literary sphere to come into being, and shape it too, were three forms of regulation, all concerned with the book: the marketplace, the library and, paradoxically perhaps, the instruments of censorship. It is easy to see that readers and audiences needed a marketplace in which, for example, publishers could invest in books but have their risk protected by a trade monopoly (the Stationers' Company). Less obvious at first is the role of the library as regulator, but the choices to be made, either for the private collection or for a large institution (such as the Bodleian Library, opened in 1602), were ones of inclusion and exclusion, whether on grounds of quality or because of subject matter or space on the shelves. Censorship took things away – passages were deleted from plays, books and pamphlets were burnt by the public hangman – but also added to them, by confirming that the undeleted and undestroyed materials were unequivocally acceptable and beyond reproach (it has been argued that in this respect early modern censorship is not merely *like* modern literary criticism, that aims to praise the good and reject the bad, rather it is the political discourse out of which modern criticism grew).[35]

The interplay of so many factors must surely have been bewildering to Shakespeare's contemporaries. The literary canon was in formation, a forum of literary judgement on what was published was becoming accessible to the many rather than just the few, and the fecundity and riotousness of the public stage threatened to overturn fundamental rules of sexual decency, law and order, and artistic decorum. The forces of the market, of the bookstack, and of limited state inspection hemmed in but also released and redirected the energies of literary writing, and created a public space for dialogues between writers and readers, and for controversies, pamphlet wars, libels, hostility and insults between rivals, and even, on occasions and however dangerous to everyone involved, political satires. Literature and drama could not be isolated

35 Burt 1993, pp. 30–54.

from the mix of everything else being written and published at the same time, of course; indeed the literary sphere, had it established and defined itself conclusively in this period, might well have become the precursor to the wider public sphere. This, according to Habermas, is in fact what happened a century later in England, in the age of Pope, Swift, Addison, and Steele:[36] a bourgeois public sphere grew out of the cosmopolitan literary culture of the essayist and poet-critic. Large questions of taste, religious and aesthetic sensibility, morality, and the constitution came to be posed, in general terms and with wider application than they had at first, as part of the critical debate about ancient and modern literature (focused on, among other things, hack writing in Grub Street, the newly arrived novel, and the search for universal principles in beauty and in the sublime). Allowance must be made, certainly, for the considerable differences between the society and book-culture of *The Dunciad* and *Gulliver's travels*, and that of *Titus Andronicus* and *The faerie queene*, but we may still find useful and fruitful the suggestion that the matter of literature might evolve into a sociopolitical forum where its participants reflected on all matters, but most of all on their own self-awareness about being part of the forum.[37]

Historical study of this phenomenon, which may have been heading towards a public sphere even before the English Civil War in the 1640s, has barely begun (how prose fiction was written and retailed is a recent starting point).[38] One thing we can be sure of, that there was indeed one writer in the early seventeenth century, Ben Jonson, who thought that the literary sphere *ought* to exist, and that he should preside over it. His disappointment that this failed to happen, at least on the scale that his genius expected, is writ large in many of his later works. The reasons for its not developing are many (among them, that there was no settled institution of the poet-critic, no coffee-houses nor clubs), but Jonson was right, from his perspective, to quarrel with one particular obstruction to the empire of letters. This was the fledgling newspaper or rather, at this date, the coranto or newsletter.[39] He attacked the new medium in several places, but especially in the play *The staple of news* (1626), in which the latest commercial venture is a shop where news (made-up stories, that is, along with fashion trivia, city gossip and novelties) is retailed, interestingly, not in printed sheets but in handwritten copies. This organ of the body politic for the most part could not be regulated (the libraries refused it, the stationers were suspicious of it, the censors unable to keep up with it), and it was inflammatory. It confounded all

36 This is part of the argument advanced by J. Habermas in *The structural transformation of the public sphere*, usefully summarized by Halasz 1997, pp. 42–5 and 162–71.

37 See further, Bruster 2000.

38 Halasz 1997, pp. 46–81.

39 See Nelson and Seccombe, below. See also Dahl 1952 and Frearson 1993a and b.

rules about authenticity, knowledge, the significance and value of the past, and it encouraged immediacy and rapidity of response. Later, in the war years and in the Interregnum, the newspaper, growing powerful, would sustain various literary and dramatic sub-genres within itself, but at this point it must have seemed like a cuckoo in the nest, about to ruin the reputation and livelihood of literary writers, and to offer a sham version of the forum, where the multitude would be fed lies and shallow opinions for the profit of a few pence.

By this time the civilizing process, through the means of poetry and stage plays, reached much further down than the court and the academy, and the prospect of literary and public spheres at least became thinkable if not yet entirely feasible. Several centuries on, we could argue that the new public urgently needed, as its heart and mind, something less upper-crust than Sidney, less trashy than the newsletter, less erudite than Spenser, and less hard to understand than Chaucer. In a while the public would find its feeling and thought realized in the epistolary novel, but arguably it found them first in a large edition of plays, thirty-seven of them, published in 1623, entitled *Mr William Shakespeares comedies, histories, & tragedies* (the First Folio). This book of Shakespeare's has become so much the secular scripture of the English-speaking world (global, talismanic and often unread), that it is hard to gauge just how important it was in the new forum, at least before the outbreak of war in 1642 and the closure of the theatres. The modern dispute about who the seventeenth century regarded as its pre-eminent dramatist – Shakespeare or Jonson or Beaumont and Fletcher – is not yet concluded, because literary historians are properly concerned not to project back into this earlier period the reputation Shakespeare subsequently enjoyed (after, say, 1740, by which time he had certainly become the Bard).[40] Yet the facts of the First Folio lead one to suspect that even in these early days it was a book already at the centre of things. Its manufacture in particular has been studied intensively, so we can estimate the print-run (probably 750 copies), the price without and with a binding (fifteen shillings and one pound sterling respectively),[41] and the time it took to print it. We know something too about the printer's output of *other* books, the manuscripts and printed texts the folio was set from, and even the identities of some of the compositors. The investment the publishers Blount and Jaggard had to make can be calculated too, and the risk they took will make us pause when we think back to those slow-selling play quartos, where it might take up to four years to sell a similar print run of a single play text costing sixpence. Thirty-seven plays

40 The evidence and conclusions presented by Bentley 1943 and 1965 are contradictory, and his assessment of reputations by simply counting allusions is far from satisfactory.

41 Blayney 1991, pp. 2 and 28–32.

for fifteen shillings was better value, but this was a lot of money for a book. The trade guessed correctly, however, that there were enough book buyers around who could afford to purchase a complete Shakespeare, since work on the Second Folio (1632), presumably with the same size print-run, was begun within seven or eight years. Viewed as a commercial venture, the First Folio was something new, and so were its contents – all plays and nothing else – but in other respects, the book was rather old-fashioned, with (for instance) the plays arranged in traditional generic groups, rather than in some order of performance or composition that purported to trace the author's development (as with Chaucer and Jonson).

Whatever the reasons, it is clear that Shakespeare and Jonson (and quite possibly Shakespeare more than Jonson) were read widely by the upper and middle classes, and in many moods. It is well known that Charles I read both writers while he was in prison awaiting execution, and a decade before, in January 1639, Mrs Anne Merrick, stuck in the country and pining for the London scene and the playhouse, wrote to a friend that 'for want of these gentile recreationes, I must content my selfe here, with the studie of Shakespeare, and the historie of woemen, All my countrie librarie.'[42] A full account of the reception of Shakespeare before the Restoration would be difficult if not impossible to write, but without it (as we are) our understanding of the literary and public spheres, incipient or not, must remain seriously incomplete. Is it possible that Shakespeare's psychological characters, his comedies of love and social manners, and the exceptional beauty and forcefulness of his writing sustained two generations of readers through a convulsive and exhausting period of English history?

Further studies of how and why other dramatists were published (the Jonson folios in 1616 and 1640–41, and Beaumont and Fletcher in 1647) may in time compel us to a different view of Shakespeare's standing among his own generation and the one that succeeded it. Something quite new does seem to have happened in the 1650s, as regards putting playbooks and poems into print. Before then canonical authors appeared in folios and quartos because of decisions made separately by particular booksellers (to what extent with or without patronage is not well understood) – Chaucer by Caxton, Spenser by Ponsonby, Daniel by Waterson, Jonson by Stansby, and Shakespeare by Jaggard and Blount. In the apparently unpromising years of the late 1640s and 1650s the publisher Humphrey Moseley not only first collected together the Beaumont

42 *The Shakespere allusion-book: a collection of allusions to Shakespere from 1591 to 1700*, ed. John Munro, 2 vols. (1909: repr. with new preface, Oxford, 1932), I, p. 443. The allusions to Charles I are on pp. 516 and 525.

and Fletcher canon, which he issued as a folio with Robinson in 1647, but recognized that there was a demand among the public for yet more collected editions of plays and poems. Moseley was a royalist and many of the collections he published, in octavo, were by courtiers – among them, the dramatists Suckling (1646), Cartwright (1651), Shirley (1651) and Brome (1653), and the poets Waller (1645), Shirley (1646), Cowley (1647), Vaughan (1651) and Carew (1651).[43]

This public interest and pleasure in drama, at the very time when the theatres had been shut by order of Parliament, has not yet been conclusively accounted for. One final question to close with here is whether some of this pleasure – whether in Shakespeare or Jonson or the others – was derived not just from plays printed in a book, but from a memory of where and how such plays had had their first life, on the public stage. Twenty, thirty, or forty years after Shakespeare's death was there a recollection through the reading, some of it sentimental perhaps, that he and his contemporaries had lived in a paradisal moment where art and the human spirit, prior to print, was as high as they had ever been, in Athens or Jerusalem or Rome? Perhaps it was just another nostalgic fantasy of a Golden Age, but if so it was one which even the radical republican John Milton, the next English literary genius, could not but acknowledge. In Book 4 of *Paradise lost*, when Satan arrives at Paradise he finds it on a hill, surrounded with an impenetrable thicket and tall trees (140–2),

> A sylvan scene, and as the ranks ascend,
> Shade above shade, a woody theatre
> Of stateliest view.

Within the theatre there is a *verdurous wall* and yet more trees and fruit, but Satan simply jumps over the wall and settles on the Tree of Life to watch. And what do his envious eyes see? What else, but Adam and Eve in bliss, watching the animals sport and play for them, where even the Elephant

> To make them mirth used all his might, and wreathed
> His lithe proboscis.

Milton draws on the printed books of the Bible and Spenser for much of this, it is true, but the inescapable, central image, remembered in his blindness, is of the Globe and the other round wooden Elizabethan public theatres on the Bankside in London, and within them uninhibited playing of every kind to please the watching spectators.

43 On Moseley, see Joad, below, and Kewes, 1995 and 1998.

17
Milton

JOAD RAYMOND

> ... it is the love I have to our own Language that hath made me diligent to collect, and set forth such *Peeces* both in Prose and Vers, as may renew the wonted honour and esteem of our English tongue.[1]

In his *Poems* of 1645 John Milton, with the assistance of the bookseller Humphrey Moseley, whose words these are, presented himself as a man of letters, an Englishman hailing his native tongue. Not only the verse but the volume spoke these ambitions. Milton was no naive and cosseted scholar, unconcerned with the commercial pathways that carried his works into the hands of readers, but a canny author, attuned to the making and selling of books and pamphlets. His relationship with the book trade suggests that he was neither a coterie author, precious of his reputation and keen to identify and maintain his connection with socially elevated circles; nor was he a prototype of the professional author, viewing his readers as a source of income; rather, he occupied the intermediary sphere of a remunerated writer who chose the marketplace as the most effective means of addressing a broad public.[2]

Milton's earliest publications and performances appeared in contexts supported by a traditional, perhaps 'courtly', emphasis on interpersonal relations. His Latin prolusions were delivered before an audience at Cambridge University; his two epitaphs on Hobson, the University Carrier, modestly circulated in manuscript.[3] His first printed work appears to have been some academic verses written *c.* 1628 on behalf of another student; his second, the poem 'On Shakespeare', appeared anonymously in the second folio of 1632.[4] 'Epitaphium Damonis', which survives in a single copy, was probably printed

1 Moseley, in Milton, *Poems* (1645), sig. a3^{r-v}.

2 Helgerson 1983; Griffin 1990; Kernan 1987; Saunders 1955; Saunders 1964, pp. 85–92; Lindenbaum 1993.

3 J. T. Shawcross, *Milton: a bibliography for the years 1624–1700* (Binghamton, 1984), nos. 2–26, 43, 46, 57, 73, 93, 200, 241, 284–6, 289, 293–5, 336; also *IELM*, II.2, pp. 86–8.

4 *Complete prose works of John Milton*, gen. ed. D. M. Wolfe (New Haven, 1953–82), I, pp. 313–14; Shawcross, *Milton: a bibliography*, nos. 27–33.

in 1639, for circulation among select friends.[5] His 'Arcades' was written as an entertainment to be performed before Alice, Dowager Countess of Derby (1633?); his *A maske presented at Ludlow Castle* was commissioned in 1634 by the Earl of Bridgewater. It was printed in 1637, at the instigation of the composer Henry Lawes, with references to the noble audience, and the familiar Renaissance formula about popular demand and the author's modesty. Lawes dedicated the volume to Bridgewater's heir, John Viscount Brackley. Milton's finest early work, 'Lycidas', appeared in *Justa Edouardo King naufrago* (1638), a collection of elegies by Cambridge students commemorating the death of an acquaintance. The circulation of these texts in print was little more than an extension of manuscript distribution.

The aristocratic or intellectual endorsement present in Milton's early writings was absent from his later writings. It was abating as early as 1641 when Milton, recently returned from Italy, intervened in public print controversy with five pamphlets on Church government, followed by four tracts on divorce and his celebrated *Of education* (1644) and *Areopagitica* (1644). This flurry of polemical activity came to an end in 1645 with the appearance of the very different volume, *Poems of Mr John Milton, both English and Latin* (plate 17.1).

These works were published by at least three booksellers and manufactured by at least six printers.[6] Milton became familiar with the London printing trade. *Areopagitica*, his censure of pre-publication licensing and of the Parliamentary Ordinance of 1643 regulating the press, speaks eloquently of a burgeoning culture of reading and writing in 1640s London. Milton praises the 'free and open encounter' between truth and falsehood, the dusty and sweaty struggle between the reader and the printed page, as the path to a disciplined, alert and thoughtful citizenry, and hence to national spiritual regeneration and the advancement of the Gospel.[7] Amongst the dense metaphors of *Areopagitica* we find sympathetic references to 'all manner of tractats', to 'an English pamphlet', to works of a mere 'three sheets'. The careful diction indicates small, inexpensive, vernacular publications, anonymous, unlicensed. He is dismissive of 'interlinearies, breviaries, *synopses*, and other loitering gear', of 'old collections in their trenches'.[8] The books Milton defends were not those chained in college libraries, but the disorderly, vociferous and sometimes radical tracts hawked on the streets.[9] Despite the careful autobiographical narratives he interlaced among his writings, assuring readers of his

5 *Ibid.*, no. 44; BL C.57.d.48.

6 Summarized in *A Milton encyclopaedia*, ed. G. K. Hunter, 9 vols. (Lewisburg, 1978–83), VII, pp. 15–18, 64–6.

7 *Complete prose*, II, p. 561; D. Norbrook, *Poetry and politics in the English Renaissance* (London, 1994).

8 *Complete prose*, II, pp. 517, 336, 537, 546–7.

9 Smith 1994; Raymond 1996b; Dobranski 1999.

cultured and gentlemanly origins, a whiff of radicalism was now attached to his name.[10]

Among all these pamphlets *Poems* comes as a surprise. Milton perhaps meant to justify the claim made in his prose tracts that his real vocation was as a poet, perhaps to clear his name after the attacks on his anti-prelatical and, especially, his divorce tracts. *Poems* was a distinctly literary volume. The epigram on the title page proclaimed his poetic and prophetic role: 'Baccare frontem / Cingite, ne vatis noceat mala lingua future' ('Bind on your brow fragrant plants, so no evil tongue may harm the future poet'). In the quotation from Virgil's seventh eclogue the shepherd and nascent poet Thyrsis requests protection from jealous rivals.[11] The engraved portrait frontispiece by William Marshall subtly bisects the poet, revealing two aspects in the same portrait: the left hand side, placed before a dark and heavy curtain, shows a cloaked, old and sombre man, 'Ore laid with black staid Wisdoms hue';[12] the right evokes a younger poet, a less worn face behind which a window reveals a pastoral scene with dancing shepherds. The antithesis perhaps reflects the contrasting dispositions of 'L'Allegro' and 'Il Penseroso'. Or perhaps Marshall wanted to capture the contrast between the present poet (aged 36 or 37) and the author Milton repeatedly evokes in the accompanying text by reminding the reader of his unripe years at the time of composition. Or perhaps the central figure is meant to look uniformly aged, and the dancing shepherds outside represent the younger Milton.[13] The engraving, however, attests that the poet is only twenty-one ('ANNO ÆTATIS ViGess: Pri:'), so Marshall may have been poking fun at the youthful pretensions of the author.[14] Whatever the case, Milton took exception to the unflattering portrait and penned a caustic Greek epigram (which Marshall presumably could not understand) and had Marshall engrave it below the portrait: 'You would say, perhaps, that this picture was drawn by an ignorant hand, when you looked at the form that nature made. Since you do not recognize the man portrayed, my friends, laugh at this rotten picture of a rotten artist.'[15] The engraving was omitted from the 1673 *Poems, &c. upon several occasions* and the epigram placed with the other Greek poems.[16]

The volume charted the intellectual growth of a poet. None of its poems had been written more recently than 1639; it was almost a volume of juvenilia,

10 See esp. *Complete prose*, I, pp. 801–23, 888–92; IV, pp. 615–6.

11 Woodall 1994; Norbrook, *Poetry and politics*, pp. 235–85; Marcus 1996, p. 208.

12 'Il Penseroso', l. 16, *Riverside Milton*, ed. R. Flannagan (Boston and New York, 1998), p. 72.

13 Marcus 1996, p. 217. 14 Johnson 1994.

15 *Milton: complete shorter poems*, ed. J. Carey (2nd edn, London and New York, 1997), pp. 245 and 293.

16 Accentual errors in the printed Greek suggest that Milton did not guide the production of the book. *Milton: complete shorter poems*, pp. 245 and 293; Hale 1995a, pp. 28–9.

revealing Milton's anxiety that 'Time the suttle theef of youth' was thwarting his ambitions.[17] He was staking a claim to respectability, demonstrating that the pamphleteer had not entirely superseded the polylingual poet.[18] In his Ode 'Ad *Joannem Roüsium*', sent to Bodley's librarian accompanying a replacement copy of the volume in 1647, Milton asks which god or hero 'might stop this damned civil war and its skirmishes and restore with holy power our vital pursuits, recall the vagrant Muses, banished now from almost every corner of England'. He imagines the Bodleian as a quiet, Parnassian refuge, which will keep his labour safe from 'the insolent babble of the ignorant . . . away from the mass of worthless readers' and preserve it for 'the children of future generations, in a wiser distant age'.[19]

Literary historians have seen royalism as the natural home of 1640s poetic endeavour, partly owing to the publishing efforts of Moseley, who sought to make a material association between the King's cause and aesthetic ability through a series of volumes of works by Waller, Fanshawe, Stanley, Carew, Shirley, Cowley, Quarles, Davenant, Denham, Howell, and, interestingly, Donne and Beaumont and Fletcher.[20] This has led to the suggestion that in 1645 Moseley kidnapped the unwilling or unwitting Milton for the Royalist cause, a suggestion that assumes a direct connection between printing and publishing formats and ideology.[21] While there are certainly consonances between Milton's *Poems* and Royalist volumes there are many significant differences in format; Moseley was far from attempting an ideologically uniform series.[22] Milton's volume includes letters by Moseley, Lawes and Wotton, which were omitted in 1673, but when compared to *bona fide* Royalist publications Milton's volume is conspicuously lacking in the courtly connections characteristic of Royalist publishing.[23]

It is misleading to sever Milton's *Poems* from the prose: the boundaries were permeable. Epigrams were also used with subtle effect on the title pages of *The Judgement of Martin Bucer* (1644), *Colasterion* (1645); and particularly in the weighty Euripidean epigraphy of *Areopagitica* and *Tetrachordon* (1645).[24]

17 Sonnet 7, *Riverside Milton* , p. 85.

18 Corns 1982 and 1984; on the multilingualism and arrangement of the 1645 volume, see Revard 1997; Hale 1995b; J. K. Hale, *Milton's languages: the impact of multilingualism on style* (Cambridge, 1997).

19 *Riverside Milton*, pp. 286–8.

20 L. Potter, *Secret rites and secret writing: Royalist literature 1641–1660* (Cambridge, 1989), pp. 20–22, 36–7, 162–3; compare the poem by John Leigh, quoted in Reed 1927–30, pp. 65–6.

21 Chernaik 1991, p. 210.

22 The most forceful connection is the mention of Lawes's musical settings on the title pages of Waller's (1645), Milton's and Carew's (1651) poems; not all of the volumes have engravings, and some have extraneous materials. This contrasts with Moseley's series of play books: see Kewes 1995, Marcus 1996, pp. 177–227.

23 Helgerson 1983, pp. 231–73.

24 D. Norbrook, 'Euripides, Milton and *Christian Doctrine*', *MQ*, 29 (1995), 37–41; Norbrook, *Poetry and politics*, pp. 15–18.

Milton would continue to use them as a propagandist, most strikingly on the title page of the second edition of *The readie & easie way* (1660), where he adapts from Juvenal: 'et nos/consilium dedimus *Syllæ*, demus populo nunc' ('And we have given counsel to Sylla, now let us do so to the people'). Like the *Poems*, *Of reformation* (1641), *The reason of Church-government*(1642) and *The doctrine and discipline of divorce* (1643), were structurally divided into two parts. Just as Milton repeatedly availed himself of the pamphleteer's prerogative of changing and republishing his texts, so he used print to reiterate and to revise his poems. The 1637 version of *A maske* was significantly changed from the earlier versions in the Trinity and Bridgewater manuscripts, and in 1645 this underwent further emendation.[25] More brazenly, a headnote was added to 'Lycidas' drawing attention to its origins in dissatisfaction with Charles I's Personal Rule in the 1630s, and suggesting that the poem had foretold 'the ruine of our corrupted Clergy then in their height'.[26]

Milton places an autobiographical digression in *Reason of Church-government* to capture the goodwill of his readers; he emphasizes his poetic aspirations, assuring them that he is no mere pamphleteer, in order to affirm his authority and integrity and the credibility of his polemic. There he mentions his welcome in the Italian 'Academies' and the 'written Encomiums' that his displays of literary wit prompted. These encomiums then appeared in *Poems*, prefacing the Latin (and Greek) section *Poemata*.[27] Perhaps *Poems* was inspired by this Italian context: not just because the works themselves were well-received, but because Italy recognized intellectuals and artists as celebrities and public servants.[28] Though the poems adopted the octavo format commonly associated with literary and devotional works, in contrast to the quarto format of prose controversy, both were nonetheless public interventions. Milton chose to have his *Poems* printed rather than circulated in manuscript in order to reach a greater and more heterogeneous readership. If the poetry was meant to redefine attitudes towards the polemicist, or to challenge the dichotomy between these modes of writing, this is because they were read by a shared audience. For Milton print bore no stigma.

Milton rechannelled his energies and published only treatises for the next two decades. In his *Second defence of the English people* (1654) he claimed that he had written his projected epic in prose:

25 *A maske: the earlier versions*, ed. S. E. Sprott (Toronto, 1973); C. C. Brown, *John Milton's aristocratic entertainments* (Cambridge, 1985), pp. 132–78.

26 *Riverside Milton*, p. 100.

27 *Complete prose*, I, pp. 809–10; Milton, *Poems* (1645), *Poemata* section, pp. 4–9.

28 Saunders 1964, pp. 87–90; though see Griffin 1991.

> I have borne witness, I might almost say I have erected a monument that will not soon pass away, to those deeds that were illustrious, that were glorious, that were almost beyond any praise, and if I have done nothing else, I have surely redeemed my pledge.[29]

Milton's poetic vocation, and his reasons for straying into 'the cool element of prose'[30] for two decades before returning to the epic he had always intended to write, have received much scholarly attention. Milton wrote eloquently about his life and ambitions, and it is easy to succumb to his rhetorical self-presentation, though he is not necessarily an entirely reliable commentator on these matters. The vocations of the prose writer and the poet were not so very opposite. During the years 1649–60 Milton rose to prominence as one of Europe's most gifted men of letters. He turned from vernacular attacks on monarchy and justifications of the regicide to the Latin defences which addressed a Continental audience. Book production was central to this project, and Milton was familiar with the trade. His name appears in the Stationers' Register as a licenser of a book in December 1649.[31] For a period beginning in 1651 he licensed the weekly newsbook *Mercurius politicus*, edited by his friend Marchamont Nedham.[32] For this some critics have indignantly accused Milton of hypocrisy.[33] Yet Milton was a less than censorious licenser: famously he was examined in 1652 for having approved for publication (in August 1650) a work known as the Racovian Catechism, a Socinian text which Parliament subsequently condemned as 'blasphemous, erroneous, and scandalous'. Milton reportedly justified himself: 'he had published a tract on the matter, that men should refrain from forbidding books – and in approving of that book he had done no more than follow his conviction'.[34]

He developed connections with the people of the trade. The Council of State used him to liaise with them.[35] Among his printers were John Field, Evan Tyler, Henry Hills, and in particular Thomas Newcombe (printer to the Council of State and by then husband to Ruth Raworth, who had printed the 1645 *Poems*), Matthew Simmons and William Dugard (Latin printer to the Council of State; though ironically he also printed Salmasius and *Eikon*

29 *Complete prose*, IV, p. 685. 30 *Complete prose*, I, p. 808.

31 W. R. Parker, *Milton: a biography*, rev. G. Campbell, 2 vols. (Oxford, 1996), I, p. 355; II, p. 960n.29.

32 The Stationers' Register records that on 17 March 1650/1 Milton registered issues dating back to January; from which time, perhaps coincidentally, his name begins to appear in the pages of the journal. The connection may have been established earlier. D. Masson, *The life of John Milton*, 7 vols. (rev. edn., London, 1875–94), IV. pp. 325–35; Parker, *Milton: a biography*, I, p. 394; II, pp. 993–4n.150.

33 F. Barker, *The tremulous private body: essays on subjection* (London, 1984), pp. 41–52; Blum 1987; cf. McKenzie 1988.

34 Parker, *Milton: a biography*, I, p. 395; II, p. 994n.153; and sources listed there.

35 *CSPD 1649–1650*, p. 474; *CSPD 1651*, p. 497; *CSPD 1651–1652*, p. 338; *CSPD 1653–1654*, p. 16.

basilike). Newcombe, Simmons and Dugard were probably numbered among Milton's acquaintance. Among Milton's publishers, as opposed to printers, were John Rothwell (who published new editions of some earlier treatises), Thomas Johnson and Livewell Chapman, though his major works of the early 1650s were instigated or sanctioned by the Council of State. When Milton was preparing a second edition of *The readie & easie way* calls went out for the arrest of Chapman, the publisher of the first edition; Milton was able to have the work fugitively printed within a few days.[36] By 1660 Milton, far from being a disinterested scholar, removed from the mechanic world of the press, had his hands dirty.

Milton broke the silence he had observed through the Restoration with the first, ten-book edition of *Paradise lost* (1667), a quarto volume that carries the faint impression of his acquired familiarity with the book trade.[37] That it was published at all is remarkable, as Milton had been reviled as an active supporter of the Cromwellian régime and a slanderer of a glorious martyred king. John Toland, one of Milton's early biographers, records that 'we had like to be eternally depriv'd of this Treasure by the Ignorance or Malice of the Licenser; who, among other frivolous Exceptions, would needs suppress the whole Poem for imaginary Treason in the following lines':

> As when the Sun new ris'n
> Looks through the Horizontal misty Air
> Shorn of his Beams, or from behind the Moon
> In dim Eclips disastrous twilight sheds
> On half the Nations, and with fear of change
> Perplexes Monarchs. (*Paradise Lost*, I, 594–9)[38]

Nevertheless Milton found in Samuel Simmons (and perhaps in Samuel's more experienced mother Mary) a printer and publisher who served him well. The contract with Samuel gave Milton £5 for the copy, and an additional £5 as each of the first three editions was sold out. A full sale of an edition was established as 1,300 copies, and each edition was contractually limited to 1,500 copies.[39] These stipulations ensured that Simmons's profits did not rise disproportionately to Milton's. Nonetheless, the £5 figure stirred the gall of

36 Raymond 1996a.

37 For historical contextualization see D. Norbrook, *Writing the English Republic: poetry, rhetoric and politics 1627–1660* (Cambridge, 1999); for competing accounts of the complex bibliography see Amory 1983; Parker, *Milton: a biography*, II. pp. 1108–112; Moyles 1985, pp. 3–28.

38 John Toland in *The early lives of John Milton*, ed. H. Darbishire (New York, 1965, orig. 1923), p. 180; *Riverside Milton*, p. 373.

39 J. M. French, *The life records of John Milton*, 5 vols. (New Brunswick, NJ, 1949–58), IV, pp. 429–31; BL, Add. MS. 18,861.

eighteenth-century editors, who, knowing the very large sums later raised for Dryden and Pope, accused Simmons of the commercial exploitation of a naive and politically beleaguered poet. It is significant that a formal agreement was struck at all, however, and this suggests commerce between relative equals.[40] Indeed Milton may have sought out Samuel as a printer because of his father Matthew's work on seven of Milton's prose tracts between 1643 and 1650.[41] Mary had taken over the business entirely upon the death of her husband, and though Samuel had finished his apprenticeship in 1662, Mary remained the more active, or more visibly active stationer. *Paradise lost* was the first book Samuel entered into the Stationers' Register under his own name. The Simmonses did a good job. Milton apparently exerted some influence over his scribes' spelling, and there is some evidence that this was partly carried over to the printing.[42] Fully blind for a decade and a half, Milton cannot have been a careful overseer, which suggests that an amanuensis may have done the job for him.[43] The Quaker circles he was now moving in, Thomas Ellwood among their number, may have assisted here: because their writings were prone to suppression or prosecution, Friends were practised in the collaborative production of books, including reading proofs.[44] Not just the poetry but the text of *Paradise lost* triumphed over darkness and adversity.

The first edition entered the world unadorned: without dedication, frontispiece, or justification. First readers turned over the title page and faced prefaceless verse: 'PARADISE LOST. / BOOK I./ Of Mans First Disobedience . . . ' This is most unusual in seventeenth-century literary works. Thomas Newton, the industrious eighteenth-century editor, wrote: 'MILTON himself prefixed no Dedication to the PARADISE LOST; for he designed it, not for a single person, but for the wise and learned of all ages.'[45] The lines of this first edition were numbered in tens between vertical rules, which was highly unusual, perhaps without precedent in English poetry. The surviving manuscript of book I, complete with printer's mark-up, is also numbered. Simmons's edition of Joseph Caryll's *An exposition, with practical observations on the book of Job* (2 vols., 1676) also has line numbers, between a double rule in the middle of the page dividing

40 McKenzie 1988; subsequently Lindenbaum 1994; Lindenbaum 1995a; Lindenbaum 1995b; Lindenbaum 1997. I am grateful to D. F. McKenzie for sending me copies of his privately printed Sandars and Lyell lectures for 1978 and 1988.

41 Excluding multiple editions. On the familial relations see McKenzie 1980; McKenzie 1988; McKenzie 1992.

42 *The poetical works of John Milton*, ed. H. Darbishire (Oxford, 1952), Introduction and appendix I; *The manuscript of Milton's* Paradise lost, *Book I* (Oxford, 1931).

43 *Pace* Darbishire (ed.), *The poetical works*, p. 311, and Moyles 1985, pp. 13–29.

44 McKenzie 1976b; for the legal hazards of proof-reading, see also Loewenstein 1994.

45 *Paradise lost: a poem*, ed. T. Newton, 2 vols. (London, 1749), I, sig. A2^{r}.

two columns of text.[46] This suggests that Simmons either punctiliously followed Milton's manuscript, or attributed to the epic a seriousness of purpose equal to Caryll's *Exposition*, or that he deliberately elevated the text to classic status by employing typographic conventions associated with ancient Greek and Latin works.

Some early readers were overwhelmed, and Milton was quickly obliged to add the arguments and a justification of 'why the Poem Rimes not'. These were inserted after the title page in the fourth issue of the first edition. In the second, twelve-book octavo edition of 1674, they were placed before each book, and the note on the verse incorporated, with commendatory poems by Samuel Barrow and Andrew Marvell, as preliminaries.[47] Milton also divided books VII and X, and added a handful of lines. Its spelling is slightly more systematic, and there are a few minor revisions of the 1667 text, though it is not certain that these were introduced by the author.[48] Into its third edition within thirteen years, this 'slender Book' with 'vast Design' as Marvell called it, sold quickly by seventeenth-century standards, and was admired. Marvell prophesied: 'no room is here for Writers left, / But to detect their Ignorance or Theft'.[49]

Though *Paradise Lost* is his consummate monument Milton was far from silent in his late years. The 1671 double-volume, *Paradise regain'd. A poem. In IV books. To which is added Samson Agonistes* (1671), was printed by Macock and published by John Starkey. Starkey had been involved in an earlier work: one of the two quite different title pages found in Milton's *Accedence commenc't grammar* (1669) specifies that it was 'Printed for S.S. and are to be sold by *John Starkey*'.[50] The works in the 1671 volume appeared without dedication, apology or introduction, except for *Samson*'s 'Argument' and 'Of that sort of Dramatic Poem which is call'd Tragedy'. *Samson* carries a curious addendum of eleven non-consecutive lines which are headed 'Omissa' (p. 102). The practice of 'casting off' makes accidental omission from a text with numbered lines very improbable, particularly as one line is coherently reattributed, and there is neither an irregularity in numbering nor any intrusive blank space in the relevant page. This suggests that the lines were added at a late stage. The inserted exchange introduces a momentary delay in the play's action, a hesitation before the cataclysm, in which the Chorus imagines that Samson's sight is restored,

46 I am indebted to John Barnard for these points. The line-numbers in *An Exposition* do not run consecutively through the text, but indicate position on each page.

47 Shawcross, *Milton: a bibliography*, nos. 291–2, 297–9, 303–3, 318. On Barrow, see Maltzahn 1995b; on the early reception, see Maltzahn 1996a.

48 Moyles 1985, pp. 12–29; Darbishire, *The poetical works*.

49 'On Paradise Lost', lines 2, 29–30, *Riverside Milton*, pp. 350–1.

50 *Complete prose*, VIII, pp. 80, 84–5. The other title page states that it was 'Printed by S. Simmons'.

and that he is 'dealing dole among his foes'. It is possible that they were an afterthought, or that Milton strategically added them, with the errata, after the text had been licensed and partly printed.[51]

For some booksellers Milton's name became a valuable property. Late works include the *Grammar*, a revision of William Lily's popular textbook, probably developed during Milton's days as a schoolmaster.[52] *The history of Britain* was commenced in early 1649 and returned to in the mid 1650s, but was not printed until 1670 by John Macock, possibly with the encouragement of the Royal Society.[53] It appeared with an engraved portrait by William Faithorne, subsequently widely reproduced. If Milton was responsible, he may have thought the author's image more appropriate to a scholarly than an imaginative work. In 1672 Milton's *Artis Logicæ*, an academic exercise in Ramist logic which had lain in manuscript for many years, was printed by Spencer Hickman, also with the Faithorne portrait.[54]

In his late publications Milton was not simply clearing his desk. These works were issued as political interventions in the marketplace of print. They commented indirectly on the régime under which Milton lived out his last years, just as the reissue of the *First defence* and the edition of *The cabinet-council* had in 1658.[55] More obviously an intervention was *Of true religion, hæresie, schism, toleration, and what best means may be us'd against the growth of Popery* (1673), which appeared without indication of its printer or publisher (Thomas Sawbridge). Whereas Milton's later works generally appeared with the plain attribution 'The Author John Milton' or 'By John Milton', this offered only initials, though this does not amount to concealment. The same year Thomas Dring published *Poems, &c.*, an expanded version of the 1645 *Poems*, with apparatus removed and the scarce tractate *Of education* added. *Epistolarum familiarium liber unus* (1674) gathered together thirty-one letters, the weight of the volume being made up, at the request of the bookseller Brabazon Aylmer, with the Cambridge prolusions.[56] Finally Aylmer published Milton's translation *A declaration, or letters patents of the election of this present King of Poland* (1674).

This left to posthumous publication only the *Literæ pseudo-senatûs Anglicani* (Amsterdam and Brussels, 1676), letters of state which were unpublishable in his lifetime; *Mr John Miltons character of the Long Parliament* (1681), a digression omitted from his *History of Britain*; *A brief history of Moscovia* (1682) an

51 *Riverside Milton*, p. 839; Dobranski 1999.

52 *Complete prose*, VII, pp. 32–83.

53 The duodecimo volume bears marks of a change in plan while at press, pages one through four having been reprinted and two leaves cut out; this may reflect an authorial modification. Maltzahn 1991; Maltzahn 1996b.

54 *Complete prose*, VIII, pp. 179–85.

55 Dzelzainis 1995.

56 Parker, *Milton: a biography*, I, p. 637.

unfinished revision of notes on Russia; and *De doctrina Christiana* (1825), a system of theology he called 'my dearest and best possession'.[57] Moves were made by Daniel Skinner to publish this not long after Milton's death, but he, and the Dutch printer Daniel Elsevier, were thwarted by the Secretary of State Sir Joseph Williamson, who found Milton's name obnoxious.[58]

Milton died in November 1674, four months after the 'Revised and augmented' *Paradise lost* appeared. Subsequent editions canonized Milton's poetry. Simmons sold off the rights to *Paradise lost* in 1680, in 1681 Jacob Tonson partially secured them from Aylmer, and in 1688 Tonson, together with Richard Bentley, published the fourth, folio edition. This prestigious volume, with fine paper and wide margins, was illustrated with 'Sculptures' by several artists and engravers and a portrait by Robert White.[59] This was the first English literary text published by subscription, and it was Tonson, not Simmons, who exploited the commercial potential of Milton's poem.[60] Isaac Disraeli wrote: 'Tonson and all his family and assignees rode in their carriages with the profits of [Milton's] five-pound epic.'[61] Milton's standing was consolidated in 1695, when the 1688 edition was re-issued by Tonson as part of *The poetical works of Mr John Milton*, dignified with extensive annotations by Patrick Hume, and by a table or index of notable passages 'Under the Three Heads of *Descriptions*, *Similes*, and *Speeches*.' Milton's epic had been given the status of a classic. Dryden commended Milton:

> *Three* Poets, in *three distant Ages born;*
> Greece, Italy, *and* England *did adorn.*
> *The* First *in loftiness of thought Surpass'd;*
> *The* Next *in Majesty; in both the* Last.
> *The force of* Nature *cou'd no farther goe:*
> *To make a* Third *she joynd the former two.*[62]

While the poetry flourished, with subsequent commentaries, annotations and editions by Joseph Addison, Richard Bentley, Francis Peck and Thomas Newton,[63] the prose remained dangerous. Even after the Revolution of 1688, Whigs wished to keep themselves clear of the republican resonances of Milton's name, which Tories might use to tar them. A collected edition of the prose did not appear until 1697, and then without imprint; a more complete version was

57 *Complete prose*, VI, p. 121.   58 Campbell *et al.* 1997.
59 Reproduced in *Riverside Milton*, pp. 296–688, *passim*.   60 See Barnard 1998.
61 McKenzie 1992, p. 409; Lindenbaum 1994, p. 189.
62 *Riverside Milton*, p. 396.   63 Walsh 1997; Levine 1991.

published with a false Amsterdam imprint in 1698.[64] Whereas the poetry represented a shared culture, the prose exposed the reality of political division. Not until the publication of David Masson's *Life of Milton* (1859–94) were the details of the poet's biography refined and the works firmly grounded in the world of seventeenth-century learning, politics and society, from which emerged a more complete understanding of the man as intellectual and republican, husband and civil servant, poet and propagandist.

64 Maltzahn 1995a; Lindenbaum 1995b; Lindenbaum 1997.

18

The Restoration poetic and dramatic canon

PAUL HAMMOND

When our great monarch into exile went,
Wit and religion sufferd banishment . . .
At length the Muses stand restord again
To that great charge which Nature did ordain.[1]

I

The idea, expressed here by Dryden, that the arts were restored in 1660 along with the Stuart monarchy was a commonplace of the day, and formed part of the mythological and ideological fashioning of this historical moment. The desire to represent the new King as a second Augustus, patron of poetry as well as bringer of peace and social order, was part of a movement by which this turning point in the nation's history was understood, by which the future was sketched out and the past rewritten. Retrospectively the republic is represented as a barbarous interlude, and Dryden himself quickly forgets that only a few months earlier he had written of Cromwell that 'in his praise no Arts can liberall be'.[2]

During the early months of 1660, the presses poured out pamphlets of all kinds.[3] In January alone, George Thomason collected two dozen verse satires against the Rump Parliament, the Army, and the leaders of the Republic; in February there were a further dozen satires, now interspersed with panegyrics to General Monck; in March verses began to be published favouring the Restoration of Charles II, and some satires took the form of miniature plays. By April it was possible to publish an elegy on Charles I. Charles II entered London on 29 May, and by the end of July Thomason had collected some thirty separate poems or collaborative volumes of verse celebrating the Restoration.

1 *To My Lord Chancellor*, lines 17–18, 23–4 in *The Poems of John Dryden*, ed. P. Hammond (London and New York, 1995), I, pp. 63–4.

2 John Dryden, *Heroic Stanzas*, line 9. 3 Thomason 1908.

The changing climate can be traced through the variety of bogus imprints used on these pamphlets, from the cautious 'Printed for Philo-Basileuticus Verax' at the beginning of March, to the bolder 'Printed for Charles Prince' and then 'Printed for Charles King' at the end of the month. Satirical imprints registered the decline of that republican and sectarian cause which had once flourished so vigorously when the printed media were opened to previously excluded political views and social classes: one pamphlet was ostensibly 'Printed at the Charge of John Lambert, Charles Fleetwood, Arthur Hesilrig and – Hewson the Cobler, and are to be distributed to the fainting Brethren.'

This is a moment at which ephemeral verses (and quasi-dramatic texts) are being rapidly produced for a wide readership in order to influence the emerging political settlement; at the same time the more literary canon is being revised as established writers hastily reposition themselves, and newcomers seize the opportunity to initiate a career. Dryden's poem to his friend and future brother-in-law Sir Robert Howard, prefixed to Howard's *Poems* (1660), admires Howard's politic relocation of himself through the publication of a volume which both praises the King and General Monck and also sets out Howard's claim to be one of the poets of the new classical age through his translations from Virgil and Statius. By contrast, George Wither appealed to the nation to keep the faith, and in his *Fides-Anglicana* (1660) he included a list of his writings, a piece of self-canonization offered in the national interest. Milton's position was much more precarious, but he saw the times as requiring a bold prose statement of his political views, the *Ready and easy way to establish a free commonwealth* (March 1660). Such visibility was dangerous: Harrington replied three weeks later with his *Censure of the rota*, while Roger L'Estrange attacked him in *No blind guides*, published in April. In May the author of *Britains triumph* gave an ominous foretaste of what might happen to prominent republican men of letters as the political tide turned: Milton, he said, should follow the example of Achitophel and hang himself, but in any case,

stab'd, hang'd or drown'd,
Will make all sure, and further good will bring,
The wretch will rail no more against his *King*.[4]

In such circumstances Edmund Waller greeted the new King with as much fervour as he had mourned Cromwell. Marvell kept silent.

4 G. S., *Britains Triumph* (London, 1660), p. 15.

II

During the Restoration period the poetry and drama of 'the last age', as it was now called, was selectively reprinted, and the canon of English literature was refashioned, both through the reprinting of works and, negatively, through what we would now regard as serious acts of oblivion. The frequency with which editions of earlier literature were issued during the Restoration period provides some indication of contemporary taste. The Royalist poets maintained some popularity for a decade or so after 1660, but then declined: Cleveland enjoyed an intense but brief vogue;[5] Carew was reprinted in 1670 and 1671, but not thereafter; Lovelace not at all after 1659; Suckling in 1676 and 1696; Herrick not at all after 1648; Henry King in 1664 but not thereafter. As for poets from earlier generations, Chaucer was given a handsome folio in 1687, and Spenser in 1679. Donne was reprinted in 1669 but not subsequently. Herbert, however, remained consistently popular, perhaps because he affected the metaphysics less outrageously than Donne, but more probably because he had become established as a devotional classic: James Duport had told his students at Cambridge in the 1650s to regard 'the divine & heavenly book Herberts Poems' as second only to the Bible.[6] Herbert's *The temple* was reprinted in 1660, 1667 (twice) 1674, 1678, 1679 and 1695. Quarles too remained popular right through this period, the emblem evidently proving to be an enduringly appealing form for religious and moral reflection: there were seven editions of his *Emblemes* between 1660 and 1696.[7] Charles Hoole selected Herbert and Quarles as suitable reading for fourth-form schoolboys.[8] It was perhaps Catholic piety which provided a readership for Crashaw, with *Steps to the temple* receiving three editions in 1670 and another *circa* 1685. But there was no demand for Henry Vaughan.

The drama of the previous age was similarly sorted and selectively preserved. The trio of Shakespeare, Jonson and Fletcher was quickly established in Restoration criticism as representing the principal achievement of the pre-war drama,[9] and this critical consensus is to some degree repeated in the republication of their works. The plays of Beaumont and Fletcher had been collected in a folio in 1647; now, no doubt due to their popularity on the Restoration stage, they were re-issued in an enlarged folio under the title *Fifty comedies and tragedies* (1679) by a consortium of booksellers, John Martyn, Henry Herringman and Richard Marriott. Their preface proudly relates how they purchased at no little

5 Morris 1967. 6 Trinity College, Cambridge MS. O. 10 A. 33. 7 Horden 1953.
8 Charles Hoole, *A new discovery of the old art of teaching schoole* (London, 1660), sig. A10^{v}.
9 Richard Flecknoe, *Love's Kingdom* (London, 1664) sig. G6^{r}; John Dryden, *Of dramatick poesie, an essay* (London, 1668).

expense an annotated copy of the previous edition from one of the playwrights' associates who had carefully corrected it, added various prologues, epilogues and songs, and no fewer than seventeen plays (sig. A^{r}–^{v}). The completeness and correctness of this weighty new folio are strongly emphasized. And the booksellers then offer the prospect that if this edition is well received they will proceed to re-issue the two folio parts of Ben Jonson's works in a single volume, 'and also to reprint Old *Shakespear*' (A^{v}). Old Shakespeare's plays had already been re-issued in the Third Folio in 1663, the second impression of which reconfigures the canon by adding *Pericles* and six other plays now regarded as spurious. The Fourth Folio, reprinting the third, appeared from Herringman, Brewster and Bentley in 1685, reset in a modernized typography which made for a more legible text. There were separate editions of some plays, including *Julius Caesar* and *Othello*, but most publications of individual plays were editions of the various adaptations by Davenant, Tate and Crowne. The Jonson folios of 1616 and 1640 were, as promised, reprinted in one volume, but not until 1692. This edition added *The new inn*, which had not been collected in the 1640 folio because it was available only in octavo format, and also supplied the *Leges convivales* together with a translation whose title proclaims: 'Rules for the Tavern academy: or, laws for the beaux esprits' – a transformation of Jonson's circle into a Restoration club of wits.

Two booksellers were particularly significant in shaping the canon of earlier poetry and drama during the Restoration period, and in adding to this the work of select contemporary writers: the lists of Henry Herringman and Jacob Tonson are in themselves almost a late seventeenth-century canon.

Herringman published poetry, drama and classical translations, together with some prose romances, theology and science.[10] His list was well established by the later 1650s, when he probably employed Dryden as an editorial assistant.[11] On the death of Cromwell he entered in the Stationers' Register his intention to publish a collection of three memorial poems by Marvell, Sprat and Dryden, but (perhaps from political caution) never proceeded with the project.[12] At the Restoration he aligned himself with the new order by publishing welcome odes by Cowley, Davenant, Dryden, Higgons, Howard and Waller. In subsequent years he signed up most of the leading contemporary poets and dramatists, publishing Cowley, Davenant, Denham, Dryden, Etherege, Fane, Howard, Killigrew, Orrery, Philips, Rochester, Roscommon, Sedley, Shadwell, Tuke, Waller and Wycherley: a mixture of professionals and aristocratic amateurs, this list virtually defines contemporary literature. The

10 Miller 1949; Plomer 1907b. 11 Osborn 1965, pp. 184–99. 12 Macdonald 1939, pp. 3–4.

works of some of these writers were collected into folio volumes, creating a highly visible and prestigious authorial canon. Cowley's *Poems* had been published in folio in 1656 by Humphrey Moseley; now in 1668 Herringman issued a folio *Works* which added Cowley's *Essays* and a preface by Thomas Sprat surveying Cowley's life and writing. This had reached its ninth edition by 1700, and there were also supplementary collections of his juvenilia and his Latin poems. A Davenant folio appeared from Herringman in 1673. But Herringman was also dominating the market for verse from the early and mid-century: he published King and Waller in 1664, Donne in 1669, Carew and Crashaw in 1670, and Suckling in 1676; the absence of Milton from this list (in spite of the fact that like Waller and Crashaw he had been published by Moseley) is no doubt a sign of Herringman's political caution. This list, together with his share in the Beaumont and Fletcher folio and in the Shakespeare Fourth Folio, makes Herringman a dominant figure in early Restoration culture. Pepys visited Herringman's shop not only to buy books but also to hear literary gossip from him and to meet his other customers: it was from Herringman that he learned of the death of Cowley, and heard that Dryden himself called *An evening's love* 'but a fifth-rate play'; it was also Herringman's shop that Pepys appointed as the place for an illicit rendezvous with Mrs Willet – a scene (and a name) straight out of the comedies which Herringman was selling.[13]

Herringman had in some respects been Moseley's successor, and in due course he was himself displaced by Jacob Tonson, who took over many of Herringman's writers.[14] Tonson's career had begun cautiously in 1675 with two conduct books, but in 1679 he published Dryden's *Troilus and Cressida*, marking the beginning of a long association between the two men. This provided Dryden with new opportunities, particularly for classical translation, and gave Tonson a prolific, popular and controversial author of the first rank to act as the mainstay of his list. Together they pioneered developments in literary publishing which would set precedents for a generation, including a new format for publishing verse in their miscellanies, and a new way of financing a major undertaking by inviting subscriptions for Dryden's Virgil.[15]

As well as cultivating Dryden (presenting him with melons, while paying him in clipped coin) Tonson added other major poets to his list. He published a *Second part of the works of Mr Abraham Cowley* in 1681, moving again into Herringman's territory. In 1691 he issued the poems of Rochester, including his adaptation of *Valentinian* which Herringman had published in 1685. He also

13 Pepys 1970–83, VIII, pp. 380, 383; IX, pp. 248, 367.
14 Papali 1968 includes a provisional checklist of Tonson's publications.
15 Barnard 1963, 1998, 2000.

made a momentous contribution to the emerging canonical status of Milton by publishing *Paradise lost* in folio in 1688, following this with Milton's shorter poems in 1695 which together made up *The poetical works of Mr John Milton*.[16] Prefaced with a handsome engraved portrait with verses by Dryden which cast Milton as the modern embodiment of Homer and Virgil, this edition was set in large clear type, and provided illustrations to each book of *Paradise lost* which would have reminded readers of the cuts included in Ogilby's Virgil. Moreover, there are 300 pages of annotation to *Paradise lost* by Patrick Hume which expound the poem's vocabulary and theology, giving it a classical scholarly treatment which at that date had been accorded to no other English poem.

Tonson seems to have been especially interested in translations from the Greek and Latin classics, including Dryden's own version of Virgil (1697), and the translations by Dryden and others of *Ovid's epistles* (1680), Plutarch (1683–6), and Juvenal and Persius (1693);[17] there were also individual works such as Talbot's translation of Seneca's *Troades*, Higden's Juvenal XIII, and L'Estrange's rendering of Cicero's *De officiis*. Tonson was evidently looking out for good translators, and signed up Creech after his Lucretius had been such a success for the Oxford bookseller Anthony Stephens,[18] publishing Creech's translations of Horace in 1684 and Manilius in 1697. He missed Oldham (published by Hindmarsh), but nevertheless found ways to associate him too with his list, printing his own memorial poem for Oldham anonymously in the miscellany *Sylvae* (1685), and including Oldham's elegy for Rochester in his 1691 edition of the Earl's poetry. Tonson also published Roscommon's *An essay on translated verse* (1684), whereas Herringman had published his translation of Horace's *Ars poetica* in 1680. Dryden is once again a key figure in this story: he knew many of the contributors to the collaborative translations of Ovid, Plutarch and Juvenal,[19] he had friendly relations with Creech, wrote a memorial poem for Oldham and a commendatory poem for Roscommon's *Essay*, and advised Tonson that he could safely venture to reprint the *Essay* in 1685.[20]

The collaboration of Dryden and Tonson was also crucial to the success of Tonson's miscellanies, which became a major influence upon Restoration and then on early eighteenth-century publishing: by providing a home for shorter poems and translations, and by collecting prologues, epilogues, epistles and commendatory poems, these volumes shaped a literary world of mutual obligation and defined a canon of contemporary writers. The series began with *Miscellany poems* in 1684, with a second part called *Sylvae* in 1685, followed

16 Bennett 1988; Maltzahn 1994; Lindenbaum 1997; Barnard 1998.
17 Gillespie 1988; Sherbo 1985. 18 Vaisey 1975. 19 Sherbo 1979; Sherbo 1985.
20 *The letters of John Dryden*, ed. Charles E. Ward (Durham, NC, 1942), pp. 22–3.

by the third part under the title *Examen poeticum* in 1693, the fourth in 1694, the fifth in 1704, and the sixth in 1709.[21] There are several indications that Tonson's ideas about this venture changed as he was putting the first two parts together:[22] *Miscellany poems* reprints three of Dryden's major poems, *Absalom and Achitophel*, *The medal*, and *Mac Flecknoe*, whereas subsequently the focus was to be on new and shorter pieces; this first volume also collects a large number of Dryden's prologues and epilogues, suggesting a connection with the earlier miscellanies which had centred around the theatre, smaller and cheaper volumes such as *Covent Garden drolery* (1672). Tonson's *Miscellany poems* includes some translations from the classics, but by the time Tonson and Dryden brought out *Sylvae*, translation had become a feature of the collection: *Sylvae* started with a major critical preface by Dryden addressing the art of translation and the literary characteristics of the classical poets from whom he was working, and then offered his selections from Virgil, Lucretius, Horace and Theocritus. Translations by other hands followed, so that purchasers who had their copies of these first two parts bound together (as many were) would have acquired a substantial selection from Ovid's *Elegies*, Horace's *Odes*, and Theocritus' *Idylls*, a complete set of Virgil's *Eclogues*, and samples of Lucretius, Catullus, Propertius, and of Virgil's *Georgics* and *Aeneid*. Tonson was thus providing his readers with a taste of the Greek and Roman poetic canon, appealing partly to a readership which had not had the benefit of a classical education (perhaps particularly to women, who were now influential in forming theatrical and poetic taste) but also to connoisseurs of the classics and of the art of translation, since some classical poems were presented in more than one version. Later, Tonson would remember the interests of such a readership by making sure that the Latin accompanied Rochester's renderings of passages from Lucretius when he published his edition in 1691.

III

I wish now to turn to some specific examples of how the canons of individual poets were shaped, and begin with Tonson's associate, Dryden.[23] It is notable that Dryden himself never collected his poems into a single volume, and the early work such as *Astraea redux* and *Annus mirabilis* remained unobtainable until Tonson began to reissue Dryden's poems in a uniform style late in his career: in 1688 several poems from the 1660s – *Annus mirabilis*, *Astraea redux*, *To His Sacred Majesty* and *To My Lord Chancellor* – were reprinted with continuous

21 Cameron 1957. 22 Hammond 1990. 23 Hammond 1992 gives a more detailed account.

pagination, and in a quarto format which made them suitable for binding up with Dryden's later poems which were published or reprinted in quarto: *Absalom and Achitophel*, *The medal* and *Mac Flecknoe* were reprinted in quarto in 1692 with continuous pagination, and Tonson also issued *Threnodia Augustalis*, *The hind and the panther* and *Britannia rediviva* in the same format.[24] Purchasers were therefore able to create their own version of Dryden's canon by having their personal selection of these works bound together. Though Dryden's conversion to Rome meant that *Religio laici* was never reprinted after 1683, it is nevertheless found bound up with the other works, so readers could override any wishes which Dryden himself may have had about what should constitute his ideal canon. The canonization of Dryden in folio had to wait until the very end of his life: following on from the handsome folio Virgil of 1697, Tonson published Dryden's *Fables ancient and modern* in folio in 1700, and after the poet's death issued a folio collection of his *Poems on various occasions; and translations from several authors* (1701): this collected the major political and religious poems (but not the *Heroic stanzas*), the translations from *Ovid's epistles* and *Sylvae* (but not from Juvenal), some of the commendatory poems (to Roscommon, Congreve and Kneller, but not the elegy on Oldham), and some of the prologues and epilogues. This volume is often found bound together with the *Fables*. A two-volume folio set of the plays also appeared in 1701 to complete the *oeuvre*.

One can perceive Dryden attaching a different status to his major poems through their differing modes of publication. In one group come the major public poems which he was happy to acknowledge: *Annus mirabilis*, *Threnodia Augustalis*, *Religio Laici*; in another, those poems which he preferred to publish anonymously,[25] *Absalom and Achitophel*, *The medal* and *The hind and the panther*, where he seems to have wished for some distance between himself and the printed text – perhaps to protect himself from the repercussions of controversial material, perhaps to provide the poems themselves with a degree of autonomy and rhetorical objectivity; and in the third category there is *Mac Flecknoe*, which circulated at first in manuscript and was never printed over Dryden's name in his lifetime. By circulating *Mac Flecknoe* in manuscript (and also, it would seem from the surviving copies, anonymously) Dryden was restricting its impact, at least initially, to those metropolitan literary circles in which its literary and theatrical topics would be particularly appreciated. Another special case is the *Heroic stanzas* on the death of Cromwell: this poem exists in what is now the only surviving autograph manuscript of a substantial work by Dryden, seemingly a fair copy intended for presentation to someone

24 Macdonald 1939, pp. 15–16. 25 Hammond 1993.

in the circle around the late Protector in 1658. The poem was first printed in 1659, and was reprinted by Dryden's enemies three times in 1681–2 (at the time of his defence of the King's interests during the Exclusion Crisis) and again in 1687 (with a rubric attributing it to 'the Author of *The H---d and the P---r*'): these were attempts to include within Dryden's canon a poem which clashed with his later political and religious convictions, and one which he might have preferred the public to forget. But he did not actually disown it, for it was re-issued *circa* 1692 by Tonson in quarto format so that readers could include it in their collections, and this looks like a brave and dignified attempt by Dryden to assert control over the canon of his work, to acknowledge his own history on his own terms at a time when, in the early years of William and Mary, he may have felt particularly vulnerable. In 1691, finding that several of his friends, 'in Buying my Plays, *&c.* Bound together, have been impos'd on by the Booksellers foisting in a Play which is not mine', he added to *King Arthur* a list of his plays and major poems, in chronological order, a canon which excludes *Heroic stanzas* and (since Shadwell was still alive) *Mac Flecknoe*, but acknowledges *Absalom and Achitophel* and *The medal*, includes *Religio laici*, and proudly concludes with *The hind and the panther* and *Britannia rediviva* on the birth of James II's son in 1688.

Besides these major poems, Dryden wrote many occasional and commendatory pieces, and these he never collected: they include one of the finest poems in the language, 'To the Memory of Mr Oldham', which could be found only in Oldham's *Remains* (1684), and the prefatory poems which he wrote for works by Howard, Lee, Roscommon and Congreve; like the prologues and epilogues which he contributed to plays by associates such as Etherege and Southerne, these too remained accessible only in the printed texts of the plays which they commended. Most of Dryden's prologues and epilogues for the King's Company in the 1670s and 1680s were gathered together in *Miscellany poems*, but generally Dryden exhibited a singular unconcern about these many occasional pieces, short but significant works in which he not only cemented friendships but often defined the classical temper and status of Restoration poetry.

Meanwhile, the circulation of poetry in manuscript allowed readers to remake the canon of individual authors, including that of Dryden. The *Heroic stanzas* were copied by readers into their personal commonplace books throughout the Restoration period, thus keeping that poem alive; similarly Dryden's verses to the Countess of Castlemaine, originally a private work for a patroness, were circulated through the medium of manuscript.[26] In this milieu a writer's canon could be significantly reshaped by speculative or mischievous attributions.

26 Hammond 1984.

Thus several scurrilous verses were attributed to Dryden in manuscript, and although we now doubt that he wrote verses on the Duchess of Portsmouth's picture, or a satire on Robert Julian, some of Dryden's contemporaries thought that he had done, and they had evidently acquired an impression of the Dryden canon which encouraged them to think of him as a likely author for topical satires and libellous lampoons. Ironically, the only work attributed to Dryden which Locke owned was the spurious *Address of John Dryden, Laureat to His Highness the Prince of Orange* (1689).[27] After the Revolution the volumes of *Poems on affairs of state* would remake Dryden's canon with more deliberate malice, as we shall see. Such reshaping of the canon could be dangerous: it is quite likely that the attack on Dryden in Rose Alley in 1679 was occasioned by a speculative attribution assigning to him the *Essay upon satire*, which was probably the work of the Earl of Mulgrave alone.

Dryden was a professional writer for whom the status of his canon had vital commercial as well as artistic significance, but most of his contemporary poets did not depend on their writing for a living, and the fortunes of their *oeuvres* show interesting variations.

John Wilmot, Earl of Rochester, did not collect his poems, and indeed very few appeared in print in his own lifetime.[28] A few love poems were printed anonymously in miscellanies, and a garbled version of *Tunbridge Wells* had been included in Richard Head's *Proteus redivivus* (1675), but apart from this the only longer poems which had been printed were *Upon nothing*, *Artemisa to Chloe* and the *Satire against reason and mankind*, each of which appeared separately in 1679. There is no indication that these publications were authorized by Rochester, and none bears his name; they were probably opportunistic publications which took their texts from whatever manuscripts came to hand. At the time of Rochester's much-publicized death in 1680, the reading public would have known his lyrics and sexually explicit poems only through manuscript circulation. Yet the substantial number of elegies for Rochester which appeared at his death (some of which even generated complimentary poems in their turn) suggests that there was already a widespread sense in literary circles as to what constituted Rochester's canon.[29] And in 1680 there began a process of canon formation which took strikingly different forms in manuscript and in print.

Several scriptorium manuscript miscellanies were compiled in 1680 or shortly thereafter, which contained a substantial selection of poems by Rochester,

27 Harrison and Laslett 1971, p. 126.

28 Vieth 1963; *IELM*, II, 2; Love 1993; Love 1996a; Love 1996b; *The works of John Wilmot, Earl of Rochester*, ed. H. Love (Oxford, 1998); Hammond 1993, pp. 130–2.

29 *Rochester: the critical heritage*, ed. David Farley-Hills (London, 1972), pp. 94–130.

including his erotic poems and the longer poems which were already in print.[30] Since all these poems were presented anonymously, there was no attempt to define a Rochester canon, even though a number of poems which we now attribute to Rochester were grouped together. Rather, the kind of canon which such manuscripts sought to present was topic-based, offering wealthy readers calligraphically written texts of erotic and satiric literature. A more deliberate attempt to define a canon for Rochester was made in the mid-1680s by the compiler of Yale University Library Osborn manuscript fb 334; this manuscript has a title page announcing 'Poem's By The Right Honourable John Earle of Rochester', with an address to the reader, and texts of *Valentinian*, the *Satire against reason and mankind*, *Artemisa to Chloe*, the *Allusion to Horace*, and some of Rochester's songs, but omits any sexually explicit pieces.

This chaste selected canon contrasts markedly with the first printed collection of Rochester's poems, *Poems on several occasions by the Right Honourable the E. of R---* ('Antwerp', 1680).[31] This volume contained sixty-one poems, of which only around a half are now accepted as his by Rochester's editors, the others being attributable with varying degrees of certainty to a range of Rochester's contemporaries, including Oldham, Behn, Scroope and Dorset. The collection capitalizes upon Rochester's notoriety to put into print an anthology which is basically much the same as the manuscript anthologies which were circulating, and so what the purchaser acquired was not so much the Rochester *oeuvre* as a canon of contemporary libertine verse: what makes it cohere is not the individual author but the persona, not John Wilmot but '*the E. of R---*' as a composite cultural fiction epitomizing the wit and the rake. Pepys made his copy the nucleus of a collection of material by and about Rochester by having it bound up with a manuscript supplement of additional poems, and Gilbert Burnet's *Some passages of the life and death of the Right Honourable John, Earl of Rochester* (1680), typically providing himself with a combination of the titillating and the edifying.[32]

This collection was reprinted through the early 1680s, though attempts were made to produce more socially respectable editions of Rochester. In 1685 a revised version of the 1680 edition appeared, with a text purged of some of the sexually explicit language. In the same year Herringman published *Valentinian* with a preface by Robert Wolseley which defended Rochester's poetry (implicitly assuming an *oeuvre* which had yet to be defined), and gave it a place in the canon by making comparisons not only with fashionable contemporary verses

30 Danielsson and Vieth 1967; Hammond 1982; Brennan and Hammond 1995.
31 Facsimile edition: *Rochester's Poems on several occasions*, edited by James Thorpe (Princeton, 1950).
32 Pepys Library, Magdalene College, Cambridge, 810.

but also with classical Roman poetry. Then in 1691 Tonson published *Poems etc. on several occasions: with Valentinian, a tragedy*. This represented a significant step in the canonization of Rochester, and once again there was an important critical preface, this time by Thomas Rymer, where comparisons were again made with Latin poetry, and also on this occasion with Boileau. The volume itself offered elegantly printed texts of Rochester's more presentable poems. Though Rymer claimed that the volume was 'a Collection of such Pieces only, as may be received in a vertuous Court, and not unbecome the Cabinet of the Severest Matron', it nevertheless includes some lyrics (such as 'Fair Chloris in a pigsty lay') which might raise eyebrows in the newly godly court of William and Mary, even though some lyrics (such as 'Love a Woman! you're an ass' and 'To a Lady, in a Letter') were edited to remove sexually explicit detail or homoerotic allusions.[33] Some of Tonson's editorial work was undoubtedly concerned with establishing a text free from obscenity, either through such local textual alterations, or by the wholesale exclusion of poems such as *A Ramble in St James's Park* and *The imperfect enjoyment*, both of which had appeared in the 1680 edition; but there were also other motives shaping this reconfiguration of Rochester's canon. Some poems (such as *Tunbridge Wells* and *Timon*) may have been excluded because of doubts about their authorship, while *An allusion to Horace* was perhaps omitted out of respect for Dryden, whom it criticizes. Some political poems by or attributed to Rochester (the *Satire on Charles II*, the *History of insipids*, or *On Rome's pardons*) would have been unacceptable on a combination of political, sexual and religious grounds. The result is that this 1691 edition presents a Rochester canon which is not only purged of his more explicit erotic writing, but also distances him from the fierce literary and political squabbles of his day.

While aristocratic disdain for print, and for the associations of professionalism which attended it, may have contributed to Rochester's lack of interest in assembling an identifiable *oeuvre*, Oldham's reticence about publication is likely to have been the caution of one who was seeking to make his way in the world as a schoolmaster and private tutor.[34] His *Satyrs upon the Jesuits*, social satires, erotic poems and libertine satires all had the potential to cause offence to prospective employers. Three of Oldham's poems (the so-called 'Satire against Virtue' and its counterpart – prompted by one of Rochester's pranks – and 'Upon the Author of a Play called *Sodom*', on a play often attributed to Rochester) appeared in the 1680 edition of '*the E. of R---*' because of their thematic links with the

33 Vieth 1960; P. Hammond, 'Rochester's homoeroticism', in N. Fisher (ed.), *That second bottle: essays on John Wilmot, Earl of Rochester* (Manchester, 2000), pp. 46–72.
34 Brooks 1936; Hammond 1993, pp. 128–30.

Earl and his milieu. The 'Satire against Virtue', 'Garnet's Ghost' (the first of the *Satyrs upon the Jesuits*), 'Upon . . . *Sodom*' and 'Sardanapalus' all circulated in manuscript, and the first two of those also appeared in print in pirated form in 1679. The subtitle of the printed edition of *Garnet's ghost* attributed the poem to 'the Author of the *Satyr against virtue*, (not yet Printed)', which suggests that the 'Satire against Virtue' had achieved sufficient notoriety through its manuscript circulation for this connection to be thought a useful selling point for *Garnet's ghost*. A canon is being assembled here without the use of an author's name. And this is in fact what Oldham himself did when he came to put his poems into print in authorized editions. The *Satyrs upon the Jesuits* appeared anonymously in 1681, and then *Some new pieces* later in the same year was attributed to 'the Author of the Satyrs upon the Jesuits'; some copies of *Poems and translations* (1683) have the same attribution, while others have a title page on which Oldham's name appears for the first time. For most readers, the first occasion on which they would have encountered Oldham's poems over his own name was in the posthumously published *Works* of 1684. In the light of this story of a canon assembled anonymously, there is an added poignancy in Dryden's description of Oldham – in his memorial poem for the 1684 volume – as 'too little and too lately known'.

Katherine Philips was also hesitant about allowing her poetry to appear in print, and its principal readership was her own circle of friends and admirers, who copied and circulated her verse.[35] She herself collected fifty-five poems into a manuscript volume of fair copies, and her friends frequently copied and circulated her verses to others: one of them transcribed ninety-six of her poems after her death and presented the volume to Mary Aubrey, who features in Philips's poems as Rosania – diplomatically excluding from this collection Philips's poem 'On Rosania's Apostacy' (National Library of Wales manuscripts 775 and 776). Philips insisted that she 'never writ any line in my life with an intention to have it printed', and was (or affected to be) horrified when an edition of her poems was published by Richard Marriott in 1664. This is generally said to have been unauthorized, but it was not pirated: Marriott was a respectable publisher who had entered the book on the Stationers' Register and had it duly licensed. The volume was soon withdrawn because of pressure from Philips's friends, but after her death one of them put together a new edition, designed in several respects to eclipse Marriott's: titled rather fulsomely *Poems by the most deservedly admired Mrs Katherine Philips the matchless Orinda*, it was in folio rather than octavo, was published by Herringman, and included a

35 *Poems*, ed. Patrick Thomas (London, 1990), 41–58; *IELM*; Hageman and Sununu 1993; Hageman and Sununu 1995; Barash 1996.

frontispiece portrait of a bust of Orinda; it had a long preface denouncing Marriott's edition, followed by commendatory poems by the Earls of Orrery and Roscommon, Cowley and others. The canon itself was expanded from seventy-four to 121 poems, and added her translations from Corneille.

The story behind the shaping of Marvell's canon is as elusive as most other aspects of this man's life. *The first anniversary of the government under O.C.* was published anonymously in 1655 as a separate quarto; the anonymity is curious, given that Marvell was on the edges of the Protectoral government and perhaps seeking advancement, for in 1653 he had been recommended by Milton for appointment as assistant Latin Secretary to the Council of State, and would actually be appointed to that office in 1657: was he hedging his bets? In 1659 Herringman registered his intention to publish three poems on Cromwell's death by Dryden, Marvell and Sprat, but when the volume eventually appeared from another bookseller Marvell's poem had been replaced by Waller's: was Marvell hedging his bets again? At the very least he seems to have exercised considerable caution about allowing a poetic canon to emerge, a caution which is evident also in the remarkable absence of any evidence of manuscript circulation for most of the poems which Marvell wrote in the 1650s, including 'An Horatian Ode'. Even 'To his coy mistress' survives in only one Restoration copy, the anonymous, shortened and probably corrupt version preserved in Bodleian manuscript don.b.8.

It was more than two years after his death that Robert Boulter published in folio the *Miscellaneous poems by Andrew Marvell, Esq; late Member of the Honourable House of Commons* (1681).[36] Boulter was primarily a publisher of political and religious works rather than poetry, though he had been one of the booksellers for *Paradise lost. Miscellaneous poems* appeared at a time of great political tension, and the reminder on the title page that Marvell had been an MP invites readers to expect a volume with some political significance. In fact the book as actually published is principally a collection of lyrical and topographical poems, and is of little topical significance, but during the printing of the book 'An Horatian ode upon Cromwell's return from Ireland', 'The first anniversary of the government under O.C.' and 'A poem upon the death of O.C.' were excised from most copies. Evidently the Marvell canon was being revised even as the book was going through the press. Though sometimes attributed to government intervention, it is more likely that this alteration was due to someone deciding that too overt a reminder of Marvell's association with the Cromwellian government would harm the Whig cause for which he had been

36 Facsimile of BL copy with MS. supplement from Bodleian copy, and anonymous bibliographical note (Menston, W. Yorks., 1969). On Marvell's posthumously created canon, see Maltzahn 1999.

such a prominent spokesman and pamphleteer. And any purchaser who expected to acquire texts of the political satires which Marvell had been writing in the late 1660s and 1670s would have been disappointed, for the *Miscellaneous poems* omits the *Last instructions to a painter* and all the other Restoration satires which had been circulating in manuscript with more or less speculative attributions to Marvell.[37] One reader remedied this omission by adding a manuscript supplement of eighteen poems to a copy of the 1681 folio (Bodleian Library manuscript Eng. Poet. d. 49), perhaps as the basis for a new edition. But the edition never materialized.

IV

During the 1650s, one of the most innovative publishers of plays had been Humphrey Moseley, who had seen a market for editions of the drama at a time when the plays were no longer being staged. He issued a series of conveniently sized octavo collections of the plays of Brome, Shirley, Massinger and Middleton.[38] But Moseley's death in 1661 prevented him from reprinting these titles or extending the series by adding contemporary plays. The distinctive mode of publication for plays in the 1660s was not the octavo but the folio collection, and works were issued in this format particularly by aristocratic amateurs: Margaret Cavendish, Duchess of Newcastle, collected her *Playes* in 1662, and her *Plays, never before printed* in 1668; Sir Robert Howard published *Four new plays* in 1665 (silently appropriating *The Indian Queen*, which he had written in collaboration with Dryden); then Sir William Killigrew's *Four new plays* appeared in 1666, followed by the Earl of Orrery's *The history of Henry the Fifth. And the tragedy of Mustapha* (1668) and *Two new plays* (1669). The folio format allowed a clear *mise-en-page* and good, legible typography, helping to dignify and canonize the contents, and particularly to establish a status for the heroic play which was the new reign's first distinctive contribution to the drama. Title pages drew attention to the writer's social status, while prefatory material often emphasized that these were the product of idle hours: there is thus a careful distancing from the professional stage. But this form of publishing did not persist beyond the 1660s, and the emerging generation of professional dramatists forged new relationships with their companies and booksellers.

Two of these writers, Cavendish and Killigrew, can be observed in the process of self-canonization. Cavendish's volumes were a form of vanity publication (the imprint of *Plays, never before printed* mentions no bookseller) and the title

37 Listed in *IELM*.

38 Kewes 1995; Kewes 1998, which provides the material for this paragraph.

page proclaims the author's status: *Playes written by the thrice noble, illustrious and excellent princess, the Lady Marchioness of Newcastle*. An engraved frontispiece portrait shows the author as a statue in a classical niche flanked by allegorical figures; there are no fewer than ten prefaces from the author to the reader, a dedication to her husband, verses in return from her husband to her, a general prologue to the plays, and yet another introduction in the form of a dramatic scene. A further address to the reader is added at the end of the volume. A more serious figure than Mad Meg was Sir William Killigrew, and in his case a rare piece of evidence survives which shows him revising his canon.[39] Killigrew took a copy of his *Four new playes* (1666), altered the title from '*Four*' to '*Five*', and had it bound up with *The imperial tragedy* (1669). The latter had been published anonymously, with this explanation on the title page: 'By a Gentleman for his own Diversion. Who, on the Importunity of Friends, has consented to have it Published; but without his Name: because many do censure Plays, according to their Opinions of the Author.' Killigrew now acknowledged his authorship of this play by signing his name on the last page. He also made substantial alterations to all five plays, ranging from small textual details to major excisions, and revised passages were written out on slips of paper pasted into the printed volume. Here we see Killigrew changing his mind about his texts, and about the shape of his public canon.

Whereas theatrical companies in the time of Shakespeare had guarded their play-texts as valuable commercial property, rarely allowing current material to be printed, in the Restoration period such texts were usually the property of the writer, and were frequently put into print soon after the play's première. Across the period the typical interval between first performance and first publication shortened: during the 1660s, the normal interval was about a year; in the 1670s, three to six months; three months in the late 1670s and the 1680s; one month in the late 1680s and 1690s.[40] Congreve's *The old batchelour* was printed concurrently with its first performance in 1693, and at some operatic performances audiences were provided with libretti. Now dramatists wished to capitalize on the success of a production through sales of a printed text, and this practice evidently relied upon there being among the theatre-going public a substantial section of literate patrons who would wish to peruse a play text; it also asserts a seriousness and value for contemporary drama, both tragic and comic. Moreover, when during the political crises of the later 1670s and early 1680s the drama began to engage with urgent constitutional and social

39 Leeds University Library Brotherton Collection MS. Lt.q.16; Horden 1984; *The Brotherton Collection, University of Leeds* (Leeds, 1986), pp. 20–1.

40 Milhous and Hume 1974.

issues, reasonably quick publication enabled a play to reach a wider audience and contribute to a quickly developing political debate.

Dryden's plays were published separately in quarto format, first by Herringman and then by Tonson. Right from the outset Dryden seized the opportunity to make the publication something more than a bare play-text, adding dedications and critical essays. His first published play, *The rival ladies* (1664), was dedicated to Roger Boyle, Earl of Orrery, himself a prominent dramatist and pioneer of the heroic play, and this dedication is no formal gesture but a short critical essay, discussing the role of the different mental faculties in composition, the problem of constructing a play, the comparative qualities of English and French writing, the characteristics of English verse in the generation of Waller and Denham, and the relative merits of rhymed and unrhymed verse. The dedication seeks to mark the entry of Dryden into the canon of English drama, and has the wider agenda of promoting discussion of the true merits and characteristics of the contemporary theatre, suggesting, in effect, the criteria by which a canon should be formed. Throughout his career Dryden would use the dedications to his plays both as a means of consolidating relations with his patrons and as an apologia for his own dramatic practice; and he often meditated on the difficulties faced both by statesmen and by writers in maintaining their integrity and spiritual freedom in the exercise of a public life. In addition, he occasionally attached substantial discourses (perhaps with an eye on Corneille's practice) which addressed questions such as rhyme in heroic drama ('A defence of an essay of dramatique poesie', added to some copies of the second edition of *The Indian Emperor*) or Jonson's linguistic faults ('Defence of the epilogue' appended to *The conquest of Granada*) or 'The grounds of criticism in tragedy' prefacing *Troilus and Cressida*: all were essays in the principles for forming a contemporary canon.

Dryden's plays continued to be popular in print throughout his career, and even those plays which might seem to belong to one specific moment in the evolution of Restoration taste stayed in demand: *The Indian Emperor* (1667) and *Aureng-Zebe* (1676), respectively his first and last rhymed heroic plays, continued to be reprinted through the 1690s. It was in 1691 that Tonson collected these quarto play-texts together into volumes which, along with the quarto poems, would form *The works of Mr John Dryden*,[41] and similar nonce-collections were assembled for other playwrights, including Orrery, Lee, Otway and Shadwell. Only after Dryden's death were his plays given classic canonical status by being reprinted in two folio volumes.

41 Macdonald 1939, pp. 146–53.

But this focus upon the publication of individual plays by individual writers neglects the important subject of co-authorship, both overt collaboration and illicit appropriation.[42] Throughout this period there was considerable sensitivity about the subject of plagiarism. Shadwell was accused by Dryden of receiving undue assistance from Sedley, and appropriating whole scenes from Etherege;[43] Dryden in turn was accused by various contemporaries of stealing his plots from French and Spanish plays. The issues of plagiarism and the canon are linked, because an increasing focus upon the *oeuvre* of individuals highlights the question of their originality, and raises the issue of their legal rights over what they put into print. And because Restoration drama and dramatic criticism is nervous about the value of contemporary plays compared with the drama of the last age or that of Continental Europe, the originality of modern drama is an issue for the culture at large. Dryden's dramatic canon, for example, included explicit adaptations of Shakespeare, Milton and Sophocles, as well as some less clearly signalled reworkings of contemporary foreign sources. And whereas collaboration had been common practice in Shakespeare's profession, it fell into disfavour during the Restoration period. The individual author was a principal focus of interest, with prologues excusing his youth or her gender, and dramatists being made to contend one against another for the laurels in the various verses called *Sessions of the poets*. By the turn of the century the emphasis is squarely upon the playwright as writer rather than dramaturge, as author rather than collaborator, and as originator rather than adaptor.

V

The formation of a contemporary canon was to some extent predicated upon the existence of a canon of classical Greek and Roman writing, and the dispute between Dryden and Shadwell in the 1670s is in part an argument over which of them is properly the heir to the classical heritage, as Shadwell places himself in a lineage which includes Horace and Jonson. But the classical canon was itself being reconfigured: a traditional canon had structured the grammar-school curriculum,[44] and now translations increasingly brought this literature within the compass of the ordinary reader.[45] Herringman had assisted in this by publishing *The poems of Horace* in English in 1666, which collected translations by a variety of writers from the mid-century; this was sufficiently successful to be revised in 1671 and again in 1680, with new translations being added. Horace was a cornerstone of the classical canon and a *point de repère* for

42 This paragraph draws upon Kewes 1998. 43 *Mac Flecknoe*, lines 163–4, 183–4.
44 Hoole, *A new discovery*. 45 CBEL; Gillespie 1991.

the contemporary canon, and writers such as Oldham and Roscommon, who were keen to promote modern translation themselves, translated the *Ars poetica* both as a demonstration of what could be done and as a way of casting into contemporary English idiom (both linguistic and conceptual) the precepts which Horace offered. Tonson in his miscellanies offered readers further examples of Horace by various hands, and published Thomas Creech's complete translation in 1684.

Ovid's *Metamorphoses* had been translated in the previous generation by George Sandys (1626, with subsequent revisions), and no one in the Restoration period succeeded in producing a new version of the complete text.[46] But several poets offered readers selected tales, often highlighting tales of sexual passion, with Oldham (1681) and Dennis (1692) both translating the story of Byblis, and Dryden rendering the tale of Cinyras and Myrrha for his *Fables ancient and modern* (1700). Many writers gave readers versions of Ovid the witty poet of love through their selections from the *Amores* and *Heroides*. While such aspects of Ovid appealed strongly to Restoration sensibilities, Dryden responded to other elements in Ovid too, for he was attracted to tales of conjugal fidelity and reverence for the gods (Baucis and Philemon, Ceyx and Alcyone; both in *Fables*) and to the extended philosophical contemplation of nature's changes (*Metamorphoses* book I, relating the creation of the world, in *Examen poeticum* (1693); and 'Of the Pythagorean Philosophy' from book XV in *Fables*).

Virgil had been translated by Ogilby in 1649 (re-issued with modifications 1650, 1654), and Dryden would translate the works again in 1697, but in between these two heroic ventures various poets published individual books: predictably book IV was the most popular, with translations by Fanshawe (1652), Harrington (1659), Howard (1660), and Denham (1668); but Denham and Harrington also translated book II (1656, 1658), with Harrington and Boys rendering book VI (1659, 1660). The fact that many of these were written by Royalist sympathizers during the Interregnum points to the use of the *Aeneid* as a source for reflection on the destruction of an empire and the experience of exile.[47] Restoration taste also relished the burlesque versions of books I and IV produced by Charles Cotton (1664–5, much reprinted).

Among those classical writers who appealed especially to Restoration taste was Anacreon: Thomas Stanley had published a complete translation of Anacreon in 1651, but in 1683 a volume called *Anacreon done into English*

46 Hopkins 1988. 47 Venuti 1993.

collected versions by various hands (including Cowley and Oldham). It was issued by Anthony Stephens, the Oxford bookseller who also published Creech's Lucretius and Theocritus. The appearance of the latter in 1684 perhaps thwarted an attempt by Tonson to assemble an English Theocritus by various hands, relics of which may be traced in *Miscellany poems* and *Sylvae*.[48] Creech's Lucretius was an extraordinarily successful translation, appearing in 1682 and being reprinted five times by 1700. It started life as an Oxford publication by an Oxford scholar, but quickly migrated into metropolitan literary circles, being taken up by Tonson, argued over in coffee-houses (Dryden was asked to settle a dispute over Creech's grammar)[49] and accumulating commendatory poems from Behn, Otway, Tate and others. As Prior remarked in his spiteful *Satire on the modern translators*,

> This pleas'd the genius of the vicious Town,
> The Wits confirm'd his Labours with Renown,
> And swear the early Atheist for their own.[50]

After Creech's death it became a canonical text in its own right, being issued in 1714 in two volumes with an extensive learned commentary in double columns elucidating the Epicurean philosophy and tracing parallels of thought and phrasing in Cowley, Milton and Dryden.[51]

Classical drama too was made available in translation, allowing readers without Latin and Greek some access to the corpus which was influencing neo-classical taste. John Wright translated Seneca's *Thyestes* in 1674 (adding a 'Mock-Thyestes, in Burlesque'), and three translations appeared of his *Troades* (1660, 1679, 1686). There were collections of the plays of Terence (by Hoole 1676; by several hands 1694) and Plautus (1694).

By the end of our period, readers without the classical languages, or those who were interested in translation as an art, would have had access to complete translations of Virgil and Persius by Dryden, and of Horace, Lucretius and Theocritus by Creech; to volumes assembling translations by various hands from Horace, Ovid and Juvenal; and to a large number of shorter translations from Latin and Greek scattered through the miscellanies. The classical and contemporary canons were each being reshaped by a process of interaction and reciprocal criticism.

48 Hammond 1990. 49 *Letters of John Dryden*, pp. 14–16.

50 Lines 122–4; *The literary works of Matthew Prior*, edited by H. Bunker Wright and Monroe K. Spears, 2 vols. (Oxford, 1971).

51 P. Hammond, 'Milton, Dryden, and Lucretius', *Seventeenth Century*, 16 (2001) 158–76.

VI

All canon formation is to some degree politically inflected, and it may be instructive to conclude with a striking instance of this from the year 1697. *Poems on affairs of state* draws principally upon the large body of satirical material which had circulated in manuscript in the reigns of Charles II and James II, providing (or so it claimed) 'a just and secret History of the former Times' (sig. A3[r]). In order to promote a strongly Whiggish and Williamite view of recent history, this volume effected an adroit reconfiguration of the canon. Its title page offered poems 'Written by the greatest Wits of the Age', whom it identified as Buckingham, Rochester, Buckhurst, Denham, Marvell, Milton, Dryden, Sprat, Waller and Ayloffe. But as we read on it soon becomes apparent that this canon is highly tendentious.

On the one hand, *Poems on affairs of state* sets out to canonize in print those satirists whose manuscript verses had advanced the Whig cause in the previous reigns. It invokes the example of Greek and Roman writers who had defended liberty, and promises 'the best Patriots, as well as Poets' (sig. A2[r]), 'Patriots' being a favourite Whig self-description. Milton is enlisted in this cause firstly through a brief defence of the prosody of *Paradise lost*, but more bizarrely by the claim that 'Directions to a Painter' is 'said to be written by Sir *John Denham*, but believed to be writ by Mr *Milton*'. The various 'Directions' are grouped together, consolidating these into a substantial attack on the misgovernment of Charles II. A clear image of a politically committed Marvell is established by the attribution to him of sixteen satires, thus correcting the impression of his *oeuvre* which had been created by the 1681 folio. His stature as a Whig hero is further confirmed by the inclusion of 'Marvell's ghost' and of an anonymous elegy which hails him as 'this Islands watchful Centinel' (p. 123). Rochester is accorded similar treatment, for five poems are attributed to him (including the notorious satire on Charles II), and the volume also includes 'Rochester's Farewell to the Court'. In the second part of *Poems on affairs of state*, published in the same year, there are further pieces attributed to Rochester, and one writer laments: 'Had the late fam'd Lord *Rochester* surviv'd,/ We'd been inform'd who all our Plots contriv'd' (p. 159). The virtually apolitical (and almost polite) image of Rochester presented in Tonson's 1691 edition is drastically revised.

On the other side, the collection mischievously reconfigures the canon of several royalist writers, notably Dryden. The preface to the first part quotes a couplet from *Absalom and Achitophel* (which had referred to the Civil War) and applies it to its own retrospect on the turmoil of the last two reigns:

And looking backward with a wise Affright,
See Seams of Wounds dishonest to the Sight.
(A3^{r})

The poems themselves begin (ostensibly simply to provide a chronologically organized documentation of recent history) with the verses on Cromwell by Waller, Sprat and Dryden; yet there is no trace of any of Marvell's three Cromwellian pieces. The anthology also attributes to Dryden the satire 'On the young statesmen' as well as the 'Essay upon satire'. Special care is taken to include much material derogatory of Dryden. In part one the speaker of 'The town life' rapidly surveys the Dryden canon with haughty moral disdain:

I cannot vere with ev'ry change of State,
Nor flatter Villains, tho' at Court they're great:
Nor will I prostitute my Pen for Hire,
Praise *Cromwell*, damn him, write the *Spanish Fryar*:
A Papist now, if next the Turk should reign,
Then piously transverse the Alcoran. (p. 190)

The second part adds a further half dozen poems which are equally derogatory of him. As *Poems on affairs of state* was being published, Dryden was putting the finishing touches to *The works of Virgil*. These two contrasting projects stand at the end of our period. The one assembles in print verses which had, for the most part, previously existed only in manuscript, circulating anonymously from hand to hand, being censored or improved upon as the transcribers thought fit: these were poems of the moment, poems shaped communally for a particular political cause. As the political climate changed, it became possible to put these poems into print in an act of partisan historiography, conserving them for posterity as a highly selective archive of the struggle, and bringing their putative authors out of the shadows. The other project is also affected by the winds of political change, as Dryden turned to translation to provide him with the living which he could no longer expect from the government. This great folio associates Dryden and Virgil in a transcultural canon, and its title page carries the words of Aeneas, turned now into a claim which is at once modest and proud: *Sequiturque patrem non passibus aequis* ('and I follow my father with steps not equal to his').[52] Here we have two appropriations of Roman poetry to define one's freedom, two kinds of historiography, two contrasting pieces of book production, two different concepts of the canon, both competing for readers in the same year.

52 P. Hammond, *Dryden and the traces of classical Rome* (Oxford, 1999), pp. 218–82.

19

Non-conformist voices and books

NIGEL SMITH

> this persecuted means of unlicenced Printing hath done more good to the people, then all the bloodie wars; the one tending to rid us quite of all slavery; but the other onely to rid us of one, and involve us into another.
> Richard Overton, *A Defiance against all Arbitrary Usurpations* (1646).[1]

Captain Lieutenant William Bray (*fl.* 1647–59) is in many ways typical of the people who wrote the books that are the concern of this chapter. He is obscure: there is little we know in any detail about his life, and he only comes to our attention because he was visible in a volatile public context for a brief period of time. We have to work by inference from his writings to glean anything of substance concerning his background and the general conditions under which he lived.[2] He served as a junior officer in the New Model Army and it would seem from his first published writings that he was immersed in the culture of godliness that so many who fought for the Parliament knew: intense Bible reading within unofficially sanctioned (and hence, before 1640 and after 1660, illegal) communities of believers. He would have known about hours and hours of prayer meetings and meetings of lay people during which the interpretation of scripture was disputed. He had a historical understanding of these godly practices that extended back into the sixteenth century, and his words are suffused with dense, seemingly spontaneously delivered millenarian terms. He wrote because he had been imprisoned on account of his sympathy with the Levellers – the popular, near-democratic movement that resisted the power of the New Model Army commanders (and their associates in Parliament) in the late 1640s. He wrote and published letters and petitions that were designed to call attention to his plight as the victim of a tyranny:

1 (Wing O626), p. 26.
2 See R. L. Greaves and R. M. Zaller, *A biographical dictionary of British Radicals in the seventeenth century*, 3 vols. (Brighton, 1982).

> I was almost three weeks imprisoned before I had any charge exhibited, which is contrary to the forme of your owne proceedings, I have declared in my narrative, the explanations and naturall causes of the Regiments distemper which if you or any godly impartiall man [do] well weigh, you will finde that fawning temporizing person had no just cause to father the distemper upon mee, because I own the Agreement of the people[3] in my Judgement, which some Officers of the Regiment subscribed at *St Albans*, and such who have carried themselves monstrously, perfideously and treacherously towards mee in charging me with a private discourse, and judgement, as in my plea is expressed, and who did not carry themselves in an honest conscientious care to your Excellencie and the Regiment as is expressed in my plea; God hath appointed a day wherein he will judge the word in righteousnesse at which time wicked deeds shall have no glory in power and rules, God will destroy *Machavell* more and more even by a Law which is like unto fire which shall enter into the inmost parts. God wil recompense vengeance into the bosome of oppressers or of those that conspire in power, [nay indeed your power] to persecute, defame and destroy, I am, and have been very much troubled [not so much in relation to my selfe, for the Lord upholds me in integrity and much comfort in more then an ordinary care] for you and the Lord hath acquainted mee in my conversation with him in an inward testimony.[4]

We should note the fusion of religious, political and juridical categories, the bridging of the most intimately private (a personal message from God known as an interior voice) and the public (the good of the nation). The indecorous, unbounded prose style, with one observation inelegantly leading onto the next, all in the service of a personal narrative, is also typical.[5] Bray was apparently not university educated, but his literacy clearly involved the reading of a wide range of materials, the reference to Machiavelli indicating the awareness of a tradition, if not a knowledge, of the texts of Italian political theory.

Just over ten years later, after the defeat of the Levellers, further periods of imprisonment for resistance to Cromwellian authority, and a period of exile in Holland, Bray re-emerged as a republican theorist on the eve of the Restoration, tying together Leveller notions with ideas of government derived from the classical tradition, partly through a dialogue with the most important republican theorist of the period, James Harrington.[6] Gone is the language of the

3 One of several documents of the same name in which the Levellers published proposals for political reform.

4 *A letter to his Excellencie Sir Thomas Fairfax* ([3 June] 1647) (Wing B4305), pp. 3–4. Wing lists sixteen works, only one of which is unsigned.

5 The best examples among Bray's contemporaries are the narratives published by John Lilburne. See, for example, Lilburne *The legall and fundamentall liberties of the people of England* (1649), in W. Haller and G. Davies (eds.), *The Leveller tracts, 1647–1653* (New York, 1944; repr. Gloucester, MA, 1964).

6 See, for example, Bray, *A plea for the peoples fundamentall liberties and Parliaments* (1659) (Wing B4306).

millennium, replaced with a secular theory of the state that is still faithful to popular rights (derived from a particular reading of the Common Law and involving annual Parliaments) and religious toleration. According to Bray, England had excellent fundamental laws, which had been corrupted by a series of alienations of popular sovereignty. He also incorporated a theory of personal reason and judgement, derived from some typical radical Puritan heresies.[7] But at the same time, Bray displayed an extensive knowledge of classical and European authorities,[8] and a subtle grasp of the history of the Civil War and Interregnum. Like many radicals at this time, Bray had matured into a sophisticated and distinctly modern-looking political thinker and operator.

Into what context do we place William Bray and his books? A possible title for this chapter might be 'Marginal and dissenting texts'. But properly speaking, Dissent can only apply after 1660 to those Protestants who refused to conform to the re-instituted Church of England. 'Marginal' is no more appropriate, since the concerns of the writers and books that are the subject of this chapter were a large part of the most pressing issues of Church and State at the time. Many religious radicals were at the centre of political power during the Interregnum. Oliver Cromwell was one of their number. 'Marginal' is often taken to mean 'non-orthodox', but the extent of unorthodoxy, if we take by that all of those who at some point between 1558 and 1685 voiced an unorthodox or unofficial belief, including Recusants, Protestant sectaries and atheists, is hardly a 'marginal' phenomenon. A particular prophet active in early seventeenth-century London may have seemed 'marginal' if considered by him or herself: add them all together and the picture is very different. Look at non-conformity in the context of the history of the book and the story becomes a rich narrative of innovation, often during tense times, involving considerable human suffering. The subject of this chapter is 'marginal' only in terms suggested by the conventional literary canon constructed much later.

No less than any other significant religious, political or intellectual group in this period, the non-conformists made specific and extensive use of the printed book: their identity and activities were partly defined by it. As we shall see, they made very special use of it. When printing and non-conformity are placed together, two phenomena in this period stand out: the Marprelate tracts (1589) and the great success of the Quakers in using the printed book to proselytize in the second half of the seventeenth century.[9] In different ways both were highly

7 For instance, Bray cited with approval the General Baptist Robert Everard's *Nature's vindication* (1652) (Wing E3540).

8 These ranged from Cassiodorus to Charron and were very possibly derived from digests rather than individual texts of each authority.

9 See below, pp. 70–5.

orchestrated and very successful attempts to exploit the powers of the press to bring a point of view to widespread public attention. Both are significant moments in the history of the development of modern press freedom. But they involved instances of press usage that surpassed in their implications the initial circumstances of their origins, and the intentions of those involved in their production and circulation.

The non-conformist use of the book emerged from the demands of radical Protestant theology and ecclesiology. The English Reformation, as is well known, was imposed from above by the monarch and his bishops. Those Protestants who remained unsatisfied with the solution offered by the 1559 religious settlement (the Puritans, who called themselves the 'godly') wanted a form of religion that they believed approximated to the primitive churches as described in the Pauline epistles. The less they believed in the justification of higher forms of Church government, the more they privileged in each individual believer the immediate presence of the Holy Spirit, a source of inspiration and a guide to godly living. They were thus relatively unsympathetic, and in extreme cases hostile to, any use of set forms in the act of worship – be it written sermons or printed prayers and catechisms. They were also opposed to the Book of Common Prayer, psalters and, in some cases, printed sermons. Their iconoclasm made them hostile to figurative written forms such as allegories. But they were not hostile (in the vast majority of cases) to the Bible. Thus, nonconformists lived with a paradox: they stressed the spontaneity and immediacy of inspired speech as the Holy Spirit moved them, but most of them accepted the printed Bible as the record of divine truth (although even this would be challenged by some in the mid-seventeenth century[10]).

How, then, did they live? In respect of worship, non-conformists tended towards separating themselves from the sinful world. This meant turning away from association with the established Church, and its complex structure and traditions of parish life. Separatists worshipped apart and, until the 1640s, mostly in secret meetings within households. Separating ministers would preach, usually from memory, and at length. The Word was readily ingested and sometimes copied down, as was the case with Puritan sermons or 'lectures' given within the established Church. In the heartland of established orthodoxy, a sermon might eventually find its way into print, thereby aiding the great print programme of the Jacobean Church. However, true separatists kept their sermons out of print. Instead, they might have been copied down and repeated thereafter in the arena of household worship. Private and

10 See in particular Samuel Fisher, *Rusticos ad academicos* (1660) (Wing F1056) and N. Smith 1989, ch. 7.

deliberately clandestine meetings of religious radicals, really a continuation of the Elizabethan prophesyings, combined Bible reading and dispute with the repetition of sermons. The early non-conformists saw it as part of a narrative of pilgrimage:

> So that when they had been conversant in these duties and pious acts of hearing the best men, repeating their notes to one another, whetting them on their hearts, and praying them over, fasting and praying together frequently, and had thus continued in so doing for about the space of twenty years, and beginning to grow somewhat numerous in that work, they had the strength to begin to go further, for the path of those truths of building up one another was well beaten.[11]

Worship was reserved for listening to sermons and Psalm-singing, with an increasing emphasis on inspired or 'gifted' singing through divine inspiration. Preaching extempore from memory was the ideal of the early Baptist John Smyth. To hostile observers the preaching of lay non-conformists (known as 'tubpreachers'), perhaps with a printed Bible to hand, looked like a gross parody of the established clergy, showing the looseness of a private meeting and, in this example, emergent signs of a non-conformist preaching 'style':

> At every place of Scripture cited, he turnes over the leaves of his Booke, more pleased with the motion of the leaves, than the matter of the Text: For hee foldes downe the leaves, though he finds not the place: his eye being still fixt on his paper, or the Pulpit: Hee lifts up the whites of his eyes towards Heaven, when he meditates on the sordid pleasures of the earth, his body being in Gods Church, when his minde is in the divels Chappell.[12]

Repetition of sermons, or disputes between educated clergy and conventiclers, was the beginning of a kind of authorship for the lay separatists. In copying down a sermon and then repeating it, powers and skills of literacy were conveyed. This process accounts for the way in which particular styles were adopted (there was even self-consciousness about this), and of course it enabled those who had been formally educated to transmit something of their achievements to those who had not. The sectary Lawrence Clarkson says that he 'went to' the Antinomian Tobias Crisp, who 'held forth against all the aforesaid churches.'[13] Crisp was but one influence upon Clarkson who could barely write when he first published a pamphlet in the mid-1640s. Also of note is

11 Underhill 1847, p. 11. This account refers to the late 1630s.
12 Thomas Heywood, *A true discourse of the two infamous upstart prophets* (1636) (*STC* 13369), p. 3.
13 Lawrence Clarkson, *The lost sheep found* (1660) (Wing c4580), p. 9.

the fact that although Clarkson appears to be recording his presence in Crisp's audience, it is not entirely clear that he did not become familiar with Crisp by reading him. Writing to the Sussex Independent, lawyer and bibliophile Samuel Jeake in 1644, John Coulton gives evidence of the influence of the printed book within the Parliamentary forces – in this example the published sermons of the Antinomian divine Tobias Crisp:

> I feare you looke for comfort wheare it is nott to be had[.] the depth saith it is nott in me: all Creature comforts saith its not in me[.] Solomon could never find any hapienes under the sunne and I am sure duties saith it is nott in me: if you look for comfort heare lett the honest Dr. Crispe teach you that sinfull weake dutyes can never afford the[e] the joy of the Holy Ghost.[14]

By the mid-century, the influence of preached, printed and repeated sermons was immense, while the sermon itself, especially in printed form, began to embody within itself the new printed forms that were so typical of those years – the newsbook and the controversial pamphlet.[15]

With the emergence of Independency (or Congregationalism), the reciting of an account of how one came to be saved (a 'confession of experience'), part of the formal act of joining a 'gathered Church', was added to the acts of authorship that non-conformist worship was inventing. The manuscript evidence of early, pre-1640 non-conformist culture that has survived consists of copies of repeatable sermons and, in a very few instances, the first conversion narratives, in addition to a few church books.

At the heart of all forms of religious non-conformity was one continuous phenomenon in the period: the intense debate of religious truth between plebeian lay people, in unremarkable environments, sometimes rural, but more often urban. Whether these were the debates between Marian exiles and Familists in Cambridgeshire inns in the 1550s, or the fierce disputes over the meaning of the text of Esdras in the parish of St Katherine Cree, London, in the early seventeenth century, the discussions of the meaning of Boehme's writings in the Thames Valley during the later 1640s and 1650s, or the Quaker confrontations with Baptists in the 1650s and 1660s, the printed book was never far from the centre of an intense form of conversation.[16]

14 John Coulton to Samuel Jeake, East Sussex County Record Office, Frewen MS. 4223, fol. 76v. This could refer to the first or second collection of Crisp's sermons, published in 1643 and 1644 respectively. A further collection was published in 1648. See also Hunter, Mandelbrote, Ovenden and Smith 1999.

15 See Rigney 1993.

16 See David Como, 'Puritans and heretics: the emergence of an antinomian underground in early Stuart England' (unpub. Ph.D. thesis, Princeton University, 1999); Peter Lake and David Como, 'Puritans, Antinomians and Laudians in Caroline London: the strange case of Peter Shaw and its contexts', *JEH*, 50 (1999), 684–715.

The extreme Puritans had an impact of no less import on the publishing activities of their enemies. In their attempt to halt the progress of forms of religion and religious opinion that had gone far beyond their own goals, several Presbyterian divines produced carefully assembled accounts of the heresies of their own times – they were the Eusebiuses of their day, and their works are now major sources for the history of the period.[17] They were in fact continuing a tradition sustained by Elizabethan divines, although their methods of intelligence-gathering and publication reflect different circumstances of communication than had previously prevailed: after 1640, a 'public sphere' existed. And by quoting so much material from the radicals (at least as much quotation was as authentic as it was 'faked'[18]), the radicals had another forum for their voice.

The heresiographers also tended to include in their lists of heretics 'atheistical' thinkers whose thought and activities lay outside the boundaries of separatism. 'Atheism' was a charge that could mean as little as denying the efficacy of an organized, public Church, or denying one of the theological fundamentals accepted by Protestant and Catholic Churches alike, such as the idea of the Holy Trinity. In the eyes of the orthodox, or the orthodox Puritan divines of the 1640s, these kinds of views were to be treated in the same way as the sectaries. We can hardly blame them: in the later sixteenth century, these kinds of opinion were the possession of privileged groups of intellectuals with court associations, and to some extent their circles intersected with those of esoteric religion, such as the Family of Love. 'Early modern atheism' owed its growth in part to the revival of scepticism, especially the Pyrrhonism found in Montaigne, and the neo-stoic revival encouraged by Dutch scholars like Justus Lipsius.[19] From the circles of Sir Thomas Harriot a group of manuscript texts began to circulate, along with sophisticated Continental scepticism, that did find a readership in some instances with influential radicals.[20] We should not be entirely surprised when the showy intellectual heresy of Marlovian drama reappears, with theatrical representation intact, inside heretical treatises of the early 1640s.[21] The roots of 'atheism' in England are traditionally seen in the

17 See, for example, Ephraim Pagitt, *Heresiography* (1645; several further editions, 1645–62) (Wing P174); Thomas Edwards, *Gangraena* (1646; 2nd edn, 1646), 3 pts (Wing E227); Robert Baillie, *Anabaptism, the true fountain of Independencie, Antinomy, Brownisme, Familisme* (1646, 2nd edn, 1647) (Wing B452).

18 Information communicated privately by Professor Ann Hughes from her project on Thomas Edwards and the making of *Gangraena*.

19 See Hunter and Wootton 1992, esp. chs. 3 and 5.

20 Christopher Hill, *Milton and the English Revolution* (London, 1977), pp. 65–6; N. Smith 1992, pp. 131–58. See also Gibbons 1995.

21 See, for example, Richard Overton, *Man's mortallitie* (1643) (Wing O629D–E), sig. ¶ 2^{v}, pp. 23–4; 2nd edn (1655), Wing O629A–C.

writings of court libertines during the Restoration. Yet here, in material often overlooked, was the beginnings of a free-thinking tradition that would be so influential on eighteenth-century intellectual life.[22]

Separately published items by religious radicals before 1640 were fairly low in number. However, between 1640 and 1660 there was an outpouring of many thousands of tracts and single sheets. This period was in turn followed by a falling off once again as the Restoration censorship tightened. The heyday of confessional and prophetic literature in print was during the Commonwealth, and especially during the republic. The radicals did not have a distinct manuscript culture (like, say, that used by court poets), although the mid-century saw the growth of the use of letters. In particular, the Quakers put letters to very significant strategic as well as pastoral use.

1 1558–1625

Part of the problem in analysing this period is in discerning the true voice of a religious radical. On the one hand, the treatises of Puritan divines adopting a position that went against that of the established church looked like Protestant interpretative polemic: part of its point was to show that its vision was more godly than that of the bishops. On the other, the statements of authentic, separated or 'simulating' sectaries are often available only through surviving records of interrogations. Thus, the voice of the sectary is defined in terms set by the interrogators. The opinions and expressions of the English Familists are particularly prone to this kind of interpretative problem. Moreover, the relationship between heresy and conformity was signalled very precisely in print terms, ones which reflected orthodox speech habits. The philo-Semite John Trask(e) (1585–1636) left no printed works behind him of his heretical opinions regarding the necessity for the strict observance of the Jewish law by believers. Instead there are a series of printed sermon-treatises (*STC* 24175.3–24178.5) that demonstrate in impeccably English Protestant terms the power of the preached word as a demonstration of the efficacy of faith and God's saving grace: radicalism could hide itself easily within the Protestant mainstream. Financial restraint was often a significant factor: the early separatists could not afford to print the kind of lengthy book that an explanation of Church government required.

Kinds of book that would become part of the hallmark of later non-conformist publishing nonetheless began to appear in a rather embryonic way. An

22 See J. Champion, *The pillars of priestcraft: the Church of England and its enemies 1660–1730* (Cambridge, 1992).

overlooked genre is the account of the congregation, schisms within it, and expulsions of members: a kind of published Church book. Here, an interesting early example is Robert Browne's *A true and short declaration, both of the gathering and Ioyning together of certaine persons: and also of the lamentable breach and division which fell amongst them* (Netherlands, ?1583[23]), an account of the breach between Robert Harrison and Browne concerning their separatist congregation in Middelburg. The tract is marred by poor presswork (a poor impression with few 'w's and odd 'f's in the font); wild spelling suggests that the compositor was probably someone who did not usually set English-language texts. The unique surviving copy with three quarto gatherings seems to be incomplete because Harrison (who had previously funded the publications of this congregation) refused to provide financial support, just as he tried to prevent the sale of other books by Browne.[24]

At the same time, and despite their remarkable use of print, the Family of Love reserved the ultimate statement of their truth for manuscript books made and kept in Holland. Nevertheless the Familists are remarkable for the way in which their beliefs spread through print (most importantly the printed prophecies of Hendrik Niclaes), giving the group a presence in the public eye out of all proportion to their number.[25] Familists habitually simulated the local established religion, hiding themselves amongst the orthodox. This resulted in Familist symbology and prophecy being hidden in relatively unremarkable works such as standard emblem books.[26] Not only did Familist books facilitate the rapid spread of Niclaes's beliefs, they also ensured the survival of Niclaes's message into the seventeenth century long after the Family of Love as an organized group had disappeared. In consequence, Niclaes's works were not only discussed by later theological luminaries like Henry More, they also played an important role in the eventual formation of late-seventeenth and early eighteenth-century mystical piety.[27]

The sixteenth-century Familist books were printed abroad, frequently with false imprints, and brought to England by travelling merchants and artisans. The importance of Continental presses (particularly those of Amsterdam) for English non-conformity should never be underestimated. A tolerant government made the United Provinces a home for Puritan and separatist

23 *STC* 23910.5.

24 *The writings of Robert Harrison and Robert Browne*, eds. A. Peel and L. H. Carlson (London, 1953), p. 396.

25 See Hamilton 1981 and Marsh 1994, esp. pp. 79–85.

26 See Wootton 2001.

27 See Marsh 1994, ch. 9; N. Smith 1989, ch. 4; D. P. Walker, *The decline of Hell: seventeenth century discusssions of eternal torment* (London, 1964), p. 124; B. J. Gibbons, *Gender in mystical and occult thought. Behmenism and its development in England* (Cambridge, 1996), ch. 8.

congregations, and the presence of an advanced printing industry made possible the safe and plentiful production of radical Puritan books.[28] The ease with which English titles, offensive to the bishops, confiscated and burned at home, could be found in Amsterdam bookshops is well attested.[29]

Niclaes's writings themselves are an extreme representative of the major features of non-conformist published discourse in this period. Niclaes believed that all forms of educated discourse, in so far as they addressed matters divine, were futile. Inspired prophecy was what mattered, and his own writings, strange enough in low German, were translated quite literally into English. To some contemporaries, they must have appeared not merely unusual, but incomprehensible, like another language entirely. Prophetic discourse was to become the distinguishing feature of mid-seventeenth-century religious radicalism, but Niclaes was not its originator. Native prophetic writing had played a vital role in English Reformation propaganda: its continuing presence as a force for further religious reform was a distinguishing mark of the Puritan who wished to reform the national Church from within. Thus religious disputes of the later-sixteenth century were in part a battle over the possession of prophetic language; after all, one form of it had been successfully appropriated for the national Church in the most widely circulated text after the Bible, John Foxe's *Actes and monuments of the English martyrs* (*STC* 11222–28). In this context, a striking precursor of the individual prophets of the mid-seventeenth century was Lady Eleanor Davies, whose early pamphlets of 1625 and 1633[30] (later followed by a large corpus of short pamphlet works) altered the gender conventions of the English language as they predicted with uncanny accuracy a number of national events, and framed an alternative apocalyptic trajectory for herself, her family, the monarchy and the nation.[31]

For the very reason that prophecy was so central to the expression of the different varieties of English Protestantism,[32] we should note that the most successful and notorious act of subversive dissent in the sixteenth century took its rhetorical lead not from the prophetic tradition, but from learned humanism and its tradition of foolish wit. The Marprelate tracts disputed Church discipline, but did so by ridicule, making bishops the targets of humour derived from contemporary jestbooks. Part of the outrageousness of Marprelate was precisely in his use of hilarious insult, a mode of religious controversy hitherto confined to learned disputes. But Marprelate gained a very wide circulation, exploiting a readership, particularly in the capital, which appreciated irreverent

28 See Sprunger 1994. 29 Sprunger 1994; Alblas 1987; Hoftijzer below, p. 739.
30 *STC* 903.5–4.5. 31 See Hindle 1935–8; see further Cope 1992; E. Davies 1995; Watt 1997.
32 See above, pp. 42–4.

jocularity, precisely the mode adopted by the newsbook writers of the Civil War and Interregnum. A stereotype of the religious radical as the half-literate artisan still prevails. Yet the college study and library (especially in Cambridge) was as much a home for non-conformity as the printshop and the cooper's yard. It was through the meeting of the two communities that non-conformity began to take its shape.

2 1625–1660

Marprelate was remembered through the first forty years of the new century even though the form of Church government he defended, Presbyterianism, had been effectively extirpated in England. This points to the survival of the Marprelate tracts inside separatist circles. When the breakdown of ecclesiastical and print censorship came after the abolition of the Court of High Commission on 11 July 1641, some Marprelate tracts were republished, and the Marprelate identity was appropriated in new works.[33] In the Restoration, Marprelate was seen as the father of a particular kind of Puritan satire, a tradition which had formed the backbone for the radicals of the 1640s, giving them a language of critical attack and dissent when they were poised between religious and political modes of understanding, even though its outright use of calumny continued to offend many godly people.

The development of political publishing for radical Puritans, and eventually political radicals, was in part a consequence of the failure of a victorious Parliament to deliver the religious toleration radicals desired. The learned separatists had formulated a response to toleration, and on the matter of obedience to the magistrate, before 1640. Robert Parker's *De politeia ecclesiastica* (Frankfurt, 1616), an extensive work, circulated in manuscript, in English translation.[34] However, the politics of the 1640s, and in particular, Parliament's decision to justify itself in print, created a context in which pamphleteering became a crucial element in popular politics. Once the New Model Army, a seedbed for radical religious sentiment, found itself in dispute with Parliament, the acquisition of a printing press was vital. Likewise, the religious radicals who launched themselves as a kind of popular political party (the Levellers) formulated an identity through the printed word – the currency that united their meetings.[35] By the time of the Putney and Whitehall Debates in 1647 and

33 Mostly the work of Richard Overton. See Wing O620, 622, 628, 630 and 638 (1645–46).

34 See Bodleian MS. Eng. th. e. 158; the translation is dated 'Finis 1634' at the end of the text, but also '1618, 2 Sep.'.

35 See N. Smith 1994, pp. 130–43; see also Freist 1997, Lindley 1997.

1648, a sophisticated political awareness was shared between grandees, officers and delegated troopers, no longer limited to scriptural interpretation alone. It was the result of the rapid growth of print culture. As the 1650s drew on, the use of printed books by radicals was even more noticeable.

The measure of Leveller print innovation was in the frustration experienced at the inefficacy of the petition, the traditional means for those from outside the political nation to have their grievances addressed. Printed petitions formed an important part of the popular politics of the 1640s: famous gatherings of crowds at Westminster presented petitions to Parliament – including groups of women. However, the decision of Parliament in 1647 not to accept a petition from Lilburne, because it had been redefined by them as a 'declaration', marked the beginning of Leveller pamphlet campaigns in earnest. Thereafter, the petition, printed or otherwise, was no longer a traditional means of communication between different parts of the social order. It became one kind of printed propaganda among many.

Petitioning was correctly viewed by Parliament as a way of gathering a crowd: it was therefore in itself a treasonable device. It was also, in its printed form, one further example of the way in which printed material became part of the iconography of popular protest in these years. Here, the most striking example was the wearing of petitions, covenants, and ultimately the Agreement of the People, by soldiers in their hatbands.

In these pamphlets, any instance that made up the life of the godly community of households, and which showed that community under stress, was represented in narrative form, thereby turning life into propaganda. As Ann Hughes has shown, in the case of the Lilburnes (it can be extended to other Levellers) this involved gender relations and the politics of the household.[36] I have argued elsewhere that this eventually put the Levellers out on a limb: once divorced from their support in the gathered Churches during the course of 1649, they were left in a 'naked space' – a pamphleteering movement with little or no support in its originating institutions.[37] At the same time, print enabled the Levellers to take lengthy legal materials, far beyond the capacity of any one person to copy, and to publish them, once interpreted in a Leveller light.

Most of the prominent Levellers had some intimate connection with the book trade: John Lilburne had been apprenticed to a printer, Richard Overton belonged to a printing family, William Larner was a bookseller. Edward Sexby was an experienced distributor of surreptitious tracts, and also practised

36 Hughes 1995, pp. 162–88. 37 Smith forthcoming; see further, Zaret 2000.

at conveying copy from imprisoned pamphleteers to printers.[38] Since the freedom to publish was one of the rights for which the Levellers campaigned, their publications often reflect intimately on the business of tract production and circulation, and its sometimes violent interruption:

> And we three were together in a Chamber discoursing, he and I intending about our business immediately to go abroad, and hearing them knock, I said, Yonder are they come for me. Whereupon, some books that lay upon the table in the room, were thrown into the beds betwixt the sheets (and the books were all the persons he found there in the beds, except that he took us for printed papers, and then there were many). . . .[39]

This was to take to an extreme the print symbolism that had already occurred in Civil War action, as we have seen. By printing a woodcut of himself with a copy of Coke's *Institutes*, speaking in his own defence at his trial, Lilburne was exemplary in using the full potential of the printed book to defend the 'freeborn Englishman's' right to buy books and read them as well as to speak freely. Leveller politics, it has been said, focus upon the treatment of information and speech acts. At their heart was also the book act.[40]

Looking back in 1669, a former army radical and republican, John Streater, could claim that it was: 'almost impossible for a Prince to rule the spirits and wills of his Subjects (since Printing came in Use) without restraining the Presse, which so evidently influences them to Evil and Good'.[41] Streater's interesting and contentious career as a popular republican activist in the 1650s (he reprinted Sexby's famous call for the assassination of Cromwell, *Killing noe murder*, 1657,[42]), and his innovative uses of print (notably his fusion of high political theory with the newsbook) are proof of the continuing hold of Leveller discoveries of print practice.[43]

At the same time, the literary life of gathered Churches and individual religious radicals flourished in an atmosphere of relative freedom, and against a background of growing diversity of confession. The confessional narrative finally came of age. In the fifteen years before 1640 there are a very few examples of narratives formally delivered, alongside a confession of faith, in

38 See J. Holstun, *'Ehud's dagger': class struggle in the English revolution* (London, 2000), ch. 8.

39 Overton, *The picture of the Counsel of State* (1649) (Wing L2154) cited Morton 1975, pp. 200–1. See further N. Smith 1994, pp. 297–304.

40 N. Smith 1994, pp. 131–48.

41 *The King's Grant of Privilege for sole-printing common-law-books, defended* (1669), p. 16. (Wing A4133).

42 Wing T1310. The tract is listed under its signatory, Silas Titus; Sexby was and is supposed to be the real author.

43 See N. Smith 1995b, pp. 137–55; Johns 1998, ch. 4.

an Independent congregation, as a condition of Church membership.[44] These examples are so obscure they have only just come to light; they are documents intended for the privacy of a particular congregation, perhaps even for a single household.[45] In the early 1650s, after the 'triumph of the saints', collections of published confessional narratives became a fashionable way of demonstrating the collective sainthood of a particular Church. No longer private, they had become highly public and part of the religious politics of the Commonwealth.[46]

The Independents were tightly organized, with a clear ecclesiology (indeed, published designs for the gathered Church represent a substantial proportion of their publications).[47] They involved Church members in acts of authorship that were also parts of worship. Other kinds of ecclesiology were more open-ended: the General Baptists encouraged lengthy theological disputes at their meetings. They are rightly seen as the source of much heretical theology in the mid-seventeenth century. Levellers wrote one way with regard to directed political campaigns: those of them who were General Baptists also produced highly original, recognizably 'free-thinking' texts, only some of which were published in print. We have little evidence of their existence as manuscript copies, but we can sometimes glimpse the co-existence of manuscript and print in troubled circumstances, as in this report by Richard Overton:

> he having ransack'd the house, found many book in the beds, and taken away all such writings, papers, and books, of what sort or kind soever, that he could finde, and given them to the souldiers, amongst which he took away certain papers which were my former Meditations upon the works of the Creation, intituled, *Gods Word confirmed by his Works*; wherein I endeavoured the probation of a God, a Creation, a State of Innocencie, a Fall, a Resurrection, a Restorer, a Day of Judgement, &c. barely from the consideration of things visible and created: and these papers I reserved to perfect and publish as soon as I could have any rest from the turmoils of this troubled Commonwealth.[48]

Inspired or 'gifted' prophetic performances were certainly part of the politics of the mid-century, and they found their way into print. Most famously, the

44 O. Watkins, *The Puritan Experience* (London, 1972), chs. 2–6; Caldwell 1983; Cohen 1986; N. Smith 1989, chs. 1–2.

45 See John Rylands Library, MS. 875, Rose Thurgood, 'A lecture of repentance', *The conversion narrative of Cecily Johnson of Colchester*, ed. Jeremy Maule (forthcoming). For an associated confessional document, significantly written in the Bermudas in 1639–40, see Norwood 1945.

46 See, for example, Henry Walker, *Spirituall experiences, of sundry beleevers* (1653) (Wing W387); John Rogers, *Ohel or Beth-Shemesh. A tabernacle for the sun* (1653) (Wing R1813); Samuel Petto, *The voice of the spirit* (1654) (Wing P1903).

47 See, for example, William Bartlet, *'Ikonographia; or a modell of the primitive congregationall way* (1647) (Wing B986); John Cotton, *The true constitution of a particular visible Church* (1642) (Wing C6468); see further G. F. Nuttall, *Visible saints: the congregational way, 1640–1660* (Oxford, 1957).

48 Overton 1649, p. 202.

recorded prophecies of women, such as Anna Trapnel, whose presence, and publications, were a focus for resistance to the Protectorate.[49] The publishing history of Trapnel's writings is still uncertainly known. Only one incomplete copy of a large body of prophetic verse survives.[50] This book points not merely to prose prophecy, and a kind of experiential narrative turned to political ends, but also the more quintessential qualities of dissenting women's culture being put to public use.

The high point of radical prophecy was at mid-century during the early days of the Commonwealth, and prophets unattached to a particular congregation voiced themselves in imitation of Old Testament prophets on the printed page. The Ranter Abiezer Coppe's writings exemplify the measure of the change wrought since the days of Marprelate. Coppe too used the rhetoric of folly to envision an alternative to selfish religious hypocrisy, and he assumed the persona of the prophet Ezekiel to do so. We should not be surprised, given his grammar-school and university education, to find him quoting classical texts occasionally too. But where Marprelate uses humanism as a vehicle for a spectacular kind of satirical attack, Coppe dismantles the very education system in the form of the grammar book (specifically those of William Lily) as his tracts proceed. He understood that the true opening to the free spirit had to be through a fundamental shift in the way in which literacy was achieved.[51] Accordingly, the tracts of the mid-century prophets created a new language that they claimed was untainted, Adamic, perfected: it could supply its readers as well as its authors with a totally liberated form of subjectivity. This was the case with the exotic writings of the prophet Thomas Tany (*fl.* 1649–55). The prophetic typography of the tracts and the associated woodcuts are striking enough, but there is further evidence of tracts copied by Tany's small band of followers in which the appearance of the printed version is exceeded in an almost incandescent writing that begins to look like the writing in William Blake's prophetic paintings.[52]

A new language was certainly the intention and the impression created by the tracts of the most successful radical religious group of the Commonwealth – the Quakers. Quaker pamphleteering grew into a stunningly successful form of proselytization, with a sophisticated infrastructure of production from more

49 Wing T2031–35. On Trapnel see H. Hinds, *God's Englishwomen: seventeenth century sectarian writing and feminist criticism* (Manchester, 1996) and *The cry of a stone*, ed. H. Hinds (Tempe, AZ, 2000).

50 Bodleian Library, s.m. s. 1. 42. Th. (lacking title page, published 1658?).

51 McDowell 1997.

52 University of Southampton, Hartley Library, Cecil Roth Papers, JSPER/R/11. The most substantial work on Tany is now Hessayon 1996. Tany's tracts are listed in Wing, T152A–158B, though T158A is by Tany's follower, William Finch.

than one press in different locations (to avoid the dangers of censorship), and with a deliberate strategy. Tracts were distributed in advance of the arrival of a particular Quaker speaker, making a trail across the country: in the wake of the tract would come the living text of the Quaker prophet.[53] In some ways, this phenomenon was a continuation and rationalization of more makeshift habits employed by earlier sectaries. Ranters seem to have carried London printed tracts with them for local distribution: their first or only impact appears to have been provincial.[54] The Muggletonians used the tract form to print letters (often of denunciation and damnation) designed to sustain the prophetic authority of their two leaders, Lodowick Muggleton and John Reeve. Many of their tracts were missed by the most avid book collectors in London even though they were specifically designed for circulation in the capital rather than the provinces.

The religious life of local communities in the late 1640s and the 1650s was accordingly marked by intense verbal battles between local incumbents (usually of a less extreme Puritan hue) and sectaries. Local communities often resented intruded ministers, who were forced to drum up popular support, and disputations with radicals were a means of achieving this end. A Baptist like John Bunyan found himself debating with both orthodox ministers and Quakers. Whereas university-trained clergy were used to the learned and highly formal conventions of debate (which had enjoyed a long vogue in Reformation Europe), the untrained radicals spoke in a way which was often incomprehensible to the educated.[55] Dispute became a colourful theatre of verbal gesture, with meaning mutually missed on all sides; it is in this context that the extensive sectarian attack on university education belongs.[56] When accounts of disputes were penned after the event, the orthodox resorted to their dialectical training, while the radicals had recourse to an uncomplicated narrative. This was derived, it has been argued, from oral forms of story telling, and the basic narrative machinery of the English Reformation: Foxean martyrology.[57] We might expect this information to belong to the history of oral culture, but these battles of the tongue were intimately involved with published materials – often the dispute was caused by a circulated pamphlet. The printed text, as much as the spoken word, was an integral part of a social drama. When Thomas Edwards was introducing his *Gangraena* in 1646, he took special care to indicate that printed books were, alongside the sermon and the disputative meeting, the means by which the radicals had their say in an amplified way.

53 See Peters 1995. 54 For instance, Thomason did not acquire all of Coppe's writings.
55 See Hughes 1990. 56 See Greaves 1969.
57 See Hughes 1990, p. 46; N. Smith 1994, pp. 130–42; see also Knott 1993, chs. 4–7.

Others made no apparent distinction between the oral and the written, as if they belonged in the same category. With the ascendency of the godly during the Interregnum, those in particular favour with the governments tended to have the advantage of the most powerful means of print representation. The Independent minister Henry Walker, who had been an important propagandist during the Civil War, consolidated his place among newsbook writers. Conversely, suspicion of print innovation remained visible in other spheres: the early Quakers resented Walker's attacks in particular. John Pennyman burned newsbooks in the Restoration.

It may seem that the contents of the debates – predestination versus free will or perfectibility; the nature of the body of Christ, and so on – had little to do with the form the debates took, in speech or writing. However, when the radicals began to challenge the status of the Bible, or human language, or any other kind of symbol, they put a premium on the medium as well as the message. Seeker and Quaker versions of the inner light made the body a 'text', an interpretable scripture that was superior to the Bible. The human body became an allegory of the Spirit's working, and forged a new relationship between the inspired prophet and the printed text.[58]

No one could doubt the intense messianism of the Quaker tract, registered most obviously in violent, apocalyptic language, and continuous with what we are able to learn of Quaker extempore preaching habits. But this should not be allowed to distort the fact that such language was but one kind of rhetoric. Many tracts were presented as letters (in imitation of a Pauline epistle), but there were many other unprinted letters sent between friends in which the living spirit, for which the Society of Friends became known, was evident. To this extent, the Quakers were realizing through their different forms of speech act a kind of community or communism of communication that had been the linguistic ideal of the scientific reformers sympathetic to the Commonwealth.[59] Indeed, what the Quakers were achieving seems to have been noticed by some of the Hartlibians. The Quakers produced a variety of writings on social themes, including social reform, concerns that border on utopianism. Seen as an aspect of a community of speech, these ideas on social organization may be regarded as part of a truly integrated communitarian vision, articulated by and embodied in the godly language of the pamphlet. In this way, the Quakers bridged the gap between the claims of prophecy and those of Christian fellowship.

58 See Smith 1990, 1995a. 59 See Hazelton 1997 and 2000.

3 1660–1695: Restoration dissent

Protestant dissent was finally excluded from established institutions by the restoration of the Church of England in 1660 and the ejection in 1662 of all ministers who refused to accept the established Church. Restoration dissenters were subject to a good deal of violent persecution. Most Churches consolidated themselves with institutional reviews, while the Quakers, remarkably, subjected themselves to a series of organizational regulations. Enthusiasm was contained. It was during this period that the first extensive histories of particular non-conformist congregations were begun,[60] and, partly for the sake of inculcating an impression of respectability, most dissenting Churches supported folio editions of the works of their more prominent members,[61] in imitation of the large format volumes containing the works of Anglicans, like Jeremy Taylor. The complicated process by which George Fox's *Journal* eventually emerged as folio text in 1694 had begun with a series of crude dictations in 1663.

But the major task was the sustaining of edification through print in the face of a hostile establishment and a State censor, the Surveyor of the Press, Sir Roger L'Estrange. Although L'Estrange could not function without the help of the Stationers' Company, when he found a target, he was brutal. For this reason, those who had been in positions of authority during the Commonwealth, when they sought to control the press, now tended to make common cause, or to appear to take up the positions, of the mid-century radicals. The freeborn Englishman was recast as the persecuted dissenter. Where the Levellers of the 1640s and the popular republicans of the 1650s had found the theatre of the trial, and its printed representation, a corridor into the language of rights, franchise reform and new constitutions, the dissenters were forced back into this earlier mode by the hostility of successive Restoration administrations. The brief and compressed pamphlets produced by erstwhile supporters of the Commonwealth in the 1660s were direct extensions and continuations of the skills, strategies and techniques learned in the previous two decades.[62] The references in so many early Restorations tracts to biblical instances of suffering suggests the very careful construction of a readership used to discerning coded messages from other godly people under duress. While the printed publication of letters in the 1650s had played a role in the establishment of identity between sects,

60 Edward Terrill's history of the Broadmead Baptist Church was begun in 1672: see Underhill 1847.
61 This was especially so of the Quakers: see William Bayly, *A collection of the several wrightings of William Bayly* (1676) (Wing B1517).
62 See, for example, anon., *The valley of Achor* (1660) (Wing V49).

and prophetic authority within them, the 1660s saw the publication of huge numbers of letters as a means of mutual support. To this extent, the letter as a genre performed a function akin to the published trial or sufferings narrative. This was especially so of the Quakers.

Where the radicals had mastered the use of newsbooks in the 1640s, some brave journalists and publishers challenged L'Estrange during the Exclusion Crisis with newsbooks that sought to influence political events. When L'Estrange decided to produce a government response in newsbook form in 1681, the scene looked very much like the battles between Royalist and Parliamentarian newsbooks in the 1640s, or more closely, between *Mercurius politicus* and its precariously situated opponents during the Protectorate. Moments of crisis were felt throughout the seventeenth century as repetition, and especially as repetitions of the crisis of 1641. To this extent, it is appropriate that Andrew Marvell should have assumed the voice of Marprelate when attacking Bishop Parker in the name of toleration.[63] Ralph Wallis, who supplied his own jocular imprimatur to some of his tracts, fused popular verse and intimately domestic dialogue between a supposed husband and wife in order to attack the bishops. He is the true heir of the Leveller satirist Richard Overton. Although his tracts contain a sophisticated narrative and dialogue skill that could only have been produced after the journalistic innovations of the Civil War and Interregnum period, he looked back to an earlier fellow cobbler, Samuel How, who had famously attacked university learning in favour of the claims of inspiration by the Holy Spirit in 1640.[64] Wallis's works and activity provide evidence of the level of dissenting engagement in surreptitious and defamatory publication – it is greater than historians have usually allowed – but the actual use of calumny was still offensive to most dissenters. They would have approved of measures to repress it, much as they disliked the ostentatious and lewd morals of Restoration society.[65] Fear and disapproval of the press was a continuing theme among religious radicals during the period: as late as the 1680s, some Quakers still burned books as an absolute gesture against worldly corruption[66] (a seemingly more extreme gesture than the government, which burned only books deemed offensive to the régime), even though the Friends made such remarkable and effective use of the press.

In a connected way, although many dissenters simply ignored the licensing laws and published unlicensed tracts or circulated manuscripts surreptitiously,

63 See especially his *The rehearsall transpos'd, the Second part* (1673) (Wing M882–3), ed. D. I. B. Smith (Oxford, 1971).

64 [Ralph Wallis], *Room for the cobler of Gloucester* (1668) (Wing W619), pp. 20–1, 40.

65 See Keeble 1987, pp. 93–126. See also Weber 1996.

66 'Phil. Ang.' [John Pennyman], *A bright shining light* (1680) (Wing M1404), p. 8.

there was a kind of self-censorship that grew among less extreme dissenters, who preferred silence on a public issue if it did not, or if they thought it would not, pass the licensers. Others still developed forms of covert circulation – seventeenth-century mail-order services in effect, a feature of Interregnum book publishing, but one that became essential for the survival of Puritanism and its emphasis upon the printed book during the Restoration. Nevertheless, Ralph Wallis flagrantly flouted the Licensing Act of 1662, the authority of the bishops and the government (and in particular L'Estrange), by printing and openly selling books in Gloucester.[67]

From the 1650s onwards, extreme Puritans, republicans and Commonwealthmen were satirized by a genre that listed titles of the books they produced and read. Some of those listed were genuine; others of course were fictitious exaggerations. The satirists were acknowledging the distinctness of Puritan book culture even before the Restoration settlement forced nonconformity to become a distinct culture by a series of legal exclusions. While any contemporary observer would have seen Puritan book culture exemplified in mainstream figures such as Richard Baxter, it is also the case that the radicals too promulgated a canon of printed works through which they claimed the Holy Spirit worked. Robert Rich, the merchant, emigrant to Barbados, and sometime disciple of James Nayler, recommended a large collection of works surprising for its ecumenical reach, from Seekers and Quakers to Roman Catholics and ancient stoics.[68] A very similar set of texts may be found in library catalogues and commonplace books assembled in the mid- and later seventeenth century. By the 1680s, the flimsy pamphlets and uncertain distribution which had characterized separatist publications (apart from a few exceptions like Henry Ainsworth's scriptural commentaries) had been replaced by a diverse, richly variegated field. Yet protest, controversy and surreptitious publication had not disappeared, and the legacy stretching back into the sixteenth century was plain to many dissenters: it showed in their writing, and framed their expectations.

The settlement of 1689 offered some mitigation of the harsh persecution of dissenters, so that when the Licensing Act was allowed to lapse in 1695, it was harder to recognize the predicament of Martin Marprelate, or John Lilburne, in the identities of contemporary dissenters. The non-conformists toned down their act, and when they took elements of their incendiary traditions into the new age, these were refashioned for a new context. Swift may have belittled

67 See *CSPD 1664–5*, pp. 309–10; see further, Keeble 1987, pp. 105–8.

68 Robert Rich, *Love without dissimulation* (1666/7) (Wing R1361), pp. 6–7; *Epistles* (1680) (Wing R1356), p. 11; *Mr Robert Rich his second letters* (1679) (Wing R1362), p. 24.

the sectaries, ridiculing their religion by suggesting that it was the product of misplaced *libido*, while simultaneously satirizing commercial publishing. Either he missed the point, or he saw it only too well: the radicals, first in worship, then in politics, had used some kinds of printed book to generate a capitalism of speech, and a democracy of the spirit, that worked against traditional forms of religious and political authority. In doing so, they bequeathed to posterity a rich literature, and a number of crucial watersheds in the history of publishing, censorship and press freedom.

20

Women writing and women written

MAUREEN BELL

Literary historians, and in particular feminist literary historians, have in recent years turned their attention to the early modern period in order to track the emergence of women writers into print and to posit a burgeoning market in 'female literature'.[1] Print's implication in the development of new literacies, particularly in the context of political and religious upheaval, is discussed elsewhere in this volume by Nigel Smith; here, the focus is on one of those many voices apparently empowered by print. I argue that existing narratives of the relationship between women and printed text in this period would benefit from a historicism sensitive to the material contexts of printing and publishing.

An enquiry of this kind is concerned not only with 'woman' as historical/biological agent but with 'woman' as sign. It must look not only to the relationship between the terms 'woman' and 'writer' but must also consider 'woman' as subject-matter for and in print. Prefatory addresses to women dedicatees, to individual women readers and exhortations to women as interest-groups, for example, may be construed as evidence of intended readers (or at least of intended *owners* or recipients); equally, however, they might be read as part of a rhetorical strategy in which 'woman' became a marketing device. There already exist several well-established contexts for the discussion of women's writing and writing about women in this period: in particular those of feminist literary history; the study of subjectivity; and the variety of theoretical approaches to gender. The value of using the history of the book as the framework for discussion is that it grounds the question of the relationship of woman and printed text in a historicism which offers a multidimensional approach.[2] Specifically, such an approach situates both women as writers and women as written in the context of the operations of the book trade, allowing women writers to be seen in relation to the intermediaries between writing and print

1 For accounts of women's writing see, for example, Hobby 1988 and Crawford 1985; for 'female literature', see Hull 1988.

2 Darnton 1982; McDonald 1997.

(transcriber, amanuensis, editor, printer, bookseller) and in relation to a growing market for books *about* women; taking into account the role of women in the material production of print (as printers, publisher/booksellers, binders, mercuries, hawkers); and bringing into view the evidence for women as consumers of print (buying, owning and using books).

Women writing

To judge the extent of women's writing on the basis of extant printed texts is inevitably misleading in a period when scribal publication was prevalent and, for both men and women, often the preferred means of circulating their work.[3] Both Love and Woudhuysen present illuminating examples of women's engagement in manuscript circulation, and in the making of verse miscellanies in particular, but the necessary detailed editorial work on establishing texts by individual women writers is still in its early stages.[4] It is indicative of the distance yet to be travelled that in the first two volumes of Beal's *Index of English literary manuscripts* only two female authors, Aphra Behn and Katherine Philips, are included.[5] The differences between these two writers in their uses of manuscript are, indeed, instructive: while, for example, 'Astrea's Booke for Songs & Satyrs', written in a variety of professional hands, suggests 'a retained, "inhouse" product of a scriptorium rather than a formal compilation actually prepared on commission for delivering to someone', the manuscript evidence for Philips suggests that her 'poems were written for limited and controlled circulation and not intended for publication'.[6] Much more cataloguing of manuscripts at this level of detail, however, is needed before a systematic survey of women's manuscript publication can be attempted. What follows, therefore, is necessarily (and narrowly) a discussion of women and *print* rather than women and *text*.

Identifying printed texts by women is not a simple matter of checking names on title pages: women's texts are frequently hidden by their mode of

3 A point made in Bell, Parfitt and Shepherd 1990, pp. xii–xvi and forcefully argued by M. J. M. Ezell (Ezell 1993).

4 On scribal publication by women, see Love 1993, pp. 54–8; Woudhuysen 1996, p. 13, notes that 'Women in particular found the use of manuscript to their advantage' and in part I gives several examples of women as dedicatees, recipients and compilers of verse miscellanies. See also Marotti 1995, pp. 48–61; and Ezell 1987, ch. 3 and *passim*.

5 *IELM*, I (1450–1625) contains no female authors. The preface to volume II (1625–1700) indicates that the principles for selection for 'a catalogue of the surviving manuscripts of those works which are accepted as constituting English literature' were established in 1974; it is presumably unlikely that were the work being planned now, such figures as Mary Sidney and Margaret Cavendish could be excluded.

6 Bodleian, Firth MS. c.16 (*IELM* BeA 18); *IELM*, II. 1, pp. 3, 133.

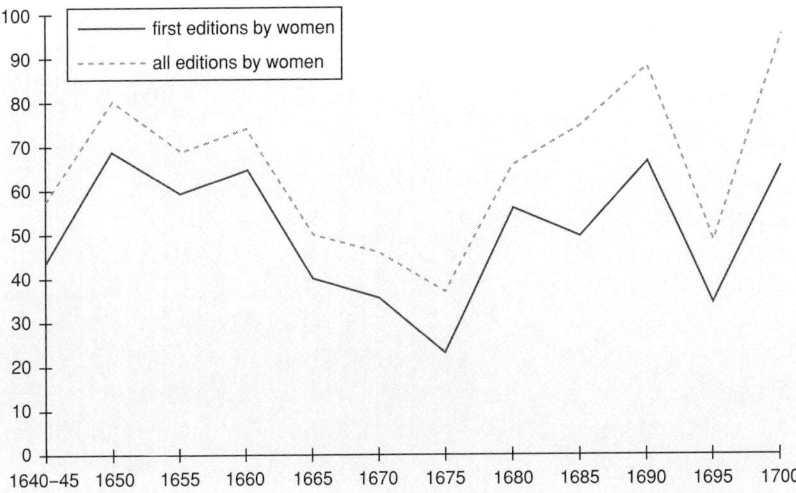

Figure 20.1 Publications by women by half-decade, 1640–1700

presentation or by their being embedded in a work with multiple authors and parts. There are many examples of such texts, especially among sectarian groups: Sarah Wight's words, spoken during a period of sustained fasting and recorded by her minister, Henry Jessey, were published in *his* text (*The exceeding riches of grace...*) and consequently she disappears, bibliographically, from view; many Quaker texts are catalogued as if written by one or two authors when in fact they contain testimonies or accounts by many more.[7] Of the 867 printed texts by women (651 first editions) identified by Crawford as published between 1600 and 1700, the vast majority occurred after 1640: indeed, only 6.5 per cent of first editions by women (and 9.1 per cent of all editions by women) were published before 1640. Of all the women known to have been writing between those dates, only about 10 per cent reached print before 1640.[8] Even after the 1640s, when the numbers of women in print began to increase significantly, still only between a half and one per cent of all printed titles were by women authors (see fig. 20.1).[9]

7 Wing J687, J688 (1647) J689, J690 (1648) and four later editions; for many Quaker examples, see Foxton 1994.

8 Figures here and in the following graphs are based on Crawford 1985. Crawford does not take account of many 'hidden' texts and consequently underestimates the extent of women's publication in the period.

9 Hobby 1988; Crawford estimates women's writing to constitute 0.5 per cent of all publications 1600–40 and 1.2 per cent of all publications 1640–1700 (Crawford 1985).

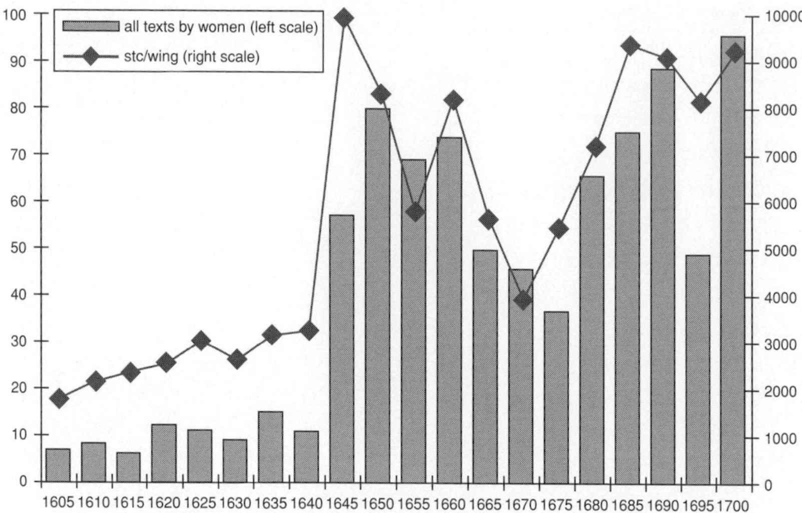

Figure 20.2 Women's published writing/all publications

Women's printed texts covered a vast range of genres and subjects: translations, saints' lives, polemic, advice, household skills, religious debate, meditation, prophecy, petitions, biography, letters and appeals as well as poetry, plays and prose fiction. In some respects the growth in published writing by women seems to have paralleled the wider development of printing (see fig. 20.2). After 1640, for example, both male and female authors below the status of gentry became more visible in print as the political and religious engagement of tradespersons and artisans (seen, for example, in the sects of the Civil War period) involved them in public actions and debates of which polemical writing formed one manifestation. So great is the variety of kinds of writing produced by women that it is reasonable to question the extent to which women writers can be seen as a 'group' at all: arguably their primary identifications and alliances were to do with class or religious/political positions, rather than gender.[10] When a group of women seem to have shared occasions, forms, tropes and motivations for writing (for example, Quaker women in the 1650s and 1660s) their collaborative writing was produced in a specific sectarian context in which the spiritual equality of male and female was a central religious tenet frequently expressed through direct action and confrontation with Church and State.

10 See, for example, Jones 1990, p. 6.

Where, then, does that leave the idea of the female author in this period? Seen through the lens of a feminist theory based on nineteenth-century literature, the seventeenth-century female author is a chimera: an effect of inappropriate and anachronistic categorization. It can be argued, however, that the idea of authorship – being transformed and forged anew in the long transition from manuscript to print – was itself a gendered concept in the early modern period. Jonathan Goldberg has demonstrated that the handwriting manuals of the sixteenth century presented the act of writing as sexualized, so that writing suggests 'feminization even as it founds the privileged male subject'.[11] Wendy Wall has argued that the Renaissance construction of the author as male in non-dramatic works printed between 1557 and 1621 is an assertion against the implicit feminization of being 'imprinted' or 'pressed'.[12] Many such examples of the sexualization of printing and publication can be found throughout the seventeenth century: the shame expressed by Margaret Cavendish's female poet who insists on sending her work to be printed is that of a woman whose distress is akin to post-coital *pudeur*:

> *But now 'tis done, with griefe repent doe I,*
> *Hang down my* head *with* shame, blush sigh, *and* cry.
> Take pitty, *and my drooping* Spirits *raise,*
> *Wipe off my* teares *with* Handkerchiefes *of* Praise.[13]

Nor were such tropes confined to 'literary' writing. In 1664 Sergeant Morton, at the trial of the bookseller Thomas Brewster, expressed his view that 'Dispersing seditious books is very near a-kin to raising of tumults; they are as like as brother and sister: raising of tumults is the more masculine; and printing and dispersing seditious books, is the feminine part of every rebellion'.[14]

A female literature?

Suzanne Hull has identified an 'emerging female literature' in the period to 1640, using the evidence of the books themselves, and in particular dedications and prefatory addresses as well as subject matter, to infer a female market (fig. 20.3).[15] Of her main sample of 163 titles, 20 per cent are translations into English. More than half (52 per cent) are practical guides (advice on education,

11 Goldberg 1990, p. 99.
12 Wall 1993, pp. 2, 4 and *passim*. See Ferguson 1996 for a useful survey of such arguments.
13 Margaret Cavendish, *Poems, and fancies* (London, 1653; repr. Menston, W. Yorks., 1972).
14 T. B. Howell, *A complete collection of state trials and proceedings for high treason and other crimes and misdemeanors*, 34 vols. (London, 1816–28), VI, col. 521.
15 Hull 1988.

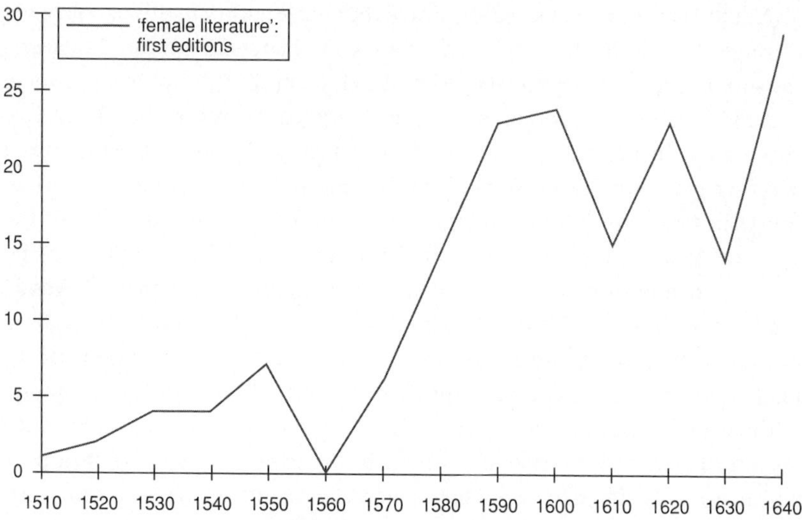

Figure 20.3 'Female literature' 1500–1640, by decade

housewifery, childbirth, cookery, medicine, needlework); about one quarter are categorized as recreational literature (romances, poetry and verse, jests, epigrams and female biography); and the remainder are equally divided between devotional works (prayer books, treatises, sermons, polemics, eulogies) and titles on the 'woman' controversy (satires, ballads, jests, defences of women). While, as she acknowledges, Hull's definitions exclude a number of types of book which, on the evidence of wills and diaries, were frequently owned and read by women (Bibles, herbals, music books, satires and plays *about* women, for example) her analysis points convincingly to a growing market from 1570 onwards (when 85 per cent of her sample were produced) and in particular demonstrates a rise in 'recreational' literature which confirms the estimates of Klotz and O'Dell for growing markets in literature and in prose fiction in the period after 1570.[16] Hull's corpus of 'female literature' includes very few books authored by women: of the nine women authors identified as writing ostensibly for women readers, three (Jane Anger, Ester Sowernam and Rachel Speght) were responding to attacks on women published by male authors, and two (Anger and Sowernam) were possibly pseudonyms for male writers.[17] Her supplementary list (of books which fail to meet Hull's specific criteria

16 Hull 1988, pp. 6, 74–5; Klotz 1937–8; O'Dell 1954.

17 The case for Anger as a woman writer is made in Shepherd 1985, pp. 30–1. Ferguson 1996, p. 152, points out that our concern with certainty on the subject is itself a potential hindrance to conceptualizing Renaissance ideas of gender and writing.

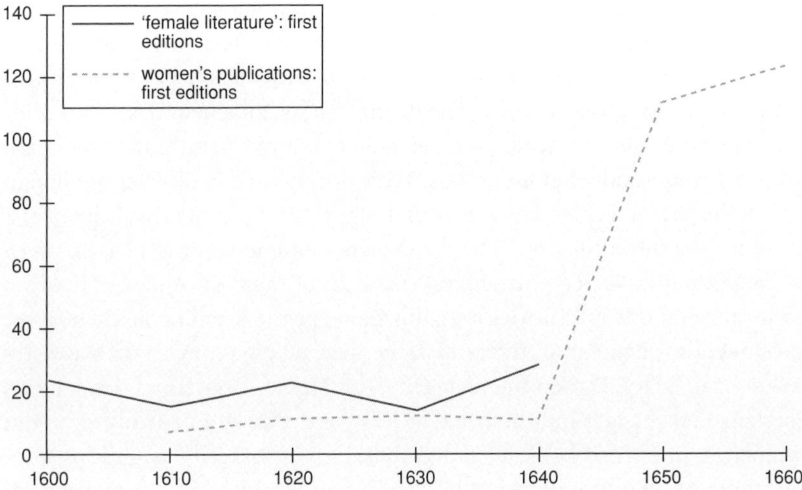

Figure 20.4 'Female literature' and women's publications 1600–1660, by decade

for 'female literature' but which have 'possible female associations') contains fourteen more texts by women, and if this list is allowed to enlarge Hull's corpus, the proportion of women writers publishing 'female literature' rises to about 8 per cent.[18]

Should printed texts by women be seen, therefore, as a sub-set of the developing market in 'female literature' as defined by Hull? Comparison of Crawford's data on texts by women with Hull's figures for 'female literature' suggests that in the period up to 1640 the increasing incidence in print of women-authored texts broadly followed the growth of 'female literature' (fig. 20.4).[19] But whereas Hull's 'female literature' emerged particularly in the period 1570–1600, the equivalent surge in women writers in print came from 1640. More detailed work needs to be done to quantify women-authored texts for the period as a whole, taking into account the hidden and embedded texts already mentioned, so as to test what currently seems a reasonable inference: that the increased interest in women-directed and women-related texts in general, observable from the 1570s, contributed to a climate in which increasing numbers of women (though still relatively few compared with the period after 1640)

18 Adding Hull's basic list of 163 to the 'Supplemental [sic] list' of 121 titles, plus a further five titles added in the reprint of 1988, brings the total to 289 first editions, of which twenty-four are, at least ostensibly, by women.

19 A rough count based on Bell, Parfitt and Shepherd 1990, supplemented by J. Todd, *A dictionary of British and American women writers 1660–1800* (London, 1987), matched with Hull's totals by decade. The data are necessarily imprecise: for example, Bell counts all editions whereas Hull lists only first editions. The comparison does no more than indicate likely trends.

came to be printed. Questions of agency, too, need to be answered: were women themselves encouraged by the publication of 'female literature' to see print as accessible to themselves as writers? Were men (husbands, widowers, editors, clergy), increasingly aware of a 'female market', encouraged to see into print those works by women which were already in limited manuscript circulation amongst family and religious groups? Were printers and booksellers willing to risk, perhaps as novelties, women-authored texts on the evidence of an interest in women as subject-matter? There is evidence – though as yet it has not been systematically collected – to suggest that each of these three parties (women as authors; men as intermediaries/editors; and printers and booksellers) were prominent as agents in different measure. Female pseudonyms such as Ester Sowernam, Mary Tattlewell, Joan Hit-Him-Home, Constantia Munda and (perhaps) Jane Anger indicate that, at least in the case of controversy about women, printers and booksellers were willing to market texts with pseudo-female voices, as well as those by biologically female authors like Rachel Speght, in order to sustain pamphlet controversies.[20] The rash of pseudo-petitions and spoofs on female parliaments appearing amongst the genuine women's petitions of the 1640s and 1650s may have been a similar phenomenon.[21]

There is no equivalent survey to Hull's for the period after 1640, so that while work on texts by women – much more plentiful in this part of the period – can be drawn on, any attempt at defining the 'female literature' remains impressionistic. Hull mentions in passing that one of the features of her pre-1641 corpus is that words like 'women', 'ladies' and 'maids' in titles became increasingly common in the early seventeenth century; and, now that electronic searching of Wing is possible, titles for the post-1640 period can be searched systematically for such terms.[22] The results of a chronological search of Wing for titles containing the words 'woman', 'women', 'lady', 'maid', 'girl', 'lass', 'wife', 'widow', 'miss or mistress', 'virgin', 'whore', female', 'femin-', 'daughter', 'sister', 'mother' and their variants can be compared with the data on women writers to indicate, at least, the broad picture for the latter part of the seventeenth century (fig. 20.5).[23] The incidence of these 'female' terms in titles rises steadily from the 1640s to the 1660s but the rate of increase in such titles is greater through the 1670s and 1680s than in previous decades; in the last decade of the century, however, there is a levelling off. Women-authored

20 See Shepherd 1985. 21 Bell, Parfitt and Shepherd 1990, pp. 263–4.
22 Hull 1988, p. 136.
23 The terms 'queen' and 'princess' were omitted since events such as coronations, deaths and births produced massive localized increases in the 1680s and 1690s. Again, this exercise is indicative rather than conclusive: there is, for example, some double counting (some titles have more than one 'female' term and Wing's use of date-ranges complicates counting by date).

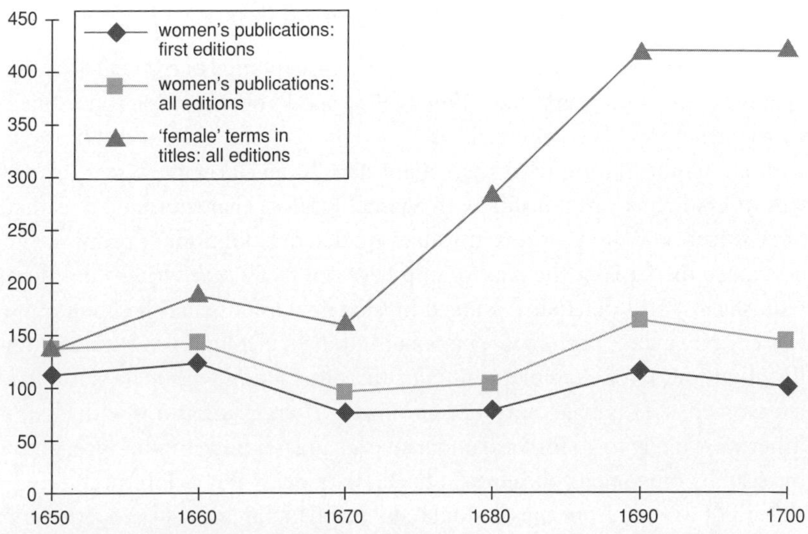

Figure 20.5 Women's publications and 'female' terms in titles 1641–1700, by decade

texts, on the other hand, show a less dramatic rate of increase across the period as a whole. There is a definite peak in women-authored texts in the 1650s (i.e. a rise from 1640s to 1650s, followed by a sharp decrease at 1660) indicating that while 'woman' as subject or addressee remained popular in titles throughout these decades, there was less of a market in works *by* women immediately after the Restoration. Since so many of the women-authored texts of the 1650s were petitions, addresses to Parliament, to Cromwell and other political leaders, and sectarian polemical works, it is perhaps not surprising that the Restoration was inimical to the publication of the very genres in which women had recently become prominent; at the same time Restoration culture can be argued to have fed, rather than damped down, the marketability of 'woman' as saleable commodity – in playhouse and brothel as well as in print. If, as was suggested in relation to the period to 1640, women's writing might be viewed as a slightly slower development of a wider market in 'female literature', then by the 1650s women's writing seems to have developed its own momentum, but one so closely allied to the specific religious and political sectarianism of the Interregnum that it falters at the Restoration. In other words, the elision of 'female literature' and women-authored literature which seemed a reasonable assumption for the earlier part of the period may be illusory: certainly from the 1650s onwards the production rates of the two diverge so as to suggest that they may be serving (or expressing) quite different social and political cultures.

Women as material producers

It is usual to characterize women as manipulated, exploited or controlled by the operations of a male book trade. Wendy Wall speaks of restrictions on women via the structures of power which 'informed the economy of book publication' without demonstrating what they might have been; Germaine Greer sexualizes Aphra Behn's relationship with Samuel Briscoe, characterizing it as that of prostitute and pimp, apparently unaware that exploitation for profit might have been the basis of the relationship between many *male* writers and their publishers.[24] It is generally assumed in such discussions that the book trade was entirely male – both in its personnel and in its ideological workings. Ann Rosalind Jones, for example, maintains that interaction with male stationers left women at a disadvantage: 'For a woman writer, negotiations with a publisher were likely to go forward under an even greater power imbalance, given the scarcity of women colleagues in the book trade'.[25] But to interpret the exclusion of women from the (undoubtedly male) hierarchies of the Stationers' Company as implying their absence from everyday involvement in the trade is to misunderstand its nature. In fact, since printing, binding and bookselling were domestic activities, women were a constant presence, working in the trade premises which were also their homes. It is ironic that even feminist literary critics have marginalized these women on the basis of an anachronistic view of women's status both within the family and within business.[26]

Women in the book trade were in fact neither 'scarce' nor passive. Of the more than 300 women identified as connected with the trade between 1557 and 1700, there may well have been some whose interest in the business was minimal and whose participation would therefore have been limited, but the everyday partnership of husband and wife in, for example, dividing responsibilities for shopkeeping or in the supervision of apprentices is well-documented. Most of the women so far identified in the London trade seem to have been involved in retail and distributive work (about 60 per cent), but women are found to have been composing and printing as well as bookselling and publishing, organizing the distribution of newspapers as mercury women and hawking papers and pamphlets on the streets. Within the records of the Stationers' Company, in the State Papers and in the proceedings of the House of Commons, the House of Lords and the courts of law they are recorded as buying, selling and assigning rights in copies; taking, transferring and freeing apprentices; arranging the

24 Wall 1993, p. 282; Greer 1995.

25 Jones 1990, p. 36; Ferguson 1996, p. 162, quotes Jones's remark uncritically.

26 Indeed, 'negotiations with a publisher' suggests an anachronistic view of the book trade itself: no separate role of 'publisher' existed in the seventeenth century.

printing of books and pirating other people's copies; being prosecuted, fined and imprisoned for illegal practices; entering into partnerships and congers; and controlling stock, workers and businesses in some cases for decades. Just over 75 per cent of those identified are known to have been the wives or widows of stationers and of those at least 20 per cent were also mothers or mothers-in-law of stationers.[27] The detailed work of reconstructing their careers, financial dealings and publishing programmes has only just begun. Several women printers, such as Anne Griffin, Gertrude Dawson, Mary Clark, Anne Maxwell, Tace Sowle and Elizabeth Flesher, ran businesses for at least ten years, some of them for much longer; only two (Tace Sowle and Mary Simmons) have so far been the object of extensive scholarly research.[28] Many independent women, usually widows, were also trading as booksellers and publishers for a decade or more: studies of, for example, Elizabeth Calvert and Hannah Allen offer grounds for inferring the women's hidden activity as wives and demonstrate the women's agency in developing the direction of the business once they take over.[29] Work on mercury women and hawkers shows the centrality of women in the developing newspaper trade of the Restoration period.[30] Our increasing awareness of the activity of women such as these throughout the period and at every level of the trade puts pressure on any neat gender division between female writer and male printer or bookseller.

Though the connections between women as writers and women as material producers of print await systematic exploration, the range and potential of such connections can be indicated here by some examples. Elinor James's prolific career as pamphleteer in support of James II and the established Church has a specific trade context, in that as the wife of a prosperous printer she had direct access to, and experience of, the business of printing and publishing. Her *Advice to all printers in general* attests her knowledge of the day-to-day running of the trade: 'I have been in the element of Printing above forty years, and I have a great love for it.' Remarks on her eccentricity by male contemporaries in the book trade such as John Dunton (who called her 'that She-State-Politician') and John Nichols (describing her as 'a very extraordinary character, a mixture of benevolence and madness') suggest that she was remarkable *not* because of being both 'woman' and 'writer', but rather because she transgressed the usual

27 Bell, 1996.

28 For Sowle, see McDowell 1998; for Simmons, see the reconstruction of the Simmons's family business (1635–78) in McKenzie 1980.

29 See Bell 1992, 1994b and 1989.

30 See Hunt 1984; McDowell 1998; M. Spufford, *The great reclothing of rural England: petty chapmen and their wares in the seventeenth century* (London, 1984) notes women peddlers and booksellers at fairs.

field of activity for a printer's wife by using her access to the printing press to publish her own words.[31] Similarly, women unconnected with the trade but known to have financed and arranged the printing and distribution of their own work (such as Lady Eleanor Davies and Margaret Cavendish) were considered eccentric or even mad by their contemporaries. Other women may have had a direct access to publication because of family connections with the trade. Mary Overton, whose petition to Parliament was published in 1647, was sister-in-law to Henry Overton, the radical bookseller–publisher, and was herself arrested for stitching copies of a seditious pamphlet.[32] Martha Simmonds, a Quaker writer and activist disowned by Fox for her part in supporting James Nayler, was the sister of Giles Calvert and sister-in-law of Elizabeth Calvert, prolific radical publishers at the sign of the Black Spread Eagle; she was also the wife of Thomas Simmonds whose bookshop at the Bull and Mouth was a centre for London Quakers. That she turned to the Calverts, rather than her husband, to publish her work may be an indication of the sectarian division which allied her more closely to the position of the Calverts than that of her husband; in any case, her own experience of the trade may have helped her to circumvent the Quakers' own informal control of their publications.[33] It is in particular in the context of sectarian publications that interconnections between women as writers and as publishers can be observed. Mary Westwood, whose biography remains obscure, appears to have published many Quaker tracts, particularly by Quakers in the south-west, between 1659 and 1663, among them several by women. She published petitions, tracts and epistles by Grace Barwick, Sarah Blackberry, Margaret Fell, Rebeckah Travers, Priscilla Cotton and Mary Cole, as well as the Quaker women's petition of 1659, *These several papers was sent to the Parliament* . . . , which was sold from the Calverts' shop.[34] Elizabeth Calvert's list of books for sale included works by women: Sarah Davy's *Heaven realize'd* and another (anonymous) conversion narrative by a woman, *Conversion exemplified*.[35] Hannah Allen, who after the death of her first husband, Benjamin, in 1646 ran their shop at the Crown in Pope's Head Alley, developed the business in the direction of radical Baptist, millenarian and republican literature and was the first to publish a number of authors who later became Fifth Monarchists. Not only did she publish and sell *Exceeding riches of grace* . . . , an account of Sarah Wight's fast and transcript of her divinely inspired words, but she is also named within the text itself as one of the visitors

31 Dunton 1705, p. 334; Nichols 1812–20, I, p. 306. McDowell 1998 makes a particular study of James.

32 Bell, Parfitt and Shepherd 1990, pp. 147, 289. 33 *Ibid.*, pp. 176, 290.

34 Wing F1605 (1659); Bell 1988; Bell, Parfitt and Shepherd 1990, pp. 212, 290.

35 Wing D444 (1670); C5980A (1663) and C5981 (1669); Bell 1994b.

to Wight's bedside who could vouch for the accuracy of the events described.[36] Tace Sowle, daughter of the Quaker printer Andrew Sowle, who took over his business when his eyesight failed, was 'the greatest Quaker printer of her generation' and 'a good Compositor herself'. She continued the business in her own name after marriage to a non-stationer, while her sister Elizabeth married their father's apprentice, William Bradford, and emigrated to set up a press in Pennsylvania. Books printed by Tace Sowle include many by Quaker women, including works by Elizabeth Bathurst, Barbara Blaugdone, Jane Fearon and Abigail Fisher and the first part of *Piety promoted*..., a collection of testimonies to Anne Whitehead.[37]

A more systematic search of imprints would no doubt yield many more examples of women's agency in the printing, publication and circulation of words *by* women. What seems likely, on the basis of the examples cited above, is that when groups of women working together appear in this way, they grow from a community of interest which is religious/political rather than gender-based. This is not, of course, a clear division: sectarian congregations were notably hospitable to women and were open to women's active and vocal participation; within such groups women's identification of their common cause involved – certainly for Quakers – consciousness and debate about a specifically female interest. Quaker women writers are disproportionately represented among women-authored texts because of the decision taken in 1672 to collect and preserve all Quaker writings. That more than one-third of all surviving printed texts by women are by Quakers does not, therefore, necessarily mean that other sectarian women were less inclined to write for print. Hannah Allen's visiting of Sarah Wight and subsequent publication of her text suggests a similar common interest among Independents, and for Fifth Monarchists it was 'the sisters, that meet together' who took charge of distributing pamphlets beyond London.[38]

It might nevertheless be argued that insertion into the picture of women as printers, booksellers and distributors does not fundamentally alter the 'maleness' of the trade: these women were marginalized by their very disempowerment from office and hierarchy within the Stationers' Company and when women did take charge of businesses, they were doing so only by permission of a structure which remained thoroughly patriarchal. But this is to impose twentieth-century theory based on nineteenth-century literature unhistorically on a period when religion, politics, family or social status may

36 By Henry Jessey, Wing J687ff. (see note 4 above); Bell 1989.

37 Wing W1885 (1686), P2217A (1686). For Sowle, see Bell, Parfitt and Shepherd 1990, p. 292 and McDowell's article on Tace and Andrew Sowle in Bracken and Silver forthcoming.

38 T. Birch, *A collection of the state papers of John Thurloe* (London, 1742), VI, p. 186.

have been more crucial for the construction of identity than gender. Instead of seeking (and failing to find) the Virago Press of the seventeenth century and consequently lamenting these women's failure to be feminists, we should be looking at the evidence of women's collaboration (and rivalries) at every level of textual production – writing, scribal copying, editing, translating, dedicating, printing, publishing, copy-owning, bookselling, hawking, distributing, peddling and advertising – to map the connections and to understand them historically.[39]

Owners and readers

The final area of study vital to our understanding of women's relationship to printed text in this period is that of the consumption and reception of texts: how did women have access to print as readers, buyers and borrowers of books? Here, however, a methodology different from that so far employed is necessary. In the absence of large surveys and of statistics which might enable even a tentative mapping of women's reading across the period, we must turn to detailed case studies of the reading practices of a handful of individual women in order to indicate the nature (and potential) of the kinds of evidence available.

Rates of literacy for women in this period are contentious and clearly readership for printed texts was limited by factors of geography, social status and, possibly, religious affiliation: for example, Puritan and sectarian women at the edges of literacy might well have been encouraged to develop their skills as readers beyond what was usual for women of their social status or region. None of this is easily quantifiable, and while a broad picture can be offered, the operations of these variables need always to be borne in mind.[40] Many more studies are needed of women's reading practices, their ownership of books, their marginalia, their records of books owned and read. Without more evidence it seems at least premature to declare, as Jones does, that 'women's low rate of literacy prevented them from forming the influential reading public to which publishers in later centuries responded'.[41] Apart from educated women of the higher gentry and aristocracy, most literate women were literate only in English, which may itself account for the early development of the 'female literature' discussed above, as part of an expansion of the market in specifically English books.[42] Saunders in 'The stigma of print' mentions

39 Rivalries and legal challenges between women certainly existed. As yet, no study of episodes of this kind has been undertaken.

40 Ferguson 1996 surveys estimates of female literacy rates.

41 Jones 1990, p. 6. For some examples of women's reading practices, see Pearson 1996.

42 The category 'women writers' includes, of course, some whose primary activity was translation. See Hull 1988 and Hannay 1985.

'the condescensions of Watson, who printed side by side a Latin poem *Meliboeus*, dedicated to a man, and its English equivalent, dedicated to a woman'.[43] The provision of the English text, though ostensibly for women to read, would of course open up the poem to those many men who were not Latin-literate, and Gabriel Harvey's equation of Latin with the 'learned' and English with the 'simple' reader performs the same manoeuvre.[44] Watson's differentiation of readers by gender is in fact one particularization of a larger discrimination which the increase in printed texts, and in particular in vernacular printing, both identified and could exploit.

Assumptions about women's reading are often made on the basis of the evidence offered by the extant books themselves. Both L. B. Wright and H. S. Bennett worked from the texts to infer public 'tastes' and interests.[45] Similarly, Hull's delineation of a 'female literature' rests on the assumption that these are 'books that authors or booksellers expected groups of women to buy, to read, or to have read to them'.[46] The trawl for women-related terms in Wing titles, reported above, works in a similar way, though looking to the books as evidence less for a female reading public than for a public interested in reading about women. For evidence of actual reading practices, however, we have to look further. One way to get closer to what women read is to look for evidence of book ownership. Private libraries have been reconstructed for a number of prominent men of the period, but women's collections of books are much harder to trace: any substantial collection is likely to have been absorbed into the larger family library in gentry or aristocratic houses. David McKitterick's identification of books with Elizabeth Puckering's name inscribed on them vividly demonstrates the problems of interpreting such inscriptions: do they indicate ownership of a discrete collection of books, the informal division of a library shared between husband and wife, or a record of individual reading?[47] Frances Wolfreston's library, reconstructed by Paul Morgan, offers evidence from signatures and annotations suggestive of both ownership and enthusiastic reading.[48] Born in 1607 in King's Norton, Wolfreston lived most of her life near Tamworth as a member of the 'middling' county gentry. That she cared about her books is obvious from her signature and comments on the books themselves and from the provision made for them in her will. Morgan demonstrates that almost half of her books were what we would call 'English literature': plays, poems and romances. Hers is the only

43 Saunders 1951.
44 G. Harvey, *Trimming of Thomas Nashe, Gentleman*, quoted in Saunders 1951, p. 162.
45 L. B. Wright, *Middle-class culture in Elizabethan England* (Ithaca, NY, 1958) and Bennett 1952, 1965 and 1970.
46 Hull 1988, p. x. 47 McKitterick 2000. 48 Morgan 1989.

known extant copy of Shakespeare's *Venus and Adonis* of 1593: a text, according to Jacqueline Pearson, 'which became . . . associated with bored, frustrated middle-class wives'.[49] Morgan identifies over 100 books, of which about a dozen (on the evidence of their short titles) would fit Hull's definition of 'female literature' by reason of their subject-matter. Wolfreston was clearly interested in the 'woman' debate, owning biographies and histories of women (Ballard's *The history of Susannah*, Elizabeth I's entertainment at Woodstock, Stubbes's *A christal glasse for christian women*) and works of controversy, including Swetnam's *The araignment of lewde, idle, froward, and unconstant women*. She also owned books *by* women, including one by Catherine of Siena and Dorothy Leigh's *The mothers blessing*.

Evidence of book ownership can also be found in wills and inventories, though such evidence is rarely unambiguous. Systematic work on wills and inventories has so far yielded relatively little evidence for women book owners. Peter Clark's study of three Kentish towns, looking at book ownership in urban populations, attempts to generalize about women's book-ownership on the basis of his relatively large-scale data collection.[50] The relative sizes of his samples for men (2,200 inventories) and women (571) mean that his findings for women are significantly less detailed than his account of book-ownership among men. Overall, he suggests that 'whereas ownership of books among men in the early seventeenth century reached about 40 per cent, among women the overall level was nearer 25 per cent'. Far fewer women than men made wills, since if they predeceased their husbands their property, apart from minor personal items, went automatically to the widower. It is likely, as Clark remarks, that certain kinds of books considered frivolous, ephemeral or otherwise unimportant were never listed in inventories at all. Nottinghamshire archives record only two seventeenth-century wills containing books of women owners. One owned a Bible and a copy of Smith's sermons; the other, Margaret Sachell of Bleasby, who died in 1665, had '2 presses full of books, with shelves and other books, £30'. Since the inventory of her husband, who had died seven years previously, had listed 'his study of books' also worth £30, it is likely that this was his library; whether or not Margaret could and did read them, we cannot know.[51] It is unlikely that establishing book ownership necessarily provides evidence of readership at all. In 1632, for example, Alexander Cooke, Vicar of Leeds, made his will which divided his substantial library between his two sons. He also made a specific bequest to his daughter: 'Item I give vnto my daughter

49 Pearson 1996, p. 83. 50 Clark 1976.

51 Inventories of Isabell Clarke (1661), Margaret Sachell (1665) and Simon Sachel (*sic*) of Bleasby (1658): Nottinghamshire Record Office PR.SW.75/14; PR.SW.79/18; PR.SW.75/46.

Elizabeth Cooke the hystory of the Counsel of Trent in folio Morisons Travels in folio and 2 great books of Acts and Monuments.'[52] Establishing precisely what this means, however, is problematical. Were they books which Cooke knew his daughter to have read and enjoyed? Had these large and expensive books some sentimental value, perhaps having been bought by or for her mother? Were they attractive objects meant for future grandsons? Whether recipients, both male and female, of bequests of this kind ever *read* the books left to them is a matter for speculation.

Marks of ownership and annotations on books can, in individual cases, help to answer questions about reading practices. Many books of poetry in the early seventeeth century carry inscriptions to women, demonstrating that husbands and brothers seem to have found poetry an appropriate gift for wives and sisters. That many such books show no marks to suggest that they were *read* is instructive negative evidence, implying the possibility of a female market constructed (prescriptively?) by male book-buyers on behalf of (resistant?) female readers. Annotations in Frances Wolfreston's books offer unequivocal evidence not only of reading but of critical enjoyment. Often her books carry only her name, in her own hand: 'Frances Wolfreston hor bouk'. Occasionally, however, she was more forthcoming. In her copy of *The good womans champion, or a defence for the weaker vessell* (*c.* 1650) she wrote after her name 'in prais of women, a good one'.[53]

Secure evidence of reading and of the ways in which women read can be found in diaries and memoirs. Lady Margaret Hoby's diary for 1599–1605, though a spiritual diary, records some details of her reading.[54] While only fourteen of the titles can be individually identified, she mentions a number of apparently favourite authors and virtually every entry in the diary records some use of a book, whether read by herself, read to her, or discussed with others: 'I gott Mr Hoby to Read some of perkines to me . . . after dinner, I red as Longe as I could my selfe . . . ' Most of the books and authors she mentions are consistent with her religious interests as a Puritan: devotional works such as *A dyet for the christian soule*; tracts and sermons by prominent ministers such as Greenham, Perkins, Rogers; Foxe's 'Booke of Marters' and Latimer's sermons.[55] Not all her reported reading was meditational or devotional, however.[56] She read works of religious controversy and 'popish' books, presumably in order to understand

52 Barnard 1992. 53 Morgan 1989, p. 204.

54 D. M. Meads (ed.), *Diary of Lady Margaret Hoby 1599–1605* (London, 1930).

55 Many books are mentioned more than once. She invited Perkins, a particular favourite, to dinner (Meads, *Diary of Lady Margaret Hoby*, p. 153).

56 Pearson 1996, p. 82, misleadingly describes her reading as 'almost exclusively religious and devout (the only exceptions being herbals and other medical works)'.

her enemies' doctrinal errors.[57] She also mentions a few secular books: as well as a herbal, referred to repeatedly, she read topical pamphlets of news, such as the *Apology of the Earl of Essex*, concerning war with Spain, which was printed in 200 copies in 1600 but suppressed. Her interest may have been a family one: Essex was her brother-in-law by her first marrige to Walter Devereux.[58] She also acquired bills of mortality from London and a proclamation issued in 1603 to prevent factious efforts to reform the Church.[59] The source of her books, however, is never mentioned. Some may have been acquired on her own or her husband's visits to York and London.[60] A more secular diary, with many references to books and reading, is that of Lady Anne Clifford for the years 1616–19. In three years she recorded the reading of thirteen books, including the Bible, Spenser's *Faerie queene*, Montaigne's *Essays*, the *Arcadia*, Ovid's *Metamorphoses* and works by Chaucer, St Augustine and Josephus. Sometimes she recorded how the book came to her hands: 'Mr *Saragol's* Book of the Supplication of the Saints which my Lord gave me'.[61] Clifford's almost obsessive documentation of her own life and lineage means that her early diary can be supplemented with other information from her written records (household account books, later diaries and memoirs) and from her 'great picture', designed by herself to document her accession to the lands and titles of the Cliffords. A triptych containing two life-size portraits of herself (aged fifteen and fifty-three respectively) and her family, the painting shows the books appropriate to her youth and age in each panel. The Bible appears in all three panels, while the 'young' portrait shows twenty-six books, their titles all identifiable, ranged neatly on shelves. On the other side panel, the older Anne Clifford is again in the presence of shelves of books, this time twenty-two volumes arranged more untidily, perhaps indicative of more constant use. There is every reason to believe that the books depicted in the painting were deliberately chosen as part of her complex self-representation as heir to the Clifford estates, and that she treasured the books of her youth as symbolic of her connection with her northern lands.[62] In her diary for May 1617, at a point when it seemed that she had lost all hope of regaining the lands and castles of Westmorland, the books

57 Meads, *Diary of Lady Margaret Hoby*, p. 120. 58 *Ibid.*, p. 132. 59 *Ibid.*, p. 208.

60 For the availability of books in York see Barnard and Bell 1994; Foster had only one woman debtor.

61 V. Sackville-West, *The diary of the Lady Anne Clifford* (London, 1923), p. 91 (20 March 1619). Sorocold's *Supplications of saints* was already in its ninth edition by 1619 (*STC* 22932ff).

62 Spence argues that, rather than representing Anne's personal library, the books constitute a family memorial, being 'her parents' books as much as her own': R. T. Spence, *Lady Anne Clifford Countess of Pembroke, Dorset and Montgomery (1590–1676)* (Stroud, 1997), p. 189. Spence lists the books depicted (pp. 190–1); see also his appendix II (pp. 257–60), 'A Catalogue of the Books in the Passage Room next the Pantry in Skipton Castle 28th August 1739'.

gave her a physical link with her youth, her relationship with her mother, and her lost inheritance: 'The 24th we set up a great many of the books that came out of the North in my closet, this being a sad day with me thinking of the troubles I have passed. I used to spend much time with Mr *Wolrich* in talking of my dear Mother and other businesses in the North.'[63] Many years later as an old lady, returned to the north at last and well settled into independence in her many castles, she bought books in the same way as she bought kid gloves – in bulk, to give out to her household and to visitors as gifts. An entry in her account book for 1673 has a payment 'for 55: Books of Devotion of Mr John Rawlet's writeing who is now minister of Kirby Stephen which I buy to give away comes to Three Pounds Five Shillings & Four Pence.' Another, in 1676, has 'And about five of the clock this Evening did George Goodgeion bring me 28 books of Devotion he bought for me at Penrith, and I then saw them paid for, and gave them all away but six to my Domestic Servants.'[64]

It is obvious from these two examples that reading and books involved a range of purposes and practices. For Margaret Hoby the book often had a specific, spiritually related use: she read books on religious subjects and made notes in them; she heard, almost daily, readings by her spiritual advisor; she set others – her 'men' and 'women' – to read aloud as they worked together; she heard sermons, took notes while listening and read printed sermons; she asked her husband to take notes of sermons she could not attend, which he then read aloud to her. Books were thus experienced orally and communally as well as being read privately, individually and, presumably, silently. Printed books, annotations, notes on reading, notes on lectures heard, conversations about books and about sermons were interwoven in her daily life as she recorded it. For Anne Clifford, a woman notably committed to documentation and record-keeping, books were a resource and a comfort, providing visual texts and mottoes in themselves and representing more than simply their contents. She surrounded herself in life, as in the great picture, with books and fragments of manuscript copied from printed books, as Bishop Carlisle's funeral sermon indicates:

> She would frequently bring out of the rich Storehouse of her memory, things new and Old, Sentences or Sayings of remark, which she had read, or learned out of Authors, and with these her Walls, her bed, her hangings and furniture must be adorned, causing her Servants to write them in papers and her Maids to pin them up that she, or they, in the time of their dressing, or as occasion

63 Sackville-West, *The diary of the Lady Anne Clifford*, p. 68.

64 G. C. Williamson, *Lady Anne Clifford Countess of Dorset, Pembroke & Montgomery. 1590–1676. Her life, letters and work*, 2nd edn (Wakefield, 1967), pp. 510 (October 1673), 268 (10 January 1676).

> served, might remember and make their descants on them, so that though she had not many books in her Chamber, yet it was dressed up with the flowers of a Library.[65]

Like Hoby, Clifford had people to read to her, including her female servants. It was her practice in the latter part of her life to record inside a book the name of the person who read it to her, the date at which they began and the date on which they finished it. In her youth, similar information was recorded in her diary. In December 1619, for example, 'The 2nd Wat. Conniston made an end of reading a book called Leicester's Common Wealth, in which there's many things concerning the reignment and death of the Queen of Scots, which was all read to me.'[66] In her youth she had been the focus of writers (including one female writer, Amelia Lanyer) who sought her favour by dedicating their own books to her. Of the 773 women recorded as the recipients of dedications in pre-1640 printed books, more than three quarters appeared only once as dedicatees.[67] Anne Clifford, however, was one of that minority of royal, aristocratic and gentry women to whom multiple dedications were addressed. Anne's total of five books dedicated to her is, however, modest when compared with her mother's apparent attractions as a potential patron: Margaret Clifford, Countess of Cumberland appears as dedicatee in seventeen printed books. The role of women as patrons is beyond my scope here, but as an important feature of aristocratic women's relationship to the development of literature in the period it has deservedly attracted scholarly attention.[68] Critical debate about the practical extent of such patronage (as, for example, about the Countess of Pembroke's *personal* influence as literary patron) does not diminish these women's importance as cultural icons of literary endeavour for contemporaries outside their social circles.[69]

While Margaret Hoby and Anne Clifford may have been untypical women readers in a number of respects (not least in their levels of literacy and in their diary-keeping) their everyday reading practices may be more generally representative of literate women's relationship to printed books. Frances Wolfreston, a woman of lower social status, left no letters or diaries but her books themselves and her will show that she used books to write in as well as to read, that she read with enjoyment, and that she cared about the eventual fate

65 Quoted by Meads in her introduction, *Diary of Lady Margaret Hoby*.

66 Sackville-West, *The diary of the Lady Anne Clifford*, p. 111.

67 F. B. Williams, 'The literary patronesses of Renaissance England', *N&Q*, 207 (1962), 364–66.

68 See, for example, Hannay 1985 and Brennan 1988.

69 M. E. Lamb's contention that 'the Countess of Pembroke's patronage has been especially exaggerated' (M. E. Lamb, 'The Countess of Pembroke's patronage' *ELR*, 12 (1982), 162) is investigated in detail by Brennan 1988.

of her collection. Further down the social scale, women's access to reading is more difficult to trace, for poor women left few records. Peter Clark mentions evidence from Kentish law suits which give an occasional glimpse of a woman reading. In 1607 Elizabeth Barker, a yeoman's wife, was said by her maid to be 'at her book reading as she uses many times to do before she goes to bed'. At around the same time one Bartholomew Dann was accused of assaulting his wife: 'when she had been reading and leaving her book in some place ... he would catch the book out of her hands and tear it in pieces or otherwise fling it away'.[70] Husbands might, indeed, be a hindrance to women's reading at all levels of society. Clifford's diary for 27 March 1617 describes how

> My Lord found me reading with Mr Ran and told me it would hinder his study so as I must leave off reading the Old Testament till I can get somebody to read it with me. This day I made an end of reading Deuteronomy.[71]

Other women writers of the period recount how their reading and writing involved either secrecy from or conflict with husbands. Jane Turner described her *Choice experiences*... as 'the fruits of my labours written at several times in my husband's absence'; Anne Wentworth's husband not only rejected her prophetic writing but confiscated and threatened to destroy the books and papers she left behind when she fled from him.[72]

This reminder of the legal, cultural and economic power of husbands over wives and men over women is a fitting point on which to end this discussion of women's relationship to printed text, for it is to the broader frame of an understanding of historical constructions of gender that the study of women and text can, finally, make an important contribution. The history of the book offers feminist literary historians a model which allows us to test our assumptions by investigating the specifics of women's agency: as writers, scribes, patrons, dedicatees, translators, editors; as printers, booksellers, bookbinders, publishers, hawkers, mercuries and peddlers; and as owners, listeners, readers and collectors of books. Moreover, in forcing us to attend to the book as product it alerts us to the ways in which print, then as now, was instrumental in the construction of gender identities, not only by the development of a female market for books but also by its representation of 'woman' as subject-matter and marketable commodity.

70 Clark 1976. 71 Sackville-West, *The diary of the Lady Anne Clifford*, p. 60.
72 Bell, Parfitt and Shepherd 1990, pp. 198, 210–11 and 280.

VERNACULAR TRADITIONS

21

The Bible trade

B.J. McMULLIN

In 1557 – a century after the publication in Mainz of the forty-two-line Bible (in the Vulgate Latin version) – the complete Bible *printed in English* was only twenty-two years old,[1] the Bible *printed in English in England* only twenty.[2] Indeed, before 1536 the *only* Bible-printing in England consisted of the first volume of a projected Vulgate edition published by Thomas Berthelet in 1535. By the end of the seventeenth century British printers had produced in Latin only about nine complete Bibles and about thirty-three New Testaments, along with a handful in Greek,[3] indicating that the demand for Bibles in those languages was not really sufficient to justify their being printed locally, the demand being met in large part by Continental editions. The story of the Bible trade in Britain is essentially, therefore, the story of the Bible in the vernacular. The earliest vernacular editions too were printed abroad, a practice dictated by ecclesiastical and political opposition at home to Tyndale's translation.[4] Domestic opposition, however, began to diminish with the worsening relations between Henry VIII and Rome and the subsequent confirmation of the King as 'only Supreme Head in earth of the Church of England', and in 1536 there appeared the first English New Testament actually printed in England – an edition of Tyndale's version – followed in 1537 by a complete Bible in Coverdale's version.[5]

With the accession of Mary in 1553 Bible printing in Britain ceased entirely, to be resumed only gradually in the early years of the reign of Elizabeth. Further editions of Tyndale's New Testament and of the Great Bible[6] were published

1 This chapter attempts to summarize existing knowledge about the Bible trade in the period, being based on published sources, which are acknowledged at appropriate points.

2 For the New Testament the respective figures are thirty-two and twenty-one; individual books have been disregarded.

3 See *STC* and Wing.

4 Accounts of the pre-Elizabethan versions are conveniently to be found in Bruce 1961 and *CHB*, III, pp. 141–74.

5 See DMH 27–33.

6 First published in 1539 – see DMH 46; so-called from its size, it was designed to be placed in churches for public reading.

in the early 1560s, but they were supplanted in use in the Church of England in 1568 by the Bishops' Bible, a revision of the Great Bible undertaken by a large group of bishops (and others) at the instance of Matthew Parker, Archbishop of Canterbury (DMH 125). Thereafter, though editions of the Bishops' Bible continued to be published until 1617 (DMH 356), two other versions dominated: the Geneva and the Authorized (or King James).

The Geneva Bible

The only English-language version of the Bible published in Mary's reign was a New Testament in octavo printed in Geneva in 1557 by Protestant exiles (DMH 106), the text – largely the work of William Whittingham – being based on Tyndale's version. This Testament was displaced in 1560 by a complete Bible in quarto, also printed in Geneva (DMH 107), which in the New Testament represented a revision of Whittingham and in the Old a revision of the Great Bible (see plate 21.1). The Geneva Bible was first printed in Britain in 1575 (DMH 141), but though it retained adherents to its text it did not long survive Elizabeth: the last complete Geneva Bible appeared in 1616 (DMH 348), the last New Testament in 1619 (DMH 371).[7]

In terms of layout the Geneva Bible was novel: it was printed in roman; it divided the text into verses, so as to facilitate the use of a concordance; words supplied in order to render the translation idiomatic were printed in italic; books and chapters were supplied with 'arguments'; and summary running titles were provided. In these respects the Geneva Bible established the typographical norms for the Bible in English, even though – in deference to a British tradition already in decline – some editions were printed in black letter, the face used for the first folio edition of the Authorized Version, 1611.[8]

The Geneva Bible is also characterized by its marginal notes, which, in explicating and commenting on the text, understandably exhibit a Protestant, anti-Roman tendency. This tendency was reinforced in Laurence Tomson's revision of the New Testament, published in octavo in London in 1576 (DMH 146), in which the notes are more overtly Calvinistic, and in the anti-Papal notes of Junius (i.e. François du Jon) to Revelation, which were first published in English

7 In fact there were editions in 1640 (DMH 545) and 1644 (DMH 579) printed in Amsterdam and an isolated London edition in 1776/8 (DMH 1246); and editions combining the text of the Authorized Version and the notes of the Geneva continued to be printed in Amsterdam until 1715 (DMH 936).

8 On the typographical and design characteristics of the Geneva Bible see Black 1961.

translation separately in 1592 (DMH 214) and later added to the Geneva–Tomson version, before finally replacing Tomson's in 1602 (DMH 272).[9]

The Authorized Version[10]

It was precisely the nature of the Geneva–Tomson–Junius notes which earned the disapproval of the new king, James: some of them he regarded as 'very partial, untrue, seditious, and savouring too much of dangerous and traitorous conceits',[11] and they therefore provided a stimulus for a new translation. At a meeting of churchmen at Hampton Court in January 1604, convened to discuss the state of the established Church, it was resolved 'That a translation be made of the whole Bible, as consonant as can be to the original Hebrew and Greek; and this to be set out and printed, without any marginal notes, and only to be used in all Churches of England in time of divine service.'[12]

The translation itself was effected by six 'companies' of translators, totalling at least forty-seven members, two companies meeting at Westminster, two at Oxford and two at Cambridge; three dealt with the Old Testament, two with the New and one with the Apocrypha. The companies were enjoined to follow the Bishops' version as far as possible, consulting the translations of Tyndale, Matthew,[13] Coverdale, the Great Bible and the Geneva whenever the Bishops' was unsatisfactory. The members of each company spent some three years working independently on their allotted span before spending a further three years coming to a consensus on a final text, which was then reviewed by a panel of twelve drawn, two each, from the six companies and finally seen through the press by Thomas Bilson (Bishop of Winchester) and Miles Smith (later Bishop of Gloucester). The black-letter folio was published in 1611 by Robert Barker, the King's Printer (plate 21.2).

In the event, the Authorized Version owes much to the Geneva and to the 'Rhemes' New Testament. The latter is the translation made by the English Roman Catholics at their College at Rheims and published there in quarto in 1582 (DMH 177). The Old Testament in the Roman Catholic translation,

9 The dating is muddied by the existence of several pirated quarto editions of the Geneva–Tomson Bible with Junius's Revelation bearing false 'London, 1599' imprints – see note 32 below.

10 I have persisted in employing the term 'Authorized Version' in deference to common usage, though, as various commentators have pointed out, in no formal sense was it 'authorized', unlike the Book of Common Prayer, the use of which was enforced in the Church of England by an Act of Parliament.

11 Quoted in Bruce 1961, p. 97.

12 Quoted in Bruce 1961, p. 96. This prescription is the closest that the new version came to being authorized.

13 DMH 34. 'Thomas Matthew' is considered to be a pseudonym of John Rogers, the Marian Martyr, who did no more than edit the translation of Tyndale for an edition printed on the Continent and published in London in 1537 by Grafton and Whitchurch.

the 'Doway', was not available to the translating companies: though translated some years earlier it was not published until 1609/10 (DMH 300), in Douai, whither the English College had returned in 1593. In general appearance the Authorized Version followed the Geneva, with the marginal notes now confined, however, to the resolution of linguistic difficulties and the pointing out of parallel passages.

With very few exceptions, for nearly three centuries from 1611 onwards the sole English translation produced in Britain was the Authorized Version. As already noted, earlier versions had been superseded by the Bishops', and the Bishops' itself was no longer published once the Authorized Version was accepted as the recommended text for use in the established Church. Likewise the Geneva ceased to be published once the essence of its text had been absorbed into the new version. The Doway–Rhemes also effectively ceased to be published: there were editions of the New Testament in 1621 (DMH 382) and 1633 (DMH 479), but not thereafter until 1738 (DMH 1041); and there was an edition of the Old Testament in 1635 (DMH 499) but not another until 1750 (DMH 1089), and no complete Bible until 1764 (DMH 1156). The Catholic translation had served as an element in the religious controversy constituting the Reformation, but once Protestantism had become entrenched and traditional Catholic practices confirmed among adherents through the Counter-Reformation there was no longer a particular need for a Bible for the laity in their own language – that is, the Vulgate was re-established as the Roman Catholics' Bible, accessible in effect only to the clergy or the educated laity. The Authorized Version therefore remained without a competitor in the English-speaking world until 1881, when the New Testament of the Revised Version appeared, to be followed in 1885 by the Old.

Printer's copy for the 1611 edition was presumably the manuscript provided by Bilson and Smith, though it is conceivable that a marked-up exemplar of an earlier edition was used by Barker. Whatever the nature of the copy, like any other work with unchanged text repeatedly reprinted, succeeding editions were set not from the copy for 1611 but from a printed version, the particular edition chosen being apparently a matter of convenience and therefore at an unknown remove from the 1611.[14] Consequently the Authorized Version suffered the same process of progressive corruption as any other reprinted text. Most of that corruption was no doubt inadvertent, resulting from lapses on the

14 However, McKitterick 1992, p. 322, notes William Kilburne's claim, made in the mid-1650s, that the manuscript copy of the Authorized Version had been defaced by interlineations and obliterations, but on what basis any such changes can have been made is not known; the claim may have been made in support of a move to have a new translation made.

part of the compositors, but occasionally it was intentional – at least such is the accepted explanation for the omission of 'not' in the seventh commandment ('Thou shalt not commit adultery') in the 'Wicked Bible', the 1631 octavo (DMH 444) – for which offence the King's Printers were fined £300. But many more of the departures from 1611 were simply the consequence of compositors modernizing the text by making it conform in accidentals with contemporary practice. None the less, as early as 1659 William Kilburne claimed to have identified nearly 20,000 errors in a single twenty-fourmo edition printed in 1653 by Hills and Field (see pp. 465–6 below).[15] And in 1833 Thomas Curtis was to claim that 'intentional departures from King James' Bible' numbered 'upwards of *Eleven Thousand*', a figure 'not at all including the general alterations of the orthography or minute punctuation'.[16]

The process of corruption was rarely interrupted: the only editions of the seventeenth century in which systematic correction has been documented are the Cambridge folios of 1629 (DMH 424, 425) and 1638 (DMH 520), in which a number of improvements were made in the wording of the 1611 and greater typographic consistency attained. The 1638 Cambridge remained the 'standard' edition, against which to judge the text of others, until displaced by the 1762 Cambridge folio/quarto and the 1769 Oxford folio/quarto. The various attempts at correction, however, met in some quarters with the accusation that the 1611, in the state that it was first published, was the standard, that any deviations from it were unacceptable, that the 1611 edition was not susceptible to improvement – no matter how well intentioned and no matter how defective the 1611 in its translation or its typographic form.

The privilege

The manuscript copy of the Authorized Version was clearly a valuable property; by virtue of a patent granted by Elizabeth in 1577 to Christopher Barker,[17] giving him the exclusive right to print the Bible and the Book of Common Prayer, it belonged to Robert Barker, son of Christopher and his successor as Queen's Printer. The Barkers also printed the Geneva Bible: in 1561 Elizabeth had granted an exclusive patent of seven years to John Bodley (father of Sir Thomas),[18] but he exercised his privilege only once, in Geneva, in 1562 (DMH 116), and when the Geneva Bible was first printed in England, in 1576 (DMH 143, 144, 146, 147), it was by Christopher Barker.

15 Kilburne 1659, p. 7. 16 Curtis 1833, p. [ii]. 17 Pollard 1911, pp. 322–6, document lvii.
18 The text is in Pollard 1911, pp. 284–5, document xlviii.

Though the potential returns on the exclusive right to publish the Authorized Version were immense, so were the costs of initial production, which included payment to the reviewing panel and to Bilson and Smith. In order to finance the production Robert Barker had to borrow from Bonham Norton and John Bill, thus instigating a series of disputes, transfers and purchases relating to the office of Queen's/King's Printer which, continuing well into the eighteenth century, are reflected in the changing imprints of Bibles.[19]

The right to publish the Authorized Version thus did not rest on actual ownership of the manuscript copy, though it remained in the possession of the King's Printers. The manuscript itself is presumed to have been destroyed in the Great Fire of 1666, but the privilege for the Authorized Version has remained with the King's/Queen's Printer.

In fact, The King's Printer's privilege in the Authorized Version was (and remains) qualified: by virtue of royal charters granted to them separately the universities of Oxford and Cambridge could also claim the right to print it and thereby to share in the considerable profits that might be made from it. The earlier of the charters was that granted to Cambridge on 20 July 1534 by Henry VIII, the crucial part of which reads, in translation: 'These Stationers or Bookprinters [i.e. the three allowed to be appointed by the University] . . . shall have lawful and incontestable power to print there all manner of books approved, or hereafter to be approved, by the aforesaid Chancellor or his deputy and three doctors there.'[20] In effect, the university did not begin to exploit its privilege until 1629, following confirmation of the 1534 charter by Charles I, on 6 February 1628. Oxford's privilege dates from 3 March 1636, in the form of a charter which absorbed earlier charters of 12 November 1632 and 13 March 1633.[21] Oxford did not begin to exercise *its* privilege until 1673–5.

The slowness with which the universities exercised their overriding privileges by printing Bibles is to be explained by reference to opposition, dating from before 1611, from the Queen's/King's Printers and the Stationers' Company.

Cambridge

John Legate, Printer to the University of Cambridge, managed to provoke both the Queen's Printer and other members of the Stationers' Company

19 There is a summary in Handover 1960, pp. 73–97, ch. 3, 'The Bible patent'. The details can be followed in Plomer 1901–02, Johnson 1948–9 and Haig 1956.

20 The full text, in the original Latin and in translation, is given in ch. 2 ('The charter of 1534') of McKitterick 1992, pp. 22–37.

21 The full texts of the 1632 and 1633 charters, in the original Latin only, are given in Madan 1895–1931, I, pp. 281–5.

in 1590–1, when he printed first a miniature edition of the Sternhold and Hopkins Psalms (*STC* 2477.5) and then an octavo Geneva Bible (DMH 208) and a miniature Geneva–Tomson New Testament (DMH 207). The Sternhold and Hopkins Psalms was considered to be the property of Richard Day, the others of Christopher Barker, who in 1588 had appointed two other Stationers, George Bishop and Ralph Newbery, as his deputies. By virtue of its powers to search for publications printed in infringement of members' rights,[22] the Company apparently seized the offending stocks, though these were quickly returned and an accommodation made whereby the University Printer was to have first choice of foreign books exhibited at the Frankfurt fairs.[23] No further editions of the Bible were to appear from Cambridge until 1629, when, in the train of the 1628 charter, a compromise was reached between the university and the Stationers' Company, 16 April 1629, when the privy council confirmed the university's right to print the Bible, but only in quarto and medium folio (formats adjudged 'unpopular' because suited neither to lectern nor to pocket), along with sufficient numbers of the Book of Common Prayer and the Sternhold and Hopkins Psalms to bind up with them. Discounting John Field's tenure, 1657–68, these were the only formats to be published at Cambridge in the seventeenth century, comprising three folios (1629, DMH 424; 1638, DMH 520; 1674, DMH 717) and sixteen quartos, ranging from 1630 (DMH 432) to 1683 (DMH 780, 783). After Field's death in 1668 the university, by reason of treaties of forbearance, was reduced to printing for the Stationers' Company, and there was no further Bible printing at Cambridge until 1743.

The response of the King's Printer to Cambridge's 1629/30 initiative had been to bring out editions in the same formats at prices which undercut those charged by the university. According to Michael Sparke, writing in 1641 about the high cost of Bibles,

> In the yeare 1629, the want of these sorts of Folio Bibles caused *Cambridge* Printers to print it, and they sold it at 10^{s} in quires: upon which the then Kings Printers set six Printing-houses at worke, and on an instant Printed one Folio Bible in the same manner, and sold with it 500. Quarto Roman Bibles, and 500. Quarto English, at 5^{s} a Book, to overthrow the *Cambridge* Printing, and so to keep all in their own hands. It were well if they would alwayes sell at this price. [side-note:] This Folio would not have bin sold under 12 or 14 *sh.* if it had not bin that *Cambridge* had Printed it: but now they sold it at 5 *sh*, which would have bin 12 *sh* at least, and the 4*to* at 5 *sh*, which was before 9 *sh.*[24]

22 Blagden 1960, pp. 65–6, 120. 23 McKitterick 1992, pp. 115–17. 24 Sparke 1641.

(There is a London folio dated 1629, DMH 423; like the 1629 Cambridge it is in roman type.)

Oxford

Having had powers the same as those of Cambridge conferred by Order in Council, 9 March 1636, Oxford deferred its venture into Bible printing until 1673, preferring in the interim to make accommodations with the Stationers' Company, whereby, in return for payments from the Company, the university agreed not to print privileged works. Archbishop Laud, Chancellor of the University 1629–41, was cautious, wanting both to establish a learned press and to avoid the controversy that Cambridge's Bible-printing had created. The university therefore entered into the first of a series of three-year covenants of forbearance on 12 March 1637, agreeing – in return for an annual payment of £200 – to not print works covered by privileges belonging to members of the Stationers' Company, including the Bible. As Laud put it, 'it will be more beneficial to the University for the Advance of a learned Press to receive £200 a Year, than to print Grammars, and Almanacks, &c., and more Honour too'.[25] In the period 1637–42 the £200 included £80 contributed by the King's Printer in consideration of the Bible; after 1642, with the outbreak of the Civil War, payments were not made until 1656, when Field and Hills entered into the first of two three-year agreements with the university, paying the same £80 a year. With the Restoration the covenant with the Stationers' Company was reinstated in 1661 and renewed in 1664 and 1669, at the old figure of £200 a year.

The arrangement with the Stationers' Company ceased on 25 March 1672, when the university farmed out its privilege – again for £200 a year – to four of its members, Dr John Fell, Dr Thomas Yate, Sir Leoline Jenkins and Joseph Williamson, under the leadership of Fell. Fell's expectation was that a learned press could be established on the profits to be won from printing the Bible (and other privileged works); though the project was not immediately successful, the Bible side, at both Oxford and Cambridge, was ultimately to provide the financial base on which the learned side could survive. The partners, however, lacked sufficient capital (despite Yate's contribution of at least £3,000), and as early as October 1672 they had to make an arrangement with the Stationers' Company, who bought their stock of privileged school books and agreed to pay them £100 a year for their forbearance. None the less, the partners clung

25 Quoted in Carter 1975, p. 33. The text is also reprinted, with different accidentals, in Johnson and Gibson 1946, p. 19.

to the notion that the Bible could be exploited in the interests of the learned press and went ahead with a quarto edition (DMH 719, 720), dated 1675 but with the colophon to the New Testament in some exemplars dated 1673. The response of the King's Printers to Oxford's initiative was the same as it had been to Cambridge's in 1629: they produced competing editions which they sold at a loss, so that the price of London quarto Bibles fell from 13*s*. 4*d*. to 5*s*. 9*d*.[26] No further English Bibles appeared from Oxford until the quarto of 1679 (DMH 744, 745, 746), by which time the partners had devised another scheme for exploiting the Bible privilege.

On 26 September 1678 the partners sold their stock to the London bookseller Moses Pitt for £3,800 and sublet the privilege for three years, at £200 a year, to Pitt and three other London booksellers: William Leake, Peter Parker and Thomas Guy. Leake died in 1681, but the others were to remain in possession of the sublease until 1691, with Parker acting as their spokesman. All except Leake already had an interest in Bibles, having been implicated in the illicit trade in Dutch-printed English Bibles; all were members of the Stationers' Company, but not part of the inner circle which controlled its operations; and all were regarded as enterprising and as speculators (Guy was sufficiently wealthy that before his death in 1724 he had founded the hospital which bears his name). As far as the four London booksellers were concerned, the arrangement with Oxford was purely commercial: it provided them with the opportunity to do legally what hitherto they had done by subterfuge – trade for profit in Bibles. In Carter's words, 'This new alliance of Oxford academics with London booksellers was for war with the King's Printers';[27] in Johnson and Gibson's, 'To Fell it was the game, as old as the world, of setting a thief to catch a thief.'[28] With the sublease the limitation which the Fell partners had imposed on themselves – to publish the Bible only in folio and quarto (in accordance with the Privy Council ruling of 1629, by which Cambridge was bound) – was abandoned: from this point on Bibles were printed in Oxford in folio, quarto, octavo and twelvemo. Oxford became particularly noted for its folios, the first of which was published in 1680 (DMH 756); and with the publication of the 1679 quarto, an octavo in 1680 (DMH 757) and a twelvemo in 1681 (DMH 762) the London partners were in direct competition with the King's Printers (Cambridge withdrew from the field in 1683), thus breaking the effective monopoly and driving down prices, thereby also removing the incentive for Dutch printers to continue their surreptitious trade (see below).

26 Madan 1895–1931, III, p. 324, on the authority of John Gutch, *Collectanea curiosa; or miscellaneous tracts, relating to the history and antiquities of England and Ireland* (Oxford, 1781), I, p. 272.

27 Carter 1975, p. 95. 28 Johnson and Gibson 1946, p. 75.

Bibles printed at Oxford between 1679 and 1691 bear various imprints, reflecting the distribution arrangements: within an edition exemplars may have simply 'Oxford, at the Theater' (the Sheldonian, used since its opening in 1669 for both ceremonial and printing purposes) or, in addition, the names of all or of one or other of the London partners (William Leake being briefly replaced after his death by his mother Ann).

The death of Fell in 1686 led directly to the university itself resuming control of printing and then making different arrangements for Bible printing. In 1688 a three-year renewal of Fell's lease was granted to his executors, and through them to Parker and Guy (Pitt, bankrupted through real estate speculation, had ceased to be active in 1683), but when the lease expired in September 1691 the Delegates of the Press accepted a proposal from the Stationers' Company whereby, in consideration of £200 a year, the Company, on behalf of the King's Printers, would add the Bible to the covenant of forbearance of October 1672 covering other privileged books. Again the Stationers agreed to buy the university's unsold stock (from the learned side), but now they also contracted 'To keep up the Printing of Bibles, Common Prayer &c.: in the Precincts of Oxford, Prices to be set by the Vice-Chancellor and Delegates.'[29] Accordingly the university purchased Parker and Guy's equipment to add to that acquired by the Oxford partners and bequeathed to the university by Fell. The Stationers' workmen were then installed in the Sheldonian in early 1692. From 1694 (an octavo New Testament, DMH 837) until 1715, when the first fruits of John Baskett's acquisition of the Oxford privilege in 1713 appeared, the imprints of Oxford Bibles carry no names, only 'the University-Printers'.

The Interregnum

When royal authority collapsed in the early 1640s the Bible privilege ceased to be of value. Though in theory any bookseller or printer could have taken advantage of the new freedom, the physical and financial resources needed to produce a work of the extent of the Bible ensured that in fact there were few competitors for the King's Printers (Cambridge published no further editions after the 1640 quarto (DMH 544); other 'Cambridge' editions purportedly dating from the 1640s are spurious). The King's Printers – various Barkers and John Bill II and his assignees – continued to publish up to the beginning of the Commonwealth, 30 January 1649, though not, it was claimed, in sufficient numbers to satisfy the demand created by the Puritan revolution for editions

29 Quoted in Carter 1975, p. 106.

for personal reading. The situation had been complicated by John Bill's flight to York with King Charles and the reluctance of Robert Barker's assignees to continue printing in the absence of an enforceable privilege.

The shortage was met in part by unauthorized editions imported from Holland, but the Westminster Assembly of Divines in 1644 appealed to the London Stationers to fill the vacuum. None, however, was willing to do so at a low enough price to satisfy the Assembly, being conscious not only of the investment required but also, no doubt, of the risk associated with a possible change in political authority or a re-instatement of the privilege in the hands of others. But the appeal was answered by William Bentley, a printer but not a member of the Stationers' Company; with the financial support of a number of London merchants, he proceeded to print several editions from his printing house at Finsbury.[30] Only two, both in octavo, seem to have survived, dated 1646 and 1648 (DMH 591, 607), though in his *Case* Bentley himself refers to five editions ('impressions'), including at least one twelvemo, and Kilburne refers to Bentley having 'imprinted several volumes by Authority of Parliament in 8°. and 12°. in the years 1646 48. 51, &c.'[31]

The involvement of the Stationers' Company itself in Bible printing dates from early 1646, when it founded the Bible Stock, paralleling the English Stock – a collection of works for which the Company as a whole owned the privilege, which was in theory exploited for the benefit of members holding shares in that stock. The Stationers had no authority to establish the Bible Stock but acted on the well-founded assumption that their combined forces would be sufficient to undercut Bentley (and any other competitors) before re-asserting a monopoly and raising prices, a tactic which was indeed successful in eliminating Bentley, who sold his stock and materials to the Company in July 1649. The Stationers' Company published an octavo Bible in 1647 (DMH 598) and at least a further thirteen editions (in quarto, octavo and twelvemo) before the venture collapsed in 1656.

The failure of the Bible Stock is attributable to the third major party involved in Bible printing in the Interregnum: John Field and Henry Hills. Since the office of King's Printer no longer existed, in 1653 the Barkers attempted – unsuccessfully – to have their right to the Authorized Version recognized by Parliament; in 1655 they attempted – again unsuccessfully – to have the manuscript copy entered to them in the Stationers' Register. Understandably

30 On Bentley and his troubles see Baillie 1997, which discusses, and reprints the texts of, *The Case of William Bentley, printer at Finsbury near London, touching his right to the printing of Bibles and Psalms* [November 1656] and the response of Field and Hills, *A Short answer to a pamphlet, entituled, The Case of William Bentley*... [November 1656].

31 Kilburne 1659, p. 6.

the Stationers rejected this attempt: to have allowed its entry would have been to render the Bible Stock immediately worthless. When the manuscript was acquired by John Field and Henry Hills sr. from Christopher Barker III and Matthew Barker, for the sum of £1,200, on 20 February 1656, Cromwell required the Stationers' Company to allow it to be entered in its Register as a conventional copy, thus indeed frustrating the Company's own venture.

Field now had a monopoly for printing the Bible: in addition to securing the right conferred by entry in the Stationers' Register, Field had been appointed Printer to Parliament (so designated in the imprint to the 1652 twelvemo, DMH 630), and then Printer to His Highness the Protector, Oliver Cromwell. Through Cromwell's influence he was subsequently also appointed as Printer to the University of Cambridge, publishing his first Bible there, an octavo, in 1657 (DMH 656), and in 1656 he and Hills had renewed the covenant of forbearance with Oxford. He continued as Printer to the University until his death in 1668, but with the Restoration Christopher Barker III and John Bill II were reinstated as King's Printers.

Piracies

One consequence of the existence of a monopoly – in this case for the printing of a work in constant demand and needed in large numbers – is the inflation of prices beyond what the informed contemporary would consider justified by the costs of production. A second consequence follows from the first: the fact of inflated prices serves to encourage interlopers – in this case the printing of the work by those unauthorized to do so. The price of Bibles printed by the King's Printers was a constant irritant in the seventeenth century – we have already noted the complaints voiced by Sparke and Kilburne. However, especially given the ineffectualness of the universities, before the 1680s there was no domestic competition to the King's Printers. For would-be British pirates the cost of laying in paper for a large edition, added to the cost of actual setting and printing off, was sufficient deterrent. In addition there were the risks of search and seizure by the aggrieved monopolists, the breaking of presses, defacing of type, fines and imprisonment.

The unauthorized printing of English Bibles was in fact probably restricted to Holland, where huge numbers, mostly in small formats, were printed for surreptitious introduction into the British Isles and the North American Plantations. It is convenient to designate these Dutch editions 'piracies', though their printers were clearly not subject to any British legislation; the penalties were felt by those importing the pirated Bibles into Britain, possessing them, distributing them or offering them for sale. The inducement to piracy for the Dutch was simply that they could produce Bibles to sell in Britain at a price below that charged by the King's Printers; for British dealers in pirated Bibles the attraction was the ability to bypass the official sources of supply to acquire cheaper stock for which there was a predictable demand. The Dutch Bibles had a reputation among the anti-monopolists for being more accurate, better printed and on better paper than their British counterparts; among the monopolists they were regarded as being inaccurate (being set by foreigners), poorly printed, and on inferior paper. In truth the general level of British printing was low in the seventeenth century and the Dutch Bibles were indistinguishable from Bibles printed in Britain in the accuracy of their texts and the quality of their production.

So indistinguishable are the Dutch-printed Bibles that we have no obvious way of identifying them; what *can* be confidently asserted is that the list provided by DMH in the 'Note on English Bibles printed abroad' (p. 187) is incomplete, possibly even seriously so (plate 21.3).

Robert Barker had occasion to complain about infringements of his privilege as early as 1601, when Andrew Hart and John Norton had an edition of the Geneva version printed in Dort (DMH 267), but the earliest documented instance of piracy – in the sense of using a false imprint – is that perpetrated by J. F. Stam,[32] who produced a series of seven quarto editions of the Geneva version, six of them (DMH 248–255) with the imprint 'London by the deputies of Christopher Barker . . . 1599', the seventh (DMH 473) – from the same setting as DMH 252 – 'Amsterdam . . . By Iohn Fredericksz Stam . . . 1633'; all seven were presumably printed in Amsterdam some time after 1625.

Stam's daughter, Anna Maria Stam, was also involved in pirating English Bibles: she and Susanna, the widow of Jan Jacobsz Schippers, were party to an agreement with Joseph Athias, dated 5 September 1673, to print English Bibles for a period of fifteen years.[33] The women contributed to the partnership two twelvemos and an eighteenmo in standing type, none of which has been identified. Athias contributed a twelvemo and an eighteenmo, set in a novel fashion; Carter and Buday concluded from the wording of the agreement and from the evidence of witnesses that the process involved was true stereotyping, and the eighteenmo has since been identified with a series of four

32 See Pocock 1883, Johnson 1954 and the letter of Sir William Boswell reproduced in Greg 1967, pp. 290–1.

33 Carter and Buday 1975, pp. 312–20.

editions (the earliest not in DMH, the others DMH 612–616) purporting to have been printed by Roger Daniel in Cambridge in 1648 but actually printed, on at least nine occasions, in Amsterdam after 1661, the year of Athias's arrival there.[34]

By the nature of the practice, the extent of piracy is unknown: as already noted, there are no clear criteria for identifying unauthorized editions. None the less some idea of its magnitude can be gathered from contemporary claims, even if they are likely to be exaggerated. Fell referred in January 1680, for example, to 'Dutch Bibles, which, to the equal shame and damage of the nation, supply half this Kingdom, all Scotland, all Ireland, and all our Plantations'.[35] The extent of Athias's involvement can be estimated from the number of impressions made from his stereotyped edition and from the number of times that the copperplate title page had to be cut afresh; he himself claimed to have printed 'more than a million English Bibles'.[36] The magnitude of the threat to the King's Printers' privilege can similarly be gauged from their response. They assumed to themselves the powers of the Stationers' Company to search for offending editions, and in the early 1670s 'They did seize from one Mansfield near 2000 Holland Bibles from another 1000 Holland'; those found with pirated Bibles were forced to compound by paying a fine, and 'In seven yeares space it is verily believed that they have seized £15000 Holland Bibles.'[37] Among the booksellers involved in the illicit trade were Pitt, Parker and, especially, Guy. The King's Printers themselves profited from the trade, not merely in fines extracted: they appear to have sold stocks of seized Bibles to Guy, who then sold them to other booksellers, only to have the King's Printers seize them afresh; and some they simply provided with a new preliminary gathering before selling them as a legitimate edition.

As already noted, the trade in pirated editions declined rapidly once the London partners operating from Oxford in the 1680s entered into direct competition with the King's Printers, driving down prices: 'Bibles in folio which had been sold for 6 pound fell in their price to one pound ten shillings; Bibles in 4° which had been sold for 13^{s} 4^{d}, were sold for 5^{s} 6^{d}, Octavos which had been sold for 6^{s}, were sold for 2^{s} 8^{d} . . . '.[38] After the turn of the century probably only a handful of English Bibles were produced in Holland, and since some were in folio it may be that they were designed for use there by English congregations.

34 McMullin 1993, pp. 184–207.
35 Quoted in Carter 1975, p. 72 from Gutch, *Collectanea*, I, p. 270.
36 Black 1963, p. 460.
37 Quoted in Johnson and Gibson 1946, pp. 78–9.
38 Quoted in Johnson and Gibson 1946, pp. 88–9.

Production

The Authorized Version continues to be produced under monopoly conditions, and its text is – at least in intent – invariant. Moreover, it is required in a variety of formats, on different qualities of paper (or in modern times in various qualities of binding) and, especially, in large numbers. In the hand-press period these various conditions led the privileged printers to devise various means to control the passage of sheets through the printing house, the bindery and the bookshop and thence into the hands of purchasers.

Press figures

It is not possible to generalize about edition quantities, and the scattered numbers which are to be found may not be typical; none the less such figures can be set against the usual edition limit of 1,500 and in that light are at least indicative of the challenges posed by the printing of Bibles. For example, Madan supposes that the first Oxford Bible was published in an edition of 5,000;[39] 20,000 is claimed by Kilburne for Field's 1656 twelvemo (DMH 651);[40] and Guy and Parker appear to have been about to start an edition of 40,000 in 1691.[41] So while the large numbers in which Bibles were produced provided economies and profits they also presented problems of production and control. The regulations of the Stationers' Company always recognized that the Queen's/King's Printer was entitled to own more presses than was any other London printer, but whereas keeping a check on the output of individual presses (and therefore of pressmen) can have presented few problems in a one- or two-press house, it did – on the evidence of the printed Bibles themselves – present problems for a printing house with as many as six (the figure for the King's Printers in 1668).[42] One aspect of control was to be able to identify the pressman or men responsible for printing a particular forme, either as a record for payment or as a means of identifying perpetrators of poor work. In a large printing establishment like the King's Printing House control was established by the use of press figures – that is, by inserting in the direction line of one of the pages in the forme a typographic symbol or an arabic number corresponding with the press at which the forme was printed.

Such, therefore, were the conditions of Bible printing that press figures were first employed at the King's Printer's in the late 1620s,[43] the device not being

39 Madan 1895–1931, III, p. 325. 40 Kilburne 1659, p. 10.
41 Johnson and Gibson 1946, p. 116. 42 Carter 1975, pp. 98–9. 43 McMullin 1979.

adopted by the trade at large until much later in the century. One economy presented by an unchanged text in constant demand – such as the Bible – is that, within the one format and the one collation, individual sheets can be reprinted in order to maintain the supply.[44] But an explanation recently advanced for the use of press figures in works produced in large numbers (and within a short time) is that rather than individual sheets being reprinted as stocks became depleted they were set concurrently in duplicate – hence the need to distinguish formes or sheets containing the same text printed at different presses, and not necessarily within the one printing house.[45]

Paper-quality marks

Editions of the Bible, and of the accompanying works with which Bibles are often bound, the Book of Common Prayer and Sternhold and Hopkins Psalms, might be produced on various qualities of paper (sometimes from the same setting of type), ranging from common to superfine and varying in price by a factor of perhaps 100 per cent or more: Michael Sparke refers to the '*Cambridge* thinne paper Folio Roman, sold at, or cheaper then 16^{s} in quires' and the '*Cambridge* Large Folio Bible Roman, of the best paper, sold at 1^{l} 10^{s} in quires, or cheaper'.[46] Sparke's reference is presumably to the 1629 edition, which is the earliest documented instance of the one edition comprising separate issues differing in quality of paper, though it is in fact to be found on seven distinct papers rather than on Sparke's three (he refers also to a 'Medyum' at £1 2*s.* 6*d.*).[47] Warehousing and distributing such a large number of issues must, one can only assume, have presented considerable difficulties, since the various qualities are not necessarily distinguishable by size and since adjacent qualities are not readily distinguishable to eye or touch.

The 1629 Cambridge folio is admittedly an extreme example, and it is doubtful if issues within any other edition of the Bible ever exceeded three. The solution to the difficulty of warehousing and distribution was to indicate on the sheets themselves what issue they belonged to, thus ensuring that exemplars would be put together made up of sheets of a uniform quality. The method of marking the sheets, apparently introduced at the Oxford Bible press in the early 1680s, was to add to the direction line of the first recto of every sheet (whether or not quired) a typographic symbol (one issue often in fact being distinguishable by lacking a symbol). Thus the three issues of the 1688 Oxford folio are distinguished, in ascending order of fineness, by the absence of a mark, by

44 McMullin 1983. 45 McMullin 1996. 46 Sparke 1641, p. 184. 47 McMullin 1984a.

¶ and by ¶¶. As with press figures, there is no contemporary reference to these symbols, but while press figures became common in general printing in the eighteenth century and survived into the nineteenth these symbols were used only rarely in the eighteenth century; the term 'paper-quality mark' is a modern coining.[48]

The privileged printers therefore were the first to face the problems encountered by large establishments engaged in producing large edition numbers of a substantial work in constant demand; in their resolution of these problems (though not invariably by the means just described) they anticipated members of the general trade. It might also be noted that Athias anticipated the use of stereotyping in the production of English Bibles but that the technique had to be re-invented before being applied at Cambridge to the production of Bibles for the British and Foreign Bible Society beginning in 1805 (DMH 1485, a New Testament).

The Bible in other British languages

By the end of the seventeenth century Bibles had been printed in Welsh and Irish (Erse), but Scottish Gaelic and Manx were to wait until the late-eighteenth for even a New Testament.[49] William Salesbury, who had compiled the first Welsh-English dictionary, published in 1547, was granted a seven-year privilege in 1563 to print the Bible in Welsh. The New Testament was published in quarto in London by Humfrey Toy in 1567 (*STC* 2960), but the whole Bible did not appear until 1588, being published in folio in London by the deputies of Christopher Barker (*STC* 2347). A revised version of the 1588 edition was published in 1620, again in folio in London, by Norton and Bill (*STC* 2348). This new version took account of the Authorized Version and has remained the standard Welsh Bible; a further five editions (two in folio, three in octavo) appeared during the seventeenth century, four from London, the fifth – the 1690 folio – from Oxford.

Queen Elizabeth had occasioned an Irish fount (actually a hybrid) to be produced in 1567 in order to promote Protestantism in Ireland, but, following an abortive attempt to print the New Testament in the late 1580s, it was not until 1602 that a New Testament in Irish was printed, in folio in Dublin by John Franckton, in an edition of 500 (*STC* 2958). No further Irish edition was published until new translations of the New Testament (1681) and the Old

48 McMullin 1984b. 49 See *CHL*, III, pp. 170–4 and below, pp. 703, 725–6, 729–30.

(1685) appeared, printed in quarto in London by Robert Everingham from a new Irish fount (Wing B2759A/C/D). This version was reprinted in twelvemo by Everingham, in an edition of 3,000, for use in the Scottish Highlands, but now in roman type (Wing B2759B/F).

The Book of Common Prayer and Sternhold and Hopkins Psalms

The privilege granted to Christopher Barker as Queen's Printer in 1577 included, in addition to the Bible, various other categories of book, including all service books required to be used in churches. Hence the Book of Common Prayer was coupled with the Bible in disputes between the Queen's/King's Printers and the universities or their agents, and when the universities' rights were confirmed but limited to Bibles in quarto and medium folio it was allowed that they should be allowed to print the Book of Common Prayer in sufficient numbers to bind up with the Bibles. Being thus often required for binding up with Bibles and therefore being printed in similarly large numbers, the Book of Common Prayer was treated in the same way in the printing house in being equipped with press figures and paper-quality marks when necessary. It differed, however, from the Bible in not apparently being pirated. The relative slightness of the text may have made it at once attractive to local pirates and unattractive to the Dutch, but one disincentive to piracy was the volatility of the text – that is, various events (notably births, deaths and marriages within the royal family) required the immediate revision of the text. The revisions were accommodated by setting the whole text anew, but also by producing cancels, ranging from paste-over slips to whole gatherings; whether the cancels were always inserted before sale or might be provided to owners to insert themselves has not been determined.[50]

Sternhold and Hopkins differed from the Book of Common Prayer in not being part of the Queen's/King's Printer's privilege. In 1577 the privilege for printing the Psalms in metre had been granted to John Day and his son Richard, but, in the face of opposition from members of the Stationers' Company at large, in 1603 it and a number of other privileges belonging to members were granted by James I to the Company as a whole, forming the English Stock. Editions of Sternhold and Hopkins were pirated to match the corresponding Bibles, but the extent of the activity has not been established. Sternhold and Hopkins was included in the various treaties of forbearance entered into by the Company

50 McMullin 1981 and McMullin 1995.

and the universities, which sometimes included provision for the Company to supply exemplars for binding up with Oxford Bibles, and when the Company dragged its feet Parker and Guy were not above printing their own supplies, as well as others for general sale. Again like the Bible and the Book of Common Prayer, Sternhold and Hopkins was equipped with press figures and paper-quality marks when necessary.

A note on the bibliography of the Bible

Numerous catalogues of collections of Bibles have been published, and one has been accepted as the standard bibliography for English Bibles, being constantly referred to in this chapter: the *Historical catalogue of printed editions of the English Bible*, first published in 1903, on the centenary of the British and Foreign Bible Society, and in a revised edition in 1968 (DMH). Despite the constant reference to it, it is a defective work. That there are numerous editions not recorded in it is a deficiency which may easily be remedied; its other deficiencies are more problematic. One such is the fact that the Bible Society collection, on which it is based, is itself based on the collection of Francis Fry, and Fry was a sophisticator, making up complete exemplars from defective originals and improving others by transferring leaves – thus the integrity of exemplars, particularly in the sixteenth century, is uncertain.[51] Moreover, the original compilers and the reviser were all lacking in bibliographical awareness sufficient to categorize, describe and distinguish items, so that the information contained and the criteria for distinction employed are alike questionable.

51 McMullin 1990.

22

English law books and legal publishing

J. H. BAKER

William Fulbecke, in 1600, divided law books into four categories: historical (law reports and statutes), explanatory (glosses on texts, such as Staunford's *Prerogative*),[1] 'miscellaneal' (abridgments), and 'monological' (monographs on particular topics).[2] Of the fourth category, which Fulbecke praised as the most orderly, few examples were then available. Besides Littleton and Perkins, on elementary land law,[3] only two on criminal law deserved mention: Sir William Staunford's *Les plees del coron* (1557) and William Lambard's *Eirenarcha* (1581). Staunford was singled out by Fulbecke for its 'force and weight, and no common kind of stile', with the hope that 'his method may be a law to the writers of the law which shall follow him'. But this was not yet the age of the advanced textbook. And older books, such as *Bracton* (first printed in 1569), though 'not unprofitable to read', were dangerous to trust. The third category was derived entirely from the first, and was designed to make the sources more accessible. Books in the second category were relatively uncommon in 1600.[4] The prime example should have been readings in the inns of court, which were commentaries on statutes, and it is a telling reflection on the change in their status that they are not mentioned in the *Direction* at all.[5]

Far more important than the other three as legal authorities were the books in Fulbecke's first category, the undigested primary sources of the law: that is, the ever growing body of acts of Parliament and reports of cases.[6] According to Fulbecke, 'The common law is for the most part contained in all the books

1 W. Staunford, *An exposition of the kings prerogative* (London, 1567) (a commentary on the 'statute' Prerogativa Regis, written before 1558).

2 *Direction or preparative to the study of the law* (London, 1600). The same scheme is adopted in W. P[hillips], *Studii legalis ratio* (London, 1662), p. 101.

3 These were very frequently reprinted. The first editions in our period were *Littletons Tenures* (1557) and *A profitable booke of Maister John Perkins* (1567), both printed by Richard Tottell.

4 Cf. E. Coke, *First Part of the Institutes* (1628) (a commentary on Littleton's *Tenures*); *Second Part* (1642) (a commentary on selected statutes); below, 491–2, 502.

5 For readings and their importance, see Baker 2001.

6 For an outline of the principal classes of law book at the beginning of our period, see also Hellinga and Trapp 1999, pp. 417–23.

called the Annals of the Law or Year-books, all of which are to be read, if the student will attain to any depth in the Law.' To them had more recently been added the reports of Edmund Plowden (*Les comentaries*, 1571; with supplement, 1578) and Sir James Dyer (*Ascuns novel cases*, 1585/6),[7] which were also essential reading. In addition to these sources of the common law, the lawyer needed to equip himself with a retrospective collection of statutes, such as Rastell's,[8] to which he could add the legislation of each new session as it was printed by the queen's printer.

Fulbecke did not mention manuscripts, and this omission is significant. By 1600 it is tacitly assumed that a student can assemble a basic library composed entirely of books in print. The story of the English law book from Elizabeth I to William III must indeed be, to a large extent, a history of the arrangements for law printing during that period, and this will be the focus of the present chapter. Yet it is all too easy for the modern observer to assume that the law manuscript was practically dead, or at best purely ornamental.[9] This would be a major error. In fact, the library of any professional lawyer in our period, from the chief justice down to the common attorney, was likely to contain manuscripts of practical value. We might well expect manuscripts ancient and modern to have filled the shelves of great judges and jurists such as Sir James Dyer (*d.* 1582),[10] Sir Edward Coke (*d.* 1634) or Sir Matthew Hale (*d.* 1676),[11] or of lawyers with antiquarian interests such as William Fletewoode (*d.* 1594) and Francis Tate (*d.* 1616).[12] Such men naturally studied and exchanged them with enthusiasm. But surviving portions of the libraries of puisne judges such as Robert Nicholas (*d.* 1667) and Thomas Twisden (*d.* 1683), or of practising serjeants at law such as Arthur Turnour (*d.* 1651) and Thomas Powys (*d.* 1671), show that substantial collections of manuscript law reports were still part of the ordinary working law library in the middle of the seventeenth century.[13] Lower down the profession, attorneys and court officers kept manuscript precedents of conveyances, pleadings and entries, frequently of their own making.[14]

7 J. H. Baker, introduction to *Reports from the lost notebooks of Sir James Dyer*, 2 vols. (Selden Society vol. 109, 1994), I.

8 W. Rastell ed., *A colleccion of all the statutes* (London, 1557). A twenty-first edn appeared in 1621.

9 Even Bennett 1965, pp. 156–66 (chapter on Law), makes no mention at all of manuscripts.

10 *Reports from the lost notebooks of Sir James Dyer*, I, pp. xxviii–xxix.

11 Coke: Hassall 1950. Hale: *ELM*, vol. II, pp. 8–18; D. E. C. Yale, introduction to *Hale's The prerogatives of the king* (Selden Society, vol. 92, 1976), pp. lix–lxxvi.

12 *CELMCUL*, intro., pp. xlvii–l.

13 For the Turnour and Powys MSS. (Harvard Law School) and the Twisden MSS. (Harvard Law School, Georgetown University), see *ELMUSA*, part II (1990). For the Nicholas MSS, see *CELMCUL*, pp. li–lii, lvii–lix.

14 *CELMCUL*, p. xxxviii.

The lawyer had to build up his own collection, since there was little reliance on the somewhat inadequate libraries of the inns of court. A law student would also make some of his books himself, by borrowing and transcribing, commonplacing, and collecting precedents. The legal commonplace book comes into particular prominence in the sixteenth century, and was still in use after our period;[15] but the many examples surviving from the period 1590–1640 suggest that for a time every student must have kept one. Most legal commonplace books are small notebooks divided into alphabetical titles, with notes entered in the course of basic reading through the yearbooks, Plowden, Dyer, Littleton and Perkins. An assiduous practitioner, such as Hale or Twisden, would use the same technique later in his career for storing notes of unpublished decisions. Other judges and practitioners kept manuscript reports in the traditional chronological form; the practice was far more widespread than the body of printed books suggests, and some of the best reports of the early seventeenth century are still unprinted.[16] Unprinted reports were not necessarily private, because some of them circulated quite widely in manuscript form,[17] and it is clear that some of the manuscript copies from the 1620s and 1630s were produced by law stationers for sale. Students also used interleaved or extra-marginated copies of Littleton – and occasionally other standard works[18] – as the basis for collecting notes on land law, and many of these survive from the Elizabethan and Jacobean periods.

More and more, however, the law student and even the practitioner came to rely on printed abridgments of case-law, especially the 'grand abridgments' of the year books by Sir Anthony Fitzherbert (reprinted in 1565 and 1577) and Sir Robert Brooke (written before 1558, but first printed in 1573–4). The standard advice given to students was that they should not rely on such books, but use them solely as finding-aids:

> Let all Professors of the Law . . . beware lest through sloathfulness, ease or negligence, they more study and make use of Abridgements . . . than of the original Law-books . . . Let them be sure to resort to the Originals themselves, and not rely upon the Abridgements alone, to prevent Mistakes, Errors, yea the loss of their Reputations, if their Abridgements should misguide them.[19]

15 D. Lemmings, *Gentlemen and barristers* (Oxford, 1990), pp. 102–3.

16 J. H. Baker, *The legal profession and the common law* (London, 1986), pp. 451–7; D. J. Ibbetson, 'Coventry's Reports', *Journal of Legal History*, 16 (1996), 281–303.

17 *CELMCUL*, pp. xli–xliii.

18 The writer has an extra-marginated copy of Fitzherbert's *La novel natura brevium* (London, 1635 ed), with copious manuscript references to yearbooks apparently transcribed from an exemplar.

19 W. Prynne, preface to R. Cotton, *An exact abridgement of the records in the Tower of London* (London, 1657), sig. A3–4 (accusing Coke of ignoring his own, similar advice). Cf. W. Phillips, *Studii legalis ratio* (1662), pp. 119–20.

However, a lawyer writing in the 1640s complained bitterly of this attitude, which he considered unrealistic. He said 'a man's life would scant suffice' for the task, and that they were in any case 'mostly filled with itterated janglinges aboute pleadinges and exceptions to writtes'. He had himself 'with a wearied spirritt and almost destroyed body' read all the law books he could find, and had come to regard the time as largely wasted; since Fitzherbert and Brooke knew the yearbooks far better than any modern student, their notes were bound to be more useful.[20] This was no doubt the counsel of despair of a less able student, but anyone who has made the like effort to conquer the yearbooks will sympathize with his predicament in a world without textbooks. Sir Matthew Hale informed a law student in 1672 that he faced a practical choice:[21]

> there were two ways of applying one's self to the study of the law: one was to attain the great learning of it which was to be had in all the old Books; but that did require great time, and would be at least seven years before a man would be fit to make any benefit by it: the other was, by fitting one's self for the practice of the Court, by reading the new Reports and the present Constitution of the Law . . . a great many of the cases seldom coming in practice, and several of them antiquated.

In the Restoration period, a few abridgments of more recent cases were published, though these were less well thought of than their precursors and were not reprinted.[22]

The printing press also supplied practitioners with more reference tools relating to practice. Elementary guides to current practice in the central courts began to appear in manuscript form in the later sixteenth century,[23] and reached the press in the seventeenth century in the form of Thomas Powell's *The attourneys academy* (1623).[24] The first notable printed work on pleading was *Doctrina placitandi ou l'art & science de bon pleading* (1677), by Sir Sampson Eure (*d.* 1659), king's serjeant under Charles I, though it is no more than an

20 Anon., 'Directions for the orderly reading of the lawe of England', Bodleian MS. Rawlinson C. 207, fo. 245 (quotations at fols. 250, 252, 256).

21 *Anecdotes of some distinguished persons*, ed. W. Seward (London, 1795–7), IV, pp. 414–15. Cf. Hale's detailed advice on reading the yearbooks: 'The Publisher's Preface directed to the Young Students of the Common-Law' in H. Rolle, *Abridgment des plusieurs cases* (London, 1668), sig. B2v; *History of the common law* (London, 1713), p. 172.

22 See below, p. 503. For the printing of Rolle, see below, pp. 485–7. For Sheppard, see below, p. 488.

23 E.g., 'Certaine instructions for an attorney' (*c.* 1588), Harvard Law School MS. 5020, unfol.; 'The offyce of an attornye', Folger Shakespeare Library MS. x. d. 483(196), fols. 3–8; 'Certaine breife noates and instructions necessarie for such as are towards the practise of an Attourney in the Comon Pleas' (*c.* 1616/18), CUL MS. Dd. 10. 49, fols. 25–88v. There are similar texts in CUL MS. Dd. 12. 27, fols. 12–37v; Lincoln's Inn MS. Misc. 586; BL, MS. Sloane 2172, fols. 46v–58; MS. Harley 1938; MS. Harley 2202, fols. 49–53v; MS. Hargrave 405, fols. 3–43; Bodleian MS. Rawlinson C. 65.

24 Note also W. Booth, *The compleat solicitor* (1660); T. Manley, *The sollicitor* (1663); T. Cory, *The course and practise of the court of Common Pleas* (1672). Cory died in 1656.

abridgment of cases on the subject.[25] These were augmented with more and more books of entries – specimens of written pleading (in Latin) taken from the plea rolls – and during the great plague of 1665 George Townesend occupied himself in the country by producing a laborious and valuable index (in 549 pages) to all the precedents contained in the printed books.[26] By 1705, so many further volumes of entries had been published that a continuation volume of equal length was required.[27] The craft of conveyancing was put on a new footing by William West's *Symbolæographia: the art, description or image of instruments* (1590–3), which combined precedents with commentary. Elementary guides to conveyancing also appeared, such as George Billinghurst's *Arcana clericalia* (1674), William Brown's *Treatise of recoveries* (1679), and Serjeant William Sheppard's more compendious and oft-reprinted *Touchstone of common assurances* (1648), together with a host of precedent-books, the most distinguished of which was the posthumous *Conveyances* (1682) of Sir Orlando Bridgman.

The law printers and their monopoly

The desirability of printing of law books was not universally accepted, because the humanistic aspiration to make the law accessible to everyone came into conflict with the more realistic – if self-serving – professional view that it would promote misunderstanding and strife if the unlearned were let loose on technical works.[28] The solution, until the 1650s, was found in language: elementary books were published in English, whereas purely professional works such as law reports or entries were preserved from vulgar eyes in their original language (law French or Latin). The printing press was therefore able to serve the different needs of the profession, of those studying to enter the profession, and of the general public. Control of legal publishing was exercised both through the law printers' monopolistic rights, granted by letters patent, and the nascent concept of intellectual property which developed alongside them, and through a judicial licensing system. Each of these will be considered in turn.

25 Note also G. Townesend, *A preparative to pleading* (1675); Sir Robert Heath (*d.* 1649), *Maxims and rules of pleading* (1694); R. Gardiner, *A method of pleading by rule* (1697).

26 *Tables to most of the printed presidents of pleadings, writs, and retorn of writs* (London: assigns of Richard and Edward Atkyns, 1667). He says in the preface that he had done the work for the common good rather than his own: 'Monie would hardly have made my Mare have gone this Journey'.

27 J. Cornwall and R. G[ardiner], *Tables to the modern printed presidents of pleadings, writs, and returns of writs, &c. at the common law: being a continuation from Mr. Townsend's Tables down to this time* (London, 1705).

28 See Ross 1998.

Richard Tottell, 1553–1593

Tottell's possession of the patent for sole printing of common-law books[29] gave him the undoubted supremacy in law publishing for forty years. As early as 1556, he invited his readers to cast their minds back a few years to the pre-Tottell era, when the books of law were imperfect, 'the most part merveloúsly mangled, and no smale part no wher to be gotten', so that the scarcity had raised the prices. He boasted that:

> ther be enow . . . that . . . can truely witnes . . . sithens I toke in hand to serve your uses, that imperfections have ben supplied, the price so eased as the scarcenes no more hindereth but that ye have them as chepe (notwithstanding the common dearth of the times) as when thei were most plentiful, the print much pleasanter to the eye in the bokes of yeres than any that ye have ben yet served with, paper and margine as good and as faire as the best, but much better and fairer than the most, no smal nomber by me set forth newly in print that before were scant to be found in writing, I nede not my self to report it.[30]

This self-assessment is not, of course, to be taken as an objective evaluation. When the printing monopolies came under attack in the 1570s and 1580s, Tottell was not immune from criticism. In fact it was alleged that, contrary to Tottell's claims, he had used the monopoly to raise prices, 'to the hinderance of a greate nomber of pore studentes'.[31] There is certainly evidence that law books commanded higher prices than other kinds of book,[32] though this might have been justified by the limited size of the market. Without access to Tottell's profit-and-loss accounts, and to particulars of the fluctuations in prices charged for law books,it is impossible to assess the truth of his assertion. The King's Printer, Christopher Barker, took the sympathetic view that Tottell's patent 'is of much lesse value then before, and is like yet to be rather worse than better, except a man should with exceading charge take another course therein then hetherto hath ben observed and as these dayes requier'.[33] The authorities seem to have accepted this assessment, and the only new restrictions placed on the law printer were that he should not have more than two presses, and that he should be liable to punishment for corrupt printing.[34]

29 See Hellinga and Trapp 1999, pp. 427–9.

30 Preface to *Magna charta cum statutis quae antiquae vocantur* (London, dated 12 June 1556), sig. *ii (abbreviations extended).

31 'The griefes of the printers . . . susteined by reson of priviledges granted to privatt persons', Burghley Papers, BL, MS. Lansdowne 48, fol. 180.

32 Johnson 1950, p. 91. For some evidence relating to the prices of yearbooks, see below, p. 496.

33 Letter to Burghley, 'A note of the state of the Company of . . . Stationers, with a valuation also of the lettres patentes concerning printing' (*c.* 1582), Burghley Papers, BL, MS. Lansdowne 48, fol. 189.

34 Greg 1967, pp. 131–2.

Although he undertook some new titles of importance, such as Staunford's *Les plees del coron* (1557), the yearbooks *1–10 Edward III* (1562) and *Henry V* (1563),[35] Plowden (1571–8), Lambard's *Eirenarcha* (1581), and Dyer (1585), much of Tottell's legal work consisted in repeatedly reprinting the haphazardly established canon of yearbooks. Bibliographers observed long ago that Tottell, like Shakespeare, 'had his name spelt very different',[36] and that the changes in spelling in the colophons were a key to identifying different printings, even when the date was left unchanged. Many of the books with colophons or title pages dated in the 1550s were actually printed in the 1560s or 1570s; indeed, two editions of *Henry VII* with a title page dated 1555 have later dates in the colophons.[37] One reason for his reluctance to change the dates may have been that he often mixed sheets from different printings. But he continued this practice even after he began to include more recent dates. For example, a copy of *Henry VII* in Peterborough Cathedral library has a 1580 title page and eighty-four sheets from the 1580 edition, a 1583 colophon and 107 sheets from the 1583/5 edition, five sheets from two earlier editions, and eight apparently new sheets (*c.* 1585).[38] Clearly it made no difference to Tottell, and probably it made no difference to his customers, how the books were made up. The divergences between printings were seldom material, and new errors were offset by corrections.[39] The system also had the positive benefit of introducing a standard foliation, which not only enabled Tottell to use up remaindered sheets but also enabled lawyers from his time onwards to cite cases by regnal year and folio. Another of his achievements in yearbook printing was to collect most of the existing individual yearbooks into composite volumes, beginning with *Henry IV* in 1554 (new style), and ending with *Henry VIII* in 1591. With Tottell, the issuing of individual years ended, with the solitary exception of the *Long quinto*.[40] This policy of consolidation may have brought to his attention the glaring gaps in the series, though it is a principal criticism of his stewardship that – with the exceptions mentioned above – he generally chose not to fill them.[41] Given the editorial standards of the time, it is perhaps as well. For example,

35 With the exception of *7 Edward III*, printed by Pynson. Tottell claimed to have collated numerous manuscripts, though only one text seems to have been printed.

36 J. Ames, *Typographical antiquities* (London, 1749), p. 288.

37 Beale, nos. R.411–12; and see *STC* 9923–4.

38 Now in CUL, shelf-mark Pet. H. 5. 12, art. 4. The editions are *STC* 9924–6; see the note to *STC* 9925.

39 For strictures on the quality of his reprints, see B. H. Putnam, *Early treatises on the practice of justices of the peace* (Oxford, 1924), p. 31; W. C. Bolland, *Manual of year book studies* (Cambridge, 1925), pp. 69–70.

40 A long report of 5 Edw. IV, in a sense outside the vulgate series, which was first printed by Powell in 1552, and was reprinted separately both by Tottell in 1587 and by More's assigns in 1638: *STC* 9802.5–9804; below, p. 484.

41 Hellinga and Trapp 1999 427–8, 431.

although his collected edition of *Henry VII* (1555) included a number of reports between 1493 and 1506 which had never before been printed, many of the additions are misdated, and some can be shown to be the work of John Caryll (*d.* 1523) whose entire reports were eventually printed in 1999.[42] Tottell also contemplated, in 1590, a volume of Richard II cases culled from Fitzherbert's *La graunde abridgement*, to rival Robinson's edition of Bellewe's *Les ans du roy Richard le second* (1585), but nothing came of it.[43] Full reports of the years used by Fitzherbert were still available in manuscript, but it seems that the general demand for old cases of that kind was far from strident.

Tottell's immediate successors, 1593–1629

Tottell did not raise a family to succeed him as law printer, and in November 1577 – fifteen years before his death – the reversion expectant upon his life interest in the monopoly was granted by letters patent to Nicasius Yetsweirt (*d.* 1586), a clerk of the signet and secretary for the French tongue to Queen Elizabeth I.[44] The terms were similar to those of the earlier patent, save that the interest was to run for thirty years from the determination of Tottell's interest. By the time the reversion fell in, on Tottell's death in 1593, Nicasius Yetsweirt had himself died. Yetsweirt's son Charles thereupon claimed that the interest had passed to him, presumably as his father's personal representative,[45] and complained about its recent infringement by the Queen's Printer (Christopher Barker) in publishing Pulton's *Abstract of all the penal statutes* (1592) and Rastell's *Collection of the statutes* (1594), the latter of which had first been printed by Tottell. Barker – whose family held the office of Queen's Printer from 1577 to 1680[46] – enjoyed the monopoly of printing Acts of Parliament, and it is difficult to see how collections of statutes could be considered to 'touche or concerne the common lawes of this ... realme'; but the difficulty was avoided by the grant of new letters patent to Charles Yetsweirt in 1594, reciting the disputes and giving him a monopoly of printing common-law books and the two statutory collections (by name), for thirty years from the date of the patent.[47] The new patent was opposed by the Stationers' Company, who offered to purchase it in 1595, though terms could not be agreed.[48] Some

42 *The reports of John Caryll*, ed. J. H. Baker (London, 1999). Cf. *Relationes ex libris Roberti Keilwey*, ed. J. Croke (London, 1602).

43 University College London, Ogden MS. 7/40.

44 For a brief biography (a pamphlet of twelve pages), see Bradford 1934.

45 The patent of 1577 granted the interest to Yetsweirt, his executors, administrators and assigns.

46 For the complex history of the Barkers' tenure, see Plomer 1901. The previous holders in our period were John Cawood (*d.* 1573) and Richard Jugge (*d.* 1577).

47 Pat. 36 Eliz. I, pt 11, mm. 6–8 (20 March 1594); Greg and Boswell 1930, p. 48.

48 Blagden 1960, p. 93.

stationers took the matter into their own hands by printing books which infringed the patent, and Yetsweirt (supported by the earl of Essex) was obliged to sue in Chancery to protect his rights. The master of the rolls is said to have granted an injunction in his favour, thereby arguably laying the foundations of later copyright protection.[49] At the height of the dispute, Charles Yetsweirt died,[50] leaving his widow and administratrix Jane to carry on the business and the litigation. She complained of her opponents' lack of humanity in harassing her in her distress, and maintained that law printing was her only livelihood; but her offer of a settlement was refused.[51] She nevertheless managed to print several law books between 1595 and 1597, including the first collected edition of *Edward V*, *Richard III*, *Henry VII* and *Henry VIII* in one volume. But in 1597 she married Sir Philip Boteler of Watton Woodhall, Hertfordshire, and became free to retire from her trade into country life.[52] In March of the following year, Jane and her husband formally surrendered the patent in Chancery.[53] It was bought soon afterwards by Thomas Wight and Bonham Norton, who had published several law books 'cum privilegio' in 1598 as 'assigns' of the Botelers, and obtained their own patent on 30 March 1599.[54] The patent gave them another thirty years, on the same terms as the Yetsweirts. Within a year, Norton left the partnership to become a leading publisher in his own right. Wight continued to print law books for about five years, and achieved some distinction as the publisher of the first four parts of Coke's *Reports* (1600–4) and of *Relationes ex libris Roberti Keilwey* (1602), being a text of John Caryll's reports edited by Serjeant John Croke from a manuscript formerly belonging to Robert Keilwey (*d.* 1581).

In 1605 Wight sold his privilege, with twenty years still to run, to the Company of Stationers, who worked it as part of their English Stock.[55] The company in September of the same year sold the 'workmanship of the privilege' to Adam Islip, during their pleasure, and he printed several law books (including most of Coke's works) before selling his interest to Robert Raworth and John Monger for £140. Not long after the transfer, these two forfeited their

49 Correspondence in BL, MS. Harley 6997, fols. 3, 18.

50 William Smith's funeral book, Folger Shakespeare Library MS. v. b. 194, pt 2, fol. 6 (*d.* 25 April 1595 and buried at Sunbury).

51 Letters from Jane Yetsweirt (to Burghley and Lord Keeper Puckering) in BL, MS. Harley 6997, fols. 18, 20; HMC, *Salisbury*, vol. 5, p. 191.

52 Parish register cited in D. Lysons, *Historical account of those parishes in Middlesex which are not described in the environs of London* (London, 1800), p. 283 (marriage on 16 June 1597).

53 Memorandum in the margin of the 1594 patent roll (m. 6), signed by Lord Keeper Egerton, Philip Boteler, and Jane Boteler, 9 March 1598/9.

54 Pat. 41 Eliz. I, pt 4, mm. 34–5. On 26 March, the patent was read out to the Stationers' Company: Greg and Boswell 1930, p. 70.

55 Jackson 1957, pp. ix, 13, 16. Wight died before 1609.

rights for infringing the copyright of another member of the company, and Raworth's place was taken by John Haviland.[56] These printers never printed law books under their own names, but always 'for the Company of Stationers'. They reprinted a number of yearbooks, continued the publication of Coke's reports, and also published Ashe's *Promptuarie* (1614)[57] – an elaborate index to the yearbooks – and Coke's monumental *Booke of entries* (1614). No doubt their greatest contribution to legal literature was to publish the first edition of *Coke upon Littleton* (1628), a word-by-word commentary on Littleton's *Tenures* by the oracular Sir Edward Coke (*d.* 1634), a difficult book which for all its faults was to remain for over two hundred years the leading textbook on the law of real property. It was the only book of the common law printed in the glossatorial manner, with Littleton's fifteenth-century text in heavy black letter and Coke's marginal commentary encrusted around it in smaller type.

John More, his assigns and successors, 1629–1680

In March 1629 the privilege granted to Wight and Norton expired. Meanwhile, on 19 January 1618, the reversion had been granted by patent to John More,[58] clerk of the signet, to run for forty years from the determination of the former privilege. More was not himself a printer, and the privilege was for him a source of revenue from his lessees. Law publishing thus became severed from law printing, and so it was to remain thereafter. A few months after his interest fell in, More leased it to Miles Flesher (a prominent stationer), John Haviland (who had already worked the patent under the Stationers) and Robert Younge, for the term of thirty-eight years. These 'assigns' – as the under-lessees describe themselves – were to pay £60 a year rent for the first seven years, and thereafter a rent to be determined by arbitration; if the arbitrators found there had been a trading loss in the first seven years, More was to refund a proportion of the rent. More was to receive in addition one third of all clear gains, which he covenanted to reinvest in the business. There was thus effectively a joint stock, to which More contributed one third and the three under-lessees the remaining two-thirds.[59] After the death of Haviland in 1638, and Younge in 1643, Flesher as the last survivor came into sole possession of the law printing[60] and produced

56 Arber, III, pp. 701, 703, 704 (citing state papers); Jackson 1957, p. 16.

57 Some copies have the imprint of John Beale as assignee of the Stationers.

58 Pat. 15 Jac. I, pt 4, mm. 21–3. The name is spelt 'Moore' in the patent, but he used the spelling 'More' in his imprints.

59 BL, MS. Harley 5903, fols. 108–15 (copy of indenture of 1 May 1629).

60 See Blagden 1960, pp. 138–45.

(amongst other law books) the first editions of the third and fourth parts of Coke's *Institutes* (1644),[61] and Selden's edition of *Fleta* (1647). By 1650 the privilege was being worked by his son James.[62]

During this period, the old trouble which had beset the Yetsweirts returned. Some Stationers objected that the privilege granted to More was a monopoly against the public interest – not to mention their own – and that More had abused it by driving up the price of law books. One pamphleteer complained that if one were to 'look but into a window of the monopolists Law-Warehouse' one would find 500 copies of the *Long quinto*, published at one shilling, priced at six shillings.[63] As early as 1636, More became involved in Chancery litigation concerning the privilege, and reasons were prepared to support the right of the Crown to grant such monopolies.[64] When More died in 1638, his reversionary interest in the privilege devolved upon his daughter Martha, wife of Colonel Richard Atkyns. His share in the joint stock, on the other hand, was sold to James Flesher, son of the last survivor of the working lessees, who thereupon became the sole owner of the stock and solely entitled to print common-law books during the term of the lease.[65] However, his rights were rendered almost worthless during the Interregnum, when an unregulated scramble to print law books brought a torrent of publications of indifferent quality. It seems from the imprints that much of the new work was carried out by Thomas Roycroft at the behest of booksellers in and around the inns of court, who presumably provided all or part of the capital outlay.[66] Other booksellers and printers acted in similar combinations.[67]

61 For these, see below, p. 491.

62 E.g. the imprint of Hobart's *Reports* (London, 1650), printed by James Flesher for William Lee and Daniel Pakeman, booksellers in Fleet Street.

63 [M. Sparke,] *Scintilla, or a light broken into darke warehouses* (London, 1641); reprinted in Arber, IV, pp. 37, 38. The 1638 *Long quinto* in the Institute of Advanced Legal Studies, London, is inscribed, 'Geo. Billingshurst prec. vj s. empt. May 22, 1652'.

64 Blagden 1960, p. 140; Greg 1967, pp. 339–40, citing state papers.

65 Chancery proceedings titled 'Reynardson', bundles 31 and 126, summarized in Plomer 1907b, p. 8. There was also a dispute with Flesher.

66 E.g. Popham's *Reports* (1656), for John Place of Furnival's Inn Gate, Hutton's *Reports* (1656) and Coke's *Reports*, pt 12 (1658), for Henry Twyford of Vine Court, Middle Temple, and Thomas Dring of the George in Fleet Street (next to Clifford's Inn); Owen's *Reports* (1656) and Ley's *Reports* (1659), for all three; Coke's *Reports*, pt 13 (1659) for Twyford, Dring and J. Sherley of The Pelican in Little Britain; Leonard's *Reports* (1658–9), for Nathaniel Ekins of the The Gun in St Paul's churchyard.

67 E.g. Hetley's *Reports* (1657), by F. L. for Matthew Walbancke of Gray's Inn Gate and Thomas Firby of Holborn (near Gray's Inn); Style's *Reports* (1658), by F. L. for W. Lee, D. Pakeman, G. Bedel and C. Adams, booksellers in Fleet Street; Croke's *Reports* temp. Car. (1657), by R. Hodgkinsonne for William Leak of The Crown in Fleet Street (between the two Temple gates) and Thomas Firby; Croke's *Reports* temp. Car. (1658), by T. Newcomb and W. Godbid for Lee, Pakeman, Abel Roper, Twyford, Bedell and Dring, of Fleet Street and the Middle Temple, George Sawbridge of Ludgate Hill, and Place (previous note).

At the Restoration, the common-law printing privilege was renewed for forty years in favour of Edward Atkyns of Lincoln's Inn,[68] apparently the colonel's younger brother,[69] presumably with the consent of and partly in trust for Colonel and Mrs Martha Atkyns. These three beneficial owners in 1664 leased the privilege for twenty-one years to the printers James Flesher, John Streater and Henry Twyford, at a fine of about £1,000 and a rent of £100 a year; Martha was also given £50 in silver plate.[70] Flesher's new partners were already well established as law booksellers, and Twyford (whose shop was in Vine Court) was arguably the most prominent legal bookseller of the period.[71] No doubt they were brought in to provide capital, since Flesher had experienced difficulties in paying his rent.

Almost as soon as the lease had been granted, the lessees found themselves embroiled in the revived Chancery litigation brought by the London Stationers, and they even spent a short time in prison.[72] Apparently the Stationers claimed some rights under More's patent (which would have expired in 1669), asserting that they had purchased it from Flesher in 1661.[73] The dispute was ended by a decree restraining the Stationers from publishing law books without the Atkyns's assent,[74] after which the lessees began to publish law books as a joint-stock partnership.[75] However, in 1668, some members of the company ignored the Chancery decree and infringed the Atkyns's rights by undertaking the publication of Rolle's *Abridgment*.[76] The owners of the privilege sought the protection of the Chancery, and Lord Keeper Bridgman referred the matter to Mr Justice Twisden and as many judges as he cared to call in. On 2 September 1668 the case was argued before all but one of the judges in Sir John Kelyng's chambers in the Inner Temple. The defendants' counsel submitted that the monopoly was an unlawful restraint of trade. Serjeant Maynard, for the plaintiffs, replied that it was more in the public interest to restrict printing – by means of patents of privilege – than to recognize a universal liberty to print

68 Pat. 12 Car. II, pt 38, mm. 25–9 (the privilege still expressly included the abridgments of Pulton and Rastell, as in the 1594 patent).

69 *Records of the Honorable Society of Lincoln's Inn: Admissions*, I (1896), p. 223 (Richard, son of Edward Atkyns of Cheshunt, Herts., admitted in 1634), 255 (Edward, the son of Edward Atkyns of Cheshunt, baron of the Exchequer, admitted in 1647).

70 Recital in Streater's bill in Chancery (1675), C5/562/32, abstracted by John Bagford in BL MS. Harley 5903, fols. 46, 58–9. (Bagford's volume contains many documents relating to the law-printing litigation of the 1660s and 1670s.)

71 Cowley 1924, p. 347. 72 Plomer 1907b, p. 8.

73 Blagden 1960, pp. 144, 179, citing a bill in Chancery (1664), PRO, C9/31/126.

74 S. Carter, *Reports of sevral special cases* (London, 1688), p. 89.

75 Streater's bill in Chancery (1675), as copied in BL, MS. Harley 5903, fol. 46.

76 H. Rolle, *Un abridgment des plusieurs cases* (London, 1668).

corruptly. Errors in printing the law, he submitted, might endanger men's lives and properties. He also urged that, in passing the statute 14 Car. II, c. 33, Parliament had recognized the validity of printing monopolies. When the matter was re-argued on 4 October, the defendants' counsel responded that the statute was intended only to give protection against piracy, and that the king could not claim a prerogative right in anything which had not existed since time immemorial. Francis North KC, for the plaintiff, countered that the king was the fountain of all the law, and that the printing of law books was analogous to printing a proclamation, which could only be done with the king's permission. This monopoly did not, he suggested, fall within the usual objections against monopolies: it did not lead to enhanced prices, because the statute 25 Hen. VIII, c. 15, restrained the increase of book prices; and it did not deter industry, because learned writers were always encouraged by the patentees. Moreover, the printing of law books required special skill, on account of the languages (law French and Latin) and the use of black-letter characters; it was reasonable to confer a monopoly on someone who had acquired such a skill. 'The judges debated the business about an hour, but came to no resolution. Then they called in the parties, and strongly and importunately pressed them to agree.'[77] The parties thereupon declining to settle, the judges in February 1669 certified their opinion to Lord Keeper Bridgman:

> That such new law-books as have been imprinted since More's patent, and acquired by any particular person or persons, are not by law restrained by More's patent; but, notwithstanding that patent, those men that acquired them may print them. But as to those law books that were printed before that patent, there is diversity of opinion among us.[78]

The Lord Keeper was therefore unable to decide in favour of the plaintiffs. From this indecision the plaintiffs appealed to the House of Lords, and the entire question was argued once again. Francis North enlarged upon his previous arguments by adding that Tottell's patent had not been in restraint of any trade, because at the time it was granted the trade was not generally exercised. It was reasonable, he said, that the Crown, which kept legal records and in whose name laws were made, and which (as he supposed) had introduced printing into England,[79] should control the printing of law. The danger of relaxing

77 'The case between the king's patentees for sole printing of law-books and some book-sellers', in Sir George Treby's MS. reports, Middle Temple Library, I, pp. 167–73. Also reported in Lincoln's Inn MS. Hill 83, p. 305. Serjeant Maynard's notes on this and the subsequent cases are in Lincoln's Inn MS. Maynard 23, fol. 233^{v}; MS. Maynard 24, fol. 56^{r}.

78 Treby MS., at pp. 190–1. The 'diversity of opinion' was limited to one dissentient.

79 He relied (Treby MS., p. 171; Carter, *Reports*, p. 191) on a document in Lambeth Palace which said printing was brought from Germany in the time of Henry VI. The same opinion is found in 4 Co.

such control had been demonstrated during the Interregnum, when 'there was no copy so absurd but somebody was found that would print it. Imperfect transcripts came out under great names that were a reproach to them; and some were so unskilfully printed that they could hardly be made use of . . .'.[80]

As to the argument that the patentees had themselves printed inaccurately, he answered that defective printing, or any other abuse, was a breach of trust and ultimately a cause of forfeiture; in any case, they could only print with the judges' *imprimatur*.[81] Common printers could not be as efficient as the patentees, because the law work was a matter of some skill; besides the law French and black letter, 'there are commonly proper termes and abbreviations which to be expert in may require a man's conversation a great while'. Persuaded by this argument, the House of Lords gave judgement for the patentees.[82] Rolle's *Abridgment* was printed with the date 1668 but no printer's name on the title page; the imprint merely lists thirteen stationers (including Roper and Sawbridge) for whom it was printed. According to the best judges, it had not been a prize worthy of the fight, being 'nothing but a collection of year-books and little things noted [by Rolle] when he made his common place book' and of no authority.[83] Sir John Vaughan said, 'he wished it had never been printed, for there are so many contradicting judgments in it that it makes the law ridiculous, and 'twas pity there was not more paines taken with it before it was printed, to expunge those judgments which were not law, or reconcile 'em to such as were law'.[84]

In 1669, the More patent having expired, the Stationers formally renounced all claim to the privilege and not long afterwards made a by-law against its infringement. But these events did not by any means put an end to controversy. In the early 1670s, Abell Roper and some other stationers brought an action in the King's Bench against the assigns for reprinting the third part of Croke's *Reports* (1669), in which they claimed the copyright by virtue of first printing. Although judgement was given for the plaintiffs, it was reversed after

Inst. 26. Offley (for the respondents) dismissed this evidence as 'pleasant, but altogether uncertain and inconclusive'.

80 Francis North's notes, BL, MS. Add. 32519, fol. 221^{v} (and cf. fol. 216). Cf. Roger North, *Discourse on the study of the laws* (London 1824 edn), pp. 31–2 ('Of later times, reports have teemed from the press, more from the profit of the copy than any good to the law . . .')

81 *The king's grant of privilege for sole printing common-law-books, defended* (London, 1669), at p. 13. This was printed by Streater, and Plomer assumed that he wrote it; but it seems to be an edited version of North's argument. The only known printed copy is in the BL, but there is a MS. text (attributed to 'a Person of Quality') in Bodleian MS. Rawlinson C. 806. For the judges' *imprimatur*, see below, p. 492.

82 *The Stationers* v. *The Patentees* 'about the printing of Roll's Abridgment' (1669) Carter, *Reports*, pp. 89–92.

83 *Anon.* (1670), Treby MS., I, p. 514, *per* Twisden J.

84 *Anon.* (1673), Roger North's MS. reports, BL, MS. Add. 32527, fol. 29.

an expensive appeal to the House of Lords in 1675.[85] But these were somewhat hollow victories for the patentees, who had to spend enormous sums defending their privileges – allegedly over £4,000 – and eventually fell out among themselves over their respective contributions to the joint stock. In 1671 they were suing each other in Chancery for accounts.[86] At around the same time, they entered into agreements 'to hold a trade or correspondency' with George Sawbridge and twelve other stationers, under which the assigns undertook to print law books solely at the behest of the stationers, who would provide the capital. But the stationers remained at loggerheads with the lessees, both before and after these financing agreements, and not only refused to make any contribution to the costs of the litigation but actually refused to appoint any law books to be printed during the dispute, so that the patent became unworkable without breaking the contracts.[87] The lessees on their part had spent so much money on the lawsuits that they could not pay their rent, and had thereby incurred a forfeiture of the 1664 lease. Their last major undertaking was the printing of Sheppard's *Grand abridgment* (1675), in four parts: according to the imprint, this was printed by Flesher, Streater and Twyford, as assigns of Richard and Edward Atkyns, for Sawbridge and twelve other booksellers.[88]

In that same year the Atkyns family took steps to obtain a forfeiture of the lease, and granted a new term of fifteen years, at the old rent, to George Sawbridge, Thomas Roycroft and William Rawlins.[89] This was, on the face of it, unconscionable conduct on the part of the lessors, since the old lessees had incurred the ruinous expenditure in defending the lessors' own title. The old lessees therefore sought relief in Chancery on the basis that the lessors had waived part of the rent pending the outcome of the appeal to the House of Lords, and that it was unfair of the lessors to allow their lessees to incur vast expenses defending their interests only to claim a forfeiture when they were unable to pay their full rent – an early application of the principle now known as equitable estoppel.[90] The Lord Keeper granted relief in the form of a decree that the lessees should pay off the arrears in a short time, and that

85 *Roper* v. *Streater* (1672–5) cited in *Modern Reports*, I, p. 257; Skinner, *Reports*, p. 234; *Chancery Cases*, II, p. 67; Streater's bill against Atkyns (below), copied BL, MS. Harley 5903, fol. 65; record cited as Mich. 22 Car. II, rot. 237; and see BL MS. Harley 5903, fols. 100, 105 (two copies of the judgement, dated 26 May 1675).

86 *Streater* v. *Twyford and Flesher*, with cross-actions by Twyford and Flesher, BL MS. Harley 5903, fols. 45–53v (imperfect copy of judgement dated 20 May 1674). James Flesher had died in 1674, and his share in the stock had been taken over by his widow Elizabeth.

87 Streater's bill in Chancery (1675), C5/562/32, copied in BL, MS. Harley 5903, at fols. 63v–65.

88 See also note 135, below.

89 Indenture of 23 March 1675, recited in *Twyford* v. *Roycroft* (below), BL, MS. Harley 5903, fol. 73.

90 *Streater and Twyford* v. *Atkyns* (1675), C5/562/32 (bill in Chancery); copy in BL, MS. Harley 5903, fols. 58–68v.

when they had done so they should be granted a new lease. In pursuance of this decree, the master certified that the arrears amounted to £335 7*s*. 3*d*., and this sum was apportioned between the partners. Such was their financial state, however, that they were still unable to pay; and, although various arrangements were discussed for raising the money, the net result was that law printing passed effectively to Sawbridge and his partners for the remainder of the period. Twyford's final suit against Sawbridge and partners does not seem to have met with any success.[91] No formal outcome has been discovered, but it may be assumed that, had Twyford won, the law-printing business would not have passed to Sawbridge.

Sawbridge, the foremost of the new farmers of the patent, was one of the principal English booksellers of the age, elected master of the Stationers' Company in 1675. Roycroft, who had printed many law books during the Interregnum, was now the King's Printer of Oriental Languages and has been praised as a printer of some merit.[92] Together they acquired beneficial interests not only in the common-law monopoly but also in the King's Printer's privilege, and so they bestowed a considerable part of their energies on law printing. Roycroft's son Samuel recalled that, after the 1675 lease, his father devoted himself wholly to law printing, 'and having beene at great charges in casting of letters and fitting his presses for printing of law books did thereby lose the greater part of his trade'.[93] Twyford, however, responded with the old lament:

> If Mr Roycroft hath lost any part of his trade by reason of the pattent, it hath been by his ill management in the disoblidging booksellers by exacting unreasonable rates, which hath been injurious to the pattent, otherwise it would have an obligation upon them whereby he increased his trade by printing other books as most booksellers in Fleetstreet can testifie.[94]

In effect, then, the arrangements for law publishing had been changed. Although the monopoly remained nominally with the Atkyns family until 1709, Sawbridge had succeeded Twyford as the chief law stationer, and Roycroft had succeeded Streater as the common-law printer. The value of the patent rose steadily with the volume of law printing, but the privilege would continue to cause strife in the eighteenth century.[95]

91 *Twyford* v. *Sawbridge, Roycroft, Rawlins, Carter and Flesher* (1678), C5/568/116 (bill and pleadings, 7 mm.); copies in BL MS. Harley 5903, fols. 73–75^{v}.

92 Plomer 1907b, pp. 158, 161.

93 Samuel Roycroft's answer to Twyford's bill, C5/568/116, m. 7, copied in BL, MS. Harley 5903, fol. 74^{v}.

94 'Some conjectures what Mr Roycroft may insist upon at last' in BL MS. Harley 5903, fol. 132^{v}, at fo. 133.

95 See Sale 1950, pp. 134–44. There is a list of all the patentees, from 1553 to 1789, in Sale 1950, pp. 352–4.

Licensing and censorship

The existence of the two monopolies in law printing rendered outside control of legal publishing largely unnecessary, and the litigation over privilege and copy were almost the only restraining influences on the monopolists. The yearbooks and precedents were not controversial in any sense that would invite governmental control. And, although some ancient books such as *Bracton* might contain matter adverse to absolutist views of monarchical authority, it is not known that any attempt was made to stop their publication on this ground – though it may be significant that *Bracton* was reprinted in 1640.[96]

There was, nevertheless, a tacit restraint upon the publication of modern law reports. Eminent judicial reporters such as Dyer and Coke, who had been privy to top-level consultations about constitutional issues and other matters of state, knew well that such material could not be printed. Dyer did not live to publish his own reports, but in 1585 his nephews as editors ruthlessly removed the sensitive matter, including even some civil cases affecting great men, so that the printed version of 'some new cases' which appeared in print lacked at least one third of the total.[97] When Coke prepared the first eleven parts of his reports for the press, he was serving as attorney-general (parts 1–5, 1600–5) and chief justice (parts 6–11, 1607–15), and he likewise was careful to omit those cases in his notebooks which might cause undue embarrassment.[98] He left out, for instance, an account of Essex's failures in northern Ireland and his eventual fate, problems over the trial of Guy Fawkes, and the murder accusation against Sir Francis Drake which the queen personally stifled, not to mention the high controversies over jurisdiction between the common-law courts on the one hand and the Chancery and prerogative courts on the other. Nevertheless, he did publish many other cases touching on the rights of the Crown, and in the year of his dismissal he was censured by the Privy Council for alleged inaccuracies searched out by his enemy Lord Ellesmere, the lord chancellor. Ellesmere claimed most unfairly that Coke 'hath as it were purposely laboured to derogate much from the rights of the Church ... and to disesteem and weaken the power of the king in the ancient use of his prerogative'.[99] Coke lived to

96 For the context of the editions of 1569 and 1640, see D. E. C. Yale, '"Of no mean authority": some later uses of Bracton' in *On the laws and customs of England*, ed. M. S. Arnold and others (Chapel Hill, NC, 1981), pp. 383–96.

97 *Ascuns novel cases, collectes per le jades tresreverend Judge, Mounsieur Jasques Dyer* (London, 1585/6); Baker ed., *Reports from the lost notebooks of Sir James Dyer*, I, pp. xliv–xlvi.

98 J. H. Baker, 'Coke's notebooks and the sources of his reports', *Cambridge Law Jnl* 30 (1972), 83–5; repr. in Baker, *Legal profession and the common law*, pp. 201–3.

99 'The Lord Chancellor Egertons observations upon the Lord Cookes reportes' (1615) BL, MS. Hargrave 254, fols. 32^{r}–50^{v}; printed in L. A. Knafla, *Law and politics in Jacobean England: the tracts of Lord Chancellor Ellesmere* (Cambridge, 1977), pp. 297–318.

see the first part of his *Institutes* through the press in 1628. *Coke upon Littleton* was hardly the stuff of political controversy, but enough was known of Coke's views on the latest trends in government, especially as a result of the Parliamentary career which followed his dismissal, to cause great concern about the nature of the other three parts of the *Institutes* which he announced in the preface. The second part, he promised, would include a commentary on Magna Carta, the third would be devoted to pleas of the Crown, and the fourth would deal with the touchy subject of jurisdiction. Only the fourth remained to be written.

Three years after the appearance of this announcement, when Coke was reported to be ill, the king ordered urgent enquiries to be made after his health:

> . . . and if hee bee in any present danger that care may be taken to seal upe his study (if hee dies) where such papers are as use may bee made of them (haveing passed thourow so many great places in the state) for his majesties service and som supressed that may disserve him.[100]

According to a contemporary, some papers were actually seized around that time 'by reason that he is about a book concerning Magna Charta', from whence it seems that it was the second *Institute* which was most feared.[101] On 26 July 1634 a royal commission issued under the royal sign a manual authorizing Sir Francis Windebank 'to repaire to the house or place or abode of the said Sir Edward Coke, and there to seize and take into your charge and bring away all such papers and manuscripts as yow shall think fitt'. This was executed a few days before Coke's death in September 1634, when a large trunk was seized from Coke's private secretary and brought before the king at Bagshot. Then, in December, Windebank authorized a clerk of the Privy Council to break into Coke's study in the Inner Temple and to seize papers there. Although many of the papers seem to have been destroyed, including 'a great buckrom bagg of the pouder treason', the drafts of the *Institutes* somehow survived. For their preservation we have to thank Sir John Finch (chief justice of the Common Pleas 1634–40) and his successor Sir Edward Littleton, who possessed them in 1640 and 1641.[102] Finch also possessed an earlier draft of the fourth institute.[103] By 1640 the danger was over, and the House of Commons at least

100 Letter from the Earl of Holland to Lord Dorchester, the king's principal secretary (24 Jan. 1630/31) State Papers 16/183/18, fol. 29.

101 Letter of Thomas Barrington (1631?) cited in HMC, *Seventh report*, App., p. 548. This may possibly refer to the 1634 seizure.

102 Baker, 'Coke's notebooks', pp. 78–80; repr. in Baker, *Legal profession and the common law*, pp. 196–8; J. H. Baker, 'The Newe Littleton', *Cambridge Law Journal*, 33 (1974) 148, 152; repr. in Baker, *Legal profession and the common law*, pp. 234, 238.

103 Bodleian MS. Ashmole 1159 was copied from the manuscript in Finch's possession in 1640.

was eager to see what Coke had written. Towards the end of that year, Sir Robert Coke petitioned the House for the return of the papers with a view to publication, and in 1641 the three draft parts of the *Institutes* were delivered to him with parliamentary encouragement to print them, coupled with a grant of copyright.[104] They were printed in 1642 and 1644, and many times since.[105] This attempt by the Crown to block publication therefore succeeded only for a few years. In 1658–9, two further parts of Coke's *Reports* were published from the autograph notebooks, including many of the great constitutional debates of James I's time. A good deal still remains unpublished.

No comparable example to Coke's is known in the field of law publishing. However, in 1637 the Star Chamber prohibited the publication of law books without the licence of the two chief justices and the chief baron.[106] The subsequent licensing practice as shown by the printed imprimaturs varied considerably. In 1650 the approval of a single puisne judge was deemed sufficient for the publication of Chief Justice Hobart's *Reports*,[107] while in 1657 the *Reports* doubtfully attributed to Sir Thomas Hetley were approved solely by John Clark, presumably the serjeant at law of that name.[108] Other law books printed in the 1650s bear no imprimatur, while some are approved by all the judges of the central courts of common law.[109] After the Restoration, it was usual for all the common-law judges to sign imprimaturs,[110] including sometimes the lord chancellor or lord keeper as well,[111] though some law books still contain no printed imprimaturs, while sometimes one judge acts alone.[112] It is a matter

104 *Journals of the House of Commons*, II, pp. 45, 80, 470, 554; 2 Co. Inst. 745b; R. Coke, *A detection of the court and state of England* (London, 1697 edn), pp. 253, 279.

105 For a document relating to the printing of the third part in 1644, see Atkinson 1926, p. 435.

106 Arber, IV, p. 529.

107 *The reports of Sir Henry Hobart* (London, 1650), sig. A4^v (imprimatur signed by Philip Jermyn, 13 June 1646).

108 *Reports and cases collected and reported, by that eminent lawyer, Sir Thomas Hetley* (London, 1657), sig. A2^v (imprimatur dated 9 Feb. 1656/7). Clark is probably the serjeant created in 1648: J. H. Baker, *The order of serjeants at law* (London, 1984), p. 505.

109 E.g. *The second part of the reports of Sir George Croke* (London, 1658), sig. A2^v (eight judges, including barons of the Exchequer). The *Second part* was printed before the first.

110 E.g. *The first part of the reports of Sir George Croke* (London, 1661), sig. A5^v (signed by eleven judges); *Plusieurs tres-bons cases colligees per Jean Latch* (London, 1661), sig. [A]2^v (signed by ten judges, who point out that these were not Latch's own reports); *The reports of Edward Bulstrode* (2nd edn, 1688), facing title (signed by twelve judges, 1 July 1687).

111 E.g. *Les reports de Sir William Jones* (London, 1675), sig. A6^v (signed by Lord Keeper Finch and twelve judges); *Les reports de Sir Gefrey Palmer* (London, 1678), sig. [A]2^v (similar); *Les reports colligees par Tho. Siderfin* (London, 1684), facing title (signed by Lord Keeper North and twelve judges, 26 Feb. 1682/3); *Reports of cases taken and collected by Sir Thomas Hardres* (London, 1693), facing title (signed by Lord Keeper Somers and twelve judges).

112 E.g. W. Sheppard, *A grand abridgment* (1675), verso of title (signed by John Vaughan); *Select cases reported by John Aleyn* (London, 1681), facing title (signed by Francis North); *Les reports de Sir John Savile* (London, 1688), facing title (sim.). Cf. *Les reports de Henry Rolle* (London, 1675), sig. A2^r (signed by Chief Justice Hale), sig. A2^v (another, signed by Lord Chancellor Finch and nine judges).

of speculation how far the licensing requirement resulted in any serious control of law printing. Whatever the judges were supposed to consider – and they usually in terms expressed approbation of the books licensed – they did not in fact impose any discernible control upon the contents of law books or the standards of editorship. The quality of the law reports published during this period was very variable, and some of the treatises and other practitioners' works were slight in the extreme.

Two case studies

Since none of the business records of the law printers or patentees have survived, most of our knowledge of the law books printed in our period is derived from the title pages, prefaces and contents of the books themselves. Needless to say, this information is not usually very comprehensive or reliable. We can therefore best explore the workings of law publishing by looking at two projects, one concerned with statutes and the other with case-law, for which background information has by chance survived.

1 Pulton's Statutes at large, 1618

Ferdinando Pulton was a former fellow of Christ's College, Cambridge, who had joined Lincoln's Inn in 1559 but, being a Roman Catholic, was never called to the Bar. Unable to practise, he devoted his life to the production of useful reference works, especially in relation to statutes. Although his work was somewhat second rate, and attracted adverse criticism at the time, his statutory projects were influential. He began with criminal law, aiming chiefly no doubt at the market for country magistrates, and edited an abridgment of statutes (*An abstract of all the penall statutes . . . in force and use*) which appeared in 1577, followed in 1609 by a treatise of little merit called *De pace regni* (1609).

In his last years he nurtured a grander project for editing all the statutes, perhaps inspired by Francis Bacon's abortive scheme of 1614–16 for consolidating the statute-book and expunging obsolete matter.[113] Bacon's scheme was inherited from his father, Sir Nicholas Bacon, who had proposed a major official consolidation in 1575;[114] and in the time of James I some work is said to have been done towards its realization by, amongst others, Heneage Finch, Sir Henry Finch, William Hakewill, Sir Henry Hobart, and William Noy.[115]

113 See 'A memorial touching the review of penal laws' (1614) in *The works of Francis Bacon*, ed. J. Spedding, XII (London, 1869) pp. 84–9; 'A proposition to His Majesty . . . touching the compiling and amendment of the laws of England' (1616) in *Works of Bacon*, ed. Spedding, XIII, pp. 61–71.

114 *Cases from the lost notebooks of Sir James Dyer*, I (Selden Society, 109, 1994), at pp. lxi–lxii.

115 *Works of Bacon*, ed. Spedding, XIII, p. 71.

But no results had appeared in public, and Pulton thought something might be done by private enterprise. Pulton's plan was to arrange the statutes alphabetically by subject, giving full texts of those still in force and abridged texts of the remainder. Moreover, 'to make this new booke at large saleable he promiseth to print the statutes first in the language the same were first wrighten and such as were originallie in French or Latine he will translate and print likewise in English'. He proposed to correct the text by the record, and for this purpose he sought free access to the records in the Tower of London, assistance in bringing rolls to his lodging near the Tower (since he was nearly eighty years old), and some clerical assistance with the transcription.

These requests were opposed by the clerk of the Parliaments (Henry Elsynge) and the Keeper of Records (Robert Bowyer). The statutes, they pointed out, were already in print in their original language in the old *Magna carta cum statutis*, a book 'well knowen to all students of the lawe', and had all been translated in the great book of statutes. A reformed edition would be possible 'yf discretion be used, but not as Mr Poulton desiereth'; many Acts of Parliament were not to be found recorded at all, 'which and the like Mr Poulton nor any man else is able to finde besides the keeper of the said recordes who hath speciallie laboured therein manie yeares, as allsoe his father before him did'. (Bowyer's predecessor, Heneage, was said to have already supervised a transcription from the record of the statutes from 4 Edward III to the end of Edward IV.) They did not think Pulton had the technical skill to read old records without their assistance. And, for good measure, they suggested that it would be politically inconvenient to reveal publicly that some statutes could not be warranted by record evidence: 'the world shalbe abused yff the secreate be opened'. In answer to his other request, they said it would be improper to lend records out of the Tower. Bowyer and Elsinge were, in effect, upset by an amateur poaching on their preserves and seeking to make money at their expense. They offered instead to do the work themselves.[116] But Pulton won this dispute, and Bowyer and Elsynge were obliged to give him the assistance he required. They subsequently sought compensation, and the dispute was referred to Sir Robert Cotton, who apparently decided that all proceeds should be divided between the three of them.[117]

Soon afterwards, Pulton wrote to Lord Chancellor Ellesmere from his home at Barton near Buckingham, referring to the latter's encouragement in the project and seeking a licence for the Oxford University Printer to produce some specimen sheets for perusal by the judges and others. In a second letter, he said that Ellesmere and other judges had encouraged him to collate the texts with

116 All the foregoing is in BL, Cotton MS. Vesp. F. IX, fols. 279–82.

117 BL, Cotton MS. Titus B. V, fol. 252, is a draft of the award with the proportions left blank.

the Tower records, and that there had been 'some difference' with Bowyer over this, but the difference had been settled and the work had now been completed; Pulton now sought some reward for himself and Bowyer for their labours.[118] This hint of judicial patronage no doubt explains the success of the project and the calming of the record keepers. The finished work, *A collection of sundrie statutes*, was finally printed in 1618, the year of Pulton's death, by Adam Islip working as the assign (under the common-law patent) of the Company of Stationers; and the company's records show that the approved print number was 1,250. As in the case of Pulton's earlier *Abstract*, and Rastell's collection, the company evidently maintained the claim that edited statutes did not fall within the monopoly of the King's Printer. The book proved a success, and was reprinted in 1632, 1636 and 1640; after the Restoration, however, it was replaced by a succession of continuously updated *Statutes at large*.

2 *The great yearbook project, 1671–80*

Access to the statute book was ensured by collections such as Pulton's and by the continuing output of the King's Printers, but the printing of law reports was another matter. Until the 1650s, modern reports circulated largely in manuscript, and the canon of older printed reports suffered from the problems facing the embattled law printers. For over forty years there were no new editions of the yearbooks,[119] Dyer,[120] or Plowden. Tottell's methods, which had at least kept those books in print, were the ways of an old world. The new way of making money was to churn out as many new titles as possible for quick sales. As a result, there was a dearth of yearbooks and other standard works in the legal profession by the time of Charles II. The books printed by Tottell had suffered from the ravages of war, fire, natural decay, and the severe wear and tear to which books are subjected in chambers. The fires in the Temple in 1666 and 1677 were particularly disastrous: for example, Sir John Vaughan (*d.* 1674), later chief justice of the Common Pleas, lost his entire library of law books and manuscripts by fire and theft.[121] For all these reasons, there were insufficient books in existence to serve the profession, and this was reflected in ever-increasing second-hand prices. Even in 1657, Prynne had complained that one could 'buy Brook's Abridgement of the Year-books for 30 or 40s. whereas the Year-books it abridgeth will cost near as many pounds'.[122] This may be an

118 H. E. Huntington Library MSS. EL 1963–4, printed in V. B. Heltzel, 'Ferdinando Pulton, Elizabethan legal editor', *HLQ* 11 (1947), 77–9.
119 The only yearbooks printed between 1620 and 1678 were *Edward IV* (London, 1640).
120 Dyer was not reprinted between 1621 and 1672.
121 BL, MS. Add. 36076, fol. 301^{v} (obituary by Serjeant Waller).
122 R. Cotton, *An exact abridgement of the records in the Tower of London* (London, 1657), preface.

exaggeration, since there is evidence that the price of a set in 1671 was more like £15.[123] But this was still six times the price of a set in 1562, when seven volumes might be appraised at £1 14*s*. 8*d*.,[124] and three times the £5 or so required to buy a set around 1615.[125] The cost would have been oppressive for a young lawyer, and the temptation to make do with abridgments must have been strong.

As early as 1671, the law printer Thomas Bassett announced that all ten volumes of the yearbooks were 'designed to be Reprinted and Sold for about half the present Price by way of Subscription', which must have represented a subscription price of about £7 or £8.[126] The scheme may have been Twyford's; at any rate, by 1675 the project was in his charge. In January 1675, Twyford successfully petitioned the king to be allowed to import the necessary paper free of customs or excise duty. The royal warrant addressed to the Lord Treasurer, the Chancellor of the Exchequer, and the commissioners of the Treasury, contains a very informative recital:

> ... Whereas our well beloved subject Henry Twyford, stationer, having undertaken the reprinting of the old Year Law Books [*sic*] being in ten volumes, and some other year books which have not yet been printed, the design whereof is particularly recommended by our now Lord Keeper of our Great Seal and by all our judges of England as very serviceable to our prerogative and revenue, and beneficial to all true students of the good laws of this our realm; and whereas the said Henry Twyford hath humbly besought us that in regard the work will be voluminous and very chargeable we would be graciously pleased for his encouragement in so great and good a work to grant him licence to import ten thousand reams of demy-royall paper without paying any custom or duty for the same; and we being willing to further so useful a work are graciously pleased to grant the petitioner's request ... [127]

The recital reveals three interesting facts. First, the scheme had been submitted to the Lord Keeper (Sir Heneage Finch) and judges as early as 1674 or 1675.

123 T. Bassett, *Catalogue of the law-books of this realm* (London, 1671), pp. 78–9 ('I have omitted the Particular Prises of the ten last mentioned Books called Year-Books; many of them being difficult to be got singly, and their Prizes uncertain: they are all in Folio, French, Price altogether 15 *l*.')

124 Inventory of William Rastell's goods (confiscated in 1562 after his flight to Louvain), *Law Magazine*, 31 (1844), 57–8. (Rastell had received the same price in 1538 for five yearbooks sold to Randle Cholmeley which are now in Lincoln's Inn: memorandum on flyleaf.) An inventory of *c*. 1572 lists the price of eight volumes of yearbooks (omitting Hen. IV–V) as 47*s*. 4*d*.: Kent Archives Office MS. U. 552. E. 1, mm. 8–9.

125 'The price of the law in quiers' (*c*. 1615), BL, MS. Harley 160, fol. 233 (8*s*. to 13*s*. 4*d*. each).

126 Bassett, *Catalogue of the law-books of this realm*, p. 79. A similar statement occurs in R. Clavell, *The general catalogue of books printed in England* (London, 1675), p. 62.

127 Copy in BL, MS. Harley 5903, fol. 95 (spelling modernized). This is undated, but the warrant from the Lord Treasurer to the Customs Commissioners recites the royal warrant as bearing date 29 Jan. 1674/5.

Secondly, the quantity of paper mentioned suggests that a very large subscription had been raised or projected. There were just over 1,250 sheets in a set of the yearbooks as ultimately printed. If five million sheets were imported, as the warrant envisaged – assuming 500 sheets to the ream, the measure used by law printers in the 1640s[128] – that would have enabled between three and four thousand sets to be printed. Some difficulties were subsequently encountered as a result of legislation against the importing of French commodities,[129] but the paper was in the event imported from France: most of the watermarks show the arms of France and Navarre within a wreath, surmounted by a crown, crudely executed. The commonest makers' names are J. Durand, P. Homo, and D. Chatel, but an eminent authority has declared the provenance of these marks to be a puzzle.[130]

Twyford was bold to gamble upon such a grand scheme while his fortunes were on the wane and his capital wasting in Chancery. No doubt he intended to raise the necessary funds by subscription from other stationers and members of the profession, hoping that success would save him from his economic difficulties. But his loss of the monopoly later in 1675 finally deprived him of the lawful means of publishing the reprint himself. The printing would now have to be done through Sawbridge and Roycroft, who were no doubt only too pleased to reap the benefits of the most ambitious law-printing project ever seen in England. Within two years, the Sawbridge partnership had undertaken the printing work. Twyford complained that two substantial printers had offered to do the work at two or three shillings in the pound cheaper than Roycroft, but he nevertheless expressed his continued support for the reprint in principle.[131] An advertisement in the *London gazette* declared that four of the volumes (those for Edward III) would be finished in Michaelmas term 1678:

> The Ten Volumes of Reports, called the Year-Books, with considerable Improvements by new References and Tables, are now Reprinting by the Approbation of the Reverend Judges, who have recommended them under their Hands to the Students of the Law, as an essential part of their study. Four of the Volumes, viz. Edward the Third, first and second Parts, Quadragesimus,

128 Atkinson 1926, p. 435 (referring to 1644). A report of 1674 on paper sizes and prices listed a demy made by A. Durand, with a similar watermark to that found in the reprint (some of which was made by J. Durand), as containing twenty-five sheets to a quire: Chapman 1927, p. 405.

129 'Advertisement concerning subscriptions for the ten volumes of year books' (Nov. 1679), which refers to 'the Extraordinary charge of Paper (since the first Proposals) occasioned by the late Act of Parliament, Prohibiting French Commodities'. The writer is grateful to Professor A. W. B. Simpson for a photocopy of the original broadsheet.

130 Heawood 1950, p. 26; p. 22, pl. 168. Cf. Churchill 1935, p. ccxliii, no. 308 (noting the 'P. Homo' version used in the reprint).

131 Heads of argument in *Twyford* v. *Roycroft* (*c.* 1677), BL, MS. Harley 5903, fol. 133 (para. 3).

> and the Book of Assizes, will be finished this Term. They are disposed of by way of Subscriptions, at little more than half the Price they have heretofore been sold for. All those that intend to have the benefit, are desired to make their Subscriptions (before the 28th of November) to any of the persons following, who will give security for the delivery thereof, and where the Proposals may be had gratis. G. Sawbridge on Ludgate-hill. H. Twyford in the Temple, F. Tyton, J. Billinger, T. Bassett, R. Pawlet, C. Wilkinson, T. Dring, C. Harper, J. Leigh, J. Amery, J. Poole in Fleetstreet and Chancery Lane, M. Place, S. Heyrick, W. Jacob, and J. Place, in Holborn .[132]

It will be noted that the name of Twyford appears immediately after that of Sawbridge in the advertisement. The advertisement proved slightly optimistic in terms of the publication date, but the ten volumes duly appeared in 1679 and 1680,[133] under the imprint of Sawbridge, Rawlins and Roycroft, but with Twyford first among the fifteen stationers who are also listed on the title page. Facing the title page is a unique recommendation signed by Lord Chancellor Finch and the judges, which has been described as 'practically the last official pronouncement on the subject of legal education for nearly a century and a half':

> We well knowing the grave use and benefit of the Year-Books, and that the scarceness of the same for some years last past hath been no small detriment to the study of the law, do well approve of the re-printing; and for satisfaction of the studious, and incouragement of the undertakers, do recommend them to the students and professors of the law, as a principal and essential part of their study.[134]

The original subscription price was £7, and in November 1679 the fifteen bookselling publishers issued a printed notice saying that the ten volumes were 'now finished', and that further advance subscriptions would be accepted until the end of the Michaelmas Term at the slightly increased rate of £7 10*s*. Thereafter the bookshop price would be £12 a set.[135] Auction prices in the 1680s

132 *London gazette*, no. 1349 (21–4 Oct. 1678). For the location of the booksellers mentioned, see note 135, below.

133 Only the two books of *Edward IV* are dated 1680, the remainder 1679.

134 'By the approbation of the reverend judges', facing the title page of *Le premier part de Edward le tierce* (London, 1679). Comment from B. W. Kelly, *A short history of the English bar* (London, 1908), p. 55.

135 'Advertisement concerning Subscriptions for the Ten Volumes of Year Books' (Nov. 1679), broadsheet issued in the names of George Sawbridge (Ludgate Hill), Henry Twyford (Temple), Francis Tyton (Fleet Street), John Billinger (Clifford's Inn Lane), Thomas Basset (Fleet Street), Robert Pawlet (Chancery Lane), Samuel Heyrick (Gray's Inn Gate), Christopher Wilkinson (Fleet Street), Thomas Dring (corner of Chancery Lane and Fleet Street), William Jacob (Barnard's Inn Gate), Charles Harper (Fleet Street), John Leigh (Fleet Street), John Ammery (Fleet Street), John Place (Furnival's Inn Gate) and John Poole (Clement's Inn Gate). (The number of law booksellers is notable: today there are only four in the same area.) The writer is grateful to Professor A. W. B. Simpson for a photocopy of the original.

show that sets retained a second-hand value of at least £6 to £8,[136] though there was a decline during the eighteenth century.[137]

The publishers used large sheets, so that both sides of the old folios could be printed on one page, preserving the old foliation in the page-numbering. There are signs of editorial work within the volumes themselves. New references were added in the margins of some of the volumes, and a new table added to the first part of Edward III. Here and there, and particularly in the last yearbooks, an attempt was made to turn the law French into something like the French of France. The result is unscholarly and confusing to the reader accustomed to older legal texts. It is hard to berate a publisher who changes *walker en son gardein* to *promener in son jardin*; but conjugations such as *jeo peux, vous pouvez, ils peuvent*, are wholly foreign to the language of the common law. Nevertheless, this was by far the most ambitious enterprise in English legal publishing before the mid-eighteenth century, and the ten volumes of 1679–80 have remained the vulgate text down to the present day for want of any better edition.

Maynard's Edward II

The royal warrant of 1675 mentioned, in addition to the proposed reprint, that it was designed to publish 'some other year books which have not yet been printed'. If this may be interpreted in the light of the outcome, it alludes to a scheme to print the years of Edward II from manuscript. The credit for this venture is usually given to Sir Matthew Hale (*d.* 1676), the Lord Chief Justice, who in 1671 had called attention to 'an excellent report of Ed. 2 in MS. in Lincolns Inn Library', adding ''tis pitty 'tis not printed'.[138] This remark was taken as a 'solemn commendation of it to the press',[139] and a year later the benchers of Lincoln's Inn appointed a committee 'to attend the Lord Chiefe Justice of England in order to the printing of the manuscript of Edward the Second, now remaineing in the Library; and to treate with the Booksellers in relacion to the printing of the said manuscript'.[140] The manuscript has been identified as 'Hale' 137(2), which of course was not part of Hale's own bequest;

136 Henry Parker's set fetched £6 3*s*. 10*d*. in 1681, John Parsons's set fetched £5 17*s*. in 1682, and John Collins's set fetched £7 19*s*. in 1683: sale catalogues in BL.

137 J. Worrall, *Bibliotheca legum* (London, 1753), p. 150 (reprint, together with Maynard's *Edward II*, priced at three guineas). Cf. *Clarke's Bibliotheca legum* (1819), p. 381 (seven guineas). The latter quotes a mere two guineas for a set of the old folios.

138 *Sacheverell* v. *Froggatt* (1671), reported in Treby MS., II, p. 634.

139 Preface to the volume as printed in 1678. Cf. M. Hale, *History of the common law*, ed. C. M. Gray (Chicago, 1971), p. 108 ('The best Copy of these Reports that I know now extant, is that in Lincoln's-Library, which gives a fair Specimen of the Learning of the Pleaders and Judges of that Time.').

140 *Records of the honorable society of Lincoln's Inn: the Black Books*, III (1899), at p. 85 (8 Nov. 1672).

it was in fact donated by George Anton.[141] In the event it was not the text used for the reprint, and one can speculate as to the reason. In 1673, or shortly thereafter, the Inn acquired a second manuscript of Edward II from the legal antiquary Charles Fairfax (*d.* 1673), and this may have brought to light divergences between the texts. At any rate, a modern editor has declared the Fairfax text to be superior to that which first caught Hale's attention and that it might have been a suitable basis for an edition.[142] However, it turned out that neither of the Lincoln's Inn manuscripts was going to be printed.

Soon after Hale's retirement in 1676, a different manuscript in the possession of Sir John Maynard (*d.* 1690), king's serjeant at law, was laid before Hale's successor, Sir Richard Raynsford, who licensed it for the press on 28 August. The manuscript is now in the British Library and contains the manuscript *imprimatur* as well as Serjeant Maynard's signature.[143] Within two years the volume was in print, and in Trinity term 1678 it could be purchased in the shops.[144] The printing had been carried out, of course, by Sawbridge, Roycroft and Rawlins. But the undertakers were not Twyford and his colleagues. The title page reveals that they were Thomas Bassett and two less well-known booksellers, J. Wright at the Crown in Ludgate Hill and James Collins in the Temple Passage from Essex Street. There is a recommendation signed by all the judges, dated 4 June 1678, saying that it was 'a Volume much and long desired by the most learned of the Gown'. There is also an anonymous preface, which relates the opinions of Hale and Selden on the value of the Edward II reports. No mention is made of Serjeant Maynard, and it has been supposed that he did no more than lend his manuscript to the printer.[145] However, the announcement in the *London gazette* states: 'There is also lately published by Sir John Maynard (with a large Table made by him) the Reports and Cases argued and adjudged in the time of Edward II', which had been 'wanting to compleat the aforesaid Ten Volumes of Reports or Year-Books' and were now available to those who subscribed to the reprint with a rebate of 5*s*.[146] This suggests that Maynard was personally responsible for the edition, as publisher,[147] and demonstrates

141 J. Hunter, *A catalogue of the manuscripts in ... Lincoln's Inn* (London, 1838), pp. 394–5; *ELM*, II, pp. 14, 42, 47.

142 G. J. Turner, introduction to *Year books 4 Edward II* (Selden Society, 26, 1914), pp. xlv–xlvi.

143 BL, MS. Add. 35094, fols. 208^{v}, 284^{v} (Maynard's name), 340^{v} (imprimatur); F. W. Maitland, introduction to *Year books 1 & 2 Edward II* (Selden Society, 17, 1903), p. xxix.

144 *A catalogue of books . . . published at London in Trinity term 1678*, reprinted in *TC*, I, p. 321.

145 F. W. Maitland, *Year books 1 & 2 Edward II* (Selden Society, 17, 1903), p. xxiii.

146 *London gazette*, no. 1349 (21–4 Oct. 1678).

147 Cf. T. Bassett, *Catalogue of the law-books of this realm* (London, 1682 edn), p. 85 ('the aforementioned Year-Book of Edward the Second was Published by Serjeant Maynard . . . '); *Exact catalogue of the common and statute law books* (London, 1684) ('Edw. II. Published by Sir John Maynard Knight'). The latter is a broadsheet in St Catharine's College Library, Cambridge, shelf-mark K. III. 22(44).

that the venture was quite separate from, though seen as an extension of, the reprint. By modern standards, the product does the learned serjeant no credit at all. It has even been called, by very high authority, a 'Nonsense Year Book made by a man who did not mind printing the merest rubbish, who knew no French and very little Latin.'[148] In castigating the edition as 'bad, very bad', Maitland spared the 'nameless editor, or rather copyist': 'We do not know how few months were allowed him for a task that demanded years; we do not know how small was his recompense; we do not know what opportunity he had of consulting any manuscripts beyond the one that belonged to Maynard . . .'[149] Maitland seems to have assumed that a medieval manuscript would have been transcribed into modern handwriting before submission to the printer; but it seems more likely that the compositor was set to work on the manuscript itself. Maynard's table to the volume still survives among the Maynard manuscripts in Lincoln's Inn;[150] but there is no trace of any transcription by him or anyone else.

Maynard's connection with the volume was well known at the time, and in his own lifetime it was known as *Maynard's Edward II*[151] or even *Maynard's reports*.[152] Some contemporary booksellers counted the volume as number I in the yearbook canon, numbering the reprint volumes II to XI, and this may account for the common misapprehension that the reprint was also connected with Maynard. It was not uncommon even in modern times for booksellers to refer to the reprint incorrectly as 'Maynard's edition',[153] and the error has infected scholars who ought to have known better.[154] The publishing history clearly shows otherwise, and in Maynard's lifetime 'compleat sets' of the reprint were often offered without his Edward II.[155]

148 From a private letter printed in *Letters of F. W. Maitland*, ed. C. H. S. Fifoot (Cambridge, 1965), p. 260, no. 331.

149 *Year books 1 & 2 Edward II*, p. xxiii.

150 Lincoln's Inn MS. Maynard 27.

151 BL MS. Harley 5903, fol. 141; *A Catalogue of the choicest, and most valuable books, of the common and statute law* (sold by Millington, 14 Feb. 1686/87), p. 2, lot 47; *Catalogue of choice books* (sold by Millington, 9 May 1687), p. 22, lot 32; *Bibliotheca Latino-Anglica* (sold by Millington, 12 July 1687), p. 52, lot 54.

152 Coventry sale catalogue (9 May 1687), p. 38, lot 1. Likewise in *Bibliotheca Stawellianae pars secunda* (sold by Bullord, 4 Feb. 1696), p. 32, lot 46; J. Worrall, *Bibliotheca legum* (1753), p. 150.

153 See W. H. Maxwell and L. F. Maxwell, *A legal bibliography*, I (2nd edn, London, 1955), p. 312. It is an old error: *Seymour* v. *Barker* (1809) in Taunton, *Reports*, II, p. 201 (Serjeant Williams cites a case of Edw. III in 'Maynard's edition'). Cf. Winfield 1925, pp. 176–7 (more cautious association with Maynard).

154 E.g. J. B. Ames, *Lectures on legal history* (Cambridge, Mass., 1913), p. 30; Winfield 1925, p. 177.

155 Six examples have been noted in sale catalogues from the 1680s: Parker sale (5 Dec. 1681), p. 10, lot 35; Parsons sale (30 Nov. 1682), p. 2, lot 46; Collins sale (2 July 1683), p. 10, lot 34; Weston sale (24 June 1686), appendix, folios, lot 23; *A catalogue containing variety of books of the common and statute law* (18 Feb. 1686/87), folios, lot 105; *Appendix to Mr Charles Mearne's catalogue* (22 Feb. 1686/87), lot 33; *Catalogue of choice books* (9 May 1687), p. 23, lot 45.

Conclusion

Towards the end of our period the necessary contents of a lawyer's library were reckoned at around fifty volumes, excluding manuscripts and minor works.[156] Sir Matthew Hale in 1668 had well over one hundred printed law books divided between home and Serjeants' Inn, and numerous manuscript volumes in both places,[157] while a serjeant at law who died in 1667 left sixty-one.[158] The range of law books had been enriched by a few major new works such as Coke's *Institutes*, and Sir Henry Finch's *Law*,[159] though the far superior major works of Sir Matthew Hale had not yet been published,[160] and most of the additions to the catalogue had been inconsequential. Many of the books recommended by Fulbecke were still basic reading, and indeed the advice on reading given by Hale in the 1660s could have been given a century earlier but for the addition of Dyer and Coke:

> First, it is convenient for a Student to spend about two or three yeares in the diligent reading of Littleton, Perkins, Doctor and Student, Fitzherbert's Natura Brevium, and especially my Lord Coke's Commentaries, and possibly his Reports; this will fit him for Exercise . . . and enable him profitably to attend the Courts at Westminster . . . Afterwards it may be fit to begin to read the Year-Books . . . and so come down in order and succession of time to the latter Law, viz. Plowden, Dyer, Coke's Reports the second time, and those other Reports lately printed . . . What he reads in the course of his Reading, let him enter the Abstract or Substance thereof, especially of Cases or Points resolved, into his Common-place-Book, under their proper Titles.[161]

Much the same advice was given by Roger North KC, at the end of our period.[162] The student should begin with the institutional works and then proceed to case-law. *Coke on Littleton* was to be deferred until the student had a good grounding, because – North was one of the first lawyers brave enough to say this in writing – 'it is the confusion of a student, and breeds more disorder in his brains than any other book can'. Despite the 'superfetation of modern reports', North still thought that 'a lawyer should know every decisive case reported in the books,

156 W. Phillips, *Studii legalis ratio* (1662), p. 121.

157 Contemporary list in Yale University, Beinecke Library, Osborn files, 'Blagden–Hale papers'.

158 Serjeant Earle (*d.* 1667): HMC, *Tenth report*, part IV, p. 219.

159 H. Finch, *Nomotechnia: cestascavoir, un description del common leys d'Angleterre* (1613), usually known by the title of the second edn (which is actually an earlier draft translated into English): *Law, or a discourse thereof, done into English* (1627); W. R. Prest, 'The dialectical origins of Finch's Law', *Cambridge Law Journal*, 36 (1977), 326–52.

160 Only two short pieces had been printed: *A summary of the pleas of the crown* (1678); and *A short treatise touching sheriffs accompts* (1683).

161 Unsigned preface to H. Rolle, *Un abridgment des plusieurs cases* (London, 1668), I, sig. b2^{v}.

162 *Discourse on the study of the laws* (London, 1824 edn).

or blush at his defect'. Here there was no short cut, because a good abridgment of modern cases was not produced until the eighteenth century. An attempt was made by William Hughes, whose *Grand abridgment of the law* was published in three parts in 1660–3, but it was not successful and copies are rare. Henry Rolle's posthumously published *Abridgment des plusieurs cases* (1668) contains material from contemporary manuscript reports (including Rolle's own), and is useful on that account as a source of case-law, but it did not digest the printed reports.[163] William Sheppard's *Grand abridgment* (1675) was really just a superficial collection of jottings and not an adequate guide to the reports at large.[164] Nor were there contemporary treatises on the substantive law, as opposed to procedure. The ever-increasing body of modern reports therefore had to be read through. On the other hand, North admitted that no one any longer read the whole of the yearbooks: 'I know the work is too immense, and the age not studious enough to promise a compensation for so much pains.' The only yearbook which he regarded as essential reading was *Henry VII*.[165] Nevertheless, a good lawyer should also be an historian, since 'generally in the law, as well as in all other human literature, antiquity is the foundation; for he that knows the elder, can distinguish what is new, but he that deals only in the new, cannot tell how fresh or stale his opinions are, nor from whence they are derived'. Legal learning was thus, in the 1690s as in the 1550s, still largely a matter of finding one's own way through the raw materials; but the availability of materials was now firmly dominated by the printing press.

163 For contemporary criticisms of it, see above, p. 487.
164 For its publication, see above, p. 488.
165 Even in 1563 this had been the first yearbook which a student tackled: 'Autobiography of Sir John Savile', ed. J. W. Clay and J. Lister, *Yorkshire Archaeological Journal*, 15 (1900), 423.

23

ABCs, almanacs, ballads, chapbooks, popular piety and textbooks

R. C. SIMMONS

Works designed and priced for a broad public which included but was not exclusively composed of the poorer and less well-educated and works printed for the education of the young were produced in very large numbers during the sixteenth and seventeenth centuries. Their cheapness, which increased in relation to wages over our period, has meant that their survival rate is in inverse proportion to the quantities produced. Hundreds of thousands of copies of ABCs and primers were printed but few are now extant. Some early single sheet almanacs and Elizabethan ABCs for example have survived only because they were used as part of the bindings of more expensive books. Street ballads and chapbooks exist in larger numbers, since they attracted early and careful collectors. During the last two decades the content and cultural significance and methods of distributing many of these works have received increasing attention, though there are still lacunae in our knowledge of aspects of their production, including editorial, printing and pricing strategies and actual numbers produced.

The growth in literacy which marked our period – and the ability to read simple texts was more widely diffused than writing skills – has been studied in a wide context, including the growth in the number of petty schools and grammar schools, the instruction of girls in reading and writing outside the school system, and the stimulus to reading that cheap and popular print itself provided.[1] The basic printed aids to literacy included the hornbook,[2] the ABC with the catechism,[3] and the primer.[4] The next stage was instruction in Latin, necessary for educational and social advancement and for entry into professional careers. Latin as well as other school books were consequently

1 Cressy 1980 is an excellent introduction to literacy. However, Spufford 1981, Barnard 1994 and others have suggested that his estimates of literacy rates are probably too low. Neuberg 1977 is also suggestive.

2 Tuer 1896. 3 Anders 1936. 4 Butterworth 1949.

printed in large numbers.[5] All these works to some extent overlapped. Typical ABCs (see plate 23.1) included the Lord's Prayer, the Creed, and the Ten Commandments, while primers, which were books of simple prayers and graces, often included an ABC. *Lily's grammar*, actually a composite work,[6] included instruction in both English and Latin grammar (plate 23.2), while many Latin school books, such as Culman's popular *Sententiae pueriles pro primis Latinae linguae*... also taught Christian precepts. Indeed, all forms of educational material, as a matter of course or of government policy, inculcated religious, family, social and political duties, including obedience to all forms of authority.

The printing and publication history of these educational works is complex.[7] Potentially highly profitable, they attracted bids for monopoly patents, which once granted were jealously defended. During Elizabeth's reign, John Daye, and Richard Daye, his son, held the right to print ABCs and William Seres, and his son, the patent for primers. Under James I the right to print ABCs was granted to the Stationers' Company. The Company in 1605 also purchased the right to publish hornbooks and by 1620 had acquired the rights to Edmund Coote's *The English scholemaister, teaching all his schollars of what age so ever the most easie, short and perfect order of distincte readinge and true writinge our English tonge*, first entered in 1596. These and other school books came to form part of its English Stock (which included Latin books). Some were also part of the privileged monopoly of the universities of Oxford and Cambridge, which themselves often granted rights of publication to the Company in return for money payments. The rights to *Lily's grammar*, a state-enjoined work, that sold in very large quantities, were held by a number of patentees; these rights were also extended to the two University Presses in the seventeenth century.

Many of these school books had first been printed overseas. Corderius's *Colloquia*, widely used in Continental Europe after its publication in 1564 was translated by Charles Hoole a hundred years later (1657) and became a 'new' book in the Stationers' Company Stock.[8] Hoole's activities seem to represent part of a policy of updating the Stock but many works were printed largely unchanged during our period and indeed into the eighteenth century.[9] In 1676/7 'Old primers' represented 75 per cent of the total value of that part of the Stock which included hornbooks, ABCs and primers. These, with one

5 Watson 1908 is still an excellent guide to the great variety of schoolbooks of the period and their printing history.

6 Allen 1954.

7 See Watson 1908, *passim*.

8 Watson 1908, pp. 337–8, 341–63; Barnard 1994, pp. 23, 30.

9 Most of the information in the rest of this paragraph is based on Barnard 1994.

other child's book, were valued at £641 13*s.* 4*d.* or 14 per cent of the Stock's total value. Thirty-nine other titles of mostly Latin school books (including Aesop's *Fables*, Culman's *Sententiae Pueriles*, and Hoole's *Corderius*) were valued at £617 17*s.* 4*d.* Both Stock categories were a declining asset for the Company, even though the market for school books was presumably increasing in the latter seventeenth century and there were large numbers of titles printed. There is no good convenient guide to the competition that they may have presented to the Stock books. The retail prices of the Stock school books were not low. While a few sold for 6*d.* or less, others cost one or two shillings. Barnard was able to provide retail prices for thirty-four titles; the average price per copy was 1*s.* 2*d.*, ranging from 3*d.* for the *Sententiae Pueriles* to 3*s.* 6*d.* for Smetius' *Prosodia.* In 1641 an attack on printing monopolies alleged that their effect on *Lily's grammar* had been to increase its selling price from 5*d.* to 8*d.*[10]

Almanacs by English or English-domiciled authors began to appear in significant numbers from the 1550s. They were either printed separately as calendars or with a prognostication which had its own title page. Typically, short chronologies of world history, English regnal tables, medical and farming advice, and other sorts of information were included in almanacs by the beginning of the seventeenth century. Most also included a 'zodiacal body', a naked human (usually male) form, showing the influence of the constellations, for instance, on different bodily parts (plate 23.3). From as early as the 1560s, more expensive almanacs provided blank pages for diary or notebook entries and, more rarely, headed (£. *s.* *d.*) columns for keeping accounts. Early market awareness on the part of authors and publishers also led to the issue of almanacs keyed to the meridians of the larger towns and cities, including a Dublin almanac as early as 1587 and, almost a century later, almanacs for Jamaica and the West Indies. During the seventeenth century, almanacs were also published for distinctive occupational groups, first mariners and seafarers, later lawyers, clergy, farriers, chapmen and constables. Many almanacs included tables of markets and fairs and information on the London distribution points for the carriage of goods to English towns and cities as well as on roads and routes. Some purchasers of almanacs bought them for their astrological content and astrology was, of course, part of the dominant belief system of early modern Europe. But it was increasingly mocked and satirized over our period, with the production of burlesque almanacs as early as 1591, and sometimes in the almanacs themselves, as in Pond's almanac for 1638:

10 Watson 1908, pp. 256–7.

Should I but dare to omit the Anatomy,
Which long since has gulled my countrey-friend,
He with contempt would straight refuse to buy
This book, and 'tis no Almanack contend.
Ask him its use, he'll say he cannot tell,
No more can I; Yet since he loves't well,
I'le let it stand, because my book should sell.

Others used almanacs as sources of information as well as entertainment. Some wealthier customers purchased bound sets of all the almanacs printed for the year, thus assuring themselves of a wide range of reference material. While almanacs made frequent references to the female sex, the first commercially successful almanacs aimed exclusively at the female reader seem not to have appeared until the early eighteenth century. However, during the efflorescence of women's writing and political activity in the Civil War period, at least one woman 'Student in Astrology' and political radical, Sarah Jinner, issued an almanac aimed at women readers.[11]

The production of almanacs and prognostications illustrates well the interaction between the state, the publisher/printer, the author and the reader in the early history of mass book production. The government was concerned to keep seditious or controversial – especially religiously controversial material – out of the almanacs and especially out of the prognostications. This was largely achieved by granting monopolies for their publication to the Stationers' Company, and by subjecting them to ecclesiastical censorship, although Capp has shown how much political and religious comment in fact appeared, especially during the Civil War and later Stuart period.[12] This government licence was invaluable and profitable. Its privileged holders were able to regulate the market, setting prices and page lengths and more or less successfully shutting out interlopers. The authors and compilers of the almanacs, often students of astronomy and astrology, often medical practitioners, were, with some notable exceptions, paid little. But their names on successful almanacs, into which advertisements for their services or for other commodities were increasingly inserted during the seventeenth century, might give them recognition, clients and status. Although about 160 names of compilers and authors appear in *STC*, the reader was thought to like the familiar and established and was largely offered these. Many almanacs appeared under the same name for many years. For example, almanacs by John Dade appeared between 1589 and 1614, and by William Dade throughout the seventeenth century, and by Schardanus

11 Capp 1979, p. 87; Hobby 1988, pp.181–2. 12 Capp 1979, ch. 3.

or Cardanus Rider, a pseudonym for Richard Saunders, from 1654 to 1699. Saunders's almanac, *Apollo Anglicanus*, was printed under his own name from 1654 to 1683 and then continued, after his death, under the same title from 1684 to 1700. The best-known seventeenth-century almanac was probably that by William Lilly, who had a successful astrological practice, and who was paid £48 per annum rather than the usual £2 to produce it. His portrait appeared on the title page, making his one of the best-known faces in the country. The reader was also assumed to be impressed either by titles that promised arcane learning (*Mercurius Cambro-Britannicus*, *Hemerologium astronomicum*) or attracted by no-nonsense plain titles, typically *A new almanac and prognostication for the year...*, titles nevertheless that used substantial amounts of red-letter printing.

The lucrative nature of the almanac trade was recognized by contemporaries from the sixteenth century onwards[13] and the Stationers' Company paid out large fees to lawyers to enforce its monopoly and also bought up and destroyed large quantities from competitors who managed to get occasional Crown grants.[14] In the sixteenth century, hundreds of thousands were printed; in the seventeenth century several millions. In 1687, for example, more than 460,000 copies of thirty different almanacs were produced. Almanac production obviously gave employment to many printers and they were certainly the largest and most profitable part of the Stationers' Company Stock during the later seventeenth century, as Blagden demonstrated in a seminal study. He calculated that the Company's profit on every £100 of sales was £39.[15] The production of different categories of almanac ('blanks' up to about forty-eight pages in length, 'sorts' or almanacs without blanks of about forty pages, and sheet almanacs) as well as the attempt to create different market segments, based on occupations, shows increasing commercial acumen. John White's *A new almanack and prognostication for... 1650* was also offered as a broadside, *A briefe and easie almanack for... 1650*.

The wholesale price of later seventeenth-century almanacs was probably around 7*d*. each and Barnard has suggested for 1676/7 a multiplier of 1.64 to get to the retail price, which seems slightly on the low side.[16] But information on retail pricing is, however, relatively sparse before the eighteenth century. A 1588 Cambridge shopkeeper's inventory valued 234 almanacs with prognostications at about 1.7*d*. each;[17] in 1611 Savage said almanacs cost 2*d*. each[18] while prices of 2½*d*. for sorts and 3*d*. for blanks have also been suggested. A 1616 York inventory priced fifty-four almanacs at 6*s*. which gives

13 Thomas Nashe wrote that they were 'readier money than ale and cakes'. Capp 1979, p. 44; Blagden 1958b discusses their profitability.

14 Capp 1979, pp. 37–40. 15 Blagden 1958b, p. 183. 16 Barnard 1994, p. 13.

17 McKitterick 1992, p. 52. 18 Bosanquet 1930, p. 366.

a price of 1.3*d*. each and 550 'Alminackes of sortes' at £34*s*. 4*d*. or 1.4*d*. each but these were probably the prices to which the shopkeeper added his own mark up, probably another 33 per cent.[19] But the production and distribution of almanacs, especially if the cheap sheet almanacs, which sold for 1*d*. in the sixteenth century, are taken into account, put them within the reach of most who wished to purchase them. Book almanacs perhaps cost 2*d*. in the sixteenth and early seventeenth centuries with their prices rising to 4*d*. later in the century, although larger bound almanacs might cost more.[20]

Almanacs were, of course, seasonal productions, distributed one or two months before the New Year. Printed ballads and chapbooks were not, although all three may have depended on the same distribution networks. The printed street ballad, previously scorned by the students of 'ballads of tradition', is now receiving renewed attention. The Bodleian Library is digitizing its complete broadside ballad collection, which numbers about 1,489 titles for the period 1557–1695. The work of Rollins and Thomson and more recent studies by Livingston, Wurzbach and Dugaw may be mentioned, while Watt's work on both ballads and chapbooks is invaluable and I have drawn heavily on it.[21] While only about 301 English and Scottish ballads are extant before 1600, the numbers entered in the Stationers' Register 1557–1600 were about 1,500 and the probable total of distinct ballad titles printed between 1550 and 1600 (allowing for under registration and gaps in the Register) was about 3,000. The numbers of new ballad titles printed in the seventeenth century is however difficult to calculate, especially if the many single-sheet theatrical and political songs printed after 1660 are considered to form part of this category. A search of Wing CD-Rom produces 187 items containing the words 'new' and 'song' of which 171 were printed after 1676. Simpson has found over 400 surviving broadside ballad tunes for the sixteenth and seventeenth centuries, although he believes that some 1,000 were actually current and he discusses the relationship between the texts and the printed music on ballad sheets. When it was provided this music was often 'fake' or 'meaningless' and in many cases only an instruction was given that the ballad should be sung to a particular tune.[22] *The trappan'd Welsh-man, sold to Virginia. Showing how a Welsh-man came to London, and went to see the Royal Exchange, where he met a handsom lass, with whom he was enamoured; who pretending to shew him the ships, carried him aboard a Virginia Man and sold him, having first got the Welsh-mans gold, to his great grief and sorrow* was to be sung 'To the Tune of, *Monsieurs misfortune*' (plate 23.4).[23] This

19 Davies 1988, p. 364, Barnard and Bell, 1994, p. 33.
20 Capp 1979, pp. 41, 114–16nn. 21 Watt 1991. 22 Simpson 1966, pp. xi–xv.
23 W. G. Day, ed. *The Pepys Ballads* (Cambridge, 1987) IV, p. 31.

single-sheet ballad was printed in four columns each headed by an illustrative woodcut. Such woodcut illustrations were a feature of ballads and all kinds of cheap print.

In an attempt to prevent the production of seditious, offensive or heretical ballads, the government required ballads to be registered, or 'entered', with the Stationers' Company. This licensing system worked erratically; unlicensed ballads were not uncommon. Unlike its control over almanacs the Stationers' Company had no legal monopoly over the printing of ballads and many printers issued a few ballads each. From about 1586 onwards ballad ownership and printing came to be concentrated among a few printers. This culminated in 1624 with the formation of a ballad 'partnership'. A partnership also entered large numbers of ballads in 1656 and Blagden has discussed the continuities which had resulted in the later seventeenth century in the formation of two large ballad partnerships and the creation of a ballad warehouse.[24] 'Old' ballads in black letter continued to be reprinted in the later seventeenth and early eighteenth centuries, although the transition to ballad-printing in roman type was evident by the end of our period. Ballads sold for $1/2$*d*. in the sixteenth and 1*d*. in the seventeenth century and the market for them was phenomenal. They were sung or declaimed on the streets, at fairs and other amusements by 'ballad-mongers' and distributed by petty-chapmen, hawkers and pedlars – often seen by the authorities as actual or potential vagrants and criminals – and displayed for sale on carts and stalls. Their purchasers pasted them up in homes, alehouses and other public places.[25]

Generalizations about the subject matter of ballads and their relationship to religious, political or social attitudes are difficult because of their numbers and because of problems of dating and context. Certainly sixteenth- and seventeenth-century ballads had a far wider range of references than chapbooks. The ballad authors, of whom the best known – and many remain unknown – are William Elderton, Thomas Deloney, Lawrence Price and Matthew Parker and the ballad printers produced almost anything they thought would sell. Parker's *When the King enjoys his own again* (1643), was according to Joseph Ritson, 'the most famous and popular air ever heard in this country' but the topics covered in most cheap print were usually less directly political. They included every kind of heterosexual and family relationship, rural and urban occupational themes, seafaring, trade and the new world, wars and rebellions, crimes and executions, fires, winds and floods, drunkenness and

24 Blagden 1954. 25 Wurzbach 1990, pp. 253–84.

gluttony, and ranged from the ultra-moralistic and godly to the bawdy and scatological.[26]

Tessa Watt has provided an invaluable survey of all forms of cheap print in relation to popular piety for the period 1550 to 1640 and has studied the godly ballads, which from the 1550s to the 1570s were produced by zealous Protestant reformers, who set new words to old lively songs. The Reverend Thomas Brice indeed wrote ballads 'out of a concern to clean up "filthy writing" and provide something more edifying for the public', attacking William Elderton's ballad, *The gods of love:*

> Tell me is Christ, or Cupide Lord?
> Doth God or Venus reigne?
> And whose are wee? Whom ought wee serve?
> I ask it, answer plaine.[27]

These godly 'moralized' ballads, although they declined as a percentage of all ballad output, appeared, like other forms of pious cheap print, in large numbers, into the two following two centuries.

Others have seen ballads as preserving popular traditions against Puritan precisionism and moralizing, while John Earle in *Micro-cosmographie* (1628) emphasized the patriotic content of the ballads of his day, writing of 'A Pot-Poet' that '... He is a man now much imploy'd in commendations of our Navy, and a bitter inveigher against the Spaniard. His frequent'st Workes goe out in single sheets, and are chanted from market to market, to a vile tune and a worse throat...' Certainly many ballads promoted a Protestant English patriotism and the ballad form was also adopted by political writers, whose works while printed on single sheets, often cost a great deal more than the street ballad, although not necessarily so when intense political excitement helped create a market for them, as during the Civil War, the Popish plot, and the Revolution of 1688. After 1660 songs from the theatres and pleasure gardens were also printed as single-sheet items as well as in little songsters. If these are taken into account the view that the ballad was replaced by the chapbook as the most popular form of cheap print may need further discussion.

Watt has produced compelling evidence that it was the ballad printers of the early seventeenth century who began the development of the commercial chapbook market.[28] Chapbooks developed as small paper-covered books or

26 In this short survey it is impossible to deal in any depth with the ballad. The best starting points for its consideration are Rollins 1919, Friedmann 1961, Shepard 1962 and 1973, Wurzbach 1990 and Watt 1991.

27 Watt 1991, p. 40.

28 Watt 1991, pp. 274–320.

pamphlets, approximately 3.5 by 6 inches, consisting usually of 4, 8, 12, 16 or 24 pages and 'almost always enlivened by the inclusion of crude woodcut illustrations'.[29] While some sixteenth-century saints' lives, sermons and news tracts had been printed to sell at from 1*d*. to 4*d*. each, there is little evidence of the specialized or mass production of such works or of the integration of production and distribution. Watt notes by contrast the activities of John Wright (1602–46), Henry Gosson (1603–41) and Francis Coles (1624–63), all active ballad printers, in producing books that were 'purposefully small, in order to reach a market of potential readers who had been hitherto unlikely to purchase the printed word, except in the form of a broadside ballad'.[30] Indeed some early chapbooks were versions of ballads (*Patient Grissel*) and others were based on more expensive godly books or traditional tales first printed before 1600, such as *A cristal glasse for christian women. Contayning an excellent discourse of the life and death of Katherine Stubbes*, published in quarto in 1591. The copyright for this was purchased by John Wright in 1620 and it subsequently appeared as a chapbook well into the eighteenth century. In a 1646 version Katherine Stubbes was said to have died on 14 December 1645, evidence of the updating of texts which has been studied for the *Bibliothèque bleue* but rather less for English cheap print.[31] Other publishers obviously commissioned new titles, including sermons and other godly books, romances, and jest books and other 'merry' books. They continued to revise their lists throughout the century, although this aspect of the chapbook trade after 1640 has not received detailed treatment. Most seventeenth-century chapbooks sold at 2*d*.–4*d*. each.

Watt's work demonstrates that early commercial chapbooks were meant to be sold and distributed alongside ballads using the same distribution networks. Spufford has discussed these distribution networks in detail and has also looked in depth at the chapbook trade to 1700, using Thackeray's trade list of *c*. 1689 and Samuel Pepys's collection of chapbooks as case studies.[32] By the time of Pepys, chapbooks appeared in the same standard formats and were advertised wholesale in specialized lists, a practice that continued through the eighteenth and into the nineteenth century. There was a large and profitable market for chapbooks, with some ballad and chapbook printers accumulating fortunes. The latter seventeenth century also saw the appearance of the specialized almanac for chapmen of which the title of *The city and countrey chapmans almanack for the year of our Lord 1685. Wherein all the marts or fairs in England and Wales,*

29 Neuberg 1977, p. 103. 30 Watt 1991, p. 278.

31 Watt 1991, pp. 267, 282–4. For the Bibliothèque bleue see, for example, Lise Andries, *La Bibliothèque bleue au dix-huitième siècle: une tradition éditoriale* in *Studies on Voltaire and the Eighteenth Century*, 270 (Oxford, 1989).

32 Spufford 1981, pp. 83–128.

are disposed in an alphabetical order in every moneth, so that both the place where, and the day on which any of them are kept, is immediately found. Also the post roads, and their several branches through England and Wales, with their distances described in a new method. And the names of all the market towns in every county in England and Wales, and on what day of the week any of them are kept... suggests the extent and importance of their trade.

Pepys divided his chapbooks into 'Penny godlinesses', 'Penny merriments', and 'Vulgaria' and each probably contained a substantial percentage of the range of English chapbooks printed in the latter seventeenth century, although it must be noted that Pepys did not collect all subjects covered by the chapbooks of his day and that Spufford's work does not cover some categories that Pepys did collect, for example, books of garlands, or collected only sparingly, as in the case of guides to practical living.[33] But the daunting and difficult task of preparing an English – certainly a British – chapbook census for the seventeenth and eighteenth centuries has not so far been attempted. Small godly books and images certainly continued to be produced in large numbers well into the eighteenth century and many publishers had separate trade lists for these. The titles from Pepys's collection of 'godlinesses' are indicative: among the themes covered are death and judgement, drunkenness and prostitution, religion and the family, the contribution of morality to prosperity, and instructional manuals and catechisms. The 'Penny merriments' included much on courtship, marriage and sexual behaviour with frequent allusions to cuckoldry, music, drink and dancing. They included song books, jest books, burlesques and guides to conjuring tricks. Anti-female, anti-Welsh and anti-Scottish material is also to be found in them. In the 'Vulgaria' Pepys placed 'penny', often 'pleasant', histories that included King Arthur, Guy of Warwick, Bevis of Southampton, St George, Robin Hood, Tom Thumb, Jack of Newbury, Thomas of Reading, the destruction of Troy and Dick Whittington, to name only the more familiar. Although Spufford has rightly noted that only one or two of these histories were not set in 'vague and idealized versions of the English past', it would perhaps be misleading to make too many assumptions about the nature of English popular culture based on such chapbooks, which were only a selection of those on offer and not the only reading matter of the poor, who increasingly were offered modern songs and images. The traditional chapbooks may by the end of our period have been aimed at a rural youth market. Certainly in the next century new chapbooks included abridgments of novels, songs from ballad operas, and other contemporary material.

33 Spufford 1981, ch. 6; Latham 1978–94, I, p. 1978.

24

Books for daily life: household, husbandry, behaviour

LYNETTE HUNTER

Many books published throughout the period are concerned with daily life. Books on household work and husbandry were often small format and appear to have been cheaply produced; more carefully printed were those relating to personal behaviour. The former include not only topics such as cookery, sewing, gardening and diets, the same material found in magazines and popular books today, but also chemistry and technology, earth sciences, botany, pharmacy, horticulture and general medicine for familial and daily use. Work inside the home involved the production of everything contained in the equivalent of a bathroom cabinet, kitchen cupboards and the contents of your desk. In addition, at particular times of year at least half of a long working day would be spent on the preservation and conservation of food. Work outside the house, while rather more varied, usually involved keeping chickens and at least a pig. It could also include maintaining horses, hives and a kitchen garden. Household work, usually part of an extended community, was the meaning of the word 'economics' at least until 1665.[1] Most things that today we might go out and buy had to be made by oneself or someone one knew. The content of books referring to this kind of daily life remains fairly constant but their publishing history is marked by a gap of nearly all new work in English between 1617 and 1650, after which an explosion of new vernacular works took place. In contrast, books relating to personal behaviour and family relationships have a continuous publishing history yet go through significant changes in status. Both kinds of book are filled with material we would recognize from the mass culture of today's periodical press.

Central to both areas are issues to do with the ownership of knowledge, and how that knowledge is controlled and mediated by the press, often working in conjunction with other interests. The account of household and husbandry books of the period is tied to an increasing fragmentation of daily work and,

1 Hunter 1999.

as noted below, the guilds' control both over various elements of domestic life and over what could or could not be published. What differentiates books on behaviour from those on daily work is largely the inappropriateness of guild control over personal lives, although civic and then nation-state authority, particularly in advice centred on attaining virtue and nobility by merit rather than by birth, came to be exercised through the printed book. Holding the two areas of publishing together is a common shift, attested to in many addresses to the reader, explicitly centred on controlling books written in the interest of the 'common good' or 'common wealth', a shift which is also tied to the rise of books written by and/or published for women.[2]

Popular books – deemed to be so usually by the vast numbers sold, gauged by their extended life and many editions – tended to be relatively cheap, small-format books for the non-specialist. Although the science in these books would be considered specialist today, it was then simply part of necessary learning. For example, the distillation of materials to isolate the active ingredients for a particular pharmaceutical would have been a central part of the work undertaken by many women on behalf of their families and larger communities. Because of changing social and commercial conditions, the status of this work for the urban dweller of the late sixteenth century differed from that of their late seventeenth-century counterpart, as it differed between city and country dwellers throughout this period. And of course the status of the work was inflected by class. For example, by 1600 sugar chemistry (then included in alchemy) and pharmacy had become accoutrements of the 'great lady' and were practised as leisure activities signifying aristocratic skill.[3] This knowledge circulated extensively in manuscript because it was the preserve of women who frequently named each other as a source, so print was not an acceptable medium because, by convention, women should remain anonymous and out of the public eye.[4] Indeed there is evidence that even when anonymous, the mere fact of publication was scandalous, because some people would have known the author.[5] Despite a brief period during the 1650s when such knowledge moved into print, and in the aftermath of the Commonwealth period, books conveying these skills were largely the province of the aristocratic men of science, of professionals (working as physicians, cooks or apothecaries), and of teachers offering vocational training in cookery and confectionery for the increasing numbers of women needing to support themselves.

2 See M. Bell, ch. 20 above. 3 Hunter 1997b.
4 See the general discussion of this issue in Hunter and Hutton 1997.
5 Dorothy Moore, undated letter to Samuel Hartlib [June,1645?], HP.

Books also establish communities. If the ordinary people flooding into London and other large towns during the period needed books in order to help them pick up a trade or skill in order to survive in an urban setting, the urban gentry, almost all of whom were 'new' in the later sixteenth century, needed books in order to find out what things were necessary for appropriate behaviour and display of position:[6] hence the advice on sugarwork, that sure indication of wealth, on the ordering of feasts, on the 'dressing' (breaking-in) of horses and on the construction of knot-gardens. It is a short step from this kind of use to the parallel books on fashion and style written precisely for the new civic man or woman. Guides to behaviour have a peculiar status. They offer a version of living which is desirable because people with status already live that way. Their readers aspire to that life, or want to identify those who are not really part of it, or simply want to learn what people will pay for and how to provide it. One thing certain about these books is that there were enough readers to make them worth printing and selling.

1557–1640

The incorporation of the Stationers' Company did something to regulate the publication of short popular works of this kind in small formats. In the 1540s and 1550s Robert Wyer had freely plagiarized the successful titles of other men, changing their titles and altering their texts:[7] thus 'Banckes Herball', first printed in 1525 with the protection of the royal privilege and frequently reprinted by Robert Banckes and his various successors, usually as a short octavo, until 1567,[8] was printed under a different title at least three times by Wyer, most outrageously as *Macers herbal. Practysyd by doctor Lynacro* (*c.* 1552).[9] Wyer never became a Stationer, and the title was finally registered by John King in 1560–1. However, in the case of titles valuable because popular, the new regulations did not prevent confusions over ownership in this competitive trade. Thomas Hill's *A most brief and pleasant treatise . . . of gardens* was first published, apparently for the author, by John Day in 1558.[10] The third edition, revised and enlarged, was entered by Thomas Marsh in the year 1567–8, who in March 1573 exchanged his rights with Henry Bynneman for the licence to

6 F. Whigham, *Ambition and privilege: the social tropes of Elizabethan courtesy theory* (London, 1984).
7 Lathrop 1914, Johnson 1944.
8 *STC* 13175.1 – .19C corrects Henrey 1975, nos. 172–92, noting three erroneous datings and two variant printings. This does not affect the argument of Johnson 1944.
9 *STC* 13175.13C: two earlier Wyer editions are 13175. 6 (1540?) and 13175. 8C (1543?).
10 *STC* 13489.5. On Hill and the book trade see Johnson 1943.

print Cato in Latin,[11] and the latter printed an edition of Hill's book in 1574. Bynneman clearly believed he still had rights in the book when he yielded them up, along with others, for the benefit of the poor of the company on 8 January 1584:[12] however, Marsh's son Edward believed he still owned the rights to Hill's book in 1591, since he assigned it to T. Onwin on 23 June, along with other titles which had belonged to his father.[13]

Edward Allde printed a large number of household and husbandry books, sometimes in partnership with the bookseller Edward White who also shared an interest in publishing plays. Allde printed for many other booksellers with whom he had a wide variety of relationships.[14] He printed, for example, nearly all the books sold by Nathaniel Fosbrooke; mathematical texts and books on sailing and navigation for John Tapp and Hugh Astley; just one work for Thomas Archer – Swetnam's *The araignment of... women* (1615), his notorious attack on women (it may be significant that Allde had a large output directed at women readers); chapbooks and ballads for Henry Gosson; and A.W.'s *A booke of cookry*, one of the first books on cooking, as distinguished from those on diet called for by Galenic medicine. Edward White also produced this kind of title, and after his death his wife reprinted *An hospital for the diseased*, acquired by White from Allde; in 1620 White's son signed his titles over to Pavier and Wright.[15] From the middle of the 1590s until 1613, when White died, Allde and White increasingly published together. Whereas in 1606 White alone re-published Markham's first work on horses *Chuse, ride, traine...*, in 1607 they together published Markham's *Cavelarice or the English horseman*.[16]

Gervase Markham (1568?–1637) is a publishing phenomenon in his own right. Initially a translator and writer of plays, from 1600 to 1620 he came to dominate the market for husbandry books.[17] Markham was one of the first writers in this field whose name became a commercial property. (John Fitzherbert's *Husbandry*, first published 1523, is commonly referred to as 'Fitzherbert's' but was so named only after Fitzherbert's death.) Markham himself was a prolific author sensitive to and self-conscious of his status, as the dedications to his *Cavelarice* (1607) and his *English husbandman* (1613–14) indicate. But it was the booksellers and printers who reprinted, abridged and vied for the rights to his books who turned his name into a guarantee of authority. Many stationers were involved in the publication of Markham's works, including White and Allde (*Cavelarice*, 1607), Okes (*Markhams maister-peece*, 1610), Roger Jackson (*Cheap and good husbandry*, 1614; *Countrey contentments*, 1615; *Markhams farwell*,

11 Arber, I, p. 359. 12 Arber, II, p. 780. 13 Arber, II, pp. 586–7.
14 McKerrow 1929. 15 Arber, IV, p. 44. 16 *STC* 17334, 17346.
17 For a full account of Markham's publications, see Poynter 1962.

1621; *Markhams method*, 1616, the last of which Jackson acquired by transfer from Langley). After Jackson's death in 1625 Michael Sparke moved in on the Markham name, publishing many editions of *Markham's faithful farrier* (1629) which, far from being a new Markham work, was in fact an abridged version of *Markhams maister-peece* and thus the property of Okes. Sparke entered it, however, in the Stationers' Register as his own, and he and his family benefited from no fewer than seven editions of the work by 1640.

The recycling of old material, sometimes abridged or with additions, is a feature of many of the works bearing Markham's name, though whether author or enterprising stationer was the source of such reworkings is not easy to distinguish. In 1616 Markham reworked existing material in *Maison rustique, or, the countrey farme* . . . , revising and enlarging Richard Surflet's translation of Charles Estienne's edition of Jean Liébault.[18] *Countrey contentments*, perhaps the best known of his works apart from the books on horsemanship, is in effect the text of his *Discourse of horsmanshippe* (first published 1593) with new matter on hunting and other sports. *Markhams method*, which ran to at least eleven editions by 1684, may have been an attempt by the bookseller Langley to cash in on the Markham name: the text is largely an abridgement of *Cheap and good husbandry*, owned by Jackson, and Langley's assignment of the copy to Jackson the same year suggests that he was forced formally to acknowledge Jackson's prior claim to the text. The extent to which an author like Markham could control the reprinting and repackaging of his texts was clearly limited: while Markham was trying to use the book trade to enhance his reputation as an author, the stationers were using him and his texts for their own profit. He complained, for example, that his *Cavalerice* had been spoilt by 'the over hastie greedinesse of a self-hurting Stationer',[19] and it is likely that the publication of *The way to get wealth* (1623) originated with the publisher, Jackson, rather than the author: it is made up of remaining copies of *Markhams farwell*, the third edition of *Cheape and good husbandry*, and the second edition of *The English huswife*.[20]

As well as demonstrating the re-use of earlier texts – via translation, revision, abridgment, addition and repackaging – typical of many publications in the period, Markham's work also signals another emerging pattern in publications of this kind: that of hinting that works were by women. Markham's *English huswife* (dedicated to the Dowager Countess of Exeter, Lady Mildred Burghley) and John Partridge's *The widows treasure* (1585) both claim, in their addresses to

18 Poynter 1962, pp. 148ff. 19 Poynter 1962, p. 100.

20 Poynter 1962, no. 34. *STC* silently disagrees with Poynter by treating *The English huswife* both as a separate publication *and* as part of this collection (*STC* 17342, 17343; 17353).

the reader, to convey the knowledge of specific women. Markham's bookseller, Roger Jackson, notes on the verso of the *English huswif* titlepage (Q1^{v}), that the writer is 'now out of his element' but that the book is based on 'an approved Manuscript which he happily light on, belonging sometime to an honorable Personage of this kingdome, who was singular amongst those of her ranke for many of the qualities here set forth'. Other works claim authority through association: Thomas Tusser's 'The book of huswifrie', published as the second part in the enlarged edition of his *A hundreth good pointes of husbandrie*[21] is dedicated to his employer Lady Elizabeth Paget, and Henry Butte's *Dyet's dry dinner* (1599) is dedicated to Lady Anne Bacon, whom Butte does not know, though he claims to be related to her. The pattern indicates that the female aristocrat, even when not claimed as the source of the text, was invoked by authors as an authority with whom the text might be appropriately associated.

Markham's career indicates one other central feature of the printing and selling of household and husbandry books: the striking gap in the production of new books on these apparently popular topics from 1617 to the early 1650s. 'Markham' books were being published with increasing regularity between 1610 and 1616, but on 14 July 1617 Markham had to promise 'never to write any more book or bookes to be printed of the Deseases or cures of any Cattle'[22] – which formed a considerable part of his works on husbandry. This may be connected to a warning added to his 1616 revision of Estienne's book, as *The country farm*, exhorting housewives to be careful not to meddle above their place in 'matters of Physicke'.[23] After 1617 there appears to be only one *new* book in English published on household preparations, 'authored' by Lord Ruthven in 1639,[24] but possibly by his wife.[25] Reprints, however, continued to appear: of the husbandry books of Leonard Mascall and Reginald Scot, for example, which were gathered together in a composite volume entitled *Countryman's recreation* (1640);[26] of William Lawson's *A new orchard and garden* (1617, 1623, 1626, 1630, 1638);[27] and of Gerard's 1597 *Herbal* (1633, 1636).[28] What new books *did* appear – such as John Parkinson's *Paradisi in sole paradisus terrestris* (1629),[29] his *Theatrum botanicum* (1640),[30] the rash of surgical texts that emerged in the 1630s – were not directed to a popular audience. Some previously popular works went out of print: Didymus Mountaine's *The gardeners labyrinth*, with at least four editions between 1577 and 1608, had no further

21 *STC* 24372.5 (1562). 22 Arber, III, p. 679, 14 July. 23 Hunter 1991, p. 47.
24 See the introduction to Davidson and Bell 1984. 25 Hunter 1997b, p. 89 and n.6.
26 *STC* 5874, reprinting Mascall (17573.5), *A booke of the art and manner, how to plante*...(1569, 1619, 1627, 1630) and Reginald Scot's *A perfite platforme of a hoppe garden*; book 3 is a re-issue of *STC* 11562, *The expert gardener* (1640), which itself reprints *STC* 18838 (*The orchard, and the garden*).
27 *STC* 15329ff. 28 *STC* 11751, 11752. 29 *STC* 19300. 30 *STC* 19302.

editions until after 1650.[31] The formation of the Society of Apothecaries in 1617, largely supported by the College of Physicians, may have been the cause of the immediate clampdown on works which contained much medicinal and pharmaceutical advice.

Incorporation of one society, however, cannot fully explain this gap, which must be part of a wider context of social change in patronage and commerce, including the ownership of knowledge. It is striking that this apparent restriction on household books which contained so much vital instruction and powerful material, occurs precisely at the time of the most virulent attacks on women in the city, which were concomitant with a growing recognition of the civic freedoms that women had a right to enjoy. Many of the books on household and husbandry matters had been published with the stated intention of providing knowledge for the common good or common wealth of the nation. For example, the physician and surgeon Peter Levens notes in his epistle to the reader in *A right profitable booke for all disseases. Called the pathway to health* that 'some . . . esteeme of nothing but that wich is most rare, or in hard or unknowne languages' and justifies his own text for its public utility: '. . . what reason is it that we should keepe secrete among a few, the thing that was made to be common to al?'[32] Similarly, John Partridge dedicates *The treasurie of commodious conceits, & hidden secrets . . . the huswives closet, of healthfull provision* to Master Richard Wistow, 'one of the Assistants of the Company of the Barbours & Surgions', commending Wistow's interest in 'publique profit and utylitie' in making 'receipts' (prescriptions or formulae) public.[33] In the same way, many of the books on behaviour from this earlier period were committed to extending the common wealth and common good by providing practical advice on self-presentation and negotiation. Others bring behaviour and household practice very close together, as in Thomas Brasbridge's *Poore man's jewell* (1578), which advises the rich who eat too much to abstain in order to give food to poorer families, to those who cannot work, or to those who have large families. Such action, he says, will be 'more healthfull for them selves, better for a Common weale, and more acceptable to GOD'.[34] In Andrew Borde's *Regyment and dietary of helthe* (1542) and *Breviary of healthe* (1547), frequently reprinted,[35] food and exercise are closely related to behaviour, as they are in Bartholomew Dowe's *A dairie booke for good huswives* (1588) which, in a dialogue between a 'South Hampshire' woman and a 'Suffolk' man, recommends dairy work to 'withdraw them [housewives] from

31 1651: Wing H2016. 32 *STC* 15532.5f (1582, 1587, 1596, 1608, 1632). 1632 ed., sigs. A2^{r-v}.

33 *STC* 19425.5 (1573), sigs. Aiii^{r}, Aiii^{v}. Eleven editions survive, 1573–1637.

34 *STC* 3548.5, sig. C2^{v}. Four more editions survive: 1578, 1579, 1580, 1592.

35 Six editions and one collection of extracts of *Regyment* survive (1542–1576, *STC* 3378.5ff.); *Breviary* survives in six editions (1547–1598, *STC* 3373.5ff.).

dumps and sullen fantasies (being a common disease amongst women)'.[36] But from the 1590s through to 1617 the connection between food and behaviour weakens: the topics begin to receive separate treatment, and references to the common good become less and less apparent.

Alongside the publication of books concerned with aspects of daily life, the entire period also generated many books of 'secrets'[37] or trade-related skills and receipts which, though similar in content, are organized not for familial use in terms of the kitchen garden, stable, brewery and dairy, but by materials. Alessio of Piedmont's *Secrets* was pre-eminent in this genre, reaching seventeen editions within four years of its first publication (including translations into French, Latin, English and Dutch).[38] Translated into English by W. Ward in 1558, the work has receipts for polish, varnish, ink, soap, metals, herbal remedies and even sugarwork for banquets, but the book is laid out in categories of stones, gems, plants and so on. Books of secrets often overlapped with books of 'novelties', using trade-related receipts for entertainment and leisure, especially at court. Together they were the butt of considerable criticism and were allied with quacks, empirics, cobblers, tanners and the like, or, in other words, anyone making a living from a basic use of chemical and physical technology. Unlike works for family use, these books not only unveiled the skills and receipts of individuals who made their money from them, but also revealed guild secrets. Take medicine, for example: from the 1540s to the 1580s there are many English-language, small-format books on diet, pharmacy, exercise, surgery and so on, but from the 1590s there is a gradual retraction of such information from both the simple guides and the more technical treatises in favour of general household and husbandry books, accompanied by a growth in Latin texts.[39]

The fate of practical and household books seems to be tied to the issue of the ownership of knowledge. The works of Hugh Plat (1552–1608) convey the difficult position felt by writers of such texts in the 1590–1617 period. Several of his shorter works, such as *Discoverie of certaine English wants* (1595)[40] and his *Sundrie new and artificiall remedies against famine* (1596),[41] offer good advice on ways to deal with crises as well as advertising his own inventions. The magnificent *Jewell house of art and nature* (1594) is dedicated to the Earl of Essex at the height of his political influence. Plat invokes the protection of

36 Sig. A2^{v}. *A dairie booke*... appears as the second part of *STC* 23703 (Kyd's translation of Tasso's *The housholders philosophie*) and has a separate title page but no separate *STC* entry.

37 Eamon 1994.

38 Eamon 1994, p. 251; table 3 (p. 252) gives twelve English editions by 1599 and two more in the seventeenth century. Altogether 104 European editions are recorded.

39 Sanderson 1999.

40 *STC* 19988.

41 *STC* 19996.

Essex against the charge of quackery, for his receipts are secrets not novelties; he is one of the few at this date still reiterating, as in many of his works, that 'the trew end of all our privat labors and studies, ought to bee the beginning of the publike and common good of our country'.[42] Yet the final parts of the book, on 'Chimicall conclusions', moulding, casting and new inventions, frequently refer to the relevant guilds. For example, Plat invented a mechanical bolter (a 'boulting hutch'), and had to show it to the Bakers of the City of London. They objected to it, but Plat sought and won approval from 'divers Cittizens of good worshippe and account'.[43] Furthermore, Plat reports in his advertising section an offer made 'of late' to the Petermen (saltpetre makers) to show them how to save half of the heat they expend on making the chemical if they will give him one third of what they save by using his advice.[44]

Plat's *Floraes paradise* (1608) was written for the profit of those 'who by their manual workes, may gaine a greater imployment, than heeretofore in their usuall callings' as well as for those who 'delight to see a raritie spring out of their own labours'.[45] In common with Thomas Lupton's *A thousand notable things* (1579), written in plain English the 'better to profit a great sorte, then to feede the fancies of a few', Plat writes in the 'plainest and most familiar phrase'.[46] Yet Plat, advised to keep some of his receipts secret from the 'common and vulgar eye',[47] used alchemical symbols for his most substantial receipt in the book. A book without a patron and written from Plat's retirement, *Floraes paradise* had to tread a very careful line with the guilds. Most of the concluding inventions and secrets are given with reference to the relevant authorities. For instance, he claims that he cannot openly give his secrets on making English wine, for he would have to be 'either free of the Vintners Company, or rather licensed by Mr Ingrams priviledge',[48] but can describe the results, with praise from worthy people. But by far the most effective protection is Plat's strategy of attributing his receipts to his manuscript and printed sources, thus undermining any charge that they might be secret. This technique is most unusual for printed books of the period, although manuscripts, because they circulated around a community of specific individuals, frequently used attributions. Virtually all the printed household and husbandry books of this earlier period, including Plat's own *Jewell house*, do not attribute sources, and have frequently been accused of plagiarism by later readers. In Plat's case, at least, the accusation is unfair: as Eamon demonstrates, Plat was himself a dedicated experimenter, recording his experiments and inventions in manuscript notebooks, several of

42 *STC* 19991, sig. A2^{r}. 43 Sig. I4^{v}. 44 Sig. K2^{v}. 45 *STC* 19990, sig. A3^{v}. 46 Sigs. A3^{v}, A4^{v}. 47 Sig. A5^{v}. 48 Sig. P3^{v}, *recte* P2^{v}.

which survive. A firm believer that the possibilities of experimental knowledge were far from exhausted, he tested and improved the receipts of Alessio and other printed books of secrets as well as gathering them from artisans, and housewives.[49] Just as today it is virtually impossible to patent a recipe, much of this collected material would have been considered 'common knowledge'. Plat's careful attribution of his receipts suggests that they were beginning to be thought of as publicly owned commodities, information held in common. Alongside his esoteric alchemical rendition of his own 'secrets', the gesture seems contradictory, but it outlines Plat's intense difficulty with areas of 'common' knowledge supposedly under guild control, and the larger paradox, felt by many later writers (see below) such as Robert Boyle, about intellectual ownership. Plat's aim in *The jewell house* of re-writing secrets into clear and accessible prose, anticipates Kenelm Digby's re-writing of Albertus Magnus's *A treatise of adhering to God* (1654) because the terse lists of ingredients for 'secrets' in the original lacked the 'form' of writing appropriate to its content for Digby's public audience; and the clear structure and plain English of the *Floraes* anticipates John Evelyn's *Acetaria* (1699) among a number of other works published in the latter half of the century.

Floraes paradise, in common with a number of books on husbandry from this period, did not appear again until the 1650s (when, in 1653, unsold sheets were re-issued with a new titlepage).[50] In contrast, Plat's *Delightes for ladies, to adorne their persons, tables, closets, and distillatories* (1600?) was in continual production throughout the period, with twenty-two editions by 1656.[51] *Delightes* lacks a dedicatee, but includes a lively epistle to the reader addressing ladies who wage war only with sugar cannonballs. There is no concern to attribute receipts here, nor any attempt to suggest that trade secrets are involved. Clearly the areas of preserves, distillation, cookery and housewifery and 'Sweet Powders' were not yet subject to guild control. Although poorly printed, this duodecimo has decorative borders on every page, giving it an aesthetic appeal, and a good index to receipts, alphabetically arranged by ingredients with page numbers for each section. Although ostensibly addressed specifically to an aristocratic and gentrified audience it was presumably cheap enough to make it a practical and affordable book for women much lower down the social scale.

What is radical about this text is the way in which it structures the knowledge appropriate for its audience into three parts: preserving, medicine and housewifery. Often found bound with Plat's *Delightes*, the anonymous *A closet*

49 Eamon 1994, pp. 311–14. 50 Wing P2384.
51 *STC* 19977.7ff. (sixteen editions [1600?]–1640); Wing P2379Aff. (six editions 1644–56).

for ladies and gentlewomen, or, the art of preserving, conserving, and candying. Also divers soveraigne medicines and salves (1608)[52] offers banqueting stuff or sugar cookery, and medicines. In at least two copies bound in the early seventeenth century[53] the two books have been assembled to bring together preserves with sugarwork, distillation with medicine, and cookery with housewifery. These three distinctive fields became the pattern for the one *new* book in this area published during the years 1617–50, Ruthven's *Ladies cabinet*, and for the two primary works (discussed below) that break the silence on new books for women, Elizabeth Grey's *Choice manuall* (1653) and W.M.'s *The Queens closet opened* (1655).

Plat's *Delightes for ladies* is one of a small number of books directed specifically to women in the opening decades of the seventeenth century. Husbandry books by definition were outside women's realm although there was a gradual acceptance that women might be interested in kitchen gardens and bee-keeping, and of course they were inextricably involved in dairy work. But most household or behaviour books, while for and about women's lives, assumed that women would get their knowledge by way of the men in their lives – or at least that they were the correct channel. We know that many manuscripts written by women in the form of diaries, novellas, verse, household receipts, as well as science and medicine, circulated among aristocratic and gentry families,[54] but apart from a few literary works they were not usually for publication outside those confines. Books on behaviour, similarly, contained information about women: whether as mothers, sisters, wives or daughters. Knowledge about and for them tended to be communicated as part of the moral and economic, as opposed to the political and ethical, realms of life, in the guides to civil and then civic personal behaviour.

Books on behaviour throw into sharp relief the inherent contradictions of texts that instruct one on how to achieve a particular status. Were these books addressed to those who already knew how to behave in order to identify interlopers and keep them out? Were they addressed to those who were aspiring to status and needed to find out what to do? Or were they conscious of and playing on both, sometimes ironizing, parodying or satirizing, and sometimes self-consciously admitting that not all people could succeed in their aspirations? From Thomas Hoby's translation of Castiglione's *The courtier* in 1561, a well-printed quarto which left little doubt that its writer intended its description

52 *STC* 5434: ten editions 1608–36.

53 The 1608 edition is bound with Plat's *Delightes* (1609) and held in the Brotherton Library Special Collections, Blanche Leigh Collection (K1); the 1611 editions of both are also found in the Preston Collection (K1). Both texts were sold by the bookseller A. Johnson.

54 See Schleiner 1994.

of behaviour for the aristocracy, early works of this kind were nearly all translations, usually from the Italian, rather than the dietaries and regiments for daily behaviour composed by English writers, and aimed at the gentry and the 'middle' people, as Bacon described the emerging bourgeoisie.

These early books aimed at status addressed an aristocracy that was being weaned from militarism by a concept of civil duty, and stressed the importance of national unity and national wars. The 1570s saw a number of translations, among them of Patrizi's book on the value of the common wealth, *A moral methode of civile policie*[55] (but not his book on the necessity for nobility); Thomas Newton's *The touchstone of complexions*[56] from Lemnius on the passions; T. Browne's version of Johan Sturm's influential work on style, rhetoric and character, *A ritch storehouse or treasurie . . . called Nobilitas literata*;[57] and R. Peterson's version of John della Casa's *Galateo* on the actions of a courtier.[58] None of these was translated by an aristocrat like Hoby, or the earlier Thomas Elyot. They were, however, closely related to the vernacular rhetorics of the period such as Thomas Wilson's *The arte of rhetorique* (1553) and *The three orations of Demosthenes* (1570), Richard Reynoldes's *Foundacion of rhetorike* (1563),[59] or Thomas Norton's *Orations, of Arsanes agaynst Philip of Macedone . . .* (1560?),[60] all of which 'English Phillipics' argued for the importance of national loyalty.[61] By the 1580s a profound distrust of style as an indication of character was setting in. New translations (for example Thomas Bowes's version of Pierre Primaudaye's *L'Academie Francaise* (1586)[62] and George Pettie's version of Guazzo's *The ciuile conversation* (1581)[63]) dealt with issues of courtly fashion, with the latter also discussing the honest behaviour of those gentry who were not part of the court. And Peacham and Puttenham each produced their vernacular rhetorical works, *The garden of eloquence* (1577) and *The arte of English poesie* (1589), on eloquence, argument and wisdom discussing behaviour in terms of deception, honesty and decorum.[64]

From 1600 the market was flooded by books such as Thomas Wright on *The passions of the minde* (1601) and Thomas Overburie's book of 'characters' (1614).[65] There was Lodowick Bryskett's translation of Giraldi Cinthio's work

55 1576, *STC* 19475. 56 1576, *STC* 15456.
57 1570, *STC* 23408. 58 1570, 1576, *STC* 4738.
59 *STC* 25799; 6578; 20925a.5. Reynoldes's *Foundacion* seems to have been issued with Kingston's 1563 edition of Wilson's *The arte of rhetorique*; *STC* notes that several copies are bound up together.
60 *STC* 785. 61 McClintock 1997. 62 *The French academie . . .*, *STC* 15233ff.
63 *STC* 12422. A translation of book 4 was added in 1586, trans. B. Young (*STC* 12423) and an adapted selection from book 3 was published as *The court of good counsell. Wherein is set downe how a man should choose a good wife and a woman a good husband* (1607, *STC* 5876).
64 *STC* 19497; 20519.
65 Wright, *STC* 26039; Overburie, *A wife, now a widowe* (*STC* 18903.5ff.): five editions in 1614, after which titles vary (in all, seventeen editions are recorded to 1638).

on a private life, *A discourse of civill life* (1606), heralding a new interest in the civic world and the 'urban, with the family' as the training ground for court life which crops up also in James Cleland's *The institution of a young noble man* (1607) and Daniel Tuvil's *Essaies politicke, and morall* (1608), both writers claiming association with tutors to the King's sons, and both arguing that nobility comes not through birth but through learning and action.[66] A new element of these civic books was 'negotiation' as elaborated in Tuvil's *The dove and the serpent* (1614),[67] a topic introduced by Bacon in his essay of that name in 1595, and lying at the heart of honest self-display rather than dissimulating fashion.

These are books of popular vernacular rhetoric, debating the differences between dialectics, logic and rhetoric that were at the centre of the academic debates on these topics in the universities of the period. The publication of academic books on rhetoric is another story completely. They were produced mainly in Latin from the presses of Oxford and Cambridge and the Continent, and destined to be scholarly textbooks rather than accessible guides to language, conversation, negotiation, style and ultimately fashion. Yet *Opinion deified* (1613)[68] by Barnaby Rich is a clear successor to Peter Ramus's marginalization of rhetoric. These more popular books are openly concerned with social and political issues, and are based on a belief that personal behaviour learned in the family trains one for civic duty and eventually, although they only gesture towards it, for service to the nation. They continually stress the direct connection between the heart and the tongue, so that what a person says is what he or she is. The focus is on decent, decorous self-display that carves out a specific place for the citizen as opposed to the courtier or the gentleman: a citizen must be 'a professor of civilitie' with appropriate habit, manner of life, conversation and phrase of speech, and the wife of a citizen 'goes at her pleasure' and 'is decked, adorned, neatly apparrelled, sits for the gaze' as a 1616 translation of della Casa attributed to Thomas Gainsford puts it in *The rich cabinet*.[69] Common wealth had ceased primarily to mean distributed wealth, and had come to mean individual access to wealth; the proper citizen is 'covetous'.

In fact these books from the early seventeenth century represent a series of guides to self-containment. If wealth and status were accessible, they could not be accessible to all. As this realization sank in, the majority of these books moved away from issues of exercise, diet, environment and display, towards private discipline; books on behaviour and religion carry this genre right through to the

66 *STC* 3958; 5393; 24396. 67 *STC* 24394. 68 *STC* 20994.
69 *STC* 11522. The complete translation of della Casa was Petersen's *Galateo*, above.

end of the century. 'Conversation' became a word delineating both the world of the family (coming later in the century to connote rhetoric associated with women), and one's relation with God, as in *The christian principle and peaceable conversation of the people . . . called Quakers . . .* (1685).[70] However, the tradition that linked personal behaviour with familial training, setting it squarely within the economics of household and husbandry issues (as seen in Thomas Tusser's *A hundreth good pointes of husbandrie* of 1557 and later in Bryskett), comes together in the monumental work by Richard Brathwaite, *The English gentleman* (1630). But this work was not for popular consumption. Its contents indicate that it was aimed at the established gentry and aristocracy, and it turns husbandry issues into a city versus country debate, in which the country is more honest and less dissimulating. It assumes that people know how to display status, and is concerned to advise on excessive or inappropriate behaviour of the private gentleman. Brathwaite's sequel, *The English gentlewoman* (1631), was the first English behaviour book directly addressed to women. In 1641 both works were printed together, as *The English gentleman and the English gentlewoman*, a volume which, appropriate to its own sense of display, was published in impressive folio format.[71] This construction of separate books for audiences of different sexes, subsequently printed as one, is a significant development in the role of the book, presaged in the publication of Hugh Plat's *Delightes for ladies* and Markham's *Countrey contentments*.

1640–1695

Although reprints of earlier household and husbandry books continued to appear between 1617 and 1640, very few were published during the 1640s. After 1650, however, one finds not only many reprints and re-issues of works from the pre-1617 period, but also numerous translations and new works by identifiable new writers. Recent work has indicated that a new pattern of publication in vernacular medical literature was possibly triggered by Nicholas Culpeper's translation of the *Pharmacopoeia* of the College of Physicians as *The London pharmacopoeia* (1649). Certainly this one book instantly became a popular work on herbal medicine. Subsequent editions far outnumber those of similar works which followed it onto the market.[72] Some booksellers appear to have developed consistent lines in books that, in the earlier period, would have been covered by husbandry but were now generated by the more specialized

70 Wing C3947. 71 *STC* 3563; 3565; Wing B4262. 72 Sanderson 1999.

areas of horticulture, or apiculture, or viticulture or botany. James Allestree and John Martyn co-published many of these titles, which is not surprising, given that they were successively publishers to the Royal Society.[73]

A central issue was the ownership of knowledge. Accounts of the interaction between the aristocratic scientists and the commercial mechanics, such as that by Johns, suggest that the scientists knew they were taking over commercial secrets in their effort to further science.[74] For some, like Robert Boyle, this was a democratization of knowledge,[75] but for others it was clearly a form of industrial espionage. John Evelyn was involved in the Royal Society's project to compile a history of trade technologies,[76] yet he never finished his contribution because he came to realize that he was potentially depriving people of their income. Joseph Moxon's *Mechanick exercises*,[77] however, details very clearly the skills involved in several trades, including the art or science of printing.

Many of the books covering a range of practical material printed in this period did not claim the scientific basis sought by members of the Royal Society. One of the booksellers interested in these more popular books was Nathaniel Brooke who sold work written by William Coles (1656 and 1657) and Robert Turner (1664). Brooke was also the seller of *The Queens closet opened* (1655), a composite work put together in the way 'Markham' titles had previously been packaged. *The Queens closet opened*, by one W. M. of the household of Queen Henrietta Maria in France, claims that the Queen herself practised the receipts.[78] This duodecimo work is in fact a group of three books which Brooke marketed both as separate works and as a composite volume: *The Queen's cabinet opened: or, The pearle of practice* (pharmacy, medicine and surgery), *A Queens delight* (preserving, conserving, distillation) and *The compleat cook* (cookery). The first two parts have individual title pages but a single register and pagination sequence, while the third part (*The compleat cook*) has its own title page, pagination and register. Brooke registered *The Queens closet* in 1654 and from the following year *The compleat cook* appeared both as a separate work[79] and as part of *The Queens closet*; the other component, *A Queens delight*, survives only as a separate work from 1668 onwards,[80] extensively rewritten in light of La Varenne's *Le parfait confiturier* which had appeared the previous year. Subsequent extant

73 Rostenberg 1965, II, pp. 237–80; Johns 1998, pp. 492–3, 496–7.
74 Johns 1991 and 1998, pp. 313–14, 470, 556–8.
75 Boyle 1655. See also Hunter 1997a, p. 190.
76 See the account in Hunter 1981, ch. 4.
77 Published in two parts, 1677 (Wing M3013) and 1683 (Wing M3014).
78 Wing M96ff.
79 Brooke registered *The Queens closet* on 2 October 1654 (ownership passing to Obadiah Blagrave, 9 February 1683). *The compleat cook*: Wing M88ff.
80 Wing Q156Bff.

editions until 1698 indicate that the *Cabinet* went through a further sixteen editions as against only four of the *Delight* and ten of *The compleat cook*. This pattern of publishing works both individually and together, as a composite work, as already noted in the cases of Plat, Markham and Brathwaite, suggests a publishing strategy of some sophistication designed to satisfy different audiences with different needs or different levels of disposable income. Other books that follow this pattern include Elizabeth Grey, Countess of Kent's *A choice manuall of rare and select secrets* (1653) usually bound with her *A true gentlewoman's delight* (1653), both 'published' (i.e. edited) by William Jarvis and printed by Gertrude Dawson. The 1656 edition prints the two as parts of the same book. By 1687 *A choice manuall* was in its nineteenth edition.

This pattern can be observed in at least one other example, the work of Hannah Wolley. *The ladies directory*, the first of her printed books, is concerned with behaviour, or what the eighteenth century called 'conduct', and is the first printed guide written in English by a woman on behaviour for women. It was printed 'for the authress' by Thomas Milbourn in 1661, and the following year was published by Peter Dring.[81] Wolley's *The cooks guide* (1664), also printed for Dring, is a fairly straightforward cookery book that promises to guide ladies and gentlewomen in the most recent fashions for making and serving food.[82] A slightly later publication is her *Gentlewoman's companion*, which Wolley began writing around 1665 although the earliest extant edition, with preface dated 1672, is 1673; this is far more varied, covering behaviour for women but also dealing with serving, cookery, medicine and conserves. In the introduction she says she has used her *Ladies directory* and *Cooks guide*, and also *The Queens closet*, Robert May's *The accomplisht cook* (1660, addressed to men going into cookery as a profession), and *The ladies companion*.[83]

In 1670 a far more sophisticated book, Wolley's *The Queen-like closet*, came out. Part one contains receipts for sugar-cookery, preservation and beauty aids, but also many of the same recipes published in the *Cook's guide*; part two adds receipts for a wider range of cookery, sauces and pickles. In 1674 a *Supplement* containing mainly medicines was printed which became, in effect, the third section of what from then on was published as a three-part work.[84] Like the late-sixteenth-century books on lifestyle written for the civic man,

81 Wing w3280 (only copy now lost); the Dring edition, Wing w3281, may be a re-issue since no more editions are known.

82 Wing w3276.

83 Wolley may have been referring to the receipt book *The ladies companion* (1654), but these receipts are not particularly interesting in the light of her own work. It is more likely that she is referring to *The ladies companion or the English midwife*, advertised in some editions of the *Gentlewoman's companion* as an octavo book, costing 2*s*., printed for and sold by Edward Thomas.

84 Wing w3282ff.

The Queen-like closet brings together behaviour, diet, exercise, medicine and housework. Wolley writes, as the title page to the second part claims, 'not confounding the Braine with multitudes of Words to little or no purpose, or vain Expressions of things which are altogether unknown to the Learned as well as the Ignorant; this is really imparted for the good of all the female sex'. Significantly, and like those earlier books aimed at men, Wolley deals with vocational and professional behaviour – but now, for women.

Wolley's books have never had a completely satisfactory bibiliographical treatment and problems of attribution are peculiarly difficult.[85] The frontispiece of the anonymous *The accomplish'd lady's delight* (1675), assigned to Wolley by Wing on slight evidence, may have been an attempt to copy Wolley's portrait at the start of *The Queen-like closet.*[86] (Increasingly these books offered a visual image of the author, whether Wolley, Queen Henrietta Maria, Nicholas Culpeper, or Alethea Talbot, Countess of Surrey and Arundel).[87] The name of the author rather than the novelty of the contents seemed to matter most: *The compleat servant-maid* (1677),[88] printed for Thomas Passinger in 1677, was taken wholly from Wolley's *Gentlewoman's companion.* Another work attributed directly to her on the title page is *The ladies delight* (1672),[89] which includes the *Exact cook* (the same as the *Cook's guide*) and the *Ladies physical closet* (containing receipts from *The Queen-like closet* of 1670). Poorly printed by Milbourn (printer of the first edition of her *The ladies directory*), *The ladies delight* is a small book quite unlike Wolley's works of the 1660s. None of these books shares the flamboyant literary style of her works prior to 1671.

The date of Wolley's death is said to be 1674, but if she died earlier, then that may be some explanation for the rash of publications in the early 1670s that use either her name, her titles or her portrait, but seem not to have originated with her. Part of the explanation is surely her popularity, leading publishers to capitalize both on her name and on her receipts; her work was certainly influential and can be traced through a number of later books. These include not only vocational guides like *The true way of preserving & candying* (1681), Mary Tillinghast's *Rare and excellent receipts* (1678)[90] for students in her confectionery school, but also fashion and lifestyle guides such as George Hartmann's *The true preserver and restorer of health* (1682) which provided occupation for

85 See, for example, Schumacher-Voelker 1981.

86 A suggestion made first by J. Ferguson, reported by Schumacher-Voelker 1981, p. 67.

87 The latter's portrait appears in *Natura exenterata* (1654, Wing N241). See Hunter 1997b for a discussion of attribution.

88 Wing W3273A. 89 Wing W3279. 90 Wing T3126A; T1182.

the leisured lady, and those which were written for the upwardly mobile, such as John Shirley's *The accomplished ladies rich closet* (1687),[91] addressed like Wolley's *The Queen-like closet* to the 'Ingenious' gentlewoman.

If the period after 1650 sees the work of earlier women writers finally being acknowledged, and contemporary women writing for a growing number of readers, it also sees the recognition of women as a rather more independent audience offering a substantial market for exploitation. Although most books in the field were still published for both men and women, many retained a mixture of guides for daily work and daily behaviour, while developing a distinct if limited pattern of 'his and her' books. John Chamberlayne is one of the first to write about work appropriate for men inside the house, as opposed to husbandry alone. He distinguishes cookery and food for men in his translation of Durante's *A treasure of health* (1686), having already translated Dufour's book on issues appropriate to women, *The manner of making of coffee, tea and chocolate* (1685).[92] By 1691 Thomas Tryon, a doctor who frequently published dietary guides as preventative medicine as well as a few simple receipts for treating illnesses and diseases among those who could not afford professional help, was also publishing gender-specific advice: *Wisdom's dictates* (1691) to men, and *The good housewife made a doctor* (1685?) to women.[93] Tryon had earlier written *Healths grand preservative or the womans best doctor* (1682), which lashes out against the abuses of drink and tobacco by women and children.[94] He also wrote a book for the family, *The waye to health, long life and happiness* (1683) which aims to advise all men and women on 'meats, drinks, air, exercise', 'English herbs' and many other topics.

It was precisely the 'voice' of these books, of the familiar advisor, which was taken up by the mushrooming periodical press after 1695. And the periodical press took over, too, the dissemination of this kind of material to a broad and popular audience during the eighteenth century. During the period from 1557 to 1695 the constitution of a 'popular' market had changed. In the sixteenth-century English vernacular advice books had been addressed largely to men of the gentry and of professional and mercantile families. Through the later sixteenth to seventeenth centuries, there was a growing audience for such books among women, artisans and the emerging urban middle class. At the same time the contents shifted in status. Some household practices and artisan secrets became aristocratic science or professional knowledge; a great deal of guidance

91 Wing H1004ff. S3498ff.

92 Wing D2682B; Wing D2454. He also wrote *The natural history of coffee, chocolate, thee* (1682), Wing C1859.

93 Wing T3205, T3180.

94 Wing T3182.

on daily behaviour became detached from awareness of diet and exercise, and was split between social and religious manners. Like their increasingly diverse audience, the books' contents became increasingly specialized and the changes in printing and marketing the works responded to that diversification, and to the pockets of customers, with the wide range of strategies that made possible the periodical press of the eighteenth century.

25
The creation of the periodical press 1620–1695

CAROLYN NELSON and MATTHEW SECCOMBE

The British periodical press developed slowly and faltered under early official controls, but flourished when political conflict created opportunities for journalists and publishers. Political journalism rose and fell depending upon events, governmental policies, and publishers' courage; nonpolitical informative or 'practical' periodicals, on the other hand, gradually became a large and stable component of the press. From negligible beginnings, by 1695 hundreds of periodicals, with tens of thousands of issues and covering a wide range of subjects, had been published in Britain (see figure 25.1).

No periodicals – defined loosely as numbered and/or dated series of pamphlets or sheets with uniform title and format – were published before 1620. (A possible exception was the weekly London bill of mortality,[1] compiled by the parish clerks and printed as early as 1603–4, but it may have been published only in times of plague.) Several factors deterred the early appearance of periodicals. Most simply, someone had to conceive of them, and the idea was not obvious. For early publishers, prayer books, sermons, treatises and ballads were known texts for a known market; periodical publications, in contrast, require planning without knowing the text in advance. The concept, therefore, involved a leap of faith, as well as the financial risks of establishing networks of sources and distribution and an ongoing printing operation – an expensive undertaking for an untested market. The major barrier, however, seems to have been the hazardous implications of the subject for which the periodical was ideally suited – the news.

News was a sensitive issue for the British state, as throughout Europe. Some kinds of news were permitted into print, featuring battles, crimes, freaks and wondrous or prophetic events. After the pamphlet *Hereafter ensue the trewe encountre or . . . batayle lately done between England and Scotland* on the battle of Flodden Field in 1513, enough news appeared in the following century to

1 *STC* 16738.5ff.

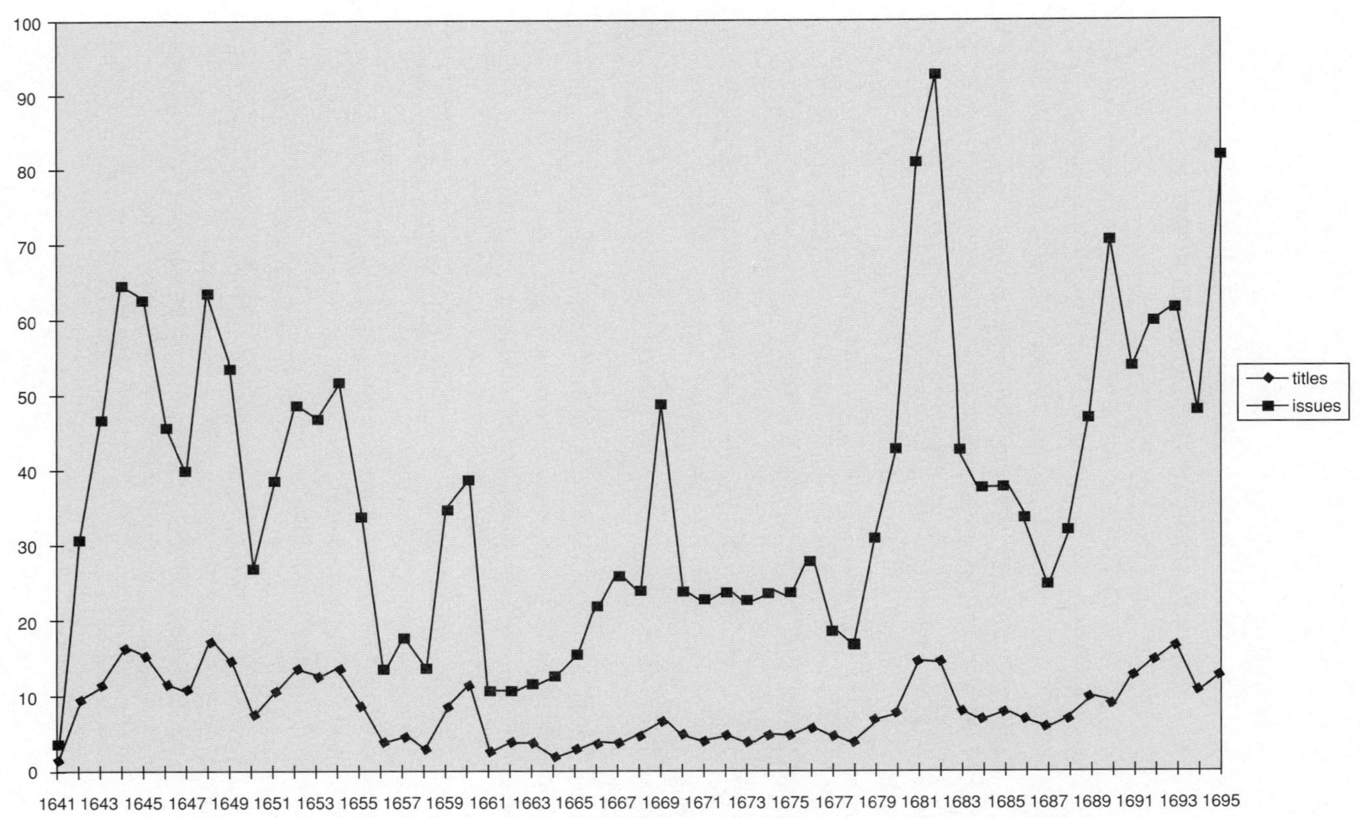

Figure 25.1 Periodical press. Titles and issues 1641–1695: mean monthly average each year

engender scepticism about its accuracy, as noted in the ballad *News good and new* (*Too good to be true*).[2] But the systematic publication of news, particularly domestic political news, was another matter. News of State was the property of the State. The public had no recognized right to political information, which was doled out selectively on a need-to-inform basis by the Crown or Parliament through authorized printers. Unauthorized publication was severely punished and rarely attempted. The development of political journalism that began in the middle of the seventeenth century would be an incremental process, advancing as competing political élites – Parliamentarians and Royalists, Whigs and Tories – used the press to seek advantage, and as the government gradually ceased to enforce prohibitions.

The start of the Thirty Years War prompted a demand for European news, and the number of news pamphlets increased, many of them published openly and entered routinely in the Stationers' Register. Early in 1620, however, the secretary to the Bishop of London, who licensed non-theological works for the Stationers' Company, withdrew his approval of a pamphlet describing 'an apparation seene over the Desertes in Arabia, together with the rayninge of Blood about Rome',[3] and until late in 1621 entries of news pamphlets ceased – whether from the authorities' refusal to endorse the copy or from the publishers' self-censorship. In the interval English-language news continued to appear, bearing either foreign imprints – a few genuine, most of them false – or no imprints at all.

Meanwhile, periodical news sheets were beginning to flourish on the Continent. The first corantos, small halfsheets printed in black-letter type, were published in Amsterdam in 1618,[4] and in December 1620 English translations began to appear in London. The first of the latter, *Corante out of Italy, Germany, &c.*, was probably a genuine Amsterdam publication,[5] but subsequent English-language corantos were almost certainly printed in London with false Dutch imprints.[6] Journalism was a hazardous trade from the start. Joseph Mead's 'courantier,' Thomas Archer, was 'set by the heels' (arrested) in August 1621 for a pamphlet that included a phrase that offended the Spanish ambassador. Mead believed that Archer's corantos were targeted for replacement by those of someone 'who hath got license to print and sell them honestly translated out of Dutch'.[7]

2 *STC* 11088.5, 18505. 3 Arber, III, p. 664 (29 January 1619/20). 4 See Dahl 1946.

5 *STC* 18507.1–17. For facsimiles of these and other English language corantos with Dutch imprints, see Stockum 1946. For a list of all surviving English-language corantos and newsbooks through 1640, see *STC* 18507 *passim*, which incorporates and extends the list in Dahl 1952.

6 *STC* 18507.8–9, 18507.13, 18507.26–28. *STC* 18507.18–25 may be genuine, but have been questioned.

7 BL, Harleian MS 389, fol. 122^{r}, 22 September 1621, cited in Lambert 1992a, pp. 8–9.

In September 1621 the *Corante, or newes from Italy, Germany* appeared, claiming to be published in London by 'N. B.'[8] Most historians have viewed these seven issues as the first genuinely English newspaper, as well as the first published by authority.[9] But the series was more English and more 'honest' than those it replaced – or rather continued – only in identifying its place of printing and its sources ('high Dutch' and 'low Dutch' corantos from Frankfurt and Amsterdam). It was not entered in the Stationers' Registers. 'N. B.' was only a partial identification of the publisher: he may well have been Nathaniel Butter, who had been publishing news pamphlets since the Gunpowder Plot,[10] but other candidates include Nicholas Bourne, Butter's future partner,[11] and Nathaniel Browne, who published three news pamphlets in 1618.[12] Whoever used the initials was surely taking advantage of their ambiguity.

That series ceased within a month, when George Cottington was appointed licenser of news.[13] He briefly favoured two other publishers, Bartholomew Downes and William Lee the younger, who entered only two books of news[14] before another interval of silence (and the appearance of more false foreign imprints). When Cottington returned to licensing in May 1622, news began to be entered in the Registers and published regularly, most frequently by Bourne and Archer, but also by Butter and others.[15] After a few months of competing with and complaining of each other, the rivals began to co-operate to produce a single numbered series,[16] and eventually Butter and Bourne emerged as the only publishers.

This collaboration may have been arranged by the series' first compiler, Captain Thomas Gainsford.[17] The title varied but most often began with or included the phrase 'weekely newes'. The publishers abandoned the half-sheet format to return to the earlier quarto of the occasional news pamphlets, and the result was the periodical 'newsbook'. Internal organization of the news was primitive and derivative. It was arranged in rough geographical/chronological order, the most distant (and therefore oldest) news first. English news – what little occurred in the Continental originals – was dropped, probably as an act of self-censorship.

Despite the crude presentation, the editor grappled with the elements and problems inherent in periodical publication. Although the newsbooks

8 *STC* 18507.29–35.

9 See, for example, Frank 1961, p. 6. For a dissenting view, see Lambert 1992a, p. 9.

10 See the entry in Arber, III, p. 308 (3 January 1606) for Butter's Gunpowder Plot pamphlet (apparently not extant).

11 *STC* 18507.45ff. 12 *STC* 4629, 11281, 24333. 13 Greg 1962. 14 *STC* 18507.35A–C.

15 *STC* 18507.36–44. 16 *STC* 18507.45–81.

17 Frank 1961, p. 10; Wayne H. Phelps, 'Thomas Gainsford (1656–1624), the "Grandfather of English Editors"', *PBSA* 73 (1979), 79–85.

advertised a weekly schedule, they could not go to press until their Dutch originals had crossed the channel (irregularly, particularly in bad weather) and had been translated into English. Delays created tension between supplier and customer: 'both the reader and the printer of these Pamphlets, agree in their expectation of weekely Newes, so that if the Printer have not wherewithall to afford satisfaction, yet will the Reader come and aske every day for new Newes'. News reports, moreover, could rarely be verified before going to press, and they often conflicted with each other. The editor sometimes offered various accounts and let his readers choose: 'in our Newes we delivered some things in severall places as wee get the tiding in severall parts to shew you how the parties agree in their relations, seeing it is knowne that many write partially'.[18]

As long as news from the front was frequent and favourable the newsbooks appeared often, but they never achieved the popularity and regularity of some of the Continental corantos. The English newsbooks faltered when Gainsford died in 1624 and once more in 1630 when England withdrew from the wars, although they recovered again briefly. In 1632, however, the King's Council banned the newsbooks for slandering a Spanish duke. By the time they were allowed to resume in 1638[19] they had apparently lost their appeal: 'if a competent number shall be [sold] weekly . . . we shall continue them; if not, we shall be forced to put a period to the Presse'. Although the publishers promised to 'keepe a constant Day every weeke', they never re-established a regular trade for their newsbooks.[20]

The English Civil War destroyed the tightly controlled, faltering foreign news-trade and gave rise to a disorderly but vigorous domestic industry. Civil conflict meant 'news' that the public wanted to read and it also reduced the power of the government to control the press. The two developments were mutually reinforcing. After the Long Parliament opened in November 1640, and even before the abolition of the Star Chamber in July 1641, a gradually increasing stream of privately (often secretly) printed pamphlets of political news and commentary began to challenge Crown and Parliamentary control of the press. The Lords' and Commons' Journals recount numerous summonses and arrests of defiant printers and publishers for whom the rewards outweighed the risks.

The ingredients for a new kind of periodical news publication were already at hand and readily combined. The earlier newsbooks of foreign news provided the format; the manuscript Parliamentary diurnals, which dated at least from the late 1620s, provided the model for organization and content. The diurnals

18 Dahl 1952, item 96n (31 January 1623); item 142 (19 March 1624), quoted in Dahl 1946, p. 19.
19 Lambert 1992a, p. 13.
20 Dahl 1952, item 361n (23 April 1640); item 367n (11 January 1641).

offered a plausible although sometimes inaccurate day-by-day account of proceedings in Parliament by weaving together summaries of official publications as well as news gathered 'without-doors' around Westminster from members' servants, from petitioners and other outsiders with temporary access to Parliamentary chambers, and occasionally from members of Parliament who had incentive to leak information.[21]

The first domestic newsbook appeared on 29 November 1641: *The heads of several proceedings in this present Parliament* (plate 25.1).[22] It bore the imprint of 'I. T.,' later identified as John Thomas; but Thomas was a servant of the printer Thomas Fawcet,[23] and Fawcet and his partner Bernard Alsop may have used Thomas's name to conceal their own identities as printers/publishers. The text was taken, and probably pirated, from the manuscript diurnal[24] compiled by Samuel Pecke, a 'scrivener in Westminster'.[25] Pecke soon became the leading print journalist, publishing with William Cooke and later Francis Coles and others.

News was urgently in demand, and the censors were temporarily overwhelmed. Other series soon followed, supplementing day-by-day Parliamentary reports with news far from the Westminster precincts disguised as 'letters read in Parliament'. None of the publishers entered their copy in the Stationers' Register; the attempt would have been useless, since Parliament was still trying to restrict printing to official publications. It was easier to copy or steal a serial title than to create a new one, and imitations and counterfeits multiplied, along with bickering about which series was the 'true' one. By January 1642 seventeen newsbook series were in print in London, and two reprinted in Edinburgh.

Some of these publications were undoubtedly sponsored and paid for as propaganda, but the economic dimension also deserves emphasis. As many competitors entered the newly opened news market, fought for survival, and gradually settled into a more stable market of a smaller number of successful competitors, they followed a classic pattern of business development.[26] The incentive was clear enough. A typical newsbook which sold for one penny might

21 Wallace Notestein and Frances Helen Relf, *Commons Debates for 1629, critically edited* (Minneapolis, 1921), pp. xliii–liv.

22 N&S, 181.101.

23 *Journals of the House of Commons [13 April 1640–14 March 1642]* (London, 1803), II, p. 518 (8 April 1642).

24 Papers of William Herbert, first Marquis of Powis (PRO 30/53).

25 *Journals of the House of Lords, beginning Anno Decimo Octavo Caroli Regis, 1642* (London, n.d.), V, p. 533 (7 January 1643). See also E&R, I, p. 59 (1 July 1643); Williams 1908, p. 38ff., and Frank 1961, p. 25.

26 Seymour 1983.

cost perhaps half as much to produce[27] – and for a periodical lucky enough to continue unchecked by government control, the profits might flow for years. Many of the publishers who entered the market in the early 1640s were men of small fortune and little luck, hungry enough to enter a risky market in pursuit of success.

The newsbooks remained unlicensed and virtually uncontrolled for over a year. The number of titles fell back to eleven in February 1642 and eight in March, at which point a Parliamentary effort to suppress them[28] was temporarily successful. At the end of the year nine newsbooks were in print, although all of the January pioneers had failed. Some order was achieved in London in June 1643 when Parliament and the Stationers' Company co-operated to institute a limited licensing system:[29] the more successful publishers registered their copies, and marginal publications ceased. The output of the news press grew and stabilized during the years of active warfare. By 1645 the news press included only half the number of titles of 1642 but double the number of issues published.

As it developed, the periodical press was affected by the consequences of its distinctive form, the most important of which was a continuing relationship among author, publisher, printer and reader. The relationship had its liabilities: whereas a pamphleteer could publish and run if his text was controversial, periodical publishers had to make their newsbooks easy for customers to find and identify each week, thus becoming more vulnerable to official control. When Parliament consolidated its power in 1643, it was relatively successful at controlling the periodical press in London; the Royalists depended on their own safe haven in Oxford.

Another consequence of periodical publication was intense deadline pressure due to competition. Whereas the coranto publisher had been able to hold the press if news from Amsterdam was delayed, the domestic newsbook had to appear on time, with enough copies to fill the market, or lose sales to a prompter rival. To save time printers resorted to standing type, double printings and shared presswork.[30] Such expedients increased production but also led to errors, such as forgetting to change the date, number or pagination each week. The haste showed: the newsbooks were homely at best and often ugly.

A third consequence was the need to find a news title that could draw fragmented issues into a whole continuous series. Publishers had to devise

27 Cotton 1971, ch. 1. 28 *CJ*, 2.500–501 (28 March 1642).

29 C. H. Firth and R. S. Rait, *Acts and Ordinances of the Interregnum, 1642–1660* (London, 1911), I, p. 184–7.

30 Nelson and Seccombe 1986, chs. 3–5.

titles that suggested both compelling subject matter and continuity – and that stood out from the field. After *Heads of proceedings* was renamed *Diurnall occurrances*,[31] half-a-dozen competitors appropriated the phrase in some form. Most added assurances that their news was *True*, or *Faithful*, or *Perfect* (i.e. complete), beginning a long and still-current tradition of self-praise. Samuel Pecke devised the best and most enduring title, *A perfect diurnall of the passages in Parliament* (plate 25.2), using it with some revisions from 1642 to 1655 and (probably) again in 1659.[32] Mirror-image periodical titles were adopted by matched pairs of antagonists, thriving on the pace of regular, frequent dialogue. *Mercurius Aulicus* (1643–5), speaking for the royal court in Oxford, was answered by *Mercurius Britanicus* (1643–6), speaking for London and Parliament; in the second Civil War the Royalist *Mercurius Pragmaticus* (1647–9) soon found its *Mercurius Anti-Pragmaticus* (1647–8).[33] Although the desire to attract buyers by emphasizing an exciting story led to experiments such as placing headlines above the title, the results were confusing and sometimes self-defeating. The norm of uniform titles prevailed, with a gradual tendency towards brevity as the familiarity of the genre reduced the need to spell out the contents.

As the 1640s progressed the periodical press stabilized considerably, unstable as many of the individual periodicals still were. Every régime tried to control the news press, but aimed to exploit it rather than eliminate it entirely. Each government had its kept journalists and privileged newsbooks to report favourable news and loyal views. Another stabilizing element was the non-partisan news press that reported news blandly and avoided offence, trying to maximize readership and stay out of trouble. These newsbooks obeyed the licensing rules and were subject to suppression whenever the government wished to give its favoured series a monopoly. In contrast, the clandestine dissenting press, such as the Royalist newsbooks in London from 1647 to 1653, could be surprisingly long-lived if the publishers kept their convictions and their courage.

Not that the industry was so mature as to be entirely rational. Henry Walker was wont to open his *Perfect occurrences* (1644–9)[34] with a word whose initial letter matched the letter in the signature of the gathering – a word which he then translated into Hebrew and then back to English to make a proverb. Readers doubtless learned to skim past such oddities.

31 N&S 181.103. 32 N&S 503–504, 507, 509, 513, 506.
33 N&S 275, 286, 369, 270. 34 N&S 465.

The periodical press had reached a remarkable state of development by 1649, eight years after the first domestic newsbook appeared. Fifty-four different periodicals were published in that year, with a mix of short-running and long-running, bland and controversial, licensed and clandestine series, and a surprising diversity of subject matter. The trade was still highly variable (see figure 25.2). Nine periodicals were published in the first week of January, peaking at twenty-one in the fourth week of May, falling to three in the second week of December, and ending with six in the final week. This rise and fall reflected both the 'news' – the regicide and the consolidation of the Commonwealth – and the new government's ability to restrict the press with a strict licensing system imposed in late September.[35]

It was a contentious year. While Parliament could speak through official declarations and reports in the licensed newsbooks and thus had no need for a purely partisan journal, the Royalists were in the opposite situation. They were powerless to control events, but their newsbooks were passionate and prolific. After Charles's execution they were briefly silenced, but regained their courage in the spring: *Mercurius Philo-Monarchicus*, *Mercurius Elencticus (for King Charles II)*, and *Mercurius Carolinus*, the last announcing that it was printed 'for the Company of State Traitors at Westminster'.[36] Another dissenting voice was the mistitled *Moderate*,[37] which published radical views from June 1648 to September 1649. By the end of the year only the Royalist *Mercurius Pragmaticus* was still in opposition.[38] The leading newsbook remained Pecke's diurnal, suitably refocused: *A perfect diurnall of some passages and proceedings of... the armies*.[39]

A significant aspect of the periodical press of 1649 was the appearance of several series that published specialized information. *A perfect narrative of... the tryal of the King* was the first criminal/legal periodical in England, and its three issues in one week indicated that the press could keep pace with rapidly developing events. Another innovation was represented by the *Irish monthly mercury* (December 1649 – February 1650), interesting for its subject, its monthly schedule, and its non-London origins, being supposedly reprinted in London from an unidentified original in Cork. Perhaps the most significant step toward specialization is exemplified by a single copy of a single issue of the *Pris courrant des marchandises a Londres*, published in November and designed to serve international commerce – the first surviving British specimen of the

35 Firth and Rait, *Acts and Ordinances*, II, p. 246, cited in Siebert 1952, pp. 222–3.
36 N&S 355, 315, 294.
37 N&S 413. Usually attributed to Gilbert Mabbott, but see Cotton 1978, p. 830 and note.
38 N&S 370. 39 N&S 503.

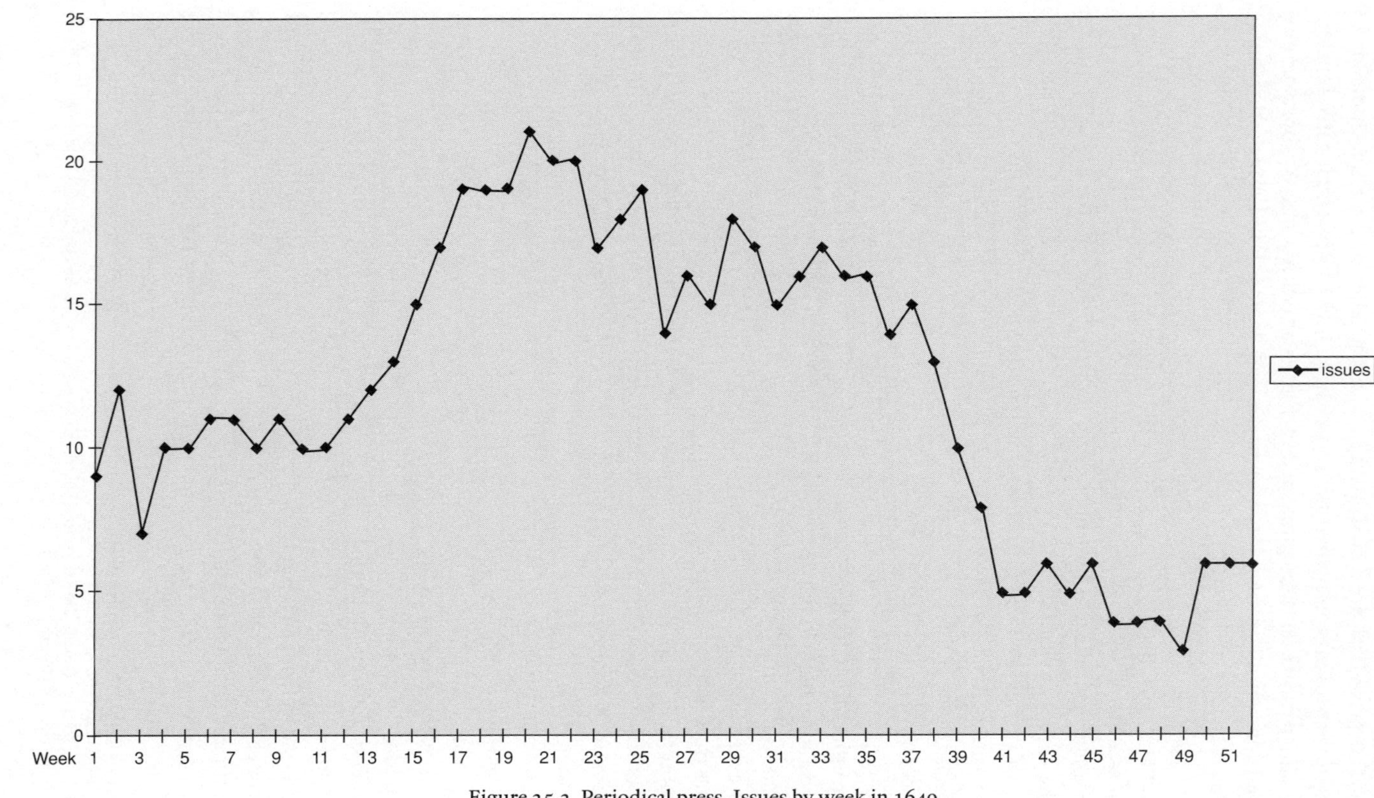

Figure 25.2 Periodical press. Issues by week in 1649

'practical press'. Not every periodical was serious. John Crouch offered humour of a sort in *Man in the moon*.[40] For the rest of the century political journalism would rise and fall, but the diversified press of business, specialized interests and entertainment would develop steadily.

The events of the next three decades extended these trends with only a few changes. In Leith, *Mercurius Scoticus* (1651–2) appeared under the watchful eye of the Parliamentary army – the first Scottish periodical other than reprints of English news. The tight control that could still be achieved by a strong government was dramatically shown by Cromwell's régime. After a gradual rise from an average of eight periodicals per month to fourteen in 1654, the government suppressed all private competition in 1655,[41] leaving only two official series, *Mercurius Politicus* (1650–60) and the *Publick intelligencer* (1655–60). From October 1655 to April 1659 no more than six periodicals appeared in any month, and often only three; not one ventured any criticism of the Lord Protector. The most notable experiment was a new kind of commercial journal. In 1657 Marchamont Nedham, a journalist who had already learned to sell himself to the highest bidder, produced the first advertising bulletin, *The publick adviser*.[42]

The collapse of the protectorate renewed the dynamics of political conflict and freer publication followed by political reconstruction and re-imposed constraints. After Richard Cromwell tumbled down in 1659 reporters and commentators sprang up, doubling the output of the periodical press. A hopeful *Royal dove* appeared in July, and the trade peaked with twenty-one titles in March 1660. The new series included William Bladen's *Account of the chief occurrences of Ireland*, the first confirmed Irish periodical. The protectorate's newsbooks quietly expired in April. Another pair of newsbooks, edited and published jointly, had begun in January 1660. *Mercurius Publicus* and *Parliamentary intelligencer*, tactfully retitled *Kingdomes intelligencer* in 1661, became the favoured newsbooks of the incoming government.[43]

The restored monarchy was quick to restore order. An attempt to report Parliamentary proceedings, *Votes of both Houses*, appeared once in June 1660[44] and was immediately silenced. The periodical press was down to six titles by the end of the year, and down it stayed: often only two or three titles each month (official news and the bills of mortality) and never more than seven titles a month from 1661 to 1678. The governing assumption had not changed. The Crown's spokesman, Sir Roger L'Estrange, warned that public information 'makes the multitude too familiar with the actions, and counsels of their superiors . . . and

40 N&S 248. 41 N&S 386; BL, E.1064(58), cited in Siebert 1952, pp. 230–1.
42 N&S 361, 575, 573, 5. 43 N&S 589, 378, 486. 44 N&S 646.

gives them, not only an itch but a colourable right, and license, to be meddling with the government'.[45]

The news press was as docile as L'Estrange could wish. In 1663 *Mercurius Publicus* and *Kingdomes intelligencer* gave way to a new team, *The intelligencer* and *The newes* under L'Estrange's direct control. Other elements of the periodical press were more adventurous. Given the character of the court, the occasional humour journals were to be expected, but a further step was the publication of mild pornography. Usually it appeared thinly clad as disapproving accounts of public indecency, but the underlying purpose was clearly served. *The wandring whore*, published occasionally from late 1660 to 1663, was an early example. As the decade progressed the 'practical press' expanded, but few copies have survived; business periodicals were usually used and discarded, not saved. *London, imported*, a daily import/export bulletin, now survives in scattered issues from 1660, with complete runs for 1668–9 and 1696–8. *Prices of merchandise* (plate 25.3) began in May 1668, followed by more specialized trade journals. Most significant for the book trade and for literary historians was the publishers' term catalogue, *Mercurius Librarius* (1668–70) and *Catalogue of books* (1670 onwards). Crime proved to be a steady seller. The Old Bailey sessions papers appeared serially first as *Inquest after blood* in 1670.[46]

In March 1665 the most important journal of the seventeenth century began, and it is still published: the *Philosophical transactions* of the Royal Society.[47] Its importance lay not only in the genius of some of its contributors – Newton, Boyle, Leeuwenhoek and others – but also in its form as a periodical. Whereas scientific books and pamphlets were published irregularly and distributed haphazardly, the *Transactions* provided a regular and widely available forum for discussion by a newly connected scientific community in Britain, Europe and even America. In successive monthly issues, discoveries and theories could be announced, tested, challenged and refined (or discarded). The common ground and the rapid dialogue that the periodical provided was crucial to scientific enterprise in the following centuries.

Although the Restoration news press continued the trends of earlier years, the format and frequency in which news was presented changed. The quarto newsbooks before 1642 had been printed on one or two sheets (diminishing briefly to a half-sheet leaflet in the late 1630s). They usually had a full title page, reducing the amount of text in a one-sheet pamphlet to six pages. This was sufficient for the contents of the manuscript diurnals from which the printed diurnals took their copies. But in the 1640s competing publishers found ways

45 N&S 201.1001. 46 N&S 201, 668, 224, 560, 337, 30, 199. 47 N&S 539.

to increase the quantity of the news they offered: smaller type, narrower margins, and a caption title on the first page to expand the text from six to eight pages. They also incorporated features of the earlier English and Continental newsbooks – numbering, continuous pagination, and continuous signing of gatherings – to encourage customers to collect the issues and have them bound in book form. In the later 1640s some long-running series expanded to one and one-half sheets (twelve pages) and to two sheets (sixteen pages). These were often official or semi-official publications, apparently trying to overwhelm private rivals by offering news in quantity. In 1663, however, the official newsbooks contracted from two sheets to one, consistent with L'Estrange's policy that less news was good news.

The *Oxford* (later *London*) *gazette*[48] decisively changed the face of news publication when it began in November 1665. It adopted the format of the 1620s corantos and of the contemporary Continental gazettes: text on both sides of a folio half-sheet in double columns, caption title and colophon. L'Estrange's newsbooks ceased in January 1666, and the *Gazette* became the dominant news outlet as well as the governmental bulletin, the function it still serves today. Its 'newspaper' format set the pattern for nearly every subsequent news publication (except for monthly journals, which were published in quarto) until the early eighteenth century. The type size was considerably smaller than that of L'Estrange's newsbooks, and the design allowed the printer to fit about two-thirds as much text into an issue as he could into a full quarto sheet. The result was symmetrical and neat; Pepys called it 'very pretty'.[49] But the *Gazette* provided its readers only a third of the news of *Mercurius Politicus* a decade earlier.

The other innovation of the *Gazette* was its twice-weekly schedule, which at first glance might seem to compensate for its limited size. In fact, however, forerunners of the twice-weekly paper date back to 1642, when Pecke published his *Perfect diurnall* on Monday and his *Continuation of certaine speciall and remarkable passages*[50] on Thursday or Friday. From 1655 to 1660 *Mercurius Politicus*, published on Thursdays, was paired with the *Parliamentary intelligencer*, published on Mondays. L'Estrange's two newsbooks were numbered, paged and signed in a single sequence. Thus the *Gazette*'s only innovation was simply to appear twice a week under the same name, giving the appearance of a more rapid flow of news.

From the mid-1660s to the late 1670s the periodical press reflected the Restoration's interests and its restrictions. In a typical month there were a handful of regular titles – the *London gazette* and its French translation *Gazette*

48 N&S 471. 49 Pepys 1970–83, VI, p. 305. 50 N&S 638.

de Londres[51] for authorized news, London's bill of mortality, and *Philosophical transactions* – plus, less reliably, a term catalogue for books, *London, imported* for commerce, and a price-current. Another category became a regular in the mid-1670s. The poet-plagiarist William Winstanley and his imitators produced *Poor Robin's intelligence*, candidly announced as being printed 'for the profit of the seller, and the pleasure of the buyer', leading to various offspring such as *Poor Gillian*. One of the century's most famous texts appeared first as a periodical in 1678: Joseph Moxon's *Mechanick exercises, or the doctrine of handy-works*, describing a variety of trades: printing, carpentry, turning.[52] Moxon soon had to suspend his publication, however, because an unexpected event 'took off the minds of my few customers from buying'.[53]

That event was the Popish Plot. The 'plot' combined all the elements required to disrupt the order of the Restoration press: serious and sensational news (real or spurious), intense public demand for news and commentary, conflict within the State, and erosion of the government's power to control the press.[54] Beginning in December 1678 Henry Care's weekly *Pacquet of advice from Rome* divulged the supposed secrets of Catholic conspiracy.[55] In mid-1679, with the crown clearly on the defensive, the *London gazette* lost its monopoly on the news. The emerging independent news press re-enacted the newsbook wars of the 1640s, with intense competition and heated arguments among antagonistic papers. Realizing that total government suppression was unlikely, given the strength of the political opposition – L'Estrange himself was targeted by the snidely titled *Snotty-Nose gazette*[56] – the Tories moved to present their side of the argument.

Some elements of the paper war were familiar from earlier conflicts, such as the jostling for profitable titles. Whig papers assured readers that they published *Protestant* news, Tory papers that they were *Loyal*. The suspicion of conspiracy was exploited by the *Weekly discoverer of the mystery of iniquity*, among others. One serial simply listed the output of the partisan press: *A compleat catalogue of... the Popish Plot*. A major change occurred in October 1680: the House of Commons, formerly jealous of the privacy of its proceedings, was now eager to publish them. The *votes of the House of Commons*,[57] licensed by the Speaker, included not only daily proceedings but also reports on the plot, charges against officials, and addresses to the King.

After Charles II defied and dismissed Parliament in 1681, L'Estrange championed the counter-offensive with his *Observator* (plate 25.4), seconded by the

51 N&S 165. 52 N&S 548, 547, 252A. 53 Moxon 1962, p. 13. 54 See Crist 1979, pp. 49–77. 55 N&S 477. 56 N&S 603. 57 N&S 681, 51A, 647.

strident Tory humour of *Heraclitus ridens*. As the tide turned the number of *Loyal* mercuries swelled and conspiracy-mongering changed sides, as in the 'the *Conventicle-courant*'.[58] When Charles triumphed and the opposition retreated, the Crown tightened its grip and the controversialists (even some Tory publishers) were forced to take cover. Care's anti-Catholic *Pacquet* ceased in mid-1683. From the cacophony of twenty-three titles in March 1681, the periodical press decreased to four familiar titles in August 1684: the bill of mortality, the *London gazette*, *Philosophical transactions*, and the *Observator*. One thing had changed: Roger L'Estrange no longer tried to keep news and commentary from the public, but simply chose to dictate them.

After the alarm of the Exclusion Crisis, the government took no chances. The accession of James II and the suppression of the Argyle and Monmouth rebellions received no notice in any periodical other than the official papers. No private newspaper, no matter how loyal, was allowed to continue for long: the *News-letter*, begun in Dublin shortly after Monmouth's defeat, lasted only a few months despite its pro-James stance.[59] The political journalists and their publishers had been silenced.

The practical press, however, continued to develop. The price bulletins, although individually short-lived, appeared as before, as did the book catalogues. The intermittent Old Bailey sessions papers became a regular periodical in 1683; the *Account of the proceedings . . . in the Old-Bayly* and its successors remained in print until the early twentieth century. It was paired the following year with the Ordinary of Newgate's *True account of the prisoners executed at Tyburn*, later known as the Newgate Calendar. *Philosophical transactions* was joined by *Medicina curiosa* in 1684 and *Observations on the weekly Bill* [of mortality] in 1686. The *Universal historical bibliotheque* (1687), a monthly book digest, reflected French cultural and literary influences in its contents as well as its title; a similar Scottish journal, *Bibliotheca universalis*, appeared in Edinburgh in 1688.[60]

The political silence of the periodical press was not broken until mid-1688.[61] In contrast to 1642, 1649, 1660, and 1678, the journalists of the Glorious Revolution followed the action at a safe distance. This failure to take the lead was partly due to the speed with which James was dispatched, but it also reflected the timidity created by the repression of the mid-1680s. The first two papers to appear, *Public occurrences truely stated* and the *Test-paper*,[62] supported James. In October James banned all privately published newspapers and

58 N&S 458, 183, 76. 59 N&S 117; *CSPD (James II)*, I, p. 281, cited in Pollard 1989, p. 252.
60 N&S 9, 613, 253, 456, 643, 25. 61 See Walker 1974, pp. 691–8. 62 N&S 577, 610.

pamphlets,[63] but after he fled London in early December a flood of newspapers and journals rushed to welcome William and Mary, including the tactfully named *Orange gazette*. A few journals published pointed commentary, such as *Observator, Tory, Trimmer, Whig, Nobs, Mob*,[64] but that appeared only once and few others tried. The boundaries of reporting were still circumscribed: in January 1689 the House of Commons refused to authorize the printing of its *Votes*, and an attempt to report the proceedings of the court and the Lords disappeared after four issues in January and February. In February the new sovereigns appointed a 'messenger of the press' to enforce the Licensing Act.[65]

If the principles of the new régime were ordered liberty and stability, the periodical press benefited from and contributed to their success. The *Gazette* simply shifted from serving James to serving William and Mary, thus emphasizing that the monarch had changed but not the State. The revolution settlement created no new rights for the press. The first attempt to publish a newspaper in America, Benjamin Harris's *Publick occurrences* (Boston, 1690) was suppressed after one issue. Although pamphleteers proceeded to justify or to condemn William and Mary's accession,[66] periodical journalists were more vulnerable to the attentions of the 'messenger' and thus more circumspect. The author of the *New Heraclitus ridens* (May 1689) promised to 'bury [16]41 and 81' and to 'avoid all reflections on persons or whole parties: to name no body, nor so much as *mean* 'em, if 'tis to be avoided'.[67] Where Charles I had provided a martyr and an heir for the Royalist periodicals of 1649–53, James II inspired no similar loyalty in 1689, and no one launched a Jacobite periodical. The outbreak of war ended the question of open dissent for the duration.

Although the pro-government *Mercurius reformatus* lasted into the 1690s,[68] genuine political dialogue would not reappear in the periodical press until the later years of Queen Anne's reign. Yet if debate did not flourish, information did – more of it, on more subjects, at a faster pace. The three broad sectors of the periodical press – general and governmental news, commercial information, and culture (high and low) – gained in numbers and diversity.

The clearest change from the beginning of the century was the regular publication of news of State. The public's right to know, never formally recognized, was partially fulfilled by the new government's need to inform in order to secure its legitimacy and win consent for wartime taxation. The privately

63 Robert Steele, *Bibliotheca Lindesiana (Vol. V), A bibliography of Royal Proclamations of the Tudor and Stuart sovereigns, 1485–1714* (Oxford, 1910), no. 3888.

64 N&S 460. 65 *CSPD (William and Mary)*, 1, p. 3, cited in Rostenberg 1965, p. 365.

66 N&S 576; Downie 1989, pp. 340–6. 67 N&S 441. 68 N&S 379.

published London newspaper *Account of the proceedings of the meeting of the Estates in Scotland* was launched in March 1689, apparently to gratify the public's interest in Parliamentary proceedings without offending the English Parliament. Parliament resumed the official publication of its *Votes* in October 1689; in 1692 the Irish Parliament published the official *Votes* of the Irish House of Commons, and 1693 the Scottish Estates followed with the official *Minuts of the proceedings*.[69]

British readers of the 1690s, like those of the 1620s and 1630s, looked to Holland for their foreign news: two monthly news summaries published in the Hague were translated as the *Present state of Europe* (1690–1738) and *Memoirs of the present state of Europe* (1692–6). The Continental-inspired digests and reviews of 'works of the learned' were complemented by a strictly domestic publication, John Dunton's *Athenian gazette* (1690–7). This question-and-answer miscellany also discussed literary and scientific subjects, but was designed for a different class of reader, intellectually curious but less well-educated than the readers of the *Philosophical transactions*. John Houghton's *Collection for the improvement of husbandry and trade* similarly posited a general reader with a diversity of interests. It provided a miscellany of information about work and commerce: stock and commodity prices, shipping news, and bills of mortality, as well as details about industrial processes and products. The *Gentleman's journal*, a leisure miscellany edited by Peter Motteux, offered verse, music and other light entertainment. Scottish and Irish publishers, still mostly following London models but expanding their periodical trade, reprinted several of these journals.[70]

The lapse of the Licensing Act of 1695 opened the door for the return of privately published newspapers in England. Within a year a trio of *Posts*[71] were published in London and distributed nationally. Compared to the unruly early newsbooks, these newspapers were more stable, long-lived and successful, and less adventurous. The cramped folio half-sheet was still a constraint, inadequate but profitable: the public resisted paying any more than a penny for a full sheet of news but was used to paying a penny for a half-sheet *Gazette* or *Post*. The growing use of supplemental issues for urgent news reflected the need and demand for more extensive coverage. That need was partly served by the new schedule of three issues per week rather than two. The point was made in the title of the *Flying post* – the news travelled fast. But not boldly: the newspapers were conventionally patriotic and carefully non-partisan. Publishers knew that they had gained the freedom to print, but not to print too freely.

69 N&S 7, 650ff., 664–5, 408.
70 N&S 557, 256, 21, 49, 170, 559, 649, 380, 558.
71 N&S 156, 554, 555.

If the periodical press of 1695 displayed more discretion than valour, it had produced the essential elements that eighteenth-century publishers and journalists would wield more courageously. The business of news, information and entertainment was firmly established. Between 1620 and 1695 nearly 700 periodical series, comprising more than 24,000 issues, were published in Britain. This steady expansion of the periodical press encouraged the general expectation of free publication that gradually became, by usage if not by law, one of England's liberties.

THE BUSINESS OF PRINT
AND
THE SPACE OF READING

26

Printing and publishing 1557–1700: constraints on the London book trades

D. F. McKENZIE

There is still no satisfactory model of the economics of the London trade which usefully structures the dense and complex relationships between writers, printers, booksellers and readers during the hand-press period. At their simplest, the elements are three: the labour force; the materials, and the skills learnt to develop and use them productively; and the national and international distribution of their products. The manner in which all three were financed, the industry's basic efficiency in selecting works, creating books and selling them, are clearly fundamental.

Yet books are different, not only from one another, but from most other manufactures. For they are, ineluctably, social products whose true value can rarely be stated only in monetary terms. They derive from an unparalleled diversity of human motives and competences, bounded only by what the mind can conceive; they deploy (despite the relatively uniform technologies of paper, type, presswork and binding) a diversity of expressive forms; and they address an exceptionally and reciprocally diversified market for which price is only a crude measure of value. The economics of choice and the applications of use, even in terms of the numbers printed and successive editions, leave us far short of that realm of intangible benefits, whether to author or reader, which any sophisticated economic model must encompass.

To say that a public community of writers could evolve only where technology could give it a voice beyond the pulpit, theatre, classroom or political assembly would imply a far too determinative role for printing. Like water, the human need to communicate finds its own level and the readiest paths down which to flow. It is salutary to bear in mind how persistent and complementary most known forms of communication still are, whether gestural, oral, graphic, written or printed. Their more recent kinetic and digitized extensions are only that: developments of a comprehensive communications industry whose prime features, for all their ostensible differences, are continuity and complementarity. That recognition helps to explain how readily members of a labour force skilled in one medium may adapt to the demands of another, either by joining it or by intersecting with it.

In London by the middle of the sixteenth century, the structure of labour in the book trades already had a long history. There is good evidence that in one form or another a mystery of stationers responsible for the commercial production of manuscripts had been formally constituted as a brotherhood by 1403.[1] It was a trade which, despite the introduction of printing, would continue to meet a vital need for manuscripts, and to do so even on a scale which justified professional scribes, and scriptoria to produce them, until at least the end of the seventeenth century.[2]

When on 4 May 1557 the Stationers became a royally incorporated fellowship, they grew from a common root. By then however their leaders had had almost a century's experience of new forms of book production and their economies of scale, and while continuing their trade in the dissemination and sale of manuscripts, they had also evolved marketing structures better adapted to handle the range and number of printed books.

The new recognition of their status and their role in controlling the trade was notable therefore mainly for the increased power it gave them to continue and refine what they and their predecessors had already begun: to control intake into the trade and the conditions of work within it, and preserve those forms of prohibitive practice which, as with any guild, sought to exclude uncontrolled competition. Their revised ordinances simply enhanced their authority to combat any subversion of the economic privileges of membership, expressed most directly in the ownership of copyrights and the limitation of the trade's productive capacity, by regulating the numbers of master printers, their presses, and their apprentices, and by a power of arrest. Resistance to patents and monopolies held outside the Company in prejudice to its interests gained force from the corporate sense of a common cause. But for present purposes the act of incorporation is also notable for the new records then begun, in particular the registration of apprentices bound and freed.[3]

It is worth stressing that the labour records of the printing and bookselling trades from the mid-sixteenth to the end of the eighteenth century probably represent the fullest account by far of any workforce in early modern England. They are not complete, but in the evidence they offer year by year of numbers, names, probable ages, origins, family connections and the social status of some

1 'Petition of the Craft of Writers of Text-Letter to the Mayor of London', 12 July 1403 (4 Hen. IV), Arber, I, pp. xxiii–xxiv. See also Blagden 1960.

2 See chapter 31 below; Love 1993. 3 McKenzie 1961 and 1974b.

17,000 individuals, they are certainly unparalleled.[4] The detail they yield of an initial relationship of identifiable individuals with a master and with fellow apprentices, and then, by virtue of their masters' trades, of their own likely skills in printing or bookselling, sets them in a complex social and industrial context. It was one from which many a future trading connection could take its start, whether in printing partnerships, the shared owning of copyrights, or the maintenance of efficient distribution networks between London, the provinces, Continental Europe, and North America.

The records of freemen are not only significant for their information about particular workmen. They provide direct evidence too of the relatively small proportion of men formally qualified to exercise their trade as journeymen, as freemen of the city, as copyright-owning booksellers, and as masters of new apprentices. With one or two exceptions where the records survive for individual printing houses, most remarkably for 1668,[5] those apprentices who never took up their freedom, whether from sickness and death, movement back to the provinces, travel abroad, change of vocation, or mere indifference, remain an imponderable element in any calculation of the total numbers actually at work in the London book trades at any one time, or indeed in any one firm. They represent over 50 per cent of those bound, and although most of them probably continued in the book trades, where and when they did so, for whom, and in exactly what numbers, are questions we can rarely answer.

Faced with such a deficiency, the economics of production can rarely be exact and will shift, either to broader characteristics of the trade which address other questions of value, or to specific instances of books for which the actual costs of acquiring the copy, of paper, of composition, proof correction, presswork and overheads, the wholesale and retail prices, edition quantities, sales and any contribution by author or patron, happen to be known. Such instances are very few, and since production was almost invariably concurrent (for the making and selling of books is always interdependent with the manufacture and sale of several others for which no such evidence exists), no economic model can claim much analytical subtlety.[6]

Yet the book trades have another singular advantage over other forms of manufacture whose economic history we might seek to understand: not only do their products survive in remarkable profusion but each one bears within it clear evidence of its making in its distinctive verbal content and in its materials. Conceptually, its generation of or reciprocity with other books implies

4 See Appendix 3: Apprentices bound in the Stationers' Company and what became of them, 1557–1700.

5 McKenzie 1974b. 6 McKenzie 1966, esp. 'Organization and production', I, pp. 94–146.

a demand for the content which justifies the investment. The risk lies in uncertainty about the extent of that demand, and the uncertainty affects in turn the material form of the book and the number printed. Except in the simple form of stab-stitched pamphlets, the one transferable cost in this period is that of binding, for binding was still a bespoke trade. For the rest, uncertainty translates into specific acts of market definition in which language, speed of production, format, paper quality, size of type (and by implication the number of sheets), decoration, illustration, preliminary matter, and pricing, all have significant but largely unquantifiable economic implications.

Evidence of marketing decisions proliferates of course within and beyond each book, first in the distinctions of edition, issue and state, next in the kinds of paper used, and most ubiquitously in the size, variety and quality of its types. But while all those features are useful indicators of value and even of meaning, in the absence of hard evidence of detailed costs for a wide range of books over a long period of time, it is virtually impossible to construct a model which can reliably incorporate all the elements that an author, printer and bookseller might have to juggle day by day in balancing expectation and risk. To complicate matters further, the language chosen (while Latin was still an option), and the economics of paper and type, like many forms of illustration, may only begin to make sense if considered in an international context, whether in terms of the reliance implied upon imported skills or for marketing abroad.

Clearly, up to a certain level, the unit cost for composition declined as the number of copies increased, and occasionally that may have influenced a bookseller into printing a larger number than the market would bear, at least within a reasonable time for the recouping of costs.[7] Hence the incidence of re-issue, and the value of its bibliographical evidence. But costs for paper and presswork being directly proportional to the size of the edition, and paper being the most expensive element and once printed not re-usable, it made better sense to test the market with small editions and then to print a work again if demand warranted it. This practice dictates caution in drawing inferences about total demand from the number of known editions. It may also help to explain, as we shall see, the trade's extensive reliance on reprints and the relatively small number of original works as a proportion of total output.

But the more crippling deficiencies in our knowledge, despite the richness of the evidence we do have, are currently three: the proportion of total production represented by the books that happen to have survived; the number printed of each edition; the number of edition-sheets any one work entailed.

7 Gaskell 1979, pp. 160–3.

To take first the number of extant works, or rather editions and issues of those works, produced in London between the years 1475 and 1700 as listed in the *Short-title catalogue* and in Wing, these total 106,829.[8] For present purposes, since I wish to focus only on the period 1556–1700, I omit those for 1475–1555. The figures for the eighty-four years 1556–1640 are 26,736, and those for the remaining period of sixty years 1641–1700 are 75,285. These relate only to books produced in London and omit the large volume of serials – over 700 titles in innumerable issues and unknown quantities, for the period 1641–1700 alone.[9]

There must I think be an *a priori* assumption that the rate of loss is greater the further back we go, and that the difference in figures across the years from, say, 148 for 1556 to 676 for 1640 simply cannot be read as a difference in output. That common-sense assumption seems all the more plausible if we extend the period to 1700, for which year the number of titles and editions of them is 1,950.

Two controls in assessing loss are the number of printers known to have been active in any year, their probable productive capacity as measured by the number of presses they had, and the intake of new labour by apprenticeship. What can be stated very briefly here is that the productive capacity of the London trade, at least in the records we have for the number of printers and presses, remained fairly stable from 1583, when there were twenty-three printing houses equipped with fifty-three presses, until 1668, when there were thirty-three printing houses with perhaps seventy-two presses.[10] Yet the number of extant books for 1583 is 240 and the number for 1668, notwithstanding the effects of the fire, is 634.[11] The number of presses, that is, went up by just over a half, but that of titles by two and a half times – an increase, not I suggest in rates of production, but of survival.

Making the other test, the rate of increase in the labour force, is less straightforward as the figures have not yet been calculated to distinguish between those bound to printers and those bound to booksellers. My impression is that the number bound to printers each year remained stable, for it was at least nominally controlled, and that the small increase in bindings is more likely to represent a slight expansion of the bookselling trade, perhaps reflecting, after 1640, its greater diversity and the increased number of titles printed. Even so, and taking only the total figures, the contrast is striking: the number bound in the decade 1601–10 was 556; the number bound in 1691–1700 was 605 – an

8 See Appendix 1, table 1. 9 See Appendix 1, table 2; and Nelson and Seccombe 1987.

10 Arber, I, p. 248, (for a 1586 list see Arber, V, p. lii, Lambert 1987, p. 3); Treadwell 1987, pp. 148, 151.

11 Bell and Barnard 1992, 1998.

increase of only 8 per cent.[12] For the first decade of the century the books we can account for number 3,294, whereas for the final decade the figure is 13,644 – an increase of 314 per cent.[13] It follows that any analysis of the output of the London trade at the end of the sixteenth century must be even more unreliable than it might be for the later years of the seventeenth.

Yet even those figures are misleading, and for three reasons. One relates to output as measured by titles and editions of those titles. Here at least we have some measure of intellectual production, the contribution made by the trade (though not by the still highly productive manuscript trade) to the dissemination of information and ideas. The loss, though substantial, is not directly proportional to the loss of editions, since a title known to have been printed many times over might still survive in a single copy. Yet the proportion of titles lost to the number that might have been printed is of course unknowable.

The evidence of compositors' output is roughly comparable, since only one surviving copy of a work produced in multiple editions is needed to attest the length and density of a text, calculated in ens, and qualified by the sizes and styles of type. The record of their work may also establish the range and state of a printer's type and ornament stock, and the likely scale of his investment in them as an element in overheads. It may enable us to identify a printer by his type or ornaments, thereby adding to our knowledge of his output, or indeed, with proof of piracy from the same evidence, subtracting from it. Such typographical traces may also yield evidence of shared production, with consequences for the calculation of the productivity of the two or more printers involved. The absolute loss of a title, however, denies us of all evidence of its composition and production. As yet another incalculable element in any analysis, it may reduce us to a point of inutility in seeking to establish the output of any particular printing house let alone of the trade as a whole.

Any argument from an unquantifiable assumption about absolute loss is of course impossible to prove. Yet as a significant element in any economic analysis it simply cannot be dismissed. Iceberg tips they may be, whose total dimensions we cannot measure, but there are odd references to books which have not survived, and there are some authors' lists of books they published which are unknown to Wing. John Pennyman, for example, compiled such a list, numbering the items from 1 to 67, but Wing has only twenty-eight entries for Pennyman.[14] Francis Bugg surveyed his writings for the years 1682

12 See Appendix 2. 13 See Appendix 1.

14 John Pennyman lists his work in a note of 'Some of the Papr:s & Bookes . . . I have been concern'd in Printing & Publishing from the Year 1670 to 1680' on a flyleaf to the Pennyman Tracts in the British Library (874. k. 26.1–17); see Wing P1401 A–P1427.

to 1714, giving thirty-five titles for the years to 1700, nine of which are not in Wing.[15] He lists another fifty for the years 1701–15, of which the ESTC knows only forty.[16] The Verney Pamphlets acquired by Cambridge University Library some years ago, number some 1,300 pamphlets all dated between 1660 and 1695, included some 200 not then in Wing.[17] Title-page edition statements are notoriously unreliable, but their evidence cannot be wholly ignored. Michael Sparke's *Crums of comfort* survives in only seven of the twenty editions published up to 1635; as Wing lists only six later editions to 1698, including a forty-second edition in 1656, that suggests that at least another sixteen have disappeared without trace.[18] At the other end of the century, an advertisement in 1697 for John Rawlet's *The Christian monitor* claimed that 95,000 copies had already been sold; yet only thirteen of the twenty-five editions published up to 1699 are recorded in Wing.[19]

Even the number of surviving titles, however, itself only a part of the whole, tells us very little about the volume of their production. For volume is measured rather by the length of a text and the total number of sheets printed, whether for any one copy of a book, as given by its collation, or for the quantity produced in one or more editions. The measure is essentially one of edition sheets. Though the work has still to be done methodically and comprehensively, it is possible to establish the number of formes set and prepared for printing across the trade as a whole, and where the work is acknowledged or identifiable, within a particular printing house. What can rarely be known is the quantity of sheets printed from those formes, and yet, as a measure of turnover, and the amount and price of paper and the cost of presswork, this is crucial information whose absence or imprecision is again deeply prejudicial to any economic analysis.

One can of course extrapolate from figures that happen to be known for some classes of book, but the fact is that, even where known, edition quantities varied so dramatically according to genre that no figure can be reliably taken as an average. A book printed for the author might run to 100 copies, probably the minimum for which it was worth going to a printer as distinct from a scribe. At the other end of the spectrum, for example in accounts of books produced by the English Stock of the Stationers' Company, the sums are dramatically different. Cyprian Blagden's analysis of the production of some thirty-six different almanacs in the 1660s, reporting as it does a total of almost 409,000

15 Francis Bugg lists his work in *The picture of Quakerism once more drawn to the life* (London, printed for the author; and sold by R. Wilkin, and Hen. Clements, 1714), pp. 164–71; Wing B5365 A–B5399 A.

16 Based on a search of the on-line ESTC in RLIN 11 September 1999.

17 Bound in thirteen volumes, CUL, Sel. 2.

18 *STC* 23015.7–23017.5; Wing S4815A–S4817 C.

19 Wing R347–R351.

copies printed in each of the five years 1664 to 1668, is a telling example.[20] The Treasurer's account of almanacs, catechisms, psalters, psalms, primers, ABCs, hornbooks, and school books ordered for the Stationers' Stock in 1676–7 tells a similar story,[21] as do the number of psalms, psalters, primers, and ABCs printed in each decade from 1663/4 to 1705/6. Some were farmed out, but of the rest an average of at least 130,000 copies were printed each year.[22] What these figures demonstrate is the extremely high loss rate of whole editions of these classes of books, especially in the smaller formats. Another reliable example of low survival rates is Thomas Dyche's *Guide to the English tongue*, printed by Charles Ackers in thirty-three editions and some 275,000 copies between 1733 and 1749.[23] Only five copies from those editions are known to be extant: a survival rate of one in 55,000.

Such reflections carry serious implications for the manner in which we interpret such phenomena as the sudden increase in the number of surviving texts for the years 1641–2, leaping as the figures do from 676 in 1640 to 3,219 in 1642. Metaphors of the trade exploding or bursting, or of books flooding or mushrooming, which lift the prose of so many historians of the period, do little to clarify its altered conditions or the exact nature of the evidence from which we infer their change. In an attempt at precision, Christopher Hill for example writes that George Thomason 'purchased twenty-two titles in 1640; in 1642, 1,966. This rate of publication was maintained for the next decade.'[24] This wording cannot of course mean that a *rate of increase* from twenty-two in 1640 to 1,966 in 1642 was maintained for the next decade: that would give an output ten years later of three and a half billion titles. But even accepting the intended meaning – that publication continued for the next decade at the high level set in 1642 – it would still be untrue. Though the number of titles extant for 1642 is actually 3,219, higher than Hill thought, it drops to half that for the next year; even lower for 1644; it remains under 1,000 for 1645; and only once again before 1685 (in 1660 when the king returned) does it even touch 2,000.

Yet the impression that the trade was unusually productive in 1642 has time and again justified an undue emphasis on censorship as a constraint on printing before the abolition of the Court of Star Chamber in July 1641, and an equally misplaced celebration of the trade's new-found but short-lived freedom from licensing after that event. One might, for example, quote Keith Thomas's fiction: 'In the 1640s, with the Civil War, all controls seemed to have lapsed altogether and the result was an extraordinary output of heterodox ideas of a kind which

20 Blagden 1958b. 21 Barnard 1994. 22 See Barnard 1999a, table 1; see also Barnard 1999b.
23 McKenzie and Ross 1968. 24 Hill 1985, I, p. 40.

would not have been allowed before or afterwards. But normally the system of state licensing, which lasted until the end of the seventeenth century, had a deeply inhibiting effect upon printed publication.'[25]

Other factors are also at play in those figures. One is of course the presence in the picture of Thomason himself, for it was his very activity of collecting ephemera, unusually so and at precisely this time, that led to their preservation in such numbers. But Thomason, even on Hill's figures, managed to collect only some 61 per cent of the titles datable to 1642. The distinct character and length of the Thomason tracts must also be carefully considered. Most are short and highly topical pamphlets which, while adding up to an impressive number of titles, did not necessarily increase the actual volume of production. By definition each pamphlet contained fewer sheets – half those published were probably only single sheets – and being as they were ephemeral, their day's life probably demanded only a small edition. In any event, what they supplied to printers was evidently far from adequate to meet complaints in 1644 about the deficiency of work caused by the restrictive practices of patentees and the importation of foreign-printed books. Such a proliferation of titles is undoubtedly important for our understanding of a significant change in the nature of public discourse, but it tells us little about the economics of the book trade in terms of its volume, or of the costs and returns to authors, printers, and booksellers as the other principal elements of an economic model.

As it happens we have a document of 1668 that makes it possible to look more closely at the operations of the printing trade and, by associating it with the extant books printed and published that year, to tease out some of its economic implications. Roger L'Estrange's survey of the London printing houses on 29 July 1668 gives us the only firm information we have about the productive capacity of the London printing trade at any point in the seventeenth century.[26] At the latest count, there are 634 products from thirty-three printing houses. Not only is the actual number of books printed uncertain – because many have not survived – but two assumptions must be made about dates and edition sizes. So, work begun in 1667 but dated 1668 is assumed to be comparable to work done in 1668 but dated 1669. And whereas the amount of typesetting and the number of formes is self-evident for surviving titles, we have to work with a quite arbitrary assumption about edition sizes. From other evidence it would

25 Thomas 1986, p. 120. For the contrary view, see Hamburger 1984–5, McKenzie 1988, and above, pp. 2–3.

26 'A Survey of the Printing Presses wth the Names & Nombers of Apprentices Officers and Workmen belonging to every perticular Presse Taken 29° Julij 1668', PRO, State Papers 29/243 (126); for an annotated transcript see appendix 2.

be just as plausible to use a figure of 500 or even 1,500, but simplicity dictates 1,000. In fact very few books are likely ever to have been printed in so many copies, but as there were vast runs of some others which provided stock work for printers, it may bring us closer to a figure for the total number of sheets printed by any one printer or by the trade as a whole. It is most important to remember, however, that it tells us absolutely nothing about the likely edition sizes of a particular book, for any of which the costs and returns might break even or shift into profit for the printer or bookseller (if not for the author) on an edition of anything from 100 to 750 copies.

On those assumptions we can do some elementary sums, although my base figure cannot be that of 634 which we now have from revised Wing but my original ones of 491 derived some time ago from unrevised Wing and the 458 of those for which, having seen them, I could establish the number of sheets in each. Despite that margin of error, certain general comments about the nature and trade contexts of text production can be offered. The first is the high incidence of anonymous proclamations, almanacs, bills of mortality, and other ephemera. Second, is the incidence of anonymous printing, which is over 54 per cent of the total: 268 items extant for the year bear no indication of the printer's name. Third, our records of type and decorative materials, their origins and the extent of their duplication, do not permit us to attribute much anonymous work to particular houses.

If we take six printing houses of medium size from the twenty-six listed by L'Estrange, calculate the amount of typesetting per book in ens set at 1,000 an hour, multiply the number of sheets in each by 1,000, and assume their printing at a maximum rate of 250 impressions an hour, we get some disturbing discrepancies. Sarah Griffiths, for example, the acknowledged printer of five books, would have required one compositor quarter-time and one pressman half-time to complete her work for the year. She was vastly over-equipped with two presses, one apprentice, and six workmen. Anne Maxwell, the acknowledged printer of twelve books, would have required one compositor and one-and-a-half press crews. Indeed she had two presses and three pressmen, which meets the hypothetical need for presswork, but she also had one apprentice (unrecorded by L'Estrange[27]) and three compositors. The paradox is that our figures for composition are more reliably inferred than those for presswork. John Redmaine, the acknowledged printer of twelve books, would have required two compositors and one pressman. He had two presses, two pressmen, one apprentice and four compositors. Robert White, the acknowledged

27 Henry Cruttenden was apprenticed to Anne Maxwell, 7 April 1668 (McKenzie 1974b, no. 2935).

printer of six books, would have needed two compositors and two pressmen, four men in all. He had three presses, three apprentices, and seven journeymen. Ellen Cotes, the acknowledged printer of thirteen books, would have required one compositor and two pressmen. She had three presses, two apprentices, and nine journeymen. Finally, Thomas Ratcliffe, the acknowledged printer of twelve books, would have needed one full-time and one half-time compositor and one-and-a-half press crews, five men in all. He had two presses, two apprentices, and seven journeymen.

But among the most interesting of the shops surveyed in 1668 is that of Mary Simmons (widow of Matthew Simmons, *d.* 1654), who only the year before had printed the first edition of *Paradise lost*. Mary is listed as having two presses, one apprentice, and five workmen apart from Mary herself and her son Samuel. But their acknowledged extant work for that year consists of only four items (one of them a re-issue of *Paradise lost*). The three new jobs contain altogether about 800,000 ens of type, all of which could have been set by two men in about six weeks, working full-time. The total number of sheets involved is only forty-eight and a half. Assuming an edition of 1,000 copies in each case, this gives a figure of 48,500 perfected sheets or 97,000 impressions. At 250 impressions an hour, they would again supply only about six weeks' work for two men working at a single press. Even if these assumptions about work rates were 100 per cent out, there would still be a great disparity between productive capacity and recorded output. What did the two compositors, two pressmen, the apprentice, and the fifth man do for the other forty-six weeks of the year? Part of the answer must be, of course, that Mary and Samuel, like all the other printers in the list, produced a great deal of other printing, certainly jobbing work, which has since disappeared entirely; but they must also have printed (or shared the printing of) a couple of dozen other titles which cannot be counted because the printer's name was omitted from them.

The list, together with the apprenticeship records, also enables us to write a profile of the age and experience of her men. Anthony Wildgoose was the most experienced, having started his apprenticeship in 1629 and been made free in 1636. He would have been about fifty-six years old in 1668. William Hall and John Warner were some ten years younger than Wildgoose: the first was bound in 1638, the second in 1641, and both were made free in 1646. By 1667–8 they must both have been in their mid-forties and thoroughly competent at their work. Of her two other journeymen, John Warner began his apprenticeship in 1653 and took up his freedom in 1661, and Thomas Westry had been bound in 1656 and freed in 1663. With the exception of William Hall, every one of her men had served his time with a master who was a printer, not a bookseller.

Mary's earlier apprentice, Thomas Harvey, probably left her just before she bound his successor John Hervey (no relation) in August 1667, the month in which the printing of *Paradise lost* is most likely to have begun.

Turning to the booksellers active in 1668 we can make some attempt to assess the extent of their share of the trade. The 458 items seen run to 8,127 signature sheets. On this basis the printer Henry Herringman's twenty-six titles account for 6 per cent of production. This would compare with 4.5 per cent for George Sawbridge were it not that Sawbridge also shared in two large enterprises involving a further 616 signature sheets, so that the scale of his operations was not far short of Herringman's.[28]

More surprising is the proportion of work printed for the author. There are twenty-one items, but they account for 1,228 sheets, which is 15 per cent of production. These figures include the books of Margaret Cavendish, Duchess of Newcastle, but exclude all other work not explicitly said to have been printed for the author. Most of those, carrying the bare imprint 'Printed in the Year 1668', would have been at the author's charge, putting their percentage of total production even higher.

In 1644 authorship is acknowledged in only 436 – or 40 per cent – of the 1,113 items I found to be now extant. My figure for 1688 is just over 43 per cent. Since only a very small proportion of the total items published could possibly have been influenced by censorship, what we must have here is simply the perpetuation of a long-established convention of authors taking a low profile in making their thoughts public. So too the anonymity of the printers and publishers has nothing whatever to do with evasion of the censorship. It simply means that the works concerned represent jobbing printing for which the author paid the primary expenses and may or may not have hoped to recoup costs.

Developing this last point, we might then ask about the extent to which innovation and commercial risk lay with authors as distinct from the booksellers. What is remarkable here is the trade's dependence upon reprints. Excluding almanacs, and re-issues, whose selling potential is only marginally different from that of any older stock, there were 117 reprints. All but three account, in signature sheets, for more than 32 per cent of total production.

The effects of the Licensing Acts are only partly reflected in the imprimaturs and entries in the Stationers' Register. Only fifty-two books bear some form of licence; there are only seventy-nine entries for the year in the Register. The

28 Sawbridge shared in Henry Rolle's *Abridgement* (Wing R1872) and Peter Heylyn's *Cosmographie* (H1692A).

more important points are that the licensing of non-controversial books could be safely evaded; and that it *had* to be evaded for controversial ones. But both licensing and registration are also a function of size. Hobbes disputed cuts with the censor because large books involve large investment and it is better to play safe; pamphlets cost less, were more easily dispersed, and their authors and printers were harder to detect. The same principle applies to the registration of copyright. Pamphlets were coming to be regarded as a distinct branch of the trade for which retailing booksellers might not even bother to keep particularized accounts, and their copyright was rarely worth registering. Very few were entered. Since for many of them, commercial gain was an irrelevant motive, there was no cause to safeguard copyright.

Attendant evidence for 1668, found largely in the books themselves, the State Papers (Domestic), the journals for the Lords and Commons, and the records of the Stationers' Company, tells us more of conditions of work and methods of distribution. There are complaints against hawkers, always at odds with the regular trade, for usurping the rights of the retail booksellers;[29] of the importation of 5,000 copies of a Dutch printed book, dispersed through Gospright in London, Burton in Yarmouth, and others in Hull and in Scotland;[30] of the part-publication and monthly delivery of *A tast[sic] of a catechetical-preaching-exercise* to each house as the weekly bills of mortality are left, with prices and delivery charges;[31] of Richard Younge's publication of books also in parts so that 'the Vendor may not want sorts, to serve his two penny customers'.[32]

Those instances of part-publication are evidence of one form of risk-averse publishing earlier than that usually cited. Subscription publishing was another form. It had been tried by Minsheu,[33] but as the means by which a bookseller secured his receipts before he spent them it would not really develop until the 1680s.[34] Another form of risk dispersal surfaces in 1668 however in the joint ownership of copyrights. The harder evidence for this is to be found much later in the activities of the congers and the trade sale-catalogues, but such combinations had a history for which the documentation is fugitive but convincing. Cornelius Bee, for example, had a half-share in John Pearson's *Critici sacri*, the remaining half being borne by five others.[35] William Barton's *Four centuries of*

29 See for example *CSPD*, *1667–8*, p. 360, *1668–9*, p. 141.
30 *CSPD*, *1667–8*, p. 282.
31 J. Batchiler ([London], 1667/8), sig. B1^{r} (Wing B1076 (formerly B1705A)).
32 *Sovereign antidote to drive out discontent: Part II* (London, 1668), p. 30 (Wing Y192).
33 The second edition of John Minsheu's 'Ηγε μωυ εις ταςγλῶσσας, *id est ductor in linguas, the guide into tongues* was published by subscription in 1625 (*STC* 17945).
34 Clapp 1931. 35 Wing P994A.

select hymns was entered without his consent to Thomas Parkhurst and Francis Eglesfield; Barton objected, asking that Francis Tyton and Octavian Pulleyn be substituted.[36] They were added, but only Parkhurst's name is in the imprint. John Place had a fourth share in Wentworth's *Office and duty of executors* but the imprint of the 1668 edition lists only the printers as assigns of Richard and Edward Atkyns.[37] George Meriton's *Touchstone of wills*, although entered only to Thomas Dring and John Place, was printed for ten booksellers, Rolle's *Abridgement* – entered to Abel Roper and Francis Tyton – for thirteen.[38]

These are clearly different from books like the fourth issue of *Paradise lost*, which lists four retail booksellers by whom the book is sold, or William Prynne's *Third tome*, printed for the author and sold by four booksellers, or Peter Heylyn's *Cosmographie*, printed for Anne Seile and sold by five others.[39] The trade combinations of 1668 however attest an already well-established share-book system in regular use by entrepreneurial booksellers.[40] In their pursuit of non-political commercial interest, their resolution of conflict by co-operation, and the restricted commitment to any one book in the spread of investment to several, they are economically stabilizing, politically neutralizing and culturally distancing agents. But the exact ownership of copyrights is rarely transparent. Imprints are little help.

Even though the Licensing Acts were largely ineffective and of little significance to the trade as a whole, many printers and booksellers were harassed, fined and imprisoned for misdemeanours under the Acts, especially when Roger L'Estrange was in business as Surveyor of the Press after 1663.

But trying to get it all into proportion, we might end with an estimate of the trade's total production for, say, the years 1641 to 1700. For London printing we have 75,285 titles or editions of them, excluding serials. Allowing a loss rate for the period of something like 25 per cent, the total output of the trade would have been about 100,000 titles or editions of them over those years.

For precisely that same period, I have recorded every book mentioned in the journals of the Lords and the Commons, the State Papers (Domestic), and the court books of the Stationers' Company. There are some 800 items, of which 400 are entirely innocent and 400 in some degree suspect. Those 400 represent 0.4 per cent of the output of the trade. Of those 400 the number which led to a charge, let alone a conviction, let alone punishment, was only the tiniest

36 Wing B1001; 8 April, 4 November 1668, E & R, II, pp. 384, 392.

37 Wing W1361A; 21 May 1668, E & R, II, p. 386.

38 Wing M1811; 26 February 1668, E & R, II, p. 384. Wing R1872; 13 May 1666, E & R, II, p. 366.

39 Wing M2139; P4104; H1692A.

40 Further discussion may be found in Mandelbrote 1997.

fraction. Sir Keith Thomas notwithstanding, fear of the courts had virtually no impact on the economy of the book trade.

This is not the chapter Don McKenzie would have written. Instead it is substantially the same paper he read at All Souls College, Oxford, 12 March 1999, which he had intended to develop for his chapter in this volume. He died before he could do that. The notes have been added by Christine Ferdinand.

27
The economic context

JAMES RAVEN

Many structural features of the early modern economy governed the working practices of the book trade. Diversity and interconnectedness marked the broader economic structure of publication and bookselling, of capitalization, productive capacity, of supplies of paper and other materials, of demand, of distribution and of trade regulation. The history of publication and its patronage ultimately begins and ends with the resources of the land and its population as a whole and, deriving from this, the wealth of particular individuals. Beyond these basic economic factors, the responses of the different crafts to the changes in economic conditions and to the changing profiles of the market were also affected by the cultural, religious and political cast of the practitioners themselves.

Publishing was driven by two economic incentives during this 140-year period: first, by the obvious possibility of immediate returns on work in hand, and second (and increasingly by the late seventeenth century), by investment opportunity. Crucial in both cases was the source of the capital to set up the business and to sustain it, and added to the early scarcity of venture funds, the difficulties in raising and managing credit heightened the importance of cash flow and steady turn-over. Even where publication can be considered as a form of speculation, the rate of sale of the products remained a primary determinant in the economic development of book and allied trades. Shared operations also became the most obvious form of risk limitation, especially where profitability was threatened by excess productive capacity.[1] The organization of publishing ranged from the bookseller-stationer collaborators in the late sixteenth century (many challenging the earlier dominance of the printers from within the Stationers' Company) through to the publishing congers of the late seventeenth century and beyond. Many stationers, printers and booksellers formed *ad hoc* associations during the sixteenth and seventeenth century. These included the

1 See above Barnard, above, p. 8.

English ballad partners who from at least the 1590s collected together the rights to print ballads. Such organization attempted the economically most efficient and least hazardous publication and distribution of print, and, where possible, to protect investments.[2]

The first main consideration is of continuing difficulties. In all parts of Britain broad resource limitations imposed crippling constraints upon business expansion – and certainly upon technological advances. Across all trades, both the sourcing of capital and the extension of credit remained problematic, and most fixed capital was invested in ways that rarely produced short-term gain.[3] Circulating capital – that is raw materials and goods – comprised whatever long-term business investment there was. By modern standards the overall result allowed a very low productivity rate, with particularly high labour-intensity, and a vast reservoir of under-employed labour. This created very little inducement for cost-reducing innovations in all trades and industries. The book trades were clearly no exception to this, and, in the particular requirement to have so much capital tied up in a particular item of production (an edition, that is) before any part of this could be sold to realize returns, the publishing sector was especially handicapped.[4]

The second main consideration is of changing opportunities. In broad terms the economy of almost all parts of Britain was transformed between 1450 and the mid 1690s. It was certainly not a story of gradual linear improvement, but one with many checks to the various components of factor growth and several clear demographic, agrarian and economic reversals, especially in the early seventeenth century.[5] The book trades contributed to these changes and were major beneficiaries of the increased wealth of the kingdoms. It is very difficult, however, to be precise about many of the constituent changes. Regular English commercial statistics were not compiled until 1696; survival rates for much that was collected are very low, and crucial considerations such as population structure, wage levels and precise price indices, are, despite many methodological advances in recent years, beyond exact historical calculation.[6]

The further general observation is that in terms of broad economic history, this period can be divided into two parts, the century after 1550, and the fifty years after about 1650. This is true of both England and Scotland, with increased (if relatively modest) urbanization north of the border and a marked economic recovery after the mid-century financial and commercial disasters

2 Greg 1956; Oastler 1975; Watt 1990.
3 Grassby 1995.
4 The economics of production are considered above McKenzie, pp. 555–6, 558–9, 562–3.
5 There were, for example, 30,000 deaths in London alone in the plague year of 1603.
6 See Wrigley and Schofield 1981, esp. appendices; Overton 1996; and, for an even broader perspective, de Vries 1984.

of the Cromwellian Union. In England increased consumption from the mid seventeenth century followed from an economic régime largely recovered from earlier price inflation, trade depression and harvest failures. The continuing move towards a money economy and price stability from about the 1650s was further related to a critical fall in the price of foodstuffs as compared to the price of industrial goods.[7]

In the context of these broader changes, the economic history of the book trades might be considered in four main and connected aspects: first, general market development and the changing profile of demand; second, new enterprise in distribution and transport; third, development of financial servicing and the role of intermediaries; and fourth, increasing regulation as part of government public policy and of the attempts to protect literary copyrights.

The structure of the British book trades changed rapidly from about 1550 to 1650. The balance between different traders and craftsmen shifted as wholesale businesses with onward-selling networks expanded in the late sixteenth century and even more markedly during the seventeenth century. The early domination of the stationers resulted from the necessarily heavy importation of paper, and at the beginning of this period the stationers and wholesalers, also importing foreign stock, were much more heavily capitalized and more strategically powerful than any other members of the book trades. By the 1580s, however, the leading London printers advanced a short-lived supremacy before publisher-booksellers consolidated their position, largely by investment in copy rights during the seventeenth century.

The changing market and, still more importantly, its evaluation, is a vital consideration in several respects. The overall economics of publication included capital start-up costs and job-specific costs of paper, the labour involved in all stages of printing, and, very rarely, whatever might have been paid to the author or begetter of the text. To an extent that became obvious by the end of this period, however, these factors alone did not explain the price structure adopted by particular publishers. Pricing, material and design considerations crucially rested upon an assessment of changes in market structures, and pricing in particular resulted from additional decisions made by the financing publisher, who might, of course, sometimes be the author, personally underwriting, for whatever reason, the printing of his or her work.[8]

Modes of sale were one aspect of this evaluation. Many printers were not, of course, selling to the public directly, but to their paying clients, publishers and authors. The imprint acted as much as anything else to inform retailers of

7 Devine 2000, p. 154, and cf. Langton 2000, map 14.1.
8 For author as publisher see above McKenzie, p. 564.

where copies might be had, although evidence relating to the character of the early bookshop and what exactly went on there is scant.[9] It does appear, however, that almost no bookseller was an exclusive retailer of books, pamphlets, stationery and prints, and usually sold other goods besides. Modes of retail and how much credit was allowed and for how long often depended as much upon customers as upon traders. The credit terms offered to customers and to the trade appear normally to have been about six months, although evidence for the early part of this period is too fragmentary to be reliable. Surviving ledgers from the mid and late seventeenth century also suggest the reluctant but often unavoidable acceptance of longer credit.[10] Not until the close of the seventeenth century, however, was there any semblance of the regularized exchange of bills of exchange and promissory notes that so characterized the development of credit and discounting in the next hundred years. This was very much a face-to-face society, in which personal trust underpinned business confidence and procedures. Reputation and good-neighbourliness still oiled the increasingly high gearing of market relations.[11]

Expansion in retailing and allied services such as the auctioning and the over-the-counter borrowing of books derived from the changing commercial potential of the audience and the successful courting of demand. Direct retailing of books and pamphlets was nothing new, but since the earliest commerce in print, off-the-shelf trading had co-existed with a client economy of producers in service to closed patronage. Much of the retailing centred on the sales of smaller productions, notably the thousands of almanacs, pamphlets and chapbooks peddled by chapmen and general traders,[12] but an increasingly active and organized second-hand market is evident by the end of the seventeenth century. In response to the greater public interest, second-hand book auctions, which appear to have been uncommon before about 1650, rapidly increased in size and frequency. Few early auctioneers bought their stock of books; instead, most were selling on behalf of others. Relatively generous credit arrangements also seem to have eased the trade, many auctioneers allowing up to a month to pay and accepting the return of any books found to be imperfect. Given that these books were second-hand, this must have been an easy let-out clause.

Increased custom from the propertied classes was mainly responsible for this remodelling of the book trade. Provincial sales outlets were extended and London booksellers launched new titles of both religious and 'entertaining and

9 For relation of imprint to trade-sign and place, see Blayney 1990.
10 Hodgson and Blagden 1953. 11 Mathias 1979, pp. 88–115; Boulton 1987; Muldrew 1997.
12 See below Barnard and Bell, pp. 666–7.

instructive' literature with no advanced assured custom. For the majority of metropolitan booksellers, the sales of open market publications became the basis for survival. The rise of a consumer society, like the rise of the middle class, has become a cliché of historical analysis, transferable between several centuries, but the effect of new consumerism upon the book trade is certainly evident from the late sixteenth century, and particularly in the decades following the Restoration.

Demographic changes remained the basic underpinning to the new demand for print. The population of England and Wales nearly doubled between 1545 and 1695, from 3 to 5.2 million. But the location of this population was also crucial. London eclipsed all other urban development. The market profile, if essentially rural, was nonetheless divided between the one great city and all other settlements, where custom was scattered. By 1680 only four towns outside London had populations in excess of 10,000, but the number of towns holding markets (however small these were) had increased from about 650 in the late sixteenth century to over 800 in the late seventeenth century.[13] By comparison, only 1.4 per cent of the Scottish population lived in towns of more than 10,000 inhabitants in 1550 (compared to 3.5 per cent in England and Wales). The medieval centres of Edinburgh, Aberdeen, Perth and Dundee maintained their ranking into the seventeenth century, but Scotland remained much more rural than England. Before the beginnings of the rise of Glasgow in the 1670s, there was no important urban area other than Edinburgh, which doubled in size between 1560 and 1640.[14]

Our problem is to assess exactly how much spending power was provided by what was an early modern, virtually subsistence economy for the most part of this period, and how this changed with increased economic activity, and modestly increasing population levels and concentrations. An expanding population is certainly not inevitably good economic news. If agricultural resources do not increase or even respond commensurately, then non-essential spending is squeezed and consumer spending decreases rather than increases. The basic régime left very little disposable income for the spending on inessential goods after the purchase of necessary items of food, shelter and clothing. It certainly left very little to be spent on books and print.

Our modelling of this is very difficult, given the imperfect and incomplete evidence of national income and wealth, output, employment levels, costs,

13 Langton 2000; Dyer 2000, p. 425 and map 13.1.

14 De Vries 1984, p. 39; Whyte 1995, pp. 174–5, Devine 2000, map 4.1, pp. 154–6 and p. 164, Griffiths *et al.* 2000, pp. 197–8.

profits and even population. This particularly frustrates our asking of questions about the relationship between demand and the supply of scarce resources – most notably paper – in which regional and local variation are often key. Other issues are identifiable, but seem only to be added on rather than integrated in a broader model. Thus, for example, in an economy with such high dependence on agriculture and without comfortable reserves in most years, seasonality in demand was marked. Lent was as much economic necessity as a matter of religious observance.

We can, then, attempt to characterize change only from very rough and ready statistics. What we can start by saying is that both the level and the elasticity of demand was extremely limited for most of this period. In this pre-industrialized society, without high mechanization, agriculture dominated the economy. The production of foodstuffs was certainly more important than the production of materials for the textile industries. Most society was rural rather than urban, with the ratio of population to land relatively low. The population, whatever its increase over the period, was also comparatively small. England had about four million inhabitants by the early seventeenth century (and Scotland just over one million), but the Italian states claimed a total population of about twelve million by 1600 and France some twenty million by 1660, although given its greater land size, the population density of France was relatively low.[15] Mortality rates were high, and, as on the Continent, inflated by sudden and recurrent crises of subsistence, when harvests failed, and by devastating epidemic disease. The plague visited with particular virulence throughout the period; not just in the Great Plague of 1665–6 but also in 1563, 1579, 1593, 1603, 1610, and 1625 (and in Scotland most markedly in 1605–6 and 1645–9).[16] In this weak, vulnerable and problematic régime, every harvest proved a pivot to the broader economy. When harvests failed all sectors of the economy suffered, as they did in the wake of the catastrophes of 1555–6, 1586, 1595–7, 1629–30, 1636–7, 1647–9, 1661 and 1693. Thereafter England was never again to suffer from catastrophic famine (except in highly localized parts), but the great Scottish famine of 1695–9 (part of the 'seven ill years' of 1696–1703), was not to be the last in that country.[17]

Although agrarian output did grow at the end of the sixteenth century and began to encourage population growth, the increase in vagabondage in both England and Scotland in the early seventeenth century must also be taken as a sign of failure to provide employment for a growing population. The

15 De Vries 1984; Wrigley 1985. 16 Slack 1985; Griffiths *et al.* 2000.
17 Schofield 1985; Flinn 1977.

resulting change in the age structure introduced further problems. Despite very high infant mortality rates, the abundance of so many young people in their pre-productive years gave a high dependency ratio to the economy.

Another constraint to demand was the long-term market weakness in England caused by the general price inflation from about 1520 (part of a Europe-wide phenomenon, it seems). The Phelps Brown and Hopkins index of general prices based on a basketful of goods selected and weighted, charts particularly rapid rises 1540–60 and again 1570–1600.[18] Thereafter the rise continued but at a slower pace. Nevertheless, by 1650 prices represented nearly 6 times what they had been before 1520, with agrarian goods showing particular increases. This was not a wage-cost inflation (usually where population is declining or where certain labour skills are in deficit); instead, in a rising population, wages lagged behind the foodstuff prices that played such a large part in the cost of living. The inflation was in part caused by the Crown's war-driven debasement of the English coinage from the 1540s, and, more contentiously, by a European inflow of bullion (it has been claimed) in the late sixteenth century.[19] Both debasement and bullion inflow increased the money supply, but these, much more significantly, were combined with population increase and urbanization. Demographic changes accelerated monetary circulation and financial transactions, leading to further inflationary pressure. The immediate consequence was a reduction in real disposable spending per capita and severely reduced market elasticity for luxury items. All resulted, in other words, in something like a basic subsistence economy in which luxuries like the print and book trades rested uneasily, and in which literary consumption proved hugely sensitive to the broader and volatile economy. It was, moreover, a stop-go, unpredictable economy repeatedly dislocated by the exogenous shocks of plague and war. The latter also added to increased and increasingly various taxation, further reducing spending on non-essential goods.

Under these conditions, book demand grew fastest amongst the middling, propertied classes, for whom the possession of luxury goods also became a sign of status.[20] The key to the growth of consumption was not simply the seventeenth-century recovery from the price inflation, but redistribution with in the economy, a process chronicled by lively contemporary reports. Under the earlier inflationary régime many landowners had benefited by marketing food surpluses in a rising market in which most of the poor and dispossessed

18 See Wrigley and Schofield 1981, app. 9, pp. 638–44.
19 For the debate see H. Kamen *European Society*, 1500–1700 (London, 1984) pp. 54–66.
20 Clark 1976.

became the real losers. The near doubling of population between 1550 and 1700 was set against a six-fold increase in price of grain, in which the gentry and some yeomanry were the real gainers, most notably following the improvement of newly acquired land in the second half of the sixteenth century.[21]

By the end of the period, there is ample evidence to suggest that British standards of living increased relative to the Continent, led by changes in agricultural productivity and a geographical expansion of the economy beyond the Severn–Wash line. Much of this geographical extension, or what has been called 'the moving frontier of the internal economy', was associated with a developing colonial market, with Scottish trade increase, and with west Midland and Newcastle coal-based industry and trades. At the same time, London continued to dominate the English economy with disproportionate growth and a population fed by immigration from the regions. Here was a market adjacent to the centres of production, with fewer distribution problems and benefiting from affluent leading-edge demand, particularly in the Parliamentary season. Together, the growth of London and broader regional developments encouraged a further expansion of urban population, diversified industries and services, and an eventual net export of foodstuffs.[22]

The growing seventeenth-century book market was to be sited in a landscape of sturdy farmhouses and coaching inns, new town houses and confident city and country gentlemen, burghers and tradesmen. The popularity of the bookplate shadowed the increase in armigerous gentry, the unprecedented building of funerary monuments in churches, and the bogus claims to gentility much reported in print.[23] This was, with obvious regional variation, an increasingly prosperous and redistributive economy in which the aggregate incomes of a rising, propertied group contributed to the development of a luxury market.[24] The change is clearly demonstrated by inventories recording increased possession of books and other print, and, by other sources, the accumulation of domestic libraries and print collections.[25] Such shifts in wealth supported the development of gentlemen's libraries, like that of Thomas Plume, vicar of Greenwich, with his library of 7–8,000 volumes, as well as the new dealers in collections. Even by 1628 the Warden of the Stationers' Company was able to list thirty-eight booksellers who dealt in 'old libraries' and this number increased three-fold by the end of the century.[26] Auctions quickened the

21 Some historians, however, have suggested that almost all the population enjoyed trickle-down benefits; see Kerridge 1973, esp. pp. 160–3.
22 Coleman 1977, p. 199. 23 See Lee 1991.
24 For the various studies of this since the 1980s see Glennie and Whyte 2000, pp. 189–90.
25 Brewer and Porter 1993; Shammas 1990; Weatherill 1988; below, ch. 14. 26 Herrmann 1991.

dispersal of gentlemens' libraries, and as one auction catalogue declared, it was now to 'be more easie for any Person of Quality, Gentlemen, or others, to Depute any one to Buy such Books for them as they shall desire'.[27] Judging by the circumstances mentioned in some of these catalogues, remarkable personal fortunes were both lost and gained at this period. Not all sales were post-mortem, and the buoyant book market was a sign of wealth reallocation as well as accumulation.

A key issue concerns the extent to which booksellers, like all businessmen, were able to stimulate demand. The structural concentration of business in London helped to focus on the recognition (not only confined to the book trades) that if a market was limited, profit margins could never be high. For booksellers especially, encouragement of demand was largely dependent upon good printed advertising. This developed from the early promotional use of title pages to the issue of printed catalogues.[28] Marketing strategies also incorporated deliberate design features, including, for example, the woodcuts in ballads. Some five-sixths of all ballads published between 1600 and 1640 used woodcut illustration, and these, as posted on tavern walls and the like, served as natural advertisers and inducements to purchase similar wares.[29]

The accuracy of market anticipation was also important because wholesale prices had to take account of the mark-ups necessary to keep retail agents in business. From what we can tell, a general perception seems to have been that market expansion was dependent on the increase of market area rather than of market depth in the sense of increased per capita income. The question of distribution was again given great emphasis therefore, and the evaluation of pricing decisions largely hinged on changes in the potential for onward selling, with the development of the discount system depending upon transport developments. Transport costs were consistently high across early modern Europe, and the transformation in the economics of distribution over this period very obviously affected book and print production. Nevertheless, evidence here is difficult to interpret, with most routes and corresponding marketing strategies most easily reconstructed from the actual print produced rather than from other, external, evidence.

London and provincial booksellers enjoyed many well-established trading connections by 1600. Cambridge and Oxford were amongst the most prominent, but York, Norwich, Exeter and Bristol, as well as Ipswich, Newcastle and several other towns are identified as established book-trading centres

27 William Cooper, 'Note to the Reader', cited in Anthony Hobson, foreword to Munby and Coral 1977.

28 See below Barnard and Bell, pp. 677–8.

29 Watt 1990, pp. 66–7.

by the beginning of the seventeenth century.[30] Nathaniel Butter, the most prominent coranto publisher, had his books sold by dozens of provincial booksellers during the 1620s, and this seems to have typified the development of wholesaler-retailer networks and London-country retailing arrangements. The establishment of the Welsh Trust in 1674 formalized more than a century-old network of contacts between London-Welsh printer-booksellers and distributors in the principality.[31] In Scotland the capital was also dominant, with widening trade. By 1620 Glasgow booksellers joined more established shops in Aberdeen, Perth, St Andrews and Stirling, in dealing in Edinburgh books.

The increased importation of books from the late sixteenth century also required new distribution and retail outlets to maintain custom, often institutional custom. This is something that needs particular attention, even though the few surviving port records for the most part of this period are frustratingly vague. Once again we have to read back from the implicit testimony of later records. A few extant business ledgers and letter books and the patchily surviving customs port books of the late seventeenth century do attest to large shipments of books, paper and equipment from the Continent, and the Netherlands in particular.[32]

The most extensive retail networks were those worked by country petty chapmen, ballad sellers and sometime minstrels, like Richard Sheale working through Staffordshire, Lancashire and routes south to London. Similar distribution systems flourished throughout the seventeenth century, and by 1696–7 some 2,500 pedlars were registered as selling chapbooks and ballads. These, however, probably represent only a fraction of the total of petty sellers of print at this date, not least, it has been suggested, because of the effects of the changing age structure of the population.[33] Most of the penny chapbook and godliness sellers were youths. They were cheap and willing labourers in what was still an under-employed economy. Many booksellers in the expanding book market proper, however, also adopted the public postal service, created in 1635.[34] For large consignments coastal shipping remained even more important. Plume's library on its first post-mortem journey, for example, was packed in barrels at a London wharf, reaching Maldon by coastal ship. Certainly, during the seventeenth century coastal shipping was developed as much as (and perhaps even more than) the pack-horse drivers and waggoners responsible for inland trade.[35]

30 See below Barnard and Bell, pp. 671–3, esp. notes 36, 39 and 45. 31 Rees 1990, p. 5.
32 Armstrong 1979; Hodgson and Blagden 1953; Needham 1999; Roberts above, ch. 6.
33 Spufford 1981; Barnard and Bell, below, p. 667. 34 Robinson 1948, chs. 2–3.
35 See Wilson 1984, esp. p. 43; Chartres 1977; Wilson 1980; Chartres 1980; and Crofts 1967.

Nevertheless, the fastest, most direct means of sending printed stock to provincial retailers and customers was by common London carrier. The management and success of the carrying trade was signalled by the publication of frequently reprinted road books like Richard Grafton's *Litle treatise*, 1571–1611, and Frank Adams's *Writing tables*, 1575–1628. As many as 200 towns are listed in John Taylor's 1637 *Carriers cosmographie*, another standard printed directory of the London carrier services. The great city coaching inns, like those at Ludgate and the Poultry, acted rather like the Victorian railway stations, located on each side of London and serving their own distinct routes. Distribution thereafter was boosted by the remarkable increase during the seventeenth century in the number of highway and market-town coaching inns.[36] This certainly supports recent studies that have demonstrated greater news circulation by weekly postal services along the London highways. In the 1620s, for example, between 250 and 850 copies of corantos were produced per week or between 12,500 and 42,400 of each series of 50 issues.[37]

Against this, economic historians have stressed continuing limits to growth, particularly emphasizing the deplorable state of the roads. Carriers travelled at only between twenty and twenty-four old English miles each day, and for many, the verdict on internal transport during much of the seventeenth century – along with rural literacy rates – is one not of progress, but of deterioration.[38] What we do need to try to determine is the cost involved in sending out books and print from London and the regional distribution points. Distribution costs were a significant add-on in financing publication (with carriage costs almost always paid for by the booksellers), and the price of poor distribution was exceptionally high. With booksellers' margins so tight, and with very little room for major capital tie-up, it was necessary to sell the full edition as quickly as possible. Nor was cheap print excluded from this assessment. Although corantos were often wrapped up in bundles of private correspondence sent by the carriers, in the early seventeenth century it cost a penny to send a letter from London to Ipswich and to Oxford. It cost two pence to send a letter to Coventry.[39]

The most important exception to these limitations was provided by both social and, by the end of this period, more commercial safety-nets. In this relatively intimate society where little institutional support existed, family and kinship support structures were vital. We have to understand the importance to business of neighbourhoods, trust and obligation and how these relationships

36 Pawson 1977, pp. 323–9. 37 Frearson 1993a, p. 5.
38 Chartres 1977; Wilson 1980; Chartres 1980; Dyer 1995. 39 Frearson 1993a, p. 7.

were policed. Goldsmiths and merchant-bankers took an early, pivotal role in support to many booksellers, but from at least the early seventeenth century members of the Stationers' Company also arranged interest-free loans between themselves. The Company's Book of Bequests, 1623–75, and Bonds for Money Lent, 1671–88, record loans and other forms of financial support. Minority communities arranged similar provision. Even after the Civil War, the effect of many Restoration Acts was to nurture sects whose inwardness extended to community and financial support. Most notable amongst these were the Quakers whose printers, as much as their bankers and, later, manufacturers, supported each other by both practical and material means.[40] By the end of the seventeenth century, however, many more financial intermediaries began to assist in the organization of publishing. At the same time, new rigour in bookkeeping and the adoption of new methods transformed the keeping of book trade accounts, even though many booksellers appear to have followed no consistent model. Most, however, attempted to ascertain costs and determine a price structure based on finer measurements than in the past. The Stationers' Company, taking a lead, adopted regular auditing from at least 1658.[41]

The elimination of high risk is a prerequisite for most modern businesses, but insurance featured very little in the book trade before the early eighteenth century. Certain overseas, long coastal, and very particular inland transport might be given rudimentary cover, but risk was usually borne even on extensive stock. This was especially so for fire, as was cruelly exposed in London by the Great Fire of 1666. Failure itself was still unprotected, and until the 1707 statute of bankruptcy there was no obvious distinction to be made between those who failed through no fault of their own or by their own ineptitude and those who failed as a result of the swindling of others.[42]

Finally, institutional support for the book trade has to be set against broader political developments. The economy was subject to recurrent government attempts to regulate and control production. Commercial resources were milked by successive governments for their own, largely war-led, needs, while at the same time the economy of both England and Scotland was variously affected by frequent political upheaval. Manufacture, distribution and custom in the book trades were all changed by action of, first, the Crown, and then, to a much greater extent, by Parliaments and the courts, while in Scotland the liberties and powers of the different burghs were fiercely guarded until at least partly curbed by legislation in the Edinburgh Parliament in 1672.[43] In an emergent

40 Hetet 1987. 41 Myers 1985, p. 15

42 See Hoppit 1987, introduction and chs. 5–7. 43 Devine 2000, p. 157.

fiscal-military state organized revenue collection supported the waging of war, and many, often desperate, attempts were made to collect levies and duties. These, in various ways impacted upon the book industry and its customers. New methods to raise revenue forced reassessments of production and distribution costings, if not with the force of the later eighteenth-century Stamp Acts. English customs rates from the late sixteenth century, for example, included duties on the importation of books as part of the regulation of overseas trade and shipping.

Much other public policy guided the internal economy. The most obvious instances were the trades licensing and apprenticeship regulations largely devolved to the guilds, and effectively amounting to multiple restrictive practices with origins that were often as much political as economic. As discussed above, the interventions most affecting book production in the late sixteenth and early seventeenth centuries were the numerous and often conflicting Crown patents, Star Chamber decrees and other monopoly grants for specific titles or genres and with varying terms of years and printing conditions. In the case of the Stationers' Company, these privileges culminated in the establishment and management of the English Stock.[44] Protectionism coupled with the Company's attempts to police entry to the book trade and to supervise its own hierarchies also created sharp economic divergences within the trade. The successive ordinances, injunctions and decrees granting Company officers authority to search and seize unauthorized books were all endorsed by the 1637 Star Chamber decree ordering the licensing and entering of books at Stationers' Hall. Star Chamber and High Commission were abolished in 1641, but two years later an ordinance restored the authority of the Stationers' Company, and a 1649 regulating Act and then the 1662 Licensing Act attempted to recreate its 1637 powers.

During the course of the seventeenth century, moreover, a small élite within the book trade benefited from the dividends of the English Stock and flourished at the expense of smaller traders and, especially, of the printers. The establishment by Royal Grant of this joint-stock of the Stationers' Company from 1603 created a financial corporation with arrangements for the successive distribution of dividends to members. Under legal protection refined and extended by successive injunctions, Company members operated a trading cartel, regulating not only the products and the manner of trade, but also access to trading and the instruments of production. By the control of their own property and by self-regulation, the Company came to offer welfare for indigent members and

44 See Barnard above, pp. 11–15.

widows, but it was thereby very rarely a force for innovation and commercial forward planning.

Nevertheless, there is also some merit in the argument that a certain protectionism was helpful to a nascent and fragile industry, and we can certainly discern a difference between the sort of engrossing monopolies granted by early modern governments that effectively deprived people of necessary commodities, and copyright protection in what was essentially a luxury goods market that safeguarded against piracies and over-production. None of that, of course, made the granting of individual printing rights any less contentious at the time. Such tensions can also be seen in the ways that government in both England and Scotland tried to furnish a framework for production and labour. In general, official regulation in traditional industries did decline by the end of the seventeenth century, but enforced labour continued in England and Wales under the 1563 Statute of Artificers, and Settlement Acts were passed from 1662 in an attempt to manage migration and labour mobility. It was in this context that the Stationers' Company exercised control over official apprenticeship and entry to trade as well as over the quality of work and wage levels.

Even more broadly, the English Navigation Acts dating from 1651, but given greatest force by those of 1660, 1663, 1673 and 1696, affected all trades including the book and stationery trades. The Acts discriminated against foreign interests generally and against Dutch interests in particular, insisting that imports from Europe had to arrive in an English ship or in a ship of the exporting country. All colonial trade was reserved to English and colonial ships. European goods were to be dispatched to the colonies only via England and certain colonial products could only be exported to England. The effects of this on book imports and exports varied between the two kingdoms: apart from the brief years of the Cromwellian Union, the Navigation Acts did not apply to Scotland until the Act of Union of 1707.

Notable in both realms was the shift in different customs duties from simple revenue-raising devices to finer instruments of commercial policy. An excise introduced by the Westminster Parliament in 1643 was retained at the Restoration, with rates increased in 1671. The hearth tax of 1660 to 1689 was followed in 1693 by the land tax. More regressive was the 1694 salt duty, with an immediate effect upon the market and the prices of ordinary consumables. By the 1690s, indeed, the state extracted an unprecedentedly large income per capita, with much of the change imposed after 1660 and in response to the demands of war.[45] If this had continued without any compensating relief, the

45 See essays in Coleman and John 1976.

wealth and income of the propertied could hardly have sustained the consumer spending of the final decades of this period. Just as the squeeze on disposable incomes began to affect the market in luxuries such as books, however, the most taxed households also began to benefit from that other result of war-induced revenue raising, the interest and investment opportunities of new government bonds and annuities. By the end of the seventeenth century the expanded resources of the two kingdoms and their populations supported an increasingly sophisticated market that was more boosted than restrained by fiscal innovation, and in which book suppliers were able to manipulate as well as service new demand.

28
French paper in English books

JOHN BIDWELL

English printers depended on imported paper until the late seventeenth century, when the government began to encourage manufacturing ventures by granting monopolies, raising tariffs, and boycotting the nation's economic enemies. A growing demand for printing paper and other economic incentives stimulated domestic production, but political measures were needed to protect it. For two hundred years the paper industry languished under pressure from foreign competition, mostly from across the Channel, where the production costs were lower and the distribution network was better organized. French mills dominated the English market, supplying far more than Italy, Germany, Holland, and the other exporting countries combined. These countries also shipped printing grades to London, but generally at higher prices and in negligible quantities except when Customs cut off French sources of supply.

Printers consumed so much French paper that they could name different types by the place of origin, like varieties of cheese. Normally they subsisted on ordinary printing grades manufactured in Normandy and Brittany, regions close enough to London to control the cost of transportation and far enough from Paris to contain the cost of labour. If times were hard, they might prefer the cheaper papers of Morlaix to those of Caen or Rouen. When they could afford it, they bought the produce of La Rochelle, but they also paid higher prices for shipments from Genoa, a leading entrepôt of paper in the pre-industrial period. On rare occasions, they might procure luxury goods from Holland to print large- or fine-paper copies for distribution to an author's friends and patrons. They associated each of these papermaking districts with a certain level of quality and price, and often ordered regional specialties by name, though not always as precisely as we might like. Some 'Dutch' papers were actually made in France; a consignment of 'Genoa' papers could include portions made in other parts of Italy; the products of the Angoumois, Périgord, and Limousin could be sold as 'Rochel' papers, even if they were shipped from Tonnay-Charente rather than from La Rochelle.[1]

Expert printers might savour this rich variety of foreign papers, and know how to pick the ones best suited to their needs, yet they would still have reason to wish for a closer, more convenient and reliable supply. Too often they had to cope with a sudden dearth of this commodity, a drop in quality, or a surge in price caused by political interference in overseas commerce, fluctuations in exchange rates, accidents at sea, adverse business conditions abroad, and other constraints on foreign trade. However, their own financial situation was so precarious that they could not afford to subsidize local manufacturing initiatives. As much as they might like to buy their supplies in Britain, they had to take their business elsewhere as long as foreigners could deliver merchandise of comparable quality at a cheaper price.

An early economic treatise recounts the plight of manufacturers, taking England's first paper mill as a prime example. Now attributed to Sir Thomas Smith, this tract was composed in 1549 in the form of a dialogue between individuals representing different social classes – a knight, merchant, capper, husbandman, and scholar, who claims to have learned about the mill in conversations with a bookbinder. Smith doesn't name the proprietor, though we now know that he was John Tate, a mercer, and that he went into business near Hertford around 1494, when he supplied paper for a papal bull printed by Wynkyn de Worde. The mill expired not long after it was founded, says Smith, because its owner 'could not forth his paper as good cheap as that came from beyond the seas and so he was forced to lay down making of paper'. Tate was not to blame for his predicament, but rather his customers who 'would give never the more for his paper because it was made here'. Since they would not renounce imported luxuries, and would not pay more for domestic wares, Smith urged the government to intervene with protective tariffs and other obstacles to foreign trade, 'for by this means, inestimable treasure should be saved within this realm'.[2]

The price war was only part of the problem. Around 1585 the law printer Richard Tottell petitioned for the exclusive right to manufacture paper in the

1 Heawood 1929; Heawood 1930; Heawood 1947. Here, and in my analysis of paper sizes and watermarks, I am greatly indebted to the work of Allan Stevenson, who died before he could complete an account of French imports into England, provisionally titled 'The unicorns of Normandy: cheap paper as a factor in English cultural development'. Several typescript drafts are in the Allan Stevenson Papers at the Princeton University Library, Collection c0630, Box 7. I am very grateful for a Bibliographical Society fellowship in support of my research on the paper trade and for advice and assistance from Maureen Bell, D. F. McKenzie, David McKitterick and Paul Needham.

2 *A discourse of the commonweal of this realm of England*, ed. M. Dewar (Charlottesville, 1969), pp. 66–7; Stevenson 1967, pp. 15–19.

kingdom, claiming that he could not raise the necessary funds from members of the Stationers' Company. They had declined to invest in his schemes on the grounds that two or three attempts to found a papermaking business had already collapsed so resoundingly as to discourage further ventures. His predecessors had failed because the French had sabotaged their efforts every step of the way, from manufacturing to sales. Tottell accused the French of cornering the supply of rags, harassing their compatriots who emigrated to work in English mills, and dumping underpriced goods on the English market to drive their rivals out of business. The government could help to combat their underhanded tactics by granting him a monopoly and forbidding the export of rags. Although he had other lucrative patents, this petition inspired no more enthusiasm in the state than his proposals did within the trade. He never obtained these royal privileges, and never forgot his dependence on imported paper, which he confessed every time he directed customers to his shop – at the sign of the Hand & Star, a common watermark in early English imprints signalling paper imported from France or Italy.[3]

While coping with cut-rate imports, British papermakers also had to keep up with the high rate of inflation during the Tudor period. Prices of industrial products were rising steeply when Tottell joined the trade in the middle of the century and were still climbing at the end of his career, when he submitted his petition. At that time, smaller printing papers cost less than 3*s.* per ream, slightly larger ones around 6*s.* or 7*s.* per ream. As a rule of thumb, printers and customs agents assumed that the cheapest papers would bring 2*s.* 8*d.* a ream.[4]

A few mills did succeed in making wrapping grades and may have sold some coarse printing papers on the side. Perhaps the best known papermaking venture is that of John Spilman, 'Ieweller to the Queenes Maiestie', whose high office gave him the means to build a mill and to obtain the prerogatives that Tottell had pursued in vain – a monopoly on paper manufacture and on the collection of raw materials. At a cost estimated between £1,400 and £1,500, Spilman converted a mill near Dartford and started production around 1588. As he could not compete against imported writing grades, he had to specialize in printing grades to recoup his investment and to comply with the terms of his patent, which obliged him to make white paper instead of brown. But he never gained a foothold in the white-paper trade, having to contend with formidable difficulties obtaining rags, defending his monopoly, and disciplining his journeymen, whose special skills were indispensable in his business. A few Spilman

3 Arber I, p. 242; Byrom 1928.
4 Gray and Palmer 1915, p. 70; Greg and Boswell 1930, p. 51; Jackson 1957, p. 54.

watermarks occur in manuscripts, but none have been found in printed matter with the exception of Ben Jonson's *Sejanus* (1605), which displays royal initials in the ordinary-paper copies. Almost certainly he took the path of least resistance, buying rags and hiring workers fit for brown paper manufacture – and little else – even at the risk of forfeiting his patent.[5]

Although forty-one mills are known to have been operating in England between 1601 and 1650, there is no evidence that any of them could supply the printing trade. In 1636 the residents of Buckingham and Middlesex denounced local papermakers in a petition to the Privy Council, alleging among other grievances that they were driving up the rents, they were attracting vagrants, their dams were flooding the streams, and their rags were spreading the plague. If bad for the neighbourhood, they were not much better in the marketplace, where they were selling defective goods at exorbitant prices – paper unfit for writing and printing because it would 'bear no ink on one side'. For all their misdeeds, they did not deserve to be reproached for poor workmanship, as they were probably making wrapping grades, an entirely different product line than white papers intended for the press and the pen.[6]

To make white papers, English papermakers had to acquire different skills and better raw materials than they were using in the manufacture of wrapping grades. White papers were only as good as their ingredients, rags collected in the vicinity or imported from other countries. Top-quality linen rags were so scarce abroad that some countries refused to export them, and they were even harder to find at home, where linen production had always lagged behind the woollen trade. Journeymen could not hope to master the White Art without learning how to sort a consignment of rags, culling the worst for wrapping grades and ranking the others by colour, purity and strength. If they were making writing and printing grades, they had to learn how to brew a gelatin size solution, and how to apply it evenly, so that each sheet would absorb the right amount to bear ink properly and attain the desired printing and handling properties. Writing grades cost twice as much as printing grades because they required greater skill, better rags, a brighter colour, a smoother finish, and a harder surface, a result of more sophisticated sizing techniques.[7]

Englishmen lacked opportunities to learn these skills, and Frenchmen were not inclined to teach them, even though they could have earned higher wages in this country. In 1713 the paper merchant Theodore Janssen calculated that

5 Coleman 1958, pp. 40–54; Calhoun and Gravell 1993.

6 Shorter 1971, p. 19; *CSPD 1636–37*, pp. 373–4.

7 Delâge 1991, p. 26. The bookseller William Churchill compared writing and printing prices in a memorial addressed to the Board of Trade, 8 April 1699, PRO CO. 388/7, fols. 194–7.

French rag sorters were paid less than a third of the salary they would receive across the Channel. Mercantilist writers like Janssen were hard pressed to explain why French workers achieved higher output on lower wages, completing more than nine reams a day while British vatmen produced no more than eight. Among other ingenious rationales, they noticed that papermakers in some districts lived amidst vast forests of chestnut trees, providing so much free nourishment 'that the common People have no other Food all the Year round, and no other Drink but Water; so that they can afford their Work very cheap, and do it next to nothing, except some of the upper Workmen, who earn a small Salary by the Week'. If, on this diet, they did not 'have as much Strength as an *Englishman with his Beef and Pudding*', then they must have superior skills, which brown papermakers would have to learn before they could match the quality and price of imported goods. In the meantime, the government would have to lend them some assistance with trade embargoes and protective tariffs. Of course, this would drive up the price of printing supplies, but these theorists were less concerned with transitory hardships than with long-term policies that would build the industrial might, financial strength, and economic independence of their country.[8]

However, higher prices did engage the full attention of printers and publishers, whose outlay on paper could amount to half of their production costs. They spent so much on paper that they often estimated presswork and other production expenses in terms of reams, a standard unit of measure in this business, each ream containing 480 to 500 sheets. For example, the publisher Thomas Walkley paid the printer John Beale 4*s*. a ream for his work on a pirated edition of Wither's poems issued in 1620. While cheating the author with his 'counterfet Impressions', Beale also swindled the publisher, who had hired him to print 1,500 copies and had supplied the paper, but had received only 700 or 800 copies, most of them imperfect. The recalcitrant printer also failed to deliver the 'ouerplus' of paper that remained after the presswork had been completed. When his customer hounded him for the missing books and the extra paper, he took the offensive and had the publisher arrested for non-payment of debts. Walkley then counter-sued and presented a petition to the king, explaining how he expected to finance his edition of Wither. As publisher, he took the responsibility of buying the paper, and duly provided eighty reams of crown (a common printing size of the period) costing him 4*s*. 6*d*. a ream, just over half of his total investment. Altogether his production expenses must have been around 5*d*. per copy, about half of his projected retail price of one

8 *The British merchant; or, commerce preserv'd* (London, 1721), I, p. 8 and II, pp. 261–5.

shilling. At 4*s*. a ream for printing, and 4*s*. 6*d*. a ream for paper, he might have made a decent profit, if he had received what he had ordered on those terms.[9]

Paper accounted for a proportionally lower share of the printing budget in publications involving greater editorial expenses and higher typesetting costs. In this category one could include the Shakespeare First Folio, printed three years after Walkley's piracy on crown of similar quality and price. Very convincingly, Peter Blayney has estimated the production cost at 6*s*. 8*d*. per copy and the retail price at about 15*s*. Each Folio consisted of 227 sheets or nearly a half a ream. If crown was still selling for 4*s*. 6*d*. a ream, then that portion of the cost per copy would have been about 2*s*. 3*d*. or a third of the total. Here the publishers' investment in paper did not equal their other expenses, which included composition charges for a text in two columns on a larger page than usual as well as the purchase of reprint rights from previous publishers of Shakespeare's plays. Nevertheless, they carefully watched the price of crown, even if it represented only a third of their unit cost; should that expenditure exceed the sum they were willing to risk on Shakespeare, they were fully prepared to adopt a cheaper format, charge a higher price, or choose another text for publication.[10]

If they did not care for the imports currently on sale, they could shop around at just a few London outlets, where they were not likely to find a better deal. By the end of the seventeenth century, the import trade had fallen into the hands of six or eight merchants, a group small and powerful enough to fix prices and restrain competition. Rightly or wrongly, they were the first to take the blame when paper was scarce or dear. During the sixteenth century, drapers, tailors, fishmongers, stationers, and other tradesmen might purchase small portions of a paper shipment, while haberdashers handled the largest amounts. Later, French immigrants dealt on a more ambitious scale, no doubt profiting from their commercial connections across the Channel. William Carbonnel bought so much from a mill near Angoulême that the master papermaker wrapped his wares with ream labels displaying the British royal arms and declaring that the contents had been made for 'M. G. Carbonel marchand à Londre et nul autre'.[11]

Sir Theodore Janssen made a fortune importing paper from Italy and France, where his grandfather had settled around 1620 and established a thriving family business, buying from local mills and selling to merchants in England and Holland. The Janssens bought their own mills to assure a regular supply and

9 McKitterick 1992, pp. 285–8; Simpson 1925.
10 Stevenson, 'Unicorns of Normandy'; Blayney 1991, pp. 25–8.
11 Johnson and Gibson 1946, plate facing p. 71.

sent their sons abroad to maximize their profits at the point of sale. Theodore set up shop in London around 1683, probably obtaining his stock from his brothers and his father Abraham Janssen, whose watermarks appear frequently in English imprints. By one account, his father sent him to England with a bankroll of £20,000. This sum is hard to believe, but his father did deal with his sons so generously that he asked them to take his consignments as their inheritance, their warehouses containing a major portion of his estate. Theodore certainly had the means and the ambition to transact business independently on a lavish scale. With his capital reserves, he invested in other trading ventures, served as paymaster for Britain's Continental allies, and provided financial support for the monumental *Suidas* published by the Cambridge University Press. He owned rental properties in London, a twenty-room townhouse in Hanover Square, and a country estate in Wimbledon. He helped to organize the Bank of England, the New East India Company, and the South Sea Company, where, unfortunately, he took a second term as director at the peak of speculative frenzy just before the crash. After the Company collapsed in 1720, Parliament charged him with a 'notorious breach of trust' and confiscated most of his personal assets, valued at £243,000.[12]

Investors in the papermaking trade naturally resented the power of these merchants and decried their influence on the market. In 1690 the Company of White-Paper-Makers accused them of trying 'to ruin the Manufacture, and to enrich themselves; the said seven or eight Paper-Sellers having more Paper than is in all *England* besides, which they hope to sell at extravagant Prices, if not prevented by the Establishment of the Manufacture here'. The complaints of manufacturers closely resemble the protests of consumers like the bookseller William Churchill, who warned the Board of Trade that 'The Great Enemys to the settling of this Manufacture must be the 5 or 6 wholesale Traders who buy all the Imported and sell it to the Retailers all over England Lett them pretend what they will.'[13]

While these merchants did control the market, and could exploit their advantages unfairly, they could also supply consumers with an impressive array of goods in different sizes, qualities, and prices. In 1674 Alexander Merreall offered the Theatre Press at Oxford a full range of printing grades obtained from mills in Normandy, Brittany, southwestern France, and Genoa. Thomas Seaward also submitted to the Oxford printers a tempting selection of imported goods, probably conveyed on his ship the *St Peter* of Calais. Their stock lists included the following varieties most frequently employed at the press:

12 Veale 1995; Delâge 1990, pp. 19–26; McKenzie 1966, I, pp. 64–5, 141 and 224–33.
13 Cameron 1964, p. 39; Churchill's memorial, fol. 195.

		Prices	
Name	*Approximate measurements*	*Ordinary*	*Fine*
Pott	12½ by 16 ins.	2*s*. 9*d*.–5*s*.	
Foolscap	13 by 17 ins.	5*s*.–5*s*. 10*d*.	6*s*. 6*d*.–7*s*. 9*d*.
Crown	13¾ by 18 ins.	4*s*.–6*s*. 6*d*.	8*s*.–8*s*. 6*d*.
Demy	15 by 19½ ins.	7*s*. 2*d*.–11*s*. 6*d*.	15*s*.–16*s*.
Royal	18 by 23½ ins.	12*s*.–24*s*.	34*s*.

Altogether they quoted prices for sixty-six different lots of paper, some of the larger varieties approaching writing quality, but even the printings could have special features that could command an extra shilling or two per ream.[14]

Merchants of Merreall's and Seaward's stature could order quantities as large as 2,000 reams. Their correspondents in France might call on several different mills to assemble this cargo (a practice that accounts for the strange multiplicity of watermarks in the Pavier quartos and other English imprints). They packed their freight in bales padded with straw and covered with canvas, the bale containing as few as eighteen or as many as seventy-two reams depending on their size and weight. A ream consisted of twenty quires, each quire composed of twenty-four or twenty-five sheets. Papermakers were allowed to include inferior sheets in the two outside quires, which helped to protect the inside quires from damage in transit, but they sometimes supplied reams composed entirely of insides, twenty-five sheets to a quire, 500 printable sheets to the ream. In 1714, some paper merchants were assuming that writings would contain twenty-four sheets to a quire and printings twenty-five sheets, the higher number probably more convenient when printers had to allocate supplies for the press and reckon the salaries of pressmen.[15]

Sometimes the merchants could not control the price of their merchandise, especially when they had to cope with higher taxes. The French trade suffered severe hardships in the 1630s after Richelieu abruptly hiked the excise duties to finance the wars against the Habsburgs. By 1638 a master papermaker in Poitou had to pay the fisc 7 sols per ream, or 15 per cent of the value of his fine papers and 21 per cent of his middling quality. Under Colbert the excise and other fees represented half the cost of smaller sizes in Paris, where prices had increased from nearly 50 to more than 100 per cent in the course of forty years. Booksellers could no longer afford paper from Angoulême, 'le plus beau du royaume', since the Dutch merchants who had taken over the trade in that region preferred to ship their products abroad than to sell them for a lower profit in Paris. These

14 Chapman 1927; *CSPD 1666–67*, p. 603.

15 Delâge 1991, pp. 42–9; Stevenson 1951–2, pp. 57–60; *Considerations relating to the intended duties on paper* (London [1714]).

obligations oppressed the trade so grievously that the government sometimes rescinded them altogether or assessed them at more lenient rates, as low as 4 per cent of the wholesale value in 1684. Nevertheless, pott, demy, and other staple printing grades cost export merchants in Angoulême twice as much in 1660 as they did in 1620.[16]

Additional taxes had to be paid when these shipments arrived in London. Like other imports, paper was subject to 5 per cent customs duty *ad valorem* or 'poundage', assessed at one shilling on the pound. Customs officials set the value of imported paper following the guidelines published in *The rates of marchandizes*, otherwise known as the Book of Rates. More than twenty editions with various titles were published between 1545 and 1675. The official valuations did not always correspond to the current market price, but are worth noting for the significant changes they reveal in the import trade as it grew in volume and prosperity in the Stuart period. Previously, white papers smaller than demy were considered a staple commodity, lumped together at a standard rate of 2*s*. 6*d*. or 2*s*. 8*d*. Under James I, however, the Book of Rates listed additional impositions, generating extra revenue and recognizing the higher quality of writing grades. Classed as one of the writings, foolscap doubled in value to 5*s*., while ordinary printing and copy papers rose less steeply to 3*s*. 6*d*. Printings advanced again to 4*s*. 6*d*. in 1635, fell back to 2*s*. 6*d*. in 1657, and then reverted in 1660 to the higher figure, where they remained to the end of the century. The Commonwealth's customs agents were expected to tell the difference between cheap papers from Brittany, moderately priced goods from Normandy, and premium wares from La Rochelle. Usually importers declared their merchandise to be ordinary printings at 4*s*. 6*d*. per ream, a bargain rate if they were entering printing royals or printing demys worth 10*s*. to 12*s*. a ream – or an arrant fraud if they were sneaking through this loophole odd-size writings worth 10*s*. to 16*s*. a ream.[17]

The Crown sometimes granted exemptions from the duty as a form of literary patronage. Authors and publishers were given the right to import large amounts of high-priced duty-free paper, which they could sell on the side to subsidize expensive publications. The Semitic scholar Edmund Castell spent his fortune and nearly lost his sight while labouring on his *Lexicon heptaglotton* (1669), a two-volume royal folio printed by Thomas Roycroft, the King's Printer in Oriental Languages. Charles II urged his subjects to subscribe to this important work and ordered the Customs to permit free passage of 5,000 reams

16 McKitterick 1992, p. 285; Martin 1969, II, pp. 583–5; Delâge 1991, pp. 21–2 and 49–57.
17 'Memorial from the Governour and Company of White Paper Makers in England', 7 Oct. 1696, PRO CO. 389/14, p. 43.

of royal, far more than Roycroft needed for this edition. Likewise, Richard Blome was allowed 8,000 reams of royal unencumbered by customs, some of which could be sold at a profit to finance his *Cosmography and geography* (1682), another ambitious subscription venture. John Ogilby petitioned for a licence to import 10,000 reams of French printing paper duty-free to compensate for losses suffered in the London Fire and to forward his business producing books adorned 'with sculpts in a more noble and heroic way than hath heretofore been done in England'. Less successful in recruiting subscribers, the theologian Peter Allix had to abandon his projected seven-volume history of the Church Councils sometime in the 1690s, but 'under that Pretence' he imported 'a great Quantity' of paper without having to pay the usual fees, which were fairly heavy at that time.[18]

The duty remained at a shilling on the pound until 1690, when Parliament authorized higher tariffs to support the campaign against France. The new law imposed specific surcharges on some grades of paper and doubled the poundage collected on the others (2 Wm. & Mary, sess. 2, c. 4), setting the customs duty at 10 per cent *ad valorem*. Parliament also fought the enemy on the economic front with an additional 25 per cent duty on French imports (4 & 5 Wm. & Mary, c. 5), soon augmented by another 25 per cent (7 & 8 Wm. III, c. 20), bringing the total due on French paper to 60 per cent in 1697. Subsequent legislation did not spare imports from other countries, and even exacted a heavy toll from domestic products, but these measures were not nearly so severe as these punitive attacks on France.

The government sometimes prohibited French importations altogether, either to redress the balance of trade or to prevent commerce with the enemy. After France declared war in 1666, the King issued a proclamation banning 'all sorts of manufactures and commodities' produced on its territories or by its citizens. The Anglo-Dutch conflict also disrupted parts of the French paper trade controlled by merchants in or from the Netherlands. Statistics compiled by D. C. Coleman show that the hostilities on these two fronts almost completely throttled the flow of imports, once reaching 120,394 reams in the two years 1662–3 but reduced to only 3,442 reams in 1667. Although probably incomplete, these figures are corroborated by a flurry of petitions from tradesmen seeking exemptions from the embargo. Merchants pleaded for permission to land this prohibited article in England, along with wine, brandy, linen, and other goods ordinarily procured across the Channel. King's Printer Christopher Barker claimed to have suffered so greatly from the ravages of

18 *CSPD 1660–61*, p. 383; *1666–67*, p. 171; *1675–76*, pp. 322–3; Clapp 1933; *The case of the paper-makers in the kingdom of England* (London, *c*. 1737?).

the Fire and from the present want of paper that he needed to buy a thousand bales 'for carrying on His Majesty's business'. Similarly afflicted, the Stationers' Company received royal warrants admitting French cargo on several ships, including one laden with sixty tons of paper, presumably for distribution to printers working on the English Stock.[19]

Trade resumed in 1668, and grew vigorously until Parliament declared another embargo in 1678 (29 & 30 Charles II, c. 1). Mercantilist principles inspired this legislation, primarily intended to retaliate against discriminatory tariffs but designed also to prevent foreign manufactures from sapping the national economy. The preamble states explicitly that drastic measures were needed to protect 'the Wealth and Treasure of this Nation [which] hath beene much exhausted by the Importation and Consumption of the French Commodities'. Retreating while they still could, British merchants began to wind down their affairs in France and turn to Holland and Italy instead. Someone with Italian connections sought to profit from the embargo by advertising in the *London gazette* large quantities of Genoa and Venetian paper just when consumers were beginning to feel the pinch. French merchants began to insert escape clauses in contracts for the sale of paper or the lease of mills, reducing or abrogating their obligations in time of war. Nevertheless, many abandoned their mills when they ran short of operating funds, while some filled their warehouses with goods they bought at discount prices, betting that the market would reopen soon. Indeed, the French trade did recover briefly when James II repealed the embargo, but foundered again after he fell from power.[20]

His successors William and Mary proclaimed another boycott lasting from 1689 until 1697, a period of re-adjustment in the marketplace while merchants cultivated new sources of supply. Shortages lasted longer than usual and pushed prices higher than booksellers were willing to pay. In this predicament they curtailed their business with printers and declined the services of authors whose works might entail an unprofitable outlay on paper. They rebuffed the proposals of the historical writer and pamphleteer Edmund Bohun, who had been seeking literary employment at that time, while trying to pay his debts, and while intriguing for the place of Licenser of the Press. 'Paper became so deare', he recalled, 'that all printing stopped, almost; and the stationers did not care to undertake anything; and there was no help that way.'[21] Almanac paper priced at 4*s*. a ream in 1671 was valued at 5*s*. 6*d*. a ream in 1693; good printing foolscap rose from 5*s*. and over in 1674 to 7*s*. 6*d*. and over in the 1690s; printing demy

19 *CSPD 1666–67*, pp. 303, 493–5, 512, 527, and 585; Coleman 1958, pp. 13 and 65.
20 Hazen 1954, pp. 325–9; Delâge 1990, pp. 164–71.
21 *The diary and autobiography of Edmund Bohun*, ed. S. Wilton Rix (Beccles, 1853), p. 88.

shot up as high as 25*s*. for a premium Dutch variety used in fine paper copies.[22] It was rumoured that some of the Dutch papers now flooding the English market were actually made in France and transshipped through Holland to evade the law. According to a more charitable explanation, the Dutch were buying French paper for their own use and were exporting their own products to England, having expanded their manufacturing capacity five-fold while their customers were at war with their suppliers.[23]

Beset by tariffs and embargoes, French merchants could no longer compete in the British market against imports from other countries and the products of British mills, by then steadily improving in quality. The papermaking business became more attractive to inventors and investors, who petitioned for royal patents similar to those solicited by Tottell and secured by Spilman. With royal approbation, Eustace Burnaby built a mill near Windsor between 1675 and 1678 and succeeded in making printing grades but eventually sold his patent for reasons that have not been ascertained. George Hagar devised a way of mixing size with rags while they were being pulped in the mortar, a promising invention that could greatly expedite the manufacture of coarse printing grades. Hagar obtained a patent in 1682, found a partner, leased a mill, raised ample capital, but lost his credit when his investors discovered that he had already gone bankrupt in the dyeing trade. His partner, William Sutton, challenged the patent of John Briscoe who claimed in 1685 to have invented a technique of making printing and writing grades 'as good and serviceable in all respects, and especially as white, as any French or Dutch paper'. Briscoe had actually learned the technique from Hagar, said Sutton, and was exploiting it in partnership with known papists. Sutton may have been slandering the competition, but his tactics prove that the prospects for making printing grades in England had improved to the point where papermaking inventions might be stolen and had to be protected.[24]

The most valuable invention introduced to England at this time was the beating engine or Hollander, developed in the Netherlands in the 1670s or perhaps as early as 1650. Instead of pounding rags in a mortar, Dutch papermakers prepared them in shorter time and in greater quantities by grinding them against a series of parallel blades mounted on a spinning cylinder enclosed in a tub of water. Stirred by the spinning blades, a constant flow of water circulated in the

22 Blagden 1958b, p. 112; Johnson and Gibson 1946, p. 186 and plate facing p. 151; Bodleian MS. Ballard 49, fol. 212.

23 'Memorial from the Governour and Company of White Paper Makers in England', p. 43; Churchill's memorial, fol. 197.

24 Hazen 1954; Cameron 1964, pp. 4–6; Overend 1909, pp. 197–8.

tub to wash the rags and draw them between the blades and a serrated metal bedplate beneath the cylinder, where they were broken and then beaten to a consistency of pulp suitable for the desired type of paper.

Two Englishmen may have learned the secret of the engine at a surprisingly early date, though their patents are so vague that they could have been referring to other methods of macerating fibre. In 1682 Nathaniel Bladen announced that he had perfected 'an engine, method, and mill, whereby hempe, flax, lynnen, cotton' and other raw materials could be 'prepared, and wrought, into paper and pastboard, much speedier and cheaper than by the milles now used'. Two years later Christopher Jackson summarily described the advantages of machinery that 'dissolveth, whiteneth, and grindeth raggs, and prepareth all other materialls whereof paper and pastboard hath been or may be made, in farr less tyme then the mills hitherto in use doe, being a new invention never yet practiced in this kingdom'. There is some question whether Bladen or Jackson really understood this invention and whether they could have exploited it successfully in commercially viable manufacturing conditions. D. C. Coleman and other historians have viewed their claims suspiciously, having found no trace of Hollanders in British mills until the early eighteenth century. However, some corroborating evidence has now come to light in an inventory that lists the components of an engine along with other paper-mill supplies shipped from London to Dublin around 1690. This Irish manufactory was established by some of Bladen's business associates, who were sufficiently familiar with his machinery to mention it without comment shortly after he obtained his patent. We can now say more confidently that this Dutch invention helped to make British mills more competitive in the 1690s, a turning-point in the paper trade.[25]

While French imports were waning, the prospects were improving for technological innovation and capital investment in manufactures. Enterprising papermakers secured twelve patents between 1665 and 1695 and formed at least six companies to exploit new commercial opportunities in various parts of the British Isles. None of these companies survived for very long, but one excited so much enthusiasm and kindled so much controversy during its brief existence that even its detractors conceded that domestic production had become possible and profitable.

The Company of White-Paper-Makers began with a core group of French immigrants, members of the Huguenot community already well established in

25 Overend 1909, pp. 196–7; Cameron 1964, pp. 43–5; Coleman 1958, pp. 60–3; Wilson 1984, p. 305; Hills 1988, p. 58.

England, but soon augmented in 1685 with thousands of refugees uprooted by the revocation of the Edict of Nantes. In that year Adam de Cardonell, Nicholas Dupin, and Elias de Gruchy petitioned for the right to display the royal arms in papers they were manufacturing in Hampshire. Nathaniel Bladen, John Briscoe, and many others soon joined this syndicate, which successfully petitioned for a charter of incorporation and a fourteen-year monopoly on the manufacture of writing and printing paper. John Dunstan was appointed Governor of the Company, Nicholas Dupin Deputy-Governor, and Bladen one of the thirteen Assistants. Later, the Company admitted William Sutton and came to terms with an investor who had purchased the patents of Eustace Burnaby and Nathaniel Bladen. It could be said, therefore, that the Company consolidated the interests of the most prominent patentees, who had pooled their knowledge, resources, and privileges to build an invincible papermaking corporation.[26]

Other papermakers feared that the Company would become so powerful that it would force them out of business, just when business was looking good. They protested vehemently against the 'Paper Act' of 1690, which, among other provisions, allowed the Company to raise additional capital and to extend its monopoly until 1704. In the spirit of compromise, Parliament divided the marketplace between brown goods and white paper, defined as any product priced at more than 4*s.* a ream. The Company had to sell above that price while its competitors had to stay below it. This conciliatory measure did not satisfy the 'Antient Paper-Makers', who claimed that they had been making white paper selling for 3*s.* to 20*s.* from time out of mind and that they were actually more experienced and better skilled in this art than the upstart patentees.[27] They did not presume to make fine writings, but they had been supplying ordinary printings for Bibles and Testaments long before the advent of the Company. They would be buying rags at a loss if they could not sort out the better ones for use in 'good middling sorts', an essential source of income, since they could not get by solely on sales of wrapping grades.[28] Furthermore, these privileges contravened the Statute of Monopolies (1624) and violated common sense, for the few mills owned by the Company could not possibly meet the growing demand for writing and printing grades throughout the kingdom. In their defence, the patentees declared that the 'brown paper men' were still incapable of making goods of acceptable quality and could not complain about illegal restraints on trade, since they were welcome to join the Company. After hearing

26 Cameron 1964, pp. 3–9.

27 *CSPD 1700–2*, pp. 552–3; HMC, *House of Lords, 1690–1*, pp. 74–6.

28 Minutes of the Board of Trade, 12 Oct. 1696, PRO CO. 391/90, fol. 116–18.

these arguments and many more, pro and con, Parliament passed the bill, and it received the royal assent on 20 May 1690, though refractory papermakers were still fighting against the monopoly as late as 1696.

Importing merchants also joined in the fray, most notably Theodore Janssen, a formidable opponent of the Company in print, in official testimony, and behind the scenes. Janssen and Alexander Merreall disputed the Company's claims at a meeting of the Board of Trade also attended by the booksellers William and Awnsham Churchill and the papermaker Rice Watkins. The merchants informed the Board that the patentees had been able to charge high prices while England was at war with France and would continue to gouge their customers even in peacetime because their labour costs were higher than those in other countries. Printing grades had become so expensive that the London trade had 'lost the impressions of many classick authors' to foreigners who paid less for their supplies.[29]

Janssen was well acquainted with the labour problems of the Company, having created some of them himself. Its managers depended on French immigrants to run its mills and eagerly recruited them despite French efforts to prevent Huguenots from leaving the country. By royal proclamation, papermakers of Auvergne were sentenced to the galleys if they were apprehended while trying to cross the border. Denis Manès started in the employment of the Company, returned to France on a recruiting mission, but was caught and sent to prison in Caen, and then turned against his employers, claiming they had extorted his share of the patent after he was released. His brother-in-law Daniel Juilhard quit the country gladly after running afoul of the law in Angoulême, where he had worked for several Dutch merchants, including Theodore Janssen's father. He had treated one of his customers so rudely that he too spent time in jail. And in this rough-and-tumble business, he endured his share of hard knocks during an altercation with his journeymen, who ganged up against him in a drunken rage, pummelled him, tore his hair, knocked him down, and kicked him for having criticized their workmanship. Upon his arrival in England, he was hired to manage one of the Company's mills but was led astray by Janssen and absconded along with two other Frenchmen subverted by the merchant. The authorities soon flushed him out of hiding, clapped him into prison, and then sent him back to work at the mill, where he remained until his employers learned that his workmen had been dumping rags in the river and had committed other acts of sabotage. They dismissed Juilhard while doing their utmost to exploit the scandal, playing on anti-French sentiments to build up

29 *Ibid.*

public sympathy for the Company. They accused Janssen of conspiring with the French ambassador, who had been given instructions and funds to persuade renegade papermakers to return to their native country. In fact, the ambassador did negotiate for Juilhard's release from jail and eventually sent him home with a reward. Janssen admitted that he had been scheming against the Company, though as a newcomer unacquainted with the laws, and acknowledged that Juilhard had been employed by his father, who could have been prosecuted for sending him to England if the son did not bring him back to France. All these excuses did not conceal his true motives for attacking the Company where it was most vulnerable, in the mills where it was trying to introduce French manufacturing techniques. The Company desperately sought to master these essential skills, even at the risk of employing treacherous personnel.[30]

However, the Company had other problems besides its troubles hiring workmen capable of making printing grades. By building new mills, it had driven up the price of rags, and it had to buy them from its own worst enemies, the brown-paper men, who could collect them more cheaply and efficiently around their mills in remote areas of the kingdom. At first the Company established a number of 'collecting houses' where it paid £4 10*s*. to £5 10*s*. per ton and sold off the brown rags for £1 10*s*. per ton. When prices began to rise, the Company abandoned its attempt to buy direct, closed down its collecting houses, and agreed with its competitors to buy their white rags at £10 per ton. This appears to have been the prevailing price through the 1690s, though the Company complained that after a year the brown-paper men went back on their bargain and jacked up the prices even higher. In turn, the Company had to charge more for its products to keep up with the cost of raw materials. But here too it failed to reach an accommodation with entrenched members of the trade, the London merchants who sold bulk quantities of paper to printers, booksellers, and other major customers. Like Janssen, many of these merchants refused to cooperate with the Company since they were still committed by family and financial ties to the import trade. Once again its directors tried to bypass the middleman by selling their wares at auction, 'by Inch of Candle', disposing by this method of 50,000 reams per year – or perhaps only 30,000 reams, depending on whether we take their word or trust the testimony of their opponents. They could not have earned very high profits by dumping their products on the market all at once in this way. A broadside catalogue for one of their sales offers a total of 4,697 reams in fifty-two lots, including several lots of printing demy, crown

30 George 1931; Delâge 1990, pp. 46–7 and 58–60; Delâge 1991, pp. 104 and 265; Cameron 1964, pp. 16–17 and 37.

imported from Morlaix, and foolscap from Caen. For them to be trading in imported goods did not bode well for their manufacturing ambitions, but these auction sales were even less auspicious, a sure sign that they lacked an adequate distribution network either because of the intransigence of the merchants or the negligence of their management.[31]

Many of the original investors in the Company were more interested in its stock than in its sales. The Company issued 400 shares at £50 per share after obtaining the patent and was authorized to increase its capital with an additional subscription in 1690. Shares trading at £60 in March 1692 dropped below par as low as £44 in June and then rose as high as £150 in March 1694. But after falling back to £140 in April, the price was no longer listed, as if there had been some kind of turmoil on the exchange. Quite possibly, the stockholders had lost confidence in the Company and decided that it was time to sell. By 1696 the original investors had almost all departed, some so suddenly that the enemies of the Company accused them of bilking the public with a stockjobbing scheme.[32]

The Company succumbed soon after 1697, when Parliament passed a bill to tax domestic paper, and when a financial crisis brought down most of the other joint-stock companies organized in its day. Papermakers later blamed its demise on 'Covetousness, Indolence and bad Management'. The Company probably was mismanaged, but it did make a dent in the printing market during the 1690s, when its watermarks appeared in English imprints such as Dryden's *Eleonora* (1692) and Congreve's *Double-dealer* (1694). Despite its monopoly privileges, it could never corner the printing market since it produced no more than 50,000 reams a year while England was still importing at least 130,000 reams a year, of which more than 75,000 reams were intended for the press. It is difficult to estimate the Company's manufacturing capacity more accurately without knowing how many mills it leased or owned and how many vats were in each mill. At various times its managers claimed to be running five, eight, nine or twelve mills. In 1696 a Company spokesman reported that it was operating twenty vats altogether, a creditable figure if we accept that each vat was working at the standard rate of 2,000 reams per year, producing a total of 40,000 reams, midway between the Company's and its competitors' estimates of its sales per year.[33]

31 Minutes of the Board of Trade, 7 and 12 Oct. 1696, PRO CO. 391/90, fol. 110–18; Hazen 1954, p. 331.

32 *A collection for improvement of husbandry and trade*, 30 March 1692 – 27 April 1694.

33 Wilson 1984, pp. 183 and 220–1; *The case of the paper-makers*; minutes of the Board of Trade, 14 Oct. 1696, PRO CO. 391/90, fol. 120; Churchill's memorial, fol. 195–6.

In the heyday of the Company, the brown-paper men owned about a hundred mills producing more than five times as much as the monopolists in quantity but only two-and-a-half times as much in value. Nevertheless, their business prospered, and by around 1712 there were twice as many mills in England with an annual output estimated at 530,000 reams, probably an optimistic figure, but not too far off the mark if, as it was conjectured, 150 mills had one vat and fifty mills had two.[34] British papermakers competed against the import trade most successfully at the lower end of the market, where they could sell cheap printing papers at a satisfactory profit. They still had much to learn before they could make printings suitable for substantial bookwork:

> *English* Paper-Works are principally employed, in making those ordinary and low priz'd Papers, which are only proper for printing *Small Tracts*, such as *News-Papers*, *Pamphlets*, and all Sorts of *stitched Books*; nor are they yet arrived to such Perfection, though Daily improving, as to make Fine or Large Papers for greater Works, in any great Quantities.[35]

Like other early industrialists, they had to start at the bottom and work up to where they could compete with foreigners who had already mastered the trades they hoped to practise in their country. They dislodged the French from the bottom of the market but still had to contend with the Dutch and the Italians, who continued to undersell them in the American colonies until the Americans established their own self-sufficient paper trade. The situation in England in the 1680s was remarkably similar to that in America in the 1780s, when local mills were producing low-quality stock for almanacs and newspapers but lacked the resources to make better printings or passable writings.[36] Skilled immigrants brought to America more advanced papermaking techniques just as the Huguenot refugees helped to introduce white-paper manufacture in the mother country. The non-importation agreements, the Revolution, the Embargo of 1807, and the War of 1812 impeded traffic in paper overseas with barriers not unlike the tariffs and embargoes that one hundred years before had blocked trade between France and England. In England and America, the papermaking business required political protection as well as financial support. Printers and booksellers ordered more paper than other customers, and ordered even more when cultural and political factors increased the demand for printed matter. The British government loosened its grip on domestic printing

34 *Proposals humbly offer'd to the consideration of the Honourable House of Commons, for raising forty thousand pounds* (London, *c.* 1712?); *The case of the paper-traders* (London, *c.* 1697?); Shorter 1971, pp. 28 and 75.

35 *The case of the manufacturers of paper, the stationers printers, &c. of this Kingdom* (London, *c.* 1712?).

36 Bidwell 2000.

with the lapse of the Licensing Act in 1695, just when it was tightening the screws on imported paper with higher tariffs on French manufactures. Papermakers could not have asked for better incentives or greater security for their trade, which grew in strength and prosperity throughout the eighteenth century, and reached a pinnacle of sorts early in the next century, when English capital perfected a French invention, the papermaking machine.

29
The old English letter foundries

NICOLAS BARKER

> I have been with all the Letter-founders in *Amsterdam*, and if I would have given *** for matrices could not persuade any of 'em but the last I went to, to part with any. so far from it that it was with much ado I could get them to let me see their business. the *Dutch* Letter-founders are the most sly and jealous people that ever I saw in my life. However this last man (being as I perceived by the strong perfume of *Geneva* waters a most profound sot) offers to sell me all his house for about ***** I mean the matrices: for the punchions with them he will not sell for any money. but there being about as much as he would have *** for, *Hebr.* and other Oriental languages, such as *Syrian Samaritan* and *Russian* characters, I would not consent to buy 'em. but the rest consisting of about 17 sets of *Rom.* and *Ital.* capitals and small letters, and about 5 sets of capital letters only, and 3 sets of *Greek*, besides a set or two of *Black* with other appurtenances, these I design to buy. he is not very fond of selling them because it will be a great while before he can furnish himself again. however I believe I shall have 'em for less than **** a matrice, which as he says is cheaper than ever they were his; but having most of the punches he can sink 'em again and so set himself to rights with little trouble and less charge.[1]

Thomas James, son of the Reverend John James, vicar of Basingstoke, after serving his apprenticeship with Robert Andrews, set up on his own in 1710. For that purpose, he went to Holland to buy equipment, whence he wrote letters to his brother, of which this, dated from Rotterdam, 22 June 1710, is the first: 'the account of his expedition is entertaining', wrote Rowe Mores, who preserved and published the letters, in his characteristic under-capitalized style. So it is, but in this passage he also touches on some of the perennial problems that faced typefounders and their customers in Britain from the outset. In considering these it is difficult to avoid the assumption, often made by bibliographers anxious to attribute unsigned work to an identifiable printer, that types were made as well as used by printers. As Rowe Mores, pondering the early silence about typefounding, put it, 'at the beginning no distinction was made between the

1 Quoted from Mores 1961, pp. 49–50. See Note on sources (pp. 618–19 below).

different operations of making the letters and using them after they were made; but the whole exercise of the profession went under the general denomination of *Printing*; a term which included every article belonging to a *printed book* from the punch to the binding'.[2]

All the evidence suggests that this was never true, even at the beginning. Gutenberg himself employed a goldsmith, Hans Dünne, and others worked for the press at Ripoli and Johann Amerbach at Basel. Specialist engravers engraved punches for printing types, Jost Bernhart for Bernhard Richel, Lautizio Perugino for Arrighi, and above all, Francesco Griffo of Bologna, who cut the Greek, roman and italic types for Aldus whose style dominated typography till the end of the eighteenth century. Other special skills were needed for striking matrices (a task long familiar in mints), justifying them, as Hans von Unkel offered to do for Amerbach,[3] and casting type. The last task was indeed a familiar feature of the printing house, though not invariably so, since it required the possession of matrices and the employment of a founder. Claude Chevallon, printer at the Golden Sun in Paris, where the great punchcutter Claude Garamond first worked, also employed a founder, Guenet, at the Fox's Brush.[4] Another founder in Paris offered to supply a printer with a fount of Garamond's 'petit romain' (a size that afterwards bore his name) in 1545.[5] Punchcutters and typefounders, among them Robert Granjon, Pierre Haultin and Ameet Tavernier, also printed books, not only to advertise their types. The existence of independent 'fondeurs de lettres' is recorded in Lyon in the first half of the sixteenth century. In the second half, there were several substantial independent foundries, among them that of François Guyot at Antwerp, Hendrik van den Keere (Henri du Tour)'s at Ghent, the Egenolff business at Frankfurt, managed by Jacob Sabon, and the Parisian foundry of three successive Guillaume Le Bés, that had grown to become substantial businesses, with several employees and a stock of matrices for use or sale, dependent on a nuclear collection of punches.

The distinguishing feature of all these businesses was the possession of punches, and the ability to create new ones to order. Engraving letters on the tip of a narrow cylinder of steel required special tools and the skill to render letters, singly or compound, with a family resemblance to each other, usually in a small size. Originally based on handwriting, printing types came to develop their own characteristics, conventions for roman and italic and the different

2 Mores 1961, p. 3.
3 Letter to Bonifacius Amerbach, 24 January 1493, *Amerbach Korrespondenz* (Basel, 1942–95), ed. A. Hartmann, I, p. 33.
4 Carter 1967, p. 19.
5 E. Coyecque, *Recueil d'actes notariés rélatifs à l'histoire de Paris et ses environs au XVIe siècle* (Paris 1923–5), no. 3137.

kinds of black letter, commonly used. These were partly external, size, colour, relation of x-height to ascenders and descenders, as demanded by the market, and partly internal, the expression of the engraver's eye and hand. At no time were there many capable of this skill, and sometimes the lack of competent punchcutters was conspicuous. It was Thomas James's misfortune to travel to Holland at such a barren period, and his complaints are echoed forty years earlier by Thomas Marshall, who had arrived there at Fell's behest just after the great Christoffel van Dijck had died. Justifying a matrix after it has been struck by the punch, that is, adjusting the four sides so that the letter cast in it sits square on the line and the right distance from its neighbours, was also a skilled task. Paterne Robelot, who justified the matrices of the *grecs du roi*, cut by Garamond, and Jean Picard were specialists in this.[6] It was customary, from very early on, to supply a mould with each set of matrices, and there were specialists in making them too. The correct alloy of type-metal was vital, both to the successful casting of types and their durability in use. If lead was its primary ingredient, other metals were required to strengthen it; after initial experiments with copper, bismuth and iron, tin and antimony became the norm, in various relative proportions, but in total about 1:4 to lead. Like all such recipes, the precise alloy was treated as a trade secret.

In the main European current of typographical development the British Isles were a backwater, and remained so until the eighteenth century. There was no punchcutter of original ability until then, and British typefounders, so far as they are known, were satellites of the main Continental centres. In this, it may be said, they were no different from the rest of the book trade. As with books, so with types, it was easier to import from abroad than to manufacture locally, and for local consumption that could not be supplied from abroad, no very high standard was required. It had not always been so. Caxton, in employing Johan Veldener, first to provide the types and print his Cologne edition of Bartholomaeus Anglicus, and then to cut the special types for his publications in English, first at Bruges and then Westminster, anticipated what was to become the norm.[7] But the dependent nature of the English trade is illustrated by the appearance of a small black letter, cast on a pica body, in the work of John Day and Robert Waldegrave between 1560 and 1590;[8] this was the work of Henric Pietersz. de Lettersnider of Rotterdam, 'the earliest punchcutter of whom there are satisfactory records',[9] one of five types that he cut at the turn of the fifteenth century in a markedly Dutch style that became deservedly popular in

6 Carter 1967, pp. 19, 29. 7 Hellinga 1999, pp. 72–9.
8 Isaac 1932, fig. 87; Isaac 1936, pl. 79. 9 Carter 1969, p. 105.

the Low Countries.[10] In the latter part of his career Caxton went to France for the black letter that became the preferred type of his successors. The prevalence of black letter for liturgical and law printing in England, long after it had ceased to be popular in France, ensured the survival of several early French types of this kind. Such a type, perhaps of Flemish rather than French origin, cast on an English body, was still available in London in the mid-seventeenth century.[11]

Whether, in fact, there were any resident typefounders in London in the early sixteenth century is open to doubt, but by the middle of the century, at least, 'there is every sign that the mechanic part of English typefounding was in the hands of resident aliens and that a demand for better designs was satisfied by imports or migrations of skilled men'.[12] The earliest known of these was Hubert d'Auvillier, apprenticed to the great Robert Granjon in 1545, who was in London in the early 1550s and remained there for forty years.[13] It may be no coincidence that Granjon's famous italics first appear in London printing at this time. Hierosme Haultin, nephew of Pierre Haultin, the distinguished Huguenot punchcutter and printer at La Rochelle, was in England by 1568, listed then as 'servant' to D'Auvillier, and stayed there until 1586, paying his uncle the substantial sum of 192 *livres tournois* for matrices in 1575–6, and supplying types to his compatriot Thomas Vautrollier.[14] Amell de Groyter, 'letter-maker for printers', is probably the same as Ameet de Gruyter, who with Herman de Gruyter founded types for Plantin after Hendrik van den Keere died in 1580.[15] Paul Rotteforde, 'founder of lettres for printers', is recorded in 1571 as having been in England for fourteen years.[16]

The most distinguished of these aliens was François Guyot, a Frenchman denizened in Antwerp from 1539 who became Plantin's first typefounder. In the list of aliens ordered by the Lord Mayor of London in 1568 appears 'ffraunces Guyott a ffrenchman, Gabriell John, Crystofor and Anne his children & James and John his servantes dowchemen they are all printemakers,

10 Kruitwagen 1923. See further Vervliet 1968.

11 It appears in the type-specimen attributable to Nicholas Nicholls, *c.* 1665, passing to Thomas Grover, from whom it was acquired by James. One hundred and one matrices were listed in the 1782 sale catalogue of the foundry (lot 88), passing later to the Reed and Stephenson Blake foundries; Mores 1961, pp. lxii, 112.

12 Mores 1961, p. lxx. The sources and usage of these types are discussed in Craig Ferguson 1989.

13 He is listed in 1571 as having been there for about twenty years in the Huguenot Society publication of the *Returns of aliens*, ed. R. E. G. and E. F. Kirk (London, 1900–8), II, p. 5. 'Antonius D'Anvillier, fusor typorum', recorded as a member of the French Church *c.* 1562–3 (*Returns of aliens.*, I, p. 291) may have been a slip of the pen. 'Hubert d'Armillier', recorded in February 1545 as Granjon's apprentice by Renouard (*Imprimeurs et libraires Parisiens du XVIe siècle* (Paris, 1964), must be the same man.

14 *Returns of aliens*, III, p. 339, Worman 1906, pp. 28–9; Mores 1961, pp. lxix–lxix.

15 *Returns of aliens*, II, p. 317.

16 *Returns of aliens*, III, p. 421.

of the Dowche churche dwellinge in the howse of John Daye printer'.[17] This is of particular interest, since a specimen of his types survives in the Folger Shakespeare Library, annotated with the prices for matrices in English.[18] It is tempting to connect his presence with the appearance of Aelfric's *A testimonie of antiquitie*, printed by Day with special Anglo-Saxon characters in 1567, followed by other works with Anglo-Saxon texts. Similarly, when a clergyman, John Karney, undertook in 1570 to supply 'stamps, formes and matrises for the printing in the Irish tongue of CC Catechisms', he was probably relying on his stationer nephew, William Kearney, who 'as well here in England as in some forraine partes, applied him self to the art and mystery of prynting . . . and lykewyse knewe howe proper letters and characters for that language might be had'; the Irish characters thus made are mixed with one of Pierre Haultin's St Augustin romans.[19] It was only such local needs that could not be supplied with existing matrices from abroad. There is a further echo of this in a letter from Archbishop Matthew Parker, the patron of Day's Anglo-Saxon printing, to Lord Burleigh: 'I have spoken to Daie the printer to cast a new Italian letter, which he is doinge, and it will cost him xl marks; and loth he and other printers be to printe any Lattin booke, because they will not heare be uttered and for that Bookes printed in Englande be in suspition abroad.'[20] François Guyot died in 1570, presumably in Antwerp,[21] but Gabriel and Christopher stayed on, at least intermittently, and are recorded in 1576 as still resident in Day's house. Gabriel may have been responsible for the pica Anglo-Saxon in Day's 1576 printing of Fox's 'Booke of martyrs'.[22] He is last recorded in London in 1588,[23] four years after Day's death, and he was back in Holland in 1590; in 1592 he was in Rotterdam, without matrices, a matter of some surprise to Frans Raphelengius,[24] although he had retrieved them by the time he died in 1610.

The sources of Day's types, all French or Flemish, confirm how dependent British typography was on alien supplies.[25] But already there were signs that native founders were beginning to take over, even if the matrices that they used came from abroad. Although there is no inventory attached to Day's will, several

17 BL, MS. Lansdowne 202, fol. 19^{v}; cited by Oastler 1975, p. 34.

18 Dreyfus 1963, no. 1. 19 Dickins 1949–53; Mores 1961, pp. lxviii–lxix.

20 *The correspondence of Matthew Parker* (Cambridge, 1853), p. 411; cited in Reed 1952, p. 94.

21 Briels 1974, p. 292.

22 His sister described him as 'lettersteker', the usual Dutch word for 'punchcutter' in 1586 (Worman 1906, s.v. 'Deise'); cf. Oastler 1975, pp. 35, 39.

23 Worman 1906, s.v. 'Guyett'. 24 Carter 1969, pp. 94–5

25 Oastler 1975, pp. 39–61. To those identified there can be added the black letters, some of which can be seen in Digges, *A boke named Tectonicon* (London, 1556). These survived to the eighteenth century (Mores 1961, nos. 68, 69–70 and 77), and two appear in the Wilson specimens of 1783 and 1786.

witnesses in the Chancery proceedings that followed mention, besides 'printing tooles' and 'lettres', 'instrumentes', a word used in Dutch for moulds.[26] Thomas Grantham, apprentice to Richard Watkins, was ordered to serve his indentures with 'Hubert Doviley', an unmistakable name, to 'learne the arte of casting of letters for printing and all the faculty which the said Hubert useth'.[27] The proceedings against Roger Ward and Robert Waldegrave for illicit printing show that their types were used as a means of identifying their work,[28] and the first record of a native founder is in the context of official control. In 1597 Benjamin Sympson was required by the Stationers' Company 'to enter into a £40 bond not to cast any letters or characters, or to deliver them, without advertising the Master and Wardens in writing, with the names of the parties forr whom they are intended'; the same Sympson is recorded as having an apprentice in 1598 (as he was not a member of the Company, his apprentice was bound to another who was), and Nashe refers to 'Beniamin the Founder'.[29] This injunction was repeated by the Company on 11 May 1622 to 'the Founders'; no names are mentioned but the plural indicates not only that there were more than one, but that they had a certain independent and collective status.[30]

This status is confirmed by the first public reference to the London typefounders by name, the notorious 'Decree' of the Court of Star Chamber regulating the trade in 1637.[31] There were five provisions in this directly relating to typefounding, infraction of which was to be punishable by the Courts of Star Chamber or High Commission. The first limited the number of founders to four, and named them as John Grismond, Thomas Wright, Arthur Nicholls and Alexander Fifield. They were, secondly, prevented from keeping more than two apprentices, their names (by implication) to be recorded in 'the Hall-booke of the Company, whereof the Master-Founder is free'. 'All Journey-men-Founders' were required to be employed by the Master-Founders, and all 'idle Journey-men be compelled to worke after the same manner' as were printers' journeymen. No other person might be employed, 'save only in the pulling off the knots of mettle hanging at the ends of letters when they are first cast, in which work it shall be lawfull . . . to employ one boy only that is not, nor hath beene bound to the trade of Founding letters'. Lastly, an earlier inhibition relating to the manufacture of presses also provided that 'no Founder shall cast

26 Oastler 1975, p. 34. Only one of the types (a great primer 'Secretary') left by the printer Henry Bynneman in 1583 was not of Continental origin (Eccles 1957, pp. 81ff.).

27 Arber, II, p. 189. 28 Reed 1952, pp. 115–18.

29 Index to the court books of the Stationers' Company, cited by Reed 1952, p. 118; Greg and Boswell 1930, p. 58; Arber, II, p. 224; T. Nashe, *Have with you to Saffron Walden* (London, 1596), sig. O1^{v}.

30 Index to the court books 1952, p. 119.

31 *A decree of Starre-Chamber, concerning printing* (London, 1637).

any Letters for any person or persons whatsoever, neither shall any person or persons bring, or cause to be brought in from any parts beyond the Seas, any Letters Founded or Cast, nor buy any such letters for Printing, Unlesse he or they respectively shall first acquaint' the Master and Wardens of the Stationers' Company. There are a number of notable features in these provisions besides the names of the four founders. It is clearly implied that typefounders might belong to other companies than the Stationers'; this was in line with common practice in all the City companies, and evidently deemed beyond government control, however desirable. The provision for a 'boy' outside the trade structure to break off the jets before the type was dressed must again reflect an established routine. Finally, the careful attempt to bring the importation of type under the same control as that cast at home shows very clearly how much the trade was still dependent on it.[32]

By an odd coincidence, the name of the first English-born typefounder for whom we have more than passing details of his career does not appear in the Star Chamber list, because he had died less than a year earlier.[33] Richard Adams had been born in London, the son of Francis Adams, a Stationer, and baptized in St Nicholas Cole Abbey on 19 January 1589. He was made free of the Stationers' Company by patrimony on 22 October 1618, and must already have been a typefounder, since he bound his first two apprentices, Abraham Bradshaw and Thomas Wright, in 1619 and 1620. They are mentioned by name in the Acts of the Privy Council for 9 January 1625, enjoining that he, then resident in Green Dragon Court and founder of letters for the King's Printing House, and his two servants are to be exempted from being pressed into the army.[34] Adams bound six more apprentices, including Alexander Fifield, who was to succeed him, and died in September 1636. He was still in Green Dragon Court, off Snow Hill in the parish of St Sepulchre, to which he left several bequests. A schedule attached to his will lists debts due to him of over £1,000, almost half from London printers and Thomas Buck at Cambridge and Leonard Lichfield at Oxford. Fifield first appears as a founder as the last name on the Star Chamber list, and he freed the last two apprentices that Adams bound. The foundry continued in Green Dragon Court until about 1640, when Fifield moved to St Andrew by the Wardrobe, close to the King's Printing House and others in Blackfriars, and remained there until his death in 1657.

32 The printer John Haviland, sent abroad to acquire Greek types and matrices about 1634 for the King's Printing House, clearly had a licence to do so, as emerges from his petition to Laud (Reed-Johnson 1952, p. 132).

33 Most of the archival records of the lives of Adams and the typefounders after him are drawn from Michael Treadwell's paper on London typefounding referred to below, see Note on sources, p. 619.

34 Reed 1952, p. 119.

Of the other Star Chamber founders, John Grismond is better known as a printer and one of the 'Ballad partners' ordered to register their stock on 6 November 1624. He was probably already a typefounder two years earlier, since the Company's injunction to 'the Founders' comes between two orders both directed to Grismond in person. Another John Grismond, possibly his son, was a printer, but there is no evidence of his founding type.[35] Thomas Wright took up his freedom on 7 May 1627 and bound his first apprentice the same year. In 1638 his foundry was in Little Britain, next to the bookseller Cornelius Bee and two doors from the printer Miles Flesher, and he probably remained there until his death in November 1646. He left one son, Daniel, then a minor, described as 'lettermaker' when he died in 1661, but neither he nor *his* son John (*d.*1696) seem to have cast type. Thomas Wright's real successor seems to have been John Goring, apprenticed to Wright on 1 June 1635 and free 4 August 1645. Before Goring's death in September 1661 he had moved to the parish of St Bartholomew the Less. He was nominally succeeded by his widow Jane (who died with debts due from four master printers, John Streeter, John Winter, James Flesher and Thomas Ratcliffe), but his apprentice Thomas Goring (not his son but perhaps a nephew, bound 31 May 1650, free 2 November 1657) in fact took over the business.

The last of the Star Chamber founders was Arthur Nicholls, made free of the City on 8 November 1632 by Royal decree 'in regard of his more than ordinary skill in making of letters'. His career seems to have taken a new turn as a result of the commutation of the fine imposed on the King's Printers for the errors of the 'Wicked Bible' into 'buying . . . Greek Letters and matrices', part of Laud's grand design for the advancement of learning in England. The capitals of the double pica Greek attributed to Nicholls, first found in 1636, show similarities with a range of roman types that appear at the same time.[36] Rejected for 'the printers place att Oxford', he petitioned Laud in 1637 'to bee a printer here in London, That soe he may make use of his owne letters for the elegant performance whereof hee doth promise to use his best care and industry'. To this petition, he attached a 'Cause of Complaint', reciting the hardship and negligible receipts of 'cuttinge the Punches and Matrices belonginge to the castinge of . . . letters', from which it appears that, unlike most of his predecessors, he cut punches as well as cast type. Collecting debts from printers was a serious problem, and in July 1640 Nicholls had to beg the Company for money to meet the fees for his release from prison. He lived as late as 1653 when he bound

35 Reed 1952, p. 155.

36 Lane 1991; the spelling 'dubbull pica Greek' on the surviving specimen (Bodleian Library, Rawlinson MS. D 317) suggests Dutch influence.

an apprentice, but before that was succeeded by his son Nicholas. The latter was born about 1612, and may be the Nicholas Nicholls who was buried in St Bartholomew the Less on 20 April 1684. If trained by his father, he was never free of the Stationers' Company and there are no records of his apprentices, not even of Thomas Grover who was to succeed him. He supplied type and punches to the Oxford University Press between 1649 and 1671, but had made over control of the foundry to Grover well before the latter's death in 1675.

About 1660, then, the four original typefoundries had all changed hands. The restrictions of 1637 were reimposed by the 1662 Licensing Act,[37] but in other respects change was in the air. In the first half of the century, the founders had been mainly dependent on imported matrices, many of them old by then. There was now a considerable impulse towards change. One cause of this was the printing of the 'London Polyglot' Bible by Thomas Roycroft, later to be made the King's Printer of Oriental Languages.[38] The first specimen of this was printed early in 1653 by James Flesher, son of Miles and neighbour of Thomas Wright, who may have supplied the original types that attracted considerable criticism. The types actually used by Roycroft come from various sources, some old, others of more recent design. Only one was new, the Samaritan, which was probably imported from Holland (perhaps from Bartholomeus or Reinhardt Voskens). The shortcomings of some of the others were criticized, and in 1654 the English Hebrew, double pica Syriac and great primer Arabic were cut with varying competence (the last being the best), perhaps by Nicholas Nicholls.[39] The English Ethiopic, still better, was cut by another contemporary hand in 1656. Ten years after the Polyglot appeared, still greater dissatisfaction with local produce made the authorities at Oxford look abroad, as they had in Laud's time. 'I se, in this Printing-designe, we English must learn to use our own hands at last to cut Letters', Thomas Marshall had written to John Fell at Oxford.[40] Fell himself had even lower expectations: 'The foundation of all successe must be layd in doing things well, and I am sure that will not be don with English letters.'[41] When Marshall reached Holland, he found the Dutch as contemptuous: 'I can observe those Masters had rather sell Letters than Formes [matrices]; and would persuade

37 This included the requirement to report to the Stationers' Company details of all founts supplied; only a fragment of one such report survives, covering the first five months of 1686 and only two of the three foundries then at work.

38 See pp. 648–51 below.

39 It is possible that at least some of these were also cut by Arthur Nicholls, but their subsequent history makes the issue doubtful (Lane 1991, pp. 321–2); on the Syriac, see Lane 1995, pp. 178–9 and n. 20.

40 Hart 1968, p. 166a.

41 To Sir Leoline Jenkins, 2 December 1672 (*CSPD*, Car. II, 294). S. Morison 1967, p. 59.

me, that, had you their Formes or Matrices, your Founders would miscast the Types or Letters.'[42]

The Dutch, as James discovered, had other reasons than aesthetic for retaining the sources of a profitable export trade, and Fell others again for preferring to remain independent of the London trade. He wanted 'some ingenious young man who would help us in the affair of letter founding . . . especially one who cutts & goes through the whole manufacture.'[43] Peter de Walpergen was German by birth (his family had earlier fled from Antwerp), but probably learnt his trade in Holland; he provided Fell with the exotic types he wanted, but was not above supplying the London trade, to Fell's irritation.[44] The Oxford experiment as a whole typified a wider impatience with existing types (some now very old), and a preference for the new Dutch style. Joseph Moxon, thanks to whom we know more about the practice of typefounding in England now than in any other country, well expressed this:

> The late made *Dutch-Letters* are so generally, and indeed most deservedly accounted the best, as for their Shape . . . which easing the Eyes in Reading, renders them more Legible . . . For my own part, I liked their *Letters* so well, especially those that were cut by *Christophel van Dijck* of *Amsterdam* . . . that I examined the biggest of his *Letters* with Glasses since common consent of Book men assign the Garland to the *Dutch-Letters* as of late *Cut*.[45]

It is ironical that the few types that Marshall and Fell got direct from the Van Dijck foundry were all old, while the rest, 'plainly inferior to Vandijkes',[46] were in fact of more recent cut, and, moreover, supplied by a founder familiar with England.

Jacques Vallet was born on 25 October 1600 in Geneva, but had moved to Amsterdam as a typefounder by 1643. He sold substantial founts to Dutch printers, and in 1650 likely acquired, with the printing equipment of Jan Fredericsz Stam, matrices from the typefounder Jacques Carpentier and his wife's previous husband, the engraver Nicolas Briot, who had supplied the Dutch trade between 1615 and 1640.[47]On 11 March 1645 he contracted an English punchcutter in Amsterdam, John Collett, to supply a small 'Hoogduits' (fraktur) type probably for a German printer in Amsterdam, Joachim Nosch.[48] By his own account, he had lived in London for seven years, probably from about 1650. He was thus an old man in 1672 when he offered all his equipment to Marshall,

42 BL, Add. MS. 22905, fol. 85.
43 To Henry Aldrich, 4 August 1673 (*CSPD 1673*, p. 478); Morison 1967, p. 39.
44 Morison 1967, p. 71. 45 Moxon 1962, pp. 22–3. 46 Hart 1968, 166b.
47 Morison, 1967, p. 67. 48 Enschedé 1978, pp. 110–11.

undertaking to come to Oxford himself, and was in London when he died in December 1672. No more is known of him or Collett, the only documented native English punchcutter before Moxon. However, the existence of such a man lends some colour to the supposition that native hands may have supplied Walton's needs for the London Polyglot, or, if not, that they were met from Holland, with which the London trade had longer and closer links than are documented. Moxon himself was cutting punches when he was visited by Marshall in August 1668,[49] and his 'Great Cannon Romain' remained popular, although his smaller sizes justify Fell's dissatisfaction. In *Mechanick exercises*, he only mentions himself and Walpergen as able to cut steel punches, and there may have been no others by then. He made a better job of the Irish type for which he cut the punches in 1680, at the instance of Robert Boyle.[50] He did not cast type, at least as a profession.

By then, too, the typefounding trade had undergone a substantial change of personnel. When Alexander Fifield died in 1657, he was succeeded by one of his apprentices, Richard Levis, who had originally been bound to Thomas Wright. Fifield had freed him in 1641, and he seems to have worked for him as a journeyman until his succession. This proved to be short-lived, for Levis, his wife and daughter died within a week during 1665, the plague year, leaving debts from four printers, among them the younger John Grismond. He was followed by another Fifield apprentice, Godfrey Head, who had been freed by Levis in 1658 and had probably worked for him, as he did for Fifield. Next year, like so many in the London trade, his premises were destroyed by the Great Fire. Typefounders' tools were portable, and St Andrew's had a day's notice of the fire, so his losses were probably not great. But the disruption to the whole commercial life of the City was great; the typefounders were generally in no position to supply Fell's needs, had he been more willing. It may have been to resolve this confusion that the court of the Stationers' Company resolved on 5 May 1668 to certify to the Archbishop of Canterbury, as required by the Star Chamber Decree and the 1662 Act, that Thomas Goring was 'fit to be one of the four present founders, there being one now wanting'.[51] What constituted this vacancy is hard to say, since there was in theory a superfluity.[52] The original founders were represented by Head, Goring, Nicholls and Grover (the last two perhaps regarded as a single business), to whom had recently been added the name of Joseph Leigh.

49 BL, Add. MS. 22905, fol. 81.
50 Lynam 1924; Maddison 1958; Mores 1961, pp. 32, 98; McGuinne, 1992, pp. 51–63.
51 Reed 1952, p. 186.
52 It may have been nominally created by the final retirement of Jane Goring.

Leigh is an exceptional figure; born in 1626, the son of the bookseller William Lee, he was freed by patrimony in 1649, and is described as a 'primer binder' when he bound apprentices, one of whom became a binder. His publications in the early 1660s give his address as in Basinghall Street, far from the other founders, from which he too must have been burnt out. He was certainly regarded as a typefounder in 1669, when the Company enjoined 'Mr Joseph Lee and Mr Goring to give at the next Court an account in writing, what sorts of letter they have made, and for whom, since the Act of Parliament in that case was provided.'[53] Only a year before, on 17 October 1668, the delegates of the Oxford University Press agreed to pay him 'in order to a fount of Greek and Latin Letters', and between then and 1672 he received some £300 for type supplied before Fell made the Press self-sufficient. Treadwell shrewdly suggests that he was not so much a professional founder as an entrepreneur who saw the commercial opportunity in re-equipping printers who had lost all by setting up a partnership with two of the other three founders. Together with Head and Goring he signed a petition to the Lord Mayor in 1672 that in view of the shortage of labour due to the 'late visitation' they may be allowed still to employ 'Journeymen Foreigners', that is, not free of the Company.[54] In January 1678 the inventory *post mortem* of the printer Andrew Clarke reveals a debt of £52 15*s.* 10*d.* to 'Mr Leigh and partners, founders', and the 1678 Poll Tax returns show all three men, plus Leigh's maid and lodgers, Goring's wife, three children, maid and apprentice, and Head's wife, two children and two apprentices, all occupying the same premises in the fourth precinct of St Botolph Aldersgate.

If Leigh was the catalyst of a restructuring of the London typefoundries that prefigured their subsequent concentration, it left out what had become the largest and most substantial, the foundry that had passed from the Nicholls family to Thomas Grover I, and then situated in Angel Alley, Aldersgate Street. The foundry must by then have owned the largest collection of different matrices, mainly ancient but some from the hands of Arthur and Nicholas Nicholls. It is probable that the elder Grover was apprenticed to Nicholas Nicholls in about 1650, since he was signing receipts for him by 1652.[55] When he apprenticed his son, Thomas Grover II, to the bookseller and printer Andrew Crooke on 3 April 1671, he was described in the Stationers' Register as 'of St Gyles Cripplegate, Founder'. When Grover died in 1675, leaving a list of debtors owing more than £1,200, including the King's Printing House at the huge sum of 'more or less £500', the total of twenty debtors was more than half of all the London

53 Reed 1952, p. 186. 54 Morison 1931, p. 20.
55 Oxford University Archives, SEP, P17b (3); Mores 1961, p. 44n.

printers, the same proportion as those listed in Adams's will. After 1675, the foundry was run by Grover's widow Cassandra until about 1680, when her son, the younger Thomas, took over until his death in 1710. The inventory of Thomas Grover II's goods, valued at £587, included 9,067 matrices, sixty-six moulds and a quantity of metal; accounts receivable added only £604 more, with debts at £103. The debtors included twenty of the seventy-odd London printers, plus six provincial printers. The reduced sum and smaller proportion of the printers' debts suggests some decline in the business.[56]

It is likely, however, that there had been an important division earlier, perhaps at Thomas Grover I's death. Nothing is known about the early career of Robert Andrews, until he was made free of the Stationers' Company in 1676, perhaps by translation from another company. But he had a connection with the Grover family, since he married Mary, daughter of Andrew Crooke (to whom Thomas Grover II was apprenticed), and half-sister of Thomas Grover I's wife Cassandra.[57] He was already married and living in the parish of St Bartholomew the Less in 1674, and was in a sufficient way of business by 1677 to be owed £47 by Thomas Roycroft at Roycroft's death that year. He stayed there until 1682, probably moving then to Charterhouse Street where he remained for the rest of his career. One of his sons, Silvester Andrews, became founder at the Oxford University Press, and another went into the Church. He was the first founder to be chosen one of the court of assistants of the Stationers' Company, and was elected master in 1709, although he pleaded indisposition and did not serve. He retired in 1733, when his foundry and his son's were bought by Thomas James, and died on 27 November 1735 at Ockham, where his son Benjamin was rector.

Both the Grover and Andrews foundries were ultimately acquired by the James foundry, and when Rowe Mores came to write his *Dissertation*, he was able to draw on detailed catalogues of the equipment of both. These were not of his own compilation,[58] and clearly precede the sale catalogue and accompanying specimen of the James foundry.[59] Both are extensive and cover a large and equally divided proportion of the types, ancient and modern, learned and current, that ended up with the Jameses. It is at least possible that this division goes back to 1675, and that the inventories on which Rowe Mores drew were prepared then. Besides the large mass of old types that both had, they each had a share of the Polyglot types, with some more modern, both Dutch and local. Andrews acquired both Moxon's and Walpergen's equipment. Andrews

56 Treadwell 1980/1, pp. 44–7. 57 This was first noted by Michael Treadwell, 1982b.

58 He notes 'a mistake of the cataloguers'; see Mores 1961, pp. 45n, 123.

59 Rowe Mores dates the Andrews catalogue '1706' and the Grover '*circ.* 1700', although the latter is so little different from the 1725/8 inventory that it may be nearer that time.

and Grover were each responsible for an innovatory type. Andrews undertook the Anglo-Saxon for Elizabeth Elstob, for which Humfrey Wanley wrote the model and was dissatisfied with the engraver's work: 'when the alphabet came into the hands of the workman (who was but a blunderer), he could not imitate the fine and regular stroke of the pen; so that the letters are not only clumsy, but unlike the letters I drew'.[60] Grover had the Alexandrian Greek, for which the punches were cut, apparently by the hydrographer John Thornton, at the instance of Cambridge University.[61]

By 1700, there were effectively only three active typefoundries in London, Grover's, Andrews's and that which went back to Richard Adams. From at least 1673 the three partners, Godfrey Head, Joseph Leigh and Thomas Goring, worked together in the parish of St Botolph Aldersgate. In 1680 they moved to Bartholomew Close; Goring died later that year, Leigh in mid-1682, but Head continued on his own until his exclusion from the Stationers' Company in 1685 and death in 1689. His widow Mary carried on the business with the help of Luke Skinner, a journeyman who had been Goring's apprentice and then Head's. Her son Edward Head took over when he came of age in about 1700, and it may be that some crude but vigorous types that appear about this time come from this source;[62] he also seems to have been the agent for Jan Bus in Amsterdam, whose deliveries to the Cambridge University Press he supplemented.[63] After his early death in 1712 his mother resumed the foundry, until her own death in 1718. Luke Skinner stayed in charge for two more years, when the foundry passed (at a valuation of £209 5*s*.) to Robert Mitchell, a former apprentice of Thomas Grover II. Mitchell moved it to Jewin Street and afterwards to Cripplegate and Paul's Alley between Aldersgate and Red Cross Streets. He bound six apprentices, the first in 1721, but none was freed. The foundry was bought jointly by William Caslon and John James on 26 July 1739.

In 1710, the year that Thomas Grover II died, Thomas James, after serving his apprenticeship to Robert Andrews, made his journey to Holland, returning with about 3,500 new matrices bought from Johannes Rolu. This was a turning point in the history of typefounding in Britain. Cambridge had followed Oxford in equipping its University Press from Holland, including its master printer, Cornelius Crownfield, rather than a typefounder.[64] Jacob Tonson had also gone

60 Nichols 1812–20, I, p. 117.

61 The crucial document on this, in Bagford's extraordinary spelling, was discovered by D. F. McKenzie and printed as a postscript by Mores 1961, p. 123. Lane 1992, p. 129, corrects 'jenken' to 'senken'.

62 These are included in Mores 1961, pp. 98 and 100 (also in the 1713 Watson specimen).

63 McKenzie 1966, I, pp. 37–9, 402, 406, 410.

64 McKenzie 1966, I, pp. 54–6.

to Holland to buy type, paper and plates. James with his new Dutch matrices was an instant success. Of his rivals, the Andrews's business came to him, the Head foundry was in decline, and the Grover foundry in desuetude. It had continued under Grover's widow, but between 1719 and 1721 she disposed of its ownership, one half passing first to her elder daughter, another Cassandra, who had married the printer Hugh Meere in 1704, the other two years later to her daughter Elizabeth. Meere's death in 1723 left it without an active manager, and a German founder, Samuel Jalleson, was brought in, but the death of Cassandra Meere in 1725 precipitated another crisis.[65] In 1728 Thomas James and William Caslon jointly valued the foundry at £464 6*s.* 6*d.*, the latter offering to buy it. The daughter thought it undervalued and refused, and the foundry remained unused in the care of the Meeres' son-in-law, another printer, Richard Nutt, until 1758 when it finally passed to Thomas James's son John. The James foundry, first at Aldermanbury, then Town Ditch off Little Britain, was from 1719 in Bartholomew Close, premises with an adjoining foundry where Roycroft had printed the London Polyglot, in the heart of the founders' traditional territory.

If this establishment typified the beginning of a new dispensation, it also reflected immemorial practice. Typefounding might be a separate profession, but it had not yet achieved a trade structure independent of the printers it supplied. If most of the founders were free of the Stationers' Company and bound apprentices in it, some were not. Whereas in the printing trade the journeymen were constantly agitating to prevent masters from employing apprentices or other unfree labour, matters in the typefoundry were much laxer. Although masters bound apprentices roughly every three years, relatively few took their freedom. Indeed, in 1675 it was the masters who complained of the shortage of free labour, claiming that there were only two free journeymen in London. This seems to have been true: in the previous twenty-five years, only seven of eighteen apprentices were freed, and of them two had become masters and three had died. The labour needed can only have come from apprentices and 'foreigners', some of them genuinely from overseas. Others besides James went to Holland, too. Thomas Grover II, according to his father's will in 1675, though bound to a London bookseller, was in fact in Holland, learning about typefounding at the source, and Alexander Fifield made his will in 1657 because he was 'intending a voyage to Sea'. If printers did not, save in exceptional circumstances like Tonson's, do likewise, it was because it was cheaper as well as more convenient to buy the home product. Although the price at source

65 Treadwell 1980/1, pp. 48–9.

was about the same, duty and freight costs increased the cost of imported type; Edward Head was thus able to undercut the prices charged by Jan Bus for the same types supplied from Amsterdam.[66] Contraband, however, cannot be underestimated. Stam, whose stock Jacques Vallet acquired, did a notable trade in English Bibles, as did Joseph Athias, another typefounder; it may have been about this business that Nicholas Kis, the Hungarian punchcutter and printer, came to grief in London in the 1680s.[67]

In the century between Richard Adams and Thomas James, the number of printers trebled, while the number of presses went up by six times. This growth explains why an otherwise stagnant typefoundry survived so well. The schedules of debts owing and receivable attached to printers' and typefounders' wills reveal the extent of their mutual interdependence. The typefounders' stock, as reflected in the inventories printed by Rowe Mores and the sale catalogue of the James foundry and its specimen, shows how evenly divided were their resources. A rough count suggests that of about 130 types shown in the 1782 specimen,[68] forty-one stem from the joint Nicholls–Grover foundry, thirty-nine from Andrews, sixteen from James's purchase from Rolu, seven from what Rowe Mores called 'The *Polyglott* Foundery' (in fact, types from different sources, later dispersed among different foundries), five or six that passed to Mitchell from the Head foundry, with ten that even Rowe Mores was forced to style '*Anonymous*'.[69] If the typefounding business as a whole did not grow, it was for lack of competent engravers to supply new punches for new types that would have introduced a degree of competition between the founders, competition that would have stimulated growth. Thomas Grover II may have attempted to reach a new market in the series of court hand, 'Union Pearl' and scriptorial types, aimed at newsletters and legal forms (few of which now survive.[70] Although rough and ready in execution, these types have a rugged vitality, and may, like the Alexandrian Greek, have been cut by Thornton.[71] But these novelties did not alter the old-fashioned appearance of books and more conventional forms of print. It was the Dutch types imported by Tonson, the Cambridge University Press and William Bowyer, as well as those cast by Thomas James in the matrices that he brought back from his Dutch expedition, that brought about the transformation.

66 McKenzie 1966, I, pp. 37–9, 402, 406, 410. 67 Haimann 1983, pp. 29–30.

68 Identifiable, that is, in the inventories printed by Edward Rowe Mores, and compared with the sale catalogue and specimen of the James foundry.

69 Mores 1961, p. 62.

70 These types appear in the James specimen, Mores 1961, pp. [16]–[18]. Their invention at the turn of the century was due to the pioneering interest of Ichabod Dawks, inherited by his former apprentice, Hugh Meere. See Morrison 1931, pp. 19–24, and Treadwell 1980/1, pp. 48–9.

71 Lane, 1992.

Thomas Marshall had realized, long before, what else was needed: 'I see, in this Printing-designe, we English must learn to use our own hands at last to cut Letters.' This finally came about one day, just about the time that Cassandra Grover was beginning to divest herself of her typefoundry, when William Bowyer

> accidentally saw in the shop of Mr Daniel Browne, bookseller, near Temple-Bar, the lettering of a book uncommonly neat; and inquiring who the artist was by whom the letters were made, Mr Caslon was introduced to his acquaintance, and was taken by him to Mr James's foundery in Bartholomew Close. Caslon had never before that time seen any part of the business; and being asked by his friend if he thought he could undertake to cut types, he requested a single day to consider the matter, and then replied he had no doubt but he could. From this answer Mr Bowyer lent him 200*l.* Mr Bettenham lent him the same sum, and Mr Watts 100*l.* and by that assistance our ingenious artist applied himself assiduously to his new pursuit, and was eminently successful. The three printers above mentioned were of course his constant customers.[72]

So James paid the penalty for his success. It was not benevolent appreciation of art, but a desire for competition rather than near monopoly in the supply of type, that induced the three printers to invest the huge sum of £500 in an outsider.[73] That they did also shows how fragile and hand-to-mouth this part of the trade still was. William Caslon took a significant step to change that too in 1720 when, the Society for Promoting Christian Knowledge having invited him to cut an Arabic type, he 'after he had finished his *Arab.* Fount cut the letters of his own name in *pica Rom.* and placed the name at the bottom of the spec.' To Rowe Mores this was a landmark in letter-cutting in this country, 'in which art *Mr Casl.* arrived to that perfection that we may without fear of contradiction assert that a fairer specimen than his cannot be found in *Europe*; that is, *Not in the world*'.[74]

NOTE

This account owes much to the work of Harry Carter and Michael Treadwell, either of whom would have better rendered it. It also depends on Talbot Baines Reed's *History of the old English Letter foundries* (1887), as edited by A. F. Johnson (1952). This is supplemented, and in places corrected, by the edition of Edward Rowe Mores's *Dissertation upon English typographical founders and founderies* by Harry Carter and Christopher

72 Nichols 1812–20, II, p. 720.

73 Treadwell recognized the importance of this episode, reinforced for me by James Mosley.

74 Mores 1961, p. 60.

Ricks (1961). Michael Treadwell's unpublished paper 'Notes on London typefounders 1620–1720', delivered in July 1982 to the Printing Historical Society in Oxford, is a mine of new information, mainly drawn from archival sources at the Stationers' Company and from printers' and typefounders' wills. It is as yet unpublished and I am deeply grateful to Florence Treadwell and Robin Myers, Archivist to the Stationers' Company, for making it available to me. I must also thank James Mosley and John Lane (to whom I owe many useful suggestions, based on his own work in Dutch archives and observation of contemporary English printing) for their advice and help.

30
Bookbinding

MIRJAM M. FOOT

On Christmas day 1534 an Act came into effect which finally brought to an end the privileged position that the alien members of the book trade had occupied since 1484.[1] Immigrant binders who had made an invaluable contribution to English binding and tool design and who had even left their mark on the way books were constructed were gradually prevented by ever more repressive regulations from carrying out their business freely and the importation for the purpose of re-sale of books bound abroad, hitherto such an enriching feature of the English book trade, was forbidden.

The incorporation of the Stationers' Company in 1557 virtually closed the book trade to foreign competition and made the position of a foreign craftsman who was not a denizen practically untenable. Nevertheless, as we shall see, foreign influences on binding and book design continued and a number of French Huguenot immigrants worked in London as bookbinders, and indeed so successfully that in 1578 the native binders demanded that no work should be given to 'forens or strangers' and that 'ffrenchmen and straungers beinge Denizens maie not haue excessiue nomber of app[re]ntic[es]'.[2] It is striking that, notwithstanding all attempts by the Stationers' Company and by the native members of the trade to keep foreign competition firmly under control, the most successful and most beautifully decorated bookbindings produced during the reign of Queen Elizabeth I were either made by French Huguenot immigrants or much influenced by French taste in design, while even the period after the Restoration, the golden age of English decorated bookbinding, owes a certain amount to those decorative techniques and styles that were the prevailing fashion in France several decades earlier.

1 A proviso added to an Act of January 1484 exempted the members of the book trade from restrictions under which foreigners could carry out business or trade in England. Duff 1905, pp. xi–xii; Foot 1993, pp. 146–50.

2 Greg and Boswell 1930, p. 4.

Foreign influences on the construction of English bindings are much harder to discern. Indeed the changes that can be observed in the materials, structures and work practices during the period from 1557 to 1695 are perhaps less immediately apparent and dramatic than those that took place during the decades that followed the introduction of printing into England. From the first quarter of the sixteenth century cheaper materials and less time-consuming structures were used to speed up production and to cut cost.[3] This tendency continued during the period under discussion here, and indeed throughout the history of hand binding. As the production of books increased and their readership grew and widened, binders adapted their work practices to cope with the ever larger number of books that needed binding but also with the demand for cheaper bound books.

At a time when the majority of books were still for sale in sheets, to be bound on demand of the purchaser either through the agency of the bookseller or by the new owner's chosen binder, we find the emergence of books apparently sold already sewn and provided with endleaves, sometimes with a wrapper to hold the sheets together and prevent loss or damage during transport or in the shop, but still awaiting the future owner's decision on a permanent binding.[4] At the same time the use of cheaper materials and simpler structures resulted in a cheaper end product. By 1550 pasteboard had become the usual material for boards, while pulpboards, made from edge trimmings and other off-cuts or from old or waste paper, 'ground in a mill to a pap'[5] may have been even cheaper to produce. In Oxford and in Scotland [6] wooden boards were still in use late in the sixteenth century, witness Thomas Thresham, writing in February 1597/8 to Dr Case, an ex-fellow of St John's College, about binding library books, 'wheather in wad [wood] or in paste bords I preferr the past bords, if they be such dooble past bords as we receaue from Paris binding'.[7]

Cheaper covering leathers included vellum and sheepskin, although in the mid-sixteenth century the Stationers' Company tried to legislate against the use of sheepskin on large or inappropriate books.[8] Limp vellum, omitting boards altogether, made its appearance on printed books[9] and became popular, mainly for books for retail during the sixteenth and seventeenth centuries. It was

3 Foot 1999. For what follows I am indebted to Pickwoad 1994 and Middleton 1996. Some is based on my own observation. Pollard 1956, although by now in part overtaken by later research, is still useful.

4 Pickwoad 1994, pp. 63–70. 5 Davenport 1902–4, p. 12. 6 Mitchell 1955, p. 66.

7 Ker 1959, p. 515. 8 Pickwoad 1994, p. 102, n. 42.

9 It was used for account books from the fourteenth century onwards and was used for printed books, first in Italy, from the early sixteenth century.

sometimes used for presentation bindings, probably commissioned by those whose purse was not deep enough to command the more expensive calf or goat.[10]

Paper was used instead of vellum for endleaves, while linen, vellum or leather ties replaced clasps, especially on smaller formats. According to Thresham apparently not only on grounds of cost, 'many make election of stringing then of clasping, in regard of avoyding the anoy of Rushing as in respect of reddylyer repayring them'.[11]

The cost of leather was considerable, witness 'A Peticion of severall Bookbinders', presented to the Master, Wardens and Assistants of the Stationers' Company at a Court meeting held on 4 March 1694/5 in which they complained of 'the lowe condition they were brought to by the lownesse of prices and dearness of Lether'.[12] The more expensive leathers, such as calf which could be sprinkled or – rarely – marbled and goatskin, were used for the more luxurious bindings, goatskin gradually becoming the norm during the Restoration period. Marbled paper was employed for endleaves in fine bindings from the middle of the seventeenth century; rope-fibre millboard was first used for fine work in the late seventeenth century, while clasps remained in use on heavy bindings in large formats, but also on smaller decorated or textile bindings on Bibles and prayer books.

The increase in book production and growing demand spurred the binders on. Sewing on single thongs and – later in the sixteenth century – on single cords took less time than the more elaborate sewing structures that were the norm for medieval bindings. Economies, such as the use of fewer sewing supports, sewing more than one section at a time and sewing on recessed or sawn-in supports, emerge and become widely used towards the end of the sixteenth and early in the seventeenth century.[13] This last practice saved time as the sewing thread could be passed over the cord instead of being wrapped round it. Stabbing or stitching through the inner margins of the book was the cheapest form of sewing of all and one that the Stationers' Company thought fit to limit to certain prescribed numbers of sheets per format.[14] From a decree issued on 25 March 1586 it is clear that the practice of stitching, or stabbing, was a relatively new one, having most likely evolved in response to the ever greater number of especially thin books that flowed from the presses. Cheaper and quicker still was the attempt to hold the sheets together with adhesive only,

10 Foot 1997. 11 Ker 1959, p. 515. 'Rushing' probably for 'Rusting'.

12 Foot 1993, pp. 20–21; Stationers' Company Court Book F., fol. 218^{b}.

13 Many of these practices were already in use in France from the middle of the sixteenth century, but took longer to reach England.

14 Foxon 1975.

and Nicholas Pickwoad has identified a group of books dating from *c.* 1670–90 that were not sewn at all, but that were made to look like conventionally sewn books.[15] The same decades also show an increase in bindings sewn on recessed supports that have been given false bands and are thus pretending to be what they are not.

Fewer supports meant less work in lacing them into the boards, while from the end of the sixteenth century onwards we find bindings where only some of the supports have been laced in, the rest having been cut off. The cores of endbands were also no longer laced in as a matter of course and other ways of cutting costs in the sewing of endbands evolved. Single cores, usually made of leather or vellum, and from the early seventeenth century of rolled up paper, were oversewn with linen or for the more expensive work with silk thread in one or more (usually two) colours, frequently worked with a bead, but no longer tied down into every section, while on the cheaper bindings they disappeared altogether. They continued to be used on fine bindings, sometimes sewn in two or more coloured silks over double cores, almost always with a bead, gradually becoming a decorative rather than a structural element. Stuck-on endbands, as found in Germany from the end of the fifteenth century, appear not to have been much used in England, although they are found occasionally at the end of the sixteenth and early in the seventeenth century. It is doubtful whether they represented an economy measure as they were quite cumbrous to produce.

Endleaves could be as simple or as elaborate as the binder had time or the owner money for. Although paper endleaves had become the norm, we still find parchment or vellum manuscript pastedowns in decorated bindings in Cambridge and Oxford until the last quarter of the sixteenth century or even a little later. The use of printers' waste as endleaves was still quite common in the sixteenth century, while from the end of the century the habit of re-enforcing endleaves gradually disappeared. White paper, folded and sewn through the fold or hooked over the edge of the first and last sections, leaving a stub, is found most frequently. The earliest English binding with marbled endpapers was made by Samuel Mearne for Cor. Pigeon in 1655;[16] one-and-a-half decades later it was commonly used for fine bindings, the marbled paper frequently backed with a white sheet, thereby hiding the sewing thread. Sometimes several pieces of marbled paper were used to make up the endpapers showing that, as much decorated paper was imported and fairly expensive, binders had to practise economy by making the most of every scrap.

15 Pickwoad 1994, p. 91; Pickwoad 1996.
16 Nixon 1974, p. 12, no. 1, first noticed by Pollard 1956, p. 79.

Although the practice of covering the backs of the sections with glue before rounding and backing the spine to give the book its shape was introduced early in the sixteenth century, it was still quite common until late in the seventeenth century to leave the spine unglued. As before, spines could be lined to give extra strength. Textile was sometimes used, especially for larger books, and still occasionally during the seventeenth century we find vellum used for lining the spine panels.

Over the centuries owners have been concerned about the width of the margins of their books and their binders' habit to trim the edges. Sir Robert Cotton frequently exhorted his binders to 'cut it as litle on the head as you can' or to 'set it even at the head because it shall nott be cut', or to 'cut it with car[e] for you cut the last Books to[o] much'. *Per contra* he sometimes asked the binder to 'cutt the Book small' or to 'cut it smo[o]th'.[17] Edges were probably trimmed (with a plough) before the boards were attached. They could also be coloured. Plain edges were the norm for cheap books, but staining in red or yellow, sprinkling in one colour, or occasionally marbling appear not to have been a great luxury, although gilt, gilt and gauffered, and painted edges were. Like so many decorative but also structural features, fashions in edge decoration moved from Italy to France and thence to England and an early description of edge gilding in English came from the Italian via the French.[18] Gauffering (tooling) on a gilt edge was usually done with pointillé tools (tools with a dotted outline) or with single dots and the design could be further embellished with paint. This technique, as well as painting underneath the gold, both dating back to *c.* 1650, added extra lustre to the fine and lavishly decorated bindings produced during the Restoration period. Marbling the edges underneath the gold was tried by the Queen's Binder A *c.* 1675–80.[19]

In 1597/8 Tresham considered a diversity of coloured edges to be one of the ways of distinguishing between books, which suggests that – in Oxford at least – books were shelved with the fore-edge outwards. The earliest known gold-tooled spine title was produced by Williamson of Eton in 1604, although decorating the spines of fine bindings with gold tooling had already become a regular feature by the mid-sixteenth century. Written spine titles continued during the early seventeenth century, but by *c.* 1660 tooled titles had become

17 Quotes from instructions on pastedowns or endleaves of the following manuscripts: B.L. Cotton MSS. Julius F. VI, fol. 315^{v}; Vespasianus E. III; Julius D. II; Titus A. XV, fol. 305^{v}; Domitian 1; Nero D. VII; see also Vitellius D. IX.

18 Alessio Piemontese, *The secretes of the reverend maister Alexis of Piemount*, London,1558–69, part 1 (1558), fol. 96.

19 Nixon 1984, no. 2073, plate 42.

common, while lettering pieces occurred sporadically during the late 1660s and 70s and then more often in the 1680s and 90s.

The subjects of edge decoration and spine titles have taken us firmly from the cheaper mass market into the realms of presentation bindings and collectors' items. The history of decorated bookbinding in England has been told elsewhere[20] in greater detail, but it should be noted that the period 1557–1695 encompasses the two brightest manifestations of English bookbinding, that which exploited the technique of gold-tooling during the reign of Queen Elizabeth I, albeit much influenced by French design fashions, and that which combined gold tooling with onlays and paint during the time immediately preceding and following the Restoration.

Decorative techniques that were already much in use during the early part of the sixteenth century continued to be employed. Tooling in blind, either with rolls, fillets, small hand tools or with larger corner and centre blocks carried on throughout the seventeenth century and well into the eighteenth. Gold tooling, already practised with success since the reign of Henry VIII, reached new heights of beauty, especially when the finely-cut solid and hatched tools, introduced from France, were used to produce the French-inspired interlace designs, but also, to good effect, in combination with larger corner and centre blocks. Huguenot immigrant binders such as Jean de Planche and the Morocco binder employed such tools in London in the 1560s and their best presentation bindings in gold-tooled calf stand comparison with those made in Paris for the famous collectors of the day (plate 30.1).

Pronounced corner and centre blocks were also used to produce heavier designs found both on plainer and on more luxurious bindings, in blind but also in gold, sometimes enhanced with coloured paint.[21] Other standard designs were carried out both in blind and in gold. 'Ovills' (oval centre blocks), 'rolles', 'fillets', 'corners' (corner blocks), 'gilt over' (all-over decoration in gold, probably with a block), 'chequer' (another way of producing an all-over design with the repeated impression of one or two small tools), and 'smale tooles ordinary' were all so common that they featured as standard decorative styles in lists of prices agreed by the bookbinders at various points during the seventeenth century.[22] These prices refer to trade work, rather than to one-off collectors' items.

The more lavish panel, fanfare, all-over, and cottage-roof designs of the Restoration period were produced in gold with small solid and dotted (pointillé)

20 Nixon and Foot 1992 (and literature quoted there).

21 Matthew Parker's binder, the MacDurnan Gospels binder, the Dudley binder and Bateman are but a few who used such designs; see Nixon and Foot 1992.

22 Foot 1993, pp. 15–67.

tools, the latter copied from French examples and probably first employed in the 1640s in Cambridge by John Houlden. Paint could be added to provide even more colour or to give emphasis to the design,

The technique of laying small, thinly pared pieces of leather either on top, or in compartments previously cut out of the cover leather was brought to England, also from France, during the reign of Queen Elizabeth I. Such onlays were particularly fashionable during the second half of the seventeenth century, already very skilfully and effectively used during Cromwell's Protectorate by binders such as the Lewis brothers and Henry Evans, but even more widely employed to enhance the cottage-roof style and to create mosaic designs following the Restoration.[23]

A technique whereby small pieces were cut out of the leather or vellum to display a lining of differently coloured silk underneath, rarely found in England, was used to cover copies of the letters and petitions of Lady Arabella Stuart written during her imprisonment in the Tower and addressed to the King, the Queen, the privy council and influential nobles, praying for her release. However, her prayers went unanswered as she died imprisoned in 1615.

Textiles and embroidery played an important role in the covering and decoration of books during the Tudor and Stuart periods. Elizabeth I is said to have preferred velvet,[24] and particularly prayer books and Bibles for private use produced during her reign and that of her successor were bound in velvet, canvas or silk, embroidered with gold and silver threads and coloured silks to a whole range of designs, varying from the conventional floral patterns and the depiction of virtues, to portraits and biblical scenes. Many were worked by professional embroiderers, some by amateur needle women, many were made for women, but by no means exclusively so.[25] Velvet could also be tooled in gold, albeit at some risk of scorching, as Daniel Boyse in Cambridge and the members of the Little Gidding lay-religious community demonstrated.[26] Canvas as a basis for embroidery seems to have disappeared at the beginning of the seventeenth century and no examples of plain canvas for cheaper retail bindings have survived – if indeed they existed before the 1760s.[27] The cheap material used instead was paper, limp or over boards, plain or decorated. A seventeenth-century publishers' binding of paper decorated with a woodblock

23 Nixon 1974; Nixon and Foot 1992.

24 P. Hentzner, *Itinerarium Germaniae*; *Galliae*; *Angliae*; *Italiae*; *etc.* (Nuremberg, 1612). The part relating to Hentzner's visit to England was translated by Richard Bentley, *A journey into England in the year 1598* (Strawberry Hill, 1757); see p. 31.

25 Davenport 1899; Foot 1986.

26 Nixon and Foot 1992, pp. 53–4, pl. 4.

27 Middleton 1996, pp. 132, 293, Pickwoad 1994, p. 89.

survives at Lambeth Palace,[28] while quarter bindings with sides of decorated paper were introduced at the very end of the period under discussion. Samuel Pepys was probably the first English collector to commission them and in his library at Magdalene College, Cambridge are a dozen quarter-leather bindings with tooled spines and either marbled or Dutch-gilt paper sides, over boards.[29] The use of marbled or Dutch-gilt paper for limp wrappers, often for pamphlets, music books, sermons or plays, also started at the end of the seventeenth century.

The questions whether and how much owners and collectors of bindings influenced the final products, how narrowly they specified both structure and decoration, and to what extent they influenced design fashions, are hard to answer. Owners of bindings can be categorized into those who bought the book for the text, those who commissioned bindings either for themselves or for presentation to others, and those who were largely on the receiving end. Scholars were probably as a rule less concerned with the physical appearance of their books, though they may have had specific wishes regarding the solidity of their structures. They are more likely either to have bought their books already bound or to have had them bound in one of the standard styles through the intermediacy of the booksellers. The lists of prices agreed between the bookbinders and booksellers of London, Westminster and Dublin for binding specific kinds of books in certain ways[30] show not only what these standard styles were, but also what kind of books, which titles even, were considered popular enough to be sold bound. Bibles, prayer books and other religious texts, classical authors, law books and history remain popular throughout the seventeenth century, but towards the middle of the century atlases, dictionaries, grammars, books on mathematics, and herbals demonstrate a widening of subjects towards the more practical side of education, while travel books, school books and reference books, humanist writers (now apparently appealing to a wider circle of readers) and translations of classical authors indicate a further widening of the reading public during the second half of the century.

Some scholars and students obviously appreciated not only the intellectual stimulus provided by their chosen text but also the aesthetic satisfaction derived from their luxurious and glittering exterior. Some may have considered a library of gold-tooled and onlaid calf and morocco suited their social position. Many owners had their bindings decorated with their armorial bearings, either simply or with the addition of some or a great deal of gold tooling. Robert Dudley, Earl

28 Foot 1993, pp. 286–7. For a tooled paper binding see Pickwoad 1994, p. 89, fig. 15.

29 Nixon 1984, p. xxi; Foot 1993, pp. 288–9.

30 Foot 1993, pp. 15–67.

of Leicester, favourite of Queen Elizabeth, was such a scholar–collector. He was well educated, probably knew Greek, Latin and Italian and was interested in mathematics as well as in classics and history. He was a patron and friend to many authors and a large number of books were dedicated to him. He owned a sizeable library and had most of his bindings decorated with his badge, showing his crest of a bear with a crescent on its shoulder holding a ragged staff, as well as a few with his coat of arms. In addition to that, the binders whom he patronized added simple frames and small fleurons, or more lavish patterns composed of gouges, interlacing fillets and finely cut solid and hatched tools, some of distinctly French appearance.[31] In particular the so-called Dudley binder, who also bound for Henry Fitzalan, twelfth Earl of Arundel and Edward Seymour, Earl of Hertford and who worked in the late 1550s, and early 1560s, used hatched tools that show a distinct similarity to those employed in Paris by Grolier's last binder. Likewise the Morocco binder, possibly a Huguenot immigrant active until at least 1576, demonstrated an admirable capacity for free-hand tooling using tools and designs reminiscent of work carried out in Paris in the 1550s and 60s. As well as for Robert Dudley, the Morocco binder also worked for his elder brother Ambrose, Earl of Warwick, for Sir Ronald Haywarde, Lord Mayor of London, for John Whitgift, Archbishop of Canterbury and his predecessor, Archbishop Matthew Parker. The latter stands out as a binding patron among his contemporaries. Not only did he on occasion provide work for almost all the best London shops of his time, among whom the MacDuman Gospels binder was one of the most consistently patronized, he also employed in his palace at Lambeth his private binders who made the standard bindings for Parker's library decorated with his coat of arms, as well as from time to time the more splendidly tooled presentation bindings.

Among the scholar–collectors of the seventeenth century Sir Robert Bruce Cotton takes an important place.[32] He showed a demonstrable interest both in the structural and the decorative aspects of his bindings, although the latter remained fairly modest. Sir Thomas Egerton, Viscount Brackley was the founder of one of the great English family libraries, later extended by his son, the first Earl of Bridgewater. A splendidly bound Saxton Atlas (1574) in gold-tooled black goatskin has large corner blocks, a sprinkling of small tools and Thomas Egerton's crest.[33] Other collectors of the first half of the seventeenth century who had their crest or coat of arms tooled on their bindings, such as Sir Christopher Hatton, Francis Bacon, Lord Verulam and Viscount St Albans,

31 E.g. the Dudley binder, the Morocco binder and the Clemens Alexandrinus binder; see Foot 1978–83, I, pp. 27–34; Nixon and Foot 1992, pp. 34–9.

32 Tite 1994; Foot 1996, pp. 37–8.

33 Nixon and Foot 1992, fig. 38.

George Villiers, Marquis and later Duke of Buckingham, may have been on the receiving as well as on the commissioning end of the chain, and so was Frances, Duchess of Richmond and Lennox, whose arms occur on the dedication copy of Captain John Smith's *Generall history of Virginia* (London, 1624).[34]

A comparatively short-lived phenomenon and one that would have appealed to those collectors who were also avid readers and who travelled a great deal, was the travelling library: a large, book-shaped box, containing rows of small vellum- or leather-bound books on a variety of subjects. Sir Thomas Egerton owned one, and so did Sir Julius Caesar, Master of the Rolls, William Hakewill presented one, possibly to John Madden Esq (attorney to James I), one was owned by a member of the Bacon family, both Prince Henry and Prince Charles owned travelling libraries, and a slightly later example belonged to a member of the Fountaine family.[35]

As we have seen, commissioners of bindings did so not only for themselves, but also to give pleasure to friends and relations or to encourage generosity in others. In the days when authorship was largely an unpaid profession, presenting one's book to a powerful patron might have been one way to secure a living. Lord Herbert of Cherbury was one of those authors who believed that a sparkling exterior would reflect well on its contents and would attract the royal patronage and scholarly recognition he craved. William Blake tried to solicit contributions for his school 'for Poor, or Fatherless Children' through issuing specially bound and decorated copies of his *Silver drops, or serious things* (*c.* 1670) to subscribers.

It was by no means unusual for publishers or editors to dedicate and present their works in fine bindings to a potential patron, and among those who were at the receiving end of such largesse was Samuel Pepys.[36] The University of Cambridge published topical verse marking suitable occasions in the life of the royal family and presented them in a range of special bindings, probably motivated by the wish to honour the king, queen or other members of the court, as well as to show political awareness and to stimulate the same among the dons. The Audit Book and the Voucher Accounts of Cambridge University contain bills for the binding of twelve such publications between 1603 and 1640. From these bills it is clear that the most elaborately bound copies were for presentation to the royal family (plate 30.2). The practice continued well into the eighteenth century.[37]

34 For illustrations of these see *Fine bindings 1500–1700 from Oxford libraries* (Oxford, 1968), nos. 131, 135, 137, 140.
35 Nixon and Jackson 1979; Nixon and Foot 1992, pp. 48–51.
36 Nixon 1984; Foot 1996, pp. 38–9. 37 Foot 1978–83, I, pp. 59–75.

Bindings as gifts, whether for gain, politically motivated, or out of friendship or generosity, reflect in the style and elaboration of their decoration not only the donor but also the recipient. Some of the most lavish products of the top craftsmen's workshops ended up on the tables and shelves of the royal libraries. Some kings and queens were demonstrably more interested in books than others,[38] but without exception all were recipients of bindings as welcome gifts. Henry, Prince of Wales was a studious prince, his personal library a mixture of the humanistic and the scientific, including not only the schoolboy classics in Latin and Greek, but also post-classical Latin and Greek authors. He owned the standard legal texts but also those by modern political thinkers. He read modern as well as classical history, books on travel, modern literature including French and Italian poets, works by German Protestant writers, and studied philosophy, geography and navigation, mathematics and mathematical theory, astronomy, engineering, military science and warfare. He possessed books on tournaments and the martial arts, as well as books on fencing and gymnastics, in short a wide-ranging, broad-based library, providing an excellent education for a Renaissance prince. The books occur in rather plain bindings of brown calf tooled in gold with the prince's coat of arms and his insignia, which nearly all seem to date from around 1610. But he also owned a few more elaborate bindings which were presumably presented to him and do not form part of the standard library. Charles I was more interested in pictures than in books, but he too owned a library bound in standard styles with a number of variants of the Stuart royal arms in the centre.[39] Charles II seems to have taken a keen interest in books and was fortunate enough to be able to employ the best English seventeenth-century binder, Samuel Mearne, who made both the standard bindings for the royal library and the lavishly decorated bindings for the king's own use which remain amongst the finest ever produced in England. He also bound for the court, for ambassadors for the Order of the Garter, and made a range of presentation bindings all of which have been well documented elsewhere.[40] Perhaps it is worth pointing out here that this most English of binders was from time to time clearly influenced by past French styles and designs, employing finely cut solid curl and pointillé tools, built-up feathery curving leafy branches, and – most strikingly – using the fanfare ribbon, developed in France a century earlier, to create both the indigenous cottage-roof style but also French-inspired all-over and mosaic designs (plate 30.3).

It is all too easy to imagine the fine binding trade during the Restoration period as centred in London, but finely tooled bindings were also produced in

38 Birrell 1986; Nixon and Foot 1992. 39 Foot 1984. 40 Nixon 1974; Nixon and Foot 1992.

Oxford and Cambridge and it is in the latter that John Houlden first introduced the new tools, copied from France, that were to become such a prominent feature during the second half of the seventeenth century.

The end of the century saw a few changes. The cottage-roof style gradually disappeared to be replaced largely by designs composed of concentric panels; a short-lived fashion emerged for service books and other pious works in blind-tooled black goatskin often with black edges; and half and quarter-leather bindings made their first appearance. The best-known collector of this period, one who both commissioned bindings for his library, bought books 'for the love of the binding', and received fine bindings as presents in the course of his distinguished civil service career was Samuel Pepys. His library is discussed in detail by the late H. M. Nixon[41] and in his own diary, but also the books themselves bear witness to his involvement in their bindings, his relationship with his binders and the interest he took in their craft.[42]

More and more people outside the educated élite learned to read; translations of the classics became popular enough to be offered for sale already bound, and so did more secular titles, more dictionaries and grammars. Nevertheless, the last bookbinders' price list of our period, that published in London in 1695, does not show any new binding styles nor the striking explosion of subjects and the clearly visible expansion of readership that took place during the next century.

41 Nixon 1984. 42 Foot 1996, pp. 38–9.

31

Mise-en-page, illustration, expressive form

INTRODUCTION

MAUREEN BELL

The study of the printed page as expressive form is a relatively recent development. The case studies presented here indicate, albeit briefly, something of the rich potential of such a study and draw attention to the physicality of the book as an agent in shaping the meaning and interpretation of text. The material form by which text reaches reader – and written texts can scarcely exist apart from their embodiment in material form[1] – is necessarily historically specific, constrained by the currently available technologies of paper, ink, print, illustration and binding. But it is also historically specific in its participation in, imitation of, or challenge to a set of typographical conventions shared and understood by the text's producers, buyers and readers.

All aspects of the text's physical form are capable of constituting meaning. Choices of paper, format, type, ornament, illustration, binding and page layout were made by one or more agents, singly or collaboratively: author, compositor, printer, publisher, editor and (especially in the case of bindings) buyer and reader. Such choices were necessarily constrained by local economic circumstances. In his study of the Cambridge University Press, for example, David McKitterick notes that the 'cramped effect, of small sizes of type occupying as much of the page as possible' of much seventeenth-century Cambridge printing was due to the 'penny-pinching' of its printers; and that the 1629 Cambridge Bible 'embodied a series of typographical decisions whose principal intention was . . . to economize within a framework established by convention.'[2] Such economies were typical of an undercapitalized English trade whose staple income came from small-format books (school books, ABCs, almanacs and prognostications) and an increasingly wide repertoire of ephemeral items

1 McKenzie 1977, pp. 81–125; Chartier 1989, pp. 154–75.
2 McKitterick 1992, p. 280.

(pamphlets, ballads, newsbooks and jobbing printing) which realized a quick return. Large and fine paper, larger formats and copperplate engravings are all indicators of deliberate and often risky investment, though not necessarily by the printer. The luxurious illustrated folios of the later seventeenth century, introduced by Ogilby's *Virgil* of 1654 and depending upon a new kind of sponsorship pioneered four years earlier by Thomas Fuller,[3] constituted a material form which is itself testimony to the commercial trade's residual need for patronage. An expensive object, the illustrated folio inscribed the cultural and social status of the buyer-sponsor whose names, arms and dedication appeared on the plate he financed.[4]

Whereas in the sixteenth century the woodcut, which could be set up in the same forme as type, was the usual method of supplying illustrations in books, during the seventeenth century the use of copperplate engravings quickly became the norm for pictorial title-pages (plates 16.1, 31.2), portraits of the author (plates 17.1, 31.4) and large illustrations. Woodcuts were increasingly relegated to cheap editions and books in which technical diagrams or stock ornaments were required (plate 23.3).[5] Tessa Watt has demonstrated the link between cheap woodcut pictures and the early seventeenth-century specialization of the ballad trade, and argues convincingly that 'in a partially literate society, the most influential media were those which combined print with non-literate forms.'[6] Series of plates designed for a specific book might have been sold as optional, and in some cases would also be sold separately as sets of decorative illustrations. The same plates might be re-used by the same or another publisher.[7] The arrangement of illustration and text on the page has particularly engaged the attention of scholars of emblem books.[8] By 1700 at least fifty books of emblems in more than 130 editions had been published in England, while numerous Continental-printed emblem books also circulated widely.[9] English printers, writers and readers interacted with their Continental counterparts: books produced by Continental printers were copied, translated and imitated in England; English emblematists were published abroad (such as

3 Fuller, *A Pisgah-sight of Palestine* (London, 1650); see Griffiths 1998, ch. 7.

4 See further Parry, pp. 183–8 above. The method of sponsorship lasted well into the eighteenth century, particularly for scientific publications (Griffiths 1998, p. 184).

5 Gaskell 1972, p. 154. 6 Watt 1991, p. 7.

7 See, for example, *STC* 11921.6 (*The nine woemen worthys*, London, *c.* 1635) and 13316 (*The exemplary lives and memorable acts of nine the most worthy women of the world*, London, 1640) in which the same set of engravings by Glover appear.

8 There is a vast literature on emblem books: see Daly and Silcox 1990. See also Watt 1991 for a detailed investigation of relationships between text and image in cheap print and ballads.

9 By comparison, more than a thousand Continental emblem books had been published by 1700 (Bath 1994, ch. 1 and appendix).

Whitney in Leiden, 1586; Hawkins in Rouen, 1633); and some English writers of emblems (like Willet and Farley) produced bilingual texts.[10] The dependence of the English trade on Continental models and skills is evident across the whole range of seventeenth-century printmaking, which relied heavily on the expertise of the Netherlands and, later, Paris. Wither's book of emblems, published in London in 1635, used plates previously published by the Antwerp engraver Crispijn de Passe in 1613, but cut down to remove the Latin text so that new verses by Wither could be supplied beneath in letterpress.[11] Although a separate technology from printing and therefore beyond the control of the Stationers' Company, printmaking increasingly contributed to the appearance of the printed book in the later seventeenth century and, notably during the Popish Plot and the Glorious Revolution, was combined with letterpress in satirical and topical broadsides.[12] Throughout the period, English publishers depended on Continental engravers and Continental plates (sometimes second-hand) and the English trade in prints was massively overshadowed by imported printed impressions. Only at the very end of the seventeenth century did an English printmaker, John Smith, establish an international reputation.[13]

Close reading of the meaning of the space of reading created by book and page, so far largely the province of scholars of emblem books, prints, ballads and broadsides in their attention to the juxtaposition of text and image, is now being extended to the non-illustrated book. Bibliographers, literary critics and theorists are investigating the materiality of the typographic text: both of the whole book and of the layout of the page itself. Walter Ong has drawn attention to the properties of the typographic text in contrast to the oral text;[14] more recently, Gérard Genette has established a taxonomy of paratextual features such as prefaces, dedications, title pages, running heads, tables of contents, marginal notes and footnotes;[15] and the hermeneutics of the footnote itself have been charted.[16] Recent critical editions of particular, mainly literary, works have

10 Bath 1994, p. 7; see also Daly 1988. Research on the ways in which sixteenth-century woodcuts were used, re-used and copied by generations of printers, having a cultural significance well beyond their printed form (for example in interior design, embroidery, architectural decoration, drama and public ceremony), is greatly facilitated by Luborsky and Ingram 1998. For a preliminary list of sets of seventeenth-century prints with similar subjects, see Griffiths 1998, appendix, pp. 307–13.

11 George Wither, *A collection of emblemes, ancient and moderne*; see Griffiths 1998, p. 18.

12 Griffiths 1998. For an account of the history of prints used for anti-Roman Catholic propaganda see O'Connell 1999, ch. 5.

13 Griffiths 1998, esp. pp. 239–43. The first English copperplate print publisher for whom catalogues survive is Peter Stent (Globe 1985).

14 Ong 1982. While Ong's view of the 'fixity' of print is put under pressure by more recent demonstrations of the *instability* of print, his relation of typographical space to the imagination and psychology of the reader remains influential.

15 Genette 1997. 16 Grafton 1997.

begun to investigate the meanings of page layout,[17] and interest amongst literary theorists in liminality and the 'marginal' has fuelled a re-evaluation of the literal margins of early modern texts by critics and textual editors.[18] The case studies which follow demonstrate how the details of physical form, from whole book to individual page, resonate with larger social, intellectual and political issues. The meaning of the early modern text inheres in its typographic expression (Campbell), the layout of the page (Barker) and the choice of type, which can be examined not only for its embodiment of textual structure and content but also for its embodiment of orality (Birrell). Format and paper alone can imply generic status (Love) and paratextual features such as prefaces construct the text's social position in a period when patronage and commercial structures existed side by side (Anderson). The combined effect of the many choices made by the producers of early modern books is thus to make permanently visible, and therefore in large part recoverable, an often complex negotiation of the text's meaning within the economic, social, political and cultural contexts and conventions current at its moment of production.

17 See, for example, D. F. McKenzie's forthcoming edition of the works of Congreve.
18 See, for example, Greetham 1997 and Tribble 1993.

❧

THE RHETORIC OF PARATEXT IN EARLY PRINTED BOOKS

RANDALL ANDERSON

> Euery booke hath his Fortune to the Capacity of his Reader; and haue mine in thee. Farewell, I could haue vsed a more mountebanque preface. But that which iudges trueth, labours least with shew.[1]

Sensitivity to the persuasive power of the ostensibly *extra*textual features of the book is hardly a novel concern of post-modern theorists.[2] Although he refers here to training in rhetoric, Francis Bacon is equally interested in the impact of such pre-emptive elements:

> Illae autem sunt, veluti Vestibula, Posticae, Ante-Camerae, Re-Camerae, Transitus, &c. Orationis; quae indiscriminatim omnibus Subiectis competere possint. Quales sunt *Praefationes*, *Conclusiones*, *Digressiones*, *Transitiones*, *Promissiones*, *Declinationes*, & plurima eiusmodi. Quemadmodùm enim in Ædificijs, plurimùm facit, & ad Voluptatem, & ad Vsum, vt Frontispicia, Gradus, Ostia, Fenestrae, Aditus, Transitus, & huiusmodi, commodè distribuantur; eodem modo, etiàm in Oratione fit, vt Additamenta & Interpositiones istae, (si decorè, & peritè formentur & collocentur) plurimum tum gratiae, tum commoditatis, vniversae Orationis Structurae adijciant.[3]

1 'To the Reader', *Lathams Falconry* (London, 1614).

2 For recent accounts, see Genette 1982 and 1997, Tribble 1993. See also Gebert 1933, Grierson and Wason 1946, and F. B. Williams 1962.

3 *De augmentis scientiarum* in *Opera* (London, 1623), sig. 2v4^r. (' I mean those parts of speech which answer to the vestibules, back doors, ante-chambers, withdrawing-chambers, passages, &c., of a house; and may serve indiscriminately for all subjects. Such are prefaces, conclusions, digressions, transitions, intimations of what is coming, excusations, and a number of the kind. For as in buildings it is a great matter both for pleasure and use that the fronts, doors, windows, approaches, passages, and the like be conveniently arranged, so also in a speech these accessory and interstitial passages (if they be handsomely and skilfully fashioned and placed) add a great deal both of ornament and effect to the whole structure', *The Works of Francis Bacon*, ed. J. Spedding, R. L. Ellis and D. D. Heath (London, 1883–92), IV, p. 492.)

Bacon's observations easily apply to the field of book production: the book-buyer harbours certain expectations of the first gathering, but these apparently peripheral features are more than merely self-indulgent ornamentation.

A preface is, literally, *prae-fatum:* that which is stated or mentioned before; that which establishes a premise. A further, important meaning of the root *fatum* – a prophetic declaration; destiny; that which is ordained – also prompts us to consider whether the operation of the preface in some measure *pre-determines* reading and response. The notion of a *premise* also invokes, phonemically, a kinship to *promise*, and suggests the ways in which a preface is also a kind of promise made with respect to future fulfilment if one reads on. In his letter 'To the Worshipfull John Stafford', Humfrey Gifford neatly captures this kinship: 'The only thing that I doubt of this in my dedication, is that your worshipp shall haue cause to account mee a deepe dissembler and one that hath byn more lauish in promise, then he is able to pay with performance.'[4] John Taylor later sets on its head the promise one might normally find in the preface:

> because I would not haue you either guld of your mony, or deceiued in expectation, I pray you take notice of my plaine dealing, for I haue not giuen my booke a swelling bumbasted title, of a promising inside of newes; therefore if you looke for any such matter from hence, take this warning hold fast your mony, and lay the booke down.

Taylor's consumer's advocacy stops there, however; before his opening paragraph ends he claims 'yet if you do buy it I dare presume you shall find somewhat in it worth part of your mony'.[5]

What happens, then, if we are deprived of the intended preface? For one opinion, we have the abuse Michael Drayton directs toward those 'Stationers, that . . . haue either despightfully left out, or at least carelessly neglected the Epistles to the Readers, and so haue cousoned the Buyers with vnperfected Bookes.'[6] For the author, at least, it appears that without these paratextual vestibules we cannot 'read' a text to its full profit, or that such reading is inherently defective or incomplete. Although sponsored by a considerably different motive – the desire to control the 'seditious, scismaticall, or offensive' potential of the press – the Star Chamber decree concerning printing confirms the *integral* nature of paratexts:

> II. *Item*, That no person or persons whatsoeuer, shall at any time print or cause to be imprinted, any Booke or Pamphlet whatsoever, vnlesse the same

4 Humfrey Gifford, *A posie of gilloflowers* (London, 1580), sig. I1^{v}.
5 *Taylor his travels* (London, 1621), sig. A2^{v}.
6 *The second part, or a continuance of Poly-Olbion* (London, 1622), sig. A2^{r}.

> Booke or Pamphlet, and also all and euery the Titles, Epistles, Prefaces, Proems, Preambles, Introductions, Tables, Dedications, and other matters and things whatsoeuer thereunto annexed, or therewith imprinted, shall be first lawfully licenced and authorized onely by such person and persons as are hereafter expressed, and by no other, and shall be also first entred into the Registers Booke of the Company of Stationers.[7]

The punishment – 'either by Fine, imprisonment, or other corporall' means – for violation of this decree extended beyond the printer, encompassing even those who merely 'bound, stitched, or sowed' the offending pages. Though not standing in the cold shadow of this Star Chamber decree, Jerome Porter makes the point a different way when he makes a plea to the reader to pay attention to all of the gatherings: 'It may please thee, good reader, before thou takest in hand to peruse this booke, to looke ouer the contents of the Preface, both for thy owne satisfaction and mine.'[8] A book's ostensibly extraneous matter clearly was not to be divorced from the text it supported.

Sometimes, however, the paratext hardly proffers an inviting gateway. John Taylor's epistle 'To Any that can Read' nicely anticipates the image of the vestibulary preface, but also suggests that the door might strike you as you pass:

> Be thou either Freind or Foe or in diferent, all's one, Read, Laugh, like or dislike, all the care is taken: The cheifest cause why I wrote this, was on set purpose to please my selfe. Yet to shew thee the meaning of this little Building, Imagine this *Epistle* to be the doore, and if thou please come in and see what stuffe the whole Frame is made off.[9]

Taylor's cavalier attitude – mirrored in Thomas Nashe's epistle 'To his Readers, hee cares not what they be',[10] and seen at its most all-encompassing in Robert Tofte's epistle 'To the Ivdiciovs Vnderstander: To the Ignorant Reader: and to the base Carper whatsoeuer' of his translation of Varchi[11] – is surprisingly common, and makes one wonder what sort of reader responds to such an address. Since rhetoric, in theory, succeeds through arrangement and amplification, and by the accordance of matter and art with occasion, we are pressed to wonder where the profit lies in such an apparently indecorous, hostile attack on the audience. It would have to be the experienced reader who can navigate ironic paratexts, but there is no such misdirection in Thomas Jordan's address 'To the Criticall Reader' (see fig. 31.1), or John Florio's letter 'To the Reader':

7 *In camera stellata*, 11 July 1637, *STC* 7757; Arber, IV, pp. 529–30.
8 *The flowers of the lives of the most renowned saincts* (London, 1632), sig. A2^{v}.
9 *Taylors revenge* (London, 1615), sig. A3^{r}. 10 *Nashes Lenten stuffe* (London, 1599), sig. A4^{v}.
11 *The blazon of iealousie* (London, 1615), sig. A3^{r}.

Sowre Sir, a word with you;
Since I am fallen into the hazzard of your infectious censure, and that I know you come to kill, not nurse my infant Muse, my language will have licence; I must tell you, you are ungently bold to trespasse on a Page of mine, seeke some knowne Author, whose applauded name selfe-loved opinion taught you to admire; The title page you censure, not the worke, I am condemn'd already by that rule, but tis no legall tryall; Is your wise knowledge so prophetick growne, that in an Authors name you reade his merit, or think you that the learned Magazin is quite exhausted from the thrifty schooles to make but one man happy. Either resolve to reade me honestly with a true purpose to be just in censure, condemning onely theft, or such blacke guilt, or fairely leave mee to my Candid Reader.

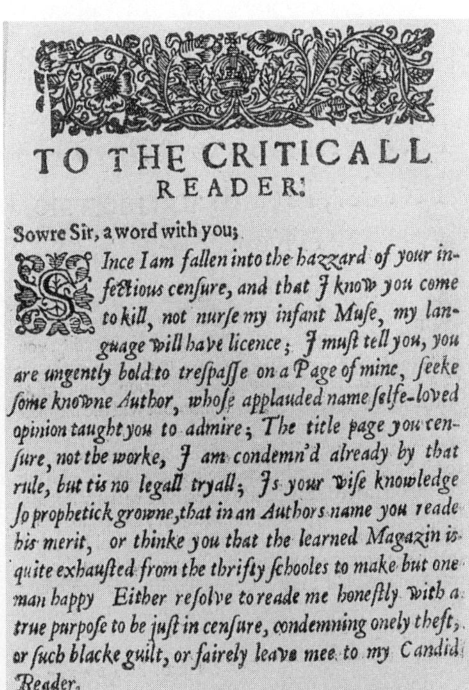

TO THE CRITICALL READER.

Sowre Sir, a word with you;

Since I am fallen into the hazzard of your infectious censure, and that I know you come to kill, not nurse my infant Muse, my language will have licence; I must tell you, you are ungently bold to trespasse on a Page of mine, seeke some knowne Author, whose applauded name selfe-loved opinion taught you to admire; The title page you censure, not the worke, I am condemn'd already by that rule, but tis no legall tryall; Is your wise knowledge so prophetick growne, that in an Authors name you reade his merit, or thinke you that the learned Magazin is quite exhausted from the thrifty schooles to make but one man happy Either resolve to reade me honestly with a true purpose to be just in censure, condemning onely theft, or such blacke guilt, or fairely leave mee to my Candid Reader.

THO. IORDAN.

A 3 TO

Figure 31.1 Thomas Jordan, *Poeticall varieties: or, varietie of fancies* (1637), sig. A3r.

> Reader, good or bad, name thy self, for I know not which to tearme thee, vnles I heard thee read, and reading iudge, or iudging exercise . . . to the first (as to my friends) I wish as gracious acceptance where they desire it most, as they extend where I deserue it least; to the second I can wish no worse than they worke themselues, though I should wish them blyndnes, deafnes, and dumbness.[12]

When Florio signs off, 'Resolute', he leaves no doubt that the epistle is often peremptory as well as prefatory: 'Farewell if thou meane well; els fare as ill, as thou wishest me to fare.'[13]

Michael Drayton takes a less aggressive, but no less accusatory, intolerant approach to the 'Generall Reader' who may be put off by his *Poly-Olbion*,

> whose vnusuall tract may perhaps seeme difficult, to the female Sex; yea, and I feare, to some that think themselues not meanly learned, being not rightly inspired by the Muses: such I meane, as had rather read the fantasies of forraine

12 *Florios second frutes* (London, 1591), sig. *1r. 13 *Florios second frutes* (London, 1591), sig. *2r.

> inuentions, then to see the Rarities & Historie of their owne Country deliuered by a true natiue Muse. Then, whosoeuer thou be, possest with such stupidity & dulnesse, that.... thou hadst rather, (because it asks thy labour) remaine, where thou wert, then straine thy selfe to walke forth with the Muses; the fault proceeds from thy idlenesse, not from any want in my industrie.[14]

Not unlike the elaborate support mechanisms which accompany John Harington's translation of Ariosto's *Orlando Furioso* – a likely target of this contempt for the 'fantasies of forraine inuentions' – Drayton also provides both graphic and explanatory paratextual aids for less capable readers – male *and* female – but will not suffer their wilfulness or autonomy (that is, their attempts to read the poem without his help or, ultimately, their arrival at any judgement other than praise for his 'industrie'). One can only wonder how many readers – 'possest with such stupidity & dulness' that they might presume to assert their preferences for reading matter – put *Poly-Olbion* aside in favour of a treatise on angling with the hook, or a description of the stars.

But nowhere is the difference between reading constituencies better revealed than in parallel epistles to the patron and the general audience. We often encounter letters, such as Samuel Pick's epistles both to his common reader and to Richard Pelham (see figs. 31.2 and 31.3), which convey essentially the same self-promoting information regarding the author's intentions. Many patrons may never read beyond the dedication – and certainly would not be expected to read the epistle to the common reader – so any point (in Pick's case, demure apology) to be made to all readers would have to be repeated in the 'personalized' epistle. Of course, the common reader is not prohibited from reading this 'private' communication – no doubt is probably *expected* to do so (especially when the author praises the protective benefits of his patronage).

Few in the early modern period were invoked for the purposes of such protection as often as Philip Sidney's sister, and no one hides behind her name more shamelessly than Thomas Howell:

> my courage... ha[s] aduentured to place in the forefrunt of this little treatise, the tytle of your name... as a sure shield to a weake Warriour, as a safe defence against any danger... [S]o if the Reader hereof, behold your name in the fyrst leafe, he will deeme the whole Booke the more fruitfull, and the framer therof the more skilfull: but if he shall once perceyue your Honor to be Patronesse to this labour, he will eyther loue it, bicause he doth honor you, or wil not dare to reproch it, bicause he perceyueth you are... ready, and knoweth you are... able to defend it... [Y]our name shall to the Reader be recompence for the greatnesse of my ignorance.[15]

14 *Poly-Olbion* (London, 1612), sig. A1^{r}. 15 *H[owell] his deuises* (London, 1581), sigs. A3^{r-v}.

TO
THE WORSHIPFVLL
His much eſteemd good Friend, Mr,
RICHARD PELHAM, Eſquire,
S.P. *Wiſheth all happines and proſperity*
here and hereafter.

WORTHY SIR,

IT may ſeeme ſomething ſtrange, that ſo meane a Muſe as mine, upon ſo unworthy a Subject as this, ſhould ſo rudely dare to ſhelter it ſelfe under the protection of your Name, or intrude upon the cenſure of ſo ſolid a judgement as reſides in your breſt; conſidering how converſant you daily are with raptures both of a higher ſtraine and better nature, daily proffered to your view and cenſure: But the perſwaſion of your courteous acceptation of ſuch wild Olives as theſe are (as of Plants which inoculated and pruned, in time may produce more mature and delicious fruites unto her foſterers) hath emboldned me to it;

A 2   and

To the Reader.

and ſhall therefore (I hope) be the better excuſed (though it want much of what I wiſh it had) becauſe it flyes to you as a Refuge, under whoſe Hands it hath both ſecurity and warrant. Expect no quaint language nor fragrant Flowers of flowing Rhetorick, but ſuch as uſe to proceed from ſpringing youth, they are the wanton fruits of idle houres, and ſo happily cannot yeeld that reliſh that may be expected from them. But yet your ingenuity and generous diſpoſition aſſures the acceptation being the firſt fruits of my Muſes ſpringing.) And that you cheriſh them, that they dye not in their Bud, but (by your promptitude) may be preferred from the blaſt of envy, and the rot of time and oblivion. The perſwaſion of your liberall acceptation vouchſafed me, not onely ympes my Muſes wings for a higher flight in the future, but vowes me to acknowledge my ſelfe now and ever

Your Worſhips moſt obſequiouſly

to be commanded,

SAMUEL PICK.

It may seeme something strange, that so meane a Muse as mine, upon so unwortby a Subject as this, sbould so rudely dare to shelter it selfe under the protection of your Name, or intrude upon the censure of so solid a judgement as resides in your brest; considering how conversant you daily are with raptures both of a higher straine and better nature, daily proffered to your view and censure: But the perswasion of your courteous acceptation of such wild Olives as these are (as of Plants which inoculated and pruned, in time may produce more mature and delicious fruites unto her fosterers) hath emboldned me to it; and shall therefore (I hope) be the better excused (though it want much of what I wish it had) because it flyes to you as a Refuge, under whose Hands it hath both security and warrant. Expect no quaint language nor fragrant Flowers of flowing Rhetorick, but such as use to proceed from springing youth, they are the wanton fruits of idle houres, and so happily cannot yeeld that relish that may be expected from them. But yet your ingenuity and generous disposition assures the acceptation being the first fruits of my Muses springing.) And that you cherish them, that they dye not in their Bud, but (by your promptitude) may be preferred from the blast of envy, and the rot of time and oblivion . . . .

Figure 31.2 Samuel Pick, *Festum voluptatis, or the banquet of pleasure* (1639), sigs. A2^{r-v}.

Although the Countess of Pembroke's favour would indeed provide a formidable shield, her son (Mr W. H.?) far outpaced her as a favourite patron (Franklin B. Williams identifies nearly one hundred titles dedicated to William Herbert,

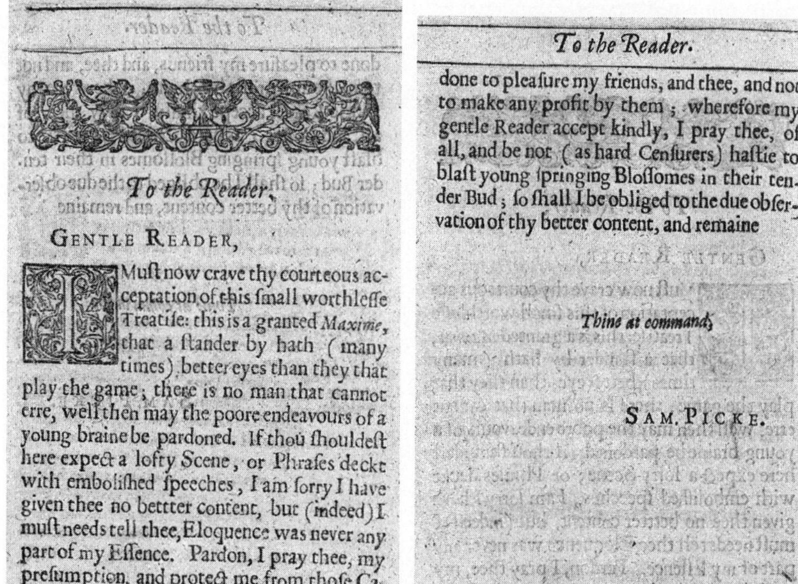

To the Reader,

GENTLE READER,

I Muſt now crave thy courteous acceptation of this ſmall worthleſſe Treatiſe: this is a granted *Maxime*, that a ſtander by hath (many times) better eyes than they that play the game; there is no man that cannot erre, well then may the poore endeavours of a young braine be pardoned. If thou ſhouldeſt here expect a lofty Scene, or Phraſes deckt with emboliſhed ſpeeches, I am ſorry I have given thee no bettter content, but (indeed) I muſt needs tell thee, Eloquence was never any part of my Eſſence. Pardon, I pray thee, my preſumption, and protect me from thoſe Cavelling finde-faults that never like well of any thing they ſee printed, though never ſo well compiled: What I have here done, I have done

To the Reader.

done to pleaſure my friends, and thee, and not to make any profit by them; wherefore my gentle Reader accept kindly, I pray thee, of all, and be not (as hard Cenſurers) haſtie to blaſt young ſpringing Bloſſomes in their tender Bud; ſo ſhall I be obliged to the due obſervation of thy better content, and remaine

Thine at command,

SAM. PICKE.

. . . If thou shouldest here expect a lofty Scene, or Phrases deckt with embolished speeches, I am sorry I have given thee no better content, but (indeed) I must needs tell thee, Eloquence was never any part of my Essence. Pardon, I pray thee, my presumption, and protect me from those Cavelling finde-faults that never like well of any thing they see printed, though never so well compiled: What I have here done, I have done to pleasure my friends, and thee, and not to make any profit by them; wherefore my gentle Reader accept kindly, I pray thee, of all, and be not (as hard Censurers) hastie to blast young springing Blossomes in their tender Bud. . . .

Figure 31.3 Samuel Pick, *Festum voluptatis, or the banquet of pleasure* (1639), sigs. A3^{r-v}.

which pales only in comparison with Queen Elizabeth, James I, and his son, Prince Henry[16]).

But the paratextual supplicant often makes these appeals without any personal assurance of the dread patron's support. No doubt this epistle 'To the Great Patroness of the World, Good Acceptance' captures the situation well:

> Cvstome (one of the great Tyrants of the Earth) hath made it as common, as Writing of Bookes; for all *Paper-Parents* . . . to commend them to the Protection

16 Williams 1962.

> of some good Patron or other, as to their carefull *Palmer*, to walk with them through the severall parts of the World, which they are to pass, much like the Penny put into the dead Man's hand . . . But for that, I have long observed, this course heares ill of the World, and Patrons most – what are frighted at the sight of a Dedication, as at the sight of a *Lord have Mercie upon us*, writ on their doore in the time of the Plague; or as at the receit of a *Privie Seale*, which they think, in good manners (though faine they would shift it) they cannot refuse. And for that, a Dedicatory Epistle is esteemed of many, no better than an Artificiall kind of *Begging*.[17]

It is significant to note that such an honest assessment of the patron's reception of a dedication is prefixed to a *pseudonymous* tract.

Despite anticipated protestations against prolixity and insincerity, and stock admissions of insufficiency, the occasions are rare on which an author or printer allows a minimum of words to mediate that boundary separating text and its pretexts, contexts, and subtexts. One particular volume does stand out, however, for both the object and sincerity of an author's dedication: George Herbert's *The Temple*. Although they claim they will let Herbert do the talking, the printers cannot keep from an intervention of their own:

> The dedication of this work having been made by the Authour to the *Divine Majestie* onely, how should we now presume to interest any mortall man in the patronage of it? Much lesse think we it meet to seek the recommendation of the Muses, for that which himself was confident to have been inspired by a diviner breath then flows from *Helicon*. The world therefore shall receive it in that naked simplicitie with which he left it, without any addition either of support or ornament, more then is included in it self.[18]

Indeed, no author or publisher could properly seek further patronage after a dedication to the Almighty. Herbert's dedicatory sexain echoes expected sentiment – 'my first fruits present themselves to thee: / Yet not mine neither: for from thee they came' – but ends in a prayerful couplet that transcends formulaic cliché: 'Turn their eyes hither, who shall make a gain: / Theirs, who shall hurt themselves or me, refrain.'[19]

These subliminal – or, if you like, transliminal – features of the Renaissance book significantly encode in bibliographical artefacts the essential issues of patronage, dissemination, demographics, and stylization of audience status. And

17 Lerimos Uthalmos, pseud., *Fasciculus florum: or, a nosegay of flowers* (London, 1636), sigs. A3^{r-v}.
18 *The Temple* (1633), sig. ¶2^{r}. The printers in fact go on to give a two-page biography.
19 *The Temple* (1633), sig. ¶4^{r}. In his revised edition of *The works of George Herbert* (Oxford, 1978), F. E. Hutchinson notes that in the two important manuscripts of *The Temple* poems, this stanza appears on the title page of one (Bodleian MS. Tanner 307) and stands alone on the first written page of the other, which lacks a half title (MS. Jones B 62).

To the great Variety of Readers.

From the most able, to him that can but spell: There you are number'd. We had rather you were weighd. Especially, when the fate of all Bookes depends vpon your capacities: and not of your heads alone, but of your purses. Well! It is now publique, & you wil stand for your priuiledges wee know: to read, and censure. . . . [I]t is not our prouince, who onely gather his works, and giue them you, to praise him. It is yours that reade him. And there we hope, to your diuers capacities, you will finde enough, both to draw, and hold you: for his wit can no more lie hid, then it could be lost. Reade hime, therefore; and againe, and againe: And if then you doe not like him, surely you are in some manifest danger, not to vnderstand him. . . .

To the great Variety of Readers.

Rom the moſt able, to him that can but ſpell: There you are number'd. We had rather you were weighd. Eſpecially, when the fate of all Bookes depends vpon your capacities: and not of your heads alone, but of your purſes. Well! It is now publique, & you wil ſtand for your priuiledges wee know: to read, and cenſure. Do ſo, but buy it firſt. That doth beſt commend a Booke, the Stationer ſaies. Then, how odde ſoeuer your braines be, or your wiſedomes, make your licence the ſame, and ſpare not. Iudge your ſixe-pen'orth, your ſhillings worth, your fiue ſhillings worth at a time, or higher, ſo you riſe to the iuſt rates, and welcome. But, what euer you do, Buy. Cenſure will not driue a Trade, or make the Iacke go. And though you be a Magiſtrate of wit, and ſit on the Stage at *Black-Friers*, or the *Cock-pit*, to arraigne Playes dailie, know, theſe Playes haue had their triall alreadie, and ſtood out all Appeales; and do now come forth quitted rather by a Decree of Court, then any purchas'd Letters of commendation.

It had bene a thing, we confeſſe, worthie to haue bene wiſhed, that the Author himſelfe had liu'd to haue ſet forth, and ouerſeen his owne writings; But ſince it hath bin ordain'd otherwiſe, and he by death departed from that right, we pray you do not envie his Friends, the office of their care, and paine, to haue collected & publiſh'd them; and ſo to haue publiſh'd them, as where (before) you were abus'd with diuerſe ſtolne, and ſurreptitious copies, maimed, and deformed by the frauds and ſtealthes of iniurious impoſtors, that expos'd them: euen thoſe, are now offer'd to your view cur'd, and perfect of their limbes; and all the reſt, abſolute in their numbers, as he conceiued thẽ. Who, as he was a happie imitator of Nature, was a moſt gentle expreſſer of it. His mind and hand went together: And what he thought, he vttered with that eaſineſſe, that wee haue ſcarſe receiued from him a blot in his papers. But it is not our prouince, who onely gather his works, and giue them you, to praiſe him. It is yours that reade him. And there we hope, to your diuers capacities, you will finde enough, both to draw, and hold you: for his wit can no more lie hid, then it could be loſt. Reade him, therefore; and againe, and againe: And if then you doe not like him, ſurely you are in ſome manifeſt danger, not to vnderſtand him. And ſo we leaue you to other of his Friends, whom if you need, can bee your guides: if you neede them not, you can leade your ſelues, and others. And ſuch Readers we wiſh him.

A 3

Iohn Heminge.
Henrie Condell.

Figure31.4 William Shakespeare, *Mr. William Shakespeares comedies, histories & tragedies. Published according to the true originall copies* (1623), sig, A3^{r}.

further encoded in this distension of text and disposition of space and resources are matters of hermeneutic and structural, as well as economic, consequence. One need only turn to the Shakespeare First Folio (fig. 31.4) to witness the manipulative eloquence one can find 'outside' of the text, and to experience both the power and the responsibilities bestowed upon literate society. In the final analysis, though, do these paratextual tactics result in a reader being challenged or intimidated or comforted? Heminge and Condell impact the potential reader in all three ways: with the challenge to embrace and activate one's 'priuiledges' as a reader; the 'manifest danger' if one does not understand; and the comfort of knowing Shakespeare will always be there to be read, 'againe, and againe'.

❧

THE TYPOGRAPHY OF HOBBES'S *LEVIATHAN*

PETER CAMPBELL

Thomas Hobbes's *Leviathan*, and other seventeenth-century treatises made to the same pattern, are examples of the typographic book, conceived of as an illustration or diagram of its contents, in full flower. The tally of parts is complete, in due hierarchical order, from title pages and contents to synoptic trees and indexes. In the differentiation of headings, paragraphs and words these books take the typographic expression of intellectual structure to the limit which is set by the number of ways of differentiating and arranging words a reader can be expected to keep in mind.

Leviathan stands at the end of the tradition in which knowledge is mapped as a series of divisions and sub-divisions. In the centuries that followed, Hobbes's kind of subject matter would be given more discursive exposition. Tree-like arrangements of arguments are still about – the decimal numbering of paragraphs in Wittgenstein's *Tractatus* is a modern example – but now only books which set out to map a whole territory – for example, dictionaries and textbooks – make a thorough, *Leviathan*-like typographic distinction between conceptual categories. By the eighteenth century the practice was quaint enough to be mocked: Slawkenbergius's vast treatise on noses, described by Sterne in *Tristram Shandy*, is clearly a book of the *Leviathan* kind.

In 1651, when the first edition was published, resources for complex typography were all there. Founders had been offering the fonts which are still the stock in trade of any book printer for more than half a century – *Leviathan* uses roman and italic in various sizes, black letter, Greek and small capitals (three fonts appear in the imprint of Leviathan alone: 'Printed for ANDREW CROOKE, at the Green Dragon in St *Pauls* Church-yard, 1651'.

All seventeenth-century printers played the variation game. Sometimes, it seems, for its own sake – they felt uneasy if a display line was followed by another in the same size and character – but in most texts, as in *Leviathan*, typographic differentiation of all save the most formal display matter is functional. It signals divisions between parts, suggests ways of reading, supplies some of the pauses and inflections of a spoken text and demonstrates relationships which would otherwise only be implied (for example that between words which explain concepts and words which name them). All this is done by MARKING – setting words or groups of words larger or smaller and in different fonts (for example setting the dedication larger than the rest of the text), by LABELLING the text and the pages which contain it with marginal, page, part and chapter headings and numbers and by using conventional POINTERS (asterisks, superior letters) to relate what is on the page to what is in the margins.

The status of a word on the page is determined by its position (headline, text, note), its font (roman, italic, small capitals, black letter, Greek), its size and its case (upper, lower).

In *Leviathan* levels of branching are distinguished by different kinds of headings (for parts, which enclose chapters and chapters which enclose paragraphs). Within paragraphs punctuation and spacing mark sentences and font changes distinguish word types. This structure could be recorded (and, indeed, perfected, for it is not entirely consistent) in a computer-orientated markup language like SGML. The typography of *Leviathan* encourages a consciousness of the text at all resolutions from the highest (word by word), through intermediate stages (as a series of propositions) to the whole text (presented in its most condensed and most general form as an illustration or diagram in a single, synoptic, engraved title page). In modern textbooks this kind of page design is intended to allow the book to be approached in non-serial modes. In *Leviathan* it seems to have a different function – to confirm for the reader, at any point in the text, not only where he or she is, but what the nature of the whole structure is. The effect is architectural. The reader is never lost, and never unaware of how each wing and the rooms it contains relate to the whole building (plate 31.1).

The typography of *Leviathan* is not unique. Burton's *Anatomy of Melancholy*, for example, is set out in much the same way – even down to the engraved title page. The fact that similar layouts were thought appropriate both for Burton's discursive text and Hobbes's avowedly axiomatic one (his excursions into mathematics were unsuccessful, but the Euclidean model strongly colours *Leviathan*) shows what any consideration of any representative group of seventeenth-century books makes clear. What we are observing is not a solution to a specific problem but a set of typographic conventions.

No matter how ill-suited the model of knowledge this structure exemplifies was to particular texts its existence was both a reflection of, and an aid to, a particular way of thinking.

Although the complexity of the typography of *Leviathan* is not matched in informal manuscripts, or in some discursive printed texts of the same period, like, say, Thomas Browne's *Urne Burial* it is mirrored in formal manuscripts. In the presentation copy on vellum of *Leviathan* in the British Library words which are set in small capitals in the printed text are written in large upper and lower case. The means are different but the same structures are being identified.

Leviathan's typography now looks over zealous, even a trifle absurd – we are with Sterne on that. But it does modulate the text string in ways which keep the reader in touch with Hobbes's argument. Simplify the typography and you lose something which is relevant, if not to the meaning of the text in the narrowest sense, at least to the flavour of its rhetoric.

THE POLYGLOT BIBLE

NICOLAS BARKER

In recent times, the great triumphs of seventeenth-century scholarship in Britain have seemed to be local. The 'Saxonists', from Archbishop Matthew Parker to George Hickes, who recovered the ancient past of the country, its Church, monuments and language, were the heroes of David Douglas's *English Scholars*.[1] At the time, however, there would have been no doubt that its greatest achievement was the multilingual edition of the Bible published in six volumes in 1657, edited by one man, Dr Brian Walton (*c.* 1600–61). It was all the more remarkable since it was conceived during the Civil War and brought to fulfilment under the Commonwealth.

The 'London Polyglot' was the fourth such edition of the Bible. The idea of publishing its texts in the original languages and scripts goes back to Aldus Manutius (*c.* 1500), but the first complete Bible was due to the initiative of Cardinal Ximenes in Spain. He employed the Greek scholar Demetrius Ducas and the printer Arnão Guillen de Brocar to produce parallel texts in Hebrew, Greek, Latin and Chaldean at Alcalá (Complutum). The 'Complutensian Polyglot' was completed in six volumes in 1517, although the New Testament was not released until 1522. Spanish gold again subsidized the 'Antwerp Polyglot', edited by Arias Montanus and printed by Christophe Plantin, which was completed in eight volumes in 1572, with a dedication to Philip II. Syriac was added to the four languages of the Complutensian, together with an apparatus, with dictionaries and grammars of the four exotic languages. Its range of exotic types was expanded by Plantin's son-in-law, Frans Raphelengius, to print Scaliger's *De emendatione temporum* (1598), and later used and further enlarged by Thomas Erpenius at Leiden.

1 Douglas 1951.

Even more sumptuous was the 'Paris Polyglot', edited by Guy-Michel le Jay and printed by Antoine Vitré, and completed in ten volumes in 1645. This went back to the initiative of François Savary de Brèves, the French ambassador at Constantinople, who promoted the publication of works in the oriental languages in Rome and at Paris. His types were used by Vitré, appointed 'Imprimeur du Roy ès langues orientales'. De Brèves died in 1627, and the competition for his types and manuscripts was strong, notably from Holland and England. This awoke Richelieu to the need to preserve the French primacy in scholarship, and led in 1640 to the foundation of the Imprimerie Royale. Le Jay, who had been associated with Savary de Brèves, determined to bring out his planned Polyglot Bible, adding the complete text in Arabic and the Pentateuch in Samaritan. His refusal to accept a subsidy from Richelieu prevented the addition of any apparatus.

These examples were not lost in England. William Bedwell, the Arabist, acquired some of the Plantin types, which he left in charge of Erpenius, and in 1625, James Ussher, Archbishop of Armagh and the foremost biblical scholar of his time, attempted to buy all the types of Erpenius, bought instead by the Elsevier brothers. Matthias Pasor began lecturing on Arabic in Oxford in 1624, and five years later William Laud, then Bishop of London, became Chancellor of the University, and set about making it a centre for such scholarship. He bestowed large gifts of books on the Bodleian and encouraged others to do likewise; in 1636 he endowed a chair of Arabic, and in 1639 retrieved Sir Henry Savile's Greek types. Oriental studies, pioneered by Abraham Whelock, found similar encouragement at Cambridge, where the second edition of Joseph Mede's *Clavis Apocalyptica* was printed in 1631, with substantial use of Hebrew type. With the war and the victory of Parliament, many of those thus encouraged were deprived of their livings or academic appointments, and in retreat or exile found solace in scholarly work.

Brian Walton was one of these.[2] He enlisted the help of others at Cambridge, Whelock and Edmund Castell of Emmanuel College. He laid his plans carefully, obtaining permission to import the necessary paper free of customs duty and the Protector's approval of the work. In 1652 he published *A brief description of an edition of the Bible in the original Hebrew, Samaritan and Greek, with the most ancient translations of the Jewish and Christian Churches, viz. the Sept. Greek, Chaldee, Syriac, Ethiopic, Arabic, Persian, etc., and the Latin versions of them all: a new apparatus, etc.*, with a specimen of the first twelve verses of Genesis on

2 For accounts of the making of the Polyglot see Todd 1821 and Reed 1952. On the Polyglot as a subscription edition, see above Parry, pp. 185–6.

facing pages, Hebrew with interlinear Latin, Vulgate Latin, Greek Septuagint with Latin, Chaldean paraphrase and Latin, Hebrew-Samaritan and Samaritan on one side, Syriac with Latin, Arabic with Latin, Latin translation of Samaritan and Persian with Latin on the other. The *Description* was printed by R. Norton for Timothy Garthwaite 'at the lesser North Gate of St Paul's Church', the specimen by James Flesher. The latter elicited a good deal of criticism from the severe Dutch scholar, Arnold Boate, and from Whelock, who wrote of it, 'I corrected at least 80 errata in it. It as yet serves to show what letters Mr Flesher, an eminent printer, my friend and printer of my booke, hath.'[3] Walton had noted on it 'Typos Hebr. et Syr. cum punctis meliores, parabimus.'[4]

This he now proceeded to do. The Hebrew, cast on an English body and complete with points and accents, was characterized as 'an ugly type' by Harry Carter, but probably of local manufacture. The Double Pica Syriac is a copy of that cut by Jacques de Sanlecque for the Paris Polyglot, and retains some of its quality; the English Samaritan and the Great Primer Arabic are also based on the Paris equivalents, the latter (if with some original features) based on that cut, apparently in the Levant, for Savary de Brèves; the English Ethiopic is a copy of the Raphelengius type, as used by Erpenius. The Greeks and roman and italic types were all types already extant, some recent, but many going back to the sixteenth century. Some idea of this progress, and the thoroughness of Walton's supervision, emerges from a letter he wrote to Ussher on 18 July 1653: 'I hope we shall shortly begin the work; yet I doubt the *founders* will make us stay a week longer than we expected ... We have resolved to have a better paper than that of 11*s*. a ream, viz., of 15*s*. a ream.'[5]

Towards the end of September that year, work began on the first volume, at the press of Thomas Roycroft in Bartholomew Close. It was completed at the beginning of September 1654, the second and third following in 1655 and 1656, and the last three volumes in 1657 (plate 31.2). In October 1654, Roycroft also printed Walton's *Introductio ad Lectionem Linguarum Orientalium, Hebraicae, Chaldaicae, Samaritanae, Syriacae, Arabicae, Persicae, Aethiopicae, Armenae, Coptae ... in usum tyronum ... praecipuè eorum qui sumptus ad Biblia Polyglotta (jam sub prelo) imprimenda contulerunt*. This useful guide had a life beyond the immediate needs of subscribers to the Bible; the Armenian and Coptic alphabets were cut on wood, as they were for the prolegomena to the great work itself. This finally contained the Old Testament in Hebrew, the Septuagint version in Greek and Latin, the Syriac version, the Chaldean in the original and Latin translation, with the complete Vulgate and almost the

3 Todd 1821, p. 56. 4 Reed 1952, p. 158. 5 Quoted by Reed 1952, p. 158.

whole Bible in Arabic. The New Testament was in the original Greek, Latin and Syriac, the Pentateuch in Samaritan and Persian, the latter with the Gospels and also a Latin translation. In Ethiopic, there was the Psalter and Canticles, again with Latin translation. The Chaldean text and the targums were in masoretic Hebrew. The sixth volume consisted entirely of variant readings.

Walton was rewarded with the bishopric of Chester and Roycroft with the title 'Orientalium Typographus Regius'. Edmund Castell, who laboured on to complete his *Lexicon Heptaglotton* in two great volumes, also printed by Roycroft, in 1669, became Professor of Arabic at Cambridge. Both this and the Polyglot Bible to which it was an adjunct remained in print until the end of the century.

The London Polyglot, though an imposing work, arguably the most distinguished as well as substantial product of the British press in the century, is not as handsome or as spacious as either of its two predecessors. But it has a greater claim than typographic elegance. Combining as it did a greater number of versions, it was a triumph of rational layout. In the words of Talbot Baines Reed, who wrote its history in *A history of the old English letter founders*, 'Each double page presents, when open, some ten or more versions of the same passage divided into parallel columns of varying width, but so set that each comprehends exactly the same amount of text as the other (plate 31.3). The regularity displayed in the general arrangement, in the references and interpolations, in the interlineations, and all the details of the composition and impression, are worthy of the undertaking and a lasting glory to the typography of the seventeenth century.'[6]

6 Reed 1952, p. 159.

THE LOOK OF NEWS: POPISH PLOT NARRATIVES 1678–1680

HAROLD LOVE

News as we know it took some time to become fully distinguished from other categories of information. Part of that perception of difference was epistemological: news is seen to differ from rumour or gossip as knowledge transmitted by the speediest of available routes and bearing the assurance, in some form or other, of accuracy. News is also knowledge about a distinct class of happenings, chiefly economic and political: information of other kinds appears in newspapers but is not taken seriously as news. Ostensibly a record of happenings of the recent past, it is by origin and intention a means of peering into the future – the only reason why it is to be preferred to the generally more satisfying productions of myth and storytelling. For this reason news always comes sifted through the judgement of a moderator, one of whose functions is to assess the likely future consequences of the information most freshly to hand. In the earliest decades of news, this moderator was the compiler of handwritten newsletters or *gazettes à main*, who would sign his name at the end of the news and whose social pose was that of one gentleman advising another. Although the early newspapers, which were a secure element of the national information network only from the 1670s, soon abandoned the epistolary convention, they continued to moderate news by sourcing it in letters or 'advices' of various dates and reliability.

Yet it was characteristic of the most interesting kinds of news that its significance was often unclear; that its accounts of events were often incomplete; and that the accompanying interpretations were often partisan. Readers quickly developed considerable sophistication in handling these materials. In *Spectator* 154 a student of journals is left in doubt for some days whether in faraway Constantinople the Grand Vizier had or had not been put to the bowstring. The satirist's implication is that to concern oneself with so remote and uncertain an event was a waste of time; yet the fate of a Grand Vizier surely did matter if one was a Turkey merchant, or had actual or prospective investments in ventures to the Ottoman lands, or simply wanted to choose the best time to buy perfume or a new carpet. Otherwise news had to be taken on trust as the product of a collective enterprise with certain inbuilt checks and balances. In this sense it became a bibliographical rather than an epistemological entity. My present concern is with kinds of publications, other than the newspaper and newsbook, that were seen at the time as falling under the category of news and which in some cases sought to indicate this through their physical appearance.

Their printed forms embrace depositions, discourses, narratives, accounts, histories, examinations, relations, informations, discoveries, and printed descriptions of public ceremonies, particularly executions. Each of these collateral genres was the bearer of topical information of a kind which could not be absorbed into the newspaper as it then existed. The period around 1680 was particularly rich in narratives. By this term we are to understand an extended account of a series of events given by an actor or intimate witness. ('Narrative' is also sometimes used for a report of a series of trials which had taken place at a particular sessions. This is a separate usage which always declares itself.) It was this personal participation which distinguished it from the more general 'Account'. It also made it less reliable, since the witness's claims were not subjected to any moderating procedure. It was therefore felt necessary to support it with every possible legitimizing gesture.

The period of the Popish Plot agitation (roughly 1678–80) was also that at which the 'Narrative' acquired a distinctive physical appearance. The major pieces were all in folio format, clearly printed on good paper. Titus Oates's *A true narrative of the horrid plot and conspiracy of the Popish party against the life of His Sacred Majesty, the government and the Protestant religion: with a list of such noblemen, gentlemen, and others that were the conspirators: and the head-officers both civil and military, that were to effect it* – the *fons et origo* of the genre – also bequathed it a rich vocabulary of validations. It is presented as the work of a clergyman of the Church of England whose name is followed on the title page by the prestigious letters D. D. (In fact Oates was a disgraced naval chaplain and his degree self awarded.) It had been twice sworn on oath: the first time on 6 September 1678 before Sir Edmund Berry Godfrey, who died shortly afterwards under mysterious circumstances, and the second time, on 28 September, before '*the Lords and others of His Majesties most Honourable Privy Council*'. On the verso facing the title page there are two certifications: the first signed by John Brown, 'Cleric. Parliamentor', authorizing Oates to print a 'Perfect Copy' of his narrative, and the second, dated 10 April 1679, signed by Oates appointing 'Thomas Parkhurst *and* Thomas Cockerill, *Citizens and Stationers of* London, *to*

Print this Narrative, containing Eighty one Paragraphs' (plate 31.4). The authority of the first certification is repeated on the title itself which notes that the work is '*Published by the Order of the Right Honourable the Lords Spiritual and Temporal in* PARLIAMENT *Assembled*'. On the line below the work is 'Humbly Presented to His Most Excellent MAJESTY'. Even the address of Parkhurst's shop at 'the Bible and Three Crowns' contributes its mite of legitimation. The title is followed by a three-page dedication addressed to the king as 'Defender of the Faith' and a letter to the 'Courteous Reader' in which Oates resumes his clerical persona, signing himself 'Thy hearty Well-wisher and Servant in Jesus Christ'. Thereafter follow fifty-seven pages of wholly invented data about the imaginary conspiracy, richly circumstantial, and delivered with a hammer-blow assertiveness that makes Oates one of the great pioneers (though this was hardly his aim) of literary realism. Finally we have a further eleven pages of lists, depositions and a summary of '*The General Design of the* POPE, *Society of* JESUS, *and their Confederates in this* PLOT', the whole comprising a fearsome cocktail of disinformation.

The folio format and various of the legitimizations were borrowed by the successors of Oates's initial volume, among them *A true narrative of the late design of the Papists to charge their horrid plot upon the Protestants*, Miles Prance's *A true narrative and discovery of several very remarkable passages relating to the horrid Popish plot*, William Bedloe's *A narrative and impartial discovery of the horrid Popish plot*, *A narrative of the depositions of Robert Jenison Esq.*, *The narrative of Robert Jenison of Grays-Inn, Esquire* (separate from the previous), *The narrative of Mr John Smith*, Thomas Blood's *A just narrative of the hellish new counter-plots of the Papists*, *Mr Thomas Dangerfields particular narrative of the late Popish design to charge those of the Presbyterian party with a pretended conspiracy against His Majesties person and government* (all 1679), and, in the following year, the narratives of Lawrence Mowbray, David Fitz Gerald and Roderick Mansell. These are merely the publications that have been examined for this chapter: others are listed in *A compleat catalogue of all the stitch'd books and single sheets printed since the first discovery of the Popish plot* (London, 1680) and its two continuations.[1] The domination of the folio in the political pamphleteering of the time is shown in the first continuation, which lists twenty-six 'Folio's Relating to the Plot' as against only four quartos and no octavos. Of the twenty-six folios, ten include the word 'narrative' in their titles, though not all fall under that category as just defined. Overall in the *Catalogue* and its two continuations there are fifty-three folio Narratives as against nine quarto ones. The tug of the folio is also seen in a play, *The excommunicated prince* (London, 1679), published under William Bedloe's

1 The continuations are reproduced in facsimile in Francis 1956.

name in that format: all other single plays of the period appear as quartos. This was another publication by Parkhurst and Cockerill, this time with Dorman Newman and Thomas Simmons. A certification by Bedloe resembling that of Oates's *Narrative* is on the verso of the title page. The major Plot narratives have wide margins, large, clear type and generous white space on the type page. Clearly paper, the major expense of printing, did not need to be husbanded: despite this they sold for the customary penny a sheet with a small premium for the larger volumes.[2] Nearly all have certifications modelled on those of Oates's *Narrative*. Narratives printed by the King's Printer add the royal arms to the title page. Oates's *The witch of Endor; or the witchcrafts of the Roman Jesebel* and the narratives of Bedloe and Prance also have copperplate portraits of the author as frontispieces, forcing the reader to meet the brazenly assured gaze of the witness before proceeding to the text. Elizabeth Cellier's self-published *Malice defeated* (London, 1680), a brave attempt to present a Catholic refutation of the Protestant allegations over the 'meal-tub' plot, was denied the legitimizing devices of the Protestant texts but used the same folio format and embellished its title page with a pious emblem and four verses from the Psalms. The effect of all this was to make the narrative a *physically* recognizable style of bookmaking.

The discrediting of the authors of the narratives (who also doubled as witnesses in the trials of the accused Catholics) had the long-term effect of depriving the genre of its status as news. Eighteenth-century works using the term in their titles are mostly travel books or retrospective memoirs. Meanwhile, the stylistic techniques used to confer plausibility on the imaginary plot were appropriated by writers of fictional memoirs, particularly Defoe. The Popish Plot narratives represent a brilliant attempt to hijack what was at the time accepted as a news medium in order to make it a vehicle of malicious untruth. But the initial success of this campaign was not simply a matter of political will: it also depended on printers, paper-merchants and booksellers being able to produce and distribute the huge amount of good-quality printed materials that the campaign required. Some of these printings were probably financed by the political groups whose cause they espoused – the Whig Green Ribbon club, or Cellier's circle of highly placed Catholics whom she had served as a midwife. Others were genuine official publications, produced at the expense of a duped Parliament. But there must also be a strong suspicion of strategic market-building on the part of the book trade at a time when better-off Londoners were at last free of the financial burdens of rebuilding the city and able to spend freely on such consumables as books.

2 For prices see Francis 1956 and Parks and Havens 1999.

The good-quality materials used for the narratives, along with the flaunting of their semi-official status, places them in a separate category from the flimsier topical pamphlets that might be purchased from a mercury-woman, stuffed into a pocket for casual reading in a coffee-house or during quiet times in Westminster Hall, and finally sacrificed to domestic uses. Indeed, it is likely that they were meant from the start for accumulation and preservation. The existence of the three printed catalogues is itself evidence for this: their re-issue as *A general catalogue of all the stitch'd books and single sheets &c. printed the two last years, commencing from the first discovery of the Popish plot* (London, 1680) advertises itself on its title page as 'Very useful for Gent. that make collections'.[3] It is also a fact that a great many copies survived as elements in bound volumes of the period, some the work of known collectors, of whom the most famous is Narcissus Luttrell, and others apparently made up by booksellers. There was a sense from the beginning that these were documents of record as well as bearers of topical news. Brought together they were intended to constitute an ongoing history of Popish intrigue against the crown and religion of England, which was greater than could be transmitted by any single one of them. Instead, their message quickly became one of the infinite corruptibility of public narrations when they were not moderated by skilled and impartial professional journalists.

3 Francis 1956, p. 6.

SIR ROGER L'ESTRANGE: THE JOURNALISM OF ORALITY

T. A. BIRRELL

Sir Roger L'Estrange (1616–1704) dominated English journalism from the Restoration to the end of the century. To be sure, he can hardly be called a 'typical' journalist. In a profession that was predominantly bourgeois and Whig, he was a totally unreconstructed Cavalier aristocrat, with a violent and unrelenting hatred of Dissenters, Whigs and Trimmers, and with a political philosophy to the right of Filmer's *Patriarcha*. But he attests to a quite distinctive phenomenon in the world of Restoration popular print.[1]

In *Toleration discuss'd* (1663) he is arguing against granting toleration to Dissenters because they use their pulpits to undermine respect for the monarchy. To enforce his point, he quotes a passage from Fulke Greville's jejeune and tedious closet-drama *Alaham* (1633) in which Alaham, the evil politician, urges Heli the priest to use the preaching of religion to bring the monarchy into contempt. What L'Estrange saw on the printed page was this:

> Preach you with firie tongue, distinguish might,
> Tyrants from Kings; duties in question bring
> Twixt God, and man; where power infinite
> Compar'd, makes finite power a scornfull thing.
> Safely so craft may with the truth give light,
> To iudge of Crownes without enammelling;
> And bring contempt upon the Monarchs State;
> Where straight unhallowed power hath peoples hate.
> Glaunce at Prerogatives indefinite,
> Taxe customes, warres and Lawes all gathering;
> Censure Kings faults, their spies and fauourites;
> Holinesse hath a priuiledge to sting.
> Men be not wise; bitternesse from zeale of spirit,

1 For a full account of all aspects of L'Estrange's remarkable career, see Kitchin 1913.

Is hardly iudge'd; the enuy of a King
Makes people like reproofe of Majesty;
Where God seemes great in Priests audacity.

What he printed in *Toleration discuss'd* was this:

Preach you with fiery tongue, distinguish Might;
Tyrants *from* Kings, *duties in question bring*
'Twixt God *and* man; *where* power infinite
Compar'd, makes finite power *a* scornfull thing.
Safely so craft may with the truth give light,
To Judge of Crowns without enammeling;
And bring contempt upon the Monarch's State;
Where straight unhallowed power hath peoples hate.
Glaunce at Prerogatives Indefinite,
Tax Customs, Warrs, and Lawes all gathering,
Censure Kings fau'ts, their Spies, and Favourites,
Holiness hath a Privilege to sting.
Men be not Wise; bitterness *from* zeal *of spirit,*
Is hardly Judg'd; the envy of a King
Makes People like reproof of Majesty.
Where God seems great in Priests audacity –

Twenty-four years later, in *A Brief history of the times* (1687) he quotes the passage again, in an even more emphatic form:

Preach you with Fiery Tongue; *Distinguish* Might;
Tyrants *from* Kings; *Duties in Question bring*
Twixt God *and* Man; *where* Power INFINITE
Compar'd, makes FINITE Power a Scornfull Thing.
Safely so, Craft *may with the* Truth give *Light,*
To Judge of Crowns, without Enammelling,
And bring Contempt *upon the* Monarchs State,
Where Streight Unhallow'd Power *has* Peoples Hate.
Glance at Prerogatives *Indefinite,*
Tax Customs, Wars, and Laws all-Gathering;
Censure Kings Faults, their Spies, and Favourites;
Holyness has a Privilege to Sting.
Men be not Wise; Bitterness *from* Zeal of Spirit
Is hardly Judg'd; *the* Envy of a King,
Makes People LIKE Reproof of Majesty,
Where GOD *seems* GREAT, *in* PRIESTS AUDACITY.

This distinctive orthographic style is not used for occasional effect: it is his essential way of writing, from first to last. He uses it for his journalism; for his translations, whether Quevedo's *Visions* (1667), Bona's *Guide to eternity* (1672), Erasmus's *Colloquies* (1679), or Aesop's *Fables* (1691); for his *Discourse of the fishery* (1674); and, above all, for his holograph correspondence. A forceful voice comes straight off the page, but it is not the contrived oratory of the pulpit or the bar, which the French thought of as orality;[2] it is the clear, easy, natural, slangy, conversational tone of the self-assured aristocrat talking to his social inferiors in Sam's Coffee-house – the nearest equivalent today would be the speech-patterns of Old Etonian racehorse trainers who spend their working lives talking to jockeys and horses. With L'Estrange the orthography, the intonation and the idiom are essential to one another:

> The Wife of *Xanthus* was well born and wealthy, but so Proud and Domineering withal, as if her Fortune and her Extraction had Entituled her to the Breeches. She was Horribly Bold, Medling, and *Expensive*; (as that sort of Women commonly are) Easily put off the Hooks, chattering at her Husband, and upon All occasions of controversy, Threatening to be gone.

This is from the Aesop of 1691 – the Glorious Revolution had no effect on L'Estrange's style. The only orthographic 'rule' is that of the modulations of the spoken voice. The capitalization of 'Horribly', the unexpected irony of the italicization of '*Expensive*', the confidential aside of the brackets – '(as that sort of Women commonly are)', all lead up to the casual and indecorous slang of 'put off the Hooks'.

L'Estrange did not speak as he thought. He thought as he spoke, he wrote as he spoke, he printed and published as he spoke. He had total authorial control over his printer and for twenty-five years he had his office in St Paul's Churchyard, above the shop of his booksellers, Henry Brome and family. He praises Brome's printer: 'first he is *Near* me, upon any Occasion of *Altering*, or *Correcting*. 2ly, He is *Carefull* of my *Work*. 3ly I'le Ask no *Pragmaticall Fopps* leave, what *Printer* I am to *Employ*' (*Observator*, 17 May 1683). There is only one example in L'Estrange's lifetime where the distinctive orthography of a first edition has been subsequently 'normalized' in later editions, and that is the difference between the first and fifth (and later) editions of the translation of Quevedo's *Visions* (1667 and 1673). But the exception proves the point, for the

2 Salazar 1995, deals with orality in virtually every genre *except* that of journalism.

Visions were published by Henry Herringman, who was a 'literary' publisher and not, like Brome, a journalistic one.

Apart from the pamphlets and translations, L'Estrange's most substantive journalistic work was *The Observator*. It began on 13 April 1681,[3] just after the Popish Plot had reached its peak, when the tide of the Whig triumph had begun to turn, and it finished on 9 March 1687. Each issue was a half-folio sheet, printed on both sides, in double column, appearing three times and, in its heyday, four times a week.[4] So in addition to his other printed pamphlets, and to his manifold activities as licenser of the press, L'Estrange was writing, and seeing through the press, a steady 8,000–10,000 words a week for six years, between the ages of sixty-five and seventy-one.

The Observator began in the form of 'Question and Answer', and then on 2 July 1681 'this Conference' was changed to a 'Dialogue betwixt Whigg and Tory', and finally, by 16 November 1682, into a dialogue between the Observator and a 'Trimmer', that is, an advocate of political compromise whom L'Estrange detested almost more than a diehard Whig:

> *Obs.* But then you must Consider that there are Severall *sorts* of **Trimmers**; as your **State-Trimmer**, Your **Law-Trimmer**; Your **Church-Trimmer**; Your **Trading-Trimmer**, &c. So that there must be a *Decorum* Observ'd, with a Respect to the *Quality* and *Condition* of the *Trimmer*, from the very *Coronet* to the *Dust-Cart*, by what *Degree* or *Title* soever he be *Dignify'd*, or *Distinguish'd*. There must be a Regard had to the Difference of *Cases* too, *Humours*, *Seasons Subjects*, &c. And now I'le begin with ye by the way of a *Tory*.
> *Trim.* And You shall Suppose *Mee* to be a *Statesman*.
> *Obs.* Ay; But of what *Magnitude?* A *Lord?* A *Knight?* Some *Overgrown Squire?* A *Citizen?* A *Bumkin?* A *Weaver?* A *Glover?* A *Costardmonger?* A *Kennell-Raker?* A *Plow-Jobber?* For there are Dablers in *Politicks*, of *all sorts*.
> *Trim.* Why truly *Nobs*, if they be all of a Price, I don't care if I be a **Lord**.
> *Obs.* We are over that Point then; And so *I am* your **Lordships** *most Humble Servant.*

The subject matter of *The Observator* varied from time to time: attacking the Popish Plot, supporting the veracity of the Rye House Plot, ridiculing the Whig printers and publishers, harassing the Dissenters, constantly calling up the spectre of 'Forty-one' and 'the Good Old Cause', and elaborating his own individualistic brand of political theory.[5] But it was all coffee-house *talk* or, at

3 The place of *The Observator* in the journalistic outburst of 1681 can be seen in the chronological tables of N&S.

4 Single half-folio sheets could be distributed within the metropolitan area by Docwra's Penny Post.

5 For instance, his sustained and unsentimental attack on Algernon Sidney's *Paper delivered to the Sheriffs* (1683).

times, coffee-house monologue – and L'Estrange is constantly at pains to stress the fact. He can be slangy, obscene, repetitive, rebarbative and allusive,[6] and he glories in it: he makes no concessions to the reader – if the reader has not the ears to *listen*, so be it. He represents no party; he sees himself as the voice of crude commonsense, commenting on the politics of his day.

For his contempories, and indeed for the modern scholar, *The Observator* can be read in two ways. Either in chronological context, day by day and week by week, alongside the other newsbooks and newsletters,[7] i.e. in the Nichols Newspapers in the Bodleian, or in the Burney Newspapers in the British Library. Or else as the solid two-volume folio dossier, complete with subject-index supplied by L'Estrange himself – and that is how it survived in gentlemen's libraries,[8] and that is how it was read by Macaulay,[9] who realized that the author he so detested was one of the primary sources for Restoration social history.

The line runs from, say, Marprelate to *The Observator* – and there it stops. In an amateurish essay on prescriptive grammar, Addison complains of the 'loquacity' of L'Estrange and of his age (*Spectator* no. 135, 4 August 1711). After L'Estrange, if a writer wishes to give the impression of talk, he assumes a *persona*, be it Mr Spectator, Sylvanus Urban, or Tristram Shandy: the solipsism of print truly begins after 1700.[10] Bourgeois respectability and the growth of a different reading public were the chief causes, but the concept of printing-house 'style', and standardized copy-editing, were also symptomatic of the change. The rot had already set in with the '*Mechanick* Exercises' (1683) of Joseph Moxon, FRS.[11] If the effect of the compositor's ideal of producing a 'normative' text, and an aesthetically satisfying printed page, was to muffle the spoken voice, then for L'Estrange it was 'Pragmaticall Foppery'. Earlier writers on the history of English book production have always stressed what was gained in the eighteenth century, without any consideration of what was lost: there is a case to be made for the Book Ugly, as well as for the Book Beautiful.

6 The manuscript marginal notes in some of the extant copies show that even contemporary readers sometimes had difficulties in identifying the allusions.

7 Even the best of them, Thomas Flatman's *Heraclitus ridens*, comes nowhere near the quality of L'Estrange.

8 N&S give locations of *The Observator* in eighteen libraries, but they give no indication that some libraries have multiple copies. Up to the late 1940s, the two-volume sets of *The Observator* were relatively easy to obtain from antiquarian booksellers.

9 Lot 671, Macaulay's auction sale, 4 March 1863.

10 Salazar 1995, p. 186 quotes from the Jansenistic Oratorian Bernard Lamy, *La rhétorique, ou l'art de parler* (Paris, 1699): 'Les paroles sur le papier sont comme un corps mort qui est étendu par terre. Dans la bouche de celui qui les profère, elles vivent, elles sont efficaces: sur le papier elles sont sans vie, incapables de produire les mêmes effets.'

11 Moxon 1962, pp. 211 and 217, urges the compositor 'to make his work show graceful to the Eye, and pleasant in Reading', and again, to be 'pleasing to a curious Eye'.

BEYOND LONDON
PRODUCTION, DISTRIBUTION, RECEPTION

32
The English provinces

JOHN BARNARD AND MAUREEN BELL

London and the provinces

The relationship between the London book trade and the provinces was for most of the sixteenth and seventeenth centuries conditioned by the power of members of the London Stationers' trade in controlling printing and distribution.[1] The relationship was, however, by no means one-way: London apprentices to the Company were, from the outset, predominantly drawn from outside the capital; bookbinders, booksellers and stationers in several towns and cities were already well established by 1600; and, although early attempts at printing outside London and the two university cities were minimal and exceptional, the end of the seventeenth century saw the beginnings of a provincial trade in printing which was to flourish in the eighteenth.[2] Thus, though the dominance of the London book trade over the whole of England and Wales was formally established by the incorporation of the Stationers' Company in 1557, that dominance was never complete, was continually challenged, and by 1695 was being significantly modified.

The main role of the provincial book trade in England and Wales from 1557 to 1695 was the distribution of vernacular books printed and published in London (which had little or no market outside Britain) and the sale of school books in Latin, printed either in London or abroad. Small in scale compared to other trades in provincial towns, the book trade rarely gave rise to its own guild, though York bookbinders and stationers obtained a charter in 1554, and in Chester stationers formed a guild with painters, glaziers and embroiderers as early as 1534. Hereford, Hull and (in 1675) Newcastle upon Tyne had guilds in which stationers were joined with other tradesmen; in most towns there were

1 We are indebted to the Leverhulme Trust without whose support this work could not have been undertaken.

2 For the provincial origins of apprentices 1555–1640 see McKenzie 1958 and Morgan 1978. Stoker 1981 discusses Anthony de Solempne's brief printing career (1568–73) in Norwich. A Royalist press was set up during the Civil War at Oxford, York, Newcastle, Worcester and Exeter.

simply too few traders in books to justify a stationers' guild.[3] The capital acted as a magnet for apprentices from all over England and Wales. D. F. McKenzie has shown that between 1562 and 1640 only 18 per cent of those apprenticed to the London trade came from the city itself.[4] From the 1640s, however, the number of Londoners apprenticed rose markedly, reaching a third of the total in the 1690s. By this time London and the home counties accounted for most of those bound (60 per cent), but the Midlands supplied the next most substantive cohort (31 per cent in the 1600s dropping to 18 per cent by the end of the century), while a small but significant number always came from Wales. Most of those freed by the Stationers' Company remained in the capital; some developed their London trade in connection with their home regions and a few, like Michael Harte of Exeter and Richard Moone of Bristol, eventually returned to set up business in their home towns.

In so far as they sought to restrict printing to London, the terms of the Stationers' Company's incorporation did no more than reflect economic reality. Earlier attempts to set up presses in York, for example, had demonstrated this only too clearly (as Oxford and Cambridge Universities, allowed the right to print, were to find out to their cost). Suitable paper for printing could only be bought from importers in London. To that cost had to be added the carriage of the raw material in one direction and of the finished products back to the capital, before they could be sold through the national distribution network. Without access to an adequate local market, co-operation of one kind or another with the London trade was inevitable. Only in the last twenty years of the seventeenth century did provincial booksellers have the capital to begin to publish in a small way with London partners. Nevertheless, the products of the London presses, over-priced and often worse produced than their Continental equivalents, were critically dependent on their sales outside the capital. At the same time, the provinces were eager for printed texts of very differing kinds.

The distribution of ballads and 'small books', whether merry or godly, presented no problem. Itinerant ballad-singers, pedlars and petty chapmen sold easily portable texts throughout the countryside at ale-houses, on the road and at fairs, and their presence is recorded as early as the 1570s.[5] London printers and booksellers quickly established their hegemony over this branch of the trade using long-established trading patterns. Inevitably, production of these lucrative and dependable genres was monopolized: from 1586 large numbers of ballads were being accumulated by a few stationers and by the 1630s the London ballad partners had gained overall control of their trade and were

3 Moran 1975. 4 Based on McKenzie 1958, table 3. See also Morgan 1978, pp. 1–2.
5 Watt 1993, p. 267; Spufford 1981, p. 116.

developing the trade in penny chapbooks which, by the late seventeenth century, had begun to take over from the ballad as the most prevalent form of cheap print.[6] Numbers of pedlars and petty chapmen increased from the 1670s onwards and in the last quarter of the century they were seen as a threat to retailers in market towns. Spufford estimates that by the 1690s there were possibly 10,000 of them, with groups concentrated around provincial towns from Newcastle upon Tyne southwards.[7] The textile manufacturing areas of the West Riding and Lancashire, the edges of the Cotswolds and the West Midlands metal area had notably high populations of itinerant traders. Successful foot pedlars (whose packs included ABCs, almanacs and ballads) might later in their careers buy horses or keep stalls, eventually settling to become shopkeepers (though usually excluded from local mercers' or drapers' companies) selling general goods with some stationery and a few books. There is evidence that both London and provincial booksellers took to the road, presumably often out of economic necessity. Nevil Simmons, who from 1692 had a shop in Sheffield, took out a hawker's licence for himself; and Samuel Johnson's father Michael, bookseller in Lichfield, kept stalls at Birmingham, Uttoxeter and Ashby-de-la-Zouche.[8] London booksellers also travelled to fairs where they both sold books direct to retail customers and dealt wholesale with other traders whose sideline was books and, increasingly, with other booksellers. Major fairs, like that at Stourbridge near Cambridge, were international in scope and attracted booksellers with considerable stocks. Stourbridge Fair, where the booksellers congregated in an area near the main road called Cooks Row, was attended both by established Cambridge booksellers (whose absence in 1593 because of plague in the town was remarked by Legate) and by those from London: in 1602 Richard Bankworth attended and in 1627 Francis Williams and John Harrison, 'one of the leading London stationers', sold Bibles there.[9] Harrison's stock included at least forty Bibles and Williams had more, many elaborately bound. In the 1680s Edward Millington held book auctions at Stourbridge and other fairs. Pollard suggests that Dunton's description of William Shrewsbury as 'perhaps . . . the only *Bookseller* that understands *Fair-keeping* to any advantage' indicates that it was almost a lost skill by the end of the seventeenth century.[10]

All this gave apparently little space for local booksellers. The traditional picture of books being sold in the provinces alongside other goods, like medicines and pills, is no doubt true;[11] it is unclear quite when London stationers began

6 Watt 1993, pp. 76, 289, 259 and below, ch. 23. 7 Spufford 1984; Spufford 1981, p. 120.
8 Spufford 1981, pp. 125, 75. 9 McKitterick 1992, pp. 16–17.
10 Pollard 1978, p. 14. 11 Alden 1952.

to favour the use of local retailers rather than going to the fairs themselves.[12] But a number of men, like John Foster of York, using their trade as binders to give added value for their customers, particularly through selling more or less elaborately bound Bibles, Testaments, psalters and Books of Common Prayer, were able to establish businesses in the larger conurbations mostly or wholly based on the sale of books. Bookbinders as well as booksellers and stationers are recorded by the 1550s in Norwich, York and Exeter as well as the two university cities and there is evidence that by 1600 there was a sustained book trade in Oxford, Cambridge, York, Newcastle, Norwich, Exeter, Ipswich and Chester. As well as supporting bookbinders, booksellers and stationers, several of these towns had also seen early attempts at printing.[13]

Oxford and Cambridge[14]

The book trade in the two university cities was on a larger scale than anywhere else outside London, and organized quite differently. Numbers of book-trade personnel in Oxford and of titles printed there seem both to have been about twice those in Cambridge.[15] It was the universities themselves, not local corporations, which licensed booksellers, binders, and, uniquely in the provinces, printers: it was in the universities' own interests to establish equitable conditions for both the trade and its own members.

Undergraduates and fellows were a dependable local clientele, whose needs increased as the universities began to grow rapidly from the 1580s and 1590s. The right to print allowed not just the official University Printer but the trade as a whole to develop to an extent not possible elsewhere. Further, both cities were only about fifty miles from London, and the Cambridge tradesmen could buy and sell to a wider market at Stourbridge Fair, while Oxford was on the route to the Cotswolds and Wales. Despite these considerable advantages the economic and legal power of the London trade meant that the booksellers and more particularly the universities and their printers had to collaborate with, or come to accommodation with, the Stationers' Company.

In the late sixteenth century native-born men took over the trade in both cities, forming a close-knit community made up of small businesses dominated by one or two larger ones. Some, particularly those of binders, were on a very

12 Pollard 1978b, p. 14.

13 We are very grateful to Peter Isaac for allowing us access to the *British Book Trade Index (BBTI)*, currently in process of compilation.

14 This account is heavily dependent on McKitterick 1992 and Philip and Morgan 1997.

15 See *BBTI* and Bell and Barnard 1998. Field's collusion with George Sawbridge probably means that more sheets, however, were printed at Cambridge (p. 200 above).

small scale: in 1606 the Oxford bookbinder Robert Billingsley left tools and materials worth only £2 13*s*.[16] Others were on a much larger scale than elsewhere in the provinces. When he died in 1581 John Sheres, never Cambridge's University Printer, but with Continental connections and himself of Dutch origin, was worth nearly £900: his book stock was valued at £150, the same scale as John Foster's stock in York thirty-five years later.[17] University Printers, who were in business on their own account and at greater risk with (sometimes) both a book shop and the expenses of a printing press, could build up substantial businesses. When Thomas Thomas died in Cambridge in 1588 his estate was valued at £920 12*s*. 9*d*., nearly half of which was invested in his business.[18] A century later his successor, John Field, was worth £1,786 2*s*. 9*d*., most of which was in books and printing equipment.[19]

The career of Joseph Barnes (*c*. 1546–1618), first Printer for the University of Oxford and so not typical of the majority of his trade, nevertheless shows the two-way relationship between the book trade and the university (a relationship already evident in the years 1450 to 1550).[20] Barnes, freed by the Stationers' Company in 1573, set up as printer in Oxford with a £100 loan from the university in 1584 and published actively until 1617. Since 1575 he had been licensed as a vintner, and on his death his High Street premises included two printing shops and a wine cellar, with books making up a quarter of his £1,128 2*s*. 9*d*. estate. His will shows his gratitude to the university: he left £5 to the University Library, 5 marks to the library of 'my loving neighboures of Brazenose College', and another 5 marks to Magdalen College's library.[21] During his lifetime his shop seems to have been a convivial meeting place for college fellows and may have circulated London newsletters, making it a precursor of later coffee-shops.[22]

The stock of booksellers in the two university cities differed markedly from that in other provincial centres. A major factor was supplying the needs of the university syllabus and the interests of senior members of the university. In consequence, a far higher proportion of their books was in Latin, many printed on the Continent. For instance, Nicolas Clifton's Oxford inventory of 1579 records only 11 per cent books in English: the rest were in Latin with a sprinkling of Greek and French books.[23] In Cambridge, Nicholas Pilgrim (1545) had only three titles in English out of 382 in all (though the three did include Chaucer's 'Opera' at 5*s*. 8*d*.); otherwise his stock was mainly of

16 Gibson 1907, p. 20.
17 McKitterick 1992, pp. 64–5; Gray and Palmer 1915. The £150 includes 'bookes in the howse'.
18 McKitterick 1992, p. 109. 19 Gray and Palmer 1915, pp. 107–9. 20 Ferdinand 1997.
21 Gibson 1907, pp. 26–7. 22 Bennett 1999. 23 Gibson 1907, pp. 10–16.

current Latin works imported from the Continent. The inventories of John Dennis (1578), of an anonymous bookseller (1588/9), and of Reignold Bridges (1590/1) show very similar proportions in their stock.[24]

Bookbinding was of considerable importance for most if not all booksellers and stationers, as elsewhere, but in both cities some craftsmen relied on binding alone for their living. Although many collectors favoured plain calf binding and textbooks were bound unpretentiously, John Dennis's Cambridge shop had the capacity for fine binding in the late 1570s: in addition to an extensive array of presses and binding materials, he had a 'gilding coushin', two corner flowers, 'printes for the cover of books' and a 'rose for the backe of a booke'.[25] Subsequently, Daniel Boyse (*fl.* 1616–30), Henry Moody (*fl.* 1612–37) and John Houlden (until 1661/2) were active, binding presentation copies for the university.[26] Houlden died in 1670 and his tools passed to his son-in-law, Titus Tillet.[27] Elaborate bindings began to be undertaken in Oxford after the Restoration where the work of Roger Bartlett in the 1680s and of Richard Sedgley in the next decade is of particular importance.[28]

Apart from the brief explosion of Royalist pamphlet printing in Oxford during the Civil War which peaked at 227 items in 1643,[29] printing in the two universities was in the hands of the University Printers. Their role as publishers for their respective institutions is discussed in an earlier chapter.[30] However, both could also print for others, either locally or from London. Oxford publications funded by Oxford or London booksellers include such ambitious works as the first five editions of Burton's *Anatomy of melancholy* (1621–38), the 1620 Bodleian catalogue, and the first English translation of Bacon's *Advancement of learning* (1640). The acquisition of a large range of exotic types (Arabic, Hebrew, Aramaic and Anglo-Saxon) enabled the publication of works like Wallis's *Opera mathematica* (1656–7) and Sommer's Anglo-Saxon dictionary (1659) to be published during the Commonwealth.[31] Although John Fell succeeded in publishing several important scholarly works in the 1670s through the university's printing house, it was the University of Cambridge which took, in 1696, 'the momentous step . . . of engaging directly in printing and bookselling',[32] setting up a true university press. Until then the local book

24 Leedham-Green 1986, nos. 25, 142, 163, 167.

25 Gray and Palmer 1915, pp. 56–7.

26 For two bindings by Daniel Boyse and some remarks on Cambridge bindings of the seventeenth century, see Foot 1978–83, I, pp. 59–75, nos. 73–5, 100, 136–8. See also Oates 1953.

27 Nixon 1974, p. 48, no. 126.

28 Philip and Morgan 1997, p. 684, citing *Fine bindings* 1968, nos. 215, 224–6, 231–2, and Foot 1978–83, II, pp. 169, 191, nos. 129, 151 and the references there cited. See also Nixon 1974, pp. 46–7, nos. 117–240.

29 Philip and Morgan 1997, p. 679.

30 McKitterick, above, pp. 201–5.

31 Philip and Morgan 1997, pp. 680–1.

32 Carter 1975, p. 142.

trade was largely responsible for publishing scholarly works by members of the university. In particular Richard Davis, made University Stationer in 1639, in a career which lasted until 1685 when it ended in debt, risked more than most to support academic publication in Oxford. In all he published or was involved in the publication of over 250 works. This output, often undertaken in partnership with other Oxford booksellers, included textbooks, sermons and other short works, but also encompassed scientific works, notably those of Robert Boyle from 1663 to 1684.[33] In publishing the medical works of Thomas Willis in 1672 and 1679 Davis '[took] over the cost and the risk of marketing books which the university delegates were glad to print but lacked the organisation to distribute'.[34]

In the last half of the seventeenth century in Cambridge, as David McKitterick points out, the 'support provided by Sawbridge and the Stationers' Company in effect subsidized local publishing, by sustaining a press of a size unwarranted by local capital'.[35] Several Cambridge booksellers were wealthier than John Hayes, University Printer since 1669. Henry Dickinson left an estate valued at £2,243 in 1694/5, including debts due to him of £1,575; William Morgan left £500 to his son, and owned freehold property in Cambridge as well as land in Suffolk. With capital to invest they were able to pay for new publications in addition to turning over stock, and from the late 1670s they turned to sharing their investment, long the case in London, though in Cambridge the need to raise capital was the driving force rather than the fair distribution of profits.[36] From the 1660s local booksellers had published books which were not wholly limited to established academic demands. In addition to textbooks, they also published works which reflected the intellectual interests in the university and works by its members, among which were scientific works like those by the oculist, William Briggs. Many of the books published (in English, Latin or, less frequently, Greek) were editions of earlier texts, but many were original. In both Oxford and Cambridge booksellers had established a viable, if relatively small, role as publishers, usually looking in the first instance to their immediate audience, but dependent upon a wider readership reached through the London trade.

Growth

Evidence for the personnel of the English provincial book trade, particularly outside Oxford and Cambridge, is inconsistent and incomplete. Apart

33 Philip and Morgan 1997, pp. 682–3. 34 *Ibid.*, pp. 367–8.
35 McKitterick 1992, p. 368. 36 *Ibid.*

from those few names which appear in imprints, usually alongside that of a London bookseller, and which show a marked increase in the last decades of the seventeenth century, the main sources are lists of freemen, the records of town corporations, and individuals' wills and inventories. There are four studies (of Norwich, Exeter, Hull, and of Bristol from 1635) which exploit these resources systematically; another has examined York from the 1590s to 1618.[37] The lists of freemen in these cities, together with those of Chester, give some idea of the way the book trade (bookbinders, stationers, and booksellers) expanded between 1557 and 1695 (see appendix 1, table 9). The first bookbinder in York was bound as early as 1452: the marked drop in the number of freemen there between 1596 and 1635 had to do with city politics, and certainly underestimates the number of men trading in that period: in 1616 there were between five and six booksellers active in the city, only one of them, Thomas Richardson, a freeman.[38] Some, like Anthony and John Foster, took advantage of the ecclesiastical liberties, so avoiding paying the city for their freedom or appearing on its rolls. This may have been true of other cities. Bristol, in any case, is underrepresented since the record there begins only in 1635: its book trade may have been on a par with Norwich or Exeter by the end of the sixteenth century. Information from the *British Book Trade Index* supplements this picture, identifying Ipswich as supporting a range of book trades (stationers from the 1530s, a bookbinder in 1556 and booksellers from 1574 onwards) and Newcastle upon Tyne as a city whose book trade was on a scale comparable to York's (ten stationers between 1496 and 1515, with booksellers from 1561 onwards).[39] Clearly, the size of the book trade was linked to the size and importance of individual cities and was often a continuation of trades which pre-dated print: Norwich had a family of bookbinders in the late fourteenth century and York supported bookbinders and stationers from at least the mid-fifteenth century.[40] Paul Morgan's remarks on the concentration of the trade 'in the area bounded by [the] Mersey, Dee, Avon and Severn' with 'another area south-west from Bristol to Plymouth' and little, with the exception of York and Newcastle, in the north seems to hold true.[41]

37 Stoker 1981–5; Maxted forthcoming; Chilton 1982; Barry 1985 and unpublished; Barnard and Bell 1994.

38 Barnard and Bell 1994, p. 4.

39 *BBTI*. Newcastle's book trade members were usually freed to another trade: two stationers, Richard Randell and Peter Maplesdon, freed in 1676, also belonged to the newly founded (1675) Newcastle Company of Upholsterers, Tinplate-Workers and Stationers; neither of the two founding members of that body, Thomas Clarke or Michael Durram, were freemen. See Hunt and Isaac 1977, pp. 165–7, Todd 1923.

40 *BBTI*: Agnes, Adam and Thomas Bookbynder of Norwich (*c.* 1375–97); in York, Thomas and John Messyngham (*c.* 1450–85) and Peter Moreux (1494), bookbinders, and Richard Garnett (1490–1502) and Frederick Freez (1495–1515), stationers.

41 Morgan 1990, p. 32.

Although the evidence is fragmentary, bookselling in provincial towns was an established fact in the 1560s and firmly in place by the 1580s. In 1571 Robert Scott of Norwich, freed there as a grocer in 1561, was sued for £12 10*s*. outstanding by the London bookseller, Abraham Veale, for goods supplied between July 1568 and November 1570.[42] In 1572/3 a 'new builded shoppe' in York Minster's Close was rented to 'the Staconer', Anthony Foster, whose business was sufficiently well developed by 1585 to sell the future Dean of Ripon, then vicar of Kirk Deighton, a 1564 Basel edition of Athanasius for 10*s*. 6*d*.[43] The shop was to remain in the hands of the Foster family until at least 1616, and it is notable that family dynasties, often continued by intermarriage within the trade, seem to have sustained businesses for decades in the provinces,[44] just as they did in London. In 1585 it was possible to buy Continental theological books in Shrewsbury as well as York. The London bookseller, Roger Ward, was unable to repay a debt of £240 to a local draper. His possessions in Shrewsbury were therefore seized. The inventory of his shop there gives a detailed list of his stock, which probably contained unauthorized editions by himself or John Wolfe,[45] and was a branch of his troubled London business, but nevertheless one selling to provincial customers. Ward himself came from Shrewsbury, an important centre for supplying books to Wales (the potential importance of this trade had been recognized when John Oswen, who had an agent in the town, was appointed King's Printer for Wales and the Marches in 1549). Ward's stock of over 2,000 books contained the same categories of books which Robert Scott was buying in Norwich in 1568–70, but in addition included many recent titles, mainly in English and dominated by religious books, but with a good range of books on other topics, along with Continental works. Anthony Foster's York stock in 1585 may well have been very similar.

Economic scale

The evidence for the economic scale of provincial booksellers' businesses is too skimpy to allow for certainty. Twenty inventories listing the value of booksellers' stock between 1538 and 1700 give variable and not easily comparable information.[46] The earliest, that of Newell Mores of York, valued his 126

42 PRO CP40/1297 m. 1668 Michaelmas 1571.

43 Mortimer 1962, p. 21. Higgin bought two further books from Foster (Basel, 1531, and Paris, 1564 (Mortimer 1962, pp. 4, 56)).

44 Barnard and Bell 1994, pp. 3–4, 7–16.

45 Rodger 1958.

46 See Barnard and Bell 1994, p. 40n. To these should be added those for Newell Mores (York, 1538), Palliser and Selwyn 1972; Roger Ward (Shrewsbury 1585), Rodger 1958; Michael Harte (Exeter, 1615) Maxted 1996; Augustyne Waitman (Lincoln 1617), Lincolnshire Archives, Inv. 120/72; James Milner (Warrington, 1639), Rylands 1885; Eden Williams (Lincoln, 1671), Johnston

copies of books at £3 3*s*. 10*d*. His stock, mainly of Continental books with some printed for York use, was aimed at clergy and theological lawyers,[47] and is the smallest in the sample. In eleven cases a minimum number of copies is given or can be calculated: the largest are those of Michael Harte (Exeter, 1615) with 4,558 and John Foster (York, 1616) with 3,374: two (Mountford, Warwick,1677) and Williams (Hereford, 1695) had less than 300 copies, while Awdley (Hull, 1644) had 832 copies in stock . Roger Ward's Shrewsbury stock amounted to over 2,000 books and in 1671 Eden Williams's 'great shopp' in Lincoln contained in excess of 2,015 books and pamphlets.[48] Two more had stocks of just over 1,000 (Booth, Warrington, 1648; Benson, Penrith, 1698). If, however, the 3,000 titles (excluding school books and over half of them Divinity) listed in William London's *Catalogue of the most vendible books* (1657), directed at the gentry and clergy in Durham, Northumberland, Cumberland and Westmorland, really represented books he had in stock, then this Newcastle bookseller, active from at least 1653 to 1660, operated on a larger scale than any other we have found. In terms of value, Augustyne Waitman of Lincoln (1617) had books worth £213 6*s*. 8*d*., Brooke of Coventry (1679) £147 3*s*. 10*d*., John Foster of York (1616) £144 16*s*. 10*d*., and Michael Harte (1615) £103 8*s*. 2*d*, with Dawkin Gove leaving books worth £29 3*s* 5*d*. in 1692 (of which books in Welsh made up a third of the value). The remainder range from just over £4 to £96 0*s*. 8*d*. In comparison, when the London bookseller and printer, Henry Bynneman, died in 1585 he had some 19,000 volumes in stock valued at just over £600 (though almost half of this is accounted for by his unfinished dictionary of Morelius).[49]

None of these men's trade, then, was on a large scale, and inventories give only a snapshot of a business. John Foster (York, 1616) was owed money (not necessarily for books) by forty-three people, mainly clergymen but including laymen, and one woman, Tomisin Wattersworth, all living within a thirty-mile radius of his shop. His debts were a tenth of the value of his book stock.[50] Robert Booth (Warrington, 1648), judging by his inventory, must have acted as a local wholesaler of school books, as more certainly did John Minshull of Chester in 1699–1700.[51] John Brooke of Coventry may also have been a wholesaler in this way, but he had other irons in the fire. His total goods and debts were worth £1,129 17*s*. 2*d*. on his death in 1679, five times his nearest rival, Augustyne Waitman (Lincoln, 1617), who was worth £257 6*s*. 4*d*. (mostly in books), and

1991, pp. 36–37; and Dawkin Gove (Carmarthen 1692), National Library of Wales, SD/1692/17, discussed and partly printed in Rees 1987, pp. xvi–vii.

47 Palliser and Selwyn 1972. 48 Johnston 1991, pp.36–7.

49 Barnard and Bell 1991, pp. 12, 24. 50 Barnard and Bell 1994, pp. 16–21.

51 Plomer 1904.

almost ten times that of John Foster in York (£163 16*s*. 2*d*.). Brooke's book stock, though, was only fractionally more valuable than Foster's: debts due to him totalled no less than £847 16*s*. 5*d*, of which the smaller part was debts for books (£136 4*s*. 8*d*. 'Sperate' and £55 11*s*. 9*d*. 'Desperate'). Although no details of the books he held are given, it seems likely that Brooke relied on a quick turnover as a local wholesaler of Stock books on long credit, and also retailed books, but was involved in other larger ventures. The steady sales of what were to become Stock titles can be inferred from Robert Scott's purchases in Norwich in 1568–70 and are clear from Brooke's 1679 inventory: they are entirely explicit in the accounts kept by the treasurer of the Stock. As Cyprian Blagden has shown, almanacs were sold annually in the hundreds of thousands,[52] but sales of other categories were also substantial. In 1676/7 catechisms, Psalters and Psalms numbered 38,923 (17 per cent in value of all Stock books), primers, ABCs and *Child's guides* amounted to 124,725, while 523,730 school books were printed (13 per cent in value).[53]

Hawkers, pedlars and petty chapmen dealing in books and ballads also relied on credit arrangements with their suppliers. They stocked up seasonally, in spring, and set off travelling for the next six or eight months, sometimes with large amounts of goods on credit. Chapbook publishers congregated around Smithfield market and on London Bridge, close to the major routes out of London, and supplied both individual pedlars and chapmen running larger businesses. Petty chapmen often worked for chapmen in London or in provincial towns who might supply them with ready-stocked packs made up of mixed goods. The chain of credit produced by such arrangements is visible from records at the point where it broke down, usually at the death of the chapman who, owing large amounts to London suppliers, was himself owed numerous small sums from customers over a wide area. Successful chapmen could, however, accumulate considerable wealth. Spufford gives the example of Joan Dant, Quaker, who began as a pedlar with a route around Friends' houses and ended, when she died aged eighty-three in 1714, with £9,000.[54] London stationers clearly developed relationships with chapmen whom they regularly supplied: Thomas Whitaker left money in his will to 'my good friends and chapmen' to buy memorial rings, and another stationer's will makes a similar provision, the money to be paid when their debts to him had been discharged.[55] Sale-or-return arrangements seem to have been usual for ballad publishers supplying chapmen.[56]

52 Blagden 1958b. 53 Barnard 1994, pp. 22–24.
54 Spufford 1984, *passim*; for Dant, see p. 46. 55 Spufford 1984, p. 80.
56 Spufford 1984.

The decline of the practice of fair-going amongst London booksellers during the seventeenth century, suggested by Dunton's praise of William Shrewsbury's fair-keeping skills, may have been a consequence of its being essentially uneconomic. Pollard quotes as evidence the Wardens of the Stationers' Company who, in accusing John Wolfe and others of piracy in 1583, remarked that they 'runne vp or down to all ye faires and markets through a great part of ye Realme, and make sale of them; whose charges in cariage with their expences in Innes and Alehouses and other places considered... they returne home more poore than they went out . . .'[57] Books, though not necessarily pamphlets, sold at fairs had to be ready bound, making carriage charges more expensive than for books sent in sheets to provincial booksellers like the Fosters who could bind them locally. As the numbers of provincial booksellers grew, London booksellers must have found it more cost-effective to sell their books wholesale and in sheets to country booksellers who might themselves retail them on their stalls at local markets and fairs.

Books and readers

There were, then, plenty of points of access for the provincial reading public. In 1571 the stock of Robert Scott's shop in Norwich included Bibles, psalters, psalms, almanacs, ballads and school books (among them an Antwerp edition of Terence), devotional works and a few miscellaneous books, including Stowe's *Chronicles*. Since Scott was ordering regularly at two-week intervals on average, there was already an established market for binding and selling these categories of books in a major provincial city. The same kinds of books were bought in 1576 and 1585 by the Taunton bookseller, John Herne, and the York bookseller, Richard Brett (not a freeman), from Francis Coldstock and Thomas Marsh respectively. Interestingly, Herne also ordered a considerable number of small law books.[58] In 1585 Thomas Marsh sued Edward Wingfield, Esquire, of Kimbolton Castle in Huntingdon for payment for a wide variety of books, mainly in the vernacular, which ranged from Stow's *Chronicles* (6*s*. 8*d*.) and Morelius's dictionary (18*s*. 6*d*.) to chapbooks.[59] It is not clear whether the debt was incurred through buying from Marsh at the local fair or from his shop in London when Wingfield was in town.

57 Arber, II, p. 779.

58 For Scott, see Stoker 1976, pp. 115–27 and appendix H (PRO CP40/1297 m. 1668 Michaelmas 1571); for Herne and Brett see Plomer 1916, pp. 324–6.

59 Plomer 1916, pp. 327–9.

Paul Morgan has shown that in the early part of the seventeenth century Frances Wolfreston could well have assembled her collection of recreational vernacular literature from local Midland booksellers alone.[60] In the last quarter of the century and in a region less well served by bookshops, a collection of more than 350 books (school books, devotional works, music, poetry and fiction, advice books) was amassed by Leonard Wheatcroft, yeoman of Ashbourne, Derbyshire.[61] In Yorkshire there was an active book culture among the gentry and clergy which depended on acquiring books through London booksellers, local booksellers, and through mutual lending, gifts and legacies.[62] If John Foster's 'Twenty-foure cattologes of the Mart' really were a series of Frankfurt book fair catalogues his customers could have ordered those Continental books not in stock through his London contacts. It is probable that Archbishop Matthew of York in part built up his very important library at the same time by using the Frankfurt catalogues still in York Minster library.[63] Sir Thomas Knyvett (c. 1539–1618) of Ashwellthorpe, Norfolk, amassed his considerable library, which had a minority of English books printed in England, through his brother, Henry, in London.[64] Others, like Drummond of Hawthornden, bought books as students during their Continental travels and, once more, when they returned to Britain.[65] At the end of the seventeenth century Richard Coffin of Portsedge, near Exeter, used his fellow countryman and bibliophile, Richard Lapthorne, as a London agent for book purchases through dealers or at auctions between 1683 and 1697. Lapthorne sent Coffin not only advice and books, but catalogues, including the *Term Catalogues*.[66]

The *Term Catalogues* raise an awkward question. How did earlier provincial readers discover the titles of books they might want to buy? The 'popular' market was easily available through itinerant dealers and fairs. After the Restoration, the *Term Catalogues* (from 1668) and the increasing number of book advertisements in the *London gazette* gave booksellers and readers a good account of new publications. Before that, aids to purchasing books were limited.[67] A few booksellers saw the need for the circulation of information within the trade: catalogues of books available for sale were published by Andrew Maunsell (1595), William Jaggard (1618) and by the Newcastle upon Tyne bookseller,

60 Morgan 1989, pp. 208–9.
61 His schoolmaster son, Titus, compiled a catalogue of his own and his father's books in 1722: Bell and Parfitt forthcoming.
62 Barnard and Bell 1994, p. 19.
63 Barnard and Bell 1994, p. 70; information from Bernard Barr.
64 McKitterick 1978, p. 10. 65 MacDonald 1971. 66 Treadwell 1997, *passim* and p. 212.
67 For access to Continental books see above p. 673.

William London (1657, 1658 and 1660). By the 1650s a few London booksellers were augmenting the brief lists of stock sometimes appearing at the back of books by circulating separate lists of their books, subdivided by subject or genre. Humphrey Moseley throughout the 1650s and Obadiah Blagrave in 1678 had separate lists printed, and specialist lists of plays, such as that issued by Francis Kirkman in 1661, also appeared.[68] Prior to that books printed in England could only have been identified by going to the shops of London booksellers when the prospective buyer (or his agent) had the time to see what they had on sale, or by visiting their stalls at fairs, or (as now) by following up references in books they were using. Nonetheless, the appearance of Jonson's 1616 *Works* in John Foster's York inventory[69] in the same year that it was published points to a swift exchange between London-produced culture and provincial readers.

A comparison of the stock of seven provincial booksellers for whom sufficiently detailed evidence survives (Shrewsbury 1585, York 1616, Hull 1644, Warrington 1648, Warwick 1677, Hereford 1695, Penrith 1698)[70] indicates that throughout this period most booksellers were catering very specifically for local clergy and schoolmasters. Inconsistencies in inventories (counting titles in some cases, copies in others) demand caution, but a broad pattern is discernible: in four cases out of the seven, more than 70 per cent of the stock consisted of religious and educational books and indeed in Warwick these constituted the entire stock. Only the Hereford and York shops (both in cathedral cities) are notable for their high proportion (more than 30 per cent) of subjects *other* than these (though Shrewsbury comes close with 29 per cent) and Foster's York bookshop is the only one of the seven whose stock is evenly balanced between the three categories of religious, educational and 'other subjects'. The market in the provinces for school books and devotional works was supplied not only by the local book trade, however: local clergy and schoolmasters may have acted as agents for London booksellers, and haberdashers and mercers sold books alongside their other wares. The inventory of Symon Sachel of Bleasby, clerk, made in 1658, includes an account of his widow's disposal of his estate, including: 'Paid to the Bookseller at London for bookes which her husband had received upon trust – £5'; these may have been ordered for personal use, but equally could have been intended for re-sale or as charitable gifts. His 'Studye of bookes' valued at £30 reappears, valued the same, in 1665

68 Greg 1939–59, III prints selections from these lists. For Moseley, see Reed 1927–30 and Kewes 1995.

69 Barnard and Bell 1994, p. 75.

70 Six of these are tabulated in Barnard and Bell 1994, p. 41; for Shrewsbury, information taken from Rodger 1958.

in the inventory of his deceased wife's goods.[71] In 1674 the goods of John Betney, a mercer of Mansfield, were inventoried. His stock, principally cloth, thread, needles and buttons, also included five dozen ABCs, twenty-one schoolbooks and four psalters.[72] It was through small shops such as Betney's that many country people living near market towns bought the means to a limited literacy.

The trade in illegal books

The discussion up to this point has dealt with the legitimate side of the provincial book trade, but the dependence of London booksellers on the country trade ensured that provincial stationers and booksellers were also involved in distributing those books which were illegally printed or imported, either because they were banned by the authorities or because they evaded the rights of patentees or the Stationers' Company. The examples which follow are less a demonstration of the Company's strictly imposed authority, as has been usually thought, than of its difficulties in exercising its powers effectively; they also suggest that the threats to its authority were of differing kinds.[73]

In 1567 the Stationers sent Thomas Purfoot I and Hugh Singleton to York to examine four York stationers suspected of selling banned Catholic books as well as ABCs, Latin primers, portasses and missals. No works by Catholic writers were found, but, among other books, a number of primers sent by the London bookseller, Thomas Marsh, to John Goldthwaite and Thomas Wraythe were impounded,[74] which suggests that the Company was concerned with copyright infringements quite as much as banned books. Banned books were, in any case, difficult to track down. For example, on 20 August 1637 the Bishop of Chester complained that although Peter Ince was the only stationer in the city (he had been freed in 1612), 'no Puritanicall bookes' are printed 'but our citizens get them as soon as any', and when Ince's premises were searched in November 'all the birds were flown ere the nest was searched'.[75] Years later, control of the trade in the same cities was still eluding the Company, but now in relation to printing. In 1685, 1686 and 1688 the Company took action against supernumerary printers in York, culminating in the appointment of John White as sole printer in York, with 'sole power of printing papers relating to revenue and courts of justice in the five northern counties'; in 1694 there was concern that pamphlets were being printed at an unsupervised press in Chester,

71 Nottingham Record Office: PRSW 75/46; PRSW 79/18. 72 PRSW 22/4a, 1674.

73 See Hunt 1997 for the serious danger posed to the Company by patentees.

74 Davies 1988, pp. 30–3. 75 Stewart-Brown 1932, p. 131.

and two years later the Company sought action against a Chester printer for printing almanacs without permission.[76]

The well-known case brought by the Stationers' Company against Roger Ward, who joined John Wolfe and others in a major revolt against the Company's wealthier members' monopoly of popular titles, also shows the importance of the provincial market, and is suggestive about the relations between the London and country trades. In 1582 Ward admitted that he had printed 10,000 *ABCs with the little catechism*. Such a large quantity obviously presented a distribution problem, the more so as speed was essential to avoid detection. In bringing its case the Company was particularly eager to find out who had sold the illegal copies: the defendants were equally determined to give away as little as possible. Ward admitted to selling 500 to the stationer, William Holmes, and another 2,000 to Abraham Draper, a draper. The rest, apart from 200 remaining imperfect copies (that is, 7,100 copies), Ward claimed he had 'sent to Shrewesburye to be ther[e] utteryd and solde in this defendantes Shoppe by JOHN LEGGE a servant to this defendant'.[77] The Stationers' Company was unable to discover anything further, but their petition to the Privy Council in 1583 against the distribution of illegally printed privileged books by men 'who runne vp or downe to all ye faires and markets through a great part of ye Realme'[78] shows the importance of the market outside London for illegal books.

A few years later a very different kind of book, the expensive folio of the third edition of Sidney's *Arcadia*, was printed for Robert Waldegrave (earlier involved in printing the Marprelate tracts) in Edinburgh and clandestinely sold in England, undercutting the price of the real third edition. When William Ponsonby, who had title to the work, took action six copies were in the shop of the Cambridge printer, John Legate; more significantly, Legate's former apprentice, William Scarlett, a bookbinder (who gave his occupation as butler and caterer to Trinity Hall) seems to have been involved two years previously in setting up the piracy with Waldegrave in Edinburgh, and admitted selling twenty copies, eighteen of them to the London bookseller, Richard Banckworth. So the Edinburgh piracy, shipped to London by sea, was in part vended through the Cambridge trade via King's Lynn and the Ouse.[79]

The distribution of Catholic books was a lucrative, if risky, business and Michael Sparke's account of his forty years in the trade as '*Stationer* and a

76 SC Court Book F, fols. 47^{v}, 57^{v}–58, 103^{v}, 166–166^{v}, 215^{v}, 263; *CSPD 1687–89*, p. 189; *1689–90*, p. 122.

77 Arber, II, p. 760; see pp. 753–86 for a fuller record, and Judge 1934, pp. 29–60, for a detailed account of Wolfe's and Ward's battle with the Company.

78 Arber, II, p. 779.

79 Judge 1934, pp. 100–5.

wholesaleman' gives some insight into its regional organization.[80] Sparke's master, Simon Pauley, 'dealt much in *Popish Books*; and in the first year of King *James* reign, spent his time in *Staffordshire* at *Worly-hall* in binding, vending, and putting to sale *Popish Books*, *Pictures*, *Beads*, and such *Trash*'.[81] Sparke refers to his own chapmen in Worcester and in particular his dealings with Francis Ash, bookbinder and 'an excellent *Workman*' who in the 1640s was 'in a manner *Agent*' for the Catholics in Worcestershire and was well known in Bristol, Gloucester, Shrewsbury and Hereford. Ash had a large Catholic trade and 'got a good considerable summe of money in his hand' by binding '*Popish* pictures' with octavo English Bibles. Based in Worcester, he supplied a whole region with Catholic books and himself travelled to France to obtain the best pictures 'as of *Vandikes Draft*', commissioning Hollar as engraver of a series.[82]

The importation of Bibles and psalms printed more cheaply abroad was a long-standing problem for the London Company. Michael Sparke, who was later to lead the fight against the Bible patentees, was accused of illegally importing Bibles in 1631 and copies were seized in 'London, Bristol, York and other towns'.[83] Despite seizures by Customs, Bibles from Scotland and from Holland continued to flood in: in the 1640s Thomas Cowper and eight others complained of the seizure by Customs of their imported Bibles (his own consignment consisted of 850 Bibles, 2,000 prayer books and 750 psalm books), William Jackson was imprisoned for importing Bibles from Amsterdam, a search was ordered for 'counterfeit' Psalms sold in the country and city, Bibles from Scotland were seized and in 1646 and 1649 Wardens of the Company were implicated in the buying of 'beyond sea psalms'.[84] Members of the Company continued to circumvent their own monopoly to make a profit: in 1684 the Bishop of Oxford complained that, because the Company's high prices and short print runs left the nation unsupplied, they in fact encouraged the importing of Holland Bibles which they then seized, sold and 'when they were retailed, they seized them again and extorted the penalty from the poor country chapmen'.[85]

The Chancery proceedings which the Company brought in 1699 against Robert Wellington, the London bookseller, and John Minshull of Chester give an insight into the mechanics and speed of national and local distribution, and

80 *A second beacon fired by Scintilla* . . ., 1652 (Wing S2259), p. 5.

81 *Ibid.*, pp. 5–6.

82 *Ibid.*, pp. 5–7.

83 Greg 1967, pp. 80–1. It is not clear whether Sparke imported the Bibles through London or used the outports of Bristol, York, and elsewhere.

84 *CSPD 1640–41*, pp. 508–9; *1641–43*, p. 34; SC Court Book C, fols. 198, 201, 206, 236–6^{v}.

85 *CSPD Oct. 1683–April 1684*, pp. 364–5. The Bishop of Oxford was not, of course, a disinterested observer.

a probable example of collusion between the London and country trades. The two men were accused of illegally printing and selling the Psalms in metre, and of selling imported copies of titles owned by the Company. John Minshull claimed that he had been a freeman of Chester for twenty-five years, and that he had been apprenticed to Peter Bodnell or Bodvell, a London bookseller burnt out by the Great Fire who had then set up business in Chester. Bodnell, who was born in Carnaervon and freed in 1663,[86] was made a freeman of Chester in 1667/8. The links here between London and the provinces are characteristic of the trade, and explain how Minshull made contact with Wellington. But the Chester bookseller also provided a schedule of the psalters and school books he had sold between January 1699 and September 1700. In twenty-one months he sold over 2,000 books worth £52 2*s.* 1½*d.* to fifteen customers. Most of these were clearly to other tradesmen selling books on a smaller scale in Wales or Cheshire. Minshull's role was that of a local wholesaler for the London trade, selling on to at least seven Welsh towns within a fifty-mile (or, if 'Whitchurch' is Whitechurch, Wales, a 100 mile) radius, as well as to a few booksellers in Cheshire. This part of his trade was divided in terms of quantity and value between psalters (30 per cent) and schoolbooks (70 per cent).[87] Even if this action was brought as a test case by the Company following the lapse of the Licensing Act in 1695, it reveals not merely the commercial importance to the Stationers of its ageing school books, but the extensiveness of a national distribution network which reached deep into Wales. In 1699 the country trade was colluding with London booksellers to distribute swiftly the cheaper versions of one kind or another (pirated or imported) of company titles just as it had when Roger Ward illegally printed and sold *ABCs with the little catechism* in 1581.

The country network was also an efficient circulator of controversial books and pamphlets which the government wished to suppress. In 1682 Sir Roger L'Estrange said:

> Of my experience of the Stationers' ways and confederacies for dispersing libels, I am more and more confirmed that the certain way of detecting and tracing them must begin from the country, for their course is this: the first thing they do on the printing of any remarkable pamphlet is to furnish the Kingdom up and down with an impression or two, before they offer at the dispersing of any [in London].[88]

Pressure could easily be applied to provincial booksellers involved in the circulation of sedition. The Secretary of State, investigating the distribution of

86 McKenzie 1974, no. 514 (bound and freed as Bodnell).

87 Based on Plomer 1904.

88 *CSPD 1682*, p. 563.

a libel in 1688, sent a series of letters to local JPs and officials directing the questioning of named booksellers in York, Chester, Norwich, Exeter, Bristol, Daventry, Oxford, Cambridge, Worcester and Hull.[89] While some provincial agents in sedition were fully aware of the source of their books, others were (or claimed to be) ignorant; and sometimes London suppliers misjudged the situation and sent books to tradesmen like the Northampton bookseller who immediately 'discovered' a parcel of *Hunt's postcripts* sent him unsolicited.[90] The spread of printed sedition was wide and swift: reports of the exiled James's *Declaration* being distributed in Bristol, Chester, Cornwall, Plymouth, Cambridge, Durham and Newcastle came within days of each other, and within a month the Earl of Shrewsbury said it had reached most parts of the kingdom.[91] In their nature the State Papers abound with investigations into libels and seditious pamphlets, although such suspect books are a statistically insignificant element of the commercial trade. Throughout the seventeenth century anxious administrations ordered searches of carriers' wagons leaving London and of ports (Yarmouth, Hull, Dover) in times of crisis. Mayors and local JPs frequently reported their suspicions of booksellers, individual 'fanatics', hawkers, pedlars and local disturbers of the peace. From Bridgwater came a report in 1683 that 'Last Thursday, a fair day, a parcel of vermin by singing and otherwise had spread amongst the common people divers scandalous ballads.'[92]

The circulation of print in the provinces overlapped with manuscript circulation in the area of news and scandal, distributed via local coffee-houses and even direct to the customer under cover of private newsletters. After the Restoration provincial coffee-houses were part of the same network of news distribution as those in London, carrying printed newspapers, displaying the latest topical pamphlets and acting as a point of exchange for letters and gossip; consequently at times of political crisis they came under similar scrutiny to houses in the capital. The coffee-houses of John Kimbar in Bristol, Mrs Daye and Fagge's in Oxford, a coffee-house in Leeds and the Dolphin in Chichester were all reported in the 1680s as involved in the spreading of printed and written news and libels and attempts were made at regulation.[93] Printed news was often enclosed with the written newsletters posted from London to individuals in the country. Writing newsletters was a profitable business: Giles Hancock charged customers as much as £6 per annum and boasted that it was worth £100 or £150 a year; another, anonymous, newswriter offered to send newsletters

89 *CSPD 1687–89*, pp. 153, 166. 90 *CSPD Oct. 1683–April 1684*, p. 129.
91 *CSPD 1689–90*, pp. 144, 145, 149, 177, 179, 180; *CJ*, x, pp. 187, 190.
92 *CSPD Jan.–June 1683*, p. 94.
93 *CSPD 1680–81*, pp. 251, 422; July–Sept. 1683, p. 87; 1689–90, p. 216.

'with the *Gazette* and what other pamphlets came out worth sending' for £10 a year.[94] Some newswriters like Gay, Robinson, Monckreive (a coffee man) and several who worked at the post office specialized in the country trade.[95] London stationers were involved in this network, too: the London bookseller Francis Smith, himself a Baptist, was accused in 1683 of supplying 'scandalous and libellous news' to newswriters who corresponded (using, apparently, a coffee-house as their office) with dissenters in Taunton, Dorchester, Lyme, Culliton, Axminster, Honiton, Tiverton, Exeter and Chard.[96]

In the 1680s the government's fear of sedition during the Exclusion crisis came together with the Stationers' Company's renegotiation of its charter, resulting in a long-running attack on hawkers, pedlars and petty chapmen. Complaints in the summer of 1683 from York of greater numbers than usual of Scotch pedlars selling 'godly bukes, as they call them' and pamphlets from Scotland began a wave of concern about pedlars and petty chapmen. Nearly forty Scotch pedlars were reported that summer in Norfolk and Suffolk, with, instead of their usual backpacks, horses to carry goods.[97] Throughout the decade and on into the 1690s Parliament, the City of London and the Company were concerned to strengthen legislation against hawkers and pedlars who, it was argued, were destructive to the trade of all corporations and market towns in England.[98]

Local audiences

Provincial audiences were not, however, simply passive recipients of a one-way trade: as writers they could engage with London printers and booksellers to the advantage of their own career, cause, or local culture. For instance, in 1583 the scholar and Chamberlain of Exeter, John Hooker, employed John Denham to print less than a hundred copies of two small quarto pamphlets about the city which he gave away as 1584 New Year's gifts to local dignitaries, ecclesiastical and lay.[99] Hooker's acquisition of local cultural capital brought financial benefit only to the London trade. In 1610, the Yorkshireman, Alexander Cooke, dedicated his *Pope Joan. A dialogue between a Protestant and a Papist* to the recently installed Archbishop of York, Tobie Matthew. This was both a contribution to Matthew's ongoing campaign against Yorkshire recusants and a part of Cooke's (successful) search for patronage (he was made Vicar of Leeds in 1615).[100] On a quite different scale, Robert Plot's *Natural history of Staffordshire* (Oxford,

94 *CSPD Oct. 1683–April 1684*, pp. 29–30, 53. 95 *CSPD Oct. 1683–April 1684*, pp. 53–4.
96 *CSPD July–Sept. 1683*, p. 218. 97 *CSPD July–Sept. 1683*, p. 97; *Oct. 1683–April 1684*, p. 260d.
98 *CJ*, XI, p. 427. 99 Snow 1977; *STC* 24885; 24889. 100 Barnard 1992, p. 82.

1686) grew from his introduction to the county by Walter Chetwynd of Ingestre, Staffordshire, who also assisted him with money and materials.[101] Local patrons could help authors to secure both readers and guaranteed sales of their works. In Westmorland Lady Anne Clifford regularly bought devotional books in bulk to give as presents to her household, estate workers and neighbours. Her account book shows, for example, that in October 1673 she paid £3 5*s*. 4*d*. for fifty-five books of devotion written by John Rawlet, minister of Kirby Stephen, 'which I buy to give away'.[102]

A particularly interesting example of the mutually beneficial interaction between the provinces and the London trade is given by the Puritan preacher, Oliver Heywood (1630–1702). After his ejection in 1662, Heywood continued his ministry in East Lancashire and West Yorkshire. Beginning with *Heart's treasure* (1667), he had published twelve books by 1701, mostly through Thomas Parkhurst the noted Presbyterian bookseller (active from 1655 to 1711). Normally Heywood paid for a number of copies at a discount (£10 for 120 copies in the case of his first work) and was given further copies in payment for his manuscript. These books, distributed gratis, were an integral part of his ministry (he gave away 286 copies of *Heart's treasure*), so that his printed words could remain with or reach out to his scattered congregation of clothworkers and farmers in his absence.[103] There are three aspects to this long-standing arrangement. For Thomas Parkhurst it meant that Heywood paid a substantial part of his production costs, which helps explain Dunton's statement that Parkhurst was known 'to sell off a whole Impression before the Book has been almost heard of in London'.[104] There was a double advantage for Heywood: his Northern flock could profit from his ministry in his absence, while the sales of the rest of the edition through Parkhurst's shop and trade connections extended his teaching, and his reputation, throughout the 'Three Kingdoms'. This arrangement suited all parties and, as Harold Love points out, may have been typical among an active minority of the 1800 ejected clergy, and even among conformist ministers. For this kind of religious book, country clergymen, he says, may 'have been an even more important force in the distribution of books outside London than the country bookseller'.[105] Furthermore, not only did Parkhurst advise Heywood to cut a politically sensitive passage from one of his books in 1682, but the author himself advised other writers.[106] The collaborative links between the provinces and London were in this case, and no doubt in others, strongly coloured by political and religious motives. Richard Baxter, in Kidderminster during the Interregnum, was especially concerned

101 *DNB*. 102 Williamson 1967, p. 510. 103 Love 1978.
104 *Ibid*., p. 230 (citing Dunton 1705, p. 281). 105 *Ibid*., p. 235. 106 *Ibid*., p. 234.

that poverty did not deprive readers of godly reading matter. He supplied 'every family in Town and Parish' with 'a Catechism, and some of my lesser Books, and of every Book I wrote usually as many as my Purse could well afford', and ensured that all families with a literate member received a Bible.[107] He made arrangements with his publishers, Underhill and Tyton, 'to facilitate the giving of books and to ensure that his own works were sold as cheaply as possible' and although after the Restoration far distant from them, he sent to his Kidderminster people 'all the Books which I wrote'.[108] Oppressed religious groupings thus used normal trade practices to spread their views to the nation at large, offering a parallel to the well-organized distribution of texts begun by the Quakers in the 1650s.[109]

Conclusion

The London trade has preoccupied most historical accounts of the press in England from 1557 to 1695. Not only was London the centre for the manufacture, import and distribution of books where many provincial booksellers learnt their trade, but its archival records, particularly those of the Stationers' Company, are fuller and better known than those for the provinces. Nevertheless, from very early on the 'country trade' was an important element of the English book trade. The apparent marginality of provincial booksellers, of pedlars and their customers, of schoolboys across the land, of educated readers lay and clergy, and the patterns of lending and borrowing books outside the metropolis, disguises their essential role in the expansion of the market for books and the creation of new readers and readerships. Together with the emergent trade with the American colonies, the establishment of clear and increasingly reciprocal distribution networks throughout the English provinces in these years[110] provided the basis for the massive increase in the new consumer economy for books of all kinds evident in the succeeding century.

107 Keeble 1987, p. 132. 108 *Ibid.*, pp. 132–3. 109 See pp. 70–5 below.

110 See, for example, the proposals in 1686 for a new edition of 'The works of King Charles' by six London booksellers which were available in twenty-two cathedral cities 'and all other Cities and Country Towns in *England* and *Wales* where there are any Booksellers', as well as in Dublin and Edinburgh (*TC*, II, p. 185).

33
Scotland

JONQUIL BEVAN

This sketch of the Scottish book trade outlines some of the principal ways in which the trade at this period, though in some ways similar, was very different from that south of the Border and, more widely, furth of and outwith Scotland.[1] The English legislation that restricted printing to London, Cambridge and Oxford created a concentration of the book-production industry in the south of England.[2] This legislation played its part in isolating that trade from the book trade in the north of England, and still more from that of Scotland. The control of the English Stationers' Company did not extend to Scotland which, like Holland, had no equivalent regulatory body. While the encouragement of Scottish printing and bookselling was, loosely, a part of government policy, the main non-governmental institutions involved in the control of the trade were the Church and, most importantly, the Scottish burghs, which played a crucial role in censorship, licensing and trade regulation.[3] This local and geographically dispersed control of the trade by the burghs of Aberdeen, Edinburgh and Glasgow resembled more closely the organization of the book trades in the Low Countries than the centralized authority of England. The unified study of book history in the British Isles has been hampered by the contrast between this relatively loose Scottish régime and the monolithic English trade, and

1 Furth of: beyond; outwith: outside. These are both terms in current use in educated Scots; I will not labour the point of continuing cultural distinctions.

2 Hillyard 1998 provides a comprehensive guide to the major work so far done in this field. The annual *Bibliography of Scotland* (1988–) is a supplementary source. See also Mann 2000b. *A history of the book in Scotland* is to be published in four volumes by Edinburgh University Press. Among associated projects is the Scottish Book Trade Archive Inventory, supported by the Edinburgh University Centre for the History of the Book, Aberdeen University Library, the British Library, Edinburgh City Archives, the Glasgow Business Archive, the National Archives of Scotland, the National Library of Scotland, and the University of Reading. Given the present state of knowledge, this chapter provides no more than a preliminary sketch. I am much indebted to Alastair Mann's research and generous help.

3 Mann 2000b, pp. 231–3. The granting of copyright remained mostly in the hands of the crown and Privy Council, while burghs granted municipal rights to publish almanacs and newspapers. The norm in the seventeenth century was to grant licences for nineteen years, a model closer to Dutch than to English practice. On Scottish copyright, see Mann 2000a and Mann 2000b, ch. 4.

by consequent differences in the records each produced: surviving Scottish records are more fragmentary and less copious than those produced by the English Stationers' Company. Scotland's own book history has itself suffered from a centralizing tendency which has focused on Edinburgh to the exclusion of Aberdeen and Glasgow; and placing it in the wider British context is frustrated by the fact that many important research projects stop on one side or other of the Border.[4] An account of the Renaissance and seventeenth-century history of the book in Scotland, placed within a history of the book in Britain, therefore requires radically altered perspectives: London seen from Edinburgh, Edinburgh seen from London, and a Scottish cultural and trade orientation towards Continental Europe rather than the south of England.

To a considerable extent cultural divisions between the Scots and the English remain, but such distinctions obviously existed far more notably at the Renaissance when England and Scotland were separate countries. Up until 1603 the two countries had separate monarchs; up to 1707 they had separate Parliaments. They still have separate legal systems, separate educational systems, separate established Churches, and separate languages. These facts, often little known to the English, will perhaps become better known as the new Scottish Parliament matures.

It is important to make some general points about the historical facts that influenced, and differentiated, book production in the two nations during the sixteenth and seventeenth centuries. First, Scotland, for most of the sixteenth century, was closer, politically and culturally, to France than to England. Secondly, printing was not introduced into Scotland until after James IV issued his patent in 1507; there is no such thing as a Scottish incunabulum. Thirdly, the official Protestant Reformation was delayed in Scotland until 1560, some twenty-five years after it came to England. Fourthly, the Protestant Reformation, when it came, was far more sweeping than the English Reformation: from the 1570s the established Church of Scotland developed the Presbyterian structure at grass roots level which it retains today, although the continuation of episcopacy until 1689 created political tensions of immense importance for much of the century. Finally, the Scots, being from a relatively small country with a weak economy, were accustomed to seek their fortunes

4 When the Bibliographical Society (London) came into being in 1892, the Bibliographical Society (founded in Edinburgh in 1890) debated whether to send a remonstrance to the new Society, suggesting that it had no right to style itself thus, without qualification of place, as if there were no other. It had the generosity not to do so; but the incident illustrates an historical lack of communication now being remedied by the various national histories of the book (of America, Australia, and Canada) which are vigorously pursuing complex cultural exchanges, not least through records of import and export.

and education on the Continent of Europe and beyond, and had long had an international outlook and widespread cultural exchange. Younger sons might become foreign merchants or mercenary soldiers. An educated Scot was multilingual, and if he survived to return to Scotland, brought his knowledge home with him. Informal networks of book acquisition from Continental centres of production accounted for much of Scottish book-buying before 1560 and demonstrate the extent to which Scottish readers were participants in the intellectual life of the Continent. The fact that educated Scottish readers, who either travelled abroad themselves or relied on friends and agents for book purchases abroad, had ready access to Continental retail markets may well have obviated the need for a home-grown printing trade, which was not sustainable until a wider public for Scots vernacular texts was available.[5]

Long before the establishment of the first Scottish press, Scots had had their works printed abroad and they continued to do so. The first Scot to have his works printed in his lifetime was James Liddell, whose *Tractatus conceptuum et signorum* was printed in Paris in 1498. Another early example of a foreign-printed Scots book is *The contemplacyon of sinners* of William of Touris, an Observant Franciscan Friar, printed in London in 1499.[6] It is likely that a number of Scottish printings abroad before 1560 have been lost. Naturally enough, the Scottish Protestant reformers also saw to it that their writings were put into print. The early vernacular writings of John Knox provide an obvious example: they have some dubious imprints, but were probably printed at London (?1554, 1554), Emden (1554), Wesel (?1556, ?1556), and Geneva (1558, 1558, 1558 (about, not by, Knox), 1559, and 1560).[7] James Watson, admittedly a biased witness, claims that the tradition of Protestant scholarly printing overseas created a lasting distrust among Scottish scholars about the accuracy of the native printing trade, and he further claims that this distrust lasted into the eighteenth century.[8] The relatively small scale of the Scottish press before the Restoration meant that it was difficult to print seditious or banned works undiscovered, and overseas printing of texts likely to attract prosecution remained important at least until the 1680s. In the early seventeenth century, for example, Leiden and Amsterdam were important centres for the publication of pro-covenanting propaganda in the 1630s and 1640s. Moreover, the undercapitalization of the Scottish trade created an open market for cheap

5 Ford 1999, pp. 197–201. 6 *STC* 5643.

7 *STC* 15059, 15074.4; 15069; 15066, 15074.6; 15067, 15070, 15063, 15064, 15060.

8 Watson 1713; but Watson, with his war against the monopolist Agnes Campbell, royal printer and widow of Andrew Anderson, had his own axe to grind and was attacking the poor quality of her printings and much else besides.

Dutch Bibles, especially from the 1630s onwards and on a massive scale after the Restoration.[9]

The long-established independence of Scots culture from England needs to be stressed. For centuries the Scots had suffered from the incursions and territorial claims of their rich and powerful English neighbour. James I, for example, had been captured at sea in 1406 and imprisoned in England until 1424. Henry VII of England made a pacific move towards Scotland when he married his elder daughter, Margaret, to James IV. The marriage and its political implications were celebrated in Dunbar's poem 'The thristle and the rois', one of the first poems to be printed in Scotland (1509). But the accession of the aggressive Henry VIII brought about a change. Having successfully fought his war with France, without the support he demanded from Scotland, Henry turned his attention to the Scots. The battle of Flodden (1513) was a devastating defeat for Scotland.[10] During the reign of James IV French and English influences had vied with each other at the royal court. After Flodden in 1513 French influences were to dominate. Henry VIII's hopes of marrying his daughter Mary to his nephew, James V, were dashed by the young King's two French marriages: the first, in 1537, to a daughter of Francis I and the second to Mary of Guise-Lorraine. In 1542 James V died, and in 1548 Mary of Guise-Lorraine, now Queen Regent, sent her six-year-old daughter, Mary Queen of Scots, to France, to be affianced to the French Dauphin. Upon her return to Scotland after the death of her husband, King of France, in 1561, Mary Queen of Scots reigned in her native kingdom until her abdication in 1567.

The court of the young dowager Queen of France, Mary – she always signed herself Marie – Queen of Scots, was inevitably French in culture.[11] Writing in Scots could expect to find little place. But the book arts might; Mary had spent her life as Dauphine at the sophisticated court at Fountainebleau where, among other arts, the art of bookbinding was greatly encouraged. The French Royal bindery flourished chiefly during the reign of François I, although it continued until about 1567. A binding, probably of 1559, was made for Mary's husband very shortly after he became King, and it is linked stylistically to another binding, now in the Municipal Library at Reims, thought to mark the Dauphin's marriage to Mary in April 1558.[12] Some of the finest sixteenth-century bindings

9 Mann 2000b, ch. 3: 'The Scottish book trade and the Low Countries'. For the situation in England, see McMullin, above, pp. 466–8, and Green and Peters, pp. 78, 80.

10 M. Lynch, *Scotland: a new history* (London, 1991), citing W. K. Emond, 'The minority of King James V, 1513–1528' (St Andrews University Ph. D., 1988).

11 It is accepted that such common Scot words as (for example) ashet, meat-dish, derives from the French *assiette*; that gigot, as in gigot-chop, lamb-chop, derives from French: *gigot*; that petticoat-tails, a form of shortbread, derives from the French: *petites gatelles*, etc.

12 Laffitte and Le Bars 1999, p. 226.

found in Scotland are not easily attributable either to French or to Scots workmanship;[13] but Helen Ross's work as embroiderer and binder to James V is well known[14] and altogether more than a dozen binders can be traced as working in Scotland in the second half of the sixteenth century, most of them in Edinburgh, some of them of foreign extraction.

The dominance of French in the literary culture of the Scottish court gave way, under James VI, to a resurgence of Scots vernacular, a driving force in the development of Scottish book production. James VI had been educated by one of the leading scholars of Europe, George Buchanan, and he retained an active interest in scholarship all his life. He was also aware of the obligations of a Renaissance prince and sought, as had his great grandfather, James IV, to create in Scotland a court that encouraged patronage of the arts. He himself wrote poetry and wrote also a short treatise explaining to his subjects the application of metre and style to the Scots language: poetry at his court was to be written in Scots, not English, and several fine poets were part of his court côterie known as the Castalian Band.[15] The succession of James VI in 1603 to the crown of England was to be a major turning point in the fortunes of the development of Scotland. The physical removal of the royal court was an important factor in seventeenth-century developments in Scottish culture, trade, politics and international relationships.

Protestantism, too, played its part in the growth of the market for Scots printed vernacular texts. In 1560 the first General Assembly of the Reformed Church of Scotland took place and within two decades Presbyterianism began to emerge. In law Protestantism replaced Roman Catholicism, and the Scottish abbeys were gradually dissolved. The Scottish abbeys had naturally been centres – not the only centres, by any means – of book culture. Scottish monastic foundations most frequently had French roots[16] and they are known to have imported French books. For example, when the Perth Charterhouse was founded in 1424, the Carthusian monks brought manuscript volumes with them from the Continent; they also borrowed others in Scotland, their intention being to copy them in order to build up a library of their own and then return the volumes to the lenders. One of these monks made a copy of Barbour's *Bruce* and Blind Harry's *Wallace*. There are references to scriptoria at Kinloss, Newbattle, Dunfermline and (1554) Pittenweem. The pre-Reformation library collection

13 Mitchell 1955, plates 11, 13, 14, 15. 14 Mann 1999, p. 137.

15 The best introduction to the Scottish literature of our period is R. D. S. Jack and P. A. T. Rozendaal (eds.), *The Mercat anthology of early Scottish Literature 1375–1707* (Edinburgh, 1997).

16 For example, the Valliscaulians only had houses in France and in Scotland: in Scotland they were at Pluscarden, Beauly and Ardchattan; M. Dilworth, *Scottish monasteries in the late middle ages* (Edinburgh, 1995), p. 7.

built up by Thomas Chrystall and Robert Reid, later Bishop of Orkney, at the Cistercian monastery of Kinloss was a particular highlight of printed and manuscript books. Another Scottish community, the Cistercians at Culross (who looked to their mother house at Citeaux), ran the only recorded business project in which monks worked: it was a scriptorium.[17]

The monasteries and their influence threw a shadow long after their dissolution. Many abbots were secular men who held their office hereditarily, and the commendators (roughly, estate managers) of some houses continued in residence after the communities of monks were dispersed. Books of monastic origin continued to be prized and cherished after the Reformation. For example, Clement Litill, a Protestant Edinburgh lawyer, who left his library of 276 volumes to 'the kirk of Edinburgh to be usit and kepit be the said kirk to the use of the ministeris, elderis and decanes thairof' in 1580, owned a number of books from monastic sources.[18] In the seventeenth century undergraduates were still able to find medieval manuscripts to present to Edinburgh University Library as the due upon graduation.[19] Perhaps, too, the fact that Scotland had, for a long time, a relatively small (and sometimes contentious) press helped encourage the development in Edinburgh of the calligraphic book, a form of art principally associated with the name of the celebrated Esther Inglis (1571–1624).[20]

When considering the importance of a surviving manuscript tradition into the age of print it must also be borne in mind, of course, that an important part of Scottish culture was not in the Scots language but in Gaelic. Although the Lordship of the Isles was forfeited to the Scottish Crown in 1493 attempts continued to be made to regain it, resistance continuing until 1545. And for long after that period Gaelic culture continued – continues – vividly alive. Originally oral, the traditional forms of literature were transmitted into manuscript, and this remained a largely manuscript culture for a considerable time to come. There was (as we shall see) one Gaelic printed book in the sixteenth century, followed by a second one in 1630, but these may be regarded as exceptions that help prove the rule. Manuscript circulation remained important throughout the seventeenth century not only for Gaelic texts but also for legal judgements and cases, the printing of which in significant numbers began only in the 1670s.

The advent of printing to Scotland was due to an act of royal patronage. Printing was not at first, as in England, a luxurious plaything enjoying court protection: it was introduced by James IV for nationalistic, cultural and patriotic reasons. On 15 September 1507 King James granted a patent for printing

17 *Ibid.*, p. 64. 18 Finlayson 1980. 19 Edinburgh University Library 1963.

20 There is a portrait of Esther Inglis and some brief account of her in the National Library of Scotland's newsletter *Quarto*, 8 (Summer 2000).

to Walter Chepman and Androw Myllar. Two points about this interesting document need to be noted. First, the patent makes reference to Chepman and Myllar's undertaking to 'bring hame ane prent with al stuf belangand tharto and expert men to use the samyne'. It is clear that these expert men came from Rouen; Myllar himself went there to learn about the trade, just as Caxton learnt the art of printing in Bruges.[21] A second point of interest is the expressed aim for this enterprise:

> It is divisit and thocht expedient be us and our consall, that in tyme cuming mess bukis, manualis, matyne bukis, and portuus bukis, efter our awin scottis use, and with legendis of Scottis sanctis, as is now gaderit and ekit be ane Reverend fader in God, and our traist consalour Williame bischope of abirdene and utheris, be usit generaly withinal al our Realme alssone as the sammyn may be imprentit and providit, and that na maner of sic bukis of Salusbery use be brocht to be sauld within our Realme in tym cuming.[22]

The first of Chepman and Myllar's productions are known as their Tracts, a collection that survives in a single copy in the National Library of Scotland.[23] These tracts are prints of poems, mostly by Dunbar and Henryson, and the earliest one that is dated bears the date 4 April 1508. It seems probable that these little leaflets were partly experimental while the new press was settling in. The *Aberdeen Breviary* as compiled by bishop Elphinstone seems to have been completed in 1510. The defeat of Flodden in 1513 may be blamed for an apparent reduction of book production.[24] Although we may list the names of John Story, of Thomas Davidson (licensed in 1540 by James V to print Acts of Parliament and printer of the celebrated edition of Hector Boece's *The hystory of croniklis of Scotland* in 1542), and of John Scott, it is not until the middle of the century that Scottish books begin to become more numerous.

In 1561 there appeared Robert Lekpruik's printing of the Confession of Faith (*The Confessione of the fayht [sic] and doctrin beleued and professed by Protestantes of the Realme of Scotland* ...) On the last leaf of the book is the date of 17 August 1560.[25] In 1567 Lekpruik had the distinction of producing the first printed book in Scots Gaelic, an edition of Knox's liturgy adapted and translated by John Carswell, Bishop of the Isles.[26] The Marian civil war which raged from 1568 to 1573, between the supporters of Mary and the boy James VI, unsettled

21 See Beattie 1950, pp. ix–xxvii.

22 For an account of Bishop William Elphinstone and the *Aberdeen Breviary* in its cultural context, see M. Lynch, *Scotland: a new history* (London, 1991), p. 96.

23 In addition to the facsimile noted in n. 15 above, the National Library has now produced an edition of the Tracts in machine-readable form.

24 The apparent reduction may in part be due to losses, rather than an actual dip in production.

25 *STC* 22018. 26 *STC* 16604.

the trade and Lekpruik's career: while Lekpruik became printer to the 'King's men', Thomas Bassandyne was printer to the 'Queen's men'. With Edinburgh under the control of Mary's supporters, Lekpruik printed at Stirling (1571) and at St Andrews (1572–3). In 1574 Lekpruik was imprisoned in Edinburgh Castle, accused of printing an unlicensed publication. The career of Thomas Bassandyne, roughly contemporary with that of Lekpruik, is chiefly celebrated for his ambitious undertaking of the Bassandyne Bible. This project, undertaken in partnership with Alexander Arbuthnot, was published in two parts, Bassandyne's name being on the New Testament title (1576) and Arbuthnot's on the Old Testament (1579).[27] This Bible was widely disseminated throughout the land and was printed in roman type, after the style of Geneva, distinguishing it from English Bibles which were still printed in black letter.[28] The strong association thus established between Scots Protestant 'tradition' and roman type became evident in 1637, when resentment at the imposition of the Prayer Book was exacerbated by its Anglicized appearance in 'alien' black letter.[29] Bassandyne was enterprising in his importation of types and employed the *civilité* type (unknown in England) in, for example, his edition of Robert Henryson's *Fables* (1571).[30]

Not surprisingly, the staunchly Protestant temper of Scotland attracted a certain number of stationers who were religious refugees from Protestant persecution elsewhere. Contrasting examples of the careers of such individuals are provided by Thomas Vautrollier (*fl.*1562–87) and Robert Waldegrave (*fl.* 1578–1603/4), both important men, in their different ways, in their contribution to the Scottish book trade. Vautrollier, a Frenchman by birth, was a Huguenot who established himself in London from 1562 as a bookseller and bookbinder, and, from 1570, as a printer. He set up a bookshop in Edinburgh 1580–3, and had a printing house there 1584–6. He had fled to Scotland in 1584 for printing the writings of the heretic Giordano Bruno (burned at the stake at Rome in 1600). Safely in Scotland, however, Vautrollier proved himself a versatile and skilled practitioner. He was repeatedly employed by King James VI, and printed, for example, James's *Essayes of a prentise* (1584).[31] His departure to Edinburgh did not impede his business, for his wife, Jacqueline, maintained the London trade and the Vautrolliers thus present us with an early example of a book business with outlets simultaneously in Edinburgh and in London. Robert Waldegrave, by contrast, was English by birth and was apprenticed to

27 *STC* 2125. 28 See Dobson 1887. 29 Mann 2000b, pp. 39–40.

30 *STC* 185.5; see *The poems and fables of Robert Henryson*, ed. H. Harvey Wood (Edinburgh, London and New York, 1968) in which some of this type is reproduced.

31 *STC* 14373.

a London Stationer.[32] He was stoutly opposed to prelatical rule and in 1581, early in his career, he published John Knox's *Confession* and other Scottish works. Deeply involved in the production of the Marprelate tracts, by 1589 he had removed – or escaped – to Edinburgh. He was made King's Printer in 1590, printing James VI's own writing, including *Basilikon doron* (1599, 1603) and introducing 'anglicized' features in language and conventions, such as the use of dedications. He accompanied his King to his new realm of England in 1603, but the records suggest that he died within the year. His Edinburgh materials passed into the hands of Thomas Finlason, who purchased from Waldegrave's widow the privilege for printing certain books.

The Scots vernacular revival of the later sixteenth century was significantly influenced by the printer and publisher Henry Charteris (*c.* 1561–99), whose publication and reprinting of vernacular poets such as Henryson, the epic poems of Bruce and Wallace, *The works of Sir David Lindsay* (1568) and the first edition of George Buchanan's controversial *De jure regni* (1579) mark him out as the greatest Scottish printer of the century. He was succeeded in the trade by his second son Robert, King's Printer in 1603; his elder son, another Henry, became Principal of the University of Edinburgh. There are a number of other family ties between the University of Edinburgh and the book trade at this period.[33] Andro Hart, who succeeded to the printing materials of Robert Charteris in 1610, continued the vernacular tradition and became the most successful Scottish printer–bookseller before the Restoration. His fine Geneva Bible of 1610, remarkable for its accuracy, was widely used as copy for Dutch Bibles imported into England and Scotland. As well as publishing the work of John Napier and William Drummond of Hawthornden, he also imported texts and commissioned printing in Amsterdam, Dort and Leiden. On Hart's death in 1621 his widow Janet Kene continued the family printing and bookselling business.

At the end of the seventeenth century the most successful Scottish book trade dynasty was that founded by George Anderson, who seems to have started printing in Edinburgh in 1637. Anderson was printer 'in King James his College' (otherwise known as 'the Tounis College', later as Edinburgh University) and in 1638 he removed to become Glasgow's first printer, acting as Town Printer until his death in 1647. Printing came briefly to St Andrews in the 1540s and 1570s and arrived in Aberdeen in 1622; Glasgow had not yet assumed the importance it was to gain from trade with the New World.[34] After Anderson's death the Glasgow town council offered to continue his subsidy, and to provide a pension for his widow and children 'swa long as they continow in prenting

32 Aldis 1910, pp. 277–9. 33 Bevan 1983, pp. 18–19. 34 *STC* III, pp. 213–15.

in the towne.'[35] This they did not do for long, returning to Edinburgh in 1649; their imprint name was changed from that of the heirs of George Anderson to Andrew Anderson, one of George's sons. In 1656 the Glasgow town council made a successful attempt to persuade Andrew and his wife, Agnes Campbell, to come back; but in 1661 they again returned to Edinburgh where, in 1663, Andrew was appointed printer to the town and the college. In 1671 he was appointed King's Printer in Scotland. The powers and privileges of this post were now considerably enlarged. They included, in theory at any rate, the supervision of all the presses and printing houses in Scotland, and the grant was for forty-one years, with remainder to Anderson's heirs and assigns in the event of his death. Anderson now took into partnership George Swintoun, James Glen, Thomas Browne and David Trench. This partnership shortly broke up, but not before they had asserted their new rights in an aggressive and highly litigious way. The other partners seem to have sold out to Anderson, but George Swintoun remained active.[36]

In 1676 Andrew Anderson died, but his widow, known, according to Scottish tradition, by her maiden name of Agnes Campbell even after her marriage and widowhood, continued the struggle to subdue the rights of other important printers, notably Robert Sanders of Glasgow and John Forbes of Aberdeen. In 1687 the Edinburgh town council, in view of Agnes Campbell's role as Printer to the College, granted her the right to erect her printing presses 'below the Bibliotheck' of the 1642 University Library building. This is a document of some interest, since it provides, among other things, detailed evidence about the demolished library buildings on the site of what is now Old College.[37] In 1711, when the original Gift to Andrew Anderson as King's Printer expired, James Watson the younger was, after a struggle, appointed as one of the Queen's Printers. In common with many other Scottish stationers he had feelings of considerable animosity towards Agnes Campbell who, in 1701, had attempted to shut down his shop. In 1713 Watson printed his *History of the art of printing*, in which he attacked Agnes Campbell violently. Her reputation has suffered ever since, probably unfairly since her litigious tactics were used equally enthusiastically by her contemporaries, including Watson himself.[38] In 1716 she succeeded in wrestling back the Gift; she died eighteen days later at the age of eighty, and her success was then overruled by the Court of Session later in 1716 and eventually by the House of Lords in 1718. The involvement of a woman in the book trade was not unusual (female printers and publishers were probably more common in Scotland, where about 10 per cent of traders were women,

35 Fairley 1925, p. 3. See also Mann 1998. 36 Fairley, pp. 4–10.
37 *Ibid.* pp. 34–6. 38 Mann 1998.

than in England); but Agnes Campbell's success was indeed remarkable, in that she was the wealthiest book trader of early modern Scotland, and the wealthiest female merchant not to have inherited her wealth.[39]

Even a very brief account of the Anderson family reminds us (as would investigation of the Charteris family, or the Hart families, to name but two) of the great value to investigators of the Scottish book trade of the inventories and detailed lists of debts owing to the dead which are part of testamentary records. These (unlike their counterparts in England) are conveniently gathered into a single repository, the Scottish Record Office in Edinburgh and have provided a firm basis for analysis of the trade.[40] A similar point must be made about customs dues, which will have much to tell us about the import and export, not only of books but also, it may be hoped, of type.[41] Investigation of the importation of books is essential for a country whose culture, trade and politics had for so long been international and Continental. In the aftermath of the Marian war direct links with France were replaced by trade with England and by the expansion of already established trading routes to Holland. As professional bookselling developed in Scotland during the 1570s and 1580s, the academic and informal networks of Continental book acquisition were gradually replaced by merchant networks. Scots who had travelled to France for university education now moved decisively away from Paris to the Low Countries. Scotland was already acquiring books from Antwerp and its Latin trade, notably with Plantin, expanded in the 1560s and 1570s until 1585 when Antwerp fell to Catholic Spain. Thereafter Continental imports came chiefly from Holland, Zeeland and the Dutch Republic and only indirectly from France. In the seventeenth century Latin books were imported from Amsterdam, Rotterdam and Leiden rather than England; and like England, Scotland imported large quantities of English language Bibles, some illegally, from Holland.[42] From the 1570s to the 1690s, as Mann has argued, 'in the provision of Latin texts and scriptures the presses and book suppliers of Antwerp and Amsterdam were more important than those of London'.[43]

The Andersons' Glasgow printing and the family's relationship with the town council is also a reminder of the way in which the development of Scottish

39 *Ibid.*; for a discussion of Campbell in the context of other women in the Scottish book trade, see Mann 1999.

40 Mann 2000b (especially ch. 7 and appendix 3) rests on the detailed analysis of the testamentary data; see also A. Mann, 'The book trade and public policy in early modern Scotland, c. 1500 to c. 1720' (unpublished PhD thesis, Stirling, 1997).

41 For references to the relatively few studies of Scottish typography, see Hillyard 1998. More is known about Scottish papermaking (see Thomson 1974) which started in Scotland in 1590 but was not firmly established until the 1670s.

42 Mann 2000b, ch.3.

43 *Ibid.*, p. 232.

printing, unfettered by the kind of legislation limiting English printing, involved individual burghs. Municipal authorities could attract and encourage local printing, often (as in Aberdeen and Glasgow) with support from universities and the church. Printing appeared only briefly in Stirling and St Andrews, but before the eighteenth century had become permanently established in Aberdeen, Glasgow and Edinburgh.[44] Aberdeen's first press was begun by Edward Raban (*fl.* 1620–50) in 1622. His Aberdeen almanac, which drew on the expertise of Aberdeen University's renowned mathematicians, became the most popular and respected of Scottish almanacs and was developed as a local product by the John Forbes, elder and younger, in the 1660s.[45] Despite close connections with the Bishop of Aberdeen, the Forbeses, father and son, were able to develop an eclectic range of religious texts, publishing not only the work of Scottish Quakers such as Robert Barclay and George Keith but also some Catholic texts. They also built on Aberdeen's long reputation for song schools, medieval in origin and continued after the Reformation in relation to the psalms, to compile a bestselling collection of *Cantus, songs and fancies*, first published in 1662. The importance for printers of support from university and Church was also apparent in Glasgow. In the later seventeenth century the Glasgow printers Robert Sanders, elder (*fl.* 1661–94) and younger (*fl.* 1695–1730), benefited from their connections with local bishops and presbyteries and with academics such as Zachary Boyd to become specialists in scripture and theology.[46] Glasgow's situation as a port also helped shape its book trade: it became the main entry point for Bibles illegally imported from Holland, in breach of the rights of Edinburgh's King's Printer, and it was well-placed to supply the Americas with religious texts as colonial trade expanded.[47]

The emphasis of book historians on the development of printing has tended to obscure the fact that bookselling, rather than book production, was the motive force in the expansion of the trade in Scotland, where the small domestic press was unable to satisfy the demand for books.[48] A retail trade in manuscript and imported printed books, conducted at burgh fairs and stationers' stalls at the universities, long pre-dated the press. Printers and bookbinders were also, of course, booksellers; but separate bookshops were being established in Edinburgh by the 1580s, in Perth (*c.*1587), Glasgow and St Andrews (*c.* 1599) and Aberdeen (*c.* 1613).[49] Despite the recession in Edinburgh during

44 For the role of these burghs see Mann 2000b, ch.1: 'Edinburgh, Aberdeen and Glasgow: the book and the burghs'. See also Mann's article 'Printing and publishing' in M. Lynch (ed.), *The Oxford companion to Scottish history* (Oxford, forthcoming).

45 Mann 2000b, pp. 15–16, 103–4. 46 *Ibid.*, p. 11.

47 *Ibid.*, pp. 93, 228. 48 *Ibid.*, p. 232.

49 A. Mann, 'Bookselling', in Lynch (ed.), *The Oxford companion to Scottish history.*

Cromwell's occupation, the 1650s in particular saw the expansion of bookselling throughout Scotland. Seventeenth-century Edinburgh booksellers increasingly developed as specialists, notably in school books (Andrew Wilson, *fl.* 1634–54) and law (John Vallange, *fl.* 1678–1712).[50]

Scotland has been well served by studies of Renaissance libraries, though the concentration has been largely on collections in Edinburgh or with Edinburgh associations.[51] Before the Reformation the universities of St Andrews, Glasgow and Aberdeen, as well as the cathedral libraries of Aberdeen, Brechin, Elgin and Glasgow had stimulated collecting. Scotland boasted the earliest pre-Reformation municipal libraries and Litill's Edinburgh library, bequeathed in 1580, was followed by the 'Common Library of New Aberdeen', founded in 1585 by burgesses, lawyers and ministers (which in 1632 passed to Marischal College) and St Mary's Church Library in Dundee (1599).[52] Individuals also amassed considerable libraries which they bequeathed to local institutions. The library of William Guild, an Aberdeen academic, was donated to St Andrews in 1657; the libraries of James Boyd, Bishop of Glasgow, and Zachary Boyd, academic and poet, were donated to Glasgow University in 1627 and 1651 respectively. A remarkable (and still intact) secular bequest is that of David Drummond, third Lord Madertie, at Innerpeffray Library near Crieff, Perthshire.[53]

The largest surviving private library from the pre-Reformation period was that of Henry Sinclair (1508–65), most of which passed to the advocate (barrister) Clement Litill. Born probably in 1527–8, Litill, the eldest son of a mercer, was educated at St Andrews and Louvain. The Latin annotations in his books suggest a gradual movement to Protestantism by 1558. He was party to the proposal to establish what was first intended to be a theological college and left his theological books to the Kirk of Edinburgh, probably with the foundation of the new college in mind (his law books are dispersed). Litill died in 1580 and his books formed the nucleus of the University of Edinburgh at its foundation in 1583.[54] It is interesting to compare his theology collection with that of Marjorie Rogers (wife – not widow – these are her own books) whose collection of thirty-one books are listed in her testamentary inventory of 1583.[55]

A very different series of collections was given to Edinburgh University over several years by the poet William Drummond of Hawthornden (1585–1649).

50 *Ibid.*

51 One of the most important sources for pre-Reformation libraries is Durkan and Ross 1961.

52 A. Mann, 'Libraries', in Lynch (ed.), *The Oxford companion to Scottish history*.

53 *Ibid.* 54 Finlayson 1980.

55 I owe this reference and a list of Marjorie Rogers's books to my colleague Professor Michael Lynch.

These are literary books, and the university demonstrated its gratitude by printing in 1627, for general circulation, a list of the books in this benefaction.[56] If this was intended *pour encourager les autres* it succeeded: Drummond's gift to the university of some 700 books was followed by the whole library of James Nairn (1,838 volumes).[57] Other Edinburgh graduates whose private libraries became public possessions were those of Robert Leighton (1611–84) whose 1,363 books became the Bibliotheca Leightoniana at Dunblane;[58] Sir Robert Sibbald (1641–1722), who left 100 of his 8,000 volumes to found the Library of the Royal College of Physicians; and the Reverend John Gray (1646–1717) who left 900 books to found a library at Haddington, East Lothian. Meanwhile, in 1698, the Edinburgh University theology students, whose access to their University Library was very restricted indeed, formed a separate library of their own for themselves and for their successors: we now know it as New College Library.[59] The Advocates' Library, created in Edinburgh in 1682, marks the high point of seventeenth-century Scottish collecting. It became a deposit library under the British Copyright Act of 1710 and in 1925 became the National Library of Scotland.

56 *STC* 7246. 57 MacDonald 1971; Simpson 1990. 58 Willis 1981.
59 Some background to a discussion of seventeenth-century Edinburgh libraries will be found in Bevan 1983.

34

The book in Ireland from the Tudor re-conquest to the battle of the Boyne

ROBERT WELCH

Authority and change

The history of the book in Ireland must, before it does anything else, take account of the continuing importance of manuscript tradition and the slow development of dependence upon the printed book in this period. Sixteenth-century Ireland became a kingdom under Henry VIII as part of a renewed attempt to bring Ireland under more complete and extensive British governance. This Tudor re-conquest was driven by two different but complementary ambitions: Henry, and subsequently his daughter Elizabeth, wanted to centralize authority throughout the islands of Britain and Ireland under their own administration in London; and they wished to further the reform of the Church in England and Ireland by making the crown the head of the Church as well as of the State. The achievement of these twin aims was to lay the foundations of a new, energetic Protestant polity; a vision in which Britain and Ireland were a conjoined imperium whose destiny was to bring into being a society which reflected the ideas of the Reformation under a settled form of authoritative government.

The printed book was one of the major instruments in the furtherance of the Reformation: people were encouraged to read the Bible for themselves and there flowed from the new presses all over Protestant Europe works of theology, philosophy, and biblical exegesis. England took a highly active part in this de-mystification of faith: for example, Richard Hooker's *Of the lawes of ecclesiasticall politie* (1593–7) framed the Tudor concept which intertwined the settlement of the state with the Church's interests and the rights and duties of the citizen.

This Protestant concept of individual liberty, structured and authorized by a nation-state free of Roman manipulation, promoted a widespread appetite for reading, thinking for oneself, and the expression of personal conviction. Predominantly Catholic countries, such as Italy and Spain, were engaged in the work of Counter-Reformation, and the practice of reading and reflection in Italy was animated by the moralizing allegories of Ariosto and Tasso. Venice was one of the great European centres of book-production and design. Such was the production of printed books that it became necessary to install some kind of regulatory system to control an exploding free market hungry for all kinds of self-expression in printed form. In this flow of energy it was quickly recognized by all persuasions that books could corrupt as well as enlighten: notoriously there were the erotic prints of Aretino. In Ben Jonson's *Volpone* (1607), these prints teach 'every quirke within lusts laborinth';[1] and there were books and pamphlets encouraging and damning all kinds of religious free-thinking – Donne's 'new philosophy' – while in The *Faerie queene*, Spenser's 'Errour' vomits up papers and books.[2]

Things could not be more different in Ireland. Its book culture was, of course, ancient: Ireland has the oldest vernacular literature in Europe, and its early medieval books, such as *The book of Durrow* (*c.* 650) and *The book of Kells* (*c.* 900) are masterpieces of illumination and of the scribal art. These and the great codices of the twelfth century, such as *The book of Leinster*, and the eleventh century *The book of the Dun Cow* reflect the refinement and cultivation of the book in medieval Irish monasteries, while law texts (dating from the seventh century), poetic texts (such as the fourteenth-century *Book of Uí Mhaine*), and various medical tracts illustrate the power and influence of learned families, such as the Mac Aodhagáins in Counties Galway and Tipperary (lawyers), the Ó Dubhagáins of County Galway (poets), and the Hickeys of Munster (physicians). This manuscript tradition was tied into the aristocratic structure of early Irish society, which survived, with very little alteration in spite of the Viking raids and the Norman invasion, down to the Tudor re-conquest.

This re-conquest was itself a reflection of a new ambition on the part of nation-states to seize territory and re-settle it with colonists who would implant their values and world-view and reform the 'savages' they encountered. It is a continuous theme in the literature of early exploration and colonization that 'the natives' had failed to realize the opportunities for enrichment that lay all around them in the form of uncultivated land or unexploited natural resources. This was how the Tudors and the Stuarts viewed Ireland, as a place of great natural plenty wasted upon a chaotic and indigent people, whose own language and culture unfitted them for the uses of society. Furthermore they

1 *Ben Jonson*, ed. C.H. Herford and P. and E. Simpson (Oxford, 1925–50), v, p. 78 (III. vii. 60–1). My thanks are due to John Barnard for his help with the London trade throughout this essay.

2 I. i. 20.

were Catholics, stubbornly allied to Rome and the Pope. The Tudor aim was the expansion of its influence from the tiny fortress of the Pale around Dublin into the wilds beyond, the *terra incognita* of Gaeldom.

The implantation and expansion of the Protestant faith by means of the efficacy of the word in stimulating the individual conscience to a recognition of its personal acceptance of God (rather than the institutional submission which Rome was said to require) was a key part of the Tudor endeavour. The word had to be primarily in English in Ireland.

In 1550 Humphrey Powell, a London printer, was paid £20 by the Privy Council to establish a printing press in Dublin, the chief purpose of which was to publish *The boke of the common praier and administracion of the Sacramentes ... of the Churche of England*. Powell styled himself King's Printer (that is, Edward VI, 1547–53), and his address is given as Dublin 'in the great toure by the Crane'.[3] This was not the beginning of an extensive development of Irish publishing and printing. The Reformation in Ireland was briefly halted during the reign of Mary Tudor (1553–8) and with it the activities of the Crown's printer. Elizabeth, however, gave the large sum of £66 13*s.* 4*d.* in 1567 'for the making of Carecter to print the New Testament in Irish', which eventually led to the creation of the first fount of Gaelic types,[4] so that the Reformation could proceed more swiftly. Translation began in the 1560s, but the work was delayed, according to Uilliam Ó Domhnaill (William Daniel, later Archbishop of Tuam) by 'Sathan' and the 'filthy frye of Roman seducers', so that the work did not appear until 1602 under the title *Tiomna Nuadh ar dtighearna agus ar slanajghtheora Josa Criosd*. Its printing was finally completed at the house of William Ussher 'near the Bridge', the printer being Seón Francke, or John Franckton,[5] made the King's Printer in 1604. This man was given explicit control of printing in Ireland, no one else being allowed to 'exercise that trade of printinge or of Stationers within this Realme' unless authorized by him.[6] The King's Printer's patent gave him 'full, sole and complete licence and authority' over not only printing in Ireland but the sale and binding of all books, imported or home produced, throughout the realm, and this authority theoretically remained in force until 1732.[7]

In 1912 C.W. Dugan in the introduction to Mc Clintock Dix's groundbreaking *Catalogue of early Dublin-printed books 1601 to 1700*, wondered why

3 *STC* 16277, Dix 1932, p. 3, plate 1, and Duff 1905. 4 Dickins 1949–53, p. 49 and *passim*.

5 See Pollard 2000 for the details and sources of Franckton's career. Pollard's *Dictionary* provides the basis for further research into Irish book trade personnel from 1550 to 1800.

6 Pollard 1989, p. 2. 7 *Ibid.*, pp. 3–16 and Pollard 1980.

printing was introduced so late into Ireland. He points out that Maurice O'Fihely (*d.* 1513), known as 'De Portu' because he came from the port of Baltimore, County Cork, had been principal corrector at Octavian Schott's press in Venice and was the author of *Enchiridion fidei* (1500) which was printed there. In 1500 O'Fihely was Archbishop of Tuam, then later of Galway. Why did O'Fihely fail to bring the arts of printing with him to Galway?[8] Neither he, nor any Irish prince or chieftain bothered to introduce this technology, although they certainly had libraries of books in English, Latin, and Italian: Hugh O'Neill, Earl of Tyrone, had a copy of Ariosto,[9] hardly surprising since O'Neill spent part of his early manhood at Sir Henry Sidney's Penshurst, a centre for the austere intellectual reform of the Sidneys and Spensers.

The obvious answer is that Ireland's Gaelic-reading population was too small to support a trade in printed books even if printers could be trained, while books in English were dominated by the London trade. Throughout this period the basic stock in trade of Irish booksellers and stationers was exactly that of the English provincial trade – Bibles, Testaments, Psalms, primers, almanacs and Latin school books[10] – all of little or no interest to the native Catholic population. Nevertheless, the 'expansion of trade and the commercialisation of the Irish economy in the early seventeenth century' encouraged the growth of the book trade, the exports from Bristol to southern Ireland, for instance, increasing five-fold between the 1590s and 1612.[11] In 1618, the London stationers, who had already invested in a small way as a corporate body in the Ulster Plantation,[12] thought the Irish market ready for commercial exploitation, and, having secured the King's Printer's patent for a twenty-one year period, made substantial investment in an Irish Stock with a view to using their monopoly over the English trade to dominate the trade throughout Ireland.[13] This was not a success: the London stationers had no real control over Irish booksellers (their influence was much greater in England), and the supply routes through outports like Bristol and Chester,[14] quite apart from imports from the Continent (which included illegal Catholic devotional works), made the trade difficult if not impossible to police. No doubt booksellers in Ireland were as adept as those in the English provinces at evading the attempts to regulate pirated and prohibited books.[15]

8 Dix 1971, I, pp. 8–9. 9 O'Faolain 1942, p. 36.
10 For the kind of titles imported see R. Gillespie 1988 and 1996.
11 Gillespie 1996, p. 2, table 1. 12 Jackson 1957, pp. ix, 44–5, 49, 63, 75, 135.
13 On the Irish Stock see Barnard, above, p. 15 and note; for information and advice on the Irish Stock I am grateful to R. J. Hunter, John Pitcher and Andrew Hadfield.
14 See Hunter 1988 and Gillespie 1996. 15 Barnard and Bell, above, pp. 679–84.

Printing was, with a few exceptions, confined to Dublin, and was exercised on behalf of the work of colonization and conversion. One apparent exception to the Dublin monopoly (and a very early one at that), is Waterford ('Portlairge') where, on 7 November 1555, John Olde's *The acquital or purgation of the most Catholyke Edward the .VI.* was 'emprinted'; however, this book seems to have been printed in Emden, by Egidius van der Erve, though issued also at Waterford.[16] Another enigmatic figure, operating in Waterford and Cork, was Peter de Pienne who printed *Eikon basilike*, an account of the 'Solitudes and sufferings' of Charles I, in Cork in 1649.

Titles such as these from presses operating outside the control of the King's Printer are an exception in sixteenth or seventeenth-century Ireland. Nevertheless, these activities reflected some threat to the monopoly in the 1640s whose patent William Bladen took over from the Company in 1641.[17] Yet there was in reality little call for printing in Ireland. In about 1620 it was said 'there is but one printer and he is scarce employed':[18] indeed, there was so little work that the Stationers' Company employed the Dublin press to print the fifth edition of Sidney's *Arcadia* in 1621.[19] The works mostly printed in Dublin throughout the century are sermons, proclamations, proposals of various kinds for relief or conversion, agricultural texts or tracts on mineral or natural resources. These all reflect the way in which the printing of books was conceived as a means of promoting the authority (and 'civility') of the Crown (or Parliament), the expansion of the reformed faith, the dissemination of English culture, and the furtherance of economic development.

The writings and activities of James Ussher, Archbishop of Armagh, offer an insight into the frame of mind that was predominant in Anglo-Ireland during and following the Tudor re-conquest. Daniel's *New Testament* had been printed in the house of William Ussher, his relative.[20] The younger Ussher helped expand the library of the recently established Trinity College, of which he was a fellow. He became Bishop of Meath in 1619 and, while in this office, came across *The book of Kells*, as noted in a gloss in the text itself, dated 4 August 1621.

Although he achieved high eminence in the Irish Church, Ussher, in his earlier days, favoured a Hibernian reformed faith more in line with the tenets of Calvinism than the more temperate accommodations Elizabeth strove to realize in her Act of Settlement. Under James I, William Laud succeeded in

16 *STC* 18797: Plomer 1910 gives an account of the 'Waterford' type.
17 Pollard 1989, p. 4.
18 R. Gillespie 1988, p. 87, citing G. O'Brien (ed.), *Advertisements for Ireland* (Dublin, 1923), p. 42.
19 *STC* 22545, Jackson 1957, pp. 116, 141, 170.
20 Dix 1971, I, p. 12.

reducing the intensity of Ussher's zeal, but the latter maintained his conviction that the reformed Irish church retained a special continuity with the early Church in Ireland, a position he defended repeatedly, and advanced in his *A discourse of the religion anciently professed by the Irish and Brittish* (1631), printed by Robert Younge 'for the Partners of the Irish Stocke', London. A corollary of this view was, of course, that papistry was in profound deviation from the true 'ancient' Irish Church. In an opening 'Epistle' he puts his case cogently, drawing upon his researches into Irish materials:

> ... as farre as I can collect by such records of the former ages as have come into my hands (eyther *manuscript* or *printed*) the religion professed by the ancient Bishops, Priests, monks, and other Christians in this land, was for substance the very same with that which now by publike authoritie is maintained therein, against the forraine doctrin brought in thither in later times by the Bishop of Romes followers.[21]

Ussher's reference here to both manuscript and printed sources identifies a crucial factor in the book culture of this phase of Irish history. The printed word was seeking, in Ireland, to advance an English authority. Ussher, in a typically adept piece of colonial obfuscation, both calculating and impassioned, claims that the faith as practised by the native Irish is in fact 'forraine' and a late import. Colonial administrators and power-brokers, and their successors, the anti-imperialists or nationalists, habitually mix assertion and appeal to origins in order to justify their positions; and from the Reformation onwards such justifications are primarily made in the printed word. Of course Ussher's manuscript sources said no such thing. There were accounts of dynastic conflicts in which the Celtic Church was deeply implicated, but there was never an attack on the authority of the Roman succession, which Ussher spends much ingenuity trying to undermine.

To place Gaelic manuscripts and English, Irish, and Latin printed sources alongside each other in the seventeenth century gives a very sharp understanding of the gulf between the level of sophistication and culture evident in the Gaelic and Hiberno-Latin traditions, and the proselytizing utilitarianism of much of the material that flowed from the English-language press. However, despite this fairly stark contrast, there are also curious interanimations and contacts operating across the languages and cultures of Ireland in this century of profound transformation.

21 Sig. A2^{v}–3^{r}.

Different traditions in seventeenth-century Ireland

In Ireland and elsewhere, though for different reasons,[22] manuscript tradition survived into the seventeenth century and beyond. Although the Tudor re-conquest and its devastating conclusion in the Battle of Kinsale and the Flight of the Earls meant the beginning of the end of the Gaelic order, native learning nevertheless persisted on a number of fronts. Poem books (*duanairí*), collections of poetry for the use of Irish nobility, continued to be compiled: in 1627 the *Duanaire Finn* (*Poem book of Fionn*) was assembled in Ostend by the scribe Aodh ō Dochartaigh for Somhairle Mac Dómhnaill from Antrim while he was soldiering in the Low Countries. This collection of Ossianic poems and tales relating to Fionn Mac Cumhail, is part of a larger collection of Fionn material which includes, most importantly, a redaction of *Acallam na Senórach* (*The colloquy of the Ancients*) which was copied by another scribe called, intriguingly, Niall Gruamdha (Niall the Morose) Ó Catháin. Mac Dómhnaill was a captain in the Spanish army fighting in the Netherlands in the years 1626–31: he served in the Irish regiment under the command of Seán O'Neill, Earl of Tyrone, and he probably died there on active service, fighting the British. His manuscripts were preserved in Louvain, at St Anthony's Irish College, a major Counter-Reformation centre, and a seminary for Franciscans. This college was also a focus for Gaelic learning and scholarship, at a time when, after the Tudor re-conquest, such an institution had become a virtual impossibility in Ireland. Mac Dómhnaill's *Duanaire Finn*, compiled for an Irish aristocrat-soldier, is now in the Franciscan Library at Killiney outside Dublin.

It took over three centuries fully to bring to light the contents of this book compiled in the Low Countries for a man of obvious taste and education but who would have made very little pretension to learning.[23] Such an example serves to emphasize the gap that separates early modern English-language books from the manuscript tradition of Gaelic culture. Before the Tudor re-conquest, say in around 1530, most of the houses of the Irish nobility whether of Gaelic, Norman, or English extraction, would have contained manuscript volumes of Irish materials, alongside printed books imported from London or Paris or any number of Continental cities. But their Irish books, their books in Irish, would have held special place, because they would have been the products of a professional caste of scribes, poets and scholars who were the keepers of each family's genealogical lore, its identity, its sense of history – Gaelic learned families like the MacAwards (or Wards), the O'Dalys, the O'Husseys,

22 See Love, above, ch. 3.
23 MacNeill and Murphy 1908–53, I, pp. xixff. and III, pp. ix–xi.

the O'Cléirighs (Clarkes), the MacEgans, the Ó Rodaighs, the O'Higgins, the Ó Neachtains, and others.

Mac Dómhnaill, in part, earned his living as a mercenary. His scribes, significantly, were not practising their art living in their ancient lands, by then in the possession of Charles Blount, Baron Mountjoy (the victor of Kinsale), and the London Companies of the Cloth Workers and others. Ó Dochartaigh and Ó Catháin were seeking protection from the Catholic countries of Europe as their own civilization was going under.

The content of Mac Dómhnaill's manuscript is curiously appropriate to the cultural context in which the transcription took place, because the Fionn tales, told and re-worked from the eleventh century onwards, mix romantic yearning for a faraway and scarcely remembered heroic past, a keenly registered sense of place, and a powerful tribal and filial loyalty. These themes of regret, melancholy, and world-weariness chime well with the realities of seventeenth-century Irish disruption and dispossession. When we read in the *Duanaire* Fionn's lament in old age, mourning the loss of his vigour and energies, a poem dating probably from *c.* 1200, we sense that Mac Dómhnaill would have shared the mood, and would have experienced emotions that were more than personal:

I once had a thick
head of yellow hair,
now my skull is covered
with a short grey crop.

I no longer have any luck
with women, they turn away;
my hair is white, I am not
as once I was.

This transformation in the fortunes of the Irish aristocracy and their learned classes did not only mean a change of ownership of the land which the plantation of Ulster began, an alteration extended in subsequent plantations. Much to the disgust of the hereditary chieftains and their learned and ecclesiastical institutions, a change also took place in the stratification of society itself. From the time of James I a new class of 'fáslaigh' (upstarts) arose, often native Irish of the meanest backgrounds, who took advantage of the seismic alterations underway in Ireland to seize opportunities, in property or trade, to advance themselves. Those literary men trained under the old system were revolted by the new order, an attitude given fierce expression in two related texts of the seventeenth century, brought together in manuscript recensions as *Páirlement Chloinne Tomáis* (*The Parliament of Clan Thomas*).

The story of this new class of interlopers is told in a set of early eighteenth-century manuscripts, the earliest of which is H.5.10 in Trinity College, Dublin, written by Shane O'Sullivan in 1703. The most complete and accurate text seems to be that known as 23.0.72 in the Royal Irish Academy, compiled by Tadhg Ua Duinnín in Dublin in 1705. These redactions were transcribed from seventeenth-century versions, now lost or as yet undiscovered.

In 1605 Arthur Chichester, now Lord Deputy, deemed that all Irish people were natural subjects of James I, and not of their local chieftains, thereby legally undermining the traditional authority of the likes of Hugh O'Neill of Tyrone, the Maguires of Fermanagh, or the MacDonnells of Dunluce. Any person who was imposed upon by these traditional lords had the right to appeal to English law and officialdom: the old policy of 'divide and rule'. This new right, designed to encourage quasi-democratic urgings in a previously disadvantaged social group, meant that 'hirelings' and 'upstarts' could take their former masters to law. These new types are the class of people which the (unknown) authors of these texts depict as 'Clan Thomas'; wheedling, big-boned, uncouth, horny-handed, unkempt, stinking, floppy-eared, stinking perversions of humanity, they are ready and willing to usurp their rightful lords. In doing so they destroy the very fabric of life itself, according to the authors, for whom tradition and ancestry are everything.

N. J. A. Williams has persuasively argued that the first of these two linked texts was probably composed not very long after Chichester's 1605 decree, so here we have a text that arises directly from the shifts taking place in Irish life due to an irreversible transformation of the ways in which Ireland was governed. The author depicts Clan Thomas as innately quarrelsome and ungovernable; wherever they assemble they brawl amongst themselves. While this registers a disgust at new social formations, the author is also describing, in a mixture of loathing and anger, involuntary spasms of violence being unleashed in social behaviour by profound change. In a fight between two of them, after flailing with rusty sickles, the combatants grab each other in a wrestling hold around their stomachs with such force that one of them, Mannarthach

> let forth a massive fart that was heard throughout the four provinces of Ireland; and for that reason his descendants after him have been known as the Kindred of Farting Mannarthach . . . a common reproach for all of Clan Thomas.[24]

24 Williams 1981, p. 72.

The Parliament of Clan Thomas is convened because they find themselves, despite their treachery, financially overstretched in trying to educate their appalling offspring in rhetoric, philosophy, and the ways of genteel living. They come to an assembly in Kerry in 1632 and 1645 (the author is almost certainly projecting forward from a date of *c.* 1615) and in doing so they are, despite their Satanic ancestry (their ancestor was Liobar Lobhtha-Rotten Flaplip, son of Beelzebub), conforming to a recognized social pattern in Gaelic society, noticed by Edmund Spenser. It was, he tells us in his *A view of the present state of Ireland* (1633), customary

> to make great assemblies together upon a Rath or hill, there to parly (as they say) about matters and wrongs between township and township, or one private person and another, but well I wot and true it hath been oftentimes approved, that in these meetings many mischiefs have been both practised and wrought. For to them do commonly resort all the scum of loose people . . .[25]

With Spenser one moves from the hidden world of Gaelic books and transcription into a public arena of politics and cultural discourse, and early formations of colonial and racial attitudes. Spenser's account was enormously influential; written in about 1596, some three years before his death, it circulated only in manuscript until it was published by Sir James Ware in 1633, together with two other similar histories, Edmund Campion's *History of Ireland* and Meredeth Hanmer's *Chronicle of Ireland.* These three texts, published as one book in a number of roughly contemporaneous issues, were printed by the Dublin Society of Stationers, under licence from the King's Printer who held the sole patent for publishing books in Ireland. It was also issued by Thomas Harper in London.[26] Spenser's *View* is an 'Irish' book, in the sense that it was amongst the relatively few books printed in Ireland in the earlier seventeenth century that were not state proclamations or religious tracts. It circulated in manuscript and it was probably in this form that Geoffrey Keating had access to it when writing his refutation of English animadversions upon Ireland, *Foras Feasa ar Éirinn* (?1616–?1634). Spenser wrote his *View* in London during his second visit there from Ireland, while he was overseeing publication of *Colin Clouts come home again* (a poem about Ireland), and the second edition of the *Faerie queene* (also a poem of Ireland, in that it was written there; sections of it are set in Ireland, and Irish affairs trouble the allegory in ways which are increasingly recognized). The *View* is the best known of a whole class of Tudor and Stuart writings to which *The Oxford companion to Irish literature* gives the generic title

25 Renwick 1970, p. 77.   26 *STC* 25067.

'Anglo-Irish Chronicles'. These are works, mostly published in England, which take the view that the Irish in their native state are ungovernable, their species of society a 'chaotic anachronism'.[27] Other such books were John Davies's *A discoverie of the true causes why Ireland was never entirely subdued, nor brought under obedience of the Crowne of England, until the beginning of his Maiesties happie raigne* (1612), and Barnabe Riche's *A new description of Ireland* (1617). Spenser, like these other commentators, promulgates the view that the Irish and the descendants of the Normans in Ireland are lazy, improvident, lecherous, godless and superstitious. The structure of Irish society, its economy, its culture, its language, arts, and mores, seemed barbaric and not reformable to civilized usages. In being dedicated to sedition its oral and manuscript learning was a perversion of moral intelligence. Spenser accuses the Irish learned classes, especially the poets, of failing in the first requirement of culture, that of moral discipline: they eulogize 'lewd liberty' and honour the kind of man who takes 'by force the spoil of other men's love'.[28] Spenser believes that Irish culture, as well as being formless and inchoate, is perverted in glorifying the rape of married women.

In fact Irish culture, in its more literary and scholarly forms, had largely been driven abroad. Bonaventura had a catechism printed at Antwerp in 1611, in a font later used at the College of St Anthony of Padua at Louvain, which became a centre for Irish culture and learning, manuscripts and print. The college was founded in 1606 by Philip III of Spain, and the poet and theologian Aodh Mac Aingil was made Guardian in 1616. In 1611 the Franciscans set up their own printing press, for the production of Irish books, amongst which were Flaithrí Ó Maolchonaire's *Desiderius* (1616), a translation of a Catalan Counter-Reformation tract and Mac Aingil's *Sgathán Shacramuinte na hAithridhe* (1618). Louvain was a centre for a range of scholarly activity in historical and hagiographical lore, linguistic study, compilation, publication, and theological and philosophical investigation and editing. The Irish friars at Louvain, many of them members of Gaelic learned families, worked on two fronts: they wished to arrest or at least obstruct the expansion of English Protestant interest in Ireland, and at the same time bring the energies of the Counter-Reformation to their native country. These labours were dedicated also to the rescue of native Irish culture, ecclesiastical and otherwise, which for them became identified with the Catholic cause.

When Aodh Mac an Bháird (another member of a learned family) became Guardian in 1626 he began a programme of research and collection with the

27 Renwick 1970, p. 177. 28 *Ibid.*, pp. 74–5.

aim of preserving the ecclesiastical, hagiographical and political records of Ireland, with Louvain as the nerve-centre. In that same year Mac an Bháird sent Míchéal Ó Cléirigh to Ireland to collect and co-ordinate anything relevant to the ancient history and dignity of the Irish people. Manuscripts, summaries, annals, calendars, in Irish and Latin, were sent back in volume to Louvain through Francis O'Mahony, a Cork Franciscan. Mac an Bháird died, and the work was taken over by John Colgan from Donegal in 1635, eventually leading to the publication, ten years later, of the *Acta Sanctorum veteris et maioris Scotiae seu Hibernia Sanctorum insulae* from the Louvain press. This volume incorporated much lore about the Irish Saints' lives whose feast-days fell between 1 January and 30 March, excepting Patrick, Brigit, and Columcille. It runs to over 900 double-column pages, a magnificent work of scholarship, industry and devotion. Colgan continued to research and write, publishing the lives of the Irish Trinity, Patrick, Brigit and Columcille, in 1647, also from Louvain, and played a major role in the renovation of the reputation of Duns Scotus in seventeenth-century Counter-Reformation theology, mistakenly believing Scotus to have been Irish. *Tractatus de vita, scriptis Johannis Scoti* (1655) by Colgan drew upon the edition published in Rome in 1639, itself inspired by a Mac Aingil commentary printed at Louvain in 1620, re-issued in Paris 1623, entitled *Apologia apologias pro Joanne Duns Scoto . . . in qua jacta in eum, eiusque vindicem convitia repullunter*. And the line goes further back: Maurice O'Fihely from Baltimore, the Venetian corrector, himself had published a commentary on Scotus in 1499.[29]

When Ó Cléirigh returned to Ireland in 1626, he based himself at the Franciscan Friary in Bundrowes, County Donegal, but also travelled all over the country to collect every kind of material for transmission back to Louvain through O'Mahoney, the secret agent in Cork. With the help of others, some of whom were to become his collaborators on the *Annals of the Four masters*, one of the truly great books of Ireland, he made recensions of the martyrologies of Donegal and Oengus; and in Lisgoole, Fermanagh, he edited and transcribed a version of the *Lebor gabála* (*Book of invasions*) under the patronage of Brian Rua Maguire in 1631. In 1632, under the patronage of Fearghal Ó Gadhra of Sligo (those of the O'Donnells who had acted as ancestral patrons of the Ó Cléirigh learned family had left the country), he and his team began work on the great undertaking, a compilation of the historical and ecclesiastical annals of Ireland from earliest times to 1616. They laboured for four years and finished on 10 August 1636. Then Brother Míchéal travelled to Flann Mac Aodhagáin

29 Walsh 1963, p. 23. I am grateful to Anne McCartney for this reference.

of the MacEgan legal family in north Tipperary to get him to check it and write a testimonial to its accuracy and worth, which was done on 2 November. Two copies were made of three volumes each, one for Ó Gadhra and the other for printing in Louvain. It appears that only two volumes of the three destined for Louvain actually arrived, and none was printed. Five of the original six volumes are now preserved in or around Dublin, in the Royal Irish Academy, the Franciscan Library at Killiney, and at Trinity. The text remained unedited, unprinted and untranslated until Owen Connellan's edition of 1846, followed by John O'Donovan's seven volumes in 1854. The text opens:

> The Age of the World, to this Year of the Deluge, 2242. Forty days before the Deluge, Ceasair came to Ireland with fifty girls and three men . . .[30]

Then it proceeds, each entry headed by its relevant year, until 1616, to the death in Rome of Hugh O'Neill, Earl of Tyrone. He is described as follows:

> a powerful, mighty lord, [endowed] with wisdom, subtlety, and profundity of mind, and intellect; a warlike, valorous, predatory enterprising lord, in defending his religion and his patrimony against his enemies; a pious and charitable lord, mild and gentle with his friends, fierce and stern towards his enemies . . .[31]

This eulogy is as nothing, however, to the heartbroken prose of the lament it contains for Hugh O'Donnell who died in Simancas, Spain.

Around the same time as Ó Cléirigh was completing his work, another cleric, this time a fully ordained priest and doctor of divinity, was putting the finishing touches to auother of the great books of Ireland: Geoffrey Keating, Seathrún Céitinn from Tipperary who, about 1634, was completing *Foras feasa ar Éirinn (Groundwork of knowledge concerning Ireland)*, a narrative history of Ireland from the earliest times to the Norman Invasion and the death of Rory O'Connor, the last high King of Ireland, in 1198. He had access to a well-resourced library,[32] and it is likely that he consulted Míchéal Ó Cléirigh. He was certainly fully acquainted with many of the sources the Four Masters drew upon. His is a polemical work, and he declares in an extensive preface that his book is intended to check the lies, ignorance, and prejudice promulgated by the Anglo-Irish chronicles. He singles out Spenser as one of the most offensive of his miscreants, but he also castigates Stanyhurst, Camden, Moryson, and Davies as calumniators of Ireland's civilization. He declares that they are like beetles in summer:

30 O'Donovan 1854, I, pp. 2–3. 31 *Ibid.*, VI, pp. 2372–5. 32 Cronin 1943–4.

> ... it is the fashion of the beetle, when it lifts it head in the summertime, to go about fluttering, not to stoop towards any delicate flower that may be in the field, or any blossom in the garden, though they be all roses and lilies, but it keeps on bustling about until it comes upon cow-dung or horse-shit, and then proceeds to roll around in it. Thus it is with the crowd named above ...[33]

This is how they, following Cambrensis, read Irish history and Irish books, Keating asserts: they ignored all the gracious deeds and activities of Irish men and women, and selectively chose material so as to shore up their own prejudices, which in any case they mimic from others, more powerful than they.

A number of manuscripts of this book survive from the seventeenth century. Manuscript A14 in the Franciscan Library at Killiney was transcribed in part by Míchéal Ó Cléirigh, work which he may have undertaken while completing the *Annals*; at any rate this book seems to have been the one used by Colgan when compiling his *Acta*, and 'ex libris conventus de Dun na ngall' (a possible reference to the friary at Bundrowes) appears in his hand at fol.53^{r}. Another copy, in Killiney, dates from *c.* 1638, while in Trinity there is a further recension by Tórna Ó Maolchonaire, a contemporary.[34]

Keating's book remained unpublished until 1811 when William Haliday printed part of it with a translation, although Dermod O'Connor had brought out a fanciful but intriguing version as early as 1723. However, in the Killiney Library there is a late recension, dated 1818,[35] which gives us an insight into the tenacity of Irish manuscript tradition and which reveals, in an autograph note by the scribe on the title page, how Gaelic learning persisted in unlikely circumstances. The scribe is Eóghan Tóibín 'a cCorcaidh', living in Blarney Lane, Cork. He has, he tells us, copied this from the text of Mícheál Ó Longáin, a well-known Cork scholar of the period, and Tobin has done this 'chuim úsáide féin' – 'for my own use'. Who was this Tobin? What was he? Living in Blarney Lane he would have been amongst the city's poor: a cobbler, a blacksmith, a criminal? We cannot tell, but we do know he revered Keating because he inscribes a prayer for him: 'go ndéana Dia grása air ar son a shaothar' – 'may God grant him grace for his work'.[36]

This account of the interconnections in the history of the Irish book in the seventeenth century concludes by returning to Sir James Ware (1594–1666), a second generation settler, antiquary and Irish historian, whose collection of books now forms the largest part of the Clarendon Collection in the Bodleian Library, Oxford. When he sponsored the publication of Spenser's *View* in 1633 he remarked that the past thirty years of peace made the ferocity of Spenser's

33 Comyn 1902, I, p. 4. 34 Dillon, Mooney and de Brún 1969, pp. 27ff.
35 *Ibid.*, no. A52. 36 *Ibid.*, pp. 116ff.

drastic prescriptions for the relief of the Irish body politic somewhat out of date. James Ussher acted as Ware's mentor, and encouraged him in his antiquarian and historical researches, introducing him to Sir Robert Cotton, the great English collector of books and manuscripts in 1626. Cotton gave him unrestricted access to his library as he did with Ussher. In 1639 Ware published, in Dublin, *De scriptoribus Hiberniae*, an account of Irish writers and scholars from the earliest times, under the imprint 'Ex Officina Typographia Societatis Bibliopolarum' (that is to say, printed for the Dublin Society of Stationers). Ware, influenced not only by Ussher, but also by the English antiquarianism of Cotton and Elias Ashmole, was animated by a desire to preserve Irish historical and literary records which seems to have all but freed itself from the preoccupation with proving the errors of the Catholic faith, and the righteousness of the Reformation. He was also anxious to advance the reputation of Dublin as a centre of research and publication. During the Commonwealth Ware was out of favour, spending some time in the Tower of London, and Henry Jones, Governor of Dublin, banished him from the islands of Britain and Ireland. However he was restored to his previous post on the Privy Council at the Restoration, and re-elected as Parliamentary representative for Trinity College. From 1660 to his death in 1666 he resumed his labours to preserve Ireland's historical remains, and to further printing and publishing in Dublin. John Crooke became the King's Printer General in Ireland from 1660, and the following year established a printing press in Dublin. Crooke's first Irish publication was, interestingly enough, Francis Synge's *Panegyrick on the most auspicious... return of... our royal Charles*, a twelve-page pamphlet, probably issued in 1661. In the following year he printed Ware's *Rerum Hibernicarum Henrico Octavo regnante annales*, historical material of Irish interest from the reign of Henry VIII, followed in 1664 by similar documents from the other Tudor monarchs prior to Elizabeth. The Gaelic historian and genealogist, Dubhaltach Mac Fhir Bhisigh from Sligo, worked as a scribe and translator at Ware's house in Castle Street in 1665–66. Mac Fhir Bhisigh's translations of Irish records informed Ware's *De praesulibus Hiberniae* (1665), an account of the Christian faith in Ireland from earliest times, also printed by John Crooke.

Ending and beginnings

Under the year '1662 [?]' in McClintock Dix's listings of Dublin printed books there is an entry on 'Abraham Cowley, *Poems*', with no details given of the printer. The following year Cowley published a London edition, with the following irate notice prefixed:

> Most of these verses which the author had not intent to publish, having lately been printed at Dublin without his consent or knowledge . . . he hath thought fit for his justification . . . to allow the reprinting of them here.[37]

'Lawfully recognized ownership of literary property' did not exist in Ireland until 1800, and the Act of Union.[38] Cowley's annoyance is only one expression of a general complaint by English printers and writers about the insouciance of the Dublin pirates of the book trade. John Dunton, in *The Dublin scuffle* (1699, published in Dublin, 'for the author', and 'to be sold by A. Baldwin'[39]) describes a classic example of such a 'pirate' or 'cormorant' of books, one Samuel Lee, who had no sense of propriety or property, and treated the produce of anyone's intellectual efforts as his own. Such was the annoyance of London booksellers during the eighteenth century, it is said, that they were reluctant to send even a single copy of a book to Dublin, for fear it would be printed. However, the picture is not so simple or so one-sided. Dublin and Ireland provided an increasingly lucrative market for London-printed books. Books were being shipped from Bristol to nine ports in southern Ireland by 1612.[40] By 1655 Ireland was importing books to the value of £1,721, of which £603 came from the Continent but the larger part from England.[41] In 1696/7 the value of books imported from London alone had nearly doubled to £2,975 and in the years 1698–1700, which continued imports at the same level mostly through Dublin, London-printed books accounted for no less than 87 per cent of the total.[42] The importance (and profitability) of the Irish market for the London trade is demonstrated by the inventory of George Sawbridge's assets made in September 1681: a quarter of the nearly £16,000 owed him had been incurred by Dublin booksellers.[43]

In 1670 a new attempt was made to regulate the book trade, clearly an indication that the market was expanding as the relatively peaceful years of Charles's reign brought greater prosperity. On 15 August 1670, at Whitehall, letters patent of the Crown authorized the Guild of St Luke the Evangelist, and amongst the beneficiaries of this authority were Mary Crooke, widow of John Crooke, Ware's printer, and Benjamin Tooke, his successor as King's Printer in Ireland. It should be emphasized, however, that this empowerment was not intended as a relaxation of controls, rather the opposite, for Tooke and his

37 Quoted Phillips 1998, p. 103 38 *Ibid.* 39 Wing D2622.
40 Gillespie 1996, p. 12. 41 R. Gillespie 1988, p. 81, Pollard 1989, p. 40.
42 Drawn from Pollard 1989, p. 41.
43 Information generously provided by Giles Mandelbrote. Sawbridge's Irish debts totalled £3,716 2*s.* 6*d.*; other creditors owed him nearly £12,000. *Inventories of the London book trade, c. 1650–c. 1720*, edited by Giles Mandelbrote, forthcoming.

colleagues were closely affiliated with the London Company of Stationers.[44] Furthermore, while granting to the Guild powers to engage and indenture apprentices, strictures were imposed relating to their demeanour, and, more importantly, their religion. They should 'be of a good Conversation and of the Protestant Religion'.[45]

The authority and control of the King's Printer was shortly to be decisively challenged. In 1680 Joseph Ray, a printer–bookseller who had served his apprenticeship in Dublin and London, set up a press in Dublin:[46] Tooke and his associates immediately sought to stop him. Ray's defence was that he was responding to an Irish demand for books, and that there was plenty of work for all concerned:

> . . . there being of late more Books wanting in this Kingdome . . . that theire is no danger but that the Complainants and this Defendant will be fully Employed.[47]

Ray's challenge was successful and the King's Printer's patent broken. Between 1681 and 1689 some fifty imprints carry his name, and he became the first official printer to the City of Dublin in 1681.[48] It is also clear that by 1681 the King's Printer no longer controlled (if he ever had) the import of books into Ireland. In that year twenty-eight people shipped in books from Chester. Although many were stationers the number included two glovers and the Archbishop of Dublin.[49]

The publications of the King's Printers to 1695 provide a marked contrast to those printed by Ray: official pronouncements and sermons as against publications such as *The Jesuits manner of consecrating both the persons and weapons imploy'd for the murdering of kings* . . . (1681), supposedly a translation; or a reprint of John Dryden's *Threnodia Augustalis* (1685), a funeral-poem on the death of Charles II, which it is highly unlikely that Jacob Tonson, Dryden's bookseller, sanctioned. Ray reprinted the *Threnodia* for Robert Thornton, a Dublin bookseller, who later became King's Stationer and a book auctioneer.[50] Already here we have, in the making, the circumstance which infuriated London publishers, especially after the Licensing Act lapsed in 1695, which allowed Irish printers to publish books legally and export them into Britain in quantity, without the bother of paying the author.

In 1690 Jonathan Swift published one of his earliest works, *A Pindarique ode to King Wm. III, to congratulate him on his great successes* in Dublin, reflecting

44 Phillips 1998, pp. 5–6. The Guild's Royal Charter was issued in October (Phillips 1998, p. 6, Pollard 1989, p. 5).

45 Pollard 1989, p. 7. 46 Pollard 1989, p. 6, and Pollard 2000. 47 Pollard 1989, p. 7.

48 *Ibid.*, p. 8. 49 Hunter 1988. 50 Pollard 2000.

Swift's own relief that the Jacobite transformations which James II had set in train in Ireland had been halted by the Williamite victory at the Battle of the Boyne in that year. Swift, with many others of the Protestant Ascendency, had to flee Trinity College and Ireland in the late 1680s as Tyrconnell imposed his Catholicizing reforms. As ever, jubilation at the securing of a Protestant State and governance in Ireland had its other side: the dismay of the Jacobites, and their champions in verse and prose, the surviving Irish literary men such as Dáibhí Ó Bruadair and Aogán Ó Rathaille, whose works were destined to continue in manuscript form, not because they wished it, but because the power of print, and of money, remained in Protestant hands. Ahead lay a glorious period for Dublin printing and publishing, George Faulkner beginning his career with the first of Swift's *Drapier's letters* on 'Wood's Copper-Money' in 1724.

At the same time, the Penal Laws, which shored up the ascendancy of a Protestant minority over a Catholic majority, ensured that Gaelic culture and learning slid even further into decline. The seventeenth century, for all its cataclysmic blows to Gaelic society, had been marked by an extraordinary energy of retrieval and recording, as if the last of the Gaelic scribes of the old order knew they were writing down what might otherwise disappear into oblivion. Their books were being written against time, in every sense of the word 'against'. The clear light of Georgian Ireland had, as its other side, a confused darkness as the Catholic Irish began to re-invent themselves in a new world, a new language. Meanwhile George Grierson was issuing his classical series, beginning with *Horace* (Dublin, 1721); and Samuel Richardson, the novelist, was, in 1753, horrified to find that, as *Sir Charles Grandison* was being printed in London, his own workmen were sending newly printed sheets to the Dublin pirates Peter Wilson, John Exshaw, and Henry Saunders, whose triumph over the English trade was to publish volumes five and six before Richardson himself, their author and printer, could do so in London.[51]

51 Pollard 1989, p. 89.

35

Wales

PHILIP HENRY JONES

Despite its small size and limited population – increasing from over a quarter of a million in the mid-sixteenth century to somewhere over 360,000 by 1670 – a complex of interrelated social, linguistic, cultural and educational differences makes it impossible to speak of 'a' history of the book in Wales during this period.

Although the great majority of the population of Wales consisted of illiterate monoglot Welsh-speakers, there were important geographical and social exceptions. The long-established Englishries such as south Gower and, more particularly, south Pembrokeshire were monoglot English areas which had little or no contact with Welsh Wales, a feature emphasized by the Pembrokeshire antiquarian George Owen (1552–1613) who noted that the inhabitants of south Pembrokeshire kept 'their language among themselves without receiving the Welsh speech or learning any part thereof'.[1] These areas were always open to printed books in English. In 1535, for example, the servant of William Barlow (Prior of Haverfordwest but soon to be the first Protestant Bishop of St David's) was seized for possessing an English New Testament and similar books.[2] In 1621 itinerants who attempted to sell books (probably the new godly chapbooks) near Haverfordwest were arrested on an unfounded suspicion of dispersing 'popishe bookes'.[3]

Welsh towns were small – in 1550 only one, Carmarthen, contained over 2,000 inhabitants and as late as 1670 the population of the largest, Wrexham, amounted to no more than about three and a quarter thousand – but they were centres where English was spoken and basic literacy in English could be acquired at petty schools such as the one in Denbigh run by the Londoner, Alice Carter, in 1574.[4] The sixty-three free schools founded under the 1650 Act for the Better Propagation and Preaching of the Gospel in Wales were conducted entirely in English (as were those supported by the Welsh Trust during the

1 Owen 1994, p. 51. 2 Williams 1967, pp. 112–13.
3 Suggett 2000, p. 26. 4 Owen 1964, p. 207.

second half of the 1670s) but may have enjoyed some measure of success in towns. Elementary schools created a demand for basic school texts, which provided Welsh mercers with a useful sideline: the 1673 probate inventory of Griffith Wynn of Caernarfon, for example, includes fourteen plain and twelve gilt hornbooks as well as ABCs, grammars and primers.[5]

Because of the prestige and value of English, the upper ranks of Welsh society had long been enthusiastic learners of the language. Its status was further reinforced by the clause in the so-called Act of Union of 1536 which disqualified from public office those who could not speak English. In practice, legal and administrative matters often had to be transacted in Welsh,[6] but the message to the upper orders was clear: as one scholar put it, 'the Tudor gentry spoke Welsh ... because they could not help it whereas they spoke English because they very much wanted to'.[7] Although English was thus established as the 'high' language in most domains, the patrons of the Welsh poets were aware of a 'high' variety of literary Welsh. The widespread scholarly use of Latin as a 'high' language further complicated matters. When Maurice Kyffin claimed that *Deffynniad Ffydd Eglwys Loegr* (1595), his Welsh translation of Jewel's *Apologia*, was for 'the unlearned'[8] he clearly equated learning with literacy in Latin. An educated gentleman in the mid-sixteenth century could often write (not merely read) Welsh, Latin and English. Scholars might add a knowledge of Greek (possibly) Hebrew and one or more modern languages; the humanist scholar William Salesbury (*c.*1520-?1599) and the clergyman-poet Edmund Prys (1543/4–1623), were reputedly fluent in eight languages.

Although the chaplains of a few gentry households kept a school for the sons of the family and promising sons of tenants (according to Sir John Wynn, the future bishop William Morgan was 'brought up in learning' in this way at Gwydir),[9] the basis for this learning was provided by the grammar schools, over two dozen of which were founded in Wales, mainly in the second half of the sixteenth century and early decades of the seventeenth.[10] These schools were the preserve of the better-off since even where a few free places were provided for poor scholars their parents had to supply writing materials and other necessaries; the poet Siôn Tudur (*c.*1522–1602) describes how a reluctant pupil was equipped with books, a satchel, splendid new clothes, and shoes.[11] The sons of the wealthier gentry were sent to English grammar schools (particularly Shrewsbury school) which offered a broader curriculum, and might prove more effective in eradicating Welsh rusticity.[12]

5 Boon 1973, pp. 45, 51. 6 Suggett 1997 and Jones 1997. 7 Williams 1964, p. 79.
8 Hughes 1967, p. 96. 9 Wynn 1990, p. 63. 10 Griffith 1989, pp. 83–4.
11 Roberts 1980, I, p. 791. 12 Griffith 1989, pp. 98–9.

The books required by grammar-school pupils were initially supplied by booksellers in nearby English towns: the chest of books landed by the *Sondaye* of Chester at Beaumaris in November 1592 may well have been intended for pupils at the town's school.[13] Later on the necessary books were sold by Welsh mercers who were themselves supplied by English booksellers such as John Minshull of Chester who in 1699–1700 provided trade customers in ten towns in North Wales with English and Latin school books, psalters, and prayer books.[14]

Higher education had to be sought outside Wales. Between 1540 and 1642 some 2,200 Welsh students were registered at Oxford and Cambridge, well over four-fifths of them at Oxford. About 700 Welsh students (over a third of whom had attended university) were admitted to the Inns of Court.[15] Recusants had to seek their education abroad. Between 1568 and 1642, 218 students from Wales and its borderland attended Continental seminaries (notably Douai), but no single centre emerged for the Welsh comparable to Louvain for the Irish.

Education at this level was of crucial importance since almost all the printed books in Welsh or relating to Wales were composed by authors who had benefited from higher education. These writers consciously employed Latin, English and Welsh for different purposes. Latin was the natural choice for scholarly works designed for an international readership: historical works such as Sir John Prise's *Historiae Brytannicae defensio* (1573); Welsh grammars, such as those by Siôn Dafydd Rhys (1592),[16] Henry Salesbury (1593), and Dr John Davies (1621); and dictionaries, notably Davies's *Dictionarium duplex* (1632). Latin was also employed for literary purposes, notably by the most popular Welsh author of the early seventeenth century, the epigrammatist John Owen (?1564–?1628).[17]

The increasing acceptability of English as an alternative to Latin for scholarly purposes meant that many Welsh-speakers composed works in that language. Scholars such as George Owen, fluent in Welsh and patrons of the poets, wrote their antiquarian and genealogical treatises in English, possibly because of the influential model provided by Camden. English was also used for social

13 Lewis 1927, pp. 267–8.

14 Plomer 1904, p. 378. Minshull dealt with retailers in Wrexham, Flint, Mold, Rhuthun, Denbigh, and St Asaph (Flintshire and Denbighshire), Bangor (Caernarfonshire), Llannerch-y-medd and Beaumaris (Anglesey), Y Bala (Merioneth).

15 Griffith 1996, table 3, p. 34.

16 In his introduction Siôn Dafydd Rhys (1534–*c.* 1619) discussed the choice of language and explained why he had written his grammar in Latin.

17 Davies 1981 provides an excellent brief introduction which may be supplemented by Davies 1995, pp. 53–84.

purposes by the gentry: surviving letters bear out the truth of Owen's observation that 'although they usually speak the Welsh tongue, yet will they write each to other in English . . . The reason is the use they have to write in the one and not using to write in the other.'[18]

But despite the growing pressure exerted by English, a small but important minority of educated Welshmen became convinced of the value of Welsh and of the urgent need for it to become a language of print. They believed that Geoffrey of Monmouth had demonstrated its antiquity by tracing the 'British tongue' back to Brutus the Trojan, and that it was also a language of ancient learning since, according to pseudo-Berosus, descendants of Samothes, son of Japhet, had founded the orders of bards and druids from which the Welsh poets originated. That so little of this learning had survived they attributed to war, treachery and, according to the Protestant myth (set out in Richard Davies's introductory epistle to the 1567 New Testament), the destruction by Augustine of Canterbury of the books of the Celtic Church including, they believed, most (if not all) of the Scriptures in the vernacular.[19]

Despite its antiquity, by the mid-sixteenth century the Welsh language was considered to be endangered. If it was to be capable of expressing the new learning and, in particular, be an adequate medium for the translation of the Scriptures, scholars had to take the Welsh language in hand. William Salesbury, stressed the urgency of the task in 1547 in the introduction to *Oll synnwyr pen Kembero ygyd* (*All the wisdom in a Welshman's head*), a collection of proverbs which was one of the first Welsh printed books. Unless the task was completed by the present generation it would be too late, partly because of the pressure of English and partly because of the fear, expressed in Salesbury's dedicatory epistle to the second edition of the work (1567), that in the absence of a standard literary language, Welsh, like Cornish and Breton, might become a mere congeries of dialects.[20]

The sense of crisis was intensified by the rapid decline of the bardic order, the traditional custodian of the Welsh language and traditions. The professional Welsh poets of the sixteenth century were the inheritors of a tradition of poetry which could be traced back for a millennium. An intensely conservative body, they jealously guarded the complex secrets of their craft and, though possessing manuscript grammars and vocabularies, instructed their pupils orally in Welsh. A few were occasionally prepared to divulge some of their secrets to their patrons[21] since knowledgeable connoisseurs might reward eulogy or elegy more generously. From the mid-sixteenth century onwards poets increasingly

18 Owen 1994, p. 40. 19 Jones, 1970, pp. 52–3.
20 Hughes 1967, p. xi. 21 Williams 1939, p. [208].

complained of a decline in patronage. The monasteries, formerly a generous source of patronage, had been dissolved. The more successful gentry gradually became anglicized through education, marriage with English heiresses, and residence in England,[22] while many of the lesser gentry, adversely affected by economic pressures and subsequently the disruption of the Civil War and its aftermath, sank to the level of yeomen, distinguishable from them only by their claim to 'better' birth. As patronage decreased, bardic itineraries which had once covered the whole of Wales contracted and poets tended to become associated with individual families which still adhered to the old traditions.

The reduction in patronage coincided with a marked decline in standards of poetic craftsmanship. New forms, particularly accentual free-metre verse, came into vogue and began to be used for subjects hitherto reserved for the strict metres. This was associated with (and probably directly linked to) a vogue for English music by the later sixteenth century.[23] At the same time, poets came to be held in lower esteem and were frequently accused of bringing their craft into disrepute by mercenary praise of the unworthy and by forging the genealogies which had become a prominent component of their poems. Despite the exhortations of the Welsh humanists, the poets made no significant attempt to embrace the new learning or to attempt new modes of poetry. Their conservatism (indeed complacency) is epitomized by the contributions of the traditional poet Wiliam Cynwal to his protracted poetic debate with Edmwnd Prys.[24] Siôn Cain, the last of the itinerant herald-bards, died about 1650[25] and in 1666 Gruffudd Phylip was mourned as the 'last of the poets'.[26] Although there were a few survivals – Siôn Dafydd La(e)s (*c.*1665–95), poet, scribe, and famous drinker, enjoyed the patronage of the house of Nannau – poetry increasingly came to be composed by craftsmen-poets such as the weaver Owen Gruffydd (*c.* 1643–1730).

In Wales the religious changes of the sixteenth century generally received little support but encountered little overt resistance. Although the 1549 English Book of Common Prayer was as unintelligible to most Welsh people as it was to the Cornish, its introduction caused no disturbance in Wales. Pre-Reformation practices remained sufficiently widespread to dismay reformers, but open recusants were a small minority increasingly confined to those areas such as Flintshire and south-east Wales where they had influential protectors. Despite

22 Bowen 1981, pp. 456–7, notes examples of poems urging sojourners in England to return home.

23 Williams 1935 reproduces a list of performers at the Christmas festivities at Lleweni in 1595: only three were poets, but ten were musicians. The same manuscript contains a contemporary list of over eighty English airs.

24 Williams 1986, pp. cxvii–cxxx; clxix–clxx.

25 Bowen 1981, pp. 492–3.

26 Bowen 1981, p. 495.

the dedication and courage of the missionary priests, the Catholic mission to Wales was on too small a scale to be effective. Self-interest and loyalty to the 'Welsh' Tudors ensured the conformity of the vast majority of the gentry.

At this point we must return to William Salesbury. He was not the first to make use of the press to provide the Welsh with basic religious texts: the first Welsh printed book, *Yny lhyvyr hwnn*,[27] published in 1546 by Sir John Prise (?1502–50), was designed to enable those 'who could read Welsh but not a word of English or Latin'[28] to familiarize themselves with key texts such as the Creed, Paternoster, and Ten Commandments. Salesbury went far beyond such Henrican objectives: as a zealous Protestant he believed that the Welsh should be provided with a printed vernacular Bible. As early as 1547 he exhorted them to

> Go on barefoot pilgrimage to the King's grace and to his Council to beg permission to have Holy Scripture in your own language, for the sake of those among you who are not able nor likely to learn English.[29]

Between 1547 and 1551 Salesbury was extraordinarily productive. He published three humanist works – *A dictionary in Englyshe and Welshe* (despite its title a Welsh–English dictionary) early in 1547, *A briefe and a playne introduction teachyng how to pronounce the letters in the British tong* in 1550, and an English translation in the same year of an astronomical work by Proclus – and also two Protestant pamphlets, one in Welsh, the other in English (both in 1550). At the same time he prepared a Welsh translation of the epistles and gospels from the Book of Common Prayer which was published in 1551 by the reformer Robert Crowley under the title *Kynniver llith a ban*. In his haste, Salesbury made some use of the English Great Bible but most of the translation (as in his later translations of the Scriptures) was based on what he believed to be the best texts of the original.[30] In his Latin dedication Salesbury urged the four Welsh bishops and the Bishop of Hereford (whose diocese contained a substantial number of Welsh-speakers) to approve *Kynniver llith a ban* for public use. The number of copies printed is not known but sufficient survived Mary's reign for the Bishop of St Asaph to require its use in 1561.[31]

Following the accession of Elizabeth, Salesbury's efforts were assisted by Richard Davies (?1501–81), appointed Bishop of St Asaph in 1560 and Bishop of St David's the following year. Influential support ensured the passage of a private Act of Parliament in 1563 which required the four Welsh bishops and

27 Gruffydd 1969 provides the fullest discussion of this important work.
28 Hughes 1967, p. 3. 29 Hughes 1967, p. 12. 30 Thomas 1976 is the definitive study.
31 Williams 1967, p. 196.

the Bishop of Hereford to ensure, on pain of a substantial fine, that the whole of the Bible was translated into Welsh by 1 March 1567.[32] Until this translation appeared, the clergy were to read the epistle and gospel in Welsh at communion (presumably using *Kynniver llith a ban*), and the Lord's Prayer, Articles of Christian Faith, Ten Commandments, and Litany weekly.[33] Although Welsh was not, unlike Irish, associated with any military threat to the state, as in Ireland there was some opposition to providing the Scriptures in the vernacular, probably on the grounds that linguistic uniformity was desirable. Thus a clause was added to the 1563 Act stipulating that an English Bible and Book of Common Prayer should be placed in every Welsh Church so that the Welsh could learn English by comparing texts in the two languages. As late as 1595 Maurice Kyffin could denounce a 'Welsh clergyman' who had maintained that it was 'not fitting to have any kind of Welsh books printed, he would rather have the people learn English and lose their Welsh . . . the Welsh Bible would do no good but a great deal of harm.'[34]

A Welsh translation of the Book of Common Prayer appeared in May 1567 and was followed by the Welsh New Testament in October. The former was (almost?) wholly Salesbury's work, as was most of the latter apart from five epistles (translated by Richard Davies) and the Book of Revelation (translated by Thomas Huet, precentor of St David's). Unfortunately Salesbury's excellence as a prose writer was obscured by his readiness to give full rein to his linguistic and orthographic theories, so that his translations were severely criticized both by his contemporaries and by later scholars.[35] For reasons which remain obscure, Salesbury and Davies failed to proceed to translate the Old Testament: a plausible (but probably apocryphal) explanation given by Sir John Wynn was that the partnership broke down because 'a variance . . . happened between [them] for the general sense and etymology of one word'.[36]

The task of providing a Welsh translation of the complete Bible passed to William Morgan (1545–1604) who, like Salesbury before him, based his translation on the best texts available rather than translating from the English. By the summer of 1587 his translation of the Old Testament and revision of the earlier translation of the Psalms and New Testament was sufficiently advanced for him to travel to London to see the Bible through the press, a process which took a year. On 22 September 1588 the Privy Council ordered that by Christmas every parish should acquire a copy of the Bible and two copies of the (separately

32 Gruffydd, 1956.

33 In 1562 John Waley had paid the Stationers' Company for a licence to print 'the latenye in Welshe'. No copy of the work has survived, but this was probably the Welsh service book purchased by Swansea churchwardens for eight pence in 1563 (Walker 1970, p. 397).

34 Hughes 1967, p. 94.

35 Williams 1997, pp. 215–16.

36 Wynn 1990, p. 62.

published) Psalms. Since there were some eight to nine hundred Welsh parishes, about a thousand copies of the Bible and two thousand of the Psalms may have been printed.[37] Despite the Privy Council decree, many parishes were slow to acquire Bibles: it was not until 26 November 1592, for example, that Bodfari bought a copy.[38] Some parishes may have acquired their Bibles as gifts. Siôn Tudur addressed a robustly Protestant poem to William Morgan requesting a copy for St Asaph Church,[39] and Siôn Phylip (d. 1620) composed a poem in the mid-1590s asking Richard Vaughan, Bishop of Bangor, for three books for Llandudwen Church: a Welsh Bible, a Welsh Book of Common Prayer, and Foxe's *Acts and monuments*.[40]

Although Morgan set about revising his translation, it was not until 1620 that the revision associated with Bishop Richard Parry (but largely the work of Dr John Davies who had earlier assisted Morgan in his 1599 revision of the Prayer Book) appeared. Other key texts also appeared in Welsh, notably Edward James's translation of the Book of Homilies (1606), and Edmwnd Prys's metrical version of the Psalms (1621), the latter being the first Welsh printed book to contain music. These works – above all the translation of the Bible – ensured that in Wales, unlike Ireland, a standard literary language was always available in print and could, indeed, be heard by the illiterate at Church every Sunday.

Catholic exiles were equally aware of the power of the printed word. Owen Lewis (1533–95) appealed in vain to Cardinal Sirleto in the late 1570s for money to print Welsh books to be 'in Angliam dextre mitti, et ibi secreta ratione spargi inter Britannos'.[41] Welsh Catholic books were printed in several places on the Continent – Milan (1567 onwards), Paris (possibly before 1600, certainly by 1609), St Omer (1618), Loreto (a broadside in 1635) – but no single centre of production emerged comparable to the press of the Irish friars at Louvain. As Owen Lewis had hoped, clandestine channels of importation were developed, some of which appear to have been extremely circuitous: Rowland Owen of Anglesey alleged that he had seen near Berwick-upon-Tweed 'a Welsh booke . . . a popish booke printed beyond sea'.[42] Within Wales, books were distributed by missionary priests and well-wishers. The system proved effective enough for sufficient copies of *Athravaeth Gristnogavl* (Milan, 1568) to have reached Wales to prompt publication of an English-language counterblast in 1571.[43] An even greater source of anxiety to the authorities were the clandestine presses in Wales itself: the one in a cave at Rhiwledin (1586–7) which printed

37 Williams 1976, p. 355. 38 Roberts 1980, II, p. 354. 39 Roberts 1980, I, p. 376.
40 Gruffydd 1984. 41 Gruffydd 1952, p. 43.
42 National Library of Wales, MS, 4554A, quoted in Gruffydd 1952, p. 42.
43 Bowen 1952, p. 388.

the first part of *Y drych Cristianogawl* (and was the first press on Welsh soil) is the best attested.[44] Catholic publications were liable to seizure throughout this period: amongst the materials seized and destroyed in 1678–9 when the Jesuit College of St Francis Xavier at Y Cwm (on the Herefordshire/Monmouthshire border) was ransacked were 'some Welsh Popish books lately printed'.[45]

Recusant works were clearly not commercial ventures, but it is legitimate to question to what extent many of the Welsh books legally published during the sixteenth and early seventeenth centuries were intended to be bought and sold in the normal course of trade. The erratic entry of Welsh books in the Stationers' register suggests that many titles were believed to be too unprofitable to require protection from piracy.[46] Certain religious texts were required to be purchased by Welsh parishes, but whether additional copies of such expensive works were produced for sale to laymen is debatable. Although a carol by the poet-parson Thomas Jones of Llandeilo Bertholau urged the Welsh to buy Morgan's Bible, it has been suggested that this probably expressed a pious aspiration rather than a practical course of action.[47] The idea of compulsory purchase by a captive market remained sufficiently strong for Dr John Davies to tell Owen Wynn of Gwydir in 1629 that the London printer, John Beale, ought not to be led to believe that every parish in Wales would be compelled to buy a copy of the *Dictionarium duplex*.[48] To what extent cheaper books were commercial ventures is also unclear. Dr John Davies had five hundred copies printed of a separate issue of the catechism included in the 1621 Book of Common Prayer for his parishioners, and had disposed of all but a dozen or so by the end of 1627.[49] Whether these were given or sold to his parishioners, and how many were presented to influential well-wishers is not known.

A commercial trade in Welsh books required a certain level of literacy in Welsh. The increasing use of writing for legal and administrative purposes but also for recording Welsh and Latin literary texts during the fourteenth and fifteenth centuries brought about, it has been claimed, 'a marked intensification of the process of creating a literate mentality'.[50] By the early seventeenth century, it is claimed, full literacy (the ability to read and write) was 'widespread among most merchants and burgesses, yeomen and substantial farmers'.[51] A recent study suggests that few of the literate 15 to 20 per cent of the population of Wales in the 1640s were literate in Welsh only.[52] The contemporary literary evidence is contradictory. Sir John Prise claimed in 1546 that 'many of

44 Gruffydd 1972.
45 Bowen 1962, p. 116. The 'Popish book' was almost certainly *Allwydd . . . Paradwys* (1670).
46 Rees 1970, p. 326. 47 Williams 1987, p. 322. 48 *Calendar* 1926, p. 510.
49 *Calendar* 1926, no. 1530. 50 Smith 1998, p. 204. 51 Williams 1987, 436.
52 Griffith 1989, p. 109.

the Welsh could read Welsh but could not read a word of English or Latin'.[53] William Salesbury maintained that a 'thousand Welshmen' would benefit from the publication of *Oll synnwyr pen*,[54] but this may reflect the print order for the book rather than his perception of the number of Welsh readers. On the other hand, the Puritan Oliver Thomas (?1598–1652) complained almost a century later that few, apart from clergymen, could read Welsh and that even some of them found it difficult.[55] A little documentary evidence survives: in 1600 the poet Huw Pennant (*fl.* 1565–1619) wrote the will of Owain Gruffydd of Penmorfa 'in the welche tongve for that as hee saied hee could not write the same in Englishe'.[56] Huw Pennant's full literacy in Welsh only is understandable since the bardic 'schools' were the only agency providing formal instruction in Welsh.

Since literacy in Welsh offered few (if any) practical benefits, its acquisition had to be based on religious considerations. Faith, as Oliver Thomas maintained in 1631, came from hearing sermons, but it was also necessary to search Scripture.[57] By reiterating over many decades the spiritual benefits to be derived from reading, a devout élite gradually convinced a growing number of monoglot Welsh people of the necessity of literacy. Their acquisition of reading skills was powerfully promoted by the popular religious verses composed mainly between 1615 and 1635 by Rhys Prichard (?1579–1644/5), vicar of Llandovery. Initially intended for oral delivery (Prichard claimed that they would be easily learnt by any one who had heard them three times),[58] the first selection of the verses was posthumously printed in 1658 and proved enormously popular, no fewer than fourteen editions appearing between 1658 and 1730.[59] Best known under the title first adopted in 1681, *Canwyll y Cymru* (*The Welshmen's candle*), the work marked a significant step in the transition from an oral to a print culture in Wales: the introduction to the 1659 edition, *Rhan o waith Mr. Rees Prichard*, urged purchasers to 'Read . . . respectfully and fearfully (Since these things have been printed to be read, not sung).' The status of print is underlined by the extensive editorial changes made to the printed text to bring it more into line with the norms of literary Welsh.[60]

Reading Welsh was a skill which had to be acquired informally. In his introduction to *Llwybr hyffordd* (1630), a translation of Arthur Dent's *The plaine man's path-way*, Robert Llwyd told the illiterate paterfamilias to 'Seek learning

53 Hughes 1967, p. 3. 54 Hughes 1967, p. 9. 55 Morgan 1981, p. [102].
56 Fisher 1919, p. 189. 57 Morgan 1981, p. [79]. 58 Richards 1994, p. 27.
59 Prichard's work is an excellent example of the way in which Welsh books were entered in the Stationers' registers only when they had proved their sales appeal: it was not registered until the fourth edition of 1672 (Rees 1970, pp. 328–9).
60 Lloyd 1996.

as soon as you can, or ensure that some one from your house learns to read, and let the others learn from him.'[61] To facilitate the process, Welsh books frequently began with an ABC and instructions on reading.[62] The introductory epistle to *Catechism Mr Perkins* (1672) suggested that children or (significantly) others learning to read should be given the first sheet only in order to prevent them from destroying the whole book.[63]

Producing a printed book necessarily involved considerable outlay before there could be any hope of return. Since, as Dr John Davies pointed out in 1623, 'the printers conceive so smalle hope of gaine by our Welshe bookes',[64] the London book trade was reluctant to venture upon them. Half a century later, according to Stephen Hughes, London booksellers maintained that as it might take fifteen years or more to dispose of an edition of the Bible in Welsh they were better off putting out their money in loans.[65]

Wealthy authors could finance the production of their own work but the great majority had to seek support from patrons. Sir William Herbert, first Earl of Pembroke, may have aided production of the first Welsh printed books,[66] and Sir Henry Sidney, Lord President of the Council of Wales from 1560 to his death in 1586, was an enthusiastic antiquarian who encouraged David Powel to prepare *The historie of Cambria* (1584) for the press.

Within Wales itself, aristocratic patrons were few. Sir Edward Stradling paid for the printing of 1250 copies of Siôn Dafydd Rhys's grammar, his generous patronage possibly enabling the work to make more extensive use of Hebrew type than any book previously printed in England.[67] Even so, Stradling's will, bequeathing fifty copies 'ready bound' to the author and instructing his cousin, Sir John Stradling, to give copies to 'such gentlemen and others as he shall think fit, for the advancement of the British tongue',[68] clearly demonstrates that publishing the grammar was intended to be a service to scholarship rather than a commercial venture.

Wealthy Welsh merchants were an important source of patronage, an early example being Humfrey Toy who financed the 1567 Welsh New Testament. Two London merchants heavily influenced by Puritanism, Thomas Myddelton (1550–1631) and Rowland Heylyn (?1562–1631), financed in 1630 the production (at a cost of £1,000) of possibly 1,500 copies of the first cheap (five shilling)

61 Hughes 1967, p. 129.
62 The importance of such material in creating a Welsh reading public in the second half of the seventeenth century is stressed by G. J. Williams in Edwards 1936, p. xxiv.
63 Williams 1969, p. 175.
64 Quoted in Burdett-Jones 1998, p. 76.
65 R. Prichard, *Gwaith Mr Rees Prichard* (London, 1672), sig. a4^{v}.
66 Gruffydd 1972, p. 5. 67 Parry 1997, p. 172. 68 G. J. Williams 1948, pp. 195–6.

Welsh Bible and also of a number of devotional works (mainly translations) such as *Llwybr hyfforddd* (1630); *Yr ymarfer o dduwioldeb* (1630); *Llyfr y resolusion* (1632); and the two versions of *Car-wr y Cymru* (1630 and 1631).

All the Welsh-language books published during this period, apart from those recusant works printed abroad or on clandestine presses, and one Welsh title printed in Dublin in 1653,[69] were printed in London or, from 1595 onwards, Oxford. Despite the considerable number of Welsh printers in London – at least 157 first-generation immigrants were apprenticed to members of the Stationers' Company before 1700 – few appear to have been significantly involved in producing Welsh-language material.[70] An ambitious scheme by a Welsh stationer, Thomas Salisbury (?1564–?1623), to print a number of humanist and Puritan works (the latter with financial assistance from Thomas Myddelton) was frustrated by Salisbury's financial problems following the plague of 1603.[71] Since Welsh books were usually printed by men wholly ignorant of the language, their authors or translators often had to spend lengthy periods of time in London in order to see them through the press.[72] Despite their care, the inevitable errors gave rise to many complaints.[73] In 1595 Maurice Kyffin maintained that 'It would have been less trouble for the workers to have printed ten times as much in a language other than Welsh since they did not know what they were about',[74] and almost a century later Thomas Jones the almanacer told his readers 'I am very sorry that some parts of this book, and my almanac for the year, 1688, have been printed so poorly; I paid as much for the worst parts as for the best parts: and indeed it is not my fault, but that of conscienceless printers.'[75] On the whole, Welsh books printed in Oxford were rather less inaccurate than those printed in London.[76]

Following the dislocation of the Civil War and Commonwealth period, Welsh-language publishing appeared to be in serious decline, only ten Welsh titles appearing between 1660 and 1669. From 1670 onwards the publishing scene was transformed by two ejected ministers, Charles Edwards (1628–?1691) and Stephen Hughes (1622–88). From 1674 to the mid-1680s their work was financed by the Welsh Trust, a London-based body supported by both moderate Anglicans and Non-conformists, largely because they feared that the ignorant

69 Davies 1938. 70 Jones 1997.

71 Gruffydd 1991, pp. 11–12. One of the manuscripts lost was that of Morgan's revised translation of the New Testament.

72 The desire of Welsh authors to take full advantage of their time in London explains why so many Welsh books from Salesbury's pioneering efforts onwards tended to appear in groups.

73 The orthographical experiments of certain Welsh humanists (noted in Crawford and Jones 1981 and Slagle 1983) may have further confused compositors.

74 Kyffin 1908, p. [xx]. 75 T. Jones, *Y Gymraeg yn ei disgleirdeb* (London, 1688), sig. X8^r.

76 Rees 1970, p. 330.

Welsh might fall easy prey to Catholicism – a fear which was powerfully reinforced by the appearance of *Allwydd . . . Paradwys* in 1670. The persuasive powers of Thomas Gouge (?1605–81) ensured that the Trust enjoyed sufficient resources to support large-scale publishing ventures. According to its report for 1675, 2,500 copies of the third edition of *Yr Ymarfer o Dduwioldeb* were 'now printing, and almost finished',[77] and almost £2,000 was forthcoming to produce 8,000 copies of the 1678 Welsh Bible.[78] A thousand copies of this edition, the largest so far, were given to those poor people who could read and make good use of it. The free distribution of religious works was an important element of the Trust's activity, a report (probably for 1678) noting those towns and parishes where books (some 5,000 volumes in all) had been given to 'poor people that could read Welsh'.[79]

As in the eighteenth and for much of the nineteenth centuries, Nonconformist clergy distributed godly books to their congregations. A list prepared by the Puritan preacher Hugh Owen (1639–1700) noted sixteen purchasers of *Y ffydd ddi-ffuant* (1671) and four of *Dadseiniad meibion y daran* (1671), and Owen was later to notify the Welsh Trust of suitable recipients of free Bibles.[80] The growing number of Welsh titles published, some in large editions, also stimulated the development of a commercial trade in Welsh books. The 1692 inventory of Dawkin Gove of Carmarthen lists over £30 worth of books (almost a third of the total value of his goods), many of which were in Welsh,[81] but Gove was an exceptionally prosperous trader. The Welsh Trust had maintained in 1675 that mercers were 'the only traders in books' in the 'chief' towns of north and south Wales,[82] but the first specialist traders in books may have emerged rather earlier. The Welsh word 'llyfrwr', defined in the *Dictionarium duplex* (1632) as 'writer of books' or 'librarian', was regularly used for 'bookseller' on the title pages of books from 1671 onwards, the earliest examples referring to booksellers in Wrexham and Llanfyllin.

The Welsh Trust was dissolved in 1684, a few years after the death of Gouge, but Stephen Hughes and his associates attempted to continue publishing Welsh books. In his introductory epistle to the first Welsh translation of *The pilgrim's progress* (1688) Hughes claimed that lack of money was now a problem.[83] More positively, he urged those who wished to learn to read Welsh to buy the primer and almanac published by Thomas Jones (1648–1713), the key figure in developing a commercial trade in popular Welsh books. By the mid-1670s Jones, who had settled in London about a decade earlier, had abandoned tailoring in

77 Jones 1937, p. 73. 78 Jenkins 1978, p. 59. 79 Jones 1937, pp. 79–80.
80 Jones 1998, pp. 117–19. 81 Rees 1988, pp. xvi–xvii. 82 Jones 1937, p. 72.
83 Williams 1969, p. 201.

favour of bookselling and, from 1676, publishing. At the beginning of 1679 Jones was granted by Letters Patent the sole right to publish a Welsh almanac. The readiness of the Stationers' Company to confirm the grant testifies to its lack of interest in the Welsh-language market. Jones then set about developing a network of distributors for his Welsh almanacs and for other popular publications, including the first cheap Welsh dictionary in 1688 and the first popular ballads which were advertised in his almanac for 1699.[84] Initially Jones relied upon wholesalers in the border towns and larger centres in Wales but also visited important Welsh fairs (such as those at Cardiff and Brecon) himself. Following his move to Shrewsbury in 1695–6 he used three main agents: Gabriel Rogers of Shrewsbury covered mid-Wales, Humphrey Page of Chester north Wales, and Samuel Rogers of Abergavenny the south. At the same time Jones extended his distribution network to smaller settlements.[85]

The upper ranks of society do not appear to have acquired scholarly English and Latin books through the Welsh book trade. Gentry letters and other sources suggest that throughout this period these were primarily acquired by sojourners in London or Oxford on behalf of friends and relations in Wales. In the mid-sixteenth century William Salesbury described how he had searched in 'Poules Churchyearde' for an English book on the spheres for his cousin, John Edwards of Chirk.[86] William Brynkir wrote from Oxford (probably in 1600) to inform his uncle, Sir William Maurice of Clenennau, that he would send him any book on astronomy or any other subject he thought would 'delight' him.[87] Following his return to Wales in 1634, Owen Wynne of Gwydir dealt with London booksellers and with 'Mr Jutes the stationer' of Chester.[88] At the beginning of 1688 Lord Herbert instructed his agent, Humphrey Owen, to hunt for his grandfather's *De religione Gentilium* in Duck Lane, 'the likeliest place for such things'.[89] These informal links also ensured that news publications rapidly reached leading families. Henry Wynn, then at the Inner Temple, sent his father, John Wynn of Gwydir, a copy of *Mercurius Gallobelgicus* on 1 May 1623.[90] The Wynn family also received copies of manuscript newsletters from London from the mid-1620s onwards.[91]

Because of the difficulty of financing the publication of Welsh books and, in many instances, a preference for the written word, the scribal tradition

84 The first Welsh ballad to appear was the enigmatic broadside *Byd y bigail* by Richard Hughes, probably published about 1620 (Lloyd 1998, pp. 84–6). This does not appear to have been a commercial venture (it was not entered in the Stationers' register) and may well have been published to mark Hughes's death in 1619.

85 Jenkins 1980, p. 94. 86 Bennett, 1969, p. 21. 87 Jones Pierce 1947, no. 423.

88 Morris 1997, p. 4. 89 Smith 1963, p. 334. 90 *Calendar* 1926, no. 1093.

91 *Calendar* 1926, no. 1392.

persisted in Wales well into the nineteenth century.[92] The historical and literary manuscripts in Welsh and Latin dispersed by the dissolution of the monasteries were collected by Welsh scholars, notably Sir John Prise, a collector ranked by Ker with Bale, Leland, and Robert Talbot.[93] During the sixteenth century poets, circles of humanist scholars (often in contact with scholars in England or on the Continent), and antiquarians collected, exchanged, and copied medieval manuscripts. In the crucial years of the mid-seventeenth century when the humanist impulse was spent and the bardic order was dying out, the greatest of all Welsh collectors, Robert Vaughan (*c.* 1592–1667)[94] assembled at Hengwrt a collection of medieval and humanist manuscripts which, over three and a half centuries later, was to form the most important of the foundation collections of the National Library of Wales.

A considerable number of original works circulated in manuscript only. Sometimes – like the many unpublished translations of Anglican devotional texts – this was because they had failed to gain sufficient patronage to be printed. Recusants had to rely largely on manuscript copies, but many other works such as George Owen's antiquarian studies were apparently not intended for publication. Like Cotton in England, scholars such as George Owen and Robert Vaughan exemplified 'the continuity of an intellectual culture grounded in the handwritten word'.[95]

Many of the gentry and clergy copied manuscripts. The most notable gentleman-scribe, John Jones of Gellilyfdy (*c.*1585–1657/8), over a hundred of whose manuscripts survive, followed a family tradition extending back over at least three generations, and pursued his interest with unchecked zeal during lengthy periods of imprisonment for debt.[96] Paid professional scribes were active in both south and north Wales. In the south, the recusants Llywelyn Siôn (1540–?1615)[97] and William Dafydd Llywelyn of Llangynidr[98] were employed by local gentlemen to copy medieval prose texts and contemporary Catholic works. In north Wales, both Dr John Davies[99] and Robert Vaughan's friend, the antiquary William Maurice of Cefn-y-Braich (*d.* 1680), are known to have employed scribes.

Printed books were also transcribed. Manuscript copies survive of lost print exemplars (such as the first edition of Robert Holland's dialogue on

92 An excellent brief outline is provided by Thomas 1997.

93 Ker 1955, p. 2. 94 Jones 1949. 95 Love 1987, p. 133.

96 Lloyd 1969 provides an outline in English of Jones's career.

97 G. J. Williams 1948, pp. 157–60. Llywelyn Siôn transcribed, *inter alia*, all three parts of the *Drych Cristianogawl.*

98 Llywelyn has been described as the 'regular copyist' of the recusant author Robert Gwyn (Bowen 1997, p. 228).

99 *Calendar* 1926, no. 1202.

witchcraft, *Ymddiddan Tudur a Gronw*, published *c.* 1595) or fill gaps in now incomplete printed texts, such as the second edition of *Oll synnwyr pen.*[100] That these works were copied so soon after their publication suggests that Welsh printed books were considered to be expensive or hard to obtain.

Despite the poverty, underdevelopment, and relative isolation of Wales, Welsh was the only Celtic language to respond positively to the challenge of print, roughly two hundred Welsh-language titles appearing during the first century and a half of Welsh-language printing. Although speakers of Irish were far more numerous, only sixteen or so Irish titles were published between 1571 and 1700, and in Brittany about twenty Breton titles had appeared by 1700.[101] The main difference between Wales and the other Celtic-speaking areas was that Welsh became the language of public worship. As well as bringing about the triumph of Protestantism this ensured that in Wales, unlike Ireland, a standard literary language was generally available[102] and could provide the basis for a prolonged Bible-based campaign to inculcate Welsh-language literacy. As literacy in Welsh became more widespread, monoglot Welsh-speakers made ever-increasing use of the printed word, a development which culminated in the flourishing vernacular press of the mid-nineteenth century.

Bibliographical note

A detailed account of Welsh-language and Welsh printed books and manuscripts during this period is provided by chapters 3 to 8 of P. H. Jones and E. Rees (eds.), *A nation and its books: a history of the book in Wales* (Aberystwyth 1998). This is usefully supplemented by the chapters on manuscripts (by G. C. G. Thomas) and printed books (by C. Parry) in R. Geraint Gruffydd (ed.), *A guide to Welsh literature c. 1530–1700*, Volume III (Cardiff, 1997). For printed books see E. Rees, 'Welsh publishing before 1717', in D. E. Rhodes (ed.), *Essays in honour of Victor Scholderer* (Mainz, 1970), pp. 323–36, and her pioneering overview, *The Welsh book-trade before 1820* (Aberystwyth, 1988). For developments from 1660 onwards G. H. Jenkins, *Literature, religion and society in Wales, 1660–1730* (Cardiff, 1978) is invaluable.

Language in early modern Wales is authoritatively covered in G. H. Jenkins (ed.), *The Welsh language before the Industrial Revolution* (Cardiff, 1997), and religion in G. Williams, *Wales and the Reformation* (Cardiff, 1999). G. Bowen, *Welsh recusant writings* (Cardiff, 1999), provides a brief overview.

100 Mathias 1952. 101 Gruffydd 1969, p. 106.
102 A contrast emphasized in Lloyd 1948, pp. 263–4.

36
British books abroad: the Continent

P. G. HOFTIJZER

From an international perspective, the slow and problematic development of the book trade in the British Isles during the sixteenth and seventeenth centuries had serious consequences. First of all, it proved very difficult to sell books printed in Britain on the European Continent. One cause was that the quality of British printing up to the end of the seventeenth century remained low. Workmanship in typesetting, proof correction, and press work was often sloppy and the printing types used were either imported fonts or cast from self-made matrices of poor design. As those in the trade knew: in 1641 the Oxford printer Leonard Lichfield apologized to the young couple Mary Stuart and the future William II of Orange in the dedication to his [προτελεια] *Anglo-Batava* (1641): 'Our Presse no *Leiden* Characters affords, / Looke then not on our Letters, but our Words.'[1]

The English language constituted another obstacle for book exports. Whereas other modern languages – French, Italian, German, Dutch – were spoken well beyond their respective language barriers, English was hardly known on mainland Europe, with the exception of mercantile ports with direct trade relations with Britain. In 1665 Denis de Sallo, editor of the *Journal des sçavants*, informed his readers that he had not included resumés from the *Philosophical transactions of the Royal Society*, because it had been impossible to find a Parisian contributor capable of undertaking their translation.[2]

The possibility of exporting British printed books in Latin was, if anything, worse. Due to the relatively high prices of books produced in Britain the export of scholarly and scientific books to the Continent was minimal. This is evident from the trade lists of Continental publishers and the catalogues of the Frankfurt book fairs. The catalogue published in 1643 by the widow of the Parisian bookseller Guillaume Pelé, for example, has among its total of 884

1 [προτελεια] *Anglo-Batava pari plusquam virgineo Guilielmo Arausii & Mariae Brittaniarum* (Oxford, 1641), p. [46].
2 *Journal des sçavants*, 30 March 1665; Ascoli 1930, II, p. 25.

titles in Latin only twenty-six British works, less than 3 per cent, compared to ninety-nine titles from France (11 per cent), 86 from the Southern Netherlands (10 per cent), 429 from the Dutch Republic (48.5 per cent), 201 from the German Empire (23 per cent), and forty-three from Italy (5 per cent).[3]

The catalogues of newly printed books published annually for the Frankfurt book fairs present an even gloomier picture. An analysis of these lists between 1564 and 1695 shows that only during the early seventeenth century did a few British publishers, almost exclusively from London, offer their books on a regular basis to Continental colleagues at the Frankfurt fairs. After 1625 numbers are down to at best only a few titles per year; for long periods no books whatsoever were on offer.[4] This may explain why William Fitzer, who served his apprenticeship in London, decided to set up his business in Germany. From there he could better reach a Continental clientele for his publications, the most notable of which was William Harvey's *Exercitatio anatomica de motu cordis* (Frankfurt, 1628).[5]

The high prices of British books had a further damaging effect. The growing interest on the Continent in British authors, particularly theological and scientific writers, encouraged foreign printers to reap the benefits of publication themselves, either by pirating these texts or having them translated into other languages. In spite of its negative connotations, book piracy, a common phenomenon in the European book trade, served as a useful corrective of poor distribution and excessive prices. British publishers, however, suffered disproportionately from this practice. Time and again their editions were undercut by cheap foreign reprints. The example of Sir Francis Bacon, one of the most esteemed and widely read English authors on the Continent, is typical. Of the eight seventeenth-century editions of Bacon's *De augmentis scientiarum*, only the first was published in London (1623); the others were printed at Paris (1624), Strasburg (1635, 1654), Leiden (1645, 1652), and Amsterdam (1662, 1694). The original London edition of Bacon's *Novum organum* (1620) was followed by four Dutch reprints, two from Leiden (1645, 1650) and two from Amsterdam (1660, 1694). Understandably, no seventeenth-century British publisher dared to venture an edition of Bacon's *Opera omnia* for fear of it being copied abroad. When it finally appeared, in 1730, four Continental editions had already been published at Frankfurt (1665), Amsterdam (1685, 1696), and Copenhagen (1694).[6]

3 Martin 1984, I, p. 302; cf. Ascoli 1930, II, pp. 19–20. Dutch catalogues from the seventeenth century show similar or even smaller percentages, cf. e.g. van Selm 1987, pp. 246–50.

4 This analysis is based on Schwetschke 1850; see also Spirgatis 1902.

5 Weil 1944. 6 Gibson 1950.

To what extent Continental translations of English books into Latin or other languages harmed the interests of British publishers is more difficult to ascertain. Sometimes it was the author rather than his publisher who complained. Robert Boyle feared that European readers might take the Latin translations of his works that were being produced on the Continent for the original editions. 'I may be suspected', he wrote to Henry Oldenburg, secretary of the Royal Society, in 1667, 'to have taken divers things from others, which indeed [they] borrowed of me.'[7] Another problem of these unauthorized Latin translations was that the text was often misinterpreted or changed.

The majority of translations of English works, however, consist of works turned into French, Dutch, German and other languages. With the exception of seventeenth-century books translated from English into Dutch, little bibliographical research has yet been done in this field. A checklist of well over 600 titles shows that by far the largest proportion of Dutch translations, nearly 80 per cent, consists of English treatises, sermons, and the like, mostly of a Puritan and pietistical character.[8] Among the most popular authors was the Puritan divine William Perkins. No less than forty-eight of his works were translated into Dutch.[9] English literary works in Dutch translation are poorly represented. Apart from a few plays, among which Shakespeare's *The taming of the shrew*, and selections and adaptations of works such as Sir Philip Sidney's *Arcadia*, there is no indication that Dutch literary taste was much affected by contemporary English literature.[10] The situation in other countries does not appear to have been different.[11]

A second important consequence of the disadvantageous condition of the British trade was that books, which for religious, political or economic reasons could not be printed in Britain itself, were produced for the British market on the Continent, sometimes by English emigré printers, but often also by indigenous publishers. At first, the motives for this activity had been predominantly commercial; as English printers were not themselves able to satisfy national demand, foreign entrepreneurs stepped in. With the success of the Reformation, religious and political considerations became increasingly important. The printing of Tyndale's English translation of the New Testament

7 Oldenburg 1965–86, IV, p. 94, letter no. 741 (29 December 1667). For bibliographical information on Continental reprints of Boyle's works, see Fulton 1961.

8 Schoneveld 1983; cf. van der Haar 1980.

9 Schoneveld 1983, nos. 437–83; op 't Hof 1987, pp. 280–388.

10 Schenkeveld-van der Dussen 1991, pp. 144–6.

11 For France, see Ascoli 1930; for Germany, Waterhouse 1914 and Oppel 1971. During the first half of the seventeenth century, however, the performances of English 'strolling players' in Central and Eastern Europe appear to have contributed significantly to the appreciation of English drama; cf. Limon 1985.

at Worms (Germany) in 1526 marks the beginning of a long tradition of Protestant as well as Catholic book production on the European mainland intended for the British market.

The location and denomination of the Continental printing presses producing English religious texts depended on the changing religious and political situations in Britain and on the Continent. In Antwerp, which had played such an important role in the production of English Protestant texts and Bibles during the 1520s and 1530s, hardly any books of this nature appeared after 1540 as a result of the harsh repression by the Habsburg government. The printing of English Catholic books in Antwerp for the British market, on the other hand, increased substantially,[12] as it did in other cities in the southern Netherlands and France. Occasionally one comes across English Catholic printers, such as John Fowler, who had gone into exile around 1561 and until his death in 1579 worked in Louvain, Antwerp, Rheims and finally Douai.[13]

Antwerp's position as a major centre for English Protestant printing was briefly taken over by Geneva during the reign of Mary Tudor, when this stronghold of calvinism offered hospitality to a group of English Puritans under the leadership of John Knox. In 1557 they produced a new English translation of the New Testament and Book of Psalms, inspired by contemporary French and Italian versions. In 1560 the printer Rowland Hall published a complete edition of the Old and New Testaments, the so-called 'Geneva Bible', which was to become the standard Bible edition for Puritans.[14]

By the end of the century the religious and political status quo which had come about in England as well as in France and the Low Countries led to an important change in the production of religious books by Continental presses for the British market. The printing of Catholic Church books, devotional literature, and recusant propaganda, now forcefully suppressed in Britain, became concentrated at Douai and St Omer thanks to the presence of two English Catholic colleges there. In continuation of the English translation of the New Testament after the Latin vulgate published in Rheims in 1582, an edition of the Old Testament appeared in Douai in 1609–10. It was printed by Laurence Kellam, who had previously worked in Louvain and Valenciennes and whose widow and sons would continue printing at Douai until 1661.[15] The press of the English Jesuit college at St Omer was active from 1608 until 1759, during which period nearly 300 works were produced.[16] However, whereas up to 80 per cent of English Catholic books printed in the period

12 Imhof, *et al.* 1994. 13 Schrickx 1976; Coppens 1993, pp. 18–20.
14 Bonnant 1999; Morison 1972; *CHB*, pp. 155–59. 15 *CHB*, pp. 161–3; Simoni 1990.
16 Walsh 1981.

1558–1640 were published abroad, this proportion declined to a mere 20 per cent between 1641 and 1700.[17]

A similar development is apparent in the printing of English Protestant books on the Continent during the seventeenth century. The persecution of Non-conformist Puritans by the Anglican Church resulted in new waves of British religious exiles. Most of them found refuge in the Dutch Republic. English separatist congregations were established first in Middelburg in the 1580s, later also in Leiden, Dordrecht, Delft, Rotterdam, and Amsterdam. All these Churches had easy access to printing facilities, through which they published theological treatises, devotional works, religious pamphlets, and Bibles, intended for local consumption as well as for export to Britain.

In Middelburg Richard Schilders (or Painter) was active. He was of southern-Netherlandish origin, but had lived in England for a long time. Besides his work as official printer to the States of Zealand, he published about ninety English titles up to his retirement in 1618.[18] In Leiden the so-called 'Pilgrim Press' was run by William Brewster between 1617 and 1619: one year later he would sail to the New World on the Mayflower.[19] Another Leiden printer of English Puritan works was Willem Christiaensz van der Boxe, a Dutchman who had married an English woman. In the 1630s and early 1640s he printed treatises by radical Puritans in English and Dutch, some of which he translated himself.[20] Little is known about the activity of James Moxon, who around 1640 worked first in Delft and later in Rotterdam.[21]

Amsterdam was the hotbed of radical English Protestant printing in the Netherlands. For about a century, English and Dutch printers and booksellers in Amsterdam were engaged in the production and distribution of large quantities of English religious and political tracts, pamphlets, liturgical works, and, in particular, Bibles.[22] The English separatist printshops in Amsterdam were small establishments. Giles Thorp, for instance, active in the early decades of the century, printed only ten identifiable publications.[23] More productive was the 'richt right' press of John Canne, minister of the Amsterdam Brownist Church. A considerable number of its forty or so publications were written by Canne himself, but he also tried his hand at editions of the Geneva Bible and the Authorized Version, to which he added his own explanatory notes.[24]

From the 1630s the printing of these 'Holland' Bibles in Amsterdam expanded rapidly, but it was Dutch, not English printers, who took the lead,

17 Allison and Rogers 1989–94; Clancy 1996. 18 Wilson 1912b.

19 Sprunger 1994, pp. 133–44. Two other English printers at Leiden, Thomas Basson and his son Govert, were mainly engaged in the academic book trade; cf. van Dorsten 1961 and 1985; Bögels 1992.

20 Sprunger 1994, pp. 144–55. 21 Moxon 1962, pp. xix–xx. 22 Sprunger 1994, ch. 4.

23 Sprunger 1994, pp. 85–93. 24 Sprunger 1994, pp. 98–105; Johnson 1951.

driven perhaps more by commercial considerations than religious zeal. The first local printer to engage in this activity was Jan Fredericksz Stam. In 1628 he had married the widow of Joris Veselaer, publisher of one of the earliest newspapers in the English language.[25] Stam produced a whole range of English Bibles in various formats, most of them with false imprints.[26] He was succeeded by his step-daughter Susanna Veselaer, better known as the widow Schippers. In the second half of the seventeenth century she became the major producer of English Bibles in the Dutch Republic. She co-operated for some time with a Jewish printer, Joseph Athias, with whom she set up a large printing establishment. Many thousands of English Bibles were printed here. Athias once boasted that he had supplied every cowhand and milkmaid in England with a Bible.[27]

The transportation and distribution of large amounts of Puritan books and Bibles in Britain was not an easy affair. The books had to be smuggled across the North Sea and sold through an extensive clandestine distribution network. The English government was very keen to put an end to this illicit trade, which threatened political and religious stability as well as the commercial interests of the English publishers. English ambassadors at the Hague were ordered to keep a watchful eye over the Puritan printshops and to put pressure on the States General and the local magistrates to bring them to a halt. Although this policy had some success, it was impossible to stop the flow of books from the Netherlands, the more so since the Dutch authorities, when it served their purposes, connived at the activities of the English fugitives.

Not all English printing establishments in the Dutch Republic in the seventeenth century, however, were run by Puritans. Around 1650 Samuel Browne, a royalist printer and bookseller, was active in the Hague. Browne, whose brother was chaplain to Mary Stuart, wife of Stadtholder William II, had come to the Netherlands in 1644 after having worked as a bookseller in London. In 1655 he moved to Heidelberg where he was appointed university printer,[28] while continuing his business in the Hague together with his son-in-law: he finally returned to England in 1662. Browne published well over a hundred books and other publications in the Hague, many of them in English dealing with events in England from a royalist perspective. He also printed a French gazette, the *Mercure anglois*, an important source of information for exiled royalists.[29]

As the Restoration made it possible for Browne to return home, so the Glorious Revolution of 1688–9 put an end to the activities of the Puritan

25 Dahl 1950; Sprunger 1994, p. 102. 26 Johnson 1954.
27 Van Eeghen 1966. 28 Weil 1951. 29 Keblusek 1997, ch. 8.

presses. As their last representatives two English widows in Amsterdam should be mentioned, Mercy Arnold and Abigael May. Both came from a Brownist background and had been married to booksellers engaged in the printing and selling of anti-Anglican and anti-Stuart publications. Mercy Arnold belonged to a group of radical Non-conformists, convinced that the end of time was drawing near. An English spy described her in 1686 as 'the retainer & printresse of all our factious pamphlets'. Yet, both women no longer worked for the most part for the English market. Many of their publications were Dutch pamphlets on the political situation in Britain or Dutch translations of popular English works, such as William Temple's *Observations upon the United Provinces* (1673), Edward Chamberlayne's *The present state of England* (1683), or the collected works of Sir Thomas Browne (1688). Abigael May also published several editions of William Sewel's successful Anglo-Dutch dictionary (first edition 1691).[30]

For a long time the shops of the exiled English printers and booksellers were the only places in the Netherlands, if not on the entire Continent, where English books could be obtained. A good impression of Mercy Arnold's assortment is provided by a stock catalogue issued by her around 1685, which contains nearly 1,400 English titles. Not surprisingly, the catalogue abounds in religious and theological works of a predominantly Puritan nature, but there are also philosophical, historical, literary, medical and scientific books, as well as travel accounts, plays and other light reading.[31] This growing interest in English affairs is also clear from other Dutch trade catalogues. Whereas a traditional wholesale bookseller like Daniel Elsevier in Amsterdam still had a small number of English books in his stock,[32] a new generation of book-trade entrepreneurs was stepping forward at the end of the seventeenth century. One of them was Pieter van der Slaart, a Rotterdam bookseller who in 1693 issued a trade catalogue of about a hundred titles, half of which are in English or of English origin. Van der Slaart's English contact may have been the London bookseller Richard Chiswell, whose publications are well represented in the list.[33] Other Dutch (and Continental) booksellers had business relations with Latin traders such as Samuel Smith, Thomas Bennet and Henry Clements. A valuable source for the history of Anglo-Continental book-trade relations are the surviving parts of their correspondence with colleagues abroad in the decades around 1700.[34]

30 Hoftijzer 1987, pp. 79–81. 31 Browning [*c.* 1685]; cf. Hoftijzer 1987, pp. 41–5.
32 Daniel Elsevier's 1674 trade catalogue contains some 20,000 titles, but has only one page with English books, listing nineteen titles.
33 Feather 1976. 34 Cf. Hodgson and Blagden 1956; also Hoftijzer 1991 and 1998.

Yet, the book trade was not the only road by which English books were brought to the mainland. Throughout the seventeenth century in every western-European country people could be found with a keen interest in British culture, religion, scholarship and science, who often knew the English language and who, through personal visits and contacts with English friends and colleagues, acquired the books they desired from Britain. Among the first Frenchmen with an outspoken admiration for the English 'new' science as advocated by Bacon and his followers in the Royal Society was Henri Justel (1620–93), a Huguenot who served as secretary to Louis XIV until his forced emigration to England in 1681. He corresponded with numerous English scholars and had a splendid library with many of their works, some of which he had ordered to be translated into Latin or French.[35] The most prominent Dutch 'anglophile' was Constantijn Huygens (1596–1687), secretary to the princes of Orange, poet, and scholar. Huygens was a regular visitor to Britain with a lively interest in English literature and science. His library contained scores of books printed in Britain – in Latin as well as in English – in all genres. Among his apparent literary favourites were Chaucer, Spenser, Shakespeare (he owned a copy of the first folio), Donne (translated by him into Dutch), Herbert, and Burton.[36]

Little is as yet known about the libraries of Englishmen living abroad, as fugitives, diplomats, merchants, or soldiers. On the basis of recent studies of the book collections of English Catholic exiles in the sixteenth-century southern Netherlands and Puritan ministers and Royalist refugees in the seventeenth-century Dutch Republic, it may be inferred that these libraries, which of course contained English as well as Continental works, functioned not only as instruments of scholarship and study, but equally as mental retreats for their owners and friends, who often had been forced to leave their country against their will.[37]

A significant role in the non-commercial traffic of books during the second half of the seventeenth century was played by the Royal Society, which through its secretary maintained an extensive European correspondence network and did much to keep foreign scholars informed about scientific progress in Britain, also by sending over issues of the *Philosophical transactions* and recent books by British scholars.[38] Being well aware of the growing importance for scientific communication of the numerous learned journals edited by Huguenot intellectuals in the Netherlands and elsewhere, the Royal Society actively tried to draw attention to new English books. In 1686 the Society's

35 Ternois 1933. 36 Colie 1956; Bachrach 1962; van Elslander and Schrikx 1952.
37 Coppens 1993; Bangs 1985; Keblusek 1995.
38 Selling 1990, ch. 4; Cavazza 1980; cf. Hall 1964.

secretary John Hoskyns sent a letter to Pierre Bayle, editor of the *Nouvelles de la Republique des Lettres* (Amsterdam, 1684–7), asking him to supply news about recently published Continental books in exchange for similar information from England. 'l'Angleterre n'est pas précisément sans savants', he wrote in impeccable French, 'et l'on fait imprimer ici fort souvent des choses dont peut-être vous feriez cas et dont la connaissance ne vous vient que fort tard, quelquefois même point du tout.'[39] Through their publication of extracts and reviews of British books these journals contributed vastly to the interest in English learning on the Continent.[40] As such they can rightly be regarded as precursors of the unprecedented anglomania that would develop in the course of the eighteenth century.

39 Quoted from Reesink 1931, p. 79. 40 Bots 1984; Almagor 1989.

37

British books abroad: the American colonies

HUGH AMORY

The historians of seventeenth-century book culture in the British colonies have traditionally focused on the advent of printing and on the private libraries of a few distinguished bookmen: the Winthrops, the Mathers, Elder Brewster, John Harvard, Isaac Norris and William Byrd, among others.[1]

This material may be fleshed out with inventories of books belonging to less distinguished owners, with the chance survivals of books with an early provenance, with auction catalogues and with anecdotal evidence, but essentially such history only begins after the books have crossed the Atlantic. The commerce that relates the English market for books with the colonies remains little explored.

Despite strong cultural, economic and demographic differences among the colonies, the book culture of the larger cities was surprisingly uniform.[2] A few private libraries, such as those of the Mathers, the Winthrops, or the Byrds, ran to more than a thousand volumes – large by any seventeenth-century standard. Most magistrates and ministers however, held no more than two or three hundred volumes, housed in a 'study' or room of its own. The New England Company that prompted the 'Great migration' of 1630–40 offered ministers £10 for books, if they would settle there, and it is clear from the libraries of Elder Brewster and John Harvard that they continued to purchase titles from Europe after their emigration. Libraries of these middling sizes belonged to persons who were in more-or-less regular official or personal communication with Europe; owners of smaller libraries contented themselves with the books that they, or their ancestors, had brought over in person. These smaller libraries were commonly described in inventories as 'a Bible and other books', the other books, when they are specified, amounting to between five and ten volumes, usually devotional and of English printing.[3]

1 Wright 1920; Korey 1976; Hayes 1997. For a fuller account of the book in America in this period see Amory and Hall 2000.

2 Wolf 1988; Morison 1956; Davis 1978.

3 Amory 1997.

The low incidence of American imprints in colonial inventories is noteworthy and probably reflects both their negligible value and the limited purposes for which they were printed. The early colonial press was official, and the bulk of the editions probably went to the ministers and magistrates who had authorized them. Liturgically, fifty copies of the Bay Psalm Book – two for every Church – and another fifty for government officialdom would have sufficed for the immediate needs of the Massachusetts Bay colony, yet 1,700 copies of the first edition (1640) and 2,000 copies of a revision (1651) were printed. The extraordinary size of these editions has suggested an extraordinary penetration of their texts at all levels of society, but if so, it proceeded at a glacial pace. A year after the first edition of the Eliot Indian Bible (1661–3) had been completed, only forty-two copies had been distributed in America, or roughly as many as the sponsors had sent to Europe; of a large second edition (2,000 copies, 1680–85), 'many hundreds' were lodged in Indian possession – which unquestionably left more hundreds behind.[4] Hundreds of copies of the early Massachusetts and Connecticut laws lingered on in the hands of officials, despite legislation mandating their distribution to every town and family.[5] Beginning with the second generation of settlers, in the 1670s, we have evidence of more vigorous distribution, particularly for books of piety, but they were typically given away. Cotton Mather and Samuel Sewall alone gave away many hundreds of sermons every year.[6]

European printing occupied the commercial sector of the market; colonial printing was subsidized, official and of small commercial value. The magistrates indeed sharply questioned a reprinting of some thirteen recent London pamphlets by the Cambridge Press in 1667–8, and this commercial experiment immediately ended, though it was clear enough that otherwise neither the magistrates nor John Eliot could provide enough material to keep the printers occupied.[7] The 'Indian press' thereafter confined itself to printing Indian, and the 'College press' to official publications, with occasional jobs on the side for Harvard students – book labels, commencement programmes, and almanacs – and for ministers. Before the establishment of printing in Boston, in 1675, the distribution of native printing was virtually monopolized by Hezekiah Usher and his son John, general merchants who incidentally dealt in books and stationery.

The Ushers were certainly selling British books before 1675, on exactly the same lines as English provincial booksellers. *The mystery of God incarnate* (1650),

4 Winship 1945, pp. 239, 355; leaves from this edition were frequently used as binder's waste.
5 *Ibid.*, pp. 110, 124; and on the 1673 Laws of Connecticut, see Bates 1900.
6 Selement 1984, ch. 4.
7 Winship 1945, pp. 282–8.

by Samuel Eaton, formerly a minister of New Haven, Connecticut appeared under four separate imprints: for Henry Cripps Junior and for Lodovic Lloyd, both in London; and with cancel title pages, to be sold by William Fugill, in Hull (Yorks), and 'to be sold by Hezekiah Usher at Boston in New England'.[8] Similarly, Michael Sparke and Anne Moore had printed a London edition of Niccolò Balbani's *Italian convert* (1635), which was re-issued with cancel title pages for English country booksellers in Salisbury, Dorchester, Coventry, Exeter and Northampton.

Eaton's provincial and colonial issues were motivated by local and sectarian interests: William Fugill was almost certainly a kinsman of Thomas Fugill, the first secretary of the New Haven colony, who had returned excommunicated and disgraced to Yorkshire in 1646. The title page of Usher's issue was apparently printed in England, and the sole surviving copy (at Harvard) was not bound in America: we may imagine him acting on behalf of some New Haven subscribers, as well as for himself. Henry Cripps Junior may also have had more than a commercial interest in the publication, for he was connected with a group of radical Protestant booksellers located in Pope's-Head Alley, London. Prominent among them were Benjamin Allen, who took refuge from Laud in Leiden, 1638–41, his wife, Hannah and his apprentice Livewell Chapman, who married Hannah after Allen's death in 1646. They reprinted the *Capital laws of Massachusetts* (1642), the laws of New Haven colony (1656), and numerous pieces by John Cotton, and they initially held the copyright to the authorized edition of the Cambridge *Platform of Church discipline* (1653).[9] John Allen, another apprentice and possibly a relation (*fl.* 1656–73), published works by New Englanders like John Cotton, John Davenport, John Norton, Increase Mather and John Eliot, as well as the *Declaration of faith and order* (1659) of the Congregational Churches of England. Cripps and Lloyd published John Norton's *Orthodox evangelist* (1654) and Cripp's apprentice, Peter Parker, took over his business after his death (and married his wife, Susan). Parker, and Matthew Simmons, who printed and published the first edition of *Paradise lost*, did most of the printing for the Allens and Chapman.

These sectarian connections, extending from 1641 to 1673, were certainly looser than the sponsorship that long supervised and sustained Quaker printing, but they must have been vital to long-distance commerce, where credit was hazardous. After the establishment of printing in Boston, in 1675, John Usher acquired new suppliers like Robert Boulter and Richard Chiswell, and John

8 Wing E123, E123A–C; on Fugill, see Chilton 1982, pp. 8–9. On Cripps, see Morgan 1975, p. 85.

9 E & R, I, pp. 333, 404; it is not clear why Hannah Allen later assigned the *Platform* to Peter Cole in 1653.

Dunton competed with them for the Boston trade.[10] Chiswell also catered to the Boston market by reprinting editions of the Bay Psalm Book and re-issuing Boston sheets of the 1672 Massachusetts laws under his own imprint. In this later phase, however, the relationship seems to have been strictly commercial. In the 1680s, Usher imported boxes and puncheons of assorted titles for private customers like the Reverend Thomas Shepard of Charlestown, Increase Mather in Boston and John Wise in Chebacco (now Essex, Mass.): Shepard's consignment included multiple copies of Psalm books that he no doubt planned to distribute among his parishioners. On his own account, Usher's orders included Lord Rochester's *Poems* (1680), that pornographic classic, *Venus in the cloyster* (1683), and *The London jilt* (1683), as well as multiple copies of 'Robert Burton's' chapbook histories and romances, titles that Benjamin Franklin later recalled reading as a child.[11] Clearly, the sectarian connection that sustained earlier trade had lapsed. By 4 November 1687, Benjamin Lynde, a future chief justice of Massachusetts, had acquired a copy of Dryden's apology for Catholicism, *The hind and the panther*, published in April of that year.[12]

The earliest evidence of the transition from religion to commerce is a copy of Edward Phillip's *New world of English words* (London: Printed by E. Tyler, for Nath. Brooke..., 1658), inscribed 'William Pearse his Booke. Cost 10s at Mr Vshers 1666'.[13] Evidently John Usher was offering the volume at the London retail price, bound (as advertised for later editions in the *Term catalogues*), which in turn implies that he had purchased it at a substantial discount – rather more, indeed, than London usually afforded English provincial booksellers. Nathaniel Brooke had reprinted the work in 1663, and it seems likely that Usher received unusually favourable terms for the remainder of the first edition. At the end of the volume is an extensive catalogue of Brooke's publications – eighty-nine titles in print, and twenty-six '*ready for printing*'. As such, the title was an ideal loss leader: Usher's copies came cheap, in order to attract orders from customers like Pearse for other titles in Brooke's catalogue.

By 1666, then John Usher had a shop where titles like Phillips's *New world of English words* were exposed for sale.[14] Governor Bellingham resorted to it around this date, as we learn from a bill in the Massachusetts archives for his purchases from 1665 to 1668. It consisted mainly of titles by the recently ejected minister from England, John Owen, whom the colony was considering for a Massachusetts pulpit, but also included a number of school books for

10 Ford 1917, pp. 88–152; Thompson 1975. 11 Thompson 1986.
12 Benjamin Lynde, Diaries, Massachusetts Historical Society, Boston.
13 I am grateful to Jerome Anderson for bringing this document in his collection to my attention.
14 For the beginnings of shops in Boston, see Bridenbaugh 1938, pp. 41–4.

the Bellingham children.[15] Other Boston shopkeepers beside the Ushers first appeared in Massachusetts Cambridge imprints around 1672: John Tappin, Edmund Ranger, Joseph Farnham, John Ratcliffe and John Griffin. Of these, only Ranger and Ratcliffe, both bookbinders, actually specialized in books and stationery, and Ratcliffe had been at work in Boston for ten years. The remainder were merchants, a class that was claiming a larger voice in public affairs at this time.[16] In the authoritative voice of John Norton (1659), echoed by John Higginson in 1663, New England had originally been 'a Plantation Religious, not a Plantation of Trade'; its declension from this ideal continued to galvanize both the ministry and the book trade.

These Bostonian developments were exceptional, however – forwarded by the largest urban concentration of seventeenth-century British America. Everywhere, including New England, merchants carried staple items like Bibles, Testaments, psalters and primers;[17] as in Boston, they might occasionally make special orders for particular customers. In the South and the West Indies, where planters might have credits in Glasgow, Bristol or London, they could exchange sugar, rice, indigo or tobacco for books and other goods, as they pleased, by direct order – but not in Boston which could only realize a profit on its salt fish, pork and beef by a triangular exchange with the West Indies and the Wine Islands. Boston merchants indeed continued their trade in staple books right up to the close of the eighteenth century: newspapers, Bibles, Testaments, psalters and primers repeatedly surface in their advertisements of shipments of cloth and other dry goods.[18] The Ushers' business expanded, and by the end of the century they and others like John Dunton were supplying English books to a number of retailers who had established tiny shops at the centre of Boston. One of them, Michael Perry, had been Usher's clerk, and his inventory of 1700 shows an impressive assortment of English books, in addition to a stock of American imprints in sheets and bound.[19] Boston merchants were as essential to long-distance credit as the Mercers, Drapers and other guilds whose commerce in Continental printing infringed the dealings of the London Stationers in sixteenth-century England.[20]

Because New England was a 'Plantation Religious', its printing was subject to stricter censorship than London's. Such censorship operated more to allocate the production of colonial books to English presses than to deny it altogether to colonial readers, however. There was little to be said for an uncontrolled liberty of printing, after all, from a purely trade point of view. Twenty to forty

15 Massachusetts Archives 100: 158. (State archives, Columbia Point, Boston, Mass.)
16 Bailyn 1955. 17 Tapley 1927, pp. 163–5. 18 Dow 1927, s.t. 'Fabrics', pp. 156–62.
19 Amory 1993. 20 Johnson 1988.

copies a year of an English edition would satisfy the colonial market as adequately as an American edition of a few hundred copies; the paper in either case would have to be brought to America, and it cost no more, and possibly a good deal less, to print it before it was sent over than to print it afterwards. The texts that required a stamp of governmental authority were few enough. The censors who prohibited the printing of the *Imitatio Christi* in 1665, but later allowed its importation from England, were ideologically inconsistent but their discrimination made good economic sense.[21] A thorough-going ban on undesirable imports in any case was impracticable: Baptist and Quaker books freely entered Rhode Island ports and spread out into Massachusetts and Connecticut, and Catholic images and prints have been found in Narragansett graves, doubtless imported from Jesuit missions to the north.[22]

Boston censors thus guaranteed the market for English books from competition by local printers, who undertook little or no printing on their own account. The separation of printing and bookselling was unique to Boston, however; elsewhere, the two trades were normally combined, and printing spread to the other colonies from London, not from Boston or Cambridge, despite a carrying trade that regularly connected New England with the South and the West Indies, and despite emigrations from the Bay colony to New Haven, and later from Connecticut to east New Jersey. Bay colony printers clung to their native base, though not for want of demand: they printed laws and election sermons for New Plymouth (1672, onwards), New Hampshire (1699), and Connecticut (1673, onwards) and they provided merchants and ministers with catechisms and almanacs for localities as distant as Bermuda and Barbados. There were no booksellers outside of Boston, and the censors prohibited a general competition with the London trade that might have stocked their shelves with cheap reprints; the Boston trade thus developed very differently from Dublin's, its closest British analogue, and it had little influence outside of New England, despite its exceptionally early start.

Though the concentration of printing in New England was certainly due to censorship, then, its meagre and belated dispersal elsewhere had other causes. In England, the lapse of the Licensing Act of 1662 spurred competition and the flight of an already overcrowded London market to the provinces; in the colonies, however, printers almost invariably moved in hopes of government business: to New York in 1693; to New London in 1708; to Jamaica in 1718; to Virginia in 1730; to Charleston in 1731. Nor were printers generally averse to

21 Winship 1945, p. 294; for the *Imitatio Christi* and many other Catholic books, see Bond and Amory 1996.

22 Amory 1996; given colonial fears of a French and Indian alliance, the collocation is striking.

the monopoly that licensing conferred: in Cambridge, Samuel Green, licensed to print English, protested at the invasion of his rights by Marmaduke Johnson, who was only licensed to print Indian; in Philadelphia, William Bradford only ventured to print forbidden texts because the Quaker authorities failed to provide an adequate supply of approved ones.[23] Sir William Berkeley, the Governor of Virginia, thanked God that there were 'no free schools nor printing' in that populous colony, and his outburst is often cited to explain the rejection of William Nuthead's petition to settle there in 1682. Nevertheless, the governor's objection was not to printing as such, but to unlicensed printing; there were in fact two free schools in the colony; he had authorized an edition of the Virginia laws from London in 1662; and his animus was clearly directed against the effects of unlicensed printing during the Civil War. Like the Governor of Jamaica in 1731, Berkeley doubted his authority to license a press independently of the privy council, but that is another matter, and colonial authorities had no basis for objecting to imports that were licensed in London. Bermuda (1621), Barbados (1654) and New Haven (1656) first printed their laws there, just like Virginia.

Unlicensed presses quickly led to cut-throat competition, the trade believed. Far from welcoming the 'freedom' that followed the lapse of the Licensing Act, the London trade launched initiatives to protect their copies that eventually led to the Copyright Act of 1710.[24] A temporary lapse of the Licensing Act from 1679 to 1685 fostered a parallel diaspora of printers and booksellers from London to the British Colonies: the Nutheads to Maryland (1682) and Virginia (1685); William Bradford to Philadelphia (1685); John Dunton, Samuel Palmer, Andrew Thorncome and Benjamin Harris, booksellers and Job and John How, and John Allen, printers, to Boston (1686–7). Other motives beside the bad market may also have been a factor: Harris and the Hows had been active in the Protestant interest during the Popish Plot, and may have feared prosecution after James II ascended the throne; the London Yearly Meeting of Friends dispatched William Bradford to supply colonists with Quaker literature; and Andrew Thorncome, a bookseller on London Bridge who appears in only two London imprints, may well have had other business interests. All of the Boston group but John Allen returned to England after the Glorious Revolution. Nevertheless, Dunton in particular remarked on the slowness of trade and hoped to collect large, overdue debts. In 1685–7, Richard Chiswell was allowing John Usher recent titles at unprecedentedly generous discounts of from a quarter to a third off the retail price. This was nearly twice the normal

23 Winship 1945, p. 283. 24 Treadwell 1996; Treadwell 1987.

eighteenth-century discount, and from two to three times the discount allowed country booksellers in the seventeenth century.[25] If the most powerful bookseller in London was so generous, trade must have been slow indeed.

The scale of the British trade to the colonies is difficult to estimate, since we have little evidence apart from a few invoices of shipments received by John Usher in Boston between 1683 and 1685, and a series of custom figures for the value of books exported from London, beginning in 1699.[26] One can roughly estimate the numbers of volumes that entered Boston in the 1680s from this data, but the figure is probably not typical of exports at other, less favourable periods; and of course, there were many other ports of entry. The overall scale depends on how reasonably we can extrapolate backwards from the early eighteenth century, and how persuasively we can convert value into volume. For the latter purposes, I shall assume that the proportion of folios, quartos, and small formats in the eighteenth-century shipments was roughly the same as in Usher's invoices, that is 1 : 3 : 36; and that the shipments, like Usher's were sent bound. A trial 'shopping basket' of seventeenth-century books made up according to this formula weighed 41.5 lb, averaging a little over a pound a volume. The English customs valued a hundred weight (112 lb) of exported books at £4.

From 1679 to 1683, then, Robert Boulter sent John Usher books and stationery worth £445 11*s.* 6*d.*; from 1678 to 1685, Richard Chiswell shipped him £655 14*s.* 6*d.*; and John Dunton's Bostonian customers owed him £500 by 1685, when he took a 'ramble' to collect their debt, with a further shipment of about the same value. Assuming that Dunton's customers had paid something on account, his sales could easily have equalled Chiswell's. In the years when these shipments overlapped (1682–3), an annual average of over £300 worth of books and stationery arrived in Boston. Though we do not have itemized invoices for these years, Usher's invoices for 1683–5 document shipments of 3,544 volumes worth about £295 and stationery worth about £35. It seems fair to conclude that between 3,500 and 4,000 volumes a year were exported to Boston from 1679 to 1685, and that they sold out, since orders would not otherwise have continued.

To select a comparable segment of colonial production, we may exclude session acts, almanacs, broadsides, analytics and variant imprints from the total recorded in the North American Imprints Project; this leaves only eighty-two

25 Barnard and Bell 1994, pp. 31–4; Feather 1985, pp. 53–59. Leedham-Green 1997, p. 17, reports a customary discount of three shillings in the pound (15 per cent) in 1592; all such 'customs', of course, were adjustable for circumstances.

26 The customs figures are taken from Barber 1976, pp. 185–224; I have corrected some minor arithmetical errors.

books printed in Boston and Cambridge between 1681 and 1689. Allowing edition sizes of 2,000 copies for the Indian Bible (1685), 1,000 for catechisms and primers, and 500 apiece for the rest, this production amounted to some 45,500 volumes. Assuming that the editions sold off steadily, and that they were exhausted in twelve years, some 19,585 of these volumes had been bound and sold by the end of 1689, an average of 2,177 volumes a year. Even as late as the 1680s, it seems that metropolitan exports were not only more prestigious but also numerically and economically more important than colonial production.

The customs records give a rather different picture of metropolitan commerce with the colonies. From 1700 to 1713, England annually exported an average of 68.82 cwt (7,708 lb) of books to New England, 29.98 cwt. to Virginia and Maryland, 9.25 cwt. to New York, 8 cwt. to Carolina, 7.61 cwt. to Pennsylvania and 60.48 cwt. to the British West Indies. Since the dockets were classed according to the first destination of the ship, these figures need not reflect the relative importance of these regional markets. In 1675, for example, a shipment of Dutch-printed Bibles reached John Usher through Barbados, late and much water-damaged; the docket would have credited the shipment to Barbados.[27] Conversely, New England dominated the shipping trade, and some proportion of its annual 7,500 volumes may well have ended up in other colonies. On the evidence of inventories, one would doubt that New England consumed roughly eight times as many books as either New York, Carolina or Pennsylvania, or that the West Indies ever approached New England's consumption (culturally, it should have been closer to Carolina's).[28]

Overall, the 20,000 books a year that were shipped to the colonies were probably distributed according to the population of Euro-American, English-speaking settlements (about 250,000 in North America by 1700); the growth of population, imports, and colonial production was certainly closely correlated. The majority of titles, though not necessarily the majority of volumes, went to the middling class of ministers, magistrates, merchants and planters, and to the five large cities, whose tastes have been well described by Edwin Wolf II. Elsewhere, and in humbler circles, colonial book culture may be equated with the Protestant doctrine of *Sola Scripta*, though few, perhaps, proceeded to the extreme of reading nothing else. We too easily forget that literacy requires no more than a single title to maintain itself, and that that title, for most of the colonists, was the Bible, eked out with books of devotion.

27 Ford 1917, p. 8, n. 2.

28 'The First Printers in Jamaica', and 'Thomas Craddock's Books: A West India Merchant's stock', in Cave 1987, pp. 179–205. See Steele 1986, for these shipping routes.

DISRUPTION AND RESTRUCTURING: THE LATE SEVENTEENTH-CENTURY BOOK TRADE

38

The stationers and the printing acts at the end of the seventeenth century

MICHAEL TREADWELL

The Act of Parliament whose expiry on 3 May 1695 provides a convenient concluding point for this volume has been called many things.[1] Legally speaking it was 14 Charles II, c. 33, and came into force on 10 June 1662. Its official title was 'An Act for Preventing the frequent Abuses in Printing Seditious, Treasonable, and Unlicensed Books and Pamphlets; and for the Regulating of Printing and Printing Presses', and contemporaries thus generally referred to it as the Printing Act. However, most subsequent scholars, following Macaulay, have called it the Licensing Act, though it has also been called the Censorship Act and, most recently, the Press Act. These labels reflect not only the varying preoccupations of those who have employed them, but also the very real variety – and confusion – of the Act itself which embodied not only the divergent general interests of its two main sponsors, but also the special interests of a number of groups or even individuals who had lobbied successfully in the Parliamentary committee to have them included.

The immediate context of the Act was the wide-ranging legislative programme undertaken during the first session of the Cavalier Parliament from 8 May 1661 to 19 May 1662, a programme which a recent historian of that Parliament has characterized as 'the reconstruction of the old regime'. This was particularly true of the Printing Act which he correctly describes as largely 'lifted directly out of the 1637 regulations'.[2] Since the Star Chamber Decree of 1637 had itself been merely the last in a long line of regulatory measures from Henry VIII's Proclamation of 1538 down through the Star Chamber Decrees of 1586 and 1637, the 1662 Act may thus be seen as the culmination of over a century of Tudor and Stuart attempts to regulate the press.

1 Michael Treadwell completed the draft of this chapter before his untimely death in April 1999. He had not fully completed the references: for his sources, see Treadwell 1987, 1992, 1996 and Maxted and Treadwell 1990.

2 Seaward 1989, title and p. 158.

There was, however, one very significant difference in this attempt and that was in the basis chosen for its authority. All significant attempts to regulate the book trade up to 1637 had ultimately been founded on the royal prerogative and enforced, latterly at least, through the prerogative courts of Star Chamber for secular or High Commission for ecclesiastical offences. Then, after the abolition of the prerogative courts in 1641 and the outbreak of hostilities in 1642, a kingless Parliament had attempted regulation through ordinances in 1643 and 1647, or through Acts in 1645 and 1653 until Cromwell reverted to the Protectorial 'prerogative' for his Orders of August 1655. In this respect therefore the 1662 Act was emphatically not an attempt to turn back the clock, since it aimed to give press regulation the full statutory authority of the King in Parliament.[3]

This major innovation apart, the Act represented a strong reaffirmation of the partnership between the government and the Stationers' Company which went back to at least 1557 when Mary's charter had granted the Stationers not merely corporate existence and rights, but broad powers, supposedly to aid the government in its ongoing battle to regulate the press. The problem had always been, however, that while the Company coveted these powers, it was far more interested in employing them in support of its own privileges and property, and in those of its leading members, than in acting on the government's behalf to suppress whatever printing might be obnoxious to the official policy of the day. And in re-establishing the old partnership the Act unfortunately did nothing to resolve this underlying tension.

The three main concerns of the Act were with what may be called licensing, trade restrictions, and printing rights, which together represent the interests of the government and the Stationers' Company. The government's interest was essentially to prevent those 'Abuses in Printing' set out in the Act's title, and to do so by restoring licensing and by 'the Regulating of Printing and Printing Presses'.[4] The interests of the Stationers' Company on the other hand were not with licensing, but with printing rights, both corporate and individual, and with the way in which its powers to regulate printing and other aspects of the trade (particularly its powers of search and seizure) might be employed in their defence. There was, of course, some overlap of interest, since the government, for example, had a serious interest in defending printing rights founded on the royal prerogative, but in general the partnership was an uneasy one.

3 Blagden 1960, p. 130.

4 Text from folio black-letter edition of the Act (1662); paragraph numbering from D. Pickering (ed.), *The Statutes at large from Magna Carta to . . . anno 1761*, 47 vols. (Cambridge, 1762–1807), VIII, pp. 137–48.

The licensing provisions of the Act were complex in practice, but simple in principle. There were long lists of specified licensers for various categories of books and elaborate rules on the number of manuscripts to be submitted and what was to become of them afterwards, but in essence the requirement was simply that every work must be licensed before it could be printed and the licence and licenser's name included in the printed version as proof. Imported books, while not requiring a formal licence, had first to be listed and the list submitted to the Archbishop of Canterbury or the Bishop of London, and the shipment then opened and inspected by a special team before being released from customs.

The rights and powers allocated to the Stationers' Company for the enforcement of these provisions were: first, that the Register of the Company was made the document of record for licensing and every licensed work required to be entered there before printing – in London at least; second, the inspection of all shipments of imported books required the presence, not only of the Bishops' representative, but also of the Master and Wardens of the Company or their nominee; and finally, that for the direct enforcement of licensing or, in the words of the Act, 'For the better discovering of printing in Corners without License' (par. 15) the Act empowered not only the King's messengers, but also the Master and Wardens of the Company to authorize searches of 'especially printing-houses, Booksellers Shops, and Warehouses & Bookbinders houses and Shops' (par. 15). Searches for printed matter smuggled past the customs are not specifically mentioned, but presumably searchers for unlicensed printing could seize any unlicensed book even though technically it had been illegally imported rather than illegally printed.

The trade-restrictive provisions of the Act begin with a preliminary rationale which notes that 'by the general licentiousness of the late times many evil-disposed persons have been encouraged to Print and sell Heretical, Schismatical, Blasphemous, Seditious, and Treasonable Books, Pamphlets, and Papers and still do continue', and concludes that 'for prevention [there]of, no surer means can be advised, than by reducing and limiting the number of Printing-Presses, and by ordering and setling... of Printing' (par. 1). As in the past this was to be accomplished by restricting printing and importing of books as much as possible to London; by restricting the London book trade as much as possible to members of the Stationers' Company; and by reducing the number of London printing houses to twenty with two presses each (three for previous Masters or Upper Wardens of the Company), the same numbers as allowed in the 1637 Decree. There were exceptions: printing was allowed in each of the universities and at York, and special licences permitted for landing books at other ports than London; freemen of other London companies could print or trade in books if their father or master had done so – or if specially licensed; and the printing houses of the soon-to-be three King's Printers and one John Streater were not counted in the twenty, nor limited as to number of presses.

These provisions in themselves constituted important concessions to the Company, and to enforce them the Company had access to the same powers of search and seizure which it was meant to employ in the enforcement of licensing. Moreover such powers might even be employed under the Act against non-Stationers engaged in trades essentially peripheral to the book trades since anyone who rented or allowed any space to be used for printing, or any 'Joyner [or] Carpenter [or] Smith' who made the wood or iron work for a printing press was now legally bound to inform the Company (par. 10), but naturally the limitation was not reciprocal and London Stationers were free to trade throughout the kingdom.

Those provisions of the Act which concern printing rights are easily the most complex and ultimately the most important since some of these rights would eventually evolve into what we now call copyrights. In 1662, however, things were confused to such a degree that it is easiest to begin with what such rights were not. Among the trade restrictive sections of the Act we noted the exception made for the right to 'the keeping and using of a Printing-Press in the City of York'. However, this allowance is quickly followed by the condition 'so as no Bibles be there Printed, nor any other Book whereof the Original Copy is or shall be belonging to the Company of Stationers in London, or any Member thereof'. The right which is granted, the simple right to print, is a right to trade; it is those rights which are explicitly withheld which are printing rights, that is, the rights to print particular books or classes of books. The reason why such care was taken in the case of York was precisely that the distinction had not always been made and that in the case of the universities the right to print had long been linked to broad printing rights which were specifically asserted in the Act, nothing in which 'shall be construed to the prejudice . . . of any of the just Rights and Priviledges of either of the two Universities . . . touching printing of Books' (par. 18).[5]

Printing rights had grown up during the sixteenth century as what were called privileges whereby the undertaker sought to protect his investment in the printing of an edition by obtaining royal letters patent granting him exclusive rights to the work for a term of years. And because such royal grants were expensive and time-consuming to obtain, the Stationers' Company had

5 McKitterick 1992, pp. 167–8.

instituted a parallel system, for its own members at least, as the royal commission report had explained in 1583:

> We find proued and confessed that the nature of bokes and printing is such, as it is not meete, nor can be without their vndoeinges of all sides, that sondrie men shold print one boke. And, therefore, where her Matie graunteth not priuilege, [the Stationers] are enforced to haue a kinde of preuileges among them selues by ordinances of the companie whereby euerie first printer of any lawefull booke, presenting it in the hall, hath the same as seuerall to him self as any man hath any boke by her Maties preuilege.[6]

Both printing rights based directly on royal prerogative patent rights and printing rights based on the by-laws of a company chartered under royal prerogative in 1557 survived to achieve statutory authority in the 1662 Act. The former rights were explicitly protected in a new clause insisting that nothing in the Act 'shall extend to prejudice the just Rights or Priviledges granted by his Majesty, or any of his Royal Predecessors to any person or persons under his Majesty's Great Seal' (par. 22). The latter were carried forward from the 1637 Decree in the insistence that no work could legally be printed, even after licensing, unless it 'be first Entered in the Book of the Register of the Company of Stationers of London' (par. 3) (with exceptions for the universities of Oxford and Cambridge). And finally, both forms of printing rights were given statutory authority in the clause of the Act (par. 6) which made it an offence to print or import any work which any person 'shall have the Right, Priviledge, Authority or Allowance, solely to Print . . . by . . . vertue of any Letters Patents . . . granted or assigned . . . or by . . . vertue of any Entry . . . thereof . . . in the Register Book of the . . . Company of Stationers', or the university Register Books for university books (par. 6). Offences under this section of the Act thus had nothing whatsoever to do with the contents of the offending work which might well have been a model of pro-Royalist, Anglican orthodoxy, and licensed to boot. Accordingly penalties for offences are contained within the section itself, quite distinct from the penalties for infringements of any other aspects of the Act.

Like all the innovations and exemptions embodied in the Act that which recognized official university Registers of printing rights is revealing of the lobbying involved. Such registers might have come to rival the Stationers' Register, but did not. Far more significant was the extension to both universities and the royal library of a formal deposit copyright in place of the bizarre clause in the 1637 Decree by which Laud had sought to enforce Bodley's agreement with the Stationers.

6 Blagden 1960, p. 42.

If the main features of the Act reflected the long-standing collaboration between the government and the Stationers' Company, some of its innovations and exemptions reflected newly emerging interests in the book trade. Clearly the universities had been lobbying since not only were all their existing rights protected by special proviso (par. 18), but their new Registers of printing rights might well have rivalled the Stationers'. In fact they came to nothing and it was instead the extension to both universities and the royal library of the right to a deposit copy of each new book published which would survive and grow.[7] Even more significant than these small university gains was the fact that York managed to keep the right to a press it had gained in the Act of 1649, thus opening a breach in the London–Oxbridge monopoly which would never be closed again.[8]

In the capital itself the Stationers had always striven to restrict trading to its own members, and though the custom of the City would normally have allowed all London freemen to trade in books, this had been narrowed by 1637 to those non-Stationers who had been freed after service to one of the book trades. The 1662 Act, however, opened the retail and even the import trade to anyone who could obtain the Archbishop or Bishop of London's licence (par. 5) and explicitly guaranteed the trade rights of the growing band of those 'who have sold Books or Papers within Westminster Hall, the Palace of Westminster' or thereabouts, from before 20 November 1661. The latter were very small fry, but they were the small fry who supplied members of Parliament with their daily ration of pamphlets and papers and the committee did not forget them. And again their exemption is more significant than it at first seems for as Sheila Lambert has noted 'it was competition from the trades operating outside the City that brought about the downfall of the livery companies in general'[9] and that although printing remained under special controls the retail book trade had already begun its inexorable slide westward and out of the control of the Stationers' Company.

There are two more exemptions to be noted. First, paragraph 9 of the Act reasserted the 1637 ban on the importation of all English-language books 'for the better encouraging [of English printing] and the prevention of divers libels [etc.]... Printed beyond the Seas in English'. Paragraph 20, however, added a new exemption for all English books more than ten years old – provided they were imported by booksellers free of the Stationers' Company. At first

7 Sir Thomas Bodley originally made an agreement as early as 1611 for the Stationers to supply his library with their output (Craster 1952, p. 19).

8 York's right to print was granted during the unsuccessful attempt to re-establish the Council of the North there: see Seaward 1989, pp. 135–7.

9 Lambert 1987, p. 2.

glance this seems designed to help the growing antiquarian trade – until one reflects that old Continental books were most unlikely to be in English. Its most important effect seems to have been a flood of Dutch-printed Bibles, all claiming to have been printed in Cambridge in 1648, just safely beyond the ten-year limit.

The final exemption is the most extraordinary of all. It provides 'That neither this Act, nor any thing therein contained shall extend to prohibit *John Streater Stationer*, from printing Books or Papers, but that he may still follow the Art and Mystery of Printing, as if this Act had never been made; Any thing therein to the contrary notwithstanding' (par. 23). Unlike the 1637 Decree which named the twenty licensed printers and four typefounders, the 1662 Act names no one other than Streater. His being singled out would thus be unusual even had he been Charles's printer in exile rather than what he was, namely a high-ranking officer in the Parliamentary army in England and Ireland, repeatedly arrested and imprisoned under the Protectorate for his republican opposition to Cromwell's 'tyrany', who had printed Harrington's *Oceana* in 1656, and plotted to seize the Tower for Parliament in 1659. True, he had changed sides just in time, and the regiment of which he was Colonel had suppressed the only armed resistance to the Restoration, but that surely qualified him for oblivion rather than for unique favour. The explanation seems to be that Streater's unlikely patron was the Royalist colonel Richard Atkyns, holder (in the right of his wife) of the law printing patent which had almost nine years to run at the Restoration. In 1660 Atkyns's influence had been sufficient to win him a forty-year reversion (1669–1709) of that patent, but he was not himself a printer, and was seriously at odds with James Flesher, the printer who had held the lease of these printing rights since the Interregnum. Flesher having sold these leased rights to the Stationers' Company in 1661 Atkyns now found himself at odds with the Company which had ample powers under the new Act to shut down any printer foolish enough to exercise on Atkyns's behalf a right which the Company now claimed for itself under the disputed lease. Atkyns's solution seems to have been to ally himself with Streater, an experienced printer known to be fiercely committed to causes, and to standing up to pressure from the Company, and then to lobby the Parliamentary committee for a clause in the Act which would protect Streater's right to print whatever he and Atkyns wished without fear of harassment from the Company.

If this hypothesis is correct then the Streater clause in the Act represents not so much a new development in the trade as a new move in the ongoing battle over printing rights to the interpretation of which under the Act we must now turn. We noted above that such rights were recognized under the Act as based either on a patent granted under the royal prerogative or an entry in the Stationers' Register. All such printing rights being, by definition, monopoly rights, as exclusive to the grantee, it is at first curious that the Crown rather than the Company was regularly accused of creating monopolies. And this is all the more remarkable given the fact that printing rights by letters patent were almost invariably for a term of years (commonly 10, 14, 21, or 31),[10] while those by entry in the Register were treated both by the Company and by their possessors as perpetual. The explanation is that although the vast majority of the rights held under both authorities were for individual titles or groups of titles, only the Crown could grant rights in whole classes of books, including therefore, books as yet unwritten. And it was these rights which were to cause the most trouble. Moreover, while most patent rights did indeed lapse (if their holders had not taken the precaution of also entering them in the Stationers' Register), the patent rights covering classes of books were regularly renewed so that they had become, *de facto*, almost as permanent as 'perpetual' Register rights.

At the time of the passing of the Act there were essentially four such patent monopoly printing rights or privileges extant: (1) those for Acts of Parliament, statutes, proclamations, the Bible in English, and English service books, all held by the King's Printers, Christopher Barker III and John Bill II; (2) those for the Latin Bible, and all Latin and Greek grammars (including the ever-popular Lilly's grammar), held by the King's Printer for Latin, Greek, and Hebrew, Roger Norton; (3) those for all books concerning the common law, and Rastell's and Poulton's *Abridgements* of the statutes, held by Richard Atkyns; and (4) those for all primers, psalters, Psalms in metre or prose, all almanacs and prognostications, and a number of classical Latin texts widely used in schools, which were held by the Stationers' Company by means of an inner joint-stock of 115 of its most-favoured members (or their widows) dominated by the Company's Court. The first two of these privileges were subject to clandestine infringement but, significantly, not to open legal challenge, at least partly because no individual could claim any rights in the Bible or the statutes.

The law-printing patent was another matter and, appropriately enough, gave rise to the most interesting challenges on points of law. J. H. Baker has already described[11] two examples which, by testing the limits of the law patent, helped demonstrate the vast reach of prerogative rights and thus bring into disrepute the Act which lent them statutory authority. In the first of these cases a group of booksellers backed by the Company, deliberately attacked the law-printing

10 Hunt 1997, pp. 39–94. 11 See pp. 485–8 above.

monopoly by printing a common-law book written since the granting of the patent. The judges consulted differed on the validity of the patent monopoly *per se*, even if limited to books which pre-dated its creation, but all agreed that it did not apply to 'such new law books as have been imprinted since More's patent'.[12] The House of Lords, however, disagreed, and affirmed the patentee's prior rights to print all texts yet unprinted and even, presumably, unwritten.

The degree of resentment likely to be generated by this judgement depended on the precise nature of the printing rights involved and it was only the second of Baker's cases which implicitly defined them. Simply put, throughout the sixteenth and early seventeenth century there existed a printing right distinct from what might, by contrast, be called a publishing right, and which is often ignored by those looking only for those early rights which evolve into modern copyright. Here is Blagden explaining the origin of this form of printing right:

> As a result of the weakening of the printers' hold on the trade there was . . . the recognition of two different rights in a book arising from the two main profits to be made from its exploitation; the first was the right to print it and the second was the right to earn what we call the publisher's profit from it. The selling of a copy by a printer to a bookseller on condition that the former might continue to have the printing of it . . . became quite common in the course of Elizabeth's reign.[13]

And here is the Attorney General in 1672 explaining to Serjeant Maynard how such printing rights applied to books of the common law:

> if you, Mr Serjeant, write a Lawbook, tis true you may give, or Sell it too whome you please, and they may keepe it by them but if either you, or they desire to print it, you must doe it by the Kings Printers for the Law.

The Attorney General, that is to say, is arguing that the law patent conveys monopoly rights in the mechanical printing of the law, rights which he presumably saw as justified by the special types and skills required, and by the need for absolute accuracy and consistency in printing the law. But what the Attorney General does not say here is what would happen if Serjeant Maynard or his purchaser should fail to keep their law book securely by them so that a copy comes into the hands of the law printers who then print it. This is the issue which was decided in the second example cited by Baker in which the law printers (Streater among them) printed without permission or payment the third part of Coke's *Reports* which belonged to others both by prior printing (during the Interregnum when the patent was in abeyance) and by entry in

12 See pp. 485–7 above on Rolle's *Abridgment* (1668).

13 Blagden 1960, p. 44.

the Stationers' Register. The rights, and thus the action, of the owners were upheld in the King's Bench, but lost on appeal to the Lords who thus defined the rights of the law printers as printing-and-publishing rights, thus implying that royal patent rights trumped the private property rights conveyed by entry in the Stationers' Register. It was not a decision designed to build support in the legal profession for an act which gave strong statutory support to such prerogative grants.[14]

The only class of patent rights granted in perpetuity were those for primers, psalters and almanacs held by the Stationers' English Stock. They were also by far the most valuable and with rare exceptions earned enough to pay the stock holders an annual dividend of 10 to 12½ per cent on their investment. Moreover it was income from the English Stock which paid the pensions of poor, disabled, or aged Stationers and their widows, a fact always prominently mentioned whenever the privilege came under attack though the dividends accounted for roughly 90 per cent of the profits and the pensions perhaps 10 per cent. Such was the financial importance of the English Stock that its affairs largely determined Company policy during the period and the vast proportion of the searches and seizures carried out by the Company under the Act involved unlawfully printed English Stock books, not unlicensed seditious or heretical ones.

The greatest threat to the Company's monopoly, however, was not such petty piracy, but two 1669 grants to the Royalist John Seymour, the first of the rights to a number of as yet unassigned classical titles and any new almanacs which might be offered to him rather than to the English Stock, and the second of the reversion of the only non-perpetual English Stock printing rights, namely those for the classical school texts. The Lords decision on patent *vs* Register rights might have protected the Stationers had Seymour merely tried to enter his rival school classical titles or almanacs in the Register – though the Company would never have permitted such entries in the first place. But Seymour's rights were founded upon a rival patent. Moreover Seymour, like Atkyns before him, had earlier enlisted the collaboration of the specially privileged John Streater to represent his interests with the Company. Faced with this threat the Company seems to have resorted to its powers of search and seizure in an attempt to intimidate Seymour. His complaint was heard by the Privy Council itself in February 1672, but while the hearing did give rise to the Attorney General's lucid explanation of printing rights, cited above, it left no recorded decision on the matter at hand. Apparently, however, Seymour's rights seemed likely to be upheld since the Company eventually agreed to pay the fines of those who had damaged

14 See pp. 487–8 above. The issue was re-opened in *Walthoe v. Walker* (1736).

Seymour's printing equipment and to buy his reversion of the school book rights for 500 guineas and his printing rights to new almanacs and school books for a hefty annuity. This was similar to the strategy which the Company had long since adopted with the universities, who were generally paid annual amounts *not* to exercise their protected rights to print books covered by other patents.[15]

The gradual determination by the courts of the way in which the printing rights sections of the Act would be applied made it clear that the Act would inevitably favour the rights of the Crown and those like the Stationers' Company and the King's Printers whom the Crown had favoured with patent rights and the powers under the Act to defend them. And a survey of the enforcement of the trade-restrictive and licensing aspects of the Act reveals the same tendencies, though here modified by greater tensions and difficulties between the Company and the Crown.

On paper the Act had assumed the old partnership between the government and the Stationers with the Company's nominee having equal rights with the Bishops' in the inspection of book imports, and the Master and Wardens as much empowered to conduct searches of printing houses and bookshops as 'the Messengers of his Majesty's Chamber, by Warrant under his Majesty's Sign Manuel or under the hand of... His Majesty's principal Secretaries of State' (par. 15). Significantly, however, it was the King's Messengers who were the innovation. Under the 1637 Decree only the Company had been nominated to conduct searches, but Charles's government was more wary than his father's had been of the good faith of a Company much of whose leadership had opposed the Crown during the recent unpleasantness.

The clearest sign of this distrust was the appointment of a rival authority to the Stationers in the enforcement of the Act. This was the ultra-Royalist Roger L'Estrange who was first named as Surveyor under Mr Secretary Nicholas in February 1662, even before the passage of the Act, and formally appointed to the office of Surveyor of the Presses by Nicholas's successor Bennet on 15 August 1663. From then until the first lapse of the Act in March 1679 and his own prudent withdrawal to Edinburgh and then the Hague in the autumn of 1680 during the Exclusion crisis, L'Estrange waged an unremitting war against the sedition of the sectaries on one hand and what he saw as the culpable inactivity of the Company on the other.

Simply put, in spite of countless arrests and seizures, licensing as a system was probably not enforceable and was certainly not successfully enforced. The Act contained no provision for the remuneration of the licensers who bore

15 Rose 1993, pp. 23–5, misunderstands both the Atkyns and Seymour cases.

such heavy responsibilities under the Act and Siebert claims that practically all the licensing done under the authority of the Secretaries of State between 1662 and 1679 had to be done by L'Estrange himself.[16] Moreover the Act also envisaged that the struggling author of every English book would produce two neat copies of the whole, including 'the Titles, Epistles, Prefaces, Tables, Dedications' (par. 4). Few authors, however orthodox their political or religious beliefs, have ever got their copy to the printer on time under such constraints, and few did. Madan long ago noted that even in Royalist Oxford fewer than half the items printed were licensed.[17] And D. F. McKenzie, who in 1974 examined 458 of the 491 items then known to have been printed in 1668 found that only fifty-two of them bore any form of the licence required by the Act – though close to half obeyed the Act by carrying some form of the printer's name, presumably because compliance was easier.[18] Finally, though 1668 saw only fifty-two books with licences, it saw seventy-nine entries in the Stationers' Register, still a small percentage of the whole, but suggestive of the fact that the book trade cared more for printing rights than for government regulations, to say nothing of the fact that the Company must have allowed the entry of unlicensed works in the Register.

This widespread evasion becomes understandable when we consider that there was never any attempt on the part of the government to enforce licensing *per se*. During the entire period the Act was in force no charges seem to have been brought against any printed matter which was not considered seditious as well as unlicensed. Indeed so consistently were the works which were prosecuted characterized as 'seditious libels' that the legal historian of seditious libel has had to take considerable pains to underline the fact that 'the defendant's crime was simply his failure to get a licence rather than seditious libel or any other form of defamation'.[19] Only in exceptional circumstances such as prevailed during the six-year lapse of the Act from 1679 to 1685 were charges brought under the law of seditious libel and even at this period the government went to great lengths to be able to charge offenders with the offence of 'publishing of books of news without licence, contrary to the declared prerogative of the King'.[20] In short, the government never tried to enforce licensing; it merely used the easily proven offence of failure to obtain a licence as its preferred weapon against those publications to which it objected on quite other grounds.

What concerned L'Estrange, however, was how much even of seditious unlicensed material slipped through the net, and he blamed the Stationers. After the first year of the Act, with the radical press still in high gear and

16 Siebert 1952, p. 243. 17 Madan 1925, pp. 121–2. 18 McKenzie 1974a.
19 Hamburger 1984–5, p. 690. 20 *Ibid.*, p. 687.

searches and seizure mounting L'Estrange noted that not a single conviction had resulted from the Company's activities. And in spite of constant exhortation and threats from L'Estrange and the government this situation changed little over the life of the Act. The Company resented L'Estrange's interference, and valued its powers of search and seizure not as weapons against sedition, but as weapons against the infringement of their printing rights and profits in the English Stock and their own private copies.[21]

At the root of the Company's failure to enforce the licensing provisions of the Act lay its unwillingness to enforce those trade-restrictive sections of the Act which were expressly designed to make licensing workable. Chief among these were the numerical restrictions on London printing which called for numbers of printing houses and presses almost identical to those in the 1637 Decree, ignoring the fact that by 1662, after twenty years of shifting authority, or none, the number of printing houses had almost tripled. Moreover, all pre-Civil War numerical restrictions on printing had been actively sought by a Company which had now come to see the advantage of some excess capacity in the printing trade. Thus the 1637 Decree had designated twenty allowed printers by name while the Act spoke vaguely of an eventual reduction to twenty 'by death or otherwise'.

'Otherwise' to L'Estrange meant active confiscation or, at the very least the buying in of presses and type from supernumerary printers or their widows, and as early as 1663 he proposed a system of fines to raise the money.[22] That was almost a year after the passing of the Act and about the same time that the Company finally got around to summoning all the master printers of whom there still turned out to be fifty-nine in business in and around London. Three years later they summoned the master printers again, this time to broach the subject of how they came by their printing houses, and this charade, punctuated with warnings, one buying in, and even the occasional indictment, continued as long as the Act was in force. As late as February 1692 the Company was still calling for a 'list of printers in and around London noting which are qualified according to the Act', but by then it was a bit late. The lowest number of master printers reached in the period was the thirty-three recorded in a count in July 1668 and that nadir was achieved by plague and fire, not by the efforts of the Stationers.

But while the numerical restrictions on the London press were used to threaten rather than reduce the London printers the geographical restrictions were ruthlessly applied. In March 1692, on the mere rumour of more presses in

21 Blagden 1960, p. 173. 22 Kitchin 1913, p. 131.

York than the Act allowed, both the Company's Wardens and a messenger of the press were immediately dispatched to seize the offending output – not seditious libels, but school books belonging to the English Stock. As for the limiting of provincial printing to York and the universities it seems to have been the one clause in the Act successfully enforced. The only rumours to the contrary concerned a private press in Chester from the mid-1680s which, if it existed, was hardly used. And when William of Orange landed in Devon in 1688 he had to bring a press with him precisely because there was none closer than Oxford.

The fact that the Company could thus enforce the Act energetically when it tried, suggested to L'Estrange and the government that in other areas it was simply not trying, and they resorted to a series of measures to force compliance. In 1663 and 1668 the King's bookseller, the King's bookbinder, and two of the three King's Printers were elected to the Court by royal command, and in 1670 the Company's resistance to reforming its by-laws to add teeth to enforcement of the Act led to the launching of *quo warranto* proceedings which could have cost the Company its charter and corporate existence. The Company complied, though reluctantly and very slowly (drafting and passing the new by-laws took seven-and-a-half more years), protesting that the real problem was the fact that the Act had done nothing to suppress hawkers and had even guaranteed the trading rights of many in the book trades who were not members of the Company and thus not subject to its by-laws, reformed or not.

Hawkers had always been harassed and were again, but forcing London freemen from one company to another challenged the long-standing custom of the City. The Crown was not yet ready for that and in 1671 contented itself with milder measures which, in any case, were not enforced. All that changed dramatically in the early 1680s, in the aftermath of the Exclusion Crisis. The Crown launched *quo warranto* proceedings, not only against the Stationers, but against the City itself and all its livery companies. The aim was to impose new civic and company charters which would make the taking of the oaths and conformity to the Church of England preconditions for office holding and also make the Companies' office holders removable at the King's pleasure. The livery companies lined up to comply, one of their motives being the hope that a renewed charter might include augmented privileges. In this the Stationers were not disappointed for they became one of a number of companies granted much extended jurisdiction which, in their case, restricted the sale and binding of books to members of the Company in London and Westminster and their suburbs for four miles around.

The new Charter was dated 22 May 1684 and the new Court of 'loyal' assistants named in it set about to assume the complete control of the London trade which the Company had always coveted. In the year between June 1684 and May 1685 they inventoried over ninety interlopers in the trade, seventy free of other companies, the rest of none, and worked to force them into the Stationers or out of business. Under the threat of loss of trading rights almost half of the complete outsiders took the freedom of the Stationers, generally by purchase, but the freemen of other City companies knew their rights and negotiations on their translation had broken down even before King James's last desperate reversal in October 1688 restored the old Charters. The Company, while content to part with an autocratic monarch was far less happy to give up its new autocratic Charter and resisted the restoration until the formal reversal of the *quo warranto* was imposed by Act of Parliament in May 1690.

This brief and ultimately fruitless episode was nevertheless important in two ways. First, the legal and other charges involved weakened the finances of the Stationers, as of many of the companies.[23] Second, the brief period in which their combined powers under the Act and the new Charter had given the Stationers total control over all aspects of the trade had alarmed not only the book traders outside the Company, but also a number of Stationers outside the magic circle of the Company's all-powerful and self-elective Court of Assistants. And it was these groups who were among those who lobbied against the renewal of the Act in 1693 and again in 1695.[24]

To understand the final lapsing of the Act in 1695 we have first to understand how it had been maintained to that point. The original Act was conceived as a stop-gap measure to run from 10 June 1662 for two years only, but the replacement bill for 'better regulating the press'[25] which was read on 10 July 1663 got nowhere, and on the last day of the Parliamentary session (17 May 1663) assent was given to a Bill to continue the Act in force until the end of the next session of Parliament. On the last day of that session (2 March 1665) it was again continued to the last day of the next (31 October 1665), but on that day the Act was renewed, not for a session only, but until the last day of the first session of the next Parliament. That new Parliament did not sit until 6 March 1679 and the session ended suddenly a week later when the king, refusing to accept the speaker proposed, prorogued Parliament for a single day. It was enough to kill the Act, and at the height of the Popish Plot, the reality of which was formally resolved by both houses on 24 March 1679, no one was in a mood to revive it.

This first lapse lasted through more than six years of recurrent crisis, during the last four of which Parliament did not sit, and during most of which the government continued to prosecute the unlicensed printing of news, the

23 C. Knight (ed.), *London*, 6 vols. (London, 1841–4), v, p. 126.
24 Treadwell 1996, pp. 10–13. 25 Seaward 1989, p. 159.

opinion having been wrung from the judges that the licensing of news was a prerogative right.[26] The Act was then revived in the first session of James II's only Parliament to run from 24 June 1685 for seven years and then to the end of the next session which came on 14 March 1693. Before that session ended the Act was renewed once again, for one year plus one session, but now, for the first time, serious opposition to the renewal was voiced in Parliament, and in that subsequent session the opposition was renewed and the Act was not. Routinely included on the list of temporary Acts slated for renewal by the committee responsible, the Printing Act alone was removed by the Commons, which instead appointed a committee to bring in a new bill – again to better regulate printing. The Lords at first objected and reinserted the Act for renewal, but after a conference with the Commons backed down, seemingly in the belief that the replacement bill would soon be sent up to them.[27] It was not, and accordingly, when the session was prorogued on 3 May 1695 the Printing Act lapsed once more, this time, as it happened, forever.

The public and private grievances and objections which eventually brought down the Act have been carefully studied by Raymond Astbury who above all emphasizes their complexity. The licensing provisions of the Act naturally drew fire, but of very different kinds, and Astbury cites, for example, the Whig opposition which, in 1693, first attacked the defective administration of the system, apparently with the aim of getting control of it into their own hands, and only began to argue against the principle of licensing when it became clear they had failed. Moreover with the Court, the Church, and many members of both houses of Parliament known to support licensing in some form such opposition was muted and the 1695 bill envisaged preserving licensing for new books on politics, religion, and law.[28]

More opposition focused on the trade restrictive provisions of the Act, and on the Stationers' Company as the great beneficiary of them. Where some opposed licensing in principle, and many its abuses in practice, far more objected to the granting of elaborate powers to a private corporation of tradesmen on the pretence that such powers were required to make licensing 'work'. Moreover, the degree to which the Company's powers of search and seizure had been used for private commercial advantage rather than against sedition was widely known. The geographical restrictions on printing drew less fire, but it is surely significant that both the 1695 draft Bill and the replacement

26 Hamburger 1984–5, p. 687.

27 Astbury 1978, p. 316, disagrees with the interpretation of these events by Lord Macaulay, *The history of England from the accession of James the Second* (London, 1873), II, p. 504.

28 An example of the complexity is the lobbying of the College of Physicians for powers to license new medical books (Astbury 1978, pp. 312–13).

Bills debated after the lapse of the Act specifically permitted printing outside the old limits of London, York, and the universities. And as for the Company's would-be monopoly of the London trade Astbury notes that among the earliest petitioners against the renewal of the Act were 'a group of independent printers, booksellers, and bookbinders who complained that the Act interfered with their freedom to practise their trades.'[29]

The Stationers' 'monopoly' was in fact the thing which most troubled opponents of the Act, though they were concerned, not so much with the Company's near-monopoly control over the working members of the trade, as about its various monopolies of printing rights, in particular the monopoly it exercised over literary property in general as long as no one had any right to print without prior entry in a register, the rules of access to which were under the complete control of the Company. And finally there were the Company's own monopoly printing rights in the titles in the English Stock, particularly almanacs. 'Monopoly' had been a bad word since the reign of James I, but it is significant that it was the Stationers' monopoly rather than the King's Printers' or law printers' monopolies which were most frequently attacked. Perhaps the latter were shielded by their implied proximity to the Crown or by their more evident public utility. But perhaps it had already been noted that while all royal patent printing rights, even those of the King's Printers, were for limited terms, the patent rights in most English Stock books, and all printing rights by virtue of entry in the Registers, were perpetual. Certainly the judges seemed to make the connection, and when perpetual rights were finally brought down in February 1774 the almanac monopoly – though not the other printing monopolies – followed them into oblivion just over a year later.

The fact that the failed 1695 Bill still sought to preserve licensing while completely abandoning the trade-restrictive aspects of the Act, as well as all reference to printing rights either by patent or entry is evidence that if the government lost its battle in the end, the Stationers had lost theirs long before. James's reign had brought a depression in trade and chaos in the livery companies from which the leadership of the Stationers' Company had never recovered. The Glorious Revolution had brought relative calm at home, a long but, costly, and initially disastrous war with France which was to last eight years and produce severe losses in shipping and thus in the fledgling insurance industry, and countless personal bankruptcies in a merchant business community where the absence of limited liability meant that most disasters caused chain reactions. It was unfortunately in this climate that the Company, acting

29 Astbury 1978, p. 301.

on behalf of the English Stock, made a very bad investment decision in bidding for Oxford University's Bible-printing rights against two of its own members, Peter Parker and Thomas Guy, who had previously held them. The Company's victory in the resulting bidding war left them saddled with a debt of over £3,000 and the bitter resentment of two powerful Stationers who subsequently supported the independent booksellers and stationers who opposed the renewal of the Act.

With this collective disaster came a series of personal ones. In 1692 the master of the Company shot himself 'in a melancholy fitt' and in 1694 the upper warden was obliged to resign from office in circumstances which led to his eventual bankruptcy.[30] Nor were these the only losses for between deaths and bankruptcies (and in one case both) the court lost ten of twenty-eight members in the twenty months immediately prior to the lapsing of the Act. And this does not include two of the four men elected in May 1694 to strengthen a beleaguered court, but obliged to withdraw before the end of the year, also by reason of financial embarrassment. Faced with widespread opposition to its previously entrenched privileges the leadership of the Company in 1694 and 1695 failed utterly to defend them, too weak to lobby and too poor to bribe.

The dramatic failure of government and Company to preserve or, in spite of several efforts after May 1695, to replace the Act, conditions us to expect a host of dramatic changes, but there were only two, neither without precedent. First, with the lapse of licensing the government lost the one power it had wielded successfully under the Act, namely that to control newspapers. At the beginning of May 1695 the government-sponsored *London gazette* was the only *news*paper in the kingdom. By the end of May there were six, and though the government theoretically possessed the same prerogative powers it had wielded from 1680 to 1685, and even ordered a prosecution, it finally chose not to test them in the courts. Second, with the lapse of trade restrictions the Stationers lost the fiercely guarded geographical limits on English printing. By May 1695 there was a printer in Bristol, by 1696 in Shrewsbury, by 1698 in Exeter, by 1701 in Norwich, and so on, and on.

If we are surprised that so little changed in the book trade in 1695 it is partly because we have forgotten that prerogative rights, though confirmed in the Act, were by no means dependent on it, and therefore did not lapse with it. Moreover the failure of any statute produced not a legal void, but rather a default to the common law or customary rights which lay beneath it. The Stationers' English

30 Ambrose Isted's suicide was reported on 25 June, N. Luttrell, *A brief historical relation of state affairs from September 1678 to April 1714* (Oxford, 1857), II, p. 494; Thomas Bassett, Upper Warden, Stationers' Company, Court Book F, 9 May 1694.

Stock held its printing rights by royal patent, but on 29 April 1695 took the added precaution of entering each individual title in its Register, after which it sued infringers as before. Individual Stationers went farther, continuing to claim that their ownership of copyrights had never depended merely on entry in the Register, being property rights at common law like any other.

The reason why there were so few dramatic changes in the book trade in 1695 is that the most significant changes had been taking place slowly over the preceding two decades or more. This period had been marked by uncertainty on a quite frightening scale. The stop on (we would say 'default of') the Exchequer in 1672 sent a chill through a London business community still recovering from the plague and fire of 1665 and 1666, but the greatest uncertainty of all hung over the succession to the throne. The Popish Plot scare of 1678 and the Exclusion Crisis which began in 1679 had been followed in the early 1680s by a sharp government counterattack on the City and the livery companies. This resulted not merely in the forced surrender and re-issue of all the City and company charters, but in a series of purges of 'loyal' assistants and liverymen which carried on while the definition of loyalty continued to shift. More than forty new assistants (three times the average for a decade in the seventeenth century) had been elected to serve, however briefly, on the court of the Stationers' Company, and while the Stationers' court had continued to function, those of some other companies had simply ceased meeting, uncertain which new decrees were now in force.

The chaos of James II's reign was ended only by William's invasion which, if it eventually brought greater political stability, brought it at the cost of a series of plots and invasion scares, and a major war with France which began badly. In particular the devastating shipping losses of the early years of the war had a domino effect in a commercial community in which every substantial merchant was a surety for others. Defoe, who failed for £17,000 in 1692, is merely the most famous bankrupt of the period; the Stationers' assistants who broke did so in good company.

It had been in March 1679, towards the beginning of this protracted crisis, that the Printing Act had lapsed for the first time, and Blagden hypothesized that the idea of the wholesaling conger had come to Richard Royston at this time 'as a measure for preserving copyrights from infringement' in the absence of statutory sanctions.[31] This may be so, but the wholesaling conger and the printing (we would say 'publishing') congers which succeeded it also served as simple insurance schemes, like those for fire and marine insurance which

31 Blagden 1960, p. 175.

developed at the same time, in which the spreading of risk was formalized in a manner which approaches that of the on-going joint-stock company. Joint-stock schemes were also in the air, the most successful being the Bank of England itself which from 1694 spread the notorious risks of lending to the government so successfully as to make the fortunes of the lenders, while incidentally securing the Revolution settlement.

The wholesaling conger, Blagden believed, shared the risk of the publisher's investment in a new *edition* among a number of fellow booksellers who had a standing agreement to take a fixed share (a fifteenth share each of a membership of sixteen in 1693, he guessed) of whatever number of copies the sixteenth (the initiator of the edition) chose to distribute in this way. The later printing congers took this idea a step farther when the contracting group agreed to share the risk of the original investment in the *copyright* itself as well as in each subsequent *edition* produced. Both systems spread the normal commercial risk of investing in a new work or a new edition which might simply fail to sell, but both also served actually to reduce the risk of piracy in an uncertain legal environment by increasing the number of those available to finance litigation or employ informal trade sanctions against a pirate.

That risk, and its management in an acutely uncertain political and thus commercial environment, was in the minds of the trade can be seen in the emergence at this same time of two other marketing innovations, one at each extreme of the market. In the mass market the hysteria of the Popish Plot and Exclusion Crisis brought with it a huge demand for political papers and pamphlets. Since these were cheap to produce and sold quickly the normal commercial risk was small. The legal risk to the bookseller of seizure, arrest, imprisonment or fine, was, however, substantial, and many members of the trade who coveted the profits, but disliked the risks, began to employ a small specialist group of poorer associates, often binders, to publish (we would say 'distribute') such works for them. These men, and often women, were the trade publishers, and their function was to let their names stand in the imprint of such works in the place of that of the actual copyright owner, to distribute the work, to account to the owner for the sales, and finally to deal with any incidental unpleasantness from the authorities – all for a small fee.[32]

At the same time the luxury end of the trade was learning to manage the risks and costs always inherent in publishing major projects like Moses Pitt's *English atlas* (1680) or Moreri's *Great historical, geographical and poetical dictionary* (1694) by pre-selling them, not to a wholesaling conger, but direct to the

32 On 'trade publishing' see Treadwell 1982a.

public. This was publishing by subscription, 'subscriber' being the appropriate Latinate word for one signing the list to buy learned and expensive books. The merchant who about this time began to sign other lists in the coffee-houses to share in the risks of commercial shipping was a plain English 'underwriter'.

But while the uncertainty of the times clearly stimulated some innovations in the late seventeenth-century trade, others seem to have developed from the normal pursuit of profit or simply with the passing of time. Given the highly visible success of the English Stock it was surely inevitable that similar though smaller joint-stocks would develop within the trade as a way of exploiting valuable copyrights. Giles Mandelbrote has recently demonstrated how far the share-book system had already progressed by this period – and how ill-equipped the Stationers' Register system was to deal with it. The catalogue of the copyrights of the bookseller Richard Bentley, disposed of by his widow after his death in 1697, included rights in 380 separate titles of which Bentley had owned only 121 in their entirety, his most common share being one twelfth (of 124 titles) and one share being as small as one forty-eighth.[33] Moreover, Bentley had only ever made ten entries in the Registers, some involving other titles entirely, presumably because he recognized that they were not an efficient vehicle for recording ownership of the growing number of ever-smaller shares inevitably created over time as valuable copyrights were divided among partners, widows, children or creditors.

The looming lapse of the Act in the spring of 1695 accordingly brought no rush to the Register on the part of the major copyright owners in the Company. They had only rarely entered their holdings before and saw even less reason why they should do so now. The court of the Company did order the entry of all English Stock books, but as Blagden noted, and as the bankruptcies perhaps confirm, the court seemed increasingly out of touch with commercial reality and power was passing from 'the ancients' to a younger group of capitalist booksellers.[34] Membership in the new wholesaling conger is unknown before 1699 and uncertain even then, but between the twenty-one men Blagden suspects as members in that year and the then twenty-five members of the court there was an overlap of only four.

In consequence, when the Act finally lapsed on 3 May 1695 leading members of the trade were not particularly disturbed. Forewarned as they had been by the earlier lapse of 1679–1685 they had already made those adjustments they considered prudent to protect their businesses in the changed conditions which seemed to be coming. A far greater concern, for Stationers as for all

33 Mandelbrote 1997, p. 68. 34 Hodgson and Blagden 1953, p. 82.

other tradesmen in the spring of 1695, was the debased state of the coinage which even caused a rift in the long-standing relation between Dryden and his publisher Jacob Tonson, already anxious about his investment in the ageing poet's great Virgil translation. For the less well established the lapse might even offer new opportunities, particularly for printers who could now set up in the provinces, or in the capital with no threat of harassment, even if they tried their hands at a newspaper. In 1695 there were about forty-five printing houses in London. Ten years later there were close to seventy.

It has in fact been argued that the government itself, after years of frustration, acquiesced in the end of licensing, though not before first testing an alternative. In 1693 they tried and executed the Jacobite printer William Anderton under the law of treason, seemingly to reassure themselves, and the trade, that there were other and more effective means than licensing to control the press.

If the government and the trade were largely undisturbed by the lapsing of the Act, others seem to have been completely oblivious. Even Macaulay was forced to admit that 'The great event passed almost unnoticed', noting that 'Evelyn and Luttrell did not think it worth mentioning in their diaries', though to Macaulay himself the vote which brought the lapse had done 'more for liberty and civilization than the Great Charter or the Bill of Rights'.[35] To the historian it was indisputably the Licensing Act, and its lapse in 1695 made an epoch. To contemporaries it remained to the end the Printing Act and when it lapsed they seem, for the most part, to have gone on about their business.

35 Lord Macaulay, *The history of England from the accession of James the Second* (London, 1873), II, pp. 504, 503.

APPENDICES

APPENDIX 1

Statistical tables

JOHN BARNARD AND MAUREEN BELL

Table 1. *Annual book production 1475–1700*[1]

Annual totals	*All*	*London*
1475	1	0
5-year	1	0
1476	6	6
1477	17	17
1478	5	4
1479	5	1
1480	15	13
5-year	48	41
Decade	49	41 (84%)
1481	12	9
1482	10	8
1483	34	24
1484	14	14
1485	14	11
5-year	84	66
1486	8	6
1487	7	6
1488	5	2
1489	9	7
1490	23	21
5-year	52	42
Decade	136	108 (79%)
1491	7	7
1492	13	8
1493	15	14
1494	25	15
1495	31	21
5-year	91	65
1496	41	40
1497	31	26
1498	31	26

1 Derived from M. Bell and J. Barnard, 'Provisional count of *STC* Titles 1475–1640', *PH*, 31 (1992), 48–64 and 'Provisional count of *Wing* Titles 1641–1700', *PH*, 44 (1998), 89–97. *STC* five-year and decade totals are here reworked for consistency with Wing figures (e.g. 1551–5, 1556–60 rather than 1550–4, 1555–9 as they appear in *PH*).

Table 1. *(cont.)*

Annual totals	*All*	*London*
1499	44	40
1500	52	45
5-year	199	177
Decade	290	242 (84%)
1501	19	14
1502	34	29
1503	30	24
1504	23	17
1505	65	54
5-year	171	138
1506	38	24
1507	33	21
1508	64	43
1509	59	50
1510	110	91
5-year	304	229
Decade	475	367 (77%)
1511	44	34
1512	41	37
1513	33	30
1514	34	28
1515	79	64
5-year	231	193
1516	52	38
1517	67	57
1518	69	54
1519	56	40
1520	110	92
5-year	354	281
Decade	585	474 (81%)
1521	78	64
1522	52	47

Annual totals	*All*	*London*
1523	59	51
1524	42	34
1525	109	87
5-year	340	283
1526	85	69
1527	93	75
1528	99	84
1529	72	59
1530	142	114
5-year	491	401
Decade	831	684 (82%)
1531	103	78
1532	92	78
1533	117	99
1534	114	93
1535	113	83
5-year	539	431
1536	91	68
1537	76	61
1538	134	97
1539	85	78
1540	118	112
5-year	504	416
Decade	1043	847 (81%)
1541	66	56
1542	95	85
1543	116	102
1544	109	98
1545	126	117
5-year	512	458

Table 1. *(cont.)*

Annual totals	*All*	*London*
1546	127	119
1547	144	139
1548	268	235
1549	170	155
1550	249	228
5-year	958	876
Decade	1470	1334 (91%)
1551	133	121
1552	153	145
1553	168	158
1554	141	122
1555	208	165
5-year	803	711
1556	191	148
1557	109	93
1558	112	92
1559	114	110
1560	172	167
5-year	698	610
Decade	1501	1321 (88%)
1561	146	137
1562	163	157
1563	154	142
1564	93	86
1565	169	141
5-year	725	663
1566	187	158
1567	168	145
1568	131	110
1569	159	149
1570	264	232
5-year	909	794
Decade	1634	1457 (89%)
1571	156	140
1572	176	154
1573	184	166
1574	186	162
1575	239	218
5-year	941	840
1576	180	171
1577	211	210
1578	220	212
1579	265	243
1580	300	276
5-year	1176	1112
Decade	2117	1952 (92%)
1581	289	271
1582	215	195
1583	250	240
1584	278	245
1585	323	270
5-year	1355	1221
1586	233	189
1587	240	210
1588	250	220
1589	293	257
1590	353	293
5-year	1369	1169
Decade	2724	2390 (88%)

Table 1. *(cont.)*

Annual totals	*All*	*London*
1591	299	273
1592	294	252
1593	211	181
1594	261	219
1595	326	288
5-year	1391	1213
1596	316	278
1597	277	233
1598	292	257
1599	329	275
1600	382	298
5-year	1596	1341
Decade	2987	2552 (86%)
1601	258	222
1602	326	268
1603	428	337
1604	406	332
1605	379	316
5-year	1797	1475
1606	407	359
1607	434	380
1608	403	327
1609	474	407
1610	420	350
5-year	2138	1823
Decade	3935	3298 (84%)
1611	401	340
1612	452	373

Annual totals	*All*	*London*
1613	510	433
1614	444	361
1615	524	447
5-year	2331	1954
1616	487	416
1617	431	356
1618	532	454
1619	511	435
1620	591	507
5-year	2552	2168
Decade	4883	4122 (84%)
1621	579	481
1622	592	507
1623	566	474
1624	605	521
1625	680	553
5-year	3022	2536
1626	417	354
1627	454	383
1628	567	474
1629	480	393
1630	695	569
5-year	2613	2173
Decade	5635	4709 (84%)
1631	636	488
1632	590	468
1633	646	462
1634	566	424
1635	689	556

Table 1. *(cont.)*

Annual totals	*All*	*London*
5-year	3127	2398
1636	535	445
1637	582	451
1638	677	501
1639	625	464
1640	848	676
5-year	3267	2537
Decade	6394	4935 (77%)
1641	2034	1789
1642	3666	3219
1643	1835	1416
1644	1206	918
1645	1174	974
5-year	9915	8316
1646	1317	1143
1647	1843	1656
1648	2309	2046
1649	1549	1327
1650	1314	1139
5-year	8332	7311
Decade	18247	15627 (86%)
1651	1072	930
1652	1113	962
1653	1284	1147
1654	1118	1002
1655	1214	1068
5-year	5801	5109

Annual totals	*All*	*London*
1656	1176	1046
1657	1176	1034
1658	1158	1026
1659	1950	1773
1660	2730	2367
5-year	8190	7246
Decade	13991	12355 (88%)
1661	1584	1348
1662	1222	1004
1663	1035	837
1664	910	768
1665	902	719
5-year	5653	4676
1666	633	478
1667	709	564
1668	761	634
1669	777	620
1670	1091	874
5-year	3971	3170
Decade	9624	7846 (82%)
1671	915	748
1672	1075	881
1673	1059	862
1674	1123	920
1675	1281	1059
5-year	5453	4470
1676	1112	930
1677	1081	909
1678	1174	957

Table 1. *(cont.)*

Annual totals	*All*	*London*
1679	1730	1448
1680	2145	1833
5-year	7242	6077
Decade	12695	10547 (83%)
1681	1978	1681
1682	1898	1659
1683	1792	1518
1684	1686	1439
1685	2034	1625
5-year	9388	7922
1686	1084	853
1687	1301	1075
1688	1941	1552
1689	2514	1997
1690	2302	1867
5-year	9142	7344
Decade	18530	15266 (82%)

Annual totals	*All*	*London*
1691	1702	1365
1692	1481	1161
1693	1563	1239
1694	1397	1142
1695	2066	1617
5-year	8209	6524
1696	1762	1373
1697	1551	1237
1698	1686	1288
1699	1672	1272
1700	2640	1950
5-year	9311	7120
Decade	17520	13644 (78%)

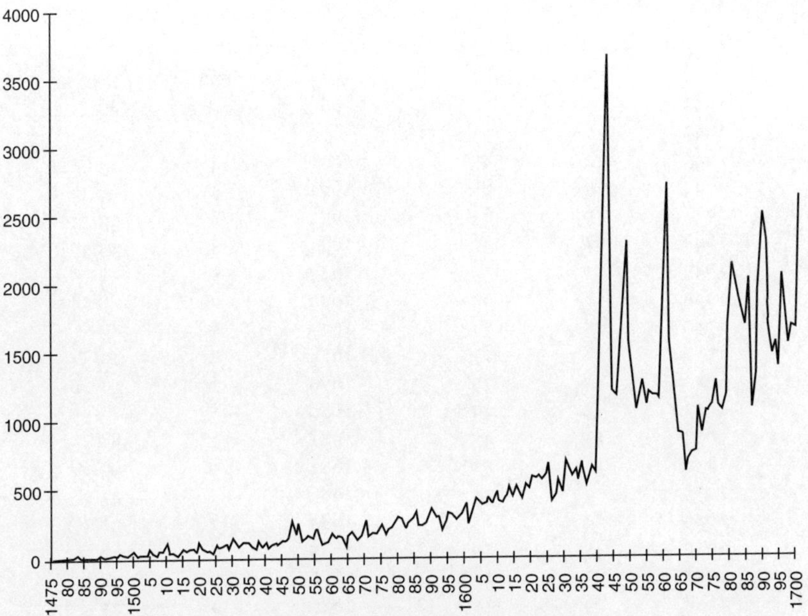

Figure A1 Annual totals 1475–1700

Table 2. *Serial publications 1641–1695: mean monthly averages*[2]

	Titles	*Issues*		*Titles*	*Issues*
1641	2	4	1669	7	49
1642	10	31	1670	5	24
1643	12	47	1671	4	23
1644	17	65	1672	5	24
1645	16	63	1673	4	23
1646	12	46	1674	5	24
1647	11	39	1675	5	24
1648	18	64	1676	6	28
1649	15	54	1677	5	19
1650	8	27	1678	4	17
1651	11	39	1679	7	31
1652	14	49	1680	8	43
1653	13	47	1681	15	81
1654	14	52	1682	15	93
1655	9	34	1683	8	43
1656	4	14	1684	7	38
1657	5	18	1685	8	38
1658	3	14	1686	7	34
1659	9	35	1687	6	25
1660	12	39	1688	7	32
1661	3	11	1689	10	47
1662	4	11	1690	9	71
1663	4	12	1691	13	54
1664	2	13	1692	15	60
1665	3	16	1693	17	62
1666	4	22	1694	11	48
1667	4	26	1695	13	82
1668	5	24			

2 Data supplied by Carolyn Nelson.

Table 3. *Serial publications: issues per week in 1649*[3]

Week	*Issues*	*Week*	*Issues*
1	9	27	16
2	12	28	15
3	7	29	18
4	10	30	17
5	10	31	15
6	11	32	16
7	11	33	17
8	10	34	16
9	11	35	16
10	10	36	14
11	10	37	15
12	11	38	13
13	12	39	10
14	13	40	8
15	15	41	5
16	17	42	5
17	19	43	6
18	19	44	5
19	19	45	6
20	21	46	4
21	20	47	4
22	20	48	4
23	17	49	3
24	18	50	6
25	19	51	6
26	14	52	6

3 Figures supplied by Carolyn Nelson.

Table 4. Term Catalogues

Subject classification of entries 1668–1709

	1668–9	1670–4	1675–9	1680–4	1685–9	1690–4	1695–9	1700–4	1705–9	Totals	
Divinity	56	398	475	742	500	762	773	825	614	5145	(30.4%)
[as % of *new* titles]	29.5%	32.4%	35.8%	39.1%	39.2%	47.7%	46%	50.5%	48.8%		41.8%
Maths	19	41	24	24	28	21	8	35	21	221	(1.3%)
History	24	104	135	224	167	196	153	146	130	1279	(7.6%)
Law	1	42	34	49	31	21	27	22	15	242	(1.4%)
Lib. Lat.	18	93	103	103	92	109	126	93	88	825	(4.9%)
Poems	14	100	132	132	103	129	116	92	88	906	(5.4%)
Physic	12	57	43	56	28	36	65	43	33	373	(2.2%)
Music	0	9	7	16	26	21	80	37	5	201	(1.2%)
Misc	41	373	364	545	347	473	331	342	263	3079	(18.2%)
Other	5	11	9	7	3	5	2	0	0	42	(0.2%)
Reprinted	77	537	526	539	482	532	708	677	477	4555	(26.9%)
Law Reprinted	0	18	22	0	0	0	0	0	0	40	(0.2%)
Totals	267	1783	1874	2437	1807	2305	2389	2312	1734	16908	

Table 5. *Translations into English 1560–1603*[5]

	Translated from				
	Latin	French	Other langs	Unknown	Totals
1560	15	1	6	2	24
1561	11	3	4	0	18
1562	7	10	1	4	22
1563	7	3	2	3	15
1564	4	4	1	0	9
1565	10	4	2	2	18
1566	8	7	5	8	28
1567	7	1	1	3	12
1568	7	6	3	4	20
1569	8	5	3	6	22
1570	9	3	8	4	24
1571	5	3	1	1	10
1572	12	2	3	0	17
1573	6	3	6	3	18
1574	9	3	13	4	29
1575	10	6	9	4	29
1576	14	7	4	4	29
1577	12	8	5	3	28
1578	12	6	6	6	30
1579	11	11	9	8	39
1580	12	9	4	7	32
1581	9	7	4	10	30
1582	10	9	6	1	26
1583	11	5	3	4	23
1584	6	3	6	3	18
1585	12	10	5	1	28
1586	7	9	5	2	23
1587	6	9	3	1	19
1588	7	7	7	6	27
1589	5	21	4	7	37
1590	11	17	6	8	42
1591	5	10	7	7	29
1592	3	15	0	5	23
1593	4	4	2	1	11
1594	3	10	6	1	20
1595	9	10	5	3	27
1596	8	4	6	1	19
1597	1	4	7	7	19
1598	7	6	17	2	32
1599	3	9	16	7	35
1600	6	3	11	4	24
1601	2	6	10	1	19
1602	4	7	10	6	27
1603	3	4	4	1	12

[5] Source: J. G. Ebel, 'A numerical survey of Elizabethan translations', *Library*, 5th ser., 22 (1967), 104–27. Ebel's totals of 43 for 1590 and 24 for 1592 are clearly slight errors in calculation.

Table 6. *Quaker publications 1652–1699*[6]

	Titles	Sheets		Titles	Sheets
1652	2	7	1676	90	460
1653	53	161	1677	63	190
1654	88	224	1678	38	299
1655	135	345	1679	59	594
1656	132	377	1680	72	343
1657	102	397	1681	72	388
1658	98	298	1682	74	336
1659	210	687	1683	92	318
1660	278	742	1684	77	304
1661	180	471	1685	64	157
1662	168	411	1686	36	134
1663	149	429	1687	45	128
1664	106	224	1688	39	75
1665	99	261	1689	49	278
1666	51	258	1690	48	125
1667	48	181	1691	43	135
1668	46	235	1692	62	200
1669	47	192	1693	39	89
1670	80	194	1694	47	265
1671	58	332	1695	45	422
1672	47	396	1696	58	157
1673	63	325	1697	41	189
1674	67	311	1698	51	249
1675	86	572	1699	62	242

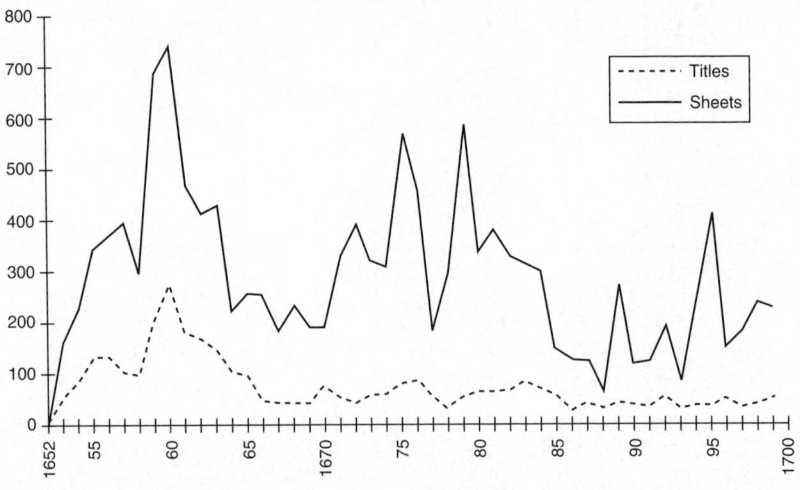

Figure A6 Quaker publications 1652–1700

6 Compiled from H. Barbour and A.O. Roberts, *Early Quaker writings 1650–1700* (Grand Rapids, Michigan, 1973), pp. 567–73. Peters (forthcoming) reconsiders these figures: see also p. 70 and n. above.

Table 7. *Analysis of published items in 1676*[7]

		% of all titles		% of all sheets
London		84		84
London first editions		56		43
Britain excluding London		12		13
Printed abroad		4		3
Formats:				
	1°	12		1
	2°	7		42
	4°	36		20
	8°	34		31
	12°	10		6
	16/24°	5		0.3
First editions		% of London titles in *Wing*		% of titles in *Term Catalogues*
Arts		9	(Poems/plays)	5.4
	History	10		7.6
	Law	5		1.4
	Religion	28	(Divinity)	30
	Science	7		?
	Other	7	(Miscellaneous)	18.2
Reprints		34		27

7 Figures taken from an unpublished analysis of the extant output dated 1676 by John Barnard.

Table 8. *Anonymous printing: 1644, 1676 and 1688*[8]
Percentages of total output

	1644	1676	1688
London printed	77	84	85
with named printer	29	29	23
no printer named	48	55	62
Britain (excl. London)	22	12	12
with named printer	16	10	8
no printer named	6	2	5
Abroad	1	4	3
with named printer	1	3	1
no printer named	<1	2	2
Total (%) items with named printer	46	42	31
Total (%) items no printer named	54	58	69

8 Derived from D. F. McKenzie's 'The economies of print', App. D, and John Barnard's unpublished analysis of 1676.

Table 9. *Freemen in the provincial book trade 1476–1695*[9]

	York	Exeter	Norwich	Bristol	Chester	Hull
1475–95	1	–	–	?	–	–
1496–1515	4	–	–	?	–	–
1516–35	4	–	–	?	–	–
1536–55	5	–	1	?	–	–
1556–75	4	1	1	?	1	–
1576–95	4	6	3	?	1	–
1596–1615	–	4	4	?	–	2
1616–35	1	3	5	?	–	2
1636–55	3	2	3	5	1	1
1656–75	9	8	5	6	3	2
1676–95	14	10	4	8	3	1
	49	34	26	19	9	8
No. of hearths 1662	(7,294)	(5,294)	(7,302)	(6,925)	(3,004)	(3,390)

9 All figures are minima. Sources: Collins 1897, 1900; Maxted (forthcoming); Millican 1934, Stoker 1981–5; Barry 1985 and unpublished, table 2; Bennett 1906; Chilton 1982, pp. 3–13; Hoskins (for number of hearths) 1984, pp. 278–9.

APPENDIX 2

Survey of printing presses, 1668 (transcription of PRO SP 29/243)[1]

D. F. McKENZIE

A Survey of the Printing Presses wth the Names & Nombers of Apprentices Officers and Workmen belonging to every perticular Presse Taken 29° Julij 1668

Att the Kings howse
Presses - 6
Compositо^{rs} - 8
o Amos Coles
x Richard Cheese
o Willm Balteum
John Sparree
x Willm Clerden
o John Milke
n John Corbett
Geo: Harvey
Pressmen - io
p Luke Norton
o Rich: Anderson
x Tho: Turner
x John Owsley
n Roger Vaughan
x Thomas Sparree
x Edw: Newcombe
x John White
x William Walker
x John Clifford

Att Mr Tylers howse
Presses - 3 & a Proofe Presse
Apprentice - i
o Richard Jon
Workmen - 6
x Willm Hughes
James Groves
o Nicholas Browne
n Willm Coltman
Willm Lichfeild
Clement Knell

Att Mr Whites house
Presses - 3
Apprentices - 3
o Isaac Lawe
x Willm White
x Franc Clarke
Workmen - 7
p Thomas Snowden
x Bernard White
o Abraham Everett
? Thomas Goodman
o Richard Hunt
r Rich: Argent
o William Wynington

Att Mr Flesshers
Presses - 5
Apprentices - 2
x Thomas Lambert
Archiball Ashburne
Workmen - i3
o Henry Lloyd
x John Richardson Senr
p John Richardson jun^{r}
x Robert Adames
Christopher Brooke
x John Watson
o Symon Heyne
x William Hill
n John Lambert
x Henry Barrow
John Croome
x Rich: Firbanke
x Rich: Jones

Att Mr Nortons
Presses - 3
Apprentices - i
William Langford
Workmen - 7
George Hopper
p Zacharie Johnson

This annotated transcript was prepared by D. F. McKenzie.

1. Twenty-nine printing houses (including the three to be 'indicted') are noted here: four more printers are omitted, the Custom House printer, Henry Brugis, John Field and Richard Hodgkinson (see Treadwell 1987, p. 151).

x John Barrow
o John Sprake
x John Cambden
John Harding
x Thomas Lambert

Att Mr Rycrofts
Presses – 4
Apprentices – 2
n William Edwards
x Nath. Sergeant
Workmen – 10
p John Harrison
x Sam: Tilbury
Steeven Lee
x Symon Chamberlayne
x Robert Battersby
Joseph Walker
Richard Meade
o John Luxford)
o Dan: Wich) not free
Willm Dowell) Stacion^{rs}

Att Mr Ratcliffs
Presses – 2
Apprentices – 2
Daniell Gregory
n Robert Daniell
Workmen – 7
Thomas Childe
p Francis Leach
x Richard Martyn
? Thom Crockett
x Ambros Hoskins
xn John Morgan
x William Cope

Att Mr Maycocks
Presses – 3
Apprentices – 3
x Robert Everingham
x Thomas Maycocke
Gabriell Brookes
Workmen 10
x Thomas Warner
Thomas Oliver
x Thomas Cooke
o Richard Berkham
o Phillipp Foxhall
o George Sparkes
Willm Macocke
Christopher Latham
? John Bayly
n William Mason

Att Mr Newcombs
Presses – 3 & a Proofe Presse
Apprentice – 1
John Joyner
Composito^{rs} – 7
x Mr Dawks Senr
p Mr Dawks Junio^{r}
Thomas James
x Thomas Hodgkin
p James Gray
x Robert Chowne
x Mathew Duckett
Pressmen – 5
x John Newby
n John Halsey
John Wever
r Geo: Croome
o Edmund Bulkeley

Att Mr Godbidds
Presses – 3
Apprentices – 2
John Playford
Richard Christmas
Workmen – 5
Anthony Izard
r Nath Thompson not free
Nich: Boyer [*not free*]
n George Horne
p Francis Leach not free

Att Mr Street^{rs}
Presses – 5
Composito^{rs} – 6
x Edw: Horton
p Willm Thomas
? Thomas Lee
x John Brent
x John Grisman
p Ben: Hicks
Pressmen – 2
? Roger Vaughan
o Charles Chamberlayne

Att Mr Milburnes
Presses – 2
Apprentices – 0
Workmen – 2
?p John Brutnell
x Richard Man

Att Mr Catterells
Presses – 2
Apprentice – 0
Composito^{rs} – 2
o Timothy Carr
?p William Dickins
Pressman
o William Hamman

Att Mrs Symons
Presses – 2
Apprentice – 1
n John Harvey
Workmen – 5
x John Warner
p John Walker
x William Hall
x Anth: Wildgos
x Tho: Westrone

Att Mr^{rs} Cotes
Presses – 3
Apprentices – 2
o Robert Higgins
x Ben Mott
Pressmen – 9
p Henry Gurney

p John: Spurrier
William Nuthead
x Matt: Morrice
x Thom: Mosse
? Rich: Balter
x Thom Almond
t Willm Wild
o Towers Castle

Att Mrs Griffins
Presses – 2
Apprentice – i
x John Dickerson
Workmen – 6
Henry Turner
x Christopher Desborowe
Edw Groves
x James Arnold
John Solden
o John Weedon not free

Att Mr Leaches
Press – i & noe more provided by Mr Graydon
Workmen – i
xn Jonath King

Att Mrs Maxwells
Presses – 2
Apprentice – o
Composito^{rs} – 3
o Robert Roberts
Clement Williams
o John Lilburne
Pressmen – 3
x Bernard Grantham
x Richard Harrice
Richard Holland

Att Mr Lillicropps
Press – i
Apprentice – i
John Whatson
Composito^{rs} – i
o Robert Ireland
Pressman
?r John Bollyn

Att Mr Redmans
Presses – 2
Apprentice – i
o Daniell Hostler
Composito^{rs} – 4
o Marmaduke Boate
x Thomas Pattingdon
o John Hearfinch
Tho: Bramston
Pressmen – 2
o Thomas Rich
o John Holland

Att Mr Cowes
Press – i

Att Mr Lloydes
Press – i

Att Mr Oakes
Presses – 2
Apprentice – o
Workmen – 2
x Rich: Dikes
o Oliver Hunt

Att Mr Purslowes
Press – i
Apprentices – o
Workman – i
o Thom: Hayley

Att Mr Johnsons
Presses – 2
Apprentice – o
Workmen – 3
o Peter Boulter
o Peter Ravishend
Dutchman
xn James Hughes not free

Mr Darby)
Mr Winter)
Mr Rawlyns)
These three Printers are to be indicted at ye next Sessions

Att Mr Crowches
Presse – i
Apprentices – o
Workman – i
William Woods

All men bound and freed unless otherwise noted

o not formally bd
x ex-London, Westminster, or Middlesex
n bd but not fd
p fd by patrimony
r fd by redemption
t translated from another Company
? identity uncertain

APPENDIX 3

Apprentices bound in the Stationers' Company and what became of them 1557–1700[1]

C. Y. FERDINAND

Year	*Bound*	*Later freed*	*Not freed*	*Freed by other means*
1557	11	3	8	15
1558	20	3	17	7
1559	20	6	14	9
1560	28	7	21	8
1561	49	12	37	9
1562	37	8	29	21
1563	21	2	19	5
1564	50	3	47	12
1565	42	3	39	8
1566	32	5	27	9
1567	27	2	25	10
1568	28	6	22	12
1569	26	10	16	5
1570	18	3	15	3
1571*	13	5	8	6
1572*	(27)	?	?	?
1573*	(37)	?	?	?
1574*	(48)	?	?	?
1575*	(33)	?	?	?

1 Detailed records for the Stationers' Company 22 July 1571 – 20 July 1576 are missing. The figures in parentheses are based on Arber's deductions and are for years from July to July, not calendar years. Other figures are based on calendar years.

Year	Bound	Later freed	Not freed	Freed by other means
1576*	(55)	?	?	?
1577	46	20	26	3
1578	32	15	17	12
1579	22	12	10	11
1580	37	15	22	19
1581	44	17	27	12
1582	23	8	15	8
1583	26	9	17	16
1584	46	15	31	22
1585	29	11	18	9
1586	26	9	17	10
1587	24	17	7	2
1588	20	11	9	4
1589	55	16	39	8
1590	23	12	11	1
1591	26	15	11	3
1592	27	13	14	2
1593	26	8	18	3
1594	62	33	29	3
1595	40	9	31	2
1596	34	7	27	3
1597	31	15	16	8
1598	40	19	21	4
1599	38	16	22	6
1600	44	20	24	16
1601	45	20	25	3
1602	58	22	36	8
1603	32	14	18	5
1604	85	41	44	13
1605	57	22	35	1
1606	45	22	23	7
1607	69	32	37	11

1608	43	21	22	4
1609	45	25	20	1
1610	76	36	40	2
1611	69	41	28	5
1612	51	29	22	6
1613	56	21	35	7
1614	54	26	28	13
1615	53	25	28	7
1616	51	22	29	4
1617	53	25	28	3
1618	58	21	37	7
1619	57	27	30	6
1620	63	31	32	5
1621	46	17	29	12
1622	46	19	27	6
1623	51	19	32	3
1624	64	21	43	1
1625	25	10	15	–
1626	100	62	38	8
1627	69	46	23	5
1628	68	40	28	7
1629	77	45	32	2
1630	60	37	23	5
1631	63	38	25	14
1632	63	26	37	8
1633	59	28	31	6
1634	78	46	32	9
1635	74	33	41	4
1636	34	12	22	4
1637	82	29	53	9
1638	105	44	61	7
1639	43	15	28	6
1640	63	23	40	4
1641	77	39	38	8
1642	49	21	28	5

Year	Bound	Later freed	Not freed	Freed by other means
1643	20	11	9	1
1644	34	11	23	2
1645	62	35	27	7
1646	105	60	45	5
1647	95	48	47	6
1648	64	27	37	13
1649	47	22	25	6
1650	69	37	32	16
1651	51	30	21	9
1652	68	32	36	9
1653	56	28	28	9
1654	95	52	43	4
1655	97	50	47	12
1656	105	58	47	8
1657	88	35	53	8
1658	70	25	45	6
1659	56	30	26	5
1660	52	23	29	6
1661	64	28	36	7
1662	46	25	21	12
1663	76	28	48	9
1664	47	13	34	11
1665	21	7	14	8
1666	48	25	23	3
1667	45	19	26	7
1668	67	28	39	4
1669	104	50	54	6
1670	89	42	47	6
1671	92	47	45	15
1672	64	29	35	12
1673	48	21	27	7
1674	66	36	30	14
1675	69	30	39	15

1676	69	24	45	17
1677	78	34	44	11
1678	68	29	39	8
1679	67	39	28	11
1680	86	40	46	17
1681	78	40	38	7
1682	94	48	46	14
1683	86	43	43	13
1684	73	31	42	23
1685	42	13	29	10
1686	52	13	39	9
1687	70	28	42	11
1688	57	28	29	17
1689	65	33	32	12
1690	55	17	38	10
1691	69	22	47	9
1692	69	27	42	14
1693	51	21	30	12
1694	54	29	25	3
1695	52	24	28	9
1696	62	32	30	3
1697	46	25	21	11
1698	63	33	30	9
1699	71	38	33	5
1700	69	34	35	6

Abbreviations

APC,	*Acts of the Privy Council, 1542–1604*, new series, 32 vols., London, 1890–1907
Arber	Arber, E. (ed.), *A transcript of the registers of the Company of Stationers of London, 1554–1640*, 5 vols., London 1875–94; rpt. Gloucester, MA, 1967
ASE	*Anglo-Saxon England*
BC	*Book Collector*
Beale	Beale, J. H., *A bibliography of early English law books*, Cambridge, MA, 1926
BL	British Library, London
BLC	*British Library catalogue of printed books*
BLJ	*British Library Journal*
BLR	*Bodleian Library Record*
Bodleian	Bodleian Library, Oxford
BQR	*Bodleian Quarterly Record*
BSANZ	Bibliographical Society of Australia and New Zealand
BSANZB	*Bibliographical Society of Australia and New Zealand Bulletin*
CBS	Cambridge Bibliographical Society
CELMCUL	Baker, J. H., *A catalogue of English legal manuscripts in Cambridge University Library*, Woodbridge and Rochester, NY, 1996.
CHB	*Cambridge History of the Bible*, Cambridge: III. Greenslade, S. L. (ed.), *The West from the Reformation to the present day*, 1963
CJ	*Journal of the House of Commons*
CLRO	City of London Record Office
CRS	Catholic Record Society
CSP	*Calendar of State Papers*
CSPD	*Calendar of State Papers Domestic*
CUL	Cambridge University Library
DMH	Darlow, T.H. and Moule, H.F., rev. Herbert, A.S., *Historical catalogue of printed editions of the English Bible 1525–1961*, London, 1968
DNB	*Dictionary of National Biography*
EcHR	*Economic History Review*
EHR	*English Historical Review*
ELH	*English Literary History*
ELM	Baker, J. H. *English legal manuscripts*, 2 vols., Zug, 1975–8

ELMUSA	Baker, J.H., *English legal manuscripts in the United States of America:* part I: *Medieval and Renaissance*, London, 1985
ELR	*English Literary Renaissance*
EMS	*English Manuscript Studies*
E & R	*A transcript of the registers of the Company of Stationers of London, 1641–1708*, 3 vols., ed. G.E.B. Eyre and C.R. Rivington, London, 1913–14
FHL	Friends' House Library
HLB	*Harvard Library Bulletin*
HLQ	*Huntington Library Quarterly*
HMC	Historical Manuscripts Commission
HP	Hartlib Papers, Sheffield University Library (for the CD-ROM version, see Greengrass and Leslie 1999)
HUO I-IV	*The History of the University of Oxford*, Oxford: I. Catto, J.I. (ed.), *The early schools*, 1984; II. Catto, J.I. and Evans, T.A.R. (eds.), *Late medieval Oxford*, 1992; III. McConica, J.K. (ed.), *The collegiate University*, 1986; IV. Tyacke, N. (ed.), *Seventeenth-century Oxford*, 1997
IELM	*Index of English Literary Manuscripts*, London and New York: I. Beal, P. (comp.), pt 1, *1450–1625 Andrewes-Donne*, 1980; pt 2, *1450–1625 Douglas-Wyatt*, 1980; II. Beal, P. (comp.), pt 1, *1625–1700 Behn-King*, 1987; pt 2, *1625–1700 Lee-Wycherley*, 1993
ITS	Irish Text Society
JEH	*Journal of Ecclesiastical History*
JFHS	*Journal of Friends' House*
JPHS	*Journal of the Printing Historical Society*
JWCI	*Journal of the Warburg and Courtauld Institute.*
Library	*The Library. Transactions of the Bibliographical Society*
MLN	*Modern Language Notes*
MLQ	*Modern Language Quarterly*
MLR	*Modern Language Review*
MP	*Modern Philology*
MQ	*Milton Quarterly*
MS	*Milton Studies*
N& Q	*Notes and Queries*
N& S	Nelson, C., and Seccombe, M., *British newspapers and periodicals, 1641–1700: a short-title catalogue of serials printed in England, scotland, Ireland and British America*, New York, 1987
NCBEL	*The new Cambridge bibliography of English literature*, Watson, G. (ed.), Cambridge: I. *600–1660*, 1974; II. *1660–1800*, 1971
OBS	Oxford Bibliographical Society
PBSA	*Papers of the Bibliographical Society of America*
PH	*Publishing History*
PLRE	Fehrenbach, R. and Leedham-Green, E.S. (eds.), *Private libraries in Renaissance England. A collection and catalogue of Tudor and early Stuart book-lists*, 5 vols. to date, 1992–98
P-MA	Plantin-Moretus Archives

PMLA	*Publications of the Modern Language Association of America*
POAS (Yale)	Lord, G. DeF (gen. ed.), *Poems of affairs of state: Augustan satirical verse, 1660–1714*, 7 vols., New Haven, CT
PRO	Public Record Office
RMA	Royal Musical Society
RenQ	*Renaissance Quarterly*
RES	*Review of English Studies*
SB	*Studies in Bibliography*
SC	Stationers' Company
SP	*Studies in Philology*
SRP	*Stuart Royal Proclamations*, Larkin, J. F. (ed.), 2 vols., Oxford 1983
STC	*A short-title catalogue of books printed in England, Scotland, and Ireland, and of English books printed abroad, 1475–1640, first compiled by A. W. Pollard and G. R. Redgrave. Second Edition, revised and enlarged, begun by W. A. Jackson and F. S. Ferguson, completed by Katharine F. Pantzer, with a chronological index by Philip R. Rider*, 3 vols., London 1976–91
STS	Scottish Text Society
TC	*Term Catalogues, 1668–1709 A. D.; with a number for Easter Term, 1711 A.D.*, Arber, E. (ed.) 3 vols., London, 1903–6
TCBS	*Transactions of the Cambridge Bibliographical Society*
TCD	Trinity College, Dublin
TRP	Hughes, P. L. and Larkin, J. F. (eds.), *Tudor Royal Proclamations*, 3 vols., New Haven, CT, 1964–9
Wing	Wing D. (comp.) *A short-title catalogue of books printed in England, Scotland, Ireland, Wales and British America and of English books printed in other countries 1641–1700*, 2nd edn, rev. and ed. Crist, T., Morrison, J. J., Nelson, C.W. *et al.*, New York, 1988–98 (CD-ROM published 1998–)

Bibliography

Alblas, J. B. H. 1987 *Johannes Brekholt (1656–1693). The first Dutch publisher of John Bunyan and other English writers: with a descriptive bibliography*, Nieuwkoop.

Alden, J. 1952 'Pills and publishing: some notes on the English book trade', *Library*, 5th ser., 7, 21–37.

Aldis, H. G., Bowes, L., Dix, E. R. *et al.* 1910 *A dictionary of printers and booksellers in England, Scotland and Ireland and of foreign printers of English books 1557–1640*, London.

Alexander, A. 1995 'The imperialist space of Elizabethan mathematics', *Studies in History and Philosophy of Science*, 26, 559–91.

Allen, R. C. (ed.) 1954 'The sources of Lily's Latin Grammar', *Library*, 5th ser., 9, 85–100.

Allison, A. F. and Rogers, D. M. (eds.) 1989–94 *The contemporary printed literature of the English Counter-Reformation between 1558 and 1640: an annotated catalogue*, vol. I. (with the collaboration of W. Lottes), *Works in languages other than English*, vol. II (with addenda and corrigenda to vol. I) *Works in English*, Aldershot. This supersedes A. F. Allison and D. M . Rogers (eds.) *A catalogue of Catholic books in England 1558–1640*, first published in *Biographical Studies 1534–1829*, 3 (1955–6). A sizeable selection of the publications listed by Allison and Rogers has been reprinted in facsimile in *English Recusant literature*, 394 volumes selected and edited by D. M. Rogers, London, 1958–79.

Almagor, J. 1989 *Pierre Des Maizeaux (1673–1745), journalist and English correspondent for Franco-Dutch periodicals, 1700–1720*, Amsterdam/Maarssen.

Alston, R. C. (ed.) 1996 *Order and connexion: studies in bibliography and book history*, Woodbridge.

Amory, H. 1983 'Things unattempted yet: a bibliography of the first edition of *Paradise lost*', *BC*, 32, 41–66.

1993 'Under the exchange: the unprofitable business of Michael Perry, a seventeenth-century Boston bookseller', *Proceedings of the American Antiquarian Society*, 103, 31–60.

1996 'The trout and the milk: an ethnobibliographical talk', *HLB*, ns, 7, 50–65.

1997 'A Bible and other books: enumerating the copies in seventeenth-century Essex county', in Alston 1996, pp. 17–37.

Amory, H. and Hall, D. (eds.) 2000 *The history of the book in America: I. The colonial book in the Atlantic world*, Cambridge and Worcester, MA.

Anders, H. 1936 'The Elizabethan ABC with the Catechism', *Library*, 4th ser., 16, 32–48.

Andrews J. H. 1987 'Sir William Petty: a tercentenary reassessment', *Map Collector*, 41, 34–9.

Andrews, K. R. 1984 *Trade, plunder and settlement: maritime enterprise and the genesis of the British Empire, 1480–1630*, Cambridge.

Andrews, K. R., Canny, N., and Hair, P. E. H. (eds.) 1978 *The Westward enterprise: English activities in Ireland, the Atlantic, and America 1480–1650*, Liverpool.

Arber, E. (ed.), 1885 *The first three English books on America, 1511–1555 A.D.*, Birmingham.

Armitage, D., Himy, A. and Skinner, Q. (eds.) 1995 *Milton and Republicanism*, Cambridge.

Armstrong, E. 1954 *Robert Estienne, royal printer*, Cambridge.

1979 'English purchases of printed books from the Continent', *EHR*, 94, 268–90.

Ascoli, G. 1930 *La Grande-Bretagne devant l'opinion française au xviie siècle*, 2 vols., Paris.

Ashbee, A. and Holman, P. (eds.) 1996 *John Jenkins and his time: studies in English consort music*, Oxford.

Astbury, R. 1978 'The renewal of the Licensing Act in 1693 and its lapse in 1695', *Library*, 5th ser., 33, 296–322.

Aston, M. 1973 'English ruins and English history: the dissolution and the sense of the past', *JWCI*, 36, 231–55.

Atkinson, W. A. 1926 'The printing of Coke's Institutes', *Law Times*, 162, 435.

Aubrey, J. 1982 *Brief lives* (ed.) R. Barber, Woodbridge.

Bachrach, A. G. H. 1962 *Sir Constantine Huygens and Britain: 1596–1687. A pattern of cultural exchange*, Leiden.

Baillie, W. M. 1997 'Printing Bibles in the Interregnum: *The case of William Bentley* and *A short answer*', *PBSA*, 91, 65–91.

Bailyn, B. 1955 *The New England merchants in the seventeenth century*, Cambridge, MA.

Baker, J. H. 2001 *Readers and reading in the Inns of Court and Chancery*, London.

Balayé, S. 1988 *La Bibliothèque Nationale des origines à 1800*, Geneva.

Bald, R. C. 1942 'Early copyright litigation and its bibliographical interest', *PBSA*, 36, 81–96.

Bale, J. (ed.) 1549 *The laboryouse journey & serche of Johan Leylande for Englandes antiquitees*, London.

Bangs, J. D. 1985 *The auction catalogue of the library of Hugh Goodyear, English reformed minister at Leiden*, Utrecht.

Bank of England 2001 'Equivalent contemporary values of the pound: A historical series', *Book Trade History Group Newsletter*, 41, 8–9.

Barash, C. 1996 *English women's poetry, 1649–1714*, Oxford.

Barber, G. 1976 'Books from the Old World and for the New: the British international trade in books in the eighteenth century', *Studies on Voltaire and the Eighteenth Century*, 151, 185–224.

Barber, P. 1983 'A Tudor mystery: Laurence Nowell's map of England and Ireland', *Map Collector*, 22, 16–21.

Barberi, F. 1965 'Libri e stampatoria nella Roma dei papi', *Studi Romani*, 13, 432–56.

Barbour, H. and Roberts, A. (eds.) 1973 *Early Quaker writings, 1650–1700*, Grand Rapids, MI.

Barker, N. 1978 *The Oxford University Press and the spread of learning, 1478–1978: an illustrated history*, Oxford.

Barnard, J. 1963 'Dryden, Tonson, and subscriptions for the 1697 *Virgil*', *PBSA*, 57, 129–51.

1992 'A Puritan controversialist and his books: the will of Alexander Cooke (1564–1632)', *PBSA*, 86, 82–6.

1994 'Some features of the Stationers' Company and its stock in 1676/7', *PH*, 36, 5–38.

1998 'The large- and small-paper copies of Dryden's *The works of Virgil (1697)*: Jacob Tonson's investment and the example of *Paradise lost (1688)*', *PBSA*, 92, 259–71.

1999a 'The Stationers' Stock 1663/4 to 1705/6: Psalms, psalters, primers and ABCs', *Library*, 6th ser., 21, 369–75.

1999b 'The survival and loss rates of Psalms, ABCs, psalters and primers from the Stationers' Stock, 1660–1700', *Library*, 6th ser., 21, 148–50.

2000 'Dryden, Tonson and the patrons of *The works of Virgil (1697)*, in P. Hammond and D. Hopkinson (eds.), *John Dryden: tercentenary essays*, Oxford, pp. 174–239.

2001 'London publishing 1640–1660: crisis, continuity and innovation', *Book History*, 4, 1–16.

Barnard, J. and Bell, M. 1991 'The inventory of Henry Bynneman (1583): a preliminary survey', *PH*, 29, 5–46.

1994 *The early seventeenth-century York book trade and John Foster's inventory of 1616*, Proceedings of the Leeds Philosophical and Literary Society, Literary and Historical Section, 24, pt 2, Leeds.

Barry, J. (unpublished) 'Impact of the printed word: Bristol 1640–1775', unpublished paper.

1985 'The cultural life of Bristol 1640–1775', unpub. D.Phil. thesis, University of Oxford.

1991 'The press and politics of culture in Bristol 1660–1775', in J. Black and J. Gregory (eds.), *Culture, politics and society in Britain 1660–1800*, Manchester, pp. 49–81.

Bartholomew, A. T. 1908 *Richard Bentley, D. D.; a bibliography*, Cambridge.

Bartholomew A. T. and Gordon, C. 1910 'On the library at King Edward VI School, Bury St Edmunds', *Library*, 3rd ser., 1, 1–27.

Bataillon, L. J., Guyot, B. G. and Rouse, R. H. (eds.) 1988 *La production du livre universitaire au moyen âge: exemplar et pecia. Actes du symposium tenu au Collegio San Bonaventura de Grottaferrata*, Paris.

Bates, A. C. 1900 *Connecticut statute laws: a bibliographical list of editions of Connecticut laws from the earliest issues to 1836*, Hartford, CT.

Bates, E. S. 1911 *Touring in 1600*, Boston, MA.

Bath, M. 1994 *Speaking pictures: English emblem books and renaissance culture*, London.

Batten, J. M. 1944 *John Dury: advocate of Christian reunion*, Chicago.

Baxter, R. 1985 *The autobiography of Richard Baxter*, ed. N. H. Keeble, London.

Beal, P. 1993 '"Notions in garrison": the seventeenth century commonplace book', in Speed Hill 1993, pp. 133–47.

1997 '"My books are the great joy of my life": Sir William Boothby, seventeenth-century bibliophile', *BC*, 46, 350–78.

1998 *In praise of scribes: manuscripts and their makers in seventeenth-century England*, Oxford.

Beale, J. H. 1926 *A bibliography of early English law books*, Cambridge, MA.

Beattie, W. (ed.) 1950 *The Chepman and Myllar prints: a facsimile with a bibliographical note*, Edinburgh.

Bell, D. N. 1994 *What nuns read: books and libraries in medieval English nunneries*, Kalamazoo, MI.

Bell, M. 1987 'Women publishers of puritan literature in the mid-seventeenth century: three case studies', unpub. Ph. D. thesis, University of Loughborough.

1988 'Mary Westwood, Quaker publisher', *PH*, 23, 5–66.

1989 'Hannah Allen and the development of a Puritan publishing business, 1646–51', *PH*, 26, 5–66.

1992 'Elizabeth Calvert and the "Confederates"', *PH*, 32, 5–49.

1994a 'Entrance in the Stationers' Register', *Library*, 6th ser., 16, 50–4.

1994b '"Her usual practices": the later career of Elizabeth Calvert, 1664–75', *PH*, 35, 5–64.

1996 'Women in the English book trade 1557–1700', *Leipziger Jahrbuch zur Buchgeschichichte* 6, 13–45.

Bell, M. and Barnard, J. 1992 'Provisional count of STC titles 1475–1648', *PH*, 31, 49–55.

1998 'Provisional count of Wing titles 1641–1700', *PH*, 44, 89–97.

Bell, M. and Parfitt, G. A. E. (forthcoming) 'Wheatcroft's books'.

Bell, M., Parfitt, G. A. E. and Shepherd, S. 1990 *A biographical dictionary of women writers 1580–1720*, Hemel Hempstead.

Bellany, A. 1993 'Libellous politics in early Stuart England', in K. Sharpe and P. Lake (eds.), *Culture and politics in early Stuart England*, Stanford, pp. 285–309.

Bennett, H. S. 1952 *English books & readers 1475 to 1557: being a study in the history of the book trade from Caxton to the incorporation of the Stationers' Company*, Cambridge.

1965 *English books & readers 1558 to 1603: being a study of the book trade in the reign of Elizabeth I*, Cambridge.

1969 *English books & readers 1475 to 1557: being a study of the book trade from Caxton to the incorporation of the Stationers' Company*, 2nd edn, Cambridge.

1970 *English books & readers 1603 to 1640: being a study in the history of the book trade in the reigns of James I and Charles I*, Cambridge.

Bennett, J. A. 1982 *The mathematical science of Christopher Wren*, Cambridge.

1986 'The mechanics' philosophy and the mechanical philosophy', *History of Science*, 24, 1–28.

1991 'The challenge of practical mathematics', in S. Pumfrey, P. L. Rossi and M. Slawinski (eds.), *Science, culture, and popular belief in Renaissance Europe*, Manchester, pp. 176–90.

Bennett, J. A. and Mandelbrote, S. 1998 *The garden, the ark, the tower, the temple. Biblical metaphors of knowledge in early modern Europe*, Oxford.

Bennett, J. H. E. (ed.) 1906 *The Rolls of the City of Chester, Part I . . . 1392–1700*, Record Society for Lancashire and Cheshire, 51.

Bennett, K. 1999 'John Aubrey, Joseph Barnes's print-shop and a sham newsletter', *Library*, 6th ser., 21, 50–8.

Bennett, S. 1988 'Jacob Tonson an early editor of *Paradise Lost?*', *Library*, 6th ser., 10, 247–52.

Bentley, G. E. 1943, 'John Cotgrave's *English treasury of wit and language* and the Elizabethan drama', *SP*, 40, 186–203.

1965 *Shakespeare and Jonson: their reputations in the seventeenth century compared*, Chicago and London.

Bevan, J. 1983 'Seventeenth-century students and their books', in G. Donaldson (ed), *Four centuries of Edinburgh University life*, Edinburgh, pp. 16–27.

Biagioli, M. 1990 'Galileo's system of patronage', *History of Science*, 28, 1–62.

1993 *Galileo, courtier: the practice of science in the culture of absolutism*, Chicago.

Bidwell, J. 1998 'Printers' supplies and capitalization', in Amory and Hall 2000, pp. 163–83.

Bill, G. 1966 'Lambeth Palace library', *Library*, 5th ser., 21, 192–206.

Binns, J. W. 1990 *Intellectual cutlure in Elizabethan and Jacobean England: the Latin writings of the age*, Leeds.

Birch, T. 1756–7 (ed.), *The history of the Royal Society of London for improving of natural knowledge*, 4 vols., London.

Birkby, A. E. 1977 *Suffolk parochial libraries: a catalogue*, London.

Birrell, T. A. 1986 *English monarchs and their books: from Henry VII to Charles II*, London.

1994 'English Counter-Reformation book culture', *Recusant History*, 22, 113–22.

Black, J. 1997 'The rhetoric of reaction: the Martin Marprelate tracts (1588–9), Anti-Martinism, and the uses of print in early modern England', *Sixteenth-Century Journal*, 28, 707–25.

Black, M. H. 1961 'The Evolution of the book-form: the octavo Bible from manuscript to the Geneva Version', *Library*, 5th ser., 16, 15–28.

1963 'The printed Bible', *CHB*, pp. 408–75.

Blades, W. 1890 *Books in chains*, London.

Blagden, C. 1953 'The genesis of the *Term Catalogues*', *Library*, 5th ser., 8, 30–5.

1954 'Notes on the ballad market in the second half of the seventeenth century', *SB*, 6, 161–80.

1957 'The English Stock of the Stationers' Company in the time of the Stuarts', *Library*, 5th ser., 12, 167–86.

1958a 'Book trade control in 1566', *Library*, 5th ser., 13, 287–92.

1958b 'The distribution of almanacks in the second half of the seventeenth century', *SB* 11, 107–16.

1958c 'The Stationers' Company in the Civil War period', *Library*, 5th ser., 13, 1–17.

1960 *The Stationers' Company: a history 1403–1959*, London.

Blair, A. 1997 *The theater of nature: Jean Bodin and Renaissance science*, Princeton, NJ.

Bland, M. 1999 'The London book-trade in 1600', in D. S. Kastan (ed.), *A companion to Shakespeare*, Oxford, pp. 450–63.

Blatchly, J. 1989 *The Town Library of Ipswich: provided for the use of town preachers in 1599: a history and catalogue*, Woodbridge.

Blayney, P. M. W. 1990 *The bookshops in Paul's Cross Churchyard*, Occassional Papers of the Bibliographical Society, London.

1991 *The First Folio of Shakespeare*, Washington DC.

1997a 'The publication of playbooks', in J. D. Cox and D. S. Kastan (eds.) *A new history of early English drama*, New York, pp. 383–422.

1997b 'William Cecil and the Stationers', in Myers and Harris 1997, pp. 11–34.

Blekastad, M. 1969 *Comenius. Versuch eines Umrisses von Levben, Werk und Schicksal des Jan Amos Komesky*, Oslo-Prague.

Blom, J. M. 1982 *The Post-Tridentine English Primer*, CRS Monograph Series, 3.

Blum, A. 1987 'The author's authority: *Areopagitica* and the labour of licensing', in M. Nyquist, and M. W. Ferguson (eds.), *Re-membering Milton: essays on the texts and traditions*, London, pp. 74–96.

Bodley, Sir T. 1926 *Letters of Sir Thomas Bodley to Thomas James, first Keeper of the Bodleian Library*, ed. and introd. by G. W. Wheeler, Oxford.

1926–8 'Letters of Sir Thomas Bodley to the University of Oxford, 1598–1611', *BQR*, 5, 46–50, 72–6, 127–30, 153–61.

Bögels, T. S. J. G. 1992 *Govert Basson, printer, bookseller, publisher. Leiden 1612–1630*, Bibliotheca bibliographica neerlandica, 29, Nieuwkoop.

Bond, W. H. and Amory, H. (eds.) 1996 *The printed catalogues of Harvard College Library, 1723–1790*, Boston, MA.

Bonnant, G. 1999 'La librairie genevoise en Grande-Bretagne jusqu'à la fin du xviiie siècle', in G. Bonnant, *Le livre genevois sous l'Ancien Régime*, Geneva, pp. 239–88.

Boon, G. C. 1973 *Welsh tokens of the seventeenth century*, Cardiff.

Bosanquet, E. 1917 *English printed almanacs and prognostications. A bibliographical history to the year 1600*, London.

1930 'English seventeenth-century almanacs', *Library*, 4th ser., 10, 361–97.

1937–8 'Notes on further addenda to English printed almanacs and Prognostications to 1600', *Library*, 4th ser., 18, 39–66.

Bossy, J. 1985 *Christianity in the West 1400–1700*, Oxford.

Bots, Hans 1984 'Jean Leclerc as journalist of the *Bibliothèques*. His contribution to the spread of English learning on the European Continent', in G. A. M. Janssens and F. G. A. M. Aarts (eds.), *Studies in seventeenth-century English literature, history and bibliography. Festschrift for Professor T. A. Birrell on the occasion of his sixtieth birthday*, Amsterdam, pp. 53–66.

Boulton, J. 1987 *Neighbourhood and society: a London suburb in the seventeenth century*, Cambridge.

Bowen, D. J. 1981 'Y cywyddwyr a'r dirywiad', *Bulletin of the Board of Celtic Studies*, 29, 453–96.

Bowen, G. 1952 'Ateb i *Athravaeth Gristnogavl* Morys Clynnog', *National Library of Wales Journal*, 7, 388.

1962 'Llyfrgell Coleg Sant Ffrancis Xavier, Y Cwm, Llanrhyddol', *Journal of the Welsh Bibliographical Society* 9, 111–32.

1997 'Roman Catholic prose and its background', in R. G. Gruffydd (ed.), *A guide to Welsh Literature c. 1530–1700*, Cardiff, pp. 210–40.

Boyer, S. and Wainwright, J. 1995 'From Barnard to Purcell: the copying activities of Stephen Bing', *Early Music*, 2, 620–48.

Boyle, R. 1655 'An epistolical discourse . . . inviting all true lovers of vertue and mankind, to a free and generous communication of their secrets and receits in physick', in S. Hartlib, *Chymical, medicinal, and chyrurgical addresses made to Samuel Hartlib, Esq.*, London, pp. 113–50.

Bracken, J. K. and Silver, J. (eds.) (forthcoming) *British literary publishers before 1820. Vol. I: 1475–1700.*

Braddick, M. J. and Greengrass, M. (eds.) 1996 *The letters of Sir Cheney Culpeper (1641–1657), seventeenth-century political and financial papers*, Camden Miscellany 33, Camden Society 5th ser., 7, pp. 105–402.

Bradford, C. A. 1934 *Nicasius Yetsweirt, secretary for the French tongue*, London.

Bradley, D. 1992 *From text to performance in the Elizabethan theatre: preparing the play for the stage*, Cambridge.

Brady, J. and Herendeen, W. H. (eds.) 1991 *Ben Jonson's 1616 folio*, Newark, NJ.

Brennan, M. 1988 *Literary patronage in the English Renaissance: the Pembroke family*, London.

Brennan, M. and Hammond, P. 1995 'The Badminton Manuscript: a new miscellany of Restoration verse', *EMS*, 5, 171–207.

Brett, C. and Carley, J. P. 1990 Introduction to *Index Britanniae scriptorum: John Bale's Index of British and other writers*, ed. R. L. Poole, and M. Bateson, Cambridge.

Brett, P. 1964 'Edward Paston (1550–1630): a Norfolk gentleman and his musical collection', *TCBS*, 4, 51–69.

Brewer, J. and Porter, R. (eds.) 1993 *Consumption and the world of goods*, London.
Bridenbaugh, C. 1938 *Cities in the wilderness: the first century of urban life in America, 1625–1742*, New York, NY.
Briels, J. G. C. A. 1974 *Zuidnederlandse boekdrukkers en boekverkopers*, Nieuwkoop.
Brooks, H. F. 1936 'A bibliography of John Oldham', *OBS Proceedings and Papers*, 5, 5–36.
Brown, C. (ed.) 1993 *Patronage, politics and literary traditions in England, 1551–1658*, Detroit.
Brown, N. P. 1989 'Paperchase: the dissemination of Catholic texts in Elizabethan England', *EMS*, 1, 120–43.
Browning, M. [c. 1685], *Catalogue of theological, historical and physical books, with other miscellanies; being a part of the books of Mercy Browning, Joseph Brownings widdow, at her shop, at the corner of the Exchange, in Amsterdam*, n.pl. [Amsterdam]. Copy BL, shelf-mark sc 11.
Bruce, F. F. 1961 *The English Bible: a history of translations*, London.
Bruster, D. 2000 'The structural transformation of print in late Elizabethan England', in A. F. Marotti and M. D. Bristol (eds.), *Print, manuscript, & performance: the changing relations of the media in early modern England*, Columbus, OH, pp. 49–89.
Burden, P. D. 1996 *The mapping of North America: a list of printed maps 1511–1670*, Rickmansworth.
Burdett-Jones, M. T. 1998 'Early Welsh dictionaries', in Jones and Rees 1998, pp. 75–81.
Burke, V. 1997 'Women and early seventeenth-century manuscript culture: four miscellanies', *The Seventeenth Century*, 12, 135–50.
Burt, R. 1993 *Licensed by authority: Ben Jonson and the discourses of censorship*, Ithaca and London.
Butterworth, C. 1949 'Early primers for the use of children', *PBSA*, 43, 374–382.
Buxton, J. 1954 *Sir Philip Sidney and the English Renaissance*, London.
Byford, M. 1988 'The price of Protestantism: assessing the impact of religious change in Elizabethan Essex', unpub. D.Phil. thesis, University of Oxford.
Byrom, H. J. 1928 'Richard Tottell – his life and work', *Library*, 4th ser., 8, 199–232.
Caldwell, P. 1983 *The Puritan conversion narrative*, Cambridge.
Caldwell, R. A. 1943 'Joseph Holand, collector and antiquary', *MP*, 40, 295–301.
Calendar 1926 *Calendar of Wynn (of Gwydir) Papers 1515–1690 in the National Library of Wales and elsewhere*, Aberystwyth.
Calhoun, T. O. and Gravell, T. L. 1993 'Paper and printing in Ben Jonson's *Sejanus* (1605)', *PBSA*, 87, 13–64.
Cameron, W. J. 1957 'Miscellany poems 1684–1716', unpub. Ph.D. thesis, University of Reading.
1964 *The Company of White-Paper-Makers of England, 1686–1696*, Auckland (Bulletin 68, Economic History Series 1).
Campbell, G., Corns, T. N., Hale, J. K., Holmes, D., and Tweedie, F., 1997 'The provenance of *De doctrina Christiana*', *MQ*, 31, 67–121.
Campbell, T. 1973 'The Drapers' Company and its school of seventeenth century chartmakers', in Wallis and Tyacke 1973, pp. 81–106.
1987 *The earliest printed maps 1472–1500*, London.
Canny, N. and Low, A. (eds.) 1998 The Oxford History of the English Empire: I. *The origins of Empire: British overseas enterprise to the close of the seventeenth century*, Oxford.
Capp, B. 1979 *English almanacs 1500–1800: astrology and the popular press*, London.

Carey, J. W. 1992 *Communication as culture*, London.

Carley, J. P. 1994 'More Pre-Conquest manuscripts from Glastonbury Abbey', *ASE*, 23, 265–81.

1997a 'Sir Thomas Bodley's Library and its acquisitions: an edition of the Nottingham benefaction of 1604', in Carley and Tite 1997, pp. 357–86.

1997b 'William Rishanger's Chronicles and history writing at St. Albans', in J. Brown and W. P. Stoneman (eds.), *A distinct voice. Medieval studies in honor of Leonard E. Boyle, O.P.*, Notre Dame, pp. 71–102.

Carley, J. P. and Tite, C. G. C. 1992 'Sir Robert Cotton as collector of manuscripts', *Library*, 6th ser., 14, 94–99.

Carley, J. P. and Tite, C. G. C. (eds.) 1997 *Books and collectors 1200–1700*, London.

Carlson, D. R. 1992 *English humanist books: writers and patrons, manuscript and print, 1475–1525*, Toronto.

Carlson, L. H. 1981 *Martin Marprelate, Gentleman: Master Job Throkmorton laid open in his colors*, San Marino.

Carlson, N. E. 1966 'Wither and the Stationers', *SB*, 18, 210–15.

Carruthers, S. W. 1957 *Three centuries of the Westminster Shorter Catechism*, Fredericton, NB.

Carter, H. 1967 *Sixteenth-century French typefounders: the Le Bé memorandum*, ed. H. Carter, Paris.

1969 *A view of early typography*, Oxford.

1975 *A history of the Oxford University Press, Volume I to the year 1780*, Oxford.

Carter, H. and Buday, G. 1975 'Stereotyping by Joseph Athias: the evidence of Nicholas Kis', *Quaerendo* 5, 312–20.

Carter, P. 1998 'Barking Abbey and the library of William Pownsett: a bibliographical conundrum', *TCBS*, 11, 263–71.

Cavazza, M. 1980 'Bologna and the Royal Society in the seventeenth century', *Notes and Records of the Royal Society of London*, 35 (1980), 105–23.

Cave, R. 1987 *Printing and the booktrade in the West Indies*, London.

Chan, M. 1979 'John Hilton's manuscript British Library Add. MS 11608', *Music & Letters*, 60, 440–5.

1990 'A mid-seventeenth-century music meeting and Playford's publishing', in J. Caldwell, E. Olleson and S. Wollenberg (eds.), *The well enchanting skill: music, poetry and drama in the culture of the Renaissance, essays in honour of F. W. Sternfeld*, Oxford, pp. 231–44.

Chaney, E. 1985 *The Grand Tour and the Great Rebellion*, Geneva.

1988 'Quo Vadis? Travel as education and the impact of Italy in the sixteenth century', *Proceedings of the 1987 Annual Conference of the History of Education Society of Great Britain*, London, 1–28.

Chapman, R. W. 1927 'An inventory of paper 1674', *Library*, 4th ser., 7, 402–8.

Chappell, E. (ed.) 1935 *The Tangier papers of Samuel Pepys*, Publications of the Navy Records Society, 73, London.

Chartier, R. 1987 *The cultural uses of print in early modern France*, trans. L. G. Cochrane, Princeton, NJ.

1989 'Texts, printings, readings', in L. Hunt (ed.), *The new cultural history*, Berkeley and Los Angeles, pp. 154–75.

1995 *Forms and meanings: texts, performances, and audiences from codex to computer*, Philadelphia.

Chartres, J. A. 1977 'Road carrying in England in the seventeenth century: myth and reality', *EcHR*, 2nd ser., 30, 73–94.

1980 'On the road with Professor Wilson', *EcHR*, 2nd ser., 33, 96–9.

Chernaik, W. 1991 'Books as memorials: the poetics of consolation', *Yearbook of English Studies* 21, 207–17.

Chiappelli, F., Allen, M. J. B., and Benson, R. L. 1976 *First images of America. The impact of the New World on the Old*, 2 vols. Berkeley, Los Angeles, London.

Chilton, C. W. 1982 *Early Hull printers and booksellers: an account of the printing, bookselling and allied trades from their beginnings to 1840*, Kingston-upon-Hull.

Christie, R. C. 1885 *The old church and school libraries of Lancashire*, Manchester (Chetham Society).

Churchill, W. A., 1935 *Watermarks in paper in Holland, England, France, etc. in the XVII and XVIII centuries*, Amsterdam.

Clair, C. 1959 'Christopher Plantin's trade-connexions with England and Scotland', *Library*, 5th ser., 14, 28–45.

Clancy, T. H. 1964 *Papist pamphleteers: the Allen-Parsons party and the political thought of the Counter-Reformation in England, 1572–1615*, Chicago.

1989 'Spiritual publications of English Jesuits', *Recusant History*, 19, 426–46.

1996 *English Catholic books 1641–1700. A bibliography*, rev. edn, Aldershot.

Clapp, S. L. C. 1931 'The beginnings of subscription publication in the seventeenth century, *MP*, 29, 199–224.

1932 'The subscription enterprises of John Ogilby and Richard Blome', *MP*, 30 (1932/3), 365–79.

1933 'Subscription publishers prior to Jacob Tonson', *Library*, 4th ser., 13, 158–83.

Clare, J. 1990 *'Art made tongue-tied by authority': Elizabethan and Jacobean dramatic censorship*, Manchester and New York.

Clark, P. 1976 'The ownership of books in England, 1560–1640: the example of some Kentish townsfolk', in Stone 1976, pp. 95–114.

2000 *The Cambridge urban history of Britain*. II. *1540–1840*, Cambridge.

Clark, S. 1983 *Popular moralistic pamphlets 1580–1640*, London.

Clegg, C. S. 1997 *Press censorship in Elizabethan England*, Cambridge.

2001 *Press censorship in Jacobean England*, Cambridge.

Clement R. W. 1997 'The beginnings of printing in Anglo-Saxon, 1565–1630', *PBSA*, 91, 192–244.

Clough, C. H. and Hair, P. E. 1994 *The European outthrust and encounter. The first phase c.1400–c.1700: essays in tribute to David Beers Quinn on his 85th birthday*, Liverpool.

Clucas, S. 1991 'Samuel Hartlib's Ephemerides, 1635–59, and the pursuit of scientific and philosophical manuscripts: the religious ethos of an intelligencer', *The Seventeenth Century*, 6, 33–55.

Cohen, C. 1986 *God's caress: the psychology of Puritan religious experience*, New York and Oxford.

Cohen, I. B. 1971 *Introduction to Newton's Principia*, Cambridge.

Coleman, D. C. 1958 *The British paper industry 1495–1860: a study in industrial growth*, Oxford.

1977 *The economy of England, 1450–1750*, London.

Coleman, D. C. and John, A. H. (eds.) 1976 *Trade, government and economy in pre-Industrial England*, London.

Coleridge, K. A. 1980 *A descriptive catalogue of the Milton Collection in the Alexander Turnbull Library, Wellington, New Zealand*, Oxford.

Colie, R. L. 1956 *'Some thankfulnesse to Constantine'. A study of English influence upon the early works of Constantijn Huygens*, The Hague.

Collins, F. (ed.) 1897, 1900 *Register of the Freemen of the City of York . . . I. 1272–1558*, Publications of the Surtees Society, vol. 96 for 1896; II. *1559–1759*, vol. 102 for 1899.

Collinson, P. 1967, 1990 *The Elizabethan Puritan movement*, London and Berkeley, 1967; Oxford 1990.

1982 *The religion of Protestants: the Church in English society 1559–1625*, Oxford.

1983 *Godly people: essays on English Protestantism and Puritanism*, London.

1986 *From iconoclasm to iconophobia: the cultural impact of the Second English Reformation*, Reading.

1988 *The birthpangs of Protestant England: religious and cultural change in the sixteenth and seventeenth centuries*, Basingstoke.

1994 'Truth and legend: the veracity of John Foxe's Book of Martyrs', *Elizabethan essays*, London and Rio Grande, pp. 151–77.

1995a 'The coherence of the text, how it hangeth together: the Bible in Reformation England', in W. P. Stephens (ed.), *The Bible, the Reformation and the Church: essays in honour of James Atkinson, Journal for the Study of the New Testament*, supp. ser., 105, pp. 84–108.

1995b 'Ecclesiastical vitriol: religious satire in the 1590s and the invention of Puritanism', in J. Guy (ed.), *The reign of Elizabeth I: court and culture in the last decade*, Cambridge, pp. 150–70.

Comyn, D. (ed.), 1902 *The history of Ireland by Geoffrey Keating D. D.*, 4 vols., ITS, London, 1902–14.

Cook, H. 1986 *The decline of the old medical regime in Stuart London*, Ithaca, NY.

Cope, E. 1992 *Handmaid of the Holy Spirit: Dame Eleanor Davies, never so mad a ladie*, Ann Arbor.

Coppens, C. 1993 *Reading in exile: the libraries of John Ramridge (d. 1568), Thomas Harding (d. 1572) and Henry Joliffe (d. 1573), recusants in Louvain*, Cambridge.

Cornforth, J. 1988 'The oldest public library', *Country Life*, 3 November.

Corns, T. N. 1982 'Milton's quest for respectability', *MLR*, 77, 769–79.

1984 'Ideology in the *Poemata* (1645)', *MS*, 19, 195–203.

Corns, T.N. and Loewenstein, D. (eds.) 1995 *The emergence of Quaker writing. Dissenting literature in seventeenth-century England*, London.

Corsten, S. 1962 'Unter dem Zeichen der "Fetten Henne". Franz Birckmann und Nachfolger', *Gutenberg-Jahrbuch*, 267–72.

Cotton, A. 1971 'London newsbooks in the Civil War: their political attitudes and sources of information', unpub. D.Phil. thesis, University of Oxford.

1978 'John Dillingham, journalist of the Middle Group', *EHR*, 93, 817–34.

Cowley, J. D. 1924 'A century of law booksellers in London 1650–1750', *Law Times*, 57, 347.

Cox, C. J. and Harvey, A. 1908 *English church furniture*, 2nd edn, London.

Craig Ferguson, W. 1989 *Pica Roman type in Elizabethan England*, London (rev. A. Weiss, *PBSA*, 73 (1989), 539–46, and J. Lane, *Library*, 6th ser., 14 (1992), 357–65).

Craster, E. 1952 *History of the Bodleian Library 1845–1945*, Oxford.

Crawford, A. and Jones, A. P. 1981 'The early typography of printed Welsh', *Library*, 6th ser., 3, 217–31.

Crawford, P. 1985 'Women's published writings 1600–1700', in M. Prior (ed.), *Women in English society 1500–1800*, London, pp, 211–82.

Cressy, D. 1977 'Levels of illiteracy in England, 1530–1630', *Historical Journal*, 20, 4–21.

1980 *Literacy and the social order: reading and writing in Tudor and Stuart England*, Cambridge.

1986 'Books as totems in seventeenth-century England and New England', *Journal of Library History*, 21, 92–106.

Crichton, J. D. 1982–3 'The Manual of 1614', *Recusant History*, 166, 159–72.

Crist, T. 1979 'Government control of the press after the expiration of the Printing Act in 1679', *PH*, 5, 49–77.

Crofts, J. 1967 *Packhorse, waggon and post: land carriage and communication under the Tudors and Stuarts*, London.

Cronin, A. 1943–4 'Sources of Keating's *Foras Feara ar Éirian*', *Éigse*, 5, 235–79.

Cross, C. 1991 'Monastic learning and libraries in sixteenth-century Yorkshire', in J. Kirk (ed.), *Humanism and reform: the Church in Europe, England, and Scotland, 1400–1643*, Oxford, pp. 255–69.

Crum, M. 1957 'A seventeenth-century collection of music belonging to Thomas Hammond, a Suffolk landowner', *BLR* 6, 373–86.

Cunningham, A. 1996 'The culture of gardens', in N. Jardine, J. A. Secord, and E. C. Spary, (eds.) *Cultures of natural history*, Cambridge, pp. 38–56.

Curtis, M. H. 1964 'William Jones: Puritan printer and propagandist', *Library*, 5th ser., 19, 38–66.

Curtis, T. 1833 *The existing monopoly, an inadequate protection of the Authorised Version of scripture... with specimens of the intentional, and other departures from the Authorised standard*, London.

Cutts, J. P. 1956 'Seventeenth-century lyrics: Oxford, Bodleian, Ms Mus. b. 1', *Musica Disciplina*, 10, 142–3.

Dahl, F. 1946 *Dutch corantos, 1618–1650: a bibliography*, The Hague.

1950 'Amsterdam, cradle of English newspapers', *Library*, 5th ser., 4, 166–79.

1952 *A bibliography of English corantos and periodical newsbooks 1620–1642*, London.

Daly, P. M. 1988 *The English emblem and the continental tradition*, New York.

Daly, P. M. and Silcox, M. V. 1990 *The English emblem: bibliography of secondary literature*, Munich.

Danielsson, B. and Vieth, D. 1967 *The Gyldenstolpe manuscript miscellany of poems by John Wilmot Earl of Rochester, and other Restoration authors*, Stockholm.

Darnton, R. 1982 'What is the history of books?', *Daedalus*, Summer, 65–83.

Davenport, C. 1899 *English embroidered bookbindings*, London.

1902–4 'Bagford's notes on bookbindings', *Transactions of the Bibliographical Society*, 8, 123–42.

Davidson, A. and Bell, M. (eds.) 1984 Lord Ruthven [?], *The ladies cabinet enlarged and opened*, London.

Davies, C. 1981 *Latin writers of the Renaissance*, Cardiff.

1995 *Welsh literature and the Classical tradition*, Cardiff.

1998 'Latin literature', in Jones and Rees 1998, pp. 67–74.

Davies, Lady E., 1995 *Prophetic writings of Lady Eleanor Davies*, E. Cope (ed.), Oxford and New York.

Davies, R. 1988 *A memoir of the York press with notices of authors, printers, and stationers, in the sixteenth, seventeenth and eighteenth centuries*, London, 1868, reprinted York.

Davies, W. Ll. 1938 'A argraffwyd Llyfr Cymraeg yn Iwerddon cyn 1700?', *Journal of the Welsh Bibliographical Society* 5, 114–19.

Davis, N. Z. 1983 'Beyond the market: books as gifts in sixteenth-century France', *Transactions of the Royal Historical Society*, 5th ser., 33, 68–88.

Davis, R. B. 1978 *Intellectual life in the colonial South, 1585–1763*, 3 vols., Knoxville, TN.

Davison, P. (ed.) 1998 *The book encompassed: studies in twentieth-century bibliography*, Winchester and New Castle, DE.

Day, C. L. and Murrie, E. B. 1940 *English Song Books 1651–1702: a bibliography with a first-line index of songs*, London.

De Hamel, C. 1991 *Syon Abbey: the library of the Bridgettine nuns and their peregrinations after the Reformation*, Edinburgh.

1997 'The dispersal of the library of Christ Church, Canterbury, from the fourteenth to the sixteenth century', in Carley and Tite 1997, pp. 263–79.

De Vries, J. 1984 *European urbanization 1500–1800*, London.

Dear, P. 1995 *Discipline and experience: the mathematical way in the scientific revolution*, Chicago.

Debus, A. G. 1966 *The English Paracelsians*, New York.

Delâge, G. 1990 *L'Angoumois au temps des marchands flamands (17e siècle)*, Paris.

1991 *Moulins à papier d'Angoumois, Périgord et Limousin (17e siècle)*, Paris.

Delano-Smith, C. 1995 'Map ownership in sixteenth century Cambridge: the evidence of probate inventories', *Imago Mundi*, 47, 67–93.

Delano-Smith, C. and Ingram, E. M. 1991 *Maps in Bibles 1500–1600*, Geneva.

Delany, P. 1969 *British autobiography in the seventeenth century*, London.

Delisle, L. 1868–91 *Le cabinet des manuscrits de la Bibliothèque Impériale*, 4 vols. Paris.

Delumeau, J. 1977 *Catholicism between Luther and Voltaire: a new view of the Counter-Reformation*, London.

Destrez, J. 1935 *La pecia dans les manuscrits universitaires du XIIIe et du XIVe siècle*, Paris.

Devine, T. M. 2000 'Scotland', in Clark 2000, pp. 151–64.

Dickins, B. 1949–53 'The Irish Broadside of 1571 and Queen Elizabeth's types', *TCBS*, 1, 48–60.

1972 'The making of the Parker Library', *TCBS*, 6, 19–34.

Dickson, D. R. 1998 *The tessera of Antilia. Utopian brotherhoods & secret societies in the early seventeenth century*, Leiden, Boston, MA, Cologne.

Dickson, R. and Edmond, J. P. 1890 *Annals of Scottish printing: from the introduction of the art in 1507 to the beginning of the seventeenth century*, Cambridge (repr. Amsterdam, 1975).

Dietz, B. (ed.) 1972 *The port and trade of early Elizabethan London: documents*, London.

Dillon, M., Mooney, C . (OFM) and de Brún, P. (eds.) 1969 *A catalogue of Irish manuscripts in the Franciscan Library, Killiney*, Dublin.

Dix, E. R. M. 1932 *Printing in Dublin prior to 1601*, 2nd edn, Dublin.

1971 *Catalogue of early Dublin-printed books 1601–1700*, 2 vols., New York, repr. of 1912 edition.

Dobbs, B. J. T. 1975 *The foundations of Newton's Alchemy: or, the hunting of the Greene Lyon*, Cambridge.

Dobranski, S. 1999 *Milton, authorship, and the book trade*, Cambridge.

Dobson, W. T. 1887 *History of the Bassandyne Bible with notices of the early printers of Edinburgh*, Edinburgh and London.

Dorsten, J. A. van 1961, *Thomas Basson 1555–1613. English printer at Leiden*, Leiden.

1981 'Literary patronage in Elizabethan England: the early phase', in G. Lytle and S. Orgel (eds.), *Patronage in the Renaissance*, Princeton, NJ.

1985 'Thomas Basson (1555–1613), English printer at Leiden', *Quaerendo*, 15, 195–224.

Douglas, D. C. 1951 *English scholars 1660–1730*, rev. edn, London.

Dow, G. F. 1927 *Arts and crafts in New England, 1704–1775: gleanings from newspapers*, Topsfield, MA.

Downie, A. 1989 'Politics and the English Press', in R. P. Maccubbin and M. Hamilton-Philips (eds.), *The age of William III and Mary II: power, politics and patronage 1688–1702*, Williamsburg, pp. 340–6.

Drake, S. (ed.) 1957 *Discoveries and opinions of Galileo*, New York.

Dreyfus, J. (ed.) 1963, *Type specimen facsimiles*, I, London.

Duff, E.G. 1905 *A century of the English booktrade*, London.

Dugaw, D. 1989 *Warrior women and popular balladry, 1650–1850*, Cambridge.

Dunn, K. 1994 'Milton among the monopolists: *Areopagitica*, intellectual property and the Hartlib circle', in Greengrass, Leslie and Raylor 1994, ch. 9.

Dunton, J. 1705 *The life and errors of John Dunton . . .* London.

1818 *The life and errors of John Dunton* [1705], ed. J. Nichols, London.

Durkan, J. and Ross, A. 1961 *Early Scottish libraries*, Glasgow.

Dury, J. 1651 *The reformed school: and the reformed library keeper*, London.

1958 Durie [var: Dury] *The reformed-school; and the reformed librarie-keeper* (London, 1651), ed. H. M. Knox, Liverpool.

Dyer, A. 1995 *Decline and growth in English towns 1400–1640*, 2nd edn, Cambridge.

2000 'Small market towns 1540–1700', in Clark 2000, pp. 425–50.

Dzelzainis, M. 1995 'Milton and the Protectorate in 1658', in Armitage, Himy and Skinner 1995, pp.181–205.

Eamon, W. 1994 *Science and the secrets of nature: books of secrets in medieval and early modern culture*, Princeton, NJ.

Ebner, D. 1971 *Autobiography in seventeenth-century England. Theology and the self*, The Hague and Paris.

Eccles, M. 1957 'Bynneman's books', *Library*, 5th ser., 12, 81–92.

Edinburgh University Library 1963 *Benefactors of the Library in five centuries: an exhibition of books and manuscripts selected from donations to the Library from the 16th to the 20th century*, Edinburgh.

Edwards, A. S. G. 1997 'Medieval manuscripts owned by William Browne of Tavistock (1590/1?-1643/5?)', in Carley and Tite 1997, pp. 441–9.

Edwards, C. 1936 *Y Ffydd Ddi-ffuant . . . argraffiad cyfatebol o gopi yn Llyfrgell Salisbury (Y trydydd argraffiad, 1677)*, Cardiff.

Edwards, P. 1988 *Last voyages. Cavendish, Hudson, Ralegh. The original narratives*, Oxford.

Eeghen, I. H. van 1966 'De befaamde drukkerij op de Herengracht over de Plantage, 1685–1755', *Jaarboek van het Genootschap Amstelodamum*, 58, 82–100.

1960–78 *De Amsterdamse boekhandel 1680–1725*, 5 vols., Amsterdam.

Eerde, K. S. van 1976 *John Ogilby and the taste of his times*, Folkestone.

Eisenstein, E. 1979 *The printing press as agent of change: communications and cultural transformations in early-modern Europe*, 2 vols., Cambridge.

Elsky, M. 1989 *Authorizing words: speech, writing and print in the English renaissance*, Ithaca, NY.

Elslander, A. van and Schrikx, W. 1952 'De Engelse werken in den catalogus van C. Huygens', *Tijdschrift voor levende talen*, 18, 35–43, 179–201.

[Elzevier, D.] 1674 *Catalogus librorum qui in bibliopolio Danielis Elsevirii venales extant*, Amsterdam. Copy BL, shelfmark 820. a. 1 (i).

Enschedé, C. 1978 *Typefoundries in the Netherlands from the fifteenth to the nineteenth centuries*, H. Carter, N. Hoeflake and L. Hellinga (eds.), Haarlem.

Estivals, R. 1961 *Le dépot légal sous l'ancien régime, de 1537 à 1791*, Paris.

Evans, I. M. and Lawrence, H. 1979 *Christopher Saxton: Elizabethan map-maker*, Wakefield and London.

Evans, J. 1956 *History of the Society of Antiquaries*, London.

Evans, R. C. 1989 *Ben Jonson and the politics of patronage*, Lewisburg.

Ezell, M. J. M. 1984 'Richard Waller, F. R. S.: "In the pursuit of nature"', *Notes and Records of the Royal Society*, 38, 215–33.

1987 *The patriarch's wife: literary evidence and the history of the family*, Chapel Hill, NC.

1993 *Writing women's literary history*, Baltimore, MD, London.

Fairley, J. A. 1925 *Agnes Campbell, Lady Roseburn, relict of Andrew Anderson the King's Printer*, Aberdeen.

Feather, J. 1976 'English books on sale in Rotterdam in 1693', *Quaerendo*, 6, 365–73.

1981 *The English provincial book trade before 1850*, OBS Occasional Publication 16.

1985 *The provincial book trade in eighteenth-century England*, Cambridge.

1988 *A history of British publishing*, London and New York.

1994 *Publishing, piracy and politics: an historical study of copyright in Britain*, London.

Febvre, L. and Martin, J. 1976 *The coming of the book: the impact of printing*, trans by D. Gerard, London.

Fehrenbach, R. J. 1992 'Sir Roger Townshend's books', *PLRE 3*, 79–135.

Feingold, M. 1990 'Isaac Barrow's library', in M. Feingold (ed.), *Before Newton: the life and times of Isaac Barrow*, Cambridge.

1997 'The mathematical sciences and new philosophies', in *HUO*, IV, pp. 359–448.

Ferdinand, C. Y. 1992 'Towards a demography of the Stationers' Company 1601–1700', *JPHS*, 21, 51–69.

1997 'Magdalen College and the book trade: the provision of books in Oxford, 1450–1550', in Hunt, Mandelbrote and Shell 1997, pp. 175–87.

Ferguson, M. W. 1996 'Renaissance concepts of the "woman writer"', in Wilcox, H. (ed.), *Women and literature in Britain 1500–1700*, Cambridge, pp. 143–68.

Findlen, P. 1994 *Possessing nature: museums, collecting, and scientific culture in early modern Italy*, Berkeley.

Fine bindings 1968 *Fine bindings 1500–1700 from Oxford libraries: a catalogue of an exhibition*, Oxford.

Finlayson, C. P. 1980 *Clement Litill and his library: the origins of Edinburgh University Library*, Edinburgh.

Finlayson, C. P. and Simpson, S. M 1967 'The library of the University of Edinburgh: the early period, 1580–1710', *Library History*, 1, 2–23.

Fisher, J. 1919 'Three Welsh wills', *Archaeologia Cambrensis*, 6th ser., 19, 181–92.

Fissell, M. 1992 'Readers, texts, and contexts: vernacular medical works in early modern England', in R. Porter (ed.), *The popularization of medicine*, 1650–1850, London, pp. 72–96.

Flinn, M. (ed.) 1977 *Scottish population history from the seventeenth century to the 1930s*, Cambridge.

Foley, H. (ed.) 1875–1883 *Records of the English Province of the Society of Jesus*, 7 vols. in 8, London.

Foot, M. M. 1978–83 *The Henry Davis gift: a collection of bookbindings*, 2 vols., London.

1984 'Some bindings for Charles I', in G. A. M. Janssens and F. G. A. M. Aarts (eds.) *Studies in Seventeenth-century English literature, history and bibliography*, Amsterdam, pp. 95–106.

1986 *Pictorial bindings*, London.

1993 *Studies in the history of bookbinding*, Aldershot.

1996 'Scholar-collectors and their binders', in Myers and Harris 1996, pp. 27–43.

1997 'For King, Earl and diplomat: some vellum bindings of the first half of the seventeenth century', in Carley and Tite 1966, pp. 403–12.

1999 'Bookbinding 1400–1557', in Hellinga and Trapp 1999, pp. 109–27.

Ford, M. 1999 'Importation of printed books', in Hellinga and Trapp 1999, pp. 179–201.

Ford, W. C. 1917 *The Boston book market, 1679–1700*, Boston, MA.

Fordham, Sir H. G. 1926 'John Ogilby (1600–1676): his *Britannia*, and the British itineraries of the eighteenth century', *Library*, 4th ser., 6,157–78.

Fox, A. 1994 'Ballads, libels and popular ridicule in Jacobean England', *Past and Present*, 145, 47–83.

1998 'Religious satire in English towns, 1570–1640', in P. Collinson and J. Craig (eds.), *The Reformation in English towns*, Basingstoke, pp. 221–40.

2000 *Oral and literate culture in England 1500–1700*, Oxford.

Fox, L. (ed.) 1956 *English historical scholarship in the sixteenth and seventeenth centuries*, London and New York.

Foxon, D. F. 1975 'Stitched books', *BC*, 24, 111–24.

Foxton, R. 1994 *'Hear the word of the Lord': a critical and bibliographical study of Quaker women's writing, 1650–1700*, BSANZ Occasional Publication, 4, Melbourne.

Francis, F. (ed.) 1956 *Narcissus Luttrell's Popish Plot catalogues*, Oxford.

Frank, J. 1961 *The beginnings of the English newspaper, 1620–1660*. Cambridge, MA.

Fraser, P. 1956 *The intelligence of the secretaries of state and their monopoly of licensed news 1660–1688*, Cambridge.

Frearson, M. 1993a 'Distribution and readership of London corantos in the 1620s', in Myers and Harris 1993, pp. 1–25.

1993b 'London corantos in the 1620s', *Studies in Newspaper and Periodical History*, 1, 3–17.

Freist, D. 1997 *Governed by opinion: politics, religion and the dynamics of communication in Stuart London, 1637–1645*, London.

Friedman, J. 1993 *Miracles and the pulp press during the English Revolution: the battle of the frogs and Fairford's flies*, London.

Friedmann, A. 1961 *The Ballad revival. Studies in the influence of popular on sophisticated poetry*, Chicago.

Fritze, R. H. 1983 '"Truth hath lacked witnesse, tyme wanted light": the dispersal of the English monastic libraries and Protestant efforts at preservation, ca. 1535–1625', *Journal of Library History*, 18, 274–91.

Fulton, J. F. 1961 *A bibliography of the Honourable Robert Boyle Fellow of the Royal Society*, Oxford.

Fussell, G. E. 1935 *The exploration of England. A select bibliography of travel and topography: 1570–1815*, London.

Gadd, I. A. 1999 '"Being like a field": corporate identity in the Stationers' Company 1557–1684', unpub. D. Phil. thesis, University of Oxford.

Gaskell, P. 1972 *A new introduction to bibliography*, reprinted with corrections, Oxford.

1980 *Trinity College library; the first 150 years*, Cambridge.

Gebert, C. L. 1933 *An anthology of Elizabethan dedications and prefaces*, New York.

Gee, J. 1624 *The foot out of the snare: with a detection of sundrey late practices and impostures of the priests and Jesuits in England. Whereunto is added a catalogue of such bookes as in this authors knowledge have been vented within two yeeres last past in London, by the priests and their agents ... [and] the names of such as disperse, print, bind or sell popish bookes*, London, 3rd edn. See also Harmsen 1992.

Genette, G. 1982 *Palimpsestes: la littérature au second degré*, Paris.

1997 *Paratexts: thresholds of interpretation*, trans. from *Seuils*, Paris, 1987, by J. E. Lewin, Cambridge.

George, R. H. 1931 'A mercantile episode', *Journal of Economic and Business History*, 3, 264–71.

Gerard, R. A. 1996 'Woutneel, de Passe and the Anglo-Netherlandish print trade', *Print Quarterly*, 13, 363–76.

Gibbons, B. J. 1995 'Richard Overton and the secularism of the Interregnum radicals', *The Seventeenth Century*, 10, 63–75.

Gibson, R. W. 1950 *Francis Bacon. A bibliography of his works and of Baconiana to the year 1750*, Oxford.

Gibson, S. 1907 *Abstracts from the wills and testamentary documents of binders, printers, and stationers of Oxford, from 1493 to 1638*, London.

Gibson, S. and Johnson, J. (eds.) 1943 *The first minute book of the Delegates of Oxford University Press, 1668–1756*, Oxford.

Gillespie, R. 1988 'Irish printing in the early seventeenth century', *Irish Economic and Social History*, 15, 81–8.

1996 'The book trade in southern Ireland, 1590–1640', in *Books beyond the Pale: aspects of the provincial book trade in Ireland before 1850*, ed. G. Long, Dublin, pp. 1–17.

Gillespie, S. 1988 'The early years of the Dryden-Tonson partnership', *Restoration*, 12, 10–19.

1991 'A checklist of Restoration English translations and adaptations of classical Greek and Latin poetry, 1660–1700', *Translation and Literature*, 1, 52–67.

Gillett, C. R. 1932 *Burned books: neglected chapters in British history and literature*, 2 vols., New York.

Girouard, M. 1978 *Life in the English country house: a social and architectural history*, 2nd printing, with corrections, New Haven.

Glenn, J. and Walsh, D. 1988 *Catalogue of the Francis Trigge chained library*, Woodbridge

Glennie, P. and Whyte, I. 2000 'Towns in an agrarian economy 1540–1700', in Clark 2000, pp. 167–93.

Globe, A. 1985 *Peter Stent, London printseller ca. 1642–1665: being a catalogue raisonnée of his engraved prints and books with a historical and bibliographical introduction*, Vancouver, BC.

Gnirrep, K. 1997 'Standing type or stereotype in the seventeenth century', *Quaerendo*, 27, 19–45.

Godzich, W. 1994 *The culture of literacy*, Cambridge, MA.

Goldberg, J. 1990 *Writing matter: from the hands of the English Renaissance*, Stanford.

Goldgar, A. 1995 *Impolite learning: conduct and community in the Republic of Letters 1680–1750*, New Haven and London.

Grafton, A. 1997 *The footnote: a curious history*, Cambridge, MA and London.

Graham, T. and Watson, A. G. (eds.) 1998 *The recovery of the past in early Elizabethan England: documents by John Bale and John Joscelyn from the circle of Matthew Parker*, Cambridge.

Grassby, R. 1995 *The business community of seventeenth-century England*, Cambridge.

Gray, G. J. and Palmer, W. M. 1915 *Abstracts from the wills and testamentary documents of printers, binders, and stationers of Cambridge, from 1504 to 1699*, London.

Greaves, R. L., 1969 *The Puritan Revolution and educational thought*, New Brunswick, NJ.

Green, I. 1981 'The first years of Queen Anne's Bounty', in R. O'Day and F. Heal (eds.), *Princes and paupers in the English Church 1500–1800*, Leicester.

1986 '"For children in yeerres and children in understanding": the emergence of the English Catechism under Elizabeth and the early Stuarts', *JEH*, 37, 397–425.

1990 'Bunyan in context: the changing face of Protestantism in seventeenth-century England', in M. van Os and G. J. Schutte (eds.), *Bunyan in England and abroad*, Amsterdam.

1996 *The Christian's ABC: catechisms and catechizing in England c.1530–1740*, Oxford.

2000 *Print and Protestantism in early modern England*, Oxford.

Greengrass, M. 1993 'Samuel Hartlib and international Calvinism', *Proceedings of the Huguenot Society* 25.5, 464–75.

1995 'The financing of a seventeenth-century intellectual: contributions for Comenius, 1637–1641', *Acta Comeniana*, 11, 71–87.

1996 'An "Intelligencer's workshop": Samuel Hartlib's Ephemerides', *Studia Comeniana et Historica* 26, 48–62.

1997 'Samuel Hartlib and scribal communication', *Acta Comeniana*, 12, 47–62.

1998 'Archive refractions: Hartlib's papers and the working of an intelligencer', in M. Hunter (ed.), *Archives of the scientific revolution. The formation and exchange of ideas in seventeenth-century Europe*, Woodbridge, pp. 35–47.

Greengrass, M. and Leslie, M. 1995 *The papers of Samuel Hartlib: the complete edition* (Ann Arbor, MI, 1995), 2 CD-ROM set.

Greengrass, M., Leslie, M., and Raylor, T. 1994 (eds.) *Samuel Hartlib and universal reformation: studies in intellectual communication*, Cambridge.

Greening, A. 1997 'A 16th-century stationer and his business connections: the Tottell family documents (1448–1719) at Stationers' Hall', in Hunt, Mandelbrote and Shell 1997, pp. 1–8.

Greer, G. 1995 'Honest Sam. Briscoe', in Myers and Harris, pp. 33–47.

Greetham, D. C. (ed.) 1997 *The margins of the text*, Ann Arbor, MI.

Greg, W. W. 1939–59 *A bibliography of the English printed drama to the Restoration*, 4 vols., London.

1956 *Some aspects and problems of London publishing between 1550 and 1650*, Oxford.
1962 *Licensers for the Press &c to 1640*. OBS Publications, ns. 10.
1966 'Entrance in the Stationers' Register: some statistics', in *W. W. Greg: Collected papers*, ed. J. C. Maxwell, pp. 341–8.
1967 *A companion to Arber*, Oxford.

Greg, W. W. and Boswell, E. (eds.) 1930 *Records of the Court of the Stationers' Company, 1576 to 1602, from Register B*, London.

Gregory, B. S. 1994 'The "True and zealous service of God": Robert Parsons, Edmund Bunny and the First booke of the Christian exercise', *JEH*, 45, 238–68.

Grell, O. P. 1989 *Dutch Calvinists in early Stuart London: the Dutch Church in Austin Friars, 1603–1642*, Leiden.

Grierson, H. J. C. and Wason, S. 1946 *The personal note: or first and last words from prefaces, introductions, dedication, and epilogues*, London.

Griffin, D. 1990 'The beginnings of modern authorship: Milton to Dryden', *MQ*, 24, 1–7.
'Milton in Italy: The making of a man of letters?', in M. A. Di Cesare (ed.), *Milton in Italy: contexts, images, contradictions*, Binghamton (Medieval and Renaissance Texts and Studies, 90), pp. 19–27.
1996 *Literary patronage in England 1650–1800*, Cambridge.

Griffith, W. P. 1989 'Schooling and society', in Jones, J. G. (ed.), *Class, community and culture in Tudor Wales*, Cardiff, pp. 79–119.
1996 *Learning, law and religion: higher education and Welsh society c.1540–1640*, Cardiff.

Griffiths, A. 1998 *The print in Stuart Britain, 1603–1689* (with the collaboration of R. A. Gerard), London.

Griffiths, D. N. 1970 'Lincoln Cathedral library', *BC*, 19, 21–30.

Griffiths, P., Landers, J., Pelling, M., and Tyson, R. 2000 'Population and disease, estrangement and belonging 1540–1700', in Clark 2000, pp. 195–233.

Gruffydd, R. G. 1952 'Dau lythyr gan Owen Lewis', *Llên Cymru*, 2, 36–45.
1956 'Humphrey Lhuyd a deddf cyfieithu'r Beibl i'r Gymraeg', *Llên Cymru*, 4, 114–15; 233.
1969 '*Yny llyvyr hwnn* (1546): the earliest Welsh printed book', *Bulletin of the Board of Celtic Studies*, 23, 105–16.
1972 *Argraffwyr cyntaf Cymru: gwasgau dirgel y Catholigion adeg Elisabeth*, Cardiff.
1984 'Cri am lyfrau newydd ar ran eglwys newydd', *Y Casglwr*, 23, 16–17.
1991 'Thomas Salisbury o Lundain a Chlocaenog: ysgolhaig-argraffydd y Dadeni Cymreig', *National Library of Wales Journal*, 27, 1–19.
1998 'The first printed books, 1546–1604', in Jones and Rees 1998, pp. 44–65.

Gulik, E. van 1975 'Drukkers en geleerden: de Leidse Officina Plantiniana (1583–1619)', in T. H. Lunsingh Scheurleer and G. H. M. Postumus Meyjes (eds.), *Leiden University in the seventeenth century*, Leiden, pp. 367–93.

Gunther, R. T. (ed.) 1923–67 *Early science in Oxford*, 15 vols., Oxford.

Haar, J. van der 1980 *From Abbadie to Young. A bibliography of English, most Puritan works, translated i/t Dutch language. Van Abbadie tot Young. Een bibliografie van Engelse, veelal puritaanse, in het Nederlands vertaalde werken*, Veenendaal.

Habermas, J. 1989 *The structural transformation of the public sphere: an inquiry into a category of bourgeois society*, trans. T. Burger with the assistance of F. Lawrence, Cambridge, MA.

Hadfield, A. and McVeagh, J. 1994 *Strangers to that land. British perceptions of Ireland from the Reformation to the Famine*, Gerrards Cross.

Hageman, E. H. and Sununu, A. 1993 'New manuscript texts of Katherine Philips', *EMS*, 4, 174–219.

1995 "More copies of it abroad than I could have imagin'd": further manuscript texts of Katherine Philips', *EMS*, 5, 127–69.

Haig, R. L. 1956 'New light on the King's Printing Office, 1680–1730', *SB*, 8, 157–67.

Haigh, C. (ed.) 1987 *The English Reformation revised*, Cambridge.

Haimann, G. 1983 *Nicholas Kis: a Hungarian punch-cutter and printer 1650–1702*, trans E. Hoch *et al.*, San Francisco.

Hair, P. E. H. 1996 'Bibliography of the Hakluyt Society 1847–1995', in R. C. Bridges and P. E. H. Hair (eds.) *'Compassing the vaste globe of the earth'. Studies in the history of the Hakluyt Society 1846–1996*, Hakluyt Society, 2nd ser., 183, 241–302.

Halasz, A. 1997 *The marketplace of print*, Cambridge.

Hale, J. K. 1995a 'Observations on Milton's accents', *Renaissance and Reformation*, 19, 23–34.

1995b 'The pre-criticism of Milton's Latin verse, illustrated from the ode "Ad Joannem Rousium"', in P. G. Stanwood (ed.), *Of poetry and politics: new essays on Milton and his world*, Binghamton, pp. 17–34.

Hall, A. R. 1964 'Oldenburg and the art of scientific communication', *British Journal of the History of Science*, 2, 277–90.

Haller, W. 1964 *Foxe's Book of martyrs and the elect nation*, London.

Hamburger, P. 1984–5 'The development of the law of seditious libel and control of the press', *Stanford Law Review*, 37, 661–765.

Hamessley, L. 1992 'The Tenbury and Ellesmere partbooks: new findings on manuscript compilation and exchange, and the reception of the Italian madrigal in Elizabethan England', *Music & Letters*, 73, 177–221.

Hamilton, A., 1981 *The Family of Love*, Cambridge.

Hammond, P. 1982 'The Robinson manuscript miscellany of Restoration verse in the Brotherton Collection, Leeds', *Proceedings of the Leeds Philosophical and Literary Society, Literary and Historical Section*, 18, 275–324.

1984 'Dryden's revision of *To the Lady Castlemain*', *PBSA*, 78, 81–90.

1990 'The printing of the Dryden-Tonson *Miscellany Poems* (1684) and *Sylvae* (1685)', *PBSA*, 84, 405–12.

1992 'The circulation of Dryden's poetry', *PBSA*, 86, 379–409.

1993 'Anonymity in Restoration poetry', *The Seventeenth Century*, 8, 123–42.

Hamper, W. (ed.), 1827 *The life, diary and correspondence of Sir William Dugdale*, London.

Hampshire, G. (ed.) 1983 *The Bodleian Library account book, 1613–1646*, OBS Publications, ns. 21.

Handover, P. M. 1960 *Printing in London from 1476 to modern times: competitive practice and technical invention in the trade of book and Bible printing, periodical production, jobbing &c*, London.

Hannaway, O. 1975 *The chemists and the word: the didactic origins of chemistry*, Baltimore, MD.

Hannay, M. P. (ed.) 1985 *Silent but for the word: Tudor women as patrons, translators, and writers of religious works*, Kent, OH.

Harkness, D. 1997 'Managing an experimental household: the Dees of Mortlake and the practice of natural philosophy', *Isis*, 88, 247–62.

Harmsen, T. H. B. (ed.) 1992 *John Gee: the foot out of the snare*, Nijmegen. See also Gee 1624.

Harrington, J. P. 1991 *The English traveller in Ireland. Accounts of Ireland and the Irish through five centuries*, Dublin.

Harris, M. 1985 'Moses Pitt and insolvency in the London book trade in the late-seventeenth century', in Myers and Harris, 1985, pp. 176–208.

Harris, P. R. (ed.) 1966 'The reports of William Udall, informer, 1605–1612', *Recusant History*, 8, 192–284.

Harrison, J. 1978 *The library of Isaac Newton*, Cambridge.

Harrison, J. P. and Laslett, P. 1971 *The library of John Locke*, 2nd edn, Oxford.

Hart, H. 1968 *Notes on a century of typography at the University Press, Oxford, 1693–1794*, Oxford.

Harvey, D. R. 1985 'Henry Playford: a bibliographical study', unpub. Ph.D thesis, University of Wellington, Victoria, NZ.

Harvey, P. D. A. 1993 *Maps in Tudor England*, London.

Hassall, W. O. (ed.) 1950 *Catalogue of the library of Sir Edward Coke*, New Haven.

Hayes, K. J. 1997 *The library of William Byrd of Westover*, Madison, WI.

Hazelton, M. 1997 '"Publishers of truth": Quakers and the public sphere, 1652–1660', unpub. M.Phil. thesis, University of Oxford.

2000 '"Money chocks": the Quaker critique of the early modern public sphere', *MP*, 98, 251–70.

Hazen, A. T. 1954 'Eustace Burnaby's manufacture of white paper in England', *PBSA*, 48, 315–33.

Heawood, E. 1929 'Sources of early English paper-supply', *Library* 4th ser., 10, 282–307 and 427–54.

1930 'Paper used in England after 1600', *Library*, 4th ser., 11, 263–99 and 466–98.

1947 'Further notes on paper used in England after 1600', *Library*, 5th ser., 2, 119–49.

1950 *Watermarks mainly of the seventeenth and eighteenth centuries*, Hilversum; *Addenda and corrigenda*, Amsterdam, 1970.

Helgerson, R. 1983 *Self-crowned Laureates: Spenser, Jonson, Milton, and the literary system*, Berkeley.

Hellinga, L. 1999 'Printing', in Hellinga and Trapp 1999, pp. 65–108.

Hellinga, L. and Trapp, J. B. (eds.) 1999 *A history of the book in Britain*, III, Cambridge.

Henrey, B. 1975 *British botanical and horticultural literature before 1800*, I. *The sixteenth and seventeenth centuries: history and bibliography*, London.

Henry, J. 1991 'Doctors and healers: popular culture and the medical profession', in S. Pumfrey, P.L. Rossi, and M. Slawinski (eds.) *Science, culture and popular belief in Renaissance Europe*, Manchester, pp. 191–221.

Herbert, A. L. 1982 'Oakham parish library', *Library History*, 6, 1–11.

Herendeen, W. H. 1988 'William Camden: historian, herald, and antiquary', *SP*, 85, 192–210.

Herrmann, F. 1991 'The emergence of the book auctioneer as a professional', in Myers and Harris 1991, pp. 1– 14.

Hessayon, A. 1996 '"Gold tried in the fire": the Prophet Theaurau, John Tany and the Puritan revolution', unpub. Ph.D. thesis, University of Cambridge.

Hessels, J. H. (ed.) 1887 *Ecclesiae Londino-Batavae archivum*, 3 vols., Cambridge, 1887–97.

Hetet, J. 1985 'The Warden's accounts of the Stationers' Company 1663–79', in Myers and Harris 1985, pp. 39–59.

1987 'A literary underground in restoration England: printers and dissenters in the context of constraint, 1660–89', unpub. Ph. D. thesis, University of Cambridge.

Hicks, L. (ed.) 1942 *Letters and memorials of Father Robert Parsons, I (to 1558)*, CRS, 29.

Higgins, P. 1973 'The reactions of women, with special reference to women petitioners', in B. Manning (ed.), *Politics, religion and the English Civil War*, London, pp. 179–97.

Hill, C. 1985 'Censorship and English literature', in *The collected essays of Christopher Hill*, 2 vols., Brighton, 1, pp. 32–71.

Hills, R.L. 1988 *Papermaking in Britain, 1488–1988*, London.

Hillyard, B. 1998 'Scottish bibliography for the period ending 1801', in Davison 1998, pp. 182–202.

Hind, A.M. 1952–64 *Engraving in England in the sixteenth and seventeenth centuries: a descriptive catalogue with introductions*, 3 vols. (vol. 3 comp. M. Corbett and M. Norton), Cambridge.

Hindle, C.J. 1935–8 *A bibliography of the printed pamphlets and broadsides of Lady Eleanor Douglas [or Davies] the seventeenth-century prophetess, Edinburgh Bibliographical Society Transactions*, 1, 65–98.

Hinton, E. M. 1935 *Ireland through Tudor eyes*,Philadelphia.

Hoare, P. 1963 'Archbishop Tenison's library, 1684–1861', unpub. diploma thesis, University College, London School of Librarianship.

Hobbs, M. 1989 'Early seventeenth-century verse miscellanies and their value for textual editors', *EMS*, 1, 182–210.

1992 *Early seventeenth-century verse miscellany manuscripts*, Aldershot.

Hobby, E. 1988 *Virtue of necessity: English women's writing, 1649–1688*, London.

Hodges, J. C. 1955 *The Library of William Congreve*, New York.

Hodgson, N. and Blagden, C. 1956 *The notebook of Thomas Bennet and Henry Clements (1686–1719), with some aspects of book trade practice*, OBS Publications, ns 6 (for 1953).

Hof, W. J. Op 't 1987 *Engelse piëtistische geschriften in het Nederlands 1598–1622*, Rotterdam.

Hoftijzer, P. G. 1987 *Engelse boekverkopers bij de Beurs. De geschiedenis van de Amsterdamse boekhandels Bruyning en Swart (1637–1724)*, Amsterdam/Maarssen.

1991 'Religious and theological books in the Anglo-Dutch book trade at the time of the Glorious Revolution', in J. van den Berg and P. G. Hoftijzer (eds.), *Church and society in change. Papers of the fourth Anglo-Dutch Church History Symposium, Exeter, 1988*, Leiden, 167–78.

1998 'Het Nederlandse boekenbedrijf en de verspreiding van Engelse wetenschap in de zeventiende en vroege achttiende eeuw', *Jaarboek voor Nederlandse boekgeschiedenis*, 5, 59–71.

Hopkins, D. 1988 'Dryden and the Garth-Tonson *Metamorphoses*', *RES*, 6th ser., 64–74.

Hoppit, J. 1987 *Risk and failure in English business 1700–1800*, Cambridge.

Horden, J. 1953 *Francis Quarles (1592–1644): a bibliography of his works to the year 1800*, OBS Publications, ns, 2, Oxford.

1984 'Sir William Killigrew's *Four new playes* (1666) with his *Imperial tragedy* (1669): a second annotated copy', *Library*, 6th ser., 6, 271–5.

Hoskins, W. G. 1984 *Local History in England*, 3rd edn, London.

Houliston, V. 1996 'Why Robert Parsons would not be pacified: Edmund Bunny's theft of the *Book of resolution*', in T. M. McCoog (ed.), *The reckoned expense: Edmund Campion and the early English Jesuits*, Woodbridge, pp. 159–77.

Houston, R. 1985 *Scottish literacy and the Scottish identity*, Cambridge.

Howard, C. 1968 *English travellers of the Renaissance*, 1914; reprinted New York.

Howell, W. S. 1956 *Logic and rhetoric in England, 1500–1700*, Princeton.

Howgego, J. 1978 *Printed maps of London circa 1553–1850*, 2nd edn, Folkestone, 1978.

Hughes, A. 1990 'The pulpit guarded: confrontations between Orthodox and Radicals in Revolutionary England', in A. Laurence, W. R. Owens and S. Sim (eds.), *John Bunyan and his England, 1628–88*, London, pp. 31–50.

1995 'Gender and politics in Leveller literature', in S. D. Amussen and M. A. Kishlansky (eds.), *Political culture and cultural politics in early modern England*, Manchester, pp. 162–88.

Hughes, G. H. (ed.) 1967 *Rhagymadroddion 1547–1659*, Cardiff.

Hull, S. W. 1988 *Chaste, silent & obedient: English books for women 1475–1640*, San Marino, CA.

Hulme, P. 1986 *Colonial encounters: Europe and the native Caribbean, 1492–1797*, London.

Hunt, A. 1997 'Book trade patents, 1630–1640', in Hunt, Mandelbrote, and Shell 1997, pp. 27–54.

Hunt, A., Mandelbrote, G. and Shell, A. (eds.) 1997 *The book trade and its customers 1450–1900*, Winchester.

Hunt, C. J. and Isaac, P. 1977 'The regulation of the booktrade in Newcastle-upon-Tyne at the beginning of the nineteenth century', *Archeologia Aeliana*, 5th ser., 5, 163–78.

Hunt, J. D. 1994 'Hortulan affairs', in Greengrass, Leslie, and Raylor 1994, pp. 321–42.

Hunt, M. 1984 'Hawkers, bawlers, and Mercuries: women and the London press in the early Enlightenment', *Women and History*, 9, 41–68.

Hunt, R. W. 1953 *A summary catalogue of Western manuscripts in the Bodleian Library at Oxford*, I, Oxford.

Hunter, D. 1997 *Opera and song books published in England 1703–1726: a descriptive bibliography*, London.

Hunter, J. P. 1997 'Protesting fiction, constructing history', in D. R. Kelley and D. H. Sacks (eds.), *The historical imagination in early modern Britain: history, rhetoric and fiction, 1500–1800*, Cambridge, pp. 298–317.

Hunter, L. 1991 'From occasional receipt to specialised book', in C. A. Wilson (ed.), *Banquetting stuffe: the fare and social background of the Tudor and Stuart banquet*, Edinburgh, pp. 36–59.

1997a 'Sisters of the Royal Society: the circle of Katherine Jones, Lady Ranelagh', in Hunter and Hutton 1997, pp. 178–97.

1997b 'Women and domestic medicine: lady experimenters, 1570–1620', in Hunter and Hutton 1997, pp. 89–107.

1999 'Civic rhetoric, 1560–1640', in F. Ames-Lewis (ed.), *Sir Thomas Gresham and Gresham College: studies in the intellectual history of London in the sixteenth and seventeenth centuries*, London, pp. 88–104.

Hunter, L. and Hutton, S. (eds.) 1997 *Women, science and medicine 1500–1700*, Stroud.

Hunter, M. 1981 *Science and society in Restoration England*, Cambridge.

Hunter, M., and Wootton, D. (eds.) 1992 *Atheism from the Reformation to the Enlightenment*, Oxford.

Hunter, M., Mandelbrote, G., Ovenden, R., and Smith, N. 1999 *A Radical's books: the library catalogue of Samuel Jeake of Rye, 1623–90*, Cambridge.

Hunter, R. J. 1988 'Chester and the Irish book trade, 1681', *Irish Economic and Social History*, 15, 89–93.

Hurst, C. 1982 *Catalogue of the Wren Library of Lincoln Cathedral; books printed before 1801*, Cambridge.

Huws, D. 1997 'Sir Thomas Mostyn and the Mostyn Manuscripts', in Carley and Tite 1997, pp. 451–72.

Hyde, R. 1980 'John Ogilby's eleventh hour', *Map Collector*, 11, 2–8.

Imhof, D. Tournoy, G., and De Nave, F. (eds.) 1994 *Antwerpen, dissident drukkerscentrum. De rol van de Antwerpse drukkers in de godsdienststrijd in Engeland (16de ee uw)*, exhibition catalogue, Museum Plantin-Moretus, Antwerp.

Ingram, E. M. 1993 'The map of the Holy Land in the Coverdale bible: a map by Holbein?', *Map Collector*, 64 (1993), 26–31.

Irving, J. 1984 'Consort playing in mid-17th-century Worcester: Thomas Tomkins and the Bodleian partbooks Mus. Sch. E.415–18', *Early Music*, 12, 337–44.

Irwin, R. 1964 *The origins of the English library*, London.

Isaac, F. 1932 *English and Scottish printing types, 1535–58, 1552–8*, London.

1936 *English printers' types of the sixteenth century*, Oxford.

Jackson, W. A. (ed.) 1957 *Records of the Court of the Stationers' Company, 1602 to 1640* [Court Book C], London.

Jagger, G. 1995 'Joseph Moxon, F. R. S., and the Royal Society', *Notes and Records of the Royal Society* 49, 193–208.

James, M. R. 1900–4 *The western manuscripts in the library of Trinity College, Cambridge*, 4 vols., Cambridge.

1909–13 *A descriptive catalogue of the manuscripts in the library of Corpus Christi College, Cambridge*, 2 vols., Cambridge.

James, T. 1605 *Catalogus librorum bibliothecae publicae quam vir ornatissimus Thomas Bodleius nuper instituit*, Oxford, reprinted in facsimile, Oxford 1986.

Jardine, L. 1996 'The triumph of the book', in *Worldly goods. A new history of the Renaissance*, London and Basingstoke, pp. 143–52.

Jardine, L. and Grafton A. 1990 '"Studied for action": how Gabriel Harvey read his Livy', *Past and Present*, 129, 30–78.

Jayne, S. 1983 *Library catalogues of the English renaissance*. 2nd edn, Winchester.

Jayne, S. and Johnson, F. R. 1956 *The Lumley Library. The catalogue of 1609*, London.

Jenkins, G. 1947–8, 'The Archpriest Controversy and the printers, 1601–1603', *Library*, 5th ser., 2, 180–6.

Jenkins, G. H. 1978 *Literature, religion and society in Wales, 1660–1730*, Cardiff.

1980 *Thomas Jones yr Almanaciwr 1648–1713*, Cardiff.

Jenkins, R. 1913 'The protection of inventions during the Commonwealth and Protectorate', *N&Q*, 11th ser., 7, 162–3.

Jenner, M. 1994 '"Another epocha?" Hartlib, John Lanyon, and the improvement of London in the 1650s', in Greengrass, Leslie, and Raylor 1994 pp. 343–56.

Johns, A. 1991 'History, science, and the history of the book: the making of natural philosophy in early modern England', *PH*, 30, 5–30.

1996 'Natural history as print culture', in N. Jardine, J. A. Secord, and E. C. Spary (eds.), *Cultures of natural history*, Cambridge, pp. 106–24.

1998 *The nature of the book: print and knowledge in the making*, Chicago.

Johnson, A. F. 1948–9 'The King's Printers, 1660–1742', *Library*, 5th ser., 3, 33–8.

1951 'The exiled English church at Amsterdam and its press', *Library*, 5th ser., 5, 219–43 (also in A. F. Johnson, *Selected essays on books and printing*, ed. P. H. Muir, Amsterdam, 1970, pp. 327–47.

1954 'J. F. Stam, Amsterdam, and English Bibles', *Library*, 5th ser., 9, 185–94. (also in A. F. Johnson, *Selected essays on books and printing*, ed. P. H. Muir, Amsterdam, 1970, pp. 348–56).

Johnson, F. R. 1943 'Thomas Hill: an Elizabethan Huxley', *HLQ*, 7, 329–51.

1944 '*A newe herball of Macer* and Banckes's *Herball*: notes on Robert Wyer and the printing of cheap handbooks of sciences in the sixteenth century', *Bulletin of the History of Medicine*, 15, 246–60.

1950 'Notes on English retail book prices 1550–1640', *Library*, 5th ser., 5, 83–178.

Johnson, G. D. 1986 'John Trundle and the book trade 1603–1626', *SB*, 39, 177–99.

1988 'The Stationers versus the Drapers: control of the press in the late sixteenth century', *Library*, 6th ser., 10, 1–17.

1992 'Succeeding as an Elizabethan publisher: the example of Cuthbert Burby', *JPHS*, 21, 71–8.

Johnson, J. and Gibson, S. 1946 *Print and privilege at Oxford to the year 1700*, Oxford.

Johnson, R. M. 1994 'The politics of publication: misrepresentation in Milton's 1645 *Poems*', *Criticism*, 36, 45–71.

Johnston, J. A. (ed.) 1991 *Probate inventories of Lincoln citizens 1661–1714*, Publications of the Lincoln Record Society, 80.

Johnston, S. 1991 'Mathematical practitioners and instruments in Elizabethan England', *Annals of Science* 48, 319–44.

Jolly, C. (ed.) 1988 *Histoire des bibliothèques françaises. Les bibliothèques sous l'ancien régime, 1530–1789*, Paris.

Jones, A. R. 1990 *The currency of Eros: women's love lyric in Europe, 1540–1620*, Bloomington.

Jones, E. D. 1949 'Robert Vaughan of Hengwrt', *Journal of the Merioneth Historical and Record Society*, 21–30.

Jones, J. G. 1997 'The Welsh language in local government: justices of the peace and the courts of quarter sessions *c.* 1536–1800', in G. H. Jenkins (ed.), *The Welsh language before the Industrial Revolution*, Cardiff, pp. 181–206.

1998 'Scribes and patrons in the seventeenth century', in Jones and Rees 1998, pp. 83–91.

Jones, M. G. 1937 'Two accounts of the Welsh Trust, 1675 and 1678(?)', *Bulletin of the Board of Celtic Studies* 9, 71–80.

Jones, N. L. 1981 'Matthew Parker, John Bale and the Magdeburg centuriators', *Sixteenth Century Journal*, 12, 35–49.

Jones, P. H. 1997 'Wales and the Stationers' Company', in Myers and Harris 1997, pp. 185–202.

Jones, P. H. and Rees, E. (eds.) 1998 *A nation and its books: a history of the book in Wales*, Aberystwyth.

Jones, R. B. 1970 *The old British tongue: the vernacular in Wales 1540–1640*, Cardiff.

Jones, R. T. 1998 *Grym y gair a fflam y ffydd: ysgrifau ar hanes crefydd yng Nghymru*, ed. D. D. Morgan, Bangor.

Jones Pierce, T. (ed.) 1947 *Clenennau letters and papers in the Brogyntyn Collection*, Aberystwyth.

Josten, C. H. (ed.) 1966 *Elias Ashmole (1617–1692): his autobiographical and historical notes, his correspondence, and other contemporary sources relating to his life and work*, 5 vols., Oxford.

Judge, C. B. 1934 *Elizabethan book-pirates*, Harvard Studies in English, 8, Cambridge, MA.
Kamen, H. 1980 *European society, 1500–1700*, London.
Karrow, R. W. 1993 *Mapmakers of the sixteenth century and their maps*, Chicago.
Kaufman, P. 1963–4 'Reading vogues at English cathedral libraries of the eighteenth century', *Bulletin of the New York Public Library*, 67, 643–72, and 68, 46–64.
Keblusek, M. 1995 'Boeken in ballingschap. De betekenis van de Bibliotheek van Michael Honywood voor de royalistische gemeenschap in de Republiek (1643–1660)', *Jaarboek voor Nederlandse boekgeschiedenis*, 2, 153–74.
1997 *Boeken in de Hofstad. Haagse boekcultuur in de Gouden eeuw*, Hilversum.
Keeble, N. H. 1987 *The literary culture of Nonconformity in the later seventeenth century*, Leicester.
1990 '"I would not tell you any tales": Marvell's constituency letters', in C. Condren and A. D. Cousins (eds.), *The political identity of Andrew Marvell*, Aldershot, pp. 111–34.
Kelliher, H. 1978 *Andrew Marvell, poet and politician 1621–78: an exhibition to commemorate the tercentenary of his death*, London.
1990a Review of W. A. Ringler's *Bibliography and index of English verse printed 1476–1558*, *Library*, 6th ser., 12, 255–60.
1990b 'Unrecorded Extracts from Shakespeare, Sidney, and Dyer', *EMS*, 2, 163–87.
Kelly, T. 1966 *Early public libraries: a history of public libraries in Great Britain before 1850*, London.
Kelly, W. 1997 *The library of Lord George Douglas (ca. 1677/8?–1693?): an early donation to the Advocates' Library*, Cambridge.
Kendrick, T. D. 1950 *British antiquity*, London.
Ker, N. R. 1949 'Medieval manuscripts from Norwich cathedral priory', *TCBS*, 1, 1–28.
1954 *Fragments of medieval manuscripts used as Pastedowns in Oxford bindings c. 1515–1620*, Oxford.
1955 'Sir John Prise', *Library* 5th ser., 10, 1–24.
1957 *Catalogue of manuscripts containing Anglo-Saxon*, Oxford; reprinted with addenda, 1990.
1959 'Oxford college libraries in the sixteenth century', *BLR*, 6, 459–515.
1964 *Medieval libraries of Great Britain. A list of surviving books*, 2nd edn, London.
1985 *Books, collectors and libraries. Studies in the medieval heritage*, ed. A. G. Watson, London.
1986 'The provision of books', *HUO*, III, pp. 441–97.
Kernan, A. P. 1987 *Printing technology, letters and Samuel Johnson*, Princeton, NJ.
Kerridge, E. 1973 *The farmers of old England*, London.
Kewes, P. 1995 '"Give me the sociable pocket-books . . .": Humphrey Moseley's serial publication of octavo play collections', *PH*, 23, 5–21.
1998 *Authorship and appropriation: conceptions of playwriting in England, 1660–1710*, Oxford.
Keynes, Sir Geoffrey 1973 *A bibliography of John Donne*, 4th edn, Oxford.
Kiessling, N. K. 1988 *The library of Robert Burton*, OBS Publication, ns. 22.
Kilburne, W. 1659 *Dangerous errors in several late printed Bibles to the great scandal, and corruption of sound and true religion*, Finsbury.
King, J. N. 1982 *English Reformation literature: the Tudor origins of the Protestant tradition*, Princeton, NJ.
King, K. R. 1994 'Jane Barker, *Poetical recreations*, and the sociable text', *ELH*, 61, 551–70.
Kirsop, W. 1984 'Les mécanismes éditoriaux', in Martin and Chartier 1984, pp. 21–33.
Kitchen, F. 1997 'John Norden (*c.* 1547–1625): estate surveyor, topographer, county mapmaker and devotional writer', *Imago Mundi*, 49, 43–61.

Kitchin, G. 1913 *Sir Roger L'Estrange: a contribution to the history of the press in the seventeenth century*, London.

Klotz, E. 1937–8 'Subject analysis of English imprints for every tenth year from 1480 to 1640', *HLQ*, 1, 417.

Knott, J. R., 1993 *Discourses of martyrdom in English Literature, 1563–1694*,

Koeman, C. 1967–85 *Atlantes Neerlandici: bibliography of terrestrial, maritime and celestial atlases and pilot books, published in the Netherlands up to 1880*, 6 vols., Amsterdam.

Korey, M. E. 1976 *The books of Isaac Norris, 1701–1766, at Dickinson College*, Carlisle, PA.

Krivatsy, N. H. and Yeandle, L. (eds.) 1992 'Sir Edward Dering', *PLRE*, 4, 137–269.

Kruitwagen, Fr. B. 1923 'De incunabeldrukker en lettersteker Henric Pieterssoen die lettersnider van Rotterdamme, *c.* 1470–1511', *De Gulden Passer*, 1, 5–44.

Krummel, D. W. 1975 *English music printing 1553–1700*, London.

Kyffin, M. 1908 *Deffynniad ffydd Eglwys Loegr a gyfieithwyd i'r Gymraeg . . . yn y flwyddyn 1595*, W. Prichard Williams (ed.), Bangor.

La Mar, V. 1960 *Travel and roads in England*, Washington, DC.

Lafitte, M.-P. and Le Bars, F., 1999 *Reliures royales de la Renaissance: la librairie de Fontainebleau 1544–1570*, Paris.

Lake, P. 1994 'Deeds against nature: cheap print, Protestantism and murder in early seventeenth century England', in K. Sharpe and P. Lake (eds.), *Culture and politics in early Stuart England*, Basingstoke, pp. 257–83.

Lambert, S. 1981 *Printing for Parliament, 1641–1700*, List and Index Society, Special Series, 20.

1984 'The beginnings of printing for the House of Commons, 1640–42', *Library*, 6th ser., 3, 43–61.

1987 'The printers and the government, 1604–1640', in Myers and Harris 1987, pp. 1–29.

1992a 'Coranto publishing in England, the first newsbooks', *Journal of Newspaper and Periodical History*, 8, 3–19.

1992b 'Journeymen and Master Printers in the early seventeenth century', *JPHS*, 21, 13–28.

Lane, J. A. 1991 'Arthur Nicolls and his Greek type for the King's Printing House', *Library*, 6th ser., 13, 297–322.

1992 'The origins of Union Pearl', *Matrix*, 12, 125–33.

1995 'Arent Corsz Hoogenacker (*c.* 1579–1636): an account of his typefoundry and a note on his types. Part two: the types', *Quaerendo*, 25, 161–91.

Lane, J. A., *et al.*, 1997 *The Arabic type specimen of Franciscus Raphelengius's Plantinian printing office (1595): a facsmile with an introduction by John A. Lane and a catalogue by R. Breugelmans & Jan Just Witkam of a Raphelengius exhibition*, Leiden.

Langham, R. 1983 *Robert Langham: a letter [1573]*, ed. R. J. P. Kuin, Medieval and Renaissance Texts, 2, Leiden.

Langton, J. 2000 'Urban growth and economic change: from the late seventeenth century to 1841', in Clark 2000, pp. 453–490.

Lanyer, A. 1993 *The poems of Aemilia Lanyer: salve deus ex Judeorum*, ed. S. Woods, New York and Oxford.

Larson, D. A. forthcoming *The verse miscellany of Constance Aston Fowler: a diplomatic edition*, Tempe, AZ.

Latham, R. (gen. ed.) 1978–94 *Catalogue of the Pepys Library at Magdalene College, Cambridge*. I. *Printed books*, by N. A. Smith. II. *Ballads*, by H. Weinstein. III. *Prints and drawings: general*, by A. W. Aspital. IV. *Music, maps, calligraphy*, by J. Stevens, S. Tyacke, R. McKitterick and J. I. Whalley. V.i. *Medieval manuscripts*, by R. McKitterick and R. Beadle. V.ii. *Modern manuscripts*, by C. S. Knighton. VI. *Bindings*, by H. M. Nixon. VII. *Facsimiles of catalogues*, ed. D. McKitterick, 2 vols., Cambridge.

Lathrop, H. B. 1914 'Some rogueries of Robert Wyer', *Library*, 5, 349–64.

Lawler, J. 1898 *Book auctions in England in the seventeenth century*, London and New York.

Lee, B. N. 1991 'Gentlemen and their book-plates', Myers and Harris 1991, pp. 43–76.

Leedham-Green, E. 1986 *Books in Cambridge inventories: book lists from Vice-Chancellor's Court probate inventories in the Tudor and Stuart periods*, 2 vols., Cambridge.

1997 'Manassess Vautrollier in Cambridge', in Hunt, Mandelbrote, and Shell 1997, pp. 9–21.

Leedham-Green, E. and McKitterick, D. 1997 'A catalogue of Cambridge University Library in 1583', in Carley and Tite 1997, pp. 153–235.

Leslie, M. and Raylor, T. (eds.) 1992 *Culture and cultivation in early modern England. Writing and the land*, Leicester and London.

Letwin, L. 1963 *The origins of scientific economics*, London.

Levine, J. M. 1987 *Humanism and history: origins of Modern English historiography*, Ithaca and London.

1991 *The Battle of the Books: history and literature in the Augustan Age*, Ithaca, NY.

Lewalski, B. F. 1993 *Writing Women in Jacobean England*, Cambridge, MA.

Lewis, E. A. (ed.) 1927 *The Welsh Port Books (1550–1603) with an analysis of the Customs revenue accounts of Wales for the same period*, London.

Lievsay, J. L. and Davis, R. B. 1954 'A Cavalier library – 1643', *SB*, 6, 141–60.

Limon, J. 1985 *Gentlemen of a company. English players in Central and Eastern Europe, 1590–1660*, Cambridge.

Lindenbaum, P. 1993 'John Milton and the republican mode of literary production', in C. C. Brown (ed.), *Patronage, politics, and literary traditions in England, 1558–1658*, Detroit, pp. 93–108. This first appeared in *The Yearbook of English Studies*, 21 (1991), 121–36.

1994 'Milton's contract', in M. Woodmansee and P. Jaszi (eds.), *The construction of authorship: textual appropriation in law and literature*, Durham and London, pp. 175–90. This first appeared in *Cardozo Arts & Entertainment Law Journal*, 10 (1992), 439–54.

1995a 'The poet in the marketplace: Milton and Samuel Simmons', in Stanwood 1995, pp. 249–62.

1995b 'Authors and publishers in the late seventeenth century: new evidence on their relations', *Library*, 6th ser., 17, 250–69.

1997 'Rematerializing Milton', *PH*, 41, 5–22.

Lindley, K. 1997 *Popular politics and religion in Civil War London*, Aldershot.

Littleboy, A. 1921 'Devonshire House Reference Library, with notes on early printers and printing in the Society of Friends', *JFHS*, 18, 1–16, 66–80.

Livingston, C. 1991 *British broadside ballads of the sixteenth century. A catalogue of extant sheets*, New York and London.

Lloyd, D. M. 1948 'The Irish, Gaelic and Welsh printed book', *Journal of the Welsh Bibliographical Society*, 6, 254–73.

Lloyd, L. J. 1967 *The library of Exeter cathedral*, Exeter.

Lloyd, N. 1969 'John Jones, Gellilyfdy', *Flintshire Historical Society Publications*, 5–18.

1996 'Sylwadau ar iaith rhai o gerddi Rhys Prichard', *National Library of Wales Journal*, 29, 257–80.

(ed.) 1998 *Ffwtman hoff: cerddi Richard Hughes Cefnllanfair* [s. l.].

Llwyd, R. 1998 'Printing and publishing in the seventeenth century', in Jones and Rees 1998, pp. 93–107.

Loades, D. (ed.) 1997 *John Foxe and the English Reformation*, Aldershot.

Loewenstein, J. F. 1991 'Printing and "The multitudinous presse": the contentious texts of Jonson's masques', in Brady and Herendeen 1991, pp. 168–91.

1994 'Legal proofs and corrected readings: press-agency and the New Bibliography', in D. L. Miller, S. O'Dair and H. Weber (eds.), *The production of English Renaissance culture*, Ithaca and London, pp. 93–122.

London, W. 1658 *A catalogue of the most vendible books in England, orderly and alphabetically digested*, London.

1660 *Catalogue of new books by way of supplement to the former*, London.

Loomie, A. B. (ed.) 1978 *Spain and the Jacobean Catholics*, II. *1613–1624*, CRS, 68.

Lough, J. 1984 *France observed in the seventeenth century by British travellers*, Stocksfield.

Love, H. 1978 'Preacher and publisher: Oliver Heywood and Thomas Parkhurst', *SB*, 31, 227–35.

1987 'Scribal publication in seventeenth-century England', *TCBS*, 9, 130–54.

1993 *Scribal publication in seventeenth-century England*, Oxford.

1995 'Hamilton's *Mémoires de la vie du comte de Grammont* and the reading of Rochester', *Restoration*, 19, 1995, 95–102.

1996a 'Refining Rochester: private texts and public readers', *HLB*, ns. 7, 40–9.

1996b 'The scribal transmission of Rochester's songs', *BSANZB*, 20, 161–80.

1997 'Rochester's "I' th' isle of Britain": decoding a textual tradition', *EMS*, 6, 75–223.

forthcoming 'Thomas Middleton: oral culture and the manuscript economy', in G. Taylor (ed.), *Thomas Middleton and early modern textual culture*.

Luborsky, R. S. and Ingram, E. M. 1998 *A guide to English illustrated books 1536–1603*, 2 vols., Tempe, AZ.

Lucas, P. J. 1997 'A testimonye of verye ancient tyme? Some manuscript models for the Parkerian Anglo-Saxon type-designs', in P. Robinson and R. Zim (eds.), *Of the making of books; medieval manuscripts, their scribes and readers. Essays presented to M. B. Parkes*, Aldershot, pp. 147–88.

Lynam, E. W. 1924 'The Irish character in print', *Library*, 4th ser., 4, 286–325.

Lynch, B. 2000 'Mr Smirke and 'Mr Filth': a bibliographic case study in Non-conformist printing', *Library*, 7th ser., 11, 46–71.

Lynch, K. M. 1971 *Jacob Tonson: Kit-Cat publisher*, Knoxville, TN.

McCart, C. 1989 'The Panmure manuscripts: a new look at an old source of Christopher Simpson's consort music', *Chelys*, 18, 18–29.

McClintock, M. 1997 'The reformation and the emergence of English vernacular rhetoric in mid-sixteenth-century England', paper given to the International Society for the History of Rhetoric, biennial conference.

Macdonald, H. 1939 *John Dryden: a bibliography of early editions and of Drydeniana*, Oxford.

McDonald, P. D. 1997 'Implicit structures and explicit interactions: Pierre Bourdieu and the history of the book', *Library*, 6th ser., 19, 106–121.

MacDonald, R. H. (ed.) 1971 *The library of Drummond of Hawthornden*, Edinburgh.

McDowell, N. 1997 'A Ranter reconsidered: Abiezer Coppe and Civil War stereotypes', *The Seventeenth Century*, 12, 173–205.

McDowell, P. 1998 *The women of Grub Street – press, politics and gender in the London literary marketplace 1678–1730*, Oxford.

Mace, N. A. 1993 'The history of the grammar patent, 1547–1620', *PBSA*, 87, 419–36.

McEntee, A. M. 1992 '"The [un]civill-sisterhood of oranges and lemons": female petitioners and demonstrators, 1642–53', in J. Holstun (ed.), *Pamphlet wars: prose in the English Revolution*, London, pp. 92–111.

McGinn, D. J. 1966 *John Penry and the Marprelate controversy*, New Brunswick, NJ.

McGuinne, D. 1992 *Irish type design*, Dublin.

MacGregor, A. (ed.) 1994 *Sir Hans Sloane*, London.

McKenzie, D. F. 1958 'Apprenticeship in the Stationers' Company, 1555–1640', *Library*, 5th ser., 13, 292–99.

1961 *Stationers' Company apprentices 1605–1640*, Charlottesville, VA.

1966 *The Cambridge University Press, 1696–1712: a bibliographical study*, 2 vols., Cambridge.

1974a 'The London book trade in 1668', *Words: Wai-te-ata Studies in Literature*, 4, 75–92.

1974b *Stationers' Company apprentices 1641–1700*, OBS, ns. 17.

1976a 'Richard Bentley's design for the Cambridge University Press c. 1696', *TCBS*, 6, 322–7.

1976b 'The London book trade in the later seventeenth century', Sandars lectures 1976, Cambridge. Typescript copies deposited in BL, Bodleian and CUL.

1977 'Typography and meaning: the case of William Congreve', in *Buch und Buchhandel in Europa im achzehnten Jahrhundert: the book and the book trade in eighteenth-century Europe* (5th Wolfenbüttel Symposium), G. Barber and B. Fabian (eds.), Hamburg.

1980 'Milton's printers: Matthew, Mary and Samuel Simmons', *MQ*, 14, 87–91.

1986 *Bibliography and the sociology of texts*, London.

1988 Lyell Lectures, privately circulated.

1992 'The economies of print, 1550–1750: scales of production and conditions of constraint', in *Produzione e commercio della carta e del libro secc. XIII–XVIII*, Prato (Istituto Internazionale di Storia Economica 'F. Datini' Prato, Serie II – Atti delle 'Settimane di Studi' e altri Convegni 23), pp. 389–425.

1997 'Stationers' Company Liber A', in Myers and Harris 1997, pp. 35–59.

forthcoming (ed.) *The works of William Congreve*, 3 vols. Oxford.

McKenzie, D. F. and Ross, J. C. (eds.) 1968 *A ledger of Charles Ackers, printer of 'The London Magazine'*, Oxford.

McKerrow, R. 1929 'Edward Allde as a typical trade printer', *Library*, 4th ser., 121–62.

McKisack, M. 1971 *Medieval History in the Tudor Age*, Oxford.

McKitterick, D. 1978 *The library of Sir Thomas Knyvett of Ashwellthorpe, c. 1539–1618*, Cambridge.

1986 *Cambridge University Library; a history. The eighteenth and nineteenth centuries*, Cambridge.

1990 'John Field in 1668: the affairs of a University Printer', *TCBS*, 9, 497–516.

(ed.) 1991 *Andrew Perne: quatercentenary studies*, Cambridge.

1992 *A history of Cambridge University Press*, I. *Printing and the book trade in Cambridge 1534–1698*, Cambridge, 1992.

(ed.) 1995 *The making of the Wren Library*, Cambridge.

1997 '"Ovid with a Littleton": the cost of English books in the early seventeenth century', *TCBS*, 9, 184–234.

2000 'Women and their books in seventeenth-century England: the case of Elizabeth Puckering', *Library*, 7th ser. pp. 359–80.

McLuhan, M. 1962 *The Gutenberg galaxy: the making of typographic man*, Toronto.

McMullin, B. J. 1979 'The origins of press figures in English printing 1629–1671', *Library*, 6th ser., 1, 307–35.

1981 'The Book of Common Prayer and the monarchy from the Restoration to the reign of George I: some bibliographical observations', *BSANZB*, 5, 81–92.

1983 'The Bible and continuous reprinting in the early seventeenth century', *Library*, 6th ser., 5, 256–63.

1984a 'The 1629 Cambridge Bible', *TCBS*, 8, 381–97.

1984b 'Paper-quality marks and the Oxford Bible Press 1682–1717', *Library*, 6th ser., 6, 39–49.

1990 'Towards a bibliography of the Oxford and Cambridge University Bible Presses in the seventeenth and eighteenth centuries', *BSANZB*, 14, 51–73.

1993 'Joseph Athias and the early history of stereotyping', *Quaerendo*, 23, 184–207.

1995 'Signing by the page', *SB*, 48, 259–68.

1996 'The lingering death of the press figure', in Alston 1996, 39–47.

MacNeill, E. (trans.) and Murphy, G. 1908–53 *Duanaire Finn: The book of the lays of Finn*, ITS, 3 vols., London.

McPherson, D. 1974 'Ben Jonson's library and marginalia: an annotated catalogue', *SP*, 71, no. 5 (Texts and Studies), 1–106.

Macray, W. D. 1890 *Annals of the Bodleian Library*, 2nd edn, Oxford.

Mączak, A. 1995 *Travel in early Modern Europe*, trans. by Ursula Phillips (from the 1978 Polish edition), Cambridge.

Madan, F. 1895–1931 *Oxford books: a bibliography relating to the University and city of Oxford, and printed or published there*, 3 vols., Oxford.

1925 'The Oxford Press, 1650–75: the struggle for a place in the sun', *Library*, 4th ser., 6, 113–47.

Madan, F. F. 1950 *A new bibliography of the* Eikon Basilike *of King Charles the First*, OBS Publications, ns. 3 (1949).

Maddison, R. E. W. 1958 'Robert Boyle and the Irish Bible', *Bulletin of the John Rylands Library*, 41, 81–101.

Maltzahn, N. von 1991 *Milton's* History of Britain*: Republican historiography in the English Revolution*, Oxford.

1994 'Wood, Allam, and the Oxford Milton', *MS*, 31, 155–77.

1995a 'The Whig Milton, 1667–1700', in Armitage, Himy, and Skinner 1995, pp. 229–53.

1995b 'Samuel Butler's Milton', *SP*, 92, 482–95.

1996a 'The first reception of *Paradise Lost* (1667)', *RES*, ns. 47, 479–99.

1996b 'The Royal Society and the provenance of Milton's *History of Britain* (1670)', *MQ*, 30, 162–7.

1999 'Marvell's ghost', in W. Chernaik and M. Dzelzainis (eds.), *Marvell and liberty*, Basingstoke, pp. 50–74.

Mandelbrote, G. 1995 'From the warehouse to the counting-house: booksellers and bookshops in late 17th-century London', in Myers and Harris 1995, pp. 49–84.

1997 'Richard Bentley's copies: the ownership of copyrights in the late 17th century', in Hunt, Mandelbrote, and Shell 1997, pp. 55–94.

(forthcoming) *Invertories of the London book trade*, c. *1650*-c. *1720*.

Manguel, A. 1996 *A history of reading*, London.

Mann, A. 1998 'Book commerce, litigation and the art of monopoly: the case of Agnes Campbell, Royal Printer, 1676–1712', *Scottish Economic and Social History*, 18, 132–156.

1999 'Embroidery to enterprise: the role of women in the book trade of early modern Scotland', in E. Ewan and M. M. Meikle (eds.), *Women in Scotland c. 1100–c. 1750*, East Linton, pp. 136–51.

2000a 'Scottish copyright before the statute of 1710', *The Juridical Review* 1, 11–25.

2000b *The Scottish book trade 1500 to 1720: print commerce and print control in early modern Scotland. An historiographical survey of the early modern book in Scotland*, East Linton

Maquerlot, J.-P. and Willems, M. (eds.) 1996 *Travel and drama in Shakespeare's time*, Cambridge.

Marcus, L. S. 1996 *Unediting the Renaissance: Shakespeare, Marlowe, Milton*, London and New York.

Marks, S. P. 1964 *The map of mid-sixteenth-century London: an investigation into the relationship between a copper-engraved map and its derivatives*, London.

Marotti, A. F. 1986 *John Donne, coterie poet*, Madison and London.

1995 *Manuscript, print, and the English renaissance lyric*, Ithaca, NY, and London.

Marsh, C. 1994 *The Family of Love in English society, 1550–1630*, Cambridge.

Martin, H.-J. 1984 *Livre, pouvoirs et société à Paris au XVIIe siècle (1598–1701)*, 2 vols., Geneva.

Martin, H.-J., and Chartier, R. (eds.) 1984 *Histoire de l'édition française*. II. *Le livre triomphant 1660–1830*, Paris.

Masson, A. 1972 *Le décor des bibliothèques du moyen âge à la Révolution*, Geneva.

1981 *The pictorial catalogue: mural decoration in libraries*, Oxford.

Mathias, P. 1979 *The transformation of England*, London.

Mathias, W. A. 1952 'Gweithiau William Salesbury', *Journal of the Welsh Bibliographical Society* 7, 125–43.

Maxted, I. 1989 *Books with Devon imprints: a handlist to 1800*, Exeter.

1996 'A common culture?: the inventory of Michael Harte, bookseller of Exeter, 1615', *Devon and Cornwall Notes and Queries*, pp. 119–28.

(forthcoming) *A good face of learning: two thousand years of the written word in Exeter and Devon*.

Maxted, I. and Treadwell, M. 1990 'The Exeter printer of 1688', *Devon and Cornwall Notes and Queries*, 36, 255–9.

Maxwell, W. H. and Maxwell, L. F. 1955 *A legal bibliography*, I, 2nd edn, London.

Mayhew, H. M. and Sharp, R. F. 1910 *Catalogue of a collection of early printed books in the library of the Royal Society*, London.

Maynard, W. 1986 *Elizabethan lyric poetry and its music*, Oxford.

Meads, D. M. (ed.) 1930 *The diary of Lady Margaret Hoby 1599–1605*, London.

Meale, C. M. 1992 'Caxton, de Worde, and the publication of romance in late Medieval England', *Library*, 6th ser., 14, 283–98.

Meli, D. B. 1993 *Equivalence and priority: Newton versus Leibniz*, Oxford.

Middleton, B. C. 1996 *A history of English craft bookbinding technique*, 4th edn, London.

Milhous, J. and Hume, R. D. 1974 'Dating play premières from publication data, 1660–1700', *HLB*, 22, 374–405.

Miller, C. W. 1949 *Henry Herringman imprints: a preliminary checklist*, Charlottesville, VA.

Millican, P. 1934 *The Register of the Freemen of Norwich 1548–1713: a transcript*, Norwich.

Milton, A. 1995 *Catholic and Reformed: the Roman and Protestant Churches in English Protestant thought, 1600–1640*, Cambridge.

Milward, P. 1977 *Religious controversies of the Elizabethan age: a survey of printed sources*, London.

1978 *Religious controversies of the Jacobean age: a survey of printed sources*, London.

Mitchell, A. F. (ed.) 1897 *A compendious book of godly and spiritual songs*, STS.

Mitchell, W. S. 1954 'The common library of New Aberdeen, 1585', *Libri*, 4, 330–44.

1955 *A history of Scottish bookbinding 1432 to 1650*, Aberdeen.

Moir, D. G. (ed.) 1973–83 *The early maps of Scotland to 1850*, 3rd edn, 2 vols., Edinburgh.

Moir, E. 1964 *The discovery of Britain. The English tourists 1540–1840*, London.

Molloy, J. 1967–8 'The devotional writings of Matthew Kellison', *Recusant History*, 9, 159–90.

Momigliano, A. 1950 'Ancient History and the antiquarian', *JWCI*, 13, 285–315.

Monson, C. 1982 *Voices and viols in England, 1600–1650: the sources and the music*, Ann Arbor, MI.

Moran, J. 1975 *Stationers' Companies of the British Isles*, Newcastle upon Tyne.

Mores, E. R. 1961 *A Dissertation upon English typographical founders and founderies* [1778], ed. H. Carter and C. Ricks, London.

Morgan, M. (ed.) 1981 *Gweithiau Oliver Thomas ac Evan Roberts, dau Biwritan cynnar*, Cardiff.

Morgan, P. 1975 'Letters relating to the Oxford book trade found in bindings in Oxford College libraries *c.* 1611–1647', in *Studies in the book trade in honour of Graham Pollard*, Oxford, pp. 71–89.

1978 *Warwickshire apprentices in the Stationers' Company of London, 1563–1700*, Dugdale Society Occasional Papers, 1.

1989 'Frances Wolfreston and "hor bouks": a seventeenth-century woman book collector', *Library*, 6th ser., 11, 197–219.

1990 'The provincial book trade in England before the end of the Licensing Act', in P. Isaac (ed.), *Six centuries of the provincial book trade in England*, Winchester, pp. 31–9.

Morison, S. 1931 *Ichabod Dawks and his newsletter*, Cambridge.

1972 *La Bible anglaise de Genève*, Geneva and Berne.

Morison, S. and Carter, H. 1967 *John Fell, the University Press and the 'Fell' types*, Oxford.

Morison, S. E. 1956 *The intellectual life of colonial New England*, 2nd edn, Ithaca, NY.

1971–4 *The European discovery of America. The Northern voyages AD 500–1600*, Oxford and New York, 1971; and *The Southern voyages AD 1492–1616*, Oxford and New York, 1974.

Morris, B. 1967 *John Cleveland (1613–1658): a bibliography of his poems*, London.

Morris, O. 1997 *The 'Chymick Bookes' of Sir Owen Wynne of Gwydir: an annotated catalogue*, Cambridge.

Morrish, P. S. 1971 'A catalogue of seventeenth-century book sale catalogues', *Quaerendo*, 1, 35–45.

1990 *Bibliotheca Higgsiana: a catalogue of the books of Dr Griffin Higgs (1589–1659)*, Oxford.

Mortimer, J. E. 1962 *The library catalogue of Anthony Higgin, Dean of Ripon (1608–1624), Proceedings of the Leeds Philosophical and Literary Society, Literary and Historical Section*, 10, 2.

Mortimer, R. 1947 'Biographical notices of printers and publishers of Friends' books to 1750: a supplement to Plomer's Dictionary', *Journal of Documentation*, 3, 107–25.

Moss, A. 1993 'Printed commonplace books in the Renaissance', *Journal of the Institute of Romance Studies*, 2, 203–13.

1996 *Printed commonplace-books and the structuring of Renaissance thought*, Oxford.

Moxon, J. 1962 *Mechanick exercises on the whole art of printing*, 2nd edn (ed.) H. Davis and H. Carter, London.

Moyles, R. G. 1985 *The text of 'Paradise lost': a study in editorial procedure*, Toronto.

Muddiman, J. G. 1971 *The King's journalist 1659–1689*, London, 1923; repr. New York.

Muldrew, C. 1997 'The currency of credit and personality: belief, trust, and the economics of reputation in early modern English society', in Fontaine, L. *et al.* (eds.) 1997 *Des personnes aux institutions*, Louvain-la-Neuve, pp. 58–79.

Munby A. N. L. 1978 'The distribution of the first edition of Newton's *Principia*', in A. N. L. Munby, *Essays and papers*, ed. N. Barker, London, pp. 43–54.

Munby, A. N. L. and Coral, L. 1977 *British book sale catalogues 1676–1800: a union list*, London.

Myers, R. 1985 'The financial records of the Stationers' Company, 1605–1811', in Myers and Harris 1985, pp. 1–31.

1990 *The Stationers' Company archives: an account of the records, 1554–1984*, Winchester.

Myers, R. and Harris, M. (eds.) 1985 *Economics of the British book trade, 1605–1939*, Cambridge.

1987 *Aspects of printing from 1600*, Oxford.

1990 *Spreading the word: the distribution networks of print 1550–1850*, Winchester.

1991 *Property of a gentleman: the formation, organisation and dispersal of the private library, 1620–1920*, Winchester.

1993 *Serials and their readers 1620–1914*, Winchester and New Castle, DE.

1994 *A millennium of the book: production, design & illustration in manuscript and print 900–1900*, Winchester and New Castle, DE.

1995 *A genius for letters: booksellers and bookselling from the 16th to the 20th century*, Winchester and New Castle, DE.

1996 *Antiquaries, book collectors and the circles of learning*, Winchester and New Castle, DE.

1997 *The Stationers' Company and the book trade 1550–1900*, Winchester and New Castle, DE.

Mynors, R. A. B and Thomson, R. M. 1993 *Catalogue of the manuscripts of Hereford Cathedral library*, Cambridge.

Needham, P. 1999 'The customs rolls as documented for the printed book trade in England', in Hellinga and Trapp 1999, pp. 148–63.

Nelson, C. and Seccombe, M. 1986 *Periodical publications 1641–1700: a survey with illustrations*, Occasional Papers of the Bibliographical Society, 2, London.

Nelson, W. 1973 *Fact of fiction, the dilemma of the Renaissance storyteller*, Cambridge, Mass.

Neuberg, V. 1972 *Chapbooks. A guide to reference material on English, Scottish and American chapbook literature of the eighteenth and nineteenth centuries*, London.

1977 *Popular literature. A history and guide*, Harmondsworth.

Newman, W. R. 1994a *Gehennical fire: the lives of George Starkey, an American alchemist in the scientific revolution*, Cambridge, MA.

1994b 'George Starkey and the selling of secrets', in Greengrass, Leslie, and Raylor 1994, pp. 193–210.

Nichols, J. 1812–20 *Literary anecdotes of the eighteenth century*, 9 vols., London.

Nischan, B. 1994 *Prince, people and confession. The Second Reformation in Brandenburg*, Philadelphia, PA.

Nixon, H. M. 1974 *English Restoration bookbinding: Samuel Mearne and his contemporaries*, London.

1984 *Bindings*, VI in Latham 1978–94.

Nixon, H. M. and Foot, M. M. 1992 *The history of decorated bookbindings in England*, Oxford.

Nixon, H. M. and Jackson, W. A. 1979 'English seventeenth-century travelling libraries', *TCBS*, 7, 294–304.

Norbrook, D. 1994 '*Areopagitica*, censorship, and the early modern public sphere', in R. Burt (ed.), *The administration of aesthetics: censorship, political criticism, and the public sphere*, Minneapolis and London (Cultural Politics, 7), pp. 3–33.

Norden, L. van 1946 'The Elizabethan College of Antiquaries', unpub. Ph.D. thesis, University of California.

1949–50 'Sir Henry Spelman on the chronology of the Elizabethan Society of Antiquaries', *HLQ*, 13, 131–60.

Norris, D. M. 1939 *A history of cataloguing and cataloguing methods, 1100–1850*, London.

Norwood, R. 1945 *The journal of Richard Norwood surveyor of Bermudas*, ed. W. F. Craven and W. B. Hayward, New York.

Nussbaum, D. 1997 'Appropriating martyrdom: fears of renewed persecution and the 1632 edition of *Acts and Monuments*', in Loades 1997, pp. 178–91.

1998, 'The reception of John Foxe's *Acts and martyrs, 1563–1641*, unpub. Ph.D. thesis, University of Cambridge.

Nuttall, G. F. 1951–2 'A transcript of Richard Baxter's Library Catalogue', *JEH*, 2, 207–21, and 3, 74–100.

Oastler, C. L. 1975 *John Day, the Elizabethan printer*, Oxford.

Oates, J. C. T. 1953 'Cambridge books of congratulatory verses 1603–1640 and their binders', *TCBS*, 1, 395–421.

1986 *Cambridge University Library; a history*. I. *From the beginnings to the Copyright Act of Queen Anne*, Cambridge.

O' Connell, S. 1999 *The popular print in England 1550–1850*, London.

O' Dell, S. 1954 *A chronological list of prose fiction in English printed in England and other countries*, Cambridge, MA.

O'Donovan, J. (ed.) 1854 *Annála Ríoghachta Éireann: Annals of the Kingdom of Ireland, by the Four Masters from the earliest period to the year 1616*, 7 vols., Dublin (repr. New York, 1966).

O'Faolain, S. 1942 *The great O'Neill: a biography of Hugh O'Neill, Earl of Tyrone, 1550–1616*, London.

Oldenburg, H. 1965–86, *The correspondence of Henry Oldenburg* (ed.) A. R. Hall, and M. B. Hall, 13 vols., Madison, WI, and London.

O'Malley, T. 1979 'The press and Quakerism, 1653–59', *JFHS*, 54, 169–84.

1982 '"Defying the powers and tempering the spirit", a review of Quaker control over their publications, 1672–89', *JEH*, 33, 72–88.

Ong, W. J. 1982 *Orality and literacy: the technologizing of the word*, London and New York.

Oppel, H. 1971 *Englisch-deutsche Literaturbeziehungen. I. Von den Anfängen bis zum Ausgang des 18. Jahrhunderts*, Berlin [Grundlagen der Anglistik und Amerikanistik, 1].

Oras, A. 1931 *Milton's editors and commentators from Patrick Hume to Henry John Todd (1695–1801): a study in critical views and methods*, London.

Osborn, J. M. 1965 *John Dryden: some biographical facts and problems*, 2nd edn, Gainesville, FL (1st edn, 1940).

O'Sullivan, W. 1995 'The Irish "remnaunt" of John Bale's manuscripts', in R. Beadle and A. J. Piper (eds.), *New Science out of old books. Studies in manuscripts and early printed books in honour of A. I. Doyle*, Aldershot, pp. 374–87.

Ovenden, R. 1994 'Jaspar Gryffyth and his books', *BLJ*, 20, 107–39.

Overend, G. H. 1909 'Notes upon the earlier history of the manufacture of paper in England', *Proceedings of the Huguenot Society of London*, 8, 177–220.

Overton, M. 1996 *Agricultural revolution in England: the transformation of the agrarian economy, 1500–1850*, Cambridge.

Overton, R. 1649 *The picture of the Councel of State*, in A. L. Morton (ed.), *Freedom in arms: a selection of Leveller writings*, London(1975), pp. 195–225.

Owen, G. 1994 *The description of Pembrokeshire*, ed. D. Miles, Llandysul.

Owen, G. D. 1964 *Elizabethan Wales: the social scene*, Cardiff.

Page, R. I. 1993 *Matthew Parker and his books*, Kalamazoo, MI.

Palliser, D. M., and Selwyn, D. G. 1972 'The stock of a York stationer, 1538', *Library*, 5th ser., 27, 207–19.

Papali, G. F. 1968 *Jacob Tonson, publisher*, Auckland.

Parker, J. 1965 *Books to build an empire. A bibliographical history of English overseas interests to 1620*, Amsterdam.

Parkes, M. B. 1997 'Archaizing hands in English Manuscripts', in Carley and Tite 1997, pp. 101–41.

Parks, S. and Havens, E. 1999 *Luttrell file: Narcissus Luttrell's dates on contemporary pamphlets 1678–1739 with a chronological index*, New Haven, CT.

Parochial libraries 1959 *The parochial libraries of the Church of England* (Central Council for the Care of Churches).

Parry, C. 1997 'From manuscript to print: II. printed books', in Gruffydd, R. G. (ed.), *A guide to Welsh literature c. 1530–1700*, Cardiff, pp. 263–76.

Parry, G. 1981 *The Golden Age restor'd: the culture of the Stuart Court 1603–1642*, Manchester.

1995 *The trophies of time: English antiquarians of the seventeenth century*, Oxford.

Pask, K. 1996 *The emergence of the English author*, Cambridge.

Patera, A. (ed.) 1892 *Jana Amosa Komenského Korrespondence*, Rozpravy Èeské Akademie Císaøe Františka Josefa, roè. 1, tø. 3, Prague.

Patterson, A. M. 1984 *Censorship and interpretation: the conditions of writing and reading in early modern England*, Madison, WI.

1993 *Reading between the lines*, Madison, WI.

Pawson, E. 1977 *Transport and economy*, London.

Pearce, E. H. 1913 *Sion College and Library*, Cambridge.

Pearson, D. 1992 'The libraries of English bishops, 1600–40', *Library*, 6th ser., 14, 221–57.

Pearson, J. 1996 'Women reading, reading women', in H. Wilcox (ed.), *Women in literature in Britain 1500–1700*, Cambridge, pp. 80–99.

Pebworth, T. -L. 1989 'John Donne, coterie poetry, and the text as performance', *Studies in English Literature 1600–1900*, 29, 61–75.

Peck, L. L. 1990 *Court patronage and corruption in early Stuart England*, London.

Peel, A. (ed.) 1915 *The seconde parte of a register: being a calendar of manuscripts under that title intended for publication by the Puritans about 1593, and now in Dr. Williams's Library, London*, 2 vols., Cambridge.

Penrose, B. 1955 *Travel and discovery in the Renaissance 1420–1620*, Cambridge, MA.

Pepys, S. 1970–83 *The diary of Samuel Pepys: a new and complete transcription*, ed. R. Latham and W. Matthews, 11 vols., London.

Peters, K. 1995 'Patterns of Quaker authorship, 1652–56', in Corns and Loewenstein 1995, pp. 6–24 (also published in *Prose Studies*, 17 (1994)).

1996 'Quaker pamphleteering and the development of the Quaker movement, 1652–1656', unpub. Ph. D. thesis, University of Cambridge.

forthcoming *Print culture and the early Quakers*, Cambridge.

Pettegree, A., Duke, A. and Lewis, G. (eds.) 1994 *Calvinism in Europe 1540–1620*, Cambridge.

Petter, H. 1974 *The Oxford almanacks*, Oxford.

Petti, A. G. (ed.) 1959 *The letters and despatches of Richard Verstegan c.1550–1640*, CRS, 52, London

Philip, I. 1983 *The Bodleian Library in the seventeenth and eighteenth centuries*, Oxford.

Philip, I. and Morgan, P. 1997 'Libraries, books and printing', in *HUO*, IV, pp. 659–85.

Phillips, J. W. 1998 *Printing and bookselling in Dublin 1670–1800: a bibliographical enquiry*, Dublin.

Pickwoad, N. 1994 'Onward and downward: how binders coped with the printing press before 1800', in Myers and Harris 1994, pp. 61–106.

1996 'Cutting corners: some deceptive practices in seventeenth-century English book-binding', in J. L. Sharpe (ed.), *Roger Powell, the compleat binder* (Turnhout, 1996), pp. 272–9.

Pierce, W. 1908 *An historical introduction to the Marprelate tracts*, London.

Pine-Coffin, R. S. 1974 *Bibliography of British and American travel in Italy to 1860*, Florence.

Pinto, D. 1990 'The music of the Hattons', *RMA Research Chronicle*, 23, 79–108.

Plomer, H. R. 1901–2 'The King's Printing House under the Stuarts', *Library*, 2nd ser., 2, 353–75.

1903 *Abstracts from the wills of English printers and stationers from 1492 to 1630*, London.

1904 'A Chester bookseller 1667–1700: some aspects of his customers and the books he sold them', *Library*, 2nd ser., 1904, 371–83.

1907a, 'Bishop Bancroft and a Catholic Press', *Library*, ns, 8, 164–7.

1907b *Dictionary of booksellers and printers who were at work in England, Scotland and Ireland from 1641 to 1667*, London.

1907c 'Some notes on the Latin and Irish Stocks of the Company of Stationers', *Library*, 2nd ser., 8, 286–97.

1910 'The Protestant press in the reign of Queen Mary', *Library*, 3rd ser., 1, 54–72.

1916 'Some Elizabethan booksales', *Library*, 3rd ser., 7, 318–29.

1922–3 'The Eliot's Court Printing House, 1584–1674', *Library*, 2nd ser., 2, 175–84; and 3, 194–209.

1924 'The importation of books into England in the fifteenth and sixteenth centuries: an examination of some customs rolls', *Library*, 4th ser., 4, 146–50.

Pocock, N. 1883 'Some notices of the Genevan Bible, part IV', *Bibliographer*, 3, 28–31.

Pol, E. H. 1975 'The library', in Th.H. Lunsingh Scheuleer and G. H. M. Postumus Meyjes (eds.), *Leiden University in the seventeenth century: an exchange of learning*, Leiden, pp. 393–459.

Pollard, A. W. (ed.) 1911 *Records of the English Bible; the documents relating to the translation and publication of the Bible in English, 1525–1611*, London. (Also included in *The Holy Bible; a facsimile in a reduced size of the Authorized Version published in the year 1611. With an introduction by A. W. Pollard and illustrative documents*, Oxford.)

Pollard, G. 1937a 'The Company of Stationers before 1557', *Library*, 4th ser., 18, 1–38.

1937b 'The early constitution of the Stationers' Company', *Library*, 4th ser., 18, 235–60.

1941 'Notes on the size of the sheet', *Library*, 4th ser., 22, 105–37.

1956 'Changes in the style of bookbinding, 1550–1830', *Library*, 5th ser., 71–94.

1978a 'The "pecia" system in the medieval universities', in M. B. Parkes and A. G. Watson (eds.) *Medieval scribes, manuscripts and libraries: essays presented to N. R. Ker*, London, pp. 145–61.

1978b 'The English market for printed books' (Sandars Lectures, 1959), *PH*, 4, 7–48.

Pollard, G. and Ehrman, A. 1965 *The distribution of books by catalogue from the invention of printing to A. D. 1800*, Cambridge.

Pollard, M. 1980 'Control of the press in Ireland through the King's Printer's Patent 1600–1800', *Irish Booklore*, 4, 79–95.

1989 *Dublin's trade in books, 1550–1800: Lyell Lectures, 1986–1987*, Oxford.

2000 *A dictionary of members of the Dublin book trade 1550–1800. Based on records of the Guild of St Luke the Evangelist*, London.

Pollen, J. H. (ed.) 1906 'The memoirs of Father Robert Persons', *Miscellanea II*, CRS, 2, London.

(ed.) 1908 *Unpublished documents relating to the English Martyrs*, I, London.

Pollen, J. H. and MacMahon, W. (eds.) 1919 *Unpublished documents relating to the English Martyrs*, II, London.

Potter, L. 1989 *Secret rites and secret writing: Royalist Literature 1641–1660*, Cambridge.

Poynter, F. 1962 *A Bibliography of Gervase Markham, 1568?–1637*, Oxford.

Price, D. C. 1976 'Gilbert Talbot, seventh earl of Shrewsbury: an Elizabethan courtier and his music', *Music & Letters*, 57, 144–51.

1981 *Patrons and musicians of the English Renaissance*, Cambridge.

Questier, M. 1996 *Conversion, politics and religion in England, 1580–1625*, Cambridge.

Quinn, D. B. 1966 *The Elizabethans and the Irish*, Ithaca, New York.

(ed.) 1974 *The Hakluyt Handbook*, 2 vols., The Hakluyt Society, 2nd ser., nos. 144–5.

1990 *Explorers and colonies: America, 1500–1625*, London and Ronceverte.

Rae, T. H. H. 1998 *John Dury and the Royal road to piety*, Studia Irenica, 37, Frankfurt am Main.

Ramsay, N. 1995 'The Cathedral archives and library', in P. Collinson, N. Ramsay and M. Sparks (eds.), *A history of Canterbury Cathedral*, Oxford.

Raven, J. 2000 'Importation of books in the eighteenth century', in Amory and Hall, 2000, pp. 183–98.

Raven, J., Small, H. and Tadmor, N. (eds.) 1996 *The practice and representation of reading in England*, Cambridge.

Ravenhill, W. 1983 'Christopher Saxton's surveying: an enigma', in S. Tyacke (ed.), *English map-making 1500–1650*, London.

(ed.) 1992 *Christopher Saxton's 16th century maps: the counties of England & Wales*, Shrewsbury.

Raylor, T. 1993 'Providence and technology in the English Civil War: Edmund Felton and his engine', *Renaissance Studies*, 7, 338–44.

1994 *Cavaliers, clubs and literary culture: Sir John Mennes, James Smith, and the Order of the Fancy*, Newark, DE.

Raymond, J. 1996a 'The cracking of the republican spokes', *Prose Studies*, 19, 255–74.

1996b *The invention of the newspaper: English newsbooks, 1641–1649*, Oxford.

Reed, J. C. 1927–30 'Humphrey Moseley, publisher', *OBS Proceedings and Papers*, 2, 57–142.

Reed, T. B. 1952 *A history of the old English letter founders with notes historical and bibliographical on the rise and progress of English typography* [1887], rev. and enlarged A. F. Johnson, London.

Rees, E. 1968 'A bibliographical note on early editions of *Canwyll y Cymry*', *Journal of the Welsh Bibliographical Society*, 10, 36–41.

1970 'Welsh publishing before 1717', in D. E. Rhodes (ed.) *Essays in honour of Victor Scholderer*, Mainz, pp. 323–36.

1987 *Libri Walliae: a catalogue of Welsh books and books printed in Wales 1546–1820*, 2 vols., Aberystwyth.

1988 *The Welsh book-trade before 1820*, Aberystwyth.

1990 'Wales and the London book trade before 1820', in Myers and Harris 1990, pp.1–20.

Reesink, H. J. 1931 *Angleterre et la littérature anglaise dans les trois plus anciens périodiques français de Hollande de 1684 à 1709*, Paris.

Reinmuth, H. S., Jr. 1973–4 'Lord William Howard (1563–1640) and his Catholic associations', *Recusant History*, 12, 226–34.

Renwick, W. L. (ed.) 1970 *A view of the present state of Ireland by Edmund Spenser*, Oxford.

Revard, S. P. 1997 *Milton and the tangle of Neaera's hair: the making of the 1645 Poems*, Columbia, MO and London.

Richards, S. N. 1994 *Y Ficer Prichard*, Caernarfon.

Rigney, J. 1993 'The English sermon 1640–1660: consuming the fire', unpub. D.Phil. thesis, University of Oxford.

Roberts, A. 1971 'The chained library, Grantham', *Library History*, 2, 75–90.

Roberts, E. (ed.) 1980 *Gwaith Siôn Tudur*, 2 vols, Cardiff.

Roberts, R. J. 1979 'John Rastell's inventory of 1538', *Library*, 6th ser., 1, 34–42.

1990 'New light on the career of Giacomo Castelvetro', *BLR*, 13, no. 5, 365–9.

1997 'Importing books for Oxford, 1500–1640', in Carley and Tite 1997, pp. 317–33.

2000 'The Latin Stock (1616–1627)', in R. Myers, M. Harris, and G. Mandelbrote (eds.), *Libraries and the book trade*, Winchester and New Castle, DE, pp. 15–28.

Roberts, R. J. and Watson, A. G. (eds.) 1990 *John Dee's Library Catalogue*, London.

Robinson, A. H. W. 1962 *Marine cartography in Britain: a history of the sea chart to 1855*, Leicester.

Robinson, B. S. 1998 '"Darke speech": Matthew Parker and the reforming of history', *Sixteenth-Century Journal*, 29, 1061–83.

Robinson, F. J. G. and Wallis, P. J. 1975 *Book subscription lists: a revised guide*, Newcastle upon Tyne.

1995– The subscription lists are available on the CD-ROM *Biography database 1680–1830*, dir. J. Cannon and F. J. G. Robinson, Newcastle upon Tyne.

Robinson, H. 1948 *The British post office*, Princeton, NJ.

Rodger, A. 1958 'Roger Ward's Shrewsbury stock: inventory of 1585', *Library*, 5th ser., 13, 247–68.

Rogers, D. 1997 'The English recusants: some medieval literary links?', *Recusant History*, 23, 483–507.

Rogers, S. 2000 'The use of Royal Licences for printing in England, 1695–1760: a bibliography', *Library*, 7th ser., 1, 145–92.

Rollins, H. 1919 'The black-letter broadside ballad', *PMLA*, 34, 259–339.

1924 *An analytical index to the ballad-entries (1557–1709) in the Register of the Company of Stationers of London*, Chapel Hill.

Rooden, P. T. van and Wesselius, J. W. 1986 'Two cases of publication by subscription in Holland and Germany: Jacob Abendana's *Mikhal Yophi* (1661) and David Cohen de Lara's *Keter Kehunna* (1668)', *Quaerendo*, 16, 110–30.

Rose, M. 1993 *Authors and owners: the invention of copyright*, Cambridge, MA.

Rosenberg, E. 1955 *Leicester, patron of letters*, New York.

Ross, R. J. 1998 'The commoning of the Common Law: the Renaissance debate over printing English law, 1520–1640', *University of Pennsylvania Law Review*, 146, 323–461.

Ross, T. 1991 'Dissolution and the making of the English literary canon: the catalogues of Leland and Bale', *Renaissance and Reformation*, 27, 57–80.

Rostenberg, L. 1954 'Robert Scott, Restoration stationer and importer, *PBSA*, 48, 49–76.

1963 *English publishers in the graphic arts 1599–1700: a study of the printsellers & publishers of engravings, art & architectural manuals, maps & copy-books*, New York.

1965 *Literary, political, scientific, religious & legal publishers, printers, and booksellers in England, 1551–1700: twelve studies*, 2 vols., New York.

1971 *The minority press and the English Crown 1558–1625: a study in repression*, Nieuwkoop.

1980 'Moses Pitt, Robert Hooke and the English Atlas', *Map Collector*, 12, 2–8.

Rotberg, R. I. and Rabb, T. K. (eds.) 1985 *Hunger and history*, Cambridge.

Rouse, E. C. 1941 'The Kederminster library', *Records of Buckinghamshire*, 14, 50–66.

Rylands, W. H. 1885 'Booksellers and stationers in Warrington, 1639 to 1657 with a full list of the contents of a stationer's stock there in 1647', *Transactions of the Historical Society of Lancashire and Cheshire*, 37 (1888 for 1885), 67–115.

Salazar, P. J. 1995 *La culte de la voix au XVIIe siècle: formes esthétiques de la parole à l' âge de l'imprimé*, Paris.

Sale W. M. 1950 *Samuel Richardson: master printer*, Ithaca, NY.

Salmon, V. 1972 *The Works of Francis Lodowick: a study of his writings in the intellectual context of the seventeenth century*, London.

Salter, J. L. 1978 'The books of an early eighteenth-century curate', *Library*, 5th ser., 33, 33–46.

Sanderson, J. 1994 'Samuel Hartlib: promoter, propagandist, and publicist', unpub. MA thesis, Institute of Bibliography and Textual Criticism, School of English, University of Leeds.

1999 'Nicholas Culpeper and the book trade: print and the promotion of vernacular medical knowledge', unpub. Ph. D. thesis, University of Leeds.

Saunders, J. W. 1951 'The stigma of print: a note on the social bases of Tudor poetry', *Essays in Criticism*, 1, 139–64.

1955 'Milton, Diomede and Amaryllis', *ELH*, 22, 254–86.

1964 *The profession of English letters*, London.

Sayle, C. E. 1916 *A catalogue of the Bradshaw Collection of Irish books in the University Library, Cambridge*, 3 vols., Cambridge.

Schenkenveld-van der Dussen, M. A. 1991 *Dutch literature in the age of Rembrandt. Themes and ideas*, Amsterdam and Philadelphia.

Schilder, G. 1985 'Jodocus Hondius, creator of the decorative map border', *Map Collector*, 32, 40–3.

1992 'An unrecorded set of thematic maps by Hondius', *Map Collector*, 59, 44–7.

Schilder, G. and Wallis, H. 1989 'Speed military maps discovered', *Map Collector*, 48, 22–6.

Schilling, H. (ed.) 1986 *Die reformierte Konfessionalisierung in Deutschland. Das Problem der 'Zweiten Reformation'*, Gütersloh.

Schleiner, L. 1994 *Tudor and Stuart women writers*, Bloomington, IL.

Schmitz, W. 1987 'Ein genealogisches Verzeichnis als buchgeschichtliche Quelle', *Jahrbuch des Kölnischen Geschichtesvereins*, 58, 185–208.

Schofield, R. S. 1985 'The impact of scarcity and plenty on population change in England, 1541–1871', in Rotberg and Rabb 1985, pp. 67–94.

Schoneveld, C. W. 1983 *Intertraffic of the mind. Studies in seventeenth-century Anglo-Dutch translation with a checklist of books translated from English into Dutch, 1600–1700*, Leiden.

Schrickx, W. 1976 'John Fowler', *De Gulden Passer*, 54, 1–48.

Schroeder, H. J. (ed.) 1978 *The Canons and Decrees of the Council of Trent*, Rockford, ILL.

Schuchard, M. 1975 *A descriptive bibliography of the works of John Ogilby and William Morgan*, Frankfurt am Main.

Schumacher-Voelker, U. 1981 'Authorship of *The accomplish'd lady's delight*, 1675', *Petit Propos Culinaires*, pp. 66–7.

Schwartz, S. B. 1994 *Implicit understandings. Observing, reporting, and reflecting on the encounters between Europeans and other peoples in the early modern era*, Cambridge.

Schwetschke, G. 1850 *Codex nundinarius Germaniae literatae bisecularis 1564–1765*, Halle; repr. Nieuwkoop, 1963.

Scouloudi, I. 1985 *Returns of Strangers in the metropolis 1593, 1627, 1635, 1639*, Huguenot Society Quarto Series, 57, London.

Seaward, P. 1989 *The Cavalier Parliament and the reconstruction of the old regime, 1661–1667*, Cambridge.

Selement, G. 1994 *Keepers of the vineyard: the Puritan ministry and collective culture in colonial New England*, London.

Selling, A. 1990 *Deutsche Gelehrten-Reisen nach England 1660–1714*, Frankfurt am Main.

Sells, A. L. 1964 *The Paradise of travellers. The Italian influence on English travellers in the seventeenth century*, London.

Selm, B. van 1987 *Een menighte treffelijcke boecken. Nederlandse boekhandelscatalogi in het begin van de zeventiende eeuw*, Utrecht.

Selwyn, D. G. 1996 *The library of Thomas Cranmer*, OBS Publications, 3rd ser., 1.

Selwyn, P. M. 1997 'Such speciall bookes of Mr Somersettes as were sould to Mr Secretory', in Carley and Tite 1997, pp. 389–401.

Sensabaugh, G. F. 1952 *That grand Whig Milton*, Stanford, CA.

Seymour, M. 1983 'Some thoughts on English Newsbooks as business enterprises in the 1640s and 50s', unpubl. paper delivered at a conference on the seventeenth-century press at Darwin College, University of Cambridge.

Shammas, C. 1990 *The pre-industrial English consumer in England and America*, Oxford.

Sharpe, K. 1979 *Sir Robert Cotton 1586–1631: history and politics in early modern England*, Oxford.

Sharpe, R. (ed.) 1996 *English Benedictine libraries: the shorter catalogues*, London.

Shepard, L. 1962 *The broadside ballad: a study in origins and meaning*, London.

1973 *The history of street literature: the story of broadside ballads, chapbooks, proclamations, news-sheets, election bills, tracts, pamphlets, cocks, catchpennies and other ephemera*, Newton Abbot.

Shepherd, S. 1985 *The women's sharp revenge*, London.

Sherbo, A. 1979 'The Dryden-Cambridge translation of Plutarch's Lives', *Études Anglaises*, 32, 177–84.

1985 'Dryden as a Cambridge editor', *SB*, 38, 251–61.

Sherman, W. 1995 *John Dee: the politics of reading and writing in the English Renaissance*, Amherst, MA.

Shire, H. M. 1969 *Song, dance and poetry of the court of Scotland under James VI*, Cambridge.

Shirley, R. W. 1980 *Early printed maps of the British Isles, a bibliography 1477–1650*, 2nd edn, London.

1983 *The mapping of the world: early printed world maps 1472–1700*, London.

1988 *Printed maps of the British Isles 1650–1750*, Tring.

1995 'The maritime maps and atlases of Seller, Thornton, Mount and Page', *Map Collector*, 73, 2–9.

Shorter, A. H. 1971 *Paper making in the British Isles: an historical and geographical study*, Newton Abbott.

Siebert, F. S. 1952 *Freedom of the press in England 1476–1776: the rise and fall of government control*, Urbana, IL; reprinted 1965.

Simoni, A. E. C. 1990 'The hidden trade-mark of Laurence Kellam, printer at Douai', *Ons geestelijk erf*, 64, 130–43.

Simpson, C. 1966 *The British broadside ballad and its music*, New Brunswick.

Simpson, E. M. 1948 *A study of the prose works of John Donne*, 2nd edn, Oxford.

Simpson, M. C. P. 1990 *A catalogue of the library of the Revd. James Nairn (1629–1678)*, Edinburgh.

Simpson, P. 1925 'Walkley's piracy of Wither's Poems in 1620', *Library*, 4th ser., 6, 271–7.

Sisson, C. J. 1940 *The judicious marriage of Mr Hooker and the birth of the 'Laws of ecclesiastical polity'*, Cambridge.

Skelton, R. A. 1966 'Bibliographical note' to *Lucas Jansz. Waghenaer: The mariners mirrour (London, 1588), Theatrum orbis terrarum*, 3rd ser., II, Amsterdam, pp. v–xi.

1970 *County atlases of the British Isles*, London.

Slack, P. 1979 'Mirrors of health and treasures of poor men: the uses of the vernacular medical literature of Tudor England', in C. Webster (ed.), *Health, medicine, and mortality in the sixteenth century*, Cambridge, pp. 237–73.

1985 *The impact of plague in Tudor and Stuart England*, London.

Slagle, G. von 1983 'A note on early Welsh orthography', *Library* 6th ser., 5, 254–6.

Smith, H. S. A. 1989 'A Manchester science library: Chetham's Library in 1684', *Library History*, 6, 110–15.

Smith, Ll. B. 1998 'Inkhorn and spectacles: the impact of literacy in late medieval Wales', in Pryce, H. (ed.), *Literacy in medieval Celtic Societies*, Cardiff, pp. 202–22.

Smith, N. 1989 *Perfection proclaimed: language and literature in English radical religion, 1640–1660*, Oxford.

1990 'Exporting enthusiasm: John Perrot and the Quaker epic', in T. F. Healy and J. Sawday (eds.), *Warre is all the world about: literature and the English Civil War*, Cambridge, pp. 248–64.

1992 'The charge of atheism and the language of radical speculation', in Hunter and Wootton 1992, 131–58 .

1994 *Literature and Revolution in England, 1640–1660*, New Haven and London.

1995a 'Hidden things brought to light', in Corns and Loewenstein 1995, pp. 57–69 (also published in *Prose Studies*, 17 (1994)).

1995b 'Popular Republicanism in the 1650s: John Streater's "heroick mechanicks"', in D. Armitage, *et al.* (eds.), *Milton and Republicanism*, Cambridge, pp. 137–55.

forthcoming '"Naked space": Radicalism, print and the public sphere', in P. Lake and S. C. A. Pincus (eds.), *The public sphere in early modern England, Manchester.*

Smith, P. H. 1994 *The business of alchemy: science and culture in the Holy Roman Empire*, Princeton, NJ.

Smith, T. R. 1978 'Manuscript and printed sea charts in seventeenth-century London: the case of the Thames School', in Thrower 1978, pp. 45–100.

Smith, W. J. (ed.) 1963 *Herbert correspondence: the sixteenth and seventeenth century letters of the Herberts of Chirbury, Powis Castle and Dolguog, formerly at Powis Castle in Montgomeryshire*, Cardiff.

Smolenaars, M. and Veenhoff, A. 1997 'Samuel Smith "an honest enough man, for a bookseller"', *Antiquarian Book Monthly*, February, 36–9.

Snow, V. F. 1977 'John Hooker's circle: evidence from his New Year's gift list of 1584', *Devon and Cornwall Notes and Queries*, 33, 273–7, 317–24.

Southern, A. C. 1950 *Elizabethan Recusant prose* 1559–1582, London and Glasgow.

Sparke, M. 1641 *Scintilla, or a light broken into darke warehouses*, London.

Speed Hill, W. 1993 *New ways of looking at old texts: papers of the Renaissance English Text Society 1985–1991*, Binghamton, NY.

Spirgatis, M. 1902 'Englische Literatur auf der Frankfurter Buchmesse von 1561–1620', *Beiträge zur Kenntnis der Schrift-, Buch- und Bibliothekwesens*, Leipzig, VII, pp. 37–89.

Sprunger, K. L. 1994 *Trumpets from the tower: English Puritan printing in the Netherlands, 1600–1640*, Leiden.

Spufford, M. 1979 'First steps in literacy', *Social History*, 4, 410–30.

1981 *Small books and pleasant histories: popular fiction and its readership in seventeenth-century England*, Cambridge.

1984 *The great reclothing of rural England: petty chapmen and their wares in the seventeenth century*, London.

1995 (ed.) *The world of rural dissenters, 1520–1725*, Cambridge.

Stanwood, P. G. 1978 'John Donne's sermon notes', *RES*, 29, 313–20.

(ed.) 1995 *Of poetry and politics: new essays on Milton and his world*, Medieval and Renaissance Texts and Studies, 126, Binghamton, NY.

Starnes, D. T. 1954 *Renaissance dictionaries: English-Latin and Latin-English*, Austin, TX and Edinburgh.

Steele, I. K. 1986 *The English Atlantic, 1675–1740*, New York.

Stevens, D. H. 1930 *A reference guide to Milton from 1800 to the present day*, Chicago.

Stevenson, A., 1951–2 'Watermarks are twins', *SB*, 4, 57–91.

1967 'Tudor roses from John Tate', *SB*, 20, 15–34.

Stewart-Brown, R. 1932 'The stationers, booksellers and printers of Chester to about 1800', *Transactions of the Historic Society of Lancashire and Cheshire*, 83, 101–52.

Stock, B. 1983 *The implications of literacy: written language and models of interpretation in the eleventh and twelfth centuries*, Princeton.

Stockum, W. P. van, Jr. 1946 *The first newspapers of England... published in Holland*, The Hague.

Stoker, D. 1976 'A History of the Norwich book trades from 1560 to 1760', unpub. Library Association Fellowship thesis.

1981 'Anthony de Solempne: attributions to his press', *Library*, 6th ser., 3, 17–32.

1981–5 'The Norwich book trades before 1800', *TCBS*, 8, 79–125.

Stone, L. (ed.) 1976 *Schooling and society*, Baltimore and London.

Stoye, J. 1989 *English travellers abroad 1604–1667*, 1952; rev. edn. New Haven and London.

Streeter, B. H. 1931 *The chained library*, London.

Strong, R. 1986 *Henry Prince of Wales and England's lost Renaissance*, London.

Suggett, R. 1997 'The Welsh language and the Court of Great Session', in G. H. Jenkins (ed.), *The Welsh language before the Industrial Revolution*, Cardiff, pp. 153–80.

2000 'Pedlars & mercers as distributors of print in 16th and 17th century Wales', in P. Isaac and B. McKay (eds.), *The mighty engine: the book trade at work*, Winchester and New Castle, DE, pp. 23–32.

Sullivan, W. W. II 1988 *The first and second Dalhousie manuscripts: poems and prose*, Columbia, MO.

1993 *The influence of John Donne: his uncollected seventeenth-century printed verse*, Columbia, MO and London.

Swift, K. 1990 '"The French-booksellers in the Strand": Huguenots in the London book trade, 1685–1730', *Proceedings of the Huguenot Society*, 25, 123–39.

Tanner, J. R. (ed.) 1926 *Samuel Pepys's naval minutes*, Publications of the Navy Records Society, 60, London.

Tapley, H. S. 1927 *Salem imprints, 1768–1825*, Salem, MA.

Taylor, A. 1966 *General subject-indexes since 1548*, Philadelphia, PA.

Temperley, N. 1972 'John Playford and the metrical psalms', *Journal of the American Musicological Society*, 25, 331–78.

Ternois, R. 1933 'Les débuts de l'anglophilie en France: Henri Justel', *Revue de littérature comparée*, 13, 588–605.

Terry, A. 1938 'Giles Calvert's publishing career', *JFHS*, 25, 45–9.

Thomas, G. C. G. 1997 'From manuscript to print: I. manuscript', in R. G. Gruffydd (ed.), *A guide to Welsh literature c. 1530–1700*, Cardiff, pp. 241–63.

Thomas, I. 1976 *Y Testament Newydd Cymraeg 1551–1620*, Cardiff.

Thomas, K. 1986 'The meaning of literacy in early modern England', in G. Baumann (ed.), *The written word: literacy in transition*, Oxford, pp. 97–131.

Thomason, G. 1908 *Catalogue of the pamphlets, books, newspapers, and manuscripts relating to the Civil War, the Commonwealth, and Restoration, collected by George Thomason, 1640–1661*, 2 vols., London.

Thompson, R. 1975 'Worthington Chauncey Ford's *Boston book market, 1679–1700: some corrections and additions*', *Proceedings of the Massachusetts Historical Society*, 86, 67–78.

1986 *Sex in Middlesex: popular mores in a Massachusetts county, 1649–1699*, Amherst, MA.

1988 'English music manuscripts and the fine paper trade, 1648–1688', unpub. Ph.D. thesis, University of London.

1989 'George Jeffreys and the "stile nuovo" in English sacred music: a new date for his autograph score, British Library, Add. MS 10338', *Music & Letters*, 70, 317–41.

1995 'Manuscript music in Purcell's London', *Early Music*, 2, 605–18.

Thomson, A. G. 1974 *The paper industry in Scotland 1590–1861*, Edinburgh.

Thomson, R. S. 1974 'The development of the broadside ballad trade and its influence on the transmission of English folksongs', unpub. Ph.D. thesis, University of Cambridge.

Thornton, D. 1997 *The scholar in his study: ownership and experience in Renaissance Italy*, New Haven, CT and London.

Thornton, P. 1978 *Seventeenth-century interior decoration in England, Holland and France*, New Haven, CT.

Thrower, N. (ed.) 1978 *The compleat plattmaker: essays on chart, map, and globe making in England in the seventeenth and eighteenth centuries*, Berkeley, CA.

Tilmouth, M. 1961 'A calendar of references to music in newspapers published in London and the provinces (1660–1719)', *RMA Research Chronicle* 1.

Tite, C. G. C. 1994 *The manuscript library of Sir Robert Cotton*, London.

1997 ' "Lost or stolen or strayed": a survey of manuscripts formerly in the Cotton Library', in Wright 1997, pp. 262–306.

Todd, J. H. 1821 *Memoirs of the life of the Right Rev. Brian Walton*, London.

Todd, M. H. 1923 *The register of Freemen of Newcastle upon Tyne*, Publications of the Newcastle upon Tyne Records Committee, 3, Newcastle upon Tyne.

Treadwell, M. 1980/1 'The Grover typefoundry', *JPHS*, 15, 36–53.

1982a 'London trade publishers 1675–1750', *Library*, 6th ser., 4, 99–134.

1982b 'Notes on London typefounders 1620–1720', unpub. paper delivered July 1982 to the Printing Historical Society in Oxford.

1987 'Lists of master printers: the size of the London printing trade, 1637–1723', in Myers and Harris, 1987, pp. 141–70. This subsumes two earlier articles.

1992 'Printers on the Court of the Stationers' Company in the seventeenth and eighteenth centuries', *JPHS*, 21, 29–42.

1996 '1695–1995: Some tercentenary thoughts on the freedoms of the press', *HLB*, ns. 7, 3–19.

1997 'Richard Lapthorne and the London retail book trade, 1683–1697', in Hunt, Mandelbrote and Shell 1977, pp. 205–22.

Trevor-Roper, H. R. 1967 *Religion, the Reformation and social change*, London.

Tribble, E. 1993 *Margins and marginality: the printed page in early modern England*, Charlottesville, VA.

Tuer, A. 1896 *The history of the horn-book*, 2 vols., London.

Turnbull, G. H. 1920 *Samuel Hartlib. A sketch of his life and his relation to J. A. Comenius*, Oxford.

1947 *Hartlib, Dury and Comenius.Gleanings from Hartlib's papers*, London.

Tyacke, N. 1990 *Anti-Calvinists: the rise of English Arminianism c. 1590–1640*, rev. edn, Oxford.

Tyacke, S. 1973 'Map-sellers and the London map trade c. 1650–1710', in Wallis and Tyacke 1973, pp. 63–80.

1978 *London map-sellers 1660–1720*, Tring.

1992 'Describing maps', in Davison 1998, pp. 130–41.

Underhill, E. B., ed. 1847 *The records of a Church of Christ meeting in Broadmead, Bristol, 1640–1687*, London.

Vaisey, D. G. 1975 'Anthony Stephens: the rise and fall of an Oxford bookseller', in *Studies in the book trade in honour of Graham Pollard*, OBS Publications, ns., 18, 91–117.

Veale, E. 1995 'Sir Theodore Janssen, Huguenot and merchant of London c. 1658–1748', *Proceedings of the Huguenot Society of Great Britain & Ireland*, 26, 264–88.

Venuti, L. 1993 '*The Destruction of Troy*: translation and Royalist cultural politics in the Interregnum', *Journal of Medieval and Renaissance Studies*, 23, 197–219.

Verner, C. 1969 'Captain Collins' Coasting Pilot: a carto-bibliographical analysis', *Map Collectors' Series*, 58, 1–56.

1978 'John Seller and the chart trade in seventeenth century England', in Thrower 1978, pp. 127–57.

Vervliet, H. D. L. 1968 *Sixteenth-century printing types of the Low Countries*, Amsterdam.

1981 *Cyrillic & oriental typography in Rome at the end of the sixteenth century: an inquiry into the later work of Robert Granjon (1578–90)*, Berkeley.

Veyrin-Forrer, J. 1987 'Aux origines de l'imprimerie française; l'atelier de la Sorbonne et ses mécènes (1470–1473)', in her *La lettre et le texte: trente années de recherches sur l'histoire du livre*, Paris, pp. 161–87.

Vieth, D. M. 1960 'A textual paradox: Rochester's "To a lady in a letter"', *PBSA*, 54, 147–62, and 55, 130–3.

1963 *Attribution in Restoration poetry: a study of Rochester's 'Poems' of 1680*, New Haven.

Voet, L. 1969–72 *The golden compasses*, 2 vols., Amsterdam.

Wabuda, S. and Litzenberger, C. (eds.) 1998 *Belief and practice in Reformation England: a tribute to Patrick Collinson by his students*, Aldershot and Brookfield, VT.

Wainwright, J. P. 1990 'George Jeffreys' copies of Italian music', *RMA Research Chronicle*, 23, 109–24.

Walker, K. 1992 'Jacob Tonson, bookseller', *The American Scholar*, 61, 424–30.

Walker, M. 1970 'Welsh books in St Mary's, Swansea, 1559–1626', *Bulletin of the Board of Celtic Studies* 23, 397–402.

Walker, R. B. 1974 'The newspaper press in the Reign of William III', *Historical Journal*, 17, 691–709.

Wall, W. 1993 *The imprint of gender: authorship and publication in the English renaissance*, Ithaca, NY.

Wallis, H. 1951 'The first English globe: a recent discovery', *Geographical Journal*, 117, 275–90.

1962 'Globes in England up to 1660', *Geographical Magazine*, 35, 267–79.

1978 'Geographie is better than divinitie. Maps, globes, and geography in the days of Samuel Pepys', in Thrower 1978, pp. 1–43.

Wallis, H. and Tyacke, S. (eds.) 1973 *My head is a map: essays & memoirs in honour of R. V. Tooley*, London.

Wallis, P. J. 1967 'An early mathematical manifesto – John Pell's *Idea of mathematics*', *Durham Research Review*, 18, 139–48.

Walsh, M. 1997 *Shakespeare, Milton, and eighteenth-century literary editing: the beginnings of interpretative scholarship*, Cambridge.

Walsh, M. J. 1981 'The publishing policy of the English press at St. Omer, 1608–1759', in K. Robbins (ed.), *Religion and humanism*, Oxford, 239–50.

Walsh, M. O'N. 1963 'Irish books printed abroad 1475–1700: an interim checklist', in L. Miller (ed.), *The Irish book*, Dublin.

Walsh, Revd P. [Breathnach, Pól], 1934 'Captain Sorley MacDonnell and his books', *Irish Book Lover*, 22, 4, 81–8.

Walsham, A. 1993 *Church Papists: Catholicism, conformity and confessional polemic in early modern England*, Royal Historical Society Studies in History, 68, Woodbridge.

1995 'Aspects of Providentialism in early modern england', unpub. Ph. D. thesis, University of Cambridge.

1998 '"A glose of godlines": Philip Stubbes, Elizabethan Grub Street and the invention of Puritanism', in Wabuda and Litzenberger 1998, pp. 177–206.

1999 *Providence in early modern England*, Oxford.

2000 '"Domme preachers": Post-Reformation English Catholicism and the culture of print', *Past & Present*, 168, 177–206.

Waterhouse, G. 1914 *The Literary relations of England and Germay in the seventeenth century*, Cambridge.

Watson, A. G. 1966 *The library of Sir Simonds D'Ewes*, London.

1986 'John Twyne of Canterbury (*d.* 1581) as a collector of medieval manuscripts: a preliminary investigation', *Library*, 6th Ser., 8, 133–51.

Watson, F. 1908 *The English Grammar Schools to 1660: their curriculum and practice*, Cambridge.

Watson, J. 1713 *The history of the art of printing* (facsimile ed., D. F. Foxon, London 1965).

Watt, D. 1997 *Sectaries of God: women prophets in late Medieval and early modern England*, Woodbridge.

Watt, T. 1990 'Publisher, pedlar, pot-poet: the changing character of the broadside trade, 1550–1640', in Myers and Harris 1990, pp. 61–81.

1991 *Cheap print and popular piety 1550–1640*, Cambridge.

1995 'Piety in the pedlar's pack: continuity and change', in Spufford 1995, pp. 235–72.

Weatherill, L. 1988 *Consumer behaviour and material culture in Britain 1660–1760*, London.

Weber, H. 1996 *Paper bullets: print and kingship under Charles II*, Lexington, KY.

Webster, C. 1975 *The Great Instauration: science, medicine and reform*, 1626–1660, London.

(ed.) 1979 *Utopian planning and the puritan revolution. Gabriel Plattes, Samuel Hartlib and 'Macaria'*, Research Publications Wellcome Unit for the History of Medicine, IL, Oxford.

1982 *From Paracelsus to Newton: magic and the making of modern science*, Cambridge.

Weil, E. 1944 'William Fitzer, the publisher of Harvey's *De motu cordis*, 1628', *Library*, 4th ser., 24, 142–64.

1951 'Samuel Browne, printer to the university of Heidelberg', *Library*, 5th ser., 5, 14–25.

Wheale, N. 1999 *Writing and society: literacy, print and politics in Britain, 1598–1660*, London.

Wheeler, G. W. 1928 *The earliest catalogues of the Bodleian Library*, Oxford.

White, H. C. 1931 *English devotional literature (prose) 1600–1640*, Madison, WI.
1951 *The Tudor books of private devotion*, Madison, WI.
1963 *Tudor books of saints and martyrs*, Madison, WI.
Whyte, I. D. 1995 *Scotland before the industrial revolution*, London.
Wilcox, P. 1994 '"The Restoration of the Church" on Calvin's "Commentaries on Isaiah the prophet"', *Archiv für Reformationsgeschichte*, 85, 68–95.
Wiles, R. M. 1957 *Serial publication in England before 1750*, Cambridge.
Wilkins, N. 1993 *Catalogue des manuscrits français de la Bibliothèque Parker*, Cambridge.
Willems, A. 1880 *Les Elzevier: histoire et annales typographiques*, 2 vols., Brussels.
Willetts, P. J. 1969 *The Henry Lawes Manuscript*, London.
1991 'John Barnard's collections of viol and vocal music', *Chelys*, 20, 28–42.
Williams, F. B. Jr. 1948 'Scholarly publication in Shakespeare's day: a leading case', in J. G. McManaway, G. E. Dawson and E. E. Willoughby (eds.), *Joseph Quincy Adams: memorial studies*, Washington, DC, pp. 755–73.
1962 *Index of dedications and commendatory verses in English books before 1641*, London.
Williams, G. 1967 *Welsh Reformation Essays*, Cardiff.
1976 'Bishop William Morgan (1545–1604) and the first Welsh Bible', *Journal of the Merioneth Historical and Record Society*, 347–72.
1987 *Recovery, reorientation and Reformation: Wales c. 1415–1642*, Oxford.
1997 'Unity of religion or unity of language? Protestants and Catholics and the Welsh language 1536–1660', in G. H. Jenkins, (ed.), *The Welsh language before the Industrial Revolution*, Cardiff, pp. 207–53.
Williams, G. A. 1986 *Ymryson Edmwnd Prys a Wiliam Chynwal: fersiwn Llawysgrif Llanstephan 43*, Cardiff.
Williams, G. J. (ed.) 1939 *Gramadeg Cymraeg gan Gruffydd Robert, yn ôl yr argraffiad y dechreuwyd ei gyhoeddi ym Milan yn 1567*, Cardiff.
1948 *Traddodiad llenyddol Morgannwg*, Cardiff.
1969 'Stephen Hughes a'i gyfnod', in A. Lewis (ed.), *Agweddau ar hanes dysg Gymraeg: detholiad o ddarlithiau G. J. Williams*, Cardiff, pp. 171–206.
Williams, I. 1935 'Cerddorion a cherddau yn Lleweni, Nadolig 1595', *Bulletin of the Board of Celtic Studies* 8, 8–10.
Williams, J. B. 1908 [J. G. Muddiman] *A history of English journalism to the foundation of the Gazette*, London.
Williams, N. J. A. (ed.) 1981 *Pairlement Chloinne Tomáis*, Dublin.
Williams, W. O. 1964 'The survival of the Welsh language after the union of England and Wales: the first phase, 1536–1642', *Welsh History Review* 2, 67–93.
Williamson, G. C. 1967 *Lady Anne Clifford, Countess of Dorset, Pembroke and Montgomery 1590–1676*, 2nd edn, Wakefield.
Willis, G. 1981 'The Leighton Library, Dunblane: its history and contents', *The Bibliotheck*, 10, 139–57.
Wilson, C. H. 1980 'Land carriage in the seventeenth century', *EcHR*, 2nd ser., 33, 92–5.
1984 *England's apprenticeship 1603–1763*, 2nd edn, London and New York.
Wilson, J. D. 1912a *Martin Marprelate and Shakespeare's Fluellen. A new theory of the authorship of the Marprelate tracts*, London.

1912b 'Richard Schilders and the English Puritans', *Transactions of the Bibliographical Society*, 11, 65–134.

Winfield, P. H. 1925 *Chief sources of English legal history*, Cambridge, MA.

Winship, G. P. 1945 *The Cambridge press, 1638–1692*, Philadelphia, PA.

Wiseman, S. 1998 *Drama and politics in the English Civil War*, Cambridge.

Wolf, E. 1988 *The book culture of a colonial American city: Philadelphia books, bookmen and booksellers*, 2nd edn, Oxford.

Wood, P. 1980 'Methodology and apologetics: Thomas Sprat's "History of the Royal Society"', *British Journal for the History of Science*, 13, 1–26.

Woodall, N. J. 1994 'Milton's Vergilian epigraphs of 1637 and 1645', in C. W. Durham and K. P. McColgan (eds.), *Spokesperson Milton: voices in contemporary criticism*, Selinsgrove, pp. 206–16.

Woodfield, D. B. 1973 *Surreptitious printing in England, 1550–1640*, New York.

Woodward, D. (ed.) 1975 *Five centuries of map printing*, Chicago, IL.

1978 'English cartography, 1650–1750: a summary', in Thrower 1978, pp. 159–193.

Woodward, G. and Christophers, R. A. 1972 *The chained library of the Royal Grammar School, Guildford*, Guildford.

Woolf, D. R. 1990 *The idea of history in early Stuart England*, Toronto.

2000 *Reading history in early modern England*, Cambridge.

Wootton, D. 1993 'The Levellers', in J. Dunn (ed.), *Democracy: the unfinished journey, 508 BC to AD 1993*, Oxford, pp. 71–89.

2001 'Reginald Scot/Abraham Fleming/The Family of Love', in S. Clark, ed., *Languages of witchcraft: narrative, ideology and meaning in early modern culture*, New York, pp. 119–38.

Wormald, F. and Wright, C. E. (eds.) 1958 *The English library before 1700: studies in history*, London.

Worman, E. J. 1906, *Alien members of the book trade during the Tudor period*, London.

Worthington, J. 1847 *Diary and correspondence*, 3 vols., Manchester, Chetham Society, vols. 13, 36 and 114, 1847–86.

Woudhuysen, H. R. 1996 *Sir Philip Sidney and the circulation of manuscripts 1558–1640*, Oxford.

Wright, C. E. 1953 'The dispersal of the monastic libraries and the beginnings of Anglo-Saxon studies', *TCBS*, 1:3, 208–37.

1958a 'The dispersal of the libraries in the sixteenth century', in Wormald and Wright 1958, pp. 148–75.

1958b 'The Elizabethan Society of Antiquaries and the formation of the Cottonian Library', in Wormald and Wright 1958, pp. 176–212.

Wright, C. J. (ed.) 1997 *Sir Robert Cotton as collector*, London.

Wright, D. H. 1967 *The Vespasian Psalter (British Museum Cotton Vespasian A 1)*, Early English Manuscripts in Facsimile, 14, Copenhagen.

Wright L. B. 1935 *Middle-class culture in Elizabethan England*, Chapel Hill.

Wright, T. G. 1920 *Literary culture in early New England, 1620–1730*, New Haven, CT.

Wrigley, E. A. 1985 'Urban growth and agricultural change: England and the Continent in the early modern period', *Journal of Interdisciplinary History*, 15, 683–728.

Wrigley, E. A. and Schofield, R. S. 1981 *The population history of England 1541–1871: a reconstruction*, London.

Wurzbach, N. 1990 *The rise of the English street ballad, 1550–1650*, Cambridge.

Wynn, J. 1990 *The history of the Gwydir family and memoirs*, ed. J. G. Jones, Llandysul.

Young, J. T. 1998 'Faith, medical alchemy and natural philosophy. Johann Moriaen, reformed intelligencer, and the Hartlib circle', in A. Cunningham and O. P. Grell (eds.), *The history of medicine in context*, Aldershot.

Young, R. F. 1932 *Comenius in England: the visit of Jan Komensky (Comenius) to London in 1641–1642*, London.

Zaret, D. 2000 *Origins of democratic culture: printing, petitions, and the public sphere in early modern England*, Princeton, NJ.

Index

THE

NEVV TESTAMENT OF IESVS CHRIST, TRANSLATED FAITHFVLLY INTO ENGLISH,

out of the authentical Latin, according to the best corrected copies of the same, diligently conferred vvith the Greeke and other editions in diuers languages: Vvith ARGVMENTS of bookes and chapters, ANNOTATIONS, and other necessarie helpes, for the better vnderstanding of the text, and specially for the discouerie of the CORRVPTIONS of diuers late translations, and for cleering the CONTROVERSIES in religion, of these daies:

IN THE ENGLISH COLLEGE OF RHEMES.

Psal. 118.

Da mihi intellectum, & scrutabor legem tuam, & custodiam illam in toto corde meo.

That is,

Giue me vnderstanding, and I vvil searche thy lavv, and vvil keepe it vvith my vvhole hart.

S. Aug. tract. 2. in Epist. Ioan.

Omnia quæ leguntur in Scripturis sanctis, ad instructionem & salutem nostram intentè oportet audire: maximè tamen memoriæ commendanda sunt, quæ aduersus Hæreticos valent plurimum: quorum insidiæ, infirmiores quosque & negligentiores circumuenire non cessant.

That is,

Al things that are readde in holy Scriptures, vve must heare vvith great attention, to our instruction and saluation: but those things specially must be commended to memorie, vvhich make most against Heretikes: vvhose deceites cease not to circumuent and beguile al the vveaker sort and the more negligent persons.

PRINTED AT RHEMES, by Iohn Fogny.

1582.

CVM PRIVILEGIO.

1.1 *The New Testament of Jesus Christ, translated faithfully into English* . . . printed at Rhemes, by John Fogny, 1582 title page. The Rheims Bible presents the translation of the New Testament made by English Catholics at their College at Rheims and published there in quarto.

5.1a Robert Jones, *The first booke of songes & ayres of four parts with tableture for the lute. So made that all the parts together, or either of them seuerally may be song to the lute, orpherian or viol de gambo*, P. Short, with the assent of T. Morley, 1600, sig. B1^{v}. A folio table book, designed so that all performers could sit around a single copy.

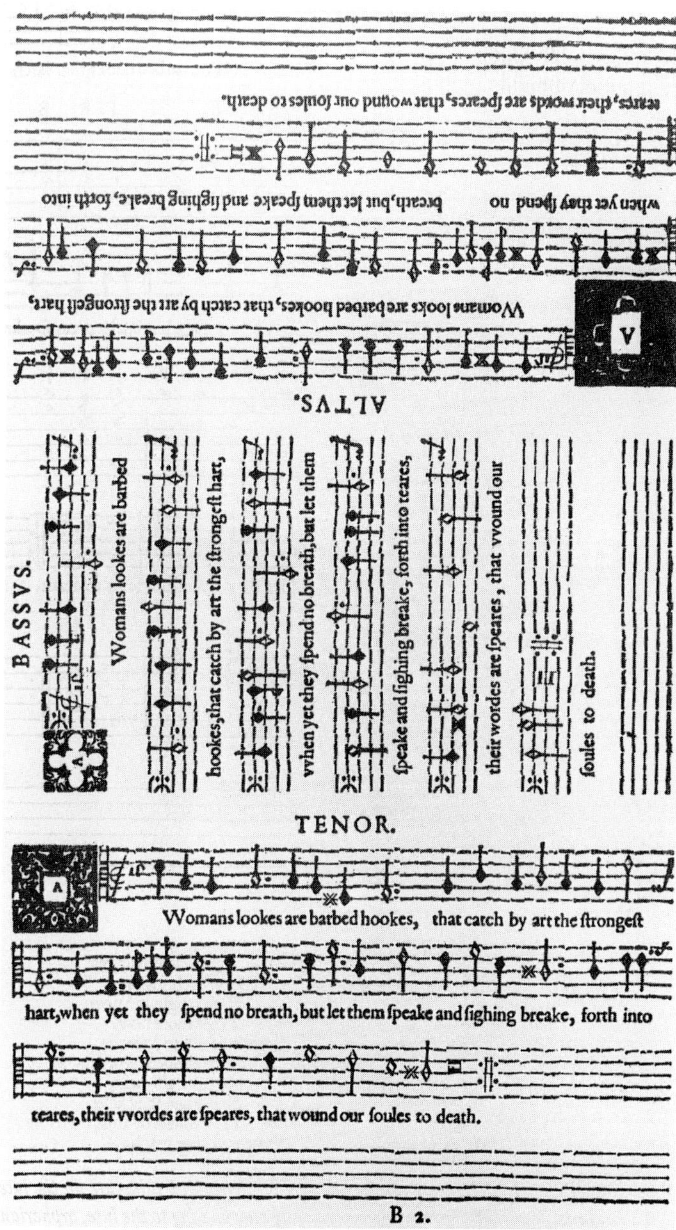

5.1b Robert Jones, *The first booke of songes & ayres of four parts with tableture for the lute. So made that all the parts together, or either of them seuerally may be song to the lute, orpherian or viol de gambo*, P. Short, with the assent of T. Morley, 1600, sig. B2^{r}.

5.2 An example of aural transcription with the words in a form of shorthand. British Library MS. Egerton 2013, fol. 60v.

10.1 Christopher Saxton, *Anglia hominu[m] numero, rerumq[ue] fere omniu[m] copiis abundans* . . . 1579. The general map of England and Wales from the first English-published and the first ever national atlas. Engraved, signed and dated in the plate by the English engraver, Augustine Ryther, and decorated both with the royal arms and those of Saxton's patron, Thomas Seckford.

12.1 Francis Willughby, *Historia piscium*, Oxford, 1686, vol. II frontispiece. Willughby's work was edited posthumously by John Ray, printed at Fell's press in Oxford, and published by the Royal Society. The Society's only substantial publishing project – works like Newton's *Principia* and the *Philosophical Transactions* remained the concern of individual members – it proved a disappointing failure in both scholarly and economic terms.

12.2 John Parkinson, *Paradisi in sole Paradisus terrestris*, London, 1629, engraved title page. Parkinson's was one of several comprehensive herbals available to wealthy mid-century landowners. It advised not only on different kinds of plants, but on the proper layout for a pleasurable garden.

A

Physical Directory:

Or a Translation of the

DISPENSATORY

Made by the

COLLEDGE of PHYSITIANS of

LONDON,

And by them imposed upon all the APOTHECARIES of *England* to make up their MEDICINES by.

Whereunto is added,

The Vertues of the SIMPLES, and COMPOUNDS.

And in this second Edition are Seven hundred eighty four Additions the general heads whereof are these: *VIZ.*

1. The Dose (or quantity to be taken at one time) and Use, both of SIMPLES and COMPOUNDS.
2. The Method of ordering the Body after sweating and purging Medicines.
3. Cautions (to all Ignorant People) upon all *Simples* or *Compounds* that are dangerous.

With many other Additions, in every Page, marked with the letter *A.*

The second Edition much enlarged, by

Nich. Culpeper Gent. Student in Physick.

Scire potestates Herbarum, usumque medendi
Maluit, & mutas agitare (inglorius) artes. Virgil.

LONDON:

Printed by *Peter Cole*, and are to be sold at his Shop at the sign of the *Printing-Press* in Cornhil, near the Royal Exchange. 1650.

12.3 Nicholas Culpeper, *A physical directory*, London, 1649, title page. Culpeper's unauthorized translation of the College of Physicians' pharmacopoeia justified itself on political grounds as well as medical: Culpeper associated the College's restriction of information to Latinate readers with the unjust oppressions of the Norman yoke. His work was extremely successful, and proved instrumental in establishing a genre of popular medical texts.

EPIGRAMMA XLV.

SOL, *fax clara poli, non corpora densa penetrat,*
Hinc illi adversis partibus umbra manet:
Vilior hæc rebus quamvis est omnibus usu
Attamen Astronomis commoda multa tulit:
Plura Sophis sed dona dedit SOL, *ejus & umbra,*
Auriferæ quoniam perficit artis opus.

Aa 3 QUE

188 FUGA XLV. in 3. sup. vertendo Bas. & incip. ab initio in clave d.

Die Sonn vnd jhr Schatten vollnbringen das Werck.

XLV. Epigrammatis Latini versio Germanica.

Die Sonn deß Himmels klares Liecht kan nicht dicke Leiber durchgehn/
Drumb bleibt ein Schatten an der Orten/ so sie nicht kan sehn/
Ob wol derselbige ist sehr gering vnter den Dingen allen/
Jedoch thut er nützlich den Astronomis gefallen/
Aber mehr Geschenck geben hat den Weisen die Sonne vnd jhr Schatt/
Dann sie die gülden Kunst vollenführen mit der That.

EMBLE-

12.4 (a) and (b) Michael Maier, *Atalanta Fugiens*, Oppenheim, 1618, Emblem 45. The combination of music, poetry, prose and images in this work exemplified alchemists' search for ways to convey many truths simultaneously. Some of Maier's harmonies were misprinted; it was assumed that a true adept would be able to perceive their errors and correct them.

PHILOSOPHIÆ

NATURALIS

PRINCIPIA

MATHEMATICA.

Autore *JS. NEWTON*, *Trin. Coll. Cantab. Soc.* Mathefeos Profeffore *Lucafiano*, & Societatis Regalis Sodali.

IMPRIMATUR.

S. PEPYS, *Reg. Soc.* PRÆSES.

Julii 5. 1686.

LONDINI,

Juffu *Societatis Regiæ* ac Typis *Jofephi Streater*. Proftat apud plures Bibliopolas. *Anno* MDCLXXXVII.

12.5 Isaac Newton, *Principia*, London, 1687, title page. Newton's work was printed in London under the watchful eye of Edmond Halley, who carefully coaxed it out of a reluctant author. Although few readers were equipped to understand its complex mathematical arguments, the *Principia* was rapidly recognized as an extraordinary achievement.

(3075) Numb. 80.

PHILOSOPHICAL TRANSACTIONS.

February 19. 16$\frac{71}{72}$.

The CONTENTS.

A Letter of Mr. Isaac Newton, *Mathematick Professor in the University of Cambridge; containing his New Theory about* Light *and* Colors: *Where* Light *is declared to be not Similar or Homogeneal, but consisting of difform rays, some of which are more refrangible than others: And* Colors *are affirm'd to be not Qualifications of Light, deriv'd from Refractions of natural Bodies, (as 'tis generally believed;) but Original and Connate properties, which in divers rays are divers: Where several Observations and Experiments are alledged to prove the said Theory. An Accompt of some Books:* I. *A Description of the EAST-INDIAN COASTS, MALABAR, COROMANDEL, CEYLON, &c. in* Dutch, *by* Phil. Baldæus. II. Antonii le Grand *INSTITUTIO PHILOSOPHIÆ,* secundùm principia Renati Des-Cartes; *novâ methodo adornata & explicata.* III. *An Essay to the Advancement of MUSICK; by* Thomas Salmon *M. A. Advertisement about* Thæon Smyrnæus. *An* Index *for the Tracts of the Year* 1671.

A Letter of Mr. Isaac Newton, *Professor of the Mathematicks in the University of Cambridge; containing his New Theory about* Light *and* Colors: *sent by the Author to the Publisher from Cambridge, Febr.* 6. 16$\frac{71}{72}$; *in order to be communicated to the* R. Society.

SIR,

TO perform my late promise to you, I shall without further ceremony acquaint you, that in the beginning of the Year 1666 (at which time I applyed my self to the grinding of Optick glasses of other figures than *Spherical*,) I procured me a Triangular glass-Prisme, to try therewith the celebrated *Phænomena* of

Gggg *Colours*.

12.6 The *Philosophical Transactions* no. 80 (19 February 1673), p. 3075. The *Transactions* was the invention of Henry Oldenburg, secretary of the Royal Society. It never generated the revenue that Oldenburg had anticipated, and for years its survival remained uncertain. Yet it endured, publishing such important work as Isaac Newton's on light, and helping to establish a new, international, community of experimental philosophers. Today it is renowned as the oldest surviving scientific periodical.

SEMPER EADEM

THE

WORKS

of

SAMVEL DANIEL

Newly augmented.

Ætas prima canat veneres
postrema tumultus.

LONDON
Printed for Simon Waterson.
1601.

16.1 Samuel Daniel, *The works of Samuel Daniel*, London, printed for Simon Waterson, 1601, engraved title page. This was the first collection by a living writer to offer such a wide range of genres as his *Works*; the design of the title page stated Daniel's credentials as an established English author.

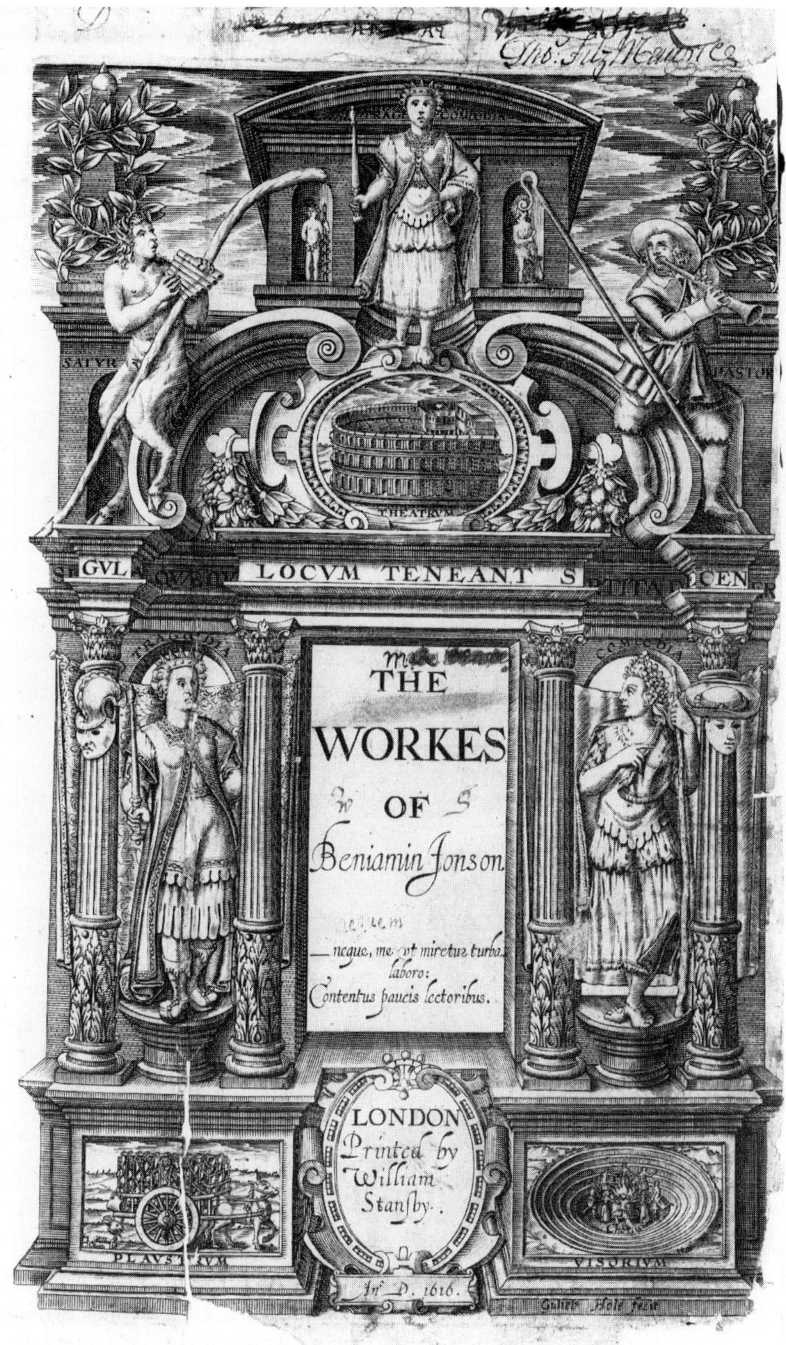

16.2 Ben Jonson, *The workes of Beniamin Jonson*, London, printed by William Stansby, 1616, engraved title page. Jonson's *Workes* proclaims the seriousness of its author in presenting himself as the foremost English writer. Its folio size and elaborate title page proclaimed its (and Jonson's) status, and its inclusion of plays alongside poetry and masques asserted the cultural importance of dramatic writing.

Melpomene · Erato · IOANNIS MILTONI ANGLI EFFIGIES ANNO ÆTATIS VIGESIMO PRI: · Urania · Clio

Α'μαθεῖ γεγράφθαι χειρὶ τήνδε μὲν εἰκόνα
Φαίης τάχ' ἄν, πρὸς εἶδος αὐτοφυὲς βλέπων
Τὸν δ' ἐκτυπωτὸν ȣ̉κ ἐπιγνόντες φίλοι
Γελᾶτε φαύλȣ δυσμίμημα ζωγράφȣ.

W.M. sculp.

POEMS
OF
Mr. John Milton,
BOTH
ENGLISH and LATIN,
Compos'd at ſeveral times.

Printed by his true Copies.

The SONGS were ſet in Muſick by Mr. HENRY LAWES Gentleman of the KINGS Chappel, and one of His MAIESTIES Private Muſick.

——*Baccare frontem*
Cingite, ne vati noceat mala lingua futuro;
Virgil, Eclog. 7.

Printed and publiſh'd according to
ORDER.

LONDON,
Printed by *Ruth Raworth* for *Humphrey Moſeley*; and are to be ſold at the ſigne of the Princes Arms in *Pauls* Church-yard. 1645.

17.1 John Milton, *Poems of Mr. John Milton, both English and Latin, compos'd at several times*, London, Ruth Raworth for Humphrey Moseley, 1645, engraved frontispiece portrait and title page. Milton's volume charted his intellectual growth as a poet and staked a claim for respectability despite his pamphleteering. Moseley, the publisher, was to become the most prominent literary publisher of his generation, issuing a series of poems and plays in small formats and coupling aesthetic sensibility with royalism.

THE REVELATION
[*]of Iohn the Diuine.

*Or, declared to Iohn.

THE ARGUMENT.

It is manifest, that the holie Gost wolde as it were gather into this moste excellent booke a summe of those prophecies, which were writen before, but shulde be fulfilled after the cōming of Christ, adding also suche things as shulde be expedient, aswel to forewarne vs of the dangers to come, as to admonish vs to beware some, and encourage vs against others. Herein therefore is liuely set forthe the Diuinitie of Christ, & the testimonies of our redēption: what things the Spirit of God alloweth in the ministers, and what things he reproueth: the prouidence of God for his elect, and of their glorie and consolation in the day of vengeance: how that the hypocrites which sting like scorpions the members of Christ, shalle destroyed, but the Lambe Christ shal defende them, which beare witnes to the trueth, who in despite of the beast and Satan wil reigne ouer all. The liuelie description of Antichrist is set forthe, whose time and power notwithstanding is limited, and albeit that he is permitted to rage against the elect, yet his power stretcheth no farther then to the hurt of their bodies: and at length he shal be destroyed by the wrath of God, when as the elect shal giue praise to God for the victorie: neuertheles for a ceason God wil permit this Antichrist, and strompet vnder colour of faire speache and pleasant doctrine to deceiue the worlde: wherefore he aduertiseth the godlie (which are but a smale portion) to auoide this harlots flateries, and bragges, whose ruine without mercie they shal se, and with the heauenlie companies sing continual praises: for the Lambe is maried: the worde of God hathe gotten the victorie: Satā that a long time was vntied, is now cast with his ministers into the pit of fyre to be tormented for euer, where as cōtrariwise the faithful (which are the holie Citie of Ierusalem, & wife of the Lambe) shal enioye perpetual glorie. Read diligently: iudge soberly, and call earnestly to God for the true vnderstanding hereof.

CHAP. I.

1 The cause of this reuelation. 3 Of them that read it. 4 Iohn writeth to the seuen Churches. 5 The maiestie and office of the Sonne of God. 20 The vision of the candlestickes and starres.

1 THe [a] reuelation of IESVS CHRIST, which
[b] God gaue vnto him, to
shewe vnto his seruants
things which must shor
tely be [c] done: which he
sent, and shewed by his
Angel vnto his seruant Iohn,
2 Who bare recorde of the worde of God,
and of the testimonie of Iesus Christ, and
of all things that he sawe.
3 Blessed *is he* that readeth, and they that
heare the wordes of this [d] prophecie, and
kepe those things which are written therein: for the time is [e] at hand.
4 Iohn, to the [f] seuē Churches which are in
Asia, Grace *be* with you & peace frō him
Which [*] is, & Which was, & Which is to
come, and from the [g] seuen Spirits which
are before his Throne,
5 And from Iesus Christ, which is a [*] faithful witnes, & [*] the first begotten of ỹ dead,
and Prince of the Kings of the earth, vnto him that loued vs, & washed vs frō our
sinnes in his [*] blood,
6 And made vs [*] Kings and Priestes vnto
God euen his Father, to him *be* glorie, &
dominion for euermore, Amen.
7 Beholde, he cometh with [*] cloudes, and
euerie eye shal se him: *yea*, euen they which
[h] pearced him through: and all kinreds of
the earth shal waile [*] before him, Euen so,
Amen.
8 I [*] am [i] α and ω, the beginning and the
ending, saith the Lord, Which is, and
Which was, and Which is to come, *euen*
the Almightie.
9 I Iohn, euen your brother, & companion
in tribulation, & in the kingdome and pa-
cience of Iesus Christ, was in the yle called Patmos, for the [*] worde of God, and
for the [*] witnessing of Iesus Christ.
10 And I was *rauished* in spirit on [k] ỹ Lords
day, and heard behinde me a great voyce,
as it had bene of a trumpet,
11 Saying, I am [l] α and ω, the first and the
last: and that which thou seest, write in a
boke, & send it vnto the [m] seuen Churches
which are in Asia, vnto Ephesus, and vnto
Smyrna, & vnto Pergamus, & vnto Thyatira, and vnto Sardi, and vnto Philadelphia, and vnto Laodicea.
12 Then I turned backe to se the [n] voyce,
that spake with me: & when I was turned,
I sawe [o] seuen golden candlestickes,
13 And in the middes of the seuen candlestickes, one like vnto the [p] Sonne of man,
clothed with a garment [q] downe to the

feete,

a Of things which were hid before.
b Christ receiued this reuelation out of his fathers bosome as his owne doctrine, but it was hid in respect of vs so that Christ as Lord and God reueiled it to Iohn his seruant by the ministerie of his Angel, to the edification of his Church
c To the good & bad.
d Which expoundeth the olde prophetes, & sheweth what shal come to passe in the newe testament.
Exo.3,14.
e And began euen then.
Psal 89.38.
1.Cor.15,21.
colos.1,18.
Ebr.9,14.
1.pet.1,19.
1 iohn.1,9.
1.Pet.2,5.
f Meaning the Church vniuersal.
g That is, from the holie Gost: or these seuen Spirits were ministers before God the Father & Christ, whome after he calleth the hornes and eyes of the Lambe, chap.5,6 In a like phrases Paul taketh God, and Christ, and the Angels to witnes, 1.Tim.5,21.

Mat.24,30.
Isa.3,14.
iude 14.
h They that contemned Christ & moste cruelly persecuted him, and put him to death, shal then acknowledge him.
Chap.21,6. & 22,13.
Or, for him
i Alpha and Omega are the first and last letters of the a b c of the Grekes.
k Which some call sunday: S Paul the first day of the weke, 1 Cor.16,2. act. 20,7. and it was established after that the Iewes Sabbath was abolished.
l I am he before whome nothing was, yea, by whome whatsoeuer is made, was made, and he that shal remaine when all thīgs shal perish, euen I am the eternal God.
m Of ỹ which some were fallen: others decayed: some were proude: others negligent: so that he sheweth remedie for all.
n That is, him whose voyce I heard.
o Meaning the Churches.
p Which was Christ the head of the Church.
q As the chief Priest.

21.1 *The Bible and holy scriptures*, Geneva, R. Hall, 1560. The Geneva Bible's layout had a lasting influence on English-Bible printing: it divided the text into verses and supplied 'arguments' and summary running titles. The opening of the Book of Revelation shows the marginal notes and anti-Roman commentary which was a feature of the Geneva version prized by Protestants.

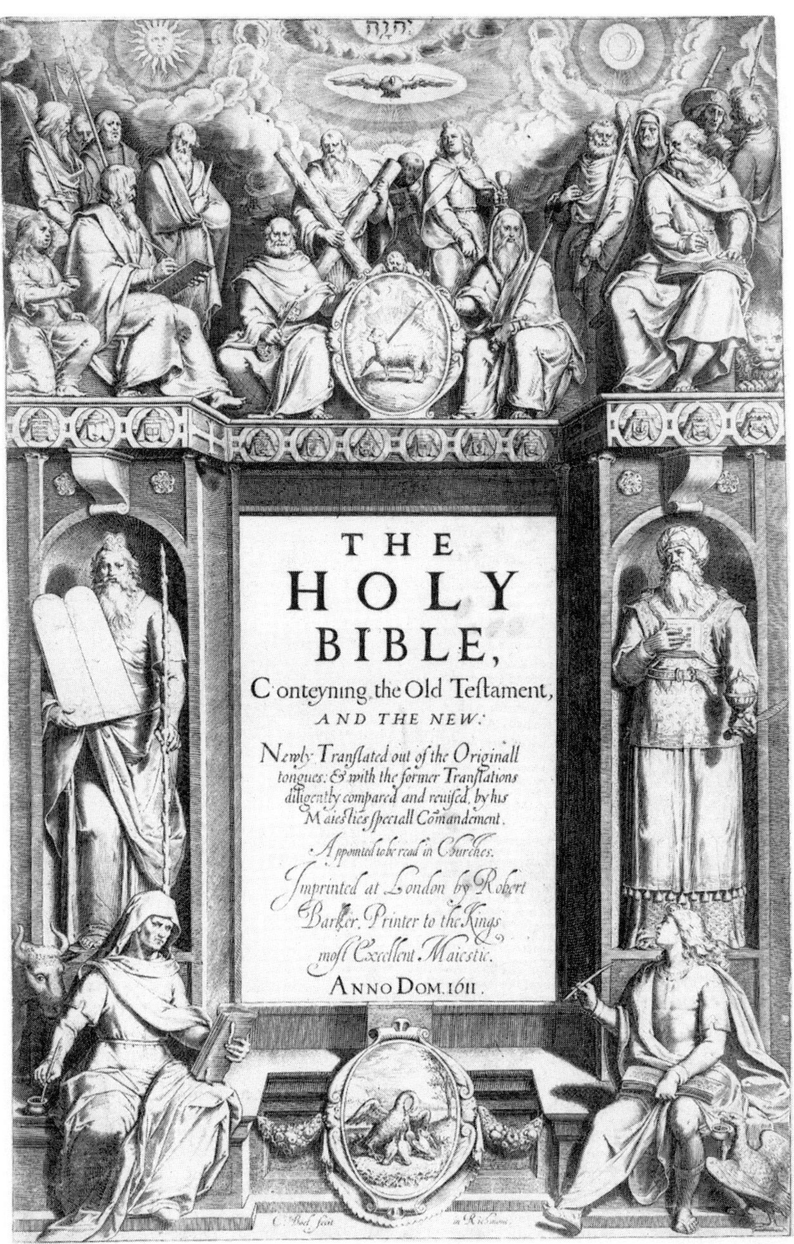

THE
HOLY
BIBLE,
Conteyning the Old Teſtament,
AND THE NEW:
Newly Tranſlated out of the Originall
tongues: & with the former Tranſlations
diligently compared and reuiſed, by his
Maieſties ſpeciall Comandement.
Appointed to be read in Churches.
Imprinted at London by Robert
Barker, Printer to the Kings
moſt Excellent Maiestie.
ANNO DOM. 1611.

21.2 *The Holy Bible, conteyning the Old Testament, and the New . . . revised, by his maiesties speciall comandement*, London, R. Barker, 1611, engraved title page. The stimulus for a new Bible translation was James I's disapproval of the Geneva text and commentaries. The Authorized Version, the work of six groups of translators, was 'to be set out and printed, without any marginal notes, and only to be used in all Churches of England.'

THE REVELATION OF SAINT IOHN THE APOSTLE AND Euangelift with the Annotations of *Francis Iunius.*

CHAP. I.

1 He declareth what kind of doctrine is here handled, 8 euen his that is the beginning and ending. 12 Then the myftery of the feuen Candleftickes and ftarres, 20 is expounded.

1 This Chapter hath two principall parts, the title or infcription, which ftandeth in ftead of an exordium: and a narration going before the whole prophecie of this booke: The infcription is double, generall and particular. The generall containeth the kind of prophecie, the authour, and matter, inftruments, and maner of communicating the fame, in the firft verfe: the moft religious faithfulneffe of the Apoftle as a publike withneffe, verfe 2. And the vfe of communicating the fame taken from the promife of God, and from the circumftance of the time, verfe the third.
a An opening of a fecret and hid thing.

THe 1 a Reuelation of b Iefus Chrift,
which God gaue vnto him, to
fhewe vnto his feruants things
which muft fhortly be done:
which hee fent, and fhewed by
his Angel vnto his feruant Iohn,
2 Who bare record of the word of God, and
of the teftimonie of Iefus Chrift, and of all things
that he faw.
3 Bleffed *is he* that readeth, and they that
heare the words of this prophecie, and keepe thofe
things which are written therein: for the time is
at hand.
4 2 Iohn to the feuen Churches which are in
Afia, Grace *be* with you, and peace 3 from him,
c Which * is, and Which was, and Which is to
come, and from 4 the d feuen Spirits which are before his Throne,
5 And from Iefus Chrift 5 which is that
* faithfull witneffe, *and* * that firft begotten of
the dead, and that Prince of the Kings of the
earth, vnto him that loued vs, and wafhed vs
from our finnes in his * blood,
6 And made vs * Kings and Priefts vnto God
euen his Father, to him, *I fay*, *be* glory, and dominion for euermore, Amen.
7 Behold, he commeth with * clouds, and
euery e eye fhall fee him: yea, euen they which
pearced him thorow: and all kindreds of the earth
fhall waile before him, Euen fo, Amen.
8 6 I * am f Alpha and Omega, the beginning
and ye ending, faith the Lord, Which is, and Which
was, and Which is to come, *euen* the Almighty.
9 7 I Iohn euen your brother and companion
in tribulation, and in the kingdome and patience
of Iefus Chrift, was in the g Ile called Patmos, for
the word of God, and for the witneffing of Iefus
Chrift.
10 And I was *rauifhed* in h fpirit on the i Lords
day, and heard behind me a great voyce, as it had
bene of a trumpet,
11 Saying, I am Alpha and Omega, that firft
and that laft: and that which thou feeft write in a
booke, and fend it vnto the feuen Churches which
are in Afia, vnto Ephefus, and vnto Smyrna, & vnto
Pergamus, and vnto Thyatira, and vnto Sardis,
and vnto Philadelphia, and vnto Laodicea.
12 8 Then I turned backe to k fee the voyce
that fpake with me: 9 and when I was turned, I
fawe feuen golden candleftickes,
13 And in the mids of the feuen candleftickes,
one like vnto the fonne of man, cloathed with a
garment downe to the feete, and girded about the
paps with a golden girdle.
14 His head and haires *vvere* white as white
wool, *&* as fnow, & his eyes *vvere* as a flame of fire,
15 And his feet like vnto fine braffe burning as
in a fornace: and his voyce as the found of many
waters.
16 And he had in his right hand feuen ftarres:
and out of his mouth went a fharpe two edged
fword, and his face *fhone* as the fonne fhineth in
his ftrength.
17 10 And when I fawe him, I fell at his feete
as dead: 11 then he laide his right hand vpon me,
faying vnto me, Feare not: 12 I am that * firft

6 A confirmation of the faluation aforegoing, taken from the words of God himfelfe: in which he auoucheth his operation in euery fingular creature, the immutable eternitie that is in himfelfe, and his omnipotencie in all things: and concludeth in the vnitie of his owne effence, that Trinitie of perfons, which was before fpoken of.
* *Chap. 21.6. and 22.13.*
f I am he before whom there is nothing, yea, by whom euery thing that is made, was made and fhall remaine though all they fhould perifh.
7 The narration opening the way to the declaring of the authoritie and calling of Saint Iohn the Euangelift in this fingular Reuelation, and to procure faith, and credit vnto this prophecie. This is the fecond part of this Chapter confifting of a propofition and an expofition. The propofition fheweth, firft who was called vnto this Reuelation, in what place, & how occupied, verfe 9. Then at what time and by what meanes, namely, by the fpirit and the word, and that on the Lords day, which day euer fince the refurrection of Chrift, was confecrated for Chriftians vnto the religion of the Sabbath: that is to fay, to be a day of reft, verfe 10. Thirdly, who is the authour that calleth him, and what is the fum of his calling. g Patmos is one of the yles of Sporas whither Iohn was banifhed as fome write. h This is that holy rauifhment expreffed, wherwith the Prophets were rauifhed, and being as it were carried out of the world were conuerfant with God, and fo Ezekiel faith often that hee was carried from place to place of the Lords Spirit, and that the Spirit of the Lord fell vpon him. i Hee calleth it the Lords day, which Paul calleth the firft day of the weeke, 1. Cor. 16, 2. 8 The expofition, declaring the third and laft point of the propofition (for the other points are euident of themfelues) wherein is fpoken firft of the authour of his calling vnto the 17. verfe. Secondly of the calling it felfe vnto the end of the Chap. And firft of all the occafion is noted in this verfe, in that S. Iohn turned himfelfe towards the vifion: after is fet downe the difcription of the authour in the verfes following 13. 14. 15. 16. k To fee him whofe voyce I had heard. 9 The defcription of the Authour, which is Chrift: by the candlefticks that ftandeth about him, that is the Churches that ftand before him, and depend vpon his direction, in this verfe: by his properties, that hee is one furnifhed with wifdome and dexteritie to the atchieuing of great things, verfe 13. and ancient grauitie and moft excellent fight of the eye, verfe 14. with ftrength inuincible and with a mightie word, verfe 15. By his operations, that he ruleth the miniftery of his feruants in the Church, giueth the effect thereunto by the fword of his word, and enlightening all things with his countenance, doeth moft mightily prouide for euery one by his diuine prouidence, verfe 16. 10 A religious feare that goeth before the calling of the Saints, and their full confirmation to take vpon them the vocation of God. 11 A diuine confirmation is this calling partly by figne and partly by word of power. 12 A moft elegant defcription of this calling conteined in three things, which are neceffary vnto a iuft vocation: firft the authoritie of him that calleth, for that he is the beginning and the end of all things, in this verfe, for that hee is eternall and omnipotent, verfe 18. Secondly, the fum of this propheticall calling, and reuelation, verfe 19. Laftly a declaration of thofe perfons vnto whom this prophecie is by the commandement of God directed in the defcription thereof, verfe 20. * *Efai. 41, 4.*

b Which the Sonne opened to vs out of his Fathers bofome by Angels. 2 This is the particular or fingular infcription, where in faluation is written vnto certaine Churches by name, which reprefent the Church Catholike: and the certainty and the trueth of the fame is declared, from the Authour thereof, vnto the eight verfe. 3 That is, from God the Father, eternall, immortall, immutable: whofe vnchangeablenefſe S. Iohn declareth by a forme of fpeach which is vndeclined. For there is no incongruitie in this place, where, of neceffitie the words muft be attempered vnto the mytteries, and not the myfteries corrupted or impaired by the word. c By thefe three times, Is, Was and fhall be, is fignified this word Iehouah, which is the proper name of God. * *Exod. 3, 14.* 4 That is, from the holy Ghoft which proceedeth from the Father and the Sonne. This Spirit is one in perfon according to his fubfiftencie: but in communication of his vertue, and in demonftration of his diuine workes in thofe feuen Churches, doeth fo perfectly manifeft himfelfe, as if there were fo many Spirits, euery one perfectly working in his owne Church, wherefore after Chap. 5. 6. they are called the feuen hornes and feuen eyes of the Lambe, as much to fay, as his moft abfolute power and wifedome: and Chap. 3, 1. Chrift is faid to haue there feuen Spirits of God: and Chap. 4. 5. it is faid, that feuen lampes doe burne before his throne, which alfo are thofe feuen Spirits of God. That this place ought to be fo vnderftood, it is thus prooued. For in grace and peace is asked by prayer of this Spirit, which is a diuine worke, and in action incommunicable, in refpect of the moft high Deitie. Secondly, he is placed betweene the Father and the Sonne, as fet in the fame degree of dignitie and operation with them. Befides he is before the throne, as of the fame fubftance with the Father and the Son: as the feuen eyes and feuen hornes of the Lambe. Moreouer, thefe fpirits are neuer fayde to adore God, as all other things are. Finally, that is the power whereby the Lambe opened the booke, and loofed the feuen feales thereof when none could be found amongft all creatures by whom the booke might be opened, Chap. 5. Of thefe things long agoe, Mafter Iohn Luid of Oxford wrote learnedly vnto mee. Now the holy Ghoft is fet in order of words before Chrift, becaufe there was in that which followeth, a long proceffe of fpeach to be vfed concerning Chrift. d Thefe are the feuen fpirits, which are afterward, Chap. 5 verfe 6. called the hornes and eyes of the Lambe, and are now made as a garde waiting vpon God. 5 A moft ample and graue commendation of Chrift, firft from his offices the Priefthood and kingdomes, fecondly from his benefits, as his loue toward vs, and wafhing vs with his blood, in this verfe, and communication of his kingdome and Priefthood with vs: thirdly from his eternall glory and power, which alwayes is to be celebrated of vs, verfe 6. Finally from the accomplifhment of all things once to be effected by him, at his fecond comming, what time hee fhall openly deftroy the wicked, and fhall comfort the godly in the trueth, verfe 7. * *Pfal. 89, 38.* * *1. Cor. 15, 21. coloff. 1. 18.* * *Heb. 9. 14. 1. pet. 1. 29. 1. Iohn 1, 9.* * *1. Pet. 2, 5.* * *Efai. 3, 14. matth. 24, 30. iude 14.* e All men.

and

21.3 *The Bible: that is the holy scriptures* . . . London, Deputies of Christopher Barker, 1599 [i.e. Amsterdam, J. Stam, ?after 1640]. An imported Bible with false English imprint. The text is that of the Geneva version and the commentary on Revelation is that by Junius, which first appeared in a complete English Bible in 1603.

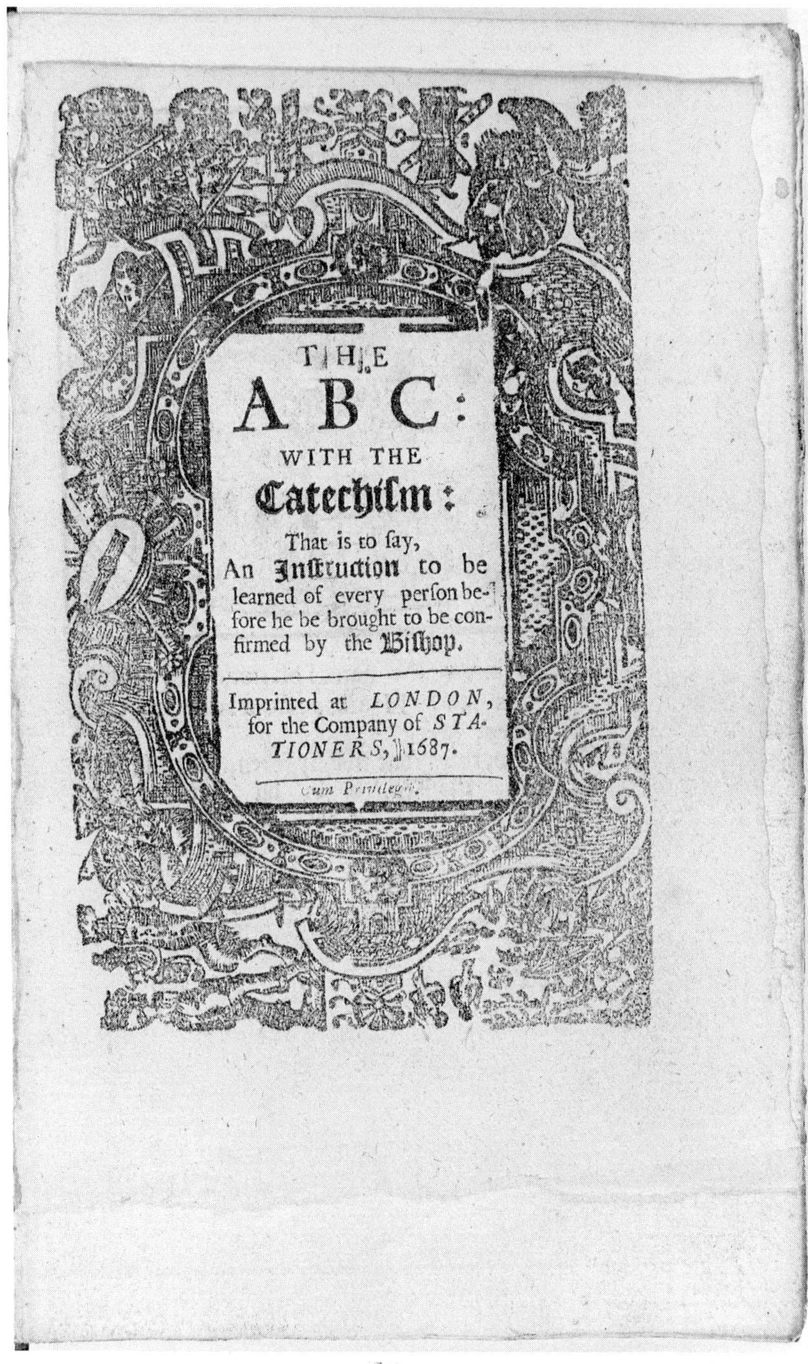
THE
ABC:
WITH THE
Catechiſm:
That is to ſay,
An Inſtruction to be
learned of every perſon be-
fore he be brought to be con-
firmed by the Biſhop.

Imprinted at *LONDON*,
for the Company of *STA-
TIONERS*, 1687.

Cum Privilegio.

23.1 *The ABC with the catechism: that is to say, An instruction to be learned of every person before he be brought to be confirmed by the bishop*, London, Company of Stationers, 1687, title page. ABCs, along with almanacs, Bibles, Psalms and school books, formed a lucrative part of the English Stock of the Stationers' Company. Thousands of copies were printed each year and ABCs were sometimes pirated by printers eager to make a quick profit.

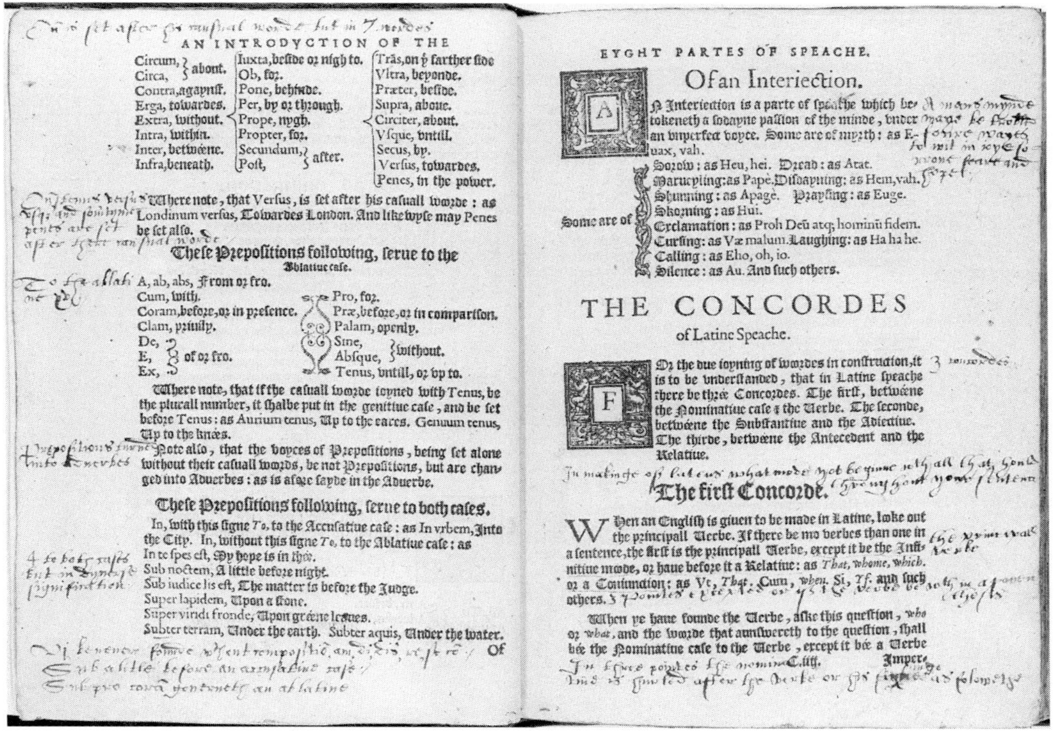
AN INTRODVCTION OF THE

Circum, Circa, about. Contra, agaynst. Erga, towardes. Extra, without. Intra, within. Inter, betwene. Infra, beneath. Iuxta, beside or nigh to. Ob, for. Pone, behinde. Per, by or through. Prope, nygh. Propter, for. Secundum, Post, after. Trãs, on ỹ farther side. Vltra, beyonde. Præter, beside. Supra, aboue. Circiter, about. Vsque, untill. Secus, by. Versus, towardes. Penes, in the power.

Where note, that Versus, is set after his casuall worde: as Londinum versus, Towardes London. And likewyse may Penes be set also.

These Prepositions following, serue to the Ablatiue case.

A, ab, abs, From or fro. Cum, with. Coram, before, or in presence. Clam, priuily. De, E, Ex, of or fro. Pro, for. Præ, before, or in comparison. Palam, openly. Sine, Absque, without. Tenus, untill, or up to.

Where note, that if the casuall worde ioyned with Tenus, be the plurall number, it shalbe put in the genitiue case, and be set before Tenus: as Aurium tenus, Up to the eares. Genuum tenus, Up to the knees.

Note also, that the voyces of Prepositions, being set alone without their casuall wordes, be not Prepositions, but are changed into Aduerbes: as is afore sayde in the Aduerbe.

These Prepositions following, serue to both cases.

In, with this signe *To*, to the Accusatiue case: as In vrbem, Into the City. In, without this signe *To*, to the Ablatiue case: as In te spes est, My hope is in thee. Sub noctem, A little before night. Sub iudice lis est, The matter is before the Iudge. Super lapidem, Upon a stone. Super viridi fronde, Upon greene leaues. Subter terram, Under the earth. Subter aquis, Under the water.

Of

EYGHT PARTES OF SPEACHE.

Of an Interiection.

An Interiection is a parte of speache which betokeneth a sodayne passion of the minde, under an unperfect voyce. Some are of myrth: as Euax, vah.

Some are of Sorow: as Heu, hei. Dread: as Atat. Marueyling: as Papæ. Disdaynyng: as Hem, vah. Shunning: as Apage. Praysing: as Euge. Skorning: as Hui. Exclamation: as Proh Deũ atq; hominũ fidem. Cursing: as Væ malum. Laughing: as Ha ha he. Calling: as Eho, oh, io. Silence: as Au. And such others.

THE CONCORDES of Latine Speache.

For the due ioyning of wordes in construction, it is to be understanded, that in Latine speache there be three Concordes. The first, betwene the Nominatiue case & the Uerbe. The seconde, betwene the Substantiue and the Adiectiue. The thirde, betwene the Antecedent and the Relatiue.

The first Concorde.

When an English is giuen to be made in Latine, loke out the principall Uerbe. If there be mo verbes than one in a sentence, the first is the principall Uerbe, except it be the Infinitiue moode, or haue before it a Relatiue: as *That, whome, which*. or a Coniunction: as Vt, *That*. Cum, *when*. Si, *If*. and such others.

When ye haue founde the Uerbe, aske this question, *who* or *what*, and the worde that aunswereth to the question, shall be the Nominatiue case to the Uerbe, except it be a Uerbe Impersonall.

23.2 William Lily [*A short introduction of grammar*], Londini, per assignationem Francisci Flor, 1575. Another stock- in-trade of the Stationers' Company, schoolbooks were often used to destruction. This copy shows the imaginative layout using roman and black-letter types, ornaments, woodcut initials and generous margins for the user's own annotations.

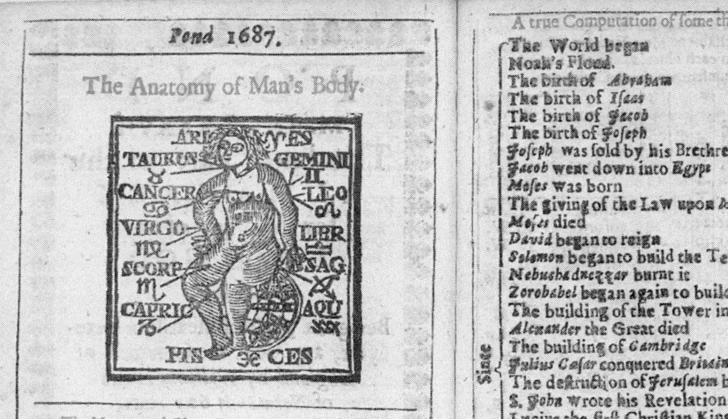

Pond 1687.

The Anatomy of Man's Body.

The Names and Characters of the twelve Signs.

♈ Aries Head and Face	♎ Libra Reins and Loyns
♉ Taurus Neck and Throat	♏ Scorpio Secret Memb.
♊ Gemini Arms and Should.	♐ Sagittarius the Thighs
♋ Cancer Breaſt and Stomach	♑ Capricornus the Knees
♌ Leo Heart and Back	♒ Aquarius the Legs
♍ Virgo Bowels and Belly	♓ Piſces the Feet

The Characters, Names and Natures of the 7 Planets.

♄ Saturn Cold and dry	♀ Venus Cold and moiſt
♃ Jupiter Hot and moiſt	☿ Mercury Variable
♂ Mars Hot and dry	☾ Luna Cold and moiſt
☉ Sol Hot and dry	

A

A true Computation of ſome things memorable.

Since

The World began	5690
Noah's Flood.	4035
The birth of *Abraham*	3682
The birth of *Iſaac*	3582
The birth of *Jacob*	3423
The birth of *Joſeph*	3431
Joſeph was ſold by his Brethren	3413
Jacob went down into *Egypt*	3392
Moſes was born	3257
The giving of the Law upon *Mount Sinai*	3177
Moſes died	3137
David began to reign	2741
Solomon began to build the Temple	2698
Nebuchadnezzar burnt it	2274
Zorobabel began again to build it	2204
The building of the Tower in *London*	2105
Alexander the Great died	2010
The building of *Cambridge*	1987
Julius Cæſar conquered *Britain*	1738
The deſtruction of *Jeruſalem* by *Titus*	1617
S. *John* wrote his Revelation	1593
Lucius the firſt Chriſtian King began	1507
Conſtantine the firſt Chriſtian Emp. began	1363
Cambridge was made an Univerſity	1053
The firſt Mayor of *London*	497
The invention of Guns	307
The invention of Printing	247
Tilbury Camp on S. *James* his day	99
The Powder Treaſon, *Novemb.* 5.	82
The beginning of the Great Froſt, *Novemb.*	82
The laſt great Plague in *London*	22
London almoſt conſumed by fire	21
S[r] *Edmund-Bury Godfry* was Murthered *Octob.*	9
The Rebellion in the *Weſt* began *June* 11.	2
The Rebells were defeated *July* 6.	2
Monmouth was beheaded *July* 15.	2

Note, that on the 6 of *February* the 3 year of our Royall K. *James* the ſecond beginneth. Whom God preſerve. *Amen.*

23.3 Edward Pond, *An almanack for the year of our Lord God 1687*, Cambridge, John Hayes, 1687. Almanacs were printed annually, usually in the autumn ready for the new year's trade, and often carried the names of their first compilers as 'brand names': thus, despite Pond's death in 1629, 'his' almanacs continued to be produced long afterwards. The woodcut astrological anatomy shown here was a standard component of the almanac's useful store of information.

The Trappan'd Welsh-man, Sold to Virginia.

Showing how a *Welsh man* came to *London*, and went to see the *Royal Exchange*, where he met a Handsom Lass, with whom he was Enamoured; who pretending to shew him the Ships, carried him aboard a *Virginia* Man and Sold him, having first got the *Welsh-mans* Gold, to his great grief and sorrow.
To the Tune of, *Monsieurs Misfortune*. This may be Printed, R. P.

NOt long ago hur came to London,
some pritty Fashions for to see,
Sure hur were mad so to be undone,
in middle of hur Bravery:
Hur knew hur got much Wit as any,
when hur arrived here from Wales,
Cots-plot, hur knew Deceivers many,
hur now be sure must tell no Tales.

Hur came to see the Exchange so neatly.
and wor no Shangling you may think,
But hur wor ser'v'd a trick compleatly,
in time that any man can wink:
But wor not this an unlucky Baggage,
a harmless Welsh-man to trappan?
She's told hur 'twor an ancient Adage,
Shack wor not born a Shentleman.

But hur had now a Sheat put on hur,
as he did view the Rarities,
A scurvy trick was put upon hur,
by one wor favour'd in hur eyes:
Plutter-a-nails, cou'd hur get home Sir
hur ne'r wou'd haf a mind to range,
wou'd hang byth' neck before hur roam sir
to London Town to see the Shange.

Looking about on ev'ry matter,
he could not chuse but all commend,
He never saw things of such nature,
and thus he did his Verdict spend:
Cou'd hur bring o're hur Habitation,
hur Pig-stye, Barn, and hur dun Cow
Hur here wou'd live so in the fashion,
like any Shentleman I vow.

By him there stood a Lass so pritty,
she was the Rarity of all,
Most wondrous handsom, fine and witty,
she to the Welsh-man then did call:
Sir, I perceive you're not so knowing,
of this so sumptuous place, as I,
Here are, kind sir, things worth the show-
if you'l accept my Courtesie. (ing,

He's very glad of that kind proffer,
and close unto her side did stick,
He heard a pritty Story of her,
of those that do Mens Pockets pick:
Plutter-a-nails, hur give 'um no money,
hur put a breakment on their Pate,
Od. she, thou canst not know't, my honey
be rul'd by me, they ne'r sh[all] ha't.

She told a Tale of Ships onth' Ocean,
which the fine Welshman might behold;
Who now was quite at her Devotion,
he gave her thirty pound in Gold,
For to lay up till they returned,
which she did never mean he should,
She play'd a prank whereat he mourned,
because he was so greatly Fool'd.

For when they came 'board the Virginny
a Ship most gay and fit for Trade,
There she did sell the harmless Ninny,
to make her Market (like a Jade:)
They call'd for Punch and other Liquor
which made the Welshman almost blind
But to conclude, she was the quicker,
and left the Welsh-man there behind.

Pray good her Worship take hur with hur
the Captain said he was too bold,
what, must hur go hur knows not whether
and to be cheated of hur Gold?
Let hur but send hur Gold unto hur,
but he could then no favour find,
What, does hur mean for to undo hur?
'splut, by St. Taffie, 'twor unkind.

God bless hur anshent Dad and Mother,
for hur must go hur knows not where,
Give sharge unto hur little Brother,
lest he unto this place repair:
God send hur ne'r may come to London,
nor never have a mind to Range,
For hur wor sure hur will be undon,
if e're hur comes unto the Shange.

Printed for C. Dennisson, at the Stationers-Arms within Aldgate.

23.4 *The trappan'd Welsh-man, sold to Virginia. Showing how a Welsh man came to London, and went to see the Royal Exchange, where he met a handsom lass, with whom he was enamoured; who pretending to shew him the ships, carried him aboard a Virginia man and sold him, having first got the Welsh-mans gold, to his great grief and sorrow. To the tune of, Monsieurs Misfortune* [London], for C. Dennisson [1685–95]. This black-letter broadsheet ballad with woodcut illustrations is an example of the cheap print available throughout the country from pedlars and hawkers in streets, markets and at fairs.

THE

HEADS OF

SEVERALL PRO-

CEEDINGS IN THIS

PRESENT PARLIAMENT,

from the 22 of *November*, to

the 29. 1 6 4 1.

VVherein is contained the ſubſtance of ſeverall Letters ſent from *Ireland*, ſhewing what diſtreſſe and miſery they are in

With divers other paſſages of moment touching the Affaires of theſe Kingdomes.

London, Printed for *I. T.* 1641.

25.1 *The heads of severall proceedings in this present parliament, from the 22 of November, to the 29, 1641*. London, for I.T. 1641. Title page of the first printed diurnal.

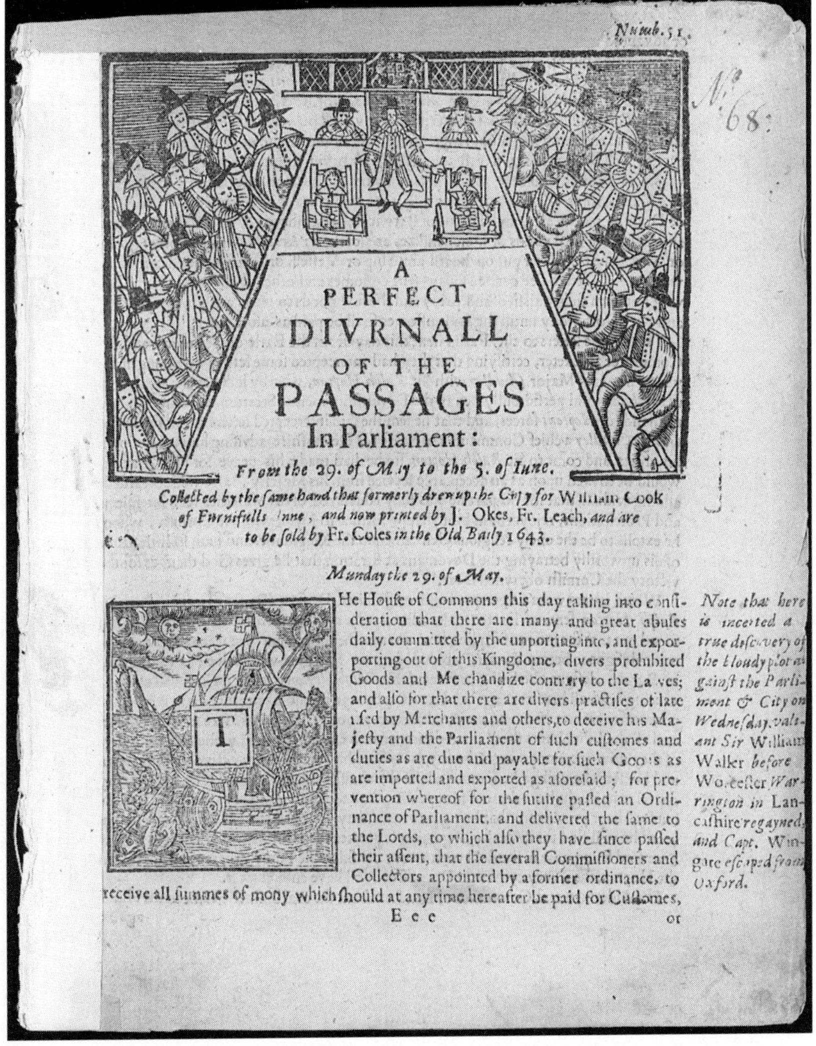

Numb. 51.

A PERFECT DIVRNALL OF THE PASSAGES In Parliament:

From the 29. of May to the 5. of Iune.

Collected by the ſame hand that formerly drew up the City for William Cook *of Furnifulls Inne, and now printed by* J. Okes, Fr. Leach, *and are to be ſold by* Fr. Coles *in the Old Baily* 1643.

Munday the 29. *of May.*

THe Houſe of Commons this day taking into conſideration that there are many and great abuſes daily committed by the importing into, and exporting out of this Kingdome, divers prohibited Goods and Merchandize contrary to the Lawes; and alſo for that there are divers practiſes of late uſed by Merchants and others, to deceive his Majeſty and the Parliament of ſuch cuſtomes and duties as are due and payable for ſuch Goods as are imported and exported as aforeſaid; for prevention whereof for the future paſſed an Ordinance of Parliament, and delivered the ſame to the Lords, to which alſo they have ſince paſſed their aſſent, that the ſeverall Commiſſioners and Collectors appointed by a former ordinance, to receive all ſummes of mony which ſhould at any time hereafter be paid for Cuſtomes,

Note that here is inserted a true diſcovery of the bloudy plot againſt the Parliament & City on Wedneſday. valiant Sir William Walker *before* Worceſter *Warrington in* Lancaſhire *regayned, and Capt.* Wingate *eſcaped from* Oxford.

E c c or

25.2 *A perfect diurnall of the passages in parliament: from the 29. of May to the 5. of June*, no. 51, sold by Fr. Coles, 1643. In order to produce sufficient copies to meet a deadline, some diurnals were printed simultaneously from two or more settings. This issue of the *Perfect diurnall* is found in two settings, distinguishable by the fact that in the other issue the woodcut is more deeply cracked.

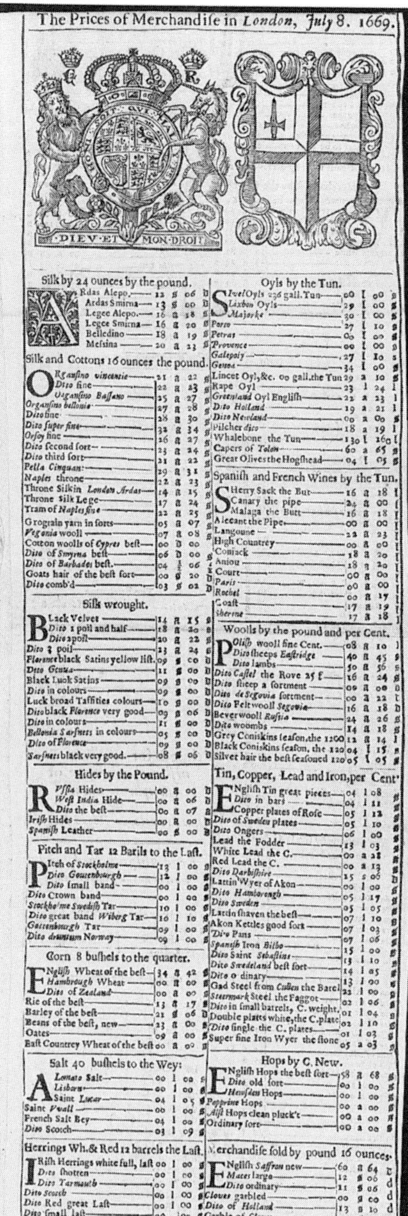

The Prices of Merchandise in *London*, *July* 8. 1669.

Silk by 24 ounces by the pound.

Ardas Alepo.	12	s	06	d
Ardas Smirna	13	s	00	d
Legee Alepo.	16	a	18	s
Legee Smirna	16	a	20	s
Belledino	18	a	19	s
Messina	20	a	23	s

Silk and Cottons 16 ounces the pound.

Organsino vincentie	21	a	22	s
Dito fine	22	a	23	s
Organsino Bassano	25	a	27	s
Organsino bellonie	27	a	28	s
Dito fine	28	a	30	s
Dito super fine	32	a	34	s
Orsoy fine	26	a	27	s
Dito second sort	23	a	24	s
Dito third sort	21	a	22	s
Pella Cinquan:	29	a	31	s
Naples throne	22	a	23	s
Throne Silk in *London Ardas*	14	a	15	s
Throne Silk Lege	17	a	24	s
Tram of *Naples fine*	22	a	25	s
Grograin yarn in sorts	05	a	07	s
Vegonia wooll	07	a	08	s
Cotton woolls of *Cypres* best	00	d	00	
Dito of *Smyrna* best	06	d	00	s
Dito of *Barbadoes* best.	04	½	06	s
Goats hair of the best sort	00	s	20	d
Dito comb'd	03	s	02	d

Silk wrought.

Black Velvet	14	a	15	s
Dito 1 poil and half	18	a	20	s
Dito 2 poil	20	a	22	s
Dito 3 poil	23	a	24	s
Florence black Satins yellow list.	09	s	00	d
Dito Genua	11	s	00	d
Black Luck Satins	09	s	00	d
Dito in colours	09	s	00	d
Luck broad Taffities colours	10	s	00	d
Dito black *Florence* very good	09	s	06	d
Dito in colours	11	s	00	d
Bellonia Sarsnets in colours	05	s	00	d
Dito of *Florence*	09	s	00	d
Sarsnets black very good.	08	s	06	d

Hides by the Pound.

Russia Hides	00	s	00	d
West India Hide	00	s	06	d
Dito the best	00	s	07	d
Irish Hides	00	s	00	d
Spanish Leather	00	s	00	d

Pitch and Tar 12 Barils to the Last.

Pitch of *Stockholme*	13	l	00	s
Dito Gottenbourgh	12	l	00	s
Dito small band	00	l	00	s
Dito Crown band	00	l	00	s
Stockholme Swedish Tar	10	l	00	s
Dito great band *Wiberg* Tar	10	l	10	s
Gottenbourgh Tar	09	l	00	s
Dito drunsum Norway	09	l	00	s

Corn 8 bushels to the quarter.

English Wheat of the best	34	a	42	s
Hambrough Wheat	00	a	00	s
Dito of *Zealand*	00	a	00	s
Rie of the best	13	a	17	s
Barley of the best	21	s	06	d
Beans of the best, new	23	a	00	s
Oates	09	a	00	s
East Countrey Wheat of the best	00	a	00	s

Salt 40 bushels to the Wey:

Lonato Salt	00	l	00	s
Lisborn	00	l	00	s
Saint *Lucar*	04	l	05	s
Saint *Vvall*	00	l	00	s
French Salt Bey	04	l	00	s
Dito Scotch	03	l	09	s

Herrings Wh. & Red 12 barrels the Last.

Irish Herrings white full, last	00	l	00	s
Dito shotten	00	l	00	s
Dito Yarmouth	00	l	00	s
Dito Scotch	00	l	00	s
Dito Red great Last	00	l	00	s
Dito small last	00	l	00	s

Oyls by the Tun.

Sivel Oyls 236 gall. Tun	00	l	00	s
Lixbon Oyls	29	l	00	s
Majorke	30	l	00	s
Porto	27	l	10	s
Petrat	00	l	00	s
Provence	00	l	00	s
Galepoly	27	l	10	s
Genoa	34	l	00	s
Lincet Oyl, &c. 00 gall. the Tun	29	a	10	s
Rape Oyl	23	l	24	l
Greenland Oyl English	22	a	23	l
Dito Holland	19	a	21	l
Dito Newland	00	a	00	s
Pilcher *dito*	18	a	19	l
Whalebone the Tun	130	l	160	l
Capers of *Tolon*	60	a	65	s
Great Olives the Hogshead	04	l	05	s

Spanish and French Wines by the Tun.

Sherry Sack the But	16	a	18	l
Canary the pipe	24	a	00	l
Malaga the Butt	16	a	18	l
Alecant the Pipe	00	a	00	l
Langoune	22	a	23	l
High Countrey	00	a	00	l
Coniack	18	a	20	l
Aniou	18	a	20	l
Court	00	a	00	l
Paris	00	a	00	l
Rochel	00	a	17	l
Coast	17	a	19	l
Sherene	17	a	18	l

Woolls by the pound and per Cent.

Polish wooll fine Cent.	08	a	10	l
Dito sheeps *Eastridge*	40	a	45	s
Dito lambs	50	a	56	s
Dito Castel the Rove 25 £	16	a	24	s
Dito sheep a sortment	09	a	00	d
Dito de Segovia sortment	00	a	22	[illegible]
Dito Felt wooll *Segovia*	16	a	18	d
Bever wooll *Russia*	24	a	26	s
Dito woombs	14	a	18	s
Grey Coniskins season, the 1200	12	a	14	l
Black Coniskins season, the 120	04	l	15	s
Silver hair the best seasoned 120	05	l	05	s

Tin, Copper, Lead and Iron, per Cent.

English Tin great pieces	04	l	08	s
Dito in bars	04	l	11	s
Copper plates of Rose	05	l	12	s
Dito of *Sweden* plates	05	l	10	s
Dito Ongers	06	l	00	s
Lead the Fodder	13	l	03	s
White Lead the C.	00	a	28	s
Red Lead the C.	00	a	13	s
Dito Darbishire	15	s	06	d
Lattin Wyer of Akon	00	l	00	s
Dito Hamborough	05	l	17	s
Dito Sweden	05	l	05	s
Lattin shaven the best	07	l	10	s
Akon Kettles good sort	07	l	03	s
Dito Pans	07	l	06	s
Spanish Iron *Bilbo*	15	l	00	s
Dito Saint *Sebastins*	13	l	10	s
Dito Swedeland best sort	14	l	05	s
Dito ordinary	13	l	00	s
Gad Steel from *Cullen* the Barel	22	l	00	s
Steermark Steel the Faggot	02	l	06	s
Dito in small barrels, C. weight.	01	l	04	s
Double platts white, the C. plate	02	l	10	s
Dito single the C. plates	01	l	03	s
Super fine Iron Wyer the stone	05	a	03	s

Hops by C. New.

English Hops the best sort	58	a	68	s
Dito old sort	00	l	00	s
Heusden Hops	00	l	00	s
Popprine Hops	00	a	00	s
Alst Hops clean pluck't	00	a	00	s
Ordinary sort	00	a	00	s

Merchandise sold by pound 16 ounces.

English *Saffron* new	60	a	64	s
Maces large	12	s	06	d
Dito ordinary	11	s	06	d
Cloves garbled	00	s	00	d
Dito of *Holland*	13	s	10	d
Garble of *Cloves*	04	s	00	d

25.3 *The prices of merchandise in London, July 8. 1669.* Financial news for the merchant in strip format, giving prices of silks, hides, pitch and tar, corn, salt, herrings, oils, wines, wools, tin, copper, lead and iron, hops etc.

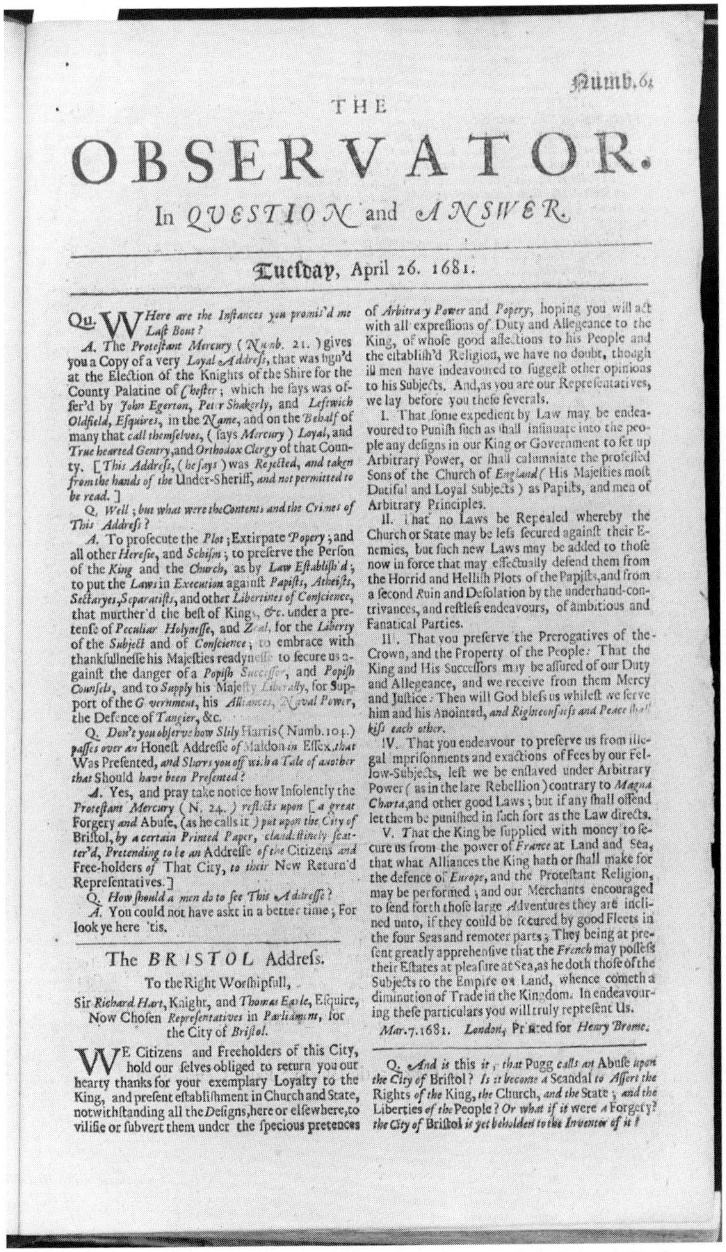

Numb. 61.

THE OBSERVATOR.

In QUESTION and ANSWER.

Tuesday, April 26. 1681.

Qu. *WHere are the Instances you promis'd me Last Bout?*

A. The *Protestant Mercury* (*Numb.* 21.) gives you a Copy of a very *Loyal Address*, that was sign'd at the Election of the Knights of the Shire for the County Palatine of *Chester*; which he says was offer'd by *John Egerton, Peter Shakerly*, and *Leftwich Oldfield, Esquires*, in the *Name*, and on the *Behalf* of many that *call themselves*, (says *Mercury*) *Loyal*, and *True hearted Gentry*, and *Orthodox Clergy* of that County. [*This Address*, (*he says*) was *Rejected, and taken from the hands of the* Under-Sheriff, *and not permitted to be read.*]

Q. *Well; but what were the Contents and the Crimes of This Address?*

A. To prosecute the *Plot*; Extirpate *Popery*; and all other *Heresie*, and *Schism*; to preserve the Person of the *King* and the *Church*, as by *Law Establish'd*; to put the *Laws* in *Execution* against *Papists, Atheists, Sectaryes, Separatists*, and other *Libertines of Conscience*, that murther'd the best of Kings, *&c.* under a pretense of *Peculiar Holynesse*, and *Zeal*, for the *Liberty* of the *Subject* and of *Conscience*; to embrace with thankfullnesse his Majesties readynesse to secure us against the danger of a *Popish Successor*, and *Popish Counsels*, and to *Supply* his Majesty *Liberally*, for Support of the *Government*, his *Alliances, Naval Power*, the Defence of *Tangier*, &c.

Q. *Don't you observe how Slily* Harris (Numb. 104.) *passes over an* Honest Addresse *of* Maldon *in* Essex, *that* Was Presented, *and Slurrs you off with a Tale of another that* Should *have been Presented?*

A. Yes, and pray take notice how Insolently the *Protestant Mercury* (N. 24.) *reflects upon* [*a great* Forgery *and* Abuse, (as he calls it) *put upon the City of* Bristol, *by a certain Printed Paper, clandestinely scatter'd, Pretending to be an* Addresse *of the* Citizens *and* Free-holders *of* That City, *to their* New Return'd Representatives.]

Q. *How should a men do to see This Addresse?*

A. You could not have askt in a better time; For look ye here 'tis.

The BRISTOL Address.

To the Right Worshipfull,

Sir *Richard Hart*, Knight, and *Thomas Earle*, Esquire, Now Chosen *Representatives* in *Parliament*, for the City of *Bristol*.

WE Citizens and Freeholders of this City, hold our selves obliged to return you our hearty thanks for your exemplary Loyalty to the King, and present establishment in Church and State, notwithstanding all the *Designs*, here or elsewhere, to vilifie or subvert them under the specious pretences of *Arbitrary Power* and *Popery*, hoping you will act with all expressions of Duty and Allegeance to the King, of whose good affections to his People and the establish'd Religion, we have no doubt, though ill men have indeavoured to suggest other opinions to his Subjects. And, as you are our Representatives, we lay before you these severals.

I. That some expedient by Law may be endeavoured to Punish such as shall insinuate into the people any designs in our King or Government to set up Arbitrary Power, or shall calumniate the professed Sons of the Church of *England* (His Majesties most Dutiful and Loyal Subjects) as Papists, and men of Arbitrary Principles.

II. That no Laws be Repealed whereby the Church or State may be less secured against their Enemies, but such new Laws may be added to those now in force that may effectually defend them from the Horrid and Hellish Plots of the Papists, and from a second *Ruin* and Desolation by the underhand-contrivances, and restless endeavours, of ambitious and Fanatical Parties.

III. That you preserve the Prerogatives of the Crown, and the Property of the People: That the King and His Successors may be assured of our Duty and Allegeance, and we receive from them Mercy and Justice: Then will God bless us whilest we serve him and his Anointed, *and Righteousness and Peace shall kiss each other.*

IV. That you endeavour to preserve us from illegal Imprisonments and exactions of Fees by our Fellow-Subjects, lest we be enslaved under Arbitrary Power (as in the late Rebellion) contrary to *Magna Charta*, and other good Laws; but if any shall offend let them be punished in such sort as the Law directs.

V. That the King be supplied with money to secure us from the power of *France* at Land and Sea, that what Alliances the King hath or shall make for the defence of *Europe*, and the Protestant Religion, may be performed; and our Merchants encouraged to send forth those large *Adventures* they are inclined unto, if they could be secured by good Fleets in the four Seas and remoter parts; They being at present greatly apprehensive that the *French* may possess their Estates at pleasure at Sea, as he doth those of the Subjects to the Empire on Land, whence cometh a diminution of Trade in the Kingdom. In endeavouring these particulars you will truly represent Us.

Mar. 7. 1681. *London*, Printed for *Henry Brome*.

Q. *And is this it, that* Pugg *calls an* Abuse *upon the City of* Bristol? *Is it become a* Scandal *to Assert the* Rights *of the* King, *the* Church, *and the* State; *and the* Liberties *of the* People? *Or what if it were a* Forgery? *the City of* Bristol *is yet beholden to the Inventor of it?*

25.4 *The Observator. In question and answer* no. 61, Tuesday, April 26. 1681. Henry Brome, the original publisher, died a month after the series began; Joanna, his widow, carried on the series as well as reprinting many issues before passing on publication to her son Charles. That this is the original edition rather than a later imprint is indicated by the nicked V in the title.

30.1 A binding by the Morocco binder, *c.* 1562. *Statutes made in the Parliament* [Edward VI and Mary], 1548–1558, London, 1558.

30.2 A presentation binding by Daniel Boyse, *c.* 1623, *Gratulatio Academiae Cantabrigiensis*, Cambridge, 1623.

30.3 A binding by Samuel Mearne , *c.* 1660. *Holy Bible*, Cambridge, 1659.

Anger for great hurt done to another, when we conceive the same to be done by Injury, INDIGNATION.

Indignation.

Desire of good to another, BENEVOLENCE, GOOD WILL, CHARITY. If to man generally, GOOD NATURE.

Benevolence. Good Nature.

Desire of Riches, COVETOUSNESSE: a name used alwayes in signification of blame; because men contending for them, are displeased with one anothers attaining them; though the desire in it selfe, be to be blamed, or allowed, according to the means by which those Riches are sought.

Covetousnesse

Desire of Office, or precedence, AMBITION: a name used also in the worse sense, for the reason before mentioned.

Ambition.

Desire of things that conduce but a little to our ends; And fear of things that are but of little hindrance, PUSILLANIMITY.

Pusillanimity.

Contempt of little helps, and hindrances, MAGNANIMITY.

Magnanimity.

Magnanimity, in danger of Death, or Wounds, VALOUR, FORTITUDE.

Valour.

Magnanimity, in the use of Riches, LIBERALITY.

Liberality.

Pusillanimity, in the same WRETCHEDNESSE, MISERABLENESSE; or PARSIMONY; as it is liked, or disliked.

Miserablenesse.

Love of Persons for society, KINDNESSE.

Kindnesse.

Love of Persons for Pleasing the sense onely, NATURALL LUST.

Naturall Lust.

Love of the same, acquired from Rumination, that is, Imagination of Pleasure past, LUXURY.

Luxury.

Love of one singularly, with desire to be singularly beloved, THE PASSION OF LOVE. The same, with fear that the love is not mutuall, JEALOUSIE.

The passion of Love. Jealousie.

Desire, by doing hurt to another, to make him condemn some fact of his own, REVENGEFULNESSE.

Revengefulnesse.

Desire, to know why, and how, CURIOSITY; such as is in no living creature but *Man*: so that Man is distinguished, not onely by his Reason; but also by this singular Passion from other *Animals*; in whom the appetite of food, and other pleasures of Sense, by prædominance, take away the care of knowing causes; which is a Lust of the mind, that by a perseverance of delight in the continuall and indefatigable generation of Knowledge, exceedeth the short vehemence of any carnall Pleasure.

Curiosity.

Feare of power invisible, feigned by the mind, or imagined from tales publiquely allowed, RELIGION; not allowed, SUPERSTITION. And when the power imagined, is truly such as we imagine, TRUE RELIGION.

Religion. Superstition. True Religion.

Feare, without the apprehension of why, or what, PANIQUE TERROR; called so from the Fables, that make *Pan* the author of them; whereas in truth, there is alwayes in him that so feareth, first, some apprehension of the cause, though the rest run away by Example; every one supposing his fellow to know why. And therefore this Passion happens to none but in a throng, or multitude of people.

Panique Terrour.

Joy, from apprehension of novelty, ADMIRATION; proper to Man, because it excites the appetite of knowing the cause.

Admiration.

Joy, arising from imagination of a mans own power and ability, is

31.1 Thomas Hobbes, *Leviathan, or, the matter, form and power of a common-wealth* . . ., London, for Andrew Crooke, 1651. The typography and layout present a text which is an illustration or diagram of its content. The use of different founts, sizes of type, labels and headings creates an architectural effect.

31.2 *Biblia sacra Polyglota*, ed. B. Walton, printed by Thomas Roycroft, 1657, engraved title page by Wenceslaus Hollar.

31.3 *Biblia sacra Polyglota*, ed. B. Walton, printed by Thomas Roycroft, 1657, double page layout. A triumph of rational layout, each double page of the Bible presents ten or more versions of the same passage. Walton closely supervised production, from the casting of type to the choice of paper.

A TRUE
NARRATIVE
OF THE
Horrid PLOT
AND
CONSPIRACY
OF THE
POPISH PARTY
Againſt the LIFE of
His Sacred Majeſty,
THE
GOVERNMENT,
AND THE
Proteſtant Religion:
With a LIST of ſuch NOBLEMEN, GENTLEMEN,
and others that were the CONSPIRATORS:
And the HEAD-OFFICERS both Civil and
Military, that were to Effect it.

Publiſhed by the Order of the Right Honourable the Lords Spiritual and Temporal in PARLIAMENT Aſſembled.

Humbly Preſented to His Moſt Excellent MAJESTY.

By *TITUS OTES*, D.D.

LONDON:
Printed for *Thomas Parkhurſt*, and *Thomas Cockerill*, at the Bible and Three Crowns in *Cheapſide* near *Mercers Chappel*, and at the Three Legs in the *Poultrey*. MDCLXXIX.

31.4 Titus Oates, *A true narrative of the horrid plot and conspiracy of the popish party against the life of his sacred majesty, the government, and the protestant religion* . . . , London, for Thomas Parkhurst and Thomas Cockerill, 1679, engraved frontispiece portrait and letterpress title page. The folio format and legitimising paratextual features were adapted by Oates's successors in publishing political narratives.

Waynesburg College/Eberly Library
3 5150 00231 2355